Health Care State Rankings 2008

Other titles in the State Fact Finder series

City Crime Rankings

Crime State Rankings

Education State Rankings

State Rankings

State Trends

Health Care State Rankings 2008

Health Care Across America

Kathleen O'Leary Morgan

and

Scott Morgan

Editors

CQ PRESS

A Division of Congressional Quarterly Inc.
Washington, D.C.

CQ Press
2300 N Street NW, Suite 800
Washington, DC 20037

Phone: 202-729-1900; toll-free, 1-866-4CQ-PRESS (1-866-427-7737)

Web: www.cqpress.com

Cover design: Silverander Communications

♾ The paper used in this publication exceeds the requirements of the American National Standard for Information Sciences—Permanence of Paper for Printed Library Materials, ANSI Z39.48-1992.

Printed and bound in the United States of America

12   11   10   09   08   1   2   3   4   5

ISBN 978-0-87289-928-5
ISSN 1065-1403

Contents

Detailed Table of Contents   vi

Preface   xiii

Healthiest State Award   xv

Subject Rankings

      Births and Reproductive Health   3
      Deaths   92
      Facilities   192
      Finance   237
      Incidence of Disease   336
      Providers   411
      Physical Fitness   495

Appendix   530

Sources   535

Index   537

Detailed Table of Contents

I. BIRTHS AND REPRODUCTIVE HEALTH

Births in 2006 3
Birth Rate in 2006 4
Percent Change in Birth Rate: 1997 to 2006 5
Births in 2005 6
Birth Rate in 2005 7
Fertility Rate in 2006 8
Births to White Women in 2006 9
White Births as a Percent of All Births in 2006 10
Births to Black Women in 2006 11
Black Births as a Percent of All Births in 2006 12
Births to Hispanic Women in 2006 13
Hispanic Births as a Percent of All Births in 2006 14
Births of Low Birthweight in 2006 15
Births of Low Birthweight as a Percent of All Births
    in 2006 16
Births of Low Birthweight to White Women in 2006 17
Births of Low Birthweight to White Women as a Percent
    of All Births to White Women in 2006. 18
Births of Low Birthweight to Black Women in 2006 19
Births of Low Birthweight to Black Women as a Percent
    of All Births to Black Women in 2006. 20
Births of Low Birthweight to Hispanic Women in 2006 ... 21
Births of Low Birthweight to Hispanic Women as a
    Percent of All Births to Hispanic Women in 2006 ... 22
Births to Unmarried Women in 2006 23
Births to Unmarried Women as a Percent of All Births
    in 2006 24
Births to Unmarried White Women in 2006 25
Births to Unmarried White Women as a Percent of
    All Births to White Women in 2006. 26
Births to Unmarried Black Women in 2006 27
Births to Unmarried Black Women as a Percent of
    All Births to Black Women in 2006. 28
Births to Unmarried Hispanic Women in 2006 29
Births to Unmarried Hispanic Women as a Percent of
    All Births to Hispanic Women in 2006 30
Pregnancy Rate in 2004 31
Teenage Pregnancy Rate in 2004 32

Percent Change in Teenage Pregnancy Rate:
    2000 to 2004 33
Births to Teenage Mothers in 2006 34
Births to Teenage Mothers as a Percent of Births
    in 2006 35
Teenage Birth Rate in 2006 36
Percent Change in Teenage Birth Rate: 2002 to 2006 37
Births to Teenage Mothers in 2005 38
Teenage Birth Rate in 2005 39
Births to White Teenage Mothers in 2005 40
White Teenage Birth Rate in 2005 41
Births to White Teenage Mothers as a Percent of
    White Births in 2005 42
Births to Black Teenage Mothers in 2005 43
Black Teenage Birth Rate in 2005 44
Births to Black Teenage Mothers as a Percent of Black
    Births in 2005 45
Births to Young Teenagers: 2003 to 2005 46
Young Teen Birthrate: 2003 to 2005 47
Births to Women 35 to 54 Years Old in 2005 48
Births to Women 35 to 54 Years Old as a Percent of
    All Births in 2005 49
Births by Vaginal Delivery in 2006 50
Percent of Births by Vaginal Delivery in 2006 51
Births by Cesarean Delivery in 2006 52
Percent of Births by Cesarean Delivery in 2006 53
Percent Change in Rate of Cesarean Births:
    2002 to 2006 54
Percent of Births That Are Pre-Term in 2006 55
Twin Birth Rate: 2002–2005 56
Assisted Reproductive Technology Procedures in 2004 ... 57
Infants Born from Assisted Reproductive Technology
    Procedures in 2004 58
Percent of Assisted Reproductive Technology Procedures
    That Resulted in Live Births in 2004. 59
Percent of Total Live Births Resulting from Assisted
    Reproductive Technology Procedures in 2004. 60
Percent of Assisted Reproductive Technology Procedure
    Infants Born in Multiple Birth Deliveries in 2004 ... 61

Percent of Mothers Beginning Prenatal Care in
  First Trimester in 2005 62
Percent of White Mothers Beginning Prenatal Care in
  First Trimester in 2005 63
Percent of Black Mothers Beginning Prenatal Care in
  First Trimester in 2005 64
Percent of Hispanic Mothers Beginning Prenatal Care in
  First Trimester in 2005 65
Percent of Mothers Receiving Late or No Prenatal Care in
  2005 66
Percent of White Mothers Receiving Late or No Prenatal
  Care in 2005 67
Percent of Black Mothers Receiving Late or No Prenatal
  Care in 2005 68
Percent of Hispanic Mothers Receiving Late or No
  Prenatal Care in 2005 69
Reported Legal Abortions in 2004 70
Percent Change in Reported Legal Abortions:
  2000 to 2004 71
Reported Legal Abortions per 1,000 Live Births in 2004 .. 72
Reported Legal Abortions per 1,000 Women Ages
  15 to 44 in 2004 73
Percent of Legal Abortions Obtained by Out-Of-State
  Residents in 2004 74
Percent of Reported Legal Abortions That Were First-Time
  Abortions: 2004 75
Percent of Reported Legal Abortions Obtained by White
  Women in 2004 76
Percent of Reported Legal Abortions Obtained by Black
  Women in 2004 77
Percent of Reported Legal Abortions Obtained by Hispanic
  Women in 2004 78
Percent of Reported Legal Abortions Obtained by Married
  Women in 2004 79
Percent of Reported Legal Abortions Obtained by
  Unmarried Women in 2004 80
Reported Legal Abortions Obtained by Teenagers
  in 2004 81
Percent of Reported Legal Abortions Obtained by
  Teenagers in 2004 82
Reported Legal Abortions Obtained by Teenagers
  17 Years and Younger in 2004 83
Percent of Reported Legal Abortions Obtained by
  Teenagers 17 Years and Younger in 2004 84
Percent of Teenage Abortions Obtained by Teenagers
  17 Years and Younger in 2004 85
Reported Legal Abortions Performed at 12 Weeks or
  Less of Gestation in 2004 86
Percent of Reported Legal Abortions Performed at
  12 Weeks or Less of Gestation in 2004 87
Reported Legal Abortions Performed at or after 21
  Weeks of Gestation in 2004 88
Percent of Reported Legal Abortions Performed at or
  after 21 Weeks of Gestation in 2004 89

II. DEATHS

Deaths in 2006 92
Death Rate in 2006 93
Deaths in 2005 94
Death Rate in 2005 95
Age-Adjusted Death Rate in 2005 96
Percent Change in Death Rate: 1996 to 2005 97
Deaths in 2004 98
Death Rate in 2004 99
Age-Adjusted Death Rate in 2004 100
Infant Deaths in 2005 101
Infant Mortality Rate in 2005 102
White Infant Deaths in 2005 103
White Infant Mortality Rate in 2005 104
Black Infant Deaths in 2005 105
Black Infant Mortality Rate in 2005 106
Neonatal Deaths in 2005 107
Neonatal Death Rate in 2005 108
White Neonatal Deaths in 2005 109
White Neonatal Death Rate in 2005 110
Black Neonatal Deaths in 2005 111
Black Neonatal Death Rate in 2005 112
Estimated Deaths by Cancer in 2007 113
Estimated Death Rate by Cancer in 2007 114
Age-Adjusted Death Rate by Cancer for Males
  in 2003 115
Age-Adjusted Death Rate by Cancer for Females
  in 2003 116
Estimated Deaths by Brain Cancer in 2007 117
Estimated Death Rate by Brain Cancer in 2007 118
Estimated Deaths by Female Breast Cancer in 2007 119
Age-Adjusted Death Rate by Female Breast Cancer
  in 2003 120
Estimated Deaths by Colon and Rectum Cancer
  in 2007 121
Estimated Death Rate by Colon and Rectum Cancer
  in 2007 122
Estimated Deaths by Leukemia in 2007 123
Estimated Death Rate by Leukemia in 2007 124
Estimated Deaths by Liver Cancer in 2007 125
Estimated Death Rate by Liver Cancer in 2007 126
Estimated Deaths by Lung Cancer in 2007 127
Estimated Death Rate by Lung Cancer in 2007 128
Estimated Deaths by Non-Hodgkin's Lymphoma
  in 2007 129
Estimated Death Rate by Non-Hodgkin's Lymphoma
  in 2007 130
Estimated Deaths by Ovarian Cancer in 2007 131
Estimated Death Rate by Ovarian Cancer in 2007 132
Estimated Deaths by Pancreatic Cancer in 2007 133
Estimated Death Rate by Pancreatic Cancer in 2007 134
Estimated Deaths by Prostate Cancer in 2007 135
Age-Adjusted Death Rate by Prostate Cancer in 2003 ... 136
Deaths by AIDS in 2004 137
Death Rate by AIDS in 2004 138
Age-Adjusted Death Rate by AIDS in 2004 139
Deaths by Alzheimer's Disease in 2004 140
Death Rate by Alzheimer's Disease in 2004 141
Age-Adjusted Death Rate by Alzheimer's Disease
  in 2004 142
Deaths by Cerebrovascular Diseases in 2004 143

Death Rate by Cerebrovascular Diseases in 2004 144

Age-Adjusted Death Rate by Cerebrovascular Diseases
in 2004 145

Deaths by Chronic Liver Disease and Cirrhosis in 2004 . . 146

Death Rate by Chronic Liver Disease and Cirrhosis
in 2004 147

Age-Adjusted Death Rate by Chronic Liver Disease and
Cirrhosis in 2004 148

Deaths by Chronic Lower Respiratory Diseases
in 2004 149

Death Rate by Chronic Lower Respiratory Diseases
in 2004 150

Age-Adjusted Death Rate by Chronic Lower Respiratory
Diseases in 2004 151

Deaths by Diabetes Mellitus in 2004 152

Death Rate by Diabetes Mellitus in 2004 153

Age-Adjusted Death Rate by Diabetes Mellitus in 2004 . . 154

Deaths by Diseases of the Heart in 2004 155

Death Rate by Diseases of the Heart in 2004 156

Age-Adjusted Death Rate by Diseases of the Heart
in 2004 157

Deaths by Malignant Neoplasms in 2004 158

Death Rate by Malignant Neoplasms in 2004 159

Age-Adjusted Death Rate by Malignant Neoplasms
in 2004 160

Deaths by Nephritis and Other Kidney Diseases
in 2004 161

Death Rate by Nephritis and Other Kidney Diseases
in 2004 162

Age-Adjusted Death Rate by Nephritis and Other Kidney
Diseases in 2004 163

Deaths by Influenza and Pneumonia in 2004 164

Death Rate by Influenza and Pneumonia in 2004 165

Age-Adjusted Death Rate by Influenza and Pneumonia
in 2004 166

Deaths by Injury in 2004 167

Death Rate by Injury in 2004 168

Age-Adjusted Death Rate by Injury in 2004 169

Deaths by Accidents in 2004 170

Death Rate by Accidents in 2004 171

Age-Adjusted Death Rate by Accidents in 2004 172

Deaths by Motor Vehicle Accidents in 2004 173

Death Rate by Motor Vehicle Accidents in 2004 174

Age-Adjusted Death Rate by Motor Vehicle Accidents
in 2004 175

Deaths by Firearm Injury in 2004 176

Death Rate by Firearm Injury in 2004 177

Age-Adjusted Death Rate by Firearm Injury in 2004 178

Deaths by Homicide in 2004 179

Death Rate by Homicide in 2004 180

Age-Adjusted Death Rate by Homicide in 2004 181

Deaths by Suicide in 2004 182

Death Rate by Suicide in 2004 183

Age-Adjusted Death Rate by Suicide in 2004 184

Alcohol-Induced Deaths in 2004 185

Death Rate by Alcohol-Induced Deaths in 2004 186

Age-Adjusted Death Rate by Alcohol-Induced Deaths
in 2004 187

Occupational Fatalities in 2006 188

Occupational Fatality Rate in 2006 189

III. FACILITIES

Community Hospitals in 2006 192

Rate of Community Hospitals in 2005 193

Community Hospitals per 1,000 Square Miles in 2006 . . . 194

Community Hospitals in Urban Areas in 2006 195

Percent of Community Hospitals in Urban Areas
in 2006 196

Community Hospitals in Rural Areas in 2006 197

Percent of Community Hospitals in Rural Areas
in 2006 198

Nongovernment Not-For-Profit Hospitals in 2006 199

Investor-Owned (For-Profit) Hospitals in 2006 200

State and Local Government-Owned Hospitals in 2006 . . 201

Beds in Community Hospitals in 2006 202

Rate of Beds in Community Hospitals in 2006 203

Average Number of Beds per Community Hospital
in 2006 204

Admissions to Community Hospitals in 2006 205

Inpatient Days in Community Hospitals in 2006 206

Average Daily Census in Community Hospitals in 2006 . . 207

Average Stay in Community Hospitals in 2006 208

Occupancy Rate in Community Hospitals in 2006 209

Outpatient Visits to Community Hospitals in 2006 210

Emergency Outpatient Visits to Community Hospitals
in 2006 211

Medicare and Medicaid Certified Facilities in 2008 212

Medicare and Medicaid Certified Hospitals in 2008 213

Beds in Medicare and Medicaid Certified Hospitals
in 2008 214

Medicare and Medicaid Certified Children's Hospitals
in 2008 215

Beds in Medicare and Medicaid Certified Children's
Hospitals in 2008 216

Medicare and Medicaid Certified Rehabilitation Hospitals
in 2008 217

Beds in Medicare and Medicaid Certified Rehabilitation
Hospitals in 2008 218

Medicare and Medicaid Certified Psychiatric Hospitals
in 2008 219

Beds in Medicare and Medicaid Certified Psychiatric
Hospitals in 2008 220

Medicare and Medicaid Certified Outpatient Surgery
Centers in 2008 221

Medicare and Medicaid Certified Community Mental
Health Centers in 2008 222

Medicare and Medicaid Certified Outpatient Physical
Therapy Facilities in 2008 223

Medicare and Medicaid Certified Rural Health Clinics
in 2008 224

Medicare and Medicaid Certified Home Health Agencies
in 2008 225

Medicare and Medicaid Certified Hospices in 2008 226

Hospice Patients in Residential Facilities in 2008 227

Medicare and Medicaid Certified Nursing Care Facilities
in 2008 228

Beds in Medicare and Medicaid Certified Nursing Care
    Facilities in 2008 229
Rate of Beds in Medicare and Medicaid Certified
    Nursing Care Facilities in 2008 230
Nursing Home Occupancy Rate in 2006 231
Nursing Home Resident Rate in 2006 232
Nursing Home Population in 2006 233
Health Care Establishments in 2005 234

IV. FINANCE

Average Medical Malpractice Payment in 2005 237
Percent of Private-Sector Establishments That Offer
    Health Insurance: 2005 238
Percent of Private-Sector Establishments with Fewer
    Than 50 Employees That Offer Health Insurance:
    2005 239
Percent of Private-Sector Establishments with More
    Than 50 Employees That Offer Health Insurance:
    2005 240
Average Annual Single Coverage Health Insurance
    Premium per Enrolled Employee in 2005 241
Average Annual Employee Contribution for Single
    Coverage Health Insurance in 2005 242
Percent of Total Premiums for Single Coverage Health
    Insurance Paid by Employees in 2005 243
Average Annual Family Coverage Health Insurance
    Premium per Enrolled Employee in 2005 244
Average Annual Employee Contribution for Family
    Coverage Health Insurance in 2005 245
Percent of Total Premiums for Family Coverage Health
    Insurance Paid by Employees in 2005 246
Persons Not Covered by Health Insurance in 2006 247
Percent of Population Not Covered by Health Insurance
    in 2006 248
Numerical Change in Persons Uninsured:
    2002 to 2006 249
Percent Change in Persons Uninsured: 2002 to 2006 250
Change in Percent of Population Uninsured:
    2002 to 2006 251
Percent of Children Not Covered by Health Insurance
    in 2006 252
Persons Covered by Health Insurance in 2006 253
Percent of Population Covered by Health Insurance
    in 2006 254
Percent of Population Covered by Private Health
    Insurance in 2006 255
Percent of Population Covered by Employment-Based
    Health Insurance in 2006 256
Percent of Population Covered by Direct Purchase Health
    Insurance in 2006 257
Percent of Population Covered by Government Health
    Insurance in 2006 258
Percent of Population Covered by Military Health Care
    in 2006 259
Percent of Children Covered by Health Insurance
    in 2006 260
Percent of Children Covered by Private Health Insurance
    in 2006 261
Percent of Children Covered by Employment-Based
    Health Insurance in 2006 262
Percent of Children Covered by Direct Purchase Health
    Insurance in 2006 263
Percent of Children Covered by Government Health
    Insurance in 2006 264
Percent of Children Covered by Military Health Care
    in 2006 265
Percent of Children Covered by Medicaid in 2006 266
State Children's Health Insurance Program (SCHIP)
    Enrollment in 2006 267
Percent Change in State Children's Health Insurance
    Program (SCHIP) Enrollment: 2005 to 2006. 268
Percent of Children Enrolled in State Children's Health
    Insurance Program (SCHIP) in 2006 269
Expenditures for State Children's Health Insurance
    Program (SCHIP) in 2006 270
Per Capita Expenditures for State Children's Health
    Insurance Program (SCHIP) in 2006 271
Expenditures per State Children's Health Insurance
    Program (SCHIP) Participant in 2006 272
Health Maintenance Organizations (HMOs) in 2007 273
Enrollees in Health Maintenance Organizations (HMOs)
    in 2007 274
Percent Change in Enrollees in Health Maintenance
    Organizations (HMOs): 2006 to 2007 275
Percent of Population Enrolled in Health Maintenance
    Organizations (HMOs) in 2007 276
Percent of Insured Population Enrolled in Health
    Maintenance Organizations (HMOs) in 2007 277
Medicare Enrollees in 2006 278
Percent Change in Medicare Enrollees: 2005 to 2006 279
Percent of Population Enrolled in Medicare in 2006 280
Percent of Medicare Enrollees in Managed Care
    Programs in 2006 281
Percent of Physicians Participating in Medicare in 2007 . . 282
Medicare Program Payments in 2006 283
Per Capita Medicare Program Payments in 2006 284
Medicare Program Payments per Enrollee in 2006 285
Medicaid Enrollment in 2006 286
Percent of Population Enrolled in Medicaid in 2006 287
Medicaid Managed Care Enrollment in 2006 288
Percent of Medicaid Enrollees in Managed Care
    in 2006 289
Estimated Medicaid Expenditures in 2007 290
Estimated Per Capita Medicaid Expenditures in 2007 . . . 291
Estimated Medicaid Expenditures as a Percent of Total
    Expenditures in 2007 292
Percent Change in Medicaid Expenditures:
    2006 to 2007 293
Medicaid Expenditures in 2006 294
Per Capita Medicaid Expenditures in 2006 295
Medicaid Expenditures per Beneficiary in 2006 296
Federal Medicaid Matching Fund Rate for 2008 297
State and Local Government Expenditures for
    Hospitals in 2005 298
Per Capita State and Local Government Expenditures for
    Hospitals in 2005 299

Percent of State and Local Government Expenditures
Used for Hospitals in 2005. 300

State and Local Government Expenditures for Health
Programs in 2005 301

Per Capita State and Local Government Expenditures
for Health Programs in 2005 302

Percent of State and Local Government Expenditures
Used for Health Programs in 2005. 303

Estimated Tobacco Settlement Revenues in Fiscal Year
2008 304

Personal Health Care Expenditures in 2004 305

Health Care Expenditures as a Percent of Gross State
Product in 2004 306

Per Capita Personal Health Care Expenditures in 2004 . . . 307

Average Annual Growth in Personal Health Care
Expenditures: 1991–2004 308

Expenditures for Hospital Care in 2004 309

Percent of Total Personal Health Care Expenditures
Spent on Hospital Care in 2004 310

Per Capita Expenditures for Hospital Care in 2004 311

Expenditures for Physician and Clinical Services
in 2004 312

Percent of Total Personal Health Care Expenditures
Spent on Physician and Clinical Services in 2004. 313

Per Capita Expenditures for Physician and Clinical
Services in 2004 314

Expenditures for Dental Services in 2004 315

Percent of Total Personal Health Care Expenditures
Spent on Dental Services in 2004 316

Per Capita Expenditures for Dental Care in 2004 317

Expenditures for Other Professional Health Care
Services in 2004 318

Percent of Total Personal Health Care Expenditures
Spent on Other Professional Health Care Services
in 2004 319

Per Capita Expenditures for Other Professional Health
Care Services in 2004 320

Expenditures for Nursing Home Care in 2004 321

Percent of Total Personal Health Care Expenditures
Spent on Nursing Home Care in 2004. 322

Per Capita Expenditures for Nursing Home Care
in 2004 323

Expenditures for Home Health Care in 2004 324

Percent of Total Personal Health Care Expenditures
Spent on Home Health Care in 2004 325

Per Capita Expenditures for Home Health Care in 2004 . . 326

Expenditures for Drugs and Other Medical Nondurables
in 2004 327

Percent of Total Personal Health Care Expenditures Spent
on Drugs and Other Medical Nondurables in 2004 328

Per Capita Expenditures for Drugs and Other Medical
Nondurables in 2004 329

Expenditures for Durable Medical Products in 2004 330

Percent of Total Personal Health Care Expenditures
Spent on Durable Medical Products in 2004 331

Per Capita Expenditures for Durable Medical Products
in 2004 332

Projected National Health Care Expenditures in 2008 . . . 333

V. INCIDENCE OF DISEASE

Estimated New Cancer Cases in 2007 336

Estimated Rate of New Cancer Cases in 2007 337

Age-Adjusted Cancer Incidence Rates for Males
in 2003 338

Age-Adjusted Cancer Incidence Rates for Females
in 2003 339

Estimated New Cases of Bladder Cancer in 2007 340

Estimated Rate of New Bladder Cancer Cases in 2007 . . . 341

Estimated New Female Breast Cancer Cases in 2007 342

Age-Adjusted Incidence Rate of Female Breast Cancer
Cases in 2003 343

Percent of Women 40 and Older Who Have Had a
Mammogram in the Past Two Years: 2006 344

Estimated New Colon and Rectum Cancer Cases
in 2007 345

Estimated Rate of New Colon and Rectum Cancer
Cases in 2007 346

Percent of Adults Who Have Ever Had a Sigmoidoscopy
or Colonoscopy Exam: 2006 347

Estimated New Leukemia Cases in 2007 348

Estimated Rate of New Leukemia Cases in 2007 349

Estimated New Lung Cancer Cases in 2007 350

Estimated Rate of New Lung Cancer Cases in 2007 351

Estimated New Non-Hodgkin's Lymphoma Cases
in 2007 352

Estimated Rate of New Non-Hodgkin's Lymphoma
Cases in 2007 353

Estimated New Prostate Cancer Cases in 2007 354

Age-Adjusted Incidence Rate of Prostate Cancer Cases
in 2003 355

Percent of Males Receiving PSA Test for Prostate Cancer:
2006 356

Estimated New Skin Melanoma Cases in 2007 357

Estimated Rate of New Skin Melanoma Cases in 2007 . . 358

Estimated New Cervical Cancer Cases in 2007 359

Estimated Rate of New Cervical Cancer Cases in 2007 . . 360

Percent of Women 18 Years Old and Older Who Had a
Pap Smear within the Past Three Years: 2006 361

Estimated New Uterine Cancer Cases in 2007 362

Estimated Rate of New Uterine Cancer Cases in 2007 . . . 363

AIDS Cases Reported in 2005 364

AIDS Rate in 2005 365

AIDS Cases Reported through December 2005 366

AIDS Cases in Children 12 Years and Younger through
December 2005 367

Chickenpox (Varicella) Cases Reported in 2007 368

Chickenpox (Varicella) Rate in 2007 369

E. Coli Cases Reported in 2007 370

E. Coli Rate in 2007 371

Hepatitis A and B Cases Reported in 2007 372

Hepatitis A and B Rate in 2007 373

Legionellosis Cases Reported in 2007 374

Legionellosis Rate in 2007 375

Lyme Disease Cases in 2007 376

Lyme Disease Rate in 2007 377

Malaria Cases Reported in 2007 378

Malaria Rate in 2007 379

Meningococcal Infections Reported in 2007 380
Meningococcal Infection Rate in 2007 381
Rabies (Animal) Cases Reported in 2007 382
Rabies (Animal) Rate in 2007 383
Rocky Mountain Spotted Fever Cases Reported in 2007 . . 384
Rocky Mountain Spotted Fever Rate in 2007 385
Salmonellosis Cases Reported in 2007 386
Salmonellosis Rate in 2007 387
Shigellosis Cases Reported in 2007 388
Shigellosis Rate in 2007 389
West Nile Virus Disease Cases Reported in 2007 390
West Nile Disease Rate in 2007 391
Whooping Cough (Pertussis) Cases Reported in 2007 . . . 392
Whooping Cough (Pertussis) Rate in 2007 393
Percent of Children Aged 19 to 35 Months Fully
    Immunized in 2006 394
Percent of Adults Aged 65 Years and Older Who
    Received Flu Shots in 2006 395
Percent of Adults Aged 65 Years and Older Who
    Have Had a Pneumonia Vaccine: 2006 396
Sexually Transmitted Diseases in 2006 397
Sexually Transmitted Disease Rate in 2006 398
Chlamydia Cases Reported in 2006 399
Chlamydia Rate in 2006 400
Gonorrhea Cases Reported in 2006 401
Gonorrhea Rate in 2006 402
Syphilis Cases Reported in 2006 403
Syphilis Rate in 2006 404
Percent of Adults Who Have Asthma: 2006 405
Percent of Adults Who Have Been Told They Have
    Arthritis: 2005 406
Percent of Adults Who Have Been Told They Have
    Diabetes: 2006 407
Percent of Adults Reporting Serious Psychological
    Distress: 2005 408

VI. PROVIDERS
Health Care Practitioners and Technicians in 2006 411
Rate of Health Care Practitioners and Technicians
    in 2006 412
Average Annual Wages of Health Care Practitioners and
    Technicians in 2006 413
Physicians in 2006 414
Rate of Physicians in 2006 415
Percent of Physicians Who Are Female: 2006 416
Percent of Physicians Under 35 Years Old in 2006 417
Percent of Physicians 65 Years Old and Older in 2006 . . . 418
Physicians in Patient Care in 2006 419
Rate of Physicians in Patient Care in 2006 420
Physicians in Primary Care in 2006 421
Rate of Physicians in Primary Care in 2006 422
Percent of Physicians in Primary Care in 2006 423
Percent of Population Lacking Access to Primary Care
    in 2007 424
Physicians in General/Family Practice in 2006 425
Rate of Physicians in General/Family Practice in 2006 . . . 426
Average Annual Wages of Family and General
    Practitioners in 2006 427

Percent of Physicians Who Are Specialists in 2006 428
Physicians in Medical Specialties in 2006 429
Rate of Nonfederal Physicians in Medical Specialties
    in 2006 430
Physicians in Internal Medicine in 2006 431
Rate of Physicians in Internal Medicine in 2006 432
Physicians in Pediatrics in 2006 433
Rate of Physicians in Pediatrics in 2006 434
Physicians in Surgical Specialties in 2006 435
Rate of Physicians in Surgical Specialties in 2006 436
Average Annual Wages of Surgeons in 2006 437
Physicians in General Surgery in 2006 438
Rate of Physicians in General Surgery in 2006 439
Physicians in Obstetrics and Gynecology in 2006 440
Rate of Physicians in Obstetrics and Gynecology
    in 2006 441
Physicians in Ophthalmology in 2006 442
Rate of Physicians in Ophthalmology in 2006 443
Physicians in Orthopedic Surgery in 2006 444
Rate of Physicians in Orthopedic Surgery in 2006 445
Physicians in Plastic Surgery in 2006 446
Rate of Physicians in Plastic Surgery in 2006 447
Physicians in Other Specialties in 2006 448
Rate of Physicians in Other Specialties in 2006 449
Physicians in Anesthesiology in 2006 450
Rate of Physicians in Anesthesiology in 2006 451
Physicians in Psychiatry in 2006 452
Rate of Physicians in Psychiatry in 2006 453
Percent of Population Lacking Access to Mental Health
    Care in 2007 454
International Medical School Graduates in 2006 455
International Medical School Graduates as a Percent of
    Physicians in 2006 456
Osteopathic Physicians in 2007 457
Rate of Osteopathic Physicians in 2007 458
Podiatrists in 2006 459
Rate of Podiatrists in 2006 460
Average Annual Wages of Podiatrists in 2006 461
Doctors of Chiropractic in 2006 462
Rate of Doctors of Chiropractic in 2006 463
Average Annual Wages of Chiropractors in 2006 464
Physician Assistants in Clinical Practice in 2008 465
Rate of Physician Assistants in Clinical Practice
    in 2007 466
Average Annual Wages of Physician Assistants
    in 2006 467
Registered Nurses in 2006 468
Rate of Registered Nurses in 2006 469
Average Annual Wages of Registered Nurses in 2006 470
Licensed Practical and Licensed Vocational Nurses
    in 2006 471
Rate of Licensed Practical and Licensed Vocational
    Nurses in 2006 472
Average Annual Wages of Licensed Practical and
    Licensed Vocational Nurses in 2006 473
Physical Therapists in 2006 474
Rate of Physical Therapists in 2006 475
Average Annual Wages of Physical Therapists in 2006 . . . 476

Dentists in 2005 477
Rate of Dentists in 2005 478
Average Annual Wages of Dentists in 2006 479
Percent of Population Lacking Access to Dental Care
    in 2007 480
Pharmacists in 2006 481
Rate of Pharmacists in 2006 482
Average Annual Wages of Pharmacists in 2006 483
Optometrists in 2006 484
Rate of Optometrists in 2006 485
Average Annual Wages of Optometrists in 2006 486
Emergency Medical Technicians and Paramedics
    in 2006 487
Rate of Emergency Medical Technicians and Paramedics
    in 2006 488
Average Annual Wages of Emergency Medical
    Technicians and Paramedics in 2006 489
Employment in Health Care Support Industries in 2006 .. 490
Rate of Employees in Health Care Support Industries
    in 2006 491
Average Annual Wages of Employees in Health Care
    Support Industries in 2006 492

VII. PHYSICAL FITNESS

Users of Exercise Equipment in 2006 495
Participants in Golf in 2006 496
Participants in Running/Jogging in 2006 497
Participants in Swimming in 2006 498
Participants in Tennis in 2006 499
Alcohol Consumption in 2005 500
Adult Per Capita Alcohol Consumption in 2005 501
Apparent Beer Consumption in 2005 502
Adult Per Capita Beer Consumption in 2005 503
Wine Consumption in 2005 504
Adult Per Capita Wine Consumption in 2005 505
Distilled Spirits Consumption in 2005 506
Adult Per Capita Distilled Spirits Consumption in 2005 .. 507
Percent of Adults Who Do Not Drink Alcohol: 2006 508
Percent of Adults Who Are Binge Drinkers: 2006 509
Percent of Adults Who Smoke: 2006 510
Percent of Men Who Smoke: 2006 511
Percent of Women Who Smoke: 2006 512
Percent of Adults Who Are Former Smokers: 2006 513
Percent of Adults Who Have Never Smoked: 2006 514
Percent of Population Who Are Illicit Drug Users: 2005 .. 515
Percent of Adults Overweight: 2006 516
Percent of Adults Obese: 2006 517
Percent of Adults Overweight or Obese: 2006 518
Percent of Adults Who Do Not Exercise: 2006 519
Percent of Adults Who Exercise Vigorously: 2005 520
Percent of Adults Who Are Disabled: 2005 521
Percent of Adults with High Blood Pressure: 2005 522
Percent of Adults with High Cholesterol: 2005 523
Percent of Adults Who Have Visited a Dentist or
    Dental Clinic: 2006 524
Percent of Adults 65 Years Old and Older Who Have
    Lost All Their Natural Teeth: 2006 525
Percent of Adults Who Average Five or More Servings of
    Fruits and Vegetables Each Day: 2005............. 526
Percent of Adults Rating Their Health as Fair or Poor
    in 2006 527
Safety Belt Usage Rate in 2006 528

VIII. APPENDIX

Population in 2007 530
Population in 2006 531
Male Population in 2006 532
Female Population in 2006 533

Preface

Health care continuously ranks as a prominent subject of consumer concern, whether in regard to an individual searching for the best quality care in a doctor, a company selecting the most cost-effective insurance for its employees, or the government subsidizing the medical care of seniors. With the 2008 presidential candidates presenting their individual health care plans, stories about wellness and obesity dominating daily newspapers, and businesses scrambling annually to find affordable health care insurance for their employees, concerns about health care garner headlines and attention across all segments of society.

Access to straightforward, unbiased, and reliable health care information is more important than ever. This newly revised edition of *Health Care State Rankings* provides a large collection of relevant, user-friendly health care data for each of the fifty United States. Information is compared state-by-state and includes births and reproductive health, deaths, disease, insurance and finance, health care providers, facilities, and physical fitness. *Health Care State Rankings* serves as an essential information tool for researchers, librarians, community leaders, and concerned citizens.

Important Notes about *Health Care State Rankings 2008*

Health Care State Rankings presents information from government and private sector sources in one user-friendly volume. Our goal is to translate complicated and often convoluted health care data into easy-to-understand tables that allow meaningful state comparisons. For each new edition, we reexamine every table and update the material as needed.

We make every effort to present the data in *Health Care State Rankings* as simply and straightforwardly as possible. Data are presented in both alphabetical and rank order, so readers can easily locate data for a particular state and just as quickly learn where that state ranks among the others. National totals, rates, and percentages are prominently displayed at the top of each table. Source information and other important notes are shown clearly at the bottom of each page. Every other line is shaded in gray for easy reading. In addition, we provide numerous information-finding tools: a thorough table of contents, table listings at the beginning of each chapter, and a detailed index.

Also included is a directory of data sources we used, providing addresses, phone numbers, and Web sites.

The statistics shown in *Health Care State Rankings 2008* require no additional calculations to convert them from millions, thousands, and so forth. All states are ranked from highest to lowest, with any ties among the states listed alphabetically for a given ranking. Negative numbers are reported in parentheses. In tables with national totals (as opposed to rates, per capita data, or the like) a separate column shows the percentage of the national total represented by each state. This column, "% of USA," is particularly interesting when compared with a state's share of the nation's population for a particular year. The appendix contains population tables to facilitate these comparisons.

Among the more interesting tables in *Health Care State Rankings* are those in which we have combined data from various sources. These tables are sourced as "CQ Press using data from. . ." Health care expenditure data, rates of disease, and alcohol consumption rates are just a few examples of these editor-generated statistical comparisons.

Which State Is Healthiest?

We take great pride in presenting straightforward and unbiased statistics. Each year, we also conduct an analysis of the numbers in an effort to determine which state is the healthiest. The results of this analysis—based on twenty-one factors reflecting the general health of each state's population, access to health care providers, affordability of health care, and such measures of preventive health care as smoking and obesity—appear on page xv.

Exciting Changes for Morgan Quitno Press

This edition of *Health Care State Rankings* ushers in a new and exciting era for our company and our customers. Effective May 2007, Morgan Quitno's reference books are published by CQ Press in Washington, D.C. A division of Congressional Quarterly Inc., CQ Press is the premier publisher of books, directories, periodicals, and electronic products on American government and politics.

While our publishing structure has changed, our commitment to bringing the highest quality publications to our customers has not. *Health Care State Rankings* is one of six titles in our series of easy-to-use, affordable reference publications.

Finally, we are so very thankful for the many librarians, government, and health care industry officials who have helped us understand and decipher data year after year. Thanks also to you, our readers, for helping us keep our books relevant and useful. We sincerely appreciate your support and look forward to providing you with top quality reference titles for many years to come.

Kathleen O'Leary Morgan and Scott Morgan
Editors

Healthiest State Award

After nine years, Minnesota is once again the Healthiest State in America. The North Star State last topped our Healthiest State rankings in 1999. It ousts Vermont, which held the title for six of the last seven years. Joining Minnesota to round out the top five states are New Hampshire, Vermont, Maine, and Massachusetts.

At the opposite end of the rankings, Mississippi falls to last place. Joining Mississippi at the less healthy end of the list are Louisiana, New Mexico, Nevada, and Florida.

Methodology

The Healthiest State designation is awarded based on twenty-one factors chosen from over 500 provided in the 2008 edition of *Health Care State Rankings*. These factors reflect access to health care providers, an emphasis on preventive care, the affordability of health care, and a generally healthy population (see box below.)

To determine this year's award, we considered the same twenty-one factors as we did for 2007. We divided the factors

---

POSITIVE (+) AND NEGATIVE (–) FACTORS CONSIDERED:

1. Births of Low Birthweight as a Percent of All Births (page 16) –
2. Teenage Birth Rate (page 36) –
3. Percent of Mothers Receiving Late or No Prenatal Care (page 66) –
4. Age-Adjusted Death Rate (page 96) –
5. Infant Mortality Rate (page 102) –
6. Age-Adjusted Death Rate by Malignant Neoplasms (page 160) –
7. Age-Adjusted Death Rate by Suicide (page 184) –
8. Average Annual Family Coverage Health Insurance Premium (page 244) –
9. Percent of Population Not Covered by Health Insurance (page 248) –
10. Percent of Children Not Covered by Health Insurance (page 252) –
11. Estimated Rate of New Cancer Cases (page 337) –
12. AIDS Rate (page 365) –
13. Sexually Transmitted Disease Rate (page 398) –
14. Percent of Population Lacking Access to Primary Care (page 424) –
15. Percent of Adults Who Are Binge Drinkers (page 509) –
16. Percent of Adults Who Smoke (page 510) –
17. Percent of Adults Obese (page 517) –
18. Percent of Adults Who Do Not Exercise (page 519) –
19. Beds in Community Hospitals per 100,000 Population (page 203) +
20. Percent of Children Aged 19–35 Months Immunized (page 394) +
21. Safety Belt Usage Rate (page 528) +

into two groups: those that are "negative"—a high ranking would be considered bad for a state—and those that are "positive"—a high ranking would be considered good for a state. We processed rates for each of the twenty-one factors through a formula that measures how a state compares to the national average for a given category. The formula also takes the positive and negative nature of each factor into account. Once these computations were made, we weighted the factors equally, then added them together to get each state's final score ("SUM" on the table that follows). This way, each state is assessed based on how it stacks up against the national average: The farther a state's health ranking is below the national average, the lower (and less healthy) the state ranks. Conversely, the farther it is above the national average, the higher (and healthier) the state ranks. We use the same methodology for our Smartest State and Safest/Most Dangerous State and City awards.

The table that follows shows how each state fared in the 2008 Healthiest State Award as well as its placement in 2007. We expect that this award will promote vigorous discussions among citizens and state leaders. While our selection of factors clearly affects the final rankings, we believe that the rankings provide a solid measurement of how states are faring with regard to health care.

Congratulations to the very healthy citizens and leaders of Minnesota!

—THE EDITORS

HEALTH SCORES

RANK	STATE	SUM*	2007	RANK	STATE	SUM*	2007
1	Minnesota	19.84	2	26	West Virginia	2.17	25
2	New Hampshire	17.46	5	27	Indiana	1.95	33
3	Vermont	15.86	1	28	Wyoming	1.16	30
4	Maine	15.81	4	29	Colorado	0.44	28
5	Massachusetts	15.68	3	30	New York	−0.16	27
6	Iowa	15.36	7	31	North Carolina	−0.20	31
7	Nebraska	14.91	6	32	Kentucky	−0.59	29
8	Hawaii	14.80	9	33	Illinois	−1.16	32
9	North Dakota	12.94	12	34	Missouri	−1.31	34
10	Rhode Island	12.58	11	35	Maryland	−1.76	35
11	Connecticut	12.05	13	36	Tennessee	−4.23	38
12	Utah	11.85	8	37	Arkansas	−5.39	37
13	Washington	10.79	14	38	Alaska	−5.81	36
14	Wisconsin	8.98	15	39	Texas	−9.18	43
15	Kansas	8.47	10	40	Arizona	−10.24	42
16	New Jersey	7.73	16	41	Delaware	−10.71	39
17	California	6.85	19	42	Alabama	−11.11	40
18	Pennsylvania	6.47	23	43	Oklahoma	−11.54	41
19	Oregon	6.44	17	44	South Carolina	−11.55	45
20	Virginia	5.18	18	45	Georgia	−11.56	44
21	Ohio	4.73	20	46	Florida	−12.15	46
22	Michigan	4.62	21	47	Nevada	−19.28	47
23	Idaho	3.95	24	48	New Mexico	−21.60	49
24	South Dakota	3.72	22	49	Louisiana	−25.72	50
25	Montana	2.55	26	50	Mississippi	−26.26	48

*Total from combining rates in the twenty-one factors considered. See page xv.

I. Births and Reproductive Health

Births in 2006 3
Birth Rate in 2006 4
Percent Change in Birth Rate: 1997 to 2006 5
Births in 2005 6
Birth Rate in 2005 7
Fertility Rate in 2006 8
Births to White Women in 2006 9
White Births as a Percent of All Births in 2006 10
Births to Black Women in 2006 11
Black Births as a Percent of All Births in 2006 12
Births to Hispanic Women in 2006 13
Hispanic Births as a Percent of All Births in 2006 14
Births of Low Birthweight in 2006 15
Births of Low Birthweight as a Percent of All Births
    in 2006 16
Births of Low Birthweight to White Women in 2006 17
Births of Low Birthweight to White Women as a Percent
    of All Births to White Women in 2006 18
Births of Low Birthweight to Black Women in 2006 19
Births of Low Birthweight to Black Women as a Percent
    of All Births to Black Women in 2006 20
Births of Low Birthweight to Hispanic Women in 2006 . . . 21
Births of Low Birthweight to Hispanic Women as a
    Percent of All Births to Hispanic Women in 2006 22
Births to Unmarried Women in 2006 23
Births to Unmarried Women as a Percent of All Births
    in 2006 24
Births to Unmarried White Women in 2006 25
Births to Unmarried White Women as a Percent of
    All Births to White Women in 2006 26
Births to Unmarried Black Women in 2006 27
Births to Unmarried Black Women as a Percent of
    All Births to Black Women in 2006 28
Births to Unmarried Hispanic Women in 2006 29
Births to Unmarried Hispanic Women as a Percent of
    All Births to Hispanic Women in 2006 30
Pregnancy Rate in 2004 31
Teenage Pregnancy Rate in 2004 32
Percent Change in Teenage Pregnancy Rate:
    2000 to 2004 33

Births to Teenage Mothers in 2006 34
Births to Teenage Mothers as a Percent of Births in 2006 . . 35
Teenage Birth Rate in 2006 36
Percent Change in Teenage Birth Rate: 2002 to 2006 37
Births to Teenage Mothers in 2005 38
Teenage Birth Rate in 2005 39
Births to White Teenage Mothers in 2005 40
White Teenage Birth Rate in 2005 41
Births to White Teenage Mothers as a Percent of White
    Births in 2005 42
Births to Black Teenage Mothers in 2005 43
Black Teenage Birth Rate in 2005 44
Births to Black Teenage Mothers as a Percent of Black
    Births in 2005 45
Births to Young Teenagers: 2003 to 2005 46
Young Teen Birthrate: 2003 to 2005 47
Births to Women 35 to 54 Years Old in 2005 48
Births to Women 35 to 54 Years Old as a Percent of All
    Births in 2005 49
Births by Vaginal Delivery in 2006 50
Percent of Births by Vaginal Delivery in 2006 51
Births by Cesarean Delivery in 2006 52
Percent of Births by Cesarean Delivery in 2006 53
Percent Change in Rate of Cesarean Births:
    2002 to 2006 54
Percent of Births That Are Pre-Term in 2006 55
Twin Birth Rate: 2002–2005 56
Assisted Reproductive Technology Procedures in 2004 . . . 57
Infants Born from Assisted Reproductive Technology
    Procedures in 2004 58
Percent of Assisted Reproductive Technology
    Procedures That Resulted in Live Births in 2004 59
Percent of Total Live Births Resulting from Assisted
    Reproductive Technology Procedures in 2004 60
Percent of Assisted Reproductive Technology Procedure
    Infants Born in Multiple Birth Deliveries in 2004 61
Percent of Mothers Beginning Prenatal Care in First
    Trimester in 2005 62
Percent of White Mothers Beginning Prenatal Care in
    First Trimester in 2005 63

Percent of Black Mothers Beginning Prenatal Care in
First Trimester in 2005 64

Percent of Hispanic Mothers Beginning Prenatal Care
in First Trimester in 2005 65

Percent of Mothers Receiving Late or No Prenatal Care
in 2005 66

Percent of White Mothers Receiving Late or No Prenatal
Care in 2005 67

Percent of Black Mothers Receiving Late or No Prenatal
Care in 2005 68

Percent of Hispanic Mothers Receiving Late or
No Prenatal Care in 2005 69

Reported Legal Abortions in 2004 70

Percent Change in Reported Legal Abortions:
2000 to 2004 71

Reported Legal Abortions per 1,000 Live Births
in 2004 72

Reported Legal Abortions per 1,000 Women Ages
15 to 44 in 2004 73

Percent of Legal Abortions Obtained by Out-Of-State
Residents in 2004 74

Percent of Reported Legal Abortions That Were
First-Time Abortions: 2004 75

Percent of Reported Legal Abortions Obtained by
White Women in 2004 76

Percent of Reported Legal Abortions Obtained by
Black Women in 2004 77

Percent of Reported Legal Abortions Obtained by
Hispanic Women in 2004 78

Percent of Reported Legal Abortions Obtained by
Married Women in 2004 79

Percent of Reported Legal Abortions Obtained by
Unmarried Women in 2004 80

Reported Legal Abortions Obtained by Teenagers
in 2004 81

Percent of Reported Legal Abortions Obtained by
Teenagers in 2004 82

Reported Legal Abortions Obtained by Teenagers
17 Years and Younger in 2004 83

Percent of Reported Legal Abortions Obtained by
Teenagers 17 Years and Younger in 2004 84

Percent of Teenage Abortions Obtained by Teenagers
17 Years and Younger in 2004 85

Reported Legal Abortions Performed at 12 Weeks or
Less of Gestation in 2004 86

Percent of Reported Legal Abortions Performed at
12 Weeks or Less of Gestation in 2004 87

Reported Legal Abortions Performed at or after
21 Weeks of Gestation in 2004 88

Percent of Reported Legal Abortions Performed at or
after 21 Weeks of Gestation in 2004 89

Births in 2006

National Total = 4,265,996 Live Births*

ALPHA ORDER

RANK	STATE	BIRTHS	% of USA
24	Alabama	63,235	1.5%
47	Alaska	10,991	0.3%
13	Arizona	102,475	2.4%
32	Arkansas	40,973	1.0%
1	California	562,431	13.2%
22	Colorado	70,750	1.7%
31	Connecticut	41,807	1.0%
45	Delaware	11,988	0.3%
4	Florida	236,882	5.6%
8	Georgia	148,619	3.5%
40	Hawaii	18,982	0.4%
38	Idaho	24,184	0.6%
5	Illinois	180,583	4.2%
14	Indiana	88,674	2.1%
34	Iowa	40,610	1.0%
33	Kansas	40,964	1.0%
26	Kentucky	58,291	1.4%
23	Louisiana	63,399	1.5%
42	Maine	14,151	0.3%
19	Maryland	77,478	1.8%
18	Massachusetts	77,769	1.8%
10	Michigan	127,476	3.0%
20	Minnesota	73,559	1.7%
30	Mississippi	46,069	1.1%
17	Missouri	81,388	1.9%
43	Montana	12,506	0.3%
37	Nebraska	26,733	0.6%
35	Nevada	40,085	0.9%
41	New Hampshire	14,380	0.3%
11	New Jersey	115,006	2.7%
36	New Mexico	29,937	0.7%
3	New York	250,091	5.9%
9	North Carolina	127,841	3.0%
48	North Dakota	8,622	0.2%
6	Ohio	150,590	3.5%
27	Oklahoma	54,018	1.3%
29	Oregon	48,717	1.1%
7	Pennsylvania	149,082	3.5%
44	Rhode Island	12,379	0.3%
25	South Carolina	62,271	1.5%
46	South Dakota	11,917	0.3%
16	Tennessee	84,345	2.0%
2	Texas	399,612	9.4%
28	Utah	53,499	1.3%
50	Vermont	6,509	0.2%
12	Virginia	107,817	2.5%
15	Washington	86,848	2.0%
39	West Virginia	20,928	0.5%
21	Wisconsin	72,335	1.7%
49	Wyoming	7,670	0.2%

RANK ORDER

RANK	STATE	BIRTHS	% of USA
1	California	562,431	13.2%
2	Texas	399,612	9.4%
3	New York	250,091	5.9%
4	Florida	236,882	5.6%
5	Illinois	180,583	4.2%
6	Ohio	150,590	3.5%
7	Pennsylvania	149,082	3.5%
8	Georgia	148,619	3.5%
9	North Carolina	127,841	3.0%
10	Michigan	127,476	3.0%
11	New Jersey	115,006	2.7%
12	Virginia	107,817	2.5%
13	Arizona	102,475	2.4%
14	Indiana	88,674	2.1%
15	Washington	86,848	2.0%
16	Tennessee	84,345	2.0%
17	Missouri	81,388	1.9%
18	Massachusetts	77,769	1.8%
19	Maryland	77,478	1.8%
20	Minnesota	73,559	1.7%
21	Wisconsin	72,335	1.7%
22	Colorado	70,750	1.7%
23	Louisiana	63,399	1.5%
24	Alabama	63,235	1.5%
25	South Carolina	62,271	1.5%
26	Kentucky	58,291	1.4%
27	Oklahoma	54,018	1.3%
28	Utah	53,499	1.3%
29	Oregon	48,717	1.1%
30	Mississippi	46,069	1.1%
31	Connecticut	41,807	1.0%
32	Arkansas	40,973	1.0%
33	Kansas	40,964	1.0%
34	Iowa	40,610	1.0%
35	Nevada	40,085	0.9%
36	New Mexico	29,937	0.7%
37	Nebraska	26,733	0.6%
38	Idaho	24,184	0.6%
39	West Virginia	20,928	0.5%
40	Hawaii	18,982	0.4%
41	New Hampshire	14,380	0.3%
42	Maine	14,151	0.3%
43	Montana	12,506	0.3%
44	Rhode Island	12,379	0.3%
45	Delaware	11,988	0.3%
46	South Dakota	11,917	0.3%
47	Alaska	10,991	0.3%
48	North Dakota	8,622	0.2%
49	Wyoming	7,670	0.2%
50	Vermont	6,509	0.2%
	District of Columbia	8,529	0.2%

Source: U.S. Department of Health and Human Services, National Center for Health Statistics
"National Vital Statistics Reports" (Vol. 56, No. 7, December 5, 2007, http://www.cdc.gov/nchs/births.htm)
*Preliminary data by state of residence.

Birth Rate in 2006

National Rate = 14.2 Live Births per 1,000 Population*

ALPHA ORDER				RANK ORDER		
RANK	STATE	RATE		RANK	STATE	RATE
31	Alabama	13.7		1	Utah	21.0
5	Alaska	16.4		2	Texas	17.0
3	Arizona	16.6		3	Arizona	16.6
19	Arkansas	14.6		4	Idaho	16.5
9	California	15.4		5	Alaska	16.4
14	Colorado	14.9		6	Nevada	16.1
45	Connecticut	11.9		7	Georgia	15.9
25	Delaware	14.0		8	Mississippi	15.8
38	Florida	13.1		9	California	15.4
7	Georgia	15.9		10	New Mexico	15.3
16	Hawaii	14.8		11	South Dakota	15.2
4	Idaho	16.5		12	Nebraska	15.1
23	Illinois	14.1		12	Oklahoma	15.1
25	Indiana	14.0		14	Colorado	14.9
32	Iowa	13.6		14	Wyoming	14.9
16	Kansas	14.8		16	Hawaii	14.8
28	Kentucky	13.9		16	Kansas	14.8
16	Louisiana	14.8		16	Louisiana	14.8
49	Maine	10.7		19	Arkansas	14.6
30	Maryland	13.8		20	North Carolina	14.4
43	Massachusetts	12.1		20	South Carolina	14.4
42	Michigan	12.6		22	Minnesota	14.2
22	Minnesota	14.2		23	Illinois	14.1
8	Mississippi	15.8		23	Virginia	14.1
28	Missouri	13.9		25	Delaware	14.0
35	Montana	13.2		25	Indiana	14.0
12	Nebraska	15.1		25	Tennessee	14.0
6	Nevada	16.1		28	Kentucky	13.9
48	New Hampshire	10.9		28	Missouri	13.9
35	New Jersey	13.2		30	Maryland	13.8
10	New Mexico	15.3		31	Alabama	13.7
40	New York	13.0		32	Iowa	13.6
20	North Carolina	14.4		32	North Dakota	13.6
32	North Dakota	13.6		32	Washington	13.6
38	Ohio	13.1		35	Montana	13.2
12	Oklahoma	15.1		35	New Jersey	13.2
35	Oregon	13.2		35	Oregon	13.2
44	Pennsylvania	12.0		38	Florida	13.1
46	Rhode Island	11.6		38	Ohio	13.1
20	South Carolina	14.4		40	New York	13.0
11	South Dakota	15.2		40	Wisconsin	13.0
25	Tennessee	14.0		42	Michigan	12.6
2	Texas	17.0		43	Massachusetts	12.1
1	Utah	21.0		44	Pennsylvania	12.0
50	Vermont	10.4		45	Connecticut	11.9
23	Virginia	14.1		46	Rhode Island	11.6
32	Washington	13.6		47	West Virginia	11.5
47	West Virginia	11.5		48	New Hampshire	10.9
40	Wisconsin	13.0		49	Maine	10.7
14	Wyoming	14.9		50	Vermont	10.4
					District of Columbia	14.7

Source: U.S. Department of Health and Human Services, National Center for Health Statistics
"National Vital Statistics Reports" (Vol. 56, No. 7, December 5, 2007, http://www.cdc.gov/nchs/births.htm)
*Preliminary data by state of residence.

Percent Change in Birth Rate: 1997 to 2006

National Percent Change = 0.0% Change*

ALPHA ORDER

RANK	STATE	PERCENT CHANGE
37	Alabama	(1.4)
31	Alaska	1.2
17	Arizona	3.8
16	Arkansas	4.3
44	California	(4.9)
8	Colorado	5.7
49	Connecticut	(7.8)
25	Delaware	2.9
22	Florida	3.1
20	Georgia	3.2
27	Hawaii	2.8
4	Idaho	9.3
43	Illinois	(4.7)
34	Indiana	0.0
6	Iowa	7.1
14	Kansas	5.0
23	Kentucky	3.0
35	Louisiana	(0.7)
39	Maine	(1.8)
29	Maryland	1.5
46	Massachusetts	(6.2)
48	Michigan	(7.4)
12	Minnesota	5.2
11	Mississippi	5.3
23	Missouri	3.0
5	Montana	8.2
3	Nebraska	9.4
12	Nevada	5.2
50	New Hampshire	(9.2)
42	New Jersey	(4.3)
30	New Mexico	1.3
45	New York	(5.8)
25	North Carolina	2.9
10	North Dakota	5.4
40	Ohio	(3.0)
9	Oklahoma	5.6
36	Oregon	(0.8)
28	Pennsylvania	1.7
41	Rhode Island	(4.1)
7	South Carolina	6.7
2	South Dakota	10.9
18	Tennessee	3.7
33	Texas	0.6
19	Utah	3.4
47	Vermont	(6.3)
15	Virginia	4.4
37	Washington	(1.4)
32	West Virginia	0.9
20	Wisconsin	3.2
1	Wyoming	14.6

RANK ORDER

RANK	STATE	PERCENT CHANGE
1	Wyoming	14.6
2	South Dakota	10.9
3	Nebraska	9.4
4	Idaho	9.3
5	Montana	8.2
6	Iowa	7.1
7	South Carolina	6.7
8	Colorado	5.7
9	Oklahoma	5.6
10	North Dakota	5.4
11	Mississippi	5.3
12	Minnesota	5.2
12	Nevada	5.2
14	Kansas	5.0
15	Virginia	4.4
16	Arkansas	4.3
17	Arizona	3.8
18	Tennessee	3.7
19	Utah	3.4
20	Georgia	3.2
20	Wisconsin	3.2
22	Florida	3.1
23	Kentucky	3.0
23	Missouri	3.0
25	Delaware	2.9
25	North Carolina	2.9
27	Hawaii	2.8
28	Pennsylvania	1.7
29	Maryland	1.5
30	New Mexico	1.3
31	Alaska	1.2
32	West Virginia	0.9
33	Texas	0.6
34	Indiana	0.0
35	Louisiana	(0.7)
36	Oregon	(0.8)
37	Alabama	(1.4)
37	Washington	(1.4)
39	Maine	(1.8)
40	Ohio	(3.0)
41	Rhode Island	(4.1)
42	New Jersey	(4.3)
43	Illinois	(4.7)
44	California	(4.9)
45	New York	(5.8)
46	Massachusetts	(6.2)
47	Vermont	(6.3)
48	Michigan	(7.4)
49	Connecticut	(7.8)
50	New Hampshire	(9.2)

| | District of Columbia | 5.0 |

Source: CQ Press using data from U.S. Department of Health and Human Services, National Center for Health Statistics
"National Vital Statistics Reports" (Vol. 56, No. 7, December 5, 2007, http://www.cdc.gov/nchs/births.htm)
"VitalStats" (http://www.cdc.gov/nchs/datawh/vitalstats/VitalStats.htm)
*By state of residence.

Births in 2005

National Total = 4,138,349 Live Births*

ALPHA ORDER

RANK	STATE	BIRTHS	% of USA
24	Alabama	60,453	1.5%
47	Alaska	10,459	0.3%
13	Arizona	96,199	2.3%
34	Arkansas	39,208	0.9%
1	California	548,882	13.3%
22	Colorado	68,944	1.7%
31	Connecticut	41,718	1.0%
44	Delaware	11,643	0.3%
4	Florida	226,240	5.5%
8	Georgia	142,200	3.4%
40	Hawaii	17,924	0.4%
38	Idaho	23,062	0.6%
5	Illinois	179,020	4.3%
14	Indiana	87,193	2.1%
33	Iowa	39,311	0.9%
32	Kansas	39,888	1.0%
26	Kentucky	56,444	1.4%
23	Louisiana	60,937	1.5%
42	Maine	14,112	0.3%
19	Maryland	74,980	1.8%
18	Massachusetts	76,865	1.9%
9	Michigan	127,706	3.1%
21	Minnesota	70,919	1.7%
30	Mississippi	42,395	1.0%
17	Missouri	78,618	1.9%
45	Montana	11,583	0.3%
37	Nebraska	26,145	0.6%
35	Nevada	37,268	0.9%
41	New Hampshire	14,420	0.3%
11	New Jersey	113,776	2.7%
36	New Mexico	28,835	0.7%
3	New York	246,351	6.0%
10	North Carolina	123,096	3.0%
48	North Dakota	8,390	0.2%
6	Ohio	148,388	3.6%
27	Oklahoma	51,801	1.3%
29	Oregon	45,922	1.1%
7	Pennsylvania	145,383	3.5%
43	Rhode Island	12,697	0.3%
25	South Carolina	57,711	1.4%
46	South Dakota	11,462	0.3%
16	Tennessee	81,747	2.0%
2	Texas	385,915	9.3%
28	Utah	51,556	1.2%
50	Vermont	6,295	0.2%
12	Virginia	104,555	2.5%
15	Washington	82,703	2.0%
39	West Virginia	20,836	0.5%
20	Wisconsin	70,984	1.7%
49	Wyoming	7,239	0.2%

RANK ORDER

RANK	STATE	BIRTHS	% of USA
1	California	548,882	13.3%
2	Texas	385,915	9.3%
3	New York	246,351	6.0%
4	Florida	226,240	5.5%
5	Illinois	179,020	4.3%
6	Ohio	148,388	3.6%
7	Pennsylvania	145,383	3.5%
8	Georgia	142,200	3.4%
9	Michigan	127,706	3.1%
10	North Carolina	123,096	3.0%
11	New Jersey	113,776	2.7%
12	Virginia	104,555	2.5%
13	Arizona	96,199	2.3%
14	Indiana	87,193	2.1%
15	Washington	82,703	2.0%
16	Tennessee	81,747	2.0%
17	Missouri	78,618	1.9%
18	Massachusetts	76,865	1.9%
19	Maryland	74,980	1.8%
20	Wisconsin	70,984	1.7%
21	Minnesota	70,919	1.7%
22	Colorado	68,944	1.7%
23	Louisiana	60,937	1.5%
24	Alabama	60,453	1.5%
25	South Carolina	57,711	1.4%
26	Kentucky	56,444	1.4%
27	Oklahoma	51,801	1.3%
28	Utah	51,556	1.2%
29	Oregon	45,922	1.1%
30	Mississippi	42,395	1.0%
31	Connecticut	41,718	1.0%
32	Kansas	39,888	1.0%
33	Iowa	39,311	0.9%
34	Arkansas	39,208	0.9%
35	Nevada	37,268	0.9%
36	New Mexico	28,835	0.7%
37	Nebraska	26,145	0.6%
38	Idaho	23,062	0.6%
39	West Virginia	20,836	0.5%
40	Hawaii	17,924	0.4%
41	New Hampshire	14,420	0.3%
42	Maine	14,112	0.3%
43	Rhode Island	12,697	0.3%
44	Delaware	11,643	0.3%
45	Montana	11,583	0.3%
46	South Dakota	11,462	0.3%
47	Alaska	10,459	0.3%
48	North Dakota	8,390	0.2%
49	Wyoming	7,239	0.2%
50	Vermont	6,295	0.2%
	District of Columbia	7,971	0.2%

Source: U.S. Department of Health and Human Services, National Center for Health Statistics
    "National Vital Statistics Reports" (Vol. 56, No. 6, December 5, 2007, http://www.cdc.gov/nchs/births.htm)
*Final data by state of residence.

Birth Rate in 2005

National Rate = 14.0 Live Births per 1,000 Population*

ALPHA ORDER

RANK	STATE	RATE
31	Alabama	13.3
5	Alaska	15.8
3	Arizona	16.2
18	Arkansas	14.1
8	California	15.2
11	Colorado	14.8
44	Connecticut	11.9
22	Delaware	13.8
39	Florida	12.7
6	Georgia	15.7
18	Hawaii	14.1
4	Idaho	16.1
20	Illinois	14.0
21	Indiana	13.9
31	Iowa	13.3
14	Kansas	14.5
28	Kentucky	13.5
28	Louisiana	13.5
49	Maine	10.7
30	Maryland	13.4
43	Massachusetts	12.0
40	Michigan	12.6
22	Minnesota	13.8
14	Mississippi	14.5
26	Missouri	13.6
42	Montana	12.4
10	Nebraska	14.9
7	Nevada	15.4
48	New Hampshire	11.0
35	New Jersey	13.1
9	New Mexico	15.0
37	New York	12.8
16	North Carolina	14.2
33	North Dakota	13.2
36	Ohio	12.9
13	Oklahoma	14.6
40	Oregon	12.6
46	Pennsylvania	11.7
45	Rhode Island	11.8
26	South Carolina	13.6
11	South Dakota	14.8
25	Tennessee	13.7
2	Texas	16.9
1	Utah	20.9
50	Vermont	10.1
22	Virginia	13.8
33	Washington	13.2
47	West Virginia	11.5
37	Wisconsin	12.8
16	Wyoming	14.2

RANK ORDER

RANK	STATE	RATE
1	Utah	20.9
2	Texas	16.9
3	Arizona	16.2
4	Idaho	16.1
5	Alaska	15.8
6	Georgia	15.7
7	Nevada	15.4
8	California	15.2
9	New Mexico	15.0
10	Nebraska	14.9
11	Colorado	14.8
11	South Dakota	14.8
13	Oklahoma	14.6
14	Kansas	14.5
14	Mississippi	14.5
16	North Carolina	14.2
16	Wyoming	14.2
18	Arkansas	14.1
18	Hawaii	14.1
20	Illinois	14.0
21	Indiana	13.9
22	Delaware	13.8
22	Minnesota	13.8
22	Virginia	13.8
25	Tennessee	13.7
26	Missouri	13.6
26	South Carolina	13.6
28	Kentucky	13.5
28	Louisiana	13.5
30	Maryland	13.4
31	Alabama	13.3
31	Iowa	13.3
33	North Dakota	13.2
33	Washington	13.2
35	New Jersey	13.1
36	Ohio	12.9
37	New York	12.8
37	Wisconsin	12.8
39	Florida	12.7
40	Michigan	12.6
40	Oregon	12.6
42	Montana	12.4
43	Massachusetts	12.0
44	Connecticut	11.9
45	Rhode Island	11.8
46	Pennsylvania	11.7
47	West Virginia	11.5
48	New Hampshire	11.0
49	Maine	10.7
50	Vermont	10.1
	District of Columbia	14.5

Source: U.S. Department of Health and Human Services, National Center for Health Statistics
"National Vital Statistics Reports" (Vol. 56, No. 6, December 5, 2007, http://www.cdc.gov/nchs/births.htm)
*Final data by state of residence.

Fertility Rate in 2006

National Rate = 68.5 Live Births per 1,000 Women 15 to 44 Years Old*

ALPHA ORDER

RANK ORDER

RANK	STATE	RATE	RANK	STATE	RATE
32	Alabama	67.0	1	Utah	94.1
7	Alaska	76.7	2	Arizona	81.6
2	Arizona	81.6	3	Idaho	80.9
16	Arkansas	72.3	4	Texas	78.8
17	California	71.8	5	South Dakota	78.4
19	Colorado	70.2	6	Nevada	78.0
45	Connecticut	58.8	7	Alaska	76.7
29	Delaware	67.3	8	Wyoming	75.9
29	Florida	67.3	9	Mississippi	75.8
15	Georgia	72.4	10	Nebraska	75.1
13	Hawaii	73.9	11	New Mexico	74.7
3	Idaho	80.9	11	Oklahoma	74.7
33	Illinois	66.8	13	Hawaii	73.9
26	Indiana	68.3	14	Kansas	73.3
22	Iowa	69.1	15	Georgia	72.4
14	Kansas	73.3	16	Arkansas	72.3
31	Kentucky	67.2	17	California	71.8
18	Louisiana	70.6	18	Louisiana	70.6
48	Maine	54.5	19	Colorado	70.2
39	Maryland	64.2	20	South Carolina	69.7
46	Massachusetts	57.0	21	Montana	69.5
41	Michigan	61.7	22	Iowa	69.1
24	Minnesota	68.7	23	North Carolina	69.0
9	Mississippi	75.8	24	Minnesota	68.7
27	Missouri	67.9	24	North Dakota	68.7
21	Montana	69.5	26	Indiana	68.3
10	Nebraska	75.1	27	Missouri	67.9
6	Nevada	78.0	28	Tennessee	67.5
49	New Hampshire	53.4	29	Delaware	67.3
38	New Jersey	64.4	29	Florida	67.3
11	New Mexico	74.7	31	Kentucky	67.2
42	New York	61.1	32	Alabama	67.0
23	North Carolina	69.0	33	Illinois	66.8
24	North Dakota	68.7	34	Virginia	66.3
37	Ohio	64.7	35	Oregon	65.5
11	Oklahoma	74.7	36	Washington	65.2
35	Oregon	65.5	37	Ohio	64.7
43	Pennsylvania	60.6	38	New Jersey	64.4
47	Rhode Island	54.6	39	Maryland	64.2
20	South Carolina	69.7	40	Wisconsin	64.0
5	South Dakota	78.4	41	Michigan	61.7
28	Tennessee	67.5	42	New York	61.1
4	Texas	78.8	43	Pennsylvania	60.6
1	Utah	94.1	44	West Virginia	59.4
50	Vermont	52.2	45	Connecticut	58.8
34	Virginia	66.3	46	Massachusetts	57.0
36	Washington	65.2	47	Rhode Island	54.6
44	West Virginia	59.4	48	Maine	54.5
40	Wisconsin	64.0	49	New Hampshire	53.4
8	Wyoming	75.9	50	Vermont	52.2
				District of Columbia	58.5

Source: U.S. Department of Health and Human Services, National Center for Health Statistics
   "National Vital Statistics Reports" (Vol. 56, No. 7, December 5, 2007, http://www.cdc.gov/nchs/births.htm)
*Preliminary data by state of residence.

Births to White Women in 2006

National Total = 3,316,474 Live Births to White Women*

ALPHA ORDER

ALPHA ORDER

RANK ORDER

RANK	STATE	BIRTHS	% of USA	RANK	STATE	BIRTHS	% of USA
26	Alabama	42,852	1.3%	1	California	453,913	13.7%
48	Alaska	6,941	0.2%	2	Texas	334,527	10.1%
11	Arizona	88,635	2.7%	3	New York	173,023	5.2%
34	Arkansas	32,143	1.0%	4	Florida	171,651	5.2%
1	California	453,913	13.7%	5	Illinois	139,380	4.2%
17	Colorado	64,570	1.9%	6	Ohio	121,608	3.7%
32	Connecticut	33,754	1.0%	7	Pennsylvania	117,631	3.5%
45	Delaware	8,393	0.3%	8	Michigan	99,016	3.0%
4	Florida	171,651	5.2%	9	Georgia	93,744	2.8%
9	Georgia	93,744	2.8%	10	North Carolina	92,444	2.8%
50	Hawaii	5,532	0.2%	11	Arizona	88,635	2.7%
38	Idaho	23,272	0.7%	12	New Jersey	82,810	2.5%
5	Illinois	139,380	4.2%	13	Indiana	76,504	2.3%
13	Indiana	76,504	2.3%	14	Virginia	76,447	2.3%
29	Iowa	37,789	1.1%	15	Washington	71,213	2.1%
31	Kansas	36,032	1.1%	16	Missouri	66,617	2.0%
22	Kentucky	51,754	1.6%	17	Colorado	64,570	1.9%
30	Louisiana	37,734	1.1%	18	Tennessee	63,703	1.9%
41	Maine	13,527	0.4%	19	Massachusetts	62,639	1.9%
24	Maryland	46,385	1.4%	20	Wisconsin	61,258	1.8%
19	Massachusetts	62,639	1.9%	21	Minnesota	59,205	1.8%
8	Michigan	99,016	3.0%	22	Kentucky	51,754	1.6%
21	Minnesota	59,205	1.8%	23	Utah	50,613	1.5%
36	Mississippi	24,219	0.7%	24	Maryland	46,385	1.4%
16	Missouri	66,617	2.0%	25	Oregon	43,926	1.3%
42	Montana	10,702	0.3%	26	Alabama	42,852	1.3%
37	Nebraska	23,574	0.7%	27	Oklahoma	41,883	1.3%
33	Nevada	33,194	1.0%	28	South Carolina	39,232	1.2%
40	New Hampshire	13,563	0.4%	29	Iowa	37,789	1.1%
12	New Jersey	82,810	2.5%	30	Louisiana	37,734	1.1%
35	New Mexico	24,815	0.7%	31	Kansas	36,032	1.1%
3	New York	173,023	5.2%	32	Connecticut	33,754	1.0%
10	North Carolina	92,444	2.8%	33	Nevada	33,194	1.0%
46	North Dakota	7,358	0.2%	34	Arkansas	32,143	1.0%
6	Ohio	121,608	3.7%	35	New Mexico	24,815	0.7%
27	Oklahoma	41,883	1.3%	36	Mississippi	24,219	0.7%
25	Oregon	43,926	1.3%	37	Nebraska	23,574	0.7%
7	Pennsylvania	117,631	3.5%	38	Idaho	23,272	0.7%
43	Rhode Island	10,460	0.3%	39	West Virginia	20,029	0.6%
28	South Carolina	39,232	1.2%	40	New Hampshire	13,563	0.4%
44	South Dakota	9,509	0.3%	41	Maine	13,527	0.4%
18	Tennessee	63,703	1.9%	42	Montana	10,702	0.3%
2	Texas	334,527	10.1%	43	Rhode Island	10,460	0.3%
23	Utah	50,613	1.5%	44	South Dakota	9,509	0.3%
49	Vermont	6,304	0.2%	45	Delaware	8,393	0.3%
14	Virginia	76,447	2.3%	46	North Dakota	7,358	0.2%
15	Washington	71,213	2.1%	47	Wyoming	7,153	0.2%
39	West Virginia	20,029	0.6%	48	Alaska	6,941	0.2%
20	Wisconsin	61,258	1.8%	49	Vermont	6,304	0.2%
47	Wyoming	7,153	0.2%	50	Hawaii	5,532	0.2%
					District of Columbia	3,295	0.1%

Source: U.S. Department of Health and Human Services, National Center for Health Statistics
   "National Vital Statistics Reports" (Vol. 56, No. 7, December 5, 2007, http://www.cdc.gov/nchs/births.htm)
*Preliminary data by state of residence. By race of mother.

White Births as a Percent of All Births in 2006

National Percent = 77.7% of Live Births*

ALPHA ORDER			RANK ORDER		
RANK	STATE	PERCENT	RANK	STATE	PERCENT
43	Alabama	67.8	1	Vermont	96.9
44	Alaska	63.2	2	Idaho	96.2
14	Arizona	86.5	3	West Virginia	95.7
32	Arkansas	78.4	4	Maine	95.6
26	California	80.7	5	Utah	94.6
9	Colorado	91.3	6	New Hampshire	94.3
26	Connecticut	80.7	7	Wyoming	93.3
41	Delaware	70.0	8	Iowa	93.1
37	Florida	72.5	9	Colorado	91.3
45	Georgia	63.1	10	Oregon	90.2
50	Hawaii	29.1	11	Kentucky	88.8
2	Idaho	96.2	12	Nebraska	88.2
35	Illinois	77.2	13	Kansas	88.0
15	Indiana	86.3	14	Arizona	86.5
8	Iowa	93.1	15	Indiana	86.3
13	Kansas	88.0	16	Montana	85.6
11	Kentucky	88.8	17	North Dakota	85.3
48	Louisiana	59.5	18	Wisconsin	84.7
4	Maine	95.6	19	Rhode Island	84.5
47	Maryland	59.9	20	Texas	83.7
28	Massachusetts	80.5	21	New Mexico	82.9
33	Michigan	77.7	22	Nevada	82.8
28	Minnesota	80.5	23	Washington	82.0
49	Mississippi	52.6	24	Missouri	81.9
24	Missouri	81.9	25	Ohio	80.8
16	Montana	85.6	26	California	80.7
12	Nebraska	88.2	26	Connecticut	80.7
22	Nevada	82.8	28	Massachusetts	80.5
6	New Hampshire	94.3	28	Minnesota	80.5
39	New Jersey	72.0	30	South Dakota	79.8
21	New Mexico	82.9	31	Pennsylvania	78.9
42	New York	69.2	32	Arkansas	78.4
38	North Carolina	72.3	33	Michigan	77.7
17	North Dakota	85.3	34	Oklahoma	77.5
25	Ohio	80.8	35	Illinois	77.2
34	Oklahoma	77.5	36	Tennessee	75.5
10	Oregon	90.2	37	Florida	72.5
31	Pennsylvania	78.9	38	North Carolina	72.3
19	Rhode Island	84.5	39	New Jersey	72.0
46	South Carolina	63.0	40	Virginia	70.9
30	South Dakota	79.8	41	Delaware	70.0
36	Tennessee	75.5	42	New York	69.2
20	Texas	83.7	43	Alabama	67.8
5	Utah	94.6	44	Alaska	63.2
1	Vermont	96.9	45	Georgia	63.1
40	Virginia	70.9	46	South Carolina	63.0
23	Washington	82.0	47	Maryland	59.9
3	West Virginia	95.7	48	Louisiana	59.5
18	Wisconsin	84.7	49	Mississippi	52.6
7	Wyoming	93.3	50	Hawaii	29.1

	District of Columbia	38.6

Source: CQ Press using data from U.S. Department of Health and Human Services, National Center for Health Statistics
    "National Vital Statistics Reports" (Vol. 56, No. 7, December 5, 2007, http://www.cdc.gov/nchs/births.htm)
*Preliminary data by state of residence. By race of mother.

Births to Black Women in 2006

National Total = 662,200 Live Births to Black Women*

ALPHA ORDER					RANK ORDER			
RANK	STATE	BIRTHS	% of USA		RANK	STATE	BIRTHS	% of USA
17	Alabama	19,362	2.9%		1	Florida	56,911	8.6%
42	Alaska	437	0.1%		2	New York	54,396	8.2%
29	Arizona	4,014	0.6%		3	Georgia	49,427	7.5%
22	Arkansas	7,912	1.2%		4	Texas	49,203	7.4%
5	California	34,281	5.2%		5	California	34,281	5.2%
32	Colorado	3,147	0.5%		6	Illinois	31,578	4.8%
25	Connecticut	5,603	0.8%		7	North Carolina	29,929	4.5%
33	Delaware	3,076	0.5%		8	Maryland	26,182	4.0%
1	Florida	56,911	8.6%		9	Ohio	25,437	3.8%
3	Georgia	49,427	7.5%		10	Pennsylvania	25,042	3.8%
39	Hawaii	611	0.1%		11	Louisiana	24,243	3.7%
46	Idaho	147	0.0%		12	Virginia	23,791	3.6%
6	Illinois	31,578	4.8%		13	Michigan	23,082	3.5%
20	Indiana	10,456	1.6%		14	South Carolina	21,505	3.2%
35	Iowa	1,619	0.2%		15	Mississippi	21,087	3.2%
31	Kansas	3,168	0.5%		16	New Jersey	20,852	3.1%
26	Kentucky	5,470	0.8%		17	Alabama	19,362	2.9%
11	Louisiana	24,243	3.7%		18	Tennessee	18,360	2.8%
43	Maine	299	0.0%		19	Missouri	12,454	1.9%
8	Maryland	26,182	4.0%		20	Indiana	10,456	1.6%
21	Massachusetts	9,303	1.4%		21	Massachusetts	9,303	1.4%
13	Michigan	23,082	3.5%		22	Arkansas	7,912	1.2%
23	Minnesota	7,586	1.1%		23	Minnesota	7,586	1.1%
15	Mississippi	21,087	3.2%		24	Wisconsin	7,109	1.1%
19	Missouri	12,454	1.9%		25	Connecticut	5,603	0.8%
50	Montana	63	0.0%		26	Kentucky	5,470	0.8%
34	Nebraska	1,886	0.3%		27	Oklahoma	4,976	0.8%
30	Nevada	3,503	0.5%		28	Washington	4,732	0.7%
44	New Hampshire	263	0.0%		29	Arizona	4,014	0.6%
16	New Jersey	20,852	3.1%		30	Nevada	3,503	0.5%
40	New Mexico	600	0.1%		31	Kansas	3,168	0.5%
2	New York	54,396	8.2%		32	Colorado	3,147	0.5%
7	North Carolina	29,929	4.5%		33	Delaware	3,076	0.5%
47	North Dakota	133	0.0%		34	Nebraska	1,886	0.3%
9	Ohio	25,437	3.8%		35	Iowa	1,619	0.2%
27	Oklahoma	4,976	0.8%		36	Rhode Island	1,189	0.2%
37	Oregon	1,150	0.2%		37	Oregon	1,150	0.2%
10	Pennsylvania	25,042	3.8%		38	West Virginia	700	0.1%
36	Rhode Island	1,189	0.2%		39	Hawaii	611	0.1%
14	South Carolina	21,505	3.2%		40	New Mexico	600	0.1%
45	South Dakota	219	0.0%		41	Utah	517	0.1%
18	Tennessee	18,360	2.8%		42	Alaska	437	0.1%
4	Texas	49,203	7.4%		43	Maine	299	0.0%
41	Utah	517	0.1%		44	New Hampshire	263	0.0%
48	Vermont	80	0.0%		45	South Dakota	219	0.0%
12	Virginia	23,791	3.6%		46	Idaho	147	0.0%
28	Washington	4,732	0.7%		47	North Dakota	133	0.0%
38	West Virginia	700	0.1%		48	Vermont	80	0.0%
24	Wisconsin	7,109	1.1%		49	Wyoming	66	0.0%
49	Wyoming	66	0.0%		50	Montana	63	0.0%
						District of Columbia	5,043	0.8%

Source: U.S. Department of Health and Human Services, National Center for Health Statistics
   "National Vital Statistics Reports" (Vol. 56, No. 7, December 5, 2007, http://www.cdc.gov/nchs/births.htm)
*Preliminary data by state of residence. By race of mother.

Black Births as a Percent of All Births in 2006

National Percent = 15.5% of Live Births*

ALPHA ORDER			RANK ORDER		
RANK	STATE	PERCENT	RANK	STATE	PERCENT
6	Alabama	30.6	1	Mississippi	45.8
35	Alaska	4.0	2	Louisiana	38.2
37	Arizona	3.9	3	South Carolina	34.5
13	Arkansas	19.3	4	Maryland	33.8
32	California	6.1	5	Georgia	33.3
34	Colorado	4.4	6	Alabama	30.6
20	Connecticut	13.4	7	Delaware	25.7
7	Delaware	25.7	8	Florida	24.0
8	Florida	24.0	9	North Carolina	23.4
5	Georgia	33.3	10	Virginia	22.1
39	Hawaii	3.2	11	New York	21.8
49	Idaho	0.6	11	Tennessee	21.8
16	Illinois	17.5	13	Arkansas	19.3
23	Indiana	11.8	14	Michigan	18.1
35	Iowa	4.0	14	New Jersey	18.1
30	Kansas	7.7	16	Illinois	17.5
27	Kentucky	9.4	17	Ohio	16.9
2	Louisiana	38.2	18	Pennsylvania	16.8
41	Maine	2.1	19	Missouri	15.3
4	Maryland	33.8	20	Connecticut	13.4
22	Massachusetts	12.0	21	Texas	12.3
14	Michigan	18.1	22	Massachusetts	12.0
24	Minnesota	10.3	23	Indiana	11.8
1	Mississippi	45.8	24	Minnesota	10.3
19	Missouri	15.3	25	Wisconsin	9.8
50	Montana	0.5	26	Rhode Island	9.6
31	Nebraska	7.1	27	Kentucky	9.4
29	Nevada	8.7	28	Oklahoma	9.2
43	New Hampshire	1.8	29	Nevada	8.7
14	New Jersey	18.1	30	Kansas	7.7
42	New Mexico	2.0	31	Nebraska	7.1
11	New York	21.8	32	California	6.1
9	North Carolina	23.4	33	Washington	5.4
45	North Dakota	1.5	34	Colorado	4.4
17	Ohio	16.9	35	Alaska	4.0
28	Oklahoma	9.2	35	Iowa	4.0
40	Oregon	2.4	37	Arizona	3.9
18	Pennsylvania	16.8	38	West Virginia	3.3
26	Rhode Island	9.6	39	Hawaii	3.2
3	South Carolina	34.5	40	Oregon	2.4
43	South Dakota	1.8	41	Maine	2.1
11	Tennessee	21.8	42	New Mexico	2.0
21	Texas	12.3	43	New Hampshire	1.8
47	Utah	1.0	43	South Dakota	1.8
46	Vermont	1.2	45	North Dakota	1.5
10	Virginia	22.1	46	Vermont	1.2
33	Washington	5.4	47	Utah	1.0
38	West Virginia	3.3	48	Wyoming	0.9
25	Wisconsin	9.8	49	Idaho	0.6
48	Wyoming	0.9	50	Montana	0.5
			District of Columbia		59.1

Source: CQ Press using data from U.S. Department of Health and Human Services, National Center for Health Statistics
"National Vital Statistics Reports" (Vol. 56, No. 7, December 5, 2007, http://www.cdc.gov/nchs/births.htm)
*Preliminary data by state of residence. By race of mother.

Births to Hispanic Women in 2006

National Total = 1,039,051 Live Births to Hispanic Women*

ALPHA ORDER

RANK	STATE	BIRTHS	% of USA
30	Alabama	4,695	0.5%
43	Alaska	752	0.1%
5	Arizona	45,534	4.4%
32	Arkansas	4,400	0.4%
1	California	293,320	28.2%
9	Colorado	22,813	2.2%
20	Connecticut	8,482	0.8%
40	Delaware	1,882	0.2%
3	Florida	70,060	6.7%
8	Georgia	23,675	2.3%
36	Hawaii	3,039	0.3%
34	Idaho	3,792	0.4%
6	Illinois	44,341	4.3%
21	Indiana	8,458	0.8%
35	Iowa	3,227	0.3%
27	Kansas	6,586	0.6%
37	Kentucky	2,777	0.3%
39	Louisiana	2,233	0.2%
49	Maine	218	0.0%
17	Maryland	10,086	1.0%
16	Massachusetts	10,755	1.0%
19	Michigan	8,682	0.8%
28	Minnesota	6,038	0.6%
41	Mississippi	1,555	0.1%
31	Missouri	4,556	0.4%
45	Montana	401	0.0%
33	Nebraska	4,000	0.4%
13	Nevada	15,621	1.5%
44	New Hampshire	585	0.1%
7	New Jersey	29,202	2.8%
11	New Mexico	16,514	1.6%
4	New York	59,331	5.7%
10	North Carolina	21,214	2.0%
47	North Dakota	249	0.0%
26	Ohio	6,736	0.6%
24	Oklahoma	7,065	0.7%
18	Oregon	9,947	1.0%
15	Pennsylvania	13,294	1.3%
38	Rhode Island	2,558	0.2%
29	South Carolina	5,888	0.6%
45	South Dakota	401	0.0%
23	Tennessee	7,938	0.8%
2	Texas	198,291	19.1%
22	Utah	8,224	0.8%
50	Vermont	74	0.0%
14	Virginia	14,463	1.4%
12	Washington	15,785	1.5%
48	West Virginia	219	0.0%
25	Wisconsin	6,870	0.7%
42	Wyoming	897	0.1%

RANK ORDER

RANK	STATE	BIRTHS	% of USA
1	California	293,320	28.2%
2	Texas	198,291	19.1%
3	Florida	70,060	6.7%
4	New York	59,331	5.7%
5	Arizona	45,534	4.4%
6	Illinois	44,341	4.3%
7	New Jersey	29,202	2.8%
8	Georgia	23,675	2.3%
9	Colorado	22,813	2.2%
10	North Carolina	21,214	2.0%
11	New Mexico	16,514	1.6%
12	Washington	15,785	1.5%
13	Nevada	15,621	1.5%
14	Virginia	14,463	1.4%
15	Pennsylvania	13,294	1.3%
16	Massachusetts	10,755	1.0%
17	Maryland	10,086	1.0%
18	Oregon	9,947	1.0%
19	Michigan	8,682	0.8%
20	Connecticut	8,482	0.8%
21	Indiana	8,458	0.8%
22	Utah	8,224	0.8%
23	Tennessee	7,938	0.8%
24	Oklahoma	7,065	0.7%
25	Wisconsin	6,870	0.7%
26	Ohio	6,736	0.6%
27	Kansas	6,586	0.6%
28	Minnesota	6,038	0.6%
29	South Carolina	5,888	0.6%
30	Alabama	4,695	0.5%
31	Missouri	4,556	0.4%
32	Arkansas	4,400	0.4%
33	Nebraska	4,000	0.4%
34	Idaho	3,792	0.4%
35	Iowa	3,227	0.3%
36	Hawaii	3,039	0.3%
37	Kentucky	2,777	0.3%
38	Rhode Island	2,558	0.2%
39	Louisiana	2,233	0.2%
40	Delaware	1,882	0.2%
41	Mississippi	1,555	0.1%
42	Wyoming	897	0.1%
43	Alaska	752	0.1%
44	New Hampshire	585	0.1%
45	Montana	401	0.0%
45	South Dakota	401	0.0%
47	North Dakota	249	0.0%
48	West Virginia	219	0.0%
49	Maine	218	0.0%
50	Vermont	74	0.0%
	District of Columbia	1,327	0.1%

Source: U.S. Department of Health and Human Services, National Center for Health Statistics
"National Vital Statistics Reports" (Vol. 56, No. 7, December 5, 2007, http://www.cdc.gov/nchs/births.htm)
*Preliminary data by state of residence. By race of mother. Persons of Hispanic origin may be of any race.

Hispanic Births as a Percent of All Births in 2006

National Percent = 24.4% of Live Births*

ALPHA ORDER

RANK	STATE	PERCENT
36	Alabama	7.4
37	Alaska	6.8
4	Arizona	44.4
28	Arkansas	10.7
2	California	52.2
6	Colorado	32.2
13	Connecticut	20.3
19	Delaware	15.7
7	Florida	29.6
18	Georgia	15.9
17	Hawaii	16.0
19	Idaho	15.7
9	Illinois	24.6
29	Indiana	9.5
35	Iowa	7.9
16	Kansas	16.1
40	Kentucky	4.8
43	Louisiana	3.5
48	Maine	1.5
26	Maryland	13.0
23	Massachusetts	13.8
37	Michigan	6.8
34	Minnesota	8.2
44	Mississippi	3.4
39	Missouri	5.6
46	Montana	3.2
22	Nebraska	15.0
5	Nevada	39.0
42	New Hampshire	4.1
8	New Jersey	25.4
1	New Mexico	55.2
10	New York	23.7
15	North Carolina	16.6
47	North Dakota	2.9
41	Ohio	4.5
25	Oklahoma	13.1
12	Oregon	20.4
33	Pennsylvania	8.9
11	Rhode Island	20.7
29	South Carolina	9.5
44	South Dakota	3.4
32	Tennessee	9.4
3	Texas	49.6
21	Utah	15.4
49	Vermont	1.1
24	Virginia	13.4
14	Washington	18.2
50	West Virginia	1.0
29	Wisconsin	9.5
27	Wyoming	11.7

RANK ORDER

RANK	STATE	PERCENT
1	New Mexico	55.2
2	California	52.2
3	Texas	49.6
4	Arizona	44.4
5	Nevada	39.0
6	Colorado	32.2
7	Florida	29.6
8	New Jersey	25.4
9	Illinois	24.6
10	New York	23.7
11	Rhode Island	20.7
12	Oregon	20.4
13	Connecticut	20.3
14	Washington	18.2
15	North Carolina	16.6
16	Kansas	16.1
17	Hawaii	16.0
18	Georgia	15.9
19	Delaware	15.7
19	Idaho	15.7
21	Utah	15.4
22	Nebraska	15.0
23	Massachusetts	13.8
24	Virginia	13.4
25	Oklahoma	13.1
26	Maryland	13.0
27	Wyoming	11.7
28	Arkansas	10.7
29	Indiana	9.5
29	South Carolina	9.5
29	Wisconsin	9.5
32	Tennessee	9.4
33	Pennsylvania	8.9
34	Minnesota	8.2
35	Iowa	7.9
36	Alabama	7.4
37	Alaska	6.8
37	Michigan	6.8
39	Missouri	5.6
40	Kentucky	4.8
41	Ohio	4.5
42	New Hampshire	4.1
43	Louisiana	3.5
44	Mississippi	3.4
44	South Dakota	3.4
46	Montana	3.2
47	North Dakota	2.9
48	Maine	1.5
49	Vermont	1.1
50	West Virginia	1.0

District of Columbia 15.6

Source: CQ Press using data from U.S. Department of Health and Human Services, National Center for Health Statistics
"National Vital Statistics Reports" (Vol. 56, No. 7, December 5, 2007, http://www.cdc.gov/nchs/births.htm)
*Preliminary data by state of residence. By race of mother. Persons of Hispanic origin may be of any race.

Births of Low Birthweight in 2006

National Total = 354,078 Live Births*

ALPHA ORDER

RANK	STATE	BIRTHS	% of USA
18	Alabama	6,640	1.9%
48	Alaska	659	0.2%
15	Arizona	7,276	2.1%
29	Arkansas	3,770	1.1%
1	California	38,245	10.8%
20	Colorado	6,297	1.8%
31	Connecticut	3,386	1.0%
41	Delaware	1,115	0.3%
4	Florida	20,609	5.8%
6	Georgia	14,267	4.0%
40	Hawaii	1,538	0.4%
39	Idaho	1,669	0.5%
5	Illinois	15,530	4.4%
16	Indiana	7,271	2.1%
35	Iowa	2,802	0.8%
34	Kansas	2,949	0.8%
25	Kentucky	5,304	1.5%
17	Louisiana	7,164	2.0%
44	Maine	962	0.3%
14	Maryland	7,283	2.1%
22	Massachusetts	6,144	1.7%
10	Michigan	10,581	3.0%
27	Minnesota	4,781	1.4%
23	Mississippi	5,713	1.6%
19	Missouri	6,592	1.9%
45	Montana	913	0.3%
38	Nebraska	1,898	0.5%
32	Nevada	3,327	0.9%
42	New Hampshire	992	0.3%
11	New Jersey	9,891	2.8%
36	New Mexico	2,664	0.8%
3	New York	20,758	5.9%
9	North Carolina	11,634	3.3%
49	North Dakota	578	0.2%
7	Ohio	13,252	3.7%
28	Oklahoma	4,483	1.3%
33	Oregon	2,972	0.8%
8	Pennsylvania	12,523	3.5%
43	Rhode Island	990	0.3%
21	South Carolina	6,289	1.8%
46	South Dakota	834	0.2%
13	Tennessee	8,097	2.3%
2	Texas	33,567	9.5%
30	Utah	3,691	1.0%
50	Vermont	449	0.1%
12	Virginia	8,949	2.5%
24	Washington	5,645	1.6%
37	West Virginia	2,030	0.6%
26	Wisconsin	4,991	1.4%
47	Wyoming	683	0.2%

RANK ORDER

RANK	STATE	BIRTHS	% of USA
1	California	38,245	10.8%
2	Texas	33,567	9.5%
3	New York	20,758	5.9%
4	Florida	20,609	5.8%
5	Illinois	15,530	4.4%
6	Georgia	14,267	4.0%
7	Ohio	13,252	3.7%
8	Pennsylvania	12,523	3.5%
9	North Carolina	11,634	3.3%
10	Michigan	10,581	3.0%
11	New Jersey	9,891	2.8%
12	Virginia	8,949	2.5%
13	Tennessee	8,097	2.3%
14	Maryland	7,283	2.1%
15	Arizona	7,276	2.1%
16	Indiana	7,271	2.1%
17	Louisiana	7,164	2.0%
18	Alabama	6,640	1.9%
19	Missouri	6,592	1.9%
20	Colorado	6,297	1.8%
21	South Carolina	6,289	1.8%
22	Massachusetts	6,144	1.7%
23	Mississippi	5,713	1.6%
24	Washington	5,645	1.6%
25	Kentucky	5,304	1.5%
26	Wisconsin	4,991	1.4%
27	Minnesota	4,781	1.4%
28	Oklahoma	4,483	1.3%
29	Arkansas	3,770	1.1%
30	Utah	3,691	1.0%
31	Connecticut	3,386	1.0%
32	Nevada	3,327	0.9%
33	Oregon	2,972	0.8%
34	Kansas	2,949	0.8%
35	Iowa	2,802	0.8%
36	New Mexico	2,664	0.8%
37	West Virginia	2,030	0.6%
38	Nebraska	1,898	0.5%
39	Idaho	1,669	0.5%
40	Hawaii	1,538	0.4%
41	Delaware	1,115	0.3%
42	New Hampshire	992	0.3%
43	Rhode Island	990	0.3%
44	Maine	962	0.3%
45	Montana	913	0.3%
46	South Dakota	834	0.2%
47	Wyoming	683	0.2%
48	Alaska	659	0.2%
49	North Dakota	578	0.2%
50	Vermont	449	0.1%
	District of Columbia	981	0.3%

Source: CQ Press using data from U.S. Department of Health and Human Services, National Center for Health Statistics
    "National Vital Statistics Reports" (Vol. 56, No. 7, December 5, 2007, http://www.cdc.gov/nchs/births.htm)
*Preliminary data by state of residence. Births of less than 2,500 grams (5 pounds 8 ounces).

Births of Low Birthweight as a Percent of All Births in 2006

National Percent = 8.3% of Live Births*

ALPHA ORDER				RANK ORDER		
RANK	STATE	PERCENT		RANK	STATE	PERCENT
3	Alabama	10.5		1	Mississippi	12.4
50	Alaska	6.0		2	Louisiana	11.3
35	Arizona	7.1		3	Alabama	10.5
10	Arkansas	9.2		4	South Carolina	10.1
44	California	6.8		5	West Virginia	9.7
13	Colorado	8.9		6	Georgia	9.6
28	Connecticut	8.1		6	Tennessee	9.6
9	Delaware	9.3		8	Maryland	9.4
17	Florida	8.7		9	Delaware	9.3
6	Georgia	9.6		10	Arkansas	9.2
28	Hawaii	8.1		11	Kentucky	9.1
38	Idaho	6.9		11	North Carolina	9.1
18	Illinois	8.6		13	Colorado	8.9
27	Indiana	8.2		13	New Mexico	8.9
38	Iowa	6.9		13	Wyoming	8.9
34	Kansas	7.2		16	Ohio	8.8
11	Kentucky	9.1		17	Florida	8.7
2	Louisiana	11.3		18	Illinois	8.6
44	Maine	6.8		18	New Jersey	8.6
8	Maryland	9.4		20	Pennsylvania	8.4
32	Massachusetts	7.9		20	Texas	8.4
22	Michigan	8.3		22	Michigan	8.3
47	Minnesota	6.5		22	Nevada	8.3
1	Mississippi	12.4		22	New York	8.3
28	Missouri	8.1		22	Oklahoma	8.3
33	Montana	7.3		22	Virginia	8.3
35	Nebraska	7.1		27	Indiana	8.2
22	Nevada	8.3		28	Connecticut	8.1
38	New Hampshire	6.9		28	Hawaii	8.1
18	New Jersey	8.6		28	Missouri	8.1
13	New Mexico	8.9		31	Rhode Island	8.0
22	New York	8.3		32	Massachusetts	7.9
11	North Carolina	9.1		33	Montana	7.3
46	North Dakota	6.7		34	Kansas	7.2
16	Ohio	8.8		35	Arizona	7.1
22	Oklahoma	8.3		35	Nebraska	7.1
49	Oregon	6.1		37	South Dakota	7.0
20	Pennsylvania	8.4		38	Idaho	6.9
31	Rhode Island	8.0		38	Iowa	6.9
4	South Carolina	10.1		38	New Hampshire	6.9
37	South Dakota	7.0		38	Utah	6.9
6	Tennessee	9.6		38	Vermont	6.9
20	Texas	8.4		38	Wisconsin	6.9
38	Utah	6.9		44	California	6.8
38	Vermont	6.9		44	Maine	6.8
22	Virginia	8.3		46	North Dakota	6.7
47	Washington	6.5		47	Minnesota	6.5
5	West Virginia	9.7		47	Washington	6.5
38	Wisconsin	6.9		49	Oregon	6.1
13	Wyoming	8.9		50	Alaska	6.0
					District of Columbia	11.5

Source: U.S. Department of Health and Human Services, National Center for Health Statistics
"Births: Preliminary data for 2006" (unpublished data)
*Preliminary data by state of residence. Births of less than 2,500 grams (5 pounds 8 ounces).

Births of Low Birthweight to White Women in 2006

National Total = 238,786 Live Births*

ALPHA ORDER				RANK ORDER			
RANK	STATE	BIRTHS	% of USA	RANK	STATE	BIRTHS	% of USA
22	Alabama	3,557	1.5%	1	California	28,597	12.0%
49	Alaska	416	0.2%	2	Texas	25,424	10.6%
12	Arizona	6,027	2.5%	3	New York	12,631	5.3%
32	Arkansas	2,507	1.0%	4	Florida	12,531	5.2%
1	California	28,597	12.0%	5	Illinois	10,175	4.3%
14	Colorado	5,553	2.3%	6	Ohio	9,242	3.9%
33	Connecticut	2,498	1.0%	7	Pennsylvania	8,705	3.6%
46	Delaware	613	0.3%	8	Michigan	6,931	2.9%
4	Florida	12,531	5.2%	9	North Carolina	6,841	2.9%
10	Georgia	6,750	2.8%	10	Georgia	6,750	2.8%
50	Hawaii	332	0.1%	11	New Jersey	6,211	2.6%
38	Idaho	1,606	0.7%	12	Arizona	6,027	2.5%
5	Illinois	10,175	4.3%	13	Indiana	5,738	2.4%
13	Indiana	5,738	2.4%	14	Colorado	5,553	2.3%
30	Iowa	2,532	1.1%	15	Tennessee	5,287	2.2%
34	Kansas	2,414	1.0%	16	Virginia	5,275	2.2%
19	Kentucky	4,451	1.9%	17	Missouri	4,730	2.0%
27	Louisiana	3,132	1.3%	18	Massachusetts	4,635	1.9%
41	Maine	920	0.4%	19	Kentucky	4,451	1.9%
25	Maryland	3,432	1.4%	20	Washington	4,344	1.8%
18	Massachusetts	4,635	1.9%	21	Wisconsin	3,798	1.6%
8	Michigan	6,931	2.9%	22	Alabama	3,557	1.5%
23	Minnesota	3,552	1.5%	23	Minnesota	3,552	1.5%
36	Mississippi	2,107	0.9%	24	Utah	3,442	1.4%
17	Missouri	4,730	2.0%	25	Maryland	3,432	1.4%
43	Montana	771	0.3%	26	Oklahoma	3,225	1.4%
39	Nebraska	1,556	0.7%	27	Louisiana	3,132	1.3%
31	Nevada	2,523	1.1%	28	South Carolina	2,982	1.2%
40	New Hampshire	936	0.4%	29	Oregon	2,592	1.1%
11	New Jersey	6,211	2.6%	30	Iowa	2,532	1.1%
35	New Mexico	2,233	0.9%	31	Nevada	2,523	1.1%
3	New York	12,631	5.3%	32	Arkansas	2,507	1.0%
9	North Carolina	6,841	2.9%	33	Connecticut	2,498	1.0%
47	North Dakota	500	0.2%	34	Kansas	2,414	1.0%
6	Ohio	9,242	3.9%	35	New Mexico	2,233	0.9%
26	Oklahoma	3,225	1.4%	36	Mississippi	2,107	0.9%
29	Oregon	2,592	1.1%	37	West Virginia	1,903	0.8%
7	Pennsylvania	8,705	3.6%	38	Idaho	1,606	0.7%
42	Rhode Island	785	0.3%	39	Nebraska	1,556	0.7%
28	South Carolina	2,982	1.2%	40	New Hampshire	936	0.4%
44	South Dakota	647	0.3%	41	Maine	920	0.4%
15	Tennessee	5,287	2.2%	42	Rhode Island	785	0.3%
2	Texas	25,424	10.6%	43	Montana	771	0.3%
24	Utah	3,442	1.4%	44	South Dakota	647	0.3%
48	Vermont	422	0.2%	45	Wyoming	622	0.3%
16	Virginia	5,275	2.2%	46	Delaware	613	0.3%
20	Washington	4,344	1.8%	47	North Dakota	500	0.2%
37	West Virginia	1,903	0.8%	48	Vermont	422	0.2%
21	Wisconsin	3,798	1.6%	49	Alaska	416	0.2%
45	Wyoming	622	0.3%	50	Hawaii	332	0.1%
					District of Columbia	241	0.1%

Source: CQ Press using data from U.S. Department of Health and Human Services, National Center for Health Statistics
    "Births: Preliminary data for 2006" (unpublished data)
*Preliminary data by state of residence. Births of less than 2,500 grams (5 pounds 8 ounces).

Births of Low Birthweight to White Women
as a Percent of All Births to White Women in 2006
National Percent = 7.2% of Live Births to White Women*

ALPHA ORDER

RANK ORDER

RANK	STATE	PERCENT	RANK	STATE	PERCENT
7	Alabama	8.3	1	West Virginia	9.5
47	Alaska	6.0	2	New Mexico	9.0
35	Arizona	6.8	3	Mississippi	8.7
10	Arkansas	7.8	3	Wyoming	8.7
44	California	6.3	5	Colorado	8.6
5	Colorado	8.6	5	Kentucky	8.6
19	Connecticut	7.4	7	Alabama	8.3
24	Delaware	7.3	7	Louisiana	8.3
24	Florida	7.3	7	Tennessee	8.3
28	Georgia	7.2	10	Arkansas	7.8
47	Hawaii	6.0	11	Oklahoma	7.7
32	Idaho	6.9	12	Nevada	7.6
24	Illinois	7.3	12	Ohio	7.6
16	Indiana	7.5	12	South Carolina	7.6
40	Iowa	6.7	12	Texas	7.6
40	Kansas	6.7	16	Indiana	7.5
5	Kentucky	8.6	16	New Jersey	7.5
7	Louisiana	8.3	16	Rhode Island	7.5
35	Maine	6.8	19	Connecticut	7.4
19	Maryland	7.4	19	Maryland	7.4
19	Massachusetts	7.4	19	Massachusetts	7.4
31	Michigan	7.0	19	North Carolina	7.4
47	Minnesota	6.0	19	Pennsylvania	7.4
3	Mississippi	8.7	24	Delaware	7.3
30	Missouri	7.1	24	Florida	7.3
28	Montana	7.2	24	Illinois	7.3
43	Nebraska	6.6	24	New York	7.3
12	Nevada	7.6	28	Georgia	7.2
32	New Hampshire	6.9	28	Montana	7.2
16	New Jersey	7.5	30	Missouri	7.1
2	New Mexico	9.0	31	Michigan	7.0
24	New York	7.3	32	Idaho	6.9
19	North Carolina	7.4	32	New Hampshire	6.9
35	North Dakota	6.8	32	Virginia	6.9
12	Ohio	7.6	35	Arizona	6.8
11	Oklahoma	7.7	35	Maine	6.8
50	Oregon	5.9	35	North Dakota	6.8
19	Pennsylvania	7.4	35	South Dakota	6.8
16	Rhode Island	7.5	35	Utah	6.8
12	South Carolina	7.6	40	Iowa	6.7
35	South Dakota	6.8	40	Kansas	6.7
7	Tennessee	8.3	40	Vermont	6.7
12	Texas	7.6	43	Nebraska	6.6
35	Utah	6.8	44	California	6.3
40	Vermont	6.7	45	Wisconsin	6.2
32	Virginia	6.9	46	Washington	6.1
46	Washington	6.1	47	Alaska	6.0
1	West Virginia	9.5	47	Hawaii	6.0
45	Wisconsin	6.2	47	Minnesota	6.0
3	Wyoming	8.7	50	Oregon	5.9
				District of Columbia	7.3

Source: U.S. Department of Health and Human Services, National Center for Health Statistics
     "Births: Preliminary data for 2006" (unpublished data)
*Preliminary data by state of residence. Births of less than 2,500 grams (5 pounds 8 ounces).

Births of Low Birthweight to Black Women in 2006

National Total = 90,059 Live Births*

RANK	STATE	BIRTHS	% of USA	RANK	STATE	BIRTHS	% of USA
16	Alabama	3,001	3.3%	1	Florida	7,398	8.2%
42	Alaska	40	0.0%	2	Georgia	7,068	7.8%
29	Arizona	498	0.6%	3	Texas	6,839	7.6%
21	Arkansas	1,187	1.3%	4	New York	6,364	7.1%
7	California	4,079	4.5%	5	Illinois	4,516	5.0%
30	Colorado	491	0.5%	6	North Carolina	4,250	4.7%
27	Connecticut	695	0.8%	7	California	4,079	4.5%
32	Delaware	458	0.5%	8	Louisiana	3,879	4.3%
1	Florida	7,398	8.2%	9	Ohio	3,612	4.0%
2	Georgia	7,068	7.8%	10	Mississippi	3,522	3.9%
41	Hawaii	59	0.1%	11	Maryland	3,456	3.8%
46	Idaho	20	0.0%	12	Pennsylvania	3,356	3.7%
5	Illinois	4,516	5.0%	13	Michigan	3,255	3.6%
20	Indiana	1,474	1.6%	14	South Carolina	3,183	3.5%
35	Iowa	168	0.2%	15	Virginia	3,069	3.4%
33	Kansas	386	0.4%	16	Alabama	3,001	3.3%
24	Kentucky	788	0.9%	17	New Jersey	2,732	3.0%
8	Louisiana	3,879	4.3%	18	Tennessee	2,644	2.9%
45	Maine	22	0.0%	19	Missouri	1,681	1.9%
11	Maryland	3,456	3.8%	20	Indiana	1,474	1.6%
22	Massachusetts	1,023	1.1%	21	Arkansas	1,187	1.3%
13	Michigan	3,255	3.6%	22	Massachusetts	1,023	1.1%
26	Minnesota	759	0.8%	23	Wisconsin	945	1.0%
10	Mississippi	3,522	3.9%	24	Kentucky	788	0.9%
19	Missouri	1,681	1.9%	25	Oklahoma	761	0.8%
NA	Montana**	NA	NA	26	Minnesota	759	0.8%
34	Nebraska	251	0.3%	27	Connecticut	695	0.8%
31	Nevada	487	0.5%	28	Washington	506	0.6%
43	New Hampshire	29	0.0%	29	Arizona	498	0.6%
17	New Jersey	2,732	3.0%	30	Colorado	491	0.5%
39	New Mexico	83	0.1%	31	Nevada	487	0.5%
4	New York	6,364	7.1%	32	Delaware	458	0.5%
6	North Carolina	4,250	4.7%	33	Kansas	386	0.4%
NA	North Dakota**	NA	NA	34	Nebraska	251	0.3%
9	Ohio	3,612	4.0%	35	Iowa	168	0.2%
25	Oklahoma	761	0.8%	36	Rhode Island	128	0.1%
38	Oregon	94	0.1%	37	West Virginia	113	0.1%
12	Pennsylvania	3,356	3.7%	38	Oregon	94	0.1%
36	Rhode Island	128	0.1%	39	New Mexico	83	0.1%
14	South Carolina	3,183	3.5%	40	Utah	61	0.1%
44	South Dakota	24	0.0%	41	Hawaii	59	0.1%
18	Tennessee	2,644	2.9%	42	Alaska	40	0.0%
3	Texas	6,839	7.6%	43	New Hampshire	29	0.0%
40	Utah	61	0.1%	44	South Dakota	24	0.0%
NA	Vermont**	NA	NA	45	Maine	22	0.0%
15	Virginia	3,069	3.4%	46	Idaho	20	0.0%
28	Washington	506	0.6%	NA	Montana**	NA	NA
37	West Virginia	113	0.1%	NA	North Dakota**	NA	NA
23	Wisconsin	945	1.0%	NA	Vermont**	NA	NA
NA	Wyoming**	NA	NA	NA	Wyoming**	NA	NA
					District of Columbia	721	0.8%

ALPHA ORDER

RANK ORDER

Source: CQ Press using data from U.S. Department of Health and Human Services, National Center for Health Statistics
   "Births: Preliminary data for 2006" (unpublished data)
*Preliminary data by state of residence. Births of less than 2,500 grams (5 pounds 8 ounces).
**Not available. Fewer than 20 births of low birthweight to black women.

Births of Low Birthweight to Black Women
as a Percent of All Births to Black Women in 2006
National Percent = 13.6% of Live Births to Black Women*

<u>ALPHA ORDER</u>

RANK	STATE	PERCENT
5	Alabama	15.5
44	Alaska	9.2
30	Arizona	12.4
7	Arkansas	15.0
33	California	11.9
4	Colorado	15.6
30	Connecticut	12.4
8	Delaware	14.9
28	Florida	13.0
12	Georgia	14.3
43	Hawaii	9.7
21	Idaho	13.7
12	Illinois	14.3
16	Indiana	14.1
41	Iowa	10.4
32	Kansas	12.2
10	Kentucky	14.4
3	Louisiana	16.0
46	Maine	7.4
26	Maryland	13.2
36	Massachusetts	11.0
16	Michigan	14.1
42	Minnesota	10.0
1	Mississippi	16.7
22	Missouri	13.5
NA	Montana**	NA
24	Nebraska	13.3
18	Nevada	13.9
36	New Hampshire	11.0
27	New Jersey	13.1
18	New Mexico	13.9
35	New York	11.7
14	North Carolina	14.2
NA	North Dakota**	NA
14	Ohio	14.2
6	Oklahoma	15.3
45	Oregon	8.2
23	Pennsylvania	13.4
39	Rhode Island	10.8
9	South Carolina	14.8
36	South Dakota	11.0
10	Tennessee	14.4
18	Texas	13.9
34	Utah	11.8
NA	Vermont**	NA
29	Virginia	12.9
40	Washington	10.7
2	West Virginia	16.2
24	Wisconsin	13.3
NA	Wyoming**	NA

<u>RANK ORDER</u>

RANK	STATE	PERCENT
1	Mississippi	16.7
2	West Virginia	16.2
3	Louisiana	16.0
4	Colorado	15.6
5	Alabama	15.5
6	Oklahoma	15.3
7	Arkansas	15.0
8	Delaware	14.9
9	South Carolina	14.8
10	Kentucky	14.4
10	Tennessee	14.4
12	Georgia	14.3
12	Illinois	14.3
14	North Carolina	14.2
14	Ohio	14.2
16	Indiana	14.1
16	Michigan	14.1
18	Nevada	13.9
18	New Mexico	13.9
18	Texas	13.9
21	Idaho	13.7
22	Missouri	13.5
23	Pennsylvania	13.4
24	Nebraska	13.3
24	Wisconsin	13.3
26	Maryland	13.2
27	New Jersey	13.1
28	Florida	13.0
29	Virginia	12.9
30	Arizona	12.4
30	Connecticut	12.4
32	Kansas	12.2
33	California	11.9
34	Utah	11.8
35	New York	11.7
36	Massachusetts	11.0
36	New Hampshire	11.0
36	South Dakota	11.0
39	Rhode Island	10.8
40	Washington	10.7
41	Iowa	10.4
42	Minnesota	10.0
43	Hawaii	9.7
44	Alaska	9.2
45	Oregon	8.2
46	Maine	7.4
NA	Montana**	NA
NA	North Dakota**	NA
NA	Vermont**	NA
NA	Wyoming**	NA

District of Columbia   14.3

Source: U.S. Department of Health and Human Services, National Center for Health Statistics
    "Births: Preliminary data for 2006" (unpublished data)
*Preliminary data by state of residence. Births of less than 2,500 grams (5 pounds 8 ounces).
**Not available. Fewer than 20 births of low birthweight to black women.

Births of Low Birthweight to Hispanic Women in 2006

National Total = 72,734 Live Births*

RANK	STATE	BIRTHS	% of USA
31	Alabama	282	0.4%
44	Alaska	37	0.1%
6	Arizona	3,142	4.3%
30	Arkansas	304	0.4%
1	California	18,479	25.4%
8	Colorado	1,916	2.6%
17	Connecticut	746	1.0%
40	Delaware	117	0.2%
3	Florida	4,904	6.7%
10	Georgia	1,444	2.0%
34	Hawaii	237	0.3%
35	Idaho	231	0.3%
5	Illinois	3,193	4.4%
22	Indiana	567	0.8%
36	Iowa	207	0.3%
28	Kansas	369	0.5%
38	Kentucky	200	0.3%
39	Louisiana	163	0.2%
48	Maine	21	0.0%
18	Maryland	686	0.9%
15	Massachusetts	914	1.3%
20	Michigan	608	0.8%
29	Minnesota	356	0.5%
41	Mississippi	110	0.2%
33	Missouri	264	0.4%
46	Montana	27	0.0%
32	Nebraska	268	0.4%
13	Nevada	1,031	1.4%
43	New Hampshire	54	0.1%
7	New Jersey	2,190	3.0%
9	New Mexico	1,503	2.1%
4	New York	4,746	6.5%
11	North Carolina	1,315	1.8%
47	North Dakota	22	0.0%
24	Ohio	485	0.7%
25	Oklahoma	466	0.6%
21	Oregon	587	0.8%
12	Pennsylvania	1,143	1.6%
37	Rhode Island	205	0.3%
27	South Carolina	371	0.5%
45	South Dakota	33	0.0%
23	Tennessee	524	0.7%
2	Texas	15,070	20.7%
19	Utah	617	0.8%
NA	Vermont**	NA	NA
16	Virginia	868	1.2%
14	Washington	994	1.4%
NA	West Virginia**	NA	NA
26	Wisconsin	426	0.6%
42	Wyoming	61	0.1%

RANK	STATE	BIRTHS	% of USA
1	California	18,479	25.4%
2	Texas	15,070	20.7%
3	Florida	4,904	6.7%
4	New York	4,746	6.5%
5	Illinois	3,193	4.4%
6	Arizona	3,142	4.3%
7	New Jersey	2,190	3.0%
8	Colorado	1,916	2.6%
9	New Mexico	1,503	2.1%
10	Georgia	1,444	2.0%
11	North Carolina	1,315	1.8%
12	Pennsylvania	1,143	1.6%
13	Nevada	1,031	1.4%
14	Washington	994	1.4%
15	Massachusetts	914	1.3%
16	Virginia	868	1.2%
17	Connecticut	746	1.0%
18	Maryland	686	0.9%
19	Utah	617	0.8%
20	Michigan	608	0.8%
21	Oregon	587	0.8%
22	Indiana	567	0.8%
23	Tennessee	524	0.7%
24	Ohio	485	0.7%
25	Oklahoma	466	0.6%
26	Wisconsin	426	0.6%
27	South Carolina	371	0.5%
28	Kansas	369	0.5%
29	Minnesota	356	0.5%
30	Arkansas	304	0.4%
31	Alabama	282	0.4%
32	Nebraska	268	0.4%
33	Missouri	264	0.4%
34	Hawaii	237	0.3%
35	Idaho	231	0.3%
36	Iowa	207	0.3%
37	Rhode Island	205	0.3%
38	Kentucky	200	0.3%
39	Louisiana	163	0.2%
40	Delaware	117	0.2%
41	Mississippi	110	0.2%
42	Wyoming	61	0.1%
43	New Hampshire	54	0.1%
44	Alaska	37	0.1%
45	South Dakota	33	0.0%
46	Montana	27	0.0%
47	North Dakota	22	0.0%
48	Maine	21	0.0%
NA	Vermont**	NA	NA
NA	West Virginia**	NA	NA
	District of Columbia	101	0.1%

Source: CQ Press using data from U.S. Department of Health and Human Services, National Center for Health Statistics
"Births: Preliminary data for 2006" (unpublished data)
*Preliminary data by state of residence. Births of less than 2,500 grams (5 pounds 8 ounces). Hispanic can be of any race.
**Not available. Fewer than 20 births of low birthweight to Hispanic women.

Births of Low Birthweight to Hispanic Women
as a Percent of All Births to Hispanic Women in 2006
National Percent = 7.0% of Live Births to Hispanic Women*

ALPHA ORDER

RANK	STATE	PERCENT
42	Alabama	6.0
48	Alaska	4.9
23	Arizona	6.9
23	Arkansas	6.9
34	California	6.3
8	Colorado	8.4
4	Connecticut	8.8
37	Delaware	6.2
21	Florida	7.0
40	Georgia	6.1
12	Hawaii	7.8
40	Idaho	6.1
17	Illinois	7.2
27	Indiana	6.7
33	Iowa	6.4
47	Kansas	5.6
17	Kentucky	7.2
16	Louisiana	7.3
1	Maine	9.6
25	Maryland	6.8
7	Massachusetts	8.5
21	Michigan	7.0
44	Minnesota	5.9
20	Mississippi	7.1
46	Missouri	5.8
27	Montana	6.7
27	Nebraska	6.7
30	Nevada	6.6
2	New Hampshire	9.3
14	New Jersey	7.5
3	New Mexico	9.1
10	New York	8.0
37	North Carolina	6.2
4	North Dakota	8.8
17	Ohio	7.2
30	Oklahoma	6.6
44	Oregon	5.9
6	Pennsylvania	8.6
10	Rhode Island	8.0
34	South Carolina	6.3
9	South Dakota	8.2
30	Tennessee	6.6
13	Texas	7.6
14	Utah	7.5
NA	Vermont**	NA
42	Virginia	6.0
34	Washington	6.3
NA	West Virginia**	NA
37	Wisconsin	6.2
25	Wyoming	6.8

RANK ORDER

RANK	STATE	PERCENT
1	Maine	9.6
2	New Hampshire	9.3
3	New Mexico	9.1
4	Connecticut	8.8
4	North Dakota	8.8
6	Pennsylvania	8.6
7	Massachusetts	8.5
8	Colorado	8.4
9	South Dakota	8.2
10	New York	8.0
10	Rhode Island	8.0
12	Hawaii	7.8
13	Texas	7.6
14	New Jersey	7.5
14	Utah	7.5
16	Louisiana	7.3
17	Illinois	7.2
17	Kentucky	7.2
17	Ohio	7.2
20	Mississippi	7.1
21	Florida	7.0
21	Michigan	7.0
23	Arizona	6.9
23	Arkansas	6.9
25	Maryland	6.8
25	Wyoming	6.8
27	Indiana	6.7
27	Montana	6.7
27	Nebraska	6.7
30	Nevada	6.6
30	Oklahoma	6.6
30	Tennessee	6.6
33	Iowa	6.4
34	California	6.3
34	South Carolina	6.3
34	Washington	6.3
37	Delaware	6.2
37	North Carolina	6.2
37	Wisconsin	6.2
40	Georgia	6.1
40	Idaho	6.1
42	Alabama	6.0
42	Virginia	6.0
44	Minnesota	5.9
44	Oregon	5.9
46	Missouri	5.8
47	Kansas	5.6
48	Alaska	4.9
NA	Vermont**	NA
NA	West Virginia**	NA

District of Columbia		7.6

Source: U.S. Department of Health and Human Services, National Center for Health Statistics
  "Births: Preliminary data for 2006" (unpublished data)
*Preliminary data by state of residence. Births of less than 2,500 grams (5 pounds 8 ounces). Hispanic can be of any race.
**Not available. Fewer than 20 births of low birthweight to Hispanic women.

Births to Unmarried Women in 2006

National Total = 1,642,408 Live Births*

ALPHA ORDER

RANK	STATE	BIRTHS	% of USA
25	Alabama	23,144	1.4%
47	Alaska	4,045	0.2%
11	Arizona	45,089	2.7%
29	Arkansas	17,127	1.0%
1	California	211,474	12.9%
28	Colorado	19,527	1.2%
34	Connecticut	14,214	0.9%
41	Delaware	5,467	0.3%
3	Florida	105,412	6.4%
6	Georgia	63,014	3.8%
39	Hawaii	6,834	0.4%
40	Idaho	5,877	0.4%
5	Illinois	69,886	4.3%
13	Indiana	36,711	2.2%
35	Iowa	13,726	0.8%
33	Kansas	14,419	0.9%
27	Kentucky	20,635	1.3%
17	Louisiana	31,129	1.9%
42	Maine	5,250	0.3%
18	Maryland	30,759	1.9%
21	Massachusetts	25,042	1.5%
10	Michigan	48,823	3.0%
24	Minnesota	23,318	1.4%
23	Mississippi	24,324	1.5%
16	Missouri	31,985	1.9%
44	Montana	4,502	0.3%
37	Nebraska	8,635	0.5%
31	Nevada	16,515	1.0%
46	New Hampshire	4,228	0.3%
12	New Jersey	37,952	2.3%
32	New Mexico	15,328	0.9%
4	New York	100,036	6.1%
9	North Carolina	51,264	3.1%
48	North Dakota	2,733	0.2%
7	Ohio	60,989	3.7%
26	Oklahoma	22,093	1.3%
30	Oregon	16,710	1.0%
8	Pennsylvania	57,098	3.5%
43	Rhode Island	5,013	0.3%
19	South Carolina	28,333	1.7%
45	South Dakota	4,421	0.3%
15	Tennessee	34,919	2.1%
2	Texas	157,447	9.6%
36	Utah	10,058	0.6%
50	Vermont	2,246	0.1%
14	Virginia	36,442	2.2%
20	Washington	27,618	1.7%
38	West Virginia	7,932	0.5%
22	Wisconsin	24,666	1.5%
49	Wyoming	2,531	0.2%

RANK ORDER

RANK	STATE	BIRTHS	% of USA
1	California	211,474	12.9%
2	Texas	157,447	9.6%
3	Florida	105,412	6.4%
4	New York	100,036	6.1%
5	Illinois	69,886	4.3%
6	Georgia	63,014	3.8%
7	Ohio	60,989	3.7%
8	Pennsylvania	57,098	3.5%
9	North Carolina	51,264	3.1%
10	Michigan	48,823	3.0%
11	Arizona	45,089	2.7%
12	New Jersey	37,952	2.3%
13	Indiana	36,711	2.2%
14	Virginia	36,442	2.2%
15	Tennessee	34,919	2.1%
16	Missouri	31,985	1.9%
17	Louisiana	31,129	1.9%
18	Maryland	30,759	1.9%
19	South Carolina	28,333	1.7%
20	Washington	27,618	1.7%
21	Massachusetts	25,042	1.5%
22	Wisconsin	24,666	1.5%
23	Mississippi	24,324	1.5%
24	Minnesota	23,318	1.4%
25	Alabama	23,144	1.4%
26	Oklahoma	22,093	1.3%
27	Kentucky	20,635	1.3%
28	Colorado	19,527	1.2%
29	Arkansas	17,127	1.0%
30	Oregon	16,710	1.0%
31	Nevada	16,515	1.0%
32	New Mexico	15,328	0.9%
33	Kansas	14,419	0.9%
34	Connecticut	14,214	0.9%
35	Iowa	13,726	0.8%
36	Utah	10,058	0.6%
37	Nebraska	8,635	0.5%
38	West Virginia	7,932	0.5%
39	Hawaii	6,834	0.4%
40	Idaho	5,877	0.4%
41	Delaware	5,467	0.3%
42	Maine	5,250	0.3%
43	Rhode Island	5,013	0.3%
44	Montana	4,502	0.3%
45	South Dakota	4,421	0.3%
46	New Hampshire	4,228	0.3%
47	Alaska	4,045	0.2%
48	North Dakota	2,733	0.2%
49	Wyoming	2,531	0.2%
50	Vermont	2,246	0.1%
	District of Columbia	4,913	0.3%

Source: CQ Press using data from U.S. Department of Health and Human Services, National Center for Health Statistics
"Births: Preliminary data for 2006" (unpublished data)
*Preliminary data by state of residence.

Births to Unmarried Women as a Percent of All Births in 2006

National Percent = 38.5% of Live Births*

RANK	STATE	PERCENT	RANK	STATE	PERCENT
	ALPHA ORDER			RANK ORDER	
29	Alabama	36.6	1	Mississippi	52.8
28	Alaska	36.8	2	New Mexico	51.2
7	Arizona	44.0	3	Louisiana	49.1
9	Arkansas	41.8	4	Delaware	45.6
25	California	37.6	5	South Carolina	45.5
48	Colorado	27.6	6	Florida	44.5
37	Connecticut	34.0	7	Arizona	44.0
4	Delaware	45.6	8	Georgia	42.4
6	Florida	44.5	9	Arkansas	41.8
8	Georgia	42.4	10	Indiana	41.4
30	Hawaii	36.0	10	Tennessee	41.4
49	Idaho	24.3	12	Nevada	41.2
21	Illinois	38.7	13	Oklahoma	40.9
10	Indiana	41.4	14	Ohio	40.5
38	Iowa	33.8	14	Rhode Island	40.5
33	Kansas	35.2	16	North Carolina	40.1
32	Kentucky	35.4	17	New York	40.0
3	Louisiana	49.1	18	Maryland	39.7
26	Maine	37.1	19	Texas	39.4
18	Maryland	39.7	20	Missouri	39.3
43	Massachusetts	32.2	21	Illinois	38.7
22	Michigan	38.3	22	Michigan	38.3
45	Minnesota	31.7	22	Pennsylvania	38.3
1	Mississippi	52.8	24	West Virginia	37.9
20	Missouri	39.3	25	California	37.6
30	Montana	36.0	26	Maine	37.1
42	Nebraska	32.3	26	South Dakota	37.1
12	Nevada	41.2	28	Alaska	36.8
47	New Hampshire	29.4	29	Alabama	36.6
40	New Jersey	33.0	30	Hawaii	36.0
2	New Mexico	51.2	30	Montana	36.0
17	New York	40.0	32	Kentucky	35.4
16	North Carolina	40.1	33	Kansas	35.2
45	North Dakota	31.7	34	Vermont	34.5
14	Ohio	40.5	35	Oregon	34.3
13	Oklahoma	40.9	36	Wisconsin	34.1
35	Oregon	34.3	37	Connecticut	34.0
22	Pennsylvania	38.3	38	Iowa	33.8
14	Rhode Island	40.5	38	Virginia	33.8
5	South Carolina	45.5	40	New Jersey	33.0
26	South Dakota	37.1	40	Wyoming	33.0
10	Tennessee	41.4	42	Nebraska	32.3
19	Texas	39.4	43	Massachusetts	32.2
50	Utah	18.8	44	Washington	31.8
34	Vermont	34.5	45	Minnesota	31.7
38	Virginia	33.8	45	North Dakota	31.7
44	Washington	31.8	47	New Hampshire	29.4
24	West Virginia	37.9	48	Colorado	27.6
36	Wisconsin	34.1	49	Idaho	24.3
40	Wyoming	33.0	50	Utah	18.8
				District of Columbia	57.6

Source: U.S. Department of Health and Human Services, National Center for Health Statistics
   "Births: Preliminary data for 2006" (unpublished data)
*Preliminary data by state of residence. By race of mother.

Births to Unmarried White Women in 2006

National Total = 1,107,702 Live Births*

ALPHA ORDER

RANK	STATE	BIRTHS	% of USA
34	Alabama	9,470	0.9%
49	Alaska	1,707	0.2%
7	Arizona	37,138	3.4%
32	Arkansas	10,671	1.0%
1	California	176,572	15.9%
20	Colorado	17,176	1.6%
33	Connecticut	10,126	0.9%
43	Delaware	3,215	0.3%
3	Florida	65,056	5.9%
10	Georgia	28,873	2.6%
50	Hawaii	1,466	0.1%
39	Idaho	5,492	0.5%
5	Illinois	44,323	4.0%
12	Indiana	28,306	2.6%
27	Iowa	12,206	1.1%
31	Kansas	11,674	1.1%
21	Kentucky	16,458	1.5%
28	Louisiana	12,075	1.1%
40	Maine	5,032	0.5%
25	Maryland	14,055	1.3%
18	Massachusetts	18,353	1.7%
9	Michigan	30,299	2.7%
22	Minnesota	15,749	1.4%
37	Mississippi	7,314	0.7%
15	Missouri	21,850	2.0%
44	Montana	3,211	0.3%
38	Nebraska	6,766	0.6%
26	Nevada	13,078	1.2%
41	New Hampshire	4,069	0.4%
13	New Jersey	23,518	2.1%
30	New Mexico	11,837	1.1%
4	New York	57,963	5.2%
11	North Carolina	28,658	2.6%
48	North Dakota	1,891	0.2%
6	Ohio	40,860	3.7%
24	Oklahoma	14,868	1.3%
23	Oregon	14,935	1.3%
8	Pennsylvania	36,701	3.3%
42	Rhode Island	3,964	0.4%
29	South Carolina	11,887	1.1%
45	South Dakota	2,596	0.2%
16	Tennessee	20,703	1.9%
2	Texas	123,106	11.1%
35	Utah	9,060	0.8%
47	Vermont	2,181	0.2%
17	Virginia	20,488	1.8%
14	Washington	21,862	2.0%
36	West Virginia	7,391	0.7%
19	Wisconsin	17,336	1.6%
46	Wyoming	2,217	0.2%

RANK ORDER

RANK	STATE	BIRTHS	% of USA
1	California	176,572	15.9%
2	Texas	123,106	11.1%
3	Florida	65,056	5.9%
4	New York	57,963	5.2%
5	Illinois	44,323	4.0%
6	Ohio	40,860	3.7%
7	Arizona	37,138	3.4%
8	Pennsylvania	36,701	3.3%
9	Michigan	30,299	2.7%
10	Georgia	28,873	2.6%
11	North Carolina	28,658	2.6%
12	Indiana	28,306	2.6%
13	New Jersey	23,518	2.1%
14	Washington	21,862	2.0%
15	Missouri	21,850	2.0%
16	Tennessee	20,703	1.9%
17	Virginia	20,488	1.8%
18	Massachusetts	18,353	1.7%
19	Wisconsin	17,336	1.6%
20	Colorado	17,176	1.6%
21	Kentucky	16,458	1.5%
22	Minnesota	15,749	1.4%
23	Oregon	14,935	1.3%
24	Oklahoma	14,868	1.3%
25	Maryland	14,055	1.3%
26	Nevada	13,078	1.2%
27	Iowa	12,206	1.1%
28	Louisiana	12,075	1.1%
29	South Carolina	11,887	1.1%
30	New Mexico	11,837	1.1%
31	Kansas	11,674	1.1%
32	Arkansas	10,671	1.0%
33	Connecticut	10,126	0.9%
34	Alabama	9,470	0.9%
35	Utah	9,060	0.8%
36	West Virginia	7,391	0.7%
37	Mississippi	7,314	0.7%
38	Nebraska	6,766	0.6%
39	Idaho	5,492	0.5%
40	Maine	5,032	0.5%
41	New Hampshire	4,069	0.4%
42	Rhode Island	3,964	0.4%
43	Delaware	3,215	0.3%
44	Montana	3,211	0.3%
45	South Dakota	2,596	0.2%
46	Wyoming	2,217	0.2%
47	Vermont	2,181	0.2%
48	North Dakota	1,891	0.2%
49	Alaska	1,707	0.2%
50	Hawaii	1,466	0.1%
	District of Columbia	906	0.1%

Source: CQ Press using data from U.S. Department of Health and Human Services, National Center for Health Statistics
    "Births: Preliminary data for 2006" (unpublished data)
*Preliminary data by state of residence. By race of mother.

Births to Unmarried White Women
as a Percent of All Births to White Women in 2006
National Percent = 33.4% of Live Births*

ALPHA ORDER

RANK	STATE	PERCENT
49	Alabama	22.1
47	Alaska	24.6
2	Arizona	41.9
17	Arkansas	33.2
4	California	38.9
43	Colorado	26.6
34	Connecticut	30.0
5	Delaware	38.3
6	Florida	37.9
28	Georgia	30.8
45	Hawaii	26.5
48	Idaho	23.6
23	Illinois	31.8
9	Indiana	37.0
21	Iowa	32.3
20	Kansas	32.4
23	Kentucky	31.8
22	Louisiana	32.0
8	Maine	37.2
31	Maryland	30.3
37	Massachusetts	29.3
30	Michigan	30.6
43	Minnesota	26.6
33	Mississippi	30.2
18	Missouri	32.8
34	Montana	30.0
38	Nebraska	28.7
3	Nevada	39.4
34	New Hampshire	30.0
39	New Jersey	28.4
1	New Mexico	47.7
16	New York	33.5
26	North Carolina	31.0
46	North Dakota	25.7
15	Ohio	33.6
12	Oklahoma	35.5
14	Oregon	34.0
25	Pennsylvania	31.2
6	Rhode Island	37.9
31	South Carolina	30.3
41	South Dakota	27.3
19	Tennessee	32.5
11	Texas	36.8
50	Utah	17.9
13	Vermont	34.6
42	Virginia	26.8
29	Washington	30.7
10	West Virginia	36.9
40	Wisconsin	28.3
26	Wyoming	31.0

RANK ORDER

RANK	STATE	PERCENT
1	New Mexico	47.7
2	Arizona	41.9
3	Nevada	39.4
4	California	38.9
5	Delaware	38.3
6	Florida	37.9
6	Rhode Island	37.9
8	Maine	37.2
9	Indiana	37.0
10	West Virginia	36.9
11	Texas	36.8
12	Oklahoma	35.5
13	Vermont	34.6
14	Oregon	34.0
15	Ohio	33.6
16	New York	33.5
17	Arkansas	33.2
18	Missouri	32.8
19	Tennessee	32.5
20	Kansas	32.4
21	Iowa	32.3
22	Louisiana	32.0
23	Illinois	31.8
23	Kentucky	31.8
25	Pennsylvania	31.2
26	North Carolina	31.0
26	Wyoming	31.0
28	Georgia	30.8
29	Washington	30.7
30	Michigan	30.6
31	Maryland	30.3
31	South Carolina	30.3
33	Mississippi	30.2
34	Connecticut	30.0
34	Montana	30.0
34	New Hampshire	30.0
37	Massachusetts	29.3
38	Nebraska	28.7
39	New Jersey	28.4
40	Wisconsin	28.3
41	South Dakota	27.3
42	Virginia	26.8
43	Colorado	26.6
43	Minnesota	26.6
45	Hawaii	26.5
46	North Dakota	25.7
47	Alaska	24.6
48	Idaho	23.6
49	Alabama	22.1
50	Utah	17.9
	District of Columbia	27.5

Source: U.S. Department of Health and Human Services, National Center for Health Statistics
    "Births: Preliminary data for 2006" (unpublished data)
*Preliminary data by state of residence. By race of mother.

Births to Unmarried Black Women in 2006

National Total = 464,864 Live Births*

ALPHA ORDER

ALPHA ORDER

RANK	STATE	BIRTHS	% of USA
18	Alabama	13,515	2.9%
41	Alaska	199	0.0%
28	Arizona	2,501	0.5%
21	Arkansas	6,195	1.3%
6	California	22,077	4.7%
33	Colorado	1,699	0.4%
26	Connecticut	3,821	0.8%
32	Delaware	2,199	0.5%
1	Florida	38,472	8.3%
3	Georgia	33,462	7.2%
42	Hawaii	165	0.0%
46	Idaho	60	0.0%
5	Illinois	24,789	5.3%
20	Indiana	8,166	1.8%
35	Iowa	1,174	0.3%
31	Kansas	2,294	0.5%
25	Kentucky	3,944	0.8%
10	Louisiana	18,643	4.0%
44	Maine	104	0.0%
13	Maryland	16,207	3.5%
23	Massachusetts	5,749	1.2%
11	Michigan	17,704	3.8%
24	Minnesota	4,605	1.0%
12	Mississippi	16,680	3.6%
19	Missouri	9,639	2.1%
50	Montana	28	0.0%
34	Nebraska	1,305	0.3%
30	Nevada	2,421	0.5%
43	New Hampshire	115	0.0%
16	New Jersey	13,762	3.0%
39	New Mexico	357	0.1%
2	New York	37,588	8.1%
7	North Carolina	21,070	4.5%
47	North Dakota	48	0.0%
8	Ohio	19,510	4.2%
27	Oklahoma	3,762	0.8%
37	Oregon	726	0.2%
9	Pennsylvania	19,182	4.1%
36	Rhode Island	759	0.2%
14	South Carolina	16,043	3.5%
45	South Dakota	103	0.0%
17	Tennessee	13,641	2.9%
4	Texas	32,130	6.9%
40	Utah	255	0.1%
49	Vermont	31	0.0%
15	Virginia	15,131	3.3%
29	Washington	2,489	0.5%
38	West Virginia	515	0.1%
22	Wisconsin	5,929	1.3%
48	Wyoming	41	0.0%

RANK ORDER

RANK	STATE	BIRTHS	% of USA
1	Florida	38,472	8.3%
2	New York	37,588	8.1%
3	Georgia	33,462	7.2%
4	Texas	32,130	6.9%
5	Illinois	24,789	5.3%
6	California	22,077	4.7%
7	North Carolina	21,070	4.5%
8	Ohio	19,510	4.2%
9	Pennsylvania	19,182	4.1%
10	Louisiana	18,643	4.0%
11	Michigan	17,704	3.8%
12	Mississippi	16,680	3.6%
13	Maryland	16,207	3.5%
14	South Carolina	16,043	3.5%
15	Virginia	15,131	3.3%
16	New Jersey	13,762	3.0%
17	Tennessee	13,641	2.9%
18	Alabama	13,515	2.9%
19	Missouri	9,639	2.1%
20	Indiana	8,166	1.8%
21	Arkansas	6,195	1.3%
22	Wisconsin	5,929	1.3%
23	Massachusetts	5,749	1.2%
24	Minnesota	4,605	1.0%
25	Kentucky	3,944	0.8%
26	Connecticut	3,821	0.8%
27	Oklahoma	3,762	0.8%
28	Arizona	2,501	0.5%
29	Washington	2,489	0.5%
30	Nevada	2,421	0.5%
31	Kansas	2,294	0.5%
32	Delaware	2,199	0.5%
33	Colorado	1,699	0.4%
34	Nebraska	1,305	0.3%
35	Iowa	1,174	0.3%
36	Rhode Island	759	0.2%
37	Oregon	726	0.2%
38	West Virginia	515	0.1%
39	New Mexico	357	0.1%
40	Utah	255	0.1%
41	Alaska	199	0.0%
42	Hawaii	165	0.0%
43	New Hampshire	115	0.0%
44	Maine	104	0.0%
45	South Dakota	103	0.0%
46	Idaho	60	0.0%
47	North Dakota	48	0.0%
48	Wyoming	41	0.0%
49	Vermont	31	0.0%
50	Montana	28	0.0%
	District of Columbia	3,979	0.9%

Source: CQ Press using data from U.S. Department of Health and Human Services, National Center for Health Statistics
    "Births: Preliminary data for 2006" (unpublished data)
*Preliminary data by state of residence. By race of mother.

Births to Unmarried Black Women
as a Percent of All Births to Black Women in 2006
National Percent = 70.2% of Live Births*

ALPHA ORDER

RANK	STATE	PERCENT
20	Alabama	69.8
43	Alaska	45.5
33	Arizona	62.3
4	Arkansas	78.3
29	California	64.4
39	Colorado	54.0
24	Connecticut	68.2
18	Delaware	71.5
26	Florida	67.6
25	Georgia	67.7
50	Hawaii	27.0
46	Idaho	40.8
3	Illinois	78.5
5	Indiana	78.1
15	Iowa	72.5
16	Kansas	72.4
17	Kentucky	72.1
7	Louisiana	76.9
49	Maine	34.8
35	Maryland	61.9
36	Massachusetts	61.8
8	Michigan	76.7
37	Minnesota	60.7
2	Mississippi	79.1
6	Missouri	77.4
44	Montana	44.4
21	Nebraska	69.2
22	Nevada	69.1
45	New Hampshire	43.7
27	New Jersey	66.0
38	New Mexico	59.5
22	New York	69.1
19	North Carolina	70.4
48	North Dakota	36.1
8	Ohio	76.7
11	Oklahoma	75.6
32	Oregon	63.1
10	Pennsylvania	76.6
30	Rhode Island	63.8
12	South Carolina	74.6
42	South Dakota	47.0
13	Tennessee	74.3
28	Texas	65.3
41	Utah	49.3
47	Vermont	38.8
31	Virginia	63.6
40	Washington	52.6
14	West Virginia	73.6
1	Wisconsin	83.4
34	Wyoming	62.1

RANK ORDER

RANK	STATE	PERCENT
1	Wisconsin	83.4
2	Mississippi	79.1
3	Illinois	78.5
4	Arkansas	78.3
5	Indiana	78.1
6	Missouri	77.4
7	Louisiana	76.9
8	Michigan	76.7
8	Ohio	76.7
10	Pennsylvania	76.6
11	Oklahoma	75.6
12	South Carolina	74.6
13	Tennessee	74.3
14	West Virginia	73.6
15	Iowa	72.5
16	Kansas	72.4
17	Kentucky	72.1
18	Delaware	71.5
19	North Carolina	70.4
20	Alabama	69.8
21	Nebraska	69.2
22	Nevada	69.1
22	New York	69.1
24	Connecticut	68.2
25	Georgia	67.7
26	Florida	67.6
27	New Jersey	66.0
28	Texas	65.3
29	California	64.4
30	Rhode Island	63.8
31	Virginia	63.6
32	Oregon	63.1
33	Arizona	62.3
34	Wyoming	62.1
35	Maryland	61.9
36	Massachusetts	61.8
37	Minnesota	60.7
38	New Mexico	59.5
39	Colorado	54.0
40	Washington	52.6
41	Utah	49.3
42	South Dakota	47.0
43	Alaska	45.5
44	Montana	44.4
45	New Hampshire	43.7
46	Idaho	40.8
47	Vermont	38.8
48	North Dakota	36.1
49	Maine	34.8
50	Hawaii	27.0
	District of Columbia	78.9

Source: U.S. Department of Health and Human Services, National Center for Health Statistics
    "Births: Preliminary data for 2006" (unpublished data)
*Preliminary data by state of residence. By race of mother.

Births to Unmarried Hispanic Women in 2006

National Total = 518,486 Live Births*

ALPHA ORDER

RANK	STATE	BIRTHS	% of USA
40	Alabama	1,005	0.2%
43	Alaska	277	0.1%
5	Arizona	25,271	4.9%
31	Arkansas	2,046	0.4%
1	California	141,380	27.3%
11	Colorado	9,445	1.8%
18	Connecticut	5,352	1.0%
38	Delaware	1,157	0.2%
4	Florida	33,489	6.5%
8	Georgia	11,506	2.2%
36	Hawaii	1,440	0.3%
35	Idaho	1,513	0.3%
6	Illinois	21,683	4.2%
19	Indiana	4,643	0.9%
33	Iowa	1,584	0.3%
28	Kansas	3,267	0.6%
37	Kentucky	1,347	0.3%
39	Louisiana	1,067	0.2%
49	Maine	93	0.0%
17	Maryland	5,436	1.0%
16	Massachusetts	7,088	1.4%
21	Michigan	4,185	0.8%
27	Minnesota	3,381	0.7%
41	Mississippi	871	0.2%
30	Missouri	2,292	0.4%
45	Montana	194	0.0%
32	Nebraska	1,952	0.4%
13	Nevada	7,686	1.5%
44	New Hampshire	268	0.1%
7	New Jersey	16,674	3.2%
10	New Mexico	9,446	1.8%
3	New York	38,031	7.3%
9	North Carolina	11,286	2.2%
47	North Dakota	116	0.0%
23	Ohio	3,833	0.7%
26	Oklahoma	3,427	0.7%
20	Oregon	4,625	0.9%
12	Pennsylvania	8,415	1.6%
34	Rhode Island	1,573	0.3%
29	South Carolina	2,703	0.5%
46	South Dakota	190	0.0%
22	Tennessee	4,152	0.8%
2	Texas	89,429	17.2%
24	Utah	3,553	0.7%
50	Vermont	27	0.0%
15	Virginia	7,246	1.4%
14	Washington	7,466	1.4%
48	West Virginia	100	0.0%
25	Wisconsin	3,449	0.7%
42	Wyoming	443	0.1%

RANK ORDER

RANK	STATE	BIRTHS	% of USA
1	California	141,380	27.3%
2	Texas	89,429	17.2%
3	New York	38,031	7.3%
4	Florida	33,489	6.5%
5	Arizona	25,271	4.9%
6	Illinois	21,683	4.2%
7	New Jersey	16,674	3.2%
8	Georgia	11,506	2.2%
9	North Carolina	11,286	2.2%
10	New Mexico	9,446	1.8%
11	Colorado	9,445	1.8%
12	Pennsylvania	8,415	1.6%
13	Nevada	7,686	1.5%
14	Washington	7,466	1.4%
15	Virginia	7,246	1.4%
16	Massachusetts	7,088	1.4%
17	Maryland	5,436	1.0%
18	Connecticut	5,352	1.0%
19	Indiana	4,643	0.9%
20	Oregon	4,625	0.9%
21	Michigan	4,185	0.8%
22	Tennessee	4,152	0.8%
23	Ohio	3,833	0.7%
24	Utah	3,553	0.7%
25	Wisconsin	3,449	0.7%
26	Oklahoma	3,427	0.7%
27	Minnesota	3,381	0.7%
28	Kansas	3,267	0.6%
29	South Carolina	2,703	0.5%
30	Missouri	2,292	0.4%
31	Arkansas	2,046	0.4%
32	Nebraska	1,952	0.4%
33	Iowa	1,584	0.3%
34	Rhode Island	1,573	0.3%
35	Idaho	1,513	0.3%
36	Hawaii	1,440	0.3%
37	Kentucky	1,347	0.3%
38	Delaware	1,157	0.2%
39	Louisiana	1,067	0.2%
40	Alabama	1,005	0.2%
41	Mississippi	871	0.2%
42	Wyoming	443	0.1%
43	Alaska	277	0.1%
44	New Hampshire	268	0.1%
45	Montana	194	0.0%
46	South Dakota	190	0.0%
47	North Dakota	116	0.0%
48	West Virginia	100	0.0%
49	Maine	93	0.0%
50	Vermont	27	0.0%
	District of Columbia	896	0.2%

Source: CQ Press using data from U.S. Department of Health and Human Services, National Center for Health Statistics
 "Births: Preliminary data for 2006" (unpublished data)
*Preliminary data by state of residence. Hispanic can be of any race.

Births to Unmarried Hispanic Women
as a Percent of All Births to Hispanic Women in 2006
National Percent = 49.9% of Live Births*

ALPHA ORDER

RANK	STATE	PERCENT
50	Alabama	21.4
48	Alaska	36.8
12	Arizona	55.5
38	Arkansas	46.5
30	California	48.2
46	Colorado	41.4
4	Connecticut	63.1
5	Delaware	61.5
32	Florida	47.8
26	Georgia	48.6
34	Hawaii	47.4
47	Idaho	39.9
24	Illinois	48.9
13	Indiana	54.9
23	Iowa	49.1
20	Kansas	49.6
27	Kentucky	48.5
32	Louisiana	47.8
45	Maine	42.7
14	Maryland	53.9
1	Massachusetts	65.9
30	Michigan	48.2
10	Minnesota	56.0
10	Mississippi	56.0
17	Missouri	50.3
29	Montana	48.4
25	Nebraska	48.8
22	Nevada	49.2
41	New Hampshire	45.8
8	New Jersey	57.1
7	New Mexico	57.2
2	New York	64.1
15	North Carolina	53.2
37	North Dakota	46.6
9	Ohio	56.9
27	Oklahoma	48.5
38	Oregon	46.5
3	Pennsylvania	63.3
5	Rhode Island	61.5
40	South Carolina	45.9
34	South Dakota	47.4
16	Tennessee	52.3
43	Texas	45.1
44	Utah	43.2
49	Vermont	36.5
19	Virginia	50.1
36	Washington	47.3
42	West Virginia	45.7
18	Wisconsin	50.2
21	Wyoming	49.4

RANK ORDER

RANK	STATE	PERCENT
1	Massachusetts	65.9
2	New York	64.1
3	Pennsylvania	63.3
4	Connecticut	63.1
5	Delaware	61.5
5	Rhode Island	61.5
7	New Mexico	57.2
8	New Jersey	57.1
9	Ohio	56.9
10	Minnesota	56.0
10	Mississippi	56.0
12	Arizona	55.5
13	Indiana	54.9
14	Maryland	53.9
15	North Carolina	53.2
16	Tennessee	52.3
17	Missouri	50.3
18	Wisconsin	50.2
19	Virginia	50.1
20	Kansas	49.6
21	Wyoming	49.4
22	Nevada	49.2
23	Iowa	49.1
24	Illinois	48.9
25	Nebraska	48.8
26	Georgia	48.6
27	Kentucky	48.5
27	Oklahoma	48.5
29	Montana	48.4
30	California	48.2
30	Michigan	48.2
32	Florida	47.8
32	Louisiana	47.8
34	Hawaii	47.4
34	South Dakota	47.4
36	Washington	47.3
37	North Dakota	46.6
38	Arkansas	46.5
38	Oregon	46.5
40	South Carolina	45.9
41	New Hampshire	45.8
42	West Virginia	45.7
43	Texas	45.1
44	Utah	43.2
45	Maine	42.7
46	Colorado	41.4
47	Idaho	39.9
48	Alaska	36.8
49	Vermont	36.5
50	Alabama	21.4
	District of Columbia	67.5

Source: U.S. Department of Health and Human Services, National Center for Health Statistics
   "Births: Preliminary data for 2006" (unpublished data)
*Preliminary data by state of residence. Hispanic can be of any race.

Pregnancy Rate in 2004

National Rate = 68.9 Births and Abortions per 1,000 Women 15-49 Years Old*

ALPHA ORDER

RANK	STATE	RATE
31	Alabama	63.4
13	Alaska	71.8
4	Arizona	77.2
27	Arkansas	65.4
NA	California**	NA
20	Colorado	67.9
34	Connecticut	62.9
6	Delaware	76.5
8	Florida	76.3
10	Georgia	73.5
11	Hawaii	72.0
16	Idaho	69.3
15	Illinois	70.1
31	Indiana	63.4
33	Iowa	63.1
7	Kansas	76.4
44	Kentucky	57.3
22	Louisiana	66.9
47	Maine	51.6
43	Maryland	58.9
37	Massachusetts	62.4
38	Michigan	62.3
25	Minnesota	66.0
30	Mississippi	63.8
41	Missouri	60.3
34	Montana	62.9
14	Nebraska	70.7
2	Nevada	80.1
NA	New Hampshire**	NA
17	New Jersey	68.6
9	New Mexico	73.7
5	New York	76.8
11	North Carolina	72.0
36	North Dakota	62.6
29	Ohio	64.7
19	Oklahoma	68.0
26	Oregon	65.6
39	Pennsylvania	60.5
24	Rhode Island	66.6
40	South Carolina	60.4
23	South Dakota	66.7
27	Tennessee	65.4
3	Texas	79.3
1	Utah	87.0
46	Vermont	54.0
21	Virginia	67.8
18	Washington	68.2
NA	West Virginia**	NA
42	Wisconsin	59.0
45	Wyoming	55.6

RANK ORDER

RANK	STATE	RATE
1	Utah	87.0
2	Nevada	80.1
3	Texas	79.3
4	Arizona	77.2
5	New York	76.8
6	Delaware	76.5
7	Kansas	76.4
8	Florida	76.3
9	New Mexico	73.7
10	Georgia	73.5
11	Hawaii	72.0
11	North Carolina	72.0
13	Alaska	71.8
14	Nebraska	70.7
15	Illinois	70.1
16	Idaho	69.3
17	New Jersey	68.6
18	Washington	68.2
19	Oklahoma	68.0
20	Colorado	67.9
21	Virginia	67.8
22	Louisiana	66.9
23	South Dakota	66.7
24	Rhode Island	66.6
25	Minnesota	66.0
26	Oregon	65.6
27	Arkansas	65.4
27	Tennessee	65.4
29	Ohio	64.7
30	Mississippi	63.8
31	Alabama	63.4
31	Indiana	63.4
33	Iowa	63.1
34	Connecticut	62.9
34	Montana	62.9
36	North Dakota	62.6
37	Massachusetts	62.4
38	Michigan	62.3
39	Pennsylvania	60.5
40	South Carolina	60.4
41	Missouri	60.3
42	Wisconsin	59.0
43	Maryland	58.9
44	Kentucky	57.3
45	Wyoming	55.6
46	Vermont	54.0
47	Maine	51.6
NA	California**	NA
NA	New Hampshire**	NA
NA	West Virginia**	NA

District of Columbia 63.0

Source: CQ Press using data from U.S. Department of Health and Human Services, Centers for Disease Control and Prevention
"Abortion Surveillance-United States, 2004" (Morbidity and Mortality Weekly Report, Vol. 56, No. SS-9, 11/23/07)
*The sum of live births and legal induced abortions per 1,000 women aged 15-49 years old. Births by state of residence, abortions by state of occurrence. Miscarriages are not included in these rates. National rate includes only states reporting abortions and births.
**Not available.

Teenage Pregnancy Rate in 2004

National Rate = 58.0 Births and Abortions per 1,000 Women 15-19 Years Old*

ALPHA ORDER

RANK	STATE	RATE
12	Alabama	66.7
14	Alaska	61.3
4	Arizona	74.0
5	Arkansas	72.2
NA	California**	NA
17	Colorado	60.2
34	Connecticut	44.4
13	Delaware	64.0
NA	Florida**	NA
6	Georgia	71.6
19	Hawaii	56.0
36	Idaho	42.6
NA	Illinois**	NA
24	Indiana	52.2
37	Iowa	41.8
15	Kansas	61.2
22	Kentucky	54.6
9	Louisiana	68.1
43	Maine	37.0
NA	Maryland**	NA
39	Massachusetts	40.0
29	Michigan	48.3
40	Minnesota	38.7
8	Mississippi	68.5
25	Missouri	51.6
27	Montana	51.3
30	Nebraska	46.1
2	Nevada	78.9
NA	New Hampshire**	NA
31	New Jersey	45.3
1	New Mexico	81.1
16	New York	60.5
7	North Carolina	69.3
42	North Dakota	37.2
20	Ohio	55.2
11	Oklahoma	67.8
26	Oregon	51.4
33	Pennsylvania	44.8
22	Rhode Island	54.6
18	South Carolina	58.9
32	South Dakota	44.9
9	Tennessee	68.1
3	Texas	77.6
41	Utah	38.2
44	Vermont	34.7
28	Virginia	51.2
21	Washington	54.7
NA	West Virginia**	NA
38	Wisconsin	40.1
34	Wyoming	44.4

RANK ORDER

RANK	STATE	RATE
1	New Mexico	81.1
2	Nevada	78.9
3	Texas	77.6
4	Arizona	74.0
5	Arkansas	72.2
6	Georgia	71.6
7	North Carolina	69.3
8	Mississippi	68.5
9	Louisiana	68.1
9	Tennessee	68.1
11	Oklahoma	67.8
12	Alabama	66.7
13	Delaware	64.0
14	Alaska	61.3
15	Kansas	61.2
16	New York	60.5
17	Colorado	60.2
18	South Carolina	58.9
19	Hawaii	56.0
20	Ohio	55.2
21	Washington	54.7
22	Kentucky	54.6
22	Rhode Island	54.6
24	Indiana	52.2
25	Missouri	51.6
26	Oregon	51.4
27	Montana	51.3
28	Virginia	51.2
29	Michigan	48.3
30	Nebraska	46.1
31	New Jersey	45.3
32	South Dakota	44.9
33	Pennsylvania	44.8
34	Connecticut	44.4
34	Wyoming	44.4
36	Idaho	42.6
37	Iowa	41.8
38	Wisconsin	40.1
39	Massachusetts	40.0
40	Minnesota	38.7
41	Utah	38.2
42	North Dakota	37.2
43	Maine	37.0
44	Vermont	34.7
NA	California**	NA
NA	Florida**	NA
NA	Illinois**	NA
NA	Maryland**	NA
NA	New Hampshire**	NA
NA	West Virginia**	NA

District of Columbia 67.3

Source: CQ Press using data from U.S. Department of Health and Human Services, Centers for Disease Control and Prevention
    "Abortion Surveillance-United States, 2004" (Morbidity and Mortality Weekly Report, Vol. 56, No. SS-9, 11/23/07)
*The sum of live births and legal induced abortions per 1,000 women aged 15-19 years old. Births by state of residence,
abortions by state of occurrence. Miscarriages are not included in these rates. National rate includes only states reporting
abortions and births.
**Not available.

Percent Change in Teenage Pregnancy Rate: 2000 to 2004

National Percent Change = 10.5% Decrease*

ALPHA ORDER			RANK ORDER		
RANK	STATE	PERCENT CHANGE	RANK	STATE	PERCENT CHANGE
31	Alabama	(13.2)	1	Wyoming	6.2
NA	Alaska**	NA	2	Colorado	4.9
9	Arizona	(6.3)	3	South Dakota	1.6
10	Arkansas	(7.0)	4	Nevada	(0.9)
NA	California**	NA	5	New Mexico	(2.2)
2	Colorado	4.9	6	Montana	(2.8)
42	Connecticut	(20.6)	7	Oklahoma	(4.6)
38	Delaware	(15.1)	8	Missouri	(6.2)
NA	Florida**	NA	9	Arizona	(6.3)
25	Georgia	(11.5)	10	Arkansas	(7.0)
41	Hawaii	(20.0)	10	Idaho	(7.0)
10	Idaho	(7.0)	12	Louisiana	(7.1)
NA	Illinois**	NA	13	Texas	(7.4)
25	Indiana	(11.5)	14	Rhode Island	(7.5)
15	Iowa	(7.7)	15	Iowa	(7.7)
28	Kansas	(12.1)	16	Nebraska	(9.4)
19	Kentucky	(10.2)	17	Pennsylvania	(9.7)
12	Louisiana	(7.1)	17	Tennessee	(9.7)
29	Maine	(12.3)	19	Kentucky	(10.2)
NA	Maryland**	NA	19	Minnesota	(10.2)
39	Massachusetts	(16.8)	21	North Dakota	(10.6)
24	Michigan	(11.2)	22	Mississippi	(10.7)
19	Minnesota	(10.2)	23	North Carolina	(10.8)
22	Mississippi	(10.7)	24	Michigan	(11.2)
8	Missouri	(6.2)	25	Georgia	(11.5)
6	Montana	(2.8)	25	Indiana	(11.5)
16	Nebraska	(9.4)	27	Wisconsin	(11.9)
4	Nevada	(0.9)	28	Kansas	(12.1)
NA	New Hampshire**	NA	29	Maine	(12.3)
40	New Jersey	(18.7)	30	Ohio	(12.7)
5	New Mexico	(2.2)	31	Alabama	(13.2)
34	New York	(13.7)	32	Utah	(13.4)
23	North Carolina	(10.8)	33	Vermont	(13.5)
21	North Dakota	(10.6)	34	New York	(13.7)
30	Ohio	(12.7)	35	South Carolina	(14.1)
7	Oklahoma	(4.6)	36	Virginia	(14.2)
43	Oregon	(22.0)	37	Washington	(14.3)
17	Pennsylvania	(9.7)	38	Delaware	(15.1)
14	Rhode Island	(7.5)	39	Massachusetts	(16.8)
35	South Carolina	(14.1)	40	New Jersey	(18.7)
3	South Dakota	1.6	41	Hawaii	(20.0)
17	Tennessee	(9.7)	42	Connecticut	(20.6)
13	Texas	(7.4)	43	Oregon	(22.0)
32	Utah	(13.4)	NA	Alaska**	NA
33	Vermont	(13.5)	NA	California**	NA
36	Virginia	(14.2)	NA	Florida**	NA
37	Washington	(14.3)	NA	Illinois**	NA
NA	West Virginia**	NA	NA	Maryland**	NA
27	Wisconsin	(11.9)	NA	New Hampshire**	NA
1	Wyoming	6.2	NA	West Virginia**	NA

District of Columbia   (41.0)

Source: CQ Press using data from U.S. Department of Health and Human Services, Centers for Disease Control and Prevention
    "Abortion Surveillance-United States, 2004" (Morbidity and Mortality Weekly Report, Vol. 56, No. SS-9, 11/23/07)
*The sum of live births and legal induced abortions per 1,000 women aged 15-19 years old. Births by state of residence,
abortions by state of occurrence. Miscarriages are not included in these rates. National rate includes only states reporting
abortions and births.
**Not available.

Births to Teenage Mothers in 2006

National Total = 443,664 Live Births*

ALPHA ORDER   RANK ORDER

RANK	STATE	BIRTHS	% of USA	RANK	STATE	BIRTHS	% of USA
17	Alabama	8,726	2.0%	1	Texas	53,948	12.2%
46	Alaska	1,110	0.3%	2	California	53,431	12.0%
10	Arizona	13,014	2.9%	3	Florida	25,820	5.8%
27	Arkansas	6,023	1.4%	4	Illinois	18,058	4.1%
2	California	53,431	12.0%	5	Georgia	17,983	4.1%
24	Colorado	6,863	1.5%	6	New York	17,756	4.0%
36	Connecticut	2,885	0.7%	7	Ohio	16,113	3.6%
42	Delaware	1,283	0.3%	8	North Carolina	14,957	3.4%
3	Florida	25,820	5.8%	9	Pennsylvania	13,865	3.1%
5	Georgia	17,983	4.1%	10	Arizona	13,014	2.9%
40	Hawaii	1,632	0.4%	11	Michigan	12,493	2.8%
38	Idaho	2,152	0.5%	12	Tennessee	10,965	2.5%
4	Illinois	18,058	4.1%	13	Indiana	9,665	2.2%
13	Indiana	9,665	2.2%	14	Missouri	9,278	2.1%
34	Iowa	3,533	0.8%	15	Virginia	9,272	2.1%
33	Kansas	4,178	0.9%	16	Louisiana	8,749	2.0%
20	Kentucky	7,520	1.7%	17	Alabama	8,726	2.0%
16	Louisiana	8,749	2.0%	18	South Carolina	8,344	1.9%
43	Maine	1,146	0.3%	19	Mississippi	7,555	1.7%
25	Maryland	6,818	1.5%	20	Kentucky	7,520	1.7%
29	Massachusetts	4,822	1.1%	21	Oklahoma	7,346	1.7%
11	Michigan	12,493	2.8%	22	New Jersey	7,245	1.6%
28	Minnesota	5,149	1.2%	23	Washington	7,208	1.6%
19	Mississippi	7,555	1.7%	24	Colorado	6,863	1.5%
14	Missouri	9,278	2.1%	25	Maryland	6,818	1.5%
41	Montana	1,288	0.3%	26	Wisconsin	6,076	1.4%
39	Nebraska	2,139	0.5%	27	Arkansas	6,023	1.4%
31	Nevada	4,369	1.0%	28	Minnesota	5,149	1.2%
47	New Hampshire	877	0.2%	29	Massachusetts	4,822	1.1%
22	New Jersey	7,245	1.6%	30	New Mexico	4,700	1.1%
30	New Mexico	4,700	1.1%	31	Nevada	4,369	1.0%
6	New York	17,756	4.0%	32	Oregon	4,336	1.0%
8	North Carolina	14,957	3.4%	33	Kansas	4,178	0.9%
49	North Dakota	638	0.1%	34	Iowa	3,533	0.8%
7	Ohio	16,113	3.6%	35	Utah	3,531	0.8%
21	Oklahoma	7,346	1.7%	36	Connecticut	2,885	0.7%
32	Oregon	4,336	1.0%	37	West Virginia	2,616	0.6%
9	Pennsylvania	13,865	3.1%	38	Idaho	2,152	0.5%
44	Rhode Island	1,139	0.3%	39	Nebraska	2,139	0.5%
18	South Carolina	8,344	1.9%	40	Hawaii	1,632	0.4%
45	South Dakota	1,132	0.3%	41	Montana	1,288	0.3%
12	Tennessee	10,965	2.5%	42	Delaware	1,283	0.3%
1	Texas	53,948	12.2%	43	Maine	1,146	0.3%
35	Utah	3,531	0.8%	44	Rhode Island	1,139	0.3%
50	Vermont	469	0.1%	45	South Dakota	1,132	0.3%
15	Virginia	9,272	2.1%	46	Alaska	1,110	0.3%
23	Washington	7,208	1.6%	47	New Hampshire	877	0.2%
37	West Virginia	2,616	0.6%	48	Wyoming	859	0.2%
26	Wisconsin	6,076	1.4%	49	North Dakota	638	0.1%
48	Wyoming	859	0.2%	50	Vermont	469	0.1%
					District of Columbia	1,023	0.2%

Source: CQ Press using data from U.S. Department of Health and Human Services, National Center for Health Statistics
 "National Vital Statistics Reports" (Vol. 56, No. 7, December 5, 2007, http://www.cdc.gov/nchs/births.htm)
*Preliminary estimates of live births to women 15 to 19 years old by state of residence.

Births to Teenage Mothers as a Percent of Births in 2006

National Percent = 10.4% of Live Births*

ALPHA ORDER			RANK ORDER		
RANK	STATE	PERCENT	RANK	STATE	PERCENT
4	Alabama	13.8	1	Mississippi	16.4
24	Alaska	10.1	2	New Mexico	15.7
11	Arizona	12.7	3	Arkansas	14.7
3	Arkansas	14.7	4	Alabama	13.8
28	California	9.5	4	Louisiana	13.8
27	Colorado	9.7	6	Oklahoma	13.6
46	Connecticut	6.9	7	Texas	13.5
20	Delaware	10.7	8	South Carolina	13.4
17	Florida	10.9	9	Tennessee	13.0
13	Georgia	12.1	10	Kentucky	12.9
36	Hawaii	8.6	11	Arizona	12.7
32	Idaho	8.9	12	West Virginia	12.5
25	Illinois	10.0	13	Georgia	12.1
17	Indiana	10.9	14	North Carolina	11.7
35	Iowa	8.7	15	Missouri	11.4
23	Kansas	10.2	16	Wyoming	11.2
10	Kentucky	12.9	17	Florida	10.9
4	Louisiana	13.8	17	Indiana	10.9
40	Maine	8.1	17	Nevada	10.9
34	Maryland	8.8	20	Delaware	10.7
49	Massachusetts	6.2	20	Ohio	10.7
26	Michigan	9.8	22	Montana	10.3
45	Minnesota	7.0	23	Kansas	10.2
1	Mississippi	16.4	24	Alaska	10.1
15	Missouri	11.4	25	Illinois	10.0
22	Montana	10.3	26	Michigan	9.8
41	Nebraska	8.0	27	Colorado	9.7
17	Nevada	10.9	28	California	9.5
50	New Hampshire	6.1	28	South Dakota	9.5
48	New Jersey	6.3	30	Pennsylvania	9.3
2	New Mexico	15.7	31	Rhode Island	9.2
44	New York	7.1	32	Idaho	8.9
14	North Carolina	11.7	32	Oregon	8.9
42	North Dakota	7.4	34	Maryland	8.8
20	Ohio	10.7	35	Iowa	8.7
6	Oklahoma	13.6	36	Hawaii	8.6
32	Oregon	8.9	36	Virginia	8.6
30	Pennsylvania	9.3	38	Wisconsin	8.4
31	Rhode Island	9.2	39	Washington	8.3
8	South Carolina	13.4	40	Maine	8.1
28	South Dakota	9.5	41	Nebraska	8.0
9	Tennessee	13.0	42	North Dakota	7.4
7	Texas	13.5	43	Vermont	7.2
47	Utah	6.6	44	New York	7.1
43	Vermont	7.2	45	Minnesota	7.0
36	Virginia	8.6	46	Connecticut	6.9
39	Washington	8.3	47	Utah	6.6
12	West Virginia	12.5	48	New Jersey	6.3
38	Wisconsin	8.4	49	Massachusetts	6.2
16	Wyoming	11.2	50	New Hampshire	6.1
				District of Columbia	12.0

Source: U.S. Department of Health and Human Services, National Center for Health Statistics
    "National Vital Statistics Reports" (Vol. 56, No. 7, December 5, 2007, http://www.cdc.gov/nchs/births.htm)
*Preliminary data. Live births to women 15 to 19 years old by state of residence.

Teenage Birth Rate in 2006

National Rate = 43.3 Live Births per 1,000 Women 15 to 19 Years Old*

ALPHA ORDER

RANK	STATE	RATE
9	Alabama	55.9
27	Alaska	39.9
4	Arizona	64.0
5	Arkansas	63.0
23	California	41.4
20	Colorado	44.0
47	Connecticut	23.9
17	Delaware	46.1
19	Florida	45.3
7	Georgia	57.2
27	Hawaii	39.9
26	Idaho	40.3
24	Illinois	40.9
21	Indiana	43.9
34	Iowa	34.6
22	Kansas	42.7
12	Kentucky	54.9
13	Louisiana	52.7
45	Maine	25.1
35	Maryland	34.5
48	Massachusetts	23.2
36	Michigan	34.4
43	Minnesota	28.1
1	Mississippi	71.3
18	Missouri	45.8
30	Montana	38.3
37	Nebraska	34.1
9	Nevada	55.9
50	New Hampshire	18.5
46	New Jersey	24.6
3	New Mexico	64.7
44	New York	27.6
14	North Carolina	52.1
42	North Dakota	28.6
25	Ohio	40.5
6	Oklahoma	59.6
33	Oregon	35.8
39	Pennsylvania	32.6
40	Rhode Island	32.0
8	South Carolina	56.9
29	South Dakota	39.3
11	Tennessee	55.8
2	Texas	64.9
31	Utah	37.0
49	Vermont	21.1
32	Virginia	36.4
38	Washington	33.2
16	West Virginia	46.3
41	Wisconsin	30.7
15	Wyoming	46.6

RANK ORDER

RANK	STATE	RATE
1	Mississippi	71.3
2	Texas	64.9
3	New Mexico	64.7
4	Arizona	64.0
5	Arkansas	63.0
6	Oklahoma	59.6
7	Georgia	57.2
8	South Carolina	56.9
9	Alabama	55.9
9	Nevada	55.9
11	Tennessee	55.8
12	Kentucky	54.9
13	Louisiana	52.7
14	North Carolina	52.1
15	Wyoming	46.6
16	West Virginia	46.3
17	Delaware	46.1
18	Missouri	45.8
19	Florida	45.3
20	Colorado	44.0
21	Indiana	43.9
22	Kansas	42.7
23	California	41.4
24	Illinois	40.9
25	Ohio	40.5
26	Idaho	40.3
27	Alaska	39.9
27	Hawaii	39.9
29	South Dakota	39.3
30	Montana	38.3
31	Utah	37.0
32	Virginia	36.4
33	Oregon	35.8
34	Iowa	34.6
35	Maryland	34.5
36	Michigan	34.4
37	Nebraska	34.1
38	Washington	33.2
39	Pennsylvania	32.6
40	Rhode Island	32.0
41	Wisconsin	30.7
42	North Dakota	28.6
43	Minnesota	28.1
44	New York	27.6
45	Maine	25.1
46	New Jersey	24.6
47	Connecticut	23.9
48	Massachusetts	23.2
49	Vermont	21.1
50	New Hampshire	18.5

District of Columbia 76.1

Source: CQ Press using data from U.S. Department of Health and Human Services, National Center for Health Statistics
"National Vital Statistics Reports" (Vol. 56, No. 7, December 5, 2007, http://www.cdc.gov/nchs/births.htm)
*Preliminary data by state of residence.

Percent Change in Teenage Birth Rate: 2002 to 2006

National Percent Change = 0.7% Increase*

ALPHA ORDER

RANK	STATE	PERCENT CHANGE
20	Alabama	2.6
25	Alaska	1.0
9	Arizona	4.6
6	Arkansas	5.2
27	California	0.7
42	Colorado	(6.4)
44	Connecticut	(7.4)
31	Delaware	(0.4)
23	Florida	1.8
19	Georgia	2.7
10	Hawaii	4.5
16	Idaho	3.1
39	Illinois	(3.1)
36	Indiana	(1.6)
5	Iowa	6.5
33	Kansas	(0.7)
3	Kentucky	7.6
48	Louisiana	(9.3)
35	Maine	(1.2)
37	Maryland	(2.5)
31	Massachusetts	(0.4)
34	Michigan	(1.1)
22	Minnesota	2.2
2	Mississippi	10.2
11	Missouri	3.9
6	Montana	5.2
46	Nebraska	(7.8)
12	Nevada	3.7
45	New Hampshire	(7.5)
47	New Jersey	(8.2)
12	New Mexico	3.7
42	New York	(6.4)
30	North Carolina	(0.2)
8	North Dakota	5.1
21	Ohio	2.5
17	Oklahoma	2.8
38	Oregon	(2.7)
15	Pennsylvania	3.2
49	Rhode Island	(10.1)
4	South Carolina	7.4
14	South Dakota	3.4
17	Tennessee	2.8
26	Texas	0.8
29	Utah	0.5
50	Vermont	(12.8)
40	Virginia	(3.2)
28	Washington	0.6
23	West Virginia	1.8
41	Wisconsin	(5.0)
1	Wyoming	16.8

RANK ORDER

RANK	STATE	PERCENT CHANGE
1	Wyoming	16.8
2	Mississippi	10.2
3	Kentucky	7.6
4	South Carolina	7.4
5	Iowa	6.5
6	Arkansas	5.2
6	Montana	5.2
8	North Dakota	5.1
9	Arizona	4.6
10	Hawaii	4.5
11	Missouri	3.9
12	Nevada	3.7
12	New Mexico	3.7
14	South Dakota	3.4
15	Pennsylvania	3.2
16	Idaho	3.1
17	Oklahoma	2.8
17	Tennessee	2.8
19	Georgia	2.7
20	Alabama	2.6
21	Ohio	2.5
22	Minnesota	2.2
23	Florida	1.8
23	West Virginia	1.8
25	Alaska	1.0
26	Texas	0.8
27	California	0.7
28	Washington	0.6
29	Utah	0.5
30	North Carolina	(0.2)
31	Delaware	(0.4)
31	Massachusetts	(0.4)
33	Kansas	(0.7)
34	Michigan	(1.1)
35	Maine	(1.2)
36	Indiana	(1.6)
37	Maryland	(2.5)
38	Oregon	(2.7)
39	Illinois	(3.1)
40	Virginia	(3.2)
41	Wisconsin	(5.0)
42	Colorado	(6.4)
42	New York	(6.4)
44	Connecticut	(7.4)
45	New Hampshire	(7.5)
46	Nebraska	(7.8)
47	New Jersey	(8.2)
48	Louisiana	(9.3)
49	Rhode Island	(10.1)
50	Vermont	(12.8)

District of Columbia   10.1

Source: CQ Press using data from U.S. Department of Health and Human Services, National Center for Health Statistics
"National Vital Statistics Reports" (Vol. 56, No. 7, December 5, 2007, http://www.cdc.gov/nchs/births.htm)
*Preliminary data by state of residence. Births to women aged 15 to 19 years old.

Births to Teenage Mothers in 2005

National Total = 414,593 Births*

ALPHA ORDER

RANK	STATE	BIRTHS	% of USA
17	Alabama	7,771	1.9%
46	Alaska	1,038	0.3%
10	Arizona	11,828	2.9%
27	Arkansas	5,646	1.4%
2	California	50,034	12.1%
23	Colorado	6,646	1.6%
36	Connecticut	2,813	0.7%
41	Delaware	1,225	0.3%
3	Florida	24,130	5.8%
6	Georgia	16,548	4.0%
40	Hawaii	1,480	0.4%
39	Idaho	2,015	0.5%
5	Illinois	17,041	4.1%
13	Indiana	9,508	2.3%
34	Iowa	3,330	0.8%
31	Kansas	4,055	1.0%
21	Kentucky	6,726	1.6%
16	Louisiana	8,151	2.0%
44	Maine	1,112	0.3%
25	Maryland	6,282	1.5%
29	Massachusetts	4,540	1.1%
11	Michigan	11,809	2.8%
28	Minnesota	4,780	1.2%
24	Mississippi	6,411	1.5%
15	Missouri	8,611	2.1%
42	Montana	1,185	0.3%
38	Nebraska	2,147	0.5%
33	Nevada	3,921	0.9%
47	New Hampshire	850	0.2%
19	New Jersey	6,874	1.7%
30	New Mexico	4,471	1.1%
4	New York	17,068	4.1%
8	North Carolina	13,933	3.4%
49	North Dakota	661	0.2%
7	Ohio	15,490	3.7%
22	Oklahoma	6,685	1.6%
32	Oregon	4,001	1.0%
9	Pennsylvania	12,910	3.1%
43	Rhode Island	1,117	0.3%
18	South Carolina	7,478	1.8%
45	South Dakota	1,082	0.3%
12	Tennessee	10,785	2.6%
1	Texas	51,180	12.3%
35	Utah	3,181	0.8%
50	Vermont	412	0.1%
14	Virginia	8,778	2.1%
20	Washington	6,746	1.6%
37	West Virginia	2,450	0.6%
26	Wisconsin	6,011	1.4%
48	Wyoming	795	0.2%

RANK ORDER

RANK	STATE	BIRTHS	% of USA
1	Texas	51,180	12.3%
2	California	50,034	12.1%
3	Florida	24,130	5.8%
4	New York	17,068	4.1%
5	Illinois	17,041	4.1%
6	Georgia	16,548	4.0%
7	Ohio	15,490	3.7%
8	North Carolina	13,933	3.4%
9	Pennsylvania	12,910	3.1%
10	Arizona	11,828	2.9%
11	Michigan	11,809	2.8%
12	Tennessee	10,785	2.6%
13	Indiana	9,508	2.3%
14	Virginia	8,778	2.1%
15	Missouri	8,611	2.1%
16	Louisiana	8,151	2.0%
17	Alabama	7,771	1.9%
18	South Carolina	7,478	1.8%
19	New Jersey	6,874	1.7%
20	Washington	6,746	1.6%
21	Kentucky	6,726	1.6%
22	Oklahoma	6,685	1.6%
23	Colorado	6,646	1.6%
24	Mississippi	6,411	1.5%
25	Maryland	6,282	1.5%
26	Wisconsin	6,011	1.4%
27	Arkansas	5,646	1.4%
28	Minnesota	4,780	1.2%
29	Massachusetts	4,540	1.1%
30	New Mexico	4,471	1.1%
31	Kansas	4,055	1.0%
32	Oregon	4,001	1.0%
33	Nevada	3,921	0.9%
34	Iowa	3,330	0.8%
35	Utah	3,181	0.8%
36	Connecticut	2,813	0.7%
37	West Virginia	2,450	0.6%
38	Nebraska	2,147	0.5%
39	Idaho	2,015	0.5%
40	Hawaii	1,480	0.4%
41	Delaware	1,225	0.3%
42	Montana	1,185	0.3%
43	Rhode Island	1,117	0.3%
44	Maine	1,112	0.3%
45	South Dakota	1,082	0.3%
46	Alaska	1,038	0.3%
47	New Hampshire	850	0.2%
48	Wyoming	795	0.2%
49	North Dakota	661	0.2%
50	Vermont	412	0.1%
	District of Columbia	852	0.2%

Source: U.S. Department of Health and Human Services, National Center for Health Statistics
"VitalStats" (http://www.cdc.gov/nchs/datawh/vitalstats/VitalStats.htm)
*Final data. Live births to women 15 to 19 years old by state of residence of mother.

Teenage Birth Rate in 2005

National Rate = 40.5 Live Births per 1,000 Women 15 to 19 Years Old*

ALPHA ORDER			RANK ORDER		
RANK	STATE	RATE	RANK	STATE	RATE
11	Alabama	49.7	1	New Mexico	61.6
28	Alaska	37.3	1	Texas	61.6
5	Arizona	58.2	3	Mississippi	60.5
4	Arkansas	59.1	4	Arkansas	59.1
24	California	38.8	5	Arizona	58.2
19	Colorado	42.6	6	Tennessee	54.9
47	Connecticut	23.3	7	Oklahoma	54.2
15	Delaware	44.0	8	Georgia	52.7
21	Florida	42.4	9	South Carolina	51.0
8	Georgia	52.7	10	Nevada	50.1
29	Hawaii	36.2	11	Alabama	49.7
26	Idaho	37.7	12	Kentucky	49.1
25	Illinois	38.6	12	Louisiana	49.1
17	Indiana	43.2	14	North Carolina	48.5
35	Iowa	32.6	15	Delaware	44.0
22	Kansas	41.4	16	West Virginia	43.4
12	Kentucky	49.1	17	Indiana	43.2
12	Louisiana	49.1	17	Wyoming	43.2
45	Maine	24.4	19	Colorado	42.6
37	Maryland	31.8	20	Missouri	42.5
48	Massachusetts	21.8	21	Florida	42.4
36	Michigan	32.5	22	Kansas	41.4
44	Minnesota	26.1	23	Ohio	38.9
3	Mississippi	60.5	24	California	38.8
20	Missouri	42.5	25	Illinois	38.6
30	Montana	35.2	26	Idaho	37.7
32	Nebraska	34.2	27	South Dakota	37.5
10	Nevada	50.1	28	Alaska	37.3
50	New Hampshire	17.9	29	Hawaii	36.2
46	New Jersey	23.4	30	Montana	35.2
1	New Mexico	61.6	31	Virginia	34.4
43	New York	26.5	32	Nebraska	34.2
14	North Carolina	48.5	33	Utah	33.4
42	North Dakota	29.7	34	Oregon	33.0
23	Ohio	38.9	35	Iowa	32.6
7	Oklahoma	54.2	36	Michigan	32.5
34	Oregon	33.0	37	Maryland	31.8
40	Pennsylvania	30.4	38	Rhode Island	31.4
38	Rhode Island	31.4	39	Washington	31.1
9	South Carolina	51.0	40	Pennsylvania	30.4
27	South Dakota	37.5	41	Wisconsin	30.3
6	Tennessee	54.9	42	North Dakota	29.7
1	Texas	61.6	43	New York	26.5
33	Utah	33.4	44	Minnesota	26.1
49	Vermont	18.6	45	Maine	24.4
31	Virginia	34.4	46	New Jersey	23.4
39	Washington	31.1	47	Connecticut	23.3
16	West Virginia	43.4	48	Massachusetts	21.8
41	Wisconsin	30.3	49	Vermont	18.6
17	Wyoming	43.2	50	New Hampshire	17.9
				District of Columbia	63.4

Source: U.S. Department of Health and Human Services, National Center for Health Statistics
   "National Vital Statistics Reports" (Vol. 56, No. 6, December 5, 2007, http://www.cdc.gov/nchs/births.htm)
*Final data by state of residence.

Births to White Teenage Mothers in 2005

National Total = 295,265 Live Births*

ALPHA ORDER

ALPHA ORDER

RANK	STATE	BIRTHS	% of USA
20	Alabama	4,440	1.5%
47	Alaska	475	0.2%
7	Arizona	9,915	3.4%
23	Arkansas	3,989	1.4%
2	California	43,178	14.6%
15	Colorado	6,000	2.0%
37	Connecticut	2,078	0.7%
45	Delaware	718	0.2%
3	Florida	14,781	5.0%
8	Georgia	9,101	3.1%
50	Hawaii	342	0.1%
38	Idaho	1,910	0.6%
4	Illinois	10,831	3.7%
11	Indiana	7,626	2.6%
32	Iowa	2,945	1.0%
29	Kansas	3,353	1.1%
16	Kentucky	5,811	2.0%
28	Louisiana	3,427	1.2%
40	Maine	1,078	0.4%
34	Maryland	2,681	0.9%
27	Massachusetts	3,474	1.2%
12	Michigan	7,532	2.6%
30	Minnesota	3,174	1.1%
35	Mississippi	2,642	0.9%
14	Missouri	6,366	2.2%
42	Montana	822	0.3%
39	Nebraska	1,695	0.6%
31	Nevada	3,153	1.1%
43	New Hampshire	817	0.3%
21	New Jersey	4,137	1.4%
24	New Mexico	3,756	1.3%
6	New York	10,460	3.5%
9	North Carolina	8,368	2.8%
48	North Dakota	457	0.2%
5	Ohio	10,734	3.6%
19	Oklahoma	4,657	1.6%
26	Oregon	3,640	1.2%
10	Pennsylvania	8,084	2.7%
41	Rhode Island	874	0.3%
25	South Carolina	3,656	1.2%
46	South Dakota	641	0.2%
13	Tennessee	7,068	2.4%
1	Texas	43,335	14.7%
33	Utah	2,943	1.0%
49	Vermont	401	0.1%
18	Virginia	5,197	1.8%
17	Washington	5,463	1.9%
36	West Virginia	2,301	0.8%
22	Wisconsin	3,990	1.4%
44	Wyoming	720	0.2%

RANK ORDER

RANK	STATE	BIRTHS	% of USA
1	Texas	43,335	14.7%
2	California	43,178	14.6%
3	Florida	14,781	5.0%
4	Illinois	10,831	3.7%
5	Ohio	10,734	3.6%
6	New York	10,460	3.5%
7	Arizona	9,915	3.4%
8	Georgia	9,101	3.1%
9	North Carolina	8,368	2.8%
10	Pennsylvania	8,084	2.7%
11	Indiana	7,626	2.6%
12	Michigan	7,532	2.6%
13	Tennessee	7,068	2.4%
14	Missouri	6,366	2.2%
15	Colorado	6,000	2.0%
16	Kentucky	5,811	2.0%
17	Washington	5,463	1.9%
18	Virginia	5,197	1.8%
19	Oklahoma	4,657	1.6%
20	Alabama	4,440	1.5%
21	New Jersey	4,137	1.4%
22	Wisconsin	3,990	1.4%
23	Arkansas	3,989	1.4%
24	New Mexico	3,756	1.3%
25	South Carolina	3,656	1.2%
26	Oregon	3,640	1.2%
27	Massachusetts	3,474	1.2%
28	Louisiana	3,427	1.2%
29	Kansas	3,353	1.1%
30	Minnesota	3,174	1.1%
31	Nevada	3,153	1.1%
32	Iowa	2,945	1.0%
33	Utah	2,943	1.0%
34	Maryland	2,681	0.9%
35	Mississippi	2,642	0.9%
36	West Virginia	2,301	0.8%
37	Connecticut	2,078	0.7%
38	Idaho	1,910	0.6%
39	Nebraska	1,695	0.6%
40	Maine	1,078	0.4%
41	Rhode Island	874	0.3%
42	Montana	822	0.3%
43	New Hampshire	817	0.3%
44	Wyoming	720	0.2%
45	Delaware	718	0.2%
46	South Dakota	641	0.2%
47	Alaska	475	0.2%
48	North Dakota	457	0.2%
49	Vermont	401	0.1%
50	Hawaii	342	0.1%
	District of Columbia	29	0.0%

Source: U.S. Department of Health and Human Services, National Center for Health Statistics
    "Vital Stats" (http://www.cdc.gov/nchs/VitalStats.htm)
*Final data. Live births to women 15 to 19 years old by state of residence.

White Teenage Birth Rate in 2005

National Rate = 36.2 Births per 1,000 White Teenage Women*

ALPHA ORDER			RANK ORDER		
RANK	STATE	RATE	RANK	STATE	RATE
12	Alabama	42.8	1	New Mexico	63.4
34	Alaska	27.5	2	Texas	62.7
3	Arizona	56.1	3	Arizona	56.1
4	Arkansas	54.3	4	Arkansas	54.3
15	California	41.5	5	Nevada	49.9
11	Colorado	43.0	6	Oklahoma	49.7
44	Connecticut	20.4	7	Kentucky	47.9
24	Delaware	33.4	8	Tennessee	47.1
23	Florida	35.2	9	Georgia	46.2
9	Georgia	46.2	10	Mississippi	46.0
50	Hawaii	18.1	11	Colorado	43.0
21	Idaho	36.2	12	Alabama	42.8
27	Illinois	31.3	13	Wyoming	42.3
17	Indiana	39.7	14	West Virginia	42.0
31	Iowa	29.2	15	California	41.5
18	Kansas	38.3	16	North Carolina	41.2
7	Kentucky	47.9	17	Indiana	39.7
21	Louisiana	36.2	18	Kansas	38.3
37	Maine	25.3	18	South Carolina	38.3
40	Maryland	22.1	20	Missouri	38.0
47	Massachusetts	18.3	21	Idaho	36.2
36	Michigan	26.1	21	Louisiana	36.2
45	Minnesota	19.6	23	Florida	35.2
10	Mississippi	46.0	24	Delaware	33.4
20	Missouri	38.0	25	Oregon	33.0
32	Montana	28.4	26	Ohio	32.4
30	Nebraska	29.3	27	Illinois	31.3
5	Nevada	49.9	28	Utah	30.4
49	New Hampshire	18.2	29	Washington	29.7
46	New Jersey	19.1	30	Nebraska	29.3
1	New Mexico	63.4	31	Iowa	29.2
42	New York	21.4	32	Montana	28.4
16	North Carolina	41.2	32	Virginia	28.4
43	North Dakota	21.1	34	Alaska	27.5
26	Ohio	32.4	35	South Dakota	26.9
6	Oklahoma	49.7	36	Michigan	26.1
25	Oregon	33.0	37	Maine	25.3
40	Pennsylvania	22.1	38	Rhode Island	24.8
38	Rhode Island	24.8	39	Wisconsin	23.3
18	South Carolina	38.3	40	Maryland	22.1
35	South Dakota	26.9	40	Pennsylvania	22.1
8	Tennessee	47.1	42	New York	21.4
2	Texas	62.7	43	North Dakota	21.1
28	Utah	30.4	44	Connecticut	20.4
47	Vermont	18.3	45	Minnesota	19.6
32	Virginia	28.4	46	New Jersey	19.1
29	Washington	29.7	47	Massachusetts	18.3
14	West Virginia	42.0	47	Vermont	18.3
39	Wisconsin	23.3	49	New Hampshire	18.2
13	Wyoming	42.3	50	Hawaii	18.1

District of Columbia   4.1

Source: CQ Press using data from U.S. Department of Health and Human Services, National Center for Health Statistics
    "Vital Stats" (http://www.cdc.gov/nchs/VitalStats.htm)
*Final data. Live births to women age 15 to 19 years old by state of residence. Rates calculated using Census 2006 estimates
for females ages 15 to 19 years old in the category of "White Alone or in Combination."

Births to White Teenage Mothers as a Percent of White Births in 2005

National Percent = 8.9% of White Live Births*

ALPHA ORDER

RANK	STATE	PERCENT
10	Alabama	10.4
36	Alaska	6.8
5	Arizona	11.2
3	Arkansas	12.4
15	California	9.5
17	Colorado	9.3
41	Connecticut	6.2
23	Delaware	8.6
23	Florida	8.6
13	Georgia	9.7
41	Hawaii	6.2
27	Idaho	8.2
29	Illinois	7.8
12	Indiana	10.0
29	Iowa	7.8
17	Kansas	9.3
5	Kentucky	11.2
20	Louisiana	9.1
28	Maine	8.0
46	Maryland	5.8
48	Massachusetts	5.5
33	Michigan	7.6
49	Minnesota	5.4
9	Mississippi	10.9
14	Missouri	9.6
31	Montana	7.7
34	Nebraska	7.2
15	Nevada	9.5
44	New Hampshire	6.0
50	New Jersey	5.0
1	New Mexico	15.1
44	New York	6.0
20	North Carolina	9.1
41	North Dakota	6.2
22	Ohio	8.8
7	Oklahoma	11.1
26	Oregon	8.3
35	Pennsylvania	6.9
25	Rhode Island	8.4
17	South Carolina	9.3
38	South Dakota	6.7
7	Tennessee	11.1
2	Texas	13.0
46	Utah	5.8
40	Vermont	6.4
36	Virginia	6.8
31	Washington	7.7
4	West Virginia	11.5
39	Wisconsin	6.5
11	Wyoming	10.1

RANK ORDER

RANK	STATE	PERCENT
1	New Mexico	15.1
2	Texas	13.0
3	Arkansas	12.4
4	West Virginia	11.5
5	Arizona	11.2
5	Kentucky	11.2
7	Oklahoma	11.1
7	Tennessee	11.1
9	Mississippi	10.9
10	Alabama	10.4
11	Wyoming	10.1
12	Indiana	10.0
13	Georgia	9.7
14	Missouri	9.6
15	California	9.5
15	Nevada	9.5
17	Colorado	9.3
17	Kansas	9.3
17	South Carolina	9.3
20	Louisiana	9.1
20	North Carolina	9.1
22	Ohio	8.8
23	Delaware	8.6
23	Florida	8.6
25	Rhode Island	8.4
26	Oregon	8.3
27	Idaho	8.2
28	Maine	8.0
29	Illinois	7.8
29	Iowa	7.8
31	Montana	7.7
31	Washington	7.7
33	Michigan	7.6
34	Nebraska	7.2
35	Pennsylvania	6.9
36	Alaska	6.8
36	Virginia	6.8
38	South Dakota	6.7
39	Wisconsin	6.5
40	Vermont	6.4
41	Connecticut	6.2
41	Hawaii	6.2
41	North Dakota	6.2
44	New Hampshire	6.0
44	New York	6.0
46	Maryland	5.8
46	Utah	5.8
48	Massachusetts	5.5
49	Minnesota	5.4
50	New Jersey	5.0

District of Columbia	0.9

Source: CQ Press using data from U.S. Department of Health and Human Services, National Center for Health Statistics
"Vital Stats" (http://www.cdc.gov/nchs/VitalStats.htm)
*Final data. Live births to women 15 to 19 years old by state of residence.

Births to Black Teenage Mothers in 2005

National Total = 103,905 Live Births*

ALPHA ORDER

RANK	STATE	BIRTHS	% of USA
17	Alabama	3,280	3.2%
41	Alaska	52	0.1%
28	Arizona	588	0.6%
21	Arkansas	1,597	1.5%
10	California	4,432	4.3%
33	Colorado	457	0.4%
27	Connecticut	696	0.7%
32	Delaware	486	0.5%
1	Florida	8,977	8.6%
3	Georgia	7,304	7.0%
42	Hawaii	32	0.0%
46	Idaho	14	0.0%
5	Illinois	6,070	5.8%
20	Indiana	1,840	1.8%
35	Iowa	291	0.3%
29	Kansas	572	0.6%
25	Kentucky	871	0.8%
8	Louisiana	4,603	4.4%
43	Maine	23	0.0%
15	Maryland	3,478	3.3%
24	Massachusetts	877	0.8%
11	Michigan	4,053	3.9%
26	Minnesota	839	0.8%
13	Mississippi	3,698	3.6%
19	Missouri	2,134	2.1%
47	Montana	9	0.0%
34	Nebraska	309	0.3%
30	Nevada	543	0.5%
44	New Hampshire	19	0.0%
18	New Jersey	2,639	2.5%
39	New Mexico	88	0.1%
4	New York	6,208	6.0%
6	North Carolina	5,081	4.9%
49	North Dakota	8	0.0%
7	Ohio	4,614	4.4%
23	Oklahoma	906	0.9%
37	Oregon	152	0.1%
9	Pennsylvania	4,571	4.4%
36	Rhode Island	171	0.2%
12	South Carolina	3,749	3.6%
45	South Dakota	17	0.0%
14	Tennessee	3,620	3.5%
2	Texas	7,424	7.1%
40	Utah	72	0.1%
50	Vermont	6	0.0%
16	Virginia	3,423	3.3%
31	Washington	518	0.5%
38	West Virginia	138	0.1%
22	Wisconsin	1,530	1.5%
47	Wyoming	9	0.0%

RANK ORDER

RANK	STATE	BIRTHS	% of USA
1	Florida	8,977	8.6%
2	Texas	7,424	7.1%
3	Georgia	7,304	7.0%
4	New York	6,208	6.0%
5	Illinois	6,070	5.8%
6	North Carolina	5,081	4.9%
7	Ohio	4,614	4.4%
8	Louisiana	4,603	4.4%
9	Pennsylvania	4,571	4.4%
10	California	4,432	4.3%
11	Michigan	4,053	3.9%
12	South Carolina	3,749	3.6%
13	Mississippi	3,698	3.6%
14	Tennessee	3,620	3.5%
15	Maryland	3,478	3.3%
16	Virginia	3,423	3.3%
17	Alabama	3,280	3.2%
18	New Jersey	2,639	2.5%
19	Missouri	2,134	2.1%
20	Indiana	1,840	1.8%
21	Arkansas	1,597	1.5%
22	Wisconsin	1,530	1.5%
23	Oklahoma	906	0.9%
24	Massachusetts	877	0.8%
25	Kentucky	871	0.8%
26	Minnesota	839	0.8%
27	Connecticut	696	0.7%
28	Arizona	588	0.6%
29	Kansas	572	0.6%
30	Nevada	543	0.5%
31	Washington	518	0.5%
32	Delaware	486	0.5%
33	Colorado	457	0.4%
34	Nebraska	309	0.3%
35	Iowa	291	0.3%
36	Rhode Island	171	0.2%
37	Oregon	152	0.1%
38	West Virginia	138	0.1%
39	New Mexico	88	0.1%
40	Utah	72	0.1%
41	Alaska	52	0.1%
42	Hawaii	32	0.0%
43	Maine	23	0.0%
44	New Hampshire	19	0.0%
45	South Dakota	17	0.0%
46	Idaho	14	0.0%
47	Montana	9	0.0%
47	Wyoming	9	0.0%
49	North Dakota	8	0.0%
50	Vermont	6	0.0%
	District of Columbia	817	0.8%

Source: U.S. Department of Health and Human Services, National Center for Health Statistics
    "Vital Stats" (http://www.cdc.gov/nchs/VitalStats.htm)
*Final data. Live births to women 15 to 19 years old by state of residence.

Black Teenage Birth Rate in 2005

National Rate = 59.2 Births per 1,000 Black Teenage Women*

ALPHA ORDER

RANK	STATE	RATE
20	Alabama	60.5
39	Alaska	37.2
27	Arizona	52.2
3	Arkansas	78.1
40	California	36.5
29	Colorado	50.1
35	Connecticut	40.0
24	Delaware	59.2
13	Florida	68.7
23	Georgia	59.5
43	Hawaii	18.9
NA	Idaho**	NA
13	Illinois	68.7
10	Indiana	70.6
8	Iowa	71.9
11	Kansas	70.1
18	Kentucky	62.4
6	Louisiana	73.4
42	Maine	32.3
30	Maryland	49.4
36	Massachusetts	39.8
25	Michigan	58.6
12	Minnesota	68.9
5	Mississippi	74.3
15	Missouri	67.7
NA	Montana**	NA
4	Nebraska	76.7
19	Nevada	61.4
NA	New Hampshire**	NA
31	New Jersey	48.3
41	New Mexico	34.7
34	New York	41.1
22	North Carolina	59.9
NA	North Dakota**	NA
7	Ohio	73.0
16	Oklahoma	65.7
37	Oregon	38.5
9	Pennsylvania	71.3
32	Rhode Island	45.3
17	South Carolina	65.4
NA	South Dakota**	NA
2	Tennessee	80.3
21	Texas	60.4
38	Utah	38.4
NA	Vermont**	NA
28	Virginia	51.6
33	Washington	42.1
26	West Virginia	52.3
1	Wisconsin	88.8
NA	Wyoming**	NA

RANK ORDER

RANK	STATE	RATE
1	Wisconsin	88.8
2	Tennessee	80.3
3	Arkansas	78.1
4	Nebraska	76.7
5	Mississippi	74.3
6	Louisiana	73.4
7	Ohio	73.0
8	Iowa	71.9
9	Pennsylvania	71.3
10	Indiana	70.6
11	Kansas	70.1
12	Minnesota	68.9
13	Florida	68.7
13	Illinois	68.7
15	Missouri	67.7
16	Oklahoma	65.7
17	South Carolina	65.4
18	Kentucky	62.4
19	Nevada	61.4
20	Alabama	60.5
21	Texas	60.4
22	North Carolina	59.9
23	Georgia	59.5
24	Delaware	59.2
25	Michigan	58.6
26	West Virginia	52.3
27	Arizona	52.2
28	Virginia	51.6
29	Colorado	50.1
30	Maryland	49.4
31	New Jersey	48.3
32	Rhode Island	45.3
33	Washington	42.1
34	New York	41.1
35	Connecticut	40.0
36	Massachusetts	39.8
37	Oregon	38.5
38	Utah	38.4
39	Alaska	37.2
40	California	36.5
41	New Mexico	34.7
42	Maine	32.3
43	Hawaii	18.9
NA	Idaho**	NA
NA	Montana**	NA
NA	New Hampshire**	NA
NA	North Dakota**	NA
NA	South Dakota**	NA
NA	Vermont**	NA
NA	Wyoming**	NA

District of Columbia   62.6

Source: CQ Press using data from U.S. Department of Health and Human Services, National Center for Health Statistics "Vital Stats" (http://www.cdc.gov/nchs/VitalStats.htm)

*Final data. Live births to women age 15 to 19 years old by state of residence. Rates calculated using Census 2006 estimates for females ages 15 to 19 years old in the category of "Black Alone or in Combination."

**Insufficient number of births for a reliable figure.

Births to Black Teenage Mothers as a Percent of Black Births in 2005

National Percent = 15.7% of Black Live Births*

ALPHA ORDER

RANK	STATE	PERCENT
18	Alabama	16.9
39	Alaska	11.9
27	Arizona	14.6
2	Arkansas	20.2
36	California	12.9
28	Colorado	14.5
38	Connecticut	12.4
21	Delaware	15.8
21	Florida	15.8
25	Georgia	14.8
50	Hawaii	5.2
43	Idaho	9.5
5	Illinois	19.2
12	Indiana	17.6
11	Iowa	18.0
9	Kansas	18.1
20	Kentucky	15.9
6	Louisiana	19.0
46	Maine	7.7
34	Maryland	13.3
44	Massachusetts	9.4
12	Michigan	17.6
41	Minnesota	11.1
14	Mississippi	17.5
16	Missouri	17.1
31	Montana	14.3
19	Nebraska	16.4
23	Nevada	15.5
48	New Hampshire	7.2
37	New Jersey	12.7
26	New Mexico	14.7
40	New York	11.4
17	North Carolina	17.0
49	North Dakota	6.0
9	Ohio	18.1
8	Oklahoma	18.2
35	Oregon	13.2
7	Pennsylvania	18.3
29	Rhode Island	14.4
15	South Carolina	17.4
45	South Dakota	7.8
3	Tennessee	19.7
24	Texas	15.1
32	Utah	13.9
47	Vermont	7.5
29	Virginia	14.4
42	Washington	10.9
3	West Virginia	19.7
1	Wisconsin	21.5
33	Wyoming	13.6

RANK ORDER

RANK	STATE	PERCENT
1	Wisconsin	21.5
2	Arkansas	20.2
3	Tennessee	19.7
3	West Virginia	19.7
5	Illinois	19.2
6	Louisiana	19.0
7	Pennsylvania	18.3
8	Oklahoma	18.2
9	Kansas	18.1
9	Ohio	18.1
11	Iowa	18.0
12	Indiana	17.6
12	Michigan	17.6
14	Mississippi	17.5
15	South Carolina	17.4
16	Missouri	17.1
17	North Carolina	17.0
18	Alabama	16.9
19	Nebraska	16.4
20	Kentucky	15.9
21	Delaware	15.8
21	Florida	15.8
23	Nevada	15.5
24	Texas	15.1
25	Georgia	14.8
26	New Mexico	14.7
27	Arizona	14.6
28	Colorado	14.5
29	Rhode Island	14.4
29	Virginia	14.4
31	Montana	14.3
32	Utah	13.9
33	Wyoming	13.6
34	Maryland	13.3
35	Oregon	13.2
36	California	12.9
37	New Jersey	12.7
38	Connecticut	12.4
39	Alaska	11.9
40	New York	11.4
41	Minnesota	11.1
42	Washington	10.9
43	Idaho	9.5
44	Massachusetts	9.4
45	South Dakota	7.8
46	Maine	7.7
47	Vermont	7.5
48	New Hampshire	7.2
49	North Dakota	6.0
50	Hawaii	5.2

District of Columbia   16.2

Source: CQ Press using data from U.S. Department of Health and Human Services, National Center for Health Statistics
   "Vital Stats" (http://www.cdc.gov/nchs/VitalStats.htm)
*Final data. Live births to women 15 to 19 years old by state of residence.

Births to Young Teenagers: 2003 to 2005

National Total = 20,164 Live Births*

ALPHA ORDER

RANK	STATE	BIRTHS	% of USA
15	Alabama	484	2.4%
43	Alaska	36	0.2%
10	Arizona	589	2.9%
21	Arkansas	316	1.6%
2	California	2,163	10.7%
23	Colorado	310	1.5%
34	Connecticut	106	0.5%
40	Delaware	58	0.3%
3	Florida	1,181	5.9%
4	Georgia	941	4.7%
41	Hawaii	55	0.3%
42	Idaho	52	0.3%
5	Illinois	892	4.4%
20	Indiana	354	1.8%
36	Iowa	92	0.5%
33	Kansas	135	0.7%
24	Kentucky	294	1.5%
13	Louisiana	543	2.7%
48	Maine	21	0.1%
18	Maryland	380	1.9%
31	Massachusetts	157	0.8%
11	Michigan	588	2.9%
30	Minnesota	189	0.9%
14	Mississippi	514	2.5%
19	Missouri	370	1.8%
44	Montana	28	0.1%
38	Nebraska	80	0.4%
29	Nevada	193	1.0%
50	New Hampshire	6	0.0%
25	New Jersey	276	1.4%
28	New Mexico	224	1.1%
7	New York	769	3.8%
6	North Carolina	799	4.0%
46	North Dakota	24	0.1%
8	Ohio	703	3.5%
22	Oklahoma	311	1.5%
32	Oregon	155	0.8%
9	Pennsylvania	665	3.3%
39	Rhode Island	62	0.3%
17	South Carolina	393	1.9%
44	South Dakota	28	0.1%
12	Tennessee	545	2.7%
1	Texas	2,838	14.1%
35	Utah	104	0.5%
49	Vermont	12	0.1%
16	Virginia	423	2.1%
26	Washington	265	1.3%
37	West Virginia	84	0.4%
27	Wisconsin	261	1.3%
46	Wyoming	24	0.1%

RANK ORDER

RANK	STATE	BIRTHS	% of USA
1	Texas	2,838	14.1%
2	California	2,163	10.7%
3	Florida	1,181	5.9%
4	Georgia	941	4.7%
5	Illinois	892	4.4%
6	North Carolina	799	4.0%
7	New York	769	3.8%
8	Ohio	703	3.5%
9	Pennsylvania	665	3.3%
10	Arizona	589	2.9%
11	Michigan	588	2.9%
12	Tennessee	545	2.7%
13	Louisiana	543	2.7%
14	Mississippi	514	2.5%
15	Alabama	484	2.4%
16	Virginia	423	2.1%
17	South Carolina	393	1.9%
18	Maryland	380	1.9%
19	Missouri	370	1.8%
20	Indiana	354	1.8%
21	Arkansas	316	1.6%
22	Oklahoma	311	1.5%
23	Colorado	310	1.5%
24	Kentucky	294	1.5%
25	New Jersey	276	1.4%
26	Washington	265	1.3%
27	Wisconsin	261	1.3%
28	New Mexico	224	1.1%
29	Nevada	193	1.0%
30	Minnesota	189	0.9%
31	Massachusetts	157	0.8%
32	Oregon	155	0.8%
33	Kansas	135	0.7%
34	Connecticut	106	0.5%
35	Utah	104	0.5%
36	Iowa	92	0.5%
37	West Virginia	84	0.4%
38	Nebraska	80	0.4%
39	Rhode Island	62	0.3%
40	Delaware	58	0.3%
41	Hawaii	55	0.3%
42	Idaho	52	0.3%
43	Alaska	36	0.2%
44	Montana	28	0.1%
44	South Dakota	28	0.1%
46	North Dakota	24	0.1%
46	Wyoming	24	0.1%
48	Maine	21	0.1%
49	Vermont	12	0.1%
50	New Hampshire	6	0.0%
	District of Columbia	72	0.4%

Source: CQ Press using data from U.S. Department of Health and Human Services, National Center for Health Statistics
   "Vital Stats" (http://www.cdc.gov/nchs/VitalStats.htm)
*Final data. Births to 10 to 14 years old during the three years of 2003 to 2005 by state of residence.

Young Teen Birthrate: 2003 to 2005

National Rate = 0.7 Live Births per 1,000 10 to 14 Year Old Females*

ALPHA ORDER				RANK ORDER		
RANK	STATE	RATE		RANK	STATE	RATE
5	Alabama	1.0		1	Mississippi	1.6
24	Alaska	0.5		2	Arkansas	1.1
5	Arizona	1.0		2	Louisiana	1.1
2	Arkansas	1.1		2	Texas	1.1
24	California	0.5		5	Alabama	1.0
14	Colorado	0.7		5	Arizona	1.0
41	Connecticut	0.3		5	Georgia	1.0
14	Delaware	0.7		5	New Mexico	1.0
14	Florida	0.7		9	North Carolina	0.9
5	Georgia	1.0		9	Oklahoma	0.9
33	Hawaii	0.4		9	South Carolina	0.9
41	Idaho	0.3		9	Tennessee	0.9
14	Illinois	0.7		13	Nevada	0.8
24	Indiana	0.5		14	Colorado	0.7
41	Iowa	0.3		14	Delaware	0.7
24	Kansas	0.5		14	Florida	0.7
14	Kentucky	0.7		14	Illinois	0.7
2	Louisiana	1.1		14	Kentucky	0.7
NA	Maine**	NA		19	Maryland	0.6
19	Maryland	0.6		19	Missouri	0.6
47	Massachusetts	0.2		19	Ohio	0.6
24	Michigan	0.5		19	Rhode Island	0.6
33	Minnesota	0.4		19	Virginia	0.6
1	Mississippi	1.6		24	Alaska	0.5
19	Missouri	0.6		24	California	0.5
41	Montana	0.3		24	Indiana	0.5
33	Nebraska	0.4		24	Kansas	0.5
13	Nevada	0.8		24	Michigan	0.5
NA	New Hampshire**	NA		24	Pennsylvania	0.5
41	New Jersey	0.3		24	West Virginia	0.5
5	New Mexico	1.0		24	Wisconsin	0.5
33	New York	0.4		24	Wyoming	0.5
9	North Carolina	0.9		33	Hawaii	0.4
33	North Dakota	0.4		33	Minnesota	0.4
19	Ohio	0.6		33	Nebraska	0.4
9	Oklahoma	0.9		33	New York	0.4
33	Oregon	0.4		33	North Dakota	0.4
24	Pennsylvania	0.5		33	Oregon	0.4
19	Rhode Island	0.6		33	Utah	0.4
9	South Carolina	0.9		33	Washington	0.4
41	South Dakota	0.3		41	Connecticut	0.3
9	Tennessee	0.9		41	Idaho	0.3
2	Texas	1.1		41	Iowa	0.3
33	Utah	0.4		41	Montana	0.3
NA	Vermont**	NA		41	New Jersey	0.3
19	Virginia	0.6		41	South Dakota	0.3
33	Washington	0.4		47	Massachusetts	0.2
24	West Virginia	0.5		NA	Maine**	NA
24	Wisconsin	0.5		NA	New Hampshire**	NA
24	Wyoming	0.5		NA	Vermont**	NA

District of Columbia   1.4

Source: CQ Press using data from U.S. Department of Health and Human Services, National Center for Health Statistics
       "Vital Stats" (http://www.cdc.gov/nchs/VitalStats.htm)
*Final data. Births to 10 to 14 years old during the three years of 2003 to 2005 by state of residence.
**Insufficient data for a reliable rate.

Births to Women 35 to 54 Years Old in 2005

National Total = 594,359 Live Births*

ALPHA ORDER

RANK	STATE	BIRTHS	% of USA
27	Alabama	5,517	0.9%
45	Alaska	1,381	0.2%
17	Arizona	10,987	1.8%
38	Arkansas	3,001	0.5%
1	California	95,164	16.0%
18	Colorado	10,544	1.8%
20	Connecticut	9,567	1.6%
44	Delaware	1,617	0.3%
4	Florida	32,768	5.5%
11	Georgia	17,424	2.9%
34	Hawaii	3,157	0.5%
41	Idaho	2,322	0.4%
5	Illinois	27,954	4.7%
21	Indiana	9,034	1.5%
32	Iowa	4,426	0.7%
31	Kansas	4,477	0.8%
28	Kentucky	5,333	0.9%
26	Louisiana	5,586	0.9%
42	Maine	2,011	0.3%
14	Maryland	14,480	2.4%
9	Massachusetts	18,260	3.1%
12	Michigan	17,195	2.9%
16	Minnesota	11,066	1.9%
35	Mississippi	3,138	0.5%
22	Missouri	8,448	1.4%
46	Montana	1,368	0.2%
36	Nebraska	3,052	0.5%
29	Nevada	4,894	0.8%
39	New Hampshire	2,622	0.4%
6	New Jersey	24,861	4.2%
37	New Mexico	3,039	0.5%
2	New York	49,777	8.4%
13	North Carolina	15,257	2.6%
49	North Dakota	847	0.1%
8	Ohio	18,280	3.1%
33	Oklahoma	4,230	0.7%
24	Oregon	6,388	1.1%
7	Pennsylvania	23,208	3.9%
40	Rhode Island	2,366	0.4%
25	South Carolina	6,176	1.0%
47	South Dakota	1,224	0.2%
23	Tennessee	8,148	1.4%
3	Texas	43,694	7.4%
30	Utah	4,686	0.8%
48	Vermont	1,093	0.2%
10	Virginia	17,556	3.0%
15	Washington	12,887	2.2%
43	West Virginia	1,863	0.3%
19	Wisconsin	9,714	1.6%
50	Wyoming	619	0.1%

RANK ORDER

RANK	STATE	BIRTHS	% of USA
1	California	95,164	16.0%
2	New York	49,777	8.4%
3	Texas	43,694	7.4%
4	Florida	32,768	5.5%
5	Illinois	27,954	4.7%
6	New Jersey	24,861	4.2%
7	Pennsylvania	23,208	3.9%
8	Ohio	18,280	3.1%
9	Massachusetts	18,260	3.1%
10	Virginia	17,556	3.0%
11	Georgia	17,424	2.9%
12	Michigan	17,195	2.9%
13	North Carolina	15,257	2.6%
14	Maryland	14,480	2.4%
15	Washington	12,887	2.2%
16	Minnesota	11,066	1.9%
17	Arizona	10,987	1.8%
18	Colorado	10,544	1.8%
19	Wisconsin	9,714	1.6%
20	Connecticut	9,567	1.6%
21	Indiana	9,034	1.5%
22	Missouri	8,448	1.4%
23	Tennessee	8,148	1.4%
24	Oregon	6,388	1.1%
25	South Carolina	6,176	1.0%
26	Louisiana	5,586	0.9%
27	Alabama	5,517	0.9%
28	Kentucky	5,333	0.9%
29	Nevada	4,894	0.8%
30	Utah	4,686	0.8%
31	Kansas	4,477	0.8%
32	Iowa	4,426	0.7%
33	Oklahoma	4,230	0.7%
34	Hawaii	3,157	0.5%
35	Mississippi	3,138	0.5%
36	Nebraska	3,052	0.5%
37	New Mexico	3,039	0.5%
38	Arkansas	3,001	0.5%
39	New Hampshire	2,622	0.4%
40	Rhode Island	2,366	0.4%
41	Idaho	2,322	0.4%
42	Maine	2,011	0.3%
43	West Virginia	1,863	0.3%
44	Delaware	1,617	0.3%
45	Alaska	1,381	0.2%
46	Montana	1,368	0.2%
47	South Dakota	1,224	0.2%
48	Vermont	1,093	0.2%
49	North Dakota	847	0.1%
50	Wyoming	619	0.1%
	District of Columbia	1,653	0.3%

Source: CQ Press using data from U.S. Department of Health and Human Services, National Center for Health Statistics
"Vital Stats" (http://www.cdc.gov/nchs/VitalStats.htm)
*Final data by state of residence.

Births to Women 35 to 54 Years Old as a Percent of All Births in 2005

National Percent = 14.4% of Live Births*

ALPHA ORDER

RANK	STATE	PERCENT
44	Alabama	9.1
23	Alaska	13.2
30	Arizona	11.4
49	Arkansas	7.7
10	California	17.3
16	Colorado	15.3
2	Connecticut	22.9
19	Delaware	13.9
17	Florida	14.5
26	Georgia	12.3
8	Hawaii	17.6
39	Idaho	10.1
13	Illinois	15.6
38	Indiana	10.4
31	Iowa	11.3
33	Kansas	11.2
42	Kentucky	9.4
43	Louisiana	9.2
18	Maine	14.3
5	Maryland	19.3
1	Massachusetts	23.8
22	Michigan	13.5
13	Minnesota	15.6
50	Mississippi	7.4
34	Missouri	10.7
28	Montana	11.8
29	Nebraska	11.7
24	Nevada	13.1
7	New Hampshire	18.2
3	New Jersey	21.9
37	New Mexico	10.5
4	New York	20.2
25	North Carolina	12.4
39	North Dakota	10.1
26	Ohio	12.3
48	Oklahoma	8.2
19	Oregon	13.9
12	Pennsylvania	16.0
6	Rhode Island	18.6
34	South Carolina	10.7
34	South Dakota	10.7
41	Tennessee	10.0
31	Texas	11.3
44	Utah	9.1
9	Vermont	17.4
11	Virginia	16.8
13	Washington	15.6
46	West Virginia	8.9
21	Wisconsin	13.7
47	Wyoming	8.6

RANK ORDER

RANK	STATE	PERCENT
1	Massachusetts	23.8
2	Connecticut	22.9
3	New Jersey	21.9
4	New York	20.2
5	Maryland	19.3
6	Rhode Island	18.6
7	New Hampshire	18.2
8	Hawaii	17.6
9	Vermont	17.4
10	California	17.3
11	Virginia	16.8
12	Pennsylvania	16.0
13	Illinois	15.6
13	Minnesota	15.6
13	Washington	15.6
16	Colorado	15.3
17	Florida	14.5
18	Maine	14.3
19	Delaware	13.9
19	Oregon	13.9
21	Wisconsin	13.7
22	Michigan	13.5
23	Alaska	13.2
24	Nevada	13.1
25	North Carolina	12.4
26	Georgia	12.3
26	Ohio	12.3
28	Montana	11.8
29	Nebraska	11.7
30	Arizona	11.4
31	Iowa	11.3
31	Texas	11.3
33	Kansas	11.2
34	Missouri	10.7
34	South Carolina	10.7
34	South Dakota	10.7
37	New Mexico	10.5
38	Indiana	10.4
39	Idaho	10.1
39	North Dakota	10.1
41	Tennessee	10.0
42	Kentucky	9.4
43	Louisiana	9.2
44	Alabama	9.1
44	Utah	9.1
46	West Virginia	8.9
47	Wyoming	8.6
48	Oklahoma	8.2
49	Arkansas	7.7
50	Mississippi	7.4

District of Columbia 20.7

Source: CQ Press using data from U.S. Department of Health and Human Services, National Center for Health Statistics
"Vital Stats" (http://www.cdc.gov/nchs/VitalStats.htm)
*Final data by state of residence.

Births by Vaginal Delivery in 2006

National Total = 2,939,271 Live Births*

ALPHA ORDER

RANK	STATE	BIRTHS	% of USA
23	Alabama	42,115	1.4%
46	Alaska	8,463	0.3%
11	Arizona	76,241	2.6%
34	Arkansas	27,370	0.9%
1	California	386,390	13.1%
20	Colorado	52,850	1.8%
33	Connecticut	27,551	0.9%
47	Delaware	8,308	0.3%
4	Florida	151,368	5.1%
8	Georgia	102,101	3.5%
39	Hawaii	14,123	0.5%
38	Idaho	18,670	0.6%
5	Illinois	127,130	4.3%
14	Indiana	62,959	2.1%
31	Iowa	29,361	1.0%
32	Kansas	28,962	1.0%
27	Kentucky	38,181	1.3%
26	Louisiana	40,956	1.4%
42	Maine	9,920	0.3%
21	Maryland	52,530	1.8%
22	Massachusetts	51,950	1.8%
10	Michigan	89,488	3.0%
18	Minnesota	54,875	1.9%
30	Mississippi	29,761	1.0%
17	Missouri	56,809	1.9%
43	Montana	9,004	0.3%
37	Nebraska	19,034	0.6%
35	Nevada	27,138	0.9%
41	New Hampshire	10,080	0.3%
13	New Jersey	71,994	2.4%
36	New Mexico	22,962	0.8%
3	New York	168,561	5.7%
9	North Carolina	89,617	3.0%
48	North Dakota	6,225	0.2%
6	Ohio	106,467	3.6%
28	Oklahoma	36,030	1.2%
29	Oregon	34,979	1.2%
7	Pennsylvania	104,805	3.6%
45	Rhode Island	8,529	0.3%
25	South Carolina	41,784	1.4%
44	South Dakota	8,699	0.3%
16	Tennessee	57,017	1.9%
2	Texas	266,941	9.1%
24	Utah	41,997	1.4%
50	Vermont	4,817	0.2%
12	Virginia	72,884	2.5%
15	Washington	62,183	2.1%
40	West Virginia	13,561	0.5%
19	Wisconsin	54,541	1.9%
49	Wyoming	5,653	0.2%

RANK ORDER

RANK	STATE	BIRTHS	% of USA
1	California	386,390	13.1%
2	Texas	266,941	9.1%
3	New York	168,561	5.7%
4	Florida	151,368	5.1%
5	Illinois	127,130	4.3%
6	Ohio	106,467	3.6%
7	Pennsylvania	104,805	3.6%
8	Georgia	102,101	3.5%
9	North Carolina	89,617	3.0%
10	Michigan	89,488	3.0%
11	Arizona	76,241	2.6%
12	Virginia	72,884	2.5%
13	New Jersey	71,994	2.4%
14	Indiana	62,959	2.1%
15	Washington	62,183	2.1%
16	Tennessee	57,017	1.9%
17	Missouri	56,809	1.9%
18	Minnesota	54,875	1.9%
19	Wisconsin	54,541	1.9%
20	Colorado	52,850	1.8%
21	Maryland	52,530	1.8%
22	Massachusetts	51,950	1.8%
23	Alabama	42,115	1.4%
24	Utah	41,997	1.4%
25	South Carolina	41,784	1.4%
26	Louisiana	40,956	1.4%
27	Kentucky	38,181	1.3%
28	Oklahoma	36,030	1.2%
29	Oregon	34,979	1.2%
30	Mississippi	29,761	1.0%
31	Iowa	29,361	1.0%
32	Kansas	28,962	1.0%
33	Connecticut	27,551	0.9%
34	Arkansas	27,370	0.9%
35	Nevada	27,138	0.9%
36	New Mexico	22,962	0.8%
37	Nebraska	19,034	0.6%
38	Idaho	18,670	0.6%
39	Hawaii	14,123	0.5%
40	West Virginia	13,561	0.5%
41	New Hampshire	10,080	0.3%
42	Maine	9,920	0.3%
43	Montana	9,004	0.3%
44	South Dakota	8,699	0.3%
45	Rhode Island	8,529	0.3%
46	Alaska	8,463	0.3%
47	Delaware	8,308	0.3%
48	North Dakota	6,225	0.2%
49	Wyoming	5,653	0.2%
50	Vermont	4,817	0.2%
	District of Columbia	5,919	0.2%

Source: CQ Press using data from U.S. Department of Health and Human Services, National Center for Health Statistics
    "National Vital Statistics Reports" (Vol. 56, No. 7, December 5, 2007, http://www.cdc.gov/nchs/births.htm)
*Preliminary estimates by state of residence.

Percent of Births by Vaginal Delivery in 2006

National Percent = 68.9% of Live Births*

ALPHA ORDER

ALPHA ORDER

RANK	STATE	PERCENT
43	Alabama	66.6
3	Alaska	77.0
8	Arizona	74.4
39	Arkansas	66.8
31	California	68.7
6	Colorado	74.7
44	Connecticut	65.9
29	Delaware	69.3
49	Florida	63.9
31	Georgia	68.7
8	Hawaii	74.4
2	Idaho	77.2
22	Illinois	70.4
19	Indiana	71.0
13	Iowa	72.3
20	Kansas	70.7
45	Kentucky	65.5
47	Louisiana	64.6
25	Maine	70.1
33	Maryland	67.8
39	Massachusetts	66.8
24	Michigan	70.2
7	Minnesota	74.6
47	Mississippi	64.6
28	Missouri	69.8
15	Montana	72.0
18	Nebraska	71.2
34	Nevada	67.7
25	New Hampshire	70.1
50	New Jersey	62.6
4	New Mexico	76.7
37	New York	67.4
25	North Carolina	70.1
14	North Dakota	72.2
20	Ohio	70.7
42	Oklahoma	66.7
16	Oregon	71.8
23	Pennsylvania	70.3
30	Rhode Island	68.9
38	South Carolina	67.1
12	South Dakota	73.0
35	Tennessee	67.6
39	Texas	66.8
1	Utah	78.5
10	Vermont	74.0
35	Virginia	67.6
17	Washington	71.6
46	West Virginia	64.8
5	Wisconsin	75.4
11	Wyoming	73.7

RANK ORDER

RANK	STATE	PERCENT
1	Utah	78.5
2	Idaho	77.2
3	Alaska	77.0
4	New Mexico	76.7
5	Wisconsin	75.4
6	Colorado	74.7
7	Minnesota	74.6
8	Arizona	74.4
8	Hawaii	74.4
10	Vermont	74.0
11	Wyoming	73.7
12	South Dakota	73.0
13	Iowa	72.3
14	North Dakota	72.2
15	Montana	72.0
16	Oregon	71.8
17	Washington	71.6
18	Nebraska	71.2
19	Indiana	71.0
20	Kansas	70.7
20	Ohio	70.7
22	Illinois	70.4
23	Pennsylvania	70.3
24	Michigan	70.2
25	Maine	70.1
25	New Hampshire	70.1
25	North Carolina	70.1
28	Missouri	69.8
29	Delaware	69.3
30	Rhode Island	68.9
31	California	68.7
31	Georgia	68.7
33	Maryland	67.8
34	Nevada	67.7
35	Tennessee	67.6
35	Virginia	67.6
37	New York	67.4
38	South Carolina	67.1
39	Arkansas	66.8
39	Massachusetts	66.8
39	Texas	66.8
42	Oklahoma	66.7
43	Alabama	66.6
44	Connecticut	65.9
45	Kentucky	65.5
46	West Virginia	64.8
47	Louisiana	64.6
47	Mississippi	64.6
49	Florida	63.9
50	New Jersey	62.6

| District of Columbia | 69.4 |

Source: CQ Press using data from U.S. Department of Health and Human Services, National Center for Health Statistics
"National Vital Statistics Reports" (Vol. 56, No. 7, December 5, 2007, http://www.cdc.gov/nchs/births.htm)
*Preliminary data by state of residence.

Births by Cesarean Delivery in 2006

National Total = 1,326,725 Live Cesarean Births*

<table>
<tr><td colspan="4">ALPHA ORDER</td><td colspan="4">RANK ORDER</td></tr>
<tr><td>RANK</td><td>STATE</td><td>BIRTHS</td><td>% of USA</td><td>RANK</td><td>STATE</td><td>BIRTHS</td><td>% of USA</td></tr>
<tr><td>21</td><td>Alabama</td><td>21,120</td><td>1.6%</td><td>1</td><td>California</td><td>176,041</td><td>13.3%</td></tr>
<tr><td>47</td><td>Alaska</td><td>2,528</td><td>0.2%</td><td>2</td><td>Texas</td><td>132,671</td><td>10.0%</td></tr>
<tr><td>14</td><td>Arizona</td><td>26,234</td><td>2.0%</td><td>3</td><td>Florida</td><td>85,514</td><td>6.4%</td></tr>
<tr><td>31</td><td>Arkansas</td><td>13,603</td><td>1.0%</td><td>4</td><td>New York</td><td>81,530</td><td>6.1%</td></tr>
<tr><td>1</td><td>California</td><td>176,041</td><td>13.3%</td><td>5</td><td>Illinois</td><td>53,453</td><td>4.0%</td></tr>
<tr><td>26</td><td>Colorado</td><td>17,900</td><td>1.3%</td><td>6</td><td>Georgia</td><td>46,518</td><td>3.5%</td></tr>
<tr><td>29</td><td>Connecticut</td><td>14,256</td><td>1.1%</td><td>7</td><td>Pennsylvania</td><td>44,277</td><td>3.3%</td></tr>
<tr><td>44</td><td>Delaware</td><td>3,680</td><td>0.3%</td><td>8</td><td>Ohio</td><td>44,123</td><td>3.3%</td></tr>
<tr><td>3</td><td>Florida</td><td>85,514</td><td>6.4%</td><td>9</td><td>New Jersey</td><td>43,012</td><td>3.2%</td></tr>
<tr><td>6</td><td>Georgia</td><td>46,518</td><td>3.5%</td><td>10</td><td>North Carolina</td><td>38,224</td><td>2.9%</td></tr>
<tr><td>40</td><td>Hawaii</td><td>4,859</td><td>0.4%</td><td>11</td><td>Michigan</td><td>37,988</td><td>2.9%</td></tr>
<tr><td>39</td><td>Idaho</td><td>5,514</td><td>0.4%</td><td>12</td><td>Virginia</td><td>34,933</td><td>2.6%</td></tr>
<tr><td>5</td><td>Illinois</td><td>53,453</td><td>4.0%</td><td>13</td><td>Tennessee</td><td>27,328</td><td>2.1%</td></tr>
<tr><td>16</td><td>Indiana</td><td>25,715</td><td>1.9%</td><td>14</td><td>Arizona</td><td>26,234</td><td>2.0%</td></tr>
<tr><td>35</td><td>Iowa</td><td>11,249</td><td>0.8%</td><td>15</td><td>Massachusetts</td><td>25,819</td><td>1.9%</td></tr>
<tr><td>33</td><td>Kansas</td><td>12,002</td><td>0.9%</td><td>16</td><td>Indiana</td><td>25,715</td><td>1.9%</td></tr>
<tr><td>23</td><td>Kentucky</td><td>20,110</td><td>1.5%</td><td>17</td><td>Maryland</td><td>24,948</td><td>1.9%</td></tr>
<tr><td>20</td><td>Louisiana</td><td>22,443</td><td>1.7%</td><td>18</td><td>Washington</td><td>24,665</td><td>1.9%</td></tr>
<tr><td>42</td><td>Maine</td><td>4,231</td><td>0.3%</td><td>19</td><td>Missouri</td><td>24,579</td><td>1.9%</td></tr>
<tr><td>17</td><td>Maryland</td><td>24,948</td><td>1.9%</td><td>20</td><td>Louisiana</td><td>22,443</td><td>1.7%</td></tr>
<tr><td>15</td><td>Massachusetts</td><td>25,819</td><td>1.9%</td><td>21</td><td>Alabama</td><td>21,120</td><td>1.6%</td></tr>
<tr><td>11</td><td>Michigan</td><td>37,988</td><td>2.9%</td><td>22</td><td>South Carolina</td><td>20,487</td><td>1.5%</td></tr>
<tr><td>24</td><td>Minnesota</td><td>18,684</td><td>1.4%</td><td>23</td><td>Kentucky</td><td>20,110</td><td>1.5%</td></tr>
<tr><td>28</td><td>Mississippi</td><td>16,308</td><td>1.2%</td><td>24</td><td>Minnesota</td><td>18,684</td><td>1.4%</td></tr>
<tr><td>19</td><td>Missouri</td><td>24,579</td><td>1.9%</td><td>25</td><td>Oklahoma</td><td>17,988</td><td>1.4%</td></tr>
<tr><td>45</td><td>Montana</td><td>3,502</td><td>0.3%</td><td>26</td><td>Colorado</td><td>17,900</td><td>1.3%</td></tr>
<tr><td>36</td><td>Nebraska</td><td>7,699</td><td>0.6%</td><td>27</td><td>Wisconsin</td><td>17,794</td><td>1.3%</td></tr>
<tr><td>32</td><td>Nevada</td><td>12,947</td><td>1.0%</td><td>28</td><td>Mississippi</td><td>16,308</td><td>1.2%</td></tr>
<tr><td>41</td><td>New Hampshire</td><td>4,300</td><td>0.3%</td><td>29</td><td>Connecticut</td><td>14,256</td><td>1.1%</td></tr>
<tr><td>9</td><td>New Jersey</td><td>43,012</td><td>3.2%</td><td>30</td><td>Oregon</td><td>13,738</td><td>1.0%</td></tr>
<tr><td>38</td><td>New Mexico</td><td>6,975</td><td>0.5%</td><td>31</td><td>Arkansas</td><td>13,603</td><td>1.0%</td></tr>
<tr><td>4</td><td>New York</td><td>81,530</td><td>6.1%</td><td>32</td><td>Nevada</td><td>12,947</td><td>1.0%</td></tr>
<tr><td>10</td><td>North Carolina</td><td>38,224</td><td>2.9%</td><td>33</td><td>Kansas</td><td>12,002</td><td>0.9%</td></tr>
<tr><td>48</td><td>North Dakota</td><td>2,397</td><td>0.2%</td><td>34</td><td>Utah</td><td>11,502</td><td>0.9%</td></tr>
<tr><td>8</td><td>Ohio</td><td>44,123</td><td>3.3%</td><td>35</td><td>Iowa</td><td>11,249</td><td>0.8%</td></tr>
<tr><td>25</td><td>Oklahoma</td><td>17,988</td><td>1.4%</td><td>36</td><td>Nebraska</td><td>7,699</td><td>0.6%</td></tr>
<tr><td>30</td><td>Oregon</td><td>13,738</td><td>1.0%</td><td>37</td><td>West Virginia</td><td>7,367</td><td>0.6%</td></tr>
<tr><td>7</td><td>Pennsylvania</td><td>44,277</td><td>3.3%</td><td>38</td><td>New Mexico</td><td>6,975</td><td>0.5%</td></tr>
<tr><td>43</td><td>Rhode Island</td><td>3,850</td><td>0.3%</td><td>39</td><td>Idaho</td><td>5,514</td><td>0.4%</td></tr>
<tr><td>22</td><td>South Carolina</td><td>20,487</td><td>1.5%</td><td>40</td><td>Hawaii</td><td>4,859</td><td>0.4%</td></tr>
<tr><td>46</td><td>South Dakota</td><td>3,218</td><td>0.2%</td><td>41</td><td>New Hampshire</td><td>4,300</td><td>0.3%</td></tr>
<tr><td>13</td><td>Tennessee</td><td>27,328</td><td>2.1%</td><td>42</td><td>Maine</td><td>4,231</td><td>0.3%</td></tr>
<tr><td>2</td><td>Texas</td><td>132,671</td><td>10.0%</td><td>43</td><td>Rhode Island</td><td>3,850</td><td>0.3%</td></tr>
<tr><td>34</td><td>Utah</td><td>11,502</td><td>0.9%</td><td>44</td><td>Delaware</td><td>3,680</td><td>0.3%</td></tr>
<tr><td>50</td><td>Vermont</td><td>1,692</td><td>0.1%</td><td>45</td><td>Montana</td><td>3,502</td><td>0.3%</td></tr>
<tr><td>12</td><td>Virginia</td><td>34,933</td><td>2.6%</td><td>46</td><td>South Dakota</td><td>3,218</td><td>0.2%</td></tr>
<tr><td>18</td><td>Washington</td><td>24,665</td><td>1.9%</td><td>47</td><td>Alaska</td><td>2,528</td><td>0.2%</td></tr>
<tr><td>37</td><td>West Virginia</td><td>7,367</td><td>0.6%</td><td>48</td><td>North Dakota</td><td>2,397</td><td>0.2%</td></tr>
<tr><td>27</td><td>Wisconsin</td><td>17,794</td><td>1.3%</td><td>49</td><td>Wyoming</td><td>2,017</td><td>0.2%</td></tr>
<tr><td>49</td><td>Wyoming</td><td>2,017</td><td>0.2%</td><td>50</td><td>Vermont</td><td>1,692</td><td>0.1%</td></tr>
<tr><td></td><td></td><td></td><td></td><td></td><td>District of Columbia</td><td>2,610</td><td>0.2%</td></tr>
</table>

Source: CQ Press using data from U.S. Department of Health and Human Services, National Center for Health Statistics
   "National Vital Statistics Reports" (Vol. 56, No. 7, December 5, 2007, http://www.cdc.gov/nchs/births.htm)
*Preliminary estimates by state of residence.

Percent of Births by Cesarean Delivery in 2006

National Percent = 31.1% of Live Births*

ALPHA ORDER			RANK ORDER		
RANK	STATE	PERCENT	RANK	STATE	PERCENT
8	Alabama	33.4	1	New Jersey	37.4
48	Alaska	23.0	2	Florida	36.1
42	Arizona	25.6	3	Louisiana	35.4
10	Arkansas	33.2	3	Mississippi	35.4
19	California	31.3	5	West Virginia	35.2
45	Colorado	25.3	6	Kentucky	34.5
7	Connecticut	34.1	7	Connecticut	34.1
22	Delaware	30.7	8	Alabama	33.4
2	Florida	36.1	9	Oklahoma	33.3
19	Georgia	31.3	10	Arkansas	33.2
42	Hawaii	25.6	10	Massachusetts	33.2
49	Idaho	22.8	10	Texas	33.2
29	Illinois	29.6	13	South Carolina	32.9
32	Indiana	29.0	14	New York	32.6
38	Iowa	27.7	15	Tennessee	32.4
30	Kansas	29.3	15	Virginia	32.4
6	Kentucky	34.5	17	Nevada	32.3
3	Louisiana	35.4	18	Maryland	32.2
24	Maine	29.9	19	California	31.3
18	Maryland	32.2	19	Georgia	31.3
10	Massachusetts	33.2	21	Rhode Island	31.1
27	Michigan	29.8	22	Delaware	30.7
44	Minnesota	25.4	23	Missouri	30.2
3	Mississippi	35.4	24	Maine	29.9
23	Missouri	30.2	24	New Hampshire	29.9
36	Montana	28.0	24	North Carolina	29.9
33	Nebraska	28.8	27	Michigan	29.8
17	Nevada	32.3	28	Pennsylvania	29.7
24	New Hampshire	29.9	29	Illinois	29.6
1	New Jersey	37.4	30	Kansas	29.3
47	New Mexico	23.3	30	Ohio	29.3
14	New York	32.6	32	Indiana	29.0
24	North Carolina	29.9	33	Nebraska	28.8
37	North Dakota	27.8	34	Washington	28.4
30	Ohio	29.3	35	Oregon	28.2
9	Oklahoma	33.3	36	Montana	28.0
35	Oregon	28.2	37	North Dakota	27.8
28	Pennsylvania	29.7	38	Iowa	27.7
21	Rhode Island	31.1	39	South Dakota	27.0
13	South Carolina	32.9	40	Wyoming	26.3
39	South Dakota	27.0	41	Vermont	26.0
15	Tennessee	32.4	42	Arizona	25.6
10	Texas	33.2	42	Hawaii	25.6
50	Utah	21.5	44	Minnesota	25.4
41	Vermont	26.0	45	Colorado	25.3
15	Virginia	32.4	46	Wisconsin	24.6
34	Washington	28.4	47	New Mexico	23.3
5	West Virginia	35.2	48	Alaska	23.0
46	Wisconsin	24.6	49	Idaho	22.8
40	Wyoming	26.3	50	Utah	21.5
				District of Columbia	30.6

Source: U.S. Department of Health and Human Services, National Center for Health Statistics
   "National Vital Statistics Reports" (Vol. 56, No. 7, December 5, 2007, http://www.cdc.gov/nchs/births.htm)
*Preliminary data by state of residence.

Percent Change in Rate of Cesarean Births: 2002 to 2006

National Percent Change = 19.6% Increase*

ALPHA ORDER

RANK	STATE	PERCENT CHANGE
36	Alabama	16.8
31	Alaska	18.6
17	Arizona	20.8
43	Arkansas	14.5
36	California	16.8
23	Colorado	19.9
1	Connecticut	31.7
48	Delaware	12.5
3	Florida	27.1
15	Georgia	21.3
20	Hawaii	20.2
40	Idaho	16.3
7	Illinois	24.4
35	Indiana	17.4
46	Iowa	12.6
31	Kansas	18.6
4	Kentucky	25.9
36	Louisiana	16.8
36	Maine	16.8
34	Maryland	17.5
28	Massachusetts	19.0
20	Michigan	20.2
42	Minnesota	16.0
44	Mississippi	14.2
33	Missouri	18.0
12	Montana	22.3
50	Nebraska	8.3
2	Nevada	27.2
9	New Hampshire	24.1
13	New Jersey	21.8
10	New Mexico	22.6
18	New York	20.7
45	North Carolina	13.7
11	North Dakota	22.5
5	Ohio	24.7
20	Oklahoma	20.2
14	Oregon	21.6
25	Pennsylvania	19.8
26	Rhode Island	19.6
40	South Carolina	16.3
49	South Dakota	10.2
30	Tennessee	18.7
23	Texas	19.9
46	Utah	12.6
7	Vermont	24.4
15	Virginia	21.3
29	Washington	18.8
19	West Virginia	20.5
27	Wisconsin	19.4
6	Wyoming	24.6

RANK ORDER

RANK	STATE	PERCENT CHANGE
1	Connecticut	31.7
2	Nevada	27.2
3	Florida	27.1
4	Kentucky	25.9
5	Ohio	24.7
6	Wyoming	24.6
7	Illinois	24.4
7	Vermont	24.4
9	New Hampshire	24.1
10	New Mexico	22.6
11	North Dakota	22.5
12	Montana	22.3
13	New Jersey	21.8
14	Oregon	21.6
15	Georgia	21.3
15	Virginia	21.3
17	Arizona	20.8
18	New York	20.7
19	West Virginia	20.5
20	Hawaii	20.2
20	Michigan	20.2
20	Oklahoma	20.2
23	Colorado	19.9
23	Texas	19.9
25	Pennsylvania	19.8
26	Rhode Island	19.6
27	Wisconsin	19.4
28	Massachusetts	19.0
29	Washington	18.8
30	Tennessee	18.7
31	Alaska	18.6
31	Kansas	18.6
33	Missouri	18.0
34	Maryland	17.5
35	Indiana	17.4
36	Alabama	16.8
36	California	16.8
36	Louisiana	16.8
36	Maine	16.8
40	Idaho	16.3
40	South Carolina	16.3
42	Minnesota	16.0
43	Arkansas	14.5
44	Mississippi	14.2
45	North Carolina	13.7
46	Iowa	12.6
46	Utah	12.6
48	Delaware	12.5
49	South Dakota	10.2
50	Nebraska	8.3

District of Columbia 15.5

Source: CQ Press using data from U.S. Department of Health and Human Services, National Center for Health Statistics
"National Vital Statistics Reports" (Vol. 56, No. 7, December 5, 2007, http://www.cdc.gov/nchs/births.htm)
*Preliminary data by state of residence.

Percent of Births That Are Pre-Term in 2006

National Percent = 12.8% of Births*

ALPHA ORDER			RANK ORDER		
RANK	STATE	PERCENT	RANK	STATE	PERCENT
2	Alabama	17.1	1	Mississippi	18.8
42	Alaska	11.2	2	Alabama	17.1
20	Arizona	13.2	3	Louisiana	16.2
13	Arkansas	13.7	4	South Carolina	15.4
45	California	10.7	5	Kentucky	15.1
30	Colorado	12.2	6	Tennessee	14.8
47	Connecticut	10.4	7	Nevada	14.4
13	Delaware	13.7	8	Georgia	14.1
12	Florida	13.8	8	New Mexico	14.1
8	Georgia	14.1	10	West Virginia	14.0
31	Hawaii	12.1	11	Oklahoma	13.9
37	Idaho	11.6	12	Florida	13.8
18	Illinois	13.3	13	Arkansas	13.7
20	Indiana	13.2	13	Delaware	13.7
37	Iowa	11.6	13	Texas	13.7
35	Kansas	11.8	16	North Carolina	13.6
5	Kentucky	15.1	17	Maryland	13.5
3	Louisiana	16.2	18	Illinois	13.3
43	Maine	11.1	18	Ohio	13.3
17	Maryland	13.5	20	Arizona	13.2
41	Massachusetts	11.3	20	Indiana	13.2
27	Michigan	12.5	22	New Jersey	12.9
46	Minnesota	10.5	23	Missouri	12.8
1	Mississippi	18.8	23	Wyoming	12.8
23	Missouri	12.8	25	South Dakota	12.7
34	Montana	11.9	26	Rhode Island	12.6
27	Nebraska	12.5	27	Michigan	12.5
7	Nevada	14.4	27	Nebraska	12.5
47	New Hampshire	10.4	29	New York	12.4
22	New Jersey	12.9	30	Colorado	12.2
8	New Mexico	14.1	31	Hawaii	12.1
29	New York	12.4	31	North Dakota	12.1
16	North Carolina	13.6	33	Virginia	12.0
31	North Dakota	12.1	34	Montana	11.9
18	Ohio	13.3	35	Kansas	11.8
11	Oklahoma	13.9	35	Pennsylvania	11.8
49	Oregon	10.3	37	Idaho	11.6
35	Pennsylvania	11.8	37	Iowa	11.6
26	Rhode Island	12.6	39	Utah	11.5
4	South Carolina	15.4	40	Wisconsin	11.4
25	South Dakota	12.7	41	Massachusetts	11.3
6	Tennessee	14.8	42	Alaska	11.2
13	Texas	13.7	43	Maine	11.1
39	Utah	11.5	44	Washington	11.0
50	Vermont	9.6	45	California	10.7
33	Virginia	12.0	46	Minnesota	10.5
44	Washington	11.0	47	Connecticut	10.4
10	West Virginia	14.0	47	New Hampshire	10.4
40	Wisconsin	11.4	49	Oregon	10.3
23	Wyoming	12.8	50	Vermont	9.6
				District of Columbia	16.0

Source: U.S. Department of Health and Human Services, National Center for Health Statistics
   "National Vital Statistics Reports" (Vol. 56, No. 7, December 5, 2007, http://www.cdc.gov/nchs/births.htm)
*Preliminary data by state of residence. Births before 37 weeks of gestation.

Twin Birth Rate: 2002-2005

National Rate = 31.9 Twins Born per 1,000 Live Births*

ALPHA ORDER

RANK	STATE	RATE
19	Alabama	32.2
47	Alaska	26.9
48	Arizona	26.5
36	Arkansas	29.4
38	California	29.0
25	Colorado	31.7
3	Connecticut	41.5
9	Delaware	35.6
33	Florida	29.9
28	Georgia	31.2
42	Hawaii	28.0
35	Idaho	29.5
8	Illinois	35.9
21	Indiana	31.9
15	Iowa	33.2
32	Kansas	30.3
31	Kentucky	30.6
27	Louisiana	31.3
16	Maine	32.8
6	Maryland	37.1
1	Massachusetts	44.5
10	Michigan	34.2
13	Minnesota	33.5
21	Mississippi	31.9
18	Missouri	32.5
43	Montana	27.6
20	Nebraska	32.1
38	Nevada	29.0
5	New Hampshire	37.2
2	New Jersey	41.8
50	New Mexico	24.2
7	New York	36.0
21	North Carolina	31.9
17	North Dakota	32.6
14	Ohio	33.4
44	Oklahoma	27.4
34	Oregon	29.8
11	Pennsylvania	33.7
4	Rhode Island	38.9
26	South Carolina	31.5
40	South Dakota	28.9
29	Tennessee	31.1
41	Texas	28.1
48	Utah	26.5
21	Vermont	31.9
12	Virginia	33.6
36	Washington	29.4
46	West Virginia	27.2
30	Wisconsin	30.8
45	Wyoming	27.3

RANK ORDER

RANK	STATE	RATE
1	Massachusetts	44.5
2	New Jersey	41.8
3	Connecticut	41.5
4	Rhode Island	38.9
5	New Hampshire	37.2
6	Maryland	37.1
7	New York	36.0
8	Illinois	35.9
9	Delaware	35.6
10	Michigan	34.2
11	Pennsylvania	33.7
12	Virginia	33.6
13	Minnesota	33.5
14	Ohio	33.4
15	Iowa	33.2
16	Maine	32.8
17	North Dakota	32.6
18	Missouri	32.5
19	Alabama	32.2
20	Nebraska	32.1
21	Indiana	31.9
21	Mississippi	31.9
21	North Carolina	31.9
21	Vermont	31.9
25	Colorado	31.7
26	South Carolina	31.5
27	Louisiana	31.3
28	Georgia	31.2
29	Tennessee	31.1
30	Wisconsin	30.8
31	Kentucky	30.6
32	Kansas	30.3
33	Florida	29.9
34	Oregon	29.8
35	Idaho	29.5
36	Arkansas	29.4
36	Washington	29.4
38	California	29.0
38	Nevada	29.0
40	South Dakota	28.9
41	Texas	28.1
42	Hawaii	28.0
43	Montana	27.6
44	Oklahoma	27.4
45	Wyoming	27.3
46	West Virginia	27.2
47	Alaska	26.9
48	Arizona	26.5
48	Utah	26.5
50	New Mexico	24.2
	District of Columbia	34.5

Source: U.S. Department of Health and Human Services, National Center for Health Statistics
    "National Vital Statistics Reports" (Vol. 56, No. 6, December 5, 2007, http://www.cdc.gov/nchs/births.htm)
*Final data by state of residence. Number of live births in twin deliveries.

Assisted Reproductive Technology Procedures in 2004

National Total = 126,952 Procedures*

ALPHA ORDER

RANK	STATE	PROCEDURES	% of USA
37	Alabama	595	0.5%
50	Alaska	48	0.0%
19	Arizona	1,715	1.4%
47	Arkansas	129	0.1%
1	California	17,303	13.6%
18	Colorado	1,815	1.4%
13	Connecticut	2,877	2.3%
38	Delaware	451	0.4%
7	Florida	5,229	4.1%
14	Georgia	2,808	2.2%
30	Hawaii	831	0.7%
40	Idaho	324	0.3%
3	Illinois	9,306	7.3%
17	Indiana	2,016	1.6%
25	Iowa	971	0.8%
34	Kansas	626	0.5%
26	Kentucky	956	0.8%
31	Louisiana	750	0.6%
43	Maine	218	0.2%
9	Maryland	4,205	3.3%
4	Massachusetts	8,906	7.0%
11	Michigan	3,498	2.8%
16	Minnesota	2,123	1.7%
39	Mississippi	416	0.3%
20	Missouri	1,589	1.3%
48	Montana	114	0.1%
32	Nebraska	702	0.6%
24	Nevada	1,045	0.8%
33	New Hampshire	669	0.5%
5	New Jersey	8,513	6.7%
41	New Mexico	250	0.2%
2	New York	16,174	12.7%
15	North Carolina	2,350	1.9%
45	North Dakota	193	0.2%
12	Ohio	3,429	2.7%
36	Oklahoma	601	0.5%
28	Oregon	894	0.7%
8	Pennsylvania	4,767	3.8%
29	Rhode Island	852	0.7%
27	South Carolina	928	0.7%
46	South Dakota	188	0.1%
23	Tennessee	1,072	0.8%
6	Texas	6,192	4.9%
35	Utah	604	0.5%
44	Vermont	202	0.2%
10	Virginia	3,757	3.0%
22	Washington	1,192	0.9%
42	West Virginia	231	0.2%
21	Wisconsin	1,553	1.2%
49	Wyoming	51	0.0%

RANK ORDER

RANK	STATE	PROCEDURES	% of USA
1	California	17,303	13.6%
2	New York	16,174	12.7%
3	Illinois	9,306	7.3%
4	Massachusetts	8,906	7.0%
5	New Jersey	8,513	6.7%
6	Texas	6,192	4.9%
7	Florida	5,229	4.1%
8	Pennsylvania	4,767	3.8%
9	Maryland	4,205	3.3%
10	Virginia	3,757	3.0%
11	Michigan	3,498	2.8%
12	Ohio	3,429	2.7%
13	Connecticut	2,877	2.3%
14	Georgia	2,808	2.2%
15	North Carolina	2,350	1.9%
16	Minnesota	2,123	1.7%
17	Indiana	2,016	1.6%
18	Colorado	1,815	1.4%
19	Arizona	1,715	1.4%
20	Missouri	1,589	1.3%
21	Wisconsin	1,553	1.2%
22	Washington	1,192	0.9%
23	Tennessee	1,072	0.8%
24	Nevada	1,045	0.8%
25	Iowa	971	0.8%
26	Kentucky	956	0.8%
27	South Carolina	928	0.7%
28	Oregon	894	0.7%
29	Rhode Island	852	0.7%
30	Hawaii	831	0.7%
31	Louisiana	750	0.6%
32	Nebraska	702	0.6%
33	New Hampshire	669	0.5%
34	Kansas	626	0.5%
35	Utah	604	0.5%
36	Oklahoma	601	0.5%
37	Alabama	595	0.5%
38	Delaware	451	0.4%
39	Mississippi	416	0.3%
40	Idaho	324	0.3%
41	New Mexico	250	0.2%
42	West Virginia	231	0.2%
43	Maine	218	0.2%
44	Vermont	202	0.2%
45	North Dakota	193	0.2%
46	South Dakota	188	0.1%
47	Arkansas	129	0.1%
48	Montana	114	0.1%
49	Wyoming	51	0.0%
50	Alaska	48	0.0%
	District of Columbia	711	0.6%

Source: U.S. Department of Health and Human Services, Centers for Disease Control and Prevention
"Assisted Reproductive Technology, 2004" (Morbidity and Mortality Weekly Report, Vol. 56, No. SS-06, 06/08/07)
*By patient's residence. Does not include 1,025 procedures for patients with residences outside the U.S. Assisted reproductive technology (ART) includes treatments in which both eggs and sperm are handled in the laboratory. In 2004, 74% of ART treatments were freshly fertilized embryos using the patient's eggs, 15% were thawed embryos using the patient's eggs, 8% were freshly fertilized embryos from donor eggs, and 4% were thawed embryos from donor eggs.

Infants Born from Assisted Reproductive Technology Procedures in 2004

National Total = 48,965 Live Births*

ALPHA ORDER

RANK	STATE	BIRTHS	% of USA
32	Alabama	286	0.6%
50	Alaska	19	0.0%
19	Arizona	678	1.4%
48	Arkansas	48	0.1%
1	California	6,536	13.3%
14	Colorado	1,074	2.2%
15	Connecticut	1,054	2.2%
38	Delaware	172	0.4%
7	Florida	1,946	4.0%
13	Georgia	1,164	2.4%
36	Hawaii	246	0.5%
39	Idaho	171	0.3%
5	Illinois	3,113	6.4%
18	Indiana	770	1.6%
28	Iowa	436	0.9%
35	Kansas	264	0.5%
23	Kentucky	463	0.9%
31	Louisiana	310	0.6%
43	Maine	79	0.2%
11	Maryland	1,457	3.0%
4	Massachusetts	3,153	6.4%
12	Michigan	1,325	2.7%
17	Minnesota	979	2.0%
40	Mississippi	162	0.3%
20	Missouri	677	1.4%
47	Montana	52	0.1%
34	Nebraska	265	0.5%
26	Nevada	442	0.9%
37	New Hampshire	236	0.5%
3	New Jersey	3,279	6.7%
41	New Mexico	159	0.3%
2	New York	5,424	11.1%
16	North Carolina	1,048	2.1%
45	North Dakota	76	0.2%
10	Ohio	1,505	3.1%
29	Oklahoma	324	0.7%
26	Oregon	442	0.9%
8	Pennsylvania	1,571	3.2%
33	Rhode Island	276	0.6%
24	South Carolina	461	0.9%
46	South Dakota	64	0.1%
25	Tennessee	456	0.9%
6	Texas	2,841	5.8%
30	Utah	317	0.6%
44	Vermont	77	0.2%
9	Virginia	1,536	3.1%
22	Washington	519	1.1%
42	West Virginia	98	0.2%
21	Wisconsin	657	1.3%
49	Wyoming	21	0.0%

RANK ORDER

RANK	STATE	BIRTHS	% of USA
1	California	6,536	13.3%
2	New York	5,424	11.1%
3	New Jersey	3,279	6.7%
4	Massachusetts	3,153	6.4%
5	Illinois	3,113	6.4%
6	Texas	2,841	5.8%
7	Florida	1,946	4.0%
8	Pennsylvania	1,571	3.2%
9	Virginia	1,536	3.1%
10	Ohio	1,505	3.1%
11	Maryland	1,457	3.0%
12	Michigan	1,325	2.7%
13	Georgia	1,164	2.4%
14	Colorado	1,074	2.2%
15	Connecticut	1,054	2.2%
16	North Carolina	1,048	2.1%
17	Minnesota	979	2.0%
18	Indiana	770	1.6%
19	Arizona	678	1.4%
20	Missouri	677	1.4%
21	Wisconsin	657	1.3%
22	Washington	519	1.1%
23	Kentucky	463	0.9%
24	South Carolina	461	0.9%
25	Tennessee	456	0.9%
26	Nevada	442	0.9%
26	Oregon	442	0.9%
28	Iowa	436	0.9%
29	Oklahoma	324	0.7%
30	Utah	317	0.6%
31	Louisiana	310	0.6%
32	Alabama	286	0.6%
33	Rhode Island	276	0.6%
34	Nebraska	265	0.5%
35	Kansas	264	0.5%
36	Hawaii	246	0.5%
37	New Hampshire	236	0.5%
38	Delaware	172	0.4%
39	Idaho	171	0.3%
40	Mississippi	162	0.3%
41	New Mexico	159	0.3%
42	West Virginia	98	0.2%
43	Maine	79	0.2%
44	Vermont	77	0.2%
45	North Dakota	76	0.2%
46	South Dakota	64	0.1%
47	Montana	52	0.1%
48	Arkansas	48	0.1%
49	Wyoming	21	0.0%
50	Alaska	19	0.0%
	District of Columbia	231	0.5%

Source: U.S. Department of Health and Human Services, Centers for Disease Control and Prevention
"Assisted Reproductive Technology, 2004" (Morbidity and Mortality Weekly Report, Vol. 56, No. SS-06, 06/08/07)
*By patient's residence. Does not include 493 births for patients with residences outside the U.S. Assisted reproductive technology (ART) includes treatments in which both eggs and sperm are handled in the laboratory. In 2004, 74% of ART treatments were freshly fertilized embryos using the patient's eggs, 15% were thawed embryos using the patient's eggs, 8% were freshly fertilized embryos from donor eggs, and 4% were thawed embryos from donor eggs.

Percent of Assisted Reproductive Technology Procedures that Resulted in Live Births in 2004
National Percent = 28.7%*

ALPHA ORDER

RANK	STATE	PERCENT
9	Alabama	35.0
31	Alaska	29.2
32	Arizona	28.9
26	Arkansas	29.5
36	California	27.9
2	Colorado	41.4
35	Connecticut	28.1
29	Delaware	29.3
39	Florida	27.7
24	Georgia	30.3
50	Hawaii	22.0
3	Idaho	39.5
48	Illinois	24.8
36	Indiana	27.9
11	Iowa	34.2
17	Kansas	31.9
12	Kentucky	33.5
24	Louisiana	30.3
42	Maine	27.1
45	Maryland	26.7
44	Massachusetts	27.0
39	Michigan	27.7
10	Minnesota	34.6
36	Mississippi	27.9
18	Missouri	31.7
8	Montana	35.1
41	Nebraska	27.4
20	Nevada	31.2
42	New Hampshire	27.1
33	New Jersey	28.8
1	New Mexico	42.4
47	New York	25.4
14	North Carolina	32.6
26	North Dakota	29.5
19	Ohio	31.6
4	Oklahoma	39.3
7	Oregon	36.9
48	Pennsylvania	24.8
46	Rhode Island	25.5
6	South Carolina	37.6
29	South Dakota	29.3
22	Tennessee	30.8
13	Texas	33.2
5	Utah	38.2
34	Vermont	28.7
23	Virginia	30.5
16	Washington	32.0
15	West Virginia	32.5
20	Wisconsin	31.2
28	Wyoming	29.4

RANK ORDER

RANK	STATE	PERCENT
1	New Mexico	42.4
2	Colorado	41.4
3	Idaho	39.5
4	Oklahoma	39.3
5	Utah	38.2
6	South Carolina	37.6
7	Oregon	36.9
8	Montana	35.1
9	Alabama	35.0
10	Minnesota	34.6
11	Iowa	34.2
12	Kentucky	33.5
13	Texas	33.2
14	North Carolina	32.6
15	West Virginia	32.5
16	Washington	32.0
17	Kansas	31.9
18	Missouri	31.7
19	Ohio	31.6
20	Nevada	31.2
20	Wisconsin	31.2
22	Tennessee	30.8
23	Virginia	30.5
24	Georgia	30.3
24	Louisiana	30.3
26	Arkansas	29.5
26	North Dakota	29.5
28	Wyoming	29.4
29	Delaware	29.3
29	South Dakota	29.3
31	Alaska	29.2
32	Arizona	28.9
33	New Jersey	28.8
34	Vermont	28.7
35	Connecticut	28.1
36	California	27.9
36	Indiana	27.9
36	Mississippi	27.9
39	Florida	27.7
39	Michigan	27.7
41	Nebraska	27.4
42	Maine	27.1
42	New Hampshire	27.1
44	Massachusetts	27.0
45	Maryland	26.7
46	Rhode Island	25.5
47	New York	25.4
48	Illinois	24.8
48	Pennsylvania	24.8
50	Hawaii	22.0

District of Columbia — 24.9

Source: CQ Press using data from U.S. Department of Health and Human Services, Centers for Disease Control and Prevention "Assisted Reproductive Technology, 2004" (Morbidity and Mortality Weekly Report, Vol. 56, No. SS-06, 06/08/07)
*By patient's residence. Assisted reproductive technology (ART) includes treatments in which both eggs and sperm are handled in the laboratory. In 2003, 74% of ART treatments were freshly fertilized embryos using the patient's eggs, 15% were thawed embryos using the patient's eggs, 8% were freshly fertilized embryos from donor eggs, and 4% were thawed embryos from donor eggs.

Percent of Total Live Births Resulting from
Assisted Reproductive Technology Procedures in 2004
National Percent = 1.2% of Live Births*

ALPHA ORDER

RANK	STATE	PERCENT
43	Alabama	0.5
49	Alaska	0.2
33	Arizona	0.7
50	Arkansas	0.1
15	California	1.2
8	Colorado	1.6
3	Connecticut	2.5
10	Delaware	1.5
23	Florida	0.9
29	Georgia	0.8
13	Hawaii	1.3
29	Idaho	0.8
7	Illinois	1.7
23	Indiana	0.9
17	Iowa	1.1
33	Kansas	0.7
29	Kentucky	0.8
43	Louisiana	0.5
36	Maine	0.6
6	Maryland	2.0
1	Massachusetts	4.0
19	Michigan	1.0
12	Minnesota	1.4
47	Mississippi	0.4
23	Missouri	0.9
43	Montana	0.5
19	Nebraska	1.0
13	Nevada	1.3
8	New Hampshire	1.6
2	New Jersey	2.8
36	New Mexico	0.6
4	New York	2.2
23	North Carolina	0.9
23	North Dakota	0.9
19	Ohio	1.0
36	Oklahoma	0.6
19	Oregon	1.0
17	Pennsylvania	1.1
4	Rhode Island	2.2
29	South Carolina	0.8
36	South Dakota	0.6
36	Tennessee	0.6
33	Texas	0.7
36	Utah	0.6
15	Vermont	1.2
10	Virginia	1.5
36	Washington	0.6
43	West Virginia	0.5
23	Wisconsin	0.9
48	Wyoming	0.3

RANK ORDER

RANK	STATE	PERCENT
1	Massachusetts	4.0
2	New Jersey	2.8
3	Connecticut	2.5
4	New York	2.2
4	Rhode Island	2.2
6	Maryland	2.0
7	Illinois	1.7
8	Colorado	1.6
8	New Hampshire	1.6
10	Delaware	1.5
10	Virginia	1.5
12	Minnesota	1.4
13	Hawaii	1.3
13	Nevada	1.3
15	California	1.2
15	Vermont	1.2
17	Iowa	1.1
17	Pennsylvania	1.1
19	Michigan	1.0
19	Nebraska	1.0
19	Ohio	1.0
19	Oregon	1.0
23	Florida	0.9
23	Indiana	0.9
23	Missouri	0.9
23	North Carolina	0.9
23	North Dakota	0.9
23	Wisconsin	0.9
29	Georgia	0.8
29	Idaho	0.8
29	Kentucky	0.8
29	South Carolina	0.8
33	Arizona	0.7
33	Kansas	0.7
33	Texas	0.7
36	Maine	0.6
36	New Mexico	0.6
36	Oklahoma	0.6
36	South Dakota	0.6
36	Tennessee	0.6
36	Utah	0.6
36	Washington	0.6
43	Alabama	0.5
43	Louisiana	0.5
43	Montana	0.5
43	West Virginia	0.5
47	Mississippi	0.4
48	Wyoming	0.3
49	Alaska	0.2
50	Arkansas	0.1

District of Columbia   2.9

Source: CQ Press using data from U.S. Department of Health and Human Services, Centers for Disease Control and Prevention
"Assisted Reproductive Technology, 2004" (Morbidity and Mortality Weekly Report, Vol. 56, No. SS-06, 06/08/07)
"National Vital Statistics Reports" (Vol. 55, No. 1, September 29, 2006)
*By patient's residence. Does not include births or procedures to patients with residences outside the U.S. Assisted reproductive technology (ART) includes treatments in which both eggs and sperm are handled in the laboratory (i.e. in vitro fertilization and related procedures).

Percent of Assisted Reproductive Technology Procedure Infants Born in Multiple Birth Deliveries in 2004
National Percent = 49.6% of Assisted Reproductive Technology Births*

ALPHA ORDER

RANK	STATE	PERCENT
5	Alabama	53.5
9	Alaska	52.6
16	Arizona	51.2
49	Arkansas	41.7
18	California	50.7
3	Colorado	58.0
45	Connecticut	44.9
43	Delaware	45.9
28	Florida	49.5
22	Georgia	50.4
23	Hawaii	50.0
34	Idaho	48.5
25	Illinois	49.8
20	Indiana	50.6
42	Iowa	46.1
35	Kansas	47.7
2	Kentucky	58.1
15	Louisiana	51.3
29	Maine	49.4
44	Maryland	45.2
41	Massachusetts	46.4
18	Michigan	50.7
33	Minnesota	48.6
4	Mississippi	54.9
25	Missouri	49.8
47	Montana	44.2
12	Nebraska	52.1
17	Nevada	50.9
40	New Hampshire	46.6
32	New Jersey	49.0
1	New Mexico	64.2
39	New York	47.2
10	North Carolina	52.3
23	North Dakota	50.0
10	Ohio	52.3
6	Oklahoma	53.4
25	Oregon	49.8
37	Pennsylvania	47.5
48	Rhode Island	42.4
38	South Carolina	47.3
50	South Dakota	28.1
14	Tennessee	51.8
6	Texas	53.4
8	Utah	52.7
29	Vermont	49.4
31	Virginia	49.3
13	Washington	52.0
45	West Virginia	44.9
21	Wisconsin	50.5
36	Wyoming	47.6

RANK ORDER

RANK	STATE	PERCENT
1	New Mexico	64.2
2	Kentucky	58.1
3	Colorado	58.0
4	Mississippi	54.9
5	Alabama	53.5
6	Oklahoma	53.4
6	Texas	53.4
8	Utah	52.7
9	Alaska	52.6
10	North Carolina	52.3
10	Ohio	52.3
12	Nebraska	52.1
13	Washington	52.0
14	Tennessee	51.8
15	Louisiana	51.3
16	Arizona	51.2
17	Nevada	50.9
18	California	50.7
18	Michigan	50.7
20	Indiana	50.6
21	Wisconsin	50.5
22	Georgia	50.4
23	Hawaii	50.0
23	North Dakota	50.0
25	Illinois	49.8
25	Missouri	49.8
25	Oregon	49.8
28	Florida	49.5
29	Maine	49.4
29	Vermont	49.4
31	Virginia	49.3
32	New Jersey	49.0
33	Minnesota	48.6
34	Idaho	48.5
35	Kansas	47.7
36	Wyoming	47.6
37	Pennsylvania	47.5
38	South Carolina	47.3
39	New York	47.2
40	New Hampshire	46.6
41	Massachusetts	46.4
42	Iowa	46.1
43	Delaware	45.9
44	Maryland	45.2
45	Connecticut	44.9
45	West Virginia	44.9
47	Montana	44.2
48	Rhode Island	42.4
49	Arkansas	41.7
50	South Dakota	28.1
	District of Columbia	45.9

Source: U.S. Department of Health and Human Services, Centers for Disease Control and Prevention
   "Assisted Reproductive Technology, 2004" (Morbidity and Mortality Weekly Report, Vol. 56, No. SS-06, 06/08/07)
*By patient's residence. Includes births and procedures to patients with residences outside the U.S. Assisted reproductive technology (ART) includes treatments in which both eggs and sperm are handled in the laboratory (i.e. in vitro fertilization and related procedures).

Percent of Mothers Beginning Prenatal Care in First Trimester in 2005

National Percent = 83.9% of Mothers*

ALPHA ORDER

RANK	STATE	RATE
22	Alabama	83.1
28	Alaska	80.2
35	Arizona	77.7
27	Arkansas	80.6
9	California	86.6
31	Colorado	80.1
8	Connecticut	86.8
23	Delaware	81.9
NA	Florida**	NA
20	Georgia	83.6
24	Hawaii	81.5
NA	Idaho**	NA
11	Illinois	86.0
32	Indiana	79.9
5	Iowa	87.6
NA	Kansas**	NA
NA	Kentucky**	NA
6	Louisiana	87.2
3	Maine	88.1
25	Maryland	81.3
1	Massachusetts	89.3
13	Michigan	85.6
10	Minnesota	86.2
18	Mississippi	84.2
4	Missouri	87.8
19	Montana	84.0
NA	Nebraska**	NA
37	Nevada	74.0
NA	New Hampshire**	NA
34	New Jersey	78.7
38	New Mexico	71.2
28	New York*	80.2
21	North Carolina	83.5
12	North Dakota	85.9
7	Ohio	87.1
36	Oklahoma	77.3
26	Oregon	80.9
NA	Pennsylvania**	NA
1	Rhode Island	89.3
NA	South Carolina**	NA
33	South Dakota	79.5
NA	Tennessee**	NA
NA	Texas**	NA
28	Utah	80.2
NA	Vermont**	NA
15	Virginia	85.0
NA	Washington**	NA
17	West Virginia	84.4
14	Wisconsin	85.5
16	Wyoming	84.9

RANK ORDER

RANK	STATE	RATE
1	Massachusetts	89.3
1	Rhode Island	89.3
3	Maine	88.1
4	Missouri	87.8
5	Iowa	87.6
6	Louisiana	87.2
7	Ohio	87.1
8	Connecticut	86.8
9	California	86.6
10	Minnesota	86.2
11	Illinois	86.0
12	North Dakota	85.9
13	Michigan	85.6
14	Wisconsin	85.5
15	Virginia	85.0
16	Wyoming	84.9
17	West Virginia	84.4
18	Mississippi	84.2
19	Montana	84.0
20	Georgia	83.6
21	North Carolina	83.5
22	Alabama	83.1
23	Delaware	81.9
24	Hawaii	81.5
25	Maryland	81.3
26	Oregon	80.9
27	Arkansas	80.6
28	Alaska	80.2
28	New York*	80.2
28	Utah	80.2
31	Colorado	80.1
32	Indiana	79.9
33	South Dakota	79.5
34	New Jersey	78.7
35	Arizona	77.7
36	Oklahoma	77.3
37	Nevada	74.0
38	New Mexico	71.2
NA	Florida**	NA
NA	Idaho**	NA
NA	Kansas**	NA
NA	Kentucky**	NA
NA	Nebraska**	NA
NA	New Hampshire**	NA
NA	Pennsylvania**	NA
NA	South Carolina**	NA
NA	Tennessee**	NA
NA	Texas**	NA
NA	Vermont**	NA
NA	Washington**	NA
	District of Columbia	77.5

Source: U.S. Department of Health and Human Services, National Center for Health Statistics
    "National Vital Statistics Reports" (Vol. 56, No. 6, December 5, 2007, http://www.cdc.gov/nchs/births.htm)
*Final data by state of residence. New York's figure is for New York City only.
**Not available. These states have implemented the 2003 Revision of the U.S. Certificate of Live Birth and their prenatal care
data are not comparable with those based on the 1989 revision.

Percent of White Mothers Beginning Prenatal Care in First Trimester in 2005

National Percent = 88.7% of White Mothers*

<u>ALPHA ORDER</u>

RANK	STATE	PERCENT
15	Alabama	89.3
27	Alaska	85.6
24	Arizona	87.5
33	Arkansas	84.2
9	California	90.1
27	Colorado	85.6
4	Connecticut	92.0
21	Delaware	88.2
NA	Florida**	NA
12	Georgia	89.6
29	Hawaii	85.2
NA	Idaho**	NA
5	Illinois	90.8
35	Indiana	83.8
12	Iowa	89.6
NA	Kansas**	NA
NA	Kentucky**	NA
1	Louisiana	92.9
20	Maine	88.3
16	Maryland	89.2
3	Massachusetts	92.1
12	Michigan	89.6
10	Minnesota	90.0
6	Mississippi	90.5
11	Missouri	89.9
25	Montana	87.1
NA	Nebraska**	NA
36	Nevada	82.4
NA	New Hampshire**	NA
22	New Jersey	88.1
38	New Mexico	79.1
22	New York*	88.1
8	North Carolina	90.2
19	North Dakota	88.7
16	Ohio	89.2
37	Oklahoma	81.5
32	Oregon	84.4
NA	Pennsylvania**	NA
2	Rhode Island	92.4
NA	South Carolina**	NA
30	South Dakota	85.0
NA	Tennessee**	NA
NA	Texas**	NA
34	Utah	84.0
NA	Vermont**	NA
6	Virginia	90.5
NA	Washington**	NA
30	West Virginia	85.0
18	Wisconsin	88.8
26	Wyoming	87.0

<u>RANK ORDER</u>

RANK	STATE	PERCENT
1	Louisiana	92.9
2	Rhode Island	92.4
3	Massachusetts	92.1
4	Connecticut	92.0
5	Illinois	90.8
6	Mississippi	90.5
6	Virginia	90.5
8	North Carolina	90.2
9	California	90.1
10	Minnesota	90.0
11	Missouri	89.9
12	Georgia	89.6
12	Iowa	89.6
12	Michigan	89.6
15	Alabama	89.3
16	Maryland	89.2
16	Ohio	89.2
18	Wisconsin	88.8
19	North Dakota	88.7
20	Maine	88.3
21	Delaware	88.2
22	New Jersey	88.1
22	New York*	88.1
24	Arizona	87.5
25	Montana	87.1
26	Wyoming	87.0
27	Alaska	85.6
27	Colorado	85.6
29	Hawaii	85.2
30	South Dakota	85.0
30	West Virginia	85.0
32	Oregon	84.4
33	Arkansas	84.2
34	Utah	84.0
35	Indiana	83.8
36	Nevada	82.4
37	Oklahoma	81.5
38	New Mexico	79.1
NA	Florida**	NA
NA	Idaho**	NA
NA	Kansas**	NA
NA	Kentucky**	NA
NA	Nebraska**	NA
NA	New Hampshire**	NA
NA	Pennsylvania**	NA
NA	South Carolina**	NA
NA	Tennessee**	NA
NA	Texas**	NA
NA	Vermont**	NA
NA	Washington**	NA
	District of Columbia	92.0

Source: U.S. Department of Health and Human Services, National Center for Health Statistics
"National Vital Statistics Reports" (Vol. 56, No. 6, December 5, 2007, http://www.cdc.gov/nchs/births.htm)
*Final data by state of residence. New York's figure is for New York City only. Does not include whites of Hispanic origin.
**Not available. These states have implemented the 2003 Revision of the U.S. Certificate of Live Birth and their prenatal care data are not comparable with those based on the 1989 revision.

Percent of Black Mothers Beginning Prenatal Care in First Trimester in 2005

National Percent = 76.5% of Black Mothers*

ALPHA ORDER

RANK	STATE	PERCENT
18	Alabama	77.0
6	Alaska	82.1
17	Arizona	77.4
28	Arkansas	74.6
4	California	82.8
23	Colorado	75.5
23	Connecticut	75.5
15	Delaware	77.9
NA	Florida**	NA
11	Georgia	79.1
5	Hawaii	82.4
NA	Idaho**	NA
22	Illinois	75.7
35	Indiana	66.0
21	Iowa	76.0
NA	Kansas**	NA
NA	Kentucky**	NA
13	Louisiana	79.0
11	Maine	79.1
27	Maryland	75.1
8	Massachusetts	80.5
30	Michigan	71.7
25	Minnesota	75.3
16	Mississippi	77.7
9	Missouri	80.3
7	Montana	81.0
NA	Nebraska**	NA
34	Nevada	68.9
NA	New Hampshire**	NA
36	New Jersey	62.9
33	New Mexico	70.8
25	New York*	75.3
20	North Carolina	76.7
3	North Dakota	83.2
14	Ohio	78.3
29	Oklahoma	71.8
32	Oregon	71.3
NA	Pennsylvania**	NA
2	Rhode Island	83.3
NA	South Carolina**	NA
37	South Dakota	58.2
NA	Tennessee**	NA
NA	Texas**	NA
38	Utah	54.9
NA	Vermont**	NA
10	Virginia	79.9
NA	Washington**	NA
30	West Virginia	71.7
19	Wisconsin	76.8
1	Wyoming	90.2

RANK ORDER

RANK	STATE	PERCENT
1	Wyoming	90.2
2	Rhode Island	83.3
3	North Dakota	83.2
4	California	82.8
5	Hawaii	82.4
6	Alaska	82.1
7	Montana	81.0
8	Massachusetts	80.5
9	Missouri	80.3
10	Virginia	79.9
11	Georgia	79.1
11	Maine	79.1
13	Louisiana	79.0
14	Ohio	78.3
15	Delaware	77.9
16	Mississippi	77.7
17	Arizona	77.4
18	Alabama	77.0
19	Wisconsin	76.8
20	North Carolina	76.7
21	Iowa	76.0
22	Illinois	75.7
23	Colorado	75.5
23	Connecticut	75.5
25	Minnesota	75.3
25	New York*	75.3
27	Maryland	75.1
28	Arkansas	74.6
29	Oklahoma	71.8
30	Michigan	71.7
30	West Virginia	71.7
32	Oregon	71.3
33	New Mexico	70.8
34	Nevada	68.9
35	Indiana	66.0
36	New Jersey	62.9
37	South Dakota	58.2
38	Utah	54.9
NA	Florida**	NA
NA	Idaho**	NA
NA	Kansas**	NA
NA	Kentucky**	NA
NA	Nebraska**	NA
NA	New Hampshire**	NA
NA	Pennsylvania**	NA
NA	South Carolina**	NA
NA	Tennessee**	NA
NA	Texas**	NA
NA	Vermont**	NA
NA	Washington**	NA

District of Columbia 73.8

Source: U.S. Department of Health and Human Services, National Center for Health Statistics
    "National Vital Statistics Reports" (Vol. 56, No. 6, December 5, 2007, http://www.cdc.gov/nchs/births.htm)
*Final data by state of residence. New York's figure is for New York City only. Does not include blacks of Hispanic origin.
**Not available. These states have implemented the 2003 Revision of the U.S. Certificate of Live Birth and their prenatal care data are not comparable with those based on the 1989 revision.

Percent of Hispanic Mothers Beginning Prenatal Care in First Trimester in 2005

National Percent = 77.6% of Hispanic Mothers*

ALPHA ORDER			RANK ORDER		
RANK	STATE	PERCENT	RANK	STATE	PERCENT
38	Alabama	51.5	1	Louisiana	85.6
10	Alaska	78.4	2	Rhode Island	85.4
25	Arizona	69.5	3	Maine	85.0
29	Arkansas	68.1	4	California	84.5
4	California	84.5	5	Massachusetts	82.5
24	Colorado	70.0	6	Illinois	82.2
16	Connecticut	76.0	7	Hawaii	81.4
36	Delaware	62.6	8	Michigan	79.0
NA	Florida**	NA	8	North Dakota	79.0
20	Georgia	72.9	10	Alaska	78.4
7	Hawaii	81.4	11	Ohio	78.2
NA	Idaho**	NA	12	New York*	77.9
6	Illinois	82.2	13	Missouri	77.5
34	Indiana	63.6	14	Montana	77.4
18	Iowa	74.2	14	Wyoming	77.4
NA	Kansas**	NA	16	Connecticut	76.0
NA	Kentucky**	NA	17	West Virginia	75.3
1	Louisiana	85.6	18	Iowa	74.2
3	Maine	85.0	19	Mississippi	73.7
35	Maryland	63.1	20	Georgia	72.9
5	Massachusetts	82.5	21	Wisconsin	72.8
8	Michigan	79.0	22	Minnesota	71.2
22	Minnesota	71.2	23	Oregon	70.1
19	Mississippi	73.7	24	Colorado	70.0
13	Missouri	77.5	25	Arizona	69.5
14	Montana	77.4	26	New Mexico	69.4
NA	Nebraska**	NA	27	North Carolina	68.8
33	Nevada	64.0	28	Virginia	68.6
NA	New Hampshire**	NA	29	Arkansas	68.1
30	New Jersey	66.6	30	New Jersey	66.6
26	New Mexico	69.4	31	Oklahoma	65.6
12	New York*	77.9	32	Utah	65.3
27	North Carolina	68.8	33	Nevada	64.0
8	North Dakota	79.0	34	Indiana	63.6
11	Ohio	78.2	35	Maryland	63.1
31	Oklahoma	65.6	36	Delaware	62.6
23	Oregon	70.1	37	South Dakota	62.4
NA	Pennsylvania**	NA	38	Alabama	51.5
2	Rhode Island	85.4	NA	Florida**	NA
NA	South Carolina**	NA	NA	Idaho**	NA
37	South Dakota	62.4	NA	Kansas**	NA
NA	Tennessee**	NA	NA	Kentucky**	NA
NA	Texas**	NA	NA	Nebraska**	NA
32	Utah	65.3	NA	New Hampshire**	NA
NA	Vermont**	NA	NA	Pennsylvania**	NA
28	Virginia	68.6	NA	South Carolina**	NA
NA	Washington**	NA	NA	Tennessee**	NA
17	West Virginia	75.3	NA	Texas**	NA
21	Wisconsin	72.8	NA	Vermont**	NA
14	Wyoming	77.4	NA	Washington**	NA
				District of Columbia	62.3

Source: U.S. Department of Health and Human Services, National Center for Health Statistics
   "National Vital Statistics Reports" (Vol. 56, No. 6, December 5, 2007, http://www.cdc.gov/nchs/births.htm)
*Final data by state of residence. New York's figure is for New York City only. Persons of Hispanic origin may be of any race.
**Not available. These states have implemented the 2003 Revision of the U.S. Certificate of Live Birth and their prenatal care data are not comparable with those based on the 1989 revision.

Percent of Mothers Receiving Late or No Prenatal Care in 2005

National Percent = 3.5% of Mothers*

<table>
<tr><td colspan="3">ALPHA ORDER</td><td colspan="3">RANK ORDER</td></tr>
<tr><td>RANK</td><td>STATE</td><td>PERCENT</td><td>RANK</td><td>STATE</td><td>PERCENT</td></tr>
<tr><td>14</td><td>Alabama</td><td>4.1</td><td>1</td><td>Nevada</td><td>8.2</td></tr>
<tr><td>5</td><td>Alaska</td><td>4.9</td><td>2</td><td>New Mexico</td><td>7.7</td></tr>
<tr><td>3</td><td>Arizona</td><td>6.2</td><td>3</td><td>Arizona</td><td>6.2</td></tr>
<tr><td>9</td><td>Arkansas</td><td>4.7</td><td>4</td><td>Oklahoma</td><td>5.5</td></tr>
<tr><td>26</td><td>California</td><td>2.7</td><td>5</td><td>Alaska</td><td>4.9</td></tr>
<tr><td>10</td><td>Colorado</td><td>4.5</td><td>5</td><td>Delaware</td><td>4.9</td></tr>
<tr><td>37</td><td>Connecticut</td><td>1.9</td><td>5</td><td>New York*</td><td>4.9</td></tr>
<tr><td>5</td><td>Delaware</td><td>4.9</td><td>8</td><td>New Jersey</td><td>4.8</td></tr>
<tr><td>NA</td><td>Florida**</td><td>NA</td><td>9</td><td>Arkansas</td><td>4.7</td></tr>
<tr><td>16</td><td>Georgia</td><td>3.8</td><td>10</td><td>Colorado</td><td>4.5</td></tr>
<tr><td>18</td><td>Hawaii</td><td>3.6</td><td>11</td><td>Maryland</td><td>4.3</td></tr>
<tr><td>NA</td><td>Idaho**</td><td>NA</td><td>11</td><td>Utah</td><td>4.3</td></tr>
<tr><td>31</td><td>Illinois</td><td>2.6</td><td>13</td><td>Indiana</td><td>4.2</td></tr>
<tr><td>13</td><td>Indiana</td><td>4.2</td><td>14</td><td>Alabama</td><td>4.1</td></tr>
<tr><td>34</td><td>Iowa</td><td>2.2</td><td>14</td><td>Oregon</td><td>4.1</td></tr>
<tr><td>NA</td><td>Kansas**</td><td>NA</td><td>16</td><td>Georgia</td><td>3.8</td></tr>
<tr><td>NA</td><td>Kentucky**</td><td>NA</td><td>16</td><td>Virginia</td><td>3.8</td></tr>
<tr><td>26</td><td>Louisiana</td><td>2.7</td><td>18</td><td>Hawaii</td><td>3.6</td></tr>
<tr><td>38</td><td>Maine</td><td>1.7</td><td>18</td><td>South Dakota</td><td>3.6</td></tr>
<tr><td>11</td><td>Maryland</td><td>4.3</td><td>20</td><td>Wyoming</td><td>3.3</td></tr>
<tr><td>34</td><td>Massachusetts</td><td>2.2</td><td>21</td><td>Michigan</td><td>3.0</td></tr>
<tr><td>21</td><td>Michigan</td><td>3.0</td><td>21</td><td>Mississippi</td><td>3.0</td></tr>
<tr><td>32</td><td>Minnesota</td><td>2.3</td><td>23</td><td>North Carolina</td><td>2.9</td></tr>
<tr><td>21</td><td>Mississippi</td><td>3.0</td><td>23</td><td>Ohio</td><td>2.9</td></tr>
<tr><td>32</td><td>Missouri</td><td>2.3</td><td>23</td><td>Wisconsin</td><td>2.9</td></tr>
<tr><td>26</td><td>Montana</td><td>2.7</td><td>26</td><td>California</td><td>2.7</td></tr>
<tr><td>NA</td><td>Nebraska**</td><td>NA</td><td>26</td><td>Louisiana</td><td>2.7</td></tr>
<tr><td>1</td><td>Nevada</td><td>8.2</td><td>26</td><td>Montana</td><td>2.7</td></tr>
<tr><td>NA</td><td>New Hampshire**</td><td>NA</td><td>26</td><td>North Dakota</td><td>2.7</td></tr>
<tr><td>8</td><td>New Jersey</td><td>4.8</td><td>26</td><td>West Virginia</td><td>2.7</td></tr>
<tr><td>2</td><td>New Mexico</td><td>7.7</td><td>31</td><td>Illinois</td><td>2.6</td></tr>
<tr><td>5</td><td>New York*</td><td>4.9</td><td>32</td><td>Minnesota</td><td>2.3</td></tr>
<tr><td>23</td><td>North Carolina</td><td>2.9</td><td>32</td><td>Missouri</td><td>2.3</td></tr>
<tr><td>26</td><td>North Dakota</td><td>2.7</td><td>34</td><td>Iowa</td><td>2.2</td></tr>
<tr><td>23</td><td>Ohio</td><td>2.9</td><td>34</td><td>Massachusetts</td><td>2.2</td></tr>
<tr><td>4</td><td>Oklahoma</td><td>5.5</td><td>34</td><td>Rhode Island</td><td>2.2</td></tr>
<tr><td>14</td><td>Oregon</td><td>4.1</td><td>37</td><td>Connecticut</td><td>1.9</td></tr>
<tr><td>NA</td><td>Pennsylvania**</td><td>NA</td><td>38</td><td>Maine</td><td>1.7</td></tr>
<tr><td>34</td><td>Rhode Island</td><td>2.2</td><td>NA</td><td>Florida**</td><td>NA</td></tr>
<tr><td>NA</td><td>South Carolina**</td><td>NA</td><td>NA</td><td>Idaho**</td><td>NA</td></tr>
<tr><td>18</td><td>South Dakota</td><td>3.6</td><td>NA</td><td>Kansas**</td><td>NA</td></tr>
<tr><td>NA</td><td>Tennessee**</td><td>NA</td><td>NA</td><td>Kentucky**</td><td>NA</td></tr>
<tr><td>NA</td><td>Texas**</td><td>NA</td><td>NA</td><td>Nebraska**</td><td>NA</td></tr>
<tr><td>11</td><td>Utah</td><td>4.3</td><td>NA</td><td>New Hampshire**</td><td>NA</td></tr>
<tr><td>NA</td><td>Vermont**</td><td>NA</td><td>NA</td><td>Pennsylvania**</td><td>NA</td></tr>
<tr><td>16</td><td>Virginia</td><td>3.8</td><td>NA</td><td>South Carolina**</td><td>NA</td></tr>
<tr><td>NA</td><td>Washington**</td><td>NA</td><td>NA</td><td>Tennessee**</td><td>NA</td></tr>
<tr><td>26</td><td>West Virginia</td><td>2.7</td><td>NA</td><td>Texas**</td><td>NA</td></tr>
<tr><td>23</td><td>Wisconsin</td><td>2.9</td><td>NA</td><td>Vermont**</td><td>NA</td></tr>
<tr><td>20</td><td>Wyoming</td><td>3.3</td><td>NA</td><td>Washington**</td><td>NA</td></tr>
<tr><td></td><td></td><td></td><td></td><td>District of Columbia</td><td>5.1</td></tr>
</table>

Source: U.S. Department of Health and Human Services, National Center for Health Statistics
"National Vital Statistics Reports" (Vol. 56, No. 6, December 5, 2007, http://www.cdc.gov/nchs/births.htm)
*Final data by state of residence. "Late" means care begun in third trimester. New York's figure is for New York City only.
**Not available. These states have implemented the 2003 Revision of the U.S. Certificate of Live Birth and their prenatal care data are not comparable with those based on the 1989 revision.

Percent of White Mothers Receiving Late or No Prenatal Care in 2005

National Percent = 2.2% of White Mothers*

ALPHA ORDER				RANK ORDER		
RANK	STATE	PERCENT		RANK	STATE	PERCENT
24	Alabama	1.9		1	Nevada	5.3
5	Alaska	3.3		2	Oklahoma	4.6
9	Arizona	2.8		3	New Mexico	4.5
4	Arkansas	3.4		4	Arkansas	3.4
19	California	2.1		5	Alaska	3.3
9	Colorado	2.8		5	Oregon	3.3
37	Connecticut	1.2		7	Indiana	3.1
15	Delaware	2.3		8	Utah	3.0
NA	Florida**	NA		9	Arizona	2.8
19	Georgia	2.1		9	Colorado	2.8
13	Hawaii	2.4		11	Wyoming	2.7
NA	Idaho**	NA		12	West Virginia	2.6
34	Illinois	1.5		13	Hawaii	2.4
7	Indiana	3.1		13	New Jersey	2.4
27	Iowa	1.7		15	Delaware	2.3
NA	Kansas**	NA		15	New York*	2.3
NA	Kentucky**	NA		15	Wisconsin	2.3
37	Louisiana	1.2		18	Ohio	2.2
29	Maine	1.6		19	California	2.1
19	Maryland	2.1		19	Georgia	2.1
29	Massachusetts	1.6		19	Maryland	2.1
23	Michigan	2.0		19	Virginia	2.1
35	Minnesota	1.4		23	Michigan	2.0
29	Mississippi	1.6		24	Alabama	1.9
26	Missouri	1.8		24	South Dakota	1.9
29	Montana	1.6		26	Missouri	1.8
NA	Nebraska**	NA		27	Iowa	1.7
1	Nevada	5.3		27	North Dakota	1.7
NA	New Hampshire**	NA		29	Maine	1.6
13	New Jersey	2.4		29	Massachusetts	1.6
3	New Mexico	4.5		29	Mississippi	1.6
15	New York*	2.3		29	Montana	1.6
29	North Carolina	1.6		29	North Carolina	1.6
27	North Dakota	1.7		34	Illinois	1.5
18	Ohio	2.2		35	Minnesota	1.4
2	Oklahoma	4.6		35	Rhode Island	1.4
5	Oregon	3.3		37	Connecticut	1.2
NA	Pennsylvania**	NA		37	Louisiana	1.2
35	Rhode Island	1.4		NA	Florida**	NA
NA	South Carolina**	NA		NA	Idaho**	NA
24	South Dakota	1.9		NA	Kansas**	NA
NA	Tennessee**	NA		NA	Kentucky**	NA
NA	Texas**	NA		NA	Nebraska**	NA
8	Utah	3.0		NA	New Hampshire**	NA
NA	Vermont**	NA		NA	Pennsylvania**	NA
19	Virginia	2.1		NA	South Carolina**	NA
NA	Washington**	NA		NA	Tennessee**	NA
12	West Virginia	2.6		NA	Texas**	NA
15	Wisconsin	2.3		NA	Vermont**	NA
11	Wyoming	2.7		NA	Washington**	NA
					District of Columbia	1.3

Source: U.S. Department of Health and Human Services, National Center for Health Statistics
  "National Vital Statistics Reports" (Vol. 56, No. 6, December 5, 2007, http://www.cdc.gov/nchs/births.htm)
*Final data by state of residence. "Late" means care begun in third trimester. New York's figure is for New York City only.
Does not include whites of Hispanic origin.
**Not available. These states have implemented the 2003 Revision of the U.S. Certificate of Live Birth and their prenatal care
data are not comparable with those based on the 1989 revision.

Percent of Black Mothers Receiving Late or No Prenatal Care in 2005

National Percent = 5.6% of Black Mothers*

<table>
<tr><td colspan="3">ALPHA ORDER</td><td colspan="3">RANK ORDER</td></tr>
<tr><td>RANK</td><td>STATE</td><td>PERCENT</td><td>RANK</td><td>STATE</td><td>PERCENT</td></tr>
<tr><td>27</td><td>Alabama</td><td>4.6</td><td>1</td><td>Utah</td><td>15.7</td></tr>
<tr><td>11</td><td>Alaska</td><td>6.0</td><td>2</td><td>Nevada</td><td>10.6</td></tr>
<tr><td>14</td><td>Arizona</td><td>5.8</td><td>3</td><td>New Jersey</td><td>10.3</td></tr>
<tr><td>6</td><td>Arkansas</td><td>7.1</td><td>4</td><td>Indiana</td><td>8.4</td></tr>
<tr><td>32</td><td>California</td><td>3.5</td><td>5</td><td>New York</td><td>7.2</td></tr>
<tr><td>9</td><td>Colorado</td><td>6.4</td><td>6</td><td>Arkansas</td><td>7.1</td></tr>
<tr><td>31</td><td>Connecticut</td><td>3.6</td><td>7</td><td>Oklahoma</td><td>7.0</td></tr>
<tr><td>22</td><td>Delaware</td><td>5.0</td><td>8</td><td>Michigan</td><td>6.9</td></tr>
<tr><td>NA</td><td>Florida**</td><td>NA</td><td>9</td><td>Colorado</td><td>6.4</td></tr>
<tr><td>24</td><td>Georgia</td><td>4.7</td><td>9</td><td>Maryland</td><td>6.4</td></tr>
<tr><td>NA</td><td>Hawaii**</td><td>NA</td><td>11</td><td>Alaska</td><td>6.0</td></tr>
<tr><td>NA</td><td>Idaho**</td><td>NA</td><td>12</td><td>Oregon</td><td>5.9</td></tr>
<tr><td>14</td><td>Illinois</td><td>5.8</td><td>12</td><td>West Virginia</td><td>5.9</td></tr>
<tr><td>4</td><td>Indiana</td><td>8.4</td><td>14</td><td>Arizona</td><td>5.8</td></tr>
<tr><td>17</td><td>Iowa</td><td>5.5</td><td>14</td><td>Illinois</td><td>5.8</td></tr>
<tr><td>NA</td><td>Kansas**</td><td>NA</td><td>14</td><td>Ohio</td><td>5.8</td></tr>
<tr><td>NA</td><td>Kentucky**</td><td>NA</td><td>17</td><td>Iowa</td><td>5.5</td></tr>
<tr><td>23</td><td>Louisiana</td><td>4.9</td><td>17</td><td>New Mexico</td><td>5.5</td></tr>
<tr><td>NA</td><td>Maine**</td><td>NA</td><td>19</td><td>Wisconsin</td><td>5.4</td></tr>
<tr><td>9</td><td>Maryland</td><td>6.4</td><td>20</td><td>Virginia</td><td>5.2</td></tr>
<tr><td>21</td><td>Massachusetts</td><td>5.1</td><td>21</td><td>Massachusetts</td><td>5.1</td></tr>
<tr><td>8</td><td>Michigan</td><td>6.9</td><td>22</td><td>Delaware</td><td>5.0</td></tr>
<tr><td>24</td><td>Minnesota</td><td>4.7</td><td>23</td><td>Louisiana</td><td>4.9</td></tr>
<tr><td>30</td><td>Mississippi</td><td>4.3</td><td>24</td><td>Georgia</td><td>4.7</td></tr>
<tr><td>29</td><td>Missouri</td><td>4.4</td><td>24</td><td>Minnesota</td><td>4.7</td></tr>
<tr><td>NA</td><td>Montana**</td><td>NA</td><td>24</td><td>North Carolina</td><td>4.7</td></tr>
<tr><td>NA</td><td>Nebraska**</td><td>NA</td><td>27</td><td>Alabama</td><td>4.6</td></tr>
<tr><td>2</td><td>Nevada</td><td>10.6</td><td>27</td><td>Rhode Island</td><td>4.6</td></tr>
<tr><td>NA</td><td>New Hampshire**</td><td>NA</td><td>29</td><td>Missouri</td><td>4.4</td></tr>
<tr><td>3</td><td>New Jersey</td><td>10.3</td><td>30</td><td>Mississippi</td><td>4.3</td></tr>
<tr><td>17</td><td>New Mexico</td><td>5.5</td><td>31</td><td>Connecticut</td><td>3.6</td></tr>
<tr><td>5</td><td>New York</td><td>7.2</td><td>32</td><td>California</td><td>3.5</td></tr>
<tr><td>24</td><td>North Carolina</td><td>4.7</td><td>NA</td><td>Florida**</td><td>NA</td></tr>
<tr><td>NA</td><td>North Dakota**</td><td>NA</td><td>NA</td><td>Hawaii**</td><td>NA</td></tr>
<tr><td>14</td><td>Ohio</td><td>5.8</td><td>NA</td><td>Idaho**</td><td>NA</td></tr>
<tr><td>7</td><td>Oklahoma</td><td>7.0</td><td>NA</td><td>Kansas**</td><td>NA</td></tr>
<tr><td>12</td><td>Oregon</td><td>5.9</td><td>NA</td><td>Kentucky**</td><td>NA</td></tr>
<tr><td>NA</td><td>Pennsylvania**</td><td>NA</td><td>NA</td><td>Maine**</td><td>NA</td></tr>
<tr><td>27</td><td>Rhode Island</td><td>4.6</td><td>NA</td><td>Montana**</td><td>NA</td></tr>
<tr><td>NA</td><td>South Carolina**</td><td>NA</td><td>NA</td><td>Nebraska**</td><td>NA</td></tr>
<tr><td>NA</td><td>South Dakota**</td><td>NA</td><td>NA</td><td>New Hampshire**</td><td>NA</td></tr>
<tr><td>NA</td><td>Tennessee**</td><td>NA</td><td>NA</td><td>North Dakota**</td><td>NA</td></tr>
<tr><td>NA</td><td>Texas**</td><td>NA</td><td>NA</td><td>Pennsylvania**</td><td>NA</td></tr>
<tr><td>1</td><td>Utah</td><td>15.7</td><td>NA</td><td>South Carolina**</td><td>NA</td></tr>
<tr><td>NA</td><td>Vermont**</td><td>NA</td><td>NA</td><td>South Dakota**</td><td>NA</td></tr>
<tr><td>20</td><td>Virginia</td><td>5.2</td><td>NA</td><td>Tennessee**</td><td>NA</td></tr>
<tr><td>NA</td><td>Washington**</td><td>NA</td><td>NA</td><td>Texas**</td><td>NA</td></tr>
<tr><td>12</td><td>West Virginia</td><td>5.9</td><td>NA</td><td>Vermont**</td><td>NA</td></tr>
<tr><td>19</td><td>Wisconsin</td><td>5.4</td><td>NA</td><td>Washington**</td><td>NA</td></tr>
<tr><td>NA</td><td>Wyoming**</td><td>NA</td><td>NA</td><td>Wyoming**</td><td>NA</td></tr>
</table>

District of Columbia   6.3

Source: U.S. Department of Health and Human Services, National Center for Health Statistics
"National Vital Statistics Reports" (Vol. 56, No. 6, December 5, 2007, http://www.cdc.gov/nchs/births.htm)
*Final data by state of residence. "Late" means care begun in third trimester. New York's figure is for New York City only.
Does not include blacks of Hispanic origin. **Not available. With the exception of Hawaii, Maine, Montana, North Dakota, South Dakota, and Wyoming, these states have implemented the 2003 Revision of the U.S. Certificate of Live Birth and their prenatal care data are not comparable with those based on the 1989 revision.

Percent of Hispanic Mothers Receiving Late or No Prenatal Care in 2005

National Percent = 5.1% of Hispanic Mothers*

<table>
<tr><th colspan="3">ALPHA ORDER</th><th colspan="3">RANK ORDER</th></tr>
<tr><th>RANK</th><th>STATE</th><th>PERCENT</th><th>RANK</th><th>STATE</th><th>PERCENT</th></tr>
<tr><td>1</td><td>Alabama</td><td>21.9</td><td>1</td><td>Alabama</td><td>21.9</td></tr>
<tr><td>10</td><td>Alaska</td><td>8.2</td><td>2</td><td>Delaware</td><td>15.3</td></tr>
<tr><td>4</td><td>Arizona</td><td>8.9</td><td>3</td><td>Nevada</td><td>11.3</td></tr>
<tr><td>6</td><td>Arkansas</td><td>8.4</td><td>4</td><td>Arizona</td><td>8.9</td></tr>
<tr><td>29</td><td>California</td><td>3.1</td><td>5</td><td>Indiana</td><td>8.6</td></tr>
<tr><td>14</td><td>Colorado</td><td>7.5</td><td>6</td><td>Arkansas</td><td>8.4</td></tr>
<tr><td>33</td><td>Connecticut</td><td>3.0</td><td>6</td><td>Mississippi</td><td>8.4</td></tr>
<tr><td>2</td><td>Delaware</td><td>15.3</td><td>6</td><td>Virginia</td><td>8.4</td></tr>
<tr><td>NA</td><td>Florida**</td><td>NA</td><td>9</td><td>Utah</td><td>8.3</td></tr>
<tr><td>13</td><td>Georgia</td><td>7.6</td><td>10</td><td>Alaska</td><td>8.2</td></tr>
<tr><td>29</td><td>Hawaii</td><td>3.1</td><td>10</td><td>New Mexico</td><td>8.2</td></tr>
<tr><td>NA</td><td>Idaho**</td><td>NA</td><td>12</td><td>Maryland</td><td>8.1</td></tr>
<tr><td>34</td><td>Illinois</td><td>2.8</td><td>13</td><td>Georgia</td><td>7.6</td></tr>
<tr><td>5</td><td>Indiana</td><td>8.6</td><td>14</td><td>Colorado</td><td>7.5</td></tr>
<tr><td>23</td><td>Iowa</td><td>5.2</td><td>15</td><td>Oklahoma</td><td>7.2</td></tr>
<tr><td>NA</td><td>Kansas**</td><td>NA</td><td>16</td><td>New Jersey</td><td>7.0</td></tr>
<tr><td>NA</td><td>Kentucky**</td><td>NA</td><td>17</td><td>Oregon</td><td>6.1</td></tr>
<tr><td>29</td><td>Louisiana</td><td>3.1</td><td>17</td><td>South Dakota</td><td>6.1</td></tr>
<tr><td>NA</td><td>Maine**</td><td>NA</td><td>19</td><td>New York*</td><td>5.5</td></tr>
<tr><td>12</td><td>Maryland</td><td>8.1</td><td>19</td><td>North Carolina</td><td>5.5</td></tr>
<tr><td>28</td><td>Massachusetts</td><td>3.4</td><td>21</td><td>Minnesota</td><td>5.3</td></tr>
<tr><td>26</td><td>Michigan</td><td>3.8</td><td>21</td><td>Ohio</td><td>5.3</td></tr>
<tr><td>21</td><td>Minnesota</td><td>5.3</td><td>23</td><td>Iowa</td><td>5.2</td></tr>
<tr><td>6</td><td>Mississippi</td><td>8.4</td><td>24</td><td>Wisconsin</td><td>4.9</td></tr>
<tr><td>27</td><td>Missouri</td><td>3.7</td><td>25</td><td>Wyoming</td><td>4.8</td></tr>
<tr><td>NA</td><td>Montana**</td><td>NA</td><td>26</td><td>Michigan</td><td>3.8</td></tr>
<tr><td>NA</td><td>Nebraska**</td><td>NA</td><td>27</td><td>Missouri</td><td>3.7</td></tr>
<tr><td>3</td><td>Nevada</td><td>11.3</td><td>28</td><td>Massachusetts</td><td>3.4</td></tr>
<tr><td>NA</td><td>New Hampshire**</td><td>NA</td><td>29</td><td>California</td><td>3.1</td></tr>
<tr><td>16</td><td>New Jersey</td><td>7.0</td><td>29</td><td>Hawaii</td><td>3.1</td></tr>
<tr><td>10</td><td>New Mexico</td><td>8.2</td><td>29</td><td>Louisiana</td><td>3.1</td></tr>
<tr><td>19</td><td>New York*</td><td>5.5</td><td>29</td><td>Rhode Island</td><td>3.1</td></tr>
<tr><td>19</td><td>North Carolina</td><td>5.5</td><td>33</td><td>Connecticut</td><td>3.0</td></tr>
<tr><td>NA</td><td>North Dakota**</td><td>NA</td><td>34</td><td>Illinois</td><td>2.8</td></tr>
<tr><td>21</td><td>Ohio</td><td>5.3</td><td>NA</td><td>Florida**</td><td>NA</td></tr>
<tr><td>15</td><td>Oklahoma</td><td>7.2</td><td>NA</td><td>Idaho**</td><td>NA</td></tr>
<tr><td>17</td><td>Oregon</td><td>6.1</td><td>NA</td><td>Kansas**</td><td>NA</td></tr>
<tr><td>NA</td><td>Pennsylvania**</td><td>NA</td><td>NA</td><td>Kentucky**</td><td>NA</td></tr>
<tr><td>29</td><td>Rhode Island</td><td>3.1</td><td>NA</td><td>Maine**</td><td>NA</td></tr>
<tr><td>NA</td><td>South Carolina**</td><td>NA</td><td>NA</td><td>Montana**</td><td>NA</td></tr>
<tr><td>17</td><td>South Dakota</td><td>6.1</td><td>NA</td><td>Nebraska**</td><td>NA</td></tr>
<tr><td>NA</td><td>Tennessee**</td><td>NA</td><td>NA</td><td>New Hampshire**</td><td>NA</td></tr>
<tr><td>NA</td><td>Texas**</td><td>NA</td><td>NA</td><td>North Dakota**</td><td>NA</td></tr>
<tr><td>9</td><td>Utah</td><td>8.3</td><td>NA</td><td>Pennsylvania**</td><td>NA</td></tr>
<tr><td>NA</td><td>Vermont**</td><td>NA</td><td>NA</td><td>South Carolina**</td><td>NA</td></tr>
<tr><td>6</td><td>Virginia</td><td>8.4</td><td>NA</td><td>Tennessee**</td><td>NA</td></tr>
<tr><td>NA</td><td>Washington**</td><td>NA</td><td>NA</td><td>Texas**</td><td>NA</td></tr>
<tr><td>NA</td><td>West Virginia**</td><td>NA</td><td>NA</td><td>Vermont**</td><td>NA</td></tr>
<tr><td>24</td><td>Wisconsin</td><td>4.9</td><td>NA</td><td>Washington**</td><td>NA</td></tr>
<tr><td>25</td><td>Wyoming</td><td>4.8</td><td>NA</td><td>West Virginia**</td><td>NA</td></tr>
<tr><td></td><td></td><td></td><td></td><td>District of Columbia</td><td>8.0</td></tr>
</table>

Source: U.S. Department of Health and Human Services, National Center for Health Statistics
"National Vital Statistics Reports" (Vol. 56, No. 6, December 5, 2007, http://www.cdc.gov/nchs/births.htm)
*Final data by state of residence. "Late" means care begun in third trimester. New York's figure is for New York City only.
Persons of Hispanic origin may be of any race. **Not available. With the exception of Hawaii, North Dakota, and West
Virginia, these states have implemented the 2003 Revision of the U.S. Certificate of Live Birth and their prenatal care data are
not comparable with those based on the 1989 revision.

Reported Legal Abortions in 2004

Reporting States' Total = 839,226 Abortions*

ALPHA ORDER

RANK	STATE	ABORTIONS	% of USA
20	Alabama	11,370	1.4%
42	Alaska	1,937	0.2%
16	Arizona	12,690	1.5%
33	Arkansas	4,644	0.6%
NA	California**	NA	NA
19	Colorado	11,415	1.4%
17	Connecticut	12,189	1.5%
34	Delaware	4,588	0.5%
2	Florida	91,710	10.9%
9	Georgia	32,513	3.9%
39	Hawaii	3,467	0.4%
45	Idaho	963	0.1%
4	Illinois	43,537	5.2%
23	Indiana	10,514	1.3%
31	Iowa	6,022	0.7%
21	Kansas	11,357	1.4%
37	Kentucky	3,557	0.4%
22	Louisiana	11,224	1.3%
40	Maine	2,593	0.3%
24	Maryland	10,096	1.2%
13	Massachusetts	24,366	2.9%
10	Michigan	26,269	3.1%
15	Minnesota	13,791	1.6%
38	Mississippi	3,500	0.4%
27	Missouri	8,072	1.0%
41	Montana	2,256	0.3%
36	Nebraska	3,584	0.4%
26	Nevada	9,856	1.2%
NA	New Hampshire**	NA	NA
8	New Jersey	32,642	3.9%
30	New Mexico	6,070	0.7%
1	New York	126,002	15.0%
7	North Carolina	33,954	4.0%
44	North Dakota	1,357	0.2%
6	Ohio	34,242	4.1%
28	Oklahoma	6,712	0.8%
18	Oregon	11,443	1.4%
5	Pennsylvania	36,030	4.3%
32	Rhode Island	5,587	0.7%
29	South Carolina	6,565	0.8%
46	South Dakota	814	0.1%
14	Tennessee	16,400	2.0%
3	Texas	74,801	8.9%
35	Utah	3,665	0.4%
43	Vermont	1,725	0.2%
11	Virginia	26,117	3.1%
12	Washington	24,664	2.9%
NA	West Virginia**	NA	NA
25	Wisconsin	9,943	1.2%
47	Wyoming	12	0.0%

RANK ORDER

RANK	STATE	ABORTIONS	% of USA
1	New York	126,002	15.0%
2	Florida	91,710	10.9%
3	Texas	74,801	8.9%
4	Illinois	43,537	5.2%
5	Pennsylvania	36,030	4.3%
6	Ohio	34,242	4.1%
7	North Carolina	33,954	4.0%
8	New Jersey	32,642	3.9%
9	Georgia	32,513	3.9%
10	Michigan	26,269	3.1%
11	Virginia	26,117	3.1%
12	Washington	24,664	2.9%
13	Massachusetts	24,366	2.9%
14	Tennessee	16,400	2.0%
15	Minnesota	13,791	1.6%
16	Arizona	12,690	1.5%
17	Connecticut	12,189	1.5%
18	Oregon	11,443	1.4%
19	Colorado	11,415	1.4%
20	Alabama	11,370	1.4%
21	Kansas	11,357	1.4%
22	Louisiana	11,224	1.3%
23	Indiana	10,514	1.3%
24	Maryland	10,096	1.2%
25	Wisconsin	9,943	1.2%
26	Nevada	9,856	1.2%
27	Missouri	8,072	1.0%
28	Oklahoma	6,712	0.8%
29	South Carolina	6,565	0.8%
30	New Mexico	6,070	0.7%
31	Iowa	6,022	0.7%
32	Rhode Island	5,587	0.7%
33	Arkansas	4,644	0.6%
34	Delaware	4,588	0.5%
35	Utah	3,665	0.4%
36	Nebraska	3,584	0.4%
37	Kentucky	3,557	0.4%
38	Mississippi	3,500	0.4%
39	Hawaii	3,467	0.4%
40	Maine	2,593	0.3%
41	Montana	2,256	0.3%
42	Alaska	1,937	0.2%
43	Vermont	1,725	0.2%
44	North Dakota	1,357	0.2%
45	Idaho	963	0.1%
46	South Dakota	814	0.1%
47	Wyoming	12	0.0%
NA	California**	NA	NA
NA	New Hampshire**	NA	NA
NA	West Virginia**	NA	NA
	District of Columbia	2,401	0.3%

Source: U.S. Department of Health and Human Services, Centers for Disease Control and Prevention
   "Abortion Surveillance-United States, 2004" (Morbidity and Mortality Weekly Report, Vol. 56, No. SS-9, 11/23/07)
*By state of occurrence. Total is for reporting states only.
**Not reported.

Percent Change in Reported Legal Abortions: 2000 to 2004

National Percent Change = 1.8% Decrease*

ALPHA ORDER			RANK ORDER		
RANK	STATE	PERCENT CHANGE	RANK	STATE	PERCENT CHANGE
43	Alabama	(16.1)	1	Colorado	170.8
NA	Alaska**	NA	2	Wyoming	100.0
4	Arizona	26.1	3	Nevada	65.0
42	Arkansas	(15.6)	4	Arizona	26.1
NA	California**	NA	5	Idaho	20.2
1	Colorado	170.8	6	North Carolina	12.6
26	Connecticut	(5.6)	7	New Mexico	11.1
34	Delaware	(9.7)	8	Iowa	4.8
10	Florida	3.6	9	Utah	4.4
12	Georgia	2.6	10	Florida	3.6
38	Hawaii	(12.0)	11	Rhode Island	3.2
5	Idaho	20.2	12	Georgia	2.6
25	Illinois	(5.1)	13	Missouri	2.4
41	Indiana	(14.3)	14	Maine	2.2
8	Iowa	4.8	15	North Dakota	1.2
31	Kansas	(7.1)	16	Pennsylvania	1.1
46	Kentucky	(23.2)	17	New Jersey	(1.2)
18	Louisiana	(1.4)	18	Louisiana	(1.4)
14	Maine	2.2	19	Texas	(1.7)
44	Maryland	(18.2)	20	Michigan	(2.0)
37	Massachusetts	(10.4)	21	New York	(2.8)
20	Michigan	(2.0)	22	Vermont	(3.1)
24	Minnesota	(4.7)	23	Washington	(4.0)
30	Mississippi	(6.9)	24	Minnesota	(4.7)
13	Missouri	2.4	25	Illinois	(5.1)
33	Montana	(7.6)	26	Connecticut	(5.6)
40	Nebraska	(14.2)	27	Tennessee	(6.2)
3	Nevada	65.0	28	Oklahoma	(6.5)
NA	New Hampshire**	NA	29	Virginia	(6.7)
17	New Jersey	(1.2)	30	Mississippi	(6.9)
7	New Mexico	11.1	31	Kansas	(7.1)
21	New York	(2.8)	32	South Dakota	(7.3)
6	North Carolina	12.6	33	Montana	(7.6)
15	North Dakota	1.2	34	Delaware	(9.7)
36	Ohio	(10.2)	35	Wisconsin	(9.9)
28	Oklahoma	(6.5)	36	Ohio	(10.2)
45	Oregon	(19.4)	37	Massachusetts	(10.4)
16	Pennsylvania	1.1	38	Hawaii	(12.0)
11	Rhode Island	3.2	39	South Carolina	(12.8)
39	South Carolina	(12.8)	40	Nebraska	(14.2)
32	South Dakota	(7.3)	41	Indiana	(14.3)
27	Tennessee	(6.2)	42	Arkansas	(15.6)
19	Texas	(1.7)	43	Alabama	(16.1)
9	Utah	4.4	44	Maryland	(18.2)
22	Vermont	(3.1)	45	Oregon	(19.4)
29	Virginia	(6.7)	46	Kentucky	(23.2)
23	Washington	(4.0)	NA	Alaska**	NA
NA	West Virginia**	NA	NA	California**	NA
35	Wisconsin	(9.9)	NA	New Hampshire**	NA
2	Wyoming	100.0	NA	West Virginia**	NA

District of Columbia   (63.9)

Source: CQ Press using data from US Dept of Health & Human Serv's, Centers for Disease Control-Prevention
    "Abortion Surveillance-United States, 2004" (Morbidity and Mortality Weekly Report, Vol. 56, No. SS-9, 11/23/07)
    "Abortion Surveillance-United States, 2000" (Morbidity and Mortality Weekly Report, Vol. 52, No. SS-12, 11/28/03)
*By state of occurrence. National percent change is only for states reporting in both years.
**Not reported.

Reported Legal Abortions per 1,000 Live Births in 2004

Reporting States' Ratio = 238 Abortions per 1,000 Live Births*

ALPHA ORDER

RANK	STATE	RATIO
25	Alabama	191
27	Alaska	187
35	Arizona	135
39	Arkansas	120
NA	California**	NA
30	Colorado	167
7	Connecticut	290
4	Delaware	404
3	Florida	421
17	Georgia	234
26	Hawaii	190
46	Idaho	43
16	Illinois	241
38	Indiana	121
32	Iowa	157
8	Kansas	286
45	Kentucky	64
29	Louisiana	172
28	Maine	186
35	Maryland	135
5	Massachusetts	311
21	Michigan	202
24	Minnesota	195
42	Mississippi	82
41	Missouri	104
22	Montana	196
34	Nebraska	136
11	Nevada	280
NA	New Hampshire**	NA
9	New Jersey	283
19	New Mexico	214
1	New York	504
9	North Carolina	283
31	North Dakota	166
18	Ohio	230
37	Oklahoma	131
13	Oregon	251
15	Pennsylvania	249
2	Rhode Island	442
40	South Carolina	116
43	South Dakota	72
20	Tennessee	206
22	Texas	196
43	Utah	72
12	Vermont	261
13	Virginia	251
6	Washington	302
NA	West Virginia**	NA
33	Wisconsin	142
NA	Wyoming**	NA

RANK ORDER

RANK	STATE	RATIO
1	New York	504
2	Rhode Island	442
3	Florida	421
4	Delaware	404
5	Massachusetts	311
6	Washington	302
7	Connecticut	290
8	Kansas	286
9	New Jersey	283
9	North Carolina	283
11	Nevada	280
12	Vermont	261
13	Oregon	251
13	Virginia	251
15	Pennsylvania	249
16	Illinois	241
17	Georgia	234
18	Ohio	230
19	New Mexico	214
20	Tennessee	206
21	Michigan	202
22	Montana	196
22	Texas	196
24	Minnesota	195
25	Alabama	191
26	Hawaii	190
27	Alaska	187
28	Maine	186
29	Louisiana	172
30	Colorado	167
31	North Dakota	166
32	Iowa	157
33	Wisconsin	142
34	Nebraska	136
35	Arizona	135
35	Maryland	135
37	Oklahoma	131
38	Indiana	121
39	Arkansas	120
40	South Carolina	116
41	Missouri	104
42	Mississippi	82
43	South Dakota	72
43	Utah	72
45	Kentucky	64
46	Idaho	43
NA	California**	NA
NA	New Hampshire**	NA
NA	West Virginia**	NA
NA	Wyoming**	NA

District of Columbia   303

Source: U.S. Department of Health and Human Services, Centers for Disease Control and Prevention
    "Abortion Surveillance-United States, 2004" (Morbidity and Mortality Weekly Report, Vol. 56, No. SS-9, 11/23/07)
*By state of occurrence. National figure is for reporting states only.
**Not reported.

Reported Legal Abortions per 1,000 Women Ages 15 to 44 in 2004

Reporting States' Rate = 16 Abortions per 1,000 Women Ages 15 to 44*

ALPHA ORDER

RANK	STATE	RATE
25	Alabama	12
18	Alaska	14
28	Arizona	11
37	Arkansas	8
NA	California**	NA
28	Colorado	11
11	Connecticut	17
3	Delaware	26
2	Florida	27
12	Georgia	16
18	Hawaii	14
46	Idaho	3
12	Illinois	16
37	Indiana	8
31	Iowa	10
5	Kansas	20
45	Kentucky	4
28	Louisiana	11
31	Maine	10
37	Maryland	8
9	Massachusetts	18
25	Michigan	12
23	Minnesota	13
43	Mississippi	6
40	Missouri	7
25	Montana	12
31	Nebraska	10
5	Nevada	20
NA	New Hampshire**	NA
9	New Jersey	18
16	New Mexico	15
1	New York	30
7	North Carolina	19
31	North Dakota	10
18	Ohio	14
35	Oklahoma	9
12	Oregon	16
18	Pennsylvania	14
4	Rhode Island	24
40	South Carolina	7
44	South Dakota	5
23	Tennessee	13
16	Texas	15
40	Utah	7
18	Vermont	14
12	Virginia	16
7	Washington	19
NA	West Virginia**	NA
35	Wisconsin	9
NA	Wyoming**	NA

RANK ORDER

RANK	STATE	RATE
1	New York	30
2	Florida	27
3	Delaware	26
4	Rhode Island	24
5	Kansas	20
5	Nevada	20
7	North Carolina	19
7	Washington	19
9	Massachusetts	18
9	New Jersey	18
11	Connecticut	17
12	Georgia	16
12	Illinois	16
12	Oregon	16
12	Virginia	16
16	New Mexico	15
16	Texas	15
18	Alaska	14
18	Hawaii	14
18	Ohio	14
18	Pennsylvania	14
18	Vermont	14
23	Minnesota	13
23	Tennessee	13
25	Alabama	12
25	Michigan	12
25	Montana	12
28	Arizona	11
28	Colorado	11
28	Louisiana	11
31	Iowa	10
31	Maine	10
31	Nebraska	10
31	North Dakota	10
35	Oklahoma	9
35	Wisconsin	9
37	Arkansas	8
37	Indiana	8
37	Maryland	8
40	Missouri	7
40	South Carolina	7
40	Utah	7
43	Mississippi	6
44	South Dakota	5
45	Kentucky	4
46	Idaho	3
NA	California**	NA
NA	New Hampshire**	NA
NA	West Virginia**	NA
NA	Wyoming**	NA
	District of Columbia	18

Source: U.S. Department of Health and Human Services, Centers for Disease Control and Prevention
    "Abortion Surveillance-United States, 2004" (Morbidity and Mortality Weekly Report, Vol. 56, No. SS-9, 11/23/07)
*By state of occurrence. National figure is for reporting states only.
**Not reported.

Percent of Legal Abortions Obtained by Out-Of-State Residents in 2004

Reporting States' Percent = 8.2% of Abortions*

ALPHA ORDER				RANK ORDER		
RANK	STATE	PERCENT		RANK	STATE	PERCENT
10	Alabama	15.2		1	Kansas	48.2
43	Alaska	0.2		2	North Dakota	37.5
38	Arizona	3.0		3	Delaware	28.9
7	Arkansas	17.4		4	Rhode Island	23.9
NA	California**	NA		5	Tennessee	21.1
18	Colorado	9.2		6	South Dakota	17.7
35	Connecticut	3.7		7	Arkansas	17.4
3	Delaware	28.9		8	Wyoming	16.7
NA	Florida**	NA		9	North Carolina	15.5
14	Georgia	12.5		10	Alabama	15.2
42	Hawaii	0.3		11	Nebraska	14.3
36	Idaho	3.6		12	Vermont	13.4
21	Illinois	7.8		13	Maryland	12.6
33	Indiana	3.9		14	Georgia	12.5
15	Iowa	11.4		15	Iowa	11.4
1	Kansas	48.2		16	Oregon	10.9
NA	Kentucky**	NA		17	Missouri	10.0
NA	Louisiana**	NA		18	Colorado	9.2
31	Maine	4.2		19	Montana	8.6
13	Maryland	12.6		20	Ohio	7.9
30	Massachusetts	4.6		21	Illinois	7.8
39	Michigan	2.9		21	Utah	7.8
23	Minnesota	7.5		23	Minnesota	7.5
40	Mississippi	2.8		24	Oklahoma	7.2
17	Missouri	10.0		25	Nevada	6.6
19	Montana	8.6		26	New Mexico	6.2
11	Nebraska	14.3		27	Virginia	5.1
25	Nevada	6.6		28	Washington	5.0
NA	New Hampshire**	NA		29	New Jersey	4.8
29	New Jersey	4.8		30	Massachusetts	4.6
26	New Mexico	6.2		31	Maine	4.2
NA	New York**	NA		31	Pennsylvania	4.2
9	North Carolina	15.5		33	Indiana	3.9
2	North Dakota	37.5		33	South Carolina	3.9
20	Ohio	7.9		35	Connecticut	3.7
24	Oklahoma	7.2		36	Idaho	3.6
16	Oregon	10.9		37	Texas	3.3
31	Pennsylvania	4.2		38	Arizona	3.0
4	Rhode Island	23.9		39	Michigan	2.9
33	South Carolina	3.9		40	Mississippi	2.8
6	South Dakota	17.7		41	Wisconsin	2.3
5	Tennessee	21.1		42	Hawaii	0.3
37	Texas	3.3		43	Alaska	0.2
21	Utah	7.8		NA	California**	NA
12	Vermont	13.4		NA	Florida**	NA
27	Virginia	5.1		NA	Kentucky**	NA
28	Washington	5.0		NA	Louisiana**	NA
NA	West Virginia**	NA		NA	New Hampshire**	NA
41	Wisconsin	2.3		NA	New York**	NA
8	Wyoming	16.7		NA	West Virginia**	NA
					District of Columbia	52.6

Source: U.S. Department of Health and Human Services, Centers for Disease Control and Prevention
  "Abortion Surveillance-United States, 2004" (Morbidity and Mortality Weekly Report, Vol. 56, No. SS-9, 11/23/07)
*By state of occurrence. National figure is for reporting states only.
**Not reported.

Percent of Reported Legal Abortions that Were First-Time Abortions: 2004

Reporting States' Percent = 53.7% of Abortions*

ALPHA ORDER				RANK ORDER		
RANK	STATE	PERCENT		RANK	STATE	PERCENT
9	Alabama	63.7		1	Oklahoma	86.8
11	Alaska	63.1		2	Wyoming	83.3
10	Arizona	63.5		3	South Dakota	75.9
13	Arkansas	62.6		4	North Dakota	71.0
NA	California**	NA		5	Nebraska	68.4
21	Colorado	58.6		6	Idaho	68.3
NA	Connecticut**	NA		7	Utah	68.2
19	Delaware	58.7		8	Iowa	64.9
NA	Florida**	NA		9	Alabama	63.7
18	Georgia	59.3		10	Arizona	63.5
23	Hawaii	57.3		11	Alaska	63.1
6	Idaho	68.3		12	Mississippi	63.0
NA	Illinois**	NA		13	Arkansas	62.6
26	Indiana	56.0		14	South Carolina	62.2
8	Iowa	64.9		15	Kansas	61.3
15	Kansas	61.3		16	New Jersey	60.3
28	Kentucky	55.0		17	Maine	59.4
NA	Louisiana**	NA		18	Georgia	59.3
17	Maine	59.4		19	Delaware	58.7
40	Maryland	28.1		19	Vermont	58.7
38	Massachusetts	48.3		21	Colorado	58.6
34	Michigan	52.1		22	Missouri	57.9
24	Minnesota	56.9		23	Hawaii	57.3
12	Mississippi	63.0		24	Minnesota	56.9
22	Missouri	57.9		25	Texas	56.3
31	Montana	53.2		26	Indiana	56.0
5	Nebraska	68.4		27	Oregon	55.6
35	Nevada	51.8		28	Kentucky	55.0
NA	New Hampshire**	NA		29	Virginia	53.9
16	New Jersey	60.3		30	Pennsylvania	53.8
NA	New Mexico**	NA		31	Montana	53.2
39	New York	44.3		32	Rhode Island	52.6
37	North Carolina	50.5		33	Washington	52.4
4	North Dakota	71.0		34	Michigan	52.1
NA	Ohio**	NA		35	Nevada	51.8
1	Oklahoma	86.8		35	Tennessee	51.8
27	Oregon	55.6		37	North Carolina	50.5
30	Pennsylvania	53.8		38	Massachusetts	48.3
32	Rhode Island	52.6		39	New York	44.3
14	South Carolina	62.2		40	Maryland	28.1
3	South Dakota	75.9		NA	California**	NA
35	Tennessee	51.8		NA	Connecticut**	NA
25	Texas	56.3		NA	Florida**	NA
7	Utah	68.2		NA	Illinois**	NA
19	Vermont	58.7		NA	Louisiana**	NA
29	Virginia	53.9		NA	New Hampshire**	NA
33	Washington	52.4		NA	New Mexico**	NA
NA	West Virginia**	NA		NA	Ohio**	NA
NA	Wisconsin**	NA		NA	West Virginia**	NA
2	Wyoming	83.3		NA	Wisconsin**	NA
				District of Columbia**		NA

Source: U.S. Department of Health and Human Services, Centers for Disease Control and Prevention
   "Abortion Surveillance-United States, 2004" (Morbidity and Mortality Weekly Report, Vol. 56, No. SS-9, 11/23/07)
*By state of occurrence. National figure is for reporting states only. Percent of abortions to women who had no previous abortions.
**Not reported.

Percent of Reported Legal Abortions Obtained by White Women in 2004

Reporting States' Percent = 52.6% of Abortions*

ALPHA ORDER

RANK	STATE	PERCENT
28	Alabama	45.9
18	Alaska	60.4
NA	Arizona**	NA
20	Arkansas	58.9
NA	California**	NA
9	Colorado	72.5
NA	Connecticut**	NA
25	Delaware	54.9
NA	Florida**	NA
31	Georgia	40.4
35	Hawaii	28.0
2	Idaho	92.8
NA	Illinois**	NA
17	Indiana	63.0
6	Iowa	78.2
12	Kansas	71.0
13	Kentucky	70.4
33	Louisiana	37.1
7	Maine	77.1
36	Maryland	24.4
27	Massachusetts	50.3
24	Michigan	56.0
16	Minnesota	63.7
37	Mississippi	23.9
22	Missouri	56.7
3	Montana	85.7
NA	Nebraska**	NA
NA	Nevada**	NA
NA	New Hampshire**	NA
34	New Jersey	29.6
NA	New Mexico**	NA
32	New York**	38.1
30	North Carolina	41.8
5	North Dakota	83.5
21	Ohio	58.3
10	Oklahoma	72.4
4	Oregon	84.2
22	Pennsylvania	56.7
14	Rhode Island	69.7
19	South Carolina	59.1
NA	South Dakota**	NA
26	Tennessee	51.5
11	Texas	71.3
NA	Utah**	NA
1	Vermont	93.2
29	Virginia	44.1
NA	Washington**	NA
NA	West Virginia**	NA
15	Wisconsin	68.9
8	Wyoming	75.0

RANK ORDER

RANK	STATE	PERCENT
1	Vermont	93.2
2	Idaho	92.8
3	Montana	85.7
4	Oregon	84.2
5	North Dakota	83.5
6	Iowa	78.2
7	Maine	77.1
8	Wyoming	75.0
9	Colorado	72.5
10	Oklahoma	72.4
11	Texas	71.3
12	Kansas	71.0
13	Kentucky	70.4
14	Rhode Island	69.7
15	Wisconsin	68.9
16	Minnesota	63.7
17	Indiana	63.0
18	Alaska	60.4
19	South Carolina	59.1
20	Arkansas	58.9
21	Ohio	58.3
22	Missouri	56.7
22	Pennsylvania	56.7
24	Michigan	56.0
25	Delaware	54.9
26	Tennessee	51.5
27	Massachusetts	50.3
28	Alabama	45.9
29	Virginia	44.1
30	North Carolina	41.8
31	Georgia	40.4
32	New York**	38.1
33	Louisiana	37.1
34	New Jersey	29.6
35	Hawaii	28.0
36	Maryland	24.4
37	Mississippi	23.9
NA	Arizona**	NA
NA	California**	NA
NA	Connecticut**	NA
NA	Florida**	NA
NA	Illinois**	NA
NA	Nebraska**	NA
NA	Nevada**	NA
NA	New Hampshire**	NA
NA	New Mexico**	NA
NA	South Dakota**	NA
NA	Utah**	NA
NA	Washington**	NA
NA	West Virginia**	NA
	District of Columbia	19.9

Source: U.S. Department of Health and Human Services, Centers for Disease Control and Prevention
     "Abortion Surveillance-United States, 2004" (Morbidity and Mortality Weekly Report, Vol. 56, No. SS-9, 11/23/07)
*By state of occurrence. Includes those of Hispanic ethnicity. National percent is for reporting states only.
**Not reported. New York's number is for New York City only.

Percent of Reported Legal Abortions Obtained by Black Women in 2004

Reporting States' Percent = 35.3% of Abortions*

ALPHA ORDER			RANK ORDER		
RANK	STATE	PERCENT	RANK	STATE	PERCENT
4	Alabama	51.5	1	Mississippi	75.7
28	Alaska	7.5	2	Maryland	64.9
NA	Arizona**	NA	3	Georgia	54.8
16	Arkansas	35.1	4	Alabama	51.5
NA	California**	NA	5	Louisiana	50.9
29	Colorado	6.2	6	New York**	45.5
NA	Connecticut**	NA	7	New Jersey	44.1
11	Delaware	41.0	8	Tennessee	44.0
NA	Florida**	NA	9	North Carolina	43.7
3	Georgia	54.8	10	Virginia	41.7
32	Hawaii	2.5	11	Delaware	41.0
34	Idaho	1.8	12	Pennsylvania	38.3
NA	Illinois**	NA	13	South Carolina	38.2
18	Indiana	28.0	14	Missouri	38.1
27	Iowa	8.9	15	Michigan	37.2
20	Kansas	23.2	16	Arkansas	35.1
23	Kentucky	20.6	16	Ohio	35.1
5	Louisiana	50.9	18	Indiana	28.0
33	Maine	2.4	19	Wisconsin	24.6
2	Maryland	64.9	20	Kansas	23.2
24	Massachusetts	19.2	21	Texas	22.4
15	Michigan	37.2	22	Minnesota	21.8
22	Minnesota	21.8	23	Kentucky	20.6
1	Mississippi	75.7	24	Massachusetts	19.2
14	Missouri	38.1	25	Oklahoma	17.5
36	Montana	0.5	26	Rhode Island	16.0
NA	Nebraska**	NA	27	Iowa	8.9
NA	Nevada**	NA	28	Alaska	7.5
NA	New Hampshire**	NA	29	Colorado	6.2
7	New Jersey	44.1	30	Oregon	5.5
NA	New Mexico**	NA	31	North Dakota	2.6
6	New York**	45.5	32	Hawaii	2.5
9	North Carolina	43.7	33	Maine	2.4
31	North Dakota	2.6	34	Idaho	1.8
16	Ohio	35.1	35	Vermont	1.7
25	Oklahoma	17.5	36	Montana	0.5
30	Oregon	5.5	NA	Arizona**	NA
12	Pennsylvania	38.3	NA	California**	NA
26	Rhode Island	16.0	NA	Connecticut**	NA
13	South Carolina	38.2	NA	Florida**	NA
NA	South Dakota**	NA	NA	Illinois**	NA
8	Tennessee	44.0	NA	Nebraska**	NA
21	Texas	22.4	NA	Nevada**	NA
NA	Utah**	NA	NA	New Hampshire**	NA
35	Vermont	1.7	NA	New Mexico**	NA
10	Virginia	41.7	NA	South Dakota**	NA
NA	Washington**	NA	NA	Utah**	NA
NA	West Virginia**	NA	NA	Washington**	NA
19	Wisconsin	24.6	NA	West Virginia**	NA
NA	Wyoming**	NA	NA	Wyoming**	NA
				District of Columbia	50.8

Source: U.S. Department of Health and Human Services, Centers for Disease Control and Prevention
   "Abortion Surveillance-United States, 2004" (Morbidity and Mortality Weekly Report, Vol. 56, No. SS-9, 11/23/07)
*By state of occurrence. National percent is for reporting states only.
**Not reported. New York's number is for New York City only.

Percent of Reported Legal Abortions Obtained by Hispanic Women in 2004

Reporting States' Percent = 18.8%*

ALPHA ORDER				RANK ORDER		
RANK	STATE	PERCENT		RANK	STATE	PERCENT
22	Alabama	2.5		1	New Mexico	50.2
NA	Alaska**	NA		2	Arizona	37.7
2	Arizona	37.7		3	Texas	37.0
19	Arkansas	3.9		4	Utah	27.5
NA	California**	NA		5	New York	25.1
7	Colorado	21.0		6	New Jersey	23.2
NA	Connecticut**	NA		7	Colorado	21.0
9	Delaware	10.9		8	Idaho	11.9
NA	Florida**	NA		9	Delaware	10.9
13	Georgia	6.4		10	Oregon	10.8
17	Hawaii	4.0		11	Kansas	9.2
8	Idaho	11.9		12	Wisconsin	8.7
NA	Illinois**	NA		13	Georgia	6.4
NA	Indiana**	NA		14	Pennsylvania	5.9
NA	Iowa**	NA		15	Minnesota	5.6
11	Kansas	9.2		16	South Carolina	4.8
NA	Kentucky**	NA		17	Hawaii	4.0
NA	Louisiana**	NA		17	Tennessee	4.0
NA	Maine**	NA		19	Arkansas	3.9
NA	Maryland**	NA		20	Ohio	3.5
NA	Massachusetts**	NA		21	Missouri	2.9
NA	Michigan**	NA		22	Alabama	2.5
15	Minnesota	5.6		23	Vermont	1.9
24	Mississippi	0.6		24	Mississippi	0.6
21	Missouri	2.9		NA	Alaska**	NA
NA	Montana**	NA		NA	California**	NA
NA	Nebraska**	NA		NA	Connecticut**	NA
NA	Nevada**	NA		NA	Florida**	NA
NA	New Hampshire**	NA		NA	Illinois**	NA
6	New Jersey	23.2		NA	Indiana**	NA
1	New Mexico	50.2		NA	Iowa**	NA
5	New York	25.1		NA	Kentucky**	NA
NA	North Carolina**	NA		NA	Louisiana**	NA
NA	North Dakota**	NA		NA	Maine**	NA
20	Ohio	3.5		NA	Maryland**	NA
NA	Oklahoma**	NA		NA	Massachusetts**	NA
10	Oregon	10.8		NA	Michigan**	NA
14	Pennsylvania	5.9		NA	Montana**	NA
NA	Rhode Island**	NA		NA	Nebraska**	NA
16	South Carolina	4.8		NA	Nevada**	NA
NA	South Dakota**	NA		NA	New Hampshire**	NA
17	Tennessee	4.0		NA	North Carolina**	NA
3	Texas	37.0		NA	North Dakota**	NA
4	Utah	27.5		NA	Oklahoma**	NA
23	Vermont	1.9		NA	Rhode Island**	NA
NA	Virginia**	NA		NA	South Dakota**	NA
NA	Washington**	NA		NA	Virginia**	NA
NA	West Virginia**	NA		NA	Washington**	NA
12	Wisconsin	8.7		NA	West Virginia**	NA
NA	Wyoming**	NA		NA	Wyoming**	NA
					District of Columbia	14.3

Source: U.S. Department of Health and Human Services, Centers for Disease Control and Prevention
　　　"Abortion Surveillance-United States, 2004" (Morbidity and Mortality Weekly Report, Vol. 56, No. SS-9, 11/23/07)
*By state of occurrence. National percent is for reporting states only. Hispanic can be of any race.
**Not reported.

Percent of Reported Legal Abortions Obtained by Married Women in 2004

Reporting States' Percent = 17.1% of Abortions*

ALPHA ORDER			RANK ORDER		
RANK	STATE	PERCENT	RANK	STATE	PERCENT
38	Alabama	13.7	1	Utah	23.2
20	Alaska	16.8	2	North Carolina	21.3
13	Arizona	18.1	2	Oklahoma	21.3
33	Arkansas	14.8	2	Oregon	21.3
NA	California**	NA	5	Montana	20.3
15	Colorado	17.6	6	Kansas	19.6
NA	Connecticut**	NA	7	Iowa	19.5
35	Delaware	14.6	8	Texas	19.4
NA	Florida**	NA	9	Hawaii	19.1
12	Georgia	18.2	9	Idaho	19.1
9	Hawaii	19.1	9	Missouri	19.1
9	Idaho	19.1	12	Georgia	18.2
20	Illinois	16.8	13	Arizona	18.1
28	Indiana	15.8	14	Tennessee	18.0
7	Iowa	19.5	15	Colorado	17.6
6	Kansas	19.6	16	Minnesota	17.5
24	Kentucky	16.3	16	Vermont	17.5
NA	Louisiana**	NA	18	Maryland	17.4
32	Maine	15.2	19	Virginia	16.9
18	Maryland	17.4	20	Alaska	16.8
25	Massachusetts	16.2	20	Illinois	16.8
37	Michigan	14.0	20	South Carolina	16.8
16	Minnesota	17.5	23	North Dakota	16.7
39	Mississippi	11.2	24	Kentucky	16.3
9	Missouri	19.1	25	Massachusetts	16.2
5	Montana	20.3	26	Ohio	16.1
NA	Nebraska**	NA	26	Wisconsin	16.1
NA	Nevada**	NA	28	Indiana	15.8
NA	New Hampshire**	NA	28	Pennsylvania	15.8
31	New Jersey	15.4	28	Rhode Island	15.8
35	New Mexico	14.6	31	New Jersey	15.4
34	New York**	14.7	32	Maine	15.2
2	North Carolina	21.3	33	Arkansas	14.8
23	North Dakota	16.7	34	New York**	14.7
26	Ohio	16.1	35	Delaware	14.6
2	Oklahoma	21.3	35	New Mexico	14.6
2	Oregon	21.3	37	Michigan	14.0
28	Pennsylvania	15.8	38	Alabama	13.7
28	Rhode Island	15.8	39	Mississippi	11.2
20	South Carolina	16.8	NA	California**	NA
NA	South Dakota**	NA	NA	Connecticut**	NA
14	Tennessee	18.0	NA	Florida**	NA
8	Texas	19.4	NA	Louisiana**	NA
1	Utah	23.2	NA	Nebraska**	NA
16	Vermont	17.5	NA	Nevada**	NA
19	Virginia	16.9	NA	New Hampshire**	NA
NA	Washington**	NA	NA	South Dakota**	NA
NA	West Virginia**	NA	NA	Washington**	NA
26	Wisconsin	16.1	NA	West Virginia**	NA
NA	Wyoming**	NA	NA	Wyoming**	NA
				District of Columbia	11.7

Source: U.S. Department of Health and Human Services, Centers for Disease Control and Prevention
  "Abortion Surveillance-United States, 2004" (Morbidity and Mortality Weekly Report, Vol. 56, No. SS-9, 11/23/07)
*By state of occurrence. National percent is for reporting states only.
**Not reported. New York's number is for New York City only.

Percent of Reported Legal Abortions Obtained by Unmarried Women in 2004

Reporting States' Percent = 80.5% of Abortions*

ALPHA ORDER				RANK ORDER		
RANK	STATE	PERCENT		RANK	STATE	PERCENT
4	Alabama	85.1		1	Mississippi	88.7
14	Alaska	82.6		2	Delaware	85.4
17	Arizona	81.9		3	Michigan	85.3
4	Arkansas	85.1		4	Alabama	85.1
NA	California**	NA		4	Arkansas	85.1
33	Colorado	77.5		6	Pennsylvania	84.2
NA	Connecticut**	NA		7	Kentucky	83.7
2	Delaware	85.4		8	New Mexico	83.6
NA	Florida**	NA		9	Wisconsin	83.4
28	Georgia	80.0		10	North Dakota	83.3
25	Hawaii	80.4		10	Wyoming	83.3
23	Idaho	80.8		12	South Carolina	83.2
17	Illinois	81.9		13	New Jersey	83.0
15	Indiana	82.4		14	Alaska	82.6
35	Iowa	74.3		15	Indiana	82.4
27	Kansas	80.3		16	New York**	82.1
7	Kentucky	83.7		17	Arizona	81.9
NA	Louisiana**	NA		17	Illinois	81.9
39	Maine	71.3		17	Ohio	81.9
20	Maryland	81.5		20	Maryland	81.5
21	Massachusetts	81.4		21	Massachusetts	81.4
3	Michigan	85.3		22	Minnesota	81.3
22	Minnesota	81.3		23	Idaho	80.8
1	Mississippi	88.7		24	Vermont	80.5
31	Missouri	78.5		25	Hawaii	80.4
37	Montana	72.5		25	Tennessee	80.4
NA	Nebraska**	NA		27	Kansas	80.3
NA	Nevada**	NA		28	Georgia	80.0
NA	New Hampshire**	NA		29	Texas	78.9
13	New Jersey	83.0		30	Oklahoma	78.7
8	New Mexico	83.6		31	Missouri	78.5
16	New York**	82.1		32	Rhode Island	78.4
36	North Carolina	73.6		33	Colorado	77.5
10	North Dakota	83.3		34	Oregon	77.3
17	Ohio	81.9		35	Iowa	74.3
30	Oklahoma	78.7		36	North Carolina	73.6
34	Oregon	77.3		37	Montana	72.5
6	Pennsylvania	84.2		38	Virginia	71.7
32	Rhode Island	78.4		39	Maine	71.3
12	South Carolina	83.2		40	Utah	67.4
NA	South Dakota**	NA		NA	California**	NA
25	Tennessee	80.4		NA	Connecticut**	NA
29	Texas	78.9		NA	Florida**	NA
40	Utah	67.4		NA	Louisiana**	NA
24	Vermont	80.5		NA	Nebraska**	NA
38	Virginia	71.7		NA	Nevada**	NA
NA	Washington**	NA		NA	New Hampshire**	NA
NA	West Virginia**	NA		NA	South Dakota**	NA
9	Wisconsin	83.4		NA	Washington**	NA
10	Wyoming	83.3		NA	West Virginia**	NA
					District of Columbia	87.6

Source: U.S. Department of Health and Human Services, Centers for Disease Control and Prevention
   "Abortion Surveillance-United States, 2004" (Morbidity and Mortality Weekly Report, Vol. 56, No. SS-9, 11/23/07)
*By state of occurrence. National percent is for reporting states only.
**Not reported. New York's number is for New York City only.

Reported Legal Abortions Obtained by Teenagers in 2004

Reporting States' Total = 118,103 Abortions Obtained by Teenagers*

<table>
<tr><td colspan="4">ALPHA ORDER</td><td colspan="4">RANK ORDER</td></tr>
<tr><th>RANK</th><th>STATE</th><th>ABORTIONS</th><th>% of USA</th><th>RANK</th><th>STATE</th><th>ABORTIONS</th><th>% of USA</th></tr>
<tr><td>16</td><td>Alabama</td><td>2,107</td><td>1.8%</td><td>1</td><td>New York</td><td>22,806</td><td>19.3%</td></tr>
<tr><td>39</td><td>Alaska</td><td>427</td><td>0.4%</td><td>2</td><td>Texas</td><td>10,107</td><td>8.6%</td></tr>
<tr><td>14</td><td>Arizona</td><td>2,278</td><td>1.9%</td><td>3</td><td>Pennsylvania</td><td>6,287</td><td>5.3%</td></tr>
<tr><td>30</td><td>Arkansas</td><td>884</td><td>0.7%</td><td>4</td><td>Ohio</td><td>6,164</td><td>5.2%</td></tr>
<tr><td>NA</td><td>California**</td><td>NA</td><td>NA</td><td>5</td><td>New Jersey</td><td>5,589</td><td>4.7%</td></tr>
<tr><td>15</td><td>Colorado</td><td>2,144</td><td>1.8%</td><td>6</td><td>North Carolina</td><td>5,391</td><td>4.6%</td></tr>
<tr><td>13</td><td>Connecticut</td><td>2,326</td><td>2.0%</td><td>7</td><td>Georgia</td><td>5,246</td><td>4.4%</td></tr>
<tr><td>32</td><td>Delaware</td><td>659</td><td>0.6%</td><td>8</td><td>Michigan</td><td>4,741</td><td>4.0%</td></tr>
<tr><td>NA</td><td>Florida**</td><td>NA</td><td>NA</td><td>9</td><td>Washington</td><td>4,598</td><td>3.9%</td></tr>
<tr><td>7</td><td>Georgia</td><td>5,246</td><td>4.4%</td><td>10</td><td>Massachusetts</td><td>4,063</td><td>3.4%</td></tr>
<tr><td>31</td><td>Hawaii</td><td>698</td><td>0.6%</td><td>11</td><td>Virginia</td><td>3,938</td><td>3.3%</td></tr>
<tr><td>42</td><td>Idaho</td><td>191</td><td>0.2%</td><td>12</td><td>Tennessee</td><td>2,657</td><td>2.2%</td></tr>
<tr><td>NA</td><td>Illinois**</td><td>NA</td><td>NA</td><td>13</td><td>Connecticut</td><td>2,326</td><td>2.0%</td></tr>
<tr><td>22</td><td>Indiana</td><td>1,674</td><td>1.4%</td><td>14</td><td>Arizona</td><td>2,278</td><td>1.9%</td></tr>
<tr><td>28</td><td>Iowa</td><td>1,158</td><td>1.0%</td><td>15</td><td>Colorado</td><td>2,144</td><td>1.8%</td></tr>
<tr><td>18</td><td>Kansas</td><td>2,009</td><td>1.7%</td><td>16</td><td>Alabama</td><td>2,107</td><td>1.8%</td></tr>
<tr><td>36</td><td>Kentucky</td><td>570</td><td>0.5%</td><td>17</td><td>Minnesota</td><td>2,080</td><td>1.8%</td></tr>
<tr><td>19</td><td>Louisiana</td><td>1,958</td><td>1.7%</td><td>18</td><td>Kansas</td><td>2,009</td><td>1.7%</td></tr>
<tr><td>37</td><td>Maine</td><td>514</td><td>0.4%</td><td>19</td><td>Louisiana</td><td>1,958</td><td>1.7%</td></tr>
<tr><td>NA</td><td>Maryland**</td><td>NA</td><td>NA</td><td>20</td><td>Oregon</td><td>1,957</td><td>1.7%</td></tr>
<tr><td>10</td><td>Massachusetts</td><td>4,063</td><td>3.4%</td><td>21</td><td>Wisconsin</td><td>1,727</td><td>1.5%</td></tr>
<tr><td>8</td><td>Michigan</td><td>4,741</td><td>4.0%</td><td>22</td><td>Indiana</td><td>1,674</td><td>1.4%</td></tr>
<tr><td>17</td><td>Minnesota</td><td>2,080</td><td>1.8%</td><td>23</td><td>Nevada</td><td>1,625</td><td>1.4%</td></tr>
<tr><td>34</td><td>Mississippi</td><td>623</td><td>0.5%</td><td>24</td><td>Missouri</td><td>1,352</td><td>1.1%</td></tr>
<tr><td>24</td><td>Missouri</td><td>1,352</td><td>1.1%</td><td>25</td><td>New Mexico</td><td>1,311</td><td>1.1%</td></tr>
<tr><td>38</td><td>Montana</td><td>452</td><td>0.4%</td><td>26</td><td>Oklahoma</td><td>1,198</td><td>1.0%</td></tr>
<tr><td>33</td><td>Nebraska</td><td>630</td><td>0.5%</td><td>27</td><td>South Carolina</td><td>1,183</td><td>1.0%</td></tr>
<tr><td>23</td><td>Nevada</td><td>1,625</td><td>1.4%</td><td>28</td><td>Iowa</td><td>1,158</td><td>1.0%</td></tr>
<tr><td>NA</td><td>New Hampshire**</td><td>NA</td><td>NA</td><td>29</td><td>Rhode Island</td><td>999</td><td>0.8%</td></tr>
<tr><td>5</td><td>New Jersey</td><td>5,589</td><td>4.7%</td><td>30</td><td>Arkansas</td><td>884</td><td>0.7%</td></tr>
<tr><td>25</td><td>New Mexico</td><td>1,311</td><td>1.1%</td><td>31</td><td>Hawaii</td><td>698</td><td>0.6%</td></tr>
<tr><td>1</td><td>New York</td><td>22,806</td><td>19.3%</td><td>32</td><td>Delaware</td><td>659</td><td>0.6%</td></tr>
<tr><td>6</td><td>North Carolina</td><td>5,391</td><td>4.6%</td><td>33</td><td>Nebraska</td><td>630</td><td>0.5%</td></tr>
<tr><td>41</td><td>North Dakota</td><td>275</td><td>0.2%</td><td>34</td><td>Mississippi</td><td>623</td><td>0.5%</td></tr>
<tr><td>4</td><td>Ohio</td><td>6,164</td><td>5.2%</td><td>35</td><td>Utah</td><td>596</td><td>0.5%</td></tr>
<tr><td>26</td><td>Oklahoma</td><td>1,198</td><td>1.0%</td><td>36</td><td>Kentucky</td><td>570</td><td>0.5%</td></tr>
<tr><td>20</td><td>Oregon</td><td>1,957</td><td>1.7%</td><td>37</td><td>Maine</td><td>514</td><td>0.4%</td></tr>
<tr><td>3</td><td>Pennsylvania</td><td>6,287</td><td>5.3%</td><td>38</td><td>Montana</td><td>452</td><td>0.4%</td></tr>
<tr><td>29</td><td>Rhode Island</td><td>999</td><td>0.8%</td><td>39</td><td>Alaska</td><td>427</td><td>0.4%</td></tr>
<tr><td>27</td><td>South Carolina</td><td>1,183</td><td>1.0%</td><td>40</td><td>Vermont</td><td>320</td><td>0.3%</td></tr>
<tr><td>43</td><td>South Dakota</td><td>150</td><td>0.1%</td><td>41</td><td>North Dakota</td><td>275</td><td>0.2%</td></tr>
<tr><td>12</td><td>Tennessee</td><td>2,657</td><td>2.2%</td><td>42</td><td>Idaho</td><td>191</td><td>0.2%</td></tr>
<tr><td>2</td><td>Texas</td><td>10,107</td><td>8.6%</td><td>43</td><td>South Dakota</td><td>150</td><td>0.1%</td></tr>
<tr><td>35</td><td>Utah</td><td>596</td><td>0.5%</td><td>44</td><td>Wyoming</td><td>2</td><td>0.0%</td></tr>
<tr><td>40</td><td>Vermont</td><td>320</td><td>0.3%</td><td>NA</td><td>California**</td><td>NA</td><td>NA</td></tr>
<tr><td>11</td><td>Virginia</td><td>3,938</td><td>3.3%</td><td>NA</td><td>Florida**</td><td>NA</td><td>NA</td></tr>
<tr><td>9</td><td>Washington</td><td>4,598</td><td>3.9%</td><td>NA</td><td>Illinois**</td><td>NA</td><td>NA</td></tr>
<tr><td>NA</td><td>West Virginia**</td><td>NA</td><td>NA</td><td>NA</td><td>Maryland**</td><td>NA</td><td>NA</td></tr>
<tr><td>21</td><td>Wisconsin</td><td>1,727</td><td>1.5%</td><td>NA</td><td>New Hampshire**</td><td>NA</td><td>NA</td></tr>
<tr><td>44</td><td>Wyoming</td><td>2</td><td>0.0%</td><td>NA</td><td>West Virginia**</td><td>NA</td><td>NA</td></tr>
<tr><td></td><td></td><td></td><td></td><td></td><td>District of Columbia</td><td>439</td><td>0.4%</td></tr>
</table>

Source: U.S. Department of Health and Human Services, Centers for Disease Control and Prevention
"Abortion Surveillance-United States, 2004" (Morbidity and Mortality Weekly Report, Vol. 56, No. SS-9, 11/23/07)
*Nineteen years old and younger by state of occurrence. National total is for reporting states only.
**Not reported.

Percent of Reported Legal Abortions Obtained by Teenagers in 2004

Reporting States' Percent = 17.0% of Abortions*

ALPHA ORDER				RANK ORDER		
RANK	STATE	PERCENT		RANK	STATE	PERCENT
14	Alabama	18.5		1	Alaska	22.0
1	Alaska	22.0		2	New Mexico	21.6
17	Arizona	18.0		3	North Dakota	20.3
10	Arkansas	19.0		4	Hawaii	20.1
NA	California**	NA		5	Montana	20.0
11	Colorado	18.8		6	Idaho	19.8
9	Connecticut	19.1		6	Maine	19.8
43	Delaware	14.4		8	Iowa	19.2
NA	Florida**	NA		9	Connecticut	19.1
37	Georgia	16.1		10	Arkansas	19.0
4	Hawaii	20.1		11	Colorado	18.8
6	Idaho	19.8		12	Vermont	18.6
NA	Illinois**	NA		12	Washington	18.6
39	Indiana	15.9		14	Alabama	18.5
8	Iowa	19.2		15	South Dakota	18.4
24	Kansas	17.7		16	New York	18.1
38	Kentucky	16.0		17	Arizona	18.0
26	Louisiana	17.4		17	Michigan	18.0
6	Maine	19.8		17	Ohio	18.0
NA	Maryland**	NA		17	South Carolina	18.0
31	Massachusetts	16.7		21	Rhode Island	17.9
17	Michigan	18.0		22	Mississippi	17.8
41	Minnesota	15.1		22	Oklahoma	17.8
22	Mississippi	17.8		24	Kansas	17.7
31	Missouri	16.7		25	Nebraska	17.6
5	Montana	20.0		26	Louisiana	17.4
25	Nebraska	17.6		26	Pennsylvania	17.4
34	Nevada	16.5		26	Wisconsin	17.4
NA	New Hampshire**	NA		29	New Jersey	17.1
29	New Jersey	17.1		29	Oregon	17.1
2	New Mexico	21.6		31	Massachusetts	16.7
16	New York	18.1		31	Missouri	16.7
39	North Carolina	15.9		31	Wyoming	16.7
3	North Dakota	20.3		34	Nevada	16.5
17	Ohio	18.0		35	Utah	16.3
22	Oklahoma	17.8		36	Tennessee	16.2
29	Oregon	17.1		37	Georgia	16.1
26	Pennsylvania	17.4		38	Kentucky	16.0
21	Rhode Island	17.9		39	Indiana	15.9
17	South Carolina	18.0		39	North Carolina	15.9
15	South Dakota	18.4		41	Minnesota	15.1
36	Tennessee	16.2		41	Virginia	15.1
44	Texas	13.5		43	Delaware	14.4
35	Utah	16.3		44	Texas	13.5
12	Vermont	18.6		NA	California**	NA
41	Virginia	15.1		NA	Florida**	NA
12	Washington	18.6		NA	Illinois**	NA
NA	West Virginia**	NA		NA	Maryland**	NA
26	Wisconsin	17.4		NA	New Hampshire**	NA
31	Wyoming	16.7		NA	West Virginia**	NA

District of Columbia   18.3

Source: CQ Press using data from U.S. Department of Health and Human Services, Centers for Disease Control and Prevention
    "Abortion Surveillance-United States, 2004" (Morbidity and Mortality Weekly Report, Vol. 56, No. SS-9, 11/23/07)
*Nineteen years old and younger by state of occurrence. National percent is for reporting states only.
**Not reported.

Reported Legal Abortions Obtained by Teenagers 17 Years and Younger in 2004

Reporting States' Total = 44,559 Abortions*

ALPHA ORDER

RANK	STATE	ABORTIONS	% of USA
14	Alabama	807	1.8%
39	Alaska	154	0.3%
17	Arizona	763	1.7%
29	Arkansas	393	0.9%
NA	California**	NA	NA
16	Colorado	781	1.8%
12	Connecticut	1,009	2.3%
32	Delaware	264	0.6%
NA	Florida**	NA	NA
6	Georgia	2,114	4.7%
30	Hawaii	329	0.7%
NA	Idaho**	NA	NA
NA	Illinois**	NA	NA
23	Indiana	562	1.3%
28	Iowa	421	0.9%
15	Kansas	785	1.8%
33	Kentucky	251	0.6%
18	Louisiana	746	1.7%
35	Maine	197	0.4%
NA	Maryland**	NA	NA
10	Massachusetts	1,405	3.2%
9	Michigan	1,770	4.0%
19	Minnesota	718	1.6%
38	Mississippi	182	0.4%
27	Missouri	440	1.0%
37	Montana	187	0.4%
34	Nebraska	232	0.5%
22	Nevada	615	1.4%
NA	New Hampshire**	NA	NA
4	New Jersey	2,292	5.1%
24	New Mexico	515	1.2%
1	New York	9,675	21.7%
7	North Carolina	1,881	4.2%
NA	North Dakota**	NA	NA
3	Ohio	2,368	5.3%
26	Oklahoma	447	1.0%
20	Oregon	713	1.6%
5	Pennsylvania	2,242	5.0%
31	Rhode Island	296	0.7%
25	South Carolina	498	1.1%
NA	South Dakota**	NA	NA
13	Tennessee	979	2.2%
2	Texas	3,255	7.3%
36	Utah	191	0.4%
40	Vermont	128	0.3%
11	Virginia	1,240	2.8%
8	Washington	1,840	4.1%
NA	West Virginia**	NA	NA
21	Wisconsin	659	1.5%
NA	Wyoming**	NA	NA

RANK ORDER

RANK	STATE	ABORTIONS	% of USA
1	New York	9,675	21.7%
2	Texas	3,255	7.3%
3	Ohio	2,368	5.3%
4	New Jersey	2,292	5.1%
5	Pennsylvania	2,242	5.0%
6	Georgia	2,114	4.7%
7	North Carolina	1,881	4.2%
8	Washington	1,840	4.1%
9	Michigan	1,770	4.0%
10	Massachusetts	1,405	3.2%
11	Virginia	1,240	2.8%
12	Connecticut	1,009	2.3%
13	Tennessee	979	2.2%
14	Alabama	807	1.8%
15	Kansas	785	1.8%
16	Colorado	781	1.8%
17	Arizona	763	1.7%
18	Louisiana	746	1.7%
19	Minnesota	718	1.6%
20	Oregon	713	1.6%
21	Wisconsin	659	1.5%
22	Nevada	615	1.4%
23	Indiana	562	1.3%
24	New Mexico	515	1.2%
25	South Carolina	498	1.1%
26	Oklahoma	447	1.0%
27	Missouri	440	1.0%
28	Iowa	421	0.9%
29	Arkansas	393	0.9%
30	Hawaii	329	0.7%
31	Rhode Island	296	0.7%
32	Delaware	264	0.6%
33	Kentucky	251	0.6%
34	Nebraska	232	0.5%
35	Maine	197	0.4%
36	Utah	191	0.4%
37	Montana	187	0.4%
38	Mississippi	182	0.4%
39	Alaska	154	0.3%
40	Vermont	128	0.3%
NA	California**	NA	NA
NA	Florida**	NA	NA
NA	Idaho**	NA	NA
NA	Illinois**	NA	NA
NA	Maryland**	NA	NA
NA	New Hampshire**	NA	NA
NA	North Dakota**	NA	NA
NA	South Dakota**	NA	NA
NA	West Virginia**	NA	NA
NA	Wyoming**	NA	NA
	District of Columbia	215	0.5%

Source: U.S. Department of Health and Human Services, Centers for Disease Control and Prevention
   "Abortion Surveillance-United States, 2004" (Morbidity and Mortality Weekly Report, Vol. 56, No. SS-9, 11/23/07)
*By state of occurrence. National total is for reporting states only.
**Not reported.

Percent of Reported Legal Abortions Obtained
by Teenagers 17 Years and Younger in 2004
Reporting States' Percent = 6.5% of Abortions*

ALPHA ORDER

RANK ORDER

RANK	STATE	PERCENT	RANK	STATE	PERCENT
12	Alabama	7.1	1	Hawaii	9.5
6	Alaska	8.0	2	Arkansas	8.5
28	Arizona	6.0	2	New Mexico	8.5
2	Arkansas	8.5	4	Connecticut	8.3
NA	California**	NA	4	Montana	8.3
18	Colorado	6.8	6	Alaska	8.0
4	Connecticut	8.3	7	New York	7.7
30	Delaware	5.8	8	Maine	7.6
NA	Florida**	NA	8	South Carolina	7.6
23	Georgia	6.5	10	Washington	7.5
1	Hawaii	9.5	11	Vermont	7.4
NA	Idaho**	NA	12	Alabama	7.1
NA	Illinois**	NA	12	Kentucky	7.1
34	Indiana	5.3	14	Iowa	7.0
14	Iowa	7.0	14	New Jersey	7.0
16	Kansas	6.9	16	Kansas	6.9
12	Kentucky	7.1	16	Ohio	6.9
21	Louisiana	6.6	18	Colorado	6.8
8	Maine	7.6	19	Michigan	6.7
NA	Maryland**	NA	19	Oklahoma	6.7
30	Massachusetts	5.8	21	Louisiana	6.6
19	Michigan	6.7	21	Wisconsin	6.6
36	Minnesota	5.2	23	Georgia	6.5
36	Mississippi	5.2	23	Nebraska	6.5
32	Missouri	5.5	25	Nevada	6.2
4	Montana	8.3	25	Oregon	6.2
23	Nebraska	6.5	25	Pennsylvania	6.2
25	Nevada	6.2	28	Arizona	6.0
NA	New Hampshire**	NA	28	Tennessee	6.0
14	New Jersey	7.0	30	Delaware	5.8
2	New Mexico	8.5	30	Massachusetts	5.8
7	New York	7.7	32	Missouri	5.5
32	North Carolina	5.5	32	North Carolina	5.5
NA	North Dakota**	NA	34	Indiana	5.3
16	Ohio	6.9	34	Rhode Island	5.3
19	Oklahoma	6.7	36	Minnesota	5.2
25	Oregon	6.2	36	Mississippi	5.2
25	Pennsylvania	6.2	36	Utah	5.2
34	Rhode Island	5.3	39	Virginia	4.7
8	South Carolina	7.6	40	Texas	4.4
NA	South Dakota**	NA	NA	California**	NA
28	Tennessee	6.0	NA	Florida**	NA
40	Texas	4.4	NA	Idaho**	NA
36	Utah	5.2	NA	Illinois**	NA
11	Vermont	7.4	NA	Maryland**	NA
39	Virginia	4.7	NA	New Hampshire**	NA
10	Washington	7.5	NA	North Dakota**	NA
NA	West Virginia**	NA	NA	South Dakota**	NA
21	Wisconsin	6.6	NA	West Virginia**	NA
NA	Wyoming**	NA	NA	Wyoming**	NA

District of Columbia   9.0

Source: CQ Press using data from U.S. Department of Health and Human Services, Centers for Disease Control and Prevention "Abortion Surveillance-United States, 2004" (Morbidity and Mortality Weekly Report, Vol. 56, No. SS-9, 11/23/07)

*By state of occurrence. National percent is for reporting states only.

**Not reported.

Percent of Teenage Abortions Obtained
by Teenagers 17 Years and Younger in 2004
Reporting States' Percent = 37.7% of Teenage Abortions*

ALPHA ORDER

RANK	STATE	PERCENT
16	Alabama	38.3
28	Alaska	36.1
34	Arizona	33.5
2	Arkansas	44.5
NA	California**	NA
25	Colorado	36.4
4	Connecticut	43.4
10	Delaware	40.1
NA	Florida**	NA
9	Georgia	40.3
1	Hawaii	47.1
NA	Idaho**	NA
NA	Illinois**	NA
33	Indiana	33.6
25	Iowa	36.4
14	Kansas	39.1
3	Kentucky	44.0
19	Louisiana	38.1
16	Maine	38.3
NA	Maryland**	NA
31	Massachusetts	34.6
21	Michigan	37.3
32	Minnesota	34.5
40	Mississippi	29.2
35	Missouri	32.5
7	Montana	41.4
23	Nebraska	36.8
20	Nevada	37.8
NA	New Hampshire**	NA
8	New Jersey	41.0
13	New Mexico	39.3
5	New York	42.4
30	North Carolina	34.9
NA	North Dakota**	NA
15	Ohio	38.4
21	Oklahoma	37.3
25	Oregon	36.4
29	Pennsylvania	35.7
39	Rhode Island	29.6
6	South Carolina	42.1
NA	South Dakota**	NA
23	Tennessee	36.8
36	Texas	32.2
37	Utah	32.0
11	Vermont	40.0
38	Virginia	31.5
11	Washington	40.0
NA	West Virginia**	NA
18	Wisconsin	38.2
NA	Wyoming**	NA

RANK ORDER

RANK	STATE	PERCENT
1	Hawaii	47.1
2	Arkansas	44.5
3	Kentucky	44.0
4	Connecticut	43.4
5	New York	42.4
6	South Carolina	42.1
7	Montana	41.4
8	New Jersey	41.0
9	Georgia	40.3
10	Delaware	40.1
11	Vermont	40.0
11	Washington	40.0
13	New Mexico	39.3
14	Kansas	39.1
15	Ohio	38.4
16	Alabama	38.3
16	Maine	38.3
18	Wisconsin	38.2
19	Louisiana	38.1
20	Nevada	37.8
21	Michigan	37.3
21	Oklahoma	37.3
23	Nebraska	36.8
23	Tennessee	36.8
25	Colorado	36.4
25	Iowa	36.4
25	Oregon	36.4
28	Alaska	36.1
29	Pennsylvania	35.7
30	North Carolina	34.9
31	Massachusetts	34.6
32	Minnesota	34.5
33	Indiana	33.6
34	Arizona	33.5
35	Missouri	32.5
36	Texas	32.2
37	Utah	32.0
38	Virginia	31.5
39	Rhode Island	29.6
40	Mississippi	29.2
NA	California**	NA
NA	Florida**	NA
NA	Idaho**	NA
NA	Illinois**	NA
NA	Maryland**	NA
NA	New Hampshire**	NA
NA	North Dakota**	NA
NA	South Dakota**	NA
NA	West Virginia**	NA
NA	Wyoming**	NA

District of Columbia — 49.0

Source: CQ Press using data from U.S. Department of Health and Human Services, Centers for Disease Control and Prevention
"Abortion Surveillance-United States, 2004" (Morbidity and Mortality Weekly Report, Vol. 56, No. SS-9, 11/23/07)

*By state of occurrence. National percent is for reporting states only.

**Not reported.

Reported Legal Abortions Performed at 12 Weeks or Less of Gestation in 2004

Reporting States' Total = 573,456 Abortions*

ALPHA ORDER

RANK	STATE	ABORTIONS	% of USA
17	Alabama	9,882	1.7%
36	Alaska	1,846	0.3%
13	Arizona	10,996	1.9%
29	Arkansas	3,765	0.7%
NA	California**	NA	NA
15	Colorado	9,992	1.7%
14	Connecticut	10,751	1.9%
33	Delaware	2,900	0.5%
NA	Florida**	NA	NA
6	Georgia	27,920	4.9%
32	Hawaii	2,952	0.5%
39	Idaho	934	0.2%
NA	Illinois**	NA	NA
19	Indiana	9,474	1.7%
26	Iowa	5,594	1.0%
18	Kansas	9,488	1.7%
31	Kentucky	3,005	0.5%
20	Louisiana	8,850	1.5%
34	Maine	2,499	0.4%
NA	Maryland**	NA	NA
NA	Massachusetts**	NA	NA
9	Michigan	23,210	4.0%
12	Minnesota	12,238	2.1%
NA	Mississippi**	NA	NA
23	Missouri	7,347	1.3%
35	Montana	1,900	0.3%
NA	Nebraska**	NA	NA
22	Nevada	7,636	1.3%
NA	New Hampshire**	NA	NA
7	New Jersey	26,268	4.6%
27	New Mexico	5,097	0.9%
1	New York	104,788	18.3%
5	North Carolina	28,051	4.9%
38	North Dakota	1,231	0.2%
4	Ohio	29,422	5.1%
25	Oklahoma	6,047	1.1%
16	Oregon	9,942	1.7%
3	Pennsylvania	31,705	5.5%
28	Rhode Island	4,996	0.9%
24	South Carolina	6,415	1.1%
40	South Dakota	779	0.1%
11	Tennessee	15,617	2.7%
2	Texas	68,638	12.0%
30	Utah	3,147	0.5%
37	Vermont	1,606	0.3%
8	Virginia	24,871	4.3%
10	Washington	21,321	3.7%
NA	West Virginia**	NA	NA
21	Wisconsin	8,342	1.5%
NA	Wyoming**	NA	NA

RANK ORDER

RANK	STATE	ABORTIONS	% of USA
1	New York	104,788	18.3%
2	Texas	68,638	12.0%
3	Pennsylvania	31,705	5.5%
4	Ohio	29,422	5.1%
5	North Carolina	28,051	4.9%
6	Georgia	27,920	4.9%
7	New Jersey	26,268	4.6%
8	Virginia	24,871	4.3%
9	Michigan	23,210	4.0%
10	Washington	21,321	3.7%
11	Tennessee	15,617	2.7%
12	Minnesota	12,238	2.1%
13	Arizona	10,996	1.9%
14	Connecticut	10,751	1.9%
15	Colorado	9,992	1.7%
16	Oregon	9,942	1.7%
17	Alabama	9,882	1.7%
18	Kansas	9,488	1.7%
19	Indiana	9,474	1.7%
20	Louisiana	8,850	1.5%
21	Wisconsin	8,342	1.5%
22	Nevada	7,636	1.3%
23	Missouri	7,347	1.3%
24	South Carolina	6,415	1.1%
25	Oklahoma	6,047	1.1%
26	Iowa	5,594	1.0%
27	New Mexico	5,097	0.9%
28	Rhode Island	4,996	0.9%
29	Arkansas	3,765	0.7%
30	Utah	3,147	0.5%
31	Kentucky	3,005	0.5%
32	Hawaii	2,952	0.5%
33	Delaware	2,900	0.5%
34	Maine	2,499	0.4%
35	Montana	1,900	0.3%
36	Alaska	1,846	0.3%
37	Vermont	1,606	0.3%
38	North Dakota	1,231	0.2%
39	Idaho	934	0.2%
40	South Dakota	779	0.1%
NA	California**	NA	NA
NA	Florida**	NA	NA
NA	Illinois**	NA	NA
NA	Maryland**	NA	NA
NA	Massachusetts**	NA	NA
NA	Mississippi**	NA	NA
NA	Nebraska**	NA	NA
NA	New Hampshire**	NA	NA
NA	West Virginia**	NA	NA
NA	Wyoming**	NA	NA
	District of Columbia	1,982	0.3%

Source: CQ Press using data from U.S. Department of Health and Human Services, Centers for Disease Control and Prevention
"Abortion Surveillance-United States, 2004" (Morbidity and Mortality Weekly Report, Vol. 56, No. SS-9, 11/23/07)
*By state of occurrence. National total is for reporting states only.
**Not reported.

Percent of Reported Legal Abortions Performed
at 12 Weeks or Less of Gestation in 2004
Reporting States' Percent = 86.3% of Abortions*

ALPHA ORDER

RANK	STATE	PERCENT
21	Alabama	86.9
5	Alaska	95.3
23	Arizona	86.7
36	Arkansas	81.1
NA	California**	NA
20	Colorado	87.5
18	Connecticut	88.2
40	Delaware	63.2
NA	Florida**	NA
25	Georgia	85.9
28	Hawaii	85.1
2	Idaho	97.0
NA	Illinois**	NA
13	Indiana	90.1
9	Iowa	92.9
33	Kansas	83.5
29	Kentucky	84.5
38	Louisiana	78.8
3	Maine	96.4
NA	Maryland**	NA
NA	Massachusetts**	NA
17	Michigan	88.4
16	Minnesota	88.7
NA	Mississippi**	NA
11	Missouri	91.0
30	Montana	84.2
NA	Nebraska**	NA
39	Nevada	77.5
NA	New Hampshire**	NA
37	New Jersey	80.5
31	New Mexico	84.0
34	New York	83.2
35	North Carolina	82.6
12	North Dakota	90.7
25	Ohio	85.9
13	Oklahoma	90.1
21	Oregon	86.9
19	Pennsylvania	88.0
15	Rhode Island	89.4
1	South Carolina	97.7
4	South Dakota	95.7
6	Tennessee	95.2
10	Texas	91.8
25	Utah	85.9
8	Vermont	93.1
6	Virginia	95.2
24	Washington	86.4
NA	West Virginia**	NA
32	Wisconsin	83.9
NA	Wyoming**	NA

RANK ORDER

RANK	STATE	PERCENT
1	South Carolina	97.7
2	Idaho	97.0
3	Maine	96.4
4	South Dakota	95.7
5	Alaska	95.3
6	Tennessee	95.2
6	Virginia	95.2
8	Vermont	93.1
9	Iowa	92.9
10	Texas	91.8
11	Missouri	91.0
12	North Dakota	90.7
13	Indiana	90.1
13	Oklahoma	90.1
15	Rhode Island	89.4
16	Minnesota	88.7
17	Michigan	88.4
18	Connecticut	88.2
19	Pennsylvania	88.0
20	Colorado	87.5
21	Alabama	86.9
21	Oregon	86.9
23	Arizona	86.7
24	Washington	86.4
25	Georgia	85.9
25	Ohio	85.9
25	Utah	85.9
28	Hawaii	85.1
29	Kentucky	84.5
30	Montana	84.2
31	New Mexico	84.0
32	Wisconsin	83.9
33	Kansas	83.5
34	New York	83.2
35	North Carolina	82.6
36	Arkansas	81.1
37	New Jersey	80.5
38	Louisiana	78.8
39	Nevada	77.5
40	Delaware	63.2
NA	California**	NA
NA	Florida**	NA
NA	Illinois**	NA
NA	Maryland**	NA
NA	Massachusetts**	NA
NA	Mississippi**	NA
NA	Nebraska**	NA
NA	New Hampshire**	NA
NA	West Virginia**	NA
NA	Wyoming**	NA

District of Columbia   82.5

Source: CQ Press using data from U.S. Department of Health and Human Services, Centers for Disease Control and Prevention
"Abortion Surveillance-United States, 2004" (Morbidity and Mortality Weekly Report, Vol. 56, No. SS-9, 11/23/07)

*By state of occurrence. National percent is for reporting states only.

**Not reported.

Reported Legal Abortions Performed at or After 21 Weeks of Gestation in 2004

Reporting States' Total = 8,365 Abortions*

ALPHA ORDER

RANK	STATE	ABORTIONS	% of USA
18	Alabama	62	0.7%
37	Alaska	0	0.0%
15	Arizona	105	1.3%
24	Arkansas	26	0.3%
NA	California**	NA	NA
9	Colorado	246	2.9%
23	Connecticut	28	0.3%
33	Delaware	5	0.1%
NA	Florida**	NA	NA
2	Georgia	1,053	12.6%
25	Hawaii	24	0.3%
33	Idaho	5	0.1%
NA	Illinois**	NA	NA
37	Indiana	0	0.0%
37	Iowa	0	0.0%
4	Kansas	584	7.0%
19	Kentucky	54	0.6%
7	Louisiana	358	4.3%
28	Maine	10	0.1%
NA	Maryland**	NA	NA
NA	Massachusetts**	NA	NA
11	Michigan	195	2.3%
17	Minnesota	67	0.8%
NA	Mississippi**	NA	NA
22	Missouri	31	0.4%
21	Montana	32	0.4%
NA	Nebraska**	NA	NA
20	Nevada	41	0.5%
NA	New Hampshire**	NA	NA
3	New Jersey	872	10.4%
13	New Mexico	117	1.4%
1	New York	2,459	29.4%
32	North Carolina	6	0.1%
37	North Dakota	0	0.0%
5	Ohio	535	6.4%
27	Oklahoma	14	0.2%
10	Oregon	234	2.8%
8	Pennsylvania	270	3.2%
33	Rhode Island	5	0.1%
28	South Carolina	10	0.1%
31	South Dakota	7	0.1%
26	Tennessee	21	0.3%
14	Texas	110	1.3%
33	Utah	5	0.1%
30	Vermont	8	0.1%
16	Virginia	78	0.9%
6	Washington	517	6.2%
NA	West Virginia**	NA	NA
12	Wisconsin	171	2.0%
NA	Wyoming**	NA	NA

RANK ORDER

RANK	STATE	ABORTIONS	% of USA
1	New York	2,459	29.4%
2	Georgia	1,053	12.6%
3	New Jersey	872	10.4%
4	Kansas	584	7.0%
5	Ohio	535	6.4%
6	Washington	517	6.2%
7	Louisiana	358	4.3%
8	Pennsylvania	270	3.2%
9	Colorado	246	2.9%
10	Oregon	234	2.8%
11	Michigan	195	2.3%
12	Wisconsin	171	2.0%
13	New Mexico	117	1.4%
14	Texas	110	1.3%
15	Arizona	105	1.3%
16	Virginia	78	0.9%
17	Minnesota	67	0.8%
18	Alabama	62	0.7%
19	Kentucky	54	0.6%
20	Nevada	41	0.5%
21	Montana	32	0.4%
22	Missouri	31	0.4%
23	Connecticut	28	0.3%
24	Arkansas	26	0.3%
25	Hawaii	24	0.3%
26	Tennessee	21	0.3%
27	Oklahoma	14	0.2%
28	Maine	10	0.1%
28	South Carolina	10	0.1%
30	Vermont	8	0.1%
31	South Dakota	7	0.1%
32	North Carolina	6	0.1%
33	Delaware	5	0.1%
33	Idaho	5	0.1%
33	Rhode Island	5	0.1%
33	Utah	5	0.1%
37	Alaska	0	0.0%
37	Indiana	0	0.0%
37	Iowa	0	0.0%
37	North Dakota	0	0.0%
NA	California**	NA	NA
NA	Florida**	NA	NA
NA	Illinois**	NA	NA
NA	Maryland**	NA	NA
NA	Massachusetts**	NA	NA
NA	Mississippi**	NA	NA
NA	Nebraska**	NA	NA
NA	New Hampshire**	NA	NA
NA	West Virginia**	NA	NA
NA	Wyoming**	NA	NA
	District of Columbia	0	0.0%

Source: U.S. Department of Health and Human Services, Centers for Disease Control and Prevention
   "Abortion Surveillance-United States, 2004" (Morbidity and Mortality Weekly Report, Vol. 56, No. SS-9, 11/23/07)
*By state of occurrence. National total is for reporting states only.
**Not reported.

Percent of Reported Legal Abortions Performed at or After 21 Weeks of Gestation in 2004
Reporting States' Percent = 1.3% of Abortions*

ALPHA ORDER

RANK	STATE	PERCENT
20	Alabama	0.5
36	Alaska	0.0
15	Arizona	0.8
19	Arkansas	0.6
NA	California**	NA
5	Colorado	2.2
28	Connecticut	0.2
31	Delaware	0.1
NA	Florida**	NA
2	Georgia	3.2
16	Hawaii	0.7
20	Idaho	0.5
NA	Illinois**	NA
36	Indiana	0.0
36	Iowa	0.0
1	Kansas	5.1
12	Kentucky	1.5
2	Louisiana	3.2
24	Maine	0.4
NA	Maryland**	NA
NA	Massachusetts**	NA
16	Michigan	0.7
20	Minnesota	0.5
NA	Mississippi**	NA
24	Missouri	0.4
13	Montana	1.4
NA	Nebraska**	NA
24	Nevada	0.4
NA	New Hampshire**	NA
4	New Jersey	2.7
9	New Mexico	1.9
7	New York	2.0
36	North Carolina	0.0
36	North Dakota	0.0
11	Ohio	1.6
28	Oklahoma	0.2
7	Oregon	2.0
16	Pennsylvania	0.7
31	Rhode Island	0.1
28	South Carolina	0.2
14	South Dakota	0.9
31	Tennessee	0.1
31	Texas	0.1
31	Utah	0.1
20	Vermont	0.5
27	Virginia	0.3
6	Washington	2.1
NA	West Virginia**	NA
10	Wisconsin	1.8
NA	Wyoming**	NA

RANK ORDER

RANK	STATE	PERCENT
1	Kansas	5.1
2	Georgia	3.2
2	Louisiana	3.2
4	New Jersey	2.7
5	Colorado	2.2
6	Washington	2.1
7	New York	2.0
7	Oregon	2.0
9	New Mexico	1.9
10	Wisconsin	1.8
11	Ohio	1.6
12	Kentucky	1.5
13	Montana	1.4
14	South Dakota	0.9
15	Arizona	0.8
16	Hawaii	0.7
16	Michigan	0.7
16	Pennsylvania	0.7
19	Arkansas	0.6
20	Alabama	0.5
20	Idaho	0.5
20	Minnesota	0.5
20	Vermont	0.5
24	Maine	0.4
24	Missouri	0.4
24	Nevada	0.4
27	Virginia	0.3
28	Connecticut	0.2
28	Oklahoma	0.2
28	South Carolina	0.2
31	Delaware	0.1
31	Rhode Island	0.1
31	Tennessee	0.1
31	Texas	0.1
31	Utah	0.1
36	Alaska	0.0
36	Indiana	0.0
36	Iowa	0.0
36	North Carolina	0.0
36	North Dakota	0.0
NA	California**	NA
NA	Florida**	NA
NA	Illinois**	NA
NA	Maryland**	NA
NA	Massachusetts**	NA
NA	Mississippi**	NA
NA	Nebraska**	NA
NA	New Hampshire**	NA
NA	West Virginia**	NA
NA	Wyoming**	NA
	District of Columbia	0.0

Source: U.S. Department of Health and Human Services, Centers for Disease Control and Prevention
"Abortion Surveillance-United States, 2004" (Morbidity and Mortality Weekly Report, Vol. 56, No. SS-9, 11/23/07)
*By state of occurrence. National percent is for reporting states only.
**Not reported.

II. Deaths

Deaths in 2006 92
Death Rate in 2006 93
Deaths in 2005 94
Death Rate in 2005 95
Age-Adjusted Death Rate in 2005 96
Percent Change in Death Rate: 1996 to 2005 97
Deaths in 2004 98
Death Rate in 2004 99
Age-Adjusted Death Rate in 2004 100
Infant Deaths in 2005 101
Infant Mortality Rate in 2005 102
White Infant Deaths in 2005 103
White Infant Mortality Rate in 2005 104
Black Infant Deaths in 2005 105
Black Infant Mortality Rate in 2005 106
Neonatal Deaths in 2005 107
Neonatal Death Rate in 2005 108
White Neonatal Deaths in 2005 109
White Neonatal Death Rate in 2005 110
Black Neonatal Deaths in 2005 111
Black Neonatal Death Rate in 2005 112
Estimated Deaths by Cancer in 2007 113
Estimated Death Rate by Cancer in 2007 114
Age-Adjusted Death Rate by Cancer for Males in 2003 . . 115
Age-Adjusted Death Rate by Cancer for Females
    in 2003 116
Estimated Deaths by Brain Cancer in 2007 117
Estimated Death Rate by Brain Cancer in 2007 118
Estimated Deaths by Female Breast Cancer in 2007 119
Age-Adjusted Death Rate by Female Breast Cancer
    in 2003 120
Estimated Deaths by Colon and Rectum Cancer
    in 2007 121
Estimated Death Rate by Colon and Rectum Cancer
    in 2007 122
Estimated Deaths by Leukemia in 2007 123
Estimated Death Rate by Leukemia in 2007 124
Estimated Deaths by Liver Cancer in 2007 125
Estimated Death Rate by Liver Cancer in 2007 126
Estimated Deaths by Lung Cancer in 2007 127

Estimated Death Rate by Lung Cancer in 2007 128
Estimated Deaths by Non-Hodgkin's Lymphoma
    in 2007 129
Estimated Death Rate by Non-Hodgkin's Lymphoma
    in 2007 130
Estimated Deaths by Ovarian Cancer in 2007 131
Estimated Death Rate by Ovarian Cancer in 2007 132
Estimated Deaths by Pancreatic Cancer in 2007 133
Estimated Death Rate by Pancreatic Cancer in 2007 134
Estimated Deaths by Prostate Cancer in 2007 135
Age-Adjusted Death Rate by Prostate Cancer in 2003 . . . 136
Deaths by AIDS in 2004 137
Death Rate by AIDS in 2004 138
Age-Adjusted Death Rate by AIDS in 2004 139
Deaths by Alzheimer's Disease in 2004 140
Death Rate by Alzheimer's Disease in 2004 141
Age-Adjusted Death Rate by Alzheimer's Disease
    in 2004 142
Deaths by Cerebrovascular Diseases in 2004 143
Death Rate by Cerebrovascular Diseases in 2004 144
Age-Adjusted Death Rate by Cerebrovascular Diseases
    in 2004 145
Deaths by Chronic Liver Disease and Cirrhosis in 2004 . . 146
Death Rate by Chronic Liver Disease and Cirrhosis
    in 2004 147
Age-Adjusted Death Rate by Chronic Liver Disease and
    Cirrhosis in 2004 148
Deaths by Chronic Lower Respiratory Diseases
    in 2004 149
Death Rate by Chronic Lower Respiratory Diseases
    in 2004 150
Age-Adjusted Death Rate by Chronic Lower Respiratory
    Diseases in 2004 151
Deaths by Diabetes Mellitus in 2004 152
Death Rate by Diabetes Mellitus in 2004 153
Age-Adjusted Death Rate by Diabetes Mellitus in 2004 . . 154
Deaths by Diseases of the Heart in 2004 155
Death Rate by Diseases of the Heart in 2004 156
Age-Adjusted Death Rate by Diseases of the Heart
    in 2004 157

Deaths by Malignant Neoplasms in 2004 158
Death Rate by Malignant Neoplasms in 2004 159
Age-Adjusted Death Rate by Malignant Neoplasms
    in 2004 160
Deaths by Nephritis and Other Kidney Diseases in 2004 . . 161
Death Rate by Nephritis and Other Kidney Diseases
    in 2004 162
Age-Adjusted Death Rate by Nephritis and Other Kidney
    Diseases in 2004 163
Deaths by Influenza and Pneumonia in 2004 164
Death Rate by Influenza and Pneumonia in 2004 165
Age-Adjusted Death Rate by Influenza and Pneumonia
    in 2004 166
Deaths by Injury in 2004 167
Death Rate by Injury in 2004 168
Age-Adjusted Death Rate by Injury in 2004 169
Deaths by Accidents in 2004 170
Death Rate by Accidents in 2004 171
Age-Adjusted Death Rate by Accidents in 2004 172

Deaths by Motor Vehicle Accidents in 2004 173
Death Rate by Motor Vehicle Accidents in 2004 174
Age-Adjusted Death Rate by Motor Vehicle Accidents
    in 2004 175
Deaths by Firearm Injury in 2004 176
Death Rate by Firearm Injury in 2004 177
Age-Adjusted Death Rate by Firearm Injury in 2004 178
Deaths by Homicide in 2004 179
Death Rate by Homicide in 2004 180
Age-Adjusted Death Rate by Homicide in 2004 181
Deaths by Suicide in 2004 182
Death Rate by Suicide in 2004 183
Age-Adjusted Death Rate by Suicide in 2004 184
Alcohol-Induced Deaths in 2004 185
Death Rate by Alcohol-Induced Deaths in 2004 186
Age-Adjusted Death Rate by Alcohol-Induced Deaths
    in 2004 187
Occupational Fatalities in 2006 188
Occupational Fatality Rate in 2006 189

Deaths in 2006

National Total = 2,416,474 Deaths*

RANK	STATE	DEATHS	% of USA
17	Alabama	47,032	1.9%
50	Alaska	3,318	0.1%
19	Arizona	46,073	1.9%
31	Arkansas	28,032	1.2%
1	California	238,011	9.8%
29	Colorado	29,502	1.2%
28	Connecticut	29,790	1.2%
45	Delaware	7,111	0.3%
2	Florida	170,007	7.0%
11	Georgia	66,335	2.7%
43	Hawaii	9,384	0.4%
40	Idaho	10,703	0.4%
7	Illinois	101,922	4.2%
14	Indiana	55,652	2.3%
32	Iowa	27,493	1.1%
33	Kansas	24,473	1.0%
22	Kentucky	40,066	1.7%
23	Louisiana	38,376	1.6%
39	Maine	12,280	0.5%
21	Maryland	43,566	1.8%
16	Massachusetts	53,631	2.2%
8	Michigan	84,716	3.5%
24	Minnesota	36,982	1.5%
30	Mississippi	28,656	1.2%
15	Missouri	54,913	2.3%
44	Montana	8,488	0.4%
37	Nebraska	14,952	0.6%
35	Nevada	18,295	0.8%
41	New Hampshire	9,901	0.4%
10	New Jersey	71,809	3.0%
36	New Mexico	14,962	0.6%
4	New York	150,329	6.2%
9	North Carolina	74,734	3.1%
47	North Dakota	5,917	0.2%
6	Ohio	106,977	4.4%
26	Oklahoma	35,585	1.5%
27	Oregon	31,361	1.3%
5	Pennsylvania	125,151	5.2%
42	Rhode Island	9,731	0.4%
25	South Carolina	36,652	1.5%
46	South Dakota	7,043	0.3%
13	Tennessee	56,687	2.3%
3	Texas	152,461	6.3%
38	Utah	13,772	0.6%
48	Vermont	5,009	0.2%
12	Virginia	57,571	2.4%
20	Washington	44,844	1.9%
34	West Virginia	20,573	0.9%
18	Wisconsin	46,188	1.9%
49	Wyoming	4,281	0.2%

RANK	STATE	DEATHS	% of USA
1	California	238,011	9.8%
2	Florida	170,007	7.0%
3	Texas	152,461	6.3%
4	New York	150,329	6.2%
5	Pennsylvania	125,151	5.2%
6	Ohio	106,977	4.4%
7	Illinois	101,922	4.2%
8	Michigan	84,716	3.5%
9	North Carolina	74,734	3.1%
10	New Jersey	71,809	3.0%
11	Georgia	66,335	2.7%
12	Virginia	57,571	2.4%
13	Tennessee	56,687	2.3%
14	Indiana	55,652	2.3%
15	Missouri	54,913	2.3%
16	Massachusetts	53,631	2.2%
17	Alabama	47,032	1.9%
18	Wisconsin	46,188	1.9%
19	Arizona	46,073	1.9%
20	Washington	44,844	1.9%
21	Maryland	43,566	1.8%
22	Kentucky	40,066	1.7%
23	Louisiana	38,376	1.6%
24	Minnesota	36,982	1.5%
25	South Carolina	36,652	1.5%
26	Oklahoma	35,585	1.5%
27	Oregon	31,361	1.3%
28	Connecticut	29,790	1.2%
29	Colorado	29,502	1.2%
30	Mississippi	28,656	1.2%
31	Arkansas	28,032	1.2%
32	Iowa	27,493	1.1%
33	Kansas	24,473	1.0%
34	West Virginia	20,573	0.9%
35	Nevada	18,295	0.8%
36	New Mexico	14,962	0.6%
37	Nebraska	14,952	0.6%
38	Utah	13,772	0.6%
39	Maine	12,280	0.5%
40	Idaho	10,703	0.4%
41	New Hampshire	9,901	0.4%
42	Rhode Island	9,731	0.4%
43	Hawaii	9,384	0.4%
44	Montana	8,488	0.4%
45	Delaware	7,111	0.3%
46	South Dakota	7,043	0.3%
47	North Dakota	5,917	0.2%
48	Vermont	5,009	0.2%
49	Wyoming	4,281	0.2%
50	Alaska	3,318	0.1%
	District of Columbia	5,177	0.2%

Source: U.S. Department of Health and Human Services, National Center for Health Statistics
"National Vital Statistics Reports" (Vol. 55, No. 20, August 28, 2007, http://www.cdc.gov/nchs/deaths.htm)
*Provisional data for 12 months ending with December by state of residence.

Death Rate in 2006

National Rate = 808.8 Deaths per 100,000 Population*

ALPHA ORDER

RANK	STATE	RATE
2	Alabama	1,024.6
50	Alaska	489.8
39	Arizona	747.2
4	Arkansas	997.9
46	California	656.6
48	Colorado	619.0
21	Connecticut	852.2
28	Delaware	833.9
8	Florida	941.5
44	Georgia	710.1
41	Hawaii	733.9
42	Idaho	731.1
33	Illinois	797.7
20	Indiana	883.0
14	Iowa	924.9
19	Kansas	888.0
7	Kentucky	952.9
16	Louisiana	904.4
10	Maine	933.9
35	Maryland	777.7
29	Massachusetts	833.5
26	Michigan	838.6
43	Minnesota	717.5
6	Mississippi	988.4
9	Missouri	940.7
17	Montana	896.5
23	Nebraska	847.7
40	Nevada	734.0
37	New Hampshire	754.8
31	New Jersey	828.6
36	New Mexico	770.3
34	New York	779.6
25	North Carolina	842.6
13	North Dakota	928.2
11	Ohio	933.2
5	Oklahoma	994.7
22	Oregon	849.6
3	Pennsylvania	1,009.1
15	Rhode Island	916.6
24	South Carolina	846.4
18	South Dakota	893.3
12	Tennessee	933.1
47	Texas	651.3
49	Utah	533.9
32	Vermont	806.9
38	Virginia	753.5
45	Washington	703.4
1	West Virginia	1,137.4
30	Wisconsin	828.8
27	Wyoming	834.9

RANK ORDER

RANK	STATE	RATE
1	West Virginia	1,137.4
2	Alabama	1,024.6
3	Pennsylvania	1,009.1
4	Arkansas	997.9
5	Oklahoma	994.7
6	Mississippi	988.4
7	Kentucky	952.9
8	Florida	941.5
9	Missouri	940.7
10	Maine	933.9
11	Ohio	933.2
12	Tennessee	933.1
13	North Dakota	928.2
14	Iowa	924.9
15	Rhode Island	916.6
16	Louisiana	904.4
17	Montana	896.5
18	South Dakota	893.3
19	Kansas	888.0
20	Indiana	883.0
21	Connecticut	852.2
22	Oregon	849.6
23	Nebraska	847.7
24	South Carolina	846.4
25	North Carolina	842.6
26	Michigan	838.6
27	Wyoming	834.9
28	Delaware	833.9
29	Massachusetts	833.5
30	Wisconsin	828.8
31	New Jersey	828.6
32	Vermont	806.9
33	Illinois	797.7
34	New York	779.6
35	Maryland	777.7
36	New Mexico	770.3
37	New Hampshire	754.8
38	Virginia	753.5
39	Arizona	747.2
40	Nevada	734.0
41	Hawaii	733.9
42	Idaho	731.1
43	Minnesota	717.5
44	Georgia	710.1
45	Washington	703.4
46	California	656.6
47	Texas	651.3
48	Colorado	619.0
49	Utah	533.9
50	Alaska	489.8

District of Columbia   884.3

Source: CQ Press using data from U.S. Department of Health and Human Services, National Center for Health Statistics
    "National Vital Statistics Reports" (Vol. 55, No. 20, August 28, 2007, http://www.cdc.gov/nchs/deaths.htm)
*Provisional data for 12 months ending with December by state of residence. Not age-adjusted.

Deaths in 2005

National Total = 2,447,903 Deaths*

ALPHA ORDER

RANK	STATE	DEATHS	% of USA
17	Alabama	47,088	1.9%
50	Alaska	3,170	0.1%
20	Arizona	45,837	1.9%
31	Arkansas	28,055	1.1%
1	California	237,079	9.7%
28	Colorado	29,628	1.2%
29	Connecticut	29,466	1.2%
45	Delaware	7,472	0.3%
2	Florida	170,787	7.0%
11	Georgia	66,735	2.7%
43	Hawaii	9,137	0.4%
40	Idaho	10,554	0.4%
7	Illinois	103,977	4.2%
14	Indiana	55,676	2.3%
32	Iowa	27,812	1.1%
33	Kansas	24,684	1.0%
23	Kentucky	40,223	1.6%
21	Louisiana	44,333	1.8%
39	Maine	12,871	0.5%
22	Maryland	43,893	1.8%
16	Massachusetts	53,872	2.2%
8	Michigan	86,868	3.5%
25	Minnesota	37,537	1.5%
30	Mississippi	29,198	1.2%
15	Missouri	54,658	2.2%
44	Montana	8,529	0.3%
37	Nebraska	14,964	0.6%
35	Nevada	19,037	0.8%
41	New Hampshire	10,194	0.4%
10	New Jersey	71,970	2.9%
36	New Mexico	14,984	0.6%
4	New York	152,427	6.2%
9	North Carolina	74,639	3.0%
47	North Dakota	5,744	0.2%
6	Ohio	109,030	4.5%
26	Oklahoma	36,181	1.5%
27	Oregon	31,099	1.3%
5	Pennsylvania	129,536	5.3%
42	Rhode Island	10,007	0.4%
24	South Carolina	38,483	1.6%
46	South Dakota	7,087	0.3%
13	Tennessee	57,270	2.3%
3	Texas	156,474	6.4%
38	Utah	13,434	0.5%
48	Vermont	5,066	0.2%
12	Virginia	57,857	2.4%
19	Washington	46,212	1.9%
34	West Virginia	20,780	0.8%
18	Wisconsin	46,709	1.9%
49	Wyoming	4,100	0.2%

RANK ORDER

RANK	STATE	DEATHS	% of USA
1	California	237,079	9.7%
2	Florida	170,787	7.0%
3	Texas	156,474	6.4%
4	New York	152,427	6.2%
5	Pennsylvania	129,536	5.3%
6	Ohio	109,030	4.5%
7	Illinois	103,977	4.2%
8	Michigan	86,868	3.5%
9	North Carolina	74,639	3.0%
10	New Jersey	71,970	2.9%
11	Georgia	66,735	2.7%
12	Virginia	57,857	2.4%
13	Tennessee	57,270	2.3%
14	Indiana	55,676	2.3%
15	Missouri	54,658	2.2%
16	Massachusetts	53,872	2.2%
17	Alabama	47,088	1.9%
18	Wisconsin	46,709	1.9%
19	Washington	46,212	1.9%
20	Arizona	45,837	1.9%
21	Louisiana	44,333	1.8%
22	Maryland	43,893	1.8%
23	Kentucky	40,223	1.6%
24	South Carolina	38,483	1.6%
25	Minnesota	37,537	1.5%
26	Oklahoma	36,181	1.5%
27	Oregon	31,099	1.3%
28	Colorado	29,628	1.2%
29	Connecticut	29,466	1.2%
30	Mississippi	29,198	1.2%
31	Arkansas	28,055	1.1%
32	Iowa	27,812	1.1%
33	Kansas	24,684	1.0%
34	West Virginia	20,780	0.8%
35	Nevada	19,037	0.8%
36	New Mexico	14,984	0.6%
37	Nebraska	14,964	0.6%
38	Utah	13,434	0.5%
39	Maine	12,871	0.5%
40	Idaho	10,554	0.4%
41	New Hampshire	10,194	0.4%
42	Rhode Island	10,007	0.4%
43	Hawaii	9,137	0.4%
44	Montana	8,529	0.3%
45	Delaware	7,472	0.3%
46	South Dakota	7,087	0.3%
47	North Dakota	5,744	0.2%
48	Vermont	5,066	0.2%
49	Wyoming	4,100	0.2%
50	Alaska	3,170	0.1%
	District of Columbia	5,483	0.2%

Source: U.S. Department of Health and Human Services, National Center for Health Statistics
"Deaths: Preliminary Data for 2005" (http://www.cdc.gov/nchs/deaths.htm)
*Preliminary data by state of residence.

Death Rate in 2005

National Rate = 825.8 Deaths per 100,000 Population*

ALPHA ORDER			RANK ORDER		
RANK	STATE	RATE	RANK	STATE	RATE
3	Alabama	1,033.1	1	West Virginia	1,143.7
50	Alaska	477.7	2	Pennsylvania	1,042.2
39	Arizona	771.8	3	Alabama	1,033.1
5	Arkansas	1,009.5	4	Oklahoma	1,019.8
47	California	656.1	5	Arkansas	1,009.5
48	Colorado	635.1	6	Mississippi	999.6
29	Connecticut	839.4	7	Louisiana	980.0
22	Delaware	885.8	8	Maine	974.0
11	Florida	960.0	9	Kentucky	963.8
42	Georgia	735.6	10	Tennessee	960.4
45	Hawaii	716.5	11	Florida	960.0
41	Idaho	738.5	12	Ohio	951.1
31	Illinois	814.7	13	Missouri	942.3
21	Indiana	887.7	14	Iowa	937.6
14	Iowa	937.6	15	Rhode Island	929.9
20	Kansas	899.3	16	South Dakota	913.4
9	Kentucky	963.8	17	Montana	911.5
7	Louisiana	980.0	18	South Carolina	904.4
8	Maine	974.0	19	North Dakota	902.2
36	Maryland	783.7	20	Kansas	899.3
28	Massachusetts	841.9	21	Indiana	887.7
24	Michigan	858.3	22	Delaware	885.8
44	Minnesota	731.3	23	North Carolina	859.6
6	Mississippi	999.6	24	Michigan	858.3
13	Missouri	942.3	25	Oregon	854.1
17	Montana	911.5	26	Nebraska	850.8
26	Nebraska	850.8	27	Wisconsin	843.7
35	Nevada	788.3	28	Massachusetts	841.9
37	New Hampshire	778.2	29	Connecticut	839.4
30	New Jersey	825.5	30	New Jersey	825.5
38	New Mexico	777.0	31	Illinois	814.7
34	New York	791.6	32	Vermont	813.1
23	North Carolina	859.6	33	Wyoming	805.0
19	North Dakota	902.2	34	New York	791.6
12	Ohio	951.1	35	Nevada	788.3
4	Oklahoma	1,019.8	36	Maryland	783.7
25	Oregon	854.1	37	New Hampshire	778.2
2	Pennsylvania	1,042.2	38	New Mexico	777.0
15	Rhode Island	929.9	39	Arizona	771.8
18	South Carolina	904.4	40	Virginia	764.5
16	South Dakota	913.4	41	Idaho	738.5
10	Tennessee	960.4	42	Georgia	735.6
46	Texas	684.5	43	Washington	735.0
49	Utah	544.0	44	Minnesota	731.3
32	Vermont	813.1	45	Hawaii	716.5
40	Virginia	764.5	46	Texas	684.5
43	Washington	735.0	47	California	656.1
1	West Virginia	1,143.7	48	Colorado	635.1
27	Wisconsin	843.7	49	Utah	544.0
33	Wyoming	805.0	50	Alaska	477.7
				District of Columbia	996.0

Source: U.S. Department of Health and Human Services, National Center for Health Statistics
"Deaths: Preliminary Data for 2005" (http://www.cdc.gov/nchs/deaths.htm)
*Preliminary data by state of residence. Not age-adjusted.

Age-Adjusted Death Rate in 2005

National Rate = 798.8 Deaths per 100,000 Population*

ALPHA ORDER

RANK	STATE	RATE
3	Alabama	997.9
33	Alaska	750.8
29	Arizona	771.8
8	Arkansas	930.2
46	California	713.1
38	Colorado	742.8
48	Connecticut	696.0
16	Delaware	830.5
35	Florida	749.4
9	Georgia	905.8
50	Hawaii	609.1
30	Idaho	766.4
25	Illinois	798.2
14	Indiana	858.7
39	Iowa	742.0
21	Kansas	806.8
7	Kentucky	958.4
2	Louisiana	1,020.6
19	Maine	813.2
26	Maryland	796.4
44	Massachusetts	721.9
20	Michigan	812.3
49	Minnesota	683.9
1	Mississippi	1,026.9
13	Missouri	869.4
24	Montana	798.4
34	Nebraska	749.5
11	Nevada	892.3
41	New Hampshire	732.3
37	New Jersey	745.9
27	New Mexico	795.0
45	New York	718.0
12	North Carolina	876.0
47	North Dakota	699.1
15	Ohio	856.8
4	Oklahoma	980.8
28	Oregon	773.7
18	Pennsylvania	814.8
36	Rhode Island	747.3
10	South Carolina	899.1
31	South Dakota	757.0
6	Tennessee	959.9
17	Texas	828.8
42	Utah	731.3
43	Vermont	728.4
22	Virginia	801.5
40	Washington	738.2
5	West Virginia	960.4
32	Wisconsin	752.2
23	Wyoming	801.4

RANK ORDER

RANK	STATE	RATE
1	Mississippi	1,026.9
2	Louisiana	1,020.6
3	Alabama	997.9
4	Oklahoma	980.8
5	West Virginia	960.4
6	Tennessee	959.9
7	Kentucky	958.4
8	Arkansas	930.2
9	Georgia	905.8
10	South Carolina	899.1
11	Nevada	892.3
12	North Carolina	876.0
13	Missouri	869.4
14	Indiana	858.7
15	Ohio	856.8
16	Delaware	830.5
17	Texas	828.8
18	Pennsylvania	814.8
19	Maine	813.2
20	Michigan	812.3
21	Kansas	806.8
22	Virginia	801.5
23	Wyoming	801.4
24	Montana	798.4
25	Illinois	798.2
26	Maryland	796.4
27	New Mexico	795.0
28	Oregon	773.7
29	Arizona	771.8
30	Idaho	766.4
31	South Dakota	757.0
32	Wisconsin	752.2
33	Alaska	750.8
34	Nebraska	749.5
35	Florida	749.4
36	Rhode Island	747.3
37	New Jersey	745.9
38	Colorado	742.8
39	Iowa	742.0
40	Washington	738.2
41	New Hampshire	732.3
42	Utah	731.3
43	Vermont	728.4
44	Massachusetts	721.9
45	New York	718.0
46	California	713.1
47	North Dakota	699.1
48	Connecticut	696.0
49	Minnesota	683.9
50	Hawaii	609.1

District of Columbia   971.4

Source: U.S. Department of Health and Human Services, National Center for Health Statistics
    "Deaths: Preliminary Data for 2005" (http://www.cdc.gov/nchs/deaths.htm)
*Preliminary data by state of residence. Age-adjusted rates eliminate the distorting effects of the aging of the population. Rates based on the year 2000 standard population.

Percent Change in Death Rate: 1996 to 2005

National Percent Change = 5.4% Decrease*

ALPHA ORDER			RANK ORDER		
RANK	STATE	PERCENT CHANGE	RANK	STATE	PERCENT CHANGE
7	Alabama	3.1	1	Alaska	12.3
1	Alaska	12.3	2	Louisiana	7.7
41	Arizona	(6.6)	3	Wyoming	7.6
32	Arkansas	(4.5)	4	Hawaii	6.7
39	California	(6.4)	4	New Mexico	6.7
37	Colorado	(5.6)	6	Montana	4.0
42	Connecticut	(7.0)	7	Alabama	3.1
16	Delaware	(1.3)	7	Maine	3.1
48	Florida	(9.9)	9	West Virginia	2.3
44	Georgia	(7.9)	10	Mississippi	1.8
4	Hawaii	6.7	11	Oklahoma	1.6
13	Idaho	0.8	12	Ohio	1.0
46	Illinois	(9.0)	13	Idaho	0.8
21	Indiana	(2.1)	14	Kentucky	0.4
30	Iowa	(4.0)	15	Tennessee	(0.6)
24	Kansas	(3.2)	16	Delaware	(1.3)
14	Kentucky	0.4	17	Michigan	(1.5)
2	Louisiana	7.7	18	South Dakota	(1.6)
7	Maine	3.1	19	Vermont	(1.7)
35	Maryland	(5.3)	20	South Carolina	(1.8)
43	Massachusetts	(7.3)	21	Indiana	(2.1)
17	Michigan	(1.5)	21	Utah	(2.1)
45	Minnesota	(8.4)	23	Pennsylvania	(2.8)
10	Mississippi	1.8	24	Kansas	(3.2)
38	Missouri	(6.3)	25	North Dakota	(3.4)
6	Montana	4.0	26	Rhode Island	(3.5)
47	Nebraska	(9.2)	27	Wisconsin	(3.6)
31	Nevada	(4.1)	28	New Hampshire	(3.7)
28	New Hampshire	(3.7)	29	Washington	(3.8)
48	New Jersey	(9.9)	30	Iowa	(4.0)
4	New Mexico	6.7	31	Nevada	(4.1)
50	New York	(12.4)	32	Arkansas	(4.5)
34	North Carolina	(5.0)	33	Virginia	(4.6)
25	North Dakota	(3.4)	34	North Carolina	(5.0)
12	Ohio	1.0	35	Maryland	(5.3)
11	Oklahoma	1.6	36	Oregon	(5.4)
36	Oregon	(5.4)	37	Colorado	(5.6)
23	Pennsylvania	(2.8)	38	Missouri	(6.3)
26	Rhode Island	(3.5)	39	California	(6.4)
20	South Carolina	(1.8)	40	Texas	(6.5)
18	South Dakota	(1.6)	41	Arizona	(6.6)
15	Tennessee	(0.6)	42	Connecticut	(7.0)
40	Texas	(6.5)	43	Massachusetts	(7.3)
21	Utah	(2.1)	44	Georgia	(7.9)
19	Vermont	(1.7)	45	Minnesota	(8.4)
33	Virginia	(4.6)	46	Illinois	(9.0)
29	Washington	(3.8)	47	Nebraska	(9.2)
9	West Virginia	2.3	48	Florida	(9.9)
27	Wisconsin	(3.6)	48	New Jersey	(9.9)
3	Wyoming	7.6	50	New York	(12.4)
				District of Columbia	(18.3)

Source: CQ Press using data from US Dept of Health & Human Services, National Center for Health Statistics
   "Deaths: Preliminary Data for 2005" (http://www.cdc.gov/nchs/deaths.htm)
   "Monthly Vital Statistics Report" (Vol. 47, No. 9, November 10, 1998)
*By state of residence. Not age-adjusted.

Deaths in 2004

National Total = 2,397,615 Deaths*

ALPHA ORDER

RANK	STATE	DEATHS	% of USA
17	Alabama	46,121	1.9%
50	Alaska	3,051	0.1%
21	Arizona	43,198	1.8%
31	Arkansas	27,528	1.1%
1	California	232,525	9.7%
29	Colorado	28,309	1.2%
28	Connecticut	29,314	1.2%
45	Delaware	7,143	0.3%
2	Florida	169,008	7.0%
11	Georgia	65,818	2.7%
43	Hawaii	9,030	0.4%
41	Idaho	10,028	0.4%
7	Illinois	102,670	4.3%
15	Indiana	54,211	2.3%
32	Iowa	26,897	1.1%
33	Kansas	23,818	1.0%
23	Kentucky	38,646	1.6%
22	Louisiana	42,215	1.8%
39	Maine	12,443	0.5%
20	Maryland	43,232	1.8%
14	Massachusetts	54,511	2.3%
8	Michigan	85,169	3.6%
25	Minnesota	37,034	1.5%
30	Mississippi	27,871	1.2%
16	Missouri	53,950	2.3%
44	Montana	8,094	0.3%
36	Nebraska	14,657	0.6%
35	Nevada	17,929	0.7%
40	New Hampshire	10,111	0.4%
10	New Jersey	71,371	3.0%
37	New Mexico	14,298	0.6%
4	New York	152,681	6.4%
9	North Carolina	72,384	3.0%
47	North Dakota	5,601	0.2%
6	Ohio	106,288	4.4%
26	Oklahoma	34,483	1.4%
27	Oregon	30,313	1.3%
5	Pennsylvania	127,640	5.3%
42	Rhode Island	9,769	0.4%
24	South Carolina	37,276	1.6%
46	South Dakota	6,833	0.3%
13	Tennessee	55,829	2.3%
3	Texas	152,870	6.4%
38	Utah	13,331	0.6%
48	Vermont	4,995	0.2%
12	Virginia	56,550	2.4%
19	Washington	44,770	1.9%
34	West Virginia	20,793	0.9%
18	Wisconsin	45,600	1.9%
49	Wyoming	3,955	0.2%

RANK ORDER

RANK	STATE	DEATHS	% of USA
1	California	232,525	9.7%
2	Florida	169,008	7.0%
3	Texas	152,870	6.4%
4	New York	152,681	6.4%
5	Pennsylvania	127,640	5.3%
6	Ohio	106,288	4.4%
7	Illinois	102,670	4.3%
8	Michigan	85,169	3.6%
9	North Carolina	72,384	3.0%
10	New Jersey	71,371	3.0%
11	Georgia	65,818	2.7%
12	Virginia	56,550	2.4%
13	Tennessee	55,829	2.3%
14	Massachusetts	54,511	2.3%
15	Indiana	54,211	2.3%
16	Missouri	53,950	2.3%
17	Alabama	46,121	1.9%
18	Wisconsin	45,600	1.9%
19	Washington	44,770	1.9%
20	Maryland	43,232	1.8%
21	Arizona	43,198	1.8%
22	Louisiana	42,215	1.8%
23	Kentucky	38,646	1.6%
24	South Carolina	37,276	1.6%
25	Minnesota	37,034	1.5%
26	Oklahoma	34,483	1.4%
27	Oregon	30,313	1.3%
28	Connecticut	29,314	1.2%
29	Colorado	28,309	1.2%
30	Mississippi	27,871	1.2%
31	Arkansas	27,528	1.1%
32	Iowa	26,897	1.1%
33	Kansas	23,818	1.0%
34	West Virginia	20,793	0.9%
35	Nevada	17,929	0.7%
36	Nebraska	14,657	0.6%
37	New Mexico	14,298	0.6%
38	Utah	13,331	0.6%
39	Maine	12,443	0.5%
40	New Hampshire	10,111	0.4%
41	Idaho	10,028	0.4%
42	Rhode Island	9,769	0.4%
43	Hawaii	9,030	0.4%
44	Montana	8,094	0.3%
45	Delaware	7,143	0.3%
46	South Dakota	6,833	0.3%
47	North Dakota	5,601	0.2%
48	Vermont	4,995	0.2%
49	Wyoming	3,955	0.2%
50	Alaska	3,051	0.1%
	District of Columbia	5,454	0.2%

Source: U.S. Department of Health and Human Services, National Center for Health Statistics
    "National Vital Statistics Reports" (Vol. 55, No. 19, August 21, 2007, http://www.cdc.gov/nchs/deaths.htm)
*Final data by state of residence.

Death Rate in 2004

National Rate = 816.5 Deaths per 100,000 Population*

ALPHA ORDER

RANK	STATE	RATE
3	Alabama	1,018.1
50	Alaska	465.5
39	Arizona	752.1
4	Arkansas	1,000.1
47	California	647.8
48	Colorado	615.2
28	Connecticut	836.7
22	Delaware	860.2
6	Florida	971.5
41	Georgia	745.4
45	Hawaii	715.1
44	Idaho	719.7
31	Illinois	807.6
21	Indiana	869.1
14	Iowa	910.4
20	Kansas	870.7
12	Kentucky	932.1
11	Louisiana	934.8
9	Maine	944.6
36	Maryland	777.8
23	Massachusetts	849.5
26	Michigan	842.2
42	Minnesota	726.0
7	Mississippi	960.1
10	Missouri	937.5
19	Montana	873.3
27	Nebraska	838.9
37	Nevada	767.9
35	New Hampshire	778.1
30	New Jersey	820.5
40	New Mexico	751.2
33	New York	794.1
24	North Carolina	847.5
18	North Dakota	882.9
13	Ohio	927.5
5	Oklahoma	978.6
25	Oregon	843.3
2	Pennsylvania	1,028.8
15	Rhode Island	904.0
16	South Carolina	887.9
17	South Dakota	886.4
8	Tennessee	946.1
46	Texas	679.7
49	Utah	558.0
32	Vermont	803.8
38	Virginia	758.1
43	Washington	721.7
1	West Virginia	1,145.4
29	Wisconsin	827.7
34	Wyoming	780.8

RANK ORDER

RANK	STATE	RATE
1	West Virginia	1,145.4
2	Pennsylvania	1,028.8
3	Alabama	1,018.1
4	Arkansas	1,000.1
5	Oklahoma	978.6
6	Florida	971.5
7	Mississippi	960.1
8	Tennessee	946.1
9	Maine	944.6
10	Missouri	937.5
11	Louisiana	934.8
12	Kentucky	932.1
13	Ohio	927.5
14	Iowa	910.4
15	Rhode Island	904.0
16	South Carolina	887.9
17	South Dakota	886.4
18	North Dakota	882.9
19	Montana	873.3
20	Kansas	870.7
21	Indiana	869.1
22	Delaware	860.2
23	Massachusetts	849.5
24	North Carolina	847.5
25	Oregon	843.3
26	Michigan	842.2
27	Nebraska	838.9
28	Connecticut	836.7
29	Wisconsin	827.7
30	New Jersey	820.5
31	Illinois	807.6
32	Vermont	803.8
33	New York	794.1
34	Wyoming	780.8
35	New Hampshire	778.1
36	Maryland	777.8
37	Nevada	767.9
38	Virginia	758.1
39	Arizona	752.1
40	New Mexico	751.2
41	Georgia	745.4
42	Minnesota	726.0
43	Washington	721.7
44	Idaho	719.7
45	Hawaii	715.1
46	Texas	679.7
47	California	647.8
48	Colorado	615.2
49	Utah	558.0
50	Alaska	465.5
	District of Columbia	985.3

Source: U.S. Department of Health and Human Services, National Center for Health Statistics
"National Vital Statistics Reports" (Vol. 55, No. 19, August 21, 2007, http://www.cdc.gov/nchs/deaths.htm)
*Final data by state of residence. Not age-adjusted.

Age-Adjusted Death Rate in 2004

National Rate = 800.8 Deaths per 100,000 Population*

<table>
<tr><td colspan="3">ALPHA ORDER</td><td colspan="3">RANK ORDER</td></tr>
<tr><td>RANK</td><td>STATE</td><td>RATE</td><td>RANK</td><td>STATE</td><td>RATE</td></tr>
<tr><td>2</td><td>Alabama</td><td>992.5</td><td>1</td><td>Mississippi</td><td>998.2</td></tr>
<tr><td>35</td><td>Alaska</td><td>750.5</td><td>2</td><td>Alabama</td><td>992.5</td></tr>
<tr><td>32</td><td>Arizona</td><td>758.1</td><td>3</td><td>Louisiana</td><td>986.1</td></tr>
<tr><td>8</td><td>Arkansas</td><td>924.7</td><td>4</td><td>West Virginia</td><td>966.0</td></tr>
<tr><td>46</td><td>California</td><td>715.6</td><td>5</td><td>Tennessee</td><td>954.0</td></tr>
<tr><td>42</td><td>Colorado</td><td>736.4</td><td>6</td><td>Oklahoma</td><td>947.7</td></tr>
<tr><td>47</td><td>Connecticut</td><td>706.2</td><td>7</td><td>Kentucky</td><td>935.1</td></tr>
<tr><td>17</td><td>Delaware</td><td>823.3</td><td>8</td><td>Arkansas</td><td>924.7</td></tr>
<tr><td>29</td><td>Florida</td><td>763.6</td><td>9</td><td>Georgia</td><td>924.6</td></tr>
<tr><td>9</td><td>Georgia</td><td>924.6</td><td>10</td><td>South Carolina</td><td>898.0</td></tr>
<tr><td>50</td><td>Hawaii</td><td>623.1</td><td>11</td><td>Nevada</td><td>880.5</td></tr>
<tr><td>33</td><td>Idaho</td><td>753.5</td><td>12</td><td>North Carolina</td><td>874.9</td></tr>
<tr><td>23</td><td>Illinois</td><td>801.4</td><td>13</td><td>Missouri</td><td>872.0</td></tr>
<tr><td>14</td><td>Indiana</td><td>849.4</td><td>14</td><td>Indiana</td><td>849.4</td></tr>
<tr><td>45</td><td>Iowa</td><td>729.4</td><td>15</td><td>Ohio</td><td>848.0</td></tr>
<tr><td>24</td><td>Kansas</td><td>793.5</td><td>16</td><td>Texas</td><td>835.6</td></tr>
<tr><td>7</td><td>Kentucky</td><td>935.1</td><td>17</td><td>Delaware</td><td>823.3</td></tr>
<tr><td>3</td><td>Louisiana</td><td>986.1</td><td>18</td><td>Pennsylvania</td><td>814.6</td></tr>
<tr><td>21</td><td>Maine</td><td>806.3</td><td>19</td><td>Michigan</td><td>812.6</td></tr>
<tr><td>22</td><td>Maryland</td><td>806.0</td><td>20</td><td>Virginia</td><td>809.2</td></tr>
<tr><td>40</td><td>Massachusetts</td><td>740.6</td><td>21</td><td>Maine</td><td>806.3</td></tr>
<tr><td>19</td><td>Michigan</td><td>812.6</td><td>22</td><td>Maryland</td><td>806.0</td></tr>
<tr><td>49</td><td>Minnesota</td><td>691.2</td><td>23</td><td>Illinois</td><td>801.4</td></tr>
<tr><td>1</td><td>Mississippi</td><td>998.2</td><td>24</td><td>Kansas</td><td>793.5</td></tr>
<tr><td>13</td><td>Missouri</td><td>872.0</td><td>25</td><td>Wyoming</td><td>789.7</td></tr>
<tr><td>27</td><td>Montana</td><td>778.6</td><td>26</td><td>New Mexico</td><td>778.9</td></tr>
<tr><td>37</td><td>Nebraska</td><td>746.9</td><td>27</td><td>Montana</td><td>778.6</td></tr>
<tr><td>11</td><td>Nevada</td><td>880.5</td><td>28</td><td>Oregon</td><td>777.7</td></tr>
<tr><td>30</td><td>New Hampshire</td><td>761.1</td><td>29</td><td>Florida</td><td>763.6</td></tr>
<tr><td>34</td><td>New Jersey</td><td>752.7</td><td>30</td><td>New Hampshire</td><td>761.1</td></tr>
<tr><td>26</td><td>New Mexico</td><td>778.9</td><td>31</td><td>Utah</td><td>760.4</td></tr>
<tr><td>43</td><td>New York</td><td>733.9</td><td>32</td><td>Arizona</td><td>758.1</td></tr>
<tr><td>12</td><td>North Carolina</td><td>874.9</td><td>33</td><td>Idaho</td><td>753.5</td></tr>
<tr><td>48</td><td>North Dakota</td><td>697.1</td><td>34</td><td>New Jersey</td><td>752.7</td></tr>
<tr><td>15</td><td>Ohio</td><td>848.0</td><td>35</td><td>Alaska</td><td>750.5</td></tr>
<tr><td>6</td><td>Oklahoma</td><td>947.7</td><td>36</td><td>Wisconsin</td><td>749.8</td></tr>
<tr><td>28</td><td>Oregon</td><td>777.7</td><td>37</td><td>Nebraska</td><td>746.9</td></tr>
<tr><td>18</td><td>Pennsylvania</td><td>814.6</td><td>38</td><td>South Dakota</td><td>746.4</td></tr>
<tr><td>39</td><td>Rhode Island</td><td>741.1</td><td>39</td><td>Rhode Island</td><td>741.1</td></tr>
<tr><td>10</td><td>South Carolina</td><td>898.0</td><td>40</td><td>Massachusetts</td><td>740.6</td></tr>
<tr><td>38</td><td>South Dakota</td><td>746.4</td><td>41</td><td>Washington</td><td>738.3</td></tr>
<tr><td>5</td><td>Tennessee</td><td>954.0</td><td>42</td><td>Colorado</td><td>736.4</td></tr>
<tr><td>16</td><td>Texas</td><td>835.6</td><td>43</td><td>New York</td><td>733.9</td></tr>
<tr><td>31</td><td>Utah</td><td>760.4</td><td>44</td><td>Vermont</td><td>731.0</td></tr>
<tr><td>44</td><td>Vermont</td><td>731.0</td><td>45</td><td>Iowa</td><td>729.4</td></tr>
<tr><td>20</td><td>Virginia</td><td>809.2</td><td>46</td><td>California</td><td>715.6</td></tr>
<tr><td>41</td><td>Washington</td><td>738.3</td><td>47</td><td>Connecticut</td><td>706.2</td></tr>
<tr><td>4</td><td>West Virginia</td><td>966.0</td><td>48</td><td>North Dakota</td><td>697.1</td></tr>
<tr><td>36</td><td>Wisconsin</td><td>749.8</td><td>49</td><td>Minnesota</td><td>691.2</td></tr>
<tr><td>25</td><td>Wyoming</td><td>789.7</td><td>50</td><td>Hawaii</td><td>623.1</td></tr>
<tr><td></td><td></td><td></td><td></td><td>District of Columbia</td><td>974.0</td></tr>
</table>

Source: U.S. Department of Health and Human Services, National Center for Health Statistics
   "National Vital Statistics Reports" (Vol. 55, No. 19, August 21, 2007, http://www.cdc.gov/nchs/deaths.htm)
*Final data by state of residence. Age-adjusted rates eliminate the distorting effects of the aging of the population. Rates based on the year 2000 standard population.

Infant Deaths in 2005

National Total = 28,440 Infant Deaths*

ALPHA ORDER

RANK	STATE	DEATHS	% of USA
18	Alabama	568	2.0%
47	Alaska	62	0.2%
14	Arizona	662	2.3%
29	Arkansas	309	1.1%
1	California	2,930	10.3%
23	Colorado	444	1.6%
32	Connecticut	243	0.9%
41	Delaware	105	0.4%
3	Florida	1,629	5.7%
7	Georgia	1,159	4.1%
40	Hawaii	116	0.4%
39	Idaho	141	0.5%
5	Illinois	1,328	4.7%
13	Indiana	698	2.5%
35	Iowa	210	0.7%
30	Kansas	294	1.0%
27	Kentucky	375	1.3%
15	Louisiana	613	2.2%
42	Maine	97	0.3%
19	Maryland	547	1.9%
26	Massachusetts	396	1.4%
10	Michigan	1,012	3.6%
28	Minnesota	362	1.3%
21	Mississippi	481	1.7%
17	Missouri	590	2.1%
45	Montana	81	0.3%
38	Nebraska	147	0.5%
34	Nevada	215	0.8%
46	New Hampshire	76	0.3%
16	New Jersey	595	2.1%
36	New Mexico	177	0.6%
4	New York	1,431	5.0%
8	North Carolina	1,083	3.8%
48	North Dakota	50	0.2%
6	Ohio	1,225	4.3%
25	Oklahoma	417	1.5%
31	Oregon	269	0.9%
9	Pennsylvania	1,061	3.7%
44	Rhode Island	82	0.3%
20	South Carolina	543	1.9%
43	South Dakota	83	0.3%
12	Tennessee	724	2.5%
2	Texas	2,537	8.9%
33	Utah	230	0.8%
50	Vermont	42	0.1%
11	Virginia	781	2.7%
24	Washington	421	1.5%
37	West Virginia	169	0.6%
22	Wisconsin	469	1.6%
49	Wyoming	49	0.2%

RANK ORDER

RANK	STATE	DEATHS	% of USA
1	California	2,930	10.3%
2	Texas	2,537	8.9%
3	Florida	1,629	5.7%
4	New York	1,431	5.0%
5	Illinois	1,328	4.7%
6	Ohio	1,225	4.3%
7	Georgia	1,159	4.1%
8	North Carolina	1,083	3.8%
9	Pennsylvania	1,061	3.7%
10	Michigan	1,012	3.6%
11	Virginia	781	2.7%
12	Tennessee	724	2.5%
13	Indiana	698	2.5%
14	Arizona	662	2.3%
15	Louisiana	613	2.2%
16	New Jersey	595	2.1%
17	Missouri	590	2.1%
18	Alabama	568	2.0%
19	Maryland	547	1.9%
20	South Carolina	543	1.9%
21	Mississippi	481	1.7%
22	Wisconsin	469	1.6%
23	Colorado	444	1.6%
24	Washington	421	1.5%
25	Oklahoma	417	1.5%
26	Massachusetts	396	1.4%
27	Kentucky	375	1.3%
28	Minnesota	362	1.3%
29	Arkansas	309	1.1%
30	Kansas	294	1.0%
31	Oregon	269	0.9%
32	Connecticut	243	0.9%
33	Utah	230	0.8%
34	Nevada	215	0.8%
35	Iowa	210	0.7%
36	New Mexico	177	0.6%
37	West Virginia	169	0.6%
38	Nebraska	147	0.5%
39	Idaho	141	0.5%
40	Hawaii	116	0.4%
41	Delaware	105	0.4%
42	Maine	97	0.3%
43	South Dakota	83	0.3%
44	Rhode Island	82	0.3%
45	Montana	81	0.3%
46	New Hampshire	76	0.3%
47	Alaska	62	0.2%
48	North Dakota	50	0.2%
49	Wyoming	49	0.2%
50	Vermont	42	0.1%
	District of Columbia	112	0.4%

Source: U.S. Department of Health and Human Services, National Center for Health Statistics
"National Vital Statistics Reports" (Vol. 56, No. 10, January 2008, http://www.cdc.gov/nchs/deaths.htm)
*Final data. Deaths under 1 year old by state of residence.

Infant Mortality Rate in 2005

National Rate = 6.9 Infant Deaths per 1,000 Live Births*

RANK	STATE	RATE
3	Alabama	9.4
37	Alaska	5.9
24	Arizona	6.9
13	Arkansas	7.9
43	California	5.3
33	Colorado	6.4
39	Connecticut	5.8
5	Delaware	9.0
21	Florida	7.2
9	Georgia	8.2
31	Hawaii	6.5
34	Idaho	6.1
17	Illinois	7.4
12	Indiana	8.0
43	Iowa	5.3
17	Kansas	7.4
28	Kentucky	6.6
2	Louisiana	10.1
24	Maine	6.9
19	Maryland	7.3
46	Massachusetts	5.2
13	Michigan	7.9
48	Minnesota	5.1
1	Mississippi	11.4
15	Missouri	7.5
23	Montana	7.0
42	Nebraska	5.6
39	Nevada	5.8
43	New Hampshire	5.3
46	New Jersey	5.2
34	New Mexico	6.1
39	New York	5.8
7	North Carolina	8.8
36	North Dakota	6.0
8	Ohio	8.3
10	Oklahoma	8.1
37	Oregon	5.9
19	Pennsylvania	7.3
31	Rhode Island	6.5
3	South Carolina	9.4
21	South Dakota	7.2
6	Tennessee	8.9
28	Texas	6.6
50	Utah	4.5
27	Vermont	6.7
15	Virginia	7.5
48	Washington	5.1
10	West Virginia	8.1
28	Wisconsin	6.6
26	Wyoming	6.8

RANK	STATE	RATE
1	Mississippi	11.4
2	Louisiana	10.1
3	Alabama	9.4
3	South Carolina	9.4
5	Delaware	9.0
6	Tennessee	8.9
7	North Carolina	8.8
8	Ohio	8.3
9	Georgia	8.2
10	Oklahoma	8.1
10	West Virginia	8.1
12	Indiana	8.0
13	Arkansas	7.9
13	Michigan	7.9
15	Missouri	7.5
15	Virginia	7.5
17	Illinois	7.4
17	Kansas	7.4
19	Maryland	7.3
19	Pennsylvania	7.3
21	Florida	7.2
21	South Dakota	7.2
23	Montana	7.0
24	Arizona	6.9
24	Maine	6.9
26	Wyoming	6.8
27	Vermont	6.7
28	Kentucky	6.6
28	Texas	6.6
28	Wisconsin	6.6
31	Hawaii	6.5
31	Rhode Island	6.5
33	Colorado	6.4
34	Idaho	6.1
34	New Mexico	6.1
36	North Dakota	6.0
37	Alaska	5.9
37	Oregon	5.9
39	Connecticut	5.8
39	Nevada	5.8
39	New York	5.8
42	Nebraska	5.6
43	California	5.3
43	Iowa	5.3
43	New Hampshire	5.3
46	Massachusetts	5.2
46	New Jersey	5.2
48	Minnesota	5.1
48	Washington	5.1
50	Utah	4.5

| | District of Columbia | 14.1 |

Source: U.S. Department of Health and Human Services, National Center for Health Statistics
   "National Vital Statistics Reports" (Vol. 56, No. 10, January 2008, http://www.cdc.gov/nchs/deaths.htm)
*Final data. Deaths under 1 year old by state of residence.

White Infant Deaths in 2005

National Total = 18,514 Deaths*

ALPHA ORDER

RANK	STATE	DEATHS	% of USA
22	Alabama	296	1.6%
50	Alaska	31	0.2%
10	Arizona	549	3.0%
31	Arkansas	196	1.1%
1	California	2,232	12.1%
16	Colorado	379	2.0%
33	Connecticut	167	0.9%
45	Delaware	49	0.3%
3	Florida	916	4.9%
11	Georgia	537	2.9%
49	Hawaii	32	0.2%
37	Idaho	134	0.7%
6	Illinois	791	4.3%
12	Indiana	526	2.8%
32	Iowa	185	1.0%
28	Kansas	233	1.3%
20	Kentucky	303	1.6%
26	Louisiana	249	1.3%
40	Maine	93	0.5%
29	Maryland	219	1.2%
21	Massachusetts	302	1.6%
9	Michigan	580	3.1%
24	Minnesota	261	1.4%
36	Mississippi	153	0.8%
15	Missouri	412	2.2%
42	Montana	66	0.4%
39	Nebraska	120	0.6%
34	Nevada	160	0.9%
41	New Hampshire	68	0.4%
17	New Jersey	332	1.8%
37	New Mexico	134	0.7%
4	New York	855	4.6%
8	North Carolina	584	3.2%
47	North Dakota	42	0.2%
5	Ohio	809	4.4%
23	Oklahoma	291	1.6%
27	Oregon	243	1.3%
7	Pennsylvania	716	3.9%
43	Rhode Island	62	0.3%
25	South Carolina	257	1.4%
44	South Dakota	56	0.3%
13	Tennessee	455	2.5%
2	Texas	1,872	10.1%
30	Utah	215	1.2%
48	Vermont	39	0.2%
14	Virginia	431	2.3%
19	Washington	327	1.8%
35	West Virginia	158	0.9%
18	Wisconsin	329	1.8%
46	Wyoming	47	0.3%

RANK ORDER

RANK	STATE	DEATHS	% of USA
1	California	2,232	12.1%
2	Texas	1,872	10.1%
3	Florida	916	4.9%
4	New York	855	4.6%
5	Ohio	809	4.4%
6	Illinois	791	4.3%
7	Pennsylvania	716	3.9%
8	North Carolina	584	3.2%
9	Michigan	580	3.1%
10	Arizona	549	3.0%
11	Georgia	537	2.9%
12	Indiana	526	2.8%
13	Tennessee	455	2.5%
14	Virginia	431	2.3%
15	Missouri	412	2.2%
16	Colorado	379	2.0%
17	New Jersey	332	1.8%
18	Wisconsin	329	1.8%
19	Washington	327	1.8%
20	Kentucky	303	1.6%
21	Massachusetts	302	1.6%
22	Alabama	296	1.6%
23	Oklahoma	291	1.6%
24	Minnesota	261	1.4%
25	South Carolina	257	1.4%
26	Louisiana	249	1.3%
27	Oregon	243	1.3%
28	Kansas	233	1.3%
29	Maryland	219	1.2%
30	Utah	215	1.2%
31	Arkansas	196	1.1%
32	Iowa	185	1.0%
33	Connecticut	167	0.9%
34	Nevada	160	0.9%
35	West Virginia	158	0.9%
36	Mississippi	153	0.8%
37	Idaho	134	0.7%
37	New Mexico	134	0.7%
39	Nebraska	120	0.6%
40	Maine	93	0.5%
41	New Hampshire	68	0.4%
42	Montana	66	0.4%
43	Rhode Island	62	0.3%
44	South Dakota	56	0.3%
45	Delaware	49	0.3%
46	Wyoming	47	0.3%
47	North Dakota	42	0.2%
48	Vermont	39	0.2%
49	Hawaii	32	0.2%
50	Alaska	31	0.2%
	District of Columbia	21	0.1%

Source: U.S. Department of Health and Human Services, National Center for Health Statistics
  "National Vital Statistics Reports" (Vol. 56, No. 10, January 2008, http://www.cdc.gov/nchs/deaths.htm)
*Final data. Deaths of infants under 1 year old, exclusive of fetal deaths. Based on race of the mother.

White Infant Mortality Rate in 2005

National Rate = 5.7 White Infant Deaths per 1,000 White Live Births*

<table>
<tr><td colspan="3">ALPHA ORDER</td><td colspan="3">RANK ORDER</td></tr>
<tr><td>RANK</td><td>STATE</td><td>RATE</td><td>RANK</td><td>STATE</td><td>RATE</td></tr>
<tr><td>4</td><td>Alabama</td><td>7.2</td><td>1</td><td>West Virginia</td><td>7.9</td></tr>
<tr><td>47</td><td>Alaska</td><td>4.7</td><td>2</td><td>Tennessee</td><td>7.4</td></tr>
<tr><td>12</td><td>Arizona</td><td>6.6</td><td>3</td><td>Oklahoma</td><td>7.3</td></tr>
<tr><td>16</td><td>Arkansas</td><td>6.4</td><td>4</td><td>Alabama</td><td>7.2</td></tr>
<tr><td>41</td><td>California</td><td>5.0</td><td>5</td><td>South Carolina</td><td>7.1</td></tr>
<tr><td>22</td><td>Colorado</td><td>6.0</td><td>6</td><td>Indiana</td><td>7.0</td></tr>
<tr><td>44</td><td>Connecticut</td><td>4.9</td><td>6</td><td>Louisiana</td><td>7.0</td></tr>
<tr><td>22</td><td>Delaware</td><td>6.0</td><td>8</td><td>Maine</td><td>6.9</td></tr>
<tr><td>32</td><td>Florida</td><td>5.7</td><td>8</td><td>Wyoming</td><td>6.9</td></tr>
<tr><td>26</td><td>Georgia</td><td>5.9</td><td>10</td><td>Montana</td><td>6.7</td></tr>
<tr><td>19</td><td>Hawaii</td><td>6.3</td><td>10</td><td>Ohio</td><td>6.7</td></tr>
<tr><td>21</td><td>Idaho</td><td>6.1</td><td>12</td><td>Arizona</td><td>6.6</td></tr>
<tr><td>32</td><td>Illinois</td><td>5.7</td><td>12</td><td>Kansas</td><td>6.6</td></tr>
<tr><td>6</td><td>Indiana</td><td>7.0</td><td>12</td><td>Mississippi</td><td>6.6</td></tr>
<tr><td>39</td><td>Iowa</td><td>5.1</td><td>15</td><td>North Carolina</td><td>6.5</td></tr>
<tr><td>12</td><td>Kansas</td><td>6.6</td><td>16</td><td>Arkansas</td><td>6.4</td></tr>
<tr><td>22</td><td>Kentucky</td><td>6.0</td><td>16</td><td>Missouri</td><td>6.4</td></tr>
<tr><td>6</td><td>Louisiana</td><td>7.0</td><td>16</td><td>Vermont</td><td>6.4</td></tr>
<tr><td>8</td><td>Maine</td><td>6.9</td><td>19</td><td>Hawaii</td><td>6.3</td></tr>
<tr><td>39</td><td>Maryland</td><td>5.1</td><td>20</td><td>Pennsylvania</td><td>6.2</td></tr>
<tr><td>45</td><td>Massachusetts</td><td>4.8</td><td>21</td><td>Idaho</td><td>6.1</td></tr>
<tr><td>28</td><td>Michigan</td><td>5.8</td><td>22</td><td>Colorado</td><td>6.0</td></tr>
<tr><td>48</td><td>Minnesota</td><td>4.5</td><td>22</td><td>Delaware</td><td>6.0</td></tr>
<tr><td>12</td><td>Mississippi</td><td>6.6</td><td>22</td><td>Kentucky</td><td>6.0</td></tr>
<tr><td>16</td><td>Missouri</td><td>6.4</td><td>22</td><td>South Dakota</td><td>6.0</td></tr>
<tr><td>10</td><td>Montana</td><td>6.7</td><td>26</td><td>Georgia</td><td>5.9</td></tr>
<tr><td>37</td><td>Nebraska</td><td>5.2</td><td>26</td><td>Oregon</td><td>5.9</td></tr>
<tr><td>37</td><td>Nevada</td><td>5.2</td><td>28</td><td>Michigan</td><td>5.8</td></tr>
<tr><td>41</td><td>New Hampshire</td><td>5.0</td><td>28</td><td>North Dakota</td><td>5.8</td></tr>
<tr><td>50</td><td>New Jersey</td><td>4.0</td><td>28</td><td>Rhode Island</td><td>5.8</td></tr>
<tr><td>35</td><td>New Mexico</td><td>5.6</td><td>28</td><td>Virginia</td><td>5.8</td></tr>
<tr><td>41</td><td>New York</td><td>5.0</td><td>32</td><td>Florida</td><td>5.7</td></tr>
<tr><td>15</td><td>North Carolina</td><td>6.5</td><td>32</td><td>Illinois</td><td>5.7</td></tr>
<tr><td>28</td><td>North Dakota</td><td>5.8</td><td>32</td><td>Texas</td><td>5.7</td></tr>
<tr><td>10</td><td>Ohio</td><td>6.7</td><td>35</td><td>New Mexico</td><td>5.6</td></tr>
<tr><td>3</td><td>Oklahoma</td><td>7.3</td><td>36</td><td>Wisconsin</td><td>5.4</td></tr>
<tr><td>26</td><td>Oregon</td><td>5.9</td><td>37</td><td>Nebraska</td><td>5.2</td></tr>
<tr><td>20</td><td>Pennsylvania</td><td>6.2</td><td>37</td><td>Nevada</td><td>5.2</td></tr>
<tr><td>28</td><td>Rhode Island</td><td>5.8</td><td>39</td><td>Iowa</td><td>5.1</td></tr>
<tr><td>5</td><td>South Carolina</td><td>7.1</td><td>39</td><td>Maryland</td><td>5.1</td></tr>
<tr><td>22</td><td>South Dakota</td><td>6.0</td><td>41</td><td>California</td><td>5.0</td></tr>
<tr><td>2</td><td>Tennessee</td><td>7.4</td><td>41</td><td>New Hampshire</td><td>5.0</td></tr>
<tr><td>32</td><td>Texas</td><td>5.7</td><td>41</td><td>New York</td><td>5.0</td></tr>
<tr><td>49</td><td>Utah</td><td>4.4</td><td>44</td><td>Connecticut</td><td>4.9</td></tr>
<tr><td>16</td><td>Vermont</td><td>6.4</td><td>45</td><td>Massachusetts</td><td>4.8</td></tr>
<tr><td>28</td><td>Virginia</td><td>5.8</td><td>45</td><td>Washington</td><td>4.8</td></tr>
<tr><td>45</td><td>Washington</td><td>4.8</td><td>47</td><td>Alaska</td><td>4.7</td></tr>
<tr><td>1</td><td>West Virginia</td><td>7.9</td><td>48</td><td>Minnesota</td><td>4.5</td></tr>
<tr><td>36</td><td>Wisconsin</td><td>5.4</td><td>49</td><td>Utah</td><td>4.4</td></tr>
<tr><td>8</td><td>Wyoming</td><td>6.9</td><td>50</td><td>New Jersey</td><td>4.0</td></tr>
<tr><td></td><td></td><td></td><td></td><td>District of Columbia</td><td>8.8</td></tr>
</table>

Source: U.S. Department of Health and Human Services, National Center for Health Statistics
   "National Vital Statistics Reports" (Vol. 56, No. 10, January 2008, http://www.cdc.gov/nchs/deaths.htm)
*Final data. Deaths of infants under 1 year old, exclusive of fetal deaths. Based on race of the mother.

Black Infant Deaths in 2005

National Total = 8,695 Deaths*

ALPHA ORDER				RANK ORDER			
RANK	STATE	DEATHS	% of USA	RANK	STATE	DEATHS	% of USA
16	Alabama	266	3.1%	1	Florida	679	7.8%
41	Alaska	4	0.0%	2	Texas	620	7.1%
31	Arizona	46	0.5%	3	Georgia	580	6.7%
22	Arkansas	111	1.3%	4	New York	507	5.8%
7	California	440	5.1%	5	Illinois	502	5.8%
30	Colorado	51	0.6%	6	North Carolina	465	5.3%
26	Connecticut	71	0.8%	7	California	440	5.1%
28	Delaware	55	0.6%	8	Michigan	411	4.7%
1	Florida	679	7.8%	9	Ohio	408	4.7%
3	Georgia	580	6.7%	10	Louisiana	359	4.1%
40	Hawaii	5	0.1%	11	Pennsylvania	329	3.8%
45	Idaho	1	0.0%	12	Virginia	323	3.7%
5	Illinois	502	5.8%	13	Mississippi	321	3.7%
20	Indiana	168	1.9%	14	Maryland	308	3.5%
34	Iowa	21	0.2%	15	South Carolina	281	3.2%
28	Kansas	55	0.6%	16	Alabama	266	3.1%
27	Kentucky	67	0.8%	17	Tennessee	258	3.0%
10	Louisiana	359	4.1%	18	New Jersey	220	2.5%
43	Maine	2	0.0%	19	Missouri	171	2.0%
14	Maryland	308	3.5%	20	Indiana	168	1.9%
25	Massachusetts	72	0.8%	21	Wisconsin	120	1.4%
8	Michigan	411	4.7%	22	Arkansas	111	1.3%
24	Minnesota	73	0.8%	23	Oklahoma	74	0.9%
13	Mississippi	321	3.7%	24	Minnesota	73	0.8%
19	Missouri	171	2.0%	25	Massachusetts	72	0.8%
48	Montana	0	0.0%	26	Connecticut	71	0.8%
35	Nebraska	18	0.2%	27	Kentucky	67	0.8%
33	Nevada	44	0.5%	28	Delaware	55	0.6%
42	New Hampshire	3	0.0%	28	Kansas	55	0.6%
18	New Jersey	220	2.5%	30	Colorado	51	0.6%
39	New Mexico	9	0.1%	31	Arizona	46	0.5%
4	New York	507	5.8%	31	Washington	46	0.5%
6	North Carolina	465	5.3%	33	Nevada	44	0.5%
48	North Dakota	0	0.0%	34	Iowa	21	0.2%
9	Ohio	408	4.7%	35	Nebraska	18	0.2%
23	Oklahoma	74	0.9%	36	Rhode Island	15	0.2%
38	Oregon	10	0.1%	37	West Virginia	11	0.1%
11	Pennsylvania	329	3.8%	38	Oregon	10	0.1%
36	Rhode Island	15	0.2%	39	New Mexico	9	0.1%
15	South Carolina	281	3.2%	40	Hawaii	5	0.1%
45	South Dakota	1	0.0%	41	Alaska	4	0.0%
17	Tennessee	258	3.0%	42	New Hampshire	3	0.0%
2	Texas	620	7.1%	43	Maine	2	0.0%
45	Utah	1	0.0%	43	Vermont	2	0.0%
43	Vermont	2	0.0%	45	Idaho	1	0.0%
12	Virginia	323	3.7%	45	South Dakota	1	0.0%
31	Washington	46	0.5%	45	Utah	1	0.0%
37	West Virginia	11	0.1%	48	Montana	0	0.0%
21	Wisconsin	120	1.4%	48	North Dakota	0	0.0%
48	Wyoming	0	0.0%	48	Wyoming	0	0.0%
					District of Columbia	91	1.0%

Source: U.S. Department of Health and Human Services, National Center for Health Statistics
"National Vital Statistics Reports" (Vol. 56, No. 10, January 2008, http://www.cdc.gov/nchs/deaths.htm)
*Final data. Deaths of infants under 1 year old, exclusive of fetal deaths. Based on race of the mother.

Black Infant Mortality Rate in 2005

National Rate = 13.7 Black Infant Deaths per 1,000 Black Live Births*

ALPHA ORDER

RANK ORDER

RANK	STATE	RATE		RANK	STATE	RATE
14	Alabama	14.7		1	Delaware	18.9
NA	Alaska**	NA		2	Michigan	18.3
26	Arizona	12.6		3	Wisconsin	17.7
12	Arkansas	14.9		4	Kansas	17.6
23	California	13.6		5	Mississippi	17.2
10	Colorado	16.3		6	Indiana	17.0
24	Connecticut	13.5		7	Ohio	16.9
1	Delaware	18.9		8	Illinois	16.4
28	Florida	12.0		8	North Carolina	16.4
26	Georgia	12.6		10	Colorado	16.3
NA	Hawaii**	NA		11	Oklahoma	15.4
NA	Idaho**	NA		12	Arkansas	14.9
8	Illinois	16.4		12	Louisiana	14.9
6	Indiana	17.0		14	Alabama	14.7
20	Iowa	13.9		15	Missouri	14.6
4	Kansas	17.6		16	Pennsylvania	14.1
25	Kentucky	13.2		16	Texas	14.1
12	Louisiana	14.9		16	Virginia	14.1
NA	Maine**	NA		19	Tennessee	14.0
29	Maryland	11.6		20	Iowa	13.9
34	Massachusetts	8.2		21	South Carolina	13.8
2	Michigan	18.3		22	Nevada	13.7
32	Minnesota	10.6		23	California	13.6
5	Mississippi	17.2		24	Connecticut	13.5
15	Missouri	14.6		25	Kentucky	13.2
NA	Montana**	NA		26	Arizona	12.6
NA	Nebraska**	NA		26	Georgia	12.6
22	Nevada	13.7		28	Florida	12.0
NA	New Hampshire**	NA		29	Maryland	11.6
30	New Jersey	11.0		30	New Jersey	11.0
NA	New Mexico**	NA		31	Washington	10.9
33	New York	9.3		32	Minnesota	10.6
8	North Carolina	16.4		33	New York	9.3
NA	North Dakota**	NA		34	Massachusetts	8.2
7	Ohio	16.9		NA	Alaska**	NA
11	Oklahoma	15.4		NA	Hawaii**	NA
NA	Oregon**	NA		NA	Idaho**	NA
16	Pennsylvania	14.1		NA	Maine**	NA
NA	Rhode Island**	NA		NA	Montana**	NA
21	South Carolina	13.8		NA	Nebraska**	NA
NA	South Dakota**	NA		NA	New Hampshire**	NA
19	Tennessee	14.0		NA	New Mexico**	NA
16	Texas	14.1		NA	North Dakota**	NA
NA	Utah**	NA		NA	Oregon**	NA
NA	Vermont**	NA		NA	Rhode Island**	NA
16	Virginia	14.1		NA	South Dakota**	NA
31	Washington	10.9		NA	Utah**	NA
NA	West Virginia**	NA		NA	Vermont**	NA
3	Wisconsin	17.7		NA	West Virginia**	NA
NA	Wyoming**	NA		NA	Wyoming**	NA
					District of Columbia	17.0

Source: U.S. Department of Health and Human Services, National Center for Health Statistics
    "National Vital Statistics Reports" (Vol. 56, No. 10, January 2008, http://www.cdc.gov/nchs/deaths.htm)
*Final data. Deaths of infants under 1 year old, exclusive of fetal deaths. Based on race of the mother.
**Not available, fewer than 20 black infant deaths.

Neonatal Deaths in 2005

National Total = 18,770 Deaths*

ALPHA ORDER				RANK ORDER			
RANK	STATE	DEATHS	% of USA	RANK	STATE	DEATHS	% of USA
19	Alabama	347	1.8%	1	California	1,991	10.6%
49	Alaska	31	0.2%	2	Texas	1,595	8.5%
14	Arizona	433	2.3%	3	Florida	1,024	5.5%
30	Arkansas	188	1.0%	4	New York	992	5.3%
1	California	1,991	10.6%	5	Illinois	891	4.7%
21	Colorado	329	1.8%	6	Ohio	828	4.4%
31	Connecticut	175	0.9%	7	Georgia	770	4.1%
40	Delaware	78	0.4%	8	North Carolina	755	4.0%
3	Florida	1,024	5.5%	9	Pennsylvania	751	4.0%
7	Georgia	770	4.1%	10	Michigan	699	3.7%
41	Hawaii	75	0.4%	11	Virginia	537	2.9%
38	Idaho	93	0.5%	12	Indiana	476	2.5%
5	Illinois	891	4.7%	13	Tennessee	462	2.5%
12	Indiana	476	2.5%	14	Arizona	433	2.3%
34	Iowa	136	0.7%	15	New Jersey	395	2.1%
29	Kansas	195	1.0%	16	Maryland	394	2.1%
28	Kentucky	226	1.2%	17	Missouri	371	2.0%
18	Louisiana	351	1.9%	18	Louisiana	351	1.9%
42	Maine	68	0.4%	19	Alabama	347	1.8%
16	Maryland	394	2.1%	20	South Carolina	336	1.8%
23	Massachusetts	286	1.5%	21	Colorado	329	1.8%
10	Michigan	699	3.7%	22	Wisconsin	318	1.7%
27	Minnesota	231	1.2%	23	Massachusetts	286	1.5%
24	Mississippi	284	1.5%	24	Mississippi	284	1.5%
17	Missouri	371	2.0%	25	Washington	254	1.4%
46	Montana	48	0.3%	26	Oklahoma	248	1.3%
39	Nebraska	86	0.5%	27	Minnesota	231	1.2%
35	Nevada	130	0.7%	28	Kentucky	226	1.2%
44	New Hampshire	62	0.3%	29	Kansas	195	1.0%
15	New Jersey	395	2.1%	30	Arkansas	188	1.0%
37	New Mexico	105	0.6%	31	Connecticut	175	0.9%
4	New York	992	5.3%	32	Oregon	174	0.9%
8	North Carolina	755	4.0%	33	Utah	155	0.8%
47	North Dakota	36	0.2%	34	Iowa	136	0.7%
6	Ohio	828	4.4%	35	Nevada	130	0.7%
26	Oklahoma	248	1.3%	36	West Virginia	106	0.6%
32	Oregon	174	0.9%	37	New Mexico	105	0.6%
9	Pennsylvania	751	4.0%	38	Idaho	93	0.5%
43	Rhode Island	64	0.3%	39	Nebraska	86	0.5%
20	South Carolina	336	1.8%	40	Delaware	78	0.4%
45	South Dakota	52	0.3%	41	Hawaii	75	0.4%
13	Tennessee	462	2.5%	42	Maine	68	0.4%
2	Texas	1,595	8.5%	43	Rhode Island	64	0.3%
33	Utah	155	0.8%	44	New Hampshire	62	0.3%
50	Vermont	26	0.1%	45	South Dakota	52	0.3%
11	Virginia	537	2.9%	46	Montana	48	0.3%
25	Washington	254	1.4%	47	North Dakota	36	0.2%
36	West Virginia	106	0.6%	48	Wyoming	34	0.2%
22	Wisconsin	318	1.7%	49	Alaska	31	0.2%
48	Wyoming	34	0.2%	50	Vermont	26	0.1%
					District of Columbia	79	0.4%

Source: U.S. Department of Health and Human Services, National Center for Health Statistics
   "National Vital Statistics Reports" (Vol. 56, No. 10, January 2008, http://www.cdc.gov/nchs/deaths.htm)
*Final data. Deaths of infants under 28 days, exclusive of fetal deaths.

Neonatal Death Rate in 2005

National Rate = 4.5 Deaths per 1,000 Live Births*

ALPHA ORDER

RANK	STATE	RATE
6	Alabama	5.7
49	Alaska	3.0
25	Arizona	4.5
19	Arkansas	4.8
41	California	3.6
19	Colorado	4.8
31	Connecticut	4.2
1	Delaware	6.7
25	Florida	4.5
11	Georgia	5.4
31	Hawaii	4.2
36	Idaho	4.0
16	Illinois	5.0
9	Indiana	5.5
43	Iowa	3.5
18	Kansas	4.9
36	Kentucky	4.0
4	Louisiana	5.8
19	Maine	4.8
12	Maryland	5.3
40	Massachusetts	3.7
9	Michigan	5.5
46	Minnesota	3.3
1	Mississippi	6.7
23	Missouri	4.7
33	Montana	4.1
46	Nebraska	3.3
43	Nevada	3.5
29	New Hampshire	4.3
43	New Jersey	3.5
41	New Mexico	3.6
36	New York	4.0
3	North Carolina	6.1
29	North Dakota	4.3
8	Ohio	5.6
19	Oklahoma	4.8
39	Oregon	3.8
13	Pennsylvania	5.2
16	Rhode Island	5.0
4	South Carolina	5.8
25	South Dakota	4.5
6	Tennessee	5.7
33	Texas	4.1
49	Utah	3.0
33	Vermont	4.1
14	Virginia	5.1
48	Washington	3.1
14	West Virginia	5.1
25	Wisconsin	4.5
23	Wyoming	4.7

RANK ORDER

RANK	STATE	RATE
1	Delaware	6.7
1	Mississippi	6.7
3	North Carolina	6.1
4	Louisiana	5.8
4	South Carolina	5.8
6	Alabama	5.7
6	Tennessee	5.7
8	Ohio	5.6
9	Indiana	5.5
9	Michigan	5.5
11	Georgia	5.4
12	Maryland	5.3
13	Pennsylvania	5.2
14	Virginia	5.1
14	West Virginia	5.1
16	Illinois	5.0
16	Rhode Island	5.0
18	Kansas	4.9
19	Arkansas	4.8
19	Colorado	4.8
19	Maine	4.8
19	Oklahoma	4.8
23	Missouri	4.7
23	Wyoming	4.7
25	Arizona	4.5
25	Florida	4.5
25	South Dakota	4.5
25	Wisconsin	4.5
29	New Hampshire	4.3
29	North Dakota	4.3
31	Connecticut	4.2
31	Hawaii	4.2
33	Montana	4.1
33	Texas	4.1
33	Vermont	4.1
36	Idaho	4.0
36	Kentucky	4.0
36	New York	4.0
39	Oregon	3.8
40	Massachusetts	3.7
41	California	3.6
41	New Mexico	3.6
43	Iowa	3.5
43	Nevada	3.5
43	New Jersey	3.5
46	Minnesota	3.3
46	Nebraska	3.3
48	Washington	3.1
49	Alaska	3.0
49	Utah	3.0
	District of Columbia	9.9

Source: U.S. Department of Health and Human Services, National Center for Health Statistics
"National Vital Statistics Reports" (Vol. 56, No. 10, January 2008, http://www.cdc.gov/nchs/deaths.htm)
*Final data. Deaths of infants under 28 days, exclusive of fetal deaths.

White Neonatal Deaths in 2005

National Total = 12,239 Deaths*

ALPHA ORDER

RANK ORDER

RANK	STATE	DEATHS	% of USA
21	Alabama	189	1.5%
50	Alaska	17	0.1%
10	Arizona	376	3.1%
33	Arkansas	114	0.9%
1	California	1,545	12.6%
14	Colorado	284	2.3%
31	Connecticut	129	1.1%
45	Delaware	37	0.3%
4	Florida	568	4.6%
12	Georgia	335	2.7%
49	Hawaii	20	0.2%
36	Idaho	88	0.7%
6	Illinois	537	4.4%
11	Indiana	349	2.9%
32	Iowa	118	1.0%
27	Kansas	156	1.3%
22	Kentucky	185	1.5%
29	Louisiana	145	1.2%
40	Maine	64	0.5%
28	Maryland	151	1.2%
19	Massachusetts	219	1.8%
8	Michigan	389	3.2%
24	Minnesota	165	1.3%
38	Mississippi	71	0.6%
16	Missouri	259	2.1%
44	Montana	41	0.3%
38	Nebraska	71	0.6%
35	Nevada	100	0.8%
41	New Hampshire	56	0.5%
17	New Jersey	229	1.9%
36	New Mexico	88	0.7%
3	New York	611	5.0%
9	North Carolina	387	3.2%
47	North Dakota	29	0.2%
5	Ohio	539	4.4%
23	Oklahoma	174	1.4%
25	Oregon	158	1.3%
7	Pennsylvania	511	4.2%
42	Rhode Island	50	0.4%
25	South Carolina	158	1.3%
43	South Dakota	42	0.3%
15	Tennessee	265	2.2%
2	Texas	1,180	9.6%
29	Utah	145	1.2%
48	Vermont	24	0.2%
13	Virginia	298	2.4%
20	Washington	197	1.6%
34	West Virginia	101	0.8%
18	Wisconsin	228	1.9%
46	Wyoming	32	0.3%

RANK	STATE	DEATHS	% of USA
1	California	1,545	12.6%
2	Texas	1,180	9.6%
3	New York	611	5.0%
4	Florida	568	4.6%
5	Ohio	539	4.4%
6	Illinois	537	4.4%
7	Pennsylvania	511	4.2%
8	Michigan	389	3.2%
9	North Carolina	387	3.2%
10	Arizona	376	3.1%
11	Indiana	349	2.9%
12	Georgia	335	2.7%
13	Virginia	298	2.4%
14	Colorado	284	2.3%
15	Tennessee	265	2.2%
16	Missouri	259	2.1%
17	New Jersey	229	1.9%
18	Wisconsin	228	1.9%
19	Massachusetts	219	1.8%
20	Washington	197	1.6%
21	Alabama	189	1.5%
22	Kentucky	185	1.5%
23	Oklahoma	174	1.4%
24	Minnesota	165	1.3%
25	Oregon	158	1.3%
25	South Carolina	158	1.3%
27	Kansas	156	1.3%
28	Maryland	151	1.2%
29	Louisiana	145	1.2%
29	Utah	145	1.2%
31	Connecticut	129	1.1%
32	Iowa	118	1.0%
33	Arkansas	114	0.9%
34	West Virginia	101	0.8%
35	Nevada	100	0.8%
36	Idaho	88	0.7%
36	New Mexico	88	0.7%
38	Mississippi	71	0.6%
38	Nebraska	71	0.6%
40	Maine	64	0.5%
41	New Hampshire	56	0.5%
42	Rhode Island	50	0.4%
43	South Dakota	42	0.3%
44	Montana	41	0.3%
45	Delaware	37	0.3%
46	Wyoming	32	0.3%
47	North Dakota	29	0.2%
48	Vermont	24	0.2%
49	Hawaii	20	0.2%
50	Alaska	17	0.1%
	District of Columbia	15	0.1%

Source: U.S. Department of Health and Human Services, National Center for Health Statistics
    "National Vital Statistics Reports" (Vol. 56, No. 10, January 2008, http://www.cdc.gov/nchs/deaths.htm)
*Final data. Deaths of infants under 28 days, exclusive of fetal deaths. Based on race of the mother.

White Neonatal Death Rate in 2005

National Rate = 3.8 White Neonatal Deaths per 1,000 White Live Births*

ALPHA ORDER

RANK	STATE	RATE
5	Alabama	4.6
NA	Alaska**	NA
7	Arizona	4.5
32	Arkansas	3.7
38	California	3.5
7	Colorado	4.5
29	Connecticut	3.8
7	Delaware	4.5
38	Florida	3.5
32	Georgia	3.7
25	Hawaii	3.9
21	Idaho	4.0
25	Illinois	3.9
5	Indiana	4.6
43	Iowa	3.2
12	Kansas	4.4
32	Kentucky	3.7
18	Louisiana	4.1
2	Maine	4.7
38	Maryland	3.5
38	Massachusetts	3.5
25	Michigan	3.9
47	Minnesota	2.9
44	Mississippi	3.1
21	Missouri	4.0
18	Montana	4.1
44	Nebraska	3.1
42	Nevada	3.3
18	New Hampshire	4.1
49	New Jersey	2.8
32	New Mexico	3.7
36	New York	3.6
16	North Carolina	4.3
21	North Dakota	4.0
7	Ohio	4.5
12	Oklahoma	4.4
29	Oregon	3.8
12	Pennsylvania	4.4
2	Rhode Island	4.7
12	South Carolina	4.4
7	South Dakota	4.5
16	Tennessee	4.3
36	Texas	3.6
46	Utah	3.0
25	Vermont	3.9
21	Virginia	4.0
47	Washington	2.9
1	West Virginia	5.1
29	Wisconsin	3.8
2	Wyoming	4.7

RANK ORDER

RANK	STATE	RATE
1	West Virginia	5.1
2	Maine	4.7
2	Rhode Island	4.7
2	Wyoming	4.7
5	Alabama	4.6
5	Indiana	4.6
7	Arizona	4.5
7	Colorado	4.5
7	Delaware	4.5
7	Ohio	4.5
7	South Dakota	4.5
12	Kansas	4.4
12	Oklahoma	4.4
12	Pennsylvania	4.4
12	South Carolina	4.4
16	North Carolina	4.3
16	Tennessee	4.3
18	Louisiana	4.1
18	Montana	4.1
18	New Hampshire	4.1
21	Idaho	4.0
21	Missouri	4.0
21	North Dakota	4.0
21	Virginia	4.0
25	Hawaii	3.9
25	Illinois	3.9
25	Michigan	3.9
25	Vermont	3.9
29	Connecticut	3.8
29	Oregon	3.8
29	Wisconsin	3.8
32	Arkansas	3.7
32	Georgia	3.7
32	Kentucky	3.7
32	New Mexico	3.7
36	New York	3.6
36	Texas	3.6
38	California	3.5
38	Florida	3.5
38	Maryland	3.5
38	Massachusetts	3.5
42	Nevada	3.3
43	Iowa	3.2
44	Mississippi	3.1
44	Nebraska	3.1
46	Utah	3.0
47	Minnesota	2.9
47	Washington	2.9
49	New Jersey	2.8
NA	Alaska**	NA
	District of Columbia**	NA

Source: U.S. Department of Health and Human Services, National Center for Health Statistics
"National Vital Statistics Reports" (Vol. 56, No. 10, January 2008, http://www.cdc.gov/nchs/deaths.htm)
*Final data. Deaths of infants under 28 days, exclusive of fetal deaths. Based on race of the mother.
**Not available. Fewer than 20 white neonatal deaths.

Black Neonatal Deaths in 2005

National Total = 5,740 Deaths*

ALPHA ORDER

RANK	STATE	DEATHS	% of USA
17	Alabama	155	2.7%
41	Alaska	2	0.0%
33	Arizona	21	0.4%
22	Arkansas	72	1.3%
9	California	269	4.7%
29	Colorado	38	0.7%
26	Connecticut	43	0.7%
27	Delaware	40	0.7%
1	Florida	436	7.6%
2	Georgia	406	7.1%
40	Hawaii	3	0.1%
47	Idaho	0	0.0%
5	Illinois	330	5.7%
19	Indiana	123	2.1%
34	Iowa	15	0.3%
30	Kansas	33	0.6%
28	Kentucky	39	0.7%
14	Louisiana	202	3.5%
41	Maine	2	0.0%
10	Maryland	227	4.0%
23	Massachusetts	54	0.9%
7	Michigan	294	5.1%
24	Minnesota	52	0.9%
13	Mississippi	209	3.6%
20	Missouri	109	1.9%
47	Montana	0	0.0%
36	Nebraska	9	0.2%
32	Nevada	24	0.4%
43	New Hampshire	1	0.0%
18	New Jersey	139	2.4%
38	New Mexico	5	0.1%
6	New York	324	5.6%
4	North Carolina	341	5.9%
47	North Dakota	0	0.0%
8	Ohio	284	4.9%
25	Oklahoma	47	0.8%
37	Oregon	6	0.1%
10	Pennsylvania	227	4.0%
35	Rhode Island	10	0.2%
16	South Carolina	175	3.0%
43	South Dakota	1	0.0%
15	Tennessee	190	3.3%
3	Texas	389	6.8%
43	Utah	1	0.0%
43	Vermont	1	0.0%
12	Virginia	219	3.8%
31	Washington	26	0.5%
38	West Virginia	5	0.1%
21	Wisconsin	78	1.4%
47	Wyoming	0	0.0%

RANK ORDER

RANK	STATE	DEATHS	% of USA
1	Florida	436	7.6%
2	Georgia	406	7.1%
3	Texas	389	6.8%
4	North Carolina	341	5.9%
5	Illinois	330	5.7%
6	New York	324	5.6%
7	Michigan	294	5.1%
8	Ohio	284	4.9%
9	California	269	4.7%
10	Maryland	227	4.0%
10	Pennsylvania	227	4.0%
12	Virginia	219	3.8%
13	Mississippi	209	3.6%
14	Louisiana	202	3.5%
15	Tennessee	190	3.3%
16	South Carolina	175	3.0%
17	Alabama	155	2.7%
18	New Jersey	139	2.4%
19	Indiana	123	2.1%
20	Missouri	109	1.9%
21	Wisconsin	78	1.4%
22	Arkansas	72	1.3%
23	Massachusetts	54	0.9%
24	Minnesota	52	0.9%
25	Oklahoma	47	0.8%
26	Connecticut	43	0.7%
27	Delaware	40	0.7%
28	Kentucky	39	0.7%
29	Colorado	38	0.7%
30	Kansas	33	0.6%
31	Washington	26	0.5%
32	Nevada	24	0.4%
33	Arizona	21	0.4%
34	Iowa	15	0.3%
35	Rhode Island	10	0.2%
36	Nebraska	9	0.2%
37	Oregon	6	0.1%
38	New Mexico	5	0.1%
38	West Virginia	5	0.1%
40	Hawaii	3	0.1%
41	Alaska	2	0.0%
41	Maine	2	0.0%
43	New Hampshire	1	0.0%
43	South Dakota	1	0.0%
43	Utah	1	0.0%
43	Vermont	1	0.0%
47	Idaho	0	0.0%
47	Montana	0	0.0%
47	North Dakota	0	0.0%
47	Wyoming	0	0.0%
	District of Columbia	64	1.1%

Source: U.S. Department of Health and Human Services, National Center for Health Statistics
   "National Vital Statistics Reports" (Vol. 56, No. 10, January 2008, http://www.cdc.gov/nchs/deaths.htm)
*Final data. Deaths of infants under 28 days, exclusive of fetal deaths. Based on race of the mother.

Black Neonatal Death Rate in 2005

National Rate = 9.1 Black Neonatal Deaths per 1,000 Black Live Births*

ALPHA ORDER

RANK	STATE	RATE
19	Alabama	8.6
NA	Alaska**	NA
33	Arizona	5.8
14	Arkansas	9.6
23	California	8.3
4	Colorado	12.2
24	Connecticut	8.1
1	Delaware	13.7
25	Florida	7.7
17	Georgia	8.8
NA	Hawaii**	NA
NA	Idaho**	NA
9	Illinois	10.8
3	Indiana	12.5
NA	Iowa**	NA
10	Kansas	10.6
25	Kentucky	7.7
22	Louisiana	8.4
NA	Maine**	NA
19	Maryland	8.6
31	Massachusetts	6.1
2	Michigan	13.1
27	Minnesota	7.5
8	Mississippi	11.2
16	Missouri	9.3
NA	Montana**	NA
NA	Nebraska**	NA
27	Nevada	7.5
NA	New Hampshire**	NA
29	New Jersey	7.0
NA	New Mexico**	NA
32	New York	6.0
5	North Carolina	12.0
NA	North Dakota**	NA
6	Ohio	11.8
12	Oklahoma	9.8
NA	Oregon**	NA
13	Pennsylvania	9.7
NA	Rhode Island**	NA
19	South Carolina	8.6
NA	South Dakota**	NA
11	Tennessee	10.3
17	Texas	8.8
NA	Utah**	NA
NA	Vermont**	NA
14	Virginia	9.6
30	Washington	6.2
NA	West Virginia**	NA
7	Wisconsin	11.5
NA	Wyoming**	NA

RANK ORDER

RANK	STATE	RATE
1	Delaware	13.7
2	Michigan	13.1
3	Indiana	12.5
4	Colorado	12.2
5	North Carolina	12.0
6	Ohio	11.8
7	Wisconsin	11.5
8	Mississippi	11.2
9	Illinois	10.8
10	Kansas	10.6
11	Tennessee	10.3
12	Oklahoma	9.8
13	Pennsylvania	9.7
14	Arkansas	9.6
14	Virginia	9.6
16	Missouri	9.3
17	Georgia	8.8
17	Texas	8.8
19	Alabama	8.6
19	Maryland	8.6
19	South Carolina	8.6
22	Louisiana	8.4
23	California	8.3
24	Connecticut	8.1
25	Florida	7.7
25	Kentucky	7.7
27	Minnesota	7.5
27	Nevada	7.5
29	New Jersey	7.0
30	Washington	6.2
31	Massachusetts	6.1
32	New York	6.0
33	Arizona	5.8
NA	Alaska**	NA
NA	Hawaii**	NA
NA	Idaho**	NA
NA	Iowa**	NA
NA	Maine**	NA
NA	Montana**	NA
NA	Nebraska**	NA
NA	New Hampshire**	NA
NA	New Mexico**	NA
NA	North Dakota**	NA
NA	Oregon**	NA
NA	Rhode Island**	NA
NA	South Dakota**	NA
NA	Utah**	NA
NA	Vermont**	NA
NA	West Virginia**	NA
NA	Wyoming**	NA
	District of Columbia	11.9

Source: U.S. Department of Health and Human Services, National Center for Health Statistics
"National Vital Statistics Reports" (Vol. 56, No. 10, January 2008, http://www.cdc.gov/nchs/deaths.htm)
*Final data. Deaths of infants under 28 days, exclusive of fetal deaths. Based on race of the mother.
**Not available. Fewer than 20 black neonatal deaths.

Estimated Deaths by Cancer in 2007

National Estimated Total = 559,650 Deaths

ALPHA ORDER					RANK ORDER			
RANK	STATE	DEATHS	% of USA		RANK	STATE	DEATHS	% of USA
21	Alabama	9,740	1.7%		1	California	54,890	9.8%
50	Alaska	810	0.1%		2	Florida	40,430	7.2%
20	Arizona	10,120	1.8%		3	New York	35,270	6.3%
31	Arkansas	6,240	1.1%		4	Texas	34,170	6.1%
1	California	54,890	9.8%		5	Pennsylvania	29,140	5.2%
29	Colorado	6,660	1.2%		6	Ohio	24,600	4.4%
28	Connecticut	6,990	1.2%		7	Illinois	23,870	4.3%
45	Delaware	1,810	0.3%		8	Michigan	19,180	3.4%
2	Florida	40,430	7.2%		9	New Jersey	17,140	3.1%
11	Georgia	14,950	2.7%		10	North Carolina	16,880	3.0%
43	Hawaii	2,260	0.4%		11	Georgia	14,950	2.7%
41	Idaho	2,370	0.4%		12	Virginia	13,740	2.5%
7	Illinois	23,870	4.3%		13	Massachusetts	13,240	2.4%
15	Indiana	12,730	2.3%		14	Tennessee	12,920	2.3%
30	Iowa	6,510	1.2%		15	Indiana	12,730	2.3%
33	Kansas	5,290	0.9%		16	Missouri	12,610	2.3%
23	Kentucky	9,390	1.7%		17	Washington	11,370	2.0%
22	Louisiana	9,550	1.7%		18	Wisconsin	10,870	1.9%
38	Maine	3,190	0.6%		19	Maryland	10,210	1.8%
19	Maryland	10,210	1.8%		20	Arizona	10,120	1.8%
13	Massachusetts	13,240	2.4%		21	Alabama	9,740	1.7%
8	Michigan	19,180	3.4%		22	Louisiana	9,550	1.7%
24	Minnesota	9,380	1.7%		23	Kentucky	9,390	1.7%
32	Mississippi	5,990	1.1%		24	Minnesota	9,380	1.7%
16	Missouri	12,610	2.3%		25	South Carolina	8,940	1.6%
44	Montana	1,920	0.3%		26	Oklahoma	7,380	1.3%
36	Nebraska	3,320	0.6%		27	Oregon	7,370	1.3%
34	Nevada	4,660	0.8%		28	Connecticut	6,990	1.2%
40	New Hampshire	2,630	0.5%		29	Colorado	6,660	1.2%
9	New Jersey	17,140	3.1%		30	Iowa	6,510	1.2%
37	New Mexico	3,270	0.6%		31	Arkansas	6,240	1.1%
3	New York	35,270	6.3%		32	Mississippi	5,990	1.1%
10	North Carolina	16,880	3.0%		33	Kansas	5,290	0.9%
47	North Dakota	1,220	0.2%		34	Nevada	4,660	0.8%
6	Ohio	24,600	4.4%		35	West Virginia	4,610	0.8%
26	Oklahoma	7,380	1.3%		36	Nebraska	3,320	0.6%
27	Oregon	7,370	1.3%		37	New Mexico	3,270	0.6%
5	Pennsylvania	29,140	5.2%		38	Maine	3,190	0.6%
41	Rhode Island	2,370	0.4%		39	Utah	2,690	0.5%
25	South Carolina	8,940	1.6%		40	New Hampshire	2,630	0.5%
46	South Dakota	1,600	0.3%		41	Idaho	2,370	0.4%
14	Tennessee	12,920	2.3%		41	Rhode Island	2,370	0.4%
4	Texas	34,170	6.1%		43	Hawaii	2,260	0.4%
39	Utah	2,690	0.5%		44	Montana	1,920	0.3%
48	Vermont	1,160	0.2%		45	Delaware	1,810	0.3%
12	Virginia	13,740	2.5%		46	South Dakota	1,600	0.3%
17	Washington	11,370	2.0%		47	North Dakota	1,220	0.2%
35	West Virginia	4,610	0.8%		48	Vermont	1,160	0.2%
18	Wisconsin	10,870	1.9%		49	Wyoming	980	0.2%
49	Wyoming	980	0.2%		50	Alaska	810	0.1%
						District of Columbia	1,020	0.2%

Source: American Cancer Society
"Cancer Facts & Figures 2007" (Copyright 2007, American Cancer Society)

Estimated Death Rate by Cancer in 2007

National Estimated Rate = 186.9 Deaths per 100,000 Population*

ALPHA ORDER

RANK	STATE	RATE
14	Alabama	211.8
49	Alaska	120.9
43	Arizona	164.1
7	Arkansas	222.0
46	California	150.6
48	Colorado	140.1
23	Connecticut	199.4
13	Delaware	212.1
4	Florida	223.5
45	Georgia	159.7
41	Hawaii	175.8
44	Idaho	161.6
34	Illinois	186.0
21	Indiana	201.6
9	Iowa	218.3
28	Kansas	191.4
5	Kentucky	223.2
6	Louisiana	222.7
2	Maine	241.4
37	Maryland	181.8
18	Massachusetts	205.7
31	Michigan	190.0
38	Minnesota	181.5
17	Mississippi	205.8
10	Missouri	215.8
20	Montana	203.3
32	Nebraska	187.7
33	Nevada	186.7
22	New Hampshire	200.0
25	New Jersey	196.5
42	New Mexico	167.3
36	New York	182.7
29	North Carolina	190.6
27	North Dakota	191.9
11	Ohio	214.3
16	Oklahoma	206.2
24	Oregon	199.1
3	Pennsylvania	234.2
7	Rhode Island	222.0
15	South Carolina	206.9
19	South Dakota	204.6
12	Tennessee	213.9
47	Texas	145.4
50	Utah	105.5
35	Vermont	185.9
39	Virginia	179.8
40	Washington	177.8
1	West Virginia	253.5
26	Wisconsin	195.6
30	Wyoming	190.3

RANK ORDER

RANK	STATE	RATE
1	West Virginia	253.5
2	Maine	241.4
3	Pennsylvania	234.2
4	Florida	223.5
5	Kentucky	223.2
6	Louisiana	222.7
7	Arkansas	222.0
7	Rhode Island	222.0
9	Iowa	218.3
10	Missouri	215.8
11	Ohio	214.3
12	Tennessee	213.9
13	Delaware	212.1
14	Alabama	211.8
15	South Carolina	206.9
16	Oklahoma	206.2
17	Mississippi	205.8
18	Massachusetts	205.7
19	South Dakota	204.6
20	Montana	203.3
21	Indiana	201.6
22	New Hampshire	200.0
23	Connecticut	199.4
24	Oregon	199.1
25	New Jersey	196.5
26	Wisconsin	195.6
27	North Dakota	191.9
28	Kansas	191.4
29	North Carolina	190.6
30	Wyoming	190.3
31	Michigan	190.0
32	Nebraska	187.7
33	Nevada	186.7
34	Illinois	186.0
35	Vermont	185.9
36	New York	182.7
37	Maryland	181.8
38	Minnesota	181.5
39	Virginia	179.8
40	Washington	177.8
41	Hawaii	175.8
42	New Mexico	167.3
43	Arizona	164.1
44	Idaho	161.6
45	Georgia	159.7
46	California	150.6
47	Texas	145.4
48	Colorado	140.1
49	Alaska	120.9
50	Utah	105.5
	District of Columbia	175.4

Source: CQ Press using data from American Cancer Society
  "Cancer Facts & Figures 2007" (Copyright 2007, American Cancer Society)
*Rates calculated using 2006 Census resident population estimates. Not age-adjusted.

Age-Adjusted Death Rate by Cancer for Males in 2003

National Rate = 243.7 Deaths per 100,000 Male Population*

ALPHA ORDER

RANK	STATE	RATE
4	Alabama	282.2
28	Alaska	237.5
46	Arizona	211.3
7	Arkansas	275.4
45	California	213.9
48	Colorado	208.1
39	Connecticut	228.5
18	Delaware	255.8
37	Florida	229.4
10	Georgia	264.5
49	Hawaii	192.5
44	Idaho	216.0
16	Illinois	256.1
9	Indiana	268.0
30	Iowa	237.2
33	Kansas	235.2
2	Kentucky	296.6
3	Louisiana	296.1
14	Maine	259.4
20	Maryland	252.5
21	Massachusetts	249.1
23	Michigan	247.4
38	Minnesota	229.1
1	Mississippi	298.4
16	Missouri	256.1
35	Montana	232.7
43	Nebraska	226.9
25	Nevada	245.4
24	New Hampshire	245.8
26	New Jersey	244.5
47	New Mexico	210.7
40	New York	228.0
11	North Carolina	263.8
41	North Dakota	227.3
12	Ohio	261.9
13	Oklahoma	260.8
34	Oregon	234.7
19	Pennsylvania	252.9
22	Rhode Island	248.1
6	South Carolina	276.6
32	South Dakota	236.6
5	Tennessee	281.6
27	Texas	243.4
50	Utah	182.2
28	Vermont	237.5
15	Virginia	256.5
36	Washington	232.0
8	West Virginia	273.7
31	Wisconsin	237.1
42	Wyoming	227.1

RANK ORDER

RANK	STATE	RATE
1	Mississippi	298.4
2	Kentucky	296.6
3	Louisiana	296.1
4	Alabama	282.2
5	Tennessee	281.6
6	South Carolina	276.6
7	Arkansas	275.4
8	West Virginia	273.7
9	Indiana	268.0
10	Georgia	264.5
11	North Carolina	263.8
12	Ohio	261.9
13	Oklahoma	260.8
14	Maine	259.4
15	Virginia	256.5
16	Illinois	256.1
16	Missouri	256.1
18	Delaware	255.8
19	Pennsylvania	252.9
20	Maryland	252.5
21	Massachusetts	249.1
22	Rhode Island	248.1
23	Michigan	247.4
24	New Hampshire	245.8
25	Nevada	245.4
26	New Jersey	244.5
27	Texas	243.4
28	Alaska	237.5
28	Vermont	237.5
30	Iowa	237.2
31	Wisconsin	237.1
32	South Dakota	236.6
33	Kansas	235.2
34	Oregon	234.7
35	Montana	232.7
36	Washington	232.0
37	Florida	229.4
38	Minnesota	229.1
39	Connecticut	228.5
40	New York	228.0
41	North Dakota	227.3
42	Wyoming	227.1
43	Nebraska	226.9
44	Idaho	216.0
45	California	213.9
46	Arizona	211.3
47	New Mexico	210.7
48	Colorado	208.1
49	Hawaii	192.5
50	Utah	182.2
	District of Columbia	299.1

Source: American Cancer Society
   "Cancer Facts & Figures 2007" (Copyright 2007, American Cancer Society)
*For 1999 to 2003. Age-adjusted to the 2000 U.S. standard population.

Age-Adjusted Death Rate by Cancer for Females in 2003

National Rate = 164.3 Deaths per 100,000 Female Population*

<table>
<tr><td colspan="3">ALPHA ORDER</td><td colspan="3">RANK ORDER</td></tr>
<tr><td>RANK</td><td>STATE</td><td>RATE</td><td>RANK</td><td>STATE</td><td>RATE</td></tr>
<tr><td>26</td><td>Alabama</td><td>165.3</td><td>1</td><td>West Virginia</td><td>182.7</td></tr>
<tr><td>25</td><td>Alaska</td><td>165.8</td><td>2</td><td>Kentucky</td><td>182.0</td></tr>
<tr><td>46</td><td>Arizona</td><td>148.3</td><td>3</td><td>Louisiana</td><td>181.1</td></tr>
<tr><td>23</td><td>Arkansas</td><td>167.0</td><td>4</td><td>Maine</td><td>178.8</td></tr>
<tr><td>42</td><td>California</td><td>155.3</td><td>5</td><td>Indiana</td><td>176.2</td></tr>
<tr><td>47</td><td>Colorado</td><td>148.2</td><td>5</td><td>Nevada</td><td>176.2</td></tr>
<tr><td>34</td><td>Connecticut</td><td>160.2</td><td>7</td><td>Delaware</td><td>175.6</td></tr>
<tr><td>7</td><td>Delaware</td><td>175.6</td><td>8</td><td>Ohio</td><td>175.2</td></tr>
<tr><td>43</td><td>Florida</td><td>154.2</td><td>9</td><td>New Jersey</td><td>175.0</td></tr>
<tr><td>27</td><td>Georgia</td><td>163.8</td><td>10</td><td>Illinois</td><td>172.6</td></tr>
<tr><td>50</td><td>Hawaii</td><td>122.7</td><td>11</td><td>Maryland</td><td>172.2</td></tr>
<tr><td>44</td><td>Idaho</td><td>151.6</td><td>12</td><td>Missouri</td><td>171.8</td></tr>
<tr><td>10</td><td>Illinois</td><td>172.6</td><td>13</td><td>Tennessee</td><td>171.6</td></tr>
<tr><td>5</td><td>Indiana</td><td>176.2</td><td>14</td><td>Pennsylvania</td><td>171.2</td></tr>
<tr><td>38</td><td>Iowa</td><td>157.1</td><td>14</td><td>Rhode Island</td><td>171.2</td></tr>
<tr><td>35</td><td>Kansas</td><td>159.3</td><td>16</td><td>Massachusetts</td><td>171.0</td></tr>
<tr><td>2</td><td>Kentucky</td><td>182.0</td><td>17</td><td>Oregon</td><td>170.2</td></tr>
<tr><td>3</td><td>Louisiana</td><td>181.1</td><td>18</td><td>Mississippi</td><td>169.7</td></tr>
<tr><td>4</td><td>Maine</td><td>178.8</td><td>19</td><td>Virginia</td><td>169.0</td></tr>
<tr><td>11</td><td>Maryland</td><td>172.2</td><td>20</td><td>Michigan</td><td>168.7</td></tr>
<tr><td>16</td><td>Massachusetts</td><td>171.0</td><td>21</td><td>Oklahoma</td><td>168.5</td></tr>
<tr><td>20</td><td>Michigan</td><td>168.7</td><td>22</td><td>New Hampshire</td><td>167.6</td></tr>
<tr><td>39</td><td>Minnesota</td><td>157.0</td><td>23</td><td>Arkansas</td><td>167.0</td></tr>
<tr><td>18</td><td>Mississippi</td><td>169.7</td><td>24</td><td>Washington</td><td>166.9</td></tr>
<tr><td>12</td><td>Missouri</td><td>171.8</td><td>25</td><td>Alaska</td><td>165.8</td></tr>
<tr><td>30</td><td>Montana</td><td>163.2</td><td>26</td><td>Alabama</td><td>165.3</td></tr>
<tr><td>40</td><td>Nebraska</td><td>156.8</td><td>27</td><td>Georgia</td><td>163.8</td></tr>
<tr><td>5</td><td>Nevada</td><td>176.2</td><td>27</td><td>South Carolina</td><td>163.8</td></tr>
<tr><td>22</td><td>New Hampshire</td><td>167.6</td><td>29</td><td>Vermont</td><td>163.3</td></tr>
<tr><td>9</td><td>New Jersey</td><td>175.0</td><td>30</td><td>Montana</td><td>163.2</td></tr>
<tr><td>48</td><td>New Mexico</td><td>142.9</td><td>30</td><td>North Carolina</td><td>163.2</td></tr>
<tr><td>32</td><td>New York</td><td>162.5</td><td>32</td><td>New York</td><td>162.5</td></tr>
<tr><td>30</td><td>North Carolina</td><td>163.2</td><td>33</td><td>Wyoming</td><td>160.9</td></tr>
<tr><td>45</td><td>North Dakota</td><td>151.1</td><td>34</td><td>Connecticut</td><td>160.2</td></tr>
<tr><td>8</td><td>Ohio</td><td>175.2</td><td>35</td><td>Kansas</td><td>159.3</td></tr>
<tr><td>21</td><td>Oklahoma</td><td>168.5</td><td>36</td><td>Texas</td><td>159.1</td></tr>
<tr><td>17</td><td>Oregon</td><td>170.2</td><td>37</td><td>Wisconsin</td><td>158.9</td></tr>
<tr><td>14</td><td>Pennsylvania</td><td>171.2</td><td>38</td><td>Iowa</td><td>157.1</td></tr>
<tr><td>14</td><td>Rhode Island</td><td>171.2</td><td>39</td><td>Minnesota</td><td>157.0</td></tr>
<tr><td>27</td><td>South Carolina</td><td>163.8</td><td>40</td><td>Nebraska</td><td>156.8</td></tr>
<tr><td>41</td><td>South Dakota</td><td>156.2</td><td>41</td><td>South Dakota</td><td>156.2</td></tr>
<tr><td>13</td><td>Tennessee</td><td>171.6</td><td>42</td><td>California</td><td>155.3</td></tr>
<tr><td>36</td><td>Texas</td><td>159.1</td><td>43</td><td>Florida</td><td>154.2</td></tr>
<tr><td>49</td><td>Utah</td><td>124.1</td><td>44</td><td>Idaho</td><td>151.6</td></tr>
<tr><td>29</td><td>Vermont</td><td>163.3</td><td>45</td><td>North Dakota</td><td>151.1</td></tr>
<tr><td>19</td><td>Virginia</td><td>169.0</td><td>46</td><td>Arizona</td><td>148.3</td></tr>
<tr><td>24</td><td>Washington</td><td>166.9</td><td>47</td><td>Colorado</td><td>148.2</td></tr>
<tr><td>1</td><td>West Virginia</td><td>182.7</td><td>48</td><td>New Mexico</td><td>142.9</td></tr>
<tr><td>37</td><td>Wisconsin</td><td>158.9</td><td>49</td><td>Utah</td><td>124.1</td></tr>
<tr><td>33</td><td>Wyoming</td><td>160.9</td><td>50</td><td>Hawaii</td><td>122.7</td></tr>
<tr><td></td><td></td><td></td><td></td><td>District of Columbia</td><td>187.8</td></tr>
</table>

Source: American Cancer Society
   "Cancer Facts & Figures 2007" (Copyright 2007, American Cancer Society)
*For 1999 to 2003. Age-adjusted to the 2000 U.S. standard population.

Estimated Deaths by Brain Cancer in 2007

National Estimated Total = 12,740 Deaths

<table>
<tr><td colspan="4">ALPHA ORDER</td><td colspan="4">RANK ORDER</td></tr>
<tr><td>RANK</td><td>STATE</td><td>DEATHS</td><td>% of USA</td><td>RANK</td><td>STATE</td><td>DEATHS</td><td>% of USA</td></tr>
<tr><td>22</td><td>Alabama</td><td>210</td><td>1.6%</td><td>1</td><td>California</td><td>1,460</td><td>11.5%</td></tr>
<tr><td>NA</td><td>Alaska*</td><td>NA</td><td>NA</td><td>2</td><td>Texas</td><td>840</td><td>6.6%</td></tr>
<tr><td>19</td><td>Arizona</td><td>250</td><td>2.0%</td><td>3</td><td>Florida</td><td>790</td><td>6.2%</td></tr>
<tr><td>32</td><td>Arkansas</td><td>140</td><td>1.1%</td><td>4</td><td>New York</td><td>720</td><td>5.7%</td></tr>
<tr><td>1</td><td>California</td><td>1,460</td><td>11.5%</td><td>5</td><td>Pennsylvania</td><td>560</td><td>4.4%</td></tr>
<tr><td>25</td><td>Colorado</td><td>190</td><td>1.5%</td><td>6</td><td>Ohio</td><td>540</td><td>4.2%</td></tr>
<tr><td>30</td><td>Connecticut</td><td>150</td><td>1.2%</td><td>7</td><td>Illinois</td><td>490</td><td>3.8%</td></tr>
<tr><td>NA</td><td>Delaware*</td><td>NA</td><td>NA</td><td>8</td><td>Michigan</td><td>450</td><td>3.5%</td></tr>
<tr><td>3</td><td>Florida</td><td>790</td><td>6.2%</td><td>9</td><td>Washington</td><td>370</td><td>2.9%</td></tr>
<tr><td>13</td><td>Georgia</td><td>280</td><td>2.2%</td><td>10</td><td>North Carolina</td><td>360</td><td>2.8%</td></tr>
<tr><td>NA</td><td>Hawaii*</td><td>NA</td><td>NA</td><td>11</td><td>Tennessee</td><td>350</td><td>2.7%</td></tr>
<tr><td>38</td><td>Idaho</td><td>80</td><td>0.6%</td><td>12</td><td>New Jersey</td><td>320</td><td>2.5%</td></tr>
<tr><td>7</td><td>Illinois</td><td>490</td><td>3.8%</td><td>13</td><td>Georgia</td><td>280</td><td>2.2%</td></tr>
<tr><td>13</td><td>Indiana</td><td>280</td><td>2.2%</td><td>13</td><td>Indiana</td><td>280</td><td>2.2%</td></tr>
<tr><td>28</td><td>Iowa</td><td>160</td><td>1.3%</td><td>13</td><td>Virginia</td><td>280</td><td>2.2%</td></tr>
<tr><td>32</td><td>Kansas</td><td>140</td><td>1.1%</td><td>16</td><td>Massachusetts</td><td>270</td><td>2.1%</td></tr>
<tr><td>30</td><td>Kentucky</td><td>150</td><td>1.2%</td><td>16</td><td>Missouri</td><td>270</td><td>2.1%</td></tr>
<tr><td>23</td><td>Louisiana</td><td>200</td><td>1.6%</td><td>18</td><td>Wisconsin</td><td>260</td><td>2.0%</td></tr>
<tr><td>38</td><td>Maine</td><td>80</td><td>0.6%</td><td>19</td><td>Arizona</td><td>250</td><td>2.0%</td></tr>
<tr><td>21</td><td>Maryland</td><td>230</td><td>1.8%</td><td>20</td><td>Minnesota</td><td>240</td><td>1.9%</td></tr>
<tr><td>16</td><td>Massachusetts</td><td>270</td><td>2.1%</td><td>21</td><td>Maryland</td><td>230</td><td>1.8%</td></tr>
<tr><td>8</td><td>Michigan</td><td>450</td><td>3.5%</td><td>22</td><td>Alabama</td><td>210</td><td>1.6%</td></tr>
<tr><td>20</td><td>Minnesota</td><td>240</td><td>1.9%</td><td>23</td><td>Louisiana</td><td>200</td><td>1.6%</td></tr>
<tr><td>28</td><td>Mississippi</td><td>160</td><td>1.3%</td><td>23</td><td>Oregon</td><td>200</td><td>1.6%</td></tr>
<tr><td>16</td><td>Missouri</td><td>270</td><td>2.1%</td><td>25</td><td>Colorado</td><td>190</td><td>1.5%</td></tr>
<tr><td>42</td><td>Montana</td><td>50</td><td>0.4%</td><td>25</td><td>South Carolina</td><td>190</td><td>1.5%</td></tr>
<tr><td>35</td><td>Nebraska</td><td>90</td><td>0.7%</td><td>27</td><td>Oklahoma</td><td>170</td><td>1.3%</td></tr>
<tr><td>34</td><td>Nevada</td><td>100</td><td>0.8%</td><td>28</td><td>Iowa</td><td>160</td><td>1.3%</td></tr>
<tr><td>41</td><td>New Hampshire</td><td>70</td><td>0.5%</td><td>28</td><td>Mississippi</td><td>160</td><td>1.3%</td></tr>
<tr><td>12</td><td>New Jersey</td><td>320</td><td>2.5%</td><td>30</td><td>Connecticut</td><td>150</td><td>1.2%</td></tr>
<tr><td>38</td><td>New Mexico</td><td>80</td><td>0.6%</td><td>30</td><td>Kentucky</td><td>150</td><td>1.2%</td></tr>
<tr><td>4</td><td>New York</td><td>720</td><td>5.7%</td><td>32</td><td>Arkansas</td><td>140</td><td>1.1%</td></tr>
<tr><td>10</td><td>North Carolina</td><td>360</td><td>2.8%</td><td>32</td><td>Kansas</td><td>140</td><td>1.1%</td></tr>
<tr><td>NA</td><td>North Dakota*</td><td>NA</td><td>NA</td><td>34</td><td>Nevada</td><td>100</td><td>0.8%</td></tr>
<tr><td>6</td><td>Ohio</td><td>540</td><td>4.2%</td><td>35</td><td>Nebraska</td><td>90</td><td>0.7%</td></tr>
<tr><td>27</td><td>Oklahoma</td><td>170</td><td>1.3%</td><td>35</td><td>Utah</td><td>90</td><td>0.7%</td></tr>
<tr><td>23</td><td>Oregon</td><td>200</td><td>1.6%</td><td>35</td><td>West Virginia</td><td>90</td><td>0.7%</td></tr>
<tr><td>5</td><td>Pennsylvania</td><td>560</td><td>4.4%</td><td>38</td><td>Idaho</td><td>80</td><td>0.6%</td></tr>
<tr><td>42</td><td>Rhode Island</td><td>50</td><td>0.4%</td><td>38</td><td>Maine</td><td>80</td><td>0.6%</td></tr>
<tr><td>25</td><td>South Carolina</td><td>190</td><td>1.5%</td><td>38</td><td>New Mexico</td><td>80</td><td>0.6%</td></tr>
<tr><td>42</td><td>South Dakota</td><td>50</td><td>0.4%</td><td>41</td><td>New Hampshire</td><td>70</td><td>0.5%</td></tr>
<tr><td>11</td><td>Tennessee</td><td>350</td><td>2.7%</td><td>42</td><td>Montana</td><td>50</td><td>0.4%</td></tr>
<tr><td>2</td><td>Texas</td><td>840</td><td>6.6%</td><td>42</td><td>Rhode Island</td><td>50</td><td>0.4%</td></tr>
<tr><td>35</td><td>Utah</td><td>90</td><td>0.7%</td><td>42</td><td>South Dakota</td><td>50</td><td>0.4%</td></tr>
<tr><td>NA</td><td>Vermont*</td><td>NA</td><td>NA</td><td>NA</td><td>Alaska*</td><td>NA</td><td>NA</td></tr>
<tr><td>13</td><td>Virginia</td><td>280</td><td>2.2%</td><td>NA</td><td>Delaware*</td><td>NA</td><td>NA</td></tr>
<tr><td>9</td><td>Washington</td><td>370</td><td>2.9%</td><td>NA</td><td>Hawaii*</td><td>NA</td><td>NA</td></tr>
<tr><td>35</td><td>West Virginia</td><td>90</td><td>0.7%</td><td>NA</td><td>North Dakota*</td><td>NA</td><td>NA</td></tr>
<tr><td>18</td><td>Wisconsin</td><td>260</td><td>2.0%</td><td>NA</td><td>Vermont*</td><td>NA</td><td>NA</td></tr>
<tr><td>NA</td><td>Wyoming*</td><td>NA</td><td>NA</td><td>NA</td><td>Wyoming*</td><td>NA</td><td>NA</td></tr>
<tr><td></td><td></td><td></td><td></td><td colspan="2">District of Columbia*</td><td>NA</td><td>NA</td></tr>
</table>

Source: American Cancer Society
"Cancer Facts & Figures 2007" (Copyright 2007, American Cancer Society)
*Fewer than 50 deaths.

Estimated Death Rate by Brain Cancer in 2007

National Estimated Rate = 4.3 Deaths per 100,000 Population*

ALPHA ORDER			RANK ORDER		
RANK	**STATE**	**RATE**	**RANK**	**STATE**	**RATE**
20	Alabama	4.6	1	South Dakota	6.4
NA	Alaska**	NA	2	Maine	6.1
30	Arizona	4.1	3	Tennessee	5.8
13	Arkansas	5.0	3	Washington	5.8
34	California	4.0	5	Idaho	5.5
34	Colorado	4.0	5	Mississippi	5.5
28	Connecticut	4.3	7	Iowa	5.4
NA	Delaware**	NA	7	Oregon	5.4
25	Florida	4.4	9	Montana	5.3
44	Georgia	3.0	9	New Hampshire	5.3
NA	Hawaii**	NA	11	Kansas	5.1
5	Idaho	5.5	11	Nebraska	5.1
37	Illinois	3.8	13	Arkansas	5.0
25	Indiana	4.4	14	West Virginia	4.9
7	Iowa	5.4	15	Louisiana	4.7
11	Kansas	5.1	15	Ohio	4.7
41	Kentucky	3.6	15	Oklahoma	4.7
15	Louisiana	4.7	15	Rhode Island	4.7
2	Maine	6.1	15	Wisconsin	4.7
30	Maryland	4.1	20	Alabama	4.6
29	Massachusetts	4.2	20	Minnesota	4.6
23	Michigan	4.5	20	Missouri	4.6
20	Minnesota	4.6	23	Michigan	4.5
5	Mississippi	5.5	23	Pennsylvania	4.5
20	Missouri	4.6	25	Florida	4.4
9	Montana	5.3	25	Indiana	4.4
11	Nebraska	5.1	25	South Carolina	4.4
34	Nevada	4.0	28	Connecticut	4.3
9	New Hampshire	5.3	29	Massachusetts	4.2
38	New Jersey	3.7	30	Arizona	4.1
30	New Mexico	4.1	30	Maryland	4.1
38	New York	3.7	30	New Mexico	4.1
30	North Carolina	4.1	30	North Carolina	4.1
NA	North Dakota**	NA	34	California	4.0
15	Ohio	4.7	34	Colorado	4.0
15	Oklahoma	4.7	34	Nevada	4.0
7	Oregon	5.4	37	Illinois	3.8
23	Pennsylvania	4.5	38	New Jersey	3.7
15	Rhode Island	4.7	38	New York	3.7
25	South Carolina	4.4	38	Virginia	3.7
1	South Dakota	6.4	41	Kentucky	3.6
3	Tennessee	5.8	41	Texas	3.6
41	Texas	3.6	43	Utah	3.5
43	Utah	3.5	44	Georgia	3.0
NA	Vermont**	NA	NA	Alaska**	NA
38	Virginia	3.7	NA	Delaware**	NA
3	Washington	5.8	NA	Hawaii**	NA
14	West Virginia	4.9	NA	North Dakota**	NA
15	Wisconsin	4.7	NA	Vermont**	NA
NA	Wyoming**	NA	NA	Wyoming**	NA
				District of Columbia**	NA

Source: CQ Press using data from American Cancer Society
"Cancer Facts & Figures 2007" (Copyright 2007, American Cancer Society)
*Rates calculated using 2006 Census resident population estimates. Not age-adjusted.
**Fewer than 50 deaths.

Estimated Deaths by Female Breast Cancer in 2007

National Estimated Total = 40,460 Deaths

ALPHA ORDER					RANK ORDER			
RANK	STATE		DEATHS	% of USA	RANK	STATE	DEATHS	% of USA
22	Alabama		680	1.7%	1	California	4,130	10.2%
50	Alaska		50	0.1%	2	Florida	2,700	6.7%
21	Arizona		710	1.8%	3	New York	2,670	6.6%
31	Arkansas		410	1.0%	4	Texas	2,480	6.1%
1	California		4,130	10.2%	5	Pennsylvania	2,470	6.1%
27	Colorado		520	1.3%	6	Ohio	1,820	4.5%
29	Connecticut		490	1.2%	7	Illinois	1,740	4.3%
45	Delaware		120	0.3%	8	New Jersey	1,350	3.3%
2	Florida		2,700	6.7%	9	Michigan	1,320	3.3%
11	Georgia		1,120	2.8%	10	North Carolina	1,240	3.1%
43	Hawaii		130	0.3%	11	Georgia	1,120	2.8%
40	Idaho		180	0.4%	12	Virginia	1,100	2.7%
7	Illinois		1,740	4.3%	13	Massachusetts	890	2.2%
16	Indiana		860	2.1%	13	Tennessee	890	2.2%
31	Iowa		410	1.0%	15	Missouri	870	2.2%
33	Kansas		380	0.9%	16	Indiana	860	2.1%
23	Kentucky		600	1.5%	17	Maryland	830	2.1%
20	Louisiana		730	1.8%	18	Washington	770	1.9%
39	Maine		190	0.5%	18	Wisconsin	770	1.9%
17	Maryland		830	2.1%	20	Louisiana	730	1.8%
13	Massachusetts		890	2.2%	21	Arizona	710	1.8%
9	Michigan		1,320	3.3%	22	Alabama	680	1.7%
23	Minnesota		600	1.5%	23	Kentucky	600	1.5%
30	Mississippi		450	1.1%	23	Minnesota	600	1.5%
15	Missouri		870	2.2%	25	South Carolina	570	1.4%
43	Montana		130	0.3%	26	Oregon	530	1.3%
38	Nebraska		220	0.5%	27	Colorado	520	1.3%
34	Nevada		330	0.8%	28	Oklahoma	510	1.3%
40	New Hampshire		180	0.4%	29	Connecticut	490	1.2%
8	New Jersey		1,350	3.3%	30	Mississippi	450	1.1%
36	New Mexico		240	0.6%	31	Arkansas	410	1.0%
3	New York		2,670	6.6%	31	Iowa	410	1.0%
10	North Carolina		1,240	3.1%	33	Kansas	380	0.9%
48	North Dakota		90	0.2%	34	Nevada	330	0.8%
6	Ohio		1,820	4.5%	35	West Virginia	280	0.7%
28	Oklahoma		510	1.3%	36	New Mexico	240	0.6%
26	Oregon		530	1.3%	36	Utah	240	0.6%
5	Pennsylvania		2,470	6.1%	38	Nebraska	220	0.5%
42	Rhode Island		140	0.3%	39	Maine	190	0.5%
25	South Carolina		570	1.4%	40	Idaho	180	0.4%
46	South Dakota		100	0.2%	40	New Hampshire	180	0.4%
13	Tennessee		890	2.2%	42	Rhode Island	140	0.3%
4	Texas		2,480	6.1%	43	Hawaii	130	0.3%
36	Utah		240	0.6%	43	Montana	130	0.3%
46	Vermont		100	0.2%	45	Delaware	120	0.3%
12	Virginia		1,100	2.7%	46	South Dakota	100	0.2%
18	Washington		770	1.9%	46	Vermont	100	0.2%
35	West Virginia		280	0.7%	48	North Dakota	90	0.2%
18	Wisconsin		770	1.9%	49	Wyoming	60	0.1%
49	Wyoming		60	0.1%	50	Alaska	50	0.1%
						District of Columbia	80	0.2%

Source: American Cancer Society
"Cancer Facts & Figures 2007" (Copyright 2007, American Cancer Society)

Age-Adjusted Death Rate by Female Breast Cancer in 2003

National Rate = 26.0 Deaths per 100,000 Female Population*

ALPHA ORDER

RANK	STATE	RATE
18	Alabama	26.3
46	Alaska	23.0
39	Arizona	24.1
36	Arkansas	24.4
35	California	24.6
45	Colorado	23.4
27	Connecticut	25.3
10	Delaware	26.8
44	Florida	23.7
22	Georgia	25.7
50	Hawaii	18.3
34	Idaho	24.7
7	Illinois	27.8
13	Indiana	26.6
38	Iowa	24.3
22	Kansas	25.7
13	Kentucky	26.6
1	Louisiana	30.1
32	Maine	24.8
4	Maryland	27.9
20	Massachusetts	26.2
13	Michigan	26.6
36	Minnesota	24.4
4	Mississippi	27.9
12	Missouri	26.7
42	Montana	23.8
42	Nebraska	23.8
18	Nevada	26.3
25	New Hampshire	25.6
2	New Jersey	29.1
49	New Mexico	22.5
9	New York	27.0
25	North Carolina	25.6
32	North Dakota	24.8
3	Ohio	28.5
16	Oklahoma	26.4
22	Oregon	25.7
4	Pennsylvania	27.9
30	Rhode Island	25.0
10	South Carolina	26.8
40	South Dakota	24.0
16	Tennessee	26.4
31	Texas	24.9
46	Utah	23.0
21	Vermont	26.1
8	Virginia	27.6
40	Washington	24.0
27	West Virginia	25.3
29	Wisconsin	25.1
46	Wyoming	23.0

RANK ORDER

RANK	STATE	RATE
1	Louisiana	30.1
2	New Jersey	29.1
3	Ohio	28.5
4	Maryland	27.9
4	Mississippi	27.9
4	Pennsylvania	27.9
7	Illinois	27.8
8	Virginia	27.6
9	New York	27.0
10	Delaware	26.8
10	South Carolina	26.8
12	Missouri	26.7
13	Indiana	26.6
13	Kentucky	26.6
13	Michigan	26.6
16	Oklahoma	26.4
16	Tennessee	26.4
18	Alabama	26.3
18	Nevada	26.3
20	Massachusetts	26.2
21	Vermont	26.1
22	Georgia	25.7
22	Kansas	25.7
22	Oregon	25.7
25	New Hampshire	25.6
25	North Carolina	25.6
27	Connecticut	25.3
27	West Virginia	25.3
29	Wisconsin	25.1
30	Rhode Island	25.0
31	Texas	24.9
32	Maine	24.8
32	North Dakota	24.8
34	Idaho	24.7
35	California	24.6
36	Arkansas	24.4
36	Minnesota	24.4
38	Iowa	24.3
39	Arizona	24.1
40	South Dakota	24.0
40	Washington	24.0
42	Montana	23.8
42	Nebraska	23.8
44	Florida	23.7
45	Colorado	23.4
46	Alaska	23.0
46	Utah	23.0
46	Wyoming	23.0
49	New Mexico	22.5
50	Hawaii	18.3
	District of Columbia	33.7

Source: American Cancer Society
    "Cancer Facts & Figures 2007" (Copyright 2007, American Cancer Society)
*For 1999 to 2003. Age-adjusted to the 2000 U.S. standard population.

Estimated Deaths by Colon and Rectum Cancer in 2007

National Estimated Total = 52,180 Deaths

ALPHA ORDER

RANK	STATE	DEATHS	% of USA
22	Alabama	880	1.7%
50	Alaska	70	0.1%
18	Arizona	970	1.9%
29	Arkansas	610	1.2%
1	California	5,230	10.0%
28	Colorado	630	1.2%
32	Connecticut	590	1.1%
44	Delaware	160	0.3%
2	Florida	3,530	6.8%
11	Georgia	1,340	2.6%
41	Hawaii	210	0.4%
43	Idaho	200	0.4%
6	Illinois	2,380	4.6%
13	Indiana	1,180	2.3%
31	Iowa	600	1.1%
33	Kansas	520	1.0%
23	Kentucky	860	1.6%
20	Louisiana	960	1.8%
38	Maine	280	0.5%
18	Maryland	970	1.9%
13	Massachusetts	1,180	2.3%
8	Michigan	1,750	3.4%
24	Minnesota	810	1.6%
29	Mississippi	610	1.2%
15	Missouri	1,170	2.2%
44	Montana	160	0.3%
36	Nebraska	350	0.7%
34	Nevada	490	0.9%
40	New Hampshire	220	0.4%
9	New Jersey	1,680	3.2%
37	New Mexico	320	0.6%
3	New York	3,350	6.4%
10	North Carolina	1,480	2.8%
47	North Dakota	120	0.2%
7	Ohio	2,350	4.5%
26	Oklahoma	720	1.4%
27	Oregon	640	1.2%
5	Pennsylvania	2,730	5.2%
41	Rhode Island	210	0.4%
25	South Carolina	790	1.5%
44	South Dakota	160	0.3%
16	Tennessee	1,160	2.2%
4	Texas	3,220	6.2%
39	Utah	240	0.5%
47	Vermont	120	0.2%
12	Virginia	1,320	2.5%
17	Washington	990	1.9%
35	West Virginia	480	0.9%
20	Wisconsin	960	1.8%
49	Wyoming	110	0.2%

RANK ORDER

RANK	STATE	DEATHS	% of USA
1	California	5,230	10.0%
2	Florida	3,530	6.8%
3	New York	3,350	6.4%
4	Texas	3,220	6.2%
5	Pennsylvania	2,730	5.2%
6	Illinois	2,380	4.6%
7	Ohio	2,350	4.5%
8	Michigan	1,750	3.4%
9	New Jersey	1,680	3.2%
10	North Carolina	1,480	2.8%
11	Georgia	1,340	2.6%
12	Virginia	1,320	2.5%
13	Indiana	1,180	2.3%
13	Massachusetts	1,180	2.3%
15	Missouri	1,170	2.2%
16	Tennessee	1,160	2.2%
17	Washington	990	1.9%
18	Arizona	970	1.9%
18	Maryland	970	1.9%
20	Louisiana	960	1.8%
20	Wisconsin	960	1.8%
22	Alabama	880	1.7%
23	Kentucky	860	1.6%
24	Minnesota	810	1.6%
25	South Carolina	790	1.5%
26	Oklahoma	720	1.4%
27	Oregon	640	1.2%
28	Colorado	630	1.2%
29	Arkansas	610	1.2%
29	Mississippi	610	1.2%
31	Iowa	600	1.1%
32	Connecticut	590	1.1%
33	Kansas	520	1.0%
34	Nevada	490	0.9%
35	West Virginia	480	0.9%
36	Nebraska	350	0.7%
37	New Mexico	320	0.6%
38	Maine	280	0.5%
39	Utah	240	0.5%
40	New Hampshire	220	0.4%
41	Hawaii	210	0.4%
41	Rhode Island	210	0.4%
43	Idaho	200	0.4%
44	Delaware	160	0.3%
44	Montana	160	0.3%
44	South Dakota	160	0.3%
47	North Dakota	120	0.2%
47	Vermont	120	0.2%
49	Wyoming	110	0.2%
50	Alaska	70	0.1%
	District of Columbia	100	0.2%

Source: American Cancer Society
"Cancer Facts & Figures 2007" (Copyright 2007, American Cancer Society)

Estimated Death Rate by Colon and Rectum Cancer in 2007

National Estimated Rate = 17.4 Deaths per 100,000 Population*

ALPHA ORDER

RANK	STATE	RATE
21	Alabama	19.1
49	Alaska	10.4
41	Arizona	15.7
4	Arkansas	21.7
44	California	14.3
48	Colorado	13.3
36	Connecticut	16.8
24	Delaware	18.7
17	Florida	19.5
44	Georgia	14.3
40	Hawaii	16.3
47	Idaho	13.6
26	Illinois	18.5
24	Indiana	18.7
11	Iowa	20.1
23	Kansas	18.8
10	Kentucky	20.4
2	Louisiana	22.4
6	Maine	21.2
30	Maryland	17.3
27	Massachusetts	18.3
30	Michigan	17.3
41	Minnesota	15.7
7	Mississippi	21.0
13	Missouri	20.0
35	Montana	16.9
14	Nebraska	19.8
16	Nevada	19.6
37	New Hampshire	16.7
18	New Jersey	19.3
39	New Mexico	16.4
29	New York	17.4
37	North Carolina	16.7
22	North Dakota	18.9
8	Ohio	20.5
11	Oklahoma	20.1
30	Oregon	17.3
3	Pennsylvania	21.9
15	Rhode Island	19.7
27	South Carolina	18.3
8	South Dakota	20.5
19	Tennessee	19.2
46	Texas	13.7
50	Utah	9.4
19	Vermont	19.2
30	Virginia	17.3
43	Washington	15.5
1	West Virginia	26.4
30	Wisconsin	17.3
5	Wyoming	21.4

RANK ORDER

RANK	STATE	RATE
1	West Virginia	26.4
2	Louisiana	22.4
3	Pennsylvania	21.9
4	Arkansas	21.7
5	Wyoming	21.4
6	Maine	21.2
7	Mississippi	21.0
8	Ohio	20.5
8	South Dakota	20.5
10	Kentucky	20.4
11	Iowa	20.1
11	Oklahoma	20.1
13	Missouri	20.0
14	Nebraska	19.8
15	Rhode Island	19.7
16	Nevada	19.6
17	Florida	19.5
18	New Jersey	19.3
19	Tennessee	19.2
19	Vermont	19.2
21	Alabama	19.1
22	North Dakota	18.9
23	Kansas	18.8
24	Delaware	18.7
24	Indiana	18.7
26	Illinois	18.5
27	Massachusetts	18.3
27	South Carolina	18.3
29	New York	17.4
30	Maryland	17.3
30	Michigan	17.3
30	Oregon	17.3
30	Virginia	17.3
30	Wisconsin	17.3
35	Montana	16.9
36	Connecticut	16.8
37	New Hampshire	16.7
37	North Carolina	16.7
39	New Mexico	16.4
40	Hawaii	16.3
41	Arizona	15.7
41	Minnesota	15.7
43	Washington	15.5
44	California	14.3
44	Georgia	14.3
46	Texas	13.7
47	Idaho	13.6
48	Colorado	13.3
49	Alaska	10.4
50	Utah	9.4

District of Columbia   17.2

Source: CQ Press using data from American Cancer Society
   "Cancer Facts & Figures 2007" (Copyright 2007, American Cancer Society)
*Rates calculated using 2006 Census resident population estimates. Not age-adjusted.

Estimated Deaths by Leukemia in 2007

National Estimated Total = 21,790 Deaths

ALPHA ORDER

RANK	STATE	DEATHS	% of USA
22	Alabama	350	1.6%
NA	Alaska*	NA	NA
19	Arizona	400	1.8%
31	Arkansas	240	1.1%
1	California	2,150	9.9%
27	Colorado	290	1.3%
29	Connecticut	270	1.2%
45	Delaware	70	0.3%
2	Florida	1,630	7.5%
11	Georgia	540	2.5%
42	Hawaii	80	0.4%
38	Idaho	120	0.6%
6	Illinois	990	4.5%
12	Indiana	510	2.3%
26	Iowa	310	1.4%
32	Kansas	230	1.1%
25	Kentucky	320	1.5%
23	Louisiana	330	1.5%
40	Maine	100	0.5%
21	Maryland	390	1.8%
14	Massachusetts	490	2.2%
8	Michigan	770	3.5%
19	Minnesota	400	1.8%
33	Mississippi	210	1.0%
18	Missouri	460	2.1%
42	Montana	80	0.4%
35	Nebraska	150	0.7%
34	Nevada	160	0.7%
40	New Hampshire	100	0.5%
9	New Jersey	680	3.1%
38	New Mexico	120	0.6%
4	New York	1,360	6.2%
10	North Carolina	610	2.8%
NA	North Dakota*	NA	NA
7	Ohio	950	4.4%
27	Oklahoma	290	1.3%
30	Oregon	260	1.2%
5	Pennsylvania	1,070	4.9%
42	Rhode Island	80	0.4%
23	South Carolina	330	1.5%
45	South Dakota	70	0.3%
17	Tennessee	480	2.2%
3	Texas	1,410	6.5%
36	Utah	130	0.6%
47	Vermont	50	0.2%
13	Virginia	500	2.3%
14	Washington	490	2.2%
36	West Virginia	130	0.6%
14	Wisconsin	490	2.2%
NA	Wyoming*	NA	NA

RANK ORDER

RANK	STATE	DEATHS	% of USA
1	California	2,150	9.9%
2	Florida	1,630	7.5%
3	Texas	1,410	6.5%
4	New York	1,360	6.2%
5	Pennsylvania	1,070	4.9%
6	Illinois	990	4.5%
7	Ohio	950	4.4%
8	Michigan	770	3.5%
9	New Jersey	680	3.1%
10	North Carolina	610	2.8%
11	Georgia	540	2.5%
12	Indiana	510	2.3%
13	Virginia	500	2.3%
14	Massachusetts	490	2.2%
14	Washington	490	2.2%
14	Wisconsin	490	2.2%
17	Tennessee	480	2.2%
18	Missouri	460	2.1%
19	Arizona	400	1.8%
19	Minnesota	400	1.8%
21	Maryland	390	1.8%
22	Alabama	350	1.6%
23	Louisiana	330	1.5%
23	South Carolina	330	1.5%
25	Kentucky	320	1.5%
26	Iowa	310	1.4%
27	Colorado	290	1.3%
27	Oklahoma	290	1.3%
29	Connecticut	270	1.2%
30	Oregon	260	1.2%
31	Arkansas	240	1.1%
32	Kansas	230	1.1%
33	Mississippi	210	1.0%
34	Nevada	160	0.7%
35	Nebraska	150	0.7%
36	Utah	130	0.6%
36	West Virginia	130	0.6%
38	Idaho	120	0.6%
38	New Mexico	120	0.6%
40	Maine	100	0.5%
40	New Hampshire	100	0.5%
42	Hawaii	80	0.4%
42	Montana	80	0.4%
42	Rhode Island	80	0.4%
45	Delaware	70	0.3%
45	South Dakota	70	0.3%
47	Vermont	50	0.2%
NA	Alaska*	NA	NA
NA	North Dakota*	NA	NA
NA	Wyoming*	NA	NA
	District of Columbia*	NA	NA

Source: American Cancer Society
"Cancer Facts & Figures 2007" (Copyright 2007, American Cancer Society)
*Fewer than 50 deaths.

Estimated Death Rate by Leukemia in 2007

National Estimated Rate = 7.3 Deaths per 100,000 Population*

ALPHA ORDER

RANK	STATE	RATE
24	Alabama	7.6
NA	Alaska**	NA
38	Arizona	6.5
6	Arkansas	8.5
45	California	5.9
42	Colorado	6.1
19	Connecticut	7.7
11	Delaware	8.2
2	Florida	9.0
46	Georgia	5.8
41	Hawaii	6.2
11	Idaho	8.2
19	Illinois	7.7
13	Indiana	8.1
1	Iowa	10.4
9	Kansas	8.3
24	Kentucky	7.6
19	Louisiana	7.7
24	Maine	7.6
36	Maryland	6.9
24	Massachusetts	7.6
24	Michigan	7.6
19	Minnesota	7.7
32	Mississippi	7.2
16	Missouri	7.9
6	Montana	8.5
6	Nebraska	8.5
40	Nevada	6.4
24	New Hampshire	7.6
18	New Jersey	7.8
42	New Mexico	6.1
34	New York	7.0
36	North Carolina	6.9
NA	North Dakota**	NA
9	Ohio	8.3
13	Oklahoma	8.1
34	Oregon	7.0
5	Pennsylvania	8.6
31	Rhode Island	7.5
24	South Carolina	7.6
2	South Dakota	9.0
16	Tennessee	7.9
44	Texas	6.0
47	Utah	5.1
15	Vermont	8.0
38	Virginia	6.5
19	Washington	7.7
33	West Virginia	7.1
4	Wisconsin	8.8
NA	Wyoming**	NA

RANK ORDER

RANK	STATE	RATE
1	Iowa	10.4
2	Florida	9.0
2	South Dakota	9.0
4	Wisconsin	8.8
5	Pennsylvania	8.6
6	Arkansas	8.5
6	Montana	8.5
6	Nebraska	8.5
9	Kansas	8.3
9	Ohio	8.3
11	Delaware	8.2
11	Idaho	8.2
13	Indiana	8.1
13	Oklahoma	8.1
15	Vermont	8.0
16	Missouri	7.9
16	Tennessee	7.9
18	New Jersey	7.8
19	Connecticut	7.7
19	Illinois	7.7
19	Louisiana	7.7
19	Minnesota	7.7
19	Washington	7.7
24	Alabama	7.6
24	Kentucky	7.6
24	Maine	7.6
24	Massachusetts	7.6
24	Michigan	7.6
24	New Hampshire	7.6
24	South Carolina	7.6
31	Rhode Island	7.5
32	Mississippi	7.2
33	West Virginia	7.1
34	New York	7.0
34	Oregon	7.0
36	Maryland	6.9
36	North Carolina	6.9
38	Arizona	6.5
38	Virginia	6.5
40	Nevada	6.4
41	Hawaii	6.2
42	Colorado	6.1
42	New Mexico	6.1
44	Texas	6.0
45	California	5.9
46	Georgia	5.8
47	Utah	5.1
NA	Alaska**	NA
NA	North Dakota**	NA
NA	Wyoming**	NA
	District of Columbia**	NA

Source: CQ Press using data from American Cancer Society
"Cancer Facts & Figures 2007" (Copyright 2007, American Cancer Society)
*Rates calculated using 2006 Census resident population estimates. Not age-adjusted.
**Fewer than 50 deaths.

Estimated Deaths by Liver Cancer in 2007

National Estimated Total = 16,780 Deaths

ALPHA ORDER

RANK	STATE	DEATHS	% of USA
20	Alabama	300	1.8%
NA	Alaska*	NA	NA
15	Arizona	330	2.0%
26	Arkansas	200	1.2%
1	California	2,270	13.5%
26	Colorado	200	1.2%
28	Connecticut	190	1.1%
NA	Delaware*	NA	NA
3	Florida	1,190	7.1%
14	Georgia	360	2.1%
36	Hawaii	110	0.7%
43	Idaho	50	0.3%
6	Illinois	650	3.9%
21	Indiana	290	1.7%
32	Iowa	140	0.8%
35	Kansas	120	0.7%
25	Kentucky	220	1.3%
15	Louisiana	330	2.0%
38	Maine	70	0.4%
22	Maryland	250	1.5%
11	Massachusetts	380	2.3%
8	Michigan	560	3.3%
23	Minnesota	240	1.4%
30	Mississippi	180	1.1%
15	Missouri	330	2.0%
NA	Montana*	NA	NA
38	Nebraska	70	0.4%
32	Nevada	140	0.8%
38	New Hampshire	70	0.4%
9	New Jersey	530	3.2%
32	New Mexico	140	0.8%
4	New York	1,090	6.5%
10	North Carolina	420	2.5%
NA	North Dakota*	NA	NA
7	Ohio	600	3.6%
30	Oklahoma	180	1.1%
28	Oregon	190	1.1%
5	Pennsylvania	790	4.7%
38	Rhode Island	70	0.4%
24	South Carolina	230	1.4%
NA	South Dakota*	NA	NA
15	Tennessee	330	2.0%
2	Texas	1,490	8.9%
38	Utah	70	0.4%
NA	Vermont*	NA	NA
13	Virginia	370	2.2%
11	Washington	380	2.3%
36	West Virginia	110	0.7%
19	Wisconsin	310	1.8%
NA	Wyoming*	NA	NA

RANK ORDER

RANK	STATE	DEATHS	% of USA
1	California	2,270	13.5%
2	Texas	1,490	8.9%
3	Florida	1,190	7.1%
4	New York	1,090	6.5%
5	Pennsylvania	790	4.7%
6	Illinois	650	3.9%
7	Ohio	600	3.6%
8	Michigan	560	3.3%
9	New Jersey	530	3.2%
10	North Carolina	420	2.5%
11	Massachusetts	380	2.3%
11	Washington	380	2.3%
13	Virginia	370	2.2%
14	Georgia	360	2.1%
15	Arizona	330	2.0%
15	Louisiana	330	2.0%
15	Missouri	330	2.0%
15	Tennessee	330	2.0%
19	Wisconsin	310	1.8%
20	Alabama	300	1.8%
21	Indiana	290	1.7%
22	Maryland	250	1.5%
23	Minnesota	240	1.4%
24	South Carolina	230	1.4%
25	Kentucky	220	1.3%
26	Arkansas	200	1.2%
26	Colorado	200	1.2%
28	Connecticut	190	1.1%
28	Oregon	190	1.1%
30	Mississippi	180	1.1%
30	Oklahoma	180	1.1%
32	Iowa	140	0.8%
32	Nevada	140	0.8%
32	New Mexico	140	0.8%
35	Kansas	120	0.7%
36	Hawaii	110	0.7%
36	West Virginia	110	0.7%
38	Maine	70	0.4%
38	Nebraska	70	0.4%
38	New Hampshire	70	0.4%
38	Rhode Island	70	0.4%
38	Utah	70	0.4%
43	Idaho	50	0.3%
NA	Alaska*	NA	NA
NA	Delaware*	NA	NA
NA	Montana*	NA	NA
NA	North Dakota*	NA	NA
NA	South Dakota*	NA	NA
NA	Vermont*	NA	NA
NA	Wyoming*	NA	NA
	District of Columbia*	NA	NA

Source: American Cancer Society
"Cancer Facts & Figures 2007" (Copyright 2007, American Cancer Society)
*Fewer than 50 deaths.

Estimated Death Rate by Liver Cancer in 2007

National Estimated Rate = 5.6 Deaths per 100,000 Population*

ALPHA ORDER

RANK	STATE	RATE
7	Alabama	6.5
NA	Alaska**	NA
22	Arizona	5.4
4	Arkansas	7.1
10	California	6.2
39	Colorado	4.2
22	Connecticut	5.4
NA	Delaware**	NA
5	Florida	6.6
41	Georgia	3.8
1	Hawaii	8.6
42	Idaho	3.4
29	Illinois	5.1
35	Indiana	4.6
33	Iowa	4.7
38	Kansas	4.3
27	Kentucky	5.2
2	Louisiana	7.7
24	Maine	5.3
37	Maryland	4.5
14	Massachusetts	5.9
20	Michigan	5.5
35	Minnesota	4.6
10	Mississippi	6.2
16	Missouri	5.6
NA	Montana**	NA
40	Nebraska	4.0
16	Nevada	5.6
24	New Hampshire	5.3
12	New Jersey	6.1
3	New Mexico	7.2
16	New York	5.6
33	North Carolina	4.7
NA	North Dakota**	NA
27	Ohio	5.2
31	Oklahoma	5.0
29	Oregon	5.1
8	Pennsylvania	6.4
5	Rhode Island	6.6
24	South Carolina	5.3
NA	South Dakota**	NA
20	Tennessee	5.5
9	Texas	6.3
43	Utah	2.7
NA	Vermont**	NA
32	Virginia	4.8
14	Washington	5.9
13	West Virginia	6.0
16	Wisconsin	5.6
NA	Wyoming**	NA

RANK ORDER

RANK	STATE	RATE
1	Hawaii	8.6
2	Louisiana	7.7
3	New Mexico	7.2
4	Arkansas	7.1
5	Florida	6.6
5	Rhode Island	6.6
7	Alabama	6.5
8	Pennsylvania	6.4
9	Texas	6.3
10	California	6.2
10	Mississippi	6.2
12	New Jersey	6.1
13	West Virginia	6.0
14	Massachusetts	5.9
14	Washington	5.9
16	Missouri	5.6
16	Nevada	5.6
16	New York	5.6
16	Wisconsin	5.6
20	Michigan	5.5
20	Tennessee	5.5
22	Arizona	5.4
22	Connecticut	5.4
24	Maine	5.3
24	New Hampshire	5.3
24	South Carolina	5.3
27	Kentucky	5.2
27	Ohio	5.2
29	Illinois	5.1
29	Oregon	5.1
31	Oklahoma	5.0
32	Virginia	4.8
33	Iowa	4.7
33	North Carolina	4.7
35	Indiana	4.6
35	Minnesota	4.6
37	Maryland	4.5
38	Kansas	4.3
39	Colorado	4.2
40	Nebraska	4.0
41	Georgia	3.8
42	Idaho	3.4
43	Utah	2.7
NA	Alaska**	NA
NA	Delaware**	NA
NA	Montana**	NA
NA	North Dakota**	NA
NA	South Dakota**	NA
NA	Vermont**	NA
NA	Wyoming**	NA
	District of Columbia**	NA

Source: CQ Press using data from American Cancer Society
"Cancer Facts & Figures 2007" (Copyright 2007, American Cancer Society)
*Rates calculated using 2006 Census resident population estimates. Not age-adjusted.
**Fewer than 50 deaths.

Estimated Deaths by Lung Cancer in 2007

National Estimated Total = 160,390 Deaths

ALPHA ORDER				RANK ORDER			
RANK	STATE	DEATHS	% of USA	RANK	STATE	DEATHS	% of USA
18	Alabama	3,240	2.0%	1	California	13,220	8.2%
50	Alaska	230	0.1%	2	Florida	12,360	7.7%
23	Arizona	2,850	1.8%	3	Texas	9,920	6.2%
27	Arkansas	2,220	1.4%	4	New York	9,500	5.9%
1	California	13,220	8.2%	5	Pennsylvania	7,780	4.9%
32	Colorado	1,650	1.0%	6	Ohio	7,310	4.6%
30	Connecticut	1,860	1.2%	7	Illinois	6,690	4.2%
41	Delaware	580	0.4%	8	Michigan	5,840	3.6%
2	Florida	12,360	7.7%	9	North Carolina	5,150	3.2%
10	Georgia	4,500	2.8%	10	Georgia	4,500	2.8%
43	Hawaii	530	0.3%	11	New Jersey	4,380	2.7%
42	Idaho	570	0.4%	12	Tennessee	4,340	2.7%
7	Illinois	6,690	4.2%	13	Virginia	4,290	2.7%
15	Indiana	3,800	2.4%	14	Missouri	4,120	2.6%
31	Iowa	1,750	1.1%	15	Indiana	3,800	2.4%
33	Kansas	1,530	1.0%	16	Massachusetts	3,630	2.3%
17	Kentucky	3,450	2.2%	17	Kentucky	3,450	2.2%
20	Louisiana	3,020	1.9%	18	Alabama	3,240	2.0%
36	Maine	970	0.6%	19	Washington	3,170	2.0%
21	Maryland	2,900	1.8%	20	Louisiana	3,020	1.9%
16	Massachusetts	3,630	2.3%	21	Maryland	2,900	1.8%
8	Michigan	5,840	3.6%	22	Wisconsin	2,890	1.8%
25	Minnesota	2,460	1.5%	23	Arizona	2,850	1.8%
29	Mississippi	2,040	1.3%	24	South Carolina	2,750	1.7%
14	Missouri	4,120	2.6%	25	Minnesota	2,460	1.5%
44	Montana	520	0.3%	26	Oklahoma	2,390	1.5%
37	Nebraska	900	0.6%	27	Arkansas	2,220	1.4%
35	Nevada	1,330	0.8%	28	Oregon	2,140	1.3%
38	New Hampshire	740	0.5%	29	Mississippi	2,040	1.3%
11	New Jersey	4,380	2.7%	30	Connecticut	1,860	1.2%
39	New Mexico	720	0.4%	31	Iowa	1,750	1.1%
4	New York	9,500	5.9%	32	Colorado	1,650	1.0%
9	North Carolina	5,150	3.2%	33	Kansas	1,530	1.0%
47	North Dakota	350	0.2%	34	West Virginia	1,450	0.9%
6	Ohio	7,310	4.6%	35	Nevada	1,330	0.8%
26	Oklahoma	2,390	1.5%	36	Maine	970	0.6%
28	Oregon	2,140	1.3%	37	Nebraska	900	0.6%
5	Pennsylvania	7,780	4.9%	38	New Hampshire	740	0.5%
40	Rhode Island	640	0.4%	39	New Mexico	720	0.4%
24	South Carolina	2,750	1.7%	40	Rhode Island	640	0.4%
46	South Dakota	420	0.3%	41	Delaware	580	0.4%
12	Tennessee	4,340	2.7%	42	Idaho	570	0.4%
3	Texas	9,920	6.2%	43	Hawaii	530	0.3%
45	Utah	470	0.3%	44	Montana	520	0.3%
47	Vermont	350	0.2%	45	Utah	470	0.3%
13	Virginia	4,290	2.7%	46	South Dakota	420	0.3%
19	Washington	3,170	2.0%	47	North Dakota	350	0.2%
34	West Virginia	1,450	0.9%	47	Vermont	350	0.2%
22	Wisconsin	2,890	1.8%	49	Wyoming	260	0.2%
49	Wyoming	260	0.2%	50	Alaska	230	0.1%
					District of Columbia	260	0.2%

Source: American Cancer Society
  "Cancer Facts & Figures 2007" (Copyright 2007, American Cancer Society)

Estimated Death Rate by Lung Cancer in 2007

National Estimated Rate = 53.6 Deaths per 100,000 Population*

ALPHA ORDER

RANK	STATE	RATE
7	Alabama	70.4
49	Alaska	34.3
42	Arizona	46.2
3	Arkansas	79.0
47	California	36.3
48	Colorado	34.7
31	Connecticut	53.1
11	Delaware	68.0
10	Florida	68.3
40	Georgia	48.1
44	Hawaii	41.2
45	Idaho	38.9
32	Illinois	52.1
16	Indiana	60.2
18	Iowa	58.7
26	Kansas	55.4
1	Kentucky	82.0
7	Louisiana	70.4
4	Maine	73.4
34	Maryland	51.6
22	Massachusetts	56.4
20	Michigan	57.8
41	Minnesota	47.6
9	Mississippi	70.1
6	Missouri	70.5
27	Montana	55.0
35	Nebraska	50.9
30	Nevada	53.3
23	New Hampshire	56.3
37	New Jersey	50.2
46	New Mexico	36.8
39	New York	49.2
19	North Carolina	58.1
27	North Dakota	55.0
13	Ohio	63.7
12	Oklahoma	66.8
20	Oregon	57.8
15	Pennsylvania	62.5
17	Rhode Island	59.9
14	South Carolina	63.6
29	South Dakota	53.7
5	Tennessee	71.9
43	Texas	42.2
50	Utah	18.4
24	Vermont	56.1
24	Virginia	56.1
38	Washington	49.6
2	West Virginia	79.7
33	Wisconsin	52.0
36	Wyoming	50.5

RANK ORDER

RANK	STATE	RATE
1	Kentucky	82.0
2	West Virginia	79.7
3	Arkansas	79.0
4	Maine	73.4
5	Tennessee	71.9
6	Missouri	70.5
7	Alabama	70.4
7	Louisiana	70.4
9	Mississippi	70.1
10	Florida	68.3
11	Delaware	68.0
12	Oklahoma	66.8
13	Ohio	63.7
14	South Carolina	63.6
15	Pennsylvania	62.5
16	Indiana	60.2
17	Rhode Island	59.9
18	Iowa	58.7
19	North Carolina	58.1
20	Michigan	57.8
20	Oregon	57.8
22	Massachusetts	56.4
23	New Hampshire	56.3
24	Vermont	56.1
24	Virginia	56.1
26	Kansas	55.4
27	Montana	55.0
27	North Dakota	55.0
29	South Dakota	53.7
30	Nevada	53.3
31	Connecticut	53.1
32	Illinois	52.1
33	Wisconsin	52.0
34	Maryland	51.6
35	Nebraska	50.9
36	Wyoming	50.5
37	New Jersey	50.2
38	Washington	49.6
39	New York	49.2
40	Georgia	48.1
41	Minnesota	47.6
42	Arizona	46.2
43	Texas	42.2
44	Hawaii	41.2
45	Idaho	38.9
46	New Mexico	36.8
47	California	36.3
48	Colorado	34.7
49	Alaska	34.3
50	Utah	18.4

District of Columbia 44.7

Source: CQ Press using data from American Cancer Society
"Cancer Facts & Figures 2007" (Copyright 2007, American Cancer Society)
*Rates calculated using 2006 Census resident population estimates. Not age-adjusted.

Estimated Deaths by Non-Hodgkin's Lymphoma in 2007

National Estimated Total = 18,660 Deaths

RANK	STATE	DEATHS	% of USA
20	Alabama	330	1.8%
NA	Alaska*	NA	NA
21	Arizona	320	1.7%
32	Arkansas	200	1.1%
1	California	1,830	9.8%
28	Colorado	240	1.3%
29	Connecticut	230	1.2%
45	Delaware	60	0.3%
2	Florida	1,300	7.0%
12	Georgia	470	2.5%
41	Hawaii	90	0.5%
40	Idaho	100	0.5%
6	Illinois	750	4.0%
14	Indiana	430	2.3%
25	Iowa	300	1.6%
30	Kansas	220	1.2%
26	Kentucky	290	1.6%
24	Louisiana	310	1.7%
38	Maine	110	0.6%
21	Maryland	320	1.7%
15	Massachusetts	420	2.3%
7	Michigan	660	3.5%
19	Minnesota	350	1.9%
33	Mississippi	170	0.9%
11	Missouri	500	2.7%
43	Montana	80	0.4%
38	Nebraska	110	0.6%
36	Nevada	130	0.7%
41	New Hampshire	90	0.5%
9	New Jersey	600	3.2%
37	New Mexico	120	0.6%
5	New York	1,030	5.5%
10	North Carolina	570	3.1%
NA	North Dakota*	NA	NA
8	Ohio	610	3.3%
31	Oklahoma	210	1.1%
17	Oregon	360	1.9%
4	Pennsylvania	1,140	6.1%
45	Rhode Island	60	0.3%
27	South Carolina	260	1.4%
43	South Dakota	80	0.4%
16	Tennessee	410	2.2%
3	Texas	1,160	6.2%
35	Utah	140	0.8%
47	Vermont	50	0.3%
17	Virginia	360	1.9%
13	Washington	440	2.4%
33	West Virginia	170	0.9%
21	Wisconsin	320	1.7%
NA	Wyoming*	NA	NA

RANK	STATE	DEATHS	% of USA
1	California	1,830	9.8%
2	Florida	1,300	7.0%
3	Texas	1,160	6.2%
4	Pennsylvania	1,140	6.1%
5	New York	1,030	5.5%
6	Illinois	750	4.0%
7	Michigan	660	3.5%
8	Ohio	610	3.3%
9	New Jersey	600	3.2%
10	North Carolina	570	3.1%
11	Missouri	500	2.7%
12	Georgia	470	2.5%
13	Washington	440	2.4%
14	Indiana	430	2.3%
15	Massachusetts	420	2.3%
16	Tennessee	410	2.2%
17	Oregon	360	1.9%
17	Virginia	360	1.9%
19	Minnesota	350	1.9%
20	Alabama	330	1.8%
21	Arizona	320	1.7%
21	Maryland	320	1.7%
21	Wisconsin	320	1.7%
24	Louisiana	310	1.7%
25	Iowa	300	1.6%
26	Kentucky	290	1.6%
27	South Carolina	260	1.4%
28	Colorado	240	1.3%
29	Connecticut	230	1.2%
30	Kansas	220	1.2%
31	Oklahoma	210	1.1%
32	Arkansas	200	1.1%
33	Mississippi	170	0.9%
33	West Virginia	170	0.9%
35	Utah	140	0.8%
36	Nevada	130	0.7%
37	New Mexico	120	0.6%
38	Maine	110	0.6%
38	Nebraska	110	0.6%
40	Idaho	100	0.5%
41	Hawaii	90	0.5%
41	New Hampshire	90	0.5%
43	Montana	80	0.4%
43	South Dakota	80	0.4%
45	Delaware	60	0.3%
45	Rhode Island	60	0.3%
47	Vermont	50	0.3%
NA	Alaska*	NA	NA
NA	North Dakota*	NA	NA
NA	Wyoming*	NA	NA
	District of Columbia*	NA	NA

Source: American Cancer Society
"Cancer Facts & Figures 2007" (Copyright 2007, American Cancer Society)
*Fewer than 50 deaths.

Estimated Death Rate by Non-Hodgkin's Lymphoma in 2007

National Estimated Rate = 6.2 Deaths per 100,000 Population*

ALPHA ORDER

RANK	STATE	RATE
11	Alabama	7.2
NA	Alaska**	NA
41	Arizona	5.2
14	Arkansas	7.1
43	California	5.0
43	Colorado	5.0
25	Connecticut	6.6
15	Delaware	7.0
11	Florida	7.2
43	Georgia	5.0
15	Hawaii	7.0
20	Idaho	6.8
33	Illinois	5.8
20	Indiana	6.8
2	Iowa	10.1
9	Kansas	8.0
17	Kentucky	6.9
11	Louisiana	7.2
8	Maine	8.3
36	Maryland	5.7
26	Massachusetts	6.5
26	Michigan	6.5
20	Minnesota	6.8
33	Mississippi	5.8
6	Missouri	8.6
7	Montana	8.5
29	Nebraska	6.2
41	Nevada	5.2
20	New Hampshire	6.8
17	New Jersey	6.9
30	New Mexico	6.1
39	New York	5.3
28	North Carolina	6.4
NA	North Dakota**	NA
39	Ohio	5.3
32	Oklahoma	5.9
3	Oregon	9.7
5	Pennsylvania	9.2
37	Rhode Island	5.6
31	South Carolina	6.0
1	South Dakota	10.2
20	Tennessee	6.8
46	Texas	4.9
38	Utah	5.5
9	Vermont	8.0
47	Virginia	4.7
17	Washington	6.9
4	West Virginia	9.3
33	Wisconsin	5.8
NA	Wyoming**	NA

RANK ORDER

RANK	STATE	RATE
1	South Dakota	10.2
2	Iowa	10.1
3	Oregon	9.7
4	West Virginia	9.3
5	Pennsylvania	9.2
6	Missouri	8.6
7	Montana	8.5
8	Maine	8.3
9	Kansas	8.0
9	Vermont	8.0
11	Alabama	7.2
11	Florida	7.2
11	Louisiana	7.2
14	Arkansas	7.1
15	Delaware	7.0
15	Hawaii	7.0
17	Kentucky	6.9
17	New Jersey	6.9
17	Washington	6.9
20	Idaho	6.8
20	Indiana	6.8
20	Minnesota	6.8
20	New Hampshire	6.8
20	Tennessee	6.8
25	Connecticut	6.6
26	Massachusetts	6.5
26	Michigan	6.5
28	North Carolina	6.4
29	Nebraska	6.2
30	New Mexico	6.1
31	South Carolina	6.0
32	Oklahoma	5.9
33	Illinois	5.8
33	Mississippi	5.8
33	Wisconsin	5.8
36	Maryland	5.7
37	Rhode Island	5.6
38	Utah	5.5
39	New York	5.3
39	Ohio	5.3
41	Arizona	5.2
41	Nevada	5.2
43	California	5.0
43	Colorado	5.0
43	Georgia	5.0
46	Texas	4.9
47	Virginia	4.7
NA	Alaska**	NA
NA	North Dakota**	NA
NA	Wyoming**	NA
	District of Columbia**	NA

Source: CQ Press using data from American Cancer Society
  "Cancer Facts & Figures 2007" (Copyright 2007, American Cancer Society)
*Rates calculated using 2006 Census resident population estimates. Not age-adjusted.
**Fewer than 50 deaths.

Estimated Deaths by Ovarian Cancer in 2007

National Estimated Total = 15,280 Deaths

ALPHA ORDER

RANK	STATE	DEATHS	% of USA
19	Alabama	290	1.9%
NA	Alaska*	NA	NA
18	Arizona	300	2.0%
33	Arkansas	140	0.9%
1	California	1,680	11.0%
24	Colorado	220	1.4%
28	Connecticut	190	1.2%
43	Delaware	50	0.3%
2	Florida	1,040	6.8%
11	Georgia	420	2.7%
43	Hawaii	50	0.3%
43	Idaho	50	0.3%
7	Illinois	620	4.1%
15	Indiana	350	2.3%
28	Iowa	190	1.2%
31	Kansas	150	1.0%
24	Kentucky	220	1.4%
24	Louisiana	220	1.4%
39	Maine	80	0.5%
21	Maryland	270	1.8%
14	Massachusetts	360	2.4%
8	Michigan	540	3.5%
22	Minnesota	250	1.6%
31	Mississippi	150	1.0%
16	Missouri	320	2.1%
40	Montana	60	0.4%
36	Nebraska	90	0.6%
35	Nevada	130	0.9%
40	New Hampshire	60	0.4%
9	New Jersey	490	3.2%
36	New Mexico	90	0.6%
3	New York	1,020	6.7%
10	North Carolina	450	2.9%
NA	North Dakota*	NA	NA
6	Ohio	650	4.3%
30	Oklahoma	170	1.1%
23	Oregon	230	1.5%
5	Pennsylvania	790	5.2%
40	Rhode Island	60	0.4%
24	South Carolina	220	1.4%
43	South Dakota	50	0.3%
16	Tennessee	320	2.1%
4	Texas	860	5.6%
36	Utah	90	0.6%
NA	Vermont*	NA	NA
12	Virginia	390	2.6%
13	Washington	370	2.4%
33	West Virginia	140	0.9%
19	Wisconsin	290	1.9%
NA	Wyoming*	NA	NA

RANK ORDER

RANK	STATE	DEATHS	% of USA
1	California	1,680	11.0%
2	Florida	1,040	6.8%
3	New York	1,020	6.7%
4	Texas	860	5.6%
5	Pennsylvania	790	5.2%
6	Ohio	650	4.3%
7	Illinois	620	4.1%
8	Michigan	540	3.5%
9	New Jersey	490	3.2%
10	North Carolina	450	2.9%
11	Georgia	420	2.7%
12	Virginia	390	2.6%
13	Washington	370	2.4%
14	Massachusetts	360	2.4%
15	Indiana	350	2.3%
16	Missouri	320	2.1%
16	Tennessee	320	2.1%
18	Arizona	300	2.0%
19	Alabama	290	1.9%
19	Wisconsin	290	1.9%
21	Maryland	270	1.8%
22	Minnesota	250	1.6%
23	Oregon	230	1.5%
24	Colorado	220	1.4%
24	Kentucky	220	1.4%
24	Louisiana	220	1.4%
24	South Carolina	220	1.4%
28	Connecticut	190	1.2%
28	Iowa	190	1.2%
30	Oklahoma	170	1.1%
31	Kansas	150	1.0%
31	Mississippi	150	1.0%
33	Arkansas	140	0.9%
33	West Virginia	140	0.9%
35	Nevada	130	0.9%
36	Nebraska	90	0.6%
36	New Mexico	90	0.6%
36	Utah	90	0.6%
39	Maine	80	0.5%
40	Montana	60	0.4%
40	New Hampshire	60	0.4%
40	Rhode Island	60	0.4%
43	Delaware	50	0.3%
43	Hawaii	50	0.3%
43	Idaho	50	0.3%
43	South Dakota	50	0.3%
NA	Alaska*	NA	NA
NA	North Dakota*	NA	NA
NA	Vermont*	NA	NA
NA	Wyoming*	NA	NA
	District of Columbia*	NA	NA

Source: American Cancer Society
"Cancer Facts & Figures 2007" (Copyright 2007, American Cancer Society)
*Fewer than 50 deaths.

Estimated Death Rate by Ovarian Cancer in 2007

National Estimated Rate = 10.2 Deaths per 100,000 Female Population*

ALPHA ORDER

RANK	STATE	RATE
6	Alabama	12.4
NA	Alaska**	NA
27	Arizona	10.1
32	Arkansas	9.9
39	California	9.3
34	Colorado	9.5
20	Connecticut	10.5
10	Delaware	11.6
11	Florida	11.5
40	Georgia	9.2
43	Hawaii	7.8
46	Idaho	7.0
34	Illinois	9.5
13	Indiana	11.0
4	Iowa	12.6
16	Kansas	10.9
23	Kentucky	10.4
34	Louisiana	9.5
8	Maine	11.8
38	Maryland	9.4
16	Massachusetts	10.9
20	Michigan	10.5
33	Minnesota	9.7
31	Mississippi	10.0
18	Missouri	10.8
2	Montana	12.8
27	Nebraska	10.1
13	Nevada	11.0
42	New Hampshire	9.0
13	New Jersey	11.0
40	New Mexico	9.2
25	New York	10.3
26	North Carolina	10.2
NA	North Dakota**	NA
12	Ohio	11.1
34	Oklahoma	9.5
4	Oregon	12.6
7	Pennsylvania	12.3
18	Rhode Island	10.8
27	South Carolina	10.1
2	South Dakota	12.8
20	Tennessee	10.5
44	Texas	7.5
45	Utah	7.3
NA	Vermont**	NA
27	Virginia	10.1
8	Washington	11.8
1	West Virginia	15.1
23	Wisconsin	10.4
NA	Wyoming**	NA

RANK ORDER

RANK	STATE	RATE
1	West Virginia	15.1
2	Montana	12.8
2	South Dakota	12.8
4	Iowa	12.6
4	Oregon	12.6
6	Alabama	12.4
7	Pennsylvania	12.3
8	Maine	11.8
8	Washington	11.8
10	Delaware	11.6
11	Florida	11.5
12	Ohio	11.1
13	Indiana	11.0
13	Nevada	11.0
13	New Jersey	11.0
16	Kansas	10.9
16	Massachusetts	10.9
18	Missouri	10.8
18	Rhode Island	10.8
20	Connecticut	10.5
20	Michigan	10.5
20	Tennessee	10.5
23	Kentucky	10.4
23	Wisconsin	10.4
25	New York	10.3
26	North Carolina	10.2
27	Arizona	10.1
27	Nebraska	10.1
27	South Carolina	10.1
27	Virginia	10.1
31	Mississippi	10.0
32	Arkansas	9.9
33	Minnesota	9.7
34	Colorado	9.5
34	Illinois	9.5
34	Louisiana	9.5
34	Oklahoma	9.5
38	Maryland	9.4
39	California	9.3
40	Georgia	9.2
40	New Mexico	9.2
42	New Hampshire	9.0
43	Hawaii	7.8
44	Texas	7.5
45	Utah	7.3
46	Idaho	7.0
NA	Alaska**	NA
NA	North Dakota**	NA
NA	Vermont**	NA
NA	Wyoming**	NA
	District of Columbia**	NA

Source: CQ Press using data from American Cancer Society
    "Cancer Facts & Figures 2007" (Copyright 2007, American Cancer Society)
*Rates calculated using 2005 Census female population estimates. Not age-adjusted.
**Fewer than 50 deaths.

Estimated Deaths by Pancreatic Cancer in 2007

National Estimated Total = 33,370 Deaths

ALPHA ORDER

RANK	STATE	DEATHS	% of USA
22	Alabama	530	1.6%
50	Alaska	50	0.1%
20	Arizona	590	1.8%
32	Arkansas	310	0.9%
1	California	3,480	10.4%
28	Colorado	410	1.2%
25	Connecticut	480	1.4%
45	Delaware	100	0.3%
2	Florida	2,350	7.0%
12	Georgia	820	2.5%
39	Hawaii	170	0.5%
42	Idaho	140	0.4%
6	Illinois	1,480	4.4%
14	Indiana	740	2.2%
29	Iowa	390	1.2%
32	Kansas	310	0.9%
26	Kentucky	460	1.4%
22	Louisiana	530	1.6%
36	Maine	190	0.6%
19	Maryland	640	1.9%
11	Massachusetts	860	2.6%
8	Michigan	1,180	3.5%
21	Minnesota	550	1.6%
31	Mississippi	340	1.0%
17	Missouri	690	2.1%
44	Montana	110	0.3%
38	Nebraska	180	0.5%
34	Nevada	260	0.8%
41	New Hampshire	150	0.4%
9	New Jersey	1,070	3.2%
36	New Mexico	190	0.6%
3	New York	2,330	7.0%
10	North Carolina	980	2.9%
47	North Dakota	80	0.2%
7	Ohio	1,370	4.1%
30	Oklahoma	370	1.1%
27	Oregon	440	1.3%
5	Pennsylvania	1,780	5.3%
42	Rhode Island	140	0.4%
24	South Carolina	510	1.5%
45	South Dakota	100	0.3%
16	Tennessee	700	2.1%
4	Texas	2,010	6.0%
39	Utah	170	0.5%
48	Vermont	70	0.2%
13	Virginia	800	2.4%
14	Washington	740	2.2%
35	West Virginia	220	0.7%
18	Wisconsin	680	2.0%
49	Wyoming	60	0.2%

RANK ORDER

RANK	STATE	DEATHS	% of USA
1	California	3,480	10.4%
2	Florida	2,350	7.0%
3	New York	2,330	7.0%
4	Texas	2,010	6.0%
5	Pennsylvania	1,780	5.3%
6	Illinois	1,480	4.4%
7	Ohio	1,370	4.1%
8	Michigan	1,180	3.5%
9	New Jersey	1,070	3.2%
10	North Carolina	980	2.9%
11	Massachusetts	860	2.6%
12	Georgia	820	2.5%
13	Virginia	800	2.4%
14	Indiana	740	2.2%
14	Washington	740	2.2%
16	Tennessee	700	2.1%
17	Missouri	690	2.1%
18	Wisconsin	680	2.0%
19	Maryland	640	1.9%
20	Arizona	590	1.8%
21	Minnesota	550	1.6%
22	Alabama	530	1.6%
22	Louisiana	530	1.6%
24	South Carolina	510	1.5%
25	Connecticut	480	1.4%
26	Kentucky	460	1.4%
27	Oregon	440	1.3%
28	Colorado	410	1.2%
29	Iowa	390	1.2%
30	Oklahoma	370	1.1%
31	Mississippi	340	1.0%
32	Arkansas	310	0.9%
32	Kansas	310	0.9%
34	Nevada	260	0.8%
35	West Virginia	220	0.7%
36	Maine	190	0.6%
36	New Mexico	190	0.6%
38	Nebraska	180	0.5%
39	Hawaii	170	0.5%
39	Utah	170	0.5%
41	New Hampshire	150	0.4%
42	Idaho	140	0.4%
42	Rhode Island	140	0.4%
44	Montana	110	0.3%
45	Delaware	100	0.3%
45	South Dakota	100	0.3%
47	North Dakota	80	0.2%
48	Vermont	70	0.2%
49	Wyoming	60	0.2%
50	Alaska	50	0.1%
	District of Columbia	60	0.2%

Source: American Cancer Society
"Cancer Facts & Figures 2007" (Copyright 2007, American Cancer Society)

Estimated Death Rate by Pancreatic Cancer in 2007

National Estimated Rate = 11.1 Deaths per 100,000 Population*

ALPHA ORDER

RANK	STATE	RATE
28	Alabama	11.5
49	Alaska	7.5
43	Arizona	9.6
35	Arkansas	11.0
44	California	9.5
47	Colorado	8.6
3	Connecticut	13.7
20	Delaware	11.7
8	Florida	13.0
46	Georgia	8.8
5	Hawaii	13.2
44	Idaho	9.5
28	Illinois	11.5
20	Indiana	11.7
6	Iowa	13.1
32	Kansas	11.2
36	Kentucky	10.9
11	Louisiana	12.4
1	Maine	14.4
30	Maryland	11.4
4	Massachusetts	13.4
20	Michigan	11.7
37	Minnesota	10.6
20	Mississippi	11.7
18	Missouri	11.8
25	Montana	11.6
41	Nebraska	10.2
39	Nevada	10.4
30	New Hampshire	11.4
12	New Jersey	12.3
42	New Mexico	9.7
14	New York	12.1
34	North Carolina	11.1
10	North Dakota	12.6
16	Ohio	11.9
40	Oklahoma	10.3
16	Oregon	11.9
2	Pennsylvania	14.3
6	Rhode Island	13.1
18	South Carolina	11.8
9	South Dakota	12.8
25	Tennessee	11.6
47	Texas	8.6
50	Utah	6.7
32	Vermont	11.2
38	Virginia	10.5
25	Washington	11.6
14	West Virginia	12.1
13	Wisconsin	12.2
20	Wyoming	11.7

RANK ORDER

RANK	STATE	RATE
1	Maine	14.4
2	Pennsylvania	14.3
3	Connecticut	13.7
4	Massachusetts	13.4
5	Hawaii	13.2
6	Iowa	13.1
6	Rhode Island	13.1
8	Florida	13.0
9	South Dakota	12.8
10	North Dakota	12.6
11	Louisiana	12.4
12	New Jersey	12.3
13	Wisconsin	12.2
14	New York	12.1
14	West Virginia	12.1
16	Ohio	11.9
16	Oregon	11.9
18	Missouri	11.8
18	South Carolina	11.8
20	Delaware	11.7
20	Indiana	11.7
20	Michigan	11.7
20	Mississippi	11.7
20	Wyoming	11.7
25	Montana	11.6
25	Tennessee	11.6
25	Washington	11.6
28	Alabama	11.5
28	Illinois	11.5
30	Maryland	11.4
30	New Hampshire	11.4
32	Kansas	11.2
32	Vermont	11.2
34	North Carolina	11.1
35	Arkansas	11.0
36	Kentucky	10.9
37	Minnesota	10.6
38	Virginia	10.5
39	Nevada	10.4
40	Oklahoma	10.3
41	Nebraska	10.2
42	New Mexico	9.7
43	Arizona	9.6
44	California	9.5
44	Idaho	9.5
46	Georgia	8.8
47	Colorado	8.6
47	Texas	8.6
49	Alaska	7.5
50	Utah	6.7
	District of Columbia	10.3

Source: CQ Press using data from American Cancer Society
"Cancer Facts & Figures 2007" (Copyright 2007, American Cancer Society)
*Rates calculated using 2006 Census resident population estimates. Not age-adjusted.

Estimated Deaths by Prostate Cancer in 2007

National Estimated Total = 27,050 Deaths

ALPHA ORDER					RANK ORDER			
RANK	STATE		DEATHS	% of USA	RANK	STATE	DEATHS	% of USA
22	Alabama		480	1.8%	1	California	3,040	11.2%
NA	Alaska*		NA	NA	2	Florida	2,180	8.1%
19	Arizona		520	1.9%	3	New York	1,630	6.0%
30	Arkansas		300	1.1%	4	Texas	1,620	6.0%
1	California		3,040	11.2%	5	Ohio	1,350	5.0%
28	Colorado		330	1.2%	6	Pennsylvania	1,310	4.8%
25	Connecticut		390	1.4%	7	Illinois	990	3.7%
47	Delaware		90	0.3%	8	Michigan	850	3.1%
2	Florida		2,180	8.1%	9	North Carolina	800	3.0%
11	Georgia		630	2.3%	10	New Jersey	750	2.8%
42	Hawaii		130	0.5%	11	Georgia	630	2.3%
39	Idaho		150	0.6%	11	Washington	630	2.3%
7	Illinois		990	3.7%	13	Indiana	600	2.2%
13	Indiana		600	2.2%	13	Virginia	600	2.2%
26	Iowa		350	1.3%	15	Massachusetts	560	2.1%
34	Kansas		220	0.8%	16	Tennessee	550	2.0%
29	Kentucky		310	1.1%	17	Maryland	540	2.0%
24	Louisiana		400	1.5%	17	Wisconsin	540	2.0%
36	Maine		180	0.7%	19	Arizona	520	1.9%
17	Maryland		540	2.0%	20	Missouri	510	1.9%
15	Massachusetts		560	2.1%	21	Minnesota	490	1.8%
8	Michigan		850	3.1%	22	Alabama	480	1.8%
21	Minnesota		490	1.8%	23	South Carolina	420	1.6%
31	Mississippi		290	1.1%	24	Louisiana	400	1.5%
20	Missouri		510	1.9%	25	Connecticut	390	1.4%
43	Montana		110	0.4%	26	Iowa	350	1.3%
37	Nebraska		170	0.6%	27	Oregon	340	1.3%
33	Nevada		230	0.9%	28	Colorado	330	1.2%
40	New Hampshire		140	0.5%	29	Kentucky	310	1.1%
10	New Jersey		750	2.8%	30	Arkansas	300	1.1%
35	New Mexico		200	0.7%	31	Mississippi	290	1.1%
3	New York		1,630	6.0%	32	Oklahoma	280	1.0%
9	North Carolina		800	3.0%	33	Nevada	230	0.9%
46	North Dakota		100	0.4%	34	Kansas	220	0.8%
5	Ohio		1,350	5.0%	35	New Mexico	200	0.7%
32	Oklahoma		280	1.0%	36	Maine	180	0.7%
27	Oregon		340	1.3%	37	Nebraska	170	0.6%
6	Pennsylvania		1,310	4.8%	38	West Virginia	160	0.6%
43	Rhode Island		110	0.4%	39	Idaho	150	0.6%
23	South Carolina		420	1.6%	40	New Hampshire	140	0.5%
43	South Dakota		110	0.4%	40	Utah	140	0.5%
16	Tennessee		550	2.0%	42	Hawaii	130	0.5%
4	Texas		1,620	6.0%	43	Montana	110	0.4%
40	Utah		140	0.5%	43	Rhode Island	110	0.4%
48	Vermont		80	0.3%	43	South Dakota	110	0.4%
13	Virginia		600	2.2%	46	North Dakota	100	0.4%
11	Washington		630	2.3%	47	Delaware	90	0.3%
38	West Virginia		160	0.6%	48	Vermont	80	0.3%
17	Wisconsin		540	2.0%	49	Wyoming	60	0.2%
49	Wyoming		60	0.2%	NA	Alaska*	NA	NA
						District of Columbia	60	0.2%

Source: American Cancer Society
"Cancer Facts & Figures 2007" (Copyright 2007, American Cancer Society)
*Fewer than 50 deaths.

Age-Adjusted Death Rate by Prostate Cancer in 2003

National Rate = 29.1 Deaths per 100,000 Male Population*

ALPHA ORDER

RANK	STATE	RATE
2	Alabama	36.9
41	Alaska	27.4
48	Arizona	25.5
9	Arkansas	31.9
46	California	26.4
33	Colorado	28.4
44	Connecticut	27.1
35	Delaware	28.3
49	Florida	24.5
5	Georgia	34.8
50	Hawaii	20.3
13	Idaho	31.1
15	Illinois	30.6
16	Indiana	30.5
19	Iowa	29.7
43	Kansas	27.2
18	Kentucky	29.9
4	Louisiana	34.9
31	Maine	28.8
12	Maryland	31.3
22	Massachusetts	29.4
22	Michigan	29.4
14	Minnesota	30.9
1	Mississippi	41.9
44	Missouri	27.1
21	Montana	29.6
47	Nebraska	26.2
32	Nevada	28.5
27	New Hampshire	29.3
33	New Jersey	28.4
27	New Mexico	29.3
37	New York	28.2
6	North Carolina	33.7
22	North Dakota	29.4
27	Ohio	29.3
40	Oklahoma	27.7
19	Oregon	29.7
30	Pennsylvania	29.2
41	Rhode Island	27.4
3	South Carolina	36.3
11	South Dakota	31.4
8	Tennessee	32.5
37	Texas	28.2
22	Utah	29.4
22	Vermont	29.4
7	Virginia	33.4
39	Washington	27.9
35	West Virginia	28.3
17	Wisconsin	30.4
10	Wyoming	31.8

RANK ORDER

RANK	STATE	RATE
1	Mississippi	41.9
2	Alabama	36.9
3	South Carolina	36.3
4	Louisiana	34.9
5	Georgia	34.8
6	North Carolina	33.7
7	Virginia	33.4
8	Tennessee	32.5
9	Arkansas	31.9
10	Wyoming	31.8
11	South Dakota	31.4
12	Maryland	31.3
13	Idaho	31.1
14	Minnesota	30.9
15	Illinois	30.6
16	Indiana	30.5
17	Wisconsin	30.4
18	Kentucky	29.9
19	Iowa	29.7
19	Oregon	29.7
21	Montana	29.6
22	Massachusetts	29.4
22	Michigan	29.4
22	North Dakota	29.4
22	Utah	29.4
22	Vermont	29.4
27	New Hampshire	29.3
27	New Mexico	29.3
27	Ohio	29.3
30	Pennsylvania	29.2
31	Maine	28.8
32	Nevada	28.5
33	Colorado	28.4
33	New Jersey	28.4
35	Delaware	28.3
35	West Virginia	28.3
37	New York	28.2
37	Texas	28.2
39	Washington	27.9
40	Oklahoma	27.7
41	Alaska	27.4
41	Rhode Island	27.4
43	Kansas	27.2
44	Connecticut	27.1
44	Missouri	27.1
46	California	26.4
47	Nebraska	26.2
48	Arizona	25.5
49	Florida	24.5
50	Hawaii	20.3
	District of Columbia	49.2

Source: American Cancer Society
    "Cancer Facts & Figures 2007" (Copyright 2007, American Cancer Society)
*For 1999 to 2003. Age-adjusted to the 2000 U.S. standard population.

Deaths by AIDS in 2004

National Total = 13,063 Deaths*

ALPHA ORDER					RANK ORDER			
RANK	STATE		DEATHS	% of USA	RANK	STATE	DEATHS	% of USA
17	Alabama		207	1.6%	1	New York	1,722	13.2%
44	Alaska		8	0.1%	2	Florida	1,719	13.2%
21	Arizona		158	1.2%	3	California	1,379	10.6%
27	Arkansas		77	0.6%	4	Texas	1,052	8.1%
3	California		1,379	10.6%	5	Georgia	700	5.4%
25	Colorado		88	0.7%	6	New Jersey	671	5.1%
18	Connecticut		189	1.4%	7	Maryland	557	4.3%
31	Delaware		58	0.4%	8	Pennsylvania	469	3.6%
2	Florida		1,719	13.2%	9	Illinois	414	3.2%
5	Georgia		700	5.4%	10	North Carolina	407	3.1%
39	Hawaii		23	0.2%	11	Louisiana	393	3.0%
48	Idaho		3	0.0%	12	Tennessee	289	2.2%
9	Illinois		414	3.2%	13	South Carolina	268	2.1%
24	Indiana		112	0.9%	14	Virginia	229	1.8%
37	Iowa		27	0.2%	15	Michigan	215	1.6%
38	Kansas		26	0.2%	16	Massachusetts	213	1.6%
29	Kentucky		66	0.5%	17	Alabama	207	1.6%
11	Louisiana		393	3.0%	18	Connecticut	189	1.4%
42	Maine		13	0.1%	19	Ohio	172	1.3%
7	Maryland		557	4.3%	20	Mississippi	164	1.3%
16	Massachusetts		213	1.6%	21	Arizona	158	1.2%
15	Michigan		215	1.6%	22	Missouri	145	1.1%
32	Minnesota		51	0.4%	23	Washington	122	0.9%
20	Mississippi		164	1.3%	24	Indiana	112	0.9%
22	Missouri		145	1.1%	25	Colorado	88	0.7%
50	Montana		0	0.0%	26	Nevada	79	0.6%
43	Nebraska		11	0.1%	27	Arkansas	77	0.6%
26	Nevada		79	0.6%	28	Oklahoma	73	0.6%
41	New Hampshire		16	0.1%	29	Kentucky	66	0.5%
6	New Jersey		671	5.1%	30	Oregon	63	0.5%
40	New Mexico		22	0.2%	31	Delaware	58	0.4%
1	New York		1,722	13.2%	32	Minnesota	51	0.4%
10	North Carolina		407	3.1%	33	Wisconsin	48	0.4%
48	North Dakota		3	0.0%	34	Utah	31	0.2%
19	Ohio		172	1.3%	34	West Virginia	31	0.2%
28	Oklahoma		73	0.6%	36	Rhode Island	28	0.2%
30	Oregon		63	0.5%	37	Iowa	27	0.2%
8	Pennsylvania		469	3.6%	38	Kansas	26	0.2%
36	Rhode Island		28	0.2%	39	Hawaii	23	0.2%
13	South Carolina		268	2.1%	40	New Mexico	22	0.2%
44	South Dakota		8	0.1%	41	New Hampshire	16	0.1%
12	Tennessee		289	2.2%	42	Maine	13	0.1%
4	Texas		1,052	8.1%	43	Nebraska	11	0.1%
34	Utah		31	0.2%	44	Alaska	8	0.1%
46	Vermont		4	0.0%	44	South Dakota	8	0.1%
14	Virginia		229	1.8%	46	Vermont	4	0.0%
23	Washington		122	0.9%	46	Wyoming	4	0.0%
34	West Virginia		31	0.2%	48	Idaho	3	0.0%
33	Wisconsin		48	0.4%	48	North Dakota	3	0.0%
46	Wyoming		4	0.0%	50	Montana	0	0.0%
						District of Columbia	236	1.8%

Source: U.S. Department of Health and Human Services, National Center for Health Statistics
"National Vital Statistics Reports" (Vol. 55, No. 19, August 21, 2007, http://www.cdc.gov/nchs/deaths.htm)
*AIDS is Acquired Immunodeficiency Syndrome. It is a specific group of diseases or conditions which are indicative of severe immunosuppression related to infection with the Human Immunodeficiency Virus (HIV).

Death Rate by AIDS in 2004

National Rate = 4.4 Deaths per 100,000 Population*

ALPHA ORDER

RANK	STATE	RATE
14	Alabama	4.6
NA	Alaska**	NA
21	Arizona	2.8
21	Arkansas	2.8
15	California	3.8
28	Colorado	1.9
10	Connecticut	5.4
7	Delaware	7.0
2	Florida	9.9
5	Georgia	7.9
29	Hawaii	1.8
NA	Idaho**	NA
18	Illinois	3.3
29	Indiana	1.8
39	Iowa	0.9
37	Kansas	1.0
33	Kentucky	1.6
4	Louisiana	8.7
NA	Maine**	NA
1	Maryland	10.0
18	Massachusetts	3.3
25	Michigan	2.1
37	Minnesota	1.0
9	Mississippi	5.6
24	Missouri	2.5
NA	Montana**	NA
NA	Nebraska**	NA
17	Nevada	3.4
NA	New Hampshire**	NA
6	New Jersey	7.7
36	New Mexico	1.2
3	New York	9.0
12	North Carolina	4.8
NA	North Dakota**	NA
34	Ohio	1.5
25	Oklahoma	2.1
29	Oregon	1.8
15	Pennsylvania	3.8
23	Rhode Island	2.6
8	South Carolina	6.4
NA	South Dakota**	NA
11	Tennessee	4.9
13	Texas	4.7
35	Utah	1.3
NA	Vermont**	NA
20	Virginia	3.1
27	Washington	2.0
32	West Virginia	1.7
39	Wisconsin	0.9
NA	Wyoming**	NA

RANK ORDER

RANK	STATE	RATE
1	Maryland	10.0
2	Florida	9.9
3	New York	9.0
4	Louisiana	8.7
5	Georgia	7.9
6	New Jersey	7.7
7	Delaware	7.0
8	South Carolina	6.4
9	Mississippi	5.6
10	Connecticut	5.4
11	Tennessee	4.9
12	North Carolina	4.8
13	Texas	4.7
14	Alabama	4.6
15	California	3.8
15	Pennsylvania	3.8
17	Nevada	3.4
18	Illinois	3.3
18	Massachusetts	3.3
20	Virginia	3.1
21	Arizona	2.8
21	Arkansas	2.8
23	Rhode Island	2.6
24	Missouri	2.5
25	Michigan	2.1
25	Oklahoma	2.1
27	Washington	2.0
28	Colorado	1.9
29	Hawaii	1.8
29	Indiana	1.8
29	Oregon	1.8
32	West Virginia	1.7
33	Kentucky	1.6
34	Ohio	1.5
35	Utah	1.3
36	New Mexico	1.2
37	Kansas	1.0
37	Minnesota	1.0
39	Iowa	0.9
39	Wisconsin	0.9
NA	Alaska**	NA
NA	Idaho**	NA
NA	Maine**	NA
NA	Montana**	NA
NA	Nebraska**	NA
NA	New Hampshire**	NA
NA	North Dakota**	NA
NA	South Dakota**	NA
NA	Vermont**	NA
NA	Wyoming**	NA

District of Columbia   42.6

Source: U.S. Department of Health and Human Services, National Center for Health Statistics
    "National Vital Statistics Reports" (Vol. 55, No. 19, August 21, 2007, http://www.cdc.gov/nchs/deaths.htm)
*AIDS is Acquired Immunodeficiency Syndrome. It is a specific group of diseases or conditions which are indicative of severe immunosuppression related to infection with the Human Immunodeficiency Virus (HIV). Not age-adjusted.
**Insufficient data to determine a reliable rate.

Age-Adjusted Death Rate by AIDS in 2004

National Rate = 4.5 Deaths per 100,000 Population*

<u>ALPHA ORDER</u>

RANK	STATE	RATE
13	Alabama	4.7
NA	Alaska**	NA
22	Arizona	2.9
20	Arkansas	3.0
15	California	3.9
27	Colorado	1.9
10	Connecticut	5.1
7	Delaware	6.8
1	Florida	10.0
5	Georgia	7.9
29	Hawaii	1.8
NA	Idaho**	NA
18	Illinois	3.3
29	Indiana	1.8
39	Iowa	0.9
37	Kansas	1.0
33	Kentucky	1.6
3	Louisiana	9.0
NA	Maine**	NA
2	Maryland	9.6
19	Massachusetts	3.2
25	Michigan	2.1
37	Minnesota	1.0
9	Mississippi	5.9
23	Missouri	2.6
NA	Montana**	NA
NA	Nebraska**	NA
17	Nevada	3.4
NA	New Hampshire**	NA
6	New Jersey	7.4
36	New Mexico	1.2
4	New York	8.7
13	North Carolina	4.7
NA	North Dakota**	NA
35	Ohio	1.5
25	Oklahoma	2.1
29	Oregon	1.8
16	Pennsylvania	3.7
23	Rhode Island	2.6
8	South Carolina	6.4
NA	South Dakota**	NA
12	Tennessee	4.8
11	Texas	4.9
33	Utah	1.6
NA	Vermont**	NA
20	Virginia	3.0
27	Washington	1.9
32	West Virginia	1.7
39	Wisconsin	0.9
NA	Wyoming**	NA

<u>RANK ORDER</u>

RANK	STATE	RATE
1	Florida	10.0
2	Maryland	9.6
3	Louisiana	9.0
4	New York	8.7
5	Georgia	7.9
6	New Jersey	7.4
7	Delaware	6.8
8	South Carolina	6.4
9	Mississippi	5.9
10	Connecticut	5.1
11	Texas	4.9
12	Tennessee	4.8
13	Alabama	4.7
13	North Carolina	4.7
15	California	3.9
16	Pennsylvania	3.7
17	Nevada	3.4
18	Illinois	3.3
19	Massachusetts	3.2
20	Arkansas	3.0
20	Virginia	3.0
22	Arizona	2.9
23	Missouri	2.6
23	Rhode Island	2.6
25	Michigan	2.1
25	Oklahoma	2.1
27	Colorado	1.9
27	Washington	1.9
29	Hawaii	1.8
29	Indiana	1.8
29	Oregon	1.8
32	West Virginia	1.7
33	Kentucky	1.6
33	Utah	1.6
35	Ohio	1.5
36	New Mexico	1.2
37	Kansas	1.0
37	Minnesota	1.0
39	Iowa	0.9
39	Wisconsin	0.9
NA	Alaska**	NA
NA	Idaho**	NA
NA	Maine**	NA
NA	Montana**	NA
NA	Nebraska**	NA
NA	New Hampshire**	NA
NA	North Dakota**	NA
NA	South Dakota**	NA
NA	Vermont**	NA
NA	Wyoming**	NA

	District of Columbia	42.0

Source: U.S. Department of Health and Human Services, National Center for Health Statistics
"National Vital Statistics Reports" (Vol. 55, No. 19, August 21, 2007, http://www.cdc.gov/nchs/deaths.htm)
*AIDS is Acquired Immunodeficiency Syndrome. It is a specific group of diseases or conditions which are indicative of severe immunosuppression related to infection with the Human Immunodeficiency Virus (HIV). Age-adjusted rates based on the year 2000 standard population.
**Insufficient data to determine a reliable rate.

Deaths by Alzheimer's Disease in 2004

National Total = 65,965 Deaths*

ALPHA ORDER

RANK	STATE	DEATHS	% of USA
19	Alabama	1,385	2.1%
50	Alaska	48	0.1%
13	Arizona	1,675	2.5%
33	Arkansas	622	0.9%
1	California	6,964	10.6%
27	Colorado	912	1.4%
31	Connecticut	684	1.0%
48	Delaware	155	0.2%
3	Florida	4,307	6.5%
12	Georgia	1,710	2.6%
47	Hawaii	171	0.3%
38	Idaho	343	0.5%
6	Illinois	2,595	3.9%
16	Indiana	1,552	2.4%
26	Iowa	968	1.5%
30	Kansas	769	1.2%
25	Kentucky	982	1.5%
21	Louisiana	1,267	1.9%
34	Maine	512	0.8%
28	Maryland	905	1.4%
14	Massachusetts	1,673	2.5%
8	Michigan	2,232	3.4%
24	Minnesota	1,231	1.9%
32	Mississippi	630	1.0%
20	Missouri	1,381	2.1%
45	Montana	228	0.3%
36	Nebraska	459	0.7%
42	Nevada	292	0.4%
39	New Hampshire	331	0.5%
11	New Jersey	1,711	2.6%
40	New Mexico	328	0.5%
10	New York	1,989	3.0%
9	North Carolina	2,188	3.3%
41	North Dakota	313	0.5%
5	Ohio	2,927	4.4%
29	Oklahoma	867	1.3%
22	Oregon	1,262	1.9%
4	Pennsylvania	3,277	5.0%
43	Rhode Island	283	0.4%
23	South Carolina	1,245	1.9%
44	South Dakota	243	0.4%
15	Tennessee	1,615	2.4%
2	Texas	4,336	6.6%
37	Utah	376	0.6%
46	Vermont	173	0.3%
17	Virginia	1,480	2.2%
7	Washington	2,233	3.4%
35	West Virginia	493	0.7%
18	Wisconsin	1,419	2.2%
49	Wyoming	105	0.2%

RANK ORDER

RANK	STATE	DEATHS	% of USA
1	California	6,964	10.6%
2	Texas	4,336	6.6%
3	Florida	4,307	6.5%
4	Pennsylvania	3,277	5.0%
5	Ohio	2,927	4.4%
6	Illinois	2,595	3.9%
7	Washington	2,233	3.4%
8	Michigan	2,232	3.4%
9	North Carolina	2,188	3.3%
10	New York	1,989	3.0%
11	New Jersey	1,711	2.6%
12	Georgia	1,710	2.6%
13	Arizona	1,675	2.5%
14	Massachusetts	1,673	2.5%
15	Tennessee	1,615	2.4%
16	Indiana	1,552	2.4%
17	Virginia	1,480	2.2%
18	Wisconsin	1,419	2.2%
19	Alabama	1,385	2.1%
20	Missouri	1,381	2.1%
21	Louisiana	1,267	1.9%
22	Oregon	1,262	1.9%
23	South Carolina	1,245	1.9%
24	Minnesota	1,231	1.9%
25	Kentucky	982	1.5%
26	Iowa	968	1.5%
27	Colorado	912	1.4%
28	Maryland	905	1.4%
29	Oklahoma	867	1.3%
30	Kansas	769	1.2%
31	Connecticut	684	1.0%
32	Mississippi	630	1.0%
33	Arkansas	622	0.9%
34	Maine	512	0.8%
35	West Virginia	493	0.7%
36	Nebraska	459	0.7%
37	Utah	376	0.6%
38	Idaho	343	0.5%
39	New Hampshire	331	0.5%
40	New Mexico	328	0.5%
41	North Dakota	313	0.5%
42	Nevada	292	0.4%
43	Rhode Island	283	0.4%
44	South Dakota	243	0.4%
45	Montana	228	0.3%
46	Vermont	173	0.3%
47	Hawaii	171	0.3%
48	Delaware	155	0.2%
49	Wyoming	105	0.2%
50	Alaska	48	0.1%
	District of Columbia	119	0.2%

Source: U.S. Department of Health and Human Services, National Center for Health Statistics
   "National Vital Statistics Reports" (Vol. 55, No. 19, August 21, 2007, http://www.cdc.gov/nchs/deaths.htm)
*Final data by state of residence. A degenerative disease of the brain cells producing loss of memory and general intellectual impairment. It usually affects people over age 65. As the disease progresses, a variety of symptoms may become apparent, including confusion, irritability, and restlessness, as well as disorientation and impaired judgment and concentration.

Death Rate by Alzheimer's Disease in 2004

National Rate = 22.5 Deaths per 100,000 Population*

ALPHA ORDER				RANK ORDER		
RANK	STATE	RATE		RANK	STATE	RATE
7	Alabama	30.6		1	North Dakota	49.3
50	Alaska	7.3		2	Maine	38.9
9	Arizona	29.2		3	Washington	36.0
31	Arkansas	22.6		4	Oregon	35.1
40	California	19.4		5	Iowa	32.8
36	Colorado	19.8		6	South Dakota	31.5
39	Connecticut	19.5		7	Alabama	30.6
43	Delaware	18.7		8	South Carolina	29.7
24	Florida	24.8		9	Arizona	29.2
40	Georgia	19.4		10	Kansas	28.1
47	Hawaii	13.5		10	Louisiana	28.1
25	Idaho	24.6		12	Vermont	27.8
35	Illinois	20.4		13	Tennessee	27.4
23	Indiana	24.9		14	West Virginia	27.2
5	Iowa	32.8		15	Pennsylvania	26.4
10	Kansas	28.1		16	Nebraska	26.3
30	Kentucky	23.7		17	Rhode Island	26.2
10	Louisiana	28.1		18	Massachusetts	26.1
2	Maine	38.9		19	Wisconsin	25.8
45	Maryland	16.3		20	North Carolina	25.6
18	Massachusetts	26.1		21	New Hampshire	25.5
32	Michigan	22.1		21	Ohio	25.5
28	Minnesota	24.1		23	Indiana	24.9
33	Mississippi	21.7		24	Florida	24.8
29	Missouri	24.0		25	Idaho	24.6
25	Montana	24.6		25	Montana	24.6
16	Nebraska	26.3		25	Oklahoma	24.6
48	Nevada	12.5		28	Minnesota	24.1
21	New Hampshire	25.5		29	Missouri	24.0
38	New Jersey	19.7		30	Kentucky	23.7
44	New Mexico	17.2		31	Arkansas	22.6
49	New York	10.3		32	Michigan	22.1
20	North Carolina	25.6		33	Mississippi	21.7
1	North Dakota	49.3		34	Wyoming	20.7
21	Ohio	25.5		35	Illinois	20.4
25	Oklahoma	24.6		36	Colorado	19.8
4	Oregon	35.1		36	Virginia	19.8
15	Pennsylvania	26.4		38	New Jersey	19.7
17	Rhode Island	26.2		39	Connecticut	19.5
8	South Carolina	29.7		40	California	19.4
6	South Dakota	31.5		40	Georgia	19.4
13	Tennessee	27.4		42	Texas	19.3
42	Texas	19.3		43	Delaware	18.7
46	Utah	15.7		44	New Mexico	17.2
12	Vermont	27.8		45	Maryland	16.3
36	Virginia	19.8		46	Utah	15.7
3	Washington	36.0		47	Hawaii	13.5
14	West Virginia	27.2		48	Nevada	12.5
19	Wisconsin	25.8		49	New York	10.3
34	Wyoming	20.7		50	Alaska	7.3
					District of Columbia	21.5

Source: U.S. Department of Health and Human Services, National Center for Health Statistics
"National Vital Statistics Reports" (Vol. 55, No. 19, August 21, 2007, http://www.cdc.gov/nchs/deaths.htm)
*Final data by state of residence. A degenerative disease of the brain cells producing loss of memory and general intellectual impairment. It usually affects people over age 65. As the disease progresses, a variety of symptoms may become apparent, including confusion, irritability, and restlessness, as well as disorientation and impaired judgment and concentration. Not age-adjusted.

Age-Adjusted Death Rate by Alzheimer's Disease in 2004

National Rate = 21.8 Deaths per 100,000 Population*

<table>
<tr><td colspan="3">ALPHA ORDER</td><td colspan="3">RANK ORDER</td></tr>
<tr><td>RANK</td><td>STATE</td><td>RATE</td><td>RANK</td><td>STATE</td><td>RATE</td></tr>
<tr><td>6</td><td>Alabama</td><td>31.1</td><td>1</td><td>Washington</td><td>36.1</td></tr>
<tr><td>44</td><td>Alaska</td><td>17.6</td><td>2</td><td>North Dakota</td><td>33.5</td></tr>
<tr><td>8</td><td>Arizona</td><td>30.0</td><td>3</td><td>Maine</td><td>32.4</td></tr>
<tr><td>36</td><td>Arkansas</td><td>20.7</td><td>4</td><td>South Carolina</td><td>32.0</td></tr>
<tr><td>29</td><td>California</td><td>21.8</td><td>5</td><td>Louisiana</td><td>31.5</td></tr>
<tr><td>13</td><td>Colorado</td><td>25.7</td><td>6</td><td>Alabama</td><td>31.1</td></tr>
<tr><td>48</td><td>Connecticut</td><td>14.7</td><td>7</td><td>Oregon</td><td>30.6</td></tr>
<tr><td>42</td><td>Delaware</td><td>18.2</td><td>8</td><td>Arizona</td><td>30.0</td></tr>
<tr><td>43</td><td>Florida</td><td>17.8</td><td>9</td><td>Tennessee</td><td>29.3</td></tr>
<tr><td>11</td><td>Georgia</td><td>27.5</td><td>10</td><td>North Carolina</td><td>27.8</td></tr>
<tr><td>49</td><td>Hawaii</td><td>10.8</td><td>11</td><td>Georgia</td><td>27.5</td></tr>
<tr><td>14</td><td>Idaho</td><td>25.4</td><td>12</td><td>Texas</td><td>26.4</td></tr>
<tr><td>38</td><td>Illinois</td><td>19.6</td><td>13</td><td>Colorado</td><td>25.7</td></tr>
<tr><td>20</td><td>Indiana</td><td>23.8</td><td>14</td><td>Idaho</td><td>25.4</td></tr>
<tr><td>23</td><td>Iowa</td><td>23.3</td><td>15</td><td>Kentucky</td><td>25.1</td></tr>
<tr><td>20</td><td>Kansas</td><td>23.8</td><td>16</td><td>Vermont</td><td>24.9</td></tr>
<tr><td>15</td><td>Kentucky</td><td>25.1</td><td>17</td><td>New Hampshire</td><td>24.8</td></tr>
<tr><td>5</td><td>Louisiana</td><td>31.5</td><td>18</td><td>Oklahoma</td><td>24.4</td></tr>
<tr><td>3</td><td>Maine</td><td>32.4</td><td>19</td><td>Mississippi</td><td>23.9</td></tr>
<tr><td>45</td><td>Maryland</td><td>17.3</td><td>20</td><td>Indiana</td><td>23.8</td></tr>
<tr><td>35</td><td>Massachusetts</td><td>20.8</td><td>20</td><td>Kansas</td><td>23.8</td></tr>
<tr><td>36</td><td>Michigan</td><td>20.7</td><td>22</td><td>South Dakota</td><td>23.5</td></tr>
<tr><td>31</td><td>Minnesota</td><td>21.7</td><td>23</td><td>Iowa</td><td>23.3</td></tr>
<tr><td>19</td><td>Mississippi</td><td>23.9</td><td>24</td><td>Utah</td><td>22.9</td></tr>
<tr><td>29</td><td>Missouri</td><td>21.8</td><td>25</td><td>West Virginia</td><td>22.8</td></tr>
<tr><td>34</td><td>Montana</td><td>21.1</td><td>26</td><td>Ohio</td><td>22.4</td></tr>
<tr><td>31</td><td>Nebraska</td><td>21.7</td><td>26</td><td>Virginia</td><td>22.4</td></tr>
<tr><td>46</td><td>Nevada</td><td>17.2</td><td>28</td><td>Wyoming</td><td>22.1</td></tr>
<tr><td>17</td><td>New Hampshire</td><td>24.8</td><td>29</td><td>California</td><td>21.8</td></tr>
<tr><td>47</td><td>New Jersey</td><td>17.0</td><td>29</td><td>Missouri</td><td>21.8</td></tr>
<tr><td>39</td><td>New Mexico</td><td>18.8</td><td>31</td><td>Minnesota</td><td>21.7</td></tr>
<tr><td>50</td><td>New York</td><td>9.2</td><td>31</td><td>Nebraska</td><td>21.7</td></tr>
<tr><td>10</td><td>North Carolina</td><td>27.8</td><td>33</td><td>Wisconsin</td><td>21.6</td></tr>
<tr><td>2</td><td>North Dakota</td><td>33.5</td><td>34</td><td>Montana</td><td>21.1</td></tr>
<tr><td>26</td><td>Ohio</td><td>22.4</td><td>35</td><td>Massachusetts</td><td>20.8</td></tr>
<tr><td>18</td><td>Oklahoma</td><td>24.4</td><td>36</td><td>Arkansas</td><td>20.7</td></tr>
<tr><td>7</td><td>Oregon</td><td>30.6</td><td>36</td><td>Michigan</td><td>20.7</td></tr>
<tr><td>41</td><td>Pennsylvania</td><td>18.6</td><td>38</td><td>Illinois</td><td>19.6</td></tr>
<tr><td>40</td><td>Rhode Island</td><td>18.7</td><td>39</td><td>New Mexico</td><td>18.8</td></tr>
<tr><td>4</td><td>South Carolina</td><td>32.0</td><td>40</td><td>Rhode Island</td><td>18.7</td></tr>
<tr><td>22</td><td>South Dakota</td><td>23.5</td><td>41</td><td>Pennsylvania</td><td>18.6</td></tr>
<tr><td>9</td><td>Tennessee</td><td>29.3</td><td>42</td><td>Delaware</td><td>18.2</td></tr>
<tr><td>12</td><td>Texas</td><td>26.4</td><td>43</td><td>Florida</td><td>17.8</td></tr>
<tr><td>24</td><td>Utah</td><td>22.9</td><td>44</td><td>Alaska</td><td>17.6</td></tr>
<tr><td>16</td><td>Vermont</td><td>24.9</td><td>45</td><td>Maryland</td><td>17.3</td></tr>
<tr><td>26</td><td>Virginia</td><td>22.4</td><td>46</td><td>Nevada</td><td>17.2</td></tr>
<tr><td>1</td><td>Washington</td><td>36.1</td><td>47</td><td>New Jersey</td><td>17.0</td></tr>
<tr><td>25</td><td>West Virginia</td><td>22.8</td><td>48</td><td>Connecticut</td><td>14.7</td></tr>
<tr><td>33</td><td>Wisconsin</td><td>21.6</td><td>49</td><td>Hawaii</td><td>10.8</td></tr>
<tr><td>28</td><td>Wyoming</td><td>22.1</td><td>50</td><td>New York</td><td>9.2</td></tr>
<tr><td></td><td></td><td></td><td></td><td>District of Columbia</td><td>20.6</td></tr>
</table>

Source: U.S. Department of Health and Human Services, National Center for Health Statistics
    "National Vital Statistics Reports" (Vol. 55, No. 19, August 21, 2007, http://www.cdc.gov/nchs/deaths.htm)
*Final data by state of residence. A degenerative disease of the brain cells producing loss of memory and general intellectual impairment. It usually affects people over age 65. As the disease progresses, a variety of symptoms may become apparent, including confusion, irritability, and restlessness, as well as disorientation and impaired judgment and concentration. Age-adjusted rates based on the year 2000 standard population.

Deaths by Cerebrovascular Diseases in 2004

National Total = 150,074 Deaths*

ALPHA ORDER

ALPHA ORDER

RANK	STATE	DEATHS	% of USA
19	Alabama	2,986	2.0%
50	Alaska	172	0.1%
24	Arizona	2,446	1.6%
29	Arkansas	1,948	1.3%
1	California	16,882	11.2%
31	Colorado	1,638	1.1%
32	Connecticut	1,635	1.1%
47	Delaware	350	0.2%
3	Florida	9,715	6.5%
10	Georgia	4,063	2.7%
40	Hawaii	714	0.5%
41	Idaho	712	0.5%
7	Illinois	6,489	4.3%
15	Indiana	3,454	2.3%
28	Iowa	1,960	1.3%
33	Kansas	1,611	1.1%
25	Kentucky	2,339	1.6%
23	Louisiana	2,489	1.7%
37	Maine	801	0.5%
20	Maryland	2,718	1.8%
16	Massachusetts	3,254	2.2%
8	Michigan	5,290	3.5%
22	Minnesota	2,542	1.7%
30	Mississippi	1,651	1.1%
14	Missouri	3,503	2.3%
44	Montana	484	0.3%
36	Nebraska	978	0.7%
35	Nevada	1,030	0.7%
42	New Hampshire	586	0.4%
12	New Jersey	3,781	2.5%
39	New Mexico	721	0.5%
5	New York	6,927	4.6%
9	North Carolina	4,955	3.3%
45	North Dakota	475	0.3%
6	Ohio	6,501	4.3%
27	Oklahoma	2,183	1.5%
26	Oregon	2,328	1.6%
4	Pennsylvania	7,792	5.2%
43	Rhode Island	522	0.3%
21	South Carolina	2,643	1.8%
46	South Dakota	469	0.3%
13	Tennessee	3,680	2.5%
2	Texas	9,853	6.6%
38	Utah	790	0.5%
48	Vermont	302	0.2%
11	Virginia	3,788	2.5%
17	Washington	3,243	2.2%
34	West Virginia	1,178	0.8%
18	Wisconsin	3,071	2.0%
49	Wyoming	214	0.1%

RANK ORDER

RANK	STATE	DEATHS	% of USA
1	California	16,882	11.2%
2	Texas	9,853	6.6%
3	Florida	9,715	6.5%
4	Pennsylvania	7,792	5.2%
5	New York	6,927	4.6%
6	Ohio	6,501	4.3%
7	Illinois	6,489	4.3%
8	Michigan	5,290	3.5%
9	North Carolina	4,955	3.3%
10	Georgia	4,063	2.7%
11	Virginia	3,788	2.5%
12	New Jersey	3,781	2.5%
13	Tennessee	3,680	2.5%
14	Missouri	3,503	2.3%
15	Indiana	3,454	2.3%
16	Massachusetts	3,254	2.2%
17	Washington	3,243	2.2%
18	Wisconsin	3,071	2.0%
19	Alabama	2,986	2.0%
20	Maryland	2,718	1.8%
21	South Carolina	2,643	1.8%
22	Minnesota	2,542	1.7%
23	Louisiana	2,489	1.7%
24	Arizona	2,446	1.6%
25	Kentucky	2,339	1.6%
26	Oregon	2,328	1.6%
27	Oklahoma	2,183	1.5%
28	Iowa	1,960	1.3%
29	Arkansas	1,948	1.3%
30	Mississippi	1,651	1.1%
31	Colorado	1,638	1.1%
32	Connecticut	1,635	1.1%
33	Kansas	1,611	1.1%
34	West Virginia	1,178	0.8%
35	Nevada	1,030	0.7%
36	Nebraska	978	0.7%
37	Maine	801	0.5%
38	Utah	790	0.5%
39	New Mexico	721	0.5%
40	Hawaii	714	0.5%
41	Idaho	712	0.5%
42	New Hampshire	586	0.4%
43	Rhode Island	522	0.3%
44	Montana	484	0.3%
45	North Dakota	475	0.3%
46	South Dakota	469	0.3%
47	Delaware	350	0.2%
48	Vermont	302	0.2%
49	Wyoming	214	0.1%
50	Alaska	172	0.1%
	District of Columbia	218	0.1%

Source: U.S. Department of Health and Human Services, National Center for Health Statistics
"National Vital Statistics Reports" (Vol. 55, No. 19, August 21, 2007, http://www.cdc.gov/nchs/deaths.htm)
*Final data by state of residence. Cerebrovascular diseases include stroke and other disorders of the blood vessels of the brain.

Death Rate by Cerebrovascular Diseases in 2004

National Rate = 51.1 Deaths per 100,000 Population*

ALPHA ORDER

RANK	STATE	RATE
4	Alabama	65.9
50	Alaska	26.2
43	Arizona	42.6
2	Arkansas	70.8
36	California	47.0
48	Colorado	35.6
37	Connecticut	46.7
44	Delaware	42.2
21	Florida	55.8
38	Georgia	46.0
18	Hawaii	56.5
28	Idaho	51.1
29	Illinois	51.0
23	Indiana	55.4
3	Iowa	66.3
14	Kansas	58.9
19	Kentucky	56.4
24	Louisiana	55.1
12	Maine	60.8
33	Maryland	48.9
31	Massachusetts	50.7
25	Michigan	52.3
32	Minnesota	49.8
16	Mississippi	56.9
11	Missouri	60.9
27	Montana	52.2
20	Nebraska	56.0
40	Nevada	44.1
39	New Hampshire	45.1
42	New Jersey	43.5
46	New Mexico	37.9
47	New York	36.0
15	North Carolina	58.0
1	North Dakota	74.9
17	Ohio	56.7
10	Oklahoma	62.0
6	Oregon	64.8
8	Pennsylvania	62.8
35	Rhode Island	48.3
7	South Carolina	63.0
12	South Dakota	60.8
9	Tennessee	62.4
41	Texas	43.8
49	Utah	33.1
34	Vermont	48.6
30	Virginia	50.8
25	Washington	52.3
5	West Virginia	64.9
22	Wisconsin	55.7
44	Wyoming	42.2

RANK ORDER

RANK	STATE	RATE
1	North Dakota	74.9
2	Arkansas	70.8
3	Iowa	66.3
4	Alabama	65.9
5	West Virginia	64.9
6	Oregon	64.8
7	South Carolina	63.0
8	Pennsylvania	62.8
9	Tennessee	62.4
10	Oklahoma	62.0
11	Missouri	60.9
12	Maine	60.8
12	South Dakota	60.8
14	Kansas	58.9
15	North Carolina	58.0
16	Mississippi	56.9
17	Ohio	56.7
18	Hawaii	56.5
19	Kentucky	56.4
20	Nebraska	56.0
21	Florida	55.8
22	Wisconsin	55.7
23	Indiana	55.4
24	Louisiana	55.1
25	Michigan	52.3
25	Washington	52.3
27	Montana	52.2
28	Idaho	51.1
29	Illinois	51.0
30	Virginia	50.8
31	Massachusetts	50.7
32	Minnesota	49.8
33	Maryland	48.9
34	Vermont	48.6
35	Rhode Island	48.3
36	California	47.0
37	Connecticut	46.7
38	Georgia	46.0
39	New Hampshire	45.1
40	Nevada	44.1
41	Texas	43.8
42	New Jersey	43.5
43	Arizona	42.6
44	Delaware	42.2
44	Wyoming	42.2
46	New Mexico	37.9
47	New York	36.0
48	Colorado	35.6
49	Utah	33.1
50	Alaska	26.2
	District of Columbia	39.4

Source: U.S. Department of Health and Human Services, National Center for Health Statistics
"National Vital Statistics Reports" (Vol. 55, No. 19, August 21, 2007, http://www.cdc.gov/nchs/deaths.htm)
*Final data by state of residence. Cerebrovascular diseases include stroke and other disorders of the blood vessels of the brain. Not age-adjusted.

Age-Adjusted Death Rate by Cerebrovascular Diseases in 2004

National Rate = 50.0 Deaths per 100,000 Population*

<table>
<tr><td colspan="3">ALPHA ORDER</td><td colspan="3">RANK ORDER</td></tr>
<tr><td>RANK</td><td>STATE</td><td>RATE</td><td>RANK</td><td>STATE</td><td>RATE</td></tr>
<tr><td>2</td><td>Alabama</td><td>65.0</td><td>1</td><td>South Carolina</td><td>65.2</td></tr>
<tr><td>22</td><td>Alaska</td><td>52.1</td><td>2</td><td>Alabama</td><td>65.0</td></tr>
<tr><td>42</td><td>Arizona</td><td>43.3</td><td>2</td><td>Arkansas</td><td>65.0</td></tr>
<tr><td>2</td><td>Arkansas</td><td>65.0</td><td>4</td><td>Tennessee</td><td>64.7</td></tr>
<tr><td>21</td><td>California</td><td>52.7</td><td>5</td><td>North Carolina</td><td>61.1</td></tr>
<tr><td>38</td><td>Colorado</td><td>44.6</td><td>6</td><td>Oklahoma</td><td>60.6</td></tr>
<tr><td>49</td><td>Connecticut</td><td>37.6</td><td>7</td><td>Georgia</td><td>60.5</td></tr>
<tr><td>45</td><td>Delaware</td><td>40.6</td><td>8</td><td>Mississippi</td><td>60.1</td></tr>
<tr><td>44</td><td>Florida</td><td>42.0</td><td>9</td><td>Louisiana</td><td>59.4</td></tr>
<tr><td>7</td><td>Georgia</td><td>60.5</td><td>10</td><td>Oregon</td><td>58.2</td></tr>
<tr><td>34</td><td>Hawaii</td><td>47.1</td><td>11</td><td>Kentucky</td><td>58.0</td></tr>
<tr><td>17</td><td>Idaho</td><td>53.8</td><td>12</td><td>Texas</td><td>56.9</td></tr>
<tr><td>27</td><td>Illinois</td><td>50.0</td><td>13</td><td>Missouri</td><td>56.0</td></tr>
<tr><td>18</td><td>Indiana</td><td>53.7</td><td>14</td><td>Virginia</td><td>55.5</td></tr>
<tr><td>29</td><td>Iowa</td><td>49.5</td><td>15</td><td>North Dakota</td><td>54.6</td></tr>
<tr><td>23</td><td>Kansas</td><td>51.8</td><td>16</td><td>West Virginia</td><td>54.1</td></tr>
<tr><td>11</td><td>Kentucky</td><td>58.0</td><td>17</td><td>Idaho</td><td>53.8</td></tr>
<tr><td>9</td><td>Louisiana</td><td>59.4</td><td>18</td><td>Indiana</td><td>53.7</td></tr>
<tr><td>25</td><td>Maine</td><td>51.0</td><td>19</td><td>Washington</td><td>53.5</td></tr>
<tr><td>24</td><td>Maryland</td><td>51.5</td><td>20</td><td>Nevada</td><td>53.4</td></tr>
<tr><td>43</td><td>Massachusetts</td><td>42.5</td><td>21</td><td>California</td><td>52.7</td></tr>
<tr><td>28</td><td>Michigan</td><td>49.9</td><td>22</td><td>Alaska</td><td>52.1</td></tr>
<tr><td>36</td><td>Minnesota</td><td>46.2</td><td>23</td><td>Kansas</td><td>51.8</td></tr>
<tr><td>8</td><td>Mississippi</td><td>60.1</td><td>24</td><td>Maryland</td><td>51.5</td></tr>
<tr><td>13</td><td>Missouri</td><td>56.0</td><td>25</td><td>Maine</td><td>51.0</td></tr>
<tr><td>37</td><td>Montana</td><td>45.7</td><td>26</td><td>Ohio</td><td>50.9</td></tr>
<tr><td>32</td><td>Nebraska</td><td>48.0</td><td>27</td><td>Illinois</td><td>50.0</td></tr>
<tr><td>20</td><td>Nevada</td><td>53.4</td><td>28</td><td>Michigan</td><td>49.9</td></tr>
<tr><td>39</td><td>New Hampshire</td><td>44.2</td><td>29</td><td>Iowa</td><td>49.5</td></tr>
<tr><td>47</td><td>New Jersey</td><td>39.2</td><td>30</td><td>Wisconsin</td><td>48.8</td></tr>
<tr><td>46</td><td>New Mexico</td><td>40.5</td><td>31</td><td>South Dakota</td><td>48.1</td></tr>
<tr><td>50</td><td>New York</td><td>32.9</td><td>32</td><td>Nebraska</td><td>48.0</td></tr>
<tr><td>5</td><td>North Carolina</td><td>61.1</td><td>33</td><td>Utah</td><td>47.7</td></tr>
<tr><td>15</td><td>North Dakota</td><td>54.6</td><td>34</td><td>Hawaii</td><td>47.1</td></tr>
<tr><td>26</td><td>Ohio</td><td>50.9</td><td>34</td><td>Pennsylvania</td><td>47.1</td></tr>
<tr><td>6</td><td>Oklahoma</td><td>60.6</td><td>36</td><td>Minnesota</td><td>46.2</td></tr>
<tr><td>10</td><td>Oregon</td><td>58.2</td><td>37</td><td>Montana</td><td>45.7</td></tr>
<tr><td>34</td><td>Pennsylvania</td><td>47.1</td><td>38</td><td>Colorado</td><td>44.6</td></tr>
<tr><td>48</td><td>Rhode Island</td><td>38.1</td><td>39</td><td>New Hampshire</td><td>44.2</td></tr>
<tr><td>1</td><td>South Carolina</td><td>65.2</td><td>40</td><td>Wyoming</td><td>43.9</td></tr>
<tr><td>31</td><td>South Dakota</td><td>48.1</td><td>41</td><td>Vermont</td><td>43.5</td></tr>
<tr><td>4</td><td>Tennessee</td><td>64.7</td><td>42</td><td>Arizona</td><td>43.3</td></tr>
<tr><td>12</td><td>Texas</td><td>56.9</td><td>43</td><td>Massachusetts</td><td>42.5</td></tr>
<tr><td>33</td><td>Utah</td><td>47.7</td><td>44</td><td>Florida</td><td>42.0</td></tr>
<tr><td>41</td><td>Vermont</td><td>43.5</td><td>45</td><td>Delaware</td><td>40.6</td></tr>
<tr><td>14</td><td>Virginia</td><td>55.5</td><td>46</td><td>New Mexico</td><td>40.5</td></tr>
<tr><td>19</td><td>Washington</td><td>53.5</td><td>47</td><td>New Jersey</td><td>39.2</td></tr>
<tr><td>16</td><td>West Virginia</td><td>54.1</td><td>48</td><td>Rhode Island</td><td>38.1</td></tr>
<tr><td>30</td><td>Wisconsin</td><td>48.8</td><td>49</td><td>Connecticut</td><td>37.6</td></tr>
<tr><td>40</td><td>Wyoming</td><td>43.9</td><td>50</td><td>New York</td><td>32.9</td></tr>
<tr><td></td><td></td><td></td><td></td><td>District of Columbia</td><td>38.9</td></tr>
</table>

Source: U.S. Department of Health and Human Services, National Center for Health Statistics
"National Vital Statistics Reports" (Vol. 55, No. 19, August 21, 2007, http://www.cdc.gov/nchs/deaths.htm)
*Final data by state of residence. Cerebrovascular diseases include stroke and other disorders of the blood vessels of the brain.
Age-adjusted rates based on the year 2000 standard population.

Deaths by Chronic Liver Disease and Cirrhosis in 2004

National Total = 27,013 Deaths*

ALPHA ORDER				RANK ORDER			
RANK	STATE	DEATHS	% of USA	RANK	STATE	DEATHS	% of USA
18	Alabama	477	1.8%	1	California	3,703	13.7%
48	Alaska	47	0.2%	2	Texas	2,281	8.4%
12	Arizona	655	2.4%	3	Florida	2,122	7.9%
34	Arkansas	231	0.9%	4	New York	1,296	4.8%
1	California	3,703	13.7%	5	Pennsylvania	1,101	4.1%
21	Colorado	427	1.6%	6	Ohio	1,063	3.9%
29	Connecticut	293	1.1%	7	Illinois	1,058	3.9%
46	Delaware	78	0.3%	8	Michigan	983	3.6%
3	Florida	2,122	7.9%	9	North Carolina	781	2.9%
11	Georgia	676	2.5%	10	New Jersey	704	2.6%
45	Hawaii	87	0.3%	11	Georgia	676	2.5%
41	Idaho	111	0.4%	12	Arizona	655	2.4%
7	Illinois	1,058	3.9%	13	Tennessee	637	2.4%
17	Indiana	509	1.9%	14	Washington	568	2.1%
36	Iowa	188	0.7%	15	Virginia	545	2.0%
35	Kansas	206	0.8%	16	Massachusetts	536	2.0%
27	Kentucky	355	1.3%	17	Indiana	509	1.9%
26	Louisiana	363	1.3%	18	Alabama	477	1.8%
38	Maine	121	0.4%	19	South Carolina	457	1.7%
23	Maryland	419	1.6%	20	Missouri	432	1.6%
16	Massachusetts	536	2.0%	21	Colorado	427	1.6%
8	Michigan	983	3.6%	22	Wisconsin	421	1.6%
28	Minnesota	333	1.2%	23	Maryland	419	1.6%
32	Mississippi	267	1.0%	24	Oregon	390	1.4%
20	Missouri	432	1.6%	25	Oklahoma	386	1.4%
43	Montana	95	0.4%	26	Louisiana	363	1.3%
40	Nebraska	116	0.4%	27	Kentucky	355	1.3%
31	Nevada	286	1.1%	28	Minnesota	333	1.2%
42	New Hampshire	100	0.4%	29	Connecticut	293	1.1%
10	New Jersey	704	2.6%	30	New Mexico	289	1.1%
30	New Mexico	289	1.1%	31	Nevada	286	1.1%
4	New York	1,296	4.8%	32	Mississippi	267	1.0%
9	North Carolina	781	2.9%	33	West Virginia	258	1.0%
47	North Dakota	58	0.2%	34	Arkansas	231	0.9%
6	Ohio	1,063	3.9%	35	Kansas	206	0.8%
25	Oklahoma	386	1.4%	36	Iowa	188	0.7%
24	Oregon	390	1.4%	37	Rhode Island	129	0.5%
5	Pennsylvania	1,101	4.1%	38	Maine	121	0.4%
37	Rhode Island	129	0.5%	39	Utah	117	0.4%
19	South Carolina	457	1.7%	40	Nebraska	116	0.4%
43	South Dakota	95	0.4%	41	Idaho	111	0.4%
13	Tennessee	637	2.4%	42	New Hampshire	100	0.4%
2	Texas	2,281	8.4%	43	Montana	95	0.4%
39	Utah	117	0.4%	43	South Dakota	95	0.4%
48	Vermont	47	0.2%	45	Hawaii	87	0.3%
15	Virginia	545	2.0%	46	Delaware	78	0.3%
14	Washington	568	2.1%	47	North Dakota	58	0.2%
33	West Virginia	258	1.0%	48	Alaska	47	0.2%
22	Wisconsin	421	1.6%	48	Vermont	47	0.2%
50	Wyoming	45	0.2%	50	Wyoming	45	0.2%
					District of Columbia	71	0.3%

Source: U.S. Department of Health and Human Services, National Center for Health Statistics
"National Vital Statistics Reports" (Vol. 55, No. 19, August 21, 2007, http://www.cdc.gov/nchs/deaths.htm)
*Final data by state of residence. Cirrhosis of the liver is characterized by the replacement of normal tissue with fibrous tissue and the loss of functional liver cells. It can result from alcohol abuse, nutritional deprivation, or infection especially by the hepatitis virus.

Death Rate by Chronic Liver Disease and Cirrhosis in 2004

National Rate = 9.2 Deaths per 100,000 Population*

ALPHA ORDER

RANK	STATE	RATE
12	Alabama	10.5
44	Alaska	7.2
7	Arizona	11.4
28	Arkansas	8.4
13	California	10.3
18	Colorado	9.3
28	Connecticut	8.4
17	Delaware	9.4
4	Florida	12.2
36	Georgia	7.7
45	Hawaii	6.9
34	Idaho	8.0
31	Illinois	8.3
32	Indiana	8.2
49	Iowa	6.4
40	Kansas	7.5
27	Kentucky	8.6
34	Louisiana	8.0
20	Maine	9.2
40	Maryland	7.5
28	Massachusetts	8.4
16	Michigan	9.7
48	Minnesota	6.5
20	Mississippi	9.2
40	Missouri	7.5
14	Montana	10.2
47	Nebraska	6.6
4	Nevada	12.2
36	New Hampshire	7.7
33	New Jersey	8.1
1	New Mexico	15.2
46	New York	6.7
23	North Carolina	9.1
23	North Dakota	9.1
18	Ohio	9.3
8	Oklahoma	11.0
10	Oregon	10.8
25	Pennsylvania	8.9
6	Rhode Island	11.9
9	South Carolina	10.9
3	South Dakota	12.3
10	Tennessee	10.8
15	Texas	10.1
50	Utah	4.9
38	Vermont	7.6
43	Virginia	7.3
20	Washington	9.2
2	West Virginia	14.2
38	Wisconsin	7.6
25	Wyoming	8.9

RANK ORDER

RANK	STATE	RATE
1	New Mexico	15.2
2	West Virginia	14.2
3	South Dakota	12.3
4	Florida	12.2
4	Nevada	12.2
6	Rhode Island	11.9
7	Arizona	11.4
8	Oklahoma	11.0
9	South Carolina	10.9
10	Oregon	10.8
10	Tennessee	10.8
12	Alabama	10.5
13	California	10.3
14	Montana	10.2
15	Texas	10.1
16	Michigan	9.7
17	Delaware	9.4
18	Colorado	9.3
18	Ohio	9.3
20	Maine	9.2
20	Mississippi	9.2
20	Washington	9.2
23	North Carolina	9.1
23	North Dakota	9.1
25	Pennsylvania	8.9
25	Wyoming	8.9
27	Kentucky	8.6
28	Arkansas	8.4
28	Connecticut	8.4
28	Massachusetts	8.4
31	Illinois	8.3
32	Indiana	8.2
33	New Jersey	8.1
34	Idaho	8.0
34	Louisiana	8.0
36	Georgia	7.7
36	New Hampshire	7.7
38	Vermont	7.6
38	Wisconsin	7.6
40	Kansas	7.5
40	Maryland	7.5
40	Missouri	7.5
43	Virginia	7.3
44	Alaska	7.2
45	Hawaii	6.9
46	New York	6.7
47	Nebraska	6.6
48	Minnesota	6.5
49	Iowa	6.4
50	Utah	4.9

District of Columbia	12.8

Source: U.S. Department of Health and Human Services, National Center for Health Statistics
    "National Vital Statistics Reports" (Vol. 55, No. 19, August 21, 2007, http://www.cdc.gov/nchs/deaths.htm)
*Final data by state of residence. Cirrhosis of the liver is characterized by the replacement of normal tissue with fibrous tissue and the loss of functional liver cells. It can result from alcohol abuse, nutritional deprivation, or infection especially by the hepatitis virus. Not age-adjusted.

Age-Adjusted Death Rate by Chronic Liver Disease and Cirrhosis in 2004

National Rate = 9.0 Deaths per 100,000 Population*

ALPHA ORDER

RANK	STATE	RATE
14	Alabama	9.9
27	Alaska	8.2
5	Arizona	11.6
32	Arkansas	7.9
8	California	10.9
15	Colorado	9.8
36	Connecticut	7.6
21	Delaware	8.8
9	Florida	10.5
23	Georgia	8.4
45	Hawaii	6.4
28	Idaho	8.1
24	Illinois	8.3
31	Indiana	8.0
50	Iowa	5.7
39	Kansas	7.3
28	Kentucky	8.1
28	Louisiana	8.1
32	Maine	7.9
38	Maryland	7.4
34	Massachusetts	7.8
16	Michigan	9.4
45	Minnesota	6.4
17	Mississippi	9.2
43	Missouri	7.0
18	Montana	9.0
45	Nebraska	6.4
2	Nevada	12.3
41	New Hampshire	7.2
36	New Jersey	7.6
1	New Mexico	15.0
45	New York	6.4
18	North Carolina	9.0
24	North Dakota	8.3
22	Ohio	8.7
11	Oklahoma	10.3
12	Oregon	10.2
35	Pennsylvania	7.7
7	Rhode Island	11.0
10	South Carolina	10.4
4	South Dakota	11.7
12	Tennessee	10.2
6	Texas	11.3
45	Utah	6.4
44	Vermont	6.8
41	Virginia	7.2
20	Washington	8.9
3	West Virginia	11.8
39	Wisconsin	7.3
24	Wyoming	8.3

RANK ORDER

RANK	STATE	RATE
1	New Mexico	15.0
2	Nevada	12.3
3	West Virginia	11.8
4	South Dakota	11.7
5	Arizona	11.6
6	Texas	11.3
7	Rhode Island	11.0
8	California	10.9
9	Florida	10.5
10	South Carolina	10.4
11	Oklahoma	10.3
12	Oregon	10.2
12	Tennessee	10.2
14	Alabama	9.9
15	Colorado	9.8
16	Michigan	9.4
17	Mississippi	9.2
18	Montana	9.0
18	North Carolina	9.0
20	Washington	8.9
21	Delaware	8.8
22	Ohio	8.7
23	Georgia	8.4
24	Illinois	8.3
24	North Dakota	8.3
24	Wyoming	8.3
27	Alaska	8.2
28	Idaho	8.1
28	Kentucky	8.1
28	Louisiana	8.1
31	Indiana	8.0
32	Arkansas	7.9
32	Maine	7.9
34	Massachusetts	7.8
35	Pennsylvania	7.7
36	Connecticut	7.6
36	New Jersey	7.6
38	Maryland	7.4
39	Kansas	7.3
39	Wisconsin	7.3
41	New Hampshire	7.2
41	Virginia	7.2
43	Missouri	7.0
44	Vermont	6.8
45	Hawaii	6.4
45	Minnesota	6.4
45	Nebraska	6.4
45	New York	6.4
45	Utah	6.4
50	Iowa	5.7

District of Columbia	12.8

Source: U.S. Department of Health and Human Services, National Center for Health Statistics
   "National Vital Statistics Reports" (Vol. 55, No. 19, August 21, 2007, http://www.cdc.gov/nchs/deaths.htm)
*Final data by state of residence. Cirrhosis of the liver is characterized by the replacement of normal tissue with fibrous tissue and the loss of functional liver cells. It can result from alcohol abuse, nutritional deprivation, or infection especially by the hepatitis virus. Age-adjusted rates based on the year 2000 standard population.

Deaths by Chronic Lower Respiratory Diseases in 2004

National Total = 121,987 Deaths*

<table>
<tr><td colspan="4">ALPHA ORDER</td><td colspan="4">RANK ORDER</td></tr>
<tr><th>RANK</th><th>STATE</th><th>DEATHS</th><th>% of USA</th><th>RANK</th><th>STATE</th><th>DEATHS</th><th>% of USA</th></tr>
<tr><td>19</td><td>Alabama</td><td>2,361</td><td>1.9%</td><td>1</td><td>California</td><td>12,522</td><td>10.3%</td></tr>
<tr><td>50</td><td>Alaska</td><td>139</td><td>0.1%</td><td>2</td><td>Florida</td><td>8,971</td><td>7.4%</td></tr>
<tr><td>18</td><td>Arizona</td><td>2,416</td><td>2.0%</td><td>3</td><td>Texas</td><td>7,402</td><td>6.1%</td></tr>
<tr><td>31</td><td>Arkansas</td><td>1,428</td><td>1.2%</td><td>4</td><td>New York</td><td>6,786</td><td>5.6%</td></tr>
<tr><td>1</td><td>California</td><td>12,522</td><td>10.3%</td><td>5</td><td>Pennsylvania</td><td>5,978</td><td>4.9%</td></tr>
<tr><td>24</td><td>Colorado</td><td>1,899</td><td>1.6%</td><td>6</td><td>Ohio</td><td>5,896</td><td>4.8%</td></tr>
<tr><td>30</td><td>Connecticut</td><td>1,432</td><td>1.2%</td><td>7</td><td>Illinois</td><td>4,723</td><td>3.9%</td></tr>
<tr><td>45</td><td>Delaware</td><td>345</td><td>0.3%</td><td>8</td><td>Michigan</td><td>4,252</td><td>3.5%</td></tr>
<tr><td>2</td><td>Florida</td><td>8,971</td><td>7.4%</td><td>9</td><td>North Carolina</td><td>3,625</td><td>3.0%</td></tr>
<tr><td>11</td><td>Georgia</td><td>3,125</td><td>2.6%</td><td>10</td><td>Indiana</td><td>3,145</td><td>2.6%</td></tr>
<tr><td>47</td><td>Hawaii</td><td>307</td><td>0.3%</td><td>11</td><td>Georgia</td><td>3,125</td><td>2.6%</td></tr>
<tr><td>42</td><td>Idaho</td><td>572</td><td>0.5%</td><td>12</td><td>New Jersey</td><td>3,031</td><td>2.5%</td></tr>
<tr><td>7</td><td>Illinois</td><td>4,723</td><td>3.9%</td><td>13</td><td>Tennessee</td><td>2,987</td><td>2.4%</td></tr>
<tr><td>10</td><td>Indiana</td><td>3,145</td><td>2.6%</td><td>14</td><td>Missouri</td><td>2,731</td><td>2.2%</td></tr>
<tr><td>29</td><td>Iowa</td><td>1,547</td><td>1.3%</td><td>15</td><td>Virginia</td><td>2,730</td><td>2.2%</td></tr>
<tr><td>33</td><td>Kansas</td><td>1,316</td><td>1.1%</td><td>16</td><td>Massachusetts</td><td>2,574</td><td>2.1%</td></tr>
<tr><td>21</td><td>Kentucky</td><td>2,265</td><td>1.9%</td><td>17</td><td>Washington</td><td>2,549</td><td>2.1%</td></tr>
<tr><td>28</td><td>Louisiana</td><td>1,615</td><td>1.3%</td><td>18</td><td>Arizona</td><td>2,416</td><td>2.0%</td></tr>
<tr><td>37</td><td>Maine</td><td>766</td><td>0.6%</td><td>19</td><td>Alabama</td><td>2,361</td><td>1.9%</td></tr>
<tr><td>23</td><td>Maryland</td><td>1,910</td><td>1.6%</td><td>20</td><td>Wisconsin</td><td>2,312</td><td>1.9%</td></tr>
<tr><td>16</td><td>Massachusetts</td><td>2,574</td><td>2.1%</td><td>21</td><td>Kentucky</td><td>2,265</td><td>1.9%</td></tr>
<tr><td>8</td><td>Michigan</td><td>4,252</td><td>3.5%</td><td>22</td><td>Oklahoma</td><td>1,985</td><td>1.6%</td></tr>
<tr><td>25</td><td>Minnesota</td><td>1,839</td><td>1.5%</td><td>23</td><td>Maryland</td><td>1,910</td><td>1.6%</td></tr>
<tr><td>32</td><td>Mississippi</td><td>1,350</td><td>1.1%</td><td>24</td><td>Colorado</td><td>1,899</td><td>1.6%</td></tr>
<tr><td>14</td><td>Missouri</td><td>2,731</td><td>2.2%</td><td>25</td><td>Minnesota</td><td>1,839</td><td>1.5%</td></tr>
<tr><td>41</td><td>Montana</td><td>578</td><td>0.5%</td><td>26</td><td>South Carolina</td><td>1,792</td><td>1.5%</td></tr>
<tr><td>36</td><td>Nebraska</td><td>815</td><td>0.7%</td><td>27</td><td>Oregon</td><td>1,778</td><td>1.5%</td></tr>
<tr><td>35</td><td>Nevada</td><td>1,124</td><td>0.9%</td><td>28</td><td>Louisiana</td><td>1,615</td><td>1.3%</td></tr>
<tr><td>39</td><td>New Hampshire</td><td>600</td><td>0.5%</td><td>29</td><td>Iowa</td><td>1,547</td><td>1.3%</td></tr>
<tr><td>12</td><td>New Jersey</td><td>3,031</td><td>2.5%</td><td>30</td><td>Connecticut</td><td>1,432</td><td>1.2%</td></tr>
<tr><td>38</td><td>New Mexico</td><td>753</td><td>0.6%</td><td>31</td><td>Arkansas</td><td>1,428</td><td>1.2%</td></tr>
<tr><td>4</td><td>New York</td><td>6,786</td><td>5.6%</td><td>32</td><td>Mississippi</td><td>1,350</td><td>1.1%</td></tr>
<tr><td>9</td><td>North Carolina</td><td>3,625</td><td>3.0%</td><td>33</td><td>Kansas</td><td>1,316</td><td>1.1%</td></tr>
<tr><td>49</td><td>North Dakota</td><td>273</td><td>0.2%</td><td>34</td><td>West Virginia</td><td>1,225</td><td>1.0%</td></tr>
<tr><td>6</td><td>Ohio</td><td>5,896</td><td>4.8%</td><td>35</td><td>Nevada</td><td>1,124</td><td>0.9%</td></tr>
<tr><td>22</td><td>Oklahoma</td><td>1,985</td><td>1.6%</td><td>36</td><td>Nebraska</td><td>815</td><td>0.7%</td></tr>
<tr><td>27</td><td>Oregon</td><td>1,778</td><td>1.5%</td><td>37</td><td>Maine</td><td>766</td><td>0.6%</td></tr>
<tr><td>5</td><td>Pennsylvania</td><td>5,978</td><td>4.9%</td><td>38</td><td>New Mexico</td><td>753</td><td>0.6%</td></tr>
<tr><td>43</td><td>Rhode Island</td><td>463</td><td>0.4%</td><td>39</td><td>New Hampshire</td><td>600</td><td>0.5%</td></tr>
<tr><td>26</td><td>South Carolina</td><td>1,792</td><td>1.5%</td><td>40</td><td>Utah</td><td>595</td><td>0.5%</td></tr>
<tr><td>44</td><td>South Dakota</td><td>391</td><td>0.3%</td><td>41</td><td>Montana</td><td>578</td><td>0.5%</td></tr>
<tr><td>13</td><td>Tennessee</td><td>2,987</td><td>2.4%</td><td>42</td><td>Idaho</td><td>572</td><td>0.5%</td></tr>
<tr><td>3</td><td>Texas</td><td>7,402</td><td>6.1%</td><td>43</td><td>Rhode Island</td><td>463</td><td>0.4%</td></tr>
<tr><td>40</td><td>Utah</td><td>595</td><td>0.5%</td><td>44</td><td>South Dakota</td><td>391</td><td>0.3%</td></tr>
<tr><td>48</td><td>Vermont</td><td>296</td><td>0.2%</td><td>45</td><td>Delaware</td><td>345</td><td>0.3%</td></tr>
<tr><td>15</td><td>Virginia</td><td>2,730</td><td>2.2%</td><td>46</td><td>Wyoming</td><td>308</td><td>0.3%</td></tr>
<tr><td>17</td><td>Washington</td><td>2,549</td><td>2.1%</td><td>47</td><td>Hawaii</td><td>307</td><td>0.3%</td></tr>
<tr><td>34</td><td>West Virginia</td><td>1,225</td><td>1.0%</td><td>48</td><td>Vermont</td><td>296</td><td>0.2%</td></tr>
<tr><td>20</td><td>Wisconsin</td><td>2,312</td><td>1.9%</td><td>49</td><td>North Dakota</td><td>273</td><td>0.2%</td></tr>
<tr><td>46</td><td>Wyoming</td><td>308</td><td>0.3%</td><td>50</td><td>Alaska</td><td>139</td><td>0.1%</td></tr>
<tr><td></td><td></td><td></td><td></td><td></td><td>District of Columbia</td><td>165</td><td>0.1%</td></tr>
</table>

Source: U.S. Department of Health and Human Services, National Center for Health Statistics
    "National Vital Statistics Reports" (Vol. 55, No. 19, August 21, 2007, http://www.cdc.gov/nchs/deaths.htm)
*Final data by state of residence. Chronic lower respiratory diseases are diseases of the lungs including bronchitis, emphysema, and asthma. Includes allied conditions.

Death Rate by Chronic Lower Respiratory Diseases in 2004

National Rate = 41.5 Deaths per 100,000 Population*

ALPHA ORDER

RANK	STATE	RATE
8	Alabama	52.1
50	Alaska	21.2
28	Arizona	42.1
9	Arkansas	51.9
44	California	34.9
32	Colorado	41.3
35	Connecticut	40.9
31	Delaware	41.5
10	Florida	51.6
42	Georgia	35.4
49	Hawaii	24.3
33	Idaho	41.1
38	Illinois	37.1
14	Indiana	50.4
7	Iowa	52.4
17	Kansas	48.1
6	Kentucky	54.6
41	Louisiana	35.8
4	Maine	58.2
46	Maryland	34.4
36	Massachusetts	40.1
29	Michigan	42.0
40	Minnesota	36.1
22	Mississippi	46.5
20	Missouri	47.5
2	Montana	62.4
21	Nebraska	46.6
17	Nevada	48.1
23	New Hampshire	46.2
45	New Jersey	34.8
37	New Mexico	39.6
43	New York	35.3
27	North Carolina	42.4
24	North Dakota	43.0
11	Ohio	51.5
5	Oklahoma	56.3
15	Oregon	49.5
16	Pennsylvania	48.2
25	Rhode Island	42.8
26	South Carolina	42.7
12	South Dakota	50.7
13	Tennessee	50.6
47	Texas	32.9
48	Utah	24.9
19	Vermont	47.6
39	Virginia	36.6
33	Washington	41.1
1	West Virginia	67.5
29	Wisconsin	42.0
3	Wyoming	60.8

RANK ORDER

RANK	STATE	RATE
1	West Virginia	67.5
2	Montana	62.4
3	Wyoming	60.8
4	Maine	58.2
5	Oklahoma	56.3
6	Kentucky	54.6
7	Iowa	52.4
8	Alabama	52.1
9	Arkansas	51.9
10	Florida	51.6
11	Ohio	51.5
12	South Dakota	50.7
13	Tennessee	50.6
14	Indiana	50.4
15	Oregon	49.5
16	Pennsylvania	48.2
17	Kansas	48.1
17	Nevada	48.1
19	Vermont	47.6
20	Missouri	47.5
21	Nebraska	46.6
22	Mississippi	46.5
23	New Hampshire	46.2
24	North Dakota	43.0
25	Rhode Island	42.8
26	South Carolina	42.7
27	North Carolina	42.4
28	Arizona	42.1
29	Michigan	42.0
29	Wisconsin	42.0
31	Delaware	41.5
32	Colorado	41.3
33	Idaho	41.1
33	Washington	41.1
35	Connecticut	40.9
36	Massachusetts	40.1
37	New Mexico	39.6
38	Illinois	37.1
39	Virginia	36.6
40	Minnesota	36.1
41	Louisiana	35.8
42	Georgia	35.4
43	New York	35.3
44	California	34.9
45	New Jersey	34.8
46	Maryland	34.4
47	Texas	32.9
48	Utah	24.9
49	Hawaii	24.3
50	Alaska	21.2

District of Columbia	29.8

Source: U.S. Department of Health and Human Services, National Center for Health Statistics
    "National Vital Statistics Reports" (Vol. 55, No. 19, August 21, 2007, http://www.cdc.gov/nchs/deaths.htm)
*Final data by state of residence. Chronic lower respiratory diseases are diseases of the lungs including bronchitis, emphysema, and asthma. Includes allied conditions. Not age-adjusted.

Age-Adjusted Death Rate by Chronic Lower Respiratory Diseases in 2004

National Rate = 41.1 Deaths per 100,000 Population*

ALPHA ORDER

RANK	STATE	RATE
9	Alabama	50.0
35	Alaska	39.4
27	Arizona	42.4
13	Arkansas	47.4
34	California	39.7
7	Colorado	51.7
46	Connecticut	34.7
33	Delaware	39.8
36	Florida	38.8
16	Georgia	45.8
50	Hawaii	21.0
19	Idaho	44.4
40	Illinois	37.5
10	Indiana	49.8
26	Iowa	42.5
18	Kansas	44.9
5	Kentucky	54.7
38	Louisiana	38.2
11	Maine	49.3
41	Maryland	36.5
45	Massachusetts	35.2
31	Michigan	41.0
43	Minnesota	35.4
12	Mississippi	48.4
20	Missouri	44.1
3	Montana	56.1
28	Nebraska	42.0
2	Nevada	56.8
16	New Hampshire	45.8
49	New Jersey	32.1
30	New Mexico	41.7
48	New York	32.8
22	North Carolina	44.0
46	North Dakota	34.7
14	Ohio	47.0
6	Oklahoma	54.0
15	Oregon	46.7
39	Pennsylvania	37.6
44	Rhode Island	35.3
24	South Carolina	43.1
25	South Dakota	42.7
8	Tennessee	50.9
29	Texas	41.9
42	Utah	35.5
20	Vermont	44.1
32	Virginia	39.9
23	Washington	43.3
4	West Virginia	55.3
37	Wisconsin	38.7
1	Wyoming	62.6

RANK ORDER

RANK	STATE	RATE
1	Wyoming	62.6
2	Nevada	56.8
3	Montana	56.1
4	West Virginia	55.3
5	Kentucky	54.7
6	Oklahoma	54.0
7	Colorado	51.7
8	Tennessee	50.9
9	Alabama	50.0
10	Indiana	49.8
11	Maine	49.3
12	Mississippi	48.4
13	Arkansas	47.4
14	Ohio	47.0
15	Oregon	46.7
16	Georgia	45.8
16	New Hampshire	45.8
18	Kansas	44.9
19	Idaho	44.4
20	Missouri	44.1
20	Vermont	44.1
22	North Carolina	44.0
23	Washington	43.3
24	South Carolina	43.1
25	South Dakota	42.7
26	Iowa	42.5
27	Arizona	42.4
28	Nebraska	42.0
29	Texas	41.9
30	New Mexico	41.7
31	Michigan	41.0
32	Virginia	39.9
33	Delaware	39.8
34	California	39.7
35	Alaska	39.4
36	Florida	38.8
37	Wisconsin	38.7
38	Louisiana	38.2
39	Pennsylvania	37.6
40	Illinois	37.5
41	Maryland	36.5
42	Utah	35.5
43	Minnesota	35.4
44	Rhode Island	35.3
45	Massachusetts	35.2
46	Connecticut	34.7
46	North Dakota	34.7
48	New York	32.8
49	New Jersey	32.1
50	Hawaii	21.0
	District of Columbia	29.5

Source: U.S. Department of Health and Human Services, National Center for Health Statistics
"National Vital Statistics Reports" (Vol. 55, No. 19, August 21, 2007, http://www.cdc.gov/nchs/deaths.htm)
*Final data by state of residence. Chronic lower respiratory diseases are diseases of the lungs including bronchitis, emphysema, and asthma. Includes allied conditions. Age-adjusted rates based on the year 2000 standard population.

Deaths by Diabetes Mellitus in 2004

National Total = 73,138 Deaths*

ALPHA ORDER

RANK	STATE	DEATHS	% of USA
18	Alabama	1,449	2.0%
50	Alaska	93	0.1%
22	Arizona	1,196	1.6%
29	Arkansas	838	1.1%
1	California	7,117	9.7%
32	Colorado	696	1.0%
30	Connecticut	767	1.0%
45	Delaware	210	0.3%
3	Florida	4,809	6.6%
14	Georgia	1,623	2.2%
47	Hawaii	194	0.3%
39	Idaho	344	0.5%
7	Illinois	3,069	4.2%
13	Indiana	1,673	2.3%
31	Iowa	700	1.0%
33	Kansas	690	0.9%
23	Kentucky	1,195	1.6%
12	Louisiana	1,717	2.3%
38	Maine	382	0.5%
19	Maryland	1,417	1.9%
20	Massachusetts	1,329	1.8%
8	Michigan	2,953	4.0%
26	Minnesota	1,130	1.5%
34	Mississippi	665	0.9%
17	Missouri	1,461	2.0%
43	Montana	237	0.3%
37	Nebraska	395	0.5%
41	Nevada	290	0.4%
40	New Hampshire	313	0.4%
9	New Jersey	2,595	3.5%
35	New Mexico	590	0.8%
4	New York	3,913	5.4%
10	North Carolina	2,253	3.1%
46	North Dakota	209	0.3%
5	Ohio	3,615	4.9%
25	Oklahoma	1,139	1.6%
27	Oregon	1,073	1.5%
6	Pennsylvania	3,579	4.9%
42	Rhode Island	280	0.4%
24	South Carolina	1,165	1.6%
44	South Dakota	229	0.3%
11	Tennessee	1,882	2.6%
2	Texas	5,435	7.4%
36	Utah	485	0.7%
48	Vermont	150	0.2%
15	Virginia	1,602	2.2%
16	Washington	1,508	2.1%
28	West Virginia	840	1.1%
21	Wisconsin	1,310	1.8%
49	Wyoming	110	0.2%

RANK ORDER

RANK	STATE	DEATHS	% of USA
1	California	7,117	9.7%
2	Texas	5,435	7.4%
3	Florida	4,809	6.6%
4	New York	3,913	5.4%
5	Ohio	3,615	4.9%
6	Pennsylvania	3,579	4.9%
7	Illinois	3,069	4.2%
8	Michigan	2,953	4.0%
9	New Jersey	2,595	3.5%
10	North Carolina	2,253	3.1%
11	Tennessee	1,882	2.6%
12	Louisiana	1,717	2.3%
13	Indiana	1,673	2.3%
14	Georgia	1,623	2.2%
15	Virginia	1,602	2.2%
16	Washington	1,508	2.1%
17	Missouri	1,461	2.0%
18	Alabama	1,449	2.0%
19	Maryland	1,417	1.9%
20	Massachusetts	1,329	1.8%
21	Wisconsin	1,310	1.8%
22	Arizona	1,196	1.6%
23	Kentucky	1,195	1.6%
24	South Carolina	1,165	1.6%
25	Oklahoma	1,139	1.6%
26	Minnesota	1,130	1.5%
27	Oregon	1,073	1.5%
28	West Virginia	840	1.1%
29	Arkansas	838	1.1%
30	Connecticut	767	1.0%
31	Iowa	700	1.0%
32	Colorado	696	1.0%
33	Kansas	690	0.9%
34	Mississippi	665	0.9%
35	New Mexico	590	0.8%
36	Utah	485	0.7%
37	Nebraska	395	0.5%
38	Maine	382	0.5%
39	Idaho	344	0.5%
40	New Hampshire	313	0.4%
41	Nevada	290	0.4%
42	Rhode Island	280	0.4%
43	Montana	237	0.3%
44	South Dakota	229	0.3%
45	Delaware	210	0.3%
46	North Dakota	209	0.3%
47	Hawaii	194	0.3%
48	Vermont	150	0.2%
49	Wyoming	110	0.2%
50	Alaska	93	0.1%
	District of Columbia	224	0.3%

Source: U.S. Department of Health and Human Services, National Center for Health Statistics
  "National Vital Statistics Reports" (Vol. 55, No. 19, August 21, 2007, http://www.cdc.gov/nchs/deaths.htm)
*Final data by state of residence. A severe, chronic form of diabetes caused by insufficient production of insulin and resulting in abnormal metabolism of carbohydrates, fats, and proteins. The disease, which typically appears in childhood or adolescence, is characterized by increased sugar levels in the blood and urine, excessive thirst, and frequent urination.

Death Rate by Diabetes Mellitus in 2004

National Rate = 24.9 Deaths per 100,000 Population*

ALPHA ORDER

RANK	STATE	RATE
5	Alabama	32.0
49	Alaska	14.2
41	Arizona	20.8
9	Arkansas	30.4
45	California	19.8
48	Colorado	15.1
38	Connecticut	21.9
25	Delaware	25.3
18	Florida	27.6
46	Georgia	18.4
47	Hawaii	15.4
27	Idaho	24.7
30	Illinois	24.1
19	Indiana	26.8
34	Iowa	23.7
26	Kansas	25.2
15	Kentucky	28.8
2	Louisiana	38.0
14	Maine	29.0
23	Maryland	25.5
42	Massachusetts	20.7
13	Michigan	29.2
37	Minnesota	22.2
35	Mississippi	22.9
24	Missouri	25.4
22	Montana	25.6
36	Nebraska	22.6
50	Nevada	12.4
30	New Hampshire	24.1
11	New Jersey	29.8
8	New Mexico	31.0
43	New York	20.4
20	North Carolina	26.4
3	North Dakota	32.9
7	Ohio	31.5
4	Oklahoma	32.3
10	Oregon	29.9
15	Pennsylvania	28.8
21	Rhode Island	25.9
17	South Carolina	27.8
12	South Dakota	29.7
6	Tennessee	31.9
29	Texas	24.2
44	Utah	20.3
30	Vermont	24.1
40	Virginia	21.5
28	Washington	24.3
1	West Virginia	46.3
33	Wisconsin	23.8
39	Wyoming	21.7

RANK ORDER

RANK	STATE	RATE
1	West Virginia	46.3
2	Louisiana	38.0
3	North Dakota	32.9
4	Oklahoma	32.3
5	Alabama	32.0
6	Tennessee	31.9
7	Ohio	31.5
8	New Mexico	31.0
9	Arkansas	30.4
10	Oregon	29.9
11	New Jersey	29.8
12	South Dakota	29.7
13	Michigan	29.2
14	Maine	29.0
15	Kentucky	28.8
15	Pennsylvania	28.8
17	South Carolina	27.8
18	Florida	27.6
19	Indiana	26.8
20	North Carolina	26.4
21	Rhode Island	25.9
22	Montana	25.6
23	Maryland	25.5
24	Missouri	25.4
25	Delaware	25.3
26	Kansas	25.2
27	Idaho	24.7
28	Washington	24.3
29	Texas	24.2
30	Illinois	24.1
30	New Hampshire	24.1
30	Vermont	24.1
33	Wisconsin	23.8
34	Iowa	23.7
35	Mississippi	22.9
36	Nebraska	22.6
37	Minnesota	22.2
38	Connecticut	21.9
39	Wyoming	21.7
40	Virginia	21.5
41	Arizona	20.8
42	Massachusetts	20.7
43	New York	20.4
44	Utah	20.3
45	California	19.8
46	Georgia	18.4
47	Hawaii	15.4
48	Colorado	15.1
49	Alaska	14.2
50	Nevada	12.4
	District of Columbia	40.5

Source: U.S. Department of Health and Human Services, National Center for Health Statistics
   "National Vital Statistics Reports" (Vol. 55, No. 19, August 21, 2007, http://www.cdc.gov/nchs/deaths.htm)
*Final data by state of residence. A severe, chronic form of diabetes caused by insufficient production of insulin and resulting in abnormal metabolism of carbohydrates, fats, and proteins. The disease, which typically appears in childhood or adolescence, is characterized by increased sugar levels in the blood and urine, excessive thirst, and frequent urination. Not age-adjusted.

Age-Adjusted Death Rate by Diabetes Mellitus in 2004

National Rate = 24.5 Deaths per 100,000 Population*

ALPHA ORDER

RANK ORDER

RANK	STATE	RATE	RANK	STATE	RATE
6	Alabama	30.7	1	Louisiana	39.9
33	Alaska	22.5	2	West Virginia	38.1
42	Arizona	20.9	3	New Mexico	31.7
12	Arkansas	28.0	4	Tennessee	31.6
36	California	22.2	5	Oklahoma	31.0
48	Colorado	18.2	6	Alabama	30.7
46	Connecticut	18.7	7	Texas	29.7
25	Delaware	24.1	8	Ohio	28.9
40	Florida	21.6	9	Kentucky	28.6
33	Georgia	22.5	9	Utah	28.6
50	Hawaii	13.4	11	Michigan	28.4
18	Idaho	26.4	12	Arkansas	28.0
24	Illinois	24.2	13	Oregon	27.9
20	Indiana	26.3	14	New Jersey	27.6
44	Iowa	19.4	14	South Carolina	27.6
28	Kansas	23.5	16	North Carolina	27.0
9	Kentucky	28.6	17	North Dakota	26.5
1	Louisiana	39.9	18	Idaho	26.4
23	Maine	24.5	18	Maryland	26.4
18	Maryland	26.4	20	Indiana	26.3
47	Massachusetts	18.4	21	South Dakota	25.2
11	Michigan	28.4	22	Washington	25.0
41	Minnesota	21.4	23	Maine	24.5
26	Mississippi	23.6	24	Illinois	24.2
26	Missouri	23.6	25	Delaware	24.1
32	Montana	22.6	26	Mississippi	23.6
43	Nebraska	20.4	26	Missouri	23.6
49	Nevada	13.9	28	Kansas	23.5
28	New Hampshire	23.5	28	New Hampshire	23.5
14	New Jersey	27.6	30	Pennsylvania	23.1
3	New Mexico	31.7	31	Virginia	22.7
45	New York	19.0	32	Montana	22.6
16	North Carolina	27.0	33	Alaska	22.5
17	North Dakota	26.5	33	Georgia	22.5
8	Ohio	28.9	35	Vermont	22.3
5	Oklahoma	31.0	36	California	22.2
13	Oregon	27.9	37	Wyoming	22.1
30	Pennsylvania	23.1	38	Rhode Island	21.9
38	Rhode Island	21.9	39	Wisconsin	21.7
14	South Carolina	27.6	40	Florida	21.6
21	South Dakota	25.2	41	Minnesota	21.4
4	Tennessee	31.6	42	Arizona	20.9
7	Texas	29.7	43	Nebraska	20.4
9	Utah	28.6	44	Iowa	19.4
35	Vermont	22.3	45	New York	19.0
31	Virginia	22.7	46	Connecticut	18.7
22	Washington	25.0	47	Massachusetts	18.4
2	West Virginia	38.1	48	Colorado	18.2
39	Wisconsin	21.7	49	Nevada	13.9
37	Wyoming	22.1	50	Hawaii	13.4

District of Columbia — 40.2

Source: U.S. Department of Health and Human Services, National Center for Health Statistics
   "National Vital Statistics Reports" (Vol. 55, No. 19, August 21, 2007, http://www.cdc.gov/nchs/deaths.htm)
*Final data by state of residence. A severe, chronic form of diabetes caused by insufficient production of insulin and resulting in abnormal metabolism of carbohydrates, fats, and proteins. The disease, which typically appears in childhood or adolescence, is characterized by increased sugar levels in the blood and urine, excessive thirst, and frequent urination. Age-adjusted rates based on the year 2000 standard population.

Deaths by Diseases of the Heart in 2004

National Total = 652,486 Deaths*

ALPHA ORDER

RANK	STATE	DEATHS	% of USA
17	Alabama	12,774	2.0%
50	Alaska	589	0.1%
22	Arizona	10,539	1.6%
29	Arkansas	7,534	1.2%
1	California	64,999	10.0%
32	Colorado	6,079	0.9%
28	Connecticut	7,868	1.2%
44	Delaware	2,015	0.3%
3	Florida	47,160	7.2%
11	Georgia	16,557	2.5%
42	Hawaii	2,457	0.4%
43	Idaho	2,450	0.4%
7	Illinois	28,284	4.3%
14	Indiana	14,636	2.2%
30	Iowa	7,299	1.1%
33	Kansas	6,048	0.9%
23	Kentucky	10,465	1.6%
20	Louisiana	10,852	1.7%
39	Maine	2,948	0.5%
19	Maryland	11,346	1.7%
16	Massachusetts	13,824	2.1%
8	Michigan	24,825	3.8%
27	Minnesota	7,891	1.2%
26	Mississippi	8,282	1.3%
12	Missouri	15,500	2.4%
45	Montana	1,838	0.3%
36	Nebraska	3,738	0.6%
35	Nevada	4,693	0.7%
41	New Hampshire	2,639	0.4%
9	New Jersey	20,560	3.2%
37	New Mexico	3,264	0.5%
2	New York	52,480	8.0%
10	North Carolina	17,607	2.7%
47	North Dakota	1,470	0.2%
6	Ohio	29,078	4.5%
24	Oklahoma	10,335	1.6%
31	Oregon	6,725	1.0%
5	Pennsylvania	36,434	5.6%
38	Rhode Island	2,969	0.5%
25	South Carolina	9,182	1.4%
46	South Dakota	1,783	0.3%
13	Tennessee	15,038	2.3%
4	Texas	40,196	6.2%
40	Utah	2,942	0.5%
48	Vermont	1,289	0.2%
15	Virginia	14,284	2.2%
21	Washington	10,644	1.6%
34	West Virginia	5,674	0.9%
18	Wisconsin	11,909	1.8%
49	Wyoming	950	0.1%

RANK ORDER

RANK	STATE	DEATHS	% of USA
1	California	64,999	10.0%
2	New York	52,480	8.0%
3	Florida	47,160	7.2%
4	Texas	40,196	6.2%
5	Pennsylvania	36,434	5.6%
6	Ohio	29,078	4.5%
7	Illinois	28,284	4.3%
8	Michigan	24,825	3.8%
9	New Jersey	20,560	3.2%
10	North Carolina	17,607	2.7%
11	Georgia	16,557	2.5%
12	Missouri	15,500	2.4%
13	Tennessee	15,038	2.3%
14	Indiana	14,636	2.2%
15	Virginia	14,284	2.2%
16	Massachusetts	13,824	2.1%
17	Alabama	12,774	2.0%
18	Wisconsin	11,909	1.8%
19	Maryland	11,346	1.7%
20	Louisiana	10,852	1.7%
21	Washington	10,644	1.6%
22	Arizona	10,539	1.6%
23	Kentucky	10,465	1.6%
24	Oklahoma	10,335	1.6%
25	South Carolina	9,182	1.4%
26	Mississippi	8,282	1.3%
27	Minnesota	7,891	1.2%
28	Connecticut	7,868	1.2%
29	Arkansas	7,534	1.2%
30	Iowa	7,299	1.1%
31	Oregon	6,725	1.0%
32	Colorado	6,079	0.9%
33	Kansas	6,048	0.9%
34	West Virginia	5,674	0.9%
35	Nevada	4,693	0.7%
36	Nebraska	3,738	0.6%
37	New Mexico	3,264	0.5%
38	Rhode Island	2,969	0.5%
39	Maine	2,948	0.5%
40	Utah	2,942	0.5%
41	New Hampshire	2,639	0.4%
42	Hawaii	2,457	0.4%
43	Idaho	2,450	0.4%
44	Delaware	2,015	0.3%
45	Montana	1,838	0.3%
46	South Dakota	1,783	0.3%
47	North Dakota	1,470	0.2%
48	Vermont	1,289	0.2%
49	Wyoming	950	0.1%
50	Alaska	589	0.1%
	District of Columbia	1,544	0.2%

Source: U.S. Department of Health and Human Services, National Center for Health Statistics
   "National Vital Statistics Reports" (Vol. 55, No. 19, August 21, 2007, http://www.cdc.gov/nchs/deaths.htm)
*Final data by state of residence.

Death Rate by Diseases of the Heart in 2004

National Rate = 222.2 Deaths per 100,000 Population*

ALPHA ORDER

RANK	STATE	RATE
5	Alabama	282.0
50	Alaska	89.9
41	Arizona	183.5
7	Arkansas	273.7
42	California	181.1
48	Colorado	132.1
22	Connecticut	224.6
16	Delaware	242.7
9	Florida	271.1
39	Georgia	187.5
36	Hawaii	194.6
44	Idaho	175.8
24	Illinois	222.5
19	Indiana	234.6
14	Iowa	247.1
25	Kansas	221.1
13	Kentucky	252.4
17	Louisiana	240.3
23	Maine	223.8
32	Maryland	204.1
28	Massachusetts	215.4
15	Michigan	245.5
47	Minnesota	154.7
4	Mississippi	285.3
10	Missouri	269.3
35	Montana	198.3
29	Nebraska	213.9
34	Nevada	201.0
33	New Hampshire	203.1
18	New Jersey	236.4
46	New Mexico	171.5
8	New York	272.9
31	North Carolina	206.1
20	North Dakota	231.7
12	Ohio	253.8
3	Oklahoma	293.3
40	Oregon	187.1
2	Pennsylvania	293.7
6	Rhode Island	274.7
26	South Carolina	218.7
21	South Dakota	231.3
11	Tennessee	254.8
43	Texas	178.7
49	Utah	123.1
30	Vermont	207.4
37	Virginia	191.5
45	Washington	171.6
1	West Virginia	312.6
27	Wisconsin	216.2
38	Wyoming	187.6

RANK ORDER

RANK	STATE	RATE
1	West Virginia	312.6
2	Pennsylvania	293.7
3	Oklahoma	293.3
4	Mississippi	285.3
5	Alabama	282.0
6	Rhode Island	274.7
7	Arkansas	273.7
8	New York	272.9
9	Florida	271.1
10	Missouri	269.3
11	Tennessee	254.8
12	Ohio	253.8
13	Kentucky	252.4
14	Iowa	247.1
15	Michigan	245.5
16	Delaware	242.7
17	Louisiana	240.3
18	New Jersey	236.4
19	Indiana	234.6
20	North Dakota	231.7
21	South Dakota	231.3
22	Connecticut	224.6
23	Maine	223.8
24	Illinois	222.5
25	Kansas	221.1
26	South Carolina	218.7
27	Wisconsin	216.2
28	Massachusetts	215.4
29	Nebraska	213.9
30	Vermont	207.4
31	North Carolina	206.1
32	Maryland	204.1
33	New Hampshire	203.1
34	Nevada	201.0
35	Montana	198.3
36	Hawaii	194.6
37	Virginia	191.5
38	Wyoming	187.6
39	Georgia	187.5
40	Oregon	187.1
41	Arizona	183.5
42	California	181.1
43	Texas	178.7
44	Idaho	175.8
45	Washington	171.6
46	New Mexico	171.5
47	Minnesota	154.7
48	Colorado	132.1
49	Utah	123.1
50	Alaska	89.9
	District of Columbia	278.9

Source: U.S. Department of Health and Human Services, National Center for Health Statistics
    "National Vital Statistics Reports" (Vol. 55, No. 19, August 21, 2007, http://www.cdc.gov/nchs/deaths.htm)
*Final data by state of residence. Not age-adjusted.

Age-Adjusted Death Rate by Diseases of the Heart in 2004

National Rate = 217.0 Deaths per 100,000 Population*

ALPHA ORDER

RANK ORDER

RANK	STATE	RATE	RANK	STATE	RATE
3	Alabama	276.3	1	Mississippi	300.1
49	Alaska	158.3	2	Oklahoma	284.3
36	Arizona	185.7	3	Alabama	276.3
8	Arkansas	250.9	4	West Virginia	260.9
27	California	202.1	5	Tennessee	259.1
48	Colorado	162.7	6	Louisiana	256.6
40	Connecticut	182.5	7	Kentucky	254.9
14	Delaware	232.3	8	Arkansas	250.9
26	Florida	204.9	9	Missouri	248.4
11	Georgia	239.7	10	New York	247.9
47	Hawaii	167.3	11	Georgia	239.7
38	Idaho	184.3	12	Nevada	236.6
20	Illinois	219.1	13	Michigan	234.3
16	Indiana	228.0	14	Delaware	232.3
30	Iowa	191.9	15	Ohio	229.0
29	Kansas	197.3	16	Indiana	228.0
7	Kentucky	254.9	17	Texas	227.0
6	Louisiana	256.6	18	Pennsylvania	223.7
33	Maine	188.3	19	South Carolina	222.0
24	Maryland	212.4	20	Illinois	219.1
39	Massachusetts	183.3	21	Rhode Island	216.0
13	Michigan	234.3	22	North Carolina	214.4
50	Minnesota	144.3	23	New Jersey	213.0
1	Mississippi	300.1	24	Maryland	212.4
9	Missouri	248.4	25	Virginia	206.5
45	Montana	173.6	26	Florida	204.9
37	Nebraska	185.3	27	California	202.1
12	Nevada	236.6	28	New Hampshire	197.6
28	New Hampshire	197.6	29	Kansas	197.3
23	New Jersey	213.0	30	Iowa	191.9
41	New Mexico	180.4	31	Wisconsin	191.8
10	New York	247.9	32	Wyoming	191.0
22	North Carolina	214.4	33	Maine	188.3
42	North Dakota	175.8	34	South Dakota	187.1
15	Ohio	229.0	35	Vermont	186.6
2	Oklahoma	284.3	36	Arizona	185.7
46	Oregon	169.3	37	Nebraska	185.3
18	Pennsylvania	223.7	38	Idaho	184.3
21	Rhode Island	216.0	39	Massachusetts	183.3
19	South Carolina	222.0	40	Connecticut	182.5
34	South Dakota	187.1	41	New Mexico	180.4
5	Tennessee	259.1	42	North Dakota	175.8
17	Texas	227.0	43	Utah	175.0
43	Utah	175.0	44	Washington	174.7
35	Vermont	186.6	45	Montana	173.6
25	Virginia	206.5	46	Oregon	169.3
44	Washington	174.7	47	Hawaii	167.3
4	West Virginia	260.9	48	Colorado	162.7
31	Wisconsin	191.8	49	Alaska	158.3
32	Wyoming	191.0	50	Minnesota	144.3

District of Columbia 274.9

Source: U.S. Department of Health and Human Services, National Center for Health Statistics
"National Vital Statistics Reports" (Vol. 55, No. 19, August 21, 2007, http://www.cdc.gov/nchs/deaths.htm)
*Final data by state of residence. Age-adjusted rates based on the year 2000 standard population.

Deaths by Malignant Neoplasms in 2004

National Total = 553,888 Deaths*

ALPHA ORDER

RANK	STATE	DEATHS	% of USA
20	Alabama	9,756	1.8%
50	Alaska	728	0.1%
21	Arizona	9,618	1.7%
30	Arkansas	6,304	1.1%
1	California	53,700	9.7%
31	Colorado	6,196	1.1%
28	Connecticut	7,175	1.3%
45	Delaware	1,827	0.3%
2	Florida	39,840	7.2%
11	Georgia	14,313	2.6%
43	Hawaii	2,088	0.4%
42	Idaho	2,227	0.4%
7	Illinois	24,289	4.4%
15	Indiana	12,552	2.3%
29	Iowa	6,340	1.1%
33	Kansas	5,312	1.0%
23	Kentucky	9,159	1.7%
22	Louisiana	9,434	1.7%
37	Maine	3,124	0.6%
19	Maryland	10,168	1.8%
13	Massachusetts	13,337	2.4%
8	Michigan	19,653	3.5%
24	Minnesota	9,093	1.6%
32	Mississippi	5,983	1.1%
16	Missouri	12,450	2.2%
44	Montana	1,867	0.3%
36	Nebraska	3,270	0.6%
35	Nevada	4,119	0.7%
39	New Hampshire	2,554	0.5%
9	New Jersey	17,208	3.1%
38	New Mexico	3,036	0.5%
3	New York	36,100	6.5%
10	North Carolina	16,477	3.0%
47	North Dakota	1,265	0.2%
6	Ohio	24,940	4.5%
26	Oklahoma	7,269	1.3%
27	Oregon	7,236	1.3%
5	Pennsylvania	29,424	5.3%
41	Rhode Island	2,418	0.4%
25	South Carolina	8,348	1.5%
46	South Dakota	1,555	0.3%
14	Tennessee	12,586	2.3%
4	Texas	33,937	6.1%
40	Utah	2,445	0.4%
48	Vermont	1,212	0.2%
12	Virginia	13,385	2.4%
17	Washington	10,989	2.0%
34	West Virginia	4,694	0.8%
18	Wisconsin	10,861	2.0%
49	Wyoming	875	0.2%

RANK ORDER

RANK	STATE	DEATHS	% of USA
1	California	53,700	9.7%
2	Florida	39,840	7.2%
3	New York	36,100	6.5%
4	Texas	33,937	6.1%
5	Pennsylvania	29,424	5.3%
6	Ohio	24,940	4.5%
7	Illinois	24,289	4.4%
8	Michigan	19,653	3.5%
9	New Jersey	17,208	3.1%
10	North Carolina	16,477	3.0%
11	Georgia	14,313	2.6%
12	Virginia	13,385	2.4%
13	Massachusetts	13,337	2.4%
14	Tennessee	12,586	2.3%
15	Indiana	12,552	2.3%
16	Missouri	12,450	2.2%
17	Washington	10,989	2.0%
18	Wisconsin	10,861	2.0%
19	Maryland	10,168	1.8%
20	Alabama	9,756	1.8%
21	Arizona	9,618	1.7%
22	Louisiana	9,434	1.7%
23	Kentucky	9,159	1.7%
24	Minnesota	9,093	1.6%
25	South Carolina	8,348	1.5%
26	Oklahoma	7,269	1.3%
27	Oregon	7,236	1.3%
28	Connecticut	7,175	1.3%
29	Iowa	6,340	1.1%
30	Arkansas	6,304	1.1%
31	Colorado	6,196	1.1%
32	Mississippi	5,983	1.1%
33	Kansas	5,312	1.0%
34	West Virginia	4,694	0.8%
35	Nevada	4,119	0.7%
36	Nebraska	3,270	0.6%
37	Maine	3,124	0.6%
38	New Mexico	3,036	0.5%
39	New Hampshire	2,554	0.5%
40	Utah	2,445	0.4%
41	Rhode Island	2,418	0.4%
42	Idaho	2,227	0.4%
43	Hawaii	2,088	0.4%
44	Montana	1,867	0.3%
45	Delaware	1,827	0.3%
46	South Dakota	1,555	0.3%
47	North Dakota	1,265	0.2%
48	Vermont	1,212	0.2%
49	Wyoming	875	0.2%
50	Alaska	728	0.1%
	District of Columbia	1,152	0.2%

Source: U.S. Department of Health and Human Services, National Center for Health Statistics
"National Vital Statistics Reports" (Vol. 55, No. 19, August 21, 2007, http://www.cdc.gov/nchs/deaths.htm)
*Final data by state of residence. Neoplasms are abnormal tissue, tumors. Includes many cancers.

Death Rate by Malignant Neoplasms in 2004

National Rate = 188.6 Deaths per 100,000 Population*

ALPHA ORDER

RANK	STATE	RATE
11	Alabama	215.4
49	Alaska	111.1
41	Arizona	167.4
4	Arkansas	229.0
47	California	149.6
48	Colorado	134.7
18	Connecticut	204.8
8	Delaware	220.0
4	Florida	229.0
43	Georgia	162.1
42	Hawaii	165.3
44	Idaho	159.8
32	Illinois	191.0
22	Indiana	201.2
12	Iowa	214.6
30	Kansas	194.2
7	Kentucky	220.9
14	Louisiana	208.9
2	Maine	237.2
35	Maryland	182.9
15	Massachusetts	207.9
29	Michigan	194.3
37	Minnesota	178.3
17	Mississippi	206.1
10	Missouri	216.3
20	Montana	201.4
34	Nebraska	187.2
39	Nevada	176.4
27	New Hampshire	196.5
25	New Jersey	197.8
45	New Mexico	159.5
33	New York	187.8
31	North Carolina	192.9
23	North Dakota	199.4
9	Ohio	217.6
16	Oklahoma	206.3
21	Oregon	201.3
2	Pennsylvania	237.2
6	Rhode Island	223.8
24	South Carolina	198.9
19	South Dakota	201.7
13	Tennessee	213.3
46	Texas	150.9
50	Utah	102.3
28	Vermont	195.0
36	Virginia	179.4
38	Washington	177.1
1	West Virginia	258.6
26	Wisconsin	197.1
40	Wyoming	172.7

RANK ORDER

RANK	STATE	RATE
1	West Virginia	258.6
2	Maine	237.2
2	Pennsylvania	237.2
4	Arkansas	229.0
4	Florida	229.0
6	Rhode Island	223.8
7	Kentucky	220.9
8	Delaware	220.0
9	Ohio	217.6
10	Missouri	216.3
11	Alabama	215.4
12	Iowa	214.6
13	Tennessee	213.3
14	Louisiana	208.9
15	Massachusetts	207.9
16	Oklahoma	206.3
17	Mississippi	206.1
18	Connecticut	204.8
19	South Dakota	201.7
20	Montana	201.4
21	Oregon	201.3
22	Indiana	201.2
23	North Dakota	199.4
24	South Carolina	198.9
25	New Jersey	197.8
26	Wisconsin	197.1
27	New Hampshire	196.5
28	Vermont	195.0
29	Michigan	194.3
30	Kansas	194.2
31	North Carolina	192.9
32	Illinois	191.0
33	New York	187.8
34	Nebraska	187.2
35	Maryland	182.9
36	Virginia	179.4
37	Minnesota	178.3
38	Washington	177.1
39	Nevada	176.4
40	Wyoming	172.7
41	Arizona	167.4
42	Hawaii	165.3
43	Georgia	162.1
44	Idaho	159.8
45	New Mexico	159.5
46	Texas	150.9
47	California	149.6
48	Colorado	134.7
49	Alaska	111.1
50	Utah	102.3
	District of Columbia	208.1

Source: U.S. Department of Health and Human Services, National Center for Health Statistics
   "National Vital Statistics Reports" (Vol. 55, No. 19, August 21, 2007, http://www.cdc.gov/nchs/deaths.htm)
*Final data by state of residence. Neoplasms are abnormal tissue, tumors. Includes many cancers. Not age-adjusted.

Age-Adjusted Death Rate by Malignant Neoplasms in 2004

National Rate = 185.8 Deaths per 100,000 Population*

ALPHA ORDER

RANK	STATE	RATE
8	Alabama	203.7
29	Alaska	183.8
44	Arizona	167.2
5	Arkansas	208.9
46	California	166.8
48	Colorado	160.1
34	Connecticut	181.5
7	Delaware	207.4
36	Florida	179.9
13	Georgia	196.3
49	Hawaii	147.8
43	Idaho	169.3
20	Illinois	193.2
12	Indiana	198.2
33	Iowa	181.8
31	Kansas	183.2
2	Kentucky	215.4
1	Louisiana	216.7
10	Maine	200.8
25	Maryland	188.6
24	Massachusetts	188.7
23	Michigan	189.5
38	Minnesota	176.4
4	Mississippi	209.8
9	Missouri	201.2
35	Montana	180.2
41	Nebraska	173.6
19	Nevada	193.4
21	New Hampshire	192.1
27	New Jersey	184.4
47	New Mexico	161.9
40	New York	176.2
16	North Carolina	195.4
45	North Dakota	166.9
11	Ohio	200.6
14	Oklahoma	196.2
22	Oregon	189.6
18	Pennsylvania	193.8
17	Rhode Island	194.1
15	South Carolina	195.5
37	South Dakota	176.8
6	Tennessee	208.6
32	Texas	182.2
50	Utah	141.2
39	Vermont	176.3
26	Virginia	187.6
30	Washington	183.6
3	West Virginia	211.7
27	Wisconsin	184.4
42	Wyoming	170.8

RANK ORDER

RANK	STATE	RATE
1	Louisiana	216.7
2	Kentucky	215.4
3	West Virginia	211.7
4	Mississippi	209.8
5	Arkansas	208.9
6	Tennessee	208.6
7	Delaware	207.4
8	Alabama	203.7
9	Missouri	201.2
10	Maine	200.8
11	Ohio	200.6
12	Indiana	198.2
13	Georgia	196.3
14	Oklahoma	196.2
15	South Carolina	195.5
16	North Carolina	195.4
17	Rhode Island	194.1
18	Pennsylvania	193.8
19	Nevada	193.4
20	Illinois	193.2
21	New Hampshire	192.1
22	Oregon	189.6
23	Michigan	189.5
24	Massachusetts	188.7
25	Maryland	188.6
26	Virginia	187.6
27	New Jersey	184.4
27	Wisconsin	184.4
29	Alaska	183.8
30	Washington	183.6
31	Kansas	183.2
32	Texas	182.2
33	Iowa	181.8
34	Connecticut	181.5
35	Montana	180.2
36	Florida	179.9
37	South Dakota	176.8
38	Minnesota	176.4
39	Vermont	176.3
40	New York	176.2
41	Nebraska	173.6
42	Wyoming	170.8
43	Idaho	169.3
44	Arizona	167.2
45	North Dakota	166.9
46	California	166.8
47	New Mexico	161.9
48	Colorado	160.1
49	Hawaii	147.8
50	Utah	141.2

	District of Columbia	207.0

Source: U.S. Department of Health and Human Services, National Center for Health Statistics
   "National Vital Statistics Reports" (Vol. 55, No. 19, August 21, 2007, http://www.cdc.gov/nchs/deaths.htm)
*Final data by state of residence. Neoplasms are abnormal tissue, tumors. Includes many cancers. Age-adjusted rates based on the year 2000 standard population.

Deaths by Nephritis and Other Kidney Diseases in 2004

National Total = 42,480 Deaths*

ALPHA ORDER

RANK ORDER

RANK	STATE	DEATHS	% of USA
17	Alabama	1,049	2.5%
50	Alaska	23	0.1%
25	Arizona	634	1.5%
28	Arkansas	562	1.3%
4	California	2,373	5.6%
32	Colorado	406	1.0%
26	Connecticut	604	1.4%
43	Delaware	128	0.3%
6	Florida	2,252	5.3%
11	Georgia	1,458	3.4%
40	Hawaii	164	0.4%
44	Idaho	109	0.3%
5	Illinois	2,339	5.5%
14	Indiana	1,244	2.9%
36	Iowa	266	0.6%
29	Kansas	554	1.3%
19	Kentucky	827	1.9%
15	Louisiana	1,110	2.6%
37	Maine	264	0.6%
21	Maryland	699	1.6%
12	Massachusetts	1,250	2.9%
9	Michigan	1,507	3.5%
23	Minnesota	669	1.6%
24	Mississippi	662	1.6%
16	Missouri	1,083	2.5%
45	Montana	108	0.3%
35	Nebraska	283	0.7%
31	Nevada	425	1.0%
41	New Hampshire	163	0.4%
8	New Jersey	1,624	3.8%
39	New Mexico	227	0.5%
3	New York	2,383	5.6%
10	North Carolina	1,470	3.5%
48	North Dakota	55	0.1%
7	Ohio	1,896	4.5%
27	Oklahoma	565	1.3%
34	Oregon	308	0.7%
1	Pennsylvania	3,067	7.2%
42	Rhode Island	131	0.3%
20	South Carolina	818	1.9%
46	South Dakota	92	0.2%
22	Tennessee	680	1.6%
2	Texas	2,561	6.0%
38	Utah	235	0.6%
47	Vermont	57	0.1%
13	Virginia	1,249	2.9%
33	Washington	348	0.8%
30	West Virginia	450	1.1%
18	Wisconsin	925	2.2%
49	Wyoming	45	0.1%

RANK	STATE	DEATHS	% of USA
1	Pennsylvania	3,067	7.2%
2	Texas	2,561	6.0%
3	New York	2,383	5.6%
4	California	2,373	5.6%
5	Illinois	2,339	5.5%
6	Florida	2,252	5.3%
7	Ohio	1,896	4.5%
8	New Jersey	1,624	3.8%
9	Michigan	1,507	3.5%
10	North Carolina	1,470	3.5%
11	Georgia	1,458	3.4%
12	Massachusetts	1,250	2.9%
13	Virginia	1,249	2.9%
14	Indiana	1,244	2.9%
15	Louisiana	1,110	2.6%
16	Missouri	1,083	2.5%
17	Alabama	1,049	2.5%
18	Wisconsin	925	2.2%
19	Kentucky	827	1.9%
20	South Carolina	818	1.9%
21	Maryland	699	1.6%
22	Tennessee	680	1.6%
23	Minnesota	669	1.6%
24	Mississippi	662	1.6%
25	Arizona	634	1.5%
26	Connecticut	604	1.4%
27	Oklahoma	565	1.3%
28	Arkansas	562	1.3%
29	Kansas	554	1.3%
30	West Virginia	450	1.1%
31	Nevada	425	1.0%
32	Colorado	406	1.0%
33	Washington	348	0.8%
34	Oregon	308	0.7%
35	Nebraska	283	0.7%
36	Iowa	266	0.6%
37	Maine	264	0.6%
38	Utah	235	0.6%
39	New Mexico	227	0.5%
40	Hawaii	164	0.4%
41	New Hampshire	163	0.4%
42	Rhode Island	131	0.3%
43	Delaware	128	0.3%
44	Idaho	109	0.3%
45	Montana	108	0.3%
46	South Dakota	92	0.2%
47	Vermont	57	0.1%
48	North Dakota	55	0.1%
49	Wyoming	45	0.1%
50	Alaska	23	0.1%
	District of Columbia	79	0.2%

Source: U.S. Department of Health and Human Services, National Center for Health Statistics
   "National Vital Statistics Reports" (Vol. 55, No. 19, August 21, 2007, http://www.cdc.gov/nchs/deaths.htm)
*Final data by state of residence. Includes nephrotic syndrome and nephrosis.

Death Rate by Nephritis and Other Kidney Diseases in 2004

National Rate = 14.5 Deaths per 100,000 Population*

ALPHA ORDER

RANK ORDER

RANK	STATE	RATE		RANK	STATE	RATE
4	Alabama	23.2		1	West Virginia	24.8
50	Alaska	3.5		2	Pennsylvania	24.7
39	Arizona	11.0		3	Louisiana	24.6
6	Arkansas	20.4		4	Alabama	23.2
48	California	6.6		5	Mississippi	22.8
44	Colorado	8.8		6	Arkansas	20.4
17	Connecticut	17.2		7	Kansas	20.3
25	Delaware	15.4		8	Maine	20.0
29	Florida	12.9		9	Indiana	19.9
21	Georgia	16.5		9	Kentucky	19.9
28	Hawaii	13.0		11	Massachusetts	19.5
47	Idaho	7.8		11	South Carolina	19.5
15	Illinois	18.4		13	Missouri	18.8
9	Indiana	19.9		14	New Jersey	18.7
42	Iowa	9.0		15	Illinois	18.4
7	Kansas	20.3		16	Nevada	18.2
9	Kentucky	19.9		17	Connecticut	17.2
3	Louisiana	24.6		17	North Carolina	17.2
8	Maine	20.0		19	Wisconsin	16.8
30	Maryland	12.6		20	Virginia	16.7
11	Massachusetts	19.5		21	Georgia	16.5
26	Michigan	14.9		21	Ohio	16.5
27	Minnesota	13.1		23	Nebraska	16.2
5	Mississippi	22.8		24	Oklahoma	16.0
13	Missouri	18.8		25	Delaware	15.4
36	Montana	11.7		26	Michigan	14.9
23	Nebraska	16.2		27	Minnesota	13.1
16	Nevada	18.2		28	Hawaii	13.0
31	New Hampshire	12.5		29	Florida	12.9
14	New Jersey	18.7		30	Maryland	12.6
34	New Mexico	11.9		31	New Hampshire	12.5
32	New York	12.4		32	New York	12.4
17	North Carolina	17.2		33	Rhode Island	12.1
45	North Dakota	8.7		34	New Mexico	11.9
21	Ohio	16.5		34	South Dakota	11.9
24	Oklahoma	16.0		36	Montana	11.7
46	Oregon	8.6		37	Tennessee	11.5
2	Pennsylvania	24.7		38	Texas	11.4
33	Rhode Island	12.1		39	Arizona	11.0
11	South Carolina	19.5		40	Utah	9.8
34	South Dakota	11.9		41	Vermont	9.2
37	Tennessee	11.5		42	Iowa	9.0
38	Texas	11.4		43	Wyoming	8.9
40	Utah	9.8		44	Colorado	8.8
41	Vermont	9.2		45	North Dakota	8.7
20	Virginia	16.7		46	Oregon	8.6
49	Washington	5.6		47	Idaho	7.8
1	West Virginia	24.8		48	California	6.6
19	Wisconsin	16.8		49	Washington	5.6
43	Wyoming	8.9		50	Alaska	3.5

District of Columbia   14.3

Source: U.S. Department of Health and Human Services, National Center for Health Statistics
   "National Vital Statistics Reports" (Vol. 55, No. 19, August 21, 2007, http://www.cdc.gov/nchs/deaths.htm)
*Final data by state of residence. Includes nephrotic syndrome and nephrosis. Not age-adjusted.

Age-Adjusted Death Rate by Nephritis and Other Kidney Diseases in 2004

National Rate = 14.2 Deaths per 100,000 Population*

ALPHA ORDER

RANK ORDER

RANK	STATE	RATE
3	Alabama	22.7
48	Alaska	7.0
36	Arizona	11.1
11	Arkansas	18.7
46	California	7.4
37	Colorado	11.0
24	Connecticut	14.4
23	Delaware	14.8
39	Florida	9.8
5	Georgia	21.2
35	Hawaii	11.3
43	Idaho	8.2
12	Illinois	18.3
9	Indiana	19.4
47	Iowa	7.1
14	Kansas	17.9
7	Kentucky	20.3
1	Louisiana	26.2
18	Maine	16.9
29	Maryland	13.2
19	Massachusetts	16.6
27	Michigan	14.3
32	Minnesota	12.3
2	Mississippi	23.9
16	Missouri	17.3
38	Montana	10.1
24	Nebraska	14.4
4	Nevada	21.5
31	New Hampshire	12.4
17	New Jersey	17.0
30	New Mexico	12.5
34	New York	11.4
14	North Carolina	17.9
49	North Dakota	6.3
21	Ohio	15.0
20	Oklahoma	15.6
45	Oregon	7.9
10	Pennsylvania	19.0
41	Rhode Island	9.5
8	South Carolina	19.8
39	South Dakota	9.8
33	Tennessee	11.7
24	Texas	14.4
28	Utah	14.1
43	Vermont	8.2
13	Virginia	18.1
50	Washington	5.7
6	West Virginia	20.5
21	Wisconsin	15.0
42	Wyoming	9.2

RANK	STATE	RATE
1	Louisiana	26.2
2	Mississippi	23.9
3	Alabama	22.7
4	Nevada	21.5
5	Georgia	21.2
6	West Virginia	20.5
7	Kentucky	20.3
8	South Carolina	19.8
9	Indiana	19.4
10	Pennsylvania	19.0
11	Arkansas	18.7
12	Illinois	18.3
13	Virginia	18.1
14	Kansas	17.9
14	North Carolina	17.9
16	Missouri	17.3
17	New Jersey	17.0
18	Maine	16.9
19	Massachusetts	16.6
20	Oklahoma	15.6
21	Ohio	15.0
21	Wisconsin	15.0
23	Delaware	14.8
24	Connecticut	14.4
24	Nebraska	14.4
24	Texas	14.4
27	Michigan	14.3
28	Utah	14.1
29	Maryland	13.2
30	New Mexico	12.5
31	New Hampshire	12.4
32	Minnesota	12.3
33	Tennessee	11.7
34	New York	11.4
35	Hawaii	11.3
36	Arizona	11.1
37	Colorado	11.0
38	Montana	10.1
39	Florida	9.8
39	South Dakota	9.8
41	Rhode Island	9.5
42	Wyoming	9.2
43	Idaho	8.2
43	Vermont	8.2
45	Oregon	7.9
46	California	7.4
47	Iowa	7.1
48	Alaska	7.0
49	North Dakota	6.3
50	Washington	5.7
	District of Columbia	14.5

Source: U.S. Department of Health and Human Services, National Center for Health Statistics
   "National Vital Statistics Reports" (Vol. 55, No. 19, August 21, 2007, http://www.cdc.gov/nchs/deaths.htm)
*Final data by state of residence. Includes nephrotic syndrome and nephrosis. Age-adjusted rates based on the year 2000 standard population.

Deaths by Influenza and Pneumonia in 2004

National Total = 59,664 Deaths*

ALPHA ORDER

RANK	STATE	DEATHS	% of USA
20	Alabama	994	1.7%
50	Alaska	42	0.1%
18	Arizona	1,111	1.9%
27	Arkansas	759	1.3%
1	California	7,323	12.3%
30	Colorado	637	1.1%
24	Connecticut	868	1.5%
47	Delaware	145	0.2%
4	Florida	3,044	5.1%
13	Georgia	1,547	2.6%
42	Hawaii	236	0.4%
43	Idaho	219	0.4%
6	Illinois	2,779	4.7%
17	Indiana	1,136	1.9%
23	Iowa	890	1.5%
32	Kansas	562	0.9%
21	Kentucky	965	1.6%
22	Louisiana	913	1.5%
38	Maine	308	0.5%
18	Maryland	1,111	1.9%
8	Massachusetts	1,959	3.3%
9	Michigan	1,957	3.3%
28	Minnesota	750	1.3%
30	Mississippi	637	1.1%
15	Missouri	1,389	2.3%
45	Montana	165	0.3%
37	Nebraska	347	0.6%
35	Nevada	402	0.7%
40	New Hampshire	271	0.5%
11	New Jersey	1,586	2.7%
38	New Mexico	308	0.5%
2	New York	5,499	9.2%
10	North Carolina	1,686	2.8%
46	North Dakota	148	0.2%
7	Ohio	2,204	3.7%
25	Oklahoma	810	1.4%
33	Oregon	558	0.9%
5	Pennsylvania	2,938	4.9%
41	Rhode Island	260	0.4%
26	South Carolina	770	1.3%
44	South Dakota	179	0.3%
12	Tennessee	1,571	2.6%
3	Texas	3,209	5.4%
36	Utah	384	0.6%
49	Vermont	86	0.1%
14	Virginia	1,449	2.4%
29	Washington	738	1.2%
34	West Virginia	474	0.8%
16	Wisconsin	1,141	1.9%
48	Wyoming	109	0.2%

RANK ORDER

RANK	STATE	DEATHS	% of USA
1	California	7,323	12.3%
2	New York	5,499	9.2%
3	Texas	3,209	5.4%
4	Florida	3,044	5.1%
5	Pennsylvania	2,938	4.9%
6	Illinois	2,779	4.7%
7	Ohio	2,204	3.7%
8	Massachusetts	1,959	3.3%
9	Michigan	1,957	3.3%
10	North Carolina	1,686	2.8%
11	New Jersey	1,586	2.7%
12	Tennessee	1,571	2.6%
13	Georgia	1,547	2.6%
14	Virginia	1,449	2.4%
15	Missouri	1,389	2.3%
16	Wisconsin	1,141	1.9%
17	Indiana	1,136	1.9%
18	Arizona	1,111	1.9%
18	Maryland	1,111	1.9%
20	Alabama	994	1.7%
21	Kentucky	965	1.6%
22	Louisiana	913	1.5%
23	Iowa	890	1.5%
24	Connecticut	868	1.5%
25	Oklahoma	810	1.4%
26	South Carolina	770	1.3%
27	Arkansas	759	1.3%
28	Minnesota	750	1.3%
29	Washington	738	1.2%
30	Colorado	637	1.1%
30	Mississippi	637	1.1%
32	Kansas	562	0.9%
33	Oregon	558	0.9%
34	West Virginia	474	0.8%
35	Nevada	402	0.7%
36	Utah	384	0.6%
37	Nebraska	347	0.6%
38	Maine	308	0.5%
38	New Mexico	308	0.5%
40	New Hampshire	271	0.5%
41	Rhode Island	260	0.4%
42	Hawaii	236	0.4%
43	Idaho	219	0.4%
44	South Dakota	179	0.3%
45	Montana	165	0.3%
46	North Dakota	148	0.2%
47	Delaware	145	0.2%
48	Wyoming	109	0.2%
49	Vermont	86	0.1%
50	Alaska	42	0.1%
	District of Columbia	91	0.2%

Source: U.S. Department of Health and Human Services, National Center for Health Statistics
"National Vital Statistics Reports" (Vol. 55, No. 19, August 21, 2007, http://www.cdc.gov/nchs/deaths.htm)
*Final data by state of residence.

Death Rate by Influenza and Pneumonia in 2004

National Rate = 20.3 Deaths per 100,000 Population*

ALPHA ORDER

RANK	STATE	RATE
16	Alabama	21.9
50	Alaska	6.4
30	Arizona	19.3
4	Arkansas	27.6
23	California	20.4
47	Colorado	13.8
7	Connecticut	24.8
37	Delaware	17.5
37	Florida	17.5
37	Georgia	17.5
32	Hawaii	18.7
43	Idaho	15.7
16	Illinois	21.9
34	Indiana	18.2
2	Iowa	30.1
22	Kansas	20.5
12	Kentucky	23.3
24	Louisiana	20.2
11	Maine	23.4
25	Maryland	20.0
1	Massachusetts	30.5
28	Michigan	19.4
45	Minnesota	14.7
16	Mississippi	21.9
8	Missouri	24.1
36	Montana	17.8
26	Nebraska	19.9
40	Nevada	17.2
20	New Hampshire	20.9
34	New Jersey	18.2
41	New Mexico	16.2
3	New York	28.6
27	North Carolina	19.7
12	North Dakota	23.3
31	Ohio	19.2
15	Oklahoma	23.0
44	Oregon	15.5
10	Pennsylvania	23.7
8	Rhode Island	24.1
33	South Carolina	18.3
14	South Dakota	23.2
5	Tennessee	26.6
46	Texas	14.3
42	Utah	16.1
47	Vermont	13.8
28	Virginia	19.4
49	Washington	11.9
6	West Virginia	26.1
21	Wisconsin	20.7
19	Wyoming	21.5

RANK ORDER

RANK	STATE	RATE
1	Massachusetts	30.5
2	Iowa	30.1
3	New York	28.6
4	Arkansas	27.6
5	Tennessee	26.6
6	West Virginia	26.1
7	Connecticut	24.8
8	Missouri	24.1
8	Rhode Island	24.1
10	Pennsylvania	23.7
11	Maine	23.4
12	Kentucky	23.3
12	North Dakota	23.3
14	South Dakota	23.2
15	Oklahoma	23.0
16	Alabama	21.9
16	Illinois	21.9
16	Mississippi	21.9
19	Wyoming	21.5
20	New Hampshire	20.9
21	Wisconsin	20.7
22	Kansas	20.5
23	California	20.4
24	Louisiana	20.2
25	Maryland	20.0
26	Nebraska	19.9
27	North Carolina	19.7
28	Michigan	19.4
28	Virginia	19.4
30	Arizona	19.3
31	Ohio	19.2
32	Hawaii	18.7
33	South Carolina	18.3
34	Indiana	18.2
34	New Jersey	18.2
36	Montana	17.8
37	Delaware	17.5
37	Florida	17.5
37	Georgia	17.5
40	Nevada	17.2
41	New Mexico	16.2
42	Utah	16.1
43	Idaho	15.7
44	Oregon	15.5
45	Minnesota	14.7
46	Texas	14.3
47	Colorado	13.8
47	Vermont	13.8
49	Washington	11.9
50	Alaska	6.4
	District of Columbia	16.4

Source: U.S. Department of Health and Human Services, National Center for Health Statistics
"National Vital Statistics Reports" (Vol. 55, No. 19, August 21, 2007, http://www.cdc.gov/nchs/deaths.htm)
*Final data by state of residence. Not age-adjusted.

Age-Adjusted Death Rate by Influenza and Pneumonia in 2004

National Rate = 19.8 Deaths per 100,000 Population*

ALPHA ORDER

RANK	STATE	RATE
14	Alabama	21.9
45	Alaska	14.7
24	Arizona	19.7
3	Arkansas	25.3
7	California	22.8
35	Colorado	17.3
25	Connecticut	19.2
39	Delaware	16.9
47	Florida	13.2
6	Georgia	23.6
43	Hawaii	15.5
41	Idaho	16.2
18	Illinois	21.2
33	Indiana	17.5
11	Iowa	22.2
32	Kansas	17.6
5	Kentucky	24.1
13	Louisiana	22.0
23	Maine	19.9
19	Maryland	21.1
4	Massachusetts	24.9
28	Michigan	18.3
47	Minnesota	13.2
16	Mississippi	21.5
12	Missouri	22.1
44	Montana	15.2
38	Nebraska	17.1
20	Nevada	21.0
22	New Hampshire	20.2
41	New Jersey	16.2
35	New Mexico	17.3
2	New York	25.9
21	North Carolina	20.9
40	North Dakota	16.6
37	Ohio	17.2
9	Oklahoma	22.6
46	Oregon	13.7
33	Pennsylvania	17.5
29	Rhode Island	18.2
26	South Carolina	19.1
30	South Dakota	17.9
1	Tennessee	27.8
27	Texas	18.6
7	Utah	22.8
49	Vermont	12.2
16	Virginia	21.5
50	Washington	11.9
14	West Virginia	21.9
31	Wisconsin	17.8
10	Wyoming	22.4

RANK ORDER

RANK	STATE	RATE
1	Tennessee	27.8
2	New York	25.9
3	Arkansas	25.3
4	Massachusetts	24.9
5	Kentucky	24.1
6	Georgia	23.6
7	California	22.8
7	Utah	22.8
9	Oklahoma	22.6
10	Wyoming	22.4
11	Iowa	22.2
12	Missouri	22.1
13	Louisiana	22.0
14	Alabama	21.9
14	West Virginia	21.9
16	Mississippi	21.5
16	Virginia	21.5
18	Illinois	21.2
19	Maryland	21.1
20	Nevada	21.0
21	North Carolina	20.9
22	New Hampshire	20.2
23	Maine	19.9
24	Arizona	19.7
25	Connecticut	19.2
26	South Carolina	19.1
27	Texas	18.6
28	Michigan	18.3
29	Rhode Island	18.2
30	South Dakota	17.9
31	Wisconsin	17.8
32	Kansas	17.6
33	Indiana	17.5
33	Pennsylvania	17.5
35	Colorado	17.3
35	New Mexico	17.3
37	Ohio	17.2
38	Nebraska	17.1
39	Delaware	16.9
40	North Dakota	16.6
41	Idaho	16.2
41	New Jersey	16.2
43	Hawaii	15.5
44	Montana	15.2
45	Alaska	14.7
46	Oregon	13.7
47	Florida	13.2
47	Minnesota	13.2
49	Vermont	12.2
50	Washington	11.9

District of Columbia	16.4

Source: U.S. Department of Health and Human Services, National Center for Health Statistics
"National Vital Statistics Reports" (Vol. 55, No. 19, August 21, 2007, http://www.cdc.gov/nchs/deaths.htm)
*Final data by state of residence. Age-adjusted rates based on the year 2000 standard population.

Deaths by Injury in 2004

National Total = 167,184 Deaths*

ALPHA ORDER

RANK	STATE	DEATHS	% of USA
19	Alabama	3,365	2.0%
45	Alaska	538	0.3%
12	Arizona	4,297	2.6%
30	Arkansas	2,101	1.3%
1	California	16,904	10.1%
24	Colorado	2,924	1.7%
32	Connecticut	1,693	1.0%
47	Delaware	436	0.3%
3	Florida	11,815	7.1%
9	Georgia	5,391	3.2%
43	Hawaii	585	0.3%
39	Idaho	889	0.5%
7	Illinois	6,136	3.7%
15	Indiana	3,667	2.2%
35	Iowa	1,543	0.9%
34	Kansas	1,674	1.0%
21	Kentucky	3,091	1.8%
16	Louisiana	3,556	2.1%
41	Maine	684	0.4%
22	Maryland	3,080	1.8%
27	Massachusetts	2,544	1.5%
10	Michigan	5,385	3.2%
26	Minnesota	2,575	1.5%
28	Mississippi	2,375	1.4%
14	Missouri	3,865	2.3%
40	Montana	768	0.5%
38	Nebraska	969	0.6%
33	Nevada	1,681	1.0%
42	New Hampshire	609	0.4%
18	New Jersey	3,385	2.0%
31	New Mexico	1,762	1.1%
5	New York	6,694	4.0%
8	North Carolina	5,716	3.4%
49	North Dakota	363	0.2%
6	Ohio	6,234	3.7%
25	Oklahoma	2,739	1.6%
29	Oregon	2,196	1.3%
4	Pennsylvania	7,446	4.5%
46	Rhode Island	509	0.3%
23	South Carolina	2,948	1.8%
44	South Dakota	561	0.3%
11	Tennessee	4,523	2.7%
2	Texas	12,312	7.4%
37	Utah	1,371	0.8%
48	Vermont	366	0.2%
13	Virginia	3,914	2.3%
17	Washington	3,508	2.1%
36	West Virginia	1,516	0.9%
20	Wisconsin	3,181	1.9%
50	Wyoming	358	0.2%

RANK ORDER

RANK	STATE	DEATHS	% of USA
1	California	16,904	10.1%
2	Texas	12,312	7.4%
3	Florida	11,815	7.1%
4	Pennsylvania	7,446	4.5%
5	New York	6,694	4.0%
6	Ohio	6,234	3.7%
7	Illinois	6,136	3.7%
8	North Carolina	5,716	3.4%
9	Georgia	5,391	3.2%
10	Michigan	5,385	3.2%
11	Tennessee	4,523	2.7%
12	Arizona	4,297	2.6%
13	Virginia	3,914	2.3%
14	Missouri	3,865	2.3%
15	Indiana	3,667	2.2%
16	Louisiana	3,556	2.1%
17	Washington	3,508	2.1%
18	New Jersey	3,385	2.0%
19	Alabama	3,365	2.0%
20	Wisconsin	3,181	1.9%
21	Kentucky	3,091	1.8%
22	Maryland	3,080	1.8%
23	South Carolina	2,948	1.8%
24	Colorado	2,924	1.7%
25	Oklahoma	2,739	1.6%
26	Minnesota	2,575	1.5%
27	Massachusetts	2,544	1.5%
28	Mississippi	2,375	1.4%
29	Oregon	2,196	1.3%
30	Arkansas	2,101	1.3%
31	New Mexico	1,762	1.1%
32	Connecticut	1,693	1.0%
33	Nevada	1,681	1.0%
34	Kansas	1,674	1.0%
35	Iowa	1,543	0.9%
36	West Virginia	1,516	0.9%
37	Utah	1,371	0.8%
38	Nebraska	969	0.6%
39	Idaho	889	0.5%
40	Montana	768	0.5%
41	Maine	684	0.4%
42	New Hampshire	609	0.4%
43	Hawaii	585	0.3%
44	South Dakota	561	0.3%
45	Alaska	538	0.3%
46	Rhode Island	509	0.3%
47	Delaware	436	0.3%
48	Vermont	366	0.2%
49	North Dakota	363	0.2%
50	Wyoming	358	0.2%
	District of Columbia	442	0.3%

Source: U.S. Department of Health and Human Services, National Center for Health Statistics
(http://wonder.cdc.gov)
*By state of residence. Injury as used here includes Accidents (including motor vehicle), Suicides, Homicides, and "Other" undetermined.

Death Rate by Injury in 2004

National Rate = 56.9 Deaths per 100,000 Population*

ALPHA ORDER

RANK	STATE	RATE
12	Alabama	74.4
5	Alaska	81.8
10	Arizona	74.9
9	Arkansas	76.4
44	California	47.2
21	Colorado	63.5
42	Connecticut	48.4
37	Delaware	52.5
17	Florida	68.0
24	Georgia	60.4
47	Hawaii	46.4
20	Idaho	63.7
43	Illinois	48.3
26	Indiana	58.9
38	Iowa	52.3
22	Kansas	61.2
11	Kentucky	74.6
6	Louisiana	78.9
40	Maine	52.0
32	Maryland	55.4
48	Massachusetts	39.7
36	Michigan	53.3
41	Minnesota	50.5
4	Mississippi	81.9
18	Missouri	67.1
3	Montana	82.9
32	Nebraska	55.4
14	Nevada	72.1
46	New Hampshire	46.9
49	New Jersey	39.0
1	New Mexico	92.6
50	New York	34.7
19	North Carolina	66.9
29	North Dakota	57.0
35	Ohio	54.4
7	Oklahoma	77.7
23	Oregon	61.1
25	Pennsylvania	60.1
45	Rhode Island	47.1
16	South Carolina	70.2
13	South Dakota	72.8
8	Tennessee	76.7
34	Texas	54.8
30	Utah	56.6
26	Vermont	58.9
38	Virginia	52.3
31	Washington	56.5
2	West Virginia	83.6
28	Wisconsin	57.8
15	Wyoming	70.8

RANK ORDER

RANK	STATE	RATE
1	New Mexico	92.6
2	West Virginia	83.6
3	Montana	82.9
4	Mississippi	81.9
5	Alaska	81.8
6	Louisiana	78.9
7	Oklahoma	77.7
8	Tennessee	76.7
9	Arkansas	76.4
10	Arizona	74.9
11	Kentucky	74.6
12	Alabama	74.4
13	South Dakota	72.8
14	Nevada	72.1
15	Wyoming	70.8
16	South Carolina	70.2
17	Florida	68.0
18	Missouri	67.1
19	North Carolina	66.9
20	Idaho	63.7
21	Colorado	63.5
22	Kansas	61.2
23	Oregon	61.1
24	Georgia	60.4
25	Pennsylvania	60.1
26	Indiana	58.9
26	Vermont	58.9
28	Wisconsin	57.8
29	North Dakota	57.0
30	Utah	56.6
31	Washington	56.5
32	Maryland	55.4
32	Nebraska	55.4
34	Texas	54.8
35	Ohio	54.4
36	Michigan	53.3
37	Delaware	52.5
38	Iowa	52.3
38	Virginia	52.3
40	Maine	52.0
41	Minnesota	50.5
42	Connecticut	48.4
43	Illinois	48.3
44	California	47.2
45	Rhode Island	47.1
46	New Hampshire	46.9
47	Hawaii	46.4
48	Massachusetts	39.7
49	New Jersey	39.0
50	New York	34.7
	District of Columbia	79.7

Source: U.S. Department of Health and Human Services, National Center for Health Statistics
   (http://wonder.cdc.gov)
*By state of residence. Injury as used here includes Accidents (including motor vehicle), Suicides, Homicides, and "Other" undetermined. Not age-adjusted.

Age-Adjusted Death Rate by Injury in 2004

National Rate = 56.4 Deaths per 100,000 Population*

ALPHA ORDER

RANK	STATE	RATE
13	Alabama	73.8
2	Alaska	87.4
10	Arizona	75.7
9	Arkansas	75.9
41	California	48.0
18	Colorado	65.9
44	Connecticut	45.6
37	Delaware	51.8
20	Florida	65.0
22	Georgia	63.6
46	Hawaii	44.3
21	Idaho	64.7
41	Illinois	48.0
26	Indiana	58.7
43	Iowa	47.4
24	Kansas	59.7
11	Kentucky	74.4
6	Louisiana	79.3
39	Maine	50.0
31	Maryland	55.5
49	Massachusetts	37.6
35	Michigan	52.8
40	Minnesota	48.7
3	Mississippi	82.7
19	Missouri	65.6
5	Montana	79.7
36	Nebraska	52.2
12	Nevada	74.0
44	New Hampshire	45.6
48	New Jersey	38.2
1	New Mexico	94.2
50	New York	33.6
17	North Carolina	67.4
38	North Dakota	51.6
33	Ohio	53.0
7	Oklahoma	77.3
25	Oregon	58.8
28	Pennsylvania	56.7
47	Rhode Island	43.4
14	South Carolina	70.2
16	South Dakota	69.5
8	Tennessee	76.2
27	Texas	57.7
23	Utah	62.8
29	Vermont	56.3
34	Virginia	52.9
30	Washington	55.9
4	West Virginia	80.9
32	Wisconsin	54.9
15	Wyoming	69.7

RANK ORDER

RANK	STATE	RATE
1	New Mexico	94.2
2	Alaska	87.4
3	Mississippi	82.7
4	West Virginia	80.9
5	Montana	79.7
6	Louisiana	79.3
7	Oklahoma	77.3
8	Tennessee	76.2
9	Arkansas	75.9
10	Arizona	75.7
11	Kentucky	74.4
12	Nevada	74.0
13	Alabama	73.8
14	South Carolina	70.2
15	Wyoming	69.7
16	South Dakota	69.5
17	North Carolina	67.4
18	Colorado	65.9
19	Missouri	65.6
20	Florida	65.0
21	Idaho	64.7
22	Georgia	63.6
23	Utah	62.8
24	Kansas	59.7
25	Oregon	58.8
26	Indiana	58.7
27	Texas	57.7
28	Pennsylvania	56.7
29	Vermont	56.3
30	Washington	55.9
31	Maryland	55.5
32	Wisconsin	54.9
33	Ohio	53.0
34	Virginia	52.9
35	Michigan	52.8
36	Nebraska	52.2
37	Delaware	51.8
38	North Dakota	51.6
39	Maine	50.0
40	Minnesota	48.7
41	California	48.0
41	Illinois	48.0
43	Iowa	47.4
44	Connecticut	45.6
44	New Hampshire	45.6
46	Hawaii	44.3
47	Rhode Island	43.4
48	New Jersey	38.2
49	Massachusetts	37.6
50	New York	33.6
	District of Columbia	78.2

Source: U.S. Department of Health and Human Services, National Center for Health Statistics
(http://wonder.cdc.gov)

*By state of residence. Injury as used here includes Accidents (including motor vehicle), Suicides, Homicides, and "Other" undetermined. Age-adjusted rates based on the year 2000 standard population.

Deaths by Accidents in 2004

National Total = 112,012 Deaths*

ALPHA ORDER

RANK	STATE	DEATHS	% of USA
15	Alabama	2,403	2.1%
45	Alaska	326	0.3%
12	Arizona	2,770	2.5%
29	Arkansas	1,406	1.3%
1	California	10,633	9.5%
25	Colorado	1,810	1.6%
31	Connecticut	1,261	1.1%
47	Delaware	294	0.3%
3	Florida	8,229	7.3%
9	Georgia	3,667	3.3%
44	Hawaii	390	0.3%
39	Idaho	593	0.5%
7	Illinois	4,133	3.7%
16	Indiana	2,395	2.1%
35	Iowa	1,108	1.0%
33	Kansas	1,144	1.0%
21	Kentucky	2,260	2.0%
20	Louisiana	2,300	2.1%
41	Maine	480	0.4%
28	Maryland	1,412	1.3%
30	Massachusetts	1,366	1.2%
10	Michigan	3,312	3.0%
24	Minnesota	1,867	1.7%
26	Mississippi	1,703	1.5%
13	Missouri	2,728	2.4%
40	Montana	535	0.5%
37	Nebraska	743	0.7%
36	Nevada	1,021	0.9%
42	New Hampshire	445	0.4%
18	New Jersey	2,324	2.1%
32	New Mexico	1,223	1.1%
5	New York	4,530	4.0%
8	North Carolina	4,019	3.6%
48	North Dakota	274	0.2%
6	Ohio	4,234	3.8%
23	Oklahoma	1,947	1.7%
27	Oregon	1,444	1.3%
4	Pennsylvania	5,200	4.6%
46	Rhode Island	298	0.3%
22	South Carolina	2,094	1.9%
43	South Dakota	416	0.4%
11	Tennessee	3,156	2.8%
2	Texas	8,323	7.4%
38	Utah	697	0.6%
49	Vermont	253	0.2%
14	Virginia	2,630	2.3%
17	Washington	2,341	2.1%
34	West Virginia	1,110	1.0%
19	Wisconsin	2,303	2.1%
50	Wyoming	243	0.2%

RANK ORDER

RANK	STATE	DEATHS	% of USA
1	California	10,633	9.5%
2	Texas	8,323	7.4%
3	Florida	8,229	7.3%
4	Pennsylvania	5,200	4.6%
5	New York	4,530	4.0%
6	Ohio	4,234	3.8%
7	Illinois	4,133	3.7%
8	North Carolina	4,019	3.6%
9	Georgia	3,667	3.3%
10	Michigan	3,312	3.0%
11	Tennessee	3,156	2.8%
12	Arizona	2,770	2.5%
13	Missouri	2,728	2.4%
14	Virginia	2,630	2.3%
15	Alabama	2,403	2.1%
16	Indiana	2,395	2.1%
17	Washington	2,341	2.1%
18	New Jersey	2,324	2.1%
19	Wisconsin	2,303	2.1%
20	Louisiana	2,300	2.1%
21	Kentucky	2,260	2.0%
22	South Carolina	2,094	1.9%
23	Oklahoma	1,947	1.7%
24	Minnesota	1,867	1.7%
25	Colorado	1,810	1.6%
26	Mississippi	1,703	1.5%
27	Oregon	1,444	1.3%
28	Maryland	1,412	1.3%
29	Arkansas	1,406	1.3%
30	Massachusetts	1,366	1.2%
31	Connecticut	1,261	1.1%
32	New Mexico	1,223	1.1%
33	Kansas	1,144	1.0%
34	West Virginia	1,110	1.0%
35	Iowa	1,108	1.0%
36	Nevada	1,021	0.9%
37	Nebraska	743	0.7%
38	Utah	697	0.6%
39	Idaho	593	0.5%
40	Montana	535	0.5%
41	Maine	480	0.4%
42	New Hampshire	445	0.4%
43	South Dakota	416	0.4%
44	Hawaii	390	0.3%
45	Alaska	326	0.3%
46	Rhode Island	298	0.3%
47	Delaware	294	0.3%
48	North Dakota	274	0.2%
49	Vermont	253	0.2%
50	Wyoming	243	0.2%
	District of Columbia	219	0.2%

Source: U.S. Department of Health and Human Services, National Center for Health Statistics
   "National Vital Statistics Reports" (Vol. 55, No. 19, August 21, 2007, http://www.cdc.gov/nchs/deaths.htm)
*Final data by state of residence. Includes motor vehicle deaths, poisoning, falls, drowning, and other accidents.

Death Rate by Accidents in 2004

National Rate = 38.1 Deaths per 100,000 Population*

ALPHA ORDER

RANK	STATE	RATE
9	Alabama	53.0
13	Alaska	49.7
14	Arizona	48.2
10	Arkansas	51.1
44	California	29.6
29	Colorado	39.3
37	Connecticut	36.0
38	Delaware	35.4
17	Florida	47.3
26	Georgia	41.5
43	Hawaii	30.9
21	Idaho	42.6
42	Illinois	32.5
30	Indiana	38.4
32	Iowa	37.5
24	Kansas	41.8
6	Kentucky	54.5
11	Louisiana	50.9
36	Maine	36.4
48	Maryland	25.4
50	Massachusetts	21.3
41	Michigan	32.8
35	Minnesota	36.6
3	Mississippi	58.7
16	Missouri	47.4
4	Montana	57.7
22	Nebraska	42.5
19	Nevada	43.7
40	New Hampshire	34.2
47	New Jersey	26.7
1	New Mexico	64.3
49	New York	23.6
18	North Carolina	47.1
20	North Dakota	43.2
34	Ohio	36.9
5	Oklahoma	55.3
28	Oregon	40.2
23	Pennsylvania	41.9
46	Rhode Island	27.6
12	South Carolina	49.9
7	South Dakota	54.0
8	Tennessee	53.5
33	Texas	37.0
45	Utah	29.2
27	Vermont	40.7
39	Virginia	35.3
31	Washington	37.7
2	West Virginia	61.1
24	Wisconsin	41.8
15	Wyoming	48.0

RANK ORDER

RANK	STATE	RATE
1	New Mexico	64.3
2	West Virginia	61.1
3	Mississippi	58.7
4	Montana	57.7
5	Oklahoma	55.3
6	Kentucky	54.5
7	South Dakota	54.0
8	Tennessee	53.5
9	Alabama	53.0
10	Arkansas	51.1
11	Louisiana	50.9
12	South Carolina	49.9
13	Alaska	49.7
14	Arizona	48.2
15	Wyoming	48.0
16	Missouri	47.4
17	Florida	47.3
18	North Carolina	47.1
19	Nevada	43.7
20	North Dakota	43.2
21	Idaho	42.6
22	Nebraska	42.5
23	Pennsylvania	41.9
24	Kansas	41.8
24	Wisconsin	41.8
26	Georgia	41.5
27	Vermont	40.7
28	Oregon	40.2
29	Colorado	39.3
30	Indiana	38.4
31	Washington	37.7
32	Iowa	37.5
33	Texas	37.0
34	Ohio	36.9
35	Minnesota	36.6
36	Maine	36.4
37	Connecticut	36.0
38	Delaware	35.4
39	Virginia	35.3
40	New Hampshire	34.2
41	Michigan	32.8
42	Illinois	32.5
43	Hawaii	30.9
44	California	29.6
45	Utah	29.2
46	Rhode Island	27.6
47	New Jersey	26.7
48	Maryland	25.4
49	New York	23.6
50	Massachusetts	21.3
	District of Columbia	39.6

Source: U.S. Department of Health and Human Services, National Center for Health Statistics
    "National Vital Statistics Reports" (Vol. 55, No. 19, August 21, 2007, http://www.cdc.gov/nchs/deaths.htm)
*Final data by state of residence. Includes motor vehicle deaths, poisoning, falls, drowning, and other accidents. Not age-adjusted.

Age-Adjusted Death Rate by Accidents in 2004

National Rate = 37.7 Deaths per 100,000 Population*

ALPHA ORDER

RANK	STATE	RATE
9	Alabama	52.8
4	Alaska	56.1
14	Arizona	48.6
12	Arkansas	50.4
44	California	30.4
22	Colorado	42.1
39	Connecticut	33.4
37	Delaware	34.9
20	Florida	44.7
19	Georgia	44.8
45	Hawaii	29.2
21	Idaho	43.1
42	Illinois	32.3
30	Indiana	38.0
41	Iowa	33.0
23	Kansas	40.3
6	Kentucky	54.6
10	Louisiana	51.6
35	Maine	35.2
46	Maryland	25.8
50	Massachusetts	19.6
43	Michigan	32.2
36	Minnesota	35.1
2	Mississippi	59.5
17	Missouri	46.1
6	Montana	54.6
25	Nebraska	39.4
18	Nevada	45.4
38	New Hampshire	33.6
46	New Jersey	25.8
1	New Mexico	65.6
49	New York	22.6
15	North Carolina	47.7
31	North Dakota	37.9
34	Ohio	35.6
5	Oklahoma	54.9
29	Oregon	38.3
28	Pennsylvania	38.6
48	Rhode Island	24.2
13	South Carolina	49.9
11	South Dakota	50.5
8	Tennessee	53.4
24	Texas	39.7
40	Utah	33.3
27	Vermont	38.7
33	Virginia	36.0
32	Washington	37.3
3	West Virginia	58.7
26	Wisconsin	39.1
16	Wyoming	47.0

RANK ORDER

RANK	STATE	RATE
1	New Mexico	65.6
2	Mississippi	59.5
3	West Virginia	58.7
4	Alaska	56.1
5	Oklahoma	54.9
6	Kentucky	54.6
6	Montana	54.6
8	Tennessee	53.4
9	Alabama	52.8
10	Louisiana	51.6
11	South Dakota	50.5
12	Arkansas	50.4
13	South Carolina	49.9
14	Arizona	48.6
15	North Carolina	47.7
16	Wyoming	47.0
17	Missouri	46.1
18	Nevada	45.4
19	Georgia	44.8
20	Florida	44.7
21	Idaho	43.1
22	Colorado	42.1
23	Kansas	40.3
24	Texas	39.7
25	Nebraska	39.4
26	Wisconsin	39.1
27	Vermont	38.7
28	Pennsylvania	38.6
29	Oregon	38.3
30	Indiana	38.0
31	North Dakota	37.9
32	Washington	37.3
33	Virginia	36.0
34	Ohio	35.6
35	Maine	35.2
36	Minnesota	35.1
37	Delaware	34.9
38	New Hampshire	33.6
39	Connecticut	33.4
40	Utah	33.3
41	Iowa	33.0
42	Illinois	32.3
43	Michigan	32.2
44	California	30.4
45	Hawaii	29.2
46	Maryland	25.8
46	New Jersey	25.8
48	Rhode Island	24.2
49	New York	22.6
50	Massachusetts	19.6
	District of Columbia	39.4

Source: U.S. Department of Health and Human Services, National Center for Health Statistics
"National Vital Statistics Reports" (Vol. 55, No. 19, August 21, 2007, http://www.cdc.gov/nchs/deaths.htm)
*Final data by state of residence. Includes motor vehicle deaths, poisoning, falls, drowning, and other accidents. Age-adjusted rates based on the year 2000 standard population.

Deaths by Motor Vehicle Accidents in 2004

National Total = 44,933 Deaths*

ALPHA ORDER

RANK	STATE	DEATHS	% of USA
12	Alabama	1,259	2.8%
47	Alaska	119	0.3%
13	Arizona	1,125	2.5%
22	Arkansas	779	1.7%
1	California	4,417	9.8%
25	Colorado	700	1.6%
36	Connecticut	336	0.7%
45	Delaware	141	0.3%
3	Florida	3,294	7.3%
8	Georgia	1,497	3.3%
44	Hawaii	142	0.3%
39	Idaho	249	0.6%
7	Illinois	1,513	3.4%
18	Indiana	1,006	2.2%
34	Iowa	418	0.9%
31	Kansas	500	1.1%
19	Kentucky	992	2.2%
16	Louisiana	1,022	2.3%
42	Maine	180	0.4%
26	Maryland	671	1.5%
29	Massachusetts	532	1.2%
11	Michigan	1,307	2.9%
28	Minnesota	652	1.5%
20	Mississippi	915	2.0%
14	Missouri	1,111	2.5%
40	Montana	241	0.5%
38	Nebraska	282	0.6%
33	Nevada	422	0.9%
43	New Hampshire	165	0.4%
23	New Jersey	771	1.7%
32	New Mexico	480	1.1%
6	New York	1,586	3.5%
4	North Carolina	1,691	3.8%
48	North Dakota	117	0.3%
10	Ohio	1,383	3.1%
24	Oklahoma	765	1.7%
30	Oregon	501	1.1%
5	Pennsylvania	1,595	3.5%
49	Rhode Island	99	0.2%
15	South Carolina	1,034	2.3%
41	South Dakota	189	0.4%
9	Tennessee	1,386	3.1%
2	Texas	3,864	8.6%
37	Utah	321	0.7%
50	Vermont	83	0.2%
17	Virginia	1,016	2.3%
27	Washington	669	1.5%
35	West Virginia	414	0.9%
21	Wisconsin	815	1.8%
46	Wyoming	121	0.3%

RANK ORDER

RANK	STATE	DEATHS	% of USA
1	California	4,417	9.8%
2	Texas	3,864	8.6%
3	Florida	3,294	7.3%
4	North Carolina	1,691	3.8%
5	Pennsylvania	1,595	3.5%
6	New York	1,586	3.5%
7	Illinois	1,513	3.4%
8	Georgia	1,497	3.3%
9	Tennessee	1,386	3.1%
10	Ohio	1,383	3.1%
11	Michigan	1,307	2.9%
12	Alabama	1,259	2.8%
13	Arizona	1,125	2.5%
14	Missouri	1,111	2.5%
15	South Carolina	1,034	2.3%
16	Louisiana	1,022	2.3%
17	Virginia	1,016	2.3%
18	Indiana	1,006	2.2%
19	Kentucky	992	2.2%
20	Mississippi	915	2.0%
21	Wisconsin	815	1.8%
22	Arkansas	779	1.7%
23	New Jersey	771	1.7%
24	Oklahoma	765	1.7%
25	Colorado	700	1.6%
26	Maryland	671	1.5%
27	Washington	669	1.5%
28	Minnesota	652	1.5%
29	Massachusetts	532	1.2%
30	Oregon	501	1.1%
31	Kansas	500	1.1%
32	New Mexico	480	1.1%
33	Nevada	422	0.9%
34	Iowa	418	0.9%
35	West Virginia	414	0.9%
36	Connecticut	336	0.7%
37	Utah	321	0.7%
38	Nebraska	282	0.6%
39	Idaho	249	0.6%
40	Montana	241	0.5%
41	South Dakota	189	0.4%
42	Maine	180	0.4%
43	New Hampshire	165	0.4%
44	Hawaii	142	0.3%
45	Delaware	141	0.3%
46	Wyoming	121	0.3%
47	Alaska	119	0.3%
48	North Dakota	117	0.3%
49	Rhode Island	99	0.2%
50	Vermont	83	0.2%
	District of Columbia	46	0.1%

Source: U.S. Department of Health and Human Services, National Center for Health Statistics
   "National Vital Statistics Reports" (Vol. 55, No. 19, August 21, 2007, http://www.cdc.gov/nchs/deaths.htm)
*Final data by state of residence. These numbers are compiled from death certificates by the Centers for Disease Control and Prevention. They may differ from motor vehicle deaths collected by the U.S. Department of Transportation from other sources.

Death Rate by Motor Vehicle Accidents in 2004

National Rate = 15.3 Deaths per 100,000 Population*

<table>
<tr><td colspan="3">ALPHA ORDER</td><td colspan="3">RANK ORDER</td></tr>
<tr><td>RANK</td><td>STATE</td><td>RATE</td><td>RANK</td><td>STATE</td><td>RATE</td></tr>
<tr><td>3</td><td>Alabama</td><td>27.8</td><td>1</td><td>Mississippi</td><td>31.5</td></tr>
<tr><td>20</td><td>Alaska</td><td>18.2</td><td>2</td><td>Arkansas</td><td>28.3</td></tr>
<tr><td>15</td><td>Arizona</td><td>19.6</td><td>3</td><td>Alabama</td><td>27.8</td></tr>
<tr><td>2</td><td>Arkansas</td><td>28.3</td><td>4</td><td>Montana</td><td>26.0</td></tr>
<tr><td>40</td><td>California</td><td>12.3</td><td>5</td><td>New Mexico</td><td>25.2</td></tr>
<tr><td>28</td><td>Colorado</td><td>15.2</td><td>6</td><td>South Carolina</td><td>24.6</td></tr>
<tr><td>46</td><td>Connecticut</td><td>9.6</td><td>7</td><td>South Dakota</td><td>24.5</td></tr>
<tr><td>24</td><td>Delaware</td><td>17.0</td><td>8</td><td>Kentucky</td><td>23.9</td></tr>
<tr><td>17</td><td>Florida</td><td>18.9</td><td>8</td><td>Wyoming</td><td>23.9</td></tr>
<tr><td>24</td><td>Georgia</td><td>17.0</td><td>10</td><td>Tennessee</td><td>23.5</td></tr>
<tr><td>44</td><td>Hawaii</td><td>11.2</td><td>11</td><td>West Virginia</td><td>22.8</td></tr>
<tr><td>22</td><td>Idaho</td><td>17.9</td><td>12</td><td>Louisiana</td><td>22.6</td></tr>
<tr><td>43</td><td>Illinois</td><td>11.9</td><td>13</td><td>Oklahoma</td><td>21.7</td></tr>
<tr><td>26</td><td>Indiana</td><td>16.1</td><td>14</td><td>North Carolina</td><td>19.8</td></tr>
<tr><td>30</td><td>Iowa</td><td>14.1</td><td>15</td><td>Arizona</td><td>19.6</td></tr>
<tr><td>19</td><td>Kansas</td><td>18.3</td><td>16</td><td>Missouri</td><td>19.3</td></tr>
<tr><td>8</td><td>Kentucky</td><td>23.9</td><td>17</td><td>Florida</td><td>18.9</td></tr>
<tr><td>12</td><td>Louisiana</td><td>22.6</td><td>18</td><td>North Dakota</td><td>18.4</td></tr>
<tr><td>32</td><td>Maine</td><td>13.7</td><td>19</td><td>Kansas</td><td>18.3</td></tr>
<tr><td>41</td><td>Maryland</td><td>12.1</td><td>20</td><td>Alaska</td><td>18.2</td></tr>
<tr><td>49</td><td>Massachusetts</td><td>8.3</td><td>21</td><td>Nevada</td><td>18.1</td></tr>
<tr><td>36</td><td>Michigan</td><td>12.9</td><td>22</td><td>Idaho</td><td>17.9</td></tr>
<tr><td>38</td><td>Minnesota</td><td>12.8</td><td>23</td><td>Texas</td><td>17.2</td></tr>
<tr><td>1</td><td>Mississippi</td><td>31.5</td><td>24</td><td>Delaware</td><td>17.0</td></tr>
<tr><td>16</td><td>Missouri</td><td>19.3</td><td>24</td><td>Georgia</td><td>17.0</td></tr>
<tr><td>4</td><td>Montana</td><td>26.0</td><td>26</td><td>Indiana</td><td>16.1</td></tr>
<tr><td>26</td><td>Nebraska</td><td>16.1</td><td>26</td><td>Nebraska</td><td>16.1</td></tr>
<tr><td>21</td><td>Nevada</td><td>18.1</td><td>28</td><td>Colorado</td><td>15.2</td></tr>
<tr><td>39</td><td>New Hampshire</td><td>12.7</td><td>29</td><td>Wisconsin</td><td>14.8</td></tr>
<tr><td>48</td><td>New Jersey</td><td>8.9</td><td>30</td><td>Iowa</td><td>14.1</td></tr>
<tr><td>5</td><td>New Mexico</td><td>25.2</td><td>31</td><td>Oregon</td><td>13.9</td></tr>
<tr><td>50</td><td>New York</td><td>8.2</td><td>32</td><td>Maine</td><td>13.7</td></tr>
<tr><td>14</td><td>North Carolina</td><td>19.8</td><td>33</td><td>Virginia</td><td>13.6</td></tr>
<tr><td>18</td><td>North Dakota</td><td>18.4</td><td>34</td><td>Utah</td><td>13.4</td></tr>
<tr><td>41</td><td>Ohio</td><td>12.1</td><td>34</td><td>Vermont</td><td>13.4</td></tr>
<tr><td>13</td><td>Oklahoma</td><td>21.7</td><td>36</td><td>Michigan</td><td>12.9</td></tr>
<tr><td>31</td><td>Oregon</td><td>13.9</td><td>36</td><td>Pennsylvania</td><td>12.9</td></tr>
<tr><td>36</td><td>Pennsylvania</td><td>12.9</td><td>38</td><td>Minnesota</td><td>12.8</td></tr>
<tr><td>47</td><td>Rhode Island</td><td>9.2</td><td>39</td><td>New Hampshire</td><td>12.7</td></tr>
<tr><td>6</td><td>South Carolina</td><td>24.6</td><td>40</td><td>California</td><td>12.3</td></tr>
<tr><td>7</td><td>South Dakota</td><td>24.5</td><td>41</td><td>Maryland</td><td>12.1</td></tr>
<tr><td>10</td><td>Tennessee</td><td>23.5</td><td>41</td><td>Ohio</td><td>12.1</td></tr>
<tr><td>23</td><td>Texas</td><td>17.2</td><td>43</td><td>Illinois</td><td>11.9</td></tr>
<tr><td>34</td><td>Utah</td><td>13.4</td><td>44</td><td>Hawaii</td><td>11.2</td></tr>
<tr><td>34</td><td>Vermont</td><td>13.4</td><td>45</td><td>Washington</td><td>10.8</td></tr>
<tr><td>33</td><td>Virginia</td><td>13.6</td><td>46</td><td>Connecticut</td><td>9.6</td></tr>
<tr><td>45</td><td>Washington</td><td>10.8</td><td>47</td><td>Rhode Island</td><td>9.2</td></tr>
<tr><td>11</td><td>West Virginia</td><td>22.8</td><td>48</td><td>New Jersey</td><td>8.9</td></tr>
<tr><td>29</td><td>Wisconsin</td><td>14.8</td><td>49</td><td>Massachusetts</td><td>8.3</td></tr>
<tr><td>8</td><td>Wyoming</td><td>23.9</td><td>50</td><td>New York</td><td>8.2</td></tr>
<tr><td></td><td></td><td></td><td></td><td>District of Columbia</td><td>8.3</td></tr>
</table>

Source: U.S. Department of Health and Human Services, National Center for Health Statistics
    "National Vital Statistics Reports" (Vol. 55, No. 19, August 21, 2007, http://www.cdc.gov/nchs/deaths.htm)
*Final data by state of residence. These numbers are compiled from death certificates by the Centers for Disease Control and Prevention. They may differ from motor vehicle deaths collected by the U.S. Department of Transportation from other sources. Not age-adjusted.

Age-Adjusted Death Rate by Motor Vehicle Accidents in 2004

National Rate = 15.2 Deaths per 100,000 Population*

ALPHA ORDER

RANK	STATE	RATE
3	Alabama	27.6
17	Alaska	18.9
15	Arizona	19.6
2	Arkansas	28.2
39	California	12.4
28	Colorado	15.3
46	Connecticut	9.6
25	Delaware	16.8
18	Florida	18.7
23	Georgia	17.4
44	Hawaii	11.2
21	Idaho	17.9
42	Illinois	11.9
26	Indiana	16.0
34	Iowa	13.5
20	Kansas	18.0
8	Kentucky	23.7
10	Louisiana	22.5
32	Maine	13.6
41	Maryland	12.1
49	Massachusetts	8.1
36	Michigan	12.8
37	Minnesota	12.6
1	Mississippi	31.3
16	Missouri	19.0
4	Montana	25.3
27	Nebraska	15.6
19	Nevada	18.3
37	New Hampshire	12.6
47	New Jersey	8.9
5	New Mexico	25.1
49	New York	8.1
14	North Carolina	19.8
22	North Dakota	17.8
42	Ohio	11.9
13	Oklahoma	21.3
31	Oregon	13.7
39	Pennsylvania	12.4
48	Rhode Island	8.8
6	South Carolina	24.4
7	South Dakota	24.2
9	Tennessee	23.2
23	Texas	17.4
30	Utah	14.1
35	Vermont	12.9
32	Virginia	13.6
45	Washington	10.6
11	West Virginia	22.4
29	Wisconsin	14.5
11	Wyoming	22.4

RANK ORDER

RANK	STATE	RATE
1	Mississippi	31.3
2	Arkansas	28.2
3	Alabama	27.6
4	Montana	25.3
5	New Mexico	25.1
6	South Carolina	24.4
7	South Dakota	24.2
8	Kentucky	23.7
9	Tennessee	23.2
10	Louisiana	22.5
11	West Virginia	22.4
11	Wyoming	22.4
13	Oklahoma	21.3
14	North Carolina	19.8
15	Arizona	19.6
16	Missouri	19.0
17	Alaska	18.9
18	Florida	18.7
19	Nevada	18.3
20	Kansas	18.0
21	Idaho	17.9
22	North Dakota	17.8
23	Georgia	17.4
23	Texas	17.4
25	Delaware	16.8
26	Indiana	16.0
27	Nebraska	15.6
28	Colorado	15.3
29	Wisconsin	14.5
30	Utah	14.1
31	Oregon	13.7
32	Maine	13.6
32	Virginia	13.6
34	Iowa	13.5
35	Vermont	12.9
36	Michigan	12.8
37	Minnesota	12.6
37	New Hampshire	12.6
39	California	12.4
39	Pennsylvania	12.4
41	Maryland	12.1
42	Illinois	11.9
42	Ohio	11.9
44	Hawaii	11.2
45	Washington	10.6
46	Connecticut	9.6
47	New Jersey	8.9
48	Rhode Island	8.8
49	Massachusetts	8.1
49	New York	8.1
	District of Columbia	8.2

Source: U.S. Department of Health and Human Services, National Center for Health Statistics
    "National Vital Statistics Reports" (Vol. 55, No. 19, August 21, 2007, http://www.cdc.gov/nchs/deaths.htm)
*Final data by state of residence. These numbers are compiled from death certificates by the Centers for Disease Control and Prevention. They may differ from motor vehicle deaths collected by the U.S. Department of Transportation from other sources. Age-adjusted rates based on the year 2000 standard population.

Deaths by Firearm Injury in 2004

National Total = 29,569 Deaths*

ALPHA ORDER

RANK	STATE	DEATHS	% of USA
15	Alabama	679	2.3%
41	Alaska	117	0.4%
12	Arizona	897	3.0%
27	Arkansas	406	1.4%
1	California	3,316	11.2%
21	Colorado	553	1.9%
38	Connecticut	173	0.6%
44	Delaware	75	0.3%
3	Florida	1,890	6.4%
5	Georgia	1,062	3.6%
49	Hawaii	41	0.1%
37	Idaho	177	0.6%
9	Illinois	994	3.4%
18	Indiana	639	2.2%
36	Iowa	195	0.7%
31	Kansas	294	1.0%
22	Kentucky	551	1.9%
11	Louisiana	902	3.1%
42	Maine	108	0.4%
17	Maryland	656	2.2%
35	Massachusetts	206	0.7%
7	Michigan	1,048	3.5%
30	Minnesota	363	1.2%
23	Mississippi	471	1.6%
16	Missouri	664	2.2%
39	Montana	125	0.4%
40	Nebraska	119	0.4%
28	Nevada	392	1.3%
45	New Hampshire	69	0.2%
25	New Jersey	454	1.5%
32	New Mexico	289	1.0%
10	New York	951	3.2%
6	North Carolina	1,055	3.6%
48	North Dakota	50	0.2%
8	Ohio	1,036	3.5%
24	Oklahoma	457	1.5%
29	Oregon	385	1.3%
4	Pennsylvania	1,270	4.3%
49	Rhode Island	41	0.1%
19	South Carolina	574	1.9%
43	South Dakota	77	0.3%
13	Tennessee	869	2.9%
2	Texas	2,342	7.9%
34	Utah	225	0.8%
46	Vermont	61	0.2%
14	Virginia	817	2.8%
20	Washington	569	1.9%
33	West Virginia	253	0.9%
26	Wisconsin	413	1.4%
47	Wyoming	56	0.2%

RANK ORDER

RANK	STATE	DEATHS	% of USA
1	California	3,316	11.2%
2	Texas	2,342	7.9%
3	Florida	1,890	6.4%
4	Pennsylvania	1,270	4.3%
5	Georgia	1,062	3.6%
6	North Carolina	1,055	3.6%
7	Michigan	1,048	3.5%
8	Ohio	1,036	3.5%
9	Illinois	994	3.4%
10	New York	951	3.2%
11	Louisiana	902	3.1%
12	Arizona	897	3.0%
13	Tennessee	869	2.9%
14	Virginia	817	2.8%
15	Alabama	679	2.3%
16	Missouri	664	2.2%
17	Maryland	656	2.2%
18	Indiana	639	2.2%
19	South Carolina	574	1.9%
20	Washington	569	1.9%
21	Colorado	553	1.9%
22	Kentucky	551	1.9%
23	Mississippi	471	1.6%
24	Oklahoma	457	1.5%
25	New Jersey	454	1.5%
26	Wisconsin	413	1.4%
27	Arkansas	406	1.4%
28	Nevada	392	1.3%
29	Oregon	385	1.3%
30	Minnesota	363	1.2%
31	Kansas	294	1.0%
32	New Mexico	289	1.0%
33	West Virginia	253	0.9%
34	Utah	225	0.8%
35	Massachusetts	206	0.7%
36	Iowa	195	0.7%
37	Idaho	177	0.6%
38	Connecticut	173	0.6%
39	Montana	125	0.4%
40	Nebraska	119	0.4%
41	Alaska	117	0.4%
42	Maine	108	0.4%
43	South Dakota	77	0.3%
44	Delaware	75	0.3%
45	New Hampshire	69	0.2%
46	Vermont	61	0.2%
47	Wyoming	56	0.2%
48	North Dakota	50	0.2%
49	Hawaii	41	0.1%
49	Rhode Island	41	0.1%
	District of Columbia	143	0.5%

Source: U.S. Department of Health and Human Services, National Center for Health Statistics
   "National Vital Statistics Reports" (Vol. 55, No. 19, August 21, 2007, http://www.cdc.gov/nchs/deaths.htm)
*Final data by state of residence.

Death Rate by Firearm Injury in 2004

National Rate = 10.1 Deaths per 100,000 Population*

ALPHA ORDER

RANK	STATE	RATE
7	Alabama	15.0
2	Alaska	17.9
5	Arizona	15.6
8	Arkansas	14.7
33	California	9.2
17	Colorado	12.0
46	Connecticut	4.9
35	Delaware	9.0
23	Florida	10.9
17	Georgia	12.0
49	Hawaii	3.2
15	Idaho	12.7
39	Illinois	7.8
28	Indiana	10.2
43	Iowa	6.6
24	Kansas	10.7
13	Kentucky	13.3
1	Louisiana	20.0
37	Maine	8.2
19	Maryland	11.8
49	Massachusetts	3.2
26	Michigan	10.4
41	Minnesota	7.1
4	Mississippi	16.2
20	Missouri	11.5
12	Montana	13.5
42	Nebraska	6.8
3	Nevada	16.8
44	New Hampshire	5.3
45	New Jersey	5.2
6	New Mexico	15.2
46	New York	4.9
16	North Carolina	12.4
38	North Dakota	7.9
35	Ohio	9.0
14	Oklahoma	13.0
24	Oregon	10.7
28	Pennsylvania	10.2
48	Rhode Island	3.8
11	South Carolina	13.7
30	South Dakota	10.0
8	Tennessee	14.7
26	Texas	10.4
32	Utah	9.4
31	Vermont	9.8
22	Virginia	11.0
33	Washington	9.2
10	West Virginia	13.9
40	Wisconsin	7.5
21	Wyoming	11.1

RANK ORDER

RANK	STATE	RATE
1	Louisiana	20.0
2	Alaska	17.9
3	Nevada	16.8
4	Mississippi	16.2
5	Arizona	15.6
6	New Mexico	15.2
7	Alabama	15.0
8	Arkansas	14.7
8	Tennessee	14.7
10	West Virginia	13.9
11	South Carolina	13.7
12	Montana	13.5
13	Kentucky	13.3
14	Oklahoma	13.0
15	Idaho	12.7
16	North Carolina	12.4
17	Colorado	12.0
17	Georgia	12.0
19	Maryland	11.8
20	Missouri	11.5
21	Wyoming	11.1
22	Virginia	11.0
23	Florida	10.9
24	Kansas	10.7
24	Oregon	10.7
26	Michigan	10.4
26	Texas	10.4
28	Indiana	10.2
28	Pennsylvania	10.2
30	South Dakota	10.0
31	Vermont	9.8
32	Utah	9.4
33	California	9.2
33	Washington	9.2
35	Delaware	9.0
35	Ohio	9.0
37	Maine	8.2
38	North Dakota	7.9
39	Illinois	7.8
40	Wisconsin	7.5
41	Minnesota	7.1
42	Nebraska	6.8
43	Iowa	6.6
44	New Hampshire	5.3
45	New Jersey	5.2
46	Connecticut	4.9
46	New York	4.9
48	Rhode Island	3.8
49	Hawaii	3.2
49	Massachusetts	3.2
	District of Columbia	25.8

Source: U.S. Department of Health and Human Services, National Center for Health Statistics
   "National Vital Statistics Reports" (Vol. 55, No. 19, August 21, 2007, http://www.cdc.gov/nchs/deaths.htm)
*Final data by state of residence. Not age-adjusted.

Age-Adjusted Death Rate by Firearm Injury in 2004

National Rate = 10.0 Deaths per 100,000 Population*

ALPHA ORDER			RANK ORDER		
RANK	STATE	RATE	RANK	STATE	RATE
7	Alabama	14.8	1	Louisiana	19.7
2	Alaska	17.7	2	Alaska	17.7
5	Arizona	15.8	3	Nevada	17.0
8	Arkansas	14.6	4	Mississippi	16.2
33	California	9.2	5	Arizona	15.8
17	Colorado	12.1	6	New Mexico	15.1
45	Connecticut	4.9	7	Alabama	14.8
36	Delaware	8.8	8	Arkansas	14.6
25	Florida	10.6	9	Tennessee	14.5
17	Georgia	12.1	10	South Carolina	13.6
49	Hawaii	3.2	11	West Virginia	13.5
14	Idaho	12.9	12	Kentucky	13.0
37	Illinois	7.7	12	Montana	13.0
28	Indiana	10.2	14	Idaho	12.9
43	Iowa	6.4	14	Oklahoma	12.9
23	Kansas	10.7	16	North Carolina	12.3
12	Kentucky	13.0	17	Colorado	12.1
1	Louisiana	19.7	17	Georgia	12.1
37	Maine	7.7	19	Maryland	11.9
19	Maryland	11.9	20	Missouri	11.4
49	Massachusetts	3.2	21	Wyoming	11.0
26	Michigan	10.4	22	Virginia	10.9
41	Minnesota	7.0	23	Kansas	10.7
4	Mississippi	16.2	23	Texas	10.7
20	Missouri	11.4	25	Florida	10.6
12	Montana	13.0	26	Michigan	10.4
42	Nebraska	6.7	26	Oregon	10.4
3	Nevada	17.0	28	Indiana	10.2
45	New Hampshire	4.9	28	Pennsylvania	10.2
44	New Jersey	5.3	28	Utah	10.2
6	New Mexico	15.1	31	South Dakota	9.9
45	New York	4.9	32	Vermont	9.3
16	North Carolina	12.3	33	California	9.2
37	North Dakota	7.7	34	Washington	9.1
35	Ohio	8.9	35	Ohio	8.9
14	Oklahoma	12.9	36	Delaware	8.8
26	Oregon	10.4	37	Illinois	7.7
28	Pennsylvania	10.2	37	Maine	7.7
48	Rhode Island	3.6	37	North Dakota	7.7
10	South Carolina	13.6	40	Wisconsin	7.3
31	South Dakota	9.9	41	Minnesota	7.0
9	Tennessee	14.5	42	Nebraska	6.7
23	Texas	10.7	43	Iowa	6.4
28	Utah	10.2	44	New Jersey	5.3
32	Vermont	9.3	45	Connecticut	4.9
22	Virginia	10.9	45	New Hampshire	4.9
34	Washington	9.1	45	New York	4.9
11	West Virginia	13.5	48	Rhode Island	3.6
40	Wisconsin	7.3	49	Hawaii	3.2
21	Wyoming	11.0	49	Massachusetts	3.2
				District of Columbia	24.7

Source: U.S. Department of Health and Human Services, National Center for Health Statistics
    "National Vital Statistics Reports" (Vol. 55, No. 19, August 21, 2007, http://www.cdc.gov/nchs/deaths.htm)
*Final data by state of residence. Age-adjusted rates based on the year 2000 standard population.

Deaths by Homicide in 2004

National Total = 17,357 Homicides*

ALPHA ORDER					RANK ORDER			
RANK	STATE		HOMICIDES	% of USA	RANK	STATE	HOMICIDES	% of USA
17	Alabama		369	2.1%	1	California	2,490	14.3%
38	Alaska		41	0.2%	2	Texas	1,416	8.2%
13	Arizona		509	2.9%	3	Florida	1,032	5.9%
26	Arkansas		211	1.2%	4	Illinois	871	5.0%
1	California		2,490	14.3%	5	New York	860	5.0%
24	Colorado		219	1.3%	6	Pennsylvania	683	3.9%
34	Connecticut		110	0.6%	7	Michigan	673	3.9%
40	Delaware		35	0.2%	8	Georgia	659	3.8%
3	Florida		1,032	5.9%	9	North Carolina	613	3.5%
8	Georgia		659	3.8%	10	Louisiana	602	3.5%
41	Hawaii		31	0.2%	11	Ohio	563	3.2%
41	Idaho		31	0.2%	12	Maryland	533	3.1%
4	Illinois		871	5.0%	13	Arizona	509	2.9%
19	Indiana		332	1.9%	14	Tennessee	417	2.4%
36	Iowa		57	0.3%	15	Virginia	407	2.3%
32	Kansas		117	0.7%	16	New Jersey	405	2.3%
22	Kentucky		228	1.3%	17	Alabama	369	2.1%
10	Louisiana		602	3.5%	17	Missouri	369	2.1%
47	Maine		21	0.1%	19	Indiana	332	1.9%
12	Maryland		533	3.1%	20	South Carolina	323	1.9%
28	Massachusetts		175	1.0%	21	Mississippi	283	1.6%
7	Michigan		673	3.9%	22	Kentucky	228	1.3%
31	Minnesota		134	0.8%	23	Oklahoma	221	1.3%
21	Mississippi		283	1.6%	24	Colorado	219	1.3%
17	Missouri		369	2.1%	25	Washington	217	1.3%
44	Montana		25	0.1%	26	Arkansas	211	1.2%
39	Nebraska		39	0.2%	27	Nevada	186	1.1%
27	Nevada		186	1.1%	28	Massachusetts	175	1.0%
46	New Hampshire		23	0.1%	29	New Mexico	173	1.0%
16	New Jersey		405	2.3%	30	Wisconsin	151	0.9%
29	New Mexico		173	1.0%	31	Minnesota	134	0.8%
5	New York		860	5.0%	32	Kansas	117	0.7%
9	North Carolina		613	3.5%	33	Oregon	112	0.6%
49	North Dakota		11	0.1%	34	Connecticut	110	0.6%
11	Ohio		563	3.2%	35	West Virginia	79	0.5%
23	Oklahoma		221	1.3%	36	Iowa	57	0.3%
33	Oregon		112	0.6%	37	Utah	45	0.3%
6	Pennsylvania		683	3.9%	38	Alaska	41	0.2%
43	Rhode Island		29	0.2%	39	Nebraska	39	0.2%
20	South Carolina		323	1.9%	40	Delaware	35	0.2%
45	South Dakota		24	0.1%	41	Hawaii	31	0.2%
14	Tennessee		417	2.4%	41	Idaho	31	0.2%
2	Texas		1,416	8.2%	43	Rhode Island	29	0.2%
37	Utah		45	0.3%	44	Montana	25	0.1%
50	Vermont		10	0.1%	45	South Dakota	24	0.1%
15	Virginia		407	2.3%	46	New Hampshire	23	0.1%
25	Washington		217	1.3%	47	Maine	21	0.1%
35	West Virginia		79	0.5%	48	Wyoming	19	0.1%
30	Wisconsin		151	0.9%	49	North Dakota	11	0.1%
48	Wyoming		19	0.1%	50	Vermont	10	0.1%
						District of Columbia	174	1.0%

Source: U.S. Department of Health and Human Services, National Center for Health Statistics
"National Vital Statistics Reports" (Vol. 55, No. 19, August 21, 2007, http://www.cdc.gov/nchs/deaths.htm)
*By state of residence. Includes legal intervention. Homicide data shown here are collected by the Centers for Disease Control and Prevention based on death certificates and differ from murder data collected by the F.B.I. from other sources.

Death Rate by Homicide in 2004

National Rate = 5.9 Deaths per 100,000 Population*

ALPHA ORDER

RANK	STATE	RATE
6	Alabama	8.1
17	Alaska	6.3
5	Arizona	8.9
8	Arkansas	7.7
13	California	6.9
26	Colorado	4.8
33	Connecticut	3.1
31	Delaware	4.2
20	Florida	5.9
10	Georgia	7.5
41	Hawaii	2.5
42	Idaho	2.2
13	Illinois	6.9
24	Indiana	5.3
44	Iowa	1.9
30	Kansas	4.3
21	Kentucky	5.5
1	Louisiana	13.3
47	Maine	1.6
3	Maryland	9.6
36	Massachusetts	2.7
15	Michigan	6.7
40	Minnesota	2.6
2	Mississippi	9.7
16	Missouri	6.4
36	Montana	2.7
42	Nebraska	2.2
7	Nevada	8.0
46	New Hampshire	1.8
27	New Jersey	4.7
4	New Mexico	9.1
28	New York	4.5
11	North Carolina	7.2
NA	North Dakota**	NA
25	Ohio	4.9
17	Oklahoma	6.3
33	Oregon	3.1
21	Pennsylvania	5.5
36	Rhode Island	2.7
8	South Carolina	7.7
33	South Dakota	3.1
12	Tennessee	7.1
17	Texas	6.3
44	Utah	1.9
NA	Vermont**	NA
21	Virginia	5.5
32	Washington	3.5
29	West Virginia	4.4
36	Wisconsin	2.7
NA	Wyoming**	NA

RANK ORDER

RANK	STATE	RATE
1	Louisiana	13.3
2	Mississippi	9.7
3	Maryland	9.6
4	New Mexico	9.1
5	Arizona	8.9
6	Alabama	8.1
7	Nevada	8.0
8	Arkansas	7.7
8	South Carolina	7.7
10	Georgia	7.5
11	North Carolina	7.2
12	Tennessee	7.1
13	California	6.9
13	Illinois	6.9
15	Michigan	6.7
16	Missouri	6.4
17	Alaska	6.3
17	Oklahoma	6.3
17	Texas	6.3
20	Florida	5.9
21	Kentucky	5.5
21	Pennsylvania	5.5
21	Virginia	5.5
24	Indiana	5.3
25	Ohio	4.9
26	Colorado	4.8
27	New Jersey	4.7
28	New York	4.5
29	West Virginia	4.4
30	Kansas	4.3
31	Delaware	4.2
32	Washington	3.5
33	Connecticut	3.1
33	Oregon	3.1
33	South Dakota	3.1
36	Massachusetts	2.7
36	Montana	2.7
36	Rhode Island	2.7
36	Wisconsin	2.7
40	Minnesota	2.6
41	Hawaii	2.5
42	Idaho	2.2
42	Nebraska	2.2
44	Iowa	1.9
44	Utah	1.9
46	New Hampshire	1.8
47	Maine	1.6
NA	North Dakota**	NA
NA	Vermont**	NA
NA	Wyoming**	NA

District of Columbia 31.4

Source: U.S. Department of Health and Human Services, National Center for Health Statistics
"National Vital Statistics Reports" (Vol. 55, No. 19, August 21, 2007, http://www.cdc.gov/nchs/deaths.htm)
*By state of residence. Includes legal intervention. Homicide data shown here are collected by the Centers for Disease Control and Prevention based on death certificates and differ from murder data collected by the F.B.I. from other sources. Not age-adjusted.
**Insufficient data to determine a reliable rate.

Age-Adjusted Death Rate by Homicide in 2004

National Rate = 5.9 Deaths per 100,000 Population*

ALPHA ORDER

RANK	STATE	RATE
6	Alabama	8.2
19	Alaska	6.1
5	Arizona	8.8
7	Arkansas	7.8
13	California	6.8
27	Colorado	4.7
33	Connecticut	3.3
31	Delaware	4.2
19	Florida	6.1
10	Georgia	7.3
41	Hawaii	2.4
42	Idaho	2.2
13	Illinois	6.8
24	Indiana	5.3
44	Iowa	1.9
30	Kansas	4.3
22	Kentucky	5.5
1	Louisiana	13.0
47	Maine	1.6
3	Maryland	9.7
36	Massachusetts	2.8
15	Michigan	6.7
40	Minnesota	2.6
2	Mississippi	9.8
16	Missouri	6.4
37	Montana	2.7
42	Nebraska	2.2
7	Nevada	7.8
46	New Hampshire	1.7
26	New Jersey	4.8
4	New Mexico	9.2
28	New York	4.5
11	North Carolina	7.1
NA	North Dakota**	NA
25	Ohio	5.0
17	Oklahoma	6.3
34	Oregon	3.1
21	Pennsylvania	5.7
37	Rhode Island	2.7
9	South Carolina	7.7
34	South Dakota	3.1
12	Tennessee	7.0
18	Texas	6.2
44	Utah	1.9
NA	Vermont**	NA
23	Virginia	5.4
32	Washington	3.5
29	West Virginia	4.4
37	Wisconsin	2.7
NA	Wyoming**	NA

RANK ORDER

RANK	STATE	RATE
1	Louisiana	13.0
2	Mississippi	9.8
3	Maryland	9.7
4	New Mexico	9.2
5	Arizona	8.8
6	Alabama	8.2
7	Arkansas	7.8
7	Nevada	7.8
9	South Carolina	7.7
10	Georgia	7.3
11	North Carolina	7.1
12	Tennessee	7.0
13	California	6.8
13	Illinois	6.8
15	Michigan	6.7
16	Missouri	6.4
17	Oklahoma	6.3
18	Texas	6.2
19	Alaska	6.1
19	Florida	6.1
21	Pennsylvania	5.7
22	Kentucky	5.5
23	Virginia	5.4
24	Indiana	5.3
25	Ohio	5.0
26	New Jersey	4.8
27	Colorado	4.7
28	New York	4.5
29	West Virginia	4.4
30	Kansas	4.3
31	Delaware	4.2
32	Washington	3.5
33	Connecticut	3.3
34	Oregon	3.1
34	South Dakota	3.1
36	Massachusetts	2.8
37	Montana	2.7
37	Rhode Island	2.7
37	Wisconsin	2.7
40	Minnesota	2.6
41	Hawaii	2.4
42	Idaho	2.2
42	Nebraska	2.2
44	Iowa	1.9
44	Utah	1.9
46	New Hampshire	1.7
47	Maine	1.6
NA	North Dakota**	NA
NA	Vermont**	NA
NA	Wyoming**	NA

District of Columbia   30.2

Source: U.S. Department of Health and Human Services, National Center for Health Statistics
 "National Vital Statistics Reports" (Vol. 55, No. 19, August 21, 2007, http://www.cdc.gov/nchs/deaths.htm)
*By state of residence. Includes legal intervention. Homicide data shown here are collected by the Centers for Disease Control and Prevention based on death certificates and differ from murder data collected by the F.B.I. from other sources. Age-adjusted rates based on the year 2000 standard population.
**Insufficient data to determine a reliable rate.

Deaths by Suicide in 2004

National Total = 32,439 Suicides*

ALPHA ORDER

RANK	STATE	SUICIDES	% of USA
22	Alabama	541	1.7%
42	Alaska	155	0.5%
11	Arizona	880	2.7%
32	Arkansas	361	1.1%
1	California	3,368	10.4%
14	Colorado	797	2.5%
36	Connecticut	294	0.9%
46	Delaware	93	0.3%
2	Florida	2,389	7.4%
10	Georgia	973	3.0%
44	Hawaii	116	0.4%
38	Idaho	236	0.7%
8	Illinois	1,028	3.2%
17	Indiana	704	2.2%
35	Iowa	343	1.1%
31	Kansas	370	1.1%
20	Kentucky	560	1.7%
23	Louisiana	537	1.7%
40	Maine	171	0.5%
26	Maryland	500	1.5%
29	Massachusetts	425	1.3%
7	Michigan	1,098	3.4%
24	Minnesota	524	1.6%
34	Mississippi	350	1.1%
16	Missouri	715	2.2%
39	Montana	175	0.5%
41	Nebraska	166	0.5%
28	Nevada	440	1.4%
43	New Hampshire	133	0.4%
19	New Jersey	597	1.8%
33	New Mexico	356	1.1%
6	New York	1,187	3.7%
9	North Carolina	1,027	3.2%
50	North Dakota	73	0.2%
5	Ohio	1,319	4.1%
25	Oklahoma	506	1.6%
21	Oregon	555	1.7%
4	Pennsylvania	1,410	4.3%
49	Rhode Island	85	0.3%
27	South Carolina	482	1.5%
45	South Dakota	112	0.3%
15	Tennessee	792	2.4%
3	Texas	2,300	7.1%
30	Utah	377	1.2%
46	Vermont	93	0.3%
13	Virginia	828	2.6%
12	Washington	830	2.6%
37	West Virginia	285	0.9%
18	Wisconsin	662	2.0%
48	Wyoming	88	0.3%

RANK ORDER

RANK	STATE	SUICIDES	% of USA
1	California	3,368	10.4%
2	Florida	2,389	7.4%
3	Texas	2,300	7.1%
4	Pennsylvania	1,410	4.3%
5	Ohio	1,319	4.1%
6	New York	1,187	3.7%
7	Michigan	1,098	3.4%
8	Illinois	1,028	3.2%
9	North Carolina	1,027	3.2%
10	Georgia	973	3.0%
11	Arizona	880	2.7%
12	Washington	830	2.6%
13	Virginia	828	2.6%
14	Colorado	797	2.5%
15	Tennessee	792	2.4%
16	Missouri	715	2.2%
17	Indiana	704	2.2%
18	Wisconsin	662	2.0%
19	New Jersey	597	1.8%
20	Kentucky	560	1.7%
21	Oregon	555	1.7%
22	Alabama	541	1.7%
23	Louisiana	537	1.7%
24	Minnesota	524	1.6%
25	Oklahoma	506	1.6%
26	Maryland	500	1.5%
27	South Carolina	482	1.5%
28	Nevada	440	1.4%
29	Massachusetts	425	1.3%
30	Utah	377	1.2%
31	Kansas	370	1.1%
32	Arkansas	361	1.1%
33	New Mexico	356	1.1%
34	Mississippi	350	1.1%
35	Iowa	343	1.1%
36	Connecticut	294	0.9%
37	West Virginia	285	0.9%
38	Idaho	236	0.7%
39	Montana	175	0.5%
40	Maine	171	0.5%
41	Nebraska	166	0.5%
42	Alaska	155	0.5%
43	New Hampshire	133	0.4%
44	Hawaii	116	0.4%
45	South Dakota	112	0.3%
46	Delaware	93	0.3%
46	Vermont	93	0.3%
48	Wyoming	88	0.3%
49	Rhode Island	85	0.3%
50	North Dakota	73	0.2%
	District of Columbia	33	0.1%

Source: U.S. Department of Health and Human Services, National Center for Health Statistics
    "National Vital Statistics Reports" (Vol. 55, No. 19, August 21, 2007, http://www.cdc.gov/nchs/deaths.htm)
*Final data by state of residence.

Death Rate by Suicide in 2004

National Rate = 11.0 Deaths per 100,000 Population*

ALPHA ORDER

RANK	STATE	RATE
26	Alabama	11.9
1	Alaska	23.6
11	Arizona	15.3
20	Arkansas	13.1
42	California	9.4
6	Colorado	17.3
45	Connecticut	8.4
34	Delaware	11.2
15	Florida	13.7
36	Georgia	11.0
43	Hawaii	9.2
7	Idaho	16.9
46	Illinois	8.1
33	Indiana	11.3
28	Iowa	11.6
16	Kansas	13.5
16	Kentucky	13.5
26	Louisiana	11.9
21	Maine	13.0
44	Maryland	9.0
49	Massachusetts	6.6
37	Michigan	10.9
38	Minnesota	10.3
23	Mississippi	12.1
22	Missouri	12.4
2	Montana	18.9
41	Nebraska	9.5
3	Nevada	18.8
39	New Hampshire	10.2
48	New Jersey	6.9
4	New Mexico	18.7
50	New York	6.2
24	North Carolina	12.0
29	North Dakota	11.5
29	Ohio	11.5
14	Oklahoma	14.4
10	Oregon	15.4
32	Pennsylvania	11.4
47	Rhode Island	7.9
29	South Carolina	11.5
13	South Dakota	14.5
18	Tennessee	13.4
39	Texas	10.2
8	Utah	15.8
12	Vermont	15.0
35	Virginia	11.1
18	Washington	13.4
9	West Virginia	15.7
24	Wisconsin	12.0
5	Wyoming	17.4

RANK ORDER

RANK	STATE	RATE
1	Alaska	23.6
2	Montana	18.9
3	Nevada	18.8
4	New Mexico	18.7
5	Wyoming	17.4
6	Colorado	17.3
7	Idaho	16.9
8	Utah	15.8
9	West Virginia	15.7
10	Oregon	15.4
11	Arizona	15.3
12	Vermont	15.0
13	South Dakota	14.5
14	Oklahoma	14.4
15	Florida	13.7
16	Kansas	13.5
16	Kentucky	13.5
18	Tennessee	13.4
18	Washington	13.4
20	Arkansas	13.1
21	Maine	13.0
22	Missouri	12.4
23	Mississippi	12.1
24	North Carolina	12.0
24	Wisconsin	12.0
26	Alabama	11.9
26	Louisiana	11.9
28	Iowa	11.6
29	North Dakota	11.5
29	Ohio	11.5
29	South Carolina	11.5
32	Pennsylvania	11.4
33	Indiana	11.3
34	Delaware	11.2
35	Virginia	11.1
36	Georgia	11.0
37	Michigan	10.9
38	Minnesota	10.3
39	New Hampshire	10.2
39	Texas	10.2
41	Nebraska	9.5
42	California	9.4
43	Hawaii	9.2
44	Maryland	9.0
45	Connecticut	8.4
46	Illinois	8.1
47	Rhode Island	7.9
48	New Jersey	6.9
49	Massachusetts	6.6
50	New York	6.2
	District of Columbia	6.0

Source: U.S. Department of Health and Human Services, National Center for Health Statistics
    "National Vital Statistics Reports" (Vol. 55, No. 19, August 21, 2007, http://www.cdc.gov/nchs/deaths.htm)
*Final data by state of residence. Not age-adjusted.

Age-Adjusted Death Rate by Suicide in 2004

National Rate = 10.9 Deaths per 100,000 Population*

ALPHA ORDER

RANK	STATE	RATE
27	Alabama	11.7
1	Alaska	23.4
9	Arizona	15.7
20	Arkansas	12.9
41	California	9.6
7	Colorado	17.3
45	Connecticut	8.1
36	Delaware	10.9
18	Florida	13.1
28	Georgia	11.3
43	Hawaii	9.0
5	Idaho	17.4
45	Illinois	8.1
28	Indiana	11.3
28	Iowa	11.3
15	Kansas	13.5
16	Kentucky	13.2
24	Louisiana	12.0
22	Maine	12.2
44	Maryland	8.9
49	Massachusetts	6.4
37	Michigan	10.8
39	Minnesota	10.1
23	Mississippi	12.1
21	Missouri	12.3
4	Montana	18.6
42	Nebraska	9.5
2	Nevada	19.2
40	New Hampshire	9.8
48	New Jersey	6.8
3	New Mexico	18.7
50	New York	6.0
24	North Carolina	12.0
33	North Dakota	11.2
28	Ohio	11.3
13	Oklahoma	14.3
11	Oregon	15.0
34	Pennsylvania	11.1
47	Rhode Island	7.5
28	South Carolina	11.3
12	South Dakota	14.7
18	Tennessee	13.1
38	Texas	10.7
7	Utah	17.3
13	Vermont	14.3
35	Virginia	11.0
16	Washington	13.2
10	West Virginia	15.3
26	Wisconsin	11.8
5	Wyoming	17.4

RANK ORDER

RANK	STATE	RATE
1	Alaska	23.4
2	Nevada	19.2
3	New Mexico	18.7
4	Montana	18.6
5	Idaho	17.4
5	Wyoming	17.4
7	Colorado	17.3
7	Utah	17.3
9	Arizona	15.7
10	West Virginia	15.3
11	Oregon	15.0
12	South Dakota	14.7
13	Oklahoma	14.3
13	Vermont	14.3
15	Kansas	13.5
16	Kentucky	13.2
16	Washington	13.2
18	Florida	13.1
18	Tennessee	13.1
20	Arkansas	12.9
21	Missouri	12.3
22	Maine	12.2
23	Mississippi	12.1
24	Louisiana	12.0
24	North Carolina	12.0
26	Wisconsin	11.8
27	Alabama	11.7
28	Georgia	11.3
28	Indiana	11.3
28	Iowa	11.3
28	Ohio	11.3
28	South Carolina	11.3
33	North Dakota	11.2
34	Pennsylvania	11.1
35	Virginia	11.0
36	Delaware	10.9
37	Michigan	10.8
38	Texas	10.7
39	Minnesota	10.1
40	New Hampshire	9.8
41	California	9.6
42	Nebraska	9.5
43	Hawaii	9.0
44	Maryland	8.9
45	Connecticut	8.1
45	Illinois	8.1
47	Rhode Island	7.5
48	New Jersey	6.8
49	Massachusetts	6.4
50	New York	6.0
	District of Columbia	5.7

Source: U.S. Department of Health and Human Services, National Center for Health Statistics
   "National Vital Statistics Reports" (Vol. 55, No. 19, August 21, 2007, http://www.cdc.gov/nchs/deaths.htm)
*Final data by state of residence. Age-adjusted rates based on the year 2000 standard population.

Alcohol-Induced Deaths in 2004

National Total = 21,081 Deaths*

ALPHA ORDER				RANK ORDER			
RANK	STATE	DEATHS	% of USA	RANK	STATE	DEATHS	% of USA
27	Alabama	250	1.2%	1	California	3,702	17.6%
39	Alaska	104	0.5%	2	Florida	1,525	7.2%
10	Arizona	590	2.8%	3	Texas	1,193	5.7%
36	Arkansas	131	0.6%	4	New York	1,065	5.1%
1	California	3,702	17.6%	5	Michigan	701	3.3%
13	Colorado	498	2.4%	6	North Carolina	681	3.2%
32	Connecticut	189	0.9%	7	Ohio	660	3.1%
50	Delaware	54	0.3%	8	Washington	633	3.0%
2	Florida	1,525	7.2%	9	Illinois	592	2.8%
11	Georgia	559	2.7%	10	Arizona	590	2.8%
47	Hawaii	66	0.3%	11	Georgia	559	2.7%
37	Idaho	119	0.6%	12	Oregon	515	2.4%
9	Illinois	592	2.8%	13	Colorado	498	2.4%
23	Indiana	327	1.6%	14	Pennsylvania	488	2.3%
34	Iowa	156	0.7%	15	New Jersey	476	2.3%
33	Kansas	167	0.8%	16	Tennessee	461	2.2%
28	Kentucky	244	1.2%	17	South Carolina	423	2.0%
30	Louisiana	216	1.0%	18	Wisconsin	417	2.0%
38	Maine	106	0.5%	19	Missouri	384	1.8%
26	Maryland	280	1.3%	20	Massachusetts	365	1.7%
20	Massachusetts	365	1.7%	21	Minnesota	358	1.7%
5	Michigan	701	3.3%	22	Virginia	332	1.6%
21	Minnesota	358	1.7%	23	Indiana	327	1.6%
31	Mississippi	192	0.9%	24	New Mexico	325	1.5%
19	Missouri	384	1.8%	25	Oklahoma	286	1.4%
43	Montana	100	0.5%	26	Maryland	280	1.3%
40	Nebraska	103	0.5%	27	Alabama	250	1.2%
29	Nevada	232	1.1%	28	Kentucky	244	1.2%
40	New Hampshire	103	0.5%	29	Nevada	232	1.1%
15	New Jersey	476	2.3%	30	Louisiana	216	1.0%
24	New Mexico	325	1.5%	31	Mississippi	192	0.9%
4	New York	1,065	5.1%	32	Connecticut	189	0.9%
6	North Carolina	681	3.2%	33	Kansas	167	0.8%
48	North Dakota	62	0.3%	34	Iowa	156	0.7%
7	Ohio	660	3.1%	35	West Virginia	134	0.6%
25	Oklahoma	286	1.4%	36	Arkansas	131	0.6%
12	Oregon	515	2.4%	37	Idaho	119	0.6%
14	Pennsylvania	488	2.3%	38	Maine	106	0.5%
45	Rhode Island	83	0.4%	39	Alaska	104	0.5%
17	South Carolina	423	2.0%	40	Nebraska	103	0.5%
42	South Dakota	101	0.5%	40	New Hampshire	103	0.5%
16	Tennessee	461	2.2%	42	South Dakota	101	0.5%
3	Texas	1,193	5.7%	43	Montana	100	0.5%
44	Utah	98	0.5%	44	Utah	98	0.5%
49	Vermont	58	0.3%	45	Rhode Island	83	0.4%
22	Virginia	332	1.6%	46	Wyoming	67	0.3%
8	Washington	633	3.0%	47	Hawaii	66	0.3%
35	West Virginia	134	0.6%	48	North Dakota	62	0.3%
18	Wisconsin	417	2.0%	49	Vermont	58	0.3%
46	Wyoming	67	0.3%	50	Delaware	54	0.3%
					District of Columbia	109	0.5%

Source: U.S. Department of Health and Human Services, National Center for Health Statistics
   (http://wonder.cdc.gov)
*By state of residence. Includes excessive blood level of alcohol, accidental poisoning by alcohol and the following
alcohol-related causes: psychoses, dependence syndrome, polyneuropathy, cardiomyopathy, gastritis, chronic liver disease, and
cirrhosis. Excludes accidents, homicides, and other causes indirectly related to alcohol use.

Death Rate by Alcohol-Induced Deaths in 2004

National Rate = 7.2 Deaths per 100,000 Population*

ALPHA ORDER

RANK	STATE	RATE
36	Alabama	5.5
2	Alaska	15.8
8	Arizona	10.3
45	Arkansas	4.8
8	California	10.3
6	Colorado	10.8
39	Connecticut	5.4
29	Delaware	6.5
15	Florida	8.8
30	Georgia	6.3
43	Hawaii	5.2
16	Idaho	8.5
47	Illinois	4.7
40	Indiana	5.3
40	Iowa	5.3
31	Kansas	6.1
32	Kentucky	5.9
45	Louisiana	4.8
17	Maine	8.1
44	Maryland	5.0
35	Massachusetts	5.7
26	Michigan	6.9
25	Minnesota	7.0
28	Mississippi	6.6
27	Missouri	6.7
6	Montana	10.8
32	Nebraska	5.9
12	Nevada	9.9
20	New Hampshire	7.9
36	New Jersey	5.5
1	New Mexico	17.1
36	New York	5.5
19	North Carolina	8.0
13	North Dakota	9.7
34	Ohio	5.8
17	Oklahoma	8.1
3	Oregon	14.3
50	Pennsylvania	3.9
22	Rhode Island	7.7
11	South Carolina	10.1
5	South Dakota	13.1
21	Tennessee	7.8
40	Texas	5.3
49	Utah	4.0
14	Vermont	9.3
48	Virginia	4.4
10	Washington	10.2
24	West Virginia	7.4
23	Wisconsin	7.6
4	Wyoming	13.2

RANK ORDER

RANK	STATE	RATE
1	New Mexico	17.1
2	Alaska	15.8
3	Oregon	14.3
4	Wyoming	13.2
5	South Dakota	13.1
6	Colorado	10.8
6	Montana	10.8
8	Arizona	10.3
8	California	10.3
10	Washington	10.2
11	South Carolina	10.1
12	Nevada	9.9
13	North Dakota	9.7
14	Vermont	9.3
15	Florida	8.8
16	Idaho	8.5
17	Maine	8.1
17	Oklahoma	8.1
19	North Carolina	8.0
20	New Hampshire	7.9
21	Tennessee	7.8
22	Rhode Island	7.7
23	Wisconsin	7.6
24	West Virginia	7.4
25	Minnesota	7.0
26	Michigan	6.9
27	Missouri	6.7
28	Mississippi	6.6
29	Delaware	6.5
30	Georgia	6.3
31	Kansas	6.1
32	Kentucky	5.9
32	Nebraska	5.9
34	Ohio	5.8
35	Massachusetts	5.7
36	Alabama	5.5
36	New Jersey	5.5
36	New York	5.5
39	Connecticut	5.4
40	Indiana	5.3
40	Iowa	5.3
40	Texas	5.3
43	Hawaii	5.2
44	Maryland	5.0
45	Arkansas	4.8
45	Louisiana	4.8
47	Illinois	4.7
48	Virginia	4.4
49	Utah	4.0
50	Pennsylvania	3.9

District of Columbia		19.7

Source: U.S. Department of Health and Human Services, National Center for Health Statistics
(http://wonder.cdc.gov)

*By state of residence. Includes excessive blood level of alcohol, accidental poisoning by alcohol and the following alcohol-related causes: psychoses, dependence syndrome, polyneuropathy, cardiomyopathy, gastritis, chronic liver disease, and cirrhosis. Excludes accidents, homicides, and other causes indirectly related to alcohol use. Not age-adjusted.

Age-Adjusted Death Rate by Alcohol-Induced Deaths in 2004

National Rate = 7.0 Deaths per 100,000 Population*

ALPHA ORDER

RANK	STATE	RATE
37	Alabama	5.2
2	Alaska	16.2
8	Arizona	10.5
47	Arkansas	4.6
7	California	10.8
6	Colorado	10.9
44	Connecticut	4.9
31	Delaware	5.8
16	Florida	8.0
27	Georgia	6.5
42	Hawaii	5.0
14	Idaho	8.6
47	Illinois	4.6
37	Indiana	5.2
42	Iowa	5.0
30	Kansas	6.1
34	Kentucky	5.6
46	Louisiana	4.7
24	Maine	6.8
45	Maryland	4.8
36	Massachusetts	5.4
25	Michigan	6.6
23	Minnesota	6.9
25	Mississippi	6.6
28	Missouri	6.4
9	Montana	9.9
31	Nebraska	5.8
11	Nevada	9.7
20	New Hampshire	7.2
40	New Jersey	5.1
1	New Mexico	16.8
37	New York	5.2
17	North Carolina	7.8
13	North Dakota	9.1
35	Ohio	5.5
17	Oklahoma	7.8
3	Oregon	13.5
50	Pennsylvania	3.6
20	Rhode Island	7.2
12	South Carolina	9.5
4	South Dakota	12.6
19	Tennessee	7.3
33	Texas	5.7
40	Utah	5.1
15	Vermont	8.4
49	Virginia	4.2
9	Washington	9.9
28	West Virginia	6.4
20	Wisconsin	7.2
5	Wyoming	12.0

RANK ORDER

RANK	STATE	RATE
1	New Mexico	16.8
2	Alaska	16.2
3	Oregon	13.5
4	South Dakota	12.6
5	Wyoming	12.0
6	Colorado	10.9
7	California	10.8
8	Arizona	10.5
9	Montana	9.9
9	Washington	9.9
11	Nevada	9.7
12	South Carolina	9.5
13	North Dakota	9.1
14	Idaho	8.6
15	Vermont	8.4
16	Florida	8.0
17	North Carolina	7.8
17	Oklahoma	7.8
19	Tennessee	7.3
20	New Hampshire	7.2
20	Rhode Island	7.2
20	Wisconsin	7.2
23	Minnesota	6.9
24	Maine	6.8
25	Michigan	6.6
25	Mississippi	6.6
27	Georgia	6.5
28	Missouri	6.4
28	West Virginia	6.4
30	Kansas	6.1
31	Delaware	5.8
31	Nebraska	5.8
33	Texas	5.7
34	Kentucky	5.6
35	Ohio	5.5
36	Massachusetts	5.4
37	Alabama	5.2
37	Indiana	5.2
37	New York	5.2
40	New Jersey	5.1
40	Utah	5.1
42	Hawaii	5.0
42	Iowa	5.0
44	Connecticut	4.9
45	Maryland	4.8
46	Louisiana	4.7
47	Arkansas	4.6
47	Illinois	4.6
49	Virginia	4.2
50	Pennsylvania	3.6
	District of Columbia	19.6

Source: U.S. Department of Health and Human Services, National Center for Health Statistics
(http://wonder.cdc.gov)

*By state of residence. Includes excessive blood level of alcohol, accidental poisoning by alcohol and the following alcohol-related causes: psychoses, dependence syndrome, polyneuropathy, cardiomyopathy, gastritis, chronic liver disease, and cirrhosis. Excludes accidents, homicides, and other causes indirectly related to alcohol use. Age-adjusted rates based on the year 2000 standard population.

Occupational Fatalities in 2006

National Total = 5,703 Deaths*

ALPHA ORDER

RANK	STATE	DEATHS	% of USA
20	Alabama	100	1.8%
39	Alaska	44	0.8%
18	Arizona	108	1.9%
29	Arkansas	78	1.4%
2	California	448	7.9%
16	Colorado	137	2.4%
40	Connecticut	38	0.7%
47	Delaware	14	0.2%
3	Florida	355	6.2%
8	Georgia	192	3.4%
45	Hawaii	30	0.5%
40	Idaho	38	0.7%
6	Illinois	207	3.6%
14	Indiana	148	2.6%
32	Iowa	71	1.2%
27	Kansas	85	1.5%
15	Kentucky	147	2.6%
17	Louisiana	118	2.1%
46	Maine	20	0.4%
19	Maryland	105	1.8%
33	Massachusetts	66	1.2%
12	Michigan	155	2.7%
29	Minnesota	78	1.4%
21	Mississippi	96	1.7%
10	Missouri	166	2.9%
38	Montana	45	0.8%
36	Nebraska	57	1.0%
37	Nevada	49	0.9%
49	New Hampshire	13	0.2%
25	New Jersey	88	1.5%
35	New Mexico	59	1.0%
5	New York	233	4.1%
9	North Carolina	167	2.9%
44	North Dakota	31	0.5%
7	Ohio	193	3.4%
23	Oklahoma	91	1.6%
31	Oregon	72	1.3%
4	Pennsylvania	240	4.2%
50	Rhode Island	10	0.2%
22	South Carolina	93	1.6%
42	South Dakota	37	0.6%
13	Tennessee	153	2.7%
1	Texas	486	8.5%
34	Utah	60	1.1%
47	Vermont	14	0.2%
11	Virginia	164	2.9%
26	Washington	87	1.5%
28	West Virginia	79	1.4%
23	Wisconsin	91	1.6%
43	Wyoming	36	0.6%

RANK ORDER

RANK	STATE	DEATHS	% of USA
1	Texas	486	8.5%
2	California	448	7.9%
3	Florida	355	6.2%
4	Pennsylvania	240	4.2%
5	New York	233	4.1%
6	Illinois	207	3.6%
7	Ohio	193	3.4%
8	Georgia	192	3.4%
9	North Carolina	167	2.9%
10	Missouri	166	2.9%
11	Virginia	164	2.9%
12	Michigan	155	2.7%
13	Tennessee	153	2.7%
14	Indiana	148	2.6%
15	Kentucky	147	2.6%
16	Colorado	137	2.4%
17	Louisiana	118	2.1%
18	Arizona	108	1.9%
19	Maryland	105	1.8%
20	Alabama	100	1.8%
21	Mississippi	96	1.7%
22	South Carolina	93	1.6%
23	Oklahoma	91	1.6%
23	Wisconsin	91	1.6%
25	New Jersey	88	1.5%
26	Washington	87	1.5%
27	Kansas	85	1.5%
28	West Virginia	79	1.4%
29	Arkansas	78	1.4%
29	Minnesota	78	1.4%
31	Oregon	72	1.3%
32	Iowa	71	1.2%
33	Massachusetts	66	1.2%
34	Utah	60	1.1%
35	New Mexico	59	1.0%
36	Nebraska	57	1.0%
37	Nevada	49	0.9%
38	Montana	45	0.8%
39	Alaska	44	0.8%
40	Connecticut	38	0.7%
40	Idaho	38	0.7%
42	South Dakota	37	0.6%
43	Wyoming	36	0.6%
44	North Dakota	31	0.5%
45	Hawaii	30	0.5%
46	Maine	20	0.4%
47	Delaware	14	0.2%
47	Vermont	14	0.2%
49	New Hampshire	13	0.2%
50	Rhode Island	10	0.2%
	District of Columbia	7	0.1%

Source: U.S. Department of Labor, Bureau of Labor Statistics
   "National Census of Fatal Occupational Injuries in 2006" (press release, August 9, 2007, http://www.bls.gov/iif/home.htm)
*Includes four fatalities that occurred within the territorial boundaries of the United States but for which a state of incident could not be determined.

Occupational Fatality Rate in 2006

National Rate = 3.9 Deaths per 100,000 Workers*

ALPHA ORDER

RANK	STATE	RATE
20	Alabama	4.6
1	Alaska	13.5
34	Arizona	3.7
12	Arkansas	5.9
44	California	2.6
15	Colorado	5.4
46	Connecticut	2.1
38	Delaware	3.2
28	Florida	4.0
26	Georgia	4.2
20	Hawaii	4.6
18	Idaho	5.2
38	Illinois	3.2
19	Indiana	4.7
25	Iowa	4.3
11	Kansas	6.0
8	Kentucky	7.5
9	Louisiana	6.6
41	Maine	2.9
35	Maryland	3.6
46	Massachusetts	2.1
37	Michigan	3.3
42	Minnesota	2.7
7	Mississippi	7.8
14	Missouri	5.7
4	Montana	9.2
12	Nebraska	5.9
32	Nevada	3.9
49	New Hampshire	1.8
48	New Jersey	2.0
10	New Mexico	6.5
44	New York	2.6
32	North Carolina	3.9
5	North Dakota	8.7
36	Ohio	3.4
15	Oklahoma	5.4
28	Oregon	4.0
28	Pennsylvania	4.0
49	Rhode Island	1.8
20	South Carolina	4.6
5	South Dakota	8.7
17	Tennessee	5.3
24	Texas	4.4
20	Utah	4.6
28	Vermont	4.0
26	Virginia	4.2
42	Washington	2.7
3	West Virginia	10.2
40	Wisconsin	3.1
2	Wyoming	12.7

RANK ORDER

RANK	STATE	RATE
1	Alaska	13.5
2	Wyoming	12.7
3	West Virginia	10.2
4	Montana	9.2
5	North Dakota	8.7
5	South Dakota	8.7
7	Mississippi	7.8
8	Kentucky	7.5
9	Louisiana	6.6
10	New Mexico	6.5
11	Kansas	6.0
12	Arkansas	5.9
12	Nebraska	5.9
14	Missouri	5.7
15	Colorado	5.4
15	Oklahoma	5.4
17	Tennessee	5.3
18	Idaho	5.2
19	Indiana	4.7
20	Alabama	4.6
20	Hawaii	4.6
20	South Carolina	4.6
20	Utah	4.6
24	Texas	4.4
25	Iowa	4.3
26	Georgia	4.2
26	Virginia	4.2
28	Florida	4.0
28	Oregon	4.0
28	Pennsylvania	4.0
28	Vermont	4.0
32	Nevada	3.9
32	North Carolina	3.9
34	Arizona	3.7
35	Maryland	3.6
36	Ohio	3.4
37	Michigan	3.3
38	Delaware	3.2
38	Illinois	3.2
40	Wisconsin	3.1
41	Maine	2.9
42	Minnesota	2.7
42	Washington	2.7
44	California	2.6
44	New York	2.6
46	Connecticut	2.1
46	Massachusetts	2.1
48	New Jersey	2.0
49	New Hampshire	1.8
49	Rhode Island	1.8

| | District of Columbia | 2.5 |

Source: CQ Press using data from U.S. Department of Labor, Bureau of Labor Statistics

"National Census of Fatal Occupational Injuries in 2006" (press release, August 9, 2007, http://www.bls.gov/iif/home.htm)

*Based on employed civilian labor force.

III. Facilities

Community Hospitals in 2006 192
Rate of Community Hospitals in 2005 193
Community Hospitals per 1,000 Square Miles in 2006 . . . 194
Community Hospitals in Urban Areas in 2006 195
Percent of Community Hospitals in Urban Areas
    in 2006 196
Community Hospitals in Rural Areas in 2006 197
Percent of Community Hospitals in Rural Areas in
    2006 198
Nongovernment Not-For-Profit Hospitals in 2006 199
Investor-Owned (For-Profit) Hospitals in 2006 200
State and Local Government-Owned Hospitals in 2006 . . 201
Beds in Community Hospitals in 2006 202
Rate of Beds in Community Hospitals in 2006 203
Average Number of Beds per Community Hospital
    in 2006 204
Admissions to Community Hospitals in 2006 205
Inpatient Days in Community Hospitals in 2006 206
Average Daily Census in Community Hospitals
    in 2006 207
Average Stay in Community Hospitals in 2006 208
Occupancy Rate in Community Hospitals in 2006 209
Outpatient Visits to Community Hospitals in 2006 210
Emergency Outpatient Visits to Community Hospitals
    in 2006 211
Medicare and Medicaid Certified Facilities in 2008 212
Medicare and Medicaid Certified Hospitals in 2008 213
Beds in Medicare and Medicaid Certified Hospitals
    in 2008 214
Medicare and Medicaid Certified Children's Hospitals
    in 2008 215
Beds in Medicare and Medicaid Certified Children's
    Hospitals in 2008 216

Medicare and Medicaid Certified Rehabilitation Hospitals
    in 2008 217
Beds in Medicare and Medicaid Certified Rehabilitation
    Hospitals in 2008 218
Medicare and Medicaid Certified Psychiatric Hospitals
    in 2008 219
Beds in Medicare and Medicaid Certified Psychiatric
    Hospitals in 2008 220
Medicare and Medicaid Certified Outpatient Surgery
    Centers in 2008 221
Medicare and Medicaid Certified Community Mental
    Health Centers in 2008 222
Medicare and Medicaid Certified Outpatient Physical
    Therapy Facilities in 2008 223
Medicare and Medicaid Certified Rural Health Clinics
    in 2008 224
Medicare and Medicaid Certified Home Health Agencies
    in 2008 225
Medicare and Medicaid Certified Hospices in 2008 226
Hospice Patients in Residential Facilities in 2008 227
Medicare and Medicaid Certified Nursing Care Facilities
    in 2008 228
Beds in Medicare and Medicaid Certified Nursing Care
    Facilities in 2008 229
Rate of Beds in Medicare and Medicaid Certified
    Nursing Care Facilities in 2008 230
Nursing Home Occupancy Rate in 2006 231
Nursing Home Resident Rate in 2006 232
Nursing Home Population in 2006 233
Health Care Establishments in 2005 234

Community Hospitals in 2006

National Total = 4,927 Hospitals*

ALPHA ORDER

RANK	STATE	HOSPITALS	% of USA	RANK	STATE	HOSPITALS	% of USA
20	Alabama	109	2.2%	1	Texas	417	8.5%
47	Alaska	22	0.4%	2	California	357	7.2%
30	Arizona	66	1.3%	3	Florida	203	4.1%
26	Arkansas	84	1.7%	3	New York	203	4.1%
2	California	357	7.2%	5	Illinois	190	3.9%
29	Colorado	73	1.5%	6	Pennsylvania	188	3.8%
42	Connecticut	35	0.7%	7	Ohio	171	3.5%
50	Delaware	6	0.1%	8	Georgia	147	3.0%
3	Florida	203	4.1%	9	Michigan	142	2.9%
8	Georgia	147	3.0%	10	Louisiana	132	2.7%
45	Hawaii	24	0.5%	11	Minnesota	131	2.7%
39	Idaho	38	0.8%	12	Tennessee	130	2.6%
5	Illinois	190	3.9%	13	Kansas	129	2.6%
17	Indiana	114	2.3%	14	Wisconsin	124	2.5%
16	Iowa	117	2.4%	15	Missouri	119	2.4%
13	Kansas	129	2.6%	16	Iowa	117	2.4%
21	Kentucky	104	2.1%	17	Indiana	114	2.3%
10	Louisiana	132	2.7%	17	North Carolina	114	2.3%
40	Maine	37	0.8%	19	Oklahoma	112	2.3%
36	Maryland	50	1.0%	20	Alabama	109	2.2%
27	Massachusetts	80	1.6%	21	Kentucky	104	2.1%
9	Michigan	142	2.9%	22	Mississippi	94	1.9%
11	Minnesota	131	2.7%	23	Virginia	88	1.8%
22	Mississippi	94	1.9%	23	Washington	88	1.8%
15	Missouri	119	2.4%	25	Nebraska	85	1.7%
34	Montana	52	1.1%	26	Arkansas	84	1.7%
25	Nebraska	85	1.7%	27	Massachusetts	80	1.6%
43	Nevada	33	0.7%	28	New Jersey	79	1.6%
44	New Hampshire	28	0.6%	29	Colorado	73	1.5%
28	New Jersey	79	1.6%	30	Arizona	66	1.3%
41	New Mexico	36	0.7%	30	South Carolina	66	1.3%
3	New York	203	4.1%	32	Oregon	58	1.2%
17	North Carolina	114	2.3%	33	West Virginia	56	1.1%
38	North Dakota	41	0.8%	34	Montana	52	1.1%
7	Ohio	171	3.5%	34	South Dakota	52	1.1%
19	Oklahoma	112	2.3%	36	Maryland	50	1.0%
32	Oregon	58	1.2%	37	Utah	43	0.9%
6	Pennsylvania	188	3.8%	38	North Dakota	41	0.8%
49	Rhode Island	11	0.2%	39	Idaho	38	0.8%
30	South Carolina	66	1.3%	40	Maine	37	0.8%
34	South Dakota	52	1.1%	41	New Mexico	36	0.7%
12	Tennessee	130	2.6%	42	Connecticut	35	0.7%
1	Texas	417	8.5%	43	Nevada	33	0.7%
37	Utah	43	0.9%	44	New Hampshire	28	0.6%
48	Vermont	14	0.3%	45	Hawaii	24	0.5%
23	Virginia	88	1.8%	45	Wyoming	24	0.5%
23	Washington	88	1.8%	47	Alaska	22	0.4%
33	West Virginia	56	1.1%	48	Vermont	14	0.3%
14	Wisconsin	124	2.5%	49	Rhode Island	11	0.2%
45	Wyoming	24	0.5%	50	Delaware	6	0.1%
					District of Columbia	11	0.2%

Source: American Hospital Association (Chicago, IL)
    "Hospital Statistics" (2008 edition)

*Community hospitals are all nonfederal, short-term, general, and special hospitals whose facilities and services are available to the public.

Rate of Community Hospitals in 2005

National Rate = 1.6 Community Hospitals per 100,000 Population*

ALPHA ORDER

RANK	STATE	RATE
18	Alabama	2.4
8	Alaska	3.2
42	Arizona	1.1
13	Arkansas	3.0
45	California	1.0
31	Colorado	1.5
45	Connecticut	1.0
50	Delaware	0.7
42	Florida	1.1
29	Georgia	1.6
24	Hawaii	1.9
15	Idaho	2.6
31	Illinois	1.5
26	Indiana	1.8
7	Iowa	3.9
5	Kansas	4.7
16	Kentucky	2.5
10	Louisiana	3.1
14	Maine	2.8
48	Maryland	0.9
40	Massachusetts	1.2
36	Michigan	1.4
16	Minnesota	2.5
8	Mississippi	3.2
23	Missouri	2.0
3	Montana	5.5
4	Nebraska	4.8
38	Nevada	1.3
21	New Hampshire	2.1
48	New Jersey	0.9
24	New Mexico	1.9
42	New York	1.1
38	North Carolina	1.3
2	North Dakota	6.4
31	Ohio	1.5
10	Oklahoma	3.1
29	Oregon	1.6
31	Pennsylvania	1.5
45	Rhode Island	1.0
31	South Carolina	1.5
1	South Dakota	6.6
21	Tennessee	2.1
26	Texas	1.8
28	Utah	1.7
19	Vermont	2.3
40	Virginia	1.2
36	Washington	1.4
10	West Virginia	3.1
20	Wisconsin	2.2
5	Wyoming	4.7

RANK ORDER

RANK	STATE	RATE
1	South Dakota	6.6
2	North Dakota	6.4
3	Montana	5.5
4	Nebraska	4.8
5	Kansas	4.7
5	Wyoming	4.7
7	Iowa	3.9
8	Alaska	3.2
8	Mississippi	3.2
10	Louisiana	3.1
10	Oklahoma	3.1
10	West Virginia	3.1
13	Arkansas	3.0
14	Maine	2.8
15	Idaho	2.6
16	Kentucky	2.5
16	Minnesota	2.5
18	Alabama	2.4
19	Vermont	2.3
20	Wisconsin	2.2
21	New Hampshire	2.1
21	Tennessee	2.1
23	Missouri	2.0
24	Hawaii	1.9
24	New Mexico	1.9
26	Indiana	1.8
26	Texas	1.8
28	Utah	1.7
29	Georgia	1.6
29	Oregon	1.6
31	Colorado	1.5
31	Illinois	1.5
31	Ohio	1.5
31	Pennsylvania	1.5
31	South Carolina	1.5
36	Michigan	1.4
36	Washington	1.4
38	Nevada	1.3
38	North Carolina	1.3
40	Massachusetts	1.2
40	Virginia	1.2
42	Arizona	1.1
42	Florida	1.1
42	New York	1.1
45	California	1.0
45	Connecticut	1.0
45	Rhode Island	1.0
48	Maryland	0.9
48	New Jersey	0.9
50	Delaware	0.7
	District of Columbia	1.9

Source: CQ Press using data from American Hospital Association (Chicago, IL)
"Hospital Statistics" (2008 edition)

*Community hospitals are all nonfederal, short-term, general, and special hospitals whose facilities and services are available to the public.

Community Hospitals per 1,000 Square Miles in 2006

National Rate = 1.3 Community Hospitals*

ALPHA ORDER

RANK	STATE	RATE
21	Alabama	2.1
50	Alaska**	0.0
41	Arizona	0.6
29	Arkansas	1.6
19	California	2.2
39	Colorado	0.7
4	Connecticut	6.3
17	Delaware	2.4
10	Florida	3.1
15	Georgia	2.5
19	Hawaii	2.2
44	Idaho	0.5
9	Illinois	3.3
10	Indiana	3.1
21	Iowa	2.1
29	Kansas	1.6
14	Kentucky	2.6
15	Louisiana	2.5
38	Maine	1.0
6	Maryland	4.0
2	Massachusetts	7.6
33	Michigan	1.5
33	Minnesota	1.5
26	Mississippi	1.9
28	Missouri	1.7
46	Montana	0.4
37	Nebraska	1.1
47	Nevada	0.3
13	New Hampshire	3.0
1	New Jersey	9.1
47	New Mexico	0.3
8	New York	3.7
21	North Carolina	2.1
41	North Dakota	0.6
7	Ohio	3.8
29	Oklahoma	1.6
41	Oregon	0.6
5	Pennsylvania	4.1
3	Rhode Island	7.1
21	South Carolina	2.1
39	South Dakota	0.7
10	Tennessee	3.1
29	Texas	1.6
44	Utah	0.5
33	Vermont	1.5
21	Virginia	2.1
36	Washington	1.2
18	West Virginia	2.3
26	Wisconsin	1.9
49	Wyoming	0.2

RANK ORDER

RANK	STATE	RATE
1	New Jersey	9.1
2	Massachusetts	7.6
3	Rhode Island	7.1
4	Connecticut	6.3
5	Pennsylvania	4.1
6	Maryland	4.0
7	Ohio	3.8
8	New York	3.7
9	Illinois	3.3
10	Florida	3.1
10	Indiana	3.1
10	Tennessee	3.1
13	New Hampshire	3.0
14	Kentucky	2.6
15	Georgia	2.5
15	Louisiana	2.5
17	Delaware	2.4
18	West Virginia	2.3
19	California	2.2
19	Hawaii	2.2
21	Alabama	2.1
21	Iowa	2.1
21	North Carolina	2.1
21	South Carolina	2.1
21	Virginia	2.1
26	Mississippi	1.9
26	Wisconsin	1.9
28	Missouri	1.7
29	Arkansas	1.6
29	Kansas	1.6
29	Oklahoma	1.6
29	Texas	1.6
33	Michigan	1.5
33	Minnesota	1.5
33	Vermont	1.5
36	Washington	1.2
37	Nebraska	1.1
38	Maine	1.0
39	Colorado	0.7
39	South Dakota	0.7
41	Arizona	0.6
41	North Dakota	0.6
41	Oregon	0.6
44	Idaho	0.5
44	Utah	0.5
46	Montana	0.4
47	Nevada	0.3
47	New Mexico	0.3
49	Wyoming	0.2
50	Alaska**	0.0

District of Columbia***   NA

Source: CQ Press using data from American Hospital Association (Chicago, IL)
       "Hospital Statistics" (2008 edition)
*Based on land and water area figures. Community hospitals are nonfederal short-term general and other special hospitals, whose facilities and services are available to the public.
**Alaska has 22 community hospitals for its 663,267 square miles.
***The District of Columbia has 11 community hospitals for its 68 square miles.

Community Hospitals in Urban Areas in 2006

National Total = 2,926 Hospitals*

ALPHA ORDER

RANK	STATE	HOSPITALS	% of USA
17	Alabama	60	2.1%
47	Alaska	5	0.2%
21	Arizona	50	1.7%
28	Arkansas	35	1.2%
1	California	324	11.1%
27	Colorado	36	1.2%
30	Connecticut	30	1.0%
48	Delaware	4	0.1%
3	Florida	173	5.9%
9	Georgia	83	2.8%
41	Hawaii	13	0.4%
39	Idaho	14	0.5%
6	Illinois	126	4.3%
13	Indiana	74	2.5%
29	Iowa	33	1.1%
31	Kansas	29	1.0%
26	Kentucky	40	1.4%
10	Louisiana	81	2.8%
38	Maine	15	0.5%
24	Maryland	44	1.5%
12	Massachusetts	78	2.7%
8	Michigan	84	2.9%
22	Minnesota	49	1.7%
33	Mississippi	27	0.9%
16	Missouri	66	2.3%
45	Montana	6	0.2%
37	Nebraska	16	0.5%
36	Nevada	22	0.8%
42	New Hampshire	11	0.4%
11	New Jersey	79	2.7%
39	New Mexico	14	0.5%
4	New York	163	5.6%
19	North Carolina	56	1.9%
45	North Dakota	6	0.2%
7	Ohio	117	4.0%
23	Oklahoma	46	1.6%
31	Oregon	29	1.0%
5	Pennsylvania	140	4.8%
42	Rhode Island	11	0.4%
25	South Carolina	41	1.4%
44	South Dakota	10	0.3%
13	Tennessee	74	2.5%
2	Texas	268	9.2%
35	Utah	25	0.9%
49	Vermont	2	0.1%
18	Virginia	58	2.0%
20	Washington	53	1.8%
34	West Virginia	26	0.9%
15	Wisconsin	67	2.3%
49	Wyoming	2	0.1%

RANK ORDER

RANK	STATE	HOSPITALS	% of USA
1	California	324	11.1%
2	Texas	268	9.2%
3	Florida	173	5.9%
4	New York	163	5.6%
5	Pennsylvania	140	4.8%
6	Illinois	126	4.3%
7	Ohio	117	4.0%
8	Michigan	84	2.9%
9	Georgia	83	2.8%
10	Louisiana	81	2.8%
11	New Jersey	79	2.7%
12	Massachusetts	78	2.7%
13	Indiana	74	2.5%
13	Tennessee	74	2.5%
15	Wisconsin	67	2.3%
16	Missouri	66	2.3%
17	Alabama	60	2.1%
18	Virginia	58	2.0%
19	North Carolina	56	1.9%
20	Washington	53	1.8%
21	Arizona	50	1.7%
22	Minnesota	49	1.7%
23	Oklahoma	46	1.6%
24	Maryland	44	1.5%
25	South Carolina	41	1.4%
26	Kentucky	40	1.4%
27	Colorado	36	1.2%
28	Arkansas	35	1.2%
29	Iowa	33	1.1%
30	Connecticut	30	1.0%
31	Kansas	29	1.0%
31	Oregon	29	1.0%
33	Mississippi	27	0.9%
34	West Virginia	26	0.9%
35	Utah	25	0.9%
36	Nevada	22	0.8%
37	Nebraska	16	0.5%
38	Maine	15	0.5%
39	Idaho	14	0.5%
39	New Mexico	14	0.5%
41	Hawaii	13	0.4%
42	New Hampshire	11	0.4%
42	Rhode Island	11	0.4%
44	South Dakota	10	0.3%
45	Montana	6	0.2%
45	North Dakota	6	0.2%
47	Alaska	5	0.2%
48	Delaware	4	0.1%
49	Vermont	2	0.1%
49	Wyoming	2	0.1%
	District of Columbia	11	0.4%

Source: American Hospital Association (Chicago, IL)
"Hospital Statistics" (2008 edition)

*Community hospitals are all nonfederal, short-term, general, and special hospitals whose facilities and services are available to the public. Urban is defined as any area inside a metropolitan statistical area as defined by the U.S. Office of Management and Budget.

Percent of Community Hospitals in Urban Areas in 2006

National Percent = 59.4% of Community Hospitals*

ALPHA ORDER

RANK	STATE	PERCENT
26	Alabama	55.0
43	Alaska	22.7
9	Arizona	75.8
33	Arkansas	41.7
4	California	90.8
30	Colorado	49.3
6	Connecticut	85.7
12	Delaware	66.7
7	Florida	85.2
24	Georgia	56.5
27	Hawaii	54.2
40	Idaho	36.8
14	Illinois	66.3
16	Indiana	64.9
42	Iowa	28.2
44	Kansas	22.5
38	Kentucky	38.5
19	Louisiana	61.4
35	Maine	40.5
5	Maryland	88.0
3	Massachusetts	97.5
21	Michigan	59.2
39	Minnesota	37.4
41	Mississippi	28.7
25	Missouri	55.5
49	Montana	11.5
46	Nebraska	18.8
12	Nevada	66.7
36	New Hampshire	39.3
1	New Jersey	100.0
37	New Mexico	38.9
8	New York	80.3
31	North Carolina	49.1
47	North Dakota	14.6
11	Ohio	68.4
34	Oklahoma	41.1
29	Oregon	50.0
10	Pennsylvania	74.5
1	Rhode Island	100.0
18	South Carolina	62.1
45	South Dakota	19.2
23	Tennessee	56.9
17	Texas	64.3
22	Utah	58.1
48	Vermont	14.3
15	Virginia	65.9
20	Washington	60.2
32	West Virginia	46.4
28	Wisconsin	54.0
50	Wyoming	8.3

RANK ORDER

RANK	STATE	PERCENT
1	New Jersey	100.0
1	Rhode Island	100.0
3	Massachusetts	97.5
4	California	90.8
5	Maryland	88.0
6	Connecticut	85.7
7	Florida	85.2
8	New York	80.3
9	Arizona	75.8
10	Pennsylvania	74.5
11	Ohio	68.4
12	Delaware	66.7
12	Nevada	66.7
14	Illinois	66.3
15	Virginia	65.9
16	Indiana	64.9
17	Texas	64.3
18	South Carolina	62.1
19	Louisiana	61.4
20	Washington	60.2
21	Michigan	59.2
22	Utah	58.1
23	Tennessee	56.9
24	Georgia	56.5
25	Missouri	55.5
26	Alabama	55.0
27	Hawaii	54.2
28	Wisconsin	54.0
29	Oregon	50.0
30	Colorado	49.3
31	North Carolina	49.1
32	West Virginia	46.4
33	Arkansas	41.7
34	Oklahoma	41.1
35	Maine	40.5
36	New Hampshire	39.3
37	New Mexico	38.9
38	Kentucky	38.5
39	Minnesota	37.4
40	Idaho	36.8
41	Mississippi	28.7
42	Iowa	28.2
43	Alaska	22.7
44	Kansas	22.5
45	South Dakota	19.2
46	Nebraska	18.8
47	North Dakota	14.6
48	Vermont	14.3
49	Montana	11.5
50	Wyoming	8.3

District of Columbia   100.0

Source: CQ Press using data from American Hospital Association (Chicago, IL)
"Hospital Statistics" (2008 edition)

*Community hospitals are all nonfederal, short-term, general, and special hospitals whose facilities and services are available to the public. Urban is defined as any area inside a metropolitan statistical area as defined by the U.S. Office of Management and Budget.

Community Hospitals in Rural Areas in 2006

National Total = 2,001 Hospitals*

RANK	STATE	HOSPITALS	% of USA
18	Alabama	49	2.4%
39	Alaska	17	0.8%
41	Arizona	16	0.8%
18	Arkansas	49	2.4%
28	California	33	1.6%
25	Colorado	37	1.8%
46	Connecticut	5	0.2%
47	Delaware	2	0.1%
29	Florida	30	1.5%
8	Georgia	64	3.2%
43	Hawaii	11	0.5%
34	Idaho	24	1.2%
8	Illinois	64	3.2%
23	Indiana	40	2.0%
3	Iowa	84	4.2%
2	Kansas	100	5.0%
8	Kentucky	64	3.2%
17	Louisiana	51	2.5%
35	Maine	22	1.1%
45	Maryland	6	0.3%
47	Massachusetts	2	0.1%
11	Michigan	58	2.9%
4	Minnesota	82	4.1%
6	Mississippi	67	3.3%
16	Missouri	53	2.6%
21	Montana	46	2.3%
5	Nebraska	69	3.4%
43	Nevada	11	0.5%
39	New Hampshire	17	0.8%
49	New Jersey	0	0.0%
35	New Mexico	22	1.1%
23	New York	40	2.0%
11	North Carolina	58	2.9%
26	North Dakota	35	1.7%
15	Ohio	54	2.7%
7	Oklahoma	66	3.3%
32	Oregon	29	1.4%
20	Pennsylvania	48	2.4%
49	Rhode Island	0	0.0%
33	South Carolina	25	1.2%
22	South Dakota	42	2.1%
14	Tennessee	56	2.8%
1	Texas	149	7.4%
38	Utah	18	0.9%
42	Vermont	12	0.6%
29	Virginia	30	1.5%
26	Washington	35	1.7%
29	West Virginia	30	1.5%
13	Wisconsin	57	2.8%
35	Wyoming	22	1.1%

RANK	STATE	HOSPITALS	% of USA
1	Texas	149	7.4%
2	Kansas	100	5.0%
3	Iowa	84	4.2%
4	Minnesota	82	4.1%
5	Nebraska	69	3.4%
6	Mississippi	67	3.3%
7	Oklahoma	66	3.3%
8	Georgia	64	3.2%
8	Illinois	64	3.2%
8	Kentucky	64	3.2%
11	Michigan	58	2.9%
11	North Carolina	58	2.9%
13	Wisconsin	57	2.8%
14	Tennessee	56	2.8%
15	Ohio	54	2.7%
16	Missouri	53	2.6%
17	Louisiana	51	2.5%
18	Alabama	49	2.4%
18	Arkansas	49	2.4%
20	Pennsylvania	48	2.4%
21	Montana	46	2.3%
22	South Dakota	42	2.1%
23	Indiana	40	2.0%
23	New York	40	2.0%
25	Colorado	37	1.8%
26	North Dakota	35	1.7%
26	Washington	35	1.7%
28	California	33	1.6%
29	Florida	30	1.5%
29	Virginia	30	1.5%
29	West Virginia	30	1.5%
32	Oregon	29	1.4%
33	South Carolina	25	1.2%
34	Idaho	24	1.2%
35	Maine	22	1.1%
35	New Mexico	22	1.1%
35	Wyoming	22	1.1%
38	Utah	18	0.9%
39	Alaska	17	0.8%
39	New Hampshire	17	0.8%
41	Arizona	16	0.8%
42	Vermont	12	0.6%
43	Hawaii	11	0.5%
43	Nevada	11	0.5%
45	Maryland	6	0.3%
46	Connecticut	5	0.2%
47	Delaware	2	0.1%
47	Massachusetts	2	0.1%
49	New Jersey	0	0.0%
49	Rhode Island	0	0.0%
	District of Columbia	0	0.0%

Source: American Hospital Association (Chicago, IL)
"Hospital Statistics" (2008 edition)

*Community hospitals are all nonfederal, short-term, general, and special hospitals whose facilities and services are available to the public. Rural is defined as any area outside a metropolitan statistical area as defined by the U.S. Office of Management and Budget.

Percent of Community Hospitals in Rural Areas in 2006

National Percent = 40.6% of Community Hospitals*

ALPHA ORDER

ALPHA ORDER

RANK	STATE	PERCENT
25	Alabama	45.0
8	Alaska	77.3
42	Arizona	24.2
18	Arkansas	58.3
47	California	9.2
21	Colorado	50.7
45	Connecticut	14.3
38	Delaware	33.3
44	Florida	14.8
27	Georgia	43.5
24	Hawaii	45.8
11	Idaho	63.2
37	Illinois	33.7
35	Indiana	35.1
9	Iowa	71.8
7	Kansas	77.5
13	Kentucky	61.5
32	Louisiana	38.6
16	Maine	59.5
46	Maryland	12.0
48	Massachusetts	2.5
30	Michigan	40.8
12	Minnesota	62.6
10	Mississippi	71.3
26	Missouri	44.5
2	Montana	88.5
5	Nebraska	81.2
38	Nevada	33.3
15	New Hampshire	60.7
49	New Jersey	0.0
14	New Mexico	61.1
43	New York	19.7
20	North Carolina	50.9
4	North Dakota	85.4
40	Ohio	31.6
17	Oklahoma	58.9
22	Oregon	50.0
41	Pennsylvania	25.5
49	Rhode Island	0.0
33	South Carolina	37.9
6	South Dakota	80.8
28	Tennessee	43.1
34	Texas	35.7
29	Utah	41.9
3	Vermont	85.7
36	Virginia	34.1
31	Washington	39.8
19	West Virginia	53.6
23	Wisconsin	46.0
1	Wyoming	91.7

RANK ORDER

RANK	STATE	PERCENT
1	Wyoming	91.7
2	Montana	88.5
3	Vermont	85.7
4	North Dakota	85.4
5	Nebraska	81.2
6	South Dakota	80.8
7	Kansas	77.5
8	Alaska	77.3
9	Iowa	71.8
10	Mississippi	71.3
11	Idaho	63.2
12	Minnesota	62.6
13	Kentucky	61.5
14	New Mexico	61.1
15	New Hampshire	60.7
16	Maine	59.5
17	Oklahoma	58.9
18	Arkansas	58.3
19	West Virginia	53.6
20	North Carolina	50.9
21	Colorado	50.7
22	Oregon	50.0
23	Wisconsin	46.0
24	Hawaii	45.8
25	Alabama	45.0
26	Missouri	44.5
27	Georgia	43.5
28	Tennessee	43.1
29	Utah	41.9
30	Michigan	40.8
31	Washington	39.8
32	Louisiana	38.6
33	South Carolina	37.9
34	Texas	35.7
35	Indiana	35.1
36	Virginia	34.1
37	Illinois	33.7
38	Delaware	33.3
38	Nevada	33.3
40	Ohio	31.6
41	Pennsylvania	25.5
42	Arizona	24.2
43	New York	19.7
44	Florida	14.8
45	Connecticut	14.3
46	Maryland	12.0
47	California	9.2
48	Massachusetts	2.5
49	New Jersey	0.0
49	Rhode Island	0.0
	District of Columbia	0.0

Source: CQ Press using data from American Hospital Association (Chicago, IL)
"Hospital Statistics" (2008 edition)

*Community hospitals are all nonfederal, short-term, general, and special hospitals whose facilities and services are available to the public. Rural is defined as any area outside a metropolitan statistical area as defined by the U.S. Office of Management and Budget.

Nongovernment Not-For-Profit Hospitals in 2006

National Total = 2,919 Hospitals*

ALPHA ORDER

RANK	STATE	HOSPITALS	% of USA
38	Alabama	26	0.9%
46	Alaska	13	0.4%
29	Arizona	41	1.4%
23	Arkansas	45	1.5%
1	California	202	6.9%
32	Colorado	35	1.2%
35	Connecticut	33	1.1%
49	Delaware	6	0.2%
10	Florida	84	2.9%
18	Georgia	59	2.0%
42	Hawaii	17	0.6%
44	Idaho	14	0.5%
4	Illinois	150	5.1%
21	Indiana	56	1.9%
19	Iowa	58	2.0%
20	Kansas	57	2.0%
13	Kentucky	71	2.4%
31	Louisiana	38	1.3%
34	Maine	34	1.2%
22	Maryland	48	1.6%
14	Massachusetts	67	2.3%
7	Michigan	120	4.1%
9	Minnesota	91	3.1%
37	Mississippi	29	1.0%
16	Missouri	62	2.1%
26	Montana	42	1.4%
25	Nebraska	43	1.5%
47	Nevada	11	0.4%
39	New Hampshire	24	0.8%
12	New Jersey	74	2.5%
43	New Mexico	15	0.5%
2	New York	177	6.1%
11	North Carolina	75	2.6%
29	North Dakota	41	1.4%
6	Ohio	136	4.7%
32	Oklahoma	35	1.2%
26	Oregon	42	1.4%
3	Pennsylvania	161	5.5%
47	Rhode Island	11	0.4%
40	South Carolina	22	0.8%
24	South Dakota	44	1.5%
17	Tennessee	60	2.1%
5	Texas	148	5.1%
40	Utah	22	0.8%
44	Vermont	14	0.5%
15	Virginia	64	2.2%
26	Washington	42	1.4%
36	West Virginia	31	1.1%
8	Wisconsin	118	4.0%
50	Wyoming	4	0.1%

RANK ORDER

RANK	STATE	HOSPITALS	% of USA
1	California	202	6.9%
2	New York	177	6.1%
3	Pennsylvania	161	5.5%
4	Illinois	150	5.1%
5	Texas	148	5.1%
6	Ohio	136	4.7%
7	Michigan	120	4.1%
8	Wisconsin	118	4.0%
9	Minnesota	91	3.1%
10	Florida	84	2.9%
11	North Carolina	75	2.6%
12	New Jersey	74	2.5%
13	Kentucky	71	2.4%
14	Massachusetts	67	2.3%
15	Virginia	64	2.2%
16	Missouri	62	2.1%
17	Tennessee	60	2.1%
18	Georgia	59	2.0%
19	Iowa	58	2.0%
20	Kansas	57	2.0%
21	Indiana	56	1.9%
22	Maryland	48	1.6%
23	Arkansas	45	1.5%
24	South Dakota	44	1.5%
25	Nebraska	43	1.5%
26	Montana	42	1.4%
26	Oregon	42	1.4%
26	Washington	42	1.4%
29	Arizona	41	1.4%
29	North Dakota	41	1.4%
31	Louisiana	38	1.3%
32	Colorado	35	1.2%
32	Oklahoma	35	1.2%
34	Maine	34	1.2%
35	Connecticut	33	1.1%
36	West Virginia	31	1.1%
37	Mississippi	29	1.0%
38	Alabama	26	0.9%
39	New Hampshire	24	0.8%
40	South Carolina	22	0.8%
40	Utah	22	0.8%
42	Hawaii	17	0.6%
43	New Mexico	15	0.5%
44	Idaho	14	0.5%
44	Vermont	14	0.5%
46	Alaska	13	0.4%
47	Nevada	11	0.4%
47	Rhode Island	11	0.4%
49	Delaware	6	0.2%
50	Wyoming	4	0.1%
	District of Columbia	7	0.2%

Source: American Hospital Association (Chicago, IL)
"Hospital Statistics" (2008 edition)
*Nongovernment not-for-profit hospitals are a subset of community hospitals.

Investor-Owned (For-Profit) Hospitals in 2006

National Total = 889 Hospitals*

ALPHA ORDER

RANK	STATE	HOSPITALS	% of USA
6	Alabama	42	4.7%
38	Alaska	2	0.2%
14	Arizona	20	2.2%
11	Arkansas	24	2.7%
3	California	79	8.9%
24	Colorado	11	1.2%
41	Connecticut	1	0.1%
44	Delaware	0	0.0%
2	Florida	95	10.7%
8	Georgia	32	3.6%
44	Hawaii	0	0.0%
33	Idaho	3	0.3%
21	Illinois	13	1.5%
17	Indiana	19	2.1%
44	Iowa	0	0.0%
24	Kansas	11	1.2%
14	Kentucky	20	2.2%
5	Louisiana	43	4.8%
41	Maine	1	0.1%
38	Maryland	2	0.2%
26	Massachusetts	10	1.1%
28	Michigan	5	0.6%
44	Minnesota	0	0.0%
11	Mississippi	24	2.7%
13	Missouri	21	2.4%
41	Montana	1	0.1%
38	Nebraska	2	0.2%
18	Nevada	15	1.7%
30	New Hampshire	4	0.4%
30	New Jersey	4	0.4%
21	New Mexico	13	1.5%
33	New York	3	0.3%
27	North Carolina	7	0.8%
44	North Dakota	0	0.0%
23	Ohio	12	1.3%
7	Oklahoma	33	3.7%
33	Oregon	3	0.3%
9	Pennsylvania	25	2.8%
44	Rhode Island	0	0.0%
9	South Carolina	25	2.8%
33	South Dakota	3	0.3%
4	Tennessee	46	5.2%
1	Texas	149	16.8%
18	Utah	15	1.7%
44	Vermont	0	0.0%
14	Virginia	20	2.2%
28	Washington	5	0.6%
18	West Virginia	15	1.7%
30	Wisconsin	4	0.4%
33	Wyoming	3	0.3%

RANK ORDER

RANK	STATE	HOSPITALS	% of USA
1	Texas	149	16.8%
2	Florida	95	10.7%
3	California	79	8.9%
4	Tennessee	46	5.2%
5	Louisiana	43	4.8%
6	Alabama	42	4.7%
7	Oklahoma	33	3.7%
8	Georgia	32	3.6%
9	Pennsylvania	25	2.8%
9	South Carolina	25	2.8%
11	Arkansas	24	2.7%
11	Mississippi	24	2.7%
13	Missouri	21	2.4%
14	Arizona	20	2.2%
14	Kentucky	20	2.2%
14	Virginia	20	2.2%
17	Indiana	19	2.1%
18	Nevada	15	1.7%
18	Utah	15	1.7%
18	West Virginia	15	1.7%
21	Illinois	13	1.5%
21	New Mexico	13	1.5%
23	Ohio	12	1.3%
24	Colorado	11	1.2%
24	Kansas	11	1.2%
26	Massachusetts	10	1.1%
27	North Carolina	7	0.8%
28	Michigan	5	0.6%
28	Washington	5	0.6%
30	New Hampshire	4	0.4%
30	New Jersey	4	0.4%
30	Wisconsin	4	0.4%
33	Idaho	3	0.3%
33	New York	3	0.3%
33	Oregon	3	0.3%
33	South Dakota	3	0.3%
33	Wyoming	3	0.3%
38	Alaska	2	0.2%
38	Maryland	2	0.2%
38	Nebraska	2	0.2%
41	Connecticut	1	0.1%
41	Maine	1	0.1%
41	Montana	1	0.1%
44	Delaware	0	0.0%
44	Hawaii	0	0.0%
44	Iowa	0	0.0%
44	Minnesota	0	0.0%
44	North Dakota	0	0.0%
44	Rhode Island	0	0.0%
44	Vermont	0	0.0%
	District of Columbia	4	0.4%

Source: American Hospital Association (Chicago, IL)
"Hospital Statistics" (2008 edition)
*Investor-owned (for-profit) hospitals are a subset of community hospitals.

State and Local Government-Owned Hospitals in 2006

National Total = 1,119 Hospitals*

ALPHA ORDER

RANK	STATE	HOSPITALS	% of USA
8	Alabama	41	3.7%
32	Alaska	7	0.6%
36	Arizona	5	0.4%
26	Arkansas	15	1.3%
2	California	76	6.8%
16	Colorado	27	2.4%
43	Connecticut	1	0.1%
45	Delaware	0	0.0%
18	Florida	24	2.1%
5	Georgia	56	5.0%
32	Hawaii	7	0.6%
22	Idaho	21	1.9%
16	Illinois	27	2.4%
13	Indiana	39	3.5%
4	Iowa	59	5.3%
3	Kansas	61	5.5%
27	Kentucky	13	1.2%
6	Louisiana	51	4.6%
40	Maine	2	0.2%
45	Maryland	0	0.0%
39	Massachusetts	3	0.3%
24	Michigan	17	1.5%
11	Minnesota	40	3.6%
8	Mississippi	41	3.7%
14	Missouri	36	3.2%
30	Montana	9	0.8%
11	Nebraska	40	3.6%
32	Nevada	7	0.6%
45	New Hampshire	0	0.0%
43	New Jersey	1	0.1%
31	New Mexico	8	0.7%
20	New York	23	2.1%
15	North Carolina	32	2.9%
45	North Dakota	0	0.0%
20	Ohio	23	2.1%
7	Oklahoma	44	3.9%
27	Oregon	13	1.2%
40	Pennsylvania	2	0.2%
45	Rhode Island	0	0.0%
23	South Carolina	19	1.7%
36	South Dakota	5	0.4%
18	Tennessee	24	2.1%
1	Texas	120	10.7%
35	Utah	6	0.5%
45	Vermont	0	0.0%
38	Virginia	4	0.4%
8	Washington	41	3.7%
29	West Virginia	10	0.9%
40	Wisconsin	2	0.2%
24	Wyoming	17	1.5%

RANK ORDER

RANK	STATE	HOSPITALS	% of USA
1	Texas	120	10.7%
2	California	76	6.8%
3	Kansas	61	5.5%
4	Iowa	59	5.3%
5	Georgia	56	5.0%
6	Louisiana	51	4.6%
7	Oklahoma	44	3.9%
8	Alabama	41	3.7%
8	Mississippi	41	3.7%
8	Washington	41	3.7%
11	Minnesota	40	3.6%
11	Nebraska	40	3.6%
13	Indiana	39	3.5%
14	Missouri	36	3.2%
15	North Carolina	32	2.9%
16	Colorado	27	2.4%
16	Illinois	27	2.4%
18	Florida	24	2.1%
18	Tennessee	24	2.1%
20	New York	23	2.1%
20	Ohio	23	2.1%
22	Idaho	21	1.9%
23	South Carolina	19	1.7%
24	Michigan	17	1.5%
24	Wyoming	17	1.5%
26	Arkansas	15	1.3%
27	Kentucky	13	1.2%
27	Oregon	13	1.2%
29	West Virginia	10	0.9%
30	Montana	9	0.8%
31	New Mexico	8	0.7%
32	Alaska	7	0.6%
32	Hawaii	7	0.6%
32	Nevada	7	0.6%
35	Utah	6	0.5%
36	Arizona	5	0.4%
36	South Dakota	5	0.4%
38	Virginia	4	0.4%
39	Massachusetts	3	0.3%
40	Maine	2	0.2%
40	Pennsylvania	2	0.2%
40	Wisconsin	2	0.2%
43	Connecticut	1	0.1%
43	New Jersey	1	0.1%
45	Delaware	0	0.0%
45	Maryland	0	0.0%
45	New Hampshire	0	0.0%
45	North Dakota	0	0.0%
45	Rhode Island	0	0.0%
45	Vermont	0	0.0%
	District of Columbia	0	0.0%

Source: American Hospital Association (Chicago, IL)
"Hospital Statistics" (2008 edition)
*State and local government-owned hospitals are a subset of community hospitals.

Beds in Community Hospitals in 2006

National Total = 802,658 Beds*

ALPHA ORDER

RANK	STATE	BEDS	% of USA
19	Alabama	15,639	1.9%
49	Alaska	1,551	0.2%
23	Arizona	11,947	1.5%
31	Arkansas	9,309	1.2%
1	California	70,021	8.7%
30	Colorado	9,518	1.2%
32	Connecticut	7,988	1.0%
47	Delaware	2,138	0.3%
4	Florida	51,423	6.4%
9	Georgia	24,772	3.1%
44	Hawaii	2,969	0.4%
43	Idaho	3,303	0.4%
6	Illinois	34,178	4.3%
14	Indiana	18,076	2.3%
28	Iowa	10,500	1.3%
29	Kansas	10,019	1.2%
20	Kentucky	14,574	1.8%
17	Louisiana	15,864	2.0%
42	Maine	3,489	0.4%
25	Maryland	11,479	1.4%
16	Massachusetts	16,344	2.0%
8	Michigan	25,945	3.2%
18	Minnesota	15,843	2.0%
22	Mississippi	12,973	1.6%
13	Missouri	18,888	2.4%
39	Montana	4,089	0.5%
33	Nebraska	7,375	0.9%
36	Nevada	4,826	0.6%
45	New Hampshire	2,825	0.4%
11	New Jersey	22,094	2.8%
41	New Mexico	3,525	0.4%
2	New York	63,591	7.9%
10	North Carolina	23,441	2.9%
40	North Dakota	3,550	0.4%
7	Ohio	32,822	4.1%
27	Oklahoma	10,773	1.3%
35	Oregon	6,609	0.8%
5	Pennsylvania	39,567	4.9%
46	Rhode Island	2,394	0.3%
24	South Carolina	11,790	1.5%
38	South Dakota	4,326	0.5%
12	Tennessee	20,328	2.5%
3	Texas	58,964	7.3%
37	Utah	4,528	0.6%
50	Vermont	1,313	0.2%
15	Virginia	17,274	2.2%
26	Washington	10,927	1.4%
34	West Virginia	7,197	0.9%
21	Wisconsin	14,123	1.8%
48	Wyoming	2,056	0.3%

RANK ORDER

RANK	STATE	BEDS	% of USA
1	California	70,021	8.7%
2	New York	63,591	7.9%
3	Texas	58,964	7.3%
4	Florida	51,423	6.4%
5	Pennsylvania	39,567	4.9%
6	Illinois	34,178	4.3%
7	Ohio	32,822	4.1%
8	Michigan	25,945	3.2%
9	Georgia	24,772	3.1%
10	North Carolina	23,441	2.9%
11	New Jersey	22,094	2.8%
12	Tennessee	20,328	2.5%
13	Missouri	18,888	2.4%
14	Indiana	18,076	2.3%
15	Virginia	17,274	2.2%
16	Massachusetts	16,344	2.0%
17	Louisiana	15,864	2.0%
18	Minnesota	15,843	2.0%
19	Alabama	15,639	1.9%
20	Kentucky	14,574	1.8%
21	Wisconsin	14,123	1.8%
22	Mississippi	12,973	1.6%
23	Arizona	11,947	1.5%
24	South Carolina	11,790	1.5%
25	Maryland	11,479	1.4%
26	Washington	10,927	1.4%
27	Oklahoma	10,773	1.3%
28	Iowa	10,500	1.3%
29	Kansas	10,019	1.2%
30	Colorado	9,518	1.2%
31	Arkansas	9,309	1.2%
32	Connecticut	7,988	1.0%
33	Nebraska	7,375	0.9%
34	West Virginia	7,197	0.9%
35	Oregon	6,609	0.8%
36	Nevada	4,826	0.6%
37	Utah	4,528	0.6%
38	South Dakota	4,326	0.5%
39	Montana	4,089	0.5%
40	North Dakota	3,550	0.4%
41	New Mexico	3,525	0.4%
42	Maine	3,489	0.4%
43	Idaho	3,303	0.4%
44	Hawaii	2,969	0.4%
45	New Hampshire	2,825	0.4%
46	Rhode Island	2,394	0.3%
47	Delaware	2,138	0.3%
48	Wyoming	2,056	0.3%
49	Alaska	1,551	0.2%
50	Vermont	1,313	0.2%
	District of Columbia	3,601	0.4%

Source: American Hospital Association (Chicago, IL)
    "Hospital Statistics" (2008 edition)
*All nonfederal short-term general and other special hospitals, whose facilities and services are available to the public. Includes beds in hospital and nursing home units.

Rate of Beds in Community Hospitals in 2006

National Rate = 269 Beds per 100,000 Population*

<table>
<tr><td colspan="3">ALPHA ORDER</td><td colspan="3">RANK ORDER</td></tr>
<tr><td>RANK</td><td>STATE</td><td>RATE</td><td>RANK</td><td>STATE</td><td>RATE</td></tr>
<tr><td>12</td><td>Alabama</td><td>341</td><td>1</td><td>North Dakota</td><td>557</td></tr>
<tr><td>35</td><td>Alaska</td><td>229</td><td>2</td><td>South Dakota</td><td>549</td></tr>
<tr><td>44</td><td>Arizona</td><td>194</td><td>3</td><td>Mississippi</td><td>447</td></tr>
<tr><td>14</td><td>Arkansas</td><td>331</td><td>4</td><td>Montana</td><td>432</td></tr>
<tr><td>46</td><td>California</td><td>193</td><td>5</td><td>Nebraska</td><td>418</td></tr>
<tr><td>43</td><td>Colorado</td><td>200</td><td>6</td><td>Wyoming</td><td>401</td></tr>
<tr><td>35</td><td>Connecticut</td><td>229</td><td>7</td><td>West Virginia</td><td>398</td></tr>
<tr><td>33</td><td>Delaware</td><td>251</td><td>8</td><td>Louisiana</td><td>374</td></tr>
<tr><td>22</td><td>Florida</td><td>285</td><td>9</td><td>Kansas</td><td>364</td></tr>
<tr><td>25</td><td>Georgia</td><td>265</td><td>10</td><td>Iowa</td><td>353</td></tr>
<tr><td>34</td><td>Hawaii</td><td>232</td><td>11</td><td>Kentucky</td><td>347</td></tr>
<tr><td>37</td><td>Idaho</td><td>226</td><td>12</td><td>Alabama</td><td>341</td></tr>
<tr><td>24</td><td>Illinois</td><td>267</td><td>13</td><td>Tennessee</td><td>335</td></tr>
<tr><td>20</td><td>Indiana</td><td>287</td><td>14</td><td>Arkansas</td><td>331</td></tr>
<tr><td>10</td><td>Iowa</td><td>353</td><td>15</td><td>New York</td><td>330</td></tr>
<tr><td>9</td><td>Kansas</td><td>364</td><td>16</td><td>Missouri</td><td>324</td></tr>
<tr><td>11</td><td>Kentucky</td><td>347</td><td>17</td><td>Pennsylvania</td><td>319</td></tr>
<tr><td>8</td><td>Louisiana</td><td>374</td><td>18</td><td>Minnesota</td><td>307</td></tr>
<tr><td>25</td><td>Maine</td><td>265</td><td>19</td><td>Oklahoma</td><td>301</td></tr>
<tr><td>42</td><td>Maryland</td><td>205</td><td>20</td><td>Indiana</td><td>287</td></tr>
<tr><td>30</td><td>Massachusetts</td><td>254</td><td>21</td><td>Ohio</td><td>286</td></tr>
<tr><td>28</td><td>Michigan</td><td>257</td><td>22</td><td>Florida</td><td>285</td></tr>
<tr><td>18</td><td>Minnesota</td><td>307</td><td>23</td><td>South Carolina</td><td>272</td></tr>
<tr><td>3</td><td>Mississippi</td><td>447</td><td>24</td><td>Illinois</td><td>267</td></tr>
<tr><td>16</td><td>Missouri</td><td>324</td><td>25</td><td>Georgia</td><td>265</td></tr>
<tr><td>4</td><td>Montana</td><td>432</td><td>25</td><td>Maine</td><td>265</td></tr>
<tr><td>5</td><td>Nebraska</td><td>418</td><td>27</td><td>North Carolina</td><td>264</td></tr>
<tr><td>44</td><td>Nevada</td><td>194</td><td>28</td><td>Michigan</td><td>257</td></tr>
<tr><td>40</td><td>New Hampshire</td><td>215</td><td>29</td><td>New Jersey</td><td>255</td></tr>
<tr><td>29</td><td>New Jersey</td><td>255</td><td>30</td><td>Massachusetts</td><td>254</td></tr>
<tr><td>47</td><td>New Mexico</td><td>181</td><td>31</td><td>Wisconsin</td><td>253</td></tr>
<tr><td>15</td><td>New York</td><td>330</td><td>32</td><td>Texas</td><td>252</td></tr>
<tr><td>27</td><td>North Carolina</td><td>264</td><td>33</td><td>Delaware</td><td>251</td></tr>
<tr><td>1</td><td>North Dakota</td><td>557</td><td>34</td><td>Hawaii</td><td>232</td></tr>
<tr><td>21</td><td>Ohio</td><td>286</td><td>35</td><td>Alaska</td><td>229</td></tr>
<tr><td>19</td><td>Oklahoma</td><td>301</td><td>35</td><td>Connecticut</td><td>229</td></tr>
<tr><td>48</td><td>Oregon</td><td>179</td><td>37</td><td>Idaho</td><td>226</td></tr>
<tr><td>17</td><td>Pennsylvania</td><td>319</td><td>37</td><td>Virginia</td><td>226</td></tr>
<tr><td>39</td><td>Rhode Island</td><td>225</td><td>39</td><td>Rhode Island</td><td>225</td></tr>
<tr><td>23</td><td>South Carolina</td><td>272</td><td>40</td><td>New Hampshire</td><td>215</td></tr>
<tr><td>2</td><td>South Dakota</td><td>549</td><td>41</td><td>Vermont</td><td>212</td></tr>
<tr><td>13</td><td>Tennessee</td><td>335</td><td>42</td><td>Maryland</td><td>205</td></tr>
<tr><td>32</td><td>Texas</td><td>252</td><td>43</td><td>Colorado</td><td>200</td></tr>
<tr><td>49</td><td>Utah</td><td>176</td><td>44</td><td>Arizona</td><td>194</td></tr>
<tr><td>41</td><td>Vermont</td><td>212</td><td>44</td><td>Nevada</td><td>194</td></tr>
<tr><td>37</td><td>Virginia</td><td>226</td><td>46</td><td>California</td><td>193</td></tr>
<tr><td>50</td><td>Washington</td><td>171</td><td>47</td><td>New Mexico</td><td>181</td></tr>
<tr><td>7</td><td>West Virginia</td><td>398</td><td>48</td><td>Oregon</td><td>179</td></tr>
<tr><td>31</td><td>Wisconsin</td><td>253</td><td>49</td><td>Utah</td><td>176</td></tr>
<tr><td>6</td><td>Wyoming</td><td>401</td><td>50</td><td>Washington</td><td>171</td></tr>
<tr><td></td><td></td><td></td><td></td><td>District of Columbia</td><td>615</td></tr>
</table>

Source: CQ Press using data from American Hospital Association (Chicago, IL)
"Hospital Statistics" (2008 edition)

*All nonfederal short-term general and other special hospitals, whose facilities and services are available to the public. Includes beds in hospital and nursing home units.

Average Number of Beds per Community Hospital in 2006

National Average = 163 Beds per Community Hospital*

ALPHA ORDER

RANK ORDER

RANK	STATE	RATE	RANK	STATE	RATE
23	Alabama	143	1	Delaware	356
50	Alaska	71	2	New York	313
15	Arizona	181	3	New Jersey	280
35	Arkansas	111	4	Florida	253
11	California	196	5	Maryland	230
27	Colorado	130	6	Connecticut	228
6	Connecticut	228	7	Rhode Island	218
1	Delaware	356	8	Pennsylvania	210
4	Florida	253	9	North Carolina	206
18	Georgia	169	10	Massachusetts	204
29	Hawaii	124	11	California	196
43	Idaho	87	11	Virginia	196
16	Illinois	180	13	Ohio	192
19	Indiana	159	14	Michigan	183
42	Iowa	90	15	Arizona	181
49	Kansas	78	16	Illinois	180
25	Kentucky	140	17	South Carolina	179
32	Louisiana	120	18	Georgia	169
40	Maine	94	19	Indiana	159
5	Maryland	230	19	Missouri	159
10	Massachusetts	204	21	Tennessee	156
14	Michigan	183	22	Nevada	146
31	Minnesota	121	23	Alabama	143
26	Mississippi	138	24	Texas	141
19	Missouri	159	25	Kentucky	140
48	Montana	79	26	Mississippi	138
43	Nebraska	87	27	Colorado	130
22	Nevada	146	28	West Virginia	129
37	New Hampshire	101	29	Hawaii	124
3	New Jersey	280	29	Washington	124
38	New Mexico	98	31	Minnesota	121
2	New York	313	32	Louisiana	120
9	North Carolina	206	33	Oregon	114
43	North Dakota	87	33	Wisconsin	114
13	Ohio	192	35	Arkansas	111
39	Oklahoma	96	36	Utah	105
33	Oregon	114	37	New Hampshire	101
8	Pennsylvania	210	38	New Mexico	98
7	Rhode Island	218	39	Oklahoma	96
17	South Carolina	179	40	Maine	94
47	South Dakota	83	40	Vermont	94
21	Tennessee	156	42	Iowa	90
24	Texas	141	43	Idaho	87
36	Utah	105	43	Nebraska	87
40	Vermont	94	43	North Dakota	87
11	Virginia	196	46	Wyoming	86
29	Washington	124	47	South Dakota	83
28	West Virginia	129	48	Montana	79
33	Wisconsin	114	49	Kansas	78
46	Wyoming	86	50	Alaska	71

District of Columbia   327

Source: CQ Press using data from American Hospital Association (Chicago, IL)
        "Hospital Statistics" (2008 edition)
*All nonfederal short-term general and other special hospitals, whose facilities and services are available to the public. Includes beds in hospital and nursing home units.

Admissions to Community Hospitals in 2006

National Total = 35,377,659 Admissions*

ALPHA ORDER

RANK	STATE	ADMISSIONS	% of USA
18	Alabama	683,726	1.9%
49	Alaska	52,357	0.1%
19	Arizona	664,773	1.9%
30	Arkansas	373,067	1.1%
1	California	3,428,885	9.7%
27	Colorado	420,547	1.2%
29	Connecticut	406,498	1.1%
45	Delaware	105,164	0.3%
4	Florida	2,373,712	6.7%
11	Georgia	956,395	2.7%
43	Hawaii	111,713	0.3%
40	Idaho	141,839	0.4%
6	Illinois	1,583,620	4.5%
16	Indiana	726,020	2.1%
31	Iowa	363,077	1.0%
33	Kansas	332,524	0.9%
22	Kentucky	612,842	1.7%
21	Louisiana	623,144	1.8%
39	Maine	150,990	0.4%
17	Maryland	690,371	2.0%
13	Massachusetts	834,895	2.4%
8	Michigan	1,205,481	3.4%
20	Minnesota	633,225	1.8%
28	Mississippi	415,577	1.2%
14	Missouri	830,882	2.3%
44	Montana	106,826	0.3%
37	Nebraska	215,219	0.6%
35	Nevada	245,649	0.7%
42	New Hampshire	118,956	0.3%
9	New Jersey	1,111,101	3.1%
38	New Mexico	160,792	0.5%
2	New York	2,571,572	7.3%
10	North Carolina	1,015,594	2.9%
47	North Dakota	88,737	0.3%
7	Ohio	1,542,333	4.4%
26	Oklahoma	454,085	1.3%
32	Oregon	341,540	1.0%
5	Pennsylvania	1,866,261	5.3%
41	Rhode Island	127,179	0.4%
25	South Carolina	521,773	1.5%
46	South Dakota	96,964	0.3%
12	Tennessee	853,304	2.4%
3	Texas	2,528,943	7.1%
36	Utah	220,750	0.6%
50	Vermont	50,402	0.1%
15	Virginia	778,680	2.2%
24	Washington	556,700	1.6%
34	West Virginia	281,766	0.8%
23	Wisconsin	609,108	1.7%
48	Wyoming	52,586	0.1%

RANK ORDER

RANK	STATE	ADMISSIONS	% of USA
1	California	3,428,885	9.7%
2	New York	2,571,572	7.3%
3	Texas	2,528,943	7.1%
4	Florida	2,373,712	6.7%
5	Pennsylvania	1,866,261	5.3%
6	Illinois	1,583,620	4.5%
7	Ohio	1,542,333	4.4%
8	Michigan	1,205,481	3.4%
9	New Jersey	1,111,101	3.1%
10	North Carolina	1,015,594	2.9%
11	Georgia	956,395	2.7%
12	Tennessee	853,304	2.4%
13	Massachusetts	834,895	2.4%
14	Missouri	830,882	2.3%
15	Virginia	778,680	2.2%
16	Indiana	726,020	2.1%
17	Maryland	690,371	2.0%
18	Alabama	683,726	1.9%
19	Arizona	664,773	1.9%
20	Minnesota	633,225	1.8%
21	Louisiana	623,144	1.8%
22	Kentucky	612,842	1.7%
23	Wisconsin	609,108	1.7%
24	Washington	556,700	1.6%
25	South Carolina	521,773	1.5%
26	Oklahoma	454,085	1.3%
27	Colorado	420,547	1.2%
28	Mississippi	415,577	1.2%
29	Connecticut	406,498	1.1%
30	Arkansas	373,067	1.1%
31	Iowa	363,077	1.0%
32	Oregon	341,540	1.0%
33	Kansas	332,524	0.9%
34	West Virginia	281,766	0.8%
35	Nevada	245,649	0.7%
36	Utah	220,750	0.6%
37	Nebraska	215,219	0.6%
38	New Mexico	160,792	0.5%
39	Maine	150,990	0.4%
40	Idaho	141,839	0.4%
41	Rhode Island	127,179	0.4%
42	New Hampshire	118,956	0.3%
43	Hawaii	111,713	0.3%
44	Montana	106,826	0.3%
45	Delaware	105,164	0.3%
46	South Dakota	96,964	0.3%
47	North Dakota	88,737	0.3%
48	Wyoming	52,586	0.1%
49	Alaska	52,357	0.1%
50	Vermont	50,402	0.1%
	District of Columbia	139,515	0.4%

Source: American Hospital Association (Chicago, IL)
    "Hospital Statistics" (2008 edition)
*Admissions to all nonfederal short-term general and other special hospitals, whose facilities and services are available to the public. Includes admissions to hospital and nursing home units.

Inpatient Days in Community Hospitals in 2006

National Total = 196,366,512 Inpatient Days*

ALPHA ORDER

RANK	STATE	DAYS	% of USA
18	Alabama	3,556,939	1.8%
50	Alaska	304,978	0.2%
24	Arizona	3,023,329	1.5%
32	Arkansas	1,943,363	1.0%
2	California	18,278,223	9.3%
30	Colorado	2,164,588	1.1%
28	Connecticut	2,303,485	1.2%
46	Delaware	669,392	0.3%
4	Florida	12,432,951	6.3%
9	Georgia	6,221,330	3.2%
41	Hawaii	841,667	0.4%
45	Idaho	678,059	0.3%
6	Illinois	8,072,145	4.1%
17	Indiana	3,801,325	1.9%
29	Iowa	2,267,449	1.2%
31	Kansas	2,024,257	1.0%
20	Kentucky	3,239,168	1.6%
19	Louisiana	3,556,169	1.8%
40	Maine	851,520	0.4%
22	Maryland	3,167,502	1.6%
13	Massachusetts	4,432,313	2.3%
8	Michigan	6,245,033	3.2%
16	Minnesota	3,955,503	2.0%
25	Mississippi	2,697,952	1.4%
15	Missouri	4,331,742	2.2%
38	Montana	975,390	0.5%
33	Nebraska	1,666,078	0.8%
36	Nevada	1,307,303	0.7%
47	New Hampshire	644,096	0.3%
11	New Jersey	5,835,422	3.0%
43	New Mexico	762,267	0.4%
1	New York	18,510,969	9.4%
10	North Carolina	6,131,924	3.1%
42	North Dakota	762,500	0.4%
7	Ohio	7,742,312	3.9%
27	Oklahoma	2,307,539	1.2%
35	Oregon	1,508,314	0.8%
5	Pennsylvania	10,110,336	5.1%
44	Rhode Island	680,881	0.3%
23	South Carolina	3,083,647	1.6%
37	South Dakota	1,022,716	0.5%
12	Tennessee	4,806,765	2.4%
3	Texas	13,045,054	6.6%
39	Utah	968,656	0.5%
49	Vermont	327,850	0.2%
14	Virginia	4,416,114	2.2%
26	Washington	2,486,577	1.3%
34	West Virginia	1,592,271	0.8%
21	Wisconsin	3,210,210	1.6%
48	Wyoming	421,089	0.2%

RANK ORDER

RANK	STATE	DAYS	% of USA
1	New York	18,510,969	9.4%
2	California	18,278,223	9.3%
3	Texas	13,045,054	6.6%
4	Florida	12,432,951	6.3%
5	Pennsylvania	10,110,336	5.1%
6	Illinois	8,072,145	4.1%
7	Ohio	7,742,312	3.9%
8	Michigan	6,245,033	3.2%
9	Georgia	6,221,330	3.2%
10	North Carolina	6,131,924	3.1%
11	New Jersey	5,835,422	3.0%
12	Tennessee	4,806,765	2.4%
13	Massachusetts	4,432,313	2.3%
14	Virginia	4,416,114	2.2%
15	Missouri	4,331,742	2.2%
16	Minnesota	3,955,503	2.0%
17	Indiana	3,801,325	1.9%
18	Alabama	3,556,939	1.8%
19	Louisiana	3,556,169	1.8%
20	Kentucky	3,239,168	1.6%
21	Wisconsin	3,210,210	1.6%
22	Maryland	3,167,502	1.6%
23	South Carolina	3,083,647	1.6%
24	Arizona	3,023,329	1.5%
25	Mississippi	2,697,952	1.4%
26	Washington	2,486,577	1.3%
27	Oklahoma	2,307,539	1.2%
28	Connecticut	2,303,485	1.2%
29	Iowa	2,267,449	1.2%
30	Colorado	2,164,588	1.1%
31	Kansas	2,024,257	1.0%
32	Arkansas	1,943,363	1.0%
33	Nebraska	1,666,078	0.8%
34	West Virginia	1,592,271	0.8%
35	Oregon	1,508,314	0.8%
36	Nevada	1,307,303	0.7%
37	South Dakota	1,022,716	0.5%
38	Montana	975,390	0.5%
39	Utah	968,656	0.5%
40	Maine	851,520	0.4%
41	Hawaii	841,667	0.4%
42	North Dakota	762,500	0.4%
43	New Mexico	762,267	0.4%
44	Rhode Island	680,881	0.3%
45	Idaho	678,059	0.3%
46	Delaware	669,392	0.3%
47	New Hampshire	644,096	0.3%
48	Wyoming	421,089	0.2%
49	Vermont	327,850	0.2%
50	Alaska	304,978	0.2%
	District of Columbia	979,850	0.5%

Source: American Hospital Association (Chicago, IL)
"Hospital Statistics" (2008 edition)
*Inpatient days in all nonfederal short-term general and other special hospitals, whose facilities and services are available to the public. Includes days in hospital and nursing home units.

Average Daily Census in Community Hospitals in 2006

National Average = 537,990 Inpatients*

ALPHA ORDER

RANK	STATE	INPATIENTS
18	Alabama	9,745
50	Alaska	836
24	Arizona	8,283
32	Arkansas	5,324
2	California	50,077
30	Colorado	5,930
28	Connecticut	6,311
46	Delaware	1,834
4	Florida	34,063
9	Georgia	17,045
41	Hawaii	2,306
45	Idaho	1,858
6	Illinois	22,115
17	Indiana	10,415
29	Iowa	6,212
31	Kansas	5,546
20	Kentucky	8,874
19	Louisiana	9,743
40	Maine	2,333
22	Maryland	8,678
13	Massachusetts	12,143
8	Michigan	17,110
16	Minnesota	10,837
25	Mississippi	7,392
15	Missouri	11,868
38	Montana	2,672
33	Nebraska	4,565
36	Nevada	3,582
47	New Hampshire	1,765
11	New Jersey	15,987
43	New Mexico	2,088
1	New York	50,715
10	North Carolina	16,800
42	North Dakota	2,089
7	Ohio	21,212
27	Oklahoma	6,322
35	Oregon	4,132
5	Pennsylvania	27,700
44	Rhode Island	1,865
23	South Carolina	8,448
37	South Dakota	2,802
12	Tennessee	13,169
3	Texas	35,740
39	Utah	2,654
49	Vermont	898
14	Virginia	12,099
26	Washington	6,813
34	West Virginia	4,362
21	Wisconsin	8,795
48	Wyoming	1,154

RANK ORDER

RANK	STATE	INPATIENTS
1	New York	50,715
2	California	50,077
3	Texas	35,740
4	Florida	34,063
5	Pennsylvania	27,700
6	Illinois	22,115
7	Ohio	21,212
8	Michigan	17,110
9	Georgia	17,045
10	North Carolina	16,800
11	New Jersey	15,987
12	Tennessee	13,169
13	Massachusetts	12,143
14	Virginia	12,099
15	Missouri	11,868
16	Minnesota	10,837
17	Indiana	10,415
18	Alabama	9,745
19	Louisiana	9,743
20	Kentucky	8,874
21	Wisconsin	8,795
22	Maryland	8,678
23	South Carolina	8,448
24	Arizona	8,283
25	Mississippi	7,392
26	Washington	6,813
27	Oklahoma	6,322
28	Connecticut	6,311
29	Iowa	6,212
30	Colorado	5,930
31	Kansas	5,546
32	Arkansas	5,324
33	Nebraska	4,565
34	West Virginia	4,362
35	Oregon	4,132
36	Nevada	3,582
37	South Dakota	2,802
38	Montana	2,672
39	Utah	2,654
40	Maine	2,333
41	Hawaii	2,306
42	North Dakota	2,089
43	New Mexico	2,088
44	Rhode Island	1,865
45	Idaho	1,858
46	Delaware	1,834
47	New Hampshire	1,765
48	Wyoming	1,154
49	Vermont	898
50	Alaska	836

District of Columbia	2,685

Source: CQ Press using data from American Hospital Association (Chicago, IL)
  "Hospital Statistics" (2008 edition)
*Average total of inpatients receiving care in all nonfederal short-term general and other special hospitals, whose facilities and services are available to the public. Excludes newborns.

Average Stay in Community Hospitals in 2006

National Average = 5.6 Days*

ALPHA ORDER				RANK ORDER		
RANK	STATE	DAYS		RANK	STATE	DAYS
33	Alabama	5.2		1	South Dakota	10.5
17	Alaska	5.8		2	Montana	9.1
47	Arizona	4.5		3	North Dakota	8.6
33	Arkansas	5.2		4	Wyoming	8.0
27	California	5.3		5	Nebraska	7.7
40	Colorado	5.1		6	Hawaii	7.5
18	Connecticut	5.7		7	New York	7.2
11	Delaware	6.4		8	Georgia	6.5
33	Florida	5.2		8	Mississippi	6.5
8	Georgia	6.5		8	Vermont	6.5
6	Hawaii	7.5		11	Delaware	6.4
44	Idaho	4.8		12	Iowa	6.2
40	Illinois	5.1		12	Minnesota	6.2
33	Indiana	5.2		14	Kansas	6.1
12	Iowa	6.2		15	North Carolina	6.0
14	Kansas	6.1		16	South Carolina	5.9
27	Kentucky	5.3		17	Alaska	5.8
18	Louisiana	5.7		18	Connecticut	5.7
22	Maine	5.6		18	Louisiana	5.7
46	Maryland	4.6		18	Virginia	5.7
27	Massachusetts	5.3		18	West Virginia	5.7
33	Michigan	5.2		22	Maine	5.6
12	Minnesota	6.2		22	Tennessee	5.6
8	Mississippi	6.5		24	New Hampshire	5.4
33	Missouri	5.2		24	Pennsylvania	5.4
2	Montana	9.1		24	Rhode Island	5.4
5	Nebraska	7.7		27	California	5.3
27	Nevada	5.3		27	Kentucky	5.3
24	New Hampshire	5.4		27	Massachusetts	5.3
27	New Jersey	5.3		27	Nevada	5.3
45	New Mexico	4.7		27	New Jersey	5.3
7	New York	7.2		27	Wisconsin	5.3
15	North Carolina	6.0		33	Alabama	5.2
3	North Dakota	8.6		33	Arkansas	5.2
43	Ohio	5.0		33	Florida	5.2
40	Oklahoma	5.1		33	Indiana	5.2
49	Oregon	4.4		33	Michigan	5.2
24	Pennsylvania	5.4		33	Missouri	5.2
24	Rhode Island	5.4		33	Texas	5.2
16	South Carolina	5.9		40	Colorado	5.1
1	South Dakota	10.5		40	Illinois	5.1
22	Tennessee	5.6		40	Oklahoma	5.1
33	Texas	5.2		43	Ohio	5.0
49	Utah	4.4		44	Idaho	4.8
8	Vermont	6.5		45	New Mexico	4.7
18	Virginia	5.7		46	Maryland	4.6
47	Washington	4.5		47	Arizona	4.5
18	West Virginia	5.7		47	Washington	4.5
27	Wisconsin	5.3		49	Oregon	4.4
4	Wyoming	8.0		49	Utah	4.4
					District of Columbia	7.0

Source: American Hospital Association (Chicago, IL)
   "Hospital Statistics" (2008 edition)
*All nonfederal short-term general and other special hospitals, whose facilities and services are available to the public.

Occupancy Rate in Community Hospitals in 2006

National Rate = 67.0% of Community Hospital Beds Occupied*

ALPHA ORDER

RANK	STATE	PERCENT
31	Alabama	62.3
50	Alaska	53.9
15	Arizona	69.3
45	Arkansas	57.2
12	California	71.5
31	Colorado	62.3
3	Connecticut	79.0
1	Delaware	85.8
20	Florida	66.2
16	Georgia	68.8
5	Hawaii	77.7
47	Idaho	56.3
25	Illinois	64.7
44	Indiana	57.6
39	Iowa	59.2
49	Kansas	55.4
36	Kentucky	60.9
35	Louisiana	61.4
19	Maine	66.9
6	Maryland	75.6
7	Massachusetts	74.3
21	Michigan	65.9
17	Minnesota	68.4
46	Mississippi	57.0
27	Missouri	62.8
22	Montana	65.3
34	Nebraska	61.9
8	Nevada	74.2
28	New Hampshire	62.5
9	New Jersey	72.4
39	New Mexico	59.2
2	New York	79.8
10	North Carolina	71.7
41	North Dakota	58.8
26	Ohio	64.6
42	Oklahoma	58.7
28	Oregon	62.5
13	Pennsylvania	70.0
4	Rhode Island	77.9
10	South Carolina	71.7
23	South Dakota	64.8
23	Tennessee	64.8
37	Texas	60.6
43	Utah	58.6
17	Vermont	68.4
13	Virginia	70.0
30	Washington	62.4
37	West Virginia	60.6
31	Wisconsin	62.3
48	Wyoming	56.1

RANK ORDER

RANK	STATE	PERCENT
1	Delaware	85.8
2	New York	79.8
3	Connecticut	79.0
4	Rhode Island	77.9
5	Hawaii	77.7
6	Maryland	75.6
7	Massachusetts	74.3
8	Nevada	74.2
9	New Jersey	72.4
10	North Carolina	71.7
10	South Carolina	71.7
12	California	71.5
13	Pennsylvania	70.0
13	Virginia	70.0
15	Arizona	69.3
16	Georgia	68.8
17	Minnesota	68.4
17	Vermont	68.4
19	Maine	66.9
20	Florida	66.2
21	Michigan	65.9
22	Montana	65.3
23	South Dakota	64.8
23	Tennessee	64.8
25	Illinois	64.7
26	Ohio	64.6
27	Missouri	62.8
28	New Hampshire	62.5
28	Oregon	62.5
30	Washington	62.4
31	Alabama	62.3
31	Colorado	62.3
31	Wisconsin	62.3
34	Nebraska	61.9
35	Louisiana	61.4
36	Kentucky	60.9
37	Texas	60.6
37	West Virginia	60.6
39	Iowa	59.2
39	New Mexico	59.2
41	North Dakota	58.8
42	Oklahoma	58.7
43	Utah	58.6
44	Indiana	57.6
45	Arkansas	57.2
46	Mississippi	57.0
47	Idaho	56.3
48	Wyoming	56.1
49	Kansas	55.4
50	Alaska	53.9

District of Columbia 74.6

Source: CQ Press using data from American Hospital Association (Chicago, IL)
    "Hospital Statistics" (2008 edition)
*Average daily census compared to number of community hospital beds.

Outpatient Visits to Community Hospitals in 2006

National Total = 599,553,025 Visits*

ALPHA ORDER

RANK	STATE	VISITS	% of USA
24	Alabama	8,023,354	1.3%
47	Alaska	1,775,920	0.3%
28	Arizona	6,555,635	1.1%
33	Arkansas	5,085,474	0.8%
2	California	53,938,435	9.0%
26	Colorado	7,264,370	1.2%
25	Connecticut	7,779,014	1.3%
46	Delaware	1,839,908	0.3%
8	Florida	22,759,029	3.8%
14	Georgia	13,782,727	2.3%
45	Hawaii	1,883,414	0.3%
41	Idaho	2,703,605	0.5%
6	Illinois	29,564,619	4.9%
12	Indiana	16,520,457	2.8%
19	Iowa	10,295,093	1.7%
30	Kansas	6,146,257	1.0%
22	Kentucky	8,815,306	1.5%
21	Louisiana	9,861,651	1.6%
37	Maine	4,205,349	0.7%
27	Maryland	7,007,817	1.2%
9	Massachusetts	19,543,928	3.3%
7	Michigan	28,125,103	4.7%
20	Minnesota	10,109,186	1.7%
36	Mississippi	4,218,371	0.7%
13	Missouri	16,338,186	2.7%
40	Montana	2,901,878	0.5%
38	Nebraska	4,049,105	0.7%
44	Nevada	2,387,808	0.4%
39	New Hampshire	3,871,017	0.6%
11	New Jersey	16,991,185	2.8%
35	New Mexico	4,344,119	0.7%
1	New York	54,029,410	9.0%
10	North Carolina	17,212,819	2.9%
49	North Dakota	1,709,284	0.3%
4	Ohio	32,686,517	5.5%
32	Oklahoma	5,334,806	0.9%
23	Oregon	8,257,876	1.4%
3	Pennsylvania	35,710,639	6.0%
43	Rhode Island	2,440,623	0.4%
31	South Carolina	6,093,696	1.0%
48	South Dakota	1,772,779	0.3%
17	Tennessee	10,861,884	1.8%
5	Texas	31,939,048	5.3%
34	Utah	4,981,695	0.8%
42	Vermont	2,500,721	0.4%
15	Virginia	13,652,744	2.3%
18	Washington	10,384,164	1.7%
29	West Virginia	6,212,146	1.0%
16	Wisconsin	12,512,050	2.1%
50	Wyoming	963,840	0.2%

RANK ORDER

RANK	STATE	VISITS	% of USA
1	New York	54,029,410	9.0%
2	California	53,938,435	9.0%
3	Pennsylvania	35,710,639	6.0%
4	Ohio	32,686,517	5.5%
5	Texas	31,939,048	5.3%
6	Illinois	29,564,619	4.9%
7	Michigan	28,125,103	4.7%
8	Florida	22,759,029	3.8%
9	Massachusetts	19,543,928	3.3%
10	North Carolina	17,212,819	2.9%
11	New Jersey	16,991,185	2.8%
12	Indiana	16,520,457	2.8%
13	Missouri	16,338,186	2.7%
14	Georgia	13,782,727	2.3%
15	Virginia	13,652,744	2.3%
16	Wisconsin	12,512,050	2.1%
17	Tennessee	10,861,884	1.8%
18	Washington	10,384,164	1.7%
19	Iowa	10,295,093	1.7%
20	Minnesota	10,109,186	1.7%
21	Louisiana	9,861,651	1.6%
22	Kentucky	8,815,306	1.5%
23	Oregon	8,257,876	1.4%
24	Alabama	8,023,354	1.3%
25	Connecticut	7,779,014	1.3%
26	Colorado	7,264,370	1.2%
27	Maryland	7,007,817	1.2%
28	Arizona	6,555,635	1.1%
29	West Virginia	6,212,146	1.0%
30	Kansas	6,146,257	1.0%
31	South Carolina	6,093,696	1.0%
32	Oklahoma	5,334,806	0.9%
33	Arkansas	5,085,474	0.8%
34	Utah	4,981,695	0.8%
35	New Mexico	4,344,119	0.7%
36	Mississippi	4,218,371	0.7%
37	Maine	4,205,349	0.7%
38	Nebraska	4,049,105	0.7%
39	New Hampshire	3,871,017	0.6%
40	Montana	2,901,878	0.5%
41	Idaho	2,703,605	0.5%
42	Vermont	2,500,721	0.4%
43	Rhode Island	2,440,623	0.4%
44	Nevada	2,387,808	0.4%
45	Hawaii	1,883,414	0.3%
46	Delaware	1,839,908	0.3%
47	Alaska	1,775,920	0.3%
48	South Dakota	1,772,779	0.3%
49	North Dakota	1,709,284	0.3%
50	Wyoming	963,840	0.2%
	District of Columbia	1,608,964	0.3%

Source: American Hospital Association (Chicago, IL)
    "Hospital Statistics" (2008 edition)
*All nonfederal short-term general and other special hospitals, whose facilities and services are available to the public. Includes emergency and other visits.

Emergency Outpatient Visits to Community Hospitals in 2006

National Total = 118,374,029 Visits*

<u>ALPHA ORDER</u>

RANK	STATE	VISITS	% of USA
18	Alabama	2,192,221	1.9%
39	Alaska	610,324	0.5%
23	Arizona	2,073,320	1.8%
30	Arkansas	1,267,198	1.1%
1	California	10,276,370	8.7%
28	Colorado	1,496,363	1.3%
29	Connecticut	1,463,125	1.2%
44	Delaware	382,935	0.3%
4	Florida	7,165,036	6.1%
10	Georgia	3,629,453	3.1%
45	Hawaii	339,863	0.3%
42	Idaho	511,381	0.4%
7	Illinois	5,079,148	4.3%
15	Indiana	2,704,727	2.3%
33	Iowa	1,122,636	0.9%
34	Kansas	972,761	0.8%
19	Kentucky	2,191,969	1.9%
21	Louisiana	2,096,962	1.8%
37	Maine	757,685	0.6%
17	Maryland	2,299,181	1.9%
12	Massachusetts	3,139,255	2.7%
8	Michigan	4,326,912	3.7%
25	Minnesota	1,711,528	1.4%
26	Mississippi	1,650,523	1.4%
16	Missouri	2,641,586	2.2%
46	Montana	333,504	0.3%
41	Nebraska	551,914	0.5%
38	Nevada	697,906	0.6%
40	New Hampshire	604,317	0.5%
11	New Jersey	3,256,298	2.8%
36	New Mexico	777,671	0.7%
3	New York	7,924,843	6.7%
9	North Carolina	3,849,736	3.3%
47	North Dakota	263,144	0.2%
5	Ohio	5,840,398	4.9%
27	Oklahoma	1,554,914	1.3%
31	Oregon	1,250,008	1.1%
6	Pennsylvania	5,583,228	4.7%
43	Rhode Island	466,720	0.4%
24	South Carolina	1,893,605	1.6%
49	South Dakota	222,244	0.2%
14	Tennessee	2,806,111	2.4%
2	Texas	8,291,213	7.0%
35	Utah	789,653	0.7%
48	Vermont	260,429	0.2%
13	Virginia	3,060,052	2.6%
20	Washington	2,147,309	1.8%
32	West Virginia	1,137,535	1.0%
22	Wisconsin	2,091,172	1.8%
50	Wyoming	221,300	0.2%

<u>RANK ORDER</u>

RANK	STATE	VISITS	% of USA
1	California	10,276,370	8.7%
2	Texas	8,291,213	7.0%
3	New York	7,924,843	6.7%
4	Florida	7,165,036	6.1%
5	Ohio	5,840,398	4.9%
6	Pennsylvania	5,583,228	4.7%
7	Illinois	5,079,148	4.3%
8	Michigan	4,326,912	3.7%
9	North Carolina	3,849,736	3.3%
10	Georgia	3,629,453	3.1%
11	New Jersey	3,256,298	2.8%
12	Massachusetts	3,139,255	2.7%
13	Virginia	3,060,052	2.6%
14	Tennessee	2,806,111	2.4%
15	Indiana	2,704,727	2.3%
16	Missouri	2,641,586	2.2%
17	Maryland	2,299,181	1.9%
18	Alabama	2,192,221	1.9%
19	Kentucky	2,191,969	1.9%
20	Washington	2,147,309	1.8%
21	Louisiana	2,096,962	1.8%
22	Wisconsin	2,091,172	1.8%
23	Arizona	2,073,320	1.8%
24	South Carolina	1,893,605	1.6%
25	Minnesota	1,711,528	1.4%
26	Mississippi	1,650,523	1.4%
27	Oklahoma	1,554,914	1.3%
28	Colorado	1,496,363	1.3%
29	Connecticut	1,463,125	1.2%
30	Arkansas	1,267,198	1.1%
31	Oregon	1,250,008	1.1%
32	West Virginia	1,137,535	1.0%
33	Iowa	1,122,636	0.9%
34	Kansas	972,761	0.8%
35	Utah	789,653	0.7%
36	New Mexico	777,671	0.7%
37	Maine	757,685	0.6%
38	Nevada	697,906	0.6%
39	Alaska	610,324	0.5%
40	New Hampshire	604,317	0.5%
41	Nebraska	551,914	0.5%
42	Idaho	511,381	0.4%
43	Rhode Island	466,720	0.4%
44	Delaware	382,935	0.3%
45	Hawaii	339,863	0.3%
46	Montana	333,504	0.3%
47	North Dakota	263,144	0.2%
48	Vermont	260,429	0.2%
49	South Dakota	222,244	0.2%
50	Wyoming	221,300	0.2%
	District of Columbia	396,343	0.3%

Source: American Hospital Association (Chicago, IL)
"Hospital Statistics" (2008 edition)

*All nonfederal short-term general and other special hospitals, whose facilities and services are available to the public.

Medicare and Medicaid Certified Facilities in 2008

National Total = 266,529 Facilities*

ALPHA ORDER

RANK	STATE	FACILITIES	% of USA
18	Alabama	4,583	1.7%
48	Alaska	628	0.2%
19	Arizona	4,540	1.7%
32	Arkansas	2,892	1.1%
2	California	24,613	9.2%
28	Colorado	3,550	1.3%
30	Connecticut	3,310	1.2%
46	Delaware	895	0.3%
3	Florida	18,212	6.8%
9	Georgia	8,347	3.1%
45	Hawaii	979	0.4%
40	Idaho	1,354	0.5%
6	Illinois	11,513	4.3%
11	Indiana	6,800	2.6%
27	Iowa	4,012	1.5%
29	Kansas	3,449	1.3%
25	Kentucky	4,284	1.6%
16	Louisiana	5,659	2.1%
39	Maine	1,369	0.5%
20	Maryland	4,412	1.7%
17	Massachusetts	4,698	1.8%
8	Michigan	8,936	3.4%
21	Minnesota	4,362	1.6%
31	Mississippi	3,250	1.2%
13	Missouri	6,436	2.4%
43	Montana	1,011	0.4%
35	Nebraska	2,321	0.9%
38	Nevada	1,679	0.6%
41	New Hampshire	1,188	0.4%
12	New Jersey	6,521	2.4%
37	New Mexico	1,723	0.6%
4	New York	12,718	4.8%
10	North Carolina	7,993	3.0%
47	North Dakota	893	0.3%
5	Ohio	12,200	4.6%
24	Oklahoma	4,296	1.6%
33	Oregon	2,784	1.0%
7	Pennsylvania	10,322	3.9%
44	Rhode Island	981	0.4%
22	South Carolina	4,310	1.6%
42	South Dakota	1,163	0.4%
14	Tennessee	5,989	2.2%
1	Texas	25,127	9.4%
36	Utah	1,779	0.7%
49	Vermont	590	0.2%
15	Virginia	5,844	2.2%
26	Washington	4,173	1.6%
34	West Virginia	2,331	0.9%
23	Wisconsin	4,303	1.6%
50	Wyoming	535	0.2%

RANK ORDER

RANK	STATE	FACILITIES	% of USA
1	Texas	25,127	9.4%
2	California	24,613	9.2%
3	Florida	18,212	6.8%
4	New York	12,718	4.8%
5	Ohio	12,200	4.6%
6	Illinois	11,513	4.3%
7	Pennsylvania	10,322	3.9%
8	Michigan	8,936	3.4%
9	Georgia	8,347	3.1%
10	North Carolina	7,993	3.0%
11	Indiana	6,800	2.6%
12	New Jersey	6,521	2.4%
13	Missouri	6,436	2.4%
14	Tennessee	5,989	2.2%
15	Virginia	5,844	2.2%
16	Louisiana	5,659	2.1%
17	Massachusetts	4,698	1.8%
18	Alabama	4,583	1.7%
19	Arizona	4,540	1.7%
20	Maryland	4,412	1.7%
21	Minnesota	4,362	1.6%
22	South Carolina	4,310	1.6%
23	Wisconsin	4,303	1.6%
24	Oklahoma	4,296	1.6%
25	Kentucky	4,284	1.6%
26	Washington	4,173	1.6%
27	Iowa	4,012	1.5%
28	Colorado	3,550	1.3%
29	Kansas	3,449	1.3%
30	Connecticut	3,310	1.2%
31	Mississippi	3,250	1.2%
32	Arkansas	2,892	1.1%
33	Oregon	2,784	1.0%
34	West Virginia	2,331	0.9%
35	Nebraska	2,321	0.9%
36	Utah	1,779	0.7%
37	New Mexico	1,723	0.6%
38	Nevada	1,679	0.6%
39	Maine	1,369	0.5%
40	Idaho	1,354	0.5%
41	New Hampshire	1,188	0.4%
42	South Dakota	1,163	0.4%
43	Montana	1,011	0.4%
44	Rhode Island	981	0.4%
45	Hawaii	979	0.4%
46	Delaware	895	0.3%
47	North Dakota	893	0.3%
48	Alaska	628	0.2%
49	Vermont	590	0.2%
50	Wyoming	535	0.2%
	District of Columbia	672	0.3%

Source: U.S. Department of Health and Human Services, Centers for Medicare and Medicaid Services
    OSCAR Report 10 (January 08, 2008)
*Certified by CMS to participate in the Medicare/Medicaid programs. All provider groups including hospitals, home health agencies, rural health centers, community mental health centers, nursing facilities, outpatient physical therapy facilities, hospices, and laboratories. National total does not include 1,460 certified facilities in U.S. territories.

Medicare and Medicaid Certified Hospitals in 2008

National Total = 6,102 Hospitals*

ALPHA ORDER

RANK	STATE	HOSPITALS	% of USA
19	Alabama	128	2.1%
47	Alaska	25	0.4%
27	Arizona	100	1.6%
26	Arkansas	103	1.7%
2	California	421	6.9%
30	Colorado	93	1.5%
42	Connecticut	45	0.7%
50	Delaware	11	0.2%
5	Florida	238	3.9%
10	Georgia	178	2.9%
46	Hawaii	27	0.4%
39	Idaho	49	0.8%
8	Illinois	211	3.5%
12	Indiana	157	2.6%
20	Iowa	122	2.0%
11	Kansas	159	2.6%
21	Kentucky	120	2.0%
6	Louisiana	230	3.8%
42	Maine	45	0.7%
34	Maryland	64	1.0%
24	Massachusetts	114	1.9%
9	Michigan	179	2.9%
15	Minnesota	146	2.4%
22	Mississippi	116	1.9%
16	Missouri	144	2.4%
34	Montana	64	1.0%
29	Nebraska	96	1.6%
41	Nevada	47	0.8%
44	New Hampshire	30	0.5%
25	New Jersey	108	1.8%
37	New Mexico	50	0.8%
3	New York	241	3.9%
18	North Carolina	133	2.2%
37	North Dakota	50	0.8%
7	Ohio	219	3.6%
13	Oklahoma	154	2.5%
36	Oregon	60	1.0%
4	Pennsylvania	239	3.9%
48	Rhode Island	15	0.2%
31	South Carolina	79	1.3%
33	South Dakota	65	1.1%
14	Tennessee	152	2.5%
1	Texas	544	8.9%
40	Utah	48	0.8%
48	Vermont	15	0.2%
23	Virginia	115	1.9%
27	Washington	100	1.6%
32	West Virginia	66	1.1%
16	Wisconsin	144	2.4%
45	Wyoming	29	0.5%

RANK ORDER

RANK	STATE	HOSPITALS	% of USA
1	Texas	544	8.9%
2	California	421	6.9%
3	New York	241	3.9%
4	Pennsylvania	239	3.9%
5	Florida	238	3.9%
6	Louisiana	230	3.8%
7	Ohio	219	3.6%
8	Illinois	211	3.5%
9	Michigan	179	2.9%
10	Georgia	178	2.9%
11	Kansas	159	2.6%
12	Indiana	157	2.6%
13	Oklahoma	154	2.5%
14	Tennessee	152	2.5%
15	Minnesota	146	2.4%
16	Missouri	144	2.4%
16	Wisconsin	144	2.4%
18	North Carolina	133	2.2%
19	Alabama	128	2.1%
20	Iowa	122	2.0%
21	Kentucky	120	2.0%
22	Mississippi	116	1.9%
23	Virginia	115	1.9%
24	Massachusetts	114	1.9%
25	New Jersey	108	1.8%
26	Arkansas	103	1.7%
27	Arizona	100	1.6%
27	Washington	100	1.6%
29	Nebraska	96	1.6%
30	Colorado	93	1.5%
31	South Carolina	79	1.3%
32	West Virginia	66	1.1%
33	South Dakota	65	1.1%
34	Maryland	64	1.0%
34	Montana	64	1.0%
36	Oregon	60	1.0%
37	New Mexico	50	0.8%
37	North Dakota	50	0.8%
39	Idaho	49	0.8%
40	Utah	48	0.8%
41	Nevada	47	0.8%
42	Connecticut	45	0.7%
42	Maine	45	0.7%
44	New Hampshire	30	0.5%
45	Wyoming	29	0.5%
46	Hawaii	27	0.4%
47	Alaska	25	0.4%
48	Rhode Island	15	0.2%
48	Vermont	15	0.2%
50	Delaware	11	0.2%
	District of Columbia	14	0.2%

Source: U.S. Department of Health and Human Services, Centers for Medicare and Medicaid Services
OSCAR Report 10 (January 08, 2008)

*Certified by CMS to participate in the Medicare/Medicaid programs. Excludes licensed facilities that do not accept federal funding and facilities managed by the Department of Veterans Affairs. National total does not include 63 certified hospitals in U.S. territories.

Beds in Medicare and Medicaid Certified Hospitals in 2008

National Total = 922,790 Beds*

ALPHA ORDER

RANK	STATE	BEDS	% of USA
16	Alabama	19,875	2.2%
49	Alaska	1,571	0.2%
24	Arizona	14,676	1.6%
31	Arkansas	10,396	1.1%
1	California	79,291	8.6%
28	Colorado	12,391	1.3%
32	Connecticut	10,199	1.1%
47	Delaware	2,520	0.3%
4	Florida	57,423	6.2%
11	Georgia	25,137	2.7%
46	Hawaii	2,718	0.3%
43	Idaho	3,301	0.4%
5	Illinois	44,493	4.8%
18	Indiana	18,708	2.0%
30	Iowa	11,174	1.2%
29	Kansas	11,414	1.2%
20	Kentucky	17,333	1.9%
14	Louisiana	21,183	2.3%
39	Maine	4,183	0.5%
21	Maryland	15,837	1.7%
17	Massachusetts	19,864	2.2%
9	Michigan	28,795	3.1%
22	Minnesota	15,593	1.7%
26	Mississippi	13,334	1.4%
13	Missouri	23,544	2.6%
45	Montana	3,099	0.3%
35	Nebraska	6,479	0.7%
36	Nevada	5,911	0.6%
41	New Hampshire	3,537	0.4%
8	New Jersey	29,728	3.2%
38	New Mexico	4,557	0.5%
2	New York	69,995	7.6%
10	North Carolina	25,461	2.8%
44	North Dakota	3,288	0.4%
6	Ohio	43,695	4.7%
23	Oklahoma	14,749	1.6%
34	Oregon	7,633	0.8%
7	Pennsylvania	35,920	3.9%
40	Rhode Island	3,657	0.4%
27	South Carolina	12,826	1.4%
42	South Dakota	3,400	0.4%
12	Tennessee	24,616	2.7%
3	Texas	66,301	7.2%
37	Utah	4,960	0.5%
48	Vermont	1,808	0.2%
15	Virginia	20,187	2.2%
25	Washington	13,479	1.5%
33	West Virginia	9,140	1.0%
19	Wisconsin	17,568	1.9%
50	Wyoming	1,474	0.2%

RANK ORDER

RANK	STATE	BEDS	% of USA
1	California	79,291	8.6%
2	New York	69,995	7.6%
3	Texas	66,301	7.2%
4	Florida	57,423	6.2%
5	Illinois	44,493	4.8%
6	Ohio	43,695	4.7%
7	Pennsylvania	35,920	3.9%
8	New Jersey	29,728	3.2%
9	Michigan	28,795	3.1%
10	North Carolina	25,461	2.8%
11	Georgia	25,137	2.7%
12	Tennessee	24,616	2.7%
13	Missouri	23,544	2.6%
14	Louisiana	21,183	2.3%
15	Virginia	20,187	2.2%
16	Alabama	19,875	2.2%
17	Massachusetts	19,864	2.2%
18	Indiana	18,708	2.0%
19	Wisconsin	17,568	1.9%
20	Kentucky	17,333	1.9%
21	Maryland	15,837	1.7%
22	Minnesota	15,593	1.7%
23	Oklahoma	14,749	1.6%
24	Arizona	14,676	1.6%
25	Washington	13,479	1.5%
26	Mississippi	13,334	1.4%
27	South Carolina	12,826	1.4%
28	Colorado	12,391	1.3%
29	Kansas	11,414	1.2%
30	Iowa	11,174	1.2%
31	Arkansas	10,396	1.1%
32	Connecticut	10,199	1.1%
33	West Virginia	9,140	1.0%
34	Oregon	7,633	0.8%
35	Nebraska	6,479	0.7%
36	Nevada	5,911	0.6%
37	Utah	4,960	0.5%
38	New Mexico	4,557	0.5%
39	Maine	4,183	0.5%
40	Rhode Island	3,657	0.4%
41	New Hampshire	3,537	0.4%
42	South Dakota	3,400	0.4%
43	Idaho	3,301	0.4%
44	North Dakota	3,288	0.4%
45	Montana	3,099	0.3%
46	Hawaii	2,718	0.3%
47	Delaware	2,520	0.3%
48	Vermont	1,808	0.2%
49	Alaska	1,571	0.2%
50	Wyoming	1,474	0.2%
	District of Columbia	4,369	0.5%

Source: U.S. Department of Health and Human Services, Centers for Medicare and Medicaid Services
    OSCAR Database (January 08, 2008)

*Beds in hospitals certified by CMS to participate in the Medicare/Medicaid programs. Excludes licensed facilities that do not accept federal funding and facilities managed by the Department of Veterans Affairs. National total does not include 11,224 beds in U.S. territories.

Medicare and Medicaid Certified Children's Hospitals in 2008

National Total = 78 Hospitals*

ALPHA ORDER

RANK	STATE	HOSPITALS	% of USA
9	Alabama	2	2.6%
33	Alaska	0	0.0%
9	Arizona	2	2.6%
21	Arkansas	1	1.3%
1	California	10	12.8%
21	Colorado	1	1.3%
21	Connecticut	1	1.3%
21	Delaware	1	1.3%
9	Florida	2	2.6%
9	Georgia	2	2.6%
21	Hawaii	1	1.3%
33	Idaho	0	0.0%
9	Illinois	2	2.6%
21	Indiana	1	1.3%
33	Iowa	0	0.0%
21	Kansas	1	1.3%
33	Kentucky	0	0.0%
21	Louisiana	1	1.3%
33	Maine	0	0.0%
9	Maryland	2	2.6%
9	Massachusetts	2	2.6%
21	Michigan	1	1.3%
5	Minnesota	3	3.8%
33	Mississippi	0	0.0%
5	Missouri	3	3.8%
33	Montana	0	0.0%
9	Nebraska	2	2.6%
33	Nevada	0	0.0%
33	New Hampshire	0	0.0%
9	New Jersey	2	2.6%
33	New Mexico	0	0.0%
21	New York	1	1.3%
33	North Carolina	0	0.0%
33	North Dakota	0	0.0%
3	Ohio	6	7.7%
9	Oklahoma	2	2.6%
33	Oregon	0	0.0%
4	Pennsylvania	5	6.4%
33	Rhode Island	0	0.0%
33	South Carolina	0	0.0%
21	South Dakota	1	1.3%
9	Tennessee	2	2.6%
2	Texas	8	10.3%
21	Utah	1	1.3%
33	Vermont	0	0.0%
5	Virginia	3	3.8%
9	Washington	2	2.6%
33	West Virginia	0	0.0%
5	Wisconsin	3	3.8%
33	Wyoming	0	0.0%

RANK ORDER

RANK	STATE	HOSPITALS	% of USA
1	California	10	12.8%
2	Texas	8	10.3%
3	Ohio	6	7.7%
4	Pennsylvania	5	6.4%
5	Minnesota	3	3.8%
5	Missouri	3	3.8%
5	Virginia	3	3.8%
5	Wisconsin	3	3.8%
9	Alabama	2	2.6%
9	Arizona	2	2.6%
9	Florida	2	2.6%
9	Georgia	2	2.6%
9	Illinois	2	2.6%
9	Maryland	2	2.6%
9	Massachusetts	2	2.6%
9	Nebraska	2	2.6%
9	New Jersey	2	2.6%
9	Oklahoma	2	2.6%
9	Tennessee	2	2.6%
9	Washington	2	2.6%
21	Arkansas	1	1.3%
21	Colorado	1	1.3%
21	Connecticut	1	1.3%
21	Delaware	1	1.3%
21	Hawaii	1	1.3%
21	Indiana	1	1.3%
21	Kansas	1	1.3%
21	Louisiana	1	1.3%
21	Michigan	1	1.3%
21	New York	1	1.3%
21	South Dakota	1	1.3%
21	Utah	1	1.3%
33	Alaska	0	0.0%
33	Idaho	0	0.0%
33	Iowa	0	0.0%
33	Kentucky	0	0.0%
33	Maine	0	0.0%
33	Mississippi	0	0.0%
33	Montana	0	0.0%
33	Nevada	0	0.0%
33	New Hampshire	0	0.0%
33	New Mexico	0	0.0%
33	North Carolina	0	0.0%
33	North Dakota	0	0.0%
33	Oregon	0	0.0%
33	Rhode Island	0	0.0%
33	South Carolina	0	0.0%
33	Vermont	0	0.0%
33	West Virginia	0	0.0%
33	Wyoming	0	0.0%
	District of Columbia	1	1.3%

Source: U.S. Department of Health and Human Services, Centers for Medicare and Medicaid Services
OSCAR Report 10 (January 08, 2008)

*Certified by CMS to participate in the Medicare/Medicaid programs. National total does not include one facility in U.S. territories.
Excludes licensed facilities that do not accept federal funding and facilities managed by the Department of Veterans Affairs.

Beds in Medicare and Medicaid Certified Children's Hospitals in 2008

National Total = 12,068 Beds*

ALPHA ORDER

RANK	STATE	BEDS	% of USA
6	Alabama	434	3.6%
33	Alaska	0	0.0%
17	Arizona	250	2.1%
13	Arkansas	280	2.3%
1	California	1,665	13.8%
16	Colorado	253	2.1%
27	Connecticut	129	1.1%
24	Delaware	180	1.5%
8	Florida	424	3.5%
5	Georgia	483	4.0%
20	Hawaii	201	1.7%
33	Idaho	0	0.0%
10	Illinois	339	2.8%
32	Indiana	20	0.2%
33	Iowa	0	0.0%
31	Kansas	34	0.3%
33	Kentucky	0	0.0%
20	Louisiana	201	1.7%
33	Maine	0	0.0%
26	Maryland	150	1.2%
9	Massachusetts	421	3.5%
19	Michigan	228	1.9%
10	Minnesota	339	2.8%
33	Mississippi	0	0.0%
7	Missouri	432	3.6%
33	Montana	0	0.0%
22	Nebraska	200	1.7%
33	Nevada	0	0.0%
33	New Hampshire	0	0.0%
28	New Jersey	104	0.9%
33	New Mexico	0	0.0%
30	New York	92	0.8%
33	North Carolina	0	0.0%
33	North Dakota	0	0.0%
3	Ohio	1,322	11.0%
25	Oklahoma	160	1.3%
33	Oregon	0	0.0%
4	Pennsylvania	742	6.1%
33	Rhode Island	0	0.0%
33	South Carolina	0	0.0%
29	South Dakota	96	0.8%
23	Tennessee	181	1.5%
2	Texas	1,385	11.5%
18	Utah	232	1.9%
33	Vermont	0	0.0%
12	Virginia	296	2.5%
14	Washington	276	2.3%
33	West Virginia	0	0.0%
14	Wisconsin	276	2.3%
33	Wyoming	0	0.0%

RANK ORDER

RANK	STATE	BEDS	% of USA
1	California	1,665	13.8%
2	Texas	1,385	11.5%
3	Ohio	1,322	11.0%
4	Pennsylvania	742	6.1%
5	Georgia	483	4.0%
6	Alabama	434	3.6%
7	Missouri	432	3.6%
8	Florida	424	3.5%
9	Massachusetts	421	3.5%
10	Illinois	339	2.8%
10	Minnesota	339	2.8%
12	Virginia	296	2.5%
13	Arkansas	280	2.3%
14	Washington	276	2.3%
14	Wisconsin	276	2.3%
16	Colorado	253	2.1%
17	Arizona	250	2.1%
18	Utah	232	1.9%
19	Michigan	228	1.9%
20	Hawaii	201	1.7%
20	Louisiana	201	1.7%
22	Nebraska	200	1.7%
23	Tennessee	181	1.5%
24	Delaware	180	1.5%
25	Oklahoma	160	1.3%
26	Maryland	150	1.2%
27	Connecticut	129	1.1%
28	New Jersey	104	0.9%
29	South Dakota	96	0.8%
30	New York	92	0.8%
31	Kansas	34	0.3%
32	Indiana	20	0.2%
33	Alaska	0	0.0%
33	Idaho	0	0.0%
33	Iowa	0	0.0%
33	Kentucky	0	0.0%
33	Maine	0	0.0%
33	Mississippi	0	0.0%
33	Montana	0	0.0%
33	Nevada	0	0.0%
33	New Hampshire	0	0.0%
33	New Mexico	0	0.0%
33	North Carolina	0	0.0%
33	North Dakota	0	0.0%
33	Oregon	0	0.0%
33	Rhode Island	0	0.0%
33	South Carolina	0	0.0%
33	Vermont	0	0.0%
33	West Virginia	0	0.0%
33	Wyoming	0	0.0%
	District of Columbia	243	2.0%

Source: U.S. Department of Health and Human Services, Centers for Medicare and Medicaid Services
    OSCAR Database (January 08, 2008)

*Certified by CMS to participate in the Medicare/Medicaid programs. National total does not include 215 beds in one facility in U.S. territories. Excludes licensed facilities that do not accept federal funding and facilities managed by the Department of Veterans Affairs.

Medicare and Medicaid Certified Rehabilitation Hospitals in 2008

National Total = 219 Hospitals*

<u>ALPHA ORDER</u>

RANK	STATE	HOSPITALS	% of USA
8	Alabama	7	3.2%
40	Alaska	0	0.0%
11	Arizona	6	2.7%
5	Arkansas	8	3.7%
11	California	6	2.7%
22	Colorado	3	1.4%
30	Connecticut	1	0.5%
40	Delaware	0	0.0%
4	Florida	14	6.4%
22	Georgia	3	1.4%
30	Hawaii	1	0.5%
30	Idaho	1	0.5%
18	Illinois	4	1.8%
8	Indiana	7	3.2%
40	Iowa	0	0.0%
18	Kansas	4	1.8%
11	Kentucky	6	2.7%
2	Louisiana	22	10.0%
30	Maine	1	0.5%
26	Maryland	2	0.9%
5	Massachusetts	8	3.7%
18	Michigan	4	1.8%
30	Minnesota	1	0.5%
40	Mississippi	0	0.0%
18	Missouri	4	1.8%
40	Montana	0	0.0%
30	Nebraska	1	0.5%
22	Nevada	3	1.4%
26	New Hampshire	2	0.9%
5	New Jersey	8	3.7%
15	New Mexico	5	2.3%
40	New York	0	0.0%
26	North Carolina	2	0.9%
40	North Dakota	0	0.0%
22	Ohio	3	1.4%
26	Oklahoma	2	0.9%
40	Oregon	0	0.0%
3	Pennsylvania	18	8.2%
30	Rhode Island	1	0.5%
15	South Carolina	5	2.3%
40	South Dakota	0	0.0%
11	Tennessee	6	2.7%
1	Texas	34	15.5%
30	Utah	1	0.5%
40	Vermont	0	0.0%
8	Virginia	7	3.2%
30	Washington	1	0.5%
15	West Virginia	5	2.3%
30	Wisconsin	1	0.5%
40	Wyoming	0	0.0%

<u>RANK ORDER</u>

RANK	STATE	HOSPITALS	% of USA
1	Texas	34	15.5%
2	Louisiana	22	10.0%
3	Pennsylvania	18	8.2%
4	Florida	14	6.4%
5	Arkansas	8	3.7%
5	Massachusetts	8	3.7%
5	New Jersey	8	3.7%
8	Alabama	7	3.2%
8	Indiana	7	3.2%
8	Virginia	7	3.2%
11	Arizona	6	2.7%
11	California	6	2.7%
11	Kentucky	6	2.7%
11	Tennessee	6	2.7%
15	New Mexico	5	2.3%
15	South Carolina	5	2.3%
15	West Virginia	5	2.3%
18	Illinois	4	1.8%
18	Kansas	4	1.8%
18	Michigan	4	1.8%
18	Missouri	4	1.8%
22	Colorado	3	1.4%
22	Georgia	3	1.4%
22	Nevada	3	1.4%
22	Ohio	3	1.4%
26	Maryland	2	0.9%
26	New Hampshire	2	0.9%
26	North Carolina	2	0.9%
26	Oklahoma	2	0.9%
30	Connecticut	1	0.5%
30	Hawaii	1	0.5%
30	Idaho	1	0.5%
30	Maine	1	0.5%
30	Minnesota	1	0.5%
30	Nebraska	1	0.5%
30	Rhode Island	1	0.5%
30	Utah	1	0.5%
30	Washington	1	0.5%
30	Wisconsin	1	0.5%
40	Alaska	0	0.0%
40	Delaware	0	0.0%
40	Iowa	0	0.0%
40	Mississippi	0	0.0%
40	Montana	0	0.0%
40	New York	0	0.0%
40	North Dakota	0	0.0%
40	Oregon	0	0.0%
40	South Dakota	0	0.0%
40	Vermont	0	0.0%
40	Wyoming	0	0.0%
	District of Columbia	1	0.5%

Source: U.S. Department of Health and Human Services, Centers for Medicare and Medicaid Services
   OSCAR Database (January 08, 2008)

*Certified by CMS to participate in the Medicare/Medicaid programs. Excludes licensed facilities that do not accept federal funding and facilities managed by the Department of Veterans Affairs. National total does not include one certified hospital in U.S. territories.

Beds in Medicare and Medicaid Certified Rehabilitation Hospitals in 2008

National Total = 14,134 Beds*

ALPHA ORDER

RANK	STATE	BEDS	% of USA
10	Alabama	392	2.8%
40	Alaska	0	0.0%
13	Arizona	331	2.3%
7	Arkansas	463	3.3%
9	California	405	2.9%
21	Colorado	226	1.6%
37	Connecticut	60	0.4%
40	Delaware	0	0.0%
3	Florida	1,102	7.8%
26	Georgia	168	1.2%
31	Hawaii	100	0.7%
38	Idaho	56	0.4%
8	Illinois	448	3.2%
12	Indiana	336	2.4%
40	Iowa	0	0.0%
19	Kansas	257	1.8%
14	Kentucky	328	2.3%
6	Louisiana	578	4.1%
31	Maine	100	0.7%
27	Maryland	131	0.9%
4	Massachusetts	1,040	7.4%
20	Michigan	240	1.7%
39	Minnesota	15	0.1%
40	Mississippi	0	0.0%
17	Missouri	282	2.0%
40	Montana	0	0.0%
36	Nebraska	72	0.5%
25	Nevada	181	1.3%
28	New Hampshire	130	0.9%
5	New Jersey	756	5.3%
23	New Mexico	212	1.5%
40	New York	0	0.0%
22	North Carolina	213	1.5%
40	North Dakota	0	0.0%
24	Ohio	199	1.4%
29	Oklahoma	107	0.8%
40	Oregon	0	0.0%
2	Pennsylvania	1,502	10.6%
34	Rhode Island	82	0.6%
15	South Carolina	301	2.1%
40	South Dakota	0	0.0%
11	Tennessee	370	2.6%
1	Texas	1,966	13.9%
33	Utah	84	0.6%
40	Vermont	0	0.0%
16	Virginia	288	2.0%
30	Washington	102	0.7%
18	West Virginia	270	1.9%
35	Wisconsin	81	0.6%
40	Wyoming	0	0.0%

RANK ORDER

RANK	STATE	BEDS	% of USA
1	Texas	1,966	13.9%
2	Pennsylvania	1,502	10.6%
3	Florida	1,102	7.8%
4	Massachusetts	1,040	7.4%
5	New Jersey	756	5.3%
6	Louisiana	578	4.1%
7	Arkansas	463	3.3%
8	Illinois	448	3.2%
9	California	405	2.9%
10	Alabama	392	2.8%
11	Tennessee	370	2.6%
12	Indiana	336	2.4%
13	Arizona	331	2.3%
14	Kentucky	328	2.3%
15	South Carolina	301	2.1%
16	Virginia	288	2.0%
17	Missouri	282	2.0%
18	West Virginia	270	1.9%
19	Kansas	257	1.8%
20	Michigan	240	1.7%
21	Colorado	226	1.6%
22	North Carolina	213	1.5%
23	New Mexico	212	1.5%
24	Ohio	199	1.4%
25	Nevada	181	1.3%
26	Georgia	168	1.2%
27	Maryland	131	0.9%
28	New Hampshire	130	0.9%
29	Oklahoma	107	0.8%
30	Washington	102	0.7%
31	Hawaii	100	0.7%
31	Maine	100	0.7%
33	Utah	84	0.6%
34	Rhode Island	82	0.6%
35	Wisconsin	81	0.6%
36	Nebraska	72	0.5%
37	Connecticut	60	0.4%
38	Idaho	56	0.4%
39	Minnesota	15	0.1%
40	Alaska	0	0.0%
40	Delaware	0	0.0%
40	Iowa	0	0.0%
40	Mississippi	0	0.0%
40	Montana	0	0.0%
40	New York	0	0.0%
40	North Dakota	0	0.0%
40	Oregon	0	0.0%
40	South Dakota	0	0.0%
40	Vermont	0	0.0%
40	Wyoming	0	0.0%
	District of Columbia	160	1.1%

Source: U.S. Department of Health and Human Services, Centers for Medicare and Medicaid Services
    OSCAR Database (January 08, 2008)

*Beds in hospitals certified by CMS to participate in the Medicare/Medicaid programs. Excludes licensed facilities that do not accept federal funding and facilities managed by the Department of Veterans Affairs. National total does not include 32 beds in U.S. territories.

Medicare and Medicaid Certified Psychiatric Hospitals in 2008

National Total = 487 Psychiatric Hospitals*

<table>
<tr><td colspan="4">ALPHA ORDER</td><td colspan="4">RANK ORDER</td></tr>
<tr><td>RANK</td><td>STATE</td><td>HOSPITALS</td><td>% of USA</td><td>RANK</td><td>STATE</td><td>HOSPITALS</td><td>% of USA</td></tr>
<tr><td>16</td><td>Alabama</td><td>10</td><td>2.1%</td><td>1</td><td>Louisiana</td><td>35</td><td>7.2%</td></tr>
<tr><td>41</td><td>Alaska</td><td>2</td><td>0.4%</td><td>1</td><td>Texas</td><td>35</td><td>7.2%</td></tr>
<tr><td>25</td><td>Arizona</td><td>7</td><td>1.4%</td><td>3</td><td>California</td><td>31</td><td>6.4%</td></tr>
<tr><td>21</td><td>Arkansas</td><td>9</td><td>1.8%</td><td>4</td><td>New York</td><td>29</td><td>6.0%</td></tr>
<tr><td>3</td><td>California</td><td>31</td><td>6.4%</td><td>5</td><td>Pennsylvania</td><td>23</td><td>4.7%</td></tr>
<tr><td>25</td><td>Colorado</td><td>7</td><td>1.4%</td><td>6</td><td>Florida</td><td>21</td><td>4.3%</td></tr>
<tr><td>25</td><td>Connecticut</td><td>7</td><td>1.4%</td><td>7</td><td>Indiana</td><td>20</td><td>4.1%</td></tr>
<tr><td>33</td><td>Delaware</td><td>4</td><td>0.8%</td><td>8</td><td>Massachusetts</td><td>16</td><td>3.3%</td></tr>
<tr><td>6</td><td>Florida</td><td>21</td><td>4.3%</td><td>8</td><td>New Jersey</td><td>16</td><td>3.3%</td></tr>
<tr><td>13</td><td>Georgia</td><td>13</td><td>2.7%</td><td>8</td><td>Ohio</td><td>16</td><td>3.3%</td></tr>
<tr><td>48</td><td>Hawaii</td><td>1</td><td>0.2%</td><td>11</td><td>Illinois</td><td>14</td><td>2.9%</td></tr>
<tr><td>29</td><td>Idaho</td><td>5</td><td>1.0%</td><td>11</td><td>Missouri</td><td>14</td><td>2.9%</td></tr>
<tr><td>11</td><td>Illinois</td><td>14</td><td>2.9%</td><td>13</td><td>Georgia</td><td>13</td><td>2.7%</td></tr>
<tr><td>7</td><td>Indiana</td><td>20</td><td>4.1%</td><td>14</td><td>Kentucky</td><td>11</td><td>2.3%</td></tr>
<tr><td>33</td><td>Iowa</td><td>4</td><td>0.8%</td><td>14</td><td>Wisconsin</td><td>11</td><td>2.3%</td></tr>
<tr><td>33</td><td>Kansas</td><td>4</td><td>0.8%</td><td>16</td><td>Alabama</td><td>10</td><td>2.1%</td></tr>
<tr><td>14</td><td>Kentucky</td><td>11</td><td>2.3%</td><td>16</td><td>Michigan</td><td>10</td><td>2.1%</td></tr>
<tr><td>1</td><td>Louisiana</td><td>35</td><td>7.2%</td><td>16</td><td>Oklahoma</td><td>10</td><td>2.1%</td></tr>
<tr><td>33</td><td>Maine</td><td>4</td><td>0.8%</td><td>16</td><td>Tennessee</td><td>10</td><td>2.1%</td></tr>
<tr><td>21</td><td>Maryland</td><td>9</td><td>1.8%</td><td>16</td><td>Virginia</td><td>10</td><td>2.1%</td></tr>
<tr><td>8</td><td>Massachusetts</td><td>16</td><td>3.3%</td><td>21</td><td>Arkansas</td><td>9</td><td>1.8%</td></tr>
<tr><td>16</td><td>Michigan</td><td>10</td><td>2.1%</td><td>21</td><td>Maryland</td><td>9</td><td>1.8%</td></tr>
<tr><td>28</td><td>Minnesota</td><td>6</td><td>1.2%</td><td>21</td><td>North Carolina</td><td>9</td><td>1.8%</td></tr>
<tr><td>29</td><td>Mississippi</td><td>5</td><td>1.0%</td><td>24</td><td>South Carolina</td><td>8</td><td>1.6%</td></tr>
<tr><td>11</td><td>Missouri</td><td>14</td><td>2.9%</td><td>25</td><td>Arizona</td><td>7</td><td>1.4%</td></tr>
<tr><td>41</td><td>Montana</td><td>2</td><td>0.4%</td><td>25</td><td>Colorado</td><td>7</td><td>1.4%</td></tr>
<tr><td>33</td><td>Nebraska</td><td>4</td><td>0.8%</td><td>25</td><td>Connecticut</td><td>7</td><td>1.4%</td></tr>
<tr><td>29</td><td>Nevada</td><td>5</td><td>1.0%</td><td>28</td><td>Minnesota</td><td>6</td><td>1.2%</td></tr>
<tr><td>41</td><td>New Hampshire</td><td>2</td><td>0.4%</td><td>29</td><td>Idaho</td><td>5</td><td>1.0%</td></tr>
<tr><td>8</td><td>New Jersey</td><td>16</td><td>3.3%</td><td>29</td><td>Mississippi</td><td>5</td><td>1.0%</td></tr>
<tr><td>41</td><td>New Mexico</td><td>2</td><td>0.4%</td><td>29</td><td>Nevada</td><td>5</td><td>1.0%</td></tr>
<tr><td>4</td><td>New York</td><td>29</td><td>6.0%</td><td>29</td><td>Washington</td><td>5</td><td>1.0%</td></tr>
<tr><td>21</td><td>North Carolina</td><td>9</td><td>1.8%</td><td>33</td><td>Delaware</td><td>4</td><td>0.8%</td></tr>
<tr><td>39</td><td>North Dakota</td><td>3</td><td>0.6%</td><td>33</td><td>Iowa</td><td>4</td><td>0.8%</td></tr>
<tr><td>8</td><td>Ohio</td><td>16</td><td>3.3%</td><td>33</td><td>Kansas</td><td>4</td><td>0.8%</td></tr>
<tr><td>16</td><td>Oklahoma</td><td>10</td><td>2.1%</td><td>33</td><td>Maine</td><td>4</td><td>0.8%</td></tr>
<tr><td>41</td><td>Oregon</td><td>2</td><td>0.4%</td><td>33</td><td>Nebraska</td><td>4</td><td>0.8%</td></tr>
<tr><td>5</td><td>Pennsylvania</td><td>23</td><td>4.7%</td><td>33</td><td>West Virginia</td><td>4</td><td>0.8%</td></tr>
<tr><td>41</td><td>Rhode Island</td><td>2</td><td>0.4%</td><td>39</td><td>North Dakota</td><td>3</td><td>0.6%</td></tr>
<tr><td>24</td><td>South Carolina</td><td>8</td><td>1.6%</td><td>39</td><td>Utah</td><td>3</td><td>0.6%</td></tr>
<tr><td>48</td><td>South Dakota</td><td>1</td><td>0.2%</td><td>41</td><td>Alaska</td><td>2</td><td>0.4%</td></tr>
<tr><td>16</td><td>Tennessee</td><td>10</td><td>2.1%</td><td>41</td><td>Montana</td><td>2</td><td>0.4%</td></tr>
<tr><td>1</td><td>Texas</td><td>35</td><td>7.2%</td><td>41</td><td>New Hampshire</td><td>2</td><td>0.4%</td></tr>
<tr><td>39</td><td>Utah</td><td>3</td><td>0.6%</td><td>41</td><td>New Mexico</td><td>2</td><td>0.4%</td></tr>
<tr><td>48</td><td>Vermont</td><td>1</td><td>0.2%</td><td>41</td><td>Oregon</td><td>2</td><td>0.4%</td></tr>
<tr><td>16</td><td>Virginia</td><td>10</td><td>2.1%</td><td>41</td><td>Rhode Island</td><td>2</td><td>0.4%</td></tr>
<tr><td>29</td><td>Washington</td><td>5</td><td>1.0%</td><td>41</td><td>Wyoming</td><td>2</td><td>0.4%</td></tr>
<tr><td>33</td><td>West Virginia</td><td>4</td><td>0.8%</td><td>48</td><td>Hawaii</td><td>1</td><td>0.2%</td></tr>
<tr><td>14</td><td>Wisconsin</td><td>11</td><td>2.3%</td><td>48</td><td>South Dakota</td><td>1</td><td>0.2%</td></tr>
<tr><td>41</td><td>Wyoming</td><td>2</td><td>0.4%</td><td>48</td><td>Vermont</td><td>1</td><td>0.2%</td></tr>
<tr><td></td><td></td><td></td><td></td><td></td><td>District of Columbia</td><td>3</td><td>0.6%</td></tr>
</table>

Source: U.S. Department of Health and Human Services, Centers for Medicare and Medicaid Services
   OSCAR Report 10 (January 08, 2008)
*Certified by CMS to participate in the Medicare/Medicaid programs. Excludes licensed facilities that do not accept federal funding and facilities managed by the Department of Veterans Affairs. National total does not include four certified psychiatric hospitals in U.S. territories.

Beds in Medicare and Medicaid Certified Psychiatric Hospitals in 2008

National Total = 53,855 Beds*

ALPHA ORDER RANK	STATE	BEDS	% of USA	RANK ORDER RANK	STATE	BEDS	% of USA
26	Alabama	698	1.3%	1	New York	6,425	11.9%
45	Alaska	169	0.3%	2	Pennsylvania	3,487	6.5%
29	Arizona	556	1.0%	3	Texas	2,922	5.4%
23	Arkansas	849	1.6%	4	New Jersey	2,849	5.3%
6	California	2,349	4.4%	5	Florida	2,559	4.8%
25	Colorado	830	1.5%	6	California	2,349	4.4%
19	Connecticut	1,081	2.0%	7	North Carolina	2,276	4.2%
38	Delaware	307	0.6%	8	Maryland	2,006	3.7%
5	Florida	2,559	4.8%	9	Louisiana	1,792	3.3%
10	Georgia	1,536	2.9%	10	Georgia	1,536	2.9%
49	Hawaii	88	0.2%	11	Illinois	1,516	2.8%
42	Idaho	243	0.5%	12	Massachusetts	1,447	2.7%
11	Illinois	1,516	2.8%	13	Wisconsin	1,407	2.6%
14	Indiana	1,314	2.4%	14	Indiana	1,314	2.4%
36	Iowa	350	0.6%	15	Kentucky	1,303	2.4%
28	Kansas	561	1.0%	16	Washington	1,283	2.4%
15	Kentucky	1,303	2.4%	17	Ohio	1,273	2.4%
9	Louisiana	1,792	3.3%	18	Michigan	1,165	2.2%
34	Maine	386	0.7%	19	Connecticut	1,081	2.0%
8	Maryland	2,006	3.7%	20	Missouri	958	1.8%
12	Massachusetts	1,447	2.7%	21	Tennessee	954	1.8%
18	Michigan	1,165	2.2%	22	Virginia	851	1.6%
31	Minnesota	491	0.9%	23	Arkansas	849	1.6%
27	Mississippi	585	1.1%	24	South Carolina	838	1.6%
20	Missouri	958	1.8%	25	Colorado	830	1.5%
43	Montana	194	0.4%	26	Alabama	698	1.3%
41	Nebraska	258	0.5%	27	Mississippi	585	1.1%
35	Nevada	378	0.7%	28	Kansas	561	1.0%
37	New Hampshire	341	0.6%	29	Arizona	556	1.0%
4	New Jersey	2,849	5.3%	30	Oklahoma	536	1.0%
46	New Mexico	151	0.3%	31	Minnesota	491	0.9%
1	New York	6,425	11.9%	32	West Virginia	485	0.9%
7	North Carolina	2,276	4.2%	33	Utah	391	0.7%
39	North Dakota	303	0.6%	34	Maine	386	0.7%
17	Ohio	1,273	2.4%	35	Nevada	378	0.7%
30	Oklahoma	536	1.0%	36	Iowa	350	0.6%
40	Oregon	281	0.5%	37	New Hampshire	341	0.6%
2	Pennsylvania	3,487	6.5%	38	Delaware	307	0.6%
44	Rhode Island	177	0.3%	39	North Dakota	303	0.6%
24	South Carolina	838	1.6%	40	Oregon	281	0.5%
48	South Dakota	133	0.2%	41	Nebraska	258	0.5%
21	Tennessee	954	1.8%	42	Idaho	243	0.5%
3	Texas	2,922	5.4%	43	Montana	194	0.4%
33	Utah	391	0.7%	44	Rhode Island	177	0.3%
47	Vermont	149	0.3%	45	Alaska	169	0.3%
22	Virginia	851	1.6%	46	New Mexico	151	0.3%
16	Washington	1,283	2.4%	47	Vermont	149	0.3%
32	West Virginia	485	0.9%	48	South Dakota	133	0.2%
13	Wisconsin	1,407	2.6%	49	Hawaii	88	0.2%
50	Wyoming	82	0.2%	50	Wyoming	82	0.2%
					District of Columbia	292	0.5%

Source: U.S. Department of Health and Human Services, Centers for Medicare and Medicaid Services
    OSCAR Database (January 08, 2008)

*Beds in hospitals certified by CMS to participate in the Medicare/Medicaid programs. Excludes licensed facilities that do not accept federal funding and facilities managed by the Department of Veterans Affairs. National total does not include 492 beds in U.S. territories.

Medicare and Medicaid Certified Outpatient Surgery Centers in 2008

National Total = 4,937 Centers*

ALPHA ORDER

RANK	STATE	CENTERS	% of USA
35	Alabama	36	0.7%
48	Alaska	9	0.2%
10	Arizona	148	3.0%
23	Arkansas	61	1.2%
1	California	654	13.2%
14	Colorado	99	2.0%
32	Connecticut	44	0.9%
37	Delaware	25	0.5%
2	Florida	360	7.3%
5	Georgia	249	5.0%
46	Hawaii	11	0.2%
26	Idaho	55	1.1%
13	Illinois	120	2.4%
12	Indiana	124	2.5%
38	Iowa	24	0.5%
22	Kansas	63	1.3%
36	Kentucky	35	0.7%
19	Louisiana	74	1.5%
41	Maine	17	0.3%
3	Maryland	353	7.2%
27	Massachusetts	54	1.1%
17	Michigan	78	1.6%
30	Minnesota	48	1.0%
21	Mississippi	64	1.3%
15	Missouri	98	2.0%
45	Montana	15	0.3%
32	Nebraska	44	0.9%
29	Nevada	50	1.0%
39	New Hampshire	21	0.4%
8	New Jersey	201	4.1%
39	New Mexico	21	0.4%
16	New York	87	1.8%
20	North Carolina	68	1.4%
41	North Dakota	17	0.3%
9	Ohio	191	3.9%
28	Oklahoma	51	1.0%
18	Oregon	76	1.5%
7	Pennsylvania	218	4.4%
49	Rhode Island	7	0.1%
23	South Carolina	61	1.2%
44	South Dakota	16	0.3%
11	Tennessee	146	3.0%
4	Texas	343	6.9%
34	Utah	43	0.9%
50	Vermont	0	0.0%
30	Virginia	48	1.0%
6	Washington	221	4.5%
46	West Virginia	11	0.2%
25	Wisconsin	57	1.2%
41	Wyoming	17	0.3%

RANK ORDER

RANK	STATE	CENTERS	% of USA
1	California	654	13.2%
2	Florida	360	7.3%
3	Maryland	353	7.2%
4	Texas	343	6.9%
5	Georgia	249	5.0%
6	Washington	221	4.5%
7	Pennsylvania	218	4.4%
8	New Jersey	201	4.1%
9	Ohio	191	3.9%
10	Arizona	148	3.0%
11	Tennessee	146	3.0%
12	Indiana	124	2.5%
13	Illinois	120	2.4%
14	Colorado	99	2.0%
15	Missouri	98	2.0%
16	New York	87	1.8%
17	Michigan	78	1.6%
18	Oregon	76	1.5%
19	Louisiana	74	1.5%
20	North Carolina	68	1.4%
21	Mississippi	64	1.3%
22	Kansas	63	1.3%
23	Arkansas	61	1.2%
23	South Carolina	61	1.2%
25	Wisconsin	57	1.2%
26	Idaho	55	1.1%
27	Massachusetts	54	1.1%
28	Oklahoma	51	1.0%
29	Nevada	50	1.0%
30	Minnesota	48	1.0%
30	Virginia	48	1.0%
32	Connecticut	44	0.9%
32	Nebraska	44	0.9%
34	Utah	43	0.9%
35	Alabama	36	0.7%
36	Kentucky	35	0.7%
37	Delaware	25	0.5%
38	Iowa	24	0.5%
39	New Hampshire	21	0.4%
39	New Mexico	21	0.4%
41	Maine	17	0.3%
41	North Dakota	17	0.3%
41	Wyoming	17	0.3%
44	South Dakota	16	0.3%
45	Montana	15	0.3%
46	Hawaii	11	0.2%
46	West Virginia	11	0.2%
48	Alaska	9	0.2%
49	Rhode Island	7	0.1%
50	Vermont	0	0.0%
	District of Columbia	4	0.1%

Source: U.S. Department of Health and Human Services, Centers for Medicare and Medicaid Services
   OSCAR Report 10 (January 08, 2008)
*Certified by CMS to participate in the Medicare/Medicaid programs. Excludes licensed facilities that do not accept federal funding and facilities managed by the Department of Veterans Affairs. National total does not include 27 certified outpatient surgery centers in U.S. territories. Also known as Ambulatory Surgical Outpatient.

Medicare and Medicaid Certified Community Mental Health Centers in 2008

National Total = 628 Centers*

ALPHA ORDER

RANK ORDER

RANK	STATE	CENTERS	% of USA
2	Alabama	58	9.2%
41	Alaska	0	0.0%
30	Arizona	3	0.5%
11	Arkansas	14	2.2%
7	California	20	3.2%
11	Colorado	14	2.2%
28	Connecticut	4	0.6%
41	Delaware	0	0.0%
1	Florida	146	23.2%
21	Georgia	9	1.4%
41	Hawaii	0	0.0%
41	Idaho	0	0.0%
20	Illinois	10	1.6%
23	Indiana	8	1.3%
27	Iowa	6	1.0%
21	Kansas	9	1.4%
18	Kentucky	11	1.8%
3	Louisiana	49	7.8%
41	Maine	0	0.0%
37	Maryland	1	0.2%
15	Massachusetts	13	2.1%
26	Michigan	7	1.1%
11	Minnesota	14	2.2%
23	Mississippi	8	1.3%
18	Missouri	11	1.8%
41	Montana	0	0.0%
37	Nebraska	1	0.2%
33	Nevada	2	0.3%
37	New Hampshire	1	0.2%
5	New Jersey	28	4.5%
11	New Mexico	14	2.2%
28	New York	4	0.6%
8	North Carolina	19	3.0%
41	North Dakota	0	0.0%
15	Ohio	13	2.1%
23	Oklahoma	8	1.3%
17	Oregon	12	1.9%
10	Pennsylvania	16	2.5%
41	Rhode Island	0	0.0%
30	South Carolina	3	0.5%
37	South Dakota	1	0.2%
9	Tennessee	17	2.7%
4	Texas	40	6.4%
33	Utah	2	0.3%
41	Vermont	0	0.0%
33	Virginia	2	0.3%
6	Washington	25	4.0%
33	West Virginia	2	0.3%
41	Wisconsin	0	0.0%
30	Wyoming	3	0.5%

RANK	STATE	CENTERS	% of USA
1	Florida	146	23.2%
2	Alabama	58	9.2%
3	Louisiana	49	7.8%
4	Texas	40	6.4%
5	New Jersey	28	4.5%
6	Washington	25	4.0%
7	California	20	3.2%
8	North Carolina	19	3.0%
9	Tennessee	17	2.7%
10	Pennsylvania	16	2.5%
11	Arkansas	14	2.2%
11	Colorado	14	2.2%
11	Minnesota	14	2.2%
11	New Mexico	14	2.2%
15	Massachusetts	13	2.1%
15	Ohio	13	2.1%
17	Oregon	12	1.9%
18	Kentucky	11	1.8%
18	Missouri	11	1.8%
20	Illinois	10	1.6%
21	Georgia	9	1.4%
21	Kansas	9	1.4%
23	Indiana	8	1.3%
23	Mississippi	8	1.3%
23	Oklahoma	8	1.3%
26	Michigan	7	1.1%
27	Iowa	6	1.0%
28	Connecticut	4	0.6%
28	New York	4	0.6%
30	Arizona	3	0.5%
30	South Carolina	3	0.5%
30	Wyoming	3	0.5%
33	Nevada	2	0.3%
33	Utah	2	0.3%
33	Virginia	2	0.3%
33	West Virginia	2	0.3%
37	Maryland	1	0.2%
37	Nebraska	1	0.2%
37	New Hampshire	1	0.2%
37	South Dakota	1	0.2%
41	Alaska	0	0.0%
41	Delaware	0	0.0%
41	Hawaii	0	0.0%
41	Idaho	0	0.0%
41	Maine	0	0.0%
41	Montana	0	0.0%
41	North Dakota	0	0.0%
41	Rhode Island	0	0.0%
41	Vermont	0	0.0%
41	Wisconsin	0	0.0%
	District of Columbia	0	0.0%

Source: U.S. Department of Health and Human Services, Centers for Medicare and Medicaid Services
    OSCAR Report 10 (January 08, 2008)

*Certified by CMS to participate in the Medicare/Medicaid programs. Excludes licensed facilities that do not accept federal funding and facilities managed by the Department of Veterans Affairs. National total does not include 13 certified mental health centers in U.S. territories.

Medicare and Medicaid Certified Outpatient Physical Therapy Facilities in 2008

National Total = 2,913 Facilities*

ALPHA ORDER

RANK	STATE	FACILITIES	% of USA
23	Alabama	38	1.3%
35	Alaska	14	0.5%
29	Arizona	26	0.9%
28	Arkansas	28	1.0%
4	California	167	5.7%
17	Colorado	55	1.9%
25	Connecticut	34	1.2%
37	Delaware	13	0.4%
1	Florida	375	12.9%
9	Georgia	101	3.5%
44	Hawaii	5	0.2%
40	Idaho	10	0.3%
8	Illinois	103	3.5%
15	Indiana	62	2.1%
25	Iowa	34	1.2%
32	Kansas	23	0.8%
10	Kentucky	100	3.4%
19	Louisiana	50	1.7%
34	Maine	17	0.6%
11	Maryland	93	3.2%
35	Massachusetts	14	0.5%
3	Michigan	240	8.2%
21	Minnesota	47	1.6%
23	Mississippi	38	1.3%
14	Missouri	67	2.3%
49	Montana	1	0.0%
41	Nebraska	9	0.3%
33	Nevada	21	0.7%
38	New Hampshire	12	0.4%
12	New Jersey	90	3.1%
27	New Mexico	30	1.0%
31	New York	25	0.9%
16	North Carolina	59	2.0%
46	North Dakota	2	0.1%
5	Ohio	129	4.4%
18	Oklahoma	51	1.8%
39	Oregon	11	0.4%
6	Pennsylvania	122	4.2%
45	Rhode Island	3	0.1%
20	South Carolina	48	1.6%
46	South Dakota	2	0.1%
13	Tennessee	77	2.6%
2	Texas	253	8.7%
43	Utah	6	0.2%
46	Vermont	2	0.1%
6	Virginia	122	4.2%
29	Washington	26	0.9%
41	West Virginia	9	0.3%
22	Wisconsin	45	1.5%
49	Wyoming	1	0.0%

RANK ORDER

RANK	STATE	FACILITIES	% of USA
1	Florida	375	12.9%
2	Texas	253	8.7%
3	Michigan	240	8.2%
4	California	167	5.7%
5	Ohio	129	4.4%
6	Pennsylvania	122	4.2%
6	Virginia	122	4.2%
8	Illinois	103	3.5%
9	Georgia	101	3.5%
10	Kentucky	100	3.4%
11	Maryland	93	3.2%
12	New Jersey	90	3.1%
13	Tennessee	77	2.6%
14	Missouri	67	2.3%
15	Indiana	62	2.1%
16	North Carolina	59	2.0%
17	Colorado	55	1.9%
18	Oklahoma	51	1.8%
19	Louisiana	50	1.7%
20	South Carolina	48	1.6%
21	Minnesota	47	1.6%
22	Wisconsin	45	1.5%
23	Alabama	38	1.3%
23	Mississippi	38	1.3%
25	Connecticut	34	1.2%
25	Iowa	34	1.2%
27	New Mexico	30	1.0%
28	Arkansas	28	1.0%
29	Arizona	26	0.9%
29	Washington	26	0.9%
31	New York	25	0.9%
32	Kansas	23	0.8%
33	Nevada	21	0.7%
34	Maine	17	0.6%
35	Alaska	14	0.5%
35	Massachusetts	14	0.5%
37	Delaware	13	0.4%
38	New Hampshire	12	0.4%
39	Oregon	11	0.4%
40	Idaho	10	0.3%
41	Nebraska	9	0.3%
41	West Virginia	9	0.3%
43	Utah	6	0.2%
44	Hawaii	5	0.2%
45	Rhode Island	3	0.1%
46	North Dakota	2	0.1%
46	South Dakota	2	0.1%
46	Vermont	2	0.1%
49	Montana	1	0.0%
49	Wyoming	1	0.0%
	District of Columbia	3	0.1%

Source: U.S. Department of Health and Human Services, Centers for Medicare and Medicaid Services
OSCAR Report 10 (January 08, 2008)

*Certified by CMS to participate in the Medicare/Medicaid programs. Excludes licensed facilities that do not accept federal funding and facilities managed by the Department of Veterans Affairs. National total does not include two certified outpatient physical therapy facilities in U.S. territories.

Medicare and Medicaid Certified Rural Health Clinics in 2008

National Total = 3,780 Rural Health Clinics*

ALPHA ORDER

RANK	STATE	CLINICS	% of USA
19	Alabama	64	1.7%
43	Alaska	3	0.1%
38	Arizona	13	0.3%
18	Arkansas	68	1.8%
3	California	256	6.8%
28	Colorado	47	1.2%
46	Connecticut	0	0.0%
46	Delaware	0	0.0%
8	Florida	149	3.9%
15	Georgia	99	2.6%
44	Hawaii	2	0.1%
28	Idaho	47	1.2%
4	Illinois	230	6.1%
24	Indiana	56	1.5%
9	Iowa	144	3.8%
5	Kansas	185	4.9%
11	Kentucky	127	3.4%
14	Louisiana	101	2.7%
32	Maine	41	1.1%
46	Maryland	0	0.0%
45	Massachusetts	1	0.0%
6	Michigan	164	4.3%
17	Minnesota	87	2.3%
7	Mississippi	152	4.0%
2	Missouri	324	8.6%
31	Montana	43	1.1%
12	Nebraska	122	3.2%
42	Nevada	6	0.2%
37	New Hampshire	15	0.4%
46	New Jersey	0	0.0%
39	New Mexico	12	0.3%
41	New York	8	0.2%
16	North Carolina	97	2.6%
19	North Dakota	64	1.7%
40	Ohio	11	0.3%
33	Oklahoma	40	1.1%
26	Oregon	54	1.4%
26	Pennsylvania	54	1.4%
46	Rhode Island	0	0.0%
13	South Carolina	102	2.7%
22	South Dakota	60	1.6%
23	Tennessee	59	1.6%
1	Texas	326	8.6%
34	Utah	18	0.5%
34	Vermont	18	0.5%
24	Virginia	56	1.5%
10	Washington	130	3.4%
21	West Virginia	61	1.6%
28	Wisconsin	47	1.2%
36	Wyoming	17	0.4%

RANK ORDER

RANK	STATE	CLINICS	% of USA
1	Texas	326	8.6%
2	Missouri	324	8.6%
3	California	256	6.8%
4	Illinois	230	6.1%
5	Kansas	185	4.9%
6	Michigan	164	4.3%
7	Mississippi	152	4.0%
8	Florida	149	3.9%
9	Iowa	144	3.8%
10	Washington	130	3.4%
11	Kentucky	127	3.4%
12	Nebraska	122	3.2%
13	South Carolina	102	2.7%
14	Louisiana	101	2.7%
15	Georgia	99	2.6%
16	North Carolina	97	2.6%
17	Minnesota	87	2.3%
18	Arkansas	68	1.8%
19	Alabama	64	1.7%
19	North Dakota	64	1.7%
21	West Virginia	61	1.6%
22	South Dakota	60	1.6%
23	Tennessee	59	1.6%
24	Indiana	56	1.5%
24	Virginia	56	1.5%
26	Oregon	54	1.4%
26	Pennsylvania	54	1.4%
28	Colorado	47	1.2%
28	Idaho	47	1.2%
28	Wisconsin	47	1.2%
31	Montana	43	1.1%
32	Maine	41	1.1%
33	Oklahoma	40	1.1%
34	Utah	18	0.5%
34	Vermont	18	0.5%
36	Wyoming	17	0.4%
37	New Hampshire	15	0.4%
38	Arizona	13	0.3%
39	New Mexico	12	0.3%
40	Ohio	11	0.3%
41	New York	8	0.2%
42	Nevada	6	0.2%
43	Alaska	3	0.1%
44	Hawaii	2	0.1%
45	Massachusetts	1	0.0%
46	Connecticut	0	0.0%
46	Delaware	0	0.0%
46	Maryland	0	0.0%
46	New Jersey	0	0.0%
46	Rhode Island	0	0.0%
	District of Columbia	0	0.0%

Source: U.S. Department of Health and Human Services, Centers for Medicare and Medicaid Services
    OSCAR Report 10 (January 08, 2008)

*Certified by CMS to participate in the Medicare/Medicaid programs. Excludes licensed facilities that do not accept federal funding and facilities managed by the Department of Veterans Affairs. There are no certified rural health centers in U.S. territories.

Medicare and Medicaid Certified Home Health Agencies in 2008

National Total = 9,230 Home Health Agencies*

ALPHA ORDER

RANK	STATE	AGENCIES	% of USA
18	Alabama	146	1.6%
48	Alaska	16	0.2%
26	Arizona	86	0.9%
15	Arkansas	174	1.9%
3	California	708	7.7%
20	Colorado	136	1.5%
27	Connecticut	85	0.9%
47	Delaware	19	0.2%
2	Florida	842	9.1%
25	Georgia	101	1.1%
49	Hawaii	14	0.2%
37	Idaho	49	0.5%
4	Illinois	498	5.4%
11	Indiana	210	2.3%
14	Iowa	177	1.9%
21	Kansas	135	1.5%
24	Kentucky	104	1.1%
8	Louisiana	221	2.4%
43	Maine	29	0.3%
37	Maryland	49	0.5%
22	Massachusetts	128	1.4%
6	Michigan	399	4.3%
9	Minnesota	214	2.3%
36	Mississippi	56	0.6%
16	Missouri	171	1.9%
41	Montana	36	0.4%
28	Nebraska	73	0.8%
30	Nevada	71	0.8%
41	New Hampshire	36	0.4%
37	New Jersey	49	0.5%
31	New Mexico	68	0.7%
12	New York	191	2.1%
17	North Carolina	169	1.8%
45	North Dakota	23	0.2%
5	Ohio	479	5.2%
9	Oklahoma	214	2.3%
35	Oregon	57	0.6%
7	Pennsylvania	325	3.5%
46	Rhode Island	22	0.2%
31	South Carolina	68	0.7%
40	South Dakota	42	0.5%
19	Tennessee	139	1.5%
1	Texas	1,827	19.8%
28	Utah	73	0.8%
50	Vermont	12	0.1%
13	Virginia	188	2.0%
34	Washington	60	0.7%
33	West Virginia	61	0.7%
22	Wisconsin	128	1.4%
44	Wyoming	27	0.3%

RANK ORDER

RANK	STATE	AGENCIES	% of USA
1	Texas	1,827	19.8%
2	Florida	842	9.1%
3	California	708	7.7%
4	Illinois	498	5.4%
5	Ohio	479	5.2%
6	Michigan	399	4.3%
7	Pennsylvania	325	3.5%
8	Louisiana	221	2.4%
9	Minnesota	214	2.3%
9	Oklahoma	214	2.3%
11	Indiana	210	2.3%
12	New York	191	2.1%
13	Virginia	188	2.0%
14	Iowa	177	1.9%
15	Arkansas	174	1.9%
16	Missouri	171	1.9%
17	North Carolina	169	1.8%
18	Alabama	146	1.6%
19	Tennessee	139	1.5%
20	Colorado	136	1.5%
21	Kansas	135	1.5%
22	Massachusetts	128	1.4%
22	Wisconsin	128	1.4%
24	Kentucky	104	1.1%
25	Georgia	101	1.1%
26	Arizona	86	0.9%
27	Connecticut	85	0.9%
28	Nebraska	73	0.8%
28	Utah	73	0.8%
30	Nevada	71	0.8%
31	New Mexico	68	0.7%
31	South Carolina	68	0.7%
33	West Virginia	61	0.7%
34	Washington	60	0.7%
35	Oregon	57	0.6%
36	Mississippi	56	0.6%
37	Idaho	49	0.5%
37	Maryland	49	0.5%
37	New Jersey	49	0.5%
40	South Dakota	42	0.5%
41	Montana	36	0.4%
41	New Hampshire	36	0.4%
43	Maine	29	0.3%
44	Wyoming	27	0.3%
45	North Dakota	23	0.2%
46	Rhode Island	22	0.2%
47	Delaware	19	0.2%
48	Alaska	16	0.2%
49	Hawaii	14	0.2%
50	Vermont	12	0.1%
	District of Columbia	25	0.3%

Source: U.S. Department of Health and Human Services, Centers for Medicare and Medicaid Services
OSCAR Report 10 (January 08, 2008)

*Certified by CMS to participate in the Medicare/Medicaid programs. Excludes agencies that do not accept federal funding. National total does not include 56 certified home health agencies in U.S. territories. A home health agency provides health services to individuals in their homes for the purpose of promoting, maintaining, or restoring health or maximizing the level of independence, while minimizing the effects of disability and illness.

Medicare and Medicaid Certified Hospices in 2008

National Total = 3,212 Hospices*

ALPHA ORDER

RANK	STATE	HOSPICES	% of USA
6	Alabama	123	3.8%
50	Alaska	5	0.2%
21	Arizona	59	1.8%
27	Arkansas	49	1.5%
2	California	211	6.6%
27	Colorado	49	1.5%
35	Connecticut	31	1.0%
47	Delaware	8	0.2%
30	Florida	41	1.3%
5	Georgia	126	3.9%
47	Hawaii	8	0.2%
32	Idaho	38	1.2%
10	Illinois	105	3.3%
13	Indiana	83	2.6%
15	Iowa	78	2.4%
23	Kansas	58	1.8%
37	Kentucky	27	0.8%
6	Louisiana	123	3.8%
40	Maine	20	0.6%
36	Maryland	28	0.9%
21	Massachusetts	59	1.8%
12	Michigan	96	3.0%
18	Minnesota	65	2.0%
8	Mississippi	120	3.7%
11	Missouri	101	3.1%
37	Montana	27	0.8%
33	Nebraska	33	1.0%
43	Nevada	15	0.5%
39	New Hampshire	21	0.7%
25	New Jersey	53	1.7%
30	New Mexico	41	1.3%
26	New York	51	1.6%
14	North Carolina	82	2.6%
45	North Dakota	14	0.4%
9	Ohio	109	3.4%
4	Oklahoma	139	4.3%
29	Oregon	48	1.5%
3	Pennsylvania	157	4.9%
47	Rhode Island	8	0.2%
18	South Carolina	65	2.0%
43	South Dakota	15	0.5%
24	Tennessee	57	1.8%
1	Texas	279	8.7%
17	Utah	68	2.1%
46	Vermont	10	0.3%
16	Virginia	75	2.3%
34	Washington	32	1.0%
41	West Virginia	18	0.6%
20	Wisconsin	63	2.0%
41	Wyoming	18	0.6%

RANK ORDER

RANK	STATE	HOSPICES	% of USA
1	Texas	279	8.7%
2	California	211	6.6%
3	Pennsylvania	157	4.9%
4	Oklahoma	139	4.3%
5	Georgia	126	3.9%
6	Alabama	123	3.8%
6	Louisiana	123	3.8%
8	Mississippi	120	3.7%
9	Ohio	109	3.4%
10	Illinois	105	3.3%
11	Missouri	101	3.1%
12	Michigan	96	3.0%
13	Indiana	83	2.6%
14	North Carolina	82	2.6%
15	Iowa	78	2.4%
16	Virginia	75	2.3%
17	Utah	68	2.1%
18	Minnesota	65	2.0%
18	South Carolina	65	2.0%
20	Wisconsin	63	2.0%
21	Arizona	59	1.8%
21	Massachusetts	59	1.8%
23	Kansas	58	1.8%
24	Tennessee	57	1.8%
25	New Jersey	53	1.7%
26	New York	51	1.6%
27	Arkansas	49	1.5%
27	Colorado	49	1.5%
29	Oregon	48	1.5%
30	Florida	41	1.3%
30	New Mexico	41	1.3%
32	Idaho	38	1.2%
33	Nebraska	33	1.0%
34	Washington	32	1.0%
35	Connecticut	31	1.0%
36	Maryland	28	0.9%
37	Kentucky	27	0.8%
37	Montana	27	0.8%
39	New Hampshire	21	0.7%
40	Maine	20	0.6%
41	West Virginia	18	0.6%
41	Wyoming	18	0.6%
43	Nevada	15	0.5%
43	South Dakota	15	0.5%
45	North Dakota	14	0.4%
46	Vermont	10	0.3%
47	Delaware	8	0.2%
47	Hawaii	8	0.2%
47	Rhode Island	8	0.2%
50	Alaska	5	0.2%
	District of Columbia	3	0.1%

Source: U.S. Department of Health and Human Services, Centers for Medicare and Medicaid Services
   OSCAR Report 10 (January 08, 2008)

*Certified by CMS to participate in the Medicare/Medicaid programs. Excludes licensed facilities that do not accept federal funding and facilities managed by the Department of Veterans Affairs. National total does not include 38 certified hospices in U.S. territories. An hospice provides specialized services for terminally ill people and their families.

Hospice Patients in Residential Facilities in 2008

National Total = 66,930 Patients*

ALPHA ORDER

RANK	STATE	PATIENTS	% of USA
16	Alabama	1,266	1.9%
50	Alaska	3	0.0%
18	Arizona	1,143	1.7%
37	Arkansas	472	0.7%
6	California	2,713	4.1%
28	Colorado	781	1.2%
22	Connecticut	1,015	1.5%
41	Delaware	208	0.3%
1	Florida	9,940	14.9%
10	Georgia	2,091	3.1%
48	Hawaii	43	0.1%
44	Idaho	155	0.2%
7	Illinois	2,422	3.6%
15	Indiana	1,388	2.1%
21	Iowa	1,029	1.5%
35	Kansas	519	0.8%
33	Kentucky	599	0.9%
32	Louisiana	612	0.9%
12	Maine	1,737	2.6%
38	Maryland	434	0.6%
5	Massachusetts	2,988	4.5%
14	Michigan	1,492	2.2%
27	Minnesota	825	1.2%
36	Mississippi	477	0.7%
9	Missouri	2,103	3.1%
24	Montana	932	1.4%
25	Nebraska	885	1.3%
43	Nevada	159	0.2%
30	New Hampshire	662	1.0%
29	New Jersey	670	1.0%
40	New Mexico	213	0.3%
17	New York	1,148	1.7%
8	North Carolina	2,251	3.4%
45	North Dakota	65	0.1%
4	Ohio	3,305	4.9%
11	Oklahoma	1,943	2.9%
23	Oregon	987	1.5%
3	Pennsylvania	4,867	7.3%
19	Rhode Island	1,113	1.7%
34	South Carolina	571	0.9%
47	South Dakota	50	0.1%
31	Tennessee	645	1.0%
2	Texas	5,775	8.6%
39	Utah	353	0.5%
46	Vermont	51	0.1%
20	Virginia	1,059	1.6%
13	Washington	1,615	2.4%
42	West Virginia	174	0.3%
26	Wisconsin	856	1.3%
49	Wyoming	32	0.0%

RANK ORDER

RANK	STATE	PATIENTS	% of USA
1	Florida	9,940	14.9%
2	Texas	5,775	8.6%
3	Pennsylvania	4,867	7.3%
4	Ohio	3,305	4.9%
5	Massachusetts	2,988	4.5%
6	California	2,713	4.1%
7	Illinois	2,422	3.6%
8	North Carolina	2,251	3.4%
9	Missouri	2,103	3.1%
10	Georgia	2,091	3.1%
11	Oklahoma	1,943	2.9%
12	Maine	1,737	2.6%
13	Washington	1,615	2.4%
14	Michigan	1,492	2.2%
15	Indiana	1,388	2.1%
16	Alabama	1,266	1.9%
17	New York	1,148	1.7%
18	Arizona	1,143	1.7%
19	Rhode Island	1,113	1.7%
20	Virginia	1,059	1.6%
21	Iowa	1,029	1.5%
22	Connecticut	1,015	1.5%
23	Oregon	987	1.5%
24	Montana	932	1.4%
25	Nebraska	885	1.3%
26	Wisconsin	856	1.3%
27	Minnesota	825	1.2%
28	Colorado	781	1.2%
29	New Jersey	670	1.0%
30	New Hampshire	662	1.0%
31	Tennessee	645	1.0%
32	Louisiana	612	0.9%
33	Kentucky	599	0.9%
34	South Carolina	571	0.9%
35	Kansas	519	0.8%
36	Mississippi	477	0.7%
37	Arkansas	472	0.7%
38	Maryland	434	0.6%
39	Utah	353	0.5%
40	New Mexico	213	0.3%
41	Delaware	208	0.3%
42	West Virginia	174	0.3%
43	Nevada	159	0.2%
44	Idaho	155	0.2%
45	North Dakota	65	0.1%
46	Vermont	51	0.1%
47	South Dakota	50	0.1%
48	Hawaii	43	0.1%
49	Wyoming	32	0.0%
50	Alaska	3	0.0%
	District of Columbia	94	0.1%

Source: U.S. Department of Health and Human Services, Centers for Medicare and Medicaid Services
   OSCAR Database (January 08, 2008)

*Patients in facilities certified by CMS to participate in the Medicare/Medicaid programs. Excludes licensed facilities that do not accept federal funding and facilities managed by the Department of Veterans Affairs. National total does not include 52 patients in U.S. territories.   A hospice provides specialized services for terminally ill people and their families.

Medicare and Medicaid Certified Nursing Care Facilities in 2008

National Total = 15,046 Nursing Care Facilities*

<u>ALPHA ORDER</u>

RANK	STATE	FACILITIES	% of USA
26	Alabama	229	1.5%
50	Alaska	15	0.1%
33	Arizona	135	0.9%
28	Arkansas	215	1.4%
1	California	1,196	7.9%
30	Colorado	193	1.3%
24	Connecticut	244	1.6%
48	Delaware	38	0.3%
6	Florida	676	4.5%
17	Georgia	357	2.4%
46	Hawaii	43	0.3%
42	Idaho	76	0.5%
5	Illinois	703	4.7%
8	Indiana	489	3.3%
12	Iowa	415	2.8%
22	Kansas	269	1.8%
19	Kentucky	292	1.9%
19	Louisiana	292	1.9%
36	Maine	113	0.8%
27	Maryland	228	1.5%
10	Massachusetts	438	2.9%
13	Michigan	404	2.7%
14	Minnesota	380	2.5%
32	Mississippi	171	1.1%
9	Missouri	485	3.2%
38	Montana	91	0.6%
29	Nebraska	196	1.3%
45	Nevada	46	0.3%
43	New Hampshire	74	0.5%
16	New Jersey	362	2.4%
44	New Mexico	67	0.4%
7	New York	655	4.4%
11	North Carolina	420	2.8%
41	North Dakota	83	0.6%
3	Ohio	956	6.4%
21	Oklahoma	280	1.9%
35	Oregon	121	0.8%
4	Pennsylvania	709	4.7%
39	Rhode Island	86	0.6%
31	South Carolina	174	1.2%
37	South Dakota	93	0.6%
18	Tennessee	299	2.0%
2	Texas	1,075	7.1%
40	Utah	85	0.6%
47	Vermont	40	0.3%
23	Virginia	257	1.7%
25	Washington	234	1.6%
34	West Virginia	123	0.8%
15	Wisconsin	372	2.5%
49	Wyoming	33	0.2%

<u>RANK ORDER</u>

RANK	STATE	FACILITIES	% of USA
1	California	1,196	7.9%
2	Texas	1,075	7.1%
3	Ohio	956	6.4%
4	Pennsylvania	709	4.7%
5	Illinois	703	4.7%
6	Florida	676	4.5%
7	New York	655	4.4%
8	Indiana	489	3.3%
9	Missouri	485	3.2%
10	Massachusetts	438	2.9%
11	North Carolina	420	2.8%
12	Iowa	415	2.8%
13	Michigan	404	2.7%
14	Minnesota	380	2.5%
15	Wisconsin	372	2.5%
16	New Jersey	362	2.4%
17	Georgia	357	2.4%
18	Tennessee	299	2.0%
19	Kentucky	292	1.9%
19	Louisiana	292	1.9%
21	Oklahoma	280	1.9%
22	Kansas	269	1.8%
23	Virginia	257	1.7%
24	Connecticut	244	1.6%
25	Washington	234	1.6%
26	Alabama	229	1.5%
27	Maryland	228	1.5%
28	Arkansas	215	1.4%
29	Nebraska	196	1.3%
30	Colorado	193	1.3%
31	South Carolina	174	1.2%
32	Mississippi	171	1.1%
33	Arizona	135	0.9%
34	West Virginia	123	0.8%
35	Oregon	121	0.8%
36	Maine	113	0.8%
37	South Dakota	93	0.6%
38	Montana	91	0.6%
39	Rhode Island	86	0.6%
40	Utah	85	0.6%
41	North Dakota	83	0.6%
42	Idaho	76	0.5%
43	New Hampshire	74	0.5%
44	New Mexico	67	0.4%
45	Nevada	46	0.3%
46	Hawaii	43	0.3%
47	Vermont	40	0.3%
48	Delaware	38	0.3%
49	Wyoming	33	0.2%
50	Alaska	15	0.1%
	District of Columbia	19	0.1%

Source: U.S. Department of Health and Human Services, Centers for Medicare and Medicaid Services
OSCAR Database (January 08, 2008)

*Certified by CMS to participate in the Medicare/Medicaid programs. Excludes licensed facilities that do not accept federal funding and facilities managed by the Department of Veterans Affairs. National total does not include 10 certified nursing facilities in U.S. territories.

Beds in Medicare and Medicaid Certified Nursing Care Facilities in 2008

National Total = 1,620,468 Beds*

RANK	STATE	BEDS	% of USA		RANK	STATE	BEDS	% of USA
23	Alabama	26,440	1.6%		1	New York	120,616	7.4%
50	Alaska	725	0.0%		2	Texas	117,024	7.2%
31	Arizona	16,205	1.0%		3	California	115,272	7.1%
26	Arkansas	22,086	1.4%		4	Ohio	92,582	5.7%
3	California	115,272	7.1%		5	Illinois	87,999	5.4%
29	Colorado	18,710	1.2%		6	Pennsylvania	87,774	5.4%
21	Connecticut	29,616	1.8%		7	Florida	81,728	5.0%
46	Delaware	4,475	0.3%		8	New Jersey	51,029	3.1%
7	Florida	81,728	5.0%		9	Massachusetts	49,117	3.0%
14	Georgia	39,682	2.4%		10	Missouri	49,042	3.0%
47	Hawaii	3,866	0.2%		11	Indiana	47,797	2.9%
43	Idaho	5,987	0.4%		12	Michigan	45,694	2.8%
5	Illinois	87,999	5.4%		13	North Carolina	43,262	2.7%
11	Indiana	47,797	2.9%		14	Georgia	39,682	2.4%
19	Iowa	29,663	1.8%		15	Louisiana	36,341	2.2%
28	Kansas	19,527	1.2%		16	Wisconsin	36,167	2.2%
25	Kentucky	25,785	1.6%		17	Tennessee	35,235	2.2%
15	Louisiana	36,341	2.2%		18	Minnesota	33,450	2.1%
38	Maine	7,279	0.4%		19	Iowa	29,663	1.8%
22	Maryland	28,969	1.8%		20	Virginia	29,634	1.8%
9	Massachusetts	49,117	3.0%		21	Connecticut	29,616	1.8%
12	Michigan	45,694	2.8%		22	Maryland	28,969	1.8%
18	Minnesota	33,450	2.1%		23	Alabama	26,440	1.6%
32	Mississippi	15,698	1.0%		24	Oklahoma	26,123	1.6%
10	Missouri	49,042	3.0%		25	Kentucky	25,785	1.6%
40	Montana	6,969	0.4%		26	Arkansas	22,086	1.4%
33	Nebraska	14,559	0.9%		27	Washington	21,816	1.3%
45	Nevada	5,383	0.3%		28	Kansas	19,527	1.2%
39	New Hampshire	7,224	0.4%		29	Colorado	18,710	1.2%
8	New Jersey	51,029	3.1%		30	South Carolina	18,108	1.1%
41	New Mexico	6,599	0.4%		31	Arizona	16,205	1.0%
1	New York	120,616	7.4%		32	Mississippi	15,698	1.0%
13	North Carolina	43,262	2.7%		33	Nebraska	14,559	0.9%
42	North Dakota	6,423	0.4%		34	Oregon	11,434	0.7%
4	Ohio	92,582	5.7%		35	West Virginia	10,160	0.6%
24	Oklahoma	26,123	1.6%		36	Rhode Island	8,738	0.5%
34	Oregon	11,434	0.7%		37	Utah	7,564	0.5%
6	Pennsylvania	87,774	5.4%		38	Maine	7,279	0.4%
36	Rhode Island	8,738	0.5%		39	New Hampshire	7,224	0.4%
30	South Carolina	18,108	1.1%		40	Montana	6,969	0.4%
44	South Dakota	5,823	0.4%		41	New Mexico	6,599	0.4%
17	Tennessee	35,235	2.2%		42	North Dakota	6,423	0.4%
2	Texas	117,024	7.2%		43	Idaho	5,987	0.4%
37	Utah	7,564	0.5%		44	South Dakota	5,823	0.4%
48	Vermont	3,299	0.2%		45	Nevada	5,383	0.3%
20	Virginia	29,634	1.8%		46	Delaware	4,475	0.3%
27	Washington	21,816	1.3%		47	Hawaii	3,866	0.2%
35	West Virginia	10,160	0.6%		48	Vermont	3,299	0.2%
16	Wisconsin	36,167	2.2%		49	Wyoming	2,826	0.2%
49	Wyoming	2,826	0.2%		50	Alaska	725	0.0%
						District of Columbia	2,944	0.2%

ALPHA ORDER

RANK ORDER

Source: U.S. Department of Health and Human Services, Centers for Medicare and Medicaid Services
    OSCAR Database (January 08, 2008)
*Beds in nursing care facilities certified by CMS to participate in the Medicare/Medicaid programs. National total does not include
393 beds in U.S. territories.

Rate of Beds in Medicare and Medicaid Certified Nursing Care Facilities in 2008

National Rate = 306 Beds per 1,000 Population 85 Years and Older*

ALPHA ORDER

RANK	STATE	RATE
21	Alabama	332
47	Alaska	175
49	Arizona	154
5	Arkansas	402
43	California	208
30	Colorado	306
8	Connecticut	388
29	Delaware	307
46	Florida	177
17	Georgia	350
50	Hawaii	144
41	Idaho	256
8	Illinois	388
3	Indiana	430
7	Iowa	395
23	Kansas	328
13	Kentucky	371
1	Louisiana	538
36	Maine	269
19	Maryland	338
16	Massachusetts	358
39	Michigan	261
22	Minnesota	329
27	Mississippi	317
2	Missouri	431
14	Montana	367
12	Nebraska	372
45	Nevada	193
28	New Hampshire	312
30	New Jersey	306
42	New Mexico	211
24	New York	325
26	North Carolina	318
11	North Dakota	382
4	Ohio	427
6	Oklahoma	398
48	Oregon	161
33	Pennsylvania	298
18	Rhode Island	348
37	South Carolina	264
32	South Dakota	305
15	Tennessee	361
10	Texas	387
40	Utah	259
34	Vermont	282
37	Virginia	264
44	Washington	204
34	West Virginia	282
24	Wisconsin	325
19	Wyoming	338

RANK ORDER

RANK	STATE	RATE
1	Louisiana	538
2	Missouri	431
3	Indiana	430
4	Ohio	427
5	Arkansas	402
6	Oklahoma	398
7	Iowa	395
8	Connecticut	388
8	Illinois	388
10	Texas	387
11	North Dakota	382
12	Nebraska	372
13	Kentucky	371
14	Montana	367
15	Tennessee	361
16	Massachusetts	358
17	Georgia	350
18	Rhode Island	348
19	Maryland	338
19	Wyoming	338
21	Alabama	332
22	Minnesota	329
23	Kansas	328
24	New York	325
24	Wisconsin	325
26	North Carolina	318
27	Mississippi	317
28	New Hampshire	312
29	Delaware	307
30	Colorado	306
30	New Jersey	306
32	South Dakota	305
33	Pennsylvania	298
34	Vermont	282
34	West Virginia	282
36	Maine	269
37	South Carolina	264
37	Virginia	264
39	Michigan	261
40	Utah	259
41	Idaho	256
42	New Mexico	211
43	California	208
44	Washington	204
45	Nevada	193
46	Florida	177
47	Alaska	175
48	Oregon	161
49	Arizona	154
50	Hawaii	144

| | District of Columbia | 273 |

Source: CQ Press using data from U.S. Department of Health and Human Services, Centers for Medicare and Medicaid Services
OSCAR Database (January 08, 2008)

*Beds in nursing care facilities certified by CMS to participate in the Medicare/Medicaid programs. National rate does not include beds or population in U.S. territories. Calculated using 2006 Census population estimate.

Nursing Home Occupancy Rate in 2006

National Rate = 83.5% of Beds in Nursing Homes Occupied

ALPHA ORDER				RANK ORDER		
RANK	**STATE**	**RATE**		**RANK**	**STATE**	**RATE**
25	Alabama	87.5		1	South Dakota	99.5
20	Alaska	88.3		2	Rhode Island	93.0
38	Arizona	77.4		3	Hawaii	92.8
44	Arkansas	72.8		3	New York	92.8
31	California	84.8		5	North Dakota	91.8
33	Colorado	83.0		6	Minnesota	91.4
8	Connecticut	90.9		7	Pennsylvania	91.1
35	Delaware	81.1		8	Connecticut	90.9
21	Florida	88.1		9	Vermont	90.6
14	Georgia	89.6		10	Maine	90.4
3	Hawaii	92.8		11	South Carolina	90.3
40	Idaho	75.0		12	New Hampshire	90.1
40	Illinois	75.0		13	West Virginia	89.9
47	Indiana	69.8		14	Georgia	89.6
37	Iowa	77.8		14	Mississippi	89.6
39	Kansas	76.4		16	Massachusetts	89.4
17	Kentucky	89.3		17	Kentucky	89.3
40	Louisiana	75.0		18	Virginia	89.2
10	Maine	90.4		19	Wisconsin	88.5
27	Maryland	87.1		20	Alaska	88.3
16	Massachusetts	89.4		21	Florida	88.1
29	Michigan	86.6		22	New Jersey	87.6
6	Minnesota	91.4		22	North Carolina	87.6
14	Mississippi	89.6		22	Tennessee	87.6
48	Missouri	69.7		25	Alabama	87.5
43	Montana	73.7		26	Ohio	87.2
34	Nebraska	82.0		27	Maryland	87.1
32	Nevada	83.1		28	New Mexico	86.7
12	New Hampshire	90.1		29	Michigan	86.6
22	New Jersey	87.6		29	Washington	86.6
28	New Mexico	86.7		31	California	84.8
3	New York	92.8		32	Nevada	83.1
22	North Carolina	87.6		33	Colorado	83.0
5	North Dakota	91.8		34	Nebraska	82.0
26	Ohio	87.2		35	Delaware	81.1
49	Oklahoma	65.8		35	Wyoming	81.1
50	Oregon	64.5		37	Iowa	77.8
7	Pennsylvania	91.1		38	Arizona	77.4
2	Rhode Island	93.0		39	Kansas	76.4
11	South Carolina	90.3		40	Idaho	75.0
1	South Dakota	99.5		40	Illinois	75.0
22	Tennessee	87.6		40	Louisiana	75.0
45	Texas	72.2		43	Montana	73.7
46	Utah	70.9		44	Arkansas	72.8
9	Vermont	90.6		45	Texas	72.2
18	Virginia	89.2		46	Utah	70.9
29	Washington	86.6		47	Indiana	69.8
13	West Virginia	89.9		48	Missouri	69.7
19	Wisconsin	88.5		49	Oklahoma	65.8
35	Wyoming	81.1		50	Oregon	64.5
					District of Columbia	92.4

Source: U.S. Department of Health and Human Services, Centers for Medicare and Medicaid Services
"Health, United States, 2007" (www.cdc.gov/nchs/data/hus/hus07.pdf)

Nursing Home Resident Rate in 2006

National Rate = 270.6 Residents per 1,000 Population Age 85 and Older*

ALPHA ORDER

RANK	STATE	RATE
26	Alabama	295.3
47	Alaska	154.3
49	Arizona	121.5
17	Arkansas	327.4
42	California	189.9
33	Colorado	270.8
3	Connecticut	358.2
35	Delaware	264.9
46	Florida	156.9
19	Georgia	315.4
48	Hawaii	142.4
40	Idaho	198.7
9	Illinois	340.0
4	Indiana	357.6
5	Iowa	357.4
13	Kansas	332.4
11	Kentucky	334.9
1	Louisiana	411.2
37	Maine	246.2
27	Maryland	294.6
16	Massachusetts	328.9
39	Michigan	235.1
18	Minnesota	322.1
14	Mississippi	331.1
12	Missouri	334.0
28	Montana	284.5
8	Nebraska	340.6
45	Nevada	167.5
22	New Hampshire	305.0
30	New Jersey	274.2
41	New Mexico	192.2
23	New York	301.7
29	North Carolina	281.6
6	North Dakota	355.2
2	Ohio	374.6
20	Oklahoma	308.7
50	Oregon	114.2
31	Pennsylvania	273.6
15	Rhode Island	329.0
38	South Carolina	242.1
7	South Dakota	350.0
10	Tennessee	335.9
24	Texas	296.7
43	Utah	187.4
34	Vermont	265.6
36	Virginia	253.1
44	Washington	182.0
32	West Virginia	272.6
21	Wisconsin	306.9
25	Wyoming	295.7

RANK ORDER

RANK	STATE	RATE
1	Louisiana	411.2
2	Ohio	374.6
3	Connecticut	358.2
4	Indiana	357.6
5	Iowa	357.4
6	North Dakota	355.2
7	South Dakota	350.0
8	Nebraska	340.6
9	Illinois	340.0
10	Tennessee	335.9
11	Kentucky	334.9
12	Missouri	334.0
13	Kansas	332.4
14	Mississippi	331.1
15	Rhode Island	329.0
16	Massachusetts	328.9
17	Arkansas	327.4
18	Minnesota	322.1
19	Georgia	315.4
20	Oklahoma	308.7
21	Wisconsin	306.9
22	New Hampshire	305.0
23	New York	301.7
24	Texas	296.7
25	Wyoming	295.7
26	Alabama	295.3
27	Maryland	294.6
28	Montana	284.5
29	North Carolina	281.6
30	New Jersey	274.2
31	Pennsylvania	273.6
32	West Virginia	272.6
33	Colorado	270.8
34	Vermont	265.6
35	Delaware	264.9
36	Virginia	253.1
37	Maine	246.2
38	South Carolina	242.1
39	Michigan	235.1
40	Idaho	198.7
41	New Mexico	192.2
42	California	189.9
43	Utah	187.4
44	Washington	182.0
45	Nevada	167.5
46	Florida	156.9
47	Alaska	154.3
48	Hawaii	142.4
49	Arizona	121.5
50	Oregon	114.2

| | District of Columbia | 256.3 |

Source: U.S. Department of Health and Human Services, Centers for Medicare and Medicaid Services
"Health, United States, 2007" (www.cdc.gov/nchs/data/hus/hus07.pdf)
*Number of nursing home residents (all ages) per 1,000 resident population 85 years of age and over.

Nursing Home Population in 2006

National Total = 1,433,523

ALPHA ORDER

RANK	STATE	POPULATION	% of USA
23	Alabama	23,488	1.6%
50	Alaska	640	0.0%
33	Arizona	12,775	0.9%
28	Arkansas	17,970	1.3%
2	California	105,458	7.4%
30	Colorado	16,579	1.2%
20	Connecticut	27,364	1.9%
46	Delaware	3,855	0.3%
7	Florida	72,552	5.1%
14	Georgia	35,755	2.5%
47	Hawaii	3,828	0.3%
45	Idaho	4,646	0.3%
6	Illinois	77,204	5.4%
11	Indiana	39,758	2.8%
21	Iowa	26,866	1.9%
26	Kansas	19,785	1.4%
24	Kentucky	23,261	1.6%
19	Louisiana	27,800	1.9%
39	Maine	6,651	0.5%
22	Maryland	25,273	1.8%
9	Massachusetts	45,068	3.1%
10	Michigan	41,090	2.9%
17	Minnesota	32,738	2.3%
31	Mississippi	16,419	1.1%
13	Missouri	38,001	2.7%
43	Montana	5,405	0.4%
32	Nebraska	13,327	0.9%
44	Nevada	4,664	0.3%
37	New Hampshire	7,052	0.5%
8	New Jersey	45,667	3.2%
40	New Mexico	6,019	0.4%
1	New York	112,141	7.8%
12	North Carolina	38,362	2.7%
41	North Dakota	5,967	0.4%
4	Ohio	81,275	5.7%
25	Oklahoma	20,242	1.4%
36	Oregon	8,108	0.6%
5	Pennsylvania	80,660	5.6%
35	Rhode Island	8,265	0.6%
29	South Carolina	16,635	1.2%
38	South Dakota	6,677	0.5%
16	Tennessee	32,819	2.3%
3	Texas	89,788	6.3%
42	Utah	5,480	0.4%
48	Vermont	3,111	0.2%
18	Virginia	28,380	2.0%
27	Washington	19,478	1.4%
34	West Virginia	9,832	0.7%
15	Wisconsin	34,111	2.4%
49	Wyoming	2,474	0.2%

RANK ORDER

RANK	STATE	POPULATION	% of USA
1	New York	112,141	7.8%
2	California	105,458	7.4%
3	Texas	89,788	6.3%
4	Ohio	81,275	5.7%
5	Pennsylvania	80,660	5.6%
6	Illinois	77,204	5.4%
7	Florida	72,552	5.1%
8	New Jersey	45,667	3.2%
9	Massachusetts	45,068	3.1%
10	Michigan	41,090	2.9%
11	Indiana	39,758	2.8%
12	North Carolina	38,362	2.7%
13	Missouri	38,001	2.7%
14	Georgia	35,755	2.5%
15	Wisconsin	34,111	2.4%
16	Tennessee	32,819	2.3%
17	Minnesota	32,738	2.3%
18	Virginia	28,380	2.0%
19	Louisiana	27,800	1.9%
20	Connecticut	27,364	1.9%
21	Iowa	26,866	1.9%
22	Maryland	25,273	1.8%
23	Alabama	23,488	1.6%
24	Kentucky	23,261	1.6%
25	Oklahoma	20,242	1.4%
26	Kansas	19,785	1.4%
27	Washington	19,478	1.4%
28	Arkansas	17,970	1.3%
29	South Carolina	16,635	1.2%
30	Colorado	16,579	1.2%
31	Mississippi	16,419	1.1%
32	Nebraska	13,327	0.9%
33	Arizona	12,775	0.9%
34	West Virginia	9,832	0.7%
35	Rhode Island	8,265	0.6%
36	Oregon	8,108	0.6%
37	New Hampshire	7,052	0.5%
38	South Dakota	6,677	0.5%
39	Maine	6,651	0.5%
40	New Mexico	6,019	0.4%
41	North Dakota	5,967	0.4%
42	Utah	5,480	0.4%
43	Montana	5,405	0.4%
44	Nevada	4,664	0.3%
45	Idaho	4,646	0.3%
46	Delaware	3,855	0.3%
47	Hawaii	3,828	0.3%
48	Vermont	3,111	0.2%
49	Wyoming	2,474	0.2%
50	Alaska	640	0.0%
	District of Columbia	2,760	0.2%

Source: U.S. Department of Health and Human Services, Centers for Medicare and Medicaid Services
"Health, United States, 2007" (www.cdc.gov/nchs/data/hus/hus07.pdf)

Health Care Establishments in 2005

National Total = 598,762 Establishments*

ALPHA ORDER

RANK	STATE	ESTABLISH'S	% of USA
26	Alabama	7,694	1.3%
47	Alaska	1,493	0.2%
16	Arizona	11,812	2.0%
32	Arkansas	5,296	0.9%
1	California	77,264	12.9%
20	Colorado	10,292	1.7%
27	Connecticut	7,629	1.3%
45	Delaware	1,694	0.3%
4	Florida	41,077	6.9%
10	Georgia	15,588	2.6%
41	Hawaii	2,782	0.5%
40	Idaho	3,222	0.5%
6	Illinois	23,925	4.0%
18	Indiana	11,299	1.9%
31	Iowa	5,656	0.9%
30	Kansas	5,692	1.0%
25	Kentucky	7,988	1.3%
23	Louisiana	8,966	1.5%
39	Maine	3,311	0.6%
15	Maryland	11,934	2.0%
12	Massachusetts	13,273	2.2%
9	Michigan	20,658	3.5%
22	Minnesota	9,941	1.7%
35	Mississippi	4,251	0.7%
17	Missouri	11,595	1.9%
44	Montana	2,271	0.4%
37	Nebraska	3,486	0.6%
34	Nevada	4,513	0.8%
43	New Hampshire	2,393	0.4%
8	New Jersey	20,733	3.5%
37	New Mexico	3,486	0.6%
3	New York	42,268	7.1%
11	North Carolina	15,052	2.5%
49	North Dakota	1,219	0.2%
7	Ohio	22,029	3.7%
28	Oklahoma	7,611	1.3%
24	Oregon	8,538	1.4%
5	Pennsylvania	27,389	4.6%
42	Rhode Island	2,504	0.4%
29	South Carolina	6,970	1.2%
46	South Dakota	1,559	0.3%
19	Tennessee	10,823	1.8%
2	Texas	42,313	7.1%
33	Utah	5,073	0.8%
48	Vermont	1,440	0.2%
14	Virginia	12,864	2.1%
13	Washington	13,221	2.2%
36	West Virginia	3,803	0.6%
21	Wisconsin	10,261	1.7%
50	Wyoming	1,199	0.2%

RANK ORDER

RANK	STATE	ESTABLISH'S	% of USA
1	California	77,264	12.9%
2	Texas	42,313	7.1%
3	New York	42,268	7.1%
4	Florida	41,077	6.9%
5	Pennsylvania	27,389	4.6%
6	Illinois	23,925	4.0%
7	Ohio	22,029	3.7%
8	New Jersey	20,733	3.5%
9	Michigan	20,658	3.5%
10	Georgia	15,588	2.6%
11	North Carolina	15,052	2.5%
12	Massachusetts	13,273	2.2%
13	Washington	13,221	2.2%
14	Virginia	12,864	2.1%
15	Maryland	11,934	2.0%
16	Arizona	11,812	2.0%
17	Missouri	11,595	1.9%
18	Indiana	11,299	1.9%
19	Tennessee	10,823	1.8%
20	Colorado	10,292	1.7%
21	Wisconsin	10,261	1.7%
22	Minnesota	9,941	1.7%
23	Louisiana	8,966	1.5%
24	Oregon	8,538	1.4%
25	Kentucky	7,988	1.3%
26	Alabama	7,694	1.3%
27	Connecticut	7,629	1.3%
28	Oklahoma	7,611	1.3%
29	South Carolina	6,970	1.2%
30	Kansas	5,692	1.0%
31	Iowa	5,656	0.9%
32	Arkansas	5,296	0.9%
33	Utah	5,073	0.8%
34	Nevada	4,513	0.8%
35	Mississippi	4,251	0.7%
36	West Virginia	3,803	0.6%
37	Nebraska	3,486	0.6%
37	New Mexico	3,486	0.6%
39	Maine	3,311	0.6%
40	Idaho	3,222	0.5%
41	Hawaii	2,782	0.5%
42	Rhode Island	2,504	0.4%
43	New Hampshire	2,393	0.4%
44	Montana	2,271	0.4%
45	Delaware	1,694	0.3%
46	South Dakota	1,559	0.3%
47	Alaska	1,493	0.2%
48	Vermont	1,440	0.2%
49	North Dakota	1,219	0.2%
50	Wyoming	1,199	0.2%
	District of Columbia	1,412	0.2%

Source: U.S. Bureau of the Census
 "County Business Patterns 2005 (NAICS)" (http://censtats.census.gov/cbpnaic/cbpnaic.shtml)
*Includes establishments exempt from as well as subject to the federal income tax. Includes those establishments within the North American Industry Classification System (NAICS) classifications 621 (ambulatory health care services), 622 (hospitals), and 623 (nursing and residential care facilities). Does not include classification 624 (social assistance facilities).

IV. Finance

Average Medical Malpractice Payment in 2005 237

Percent of Private-Sector Establishments That Offer
Health Insurance: 2005 238

Percent of Private-Sector Establishments with Fewer
Than 50 Employees That Offer Health Insurance:
2005 239

Percent of Private-Sector Establishments with More
Than 50 Employees That Offer Health Insurance:
2005 240

Average Annual Single Coverage Health Insurance
Premium per Enrolled Employee in 2005 241

Average Annual Employee Contribution for Single
Coverage Health Insurance in 2005 242

Percent of Total Premiums for Single Coverage Health
Insurance Paid by Employees in 2005 243

Average Annual Family Coverage Health Insurance
Premium per Enrolled Employee in 2005 244

Average Annual Employee Contribution for Family
Coverage Health Insurance in 2005 245

Percent of Total Premiums for Family Coverage Health
Insurance Paid by Employees in 2005 246

Persons Not Covered by Health Insurance in 2006 247

Percent of Population Not Covered by Health Insurance
in 2006 248

Numerical Change in Persons Uninsured: 2002 to 2006 . . 249

Percent Change in Persons Uninsured: 2002 to 2006 250

Change in Percent of Population Uninsured:
2002 to 2006 251

Percent of Children Not Covered by Health Insurance
in 2006 252

Persons Covered by Health Insurance in 2006 253

Percent of Population Covered by Health Insurance
in 2006 254

Percent of Population Covered by Private Health
Insurance in 2006 255

Percent of Population Covered by Employment-Based
Health Insurance in 2006 256

Percent of Population Covered by Direct Purchase
Health Insurance in 2006 257

Percent of Population Covered by Government Health
Insurance in 2006 258

Percent of Population Covered by Military Health Care
in 2006 259

Percent of Children Covered by Health Insurance
in 2006 260

Percent of Children Covered by Private Health Insurance
in 2006 261

Percent of Children Covered by Employment-Based
Health Insurance in 2006 262

Percent of Children Covered by Direct Purchase Health
Insurance in 2006 263

Percent of Children Covered by Government Health
Insurance in 2006 264

Percent of Children Covered by Military Health Care
in 2006 265

Percent of Children Covered by Medicaid in 2006 266

State Children's Health Insurance Program (SCHIP)
Enrollment in 2006 267

Percent Change in State Children's Health Insurance
Program (SCHIP) Enrollment: 2005 to 2006 268

Percent of Children Enrolled in State Children's Health
Insurance Program (SCHIP) in 2006 269

Expenditures for State Children's Health Insurance
Program (SCHIP) in 2006 270

Per Capita Expenditures for State Children's Health
Insurance Program (SCHIP) in 2006 271

Expenditures per State Children's Health Insurance
Program (SCHIP) Participant in 2006 272

Health Maintenance Organizations (HMOs) in 2007 273

Enrollees in Health Maintenance Organizations (HMOs)
in 2007 274

Percent Change in Enrollees in Health Maintenance
Organizations (HMOs): 2006 to 2007 275

Percent of Population Enrolled in Health Maintenance
Organizations (HMOs) in 2007 276

Percent of Insured Population Enrolled in Health
Maintenance Organizations (HMOs) in 2007 277

Medicare Enrollees in 2006 278

Percent Change in Medicare Enrollees: 2005 to 2006 279
Percent of Population Enrolled in Medicare in 2006 280
Percent of Medicare Enrollees in Managed Care
    Programs in 2006 281
Percent of Physicians Participating in Medicare
    in 2007 282
Medicare Program Payments in 2006 283
Per Capita Medicare Program Payments in 2006 284
Medicare Program Payments per Enrollee in 2006 285
Medicaid Enrollment in 2006 286
Percent of Population Enrolled in Medicaid in 2006 287
Medicaid Managed Care Enrollment in 2006 288
Percent of Medicaid Enrollees in Managed Care
    in 2006 289
Estimated Medicaid Expenditures in 2007 290
Estimated Per Capita Medicaid Expenditures in 2007 ... 291
Estimated Medicaid Expenditures as a Percent of
    Total Expenditures in 2007 292
Percent Change in Medicaid Expenditures:
    2006 to 2007 293
Medicaid Expenditures in 2006 294
Per Capita Medicaid Expenditures in 2006 295
Medicaid Expenditures per Beneficiary in 2006 296
Federal Medicaid Matching Fund Rate for 2008 297
State and Local Government Expenditures for Hospitals
    in 2005 298
Per Capita State and Local Government Expenditures
    for Hospitals in 2005 299
Percent of State and Local Government Expenditures
    Used for Hospitals in 2005. 300
State and Local Government Expenditures for Health
    Programs in 2005 301
Per Capita State and Local Government Expenditures
    for Health Programs in 2005 302
Percent of State and Local Government Expenditures
    Used for Health Programs in 2005. 303
Estimated Tobacco Settlement Revenues in Fiscal Year
    2008 304
Personal Health Care Expenditures in 2004 305
Health Care Expenditures as a Percent of Gross State
    Product in 2004 306
Per Capita Personal Health Care Expenditures in 2004 ... 307
Average Annual Growth in Personal Health Care
    Expenditures: 1991–2004 308

Expenditures for Hospital Care in 2004 309
Percent of Total Personal Health Care Expenditures
    Spent on Hospital Care in 2004 310
Per Capita Expenditures for Hospital Care in 2004 311
Expenditures for Physician and Clinical Services
    in 2004 312
Percent of Total Personal Health Care Expenditures
    Spent on Physician and Clinical Services in 2004..... 313
Per Capita Expenditures for Physician and Clinical
    Services in 2004 314
Expenditures for Dental Services in 2004 315
Percent of Total Personal Health Care Expenditures
    Spent on Dental Services in 2004 316
Per Capita Expenditures for Dental Care in 2004 317
Expenditures for Other Professional Health Care Services
    in 2004 318
Percent of Total Personal Health Care Expenditures
    Spent on Other Professional Health Care Services
    in 2004 319
Per Capita Expenditures for Other Professional Health
    Care Services in 2004 320
Expenditures for Nursing Home Care in 2004 321
Percent of Total Personal Health Care Expenditures
    Spent on Nursing Home Care in 2004 322
Per Capita Expenditures for Nursing Home Care
    in 2004 323
Expenditures for Home Health Care in 2004 324
Percent of Total Personal Health Care Expenditures
    Spent on Home Health Care in 2004 325
Per Capita Expenditures for Home Health Care in 2004 .. 326
Expenditures for Drugs and Other Medical Nondurables
    in 2004 327
Percent of Total Personal Health Care Expenditures
    Spent on Drugs and Other Medical Nondurables
    in 2004 328
Per Capita Expenditures for Drugs and Other Medical
    Nondurables in 2004 329
Expenditures for Durable Medical Products in 2004 330
Percent of Total Personal Health Care Expenditures
    Spent on Durable Medical Products in 2004 331
Per Capita Expenditures for Durable Medical Products
    in 2004 332
Projected National Health Care Expenditures in 2008 ... 333

Average Medical Malpractice Payment in 2005

National Average = $294,153*

ALPHA ORDER			RANK ORDER		
RANK	STATE	AVERAGE PAYMENT	RANK	STATE	AVERAGE PAYMENT
29	Alabama	$256,056	1	Connecticut	$735,569
3	Alaska	533,524	2	Hawaii	577,834
22	Arizona	304,851	3	Alaska	533,524
19	Arkansas	311,623	4	Illinois	510,668
39	California	210,060	5	Massachusetts	476,428
25	Colorado	277,620	6	Delaware	456,677
1	Connecticut	735,569	7	Minnesota	449,819
6	Delaware	456,677	8	New York	390,802
34	Florida**	240,256	9	New Jersey	374,247
16	Georgia	337,322	10	Maryland	371,299
2	Hawaii	577,834	11	Wisconsin**	370,236
43	Idaho	190,122	12	Rhode Island	362,268
4	Illinois	510,668	13	New Hampshire	358,227
26	Indiana**	271,139	14	Virginia	353,882
40	Iowa	199,179	15	Pennsylvania**	346,832
47	Kansas**	156,552	16	Georgia	337,322
37	Kentucky	234,316	17	Washington	331,034
44	Louisiana**	181,897	18	Oregon	314,973
35	Maine	239,414	19	Arkansas	311,623
10	Maryland	371,299	20	North Carolina	308,528
5	Massachusetts	476,428	21	Ohio	305,501
49	Michigan	134,837	22	Arizona	304,851
7	Minnesota	449,819	23	Missouri	303,064
41	Mississippi	199,155	24	Wyoming	290,464
23	Missouri	303,064	25	Colorado	277,620
28	Montana	259,141	26	Indiana**	271,139
50	Nebraska**	98,998	27	South Dakota	268,200
32	Nevada	245,924	28	Montana	259,141
13	New Hampshire	358,227	29	Alabama	256,056
9	New Jersey	374,247	30	Tennessee	254,960
36	New Mexico**	239,150	31	North Dakota	254,147
8	New York	390,802	32	Nevada	245,924
20	North Carolina	308,528	33	Oklahoma	243,224
31	North Dakota	254,147	34	Florida**	240,256
21	Ohio	305,501	35	Maine	239,414
33	Oklahoma	243,224	36	New Mexico**	239,150
18	Oregon	314,973	37	Kentucky	234,316
15	Pennsylvania**	346,832	38	West Virginia	231,753
12	Rhode Island	362,268	39	California	210,060
45	South Carolina**	167,587	40	Iowa	199,179
27	South Dakota	268,200	41	Mississippi	199,155
30	Tennessee	254,960	42	Texas	191,060
42	Texas	191,060	43	Idaho	190,122
48	Utah	153,393	44	Louisiana**	181,897
46	Vermont	161,478	45	South Carolina**	167,587
14	Virginia	353,882	46	Vermont	161,478
17	Washington	331,034	47	Kansas**	156,552
38	West Virginia	231,753	48	Utah	153,393
11	Wisconsin**	370,236	49	Michigan	134,837
24	Wyoming	290,464	50	Nebraska**	98,998
				District of Columbia	367,541

Source: U.S. Department of Health and Human Services, Bureau of Health Professions
   "National Practitioner Data Bank, 2005 Annual Report" (http://www.npdb-hipdb.com/annualrpt.html)
*National figure includes U.S. territories and U.S. Armed Forces locations overseas.
**The figures for these states have not been adjusted for payments by state compensation funds and other similar funds.
Average payments for these states understate the actual average amounts received by claimants.

Percent of Private-Sector Establishments That Offer Health Insurance: 2005

National Percent = 56.3%

ALPHA ORDER

RANK	STATE	PERCENT
11	Alabama	59.8
47	Alaska	42.4
23	Arizona	55.0
48	Arkansas	40.8
11	California	59.8
26	Colorado	54.1
4	Connecticut	63.8
15	Delaware	57.6
33	Florida	51.2
32	Georgia	52.3
1	Hawaii	89.6
46	Idaho	43.8
28	Illinois	53.3
21	Indiana	55.9
42	Iowa	47.9
35	Kansas	50.8
16	Kentucky	57.1
31	Louisiana	52.6
22	Maine	55.6
3	Maryland	64.1
5	Massachusetts	63.3
10	Michigan	59.9
25	Minnesota	54.3
43	Mississippi	45.3
36	Missouri	50.6
49	Montana	39.2
44	Nebraska	45.2
30	Nevada	52.8
7	New Hampshire	62.0
2	New Jersey	69.3
33	New Mexico	51.2
9	New York	60.1
18	North Carolina	56.7
38	North Dakota	49.1
6	Ohio	62.8
40	Oklahoma	48.3
18	Oregon	56.7
8	Pennsylvania	61.5
13	Rhode Island	59.5
29	South Carolina	53.2
41	South Dakota	48.1
24	Tennessee	54.7
37	Texas	50.1
45	Utah	44.1
17	Vermont	56.8
18	Virginia	56.7
27	Washington	53.8
39	West Virginia	48.8
14	Wisconsin	59.3
50	Wyoming	38.6

RANK ORDER

RANK	STATE	PERCENT
1	Hawaii	89.6
2	New Jersey	69.3
3	Maryland	64.1
4	Connecticut	63.8
5	Massachusetts	63.3
6	Ohio	62.8
7	New Hampshire	62.0
8	Pennsylvania	61.5
9	New York	60.1
10	Michigan	59.9
11	Alabama	59.8
11	California	59.8
13	Rhode Island	59.5
14	Wisconsin	59.3
15	Delaware	57.6
16	Kentucky	57.1
17	Vermont	56.8
18	North Carolina	56.7
18	Oregon	56.7
18	Virginia	56.7
21	Indiana	55.9
22	Maine	55.6
23	Arizona	55.0
24	Tennessee	54.7
25	Minnesota	54.3
26	Colorado	54.1
27	Washington	53.8
28	Illinois	53.3
29	South Carolina	53.2
30	Nevada	52.8
31	Louisiana	52.6
32	Georgia	52.3
33	Florida	51.2
33	New Mexico	51.2
35	Kansas	50.8
36	Missouri	50.6
37	Texas	50.1
38	North Dakota	49.1
39	West Virginia	48.8
40	Oklahoma	48.3
41	South Dakota	48.1
42	Iowa	47.9
43	Mississippi	45.3
44	Nebraska	45.2
45	Utah	44.1
46	Idaho	43.8
47	Alaska	42.4
48	Arkansas	40.8
49	Montana	39.2
50	Wyoming	38.6

District of Columbia	74.3

Source: U.S. Department of Health and Human Services, Agency for Healthcare Research and Quality
"Private-Sector Data by Firm Size and State" (Table II Series, Medical Expenditures Panel Survey)
(http://www.meps.ahrq.gov/mepsweb/survey_comp/Insurance.jsp)

Percent of Private-Sector Establishments with Fewer Than 50 Employees That Offer Health Insurance: 2005
National Percent = 43.4%

ALPHA ORDER

RANK	STATE	PERCENT
15	Alabama	46.3
48	Alaska	27.1
28	Arizona	37.9
50	Arkansas	22.2
11	California	49.0
25	Colorado	40.6
3	Connecticut	53.5
20	Delaware	42.7
27	Florida	38.0
37	Georgia	35.7
1	Hawaii	85.8
44	Idaho	30.8
26	Illinois	40.2
23	Indiana	41.4
39	Iowa	33.8
32	Kansas	37.0
18	Kentucky	43.5
34	Louisiana	36.6
16	Maine	44.9
5	Maryland	51.0
4	Massachusetts	52.7
8	Michigan	50.0
24	Minnesota	41.3
46	Mississippi	28.1
33	Missouri	36.9
47	Montana	27.7
43	Nebraska	31.3
36	Nevada	36.2
6	New Hampshire	50.6
2	New Jersey	62.3
35	New Mexico	36.3
6	New York	50.6
22	North Carolina	42.2
29	North Dakota	37.6
9	Ohio	49.1
41	Oklahoma	32.7
16	Oregon	44.9
12	Pennsylvania	48.5
9	Rhode Island	49.1
31	South Carolina	37.1
30	South Dakota	37.3
38	Tennessee	35.4
40	Texas	33.6
45	Utah	29.1
13	Vermont	48.4
19	Virginia	43.2
20	Washington	42.7
42	West Virginia	32.2
14	Wisconsin	47.2
49	Wyoming	25.2

RANK ORDER

RANK	STATE	PERCENT
1	Hawaii	85.8
2	New Jersey	62.3
3	Connecticut	53.5
4	Massachusetts	52.7
5	Maryland	51.0
6	New Hampshire	50.6
6	New York	50.6
8	Michigan	50.0
9	Ohio	49.1
9	Rhode Island	49.1
11	California	49.0
12	Pennsylvania	48.5
13	Vermont	48.4
14	Wisconsin	47.2
15	Alabama	46.3
16	Maine	44.9
16	Oregon	44.9
18	Kentucky	43.5
19	Virginia	43.2
20	Delaware	42.7
20	Washington	42.7
22	North Carolina	42.2
23	Indiana	41.4
24	Minnesota	41.3
25	Colorado	40.6
26	Illinois	40.2
27	Florida	38.0
28	Arizona	37.9
29	North Dakota	37.6
30	South Dakota	37.3
31	South Carolina	37.1
32	Kansas	37.0
33	Missouri	36.9
34	Louisiana	36.6
35	New Mexico	36.3
36	Nevada	36.2
37	Georgia	35.7
38	Tennessee	35.4
39	Iowa	33.8
40	Texas	33.6
41	Oklahoma	32.7
42	West Virginia	32.2
43	Nebraska	31.3
44	Idaho	30.8
45	Utah	29.1
46	Mississippi	28.1
47	Montana	27.7
48	Alaska	27.1
49	Wyoming	25.2
50	Arkansas	22.2
	District of Columbia	61.8

Source: U.S. Department of Health and Human Services, Agency for Healthcare Research and Quality
"Private-Sector Data by Firm Size and State" (Table II Series, Medical Expenditures Panel Survey)
(http://www.meps.ahrq.gov/mepsweb/survey_comp/Insurance.jsp)

Percent of Private-Sector Establishments with More Than 50 Employees That Offer Health Insurance: 2005
National Percent = 95.7%

ALPHA ORDER

RANK	STATE	PERCENT
16	Alabama	96.9
30	Alaska	95.2
14	Arizona	97.2
43	Arkansas	93.4
21	California	96.2
4	Colorado	98.9
4	Connecticut	98.9
47	Delaware	93.1
38	Florida	94.4
34	Georgia	94.9
1	Hawaii	100.0
30	Idaho	95.2
36	Illinois	94.6
43	Indiana	93.4
18	Iowa	96.5
27	Kansas	95.5
42	Kentucky	93.5
43	Louisiana	93.4
11	Maine	97.4
13	Maryland	97.3
19	Massachusetts	96.3
40	Michigan	94.1
3	Minnesota	99.0
48	Mississippi	93.0
29	Missouri	95.4
50	Montana	91.0
21	Nebraska	96.2
15	Nevada	97.0
9	New Hampshire	97.5
38	New Jersey	94.4
49	New Mexico	92.6
6	New York	98.5
27	North Carolina	95.5
19	North Dakota	96.3
23	Ohio	96.1
35	Oklahoma	94.7
25	Oregon	95.7
26	Pennsylvania	95.6
2	Rhode Island	99.2
30	South Carolina	95.2
8	South Dakota	97.8
7	Tennessee	98.0
43	Texas	93.4
33	Utah	95.1
16	Vermont	96.9
11	Virginia	97.4
41	Washington	93.7
37	West Virginia	94.5
9	Wisconsin	97.5
24	Wyoming	95.8

RANK ORDER

RANK	STATE	PERCENT
1	Hawaii	100.0
2	Rhode Island	99.2
3	Minnesota	99.0
4	Colorado	98.9
4	Connecticut	98.9
6	New York	98.5
7	Tennessee	98.0
8	South Dakota	97.8
9	New Hampshire	97.5
9	Wisconsin	97.5
11	Maine	97.4
11	Virginia	97.4
13	Maryland	97.3
14	Arizona	97.2
15	Nevada	97.0
16	Alabama	96.9
16	Vermont	96.9
18	Iowa	96.5
19	Massachusetts	96.3
19	North Dakota	96.3
21	California	96.2
21	Nebraska	96.2
23	Ohio	96.1
24	Wyoming	95.8
25	Oregon	95.7
26	Pennsylvania	95.6
27	Kansas	95.5
27	North Carolina	95.5
29	Missouri	95.4
30	Alaska	95.2
30	Idaho	95.2
30	South Carolina	95.2
33	Utah	95.1
34	Georgia	94.9
35	Oklahoma	94.7
36	Illinois	94.6
37	West Virginia	94.5
38	Florida	94.4
38	New Jersey	94.4
40	Michigan	94.1
41	Washington	93.7
42	Kentucky	93.5
43	Arkansas	93.4
43	Indiana	93.4
43	Louisiana	93.4
43	Texas	93.4
47	Delaware	93.1
48	Mississippi	93.0
49	New Mexico	92.6
50	Montana	91.0

District of Columbia	95.9

Source: U.S. Department of Health and Human Services, Agency for Healthcare Research and Quality
"Private-Sector Data by Firm Size and State" (Table II Series, Medical Expenditures Panel Survey)
(http://www.meps.ahrq.gov/mepsweb/survey_comp/Insurance.jsp)

Average Annual Single Coverage Health Insurance Premium per Enrolled Employee in 2005
National Average = $3,991*

ALPHA ORDER				RANK ORDER		
RANK	STATE	PREMIUM		RANK	STATE	PREMIUM
48	Alabama	$3,419		1	Alaska	$5,088
1	Alaska	5,088		2	Delaware	4,623
8	Arizona	4,294		3	Rhode Island	4,417
46	Arkansas	3,590		4	Vermont	4,392
33	California	3,823		5	Connecticut	4,390
30	Colorado	3,891		6	Wyoming	4,388
5	Connecticut	4,390		7	New Jersey	4,332
2	Delaware	4,623		8	Arizona	4,294
23	Florida	4,003		9	Maine	4,290
31	Georgia	3,861		10	Michigan	4,287
50	Hawaii	3,339		11	New York	4,239
19	Idaho	4,078		12	Massachusetts	4,235
21	Illinois	4,049		13	Wisconsin	4,223
22	Indiana	4,042		14	Pennsylvania	4,195
44	Iowa	3,686		15	New Hampshire	4,175
40	Kansas	3,755		16	West Virginia	4,128
33	Kentucky	3,823		17	Texas	4,108
27	Louisiana	3,931		18	Oklahoma	4,088
9	Maine	4,290		19	Idaho	4,078
32	Maryland	3,834		20	Oregon	4,051
12	Massachusetts	4,235		21	Illinois	4,049
10	Michigan	4,287		22	Indiana	4,042
26	Minnesota	3,932		23	Florida	4,003
49	Mississippi	3,402		24	Washington	3,975
42	Missouri	3,741		25	South Carolina	3,943
29	Montana	3,898		26	Minnesota	3,932
39	Nebraska	3,777		27	Louisiana	3,931
41	Nevada	3,752		28	Ohio	3,928
15	New Hampshire	4,175		29	Montana	3,898
7	New Jersey	4,332		30	Colorado	3,891
36	New Mexico	3,813		31	Georgia	3,861
11	New York	4,239		32	Maryland	3,834
37	North Carolina	3,802		33	California	3,823
47	North Dakota	3,438		33	Kentucky	3,823
28	Ohio	3,928		35	Tennessee	3,822
18	Oklahoma	4,088		36	New Mexico	3,813
20	Oregon	4,051		37	North Carolina	3,802
14	Pennsylvania	4,195		38	South Dakota	3,796
3	Rhode Island	4,417		39	Nebraska	3,777
25	South Carolina	3,943		40	Kansas	3,755
38	South Dakota	3,796		41	Nevada	3,752
35	Tennessee	3,822		42	Missouri	3,741
17	Texas	4,108		43	Virginia	3,734
45	Utah	3,633		44	Iowa	3,686
4	Vermont	4,392		45	Utah	3,633
43	Virginia	3,734		46	Arkansas	3,590
24	Washington	3,975		47	North Dakota	3,438
16	West Virginia	4,128		48	Alabama	3,419
13	Wisconsin	4,223		49	Mississippi	3,402
6	Wyoming	4,388		50	Hawaii	3,339
					District of Columbia	4,220

Source: U.S. Department of Health and Human Services, Agency for Healthcare Research and Quality
   "Private-Sector Data by Firm Size and State" (Table II Series, Medical Expenditures Panel Survey)
      (http://www.meps.ahrq.gov/mepsweb/survey_comp/Insurance.jsp)
*Enrolled employees at private-sector establishments that offer health insurance coverage.

Average Annual Employee Contribution for
Single Coverage Health Insurance in 2005
National Average = $723*

ALPHA ORDER

RANK	STATE	PREMIUM
11	Alabama	$838
5	Alaska	895
24	Arizona	752
16	Arkansas	796
46	California	592
27	Colorado	741
26	Connecticut	749
3	Delaware	905
6	Florida	892
33	Georgia	707
50	Hawaii	302
29	Idaho	737
9	Illinois	846
35	Indiana	701
23	Iowa	762
31	Kansas	721
30	Kentucky	731
14	Louisiana	803
19	Maine	792
4	Maryland	896
2	Massachusetts	918
34	Michigan	704
12	Minnesota	809
44	Mississippi	648
41	Missouri	665
47	Montana	548
21	Nebraska	776
36	Nevada	691
1	New Hampshire	965
8	New Jersey	847
18	New Mexico	794
20	New York	781
37	North Carolina	681
31	North Dakota	721
39	Ohio	674
38	Oklahoma	680
48	Oregon	503
42	Pennsylvania	659
10	Rhode Island	840
21	South Carolina	776
13	South Dakota	807
15	Tennessee	800
45	Texas	617
16	Utah	796
28	Vermont	739
24	Virginia	752
49	Washington	384
43	West Virginia	656
7	Wisconsin	859
40	Wyoming	673

RANK ORDER

RANK	STATE	PREMIUM
1	New Hampshire	$965
2	Massachusetts	918
3	Delaware	905
4	Maryland	896
5	Alaska	895
6	Florida	892
7	Wisconsin	859
8	New Jersey	847
9	Illinois	846
10	Rhode Island	840
11	Alabama	838
12	Minnesota	809
13	South Dakota	807
14	Louisiana	803
15	Tennessee	800
16	Arkansas	796
16	Utah	796
18	New Mexico	794
19	Maine	792
20	New York	781
21	Nebraska	776
21	South Carolina	776
23	Iowa	762
24	Arizona	752
24	Virginia	752
26	Connecticut	749
27	Colorado	741
28	Vermont	739
29	Idaho	737
30	Kentucky	731
31	Kansas	721
31	North Dakota	721
33	Georgia	707
34	Michigan	704
35	Indiana	701
36	Nevada	691
37	North Carolina	681
38	Oklahoma	680
39	Ohio	674
40	Wyoming	673
41	Missouri	665
42	Pennsylvania	659
43	West Virginia	656
44	Mississippi	648
45	Texas	617
46	California	592
47	Montana	548
48	Oregon	503
49	Washington	384
50	Hawaii	302

District of Columbia   765

Source: U.S. Department of Health and Human Services, Agency for Healthcare Research and Quality
"Private-Sector Data by Firm Size and State" (Table II Series, Medical Expenditures Panel Survey)
(http://www.meps.ahrq.gov/mepsweb/survey_comp/Insurance.jsp)
*Enrolled employees at private-sector establishments that offer health insurance coverage.

Percent of Total Premiums for Single Coverage
Health Insurance Paid by Employees in 2005
National Average = 18.1%*

ALPHA ORDER

RANK	STATE	PERCENT
1	Alabama	24.5
34	Alaska	17.6
35	Arizona	17.5
5	Arkansas	22.2
44	California	15.5
24	Colorado	19.0
37	Connecticut	17.1
20	Delaware	19.6
4	Florida	22.3
30	Georgia	18.3
50	Hawaii	9.0
31	Idaho	18.1
10	Illinois	20.9
36	Indiana	17.3
13	Iowa	20.7
22	Kansas	19.2
23	Kentucky	19.1
16	Louisiana	20.4
27	Maine	18.5
2	Maryland	23.4
7	Massachusetts	21.7
41	Michigan	16.4
14	Minnesota	20.6
24	Mississippi	19.0
33	Missouri	17.8
47	Montana	14.1
15	Nebraska	20.5
28	Nevada	18.4
3	New Hampshire	23.1
20	New Jersey	19.6
12	New Mexico	20.8
28	New York	18.4
32	North Carolina	17.9
9	North Dakota	21.0
37	Ohio	17.1
40	Oklahoma	16.6
48	Oregon	12.4
43	Pennsylvania	15.7
24	Rhode Island	19.0
19	South Carolina	19.7
8	South Dakota	21.2
10	Tennessee	20.9
46	Texas	15.0
6	Utah	21.9
39	Vermont	16.8
18	Virginia	20.1
49	Washington	9.7
42	West Virginia	15.9
17	Wisconsin	20.3
45	Wyoming	15.3

RANK ORDER

RANK	STATE	PERCENT
1	Alabama	24.5
2	Maryland	23.4
3	New Hampshire	23.1
4	Florida	22.3
5	Arkansas	22.2
6	Utah	21.9
7	Massachusetts	21.7
8	South Dakota	21.2
9	North Dakota	21.0
10	Illinois	20.9
10	Tennessee	20.9
12	New Mexico	20.8
13	Iowa	20.7
14	Minnesota	20.6
15	Nebraska	20.5
16	Louisiana	20.4
17	Wisconsin	20.3
18	Virginia	20.1
19	South Carolina	19.7
20	Delaware	19.6
20	New Jersey	19.6
22	Kansas	19.2
23	Kentucky	19.1
24	Colorado	19.0
24	Mississippi	19.0
24	Rhode Island	19.0
27	Maine	18.5
28	Nevada	18.4
28	New York	18.4
30	Georgia	18.3
31	Idaho	18.1
32	North Carolina	17.9
33	Missouri	17.8
34	Alaska	17.6
35	Arizona	17.5
36	Indiana	17.3
37	Connecticut	17.1
37	Ohio	17.1
39	Vermont	16.8
40	Oklahoma	16.6
41	Michigan	16.4
42	West Virginia	15.9
43	Pennsylvania	15.7
44	California	15.5
45	Wyoming	15.3
46	Texas	15.0
47	Montana	14.1
48	Oregon	12.4
49	Washington	9.7
50	Hawaii	9.0
	District of Columbia	18.1

Source: U.S. Department of Health and Human Services, Agency for Healthcare Research and Quality
"Private-Sector Data by Firm Size and State" (Table II Series, Medical Expenditures Panel Survey)
(http://www.meps.ahrq.gov/mepsweb/survey_comp/Insurance.jsp)
*Enrolled employees at private-sector establishments that offer health insurance coverage.

Average Annual Family Coverage Health Insurance Premium per Enrolled Employee in 2005
National Average = $10,728*

ALPHA ORDER

RANK	STATE	PREMIUM
46	Alabama	$9,420
4	Alaska	11,542
37	Arizona	10,268
49	Arkansas	9,190
29	California	10,551
21	Colorado	10,850
3	Connecticut	11,717
17	Delaware	10,964
20	Florida	10,852
38	Georgia	10,262
47	Hawaii	9,392
32	Idaho	10,398
28	Illinois	10,574
23	Indiana	10,678
48	Iowa	9,359
44	Kansas	9,734
26	Kentucky	10,617
27	Louisiana	10,602
10	Maine	11,289
30	Maryland	10,528
7	Massachusetts	11,435
14	Michigan	11,005
22	Minnesota	10,846
41	Mississippi	9,987
42	Missouri	9,948
39	Montana	10,058
43	Nebraska	9,805
40	Nevada	10,011
2	New Hampshire	11,835
9	New Jersey	11,403
25	New Mexico	10,637
11	New York	11,280
45	North Carolina	9,657
50	North Dakota	8,334
24	Ohio	10,662
15	Oklahoma	10,985
19	Oregon	10,898
12	Pennsylvania	11,108
1	Rhode Island	11,924
31	South Carolina	10,436
34	South Dakota	10,312
33	Tennessee	10,361
5	Texas	11,533
36	Utah	10,282
8	Vermont	11,420
35	Virginia	10,292
13	Washington	11,018
18	West Virginia	10,900
16	Wisconsin	10,983
6	Wyoming	11,467

RANK ORDER

RANK	STATE	PREMIUM
1	Rhode Island	$11,924
2	New Hampshire	11,835
3	Connecticut	11,717
4	Alaska	11,542
5	Texas	11,533
6	Wyoming	11,467
7	Massachusetts	11,435
8	Vermont	11,420
9	New Jersey	11,403
10	Maine	11,289
11	New York	11,280
12	Pennsylvania	11,108
13	Washington	11,018
14	Michigan	11,005
15	Oklahoma	10,985
16	Wisconsin	10,983
17	Delaware	10,964
18	West Virginia	10,900
19	Oregon	10,898
20	Florida	10,852
21	Colorado	10,850
22	Minnesota	10,846
23	Indiana	10,678
24	Ohio	10,662
25	New Mexico	10,637
26	Kentucky	10,617
27	Louisiana	10,602
28	Illinois	10,574
29	California	10,551
30	Maryland	10,528
31	South Carolina	10,436
32	Idaho	10,398
33	Tennessee	10,361
34	South Dakota	10,312
35	Virginia	10,292
36	Utah	10,282
37	Arizona	10,268
38	Georgia	10,262
39	Montana	10,058
40	Nevada	10,011
41	Mississippi	9,987
42	Missouri	9,948
43	Nebraska	9,805
44	Kansas	9,734
45	North Carolina	9,657
46	Alabama	9,420
47	Hawaii	9,392
48	Iowa	9,359
49	Arkansas	9,190
50	North Dakota	8,334
	District of Columbia	11,623

Source: U.S. Department of Health and Human Services, Agency for Healthcare Research and Quality
"Private-Sector Data by Firm Size and State" (Table II Series, Medical Expenditures Panel Survey)
(http://www.meps.ahrq.gov/mepsweb/survey_comp/Insurance.jsp)
*Enrolled employees at private-sector establishments that offer health insurance coverage.

Average Annual Employee Contribution for Family Coverage Health Insurance in 2005
National Average = $2,585*

	ALPHA ORDER				RANK ORDER	
RANK	**STATE**	**PREMIUM**		**RANK**	**STATE**	**PREMIUM**
24	Alabama	$2,719		1	Florida	$3,497
10	Alaska	2,850		2	South Dakota	3,374
8	Arizona	2,873		3	Maine	3,303
31	Arkansas	2,523		4	Louisiana	3,160
37	California	2,390		5	Massachusetts	3,040
11	Colorado	2,845		6	Maryland	3,011
33	Connecticut	2,471		7	New Hampshire	2,882
39	Delaware	2,324		8	Arizona	2,873
1	Florida	3,497		9	Oklahoma	2,860
14	Georgia	2,830		10	Alaska	2,850
44	Hawaii	2,193		11	Colorado	2,845
21	Idaho	2,726		12	Oregon	2,838
40	Illinois	2,265		13	Texas	2,834
45	Indiana	2,188		14	Georgia	2,830
36	Iowa	2,436		15	Mississippi	2,811
35	Kansas	2,443		16	Nevada	2,800
38	Kentucky	2,342		17	Tennessee	2,752
4	Louisiana	3,160		18	New Jersey	2,742
3	Maine	3,303		19	Minnesota	2,734
6	Maryland	3,011		19	New Mexico	2,734
5	Massachusetts	3,040		21	Idaho	2,726
50	Michigan	1,891		22	North Dakota	2,723
19	Minnesota	2,734		22	Virginia	2,723
15	Mississippi	2,811		24	Alabama	2,719
34	Missouri	2,447		25	North Carolina	2,659
46	Montana	2,144		26	New York	2,609
27	Nebraska	2,605		27	Nebraska	2,605
16	Nevada	2,800		28	Utah	2,585
7	New Hampshire	2,882		29	Rhode Island	2,581
18	New Jersey	2,742		30	Vermont	2,541
19	New Mexico	2,734		31	Arkansas	2,523
26	New York	2,609		32	Washington	2,474
25	North Carolina	2,659		33	Connecticut	2,471
22	North Dakota	2,723		34	Missouri	2,447
43	Ohio	2,220		35	Kansas	2,443
9	Oklahoma	2,860		36	Iowa	2,436
12	Oregon	2,838		37	California	2,390
47	Pennsylvania	2,120		38	Kentucky	2,342
29	Rhode Island	2,581		39	Delaware	2,324
48	South Carolina	2,112		40	Illinois	2,265
2	South Dakota	3,374		41	Wisconsin	2,251
17	Tennessee	2,752		42	Wyoming	2,221
13	Texas	2,834		43	Ohio	2,220
28	Utah	2,585		44	Hawaii	2,193
30	Vermont	2,541		45	Indiana	2,188
22	Virginia	2,723		46	Montana	2,144
32	Washington	2,474		47	Pennsylvania	2,120
49	West Virginia	1,945		48	South Carolina	2,112
41	Wisconsin	2,251		49	West Virginia	1,945
42	Wyoming	2,221		50	Michigan	1,891
					District of Columbia	3,701

Source: U.S. Department of Health and Human Services, Agency for Healthcare Research and Quality
  "Private-Sector Data by Firm Size and State" (Table II Series, Medical Expenditures Panel Survey)
  (http://www.meps.ahrq.gov/mepsweb/survey_comp/Insurance.jsp)
*Enrolled employees at private-sector establishments that offer health insurance coverage.

Percent of Total Premiums for Family Coverage
Health Insurance Paid by Employees in 2005
National Average = 24.1%*

ALPHA ORDER

RANK	STATE	PERCENT
6	Alabama	28.9
27	Alaska	24.7
9	Arizona	28.0
12	Arkansas	27.5
34	California	22.7
18	Colorado	26.2
42	Connecticut	21.1
41	Delaware	21.2
3	Florida	32.2
11	Georgia	27.6
32	Hawaii	23.3
18	Idaho	26.2
39	Illinois	21.4
44	Indiana	20.5
20	Iowa	26.0
25	Kansas	25.1
37	Kentucky	22.1
4	Louisiana	29.8
5	Maine	29.3
7	Maryland	28.6
14	Massachusetts	26.6
50	Michigan	17.2
24	Minnesota	25.2
8	Mississippi	28.1
28	Missouri	24.6
40	Montana	21.3
14	Nebraska	26.6
9	Nevada	28.0
30	New Hampshire	24.4
31	New Jersey	24.0
23	New Mexico	25.7
33	New York	23.1
12	North Carolina	27.5
1	North Dakota	32.7
43	Ohio	20.8
20	Oklahoma	26.0
20	Oregon	26.0
48	Pennsylvania	19.1
38	Rhode Island	21.6
46	South Carolina	20.2
1	South Dakota	32.7
14	Tennessee	26.6
28	Texas	24.6
25	Utah	25.1
36	Vermont	22.3
17	Virginia	26.5
35	Washington	22.5
49	West Virginia	17.8
44	Wisconsin	20.5
47	Wyoming	19.4

RANK ORDER

RANK	STATE	PERCENT
1	North Dakota	32.7
1	South Dakota	32.7
3	Florida	32.2
4	Louisiana	29.8
5	Maine	29.3
6	Alabama	28.9
7	Maryland	28.6
8	Mississippi	28.1
9	Arizona	28.0
9	Nevada	28.0
11	Georgia	27.6
12	Arkansas	27.5
12	North Carolina	27.5
14	Massachusetts	26.6
14	Nebraska	26.6
14	Tennessee	26.6
17	Virginia	26.5
18	Colorado	26.2
18	Idaho	26.2
20	Iowa	26.0
20	Oklahoma	26.0
20	Oregon	26.0
23	New Mexico	25.7
24	Minnesota	25.2
25	Kansas	25.1
25	Utah	25.1
27	Alaska	24.7
28	Missouri	24.6
28	Texas	24.6
30	New Hampshire	24.4
31	New Jersey	24.0
32	Hawaii	23.3
33	New York	23.1
34	California	22.7
35	Washington	22.5
36	Vermont	22.3
37	Kentucky	22.1
38	Rhode Island	21.6
39	Illinois	21.4
40	Montana	21.3
41	Delaware	21.2
42	Connecticut	21.1
43	Ohio	20.8
44	Indiana	20.5
44	Wisconsin	20.5
46	South Carolina	20.2
47	Wyoming	19.4
48	Pennsylvania	19.1
49	West Virginia	17.8
50	Michigan	17.2

District of Columbia — 31.8

Source: U.S. Department of Health and Human Services, Agency for Healthcare Research and Quality
   "Private-Sector Data by Firm Size and State" (Table II Series, Medical Expenditures Panel Survey)
      (http://www.meps.ahrq.gov/mepsweb/survey_comp/Insurance.jsp)
*Enrolled employees at private-sector establishments that offer health insurance coverage.

Persons Not Covered by Health Insurance in 2006

National Total = 46,995,000 Uninsured

ALPHA ORDER

RANK	STATE	UNINSURED	% of USA
21	Alabama	689,000	1.5%
44	Alaska	109,000	0.2%
9	Arizona	1,311,000	2.8%
28	Arkansas	521,000	1.1%
1	California	6,791,000	14.5%
15	Colorado	826,000	1.8%
35	Connecticut	325,000	0.7%
45	Delaware	105,000	0.2%
3	Florida	3,828,000	8.1%
6	Georgia	1,659,000	3.5%
43	Hawaii	110,000	0.2%
38	Idaho	227,000	0.5%
5	Illinois	1,776,000	3.8%
19	Indiana	748,000	1.6%
36	Iowa	307,000	0.7%
34	Kansas	335,000	0.7%
26	Kentucky	639,000	1.4%
14	Louisiana	921,000	2.0%
42	Maine	122,000	0.3%
17	Maryland	776,000	1.7%
25	Massachusetts	657,000	1.4%
12	Michigan	1,043,000	2.2%
31	Minnesota	475,000	1.0%
27	Mississippi	600,000	1.3%
18	Missouri	772,000	1.6%
40	Montana	160,000	0.3%
39	Nebraska	217,000	0.5%
29	Nevada	496,000	1.1%
41	New Hampshire	150,000	0.3%
8	New Jersey	1,341,000	2.9%
32	New Mexico	445,000	0.9%
4	New York	2,662,000	5.7%
7	North Carolina	1,585,000	3.4%
48	North Dakota	75,000	0.2%
11	Ohio	1,138,000	2.4%
24	Oklahoma	661,000	1.4%
23	Oregon	665,000	1.4%
10	Pennsylvania	1,237,000	2.6%
46	Rhode Island	91,000	0.2%
22	South Carolina	672,000	1.4%
46	South Dakota	91,000	0.2%
16	Tennessee	809,000	1.7%
2	Texas	5,704,000	12.1%
33	Utah	442,000	0.9%
50	Vermont	63,000	0.1%
13	Virginia	1,006,000	2.1%
20	Washington	746,000	1.6%
37	West Virginia	245,000	0.5%
30	Wisconsin	481,000	1.0%
48	Wyoming	75,000	0.2%

RANK ORDER

RANK	STATE	UNINSURED	% of USA
1	California	6,791,000	14.5%
2	Texas	5,704,000	12.1%
3	Florida	3,828,000	8.1%
4	New York	2,662,000	5.7%
5	Illinois	1,776,000	3.8%
6	Georgia	1,659,000	3.5%
7	North Carolina	1,585,000	3.4%
8	New Jersey	1,341,000	2.9%
9	Arizona	1,311,000	2.8%
10	Pennsylvania	1,237,000	2.6%
11	Ohio	1,138,000	2.4%
12	Michigan	1,043,000	2.2%
13	Virginia	1,006,000	2.1%
14	Louisiana	921,000	2.0%
15	Colorado	826,000	1.8%
16	Tennessee	809,000	1.7%
17	Maryland	776,000	1.7%
18	Missouri	772,000	1.6%
19	Indiana	748,000	1.6%
20	Washington	746,000	1.6%
21	Alabama	689,000	1.5%
22	South Carolina	672,000	1.4%
23	Oregon	665,000	1.4%
24	Oklahoma	661,000	1.4%
25	Massachusetts	657,000	1.4%
26	Kentucky	639,000	1.4%
27	Mississippi	600,000	1.3%
28	Arkansas	521,000	1.1%
29	Nevada	496,000	1.1%
30	Wisconsin	481,000	1.0%
31	Minnesota	475,000	1.0%
32	New Mexico	445,000	0.9%
33	Utah	442,000	0.9%
34	Kansas	335,000	0.7%
35	Connecticut	325,000	0.7%
36	Iowa	307,000	0.7%
37	West Virginia	245,000	0.5%
38	Idaho	227,000	0.5%
39	Nebraska	217,000	0.5%
40	Montana	160,000	0.3%
41	New Hampshire	150,000	0.3%
42	Maine	122,000	0.3%
43	Hawaii	110,000	0.2%
44	Alaska	109,000	0.2%
45	Delaware	105,000	0.2%
46	Rhode Island	91,000	0.2%
46	South Dakota	91,000	0.2%
48	North Dakota	75,000	0.2%
48	Wyoming	75,000	0.2%
50	Vermont	63,000	0.1%
	District of Columbia	66,000	0.1%

Source: U.S. Bureau of the Census
"Health Insurance Coverage Status by State for All People: 2006" (http://www.census.gov/hhes/www/hlthins/hlthin06.html)

Percent of Population Not Covered by Health Insurance in 2006

National Percent = 15.3% of Population*

ALPHA ORDER

RANK	STATE	PERCENT
22	Alabama	14.1
13	Alaska	16.7
4	Arizona	19.0
11	Arkansas	17.5
6	California	18.5
14	Colorado	16.6
41	Connecticut	10.4
31	Delaware	12.5
3	Florida	20.3
10	Georgia	17.6
49	Hawaii	8.6
20	Idaho	14.9
25	Illinois	13.6
30	Indiana	13.1
48	Iowa	9.3
35	Kansas	11.1
24	Kentucky	13.8
6	Louisiana	18.5
46	Maine	9.5
26	Maryland	13.5
43	Massachusetts	10.3
40	Michigan	10.6
50	Minnesota	8.5
9	Mississippi	18.1
33	Missouri	12.3
12	Montana	17.0
35	Nebraska	11.1
8	Nevada	18.3
41	New Hampshire	10.4
21	New Jersey	14.6
2	New Mexico	21.0
28	New York	13.2
16	North Carolina	16.0
35	North Dakota	11.1
39	Ohio	10.7
5	Oklahoma	18.7
14	Oregon	16.6
44	Pennsylvania	10.2
44	Rhode Island	10.2
16	South Carolina	16.0
34	South Dakota	11.6
27	Tennessee	13.4
1	Texas	24.1
18	Utah	15.7
38	Vermont	10.8
28	Virginia	13.2
31	Washington	12.5
19	West Virginia	15.5
47	Wisconsin	9.4
23	Wyoming	14.0

RANK ORDER

RANK	STATE	PERCENT
1	Texas	24.1
2	New Mexico	21.0
3	Florida	20.3
4	Arizona	19.0
5	Oklahoma	18.7
6	California	18.5
6	Louisiana	18.5
8	Nevada	18.3
9	Mississippi	18.1
10	Georgia	17.6
11	Arkansas	17.5
12	Montana	17.0
13	Alaska	16.7
14	Colorado	16.6
14	Oregon	16.6
16	North Carolina	16.0
16	South Carolina	16.0
18	Utah	15.7
19	West Virginia	15.5
20	Idaho	14.9
21	New Jersey	14.6
22	Alabama	14.1
23	Wyoming	14.0
24	Kentucky	13.8
25	Illinois	13.6
26	Maryland	13.5
27	Tennessee	13.4
28	New York	13.2
28	Virginia	13.2
30	Indiana	13.1
31	Delaware	12.5
31	Washington	12.5
33	Missouri	12.3
34	South Dakota	11.6
35	Kansas	11.1
35	Nebraska	11.1
35	North Dakota	11.1
38	Vermont	10.8
39	Ohio	10.7
40	Michigan	10.6
41	Connecticut	10.4
41	New Hampshire	10.4
43	Massachusetts	10.3
44	Pennsylvania	10.2
44	Rhode Island	10.2
46	Maine	9.5
47	Wisconsin	9.4
48	Iowa	9.3
49	Hawaii	8.6
50	Minnesota	8.5

| | District of Columbia | 12.4 |

Source: U.S. Bureau of the Census

"Health Insurance Coverage Status by State for All People: 2006" (http://www.census.gov/hhes/www/hlthins/hlthin06.html)

*Three-year average for 2004 through 2006.

Numerical Change in Persons Uninsured: 2002 to 2006

National Change = 3,421,000 Increase

ALPHA ORDER

RANK	STATE	UNINSURED
14	Alabama	125,000
37	Alaska	(10,000)
2	Arizona	395,000
18	Arkansas	81,000
3	California	393,000
15	Colorado	106,000
43	Connecticut	(31,000)
28	Delaware	26,000
1	Florida	985,000
4	Georgia	305,000
40	Hawaii	(13,000)
36	Idaho	(6,000)
32	Illinois	9,000
44	Indiana	(49,000)
27	Iowa	30,000
23	Kansas	55,000
17	Kentucky	91,000
16	Louisiana	101,000
42	Maine	(22,000)
24	Maryland	46,000
31	Massachusetts	13,000
47	Michigan	(115,000)
19	Minnesota	78,000
11	Mississippi	135,000
13	Missouri	126,000
30	Montana	21,000
26	Nebraska	43,000
19	Nevada	78,000
29	New Hampshire	25,000
10	New Jersey	144,000
22	New Mexico	57,000
50	New York	(380,000)
5	North Carolina	217,000
33	North Dakota	6,000
49	Ohio	(206,000)
21	Oklahoma	60,000
8	Oregon	154,000
48	Pennsylvania	(143,000)
40	Rhode Island	(13,000)
7	South Carolina	172,000
33	South Dakota	6,000
6	Tennessee	195,000
9	Texas	148,000
12	Utah	132,000
35	Vermont	(3,000)
25	Virginia	44,000
46	Washington	(104,000)
37	West Virginia	(10,000)
45	Wisconsin	(57,000)
39	Wyoming	(11,000)

RANK ORDER

RANK	STATE	UNINSURED
1	Florida	985,000
2	Arizona	395,000
3	California	393,000
4	Georgia	305,000
5	North Carolina	217,000
6	Tennessee	195,000
7	South Carolina	172,000
8	Oregon	154,000
9	Texas	148,000
10	New Jersey	144,000
11	Mississippi	135,000
12	Utah	132,000
13	Missouri	126,000
14	Alabama	125,000
15	Colorado	106,000
16	Louisiana	101,000
17	Kentucky	91,000
18	Arkansas	81,000
19	Minnesota	78,000
19	Nevada	78,000
21	Oklahoma	60,000
22	New Mexico	57,000
23	Kansas	55,000
24	Maryland	46,000
25	Virginia	44,000
26	Nebraska	43,000
27	Iowa	30,000
28	Delaware	26,000
29	New Hampshire	25,000
30	Montana	21,000
31	Massachusetts	13,000
32	Illinois	9,000
33	North Dakota	6,000
33	South Dakota	6,000
35	Vermont	(3,000)
36	Idaho	(6,000)
37	Alaska	(10,000)
37	West Virginia	(10,000)
39	Wyoming	(11,000)
40	Hawaii	(13,000)
40	Rhode Island	(13,000)
42	Maine	(22,000)
43	Connecticut	(31,000)
44	Indiana	(49,000)
45	Wisconsin	(57,000)
46	Washington	(104,000)
47	Michigan	(115,000)
48	Pennsylvania	(143,000)
49	Ohio	(206,000)
50	New York	(380,000)

District of Columbia (8,000)

Source: CQ Press using data from U.S. Bureau of the Census
  "Health Insurance Coverage Status by State for All People: 2006" (http://www.census.gov/hhes/www/hlthins/hlthin06.html)
  "Health Insurance Coverage Status by State for All People: 2002"

Percent Change in Persons Uninsured: 2002 to 2006

National Percent Change = 7.9% Increase

ALPHA ORDER

RANK	STATE	PERCENT CHANGE
11	Alabama	22.2
39	Alaska	(8.4)
1	Arizona	43.1
17	Arkansas	18.4
30	California	6.1
21	Colorado	14.7
40	Connecticut	(8.7)
5	Delaware	32.9
3	Florida	34.6
10	Georgia	22.5
43	Hawaii	(10.6)
35	Idaho	(2.6)
34	Illinois	0.5
38	Indiana	(6.1)
25	Iowa	10.8
13	Kansas	19.6
18	Kentucky	16.6
23	Louisiana	12.3
49	Maine	(15.3)
29	Maryland	6.3
33	Massachusetts	2.0
41	Michigan	(9.9)
13	Minnesota	19.6
8	Mississippi	29.0
15	Missouri	19.5
20	Montana	15.1
9	Nebraska	24.7
16	Nevada	18.7
12	New Hampshire	20.0
24	New Jersey	12.0
21	New Mexico	14.7
46	New York	(12.5)
19	North Carolina	15.9
27	North Dakota	8.7
49	Ohio	(15.3)
26	Oklahoma	10.0
7	Oregon	30.1
42	Pennsylvania	(10.4)
46	Rhode Island	(12.5)
4	South Carolina	34.4
28	South Dakota	7.1
6	Tennessee	31.8
32	Texas	2.7
2	Utah	42.6
37	Vermont	(4.5)
31	Virginia	4.6
45	Washington	(12.2)
36	West Virginia	(3.9)
43	Wisconsin	(10.6)
48	Wyoming	(12.8)

RANK ORDER

RANK	STATE	PERCENT CHANGE
1	Arizona	43.1
2	Utah	42.6
3	Florida	34.6
4	South Carolina	34.4
5	Delaware	32.9
6	Tennessee	31.8
7	Oregon	30.1
8	Mississippi	29.0
9	Nebraska	24.7
10	Georgia	22.5
11	Alabama	22.2
12	New Hampshire	20.0
13	Kansas	19.6
13	Minnesota	19.6
15	Missouri	19.5
16	Nevada	18.7
17	Arkansas	18.4
18	Kentucky	16.6
19	North Carolina	15.9
20	Montana	15.1
21	Colorado	14.7
21	New Mexico	14.7
23	Louisiana	12.3
24	New Jersey	12.0
25	Iowa	10.8
26	Oklahoma	10.0
27	North Dakota	8.7
28	South Dakota	7.1
29	Maryland	6.3
30	California	6.1
31	Virginia	4.6
32	Texas	2.7
33	Massachusetts	2.0
34	Illinois	0.5
35	Idaho	(2.6)
36	West Virginia	(3.9)
37	Vermont	(4.5)
38	Indiana	(6.1)
39	Alaska	(8.4)
40	Connecticut	(8.7)
41	Michigan	(9.9)
42	Pennsylvania	(10.4)
43	Hawaii	(10.6)
43	Wisconsin	(10.6)
45	Washington	(12.2)
46	New York	(12.5)
46	Rhode Island	(12.5)
48	Wyoming	(12.8)
49	Maine	(15.3)
49	Ohio	(15.3)
	District of Columbia	(10.8)

Source: CQ Press using data from U.S. Bureau of the Census
"Health Insurance Coverage Status by State for All People: 2006" (http://www.census.gov/hhes/www/hlthins/hlthin06.html)
"Health Insurance Coverage Status by State for All People: 2002"

Change in Percent of Population Uninsured: 2002 to 2006

National Percent Change = 4.1% Increase*

ALPHA ORDER			RANK ORDER		
RANK	STATE	PERCENT CHANGE	RANK	STATE	PERCENT CHANGE
25	Alabama	8.5	1	Delaware	31.6
44	Alaska	(6.2)	2	South Carolina	30.1
20	Arizona	11.1	3	Oregon	24.8
15	Arkansas	12.2	4	Rhode Island	22.9
40	California	(1.1)	5	Tennessee	21.8
25	Colorado	8.5	6	Missouri	18.3
35	Connecticut	2.0	7	Florida	16.0
1	Delaware	31.6	7	Mississippi	16.0
7	Florida	16.0	9	Nebraska	15.6
16	Georgia	12.1	10	Utah	15.4
47	Hawaii	(11.3)	11	Massachusetts	14.4
46	Idaho	(9.1)	12	New Hampshire	13.0
41	Illinois	(2.2)	13	Maryland	12.5
24	Indiana	9.2	13	Vermont	12.5
27	Iowa	8.1	15	Arkansas	12.2
37	Kansas	1.8	16	Georgia	12.1
32	Kentucky	4.5	17	Wisconsin	11.9
39	Louisiana	(0.5)	18	Montana	11.8
48	Maine	(12.0)	19	New Jersey	11.5
13	Maryland	12.5	20	Arizona	11.1
11	Massachusetts	14.4	21	West Virginia	10.7
36	Michigan	1.9	22	Virginia	10.0
29	Minnesota	6.3	23	South Dakota	9.4
7	Mississippi	16.0	24	Indiana	9.2
6	Missouri	18.3	25	Alabama	8.5
18	Montana	11.8	25	Colorado	8.5
9	Nebraska	15.6	27	Iowa	8.1
31	Nevada	4.6	28	North Carolina	7.4
12	New Hampshire	13.0	29	Minnesota	6.3
19	New Jersey	11.5	30	Pennsylvania	5.2
42	New Mexico	(4.5)	31	Nevada	4.6
50	New York	(16.5)	32	Kentucky	4.5
28	North Carolina	7.4	33	North Dakota	3.7
33	North Dakota	3.7	34	Oklahoma	2.7
43	Ohio	(6.1)	35	Connecticut	2.0
34	Oklahoma	2.7	36	Michigan	1.9
3	Oregon	24.8	37	Kansas	1.8
30	Pennsylvania	5.2	38	Texas	0.0
4	Rhode Island	22.9	39	Louisiana	(0.5)
2	South Carolina	30.1	40	California	(1.1)
23	South Dakota	9.4	41	Illinois	(2.2)
5	Tennessee	21.8	42	New Mexico	(4.5)
38	Texas	0.0	43	Ohio	(6.1)
10	Utah	15.4	44	Alaska	(6.2)
13	Vermont	12.5	45	Washington	(8.1)
22	Virginia	10.0	46	Idaho	(9.1)
45	Washington	(8.1)	47	Hawaii	(11.3)
21	West Virginia	10.7	48	Maine	(12.0)
17	Wisconsin	11.9	49	Wyoming	(14.6)
49	Wyoming	(14.6)	50	New York	(16.5)

District of Columbia (6.1)

Source: CQ Press using data from U.S. Bureau of the Census
"Health Insurance Coverage Status by State for All People: 2006" (http://www.census.gov/hhes/www/hlthins/hlthin06.html)
"Health Insurance Coverage Status by State for All People: 2002"
*Based on three-year averages for 2004 through 2006 and 2000 through 2002.

Percent of Children Not Covered by Health Insurance in 2006

National Percent = 11.7% of Children*

<table>
<tr><td colspan="3">ALPHA ORDER</td><td colspan="3">RANK ORDER</td></tr>
<tr><td>RANK</td><td>STATE</td><td>PERCENT</td><td>RANK</td><td>STATE</td><td>PERCENT</td></tr>
<tr><td>37</td><td>Alabama</td><td>7.4</td><td>1</td><td>Texas</td><td>21.2</td></tr>
<tr><td>20</td><td>Alaska</td><td>10.3</td><td>2</td><td>Florida</td><td>18.9</td></tr>
<tr><td>6</td><td>Arizona</td><td>17.0</td><td>2</td><td>Mississippi</td><td>18.9</td></tr>
<tr><td>27</td><td>Arkansas</td><td>9.3</td><td>4</td><td>Nevada</td><td>18.8</td></tr>
<tr><td>15</td><td>California</td><td>12.8</td><td>5</td><td>New Mexico</td><td>17.9</td></tr>
<tr><td>9</td><td>Colorado</td><td>14.6</td><td>6</td><td>Arizona</td><td>17.0</td></tr>
<tr><td>46</td><td>Connecticut</td><td>6.0</td><td>7</td><td>Louisiana</td><td>15.9</td></tr>
<tr><td>18</td><td>Delaware</td><td>11.7</td><td>8</td><td>Utah</td><td>15.0</td></tr>
<tr><td>2</td><td>Florida</td><td>18.9</td><td>9</td><td>Colorado</td><td>14.6</td></tr>
<tr><td>15</td><td>Georgia</td><td>12.8</td><td>10</td><td>Montana</td><td>14.5</td></tr>
<tr><td>44</td><td>Hawaii</td><td>6.3</td><td>11</td><td>North Carolina</td><td>14.0</td></tr>
<tr><td>14</td><td>Idaho</td><td>13.0</td><td>12</td><td>New Jersey</td><td>13.3</td></tr>
<tr><td>26</td><td>Illinois</td><td>9.5</td><td>13</td><td>Oregon</td><td>13.1</td></tr>
<tr><td>35</td><td>Indiana</td><td>7.8</td><td>14</td><td>Idaho</td><td>13.0</td></tr>
<tr><td>44</td><td>Iowa</td><td>6.3</td><td>15</td><td>California</td><td>12.8</td></tr>
<tr><td>38</td><td>Kansas</td><td>7.3</td><td>15</td><td>Georgia</td><td>12.8</td></tr>
<tr><td>25</td><td>Kentucky</td><td>9.7</td><td>17</td><td>Oklahoma</td><td>12.5</td></tr>
<tr><td>7</td><td>Louisiana</td><td>15.9</td><td>18</td><td>Delaware</td><td>11.7</td></tr>
<tr><td>42</td><td>Maine</td><td>6.4</td><td>19</td><td>South Carolina</td><td>10.7</td></tr>
<tr><td>24</td><td>Maryland</td><td>9.9</td><td>20</td><td>Alaska</td><td>10.3</td></tr>
<tr><td>40</td><td>Massachusetts</td><td>7.0</td><td>20</td><td>North Dakota</td><td>10.3</td></tr>
<tr><td>49</td><td>Michigan</td><td>4.7</td><td>22</td><td>Nebraska</td><td>10.1</td></tr>
<tr><td>32</td><td>Minnesota</td><td>8.3</td><td>22</td><td>Virginia</td><td>10.1</td></tr>
<tr><td>2</td><td>Mississippi</td><td>18.9</td><td>24</td><td>Maryland</td><td>9.9</td></tr>
<tr><td>29</td><td>Missouri</td><td>9.1</td><td>25</td><td>Kentucky</td><td>9.7</td></tr>
<tr><td>10</td><td>Montana</td><td>14.5</td><td>26</td><td>Illinois</td><td>9.5</td></tr>
<tr><td>22</td><td>Nebraska</td><td>10.1</td><td>27</td><td>Arkansas</td><td>9.3</td></tr>
<tr><td>4</td><td>Nevada</td><td>18.8</td><td>28</td><td>South Dakota</td><td>9.2</td></tr>
<tr><td>36</td><td>New Hampshire</td><td>7.5</td><td>29</td><td>Missouri</td><td>9.1</td></tr>
<tr><td>12</td><td>New Jersey</td><td>13.3</td><td>30</td><td>West Virginia</td><td>8.5</td></tr>
<tr><td>5</td><td>New Mexico</td><td>17.9</td><td>31</td><td>New York</td><td>8.4</td></tr>
<tr><td>31</td><td>New York</td><td>8.4</td><td>32</td><td>Minnesota</td><td>8.3</td></tr>
<tr><td>11</td><td>North Carolina</td><td>14.0</td><td>33</td><td>Wyoming</td><td>8.2</td></tr>
<tr><td>20</td><td>North Dakota</td><td>10.3</td><td>34</td><td>Vermont</td><td>8.0</td></tr>
<tr><td>47</td><td>Ohio</td><td>5.7</td><td>35</td><td>Indiana</td><td>7.8</td></tr>
<tr><td>17</td><td>Oklahoma</td><td>12.5</td><td>36</td><td>New Hampshire</td><td>7.5</td></tr>
<tr><td>13</td><td>Oregon</td><td>13.1</td><td>37</td><td>Alabama</td><td>7.4</td></tr>
<tr><td>38</td><td>Pennsylvania</td><td>7.3</td><td>38</td><td>Kansas</td><td>7.3</td></tr>
<tr><td>50</td><td>Rhode Island</td><td>4.1</td><td>38</td><td>Pennsylvania</td><td>7.3</td></tr>
<tr><td>19</td><td>South Carolina</td><td>10.7</td><td>40</td><td>Massachusetts</td><td>7.0</td></tr>
<tr><td>28</td><td>South Dakota</td><td>9.2</td><td>41</td><td>Washington</td><td>6.9</td></tr>
<tr><td>42</td><td>Tennessee</td><td>6.4</td><td>42</td><td>Maine</td><td>6.4</td></tr>
<tr><td>1</td><td>Texas</td><td>21.2</td><td>42</td><td>Tennessee</td><td>6.4</td></tr>
<tr><td>8</td><td>Utah</td><td>15.0</td><td>44</td><td>Hawaii</td><td>6.3</td></tr>
<tr><td>34</td><td>Vermont</td><td>8.0</td><td>44</td><td>Iowa</td><td>6.3</td></tr>
<tr><td>22</td><td>Virginia</td><td>10.1</td><td>46</td><td>Connecticut</td><td>6.0</td></tr>
<tr><td>41</td><td>Washington</td><td>6.9</td><td>47</td><td>Ohio</td><td>5.7</td></tr>
<tr><td>30</td><td>West Virginia</td><td>8.5</td><td>48</td><td>Wisconsin</td><td>4.9</td></tr>
<tr><td>48</td><td>Wisconsin</td><td>4.9</td><td>49</td><td>Michigan</td><td>4.7</td></tr>
<tr><td>33</td><td>Wyoming</td><td>8.2</td><td>50</td><td>Rhode Island</td><td>4.1</td></tr>
<tr><td></td><td></td><td></td><td></td><td>District of Columbia</td><td>8.7</td></tr>
</table>

Source: U.S. Bureau of the Census
    "Health Insurance Coverage Status" (http://www.census.gov/hhes/www/hlthins/historic/hihistt6.html)
*Children under 18 years old.

Persons Covered by Health Insurance in 2006

National Total = 249,829,000 Insured

ALPHA ORDER

RANK	STATE	INSURED	% of USA
23	Alabama	3,843,000	1.5%
48	Alaska	550,000	0.2%
19	Arizona	4,958,000	2.0%
33	Arkansas	2,237,000	0.9%
1	California	29,417,000	11.8%
22	Colorado	3,977,000	1.6%
27	Connecticut	3,137,000	1.3%
45	Delaware	757,000	0.3%
4	Florida	14,233,000	5.7%
9	Georgia	7,688,000	3.1%
42	Hawaii	1,144,000	0.5%
39	Idaho	1,248,000	0.5%
6	Illinois	10,867,000	4.3%
14	Indiana	5,590,000	2.2%
30	Iowa	2,612,000	1.0%
31	Kansas	2,387,000	1.0%
25	Kentucky	3,467,000	1.4%
26	Louisiana	3,291,000	1.3%
40	Maine	1,192,000	0.5%
20	Maryland	4,836,000	1.9%
13	Massachusetts	5,678,000	2.3%
8	Michigan	8,928,000	3.6%
21	Minnesota	4,675,000	1.9%
32	Mississippi	2,292,000	0.9%
17	Missouri	5,028,000	2.0%
44	Montana	772,000	0.3%
37	Nebraska	1,549,000	0.6%
35	Nevada	2,039,000	0.8%
41	New Hampshire	1,159,000	0.5%
10	New Jersey	7,319,000	2.9%
38	New Mexico	1,498,000	0.6%
3	New York	16,378,000	6.6%
11	North Carolina	7,266,000	2.9%
49	North Dakota	541,000	0.2%
7	Ohio	10,181,000	4.1%
29	Oklahoma	2,831,000	1.1%
28	Oregon	3,051,000	1.2%
5	Pennsylvania	11,108,000	4.4%
43	Rhode Island	963,000	0.4%
24	South Carolina	3,553,000	1.4%
46	South Dakota	679,000	0.3%
16	Tennessee	5,111,000	2.0%
2	Texas	17,533,000	7.0%
34	Utah	2,094,000	0.8%
47	Vermont	557,000	0.2%
12	Virginia	6,532,000	2.6%
15	Washington	5,572,000	2.2%
36	West Virginia	1,570,000	0.6%
18	Wisconsin	4,995,000	2.0%
50	Wyoming	441,000	0.2%

RANK ORDER

RANK	STATE	INSURED	% of USA
1	California	29,417,000	11.8%
2	Texas	17,533,000	7.0%
3	New York	16,378,000	6.6%
4	Florida	14,233,000	5.7%
5	Pennsylvania	11,108,000	4.4%
6	Illinois	10,867,000	4.3%
7	Ohio	10,181,000	4.1%
8	Michigan	8,928,000	3.6%
9	Georgia	7,688,000	3.1%
10	New Jersey	7,319,000	2.9%
11	North Carolina	7,266,000	2.9%
12	Virginia	6,532,000	2.6%
13	Massachusetts	5,678,000	2.3%
14	Indiana	5,590,000	2.2%
15	Washington	5,572,000	2.2%
16	Tennessee	5,111,000	2.0%
17	Missouri	5,028,000	2.0%
18	Wisconsin	4,995,000	2.0%
19	Arizona	4,958,000	2.0%
20	Maryland	4,836,000	1.9%
21	Minnesota	4,675,000	1.9%
22	Colorado	3,977,000	1.6%
23	Alabama	3,843,000	1.5%
24	South Carolina	3,553,000	1.4%
25	Kentucky	3,467,000	1.4%
26	Louisiana	3,291,000	1.3%
27	Connecticut	3,137,000	1.3%
28	Oregon	3,051,000	1.2%
29	Oklahoma	2,831,000	1.1%
30	Iowa	2,612,000	1.0%
31	Kansas	2,387,000	1.0%
32	Mississippi	2,292,000	0.9%
33	Arkansas	2,237,000	0.9%
34	Utah	2,094,000	0.8%
35	Nevada	2,039,000	0.8%
36	West Virginia	1,570,000	0.6%
37	Nebraska	1,549,000	0.6%
38	New Mexico	1,498,000	0.6%
39	Idaho	1,248,000	0.5%
40	Maine	1,192,000	0.5%
41	New Hampshire	1,159,000	0.5%
42	Hawaii	1,144,000	0.5%
43	Rhode Island	963,000	0.4%
44	Montana	772,000	0.3%
45	Delaware	757,000	0.3%
46	South Dakota	679,000	0.3%
47	Vermont	557,000	0.2%
48	Alaska	550,000	0.2%
49	North Dakota	541,000	0.2%
50	Wyoming	441,000	0.2%
	District of Columbia	503,000	0.2%

Source: U.S. Bureau of the Census
"Health Insurance Coverage Status by State for All People: 2006" (http://www.census.gov/hhes/www/hlthins/hlthin06.html)

Percent of Population Covered by Health Insurance in 2006

National Percent = 84.2% of Population

ALPHA ORDER

RANK	STATE	PERCENT
29	Alabama	84.8
34	Alaska	83.5
46	Arizona	79.1
42	Arkansas	81.1
41	California	81.2
36	Colorado	82.8
6	Connecticut	90.6
17	Delaware	87.9
47	Florida	78.8
38	Georgia	82.3
2	Hawaii	91.2
30	Idaho	84.6
26	Illinois	86.0
14	Indiana	88.2
11	Iowa	89.5
19	Kansas	87.7
32	Kentucky	84.4
48	Louisiana	78.1
5	Maine	90.7
25	Maryland	86.2
10	Massachusetts	89.6
11	Michigan	89.5
4	Minnesota	90.8
45	Mississippi	79.2
21	Missouri	86.7
35	Montana	82.9
19	Nebraska	87.7
44	Nevada	80.4
13	New Hampshire	88.5
31	New Jersey	84.5
49	New Mexico	77.1
26	New York	86.0
39	North Carolina	82.1
18	North Dakota	87.8
8	Ohio	89.9
42	Oklahoma	81.1
39	Oregon	82.1
7	Pennsylvania	90.0
1	Rhode Island	91.4
33	South Carolina	84.1
14	South Dakota	88.2
24	Tennessee	86.3
50	Texas	75.5
37	Utah	82.6
9	Vermont	89.8
21	Virginia	86.7
14	Washington	88.2
23	West Virginia	86.5
2	Wisconsin	91.2
28	Wyoming	85.4

RANK ORDER

RANK	STATE	PERCENT
1	Rhode Island	91.4
2	Hawaii	91.2
2	Wisconsin	91.2
4	Minnesota	90.8
5	Maine	90.7
6	Connecticut	90.6
7	Pennsylvania	90.0
8	Ohio	89.9
9	Vermont	89.8
10	Massachusetts	89.6
11	Iowa	89.5
11	Michigan	89.5
13	New Hampshire	88.5
14	Indiana	88.2
14	South Dakota	88.2
14	Washington	88.2
17	Delaware	87.9
18	North Dakota	87.8
19	Kansas	87.7
19	Nebraska	87.7
21	Missouri	86.7
21	Virginia	86.7
23	West Virginia	86.5
24	Tennessee	86.3
25	Maryland	86.2
26	Illinois	86.0
26	New York	86.0
28	Wyoming	85.4
29	Alabama	84.8
30	Idaho	84.6
31	New Jersey	84.5
32	Kentucky	84.4
33	South Carolina	84.1
34	Alaska	83.5
35	Montana	82.9
36	Colorado	82.8
37	Utah	82.6
38	Georgia	82.3
39	North Carolina	82.1
39	Oregon	82.1
41	California	81.2
42	Arkansas	81.1
42	Oklahoma	81.1
44	Nevada	80.4
45	Mississippi	79.2
46	Arizona	79.1
47	Florida	78.8
48	Louisiana	78.1
49	New Mexico	77.1
50	Texas	75.5
	District of Columbia	88.4

Source: U.S. Bureau of the Census

"Health Insurance Coverage Status by State for All People: 2006" (http://www.census.gov/hhes/www/hlthins/hlthin06.html)

Percent of Population Covered by Private Health Insurance in 2006

National Percent = 67.9% of Population*

ALPHA ORDER

RANK	STATE	PERCENT
30	Alabama	68.5
38	Alaska	65.0
46	Arizona	60.1
45	Arkansas	60.3
43	California	62.6
28	Colorado	70.6
5	Connecticut	76.2
14	Delaware	74.0
42	Florida	62.7
37	Georgia	65.1
11	Hawaii	74.7
29	Idaho	69.1
21	Illinois	72.8
7	Indiana	75.3
6	Iowa	75.9
11	Kansas	74.7
33	Kentucky	66.7
49	Louisiana	58.6
27	Maine	70.7
10	Maryland	75.0
14	Massachusetts	74.0
11	Michigan	74.7
2	Minnesota	78.1
48	Mississippi	59.2
26	Missouri	70.9
32	Montana	67.6
8	Nebraska	75.1
34	Nevada	66.5
1	New Hampshire	78.9
18	New Jersey	73.5
50	New Mexico	55.6
35	New York	66.4
40	North Carolina	64.6
4	North Dakota	76.7
16	Ohio	73.7
44	Oklahoma	61.4
31	Oregon	68.2
8	Pennsylvania	75.1
19	Rhode Island	73.4
38	South Carolina	65.0
16	South Dakota	73.7
36	Tennessee	66.2
47	Texas	59.3
24	Utah	71.9
25	Vermont	71.3
23	Virginia	72.1
22	Washington	72.7
41	West Virginia	64.0
3	Wisconsin	77.1
20	Wyoming	73.2

RANK ORDER

RANK	STATE	PERCENT
1	New Hampshire	78.9
2	Minnesota	78.1
3	Wisconsin	77.1
4	North Dakota	76.7
5	Connecticut	76.2
6	Iowa	75.9
7	Indiana	75.3
8	Nebraska	75.1
8	Pennsylvania	75.1
10	Maryland	75.0
11	Hawaii	74.7
11	Kansas	74.7
11	Michigan	74.7
14	Delaware	74.0
14	Massachusetts	74.0
16	Ohio	73.7
16	South Dakota	73.7
18	New Jersey	73.5
19	Rhode Island	73.4
20	Wyoming	73.2
21	Illinois	72.8
22	Washington	72.7
23	Virginia	72.1
24	Utah	71.9
25	Vermont	71.3
26	Missouri	70.9
27	Maine	70.7
28	Colorado	70.6
29	Idaho	69.1
30	Alabama	68.5
31	Oregon	68.2
32	Montana	67.6
33	Kentucky	66.7
34	Nevada	66.5
35	New York	66.4
36	Tennessee	66.2
37	Georgia	65.1
38	Alaska	65.0
38	South Carolina	65.0
40	North Carolina	64.6
41	West Virginia	64.0
42	Florida	62.7
43	California	62.6
44	Oklahoma	61.4
45	Arkansas	60.3
46	Arizona	60.1
47	Texas	59.3
48	Mississippi	59.2
49	Louisiana	58.6
50	New Mexico	55.6
	District of Columbia	67.0

Source: U.S. Bureau of the Census
"Health Insurance Coverage Status" (http://www.census.gov/hhes/www/hlthins/historic/hihistt6.html)
*Private health insurance is coverage by a health plan provided through an employer or union or purchased by an individual from a private health insurance company.

Percent of Population Covered by
Employment-Based Health Insurance in 2006
National Percent = 59.7% of Population*

ALPHA ORDER

RANK	STATE	PERCENT
34	Alabama	59.5
32	Alaska	59.6
41	Arizona	54.1
47	Arkansas	51.7
43	California	53.2
23	Colorado	60.8
4	Connecticut	68.4
2	Delaware	68.9
45	Florida	52.7
32	Georgia	59.6
6	Hawaii	68.1
30	Idaho	60.0
17	Illinois	64.1
7	Indiana	67.5
16	Iowa	64.4
22	Kansas	61.2
35	Kentucky	58.7
49	Louisiana	50.2
26	Maine	60.3
2	Maryland	68.9
12	Massachusetts	65.9
5	Michigan	68.2
13	Minnesota	65.7
48	Mississippi	50.3
24	Missouri	60.6
42	Montana	54.0
21	Nebraska	61.8
27	Nevada	60.2
1	New Hampshire	70.9
7	New Jersey	67.5
50	New Mexico	49.6
24	New York	60.6
40	North Carolina	56.3
30	North Dakota	60.0
10	Ohio	66.9
44	Oklahoma	53.1
37	Oregon	58.0
18	Pennsylvania	63.9
14	Rhode Island	64.9
39	South Carolina	57.0
36	South Dakota	58.2
38	Tennessee	57.7
46	Texas	52.2
20	Utah	62.8
19	Vermont	63.2
11	Virginia	66.7
15	Washington	64.6
28	West Virginia	60.1
9	Wisconsin	67.1
28	Wyoming	60.1

RANK ORDER

RANK	STATE	PERCENT
1	New Hampshire	70.9
2	Delaware	68.9
2	Maryland	68.9
4	Connecticut	68.4
5	Michigan	68.2
6	Hawaii	68.1
7	Indiana	67.5
7	New Jersey	67.5
9	Wisconsin	67.1
10	Ohio	66.9
11	Virginia	66.7
12	Massachusetts	65.9
13	Minnesota	65.7
14	Rhode Island	64.9
15	Washington	64.6
16	Iowa	64.4
17	Illinois	64.1
18	Pennsylvania	63.9
19	Vermont	63.2
20	Utah	62.8
21	Nebraska	61.8
22	Kansas	61.2
23	Colorado	60.8
24	Missouri	60.6
24	New York	60.6
26	Maine	60.3
27	Nevada	60.2
28	West Virginia	60.1
28	Wyoming	60.1
30	Idaho	60.0
30	North Dakota	60.0
32	Alaska	59.6
32	Georgia	59.6
34	Alabama	59.5
35	Kentucky	58.7
36	South Dakota	58.2
37	Oregon	58.0
38	Tennessee	57.7
39	South Carolina	57.0
40	North Carolina	56.3
41	Arizona	54.1
42	Montana	54.0
43	California	53.2
44	Oklahoma	53.1
45	Florida	52.7
46	Texas	52.2
47	Arkansas	51.7
48	Mississippi	50.3
49	Louisiana	50.2
50	New Mexico	49.6

| | District of Columbia | 60.2 |

Source: U.S. Bureau of the Census
   "Health Insurance Coverage Status" (http://www.census.gov/hhes/www/hlthins/historic/hihistt6.html)
*Employment-based health insurance is private insurance coverage offered through one's own employment or a relative's. It may be offered by an employer or by a union.

Percent of Population Covered by Direct Purchase Health Insurance in 2006

National Percent = 9.1% of Population*

ALPHA ORDER

RANK	STATE	PERCENT
16	Alabama	10.3
45	Alaska	6.8
42	Arizona	7.1
21	Arkansas	9.4
18	California	10.2
11	Colorado	11.9
28	Connecticut	9.1
48	Delaware	6.2
12	Florida	11.2
48	Georgia	6.2
35	Hawaii	8.0
19	Idaho	9.8
20	Illinois	9.6
28	Indiana	9.1
10	Iowa	12.0
3	Kansas	14.9
34	Kentucky	8.5
21	Louisiana	9.4
14	Maine	10.9
37	Maryland	7.6
35	Massachusetts	8.0
44	Michigan	6.9
7	Minnesota	12.3
15	Mississippi	10.4
13	Missouri	11.1
4	Montana	14.3
5	Nebraska	12.6
39	Nevada	7.3
24	New Hampshire	9.3
47	New Jersey	6.6
46	New Mexico	6.7
43	New York	7.0
33	North Carolina	8.6
1	North Dakota	16.8
39	Ohio	7.3
24	Oklahoma	9.3
7	Oregon	12.3
5	Pennsylvania	12.6
21	Rhode Island	9.4
24	South Carolina	9.3
2	South Dakota	16.7
30	Tennessee	8.8
38	Texas	7.5
24	Utah	9.3
30	Vermont	8.8
41	Virginia	7.2
32	Washington	8.7
50	West Virginia	5.0
16	Wisconsin	10.3
9	Wyoming	12.1

RANK ORDER

RANK	STATE	PERCENT
1	North Dakota	16.8
2	South Dakota	16.7
3	Kansas	14.9
4	Montana	14.3
5	Nebraska	12.6
5	Pennsylvania	12.6
7	Minnesota	12.3
7	Oregon	12.3
9	Wyoming	12.1
10	Iowa	12.0
11	Colorado	11.9
12	Florida	11.2
13	Missouri	11.1
14	Maine	10.9
15	Mississippi	10.4
16	Alabama	10.3
16	Wisconsin	10.3
18	California	10.2
19	Idaho	9.8
20	Illinois	9.6
21	Arkansas	9.4
21	Louisiana	9.4
21	Rhode Island	9.4
24	New Hampshire	9.3
24	Oklahoma	9.3
24	South Carolina	9.3
24	Utah	9.3
28	Connecticut	9.1
28	Indiana	9.1
30	Tennessee	8.8
30	Vermont	8.8
32	Washington	8.7
33	North Carolina	8.6
34	Kentucky	8.5
35	Hawaii	8.0
35	Massachusetts	8.0
37	Maryland	7.6
38	Texas	7.5
39	Nevada	7.3
39	Ohio	7.3
41	Virginia	7.2
42	Arizona	7.1
43	New York	7.0
44	Michigan	6.9
45	Alaska	6.8
46	New Mexico	6.7
47	New Jersey	6.6
48	Delaware	6.2
48	Georgia	6.2
50	West Virginia	5.0

District of Columbia   7.9

Source: U.S. Bureau of the Census
  "Health Insurance Coverage Status" (http://www.census.gov/hhes/www/hlthins/historic/hihistt6.html)
*Direct-purchase health insurance is private insurance coverage though a plan purchased by an individual from a private company.

Percent of Population Covered by Government Health Insurance in 2006

National Percent = 27.0% of Population*

ALPHA ORDER

RANK	STATE	PERCENT
18	Alabama	29.1
9	Alaska	30.9
16	Arizona	29.6
8	Arkansas	31.1
32	California	26.7
48	Colorado	20.8
27	Connecticut	27.2
27	Delaware	27.2
21	Florida	28.3
35	Georgia	26.3
13	Hawaii	30.2
33	Idaho	26.6
43	Illinois	23.3
42	Indiana	23.4
23	Iowa	27.8
27	Kansas	27.2
17	Kentucky	29.4
13	Louisiana	30.2
2	Maine	34.4
43	Maryland	23.3
36	Massachusetts	25.9
23	Michigan	27.8
38	Minnesota	25.1
10	Mississippi	30.6
25	Missouri	27.7
25	Montana	27.7
41	Nebraska	24.5
47	Nevada	21.2
46	New Hampshire	21.6
49	New Jersey	20.4
3	New Mexico	32.5
12	New York	30.4
21	North Carolina	28.3
43	North Dakota	23.3
19	Ohio	28.7
7	Oklahoma	31.6
40	Oregon	24.8
31	Pennsylvania	26.8
5	Rhode Island	32.0
10	South Carolina	30.6
19	South Dakota	28.7
4	Tennessee	32.2
39	Texas	24.9
50	Utah	19.6
6	Vermont	31.7
27	Virginia	27.2
15	Washington	29.8
1	West Virginia	35.1
37	Wisconsin	25.6
33	Wyoming	26.6

RANK ORDER

RANK	STATE	PERCENT
1	West Virginia	35.1
2	Maine	34.4
3	New Mexico	32.5
4	Tennessee	32.2
5	Rhode Island	32.0
6	Vermont	31.7
7	Oklahoma	31.6
8	Arkansas	31.1
9	Alaska	30.9
10	Mississippi	30.6
10	South Carolina	30.6
12	New York	30.4
13	Hawaii	30.2
13	Louisiana	30.2
15	Washington	29.8
16	Arizona	29.6
17	Kentucky	29.4
18	Alabama	29.1
19	Ohio	28.7
19	South Dakota	28.7
21	Florida	28.3
21	North Carolina	28.3
23	Iowa	27.8
23	Michigan	27.8
25	Missouri	27.7
25	Montana	27.7
27	Connecticut	27.2
27	Delaware	27.2
27	Kansas	27.2
27	Virginia	27.2
31	Pennsylvania	26.8
32	California	26.7
33	Idaho	26.6
33	Wyoming	26.6
35	Georgia	26.3
36	Massachusetts	25.9
37	Wisconsin	25.6
38	Minnesota	25.1
39	Texas	24.9
40	Oregon	24.8
41	Nebraska	24.5
42	Indiana	23.4
43	Illinois	23.3
43	Maryland	23.3
43	North Dakota	23.3
46	New Hampshire	21.6
47	Nevada	21.2
48	Colorado	20.8
49	New Jersey	20.4
50	Utah	19.6
	District of Columbia	31.3

Source: U.S. Bureau of the Census

"Health Insurance Coverage Status" (http://www.census.gov/hhes/www/hlthins/historic/hihistt6.html)

*Includes Medicaid, Medicare, State Children's Health Insurance Program (SCHIP) and military health care.

Percent of Population Covered by Military Health Care in 2006

National Percent = 3.6% of Population*

ALPHA ORDER

RANK	STATE	PERCENT
18	Alabama	4.8
1	Alaska	13.8
22	Arizona	4.2
16	Arkansas	4.9
40	California	2.6
23	Colorado	4.0
40	Connecticut	2.6
16	Delaware	4.9
13	Florida	5.4
11	Georgia	5.8
3	Hawaii	9.6
27	Idaho	3.8
45	Illinois	1.6
35	Indiana	2.9
38	Iowa	2.8
29	Kansas	3.3
25	Kentucky	3.9
44	Louisiana	2.3
15	Maine	5.1
20	Maryland	4.4
47	Massachusetts	1.3
45	Michigan	1.6
43	Minnesota	2.4
19	Mississippi	4.6
33	Missouri	3.0
14	Montana	5.2
7	Nebraska	6.6
23	Nevada	4.0
31	New Hampshire	3.2
49	New Jersey	1.0
10	New Mexico	5.9
49	New York	1.0
25	North Carolina	3.9
29	North Dakota	3.3
32	Ohio	3.1
4	Oklahoma	7.8
35	Oregon	2.9
47	Pennsylvania	1.3
39	Rhode Island	2.7
12	South Carolina	5.5
6	South Dakota	6.8
7	Tennessee	6.6
28	Texas	3.4
35	Utah	2.9
33	Vermont	3.0
2	Virginia	10.5
5	Washington	7.3
20	West Virginia	4.4
40	Wisconsin	2.6
9	Wyoming	6.1

RANK ORDER

RANK	STATE	PERCENT
1	Alaska	13.8
2	Virginia	10.5
3	Hawaii	9.6
4	Oklahoma	7.8
5	Washington	7.3
6	South Dakota	6.8
7	Nebraska	6.6
7	Tennessee	6.6
9	Wyoming	6.1
10	New Mexico	5.9
11	Georgia	5.8
12	South Carolina	5.5
13	Florida	5.4
14	Montana	5.2
15	Maine	5.1
16	Arkansas	4.9
16	Delaware	4.9
18	Alabama	4.8
19	Mississippi	4.6
20	Maryland	4.4
20	West Virginia	4.4
22	Arizona	4.2
23	Colorado	4.0
23	Nevada	4.0
25	Kentucky	3.9
25	North Carolina	3.9
27	Idaho	3.8
28	Texas	3.4
29	Kansas	3.3
29	North Dakota	3.3
31	New Hampshire	3.2
32	Ohio	3.1
33	Missouri	3.0
33	Vermont	3.0
35	Indiana	2.9
35	Oregon	2.9
35	Utah	2.9
38	Iowa	2.8
39	Rhode Island	2.7
40	California	2.6
40	Connecticut	2.6
40	Wisconsin	2.6
43	Minnesota	2.4
44	Louisiana	2.3
45	Illinois	1.6
45	Michigan	1.6
47	Massachusetts	1.3
47	Pennsylvania	1.3
49	New Jersey	1.0
49	New York	1.0
	District of Columbia	2.0

Source: U.S. Bureau of the Census
 "Health Insurance Coverage Status" (http://www.census.gov/hhes/www/hlthins/historic/hihistt6.html)
*Includes CHAMPUS (Comprehensive Health and Medical Plan for Uniformed Services)/Tricare, Veterans, and military health care.

Percent of Children Covered by Health Insurance in 2006

National Percent = 88.3% of Children*

ALPHA ORDER

RANK	STATE	PERCENT
14	Alabama	92.6
30	Alaska	89.7
45	Arizona	83.0
24	Arkansas	90.7
35	California	87.2
42	Colorado	85.4
5	Connecticut	94.0
33	Delaware	88.3
48	Florida	81.1
35	Georgia	87.2
6	Hawaii	93.7
37	Idaho	87.0
25	Illinois	90.5
16	Indiana	92.2
6	Iowa	93.7
12	Kansas	92.7
26	Kentucky	90.3
44	Louisiana	84.1
8	Maine	93.6
27	Maryland	90.1
11	Massachusetts	93.0
2	Michigan	95.3
19	Minnesota	91.7
48	Mississippi	81.1
22	Missouri	90.9
41	Montana	85.5
28	Nebraska	89.9
47	Nevada	81.2
15	New Hampshire	92.5
39	New Jersey	86.7
46	New Mexico	82.1
20	New York	91.6
40	North Carolina	86.0
30	North Dakota	89.7
4	Ohio	94.3
34	Oklahoma	87.5
38	Oregon	86.9
12	Pennsylvania	92.7
1	Rhode Island	95.9
32	South Carolina	89.3
23	South Dakota	90.8
8	Tennessee	93.6
50	Texas	78.8
43	Utah	85.0
17	Vermont	92.0
28	Virginia	89.9
10	Washington	93.1
21	West Virginia	91.5
3	Wisconsin	95.1
18	Wyoming	91.8

RANK ORDER

RANK	STATE	PERCENT
1	Rhode Island	95.9
2	Michigan	95.3
3	Wisconsin	95.1
4	Ohio	94.3
5	Connecticut	94.0
6	Hawaii	93.7
6	Iowa	93.7
8	Maine	93.6
8	Tennessee	93.6
10	Washington	93.1
11	Massachusetts	93.0
12	Kansas	92.7
12	Pennsylvania	92.7
14	Alabama	92.6
15	New Hampshire	92.5
16	Indiana	92.2
17	Vermont	92.0
18	Wyoming	91.8
19	Minnesota	91.7
20	New York	91.6
21	West Virginia	91.5
22	Missouri	90.9
23	South Dakota	90.8
24	Arkansas	90.7
25	Illinois	90.5
26	Kentucky	90.3
27	Maryland	90.1
28	Nebraska	89.9
28	Virginia	89.9
30	Alaska	89.7
30	North Dakota	89.7
32	South Carolina	89.3
33	Delaware	88.3
34	Oklahoma	87.5
35	California	87.2
35	Georgia	87.2
37	Idaho	87.0
38	Oregon	86.9
39	New Jersey	86.7
40	North Carolina	86.0
41	Montana	85.5
42	Colorado	85.4
43	Utah	85.0
44	Louisiana	84.1
45	Arizona	83.0
46	New Mexico	82.1
47	Nevada	81.2
48	Florida	81.1
48	Mississippi	81.1
50	Texas	78.8
	District of Columbia	91.3

Source: U.S. Bureau of the Census
 "Health Insurance Coverage Status" (http://www.census.gov/hhes/www/hlthins/historic/hihistt6.html)
*Children under 18 covered by either private or government health insurance.

Percent of Children Covered by Private Health Insurance in 2006

National Percent = 64.6% of Children*

ALPHA ORDER

RANK	STATE	PERCENT
38	Alabama	63.3
32	Alaska	64.9
44	Arizona	56.8
46	Arkansas	54.2
41	California	59.1
17	Colorado	70.3
6	Connecticut	73.6
22	Delaware	69.5
39	Florida	60.1
40	Georgia	59.9
20	Hawaii	70.0
33	Idaho	64.6
19	Illinois	70.2
10	Indiana	72.5
9	Iowa	72.9
28	Kansas	67.3
35	Kentucky	63.6
48	Louisiana	53.3
25	Maine	68.7
4	Maryland	74.5
2	Massachusetts	77.5
8	Michigan	73.1
3	Minnesota	75.9
47	Mississippi	53.8
24	Missouri	68.8
34	Montana	64.0
6	Nebraska	73.6
26	Nevada	68.5
1	New Hampshire	80.3
15	New Jersey	70.9
50	New Mexico	50.9
30	New York	66.6
41	North Carolina	59.1
13	North Dakota	71.4
14	Ohio	71.1
45	Oklahoma	55.6
28	Oregon	67.3
17	Pennsylvania	70.3
12	Rhode Island	71.8
35	South Carolina	63.6
27	South Dakota	67.6
31	Tennessee	65.8
49	Texas	52.9
15	Utah	70.9
35	Vermont	63.6
21	Virginia	69.9
23	Washington	69.2
43	West Virginia	57.2
5	Wisconsin	74.0
11	Wyoming	71.9

RANK ORDER

RANK	STATE	PERCENT
1	New Hampshire	80.3
2	Massachusetts	77.5
3	Minnesota	75.9
4	Maryland	74.5
5	Wisconsin	74.0
6	Connecticut	73.6
6	Nebraska	73.6
8	Michigan	73.1
9	Iowa	72.9
10	Indiana	72.5
11	Wyoming	71.9
12	Rhode Island	71.8
13	North Dakota	71.4
14	Ohio	71.1
15	New Jersey	70.9
15	Utah	70.9
17	Colorado	70.3
17	Pennsylvania	70.3
19	Illinois	70.2
20	Hawaii	70.0
21	Virginia	69.9
22	Delaware	69.5
23	Washington	69.2
24	Missouri	68.8
25	Maine	68.7
26	Nevada	68.5
27	South Dakota	67.6
28	Kansas	67.3
28	Oregon	67.3
30	New York	66.6
31	Tennessee	65.8
32	Alaska	64.9
33	Idaho	64.6
34	Montana	64.0
35	Kentucky	63.6
35	South Carolina	63.6
35	Vermont	63.6
38	Alabama	63.3
39	Florida	60.1
40	Georgia	59.9
41	California	59.1
41	North Carolina	59.1
43	West Virginia	57.2
44	Arizona	56.8
45	Oklahoma	55.6
46	Arkansas	54.2
47	Mississippi	53.8
48	Louisiana	53.3
49	Texas	52.9
50	New Mexico	50.9
	District of Columbia	51.5

Source: U.S. Bureau of the Census
   "Health Insurance Coverage Status" (http://www.census.gov/hhes/www/hlthins/historic/hihistt6.html)
*Children under 18. Private health insurance is coverage by a health plan provided through an employer or union or purchased by an individual from a private health insurance company.

Percent of Children Covered by Employment-Based Health Insurance in 2006

National Percent = 59.7% of Children*

ALPHA ORDER

RANK	STATE	PERCENT
32	Alabama	60.3
28	Alaska	61.1
41	Arizona	54.0
46	Arkansas	49.1
44	California	51.9
25	Colorado	63.1
3	Connecticut	71.1
11	Delaware	67.7
42	Florida	53.9
39	Georgia	56.5
14	Hawaii	66.9
37	Idaho	57.7
17	Illinois	66.2
9	Indiana	68.1
12	Iowa	67.3
31	Kansas	60.7
36	Kentucky	58.2
49	Louisiana	47.4
20	Maine	65.0
4	Maryland	70.1
2	Massachusetts	73.2
6	Michigan	69.2
4	Minnesota	70.1
50	Mississippi	47.3
27	Missouri	61.2
38	Montana	57.0
15	Nebraska	66.8
23	Nevada	64.1
1	New Hampshire	76.6
8	New Jersey	69.0
48	New Mexico	47.5
26	New York	62.9
43	North Carolina	53.5
21	North Dakota	64.5
12	Ohio	67.3
45	Oklahoma	50.2
34	Oregon	59.1
19	Pennsylvania	65.8
10	Rhode Island	68.0
35	South Carolina	58.4
29	South Dakota	61.0
33	Tennessee	59.4
47	Texas	49.0
24	Utah	63.5
29	Vermont	61.0
16	Virginia	66.5
21	Washington	64.5
40	West Virginia	55.9
6	Wisconsin	69.2
18	Wyoming	66.0

RANK ORDER

RANK	STATE	PERCENT
1	New Hampshire	76.6
2	Massachusetts	73.2
3	Connecticut	71.1
4	Maryland	70.1
4	Minnesota	70.1
6	Michigan	69.2
6	Wisconsin	69.2
8	New Jersey	69.0
9	Indiana	68.1
10	Rhode Island	68.0
11	Delaware	67.7
12	Iowa	67.3
12	Ohio	67.3
14	Hawaii	66.9
15	Nebraska	66.8
16	Virginia	66.5
17	Illinois	66.2
18	Wyoming	66.0
19	Pennsylvania	65.8
20	Maine	65.0
21	North Dakota	64.5
21	Washington	64.5
23	Nevada	64.1
24	Utah	63.5
25	Colorado	63.1
26	New York	62.9
27	Missouri	61.2
28	Alaska	61.1
29	South Dakota	61.0
29	Vermont	61.0
31	Kansas	60.7
32	Alabama	60.3
33	Tennessee	59.4
34	Oregon	59.1
35	South Carolina	58.4
36	Kentucky	58.2
37	Idaho	57.7
38	Montana	57.0
39	Georgia	56.5
40	West Virginia	55.9
41	Arizona	54.0
42	Florida	53.9
43	North Carolina	53.5
44	California	51.9
45	Oklahoma	50.2
46	Arkansas	49.1
47	Texas	49.0
48	New Mexico	47.5
49	Louisiana	47.4
50	Mississippi	47.3
	District of Columbia	49.6

Source: U.S. Bureau of the Census
   "Health Insurance Coverage Status" (http://www.census.gov/hhes/www/hlthins/historic/hihistt6.html)
*Children under 18. Employment-based health insurance is private insurance coverage offered through one's own employment or a relative's. It may be offered by an employer or by a union.

Percent of Children Covered by Direct Purchase Health Insurance in 2006

National Percent = 5.3% of Children*

ALPHA ORDER

RANK	STATE	PERCENT
35	Alabama	4.1
26	Alaska	4.7
44	Arizona	3.3
17	Arkansas	5.6
5	California	7.8
2	Colorado	9.0
46	Connecticut	2.8
49	Delaware	1.9
8	Florida	7.1
42	Georgia	3.4
35	Hawaii	4.1
17	Idaho	5.6
23	Illinois	5.3
24	Indiana	5.0
17	Iowa	5.6
8	Kansas	7.1
21	Kentucky	5.5
14	Louisiana	6.4
40	Maine	3.6
28	Maryland	4.5
42	Massachusetts	3.4
37	Michigan	4.0
15	Minnesota	5.9
3	Mississippi	8.5
11	Missouri	6.9
7	Montana	7.3
13	Nebraska	6.6
17	Nevada	5.6
34	New Hampshire	4.2
47	New Jersey	2.1
41	New Mexico	3.5
32	New York	4.4
27	North Carolina	4.6
6	North Dakota	7.5
45	Ohio	2.9
15	Oklahoma	5.9
1	Oregon	9.4
28	Pennsylvania	4.5
32	Rhode Island	4.4
28	South Carolina	4.5
8	South Dakota	7.1
12	Tennessee	6.7
37	Texas	4.0
4	Utah	8.1
48	Vermont	2.0
28	Virginia	4.5
37	Washington	4.0
50	West Virginia	1.4
21	Wisconsin	5.5
25	Wyoming	4.9

RANK ORDER

RANK	STATE	PERCENT
1	Oregon	9.4
2	Colorado	9.0
3	Mississippi	8.5
4	Utah	8.1
5	California	7.8
6	North Dakota	7.5
7	Montana	7.3
8	Florida	7.1
8	Kansas	7.1
8	South Dakota	7.1
11	Missouri	6.9
12	Tennessee	6.7
13	Nebraska	6.6
14	Louisiana	6.4
15	Minnesota	5.9
15	Oklahoma	5.9
17	Arkansas	5.6
17	Idaho	5.6
17	Iowa	5.6
17	Nevada	5.6
21	Kentucky	5.5
21	Wisconsin	5.5
23	Illinois	5.3
24	Indiana	5.0
25	Wyoming	4.9
26	Alaska	4.7
27	North Carolina	4.6
28	Maryland	4.5
28	Pennsylvania	4.5
28	South Carolina	4.5
28	Virginia	4.5
32	New York	4.4
32	Rhode Island	4.4
34	New Hampshire	4.2
35	Alabama	4.1
35	Hawaii	4.1
37	Michigan	4.0
37	Texas	4.0
37	Washington	4.0
40	Maine	3.6
41	New Mexico	3.5
42	Georgia	3.4
42	Massachusetts	3.4
44	Arizona	3.3
45	Ohio	2.9
46	Connecticut	2.8
47	New Jersey	2.1
48	Vermont	2.0
49	Delaware	1.9
50	West Virginia	1.4

District of Columbia   1.9

Source: U.S. Bureau of the Census
   "Health Insurance Coverage Status" (http://www.census.gov/hhes/www/hlthins/historic/hihistt6.html)
*Children under 18. Direct-purchase health insurance is private insurance coverage though a plan purchased by an individual from a private company.

Percent of Children Covered by Government Health Insurance in 2006

National Percent = 29.8% of Children*

RANK	STATE	PERCENT
18	Alabama	33.0
6	Alaska	37.3
11	Arizona	34.6
1	Arkansas	44.7
17	California	33.2
48	Colorado	19.4
36	Connecticut	26.5
38	Delaware	24.7
34	Florida	27.6
9	Georgia	35.6
8	Hawaii	35.8
25	Idaho	30.7
39	Illinois	24.6
42	Indiana	23.4
29	Iowa	29.7
20	Kansas	32.6
14	Kentucky	33.9
12	Louisiana	34.5
19	Maine	32.8
43	Maryland	22.0
44	Massachusetts	21.0
27	Michigan	29.9
45	Minnesota	20.8
10	Mississippi	35.5
26	Missouri	30.6
32	Montana	27.9
41	Nebraska	23.9
50	Nevada	15.9
46	New Hampshire	20.0
49	New Jersey	19.0
3	New Mexico	40.3
21	New York	32.4
16	North Carolina	33.3
37	North Dakota	25.3
23	Ohio	31.0
5	Oklahoma	38.4
40	Oregon	24.4
35	Pennsylvania	26.7
13	Rhode Island	34.1
15	South Carolina	33.7
23	South Dakota	31.0
7	Tennessee	36.5
27	Texas	29.9
47	Utah	19.9
4	Vermont	38.5
30	Virginia	29.5
22	Washington	31.6
2	West Virginia	42.2
33	Wisconsin	27.7
31	Wyoming	28.0

RANK	STATE	PERCENT
1	Arkansas	44.7
2	West Virginia	42.2
3	New Mexico	40.3
4	Vermont	38.5
5	Oklahoma	38.4
6	Alaska	37.3
7	Tennessee	36.5
8	Hawaii	35.8
9	Georgia	35.6
10	Mississippi	35.5
11	Arizona	34.6
12	Louisiana	34.5
13	Rhode Island	34.1
14	Kentucky	33.9
15	South Carolina	33.7
16	North Carolina	33.3
17	California	33.2
18	Alabama	33.0
19	Maine	32.8
20	Kansas	32.6
21	New York	32.4
22	Washington	31.6
23	Ohio	31.0
23	South Dakota	31.0
25	Idaho	30.7
26	Missouri	30.6
27	Michigan	29.9
27	Texas	29.9
29	Iowa	29.7
30	Virginia	29.5
31	Wyoming	28.0
32	Montana	27.9
33	Wisconsin	27.7
34	Florida	27.6
35	Pennsylvania	26.7
36	Connecticut	26.5
37	North Dakota	25.3
38	Delaware	24.7
39	Illinois	24.6
40	Oregon	24.4
41	Nebraska	23.9
42	Indiana	23.4
43	Maryland	22.0
44	Massachusetts	21.0
45	Minnesota	20.8
46	New Hampshire	20.0
47	Utah	19.9
48	Colorado	19.4
49	New Jersey	19.0
50	Nevada	15.9

	District of Columbia	48.6

Source: U.S. Bureau of the Census
"Health Insurance Coverage Status" (http://www.census.gov/hhes/www/hlthins/historic/hihistt6.html)
*Children under 18. Includes Medicaid, Medicare, State Children's Health Insurance Program (SCHIP) and military health care.

Percent of Children Covered by Military Health Care in 2006

National Percent = 2.8% of Children*

ALPHA ORDER				RANK ORDER		
RANK	STATE	PERCENT		RANK	STATE	PERCENT
17	Alabama	3.7		1	Alaska	15.4
1	Alaska	15.4		2	Hawaii	13.5
13	Arizona	3.8		3	Virginia	10.9
21	Arkansas	3.3		4	Georgia	6.4
31	California	2.4		5	Nebraska	5.9
23	Colorado	3.2		5	Washington	5.9
27	Connecticut	2.8		7	Tennessee	5.5
11	Delaware	4.2		8	Oklahoma	5.3
13	Florida	3.8		9	New Mexico	5.2
4	Georgia	6.4		10	Wyoming	5.1
2	Hawaii	13.5		11	Delaware	4.2
29	Idaho	2.5		11	Maine	4.2
42	Illinois	1.1		13	Arizona	3.8
45	Indiana	0.8		13	Florida	3.8
38	Iowa	1.6		13	Maryland	3.8
21	Kansas	3.3		13	Mississippi	3.8
19	Kentucky	3.5		17	Alabama	3.7
36	Louisiana	1.7		18	North Dakota	3.6
11	Maine	4.2		19	Kentucky	3.5
13	Maryland	3.8		19	South Dakota	3.5
49	Massachusetts	0.5		21	Arkansas	3.3
41	Michigan	1.3		21	Kansas	3.3
48	Minnesota	0.6		23	Colorado	3.2
13	Mississippi	3.8		24	West Virginia	3.1
43	Missouri	1.0		25	North Carolina	2.9
29	Montana	2.5		25	Vermont	2.9
5	Nebraska	5.9		27	Connecticut	2.8
43	Nevada	1.0		28	Texas	2.7
32	New Hampshire	2.3		29	Idaho	2.5
45	New Jersey	0.8		29	Montana	2.5
9	New Mexico	5.2		31	California	2.4
47	New York	0.7		32	New Hampshire	2.3
25	North Carolina	2.9		32	South Carolina	2.3
18	North Dakota	3.6		34	Rhode Island	2.0
35	Ohio	1.8		35	Ohio	1.8
8	Oklahoma	5.3		36	Louisiana	1.7
40	Oregon	1.5		36	Utah	1.7
50	Pennsylvania	0.4		38	Iowa	1.6
34	Rhode Island	2.0		38	Wisconsin	1.6
32	South Carolina	2.3		40	Oregon	1.5
19	South Dakota	3.5		41	Michigan	1.3
7	Tennessee	5.5		42	Illinois	1.1
28	Texas	2.7		43	Missouri	1.0
36	Utah	1.7		43	Nevada	1.0
25	Vermont	2.9		45	Indiana	0.8
3	Virginia	10.9		45	New Jersey	0.8
5	Washington	5.9		47	New York	0.7
24	West Virginia	3.1		48	Minnesota	0.6
38	Wisconsin	1.6		49	Massachusetts	0.5
10	Wyoming	5.1		50	Pennsylvania	0.4
					District of Columbia	0.9

Source: U.S. Bureau of the Census

"Health Insurance Coverage Status" (http://www.census.gov/hhes/www/hlthins/historic/hihistt6.html)

*Children under 18. Includes CHAMPUS (Comprehensive Health and Medical Plan for Uniformed Services)/Tricare, Veterans, and military health care.

Percent of Children Covered by Medicaid in 2006

National Percent = 27.1% of Children*

ALPHA ORDER			RANK ORDER		
RANK	STATE	PERCENT	RANK	STATE	PERCENT
19	Alabama	28.9	1	Arkansas	41.9
32	Alaska	24.0	2	West Virginia	39.5
8	Arizona	32.1	3	New Mexico	36.4
1	Arkansas	41.9	4	Vermont	36.3
13	California	30.7	5	Oklahoma	33.6
49	Colorado	15.8	6	Louisiana	33.3
34	Connecticut	23.7	7	Rhode Island	32.2
41	Delaware	20.0	8	Arizona	32.1
31	Florida	24.3	9	Mississippi	32.0
19	Georgia	28.9	10	New York	31.7
38	Hawaii	22.4	11	Tennessee	31.5
24	Idaho	28.0	12	South Carolina	31.0
33	Illinois	23.8	13	California	30.7
37	Indiana	22.6	14	Kentucky	30.2
24	Iowa	28.0	15	North Carolina	29.8
18	Kansas	29.4	16	Missouri	29.6
14	Kentucky	30.2	17	Ohio	29.5
6	Louisiana	33.3	18	Kansas	29.4
21	Maine	28.8	19	Alabama	28.9
45	Maryland	18.4	19	Georgia	28.9
40	Massachusetts	20.3	21	Maine	28.8
22	Michigan	28.3	22	Michigan	28.3
42	Minnesota	19.7	22	South Dakota	28.3
9	Mississippi	32.0	24	Idaho	28.0
16	Missouri	29.6	24	Iowa	28.0
30	Montana	25.3	26	Texas	26.8
44	Nebraska	18.5	27	Pennsylvania	26.4
50	Nevada	14.8	28	Washington	26.0
47	New Hampshire	18.1	28	Wisconsin	26.0
46	New Jersey	18.2	30	Montana	25.3
3	New Mexico	36.4	31	Florida	24.3
10	New York	31.7	32	Alaska	24.0
15	North Carolina	29.8	33	Illinois	23.8
39	North Dakota	21.9	34	Connecticut	23.7
17	Ohio	29.5	35	Wyoming	23.1
5	Oklahoma	33.6	36	Oregon	23.0
36	Oregon	23.0	37	Indiana	22.6
27	Pennsylvania	26.4	38	Hawaii	22.4
7	Rhode Island	32.2	39	North Dakota	21.9
12	South Carolina	31.0	40	Massachusetts	20.3
22	South Dakota	28.3	41	Delaware	20.0
11	Tennessee	31.5	42	Minnesota	19.7
26	Texas	26.8	43	Virginia	18.7
48	Utah	17.9	44	Nebraska	18.5
4	Vermont	36.3	45	Maryland	18.4
43	Virginia	18.7	46	New Jersey	18.2
28	Washington	26.0	47	New Hampshire	18.1
2	West Virginia	39.5	48	Utah	17.9
28	Wisconsin	26.0	49	Colorado	15.8
35	Wyoming	23.1	50	Nevada	14.8
				District of Columbia	47.7

Source: U.S. Bureau of the Census
    "Health Insurance Coverage Status" (http://www.census.gov/hhes/www/hlthins/historic/hihistt6.html)
*Children under 18 years old. Medicaid is a form of government insurance.

State Children's Health Insurance Program (SCHIP) Enrollment in 2006

National Total = 6,624,152 Children*

ALPHA ORDER

RANK	STATE	CHILDREN	% of USA
20	Alabama	84,257	1.3%
38	Alaska	22,227	0.3%
19	Arizona	96,669	1.5%
49	Arkansas	3,440	0.1%
1	California	1,391,405	21.0%
22	Colorado	69,997	1.1%
37	Connecticut	23,110	0.3%
44	Delaware	10,751	0.2%
6	Florida	303,595	4.6%
4	Georgia	343,690	5.2%
39	Hawaii	22,031	0.3%
36	Idaho	24,727	0.4%
5	Illinois	316,781	4.8%
14	Indiana	133,696	2.0%
28	Iowa	49,575	0.7%
29	Kansas	48,934	0.7%
24	Kentucky	64,861	1.0%
11	Louisiana	142,389	2.1%
33	Maine	31,114	0.5%
13	Maryland	136,034	2.1%
9	Massachusetts	190,640	2.9%
16	Michigan	118,501	1.8%
48	Minnesota	5,343	0.1%
21	Mississippi	83,359	1.3%
18	Missouri	106,577	1.6%
40	Montana	17,304	0.3%
30	Nebraska	44,981	0.7%
32	Nevada	39,317	0.6%
43	New Hampshire	12,393	0.2%
15	New Jersey	120,884	1.8%
35	New Mexico	25,155	0.4%
2	New York	688,362	10.4%
7	North Carolina	247,991	3.7%
46	North Dakota	6,318	0.1%
8	Ohio	218,529	3.3%
17	Oklahoma	116,012	1.8%
25	Oregon	59,039	0.9%
10	Pennsylvania	188,765	2.8%
34	Rhode Island	25,492	0.4%
23	South Carolina	68,870	1.0%
42	South Dakota	14,584	0.2%
NA	Tennessee **	NA	NA
3	Texas	585,461	8.8%
27	Utah	51,967	0.8%
47	Vermont	6,314	0.1%
12	Virginia	137,182	2.1%
41	Washington	15,000	0.2%
31	West Virginia	39,855	0.6%
26	Wisconsin	56,627	0.9%
45	Wyoming	7,715	0.1%

RANK ORDER

RANK	STATE	CHILDREN	% of USA
1	California	1,391,405	21.0%
2	New York	688,362	10.4%
3	Texas	585,461	8.8%
4	Georgia	343,690	5.2%
5	Illinois	316,781	4.8%
6	Florida	303,595	4.6%
7	North Carolina	247,991	3.7%
8	Ohio	218,529	3.3%
9	Massachusetts	190,640	2.9%
10	Pennsylvania	188,765	2.8%
11	Louisiana	142,389	2.1%
12	Virginia	137,182	2.1%
13	Maryland	136,034	2.1%
14	Indiana	133,696	2.0%
15	New Jersey	120,884	1.8%
16	Michigan	118,501	1.8%
17	Oklahoma	116,012	1.8%
18	Missouri	106,577	1.6%
19	Arizona	96,669	1.5%
20	Alabama	84,257	1.3%
21	Mississippi	83,359	1.3%
22	Colorado	69,997	1.1%
23	South Carolina	68,870	1.0%
24	Kentucky	64,861	1.0%
25	Oregon	59,039	0.9%
26	Wisconsin	56,627	0.9%
27	Utah	51,967	0.8%
28	Iowa	49,575	0.7%
29	Kansas	48,934	0.7%
30	Nebraska	44,981	0.7%
31	West Virginia	39,855	0.6%
32	Nevada	39,317	0.6%
33	Maine	31,114	0.5%
34	Rhode Island	25,492	0.4%
35	New Mexico	25,155	0.4%
36	Idaho	24,727	0.4%
37	Connecticut	23,110	0.3%
38	Alaska	22,227	0.3%
39	Hawaii	22,031	0.3%
40	Montana	17,304	0.3%
41	Washington	15,000	0.2%
42	South Dakota	14,584	0.2%
43	New Hampshire	12,393	0.2%
44	Delaware	10,751	0.2%
45	Wyoming	7,715	0.1%
46	North Dakota	6,318	0.1%
47	Vermont	6,314	0.1%
48	Minnesota	5,343	0.1%
49	Arkansas	3,440	0.1%
NA	Tennessee **	NA	NA
	District of Columbia	6,332	0.1%

Source: U.S. Department of Health and Human Services, Centers for Medicare and Medicaid Services
"Children's Health Insurance Program Annual Enrollment Report" (http://www.cms.hhs.gov/NationalSCHIPPolicy/)
*Figures for fiscal year 2006. The State Children's Health Insurance Program (SCHIP) was created in 1997 to help states expand health insurance to children whose families earn too much to qualify for Medicaid, yet not enough to afford private health insurance.
**Not available.

Percent Change in State Children's Health Insurance Program (SCHIP) Enrollment: 2005 to 2006
National Percent Change = 7.7% Increase*

ALPHA ORDER

RANK	STATE	PERCENT CHANGE
34	Alabama	2.9
40	Alaska	(0.4)
18	Arizona	9.8
1	Arkansas	183.4
8	California	13.7
6	Colorado	17.6
29	Connecticut	3.7
28	Delaware	3.8
49	Florida	(21.1)
12	Georgia	12.0
21	Hawaii	6.9
9	Idaho	13.2
11	Illinois	12.6
32	Indiana	3.2
22	Iowa	6.5
31	Kansas	3.4
35	Kentucky	1.8
42	Louisiana	(2.7)
36	Maine	1.5
10	Maryland	13.1
7	Massachusetts	17.2
2	Michigan	32.8
23	Minnesota	5.3
24	Mississippi	5.0
47	Missouri	(7.6)
19	Montana	9.2
38	Nebraska	0.6
39	Nevada	0.0
26	New Hampshire	4.2
46	New Jersey	(6.7)
30	New Mexico	3.5
14	New York	11.2
3	North Carolina	26.4
17	North Dakota	10.4
37	Ohio	0.9
20	Oklahoma	7.3
12	Oregon	12.0
24	Pennsylvania	5.0
45	Rhode Island	(6.1)
48	South Carolina	(14.6)
27	South Dakota	3.9
NA	Tennessee **	NA
14	Texas	11.2
5	Utah	18.3
44	Vermont	(4.5)
16	Virginia	10.6
43	Washington	(3.5)
32	West Virginia	3.2
41	Wisconsin	(0.9)
4	Wyoming	26.1

RANK ORDER

RANK	STATE	PERCENT CHANGE
1	Arkansas	183.4
2	Michigan	32.8
3	North Carolina	26.4
4	Wyoming	26.1
5	Utah	18.3
6	Colorado	17.6
7	Massachusetts	17.2
8	California	13.7
9	Idaho	13.2
10	Maryland	13.1
11	Illinois	12.6
12	Georgia	12.0
12	Oregon	12.0
14	New York	11.2
14	Texas	11.2
16	Virginia	10.6
17	North Dakota	10.4
18	Arizona	9.8
19	Montana	9.2
20	Oklahoma	7.3
21	Hawaii	6.9
22	Iowa	6.5
23	Minnesota	5.3
24	Mississippi	5.0
24	Pennsylvania	5.0
26	New Hampshire	4.2
27	South Dakota	3.9
28	Delaware	3.8
29	Connecticut	3.7
30	New Mexico	3.5
31	Kansas	3.4
32	Indiana	3.2
32	West Virginia	3.2
34	Alabama	2.9
35	Kentucky	1.8
36	Maine	1.5
37	Ohio	0.9
38	Nebraska	0.6
39	Nevada	0.0
40	Alaska	(0.4)
41	Wisconsin	(0.9)
42	Louisiana	(2.7)
43	Washington	(3.5)
44	Vermont	(4.5)
45	Rhode Island	(6.1)
46	New Jersey	(6.7)
47	Missouri	(7.6)
48	South Carolina	(14.6)
49	Florida	(21.1)
NA	Tennessee **	NA

District of Columbia   (4.5)

Source: CQ Press using data from U.S. Department of Health and Human Services, Centers for Medicare and Medicaid Services "Children's Health Insurance Program Annual Enrollment Report" (http://www.cms.hhs.gov/NationalSCHIPPolicy/)

*Figures for fiscal years. The State Children's Health Insurance Program (SCHIP) was created in 1997 to help states expand health insurance to children whose families earn too much to qualify for Medicaid, yet not enough to afford private health insurance.

**Not available.

Percent of Children Enrolled in State Children's Health Insurance Program (SCHIP) in 2006
National Percent = 9.2% of Children 17 Years and Younger*

ALPHA ORDER

RANK	STATE	PERCENT
20	Alabama	7.6
7	Alaska	12.3
37	Arizona	5.9
48	Arkansas	0.5
2	California	14.6
36	Colorado	6.0
46	Connecticut	2.8
39	Delaware	5.3
22	Florida	7.5
3	Georgia	14.0
25	Hawaii	7.4
33	Idaho	6.3
15	Illinois	9.9
17	Indiana	8.5
26	Iowa	7.0
26	Kansas	7.0
32	Kentucky	6.5
5	Louisiana	13.1
9	Maine	11.1
14	Maryland	10.0
4	Massachusetts	13.2
41	Michigan	4.8
49	Minnesota	0.4
10	Mississippi	11.0
22	Missouri	7.5
18	Montana	7.9
13	Nebraska	10.1
35	Nevada	6.2
45	New Hampshire	4.2
38	New Jersey	5.8
40	New Mexico	4.9
1	New York	15.2
8	North Carolina	11.5
43	North Dakota	4.4
18	Ohio	7.9
6	Oklahoma	13.0
28	Oregon	6.9
29	Pennsylvania	6.7
11	Rhode Island	10.7
30	South Carolina	6.6
22	South Dakota	7.5
NA	Tennessee **	NA
16	Texas	9.0
30	Utah	6.6
42	Vermont	4.7
20	Virginia	7.6
47	Washington	1.0
12	West Virginia	10.2
44	Wisconsin	4.3
33	Wyoming	6.3

RANK ORDER

RANK	STATE	PERCENT
1	New York	15.2
2	California	14.6
3	Georgia	14.0
4	Massachusetts	13.2
5	Louisiana	13.1
6	Oklahoma	13.0
7	Alaska	12.3
8	North Carolina	11.5
9	Maine	11.1
10	Mississippi	11.0
11	Rhode Island	10.7
12	West Virginia	10.2
13	Nebraska	10.1
14	Maryland	10.0
15	Illinois	9.9
16	Texas	9.0
17	Indiana	8.5
18	Montana	7.9
18	Ohio	7.9
20	Alabama	7.6
20	Virginia	7.6
22	Florida	7.5
22	Missouri	7.5
22	South Dakota	7.5
25	Hawaii	7.4
26	Iowa	7.0
26	Kansas	7.0
28	Oregon	6.9
29	Pennsylvania	6.7
30	South Carolina	6.6
30	Utah	6.6
32	Kentucky	6.5
33	Idaho	6.3
33	Wyoming	6.3
35	Nevada	6.2
36	Colorado	6.0
37	Arizona	5.9
38	New Jersey	5.8
39	Delaware	5.3
40	New Mexico	4.9
41	Michigan	4.8
42	Vermont	4.7
43	North Dakota	4.4
44	Wisconsin	4.3
45	New Hampshire	4.2
46	Connecticut	2.8
47	Washington	1.0
48	Arkansas	0.5
49	Minnesota	0.4
NA	Tennessee **	NA

District of Columbia   5.5

Source: CQ Press using data from U.S. Department of Health and Human Services, Centers for Medicare and Medicaid Services "Children's Health Insurance Program Annual Enrollment Report" (http://www.cms.hhs.gov/NationalSCHIPPolicy/)
*Figures for fiscal year 2006. The State Children's Health Insurance Program (SCHIP) was created in 1997 to help states expand health insurance to children whose families earn too much to qualify for Medicaid, yet not enough to afford private health insurance. Calculated using 2006 Census estimates for 17 and younger for reporting states.
**Not available.

Expenditures for State Children's Health Insurance Program (SCHIP) in 2006

National Total = $7,034,300,000*

ALPHA ORDER

RANK	STATE	EXPENDITURES	% of USA
16	Alabama	$111,100,000	1.6%
39	Alaska	27,800,000	0.4%
21	Arizona	95,800,000	1.4%
28	Arkansas	60,400,000	0.9%
1	California	1,801,100,000	25.6%
23	Colorado	77,100,000	1.1%
37	Connecticut	31,500,000	0.4%
47	Delaware	10,800,000	0.2%
5	Florida	300,600,000	4.3%
7	Georgia	265,200,000	3.8%
43	Hawaii	19,300,000	0.3%
41	Idaho	23,000,000	0.3%
4	Illinois	312,100,000	4.4%
18	Indiana	106,300,000	1.5%
26	Iowa	64,200,000	0.9%
25	Kansas	67,200,000	1.0%
20	Kentucky	98,300,000	1.4%
15	Louisiana	122,400,000	1.7%
36	Maine	33,100,000	0.5%
11	Maryland	212,400,000	3.0%
10	Massachusetts	233,500,000	3.3%
22	Michigan	95,500,000	1.4%
34	Minnesota	39,400,000	0.6%
14	Mississippi	124,200,000	1.8%
17	Missouri	106,400,000	1.5%
42	Montana	21,800,000	0.3%
38	Nebraska	29,900,000	0.4%
33	Nevada	40,200,000	0.6%
46	New Hampshire	11,600,000	0.2%
12	New Jersey	190,600,000	2.7%
40	New Mexico	23,800,000	0.3%
2	New York	505,400,000	7.2%
6	North Carolina	271,900,000	3.9%
44	North Dakota	14,100,000	0.2%
9	Ohio	236,100,000	3.4%
19	Oklahoma	105,000,000	1.5%
24	Oregon	72,500,000	1.0%
8	Pennsylvania	239,800,000	3.4%
30	Rhode Island	42,100,000	0.6%
27	South Carolina	62,600,000	0.9%
45	South Dakota	14,000,000	0.2%
NA	Tennessee **	NA	NA
3	Texas	371,800,000	5.3%
29	Utah	56,900,000	0.8%
49	Vermont	4,700,000	0.1%
13	Virginia	145,900,000	2.1%
32	Washington	40,300,000	0.6%
31	West Virginia	41,600,000	0.6%
35	Wisconsin	33,400,000	0.5%
48	Wyoming	9,400,000	0.1%

RANK ORDER

RANK	STATE	EXPENDITURES	% of USA
1	California	$1,801,100,000	25.6%
2	New York	505,400,000	7.2%
3	Texas	371,800,000	5.3%
4	Illinois	312,100,000	4.4%
5	Florida	300,600,000	4.3%
6	North Carolina	271,900,000	3.9%
7	Georgia	265,200,000	3.8%
8	Pennsylvania	239,800,000	3.4%
9	Ohio	236,100,000	3.4%
10	Massachusetts	233,500,000	3.3%
11	Maryland	212,400,000	3.0%
12	New Jersey	190,600,000	2.7%
13	Virginia	145,900,000	2.1%
14	Mississippi	124,200,000	1.8%
15	Louisiana	122,400,000	1.7%
16	Alabama	111,100,000	1.6%
17	Missouri	106,400,000	1.5%
18	Indiana	106,300,000	1.5%
19	Oklahoma	105,000,000	1.5%
20	Kentucky	98,300,000	1.4%
21	Arizona	95,800,000	1.4%
22	Michigan	95,500,000	1.4%
23	Colorado	77,100,000	1.1%
24	Oregon	72,500,000	1.0%
25	Kansas	67,200,000	1.0%
26	Iowa	64,200,000	0.9%
27	South Carolina	62,600,000	0.9%
28	Arkansas	60,400,000	0.9%
29	Utah	56,900,000	0.8%
30	Rhode Island	42,100,000	0.6%
31	West Virginia	41,600,000	0.6%
32	Washington	40,300,000	0.6%
33	Nevada	40,200,000	0.6%
34	Minnesota	39,400,000	0.6%
35	Wisconsin	33,400,000	0.5%
36	Maine	33,100,000	0.5%
37	Connecticut	31,500,000	0.4%
38	Nebraska	29,900,000	0.4%
39	Alaska	27,800,000	0.4%
40	New Mexico	23,800,000	0.3%
41	Idaho	23,000,000	0.3%
42	Montana	21,800,000	0.3%
43	Hawaii	19,300,000	0.3%
44	North Dakota	14,100,000	0.2%
45	South Dakota	14,000,000	0.2%
46	New Hampshire	11,600,000	0.2%
47	Delaware	10,800,000	0.2%
48	Wyoming	9,400,000	0.1%
49	Vermont	4,700,000	0.1%
NA	Tennessee **	NA	NA
	District of Columbia	9,900,000	0.1%

Source: U.S. Department of Health and Human Services, Centers for Medicare and Medicaid Services
"Statement of Expenditures for the SCHIP Program" (CMS-21 Report)
*Federal and state expenditures for fiscal year 2006. National total does not include funds spent in U.S. territories. The State Children's Health Insurance Program (SCHIP) was created in 1997 to help states expand health insurance to children whose families earn too much to qualify for Medicaid, yet not enough to afford private health insurance.
**Not available.

Per Capita Expenditures for State Children's Health Insurance Program (SCHIP) in 2006
National Per Capita = $23.55*

ALPHA ORDER

RANK	STATE	PER CAPITA
15	Alabama	$24.20
3	Alaska	41.04
38	Arizona	15.54
23	Arkansas	21.50
1	California	49.69
34	Colorado	16.18
44	Connecticut	9.01
41	Delaware	12.66
33	Florida	16.65
10	Georgia	28.39
39	Hawaii	15.09
37	Idaho	15.71
13	Illinois	24.43
32	Indiana	16.87
22	Iowa	21.60
14	Kansas	24.38
16	Kentucky	23.38
9	Louisiana	28.85
12	Maine	25.17
5	Maryland	37.91
6	Massachusetts	36.29
43	Michigan	9.45
46	Minnesota	7.64
2	Mississippi	42.84
29	Missouri	18.23
17	Montana	23.03
31	Nebraska	16.95
35	Nevada	16.13
45	New Hampshire	8.84
21	New Jersey	21.99
42	New Mexico	12.25
11	New York	26.21
7	North Carolina	30.66
19	North Dakota	22.12
24	Ohio	20.60
8	Oklahoma	29.35
25	Oregon	19.64
26	Pennsylvania	19.33
4	Rhode Island	39.66
40	South Carolina	14.46
30	South Dakota	17.76
NA	Tennessee **	NA
36	Texas	15.88
20	Utah	22.06
47	Vermont	7.57
27	Virginia	19.10
48	Washington	6.32
18	West Virginia	23.00
49	Wisconsin	5.99
28	Wyoming	18.33

RANK ORDER

RANK	STATE	PER CAPITA
1	California	$49.69
2	Mississippi	42.84
3	Alaska	41.04
4	Rhode Island	39.66
5	Maryland	37.91
6	Massachusetts	36.29
7	North Carolina	30.66
8	Oklahoma	29.35
9	Louisiana	28.85
10	Georgia	28.39
11	New York	26.21
12	Maine	25.17
13	Illinois	24.43
14	Kansas	24.38
15	Alabama	24.20
16	Kentucky	23.38
17	Montana	23.03
18	West Virginia	23.00
19	North Dakota	22.12
20	Utah	22.06
21	New Jersey	21.99
22	Iowa	21.60
23	Arkansas	21.50
24	Ohio	20.60
25	Oregon	19.64
26	Pennsylvania	19.33
27	Virginia	19.10
28	Wyoming	18.33
29	Missouri	18.23
30	South Dakota	17.76
31	Nebraska	16.95
32	Indiana	16.87
33	Florida	16.65
34	Colorado	16.18
35	Nevada	16.13
36	Texas	15.88
37	Idaho	15.71
38	Arizona	15.54
39	Hawaii	15.09
40	South Carolina	14.46
41	Delaware	12.66
42	New Mexico	12.25
43	Michigan	9.45
44	Connecticut	9.01
45	New Hampshire	8.84
46	Minnesota	7.64
47	Vermont	7.57
48	Washington	6.32
49	Wisconsin	5.99
NA	Tennessee **	NA

District of Columbia   16.91

Source: CQ Press using data from U.S. Department of Health and Human Services, Centers for Medicare and Medicaid Services
    "Statement of Expenditures for the SCHIP Program" (CMS-21 Report)

*Federal and state expenditures for fiscal year 2006. National figure does not include funds spent in U.S. territories. The State Children's Health Insurance Program (SCHIP) was created in 1997 to help states expand health insurance to children whose families earn too much to qualify for Medicaid, yet not enough to afford private health insurance.
**Not available.

Expenditures per State Children's Health Insurance Program (SCHIP) Participant in 2006
National Per Participant = $1,062*

ALPHA ORDER				RANK ORDER		
RANK	STATE	PER PARTICIPANT		RANK	STATE	PER PARTICIPANT
12	Alabama	$1,319		1	Arkansas	$17,558
17	Alaska	1,251		2	Minnesota	7,374
31	Arizona	991		3	Washington	2,687
1	Arkansas	17,558		4	North Dakota	2,232
14	California	1,294		5	Rhode Island	1,651
21	Colorado	1,101		6	New Jersey	1,577
11	Connecticut	1,363		7	Maryland	1,561
29	Delaware	1,005		8	Kentucky	1,516
32	Florida	990		9	Mississippi	1,490
44	Georgia	772		10	Kansas	1,373
40	Hawaii	876		11	Connecticut	1,363
37	Idaho	930		12	Alabama	1,319
33	Illinois	985		13	Iowa	1,295
43	Indiana	795		14	California	1,294
13	Iowa	1,295		15	Pennsylvania	1,270
10	Kansas	1,373		16	Montana	1,260
8	Kentucky	1,516		17	Alaska	1,251
41	Louisiana	860		18	Oregon	1,228
25	Maine	1,064		19	Massachusetts	1,225
7	Maryland	1,561		20	Wyoming	1,218
19	Massachusetts	1,225		21	Colorado	1,101
42	Michigan	806		22	North Carolina	1,096
2	Minnesota	7,374		23	Utah	1,095
9	Mississippi	1,490		24	Ohio	1,080
30	Missouri	998		25	Maine	1,064
16	Montana	1,260		25	Virginia	1,064
47	Nebraska	665		27	West Virginia	1,044
28	Nevada	1,022		28	Nevada	1,022
36	New Hampshire	936		29	Delaware	1,005
6	New Jersey	1,577		30	Missouri	998
35	New Mexico	946		31	Arizona	991
46	New York	734		32	Florida	990
22	North Carolina	1,096		33	Illinois	985
4	North Dakota	2,232		34	South Dakota	960
24	Ohio	1,080		35	New Mexico	946
39	Oklahoma	905		36	New Hampshire	936
18	Oregon	1,228		37	Idaho	930
15	Pennsylvania	1,270		38	South Carolina	909
5	Rhode Island	1,651		39	Oklahoma	905
38	South Carolina	909		40	Hawaii	876
34	South Dakota	960		41	Louisiana	860
NA	Tennessee **	NA		42	Michigan	806
48	Texas	635		43	Indiana	795
23	Utah	1,095		44	Georgia	772
45	Vermont	744		45	Vermont	744
25	Virginia	1,064		46	New York	734
3	Washington	2,687		47	Nebraska	665
27	West Virginia	1,044		48	Texas	635
49	Wisconsin	590		49	Wisconsin	590
20	Wyoming	1,218		NA	Tennessee **	NA
					District of Columbia	1,563

Source: CQ Press using data from U.S. Department of Health and Human Services, Centers for Medicare and Medicaid Services
  "Statement of Expenditures for the SCHIP Program" (CMS-21 Report)
*Federal and state expenditures for fiscal year 2006. National figure does not include funds spent in U.S. territories. The State Children's Health Insurance Program (SCHIP) was created in 1997 to help states expand health insurance to children whose families earn too much to qualify for Medicaid, yet not enough to afford private health insurance.
**Not available.

Health Maintenance Organizations (HMOs) in 2007

National Total = 629 HMOs*

ALPHA ORDER

RANK	STATE	HMOs	% of USA
37	Alabama	17	2.7%
50	Alaska	5	0.8%
5	Arizona	51	8.1%
31	Arkansas	19	3.0%
1	California	78	12.4%
28	Colorado	22	3.5%
14	Connecticut	32	5.1%
34	Delaware	18	2.9%
2	Florida	70	11.1%
21	Georgia	30	4.8%
44	Hawaii	11	1.7%
31	Idaho	19	3.0%
7	Illinois	43	6.8%
14	Indiana	32	5.1%
34	Iowa	18	2.9%
24	Kansas	23	3.7%
30	Kentucky	21	3.3%
31	Louisiana	19	3.0%
38	Maine	14	2.2%
20	Maryland	31	4.9%
14	Massachusetts	32	5.1%
8	Michigan	41	6.5%
24	Minnesota	23	3.7%
42	Mississippi	12	1.9%
10	Missouri	36	5.7%
44	Montana	11	1.7%
40	Nebraska	13	2.1%
12	Nevada	35	5.6%
42	New Hampshire	12	1.9%
10	New Jersey	36	5.7%
24	New Mexico	23	3.7%
3	New York	67	10.7%
24	North Carolina	23	3.7%
48	North Dakota	8	1.3%
6	Ohio	46	7.3%
28	Oklahoma	22	3.5%
13	Oregon	34	5.4%
9	Pennsylvania	39	6.2%
40	Rhode Island	13	2.1%
23	South Carolina	26	4.1%
46	South Dakota	10	1.6%
22	Tennessee	28	4.5%
4	Texas	59	9.4%
34	Utah	18	2.9%
49	Vermont	7	1.1%
14	Virginia	32	5.1%
14	Washington	32	5.1%
38	West Virginia	14	2.2%
14	Wisconsin	32	5.1%
46	Wyoming	10	1.6%

RANK ORDER

RANK	STATE	HMOs	% of USA
1	California	78	12.4%
2	Florida	70	11.1%
3	New York	67	10.7%
4	Texas	59	9.4%
5	Arizona	51	8.1%
6	Ohio	46	7.3%
7	Illinois	43	6.8%
8	Michigan	41	6.5%
9	Pennsylvania	39	6.2%
10	Missouri	36	5.7%
10	New Jersey	36	5.7%
12	Nevada	35	5.6%
13	Oregon	34	5.4%
14	Connecticut	32	5.1%
14	Indiana	32	5.1%
14	Massachusetts	32	5.1%
14	Virginia	32	5.1%
14	Washington	32	5.1%
14	Wisconsin	32	5.1%
20	Maryland	31	4.9%
21	Georgia	30	4.8%
22	Tennessee	28	4.5%
23	South Carolina	26	4.1%
24	Kansas	23	3.7%
24	Minnesota	23	3.7%
24	New Mexico	23	3.7%
24	North Carolina	23	3.7%
28	Colorado	22	3.5%
28	Oklahoma	22	3.5%
30	Kentucky	21	3.3%
31	Arkansas	19	3.0%
31	Idaho	19	3.0%
31	Louisiana	19	3.0%
34	Delaware	18	2.9%
34	Iowa	18	2.9%
34	Utah	18	2.9%
37	Alabama	17	2.7%
38	Maine	14	2.2%
38	West Virginia	14	2.2%
40	Nebraska	13	2.1%
40	Rhode Island	13	2.1%
42	Mississippi	12	1.9%
42	New Hampshire	12	1.9%
44	Hawaii	11	1.7%
44	Montana	11	1.7%
46	South Dakota	10	1.6%
46	Wyoming	10	1.6%
48	North Dakota	8	1.3%
49	Vermont	7	1.1%
50	Alaska	5	0.8%
	District of Columbia	19	3.0%

Source: Lance Wolkenbrod, Data Analyst
    HealthLeaders - InterStudy (Nashville, TN)
*As of January 2007. National total reflects the total HMOs nationwide and does not count HMOs in more than one state as multiple HMOs. The total for all HMO programs by state is 1,386.

Enrollees in Health Maintenance Organizations (HMOs) in 2007

National Total = 66,810,392 Enrollees*

ALPHA ORDER

RANK	STATE	ENROLLEES	% of USA
40	Alabama	127,234	0.2%
50	Alaska	56	0.0%
12	Arizona	1,567,920	2.3%
42	Arkansas	92,023	0.1%
1	California	16,948,843	25.4%
21	Colorado	938,596	1.4%
18	Connecticut	1,178,552	1.8%
39	Delaware	171,612	0.3%
3	Florida	3,505,537	5.2%
9	Georgia	2,069,589	3.1%
26	Hawaii	590,307	0.9%
44	Idaho	65,835	0.1%
11	Illinois	1,660,972	2.5%
20	Indiana	956,542	1.4%
34	Iowa	267,470	0.4%
29	Kansas	405,603	0.6%
33	Kentucky	293,704	0.4%
32	Louisiana	305,493	0.5%
30	Maine	357,806	0.5%
14	Maryland	1,430,333	2.1%
7	Massachusetts	2,274,586	3.4%
6	Michigan	2,768,991	4.1%
24	Minnesota	716,467	1.1%
48	Mississippi	4,411	0.0%
19	Missouri	974,189	1.5%
46	Montana	48,678	0.1%
41	Nebraska	96,065	0.1%
25	Nevada	611,422	0.9%
37	New Hampshire	194,910	0.3%
10	New Jersey	1,953,227	2.9%
27	New Mexico	492,394	0.7%
2	New York	6,449,125	9.7%
28	North Carolina	424,759	0.6%
49	North Dakota	1,914	0.0%
8	Ohio	2,160,673	3.2%
35	Oklahoma	227,944	0.3%
22	Oregon	890,260	1.3%
4	Pennsylvania	3,284,190	4.9%
38	Rhode Island	193,874	0.3%
31	South Carolina	313,162	0.5%
43	South Dakota	69,334	0.1%
13	Tennessee	1,522,429	2.3%
5	Texas	2,903,311	4.3%
23	Utah	762,082	1.1%
45	Vermont	55,117	0.1%
16	Virginia	1,324,430	2.0%
17	Washington	1,218,465	1.8%
36	West Virginia	209,014	0.3%
15	Wisconsin	1,366,217	2.0%
47	Wyoming	12,916	0.0%

RANK ORDER

RANK	STATE	ENROLLEES	% of USA
1	California	16,948,843	25.4%
2	New York	6,449,125	9.7%
3	Florida	3,505,537	5.2%
4	Pennsylvania	3,284,190	4.9%
5	Texas	2,903,311	4.3%
6	Michigan	2,768,991	4.1%
7	Massachusetts	2,274,586	3.4%
8	Ohio	2,160,673	3.2%
9	Georgia	2,069,589	3.1%
10	New Jersey	1,953,227	2.9%
11	Illinois	1,660,972	2.5%
12	Arizona	1,567,920	2.3%
13	Tennessee	1,522,429	2.3%
14	Maryland	1,430,333	2.1%
15	Wisconsin	1,366,217	2.0%
16	Virginia	1,324,430	2.0%
17	Washington	1,218,465	1.8%
18	Connecticut	1,178,552	1.8%
19	Missouri	974,189	1.5%
20	Indiana	956,542	1.4%
21	Colorado	938,596	1.4%
22	Oregon	890,260	1.3%
23	Utah	762,082	1.1%
24	Minnesota	716,467	1.1%
25	Nevada	611,422	0.9%
26	Hawaii	590,307	0.9%
27	New Mexico	492,394	0.7%
28	North Carolina	424,759	0.6%
29	Kansas	405,603	0.6%
30	Maine	357,806	0.5%
31	South Carolina	313,162	0.5%
32	Louisiana	305,493	0.5%
33	Kentucky	293,704	0.4%
34	Iowa	267,470	0.4%
35	Oklahoma	227,944	0.3%
36	West Virginia	209,014	0.3%
37	New Hampshire	194,910	0.3%
38	Rhode Island	193,874	0.3%
39	Delaware	171,612	0.3%
40	Alabama	127,234	0.2%
41	Nebraska	96,065	0.1%
42	Arkansas	92,023	0.1%
43	South Dakota	69,334	0.1%
44	Idaho	65,835	0.1%
45	Vermont	55,117	0.1%
46	Montana	48,678	0.1%
47	Wyoming	12,916	0.0%
48	Mississippi	4,411	0.0%
49	North Dakota	1,914	0.0%
50	Alaska	56	0.0%
	District of Columbia	351,809	0.5%

Source: Lance Wolkenbrod, Data Analyst
      HealthLeaders - InterStudy (Nashville, TN)
*As of January 2007.

Percent Change in Enrollees in Health Maintenance Organizations (HMOs): 2006 to 2007
National Percent Change = 7.6% Decrease*

ALPHA ORDER

RANK	STATE	PERCENT CHANGE
31	Alabama	(10.7)
NA	Alaska **	NA
40	Arizona	(22.8)
24	Arkansas	(4.4)
25	California	(4.6)
39	Colorado	(22.2)
12	Connecticut	7.1
3	Delaware	31.2
37	Florida	(19.7)
2	Georgia	48.1
20	Hawaii	(1.0)
1	Idaho	56.8
33	Illinois	(14.4)
46	Indiana	(40.7)
38	Iowa	(21.7)
18	Kansas	0.2
10	Kentucky	12.8
43	Louisiana	(29.2)
41	Maine	(26.1)
32	Maryland	(12.4)
36	Massachusetts	(19.6)
16	Michigan	3.0
14	Minnesota	5.0
49	Mississippi	(80.6)
29	Missouri	(9.9)
5	Montana	28.4
44	Nebraska	(30.6)
17	Nevada	2.3
45	New Hampshire	(30.7)
27	New Jersey	(8.3)
11	New Mexico	7.5
7	New York	21.6
47	North Carolina	(50.3)
34	North Dakota	(17.9)
35	Ohio	(18.6)
28	Oklahoma	(8.8)
22	Oregon	(1.5)
23	Pennsylvania	(1.9)
42	Rhode Island	(28.1)
19	South Carolina	(0.3)
8	South Dakota	18.7
21	Tennessee	(1.1)
14	Texas	5.0
9	Utah	18.0
48	Vermont	(63.9)
30	Virginia	(10.3)
13	Washington	6.0
4	West Virginia	29.8
26	Wisconsin	(6.1)
6	Wyoming	24.9

RANK ORDER

RANK	STATE	PERCENT CHANGE
1	Idaho	56.8
2	Georgia	48.1
3	Delaware	31.2
4	West Virginia	29.8
5	Montana	28.4
6	Wyoming	24.9
7	New York	21.6
8	South Dakota	18.7
9	Utah	18.0
10	Kentucky	12.8
11	New Mexico	7.5
12	Connecticut	7.1
13	Washington	6.0
14	Minnesota	5.0
14	Texas	5.0
16	Michigan	3.0
17	Nevada	2.3
18	Kansas	0.2
19	South Carolina	(0.3)
20	Hawaii	(1.0)
21	Tennessee	(1.1)
22	Oregon	(1.5)
23	Pennsylvania	(1.9)
24	Arkansas	(4.4)
25	California	(4.6)
26	Wisconsin	(6.1)
27	New Jersey	(8.3)
28	Oklahoma	(8.8)
29	Missouri	(9.9)
30	Virginia	(10.3)
31	Alabama	(10.7)
32	Maryland	(12.4)
33	Illinois	(14.4)
34	North Dakota	(17.9)
35	Ohio	(18.6)
36	Massachusetts	(19.6)
37	Florida	(19.7)
38	Iowa	(21.7)
39	Colorado	(22.2)
40	Arizona	(22.8)
41	Maine	(26.1)
42	Rhode Island	(28.1)
43	Louisiana	(29.2)
44	Nebraska	(30.6)
45	New Hampshire	(30.7)
46	Indiana	(40.7)
47	North Carolina	(50.3)
48	Vermont	(63.9)
49	Mississippi	(80.6)
NA	Alaska **	NA

District of Columbia   15.4

Source: CQ Press using data from Lance Wolkenbrod, Data Analyst
    HealthLeaders - InterStudy (Nashville, TN)
*As of January 2007. National figure does not include enrollees in U.S. territories.
**Not available.

Percent of Population Enrolled in Health Maintenance Organizations (HMOs) in 2007
National Percent = 22.3% Enrolled in HMOs*

ALPHA ORDER

RANK	STATE	PERCENT
46	Alabama	2.8
50	Alaska	0.0
11	Arizona	25.4
45	Arkansas	3.3
1	California	46.5
20	Colorado	19.7
4	Connecticut	33.6
19	Delaware	20.1
21	Florida	19.4
18	Georgia	22.1
2	Hawaii	45.9
44	Idaho	4.5
31	Illinois	12.9
27	Indiana	15.2
34	Iowa	9.0
29	Kansas	14.7
39	Kentucky	7.0
38	Louisiana	7.1
8	Maine	27.1
10	Maryland	25.5
3	Massachusetts	35.3
7	Michigan	27.4
30	Minnesota	13.9
49	Mississippi	0.2
26	Missouri	16.7
42	Montana	5.2
41	Nebraska	5.4
15	Nevada	24.5
28	New Hampshire	14.8
17	New Jersey	22.4
12	New Mexico	25.2
5	New York	33.4
43	North Carolina	4.8
48	North Dakota	0.3
23	Ohio	18.8
40	Oklahoma	6.4
16	Oregon	24.1
9	Pennsylvania	26.4
24	Rhode Island	18.2
37	South Carolina	7.2
35	South Dakota	8.9
12	Tennessee	25.2
32	Texas	12.4
6	Utah	29.9
36	Vermont	8.8
25	Virginia	17.3
22	Washington	19.1
33	West Virginia	11.5
14	Wisconsin	24.6
47	Wyoming	2.5

RANK ORDER

RANK	STATE	PERCENT
1	California	46.5
2	Hawaii	45.9
3	Massachusetts	35.3
4	Connecticut	33.6
5	New York	33.4
6	Utah	29.9
7	Michigan	27.4
8	Maine	27.1
9	Pennsylvania	26.4
10	Maryland	25.5
11	Arizona	25.4
12	New Mexico	25.2
12	Tennessee	25.2
14	Wisconsin	24.6
15	Nevada	24.5
16	Oregon	24.1
17	New Jersey	22.4
18	Georgia	22.1
19	Delaware	20.1
20	Colorado	19.7
21	Florida	19.4
22	Washington	19.1
23	Ohio	18.8
24	Rhode Island	18.2
25	Virginia	17.3
26	Missouri	16.7
27	Indiana	15.2
28	New Hampshire	14.8
29	Kansas	14.7
30	Minnesota	13.9
31	Illinois	12.9
32	Texas	12.4
33	West Virginia	11.5
34	Iowa	9.0
35	South Dakota	8.9
36	Vermont	8.8
37	South Carolina	7.2
38	Louisiana	7.1
39	Kentucky	7.0
40	Oklahoma	6.4
41	Nebraska	5.4
42	Montana	5.2
43	North Carolina	4.8
44	Idaho	4.5
45	Arkansas	3.3
46	Alabama	2.8
47	Wyoming	2.5
48	North Dakota	0.3
49	Mississippi	0.2
50	Alaska	0.0
	District of Columbia	60.5

Source: Lance Wolkenbrod, Data Analyst
     HealthLeaders - InterStudy (Nashville, TN)
*As of January 2007.

Percent of Insured Population Enrolled in
Health Maintenance Organizations (HMOs) in 2007
National Percent = 26.7% of Insured are Enrolled in HMOs*

RANK	STATE	PERCENT
46	Alabama	3.3
50	Alaska	0.0
8	Arizona	31.6
45	Arkansas	4.1
1	California	57.6
20	Colorado	23.6
5	Connecticut	37.6
21	Delaware	22.7
19	Florida	24.6
17	Georgia	26.9
2	Hawaii	51.6
44	Idaho	5.3
31	Illinois	15.3
27	Indiana	17.1
34	Iowa	10.2
28	Kansas	17.0
39	Kentucky	8.5
37	Louisiana	9.3
10	Maine	30.0
13	Maryland	29.6
3	Massachusetts	40.1
9	Michigan	31.0
31	Minnesota	15.3
49	Mississippi	0.2
26	Missouri	19.4
41	Montana	6.3
42	Nebraska	6.2
10	Nevada	30.0
29	New Hampshire	16.8
18	New Jersey	26.7
7	New Mexico	32.9
4	New York	39.4
43	North Carolina	5.8
48	North Dakota	0.4
23	Ohio	21.2
40	Oklahoma	8.1
15	Oregon	29.2
13	Pennsylvania	29.6
25	Rhode Island	20.1
38	South Carolina	8.8
34	South Dakota	10.2
12	Tennessee	29.8
30	Texas	16.6
6	Utah	36.4
36	Vermont	9.9
24	Virginia	20.3
22	Washington	21.9
33	West Virginia	13.3
16	Wisconsin	27.4
47	Wyoming	2.9

RANK	STATE	PERCENT
1	California	57.6
2	Hawaii	51.6
3	Massachusetts	40.1
4	New York	39.4
5	Connecticut	37.6
6	Utah	36.4
7	New Mexico	32.9
8	Arizona	31.6
9	Michigan	31.0
10	Maine	30.0
10	Nevada	30.0
12	Tennessee	29.8
13	Maryland	29.6
13	Pennsylvania	29.6
15	Oregon	29.2
16	Wisconsin	27.4
17	Georgia	26.9
18	New Jersey	26.7
19	Florida	24.6
20	Colorado	23.6
21	Delaware	22.7
22	Washington	21.9
23	Ohio	21.2
24	Virginia	20.3
25	Rhode Island	20.1
26	Missouri	19.4
27	Indiana	17.1
28	Kansas	17.0
29	New Hampshire	16.8
30	Texas	16.6
31	Illinois	15.3
31	Minnesota	15.3
33	West Virginia	13.3
34	Iowa	10.2
34	South Dakota	10.2
36	Vermont	9.9
37	Louisiana	9.3
38	South Carolina	8.8
39	Kentucky	8.5
40	Oklahoma	8.1
41	Montana	6.3
42	Nebraska	6.2
43	North Carolina	5.8
44	Idaho	5.3
45	Arkansas	4.1
46	Alabama	3.3
47	Wyoming	2.9
48	North Dakota	0.4
49	Mississippi	0.2
50	Alaska	0.0

| | District of Columbia | 69.9 |

Source: CQ Press using data from Lance Wolkenbrod, Data Analyst
        HealthLeaders - InterStudy (Nashville, TN)
*As of January 2007. Calculated using estimated number of insured as of 2006 from the U.S. Census Bureau.

Medicare Enrollees in 2006

National Total = 43,338,571 Enrollees*

ALPHA ORDER					RANK ORDER			

RANK	STATE	ENROLLEES	% of USA		RANK	STATE	ENROLLEES	% of USA
20	Alabama	772,280	1.8%		1	California	4,275,113	9.9%
50	Alaska	54,305	0.1%		2	Florida	3,079,554	7.1%
19	Arizona	815,115	1.9%		3	New York	2,804,725	6.5%
31	Arkansas	484,836	1.1%		4	Texas	2,625,612	6.1%
1	California	4,275,113	9.9%		5	Pennsylvania	2,155,832	5.0%
28	Colorado	539,883	1.2%		6	Ohio	1,778,058	4.1%
29	Connecticut	530,034	1.2%		7	Illinois	1,712,828	4.0%
45	Delaware	131,832	0.3%		8	Michigan	1,510,532	3.5%
2	Florida	3,079,554	7.1%		9	North Carolina	1,317,754	3.0%
11	Georgia	1,075,265	2.5%		10	New Jersey	1,241,698	2.9%
42	Hawaii	185,449	0.4%		11	Georgia	1,075,265	2.5%
40	Idaho	199,505	0.5%		12	Virginia	1,017,880	2.3%
7	Illinois	1,712,828	4.0%		13	Massachusetts	981,691	2.3%
16	Indiana	922,553	2.1%		14	Tennessee	949,263	2.2%
30	Iowa	494,523	1.1%		15	Missouri	929,501	2.1%
33	Kansas	406,456	0.9%		16	Indiana	922,553	2.1%
23	Kentucky	694,894	1.6%		17	Washington	846,793	2.0%
25	Louisiana	624,151	1.4%		18	Wisconsin	839,806	1.9%
39	Maine	240,568	0.6%		19	Arizona	815,115	1.9%
22	Maryland	708,049	1.6%		20	Alabama	772,280	1.8%
13	Massachusetts	981,691	2.3%		21	Minnesota	713,242	1.6%
8	Michigan	1,510,532	3.5%		22	Maryland	708,049	1.6%
21	Minnesota	713,242	1.6%		23	Kentucky	694,894	1.6%
32	Mississippi	461,641	1.1%		24	South Carolina	673,965	1.6%
15	Missouri	929,501	2.1%		25	Louisiana	624,151	1.4%
44	Montana	151,738	0.4%		26	Oklahoma	553,545	1.3%
37	Nebraska	264,307	0.6%		27	Oregon	552,856	1.3%
35	Nevada	306,777	0.7%		28	Colorado	539,883	1.2%
41	New Hampshire	197,821	0.5%		29	Connecticut	530,034	1.2%
10	New Jersey	1,241,698	2.9%		30	Iowa	494,523	1.1%
36	New Mexico	275,806	0.6%		31	Arkansas	484,836	1.1%
3	New York	2,804,725	6.5%		32	Mississippi	461,641	1.1%
9	North Carolina	1,317,754	3.0%		33	Kansas	406,456	0.9%
47	North Dakota	104,418	0.2%		34	West Virginia	361,308	0.8%
6	Ohio	1,778,058	4.1%		35	Nevada	306,777	0.7%
26	Oklahoma	553,545	1.3%		36	New Mexico	275,806	0.6%
27	Oregon	552,856	1.3%		37	Nebraska	264,307	0.6%
5	Pennsylvania	2,155,832	5.0%		38	Utah	245,960	0.6%
43	Rhode Island	173,776	0.4%		39	Maine	240,568	0.6%
24	South Carolina	673,965	1.6%		40	Idaho	199,505	0.5%
46	South Dakota	127,044	0.3%		41	New Hampshire	197,821	0.5%
14	Tennessee	949,263	2.2%		42	Hawaii	185,449	0.4%
4	Texas	2,625,612	6.1%		43	Rhode Island	173,776	0.4%
38	Utah	245,960	0.6%		44	Montana	151,738	0.4%
48	Vermont	99,071	0.2%		45	Delaware	131,832	0.3%
12	Virginia	1,017,880	2.3%		46	South Dakota	127,044	0.3%
17	Washington	846,793	2.0%		47	North Dakota	104,418	0.2%
34	West Virginia	361,308	0.8%		48	Vermont	99,071	0.2%
18	Wisconsin	839,806	1.9%		49	Wyoming	72,402	0.2%
49	Wyoming	72,402	0.2%		50	Alaska	54,305	0.1%
						District of Columbia	73,575	0.2%

Source: U.S. Department of Health and Human Services, Centers for Medicare and Medicaid Services
"2007 Data Compendium" (http://www.cms.hhs.gov/DataCompendium/)
*Includes aged and disabled enrollees. Total includes 609,956 enrollees in Puerto Rico and other outlying areas, foreign countries
or whose address is unknown.

Percent Change in Medicare Enrollees: 2005 to 2006

National Percent Change = 2.0% Increase

ALPHA ORDER				RANK ORDER		
RANK	STATE	PERCENT CHANGE		RANK	STATE	PERCENT CHANGE
22	Alabama	2.3		1	Alaska	4.7
1	Alaska	4.7		2	Idaho	3.7
16	Arizona	2.7		2	Utah	3.7
17	Arkansas	2.6		4	Georgia	3.5
33	California	1.8		4	South Carolina	3.5
6	Colorado	3.4		6	Colorado	3.4
48	Connecticut	0.9		6	Nevada	3.4
9	Delaware	3.2		8	New Mexico	3.3
42	Florida	1.1		9	Delaware	3.2
4	Georgia	3.5		9	North Carolina	3.2
27	Hawaii	2.1		9	Texas	3.2
2	Idaho	3.7		12	New Hampshire	3.1
39	Illinois	1.3		12	Washington	3.1
29	Indiana	1.9		14	Tennessee	3.0
46	Iowa	1.0		15	Vermont	2.8
42	Kansas	1.1		16	Arizona	2.7
20	Kentucky	2.4		17	Arkansas	2.6
22	Louisiana	2.3		18	Montana	2.5
25	Maine	2.2		18	Virginia	2.5
29	Maryland	1.9		20	Kentucky	2.4
40	Massachusetts	1.2		20	Oregon	2.4
29	Michigan	1.9		22	Alabama	2.3
22	Minnesota	2.3		22	Louisiana	2.3
37	Mississippi	1.6		22	Minnesota	2.3
29	Missouri	1.9		25	Maine	2.2
18	Montana	2.5		25	Oklahoma	2.2
42	Nebraska	1.1		27	Hawaii	2.1
6	Nevada	3.4		28	Wyoming	2.0
12	New Hampshire	3.1		29	Indiana	1.9
40	New Jersey	1.2		29	Maryland	1.9
8	New Mexico	3.3		29	Michigan	1.9
46	New York	1.0		29	Missouri	1.9
9	North Carolina	3.2		33	California	1.8
50	North Dakota	0.6		34	South Dakota	1.7
38	Ohio	1.4		34	West Virginia	1.7
25	Oklahoma	2.2		34	Wisconsin	1.7
20	Oregon	2.4		37	Mississippi	1.6
42	Pennsylvania	1.1		38	Ohio	1.4
49	Rhode Island	0.8		39	Illinois	1.3
4	South Carolina	3.5		40	Massachusetts	1.2
34	South Dakota	1.7		40	New Jersey	1.2
14	Tennessee	3.0		42	Florida	1.1
9	Texas	3.2		42	Kansas	1.1
2	Utah	3.7		42	Nebraska	1.1
15	Vermont	2.8		42	Pennsylvania	1.1
18	Virginia	2.5		46	Iowa	1.0
12	Washington	3.1		46	New York	1.0
34	West Virginia	1.7		48	Connecticut	0.9
34	Wisconsin	1.7		49	Rhode Island	0.8
28	Wyoming	2.0		50	North Dakota	0.6
					District of Columbia	0.4

Source: CQ Press using data from U.S. Department of Health and Human Services, Centers for Medicare and Medicaid Services
"2007 Data Compendium" (http://www.cms.hhs.gov/DataCompendium/)
*Includes aged and disabled enrollees. National rate includes enrollees in Puerto Rico and other outlying areas, foreign countries
or whose address is unknown.

Percent of Population Enrolled in Medicare in 2006

National Percent = 14.3% of Population*

ALPHA ORDER

RANK	STATE	PERCENT
6	Alabama	16.9
50	Alaska	8.2
39	Arizona	13.7
3	Arkansas	17.4
46	California	11.8
47	Colorado	11.6
25	Connecticut	15.1
18	Delaware	15.6
4	Florida	17.3
45	Georgia	11.9
32	Hawaii	14.5
36	Idaho	14.0
42	Illinois	13.4
30	Indiana	14.7
7	Iowa	16.7
29	Kansas	14.8
7	Kentucky	16.7
38	Louisiana	13.8
2	Maine	18.2
44	Maryland	12.6
21	Massachusetts	15.3
28	Michigan	14.9
37	Minnesota	13.9
16	Mississippi	15.8
13	Missouri	16.0
11	Montana	16.2
27	Nebraska	15.0
43	Nevada	12.7
25	New Hampshire	15.1
34	New Jersey	14.2
33	New Mexico	14.3
31	New York	14.6
22	North Carolina	15.2
9	North Dakota	16.4
20	Ohio	15.5
18	Oklahoma	15.6
22	Oregon	15.2
4	Pennsylvania	17.3
12	Rhode Island	16.1
16	South Carolina	15.8
9	South Dakota	16.4
14	Tennessee	15.9
48	Texas	11.5
49	Utah	10.0
14	Vermont	15.9
40	Virginia	13.5
40	Washington	13.5
1	West Virginia	19.9
22	Wisconsin	15.2
34	Wyoming	14.2

RANK ORDER

RANK	STATE	PERCENT
1	West Virginia	19.9
2	Maine	18.2
3	Arkansas	17.4
4	Florida	17.3
4	Pennsylvania	17.3
6	Alabama	16.9
7	Iowa	16.7
7	Kentucky	16.7
9	North Dakota	16.4
9	South Dakota	16.4
11	Montana	16.2
12	Rhode Island	16.1
13	Missouri	16.0
14	Tennessee	15.9
14	Vermont	15.9
16	Mississippi	15.8
16	South Carolina	15.8
18	Delaware	15.6
18	Oklahoma	15.6
20	Ohio	15.5
21	Massachusetts	15.3
22	North Carolina	15.2
22	Oregon	15.2
22	Wisconsin	15.2
25	Connecticut	15.1
25	New Hampshire	15.1
27	Nebraska	15.0
28	Michigan	14.9
29	Kansas	14.8
30	Indiana	14.7
31	New York	14.6
32	Hawaii	14.5
33	New Mexico	14.3
34	New Jersey	14.2
34	Wyoming	14.2
36	Idaho	14.0
37	Minnesota	13.9
38	Louisiana	13.8
39	Arizona	13.7
40	Virginia	13.5
40	Washington	13.5
42	Illinois	13.4
43	Nevada	12.7
44	Maryland	12.6
45	Georgia	11.9
46	California	11.8
47	Colorado	11.6
48	Texas	11.5
49	Utah	10.0
50	Alaska	8.2
	District of Columbia	13.4

Source: U.S. Department of Health and Human Services, Centers for Medicare and Medicaid Services
"2007 Data Compendium" (http://www.cms.hhs.gov/DataCompendium/)
*Includes aged and disabled enrollees. National rate includes only residents of the 50 states and the District of Columbia.

Percent of Medicare Enrollees in Managed Care Programs in 2006

National Percent = 17.3% of Medicare Enrollees*

ALPHA ORDER

RANK	STATE	PERCENT
22	Alabama	12.8
49	Alaska	0.4
3	Arizona	34.9
40	Arkansas	5.4
5	California	33.1
7	Colorado	29.8
31	Connecticut	7.4
46	Delaware	1.5
10	Florida	23.0
33	Georgia	7.1
2	Hawaii	36.1
16	Idaho	16.6
35	Illinois	6.9
36	Indiana	6.5
26	Iowa	9.6
37	Kansas	6.2
34	Kentucky	7.0
19	Louisiana	15.0
47	Maine	1.0
41	Maryland	5.2
15	Massachusetts	16.7
39	Michigan	5.9
9	Minnesota	26.0
44	Mississippi	4.0
21	Missouri	14.7
30	Montana	7.7
29	Nebraska	8.0
8	Nevada	29.1
47	New Hampshire	1.0
27	New Jersey	8.9
12	New Mexico	20.6
11	New York	22.3
24	North Carolina	11.0
42	North Dakota	5.1
18	Ohio	15.7
25	Oklahoma	10.5
1	Oregon	37.4
6	Pennsylvania	31.2
4	Rhode Island	34.7
37	South Carolina	6.2
45	South Dakota	2.7
20	Tennessee	14.8
23	Texas	12.2
13	Utah	17.5
49	Vermont	0.4
32	Virginia	7.2
14	Washington	17.4
28	West Virginia	8.7
17	Wisconsin	15.9
43	Wyoming	4.1

RANK ORDER

RANK	STATE	PERCENT
1	Oregon	37.4
2	Hawaii	36.1
3	Arizona	34.9
4	Rhode Island	34.7
5	California	33.1
6	Pennsylvania	31.2
7	Colorado	29.8
8	Nevada	29.1
9	Minnesota	26.0
10	Florida	23.0
11	New York	22.3
12	New Mexico	20.6
13	Utah	17.5
14	Washington	17.4
15	Massachusetts	16.7
16	Idaho	16.6
17	Wisconsin	15.9
18	Ohio	15.7
19	Louisiana	15.0
20	Tennessee	14.8
21	Missouri	14.7
22	Alabama	12.8
23	Texas	12.2
24	North Carolina	11.0
25	Oklahoma	10.5
26	Iowa	9.6
27	New Jersey	8.9
28	West Virginia	8.7
29	Nebraska	8.0
30	Montana	7.7
31	Connecticut	7.4
32	Virginia	7.2
33	Georgia	7.1
34	Kentucky	7.0
35	Illinois	6.9
36	Indiana	6.5
37	Kansas	6.2
37	South Carolina	6.2
39	Michigan	5.9
40	Arkansas	5.4
41	Maryland	5.2
42	North Dakota	5.1
43	Wyoming	4.1
44	Mississippi	4.0
45	South Dakota	2.7
46	Delaware	1.5
47	Maine	1.0
47	New Hampshire	1.0
49	Alaska	0.4
49	Vermont	0.4
	District of Columbia	7.7

Source: U.S. Department of Health and Human Services, Centers for Medicare and Medicaid Services
   "Medicare Managed Care Report"
*As of December 2006. National rate is a weighted average calculated by the editors. Includes Medicare Advantage and Employer Direct Plans. Regional Preferred Provider Organizations, Special Needs Plans, and employer only plans are also included.

Percent of Physicians Participating in Medicare in 2007

National Percent = 93.3% of Physicians Participate in Medicare*

ALPHA ORDER

RANK	STATE	PERCENT
5	Alabama	97.4
48	Alaska	89.7
36	Arizona	92.8
9	Arkansas	97.0
49	California	84.7
39	Colorado	92.2
28	Connecticut	95.0
16	Delaware	96.1
28	Florida	95.0
34	Georgia	93.4
25	Hawaii	95.4
46	Idaho	90.1
27	Illinois	95.1
22	Indiana	95.5
21	Iowa	95.6
6	Kansas	97.3
22	Kentucky	95.5
30	Louisiana	94.4
43	Maine	91.7
22	Maryland	95.5
40	Massachusetts	92.0
2	Michigan	97.8
50	Minnesota	81.2
40	Mississippi	92.0
30	Missouri	94.4
32	Montana	94.0
11	Nebraska	96.8
12	Nevada	96.7
47	New Hampshire	90.0
42	New Jersey	91.9
19	New Mexico	95.9
36	New York	92.8
17	North Carolina	96.0
3	North Dakota	97.6
10	Ohio	96.9
17	Oklahoma	96.0
32	Oregon	94.0
6	Pennsylvania	97.3
1	Rhode Island	98.2
19	South Carolina	95.9
35	South Dakota	93.2
15	Tennessee	96.3
38	Texas	92.7
4	Utah	97.5
45	Vermont	91.5
26	Virginia	95.3
13	Washington	96.5
8	West Virginia	97.1
14	Wisconsin	96.4
44	Wyoming	91.6

RANK ORDER

RANK	STATE	PERCENT
1	Rhode Island	98.2
2	Michigan	97.8
3	North Dakota	97.6
4	Utah	97.5
5	Alabama	97.4
6	Kansas	97.3
6	Pennsylvania	97.3
8	West Virginia	97.1
9	Arkansas	97.0
10	Ohio	96.9
11	Nebraska	96.8
12	Nevada	96.7
13	Washington	96.5
14	Wisconsin	96.4
15	Tennessee	96.3
16	Delaware	96.1
17	North Carolina	96.0
17	Oklahoma	96.0
19	New Mexico	95.9
19	South Carolina	95.9
21	Iowa	95.6
22	Indiana	95.5
22	Kentucky	95.5
22	Maryland	95.5
25	Hawaii	95.4
26	Virginia	95.3
27	Illinois	95.1
28	Connecticut	95.0
28	Florida	95.0
30	Louisiana	94.4
30	Missouri	94.4
32	Montana	94.0
32	Oregon	94.0
34	Georgia	93.4
35	South Dakota	93.2
36	Arizona	92.8
36	New York	92.8
38	Texas	92.7
39	Colorado	92.2
40	Massachusetts	92.0
40	Mississippi	92.0
42	New Jersey	91.9
43	Maine	91.7
44	Wyoming	91.6
45	Vermont	91.5
46	Idaho	90.1
47	New Hampshire	90.0
48	Alaska	89.7
49	California	84.7
50	Minnesota	81.2

District of Columbia	92.7

Source: U.S. Department of Health and Human Services, Centers for Medicare and Medicaid Services
   "2007 Data Compendium" (http://www.cms.hhs.gov/DataCompendium/)
*As of January 2007. Refers to Medicare Part B. Physicians include MDs, DOs, limited license practitioners, and non-physician practitioners. National average is a weighted average based on state population.

Medicare Program Payments in 2006

National Total = $279,452,000,000*

ALPHA ORDER

RANK	STATE	BENEFITS	% of USA
18	Alabama	$5,052,000,000	1.8%
50	Alaska	350,000,000	0.1%
26	Arizona	3,772,000,000	1.3%
29	Arkansas	3,137,000,000	1.1%
1	California	23,204,000,000	8.3%
32	Colorado	2,705,000,000	1.0%
24	Connecticut	4,235,000,000	1.5%
42	Delaware	995,000,000	0.4%
2	Florida	21,997,000,000	7.9%
11	Georgia	7,388,000,000	2.6%
47	Hawaii	599,000,000	0.2%
41	Idaho	1,013,000,000	0.4%
5	Illinois	13,124,000,000	4.7%
13	Indiana	6,407,000,000	2.3%
30	Iowa	2,869,000,000	1.0%
31	Kansas	2,731,000,000	1.0%
21	Kentucky	4,766,000,000	1.7%
19	Louisiana	4,947,000,000	1.8%
37	Maine	1,466,000,000	0.5%
15	Maryland	6,350,000,000	2.3%
12	Massachusetts	6,957,000,000	2.5%
7	Michigan	12,073,000,000	4.3%
27	Minnesota	3,674,000,000	1.3%
28	Mississippi	3,555,000,000	1.3%
17	Missouri	5,883,000,000	2.1%
44	Montana	840,000,000	0.3%
35	Nebraska	1,679,000,000	0.6%
36	Nevada	1,631,000,000	0.6%
39	New Hampshire	1,337,000,000	0.5%
9	New Jersey	10,356,000,000	3.7%
38	New Mexico	1,353,000,000	0.5%
4	New York	19,313,000,000	6.9%
10	North Carolina	8,673,000,000	3.1%
48	North Dakota	591,000,000	0.2%
6	Ohio	12,104,000,000	4.3%
25	Oklahoma	3,854,000,000	1.4%
34	Oregon	2,141,000,000	0.8%
8	Pennsylvania	11,818,000,000	4.2%
43	Rhode Island	858,000,000	0.3%
22	South Carolina	4,718,000,000	1.7%
45	South Dakota	720,000,000	0.3%
16	Tennessee	6,261,000,000	2.2%
3	Texas	20,915,000,000	7.5%
40	Utah	1,300,000,000	0.5%
46	Vermont	655,000,000	0.2%
14	Virginia	6,352,000,000	2.3%
23	Washington	4,507,000,000	1.6%
33	West Virginia	2,367,000,000	0.8%
20	Wisconsin	4,788,000,000	1.7%
49	Wyoming	444,000,000	0.2%

RANK ORDER

RANK	STATE	BENEFITS	% of USA
1	California	$23,204,000,000	8.3%
2	Florida	21,997,000,000	7.9%
3	Texas	20,915,000,000	7.5%
4	New York	19,313,000,000	6.9%
5	Illinois	13,124,000,000	4.7%
6	Ohio	12,104,000,000	4.3%
7	Michigan	12,073,000,000	4.3%
8	Pennsylvania	11,818,000,000	4.2%
9	New Jersey	10,356,000,000	3.7%
10	North Carolina	8,673,000,000	3.1%
11	Georgia	7,388,000,000	2.6%
12	Massachusetts	6,957,000,000	2.5%
13	Indiana	6,407,000,000	2.3%
14	Virginia	6,352,000,000	2.3%
15	Maryland	6,350,000,000	2.3%
16	Tennessee	6,261,000,000	2.2%
17	Missouri	5,883,000,000	2.1%
18	Alabama	5,052,000,000	1.8%
19	Louisiana	4,947,000,000	1.8%
20	Wisconsin	4,788,000,000	1.7%
21	Kentucky	4,766,000,000	1.7%
22	South Carolina	4,718,000,000	1.7%
23	Washington	4,507,000,000	1.6%
24	Connecticut	4,235,000,000	1.5%
25	Oklahoma	3,854,000,000	1.4%
26	Arizona	3,772,000,000	1.3%
27	Minnesota	3,674,000,000	1.3%
28	Mississippi	3,555,000,000	1.3%
29	Arkansas	3,137,000,000	1.1%
30	Iowa	2,869,000,000	1.0%
31	Kansas	2,731,000,000	1.0%
32	Colorado	2,705,000,000	1.0%
33	West Virginia	2,367,000,000	0.8%
34	Oregon	2,141,000,000	0.8%
35	Nebraska	1,679,000,000	0.6%
36	Nevada	1,631,000,000	0.6%
37	Maine	1,466,000,000	0.5%
38	New Mexico	1,353,000,000	0.5%
39	New Hampshire	1,337,000,000	0.5%
40	Utah	1,300,000,000	0.5%
41	Idaho	1,013,000,000	0.4%
42	Delaware	995,000,000	0.4%
43	Rhode Island	858,000,000	0.3%
44	Montana	840,000,000	0.3%
45	South Dakota	720,000,000	0.3%
46	Vermont	655,000,000	0.2%
47	Hawaii	599,000,000	0.2%
48	North Dakota	591,000,000	0.2%
49	Wyoming	444,000,000	0.2%
50	Alaska	350,000,000	0.1%
	District of Columbia	630,000,000	0.2%

Source: U.S. Department of Health and Human Services, Centers for Medicare and Medicaid Services
"Health Care Financing Review, 2007 Statistical Supplement" (http://cms.hhs.gov/MedicareMedicaidStatSupp)
*Figures for calendar year 2006. Includes payments to aged and disabled enrollees. Total does not include payments to beneficiaries in Puerto Rico and other outlying areas.

Per Capita Medicare Program Payments in 2006

National Per Capita = $935*

ALPHA ORDER

RANK	STATE	PER CAPITA
13	Alabama	$1,101
48	Alaska	517
45	Arizona	612
11	Arkansas	1,117
44	California	640
47	Colorado	568
4	Connecticut	1,211
7	Delaware	1,167
3	Florida	1,218
38	Georgia	791
50	Hawaii	468
42	Idaho	692
20	Illinois	1,027
22	Indiana	1,017
27	Iowa	965
25	Kansas	991
9	Kentucky	1,134
8	Louisiana	1,166
12	Maine	1,115
9	Maryland	1,134
15	Massachusetts	1,081
5	Michigan	1,195
39	Minnesota	713
2	Mississippi	1,226
23	Missouri	1,008
33	Montana	887
29	Nebraska	952
43	Nevada	654
21	New Hampshire	1,019
5	New Jersey	1,195
41	New Mexico	697
24	New York	1,002
26	North Carolina	978
30	North Dakota	927
17	Ohio	1,056
16	Oklahoma	1,077
46	Oregon	580
28	Pennsylvania	953
37	Rhode Island	808
14	South Carolina	1,090
31	South Dakota	913
19	Tennessee	1,031
32	Texas	894
49	Utah	504
18	Vermont	1,055
36	Virginia	831
40	Washington	707
1	West Virginia	1,309
35	Wisconsin	859
34	Wyoming	866

RANK ORDER

RANK	STATE	PER CAPITA
1	West Virginia	$1,309
2	Mississippi	1,226
3	Florida	1,218
4	Connecticut	1,211
5	Michigan	1,195
5	New Jersey	1,195
7	Delaware	1,167
8	Louisiana	1,166
9	Kentucky	1,134
9	Maryland	1,134
11	Arkansas	1,117
12	Maine	1,115
13	Alabama	1,101
14	South Carolina	1,090
15	Massachusetts	1,081
16	Oklahoma	1,077
17	Ohio	1,056
18	Vermont	1,055
19	Tennessee	1,031
20	Illinois	1,027
21	New Hampshire	1,019
22	Indiana	1,017
23	Missouri	1,008
24	New York	1,002
25	Kansas	991
26	North Carolina	978
27	Iowa	965
28	Pennsylvania	953
29	Nebraska	952
30	North Dakota	927
31	South Dakota	913
32	Texas	894
33	Montana	887
34	Wyoming	866
35	Wisconsin	859
36	Virginia	831
37	Rhode Island	808
38	Georgia	791
39	Minnesota	713
40	Washington	707
41	New Mexico	697
42	Idaho	692
43	Nevada	654
44	California	640
45	Arizona	612
46	Oregon	580
47	Colorado	568
48	Alaska	517
49	Utah	504
50	Hawaii	468

District of Columbia   1,076

Source: CQ Press using data from U.S. Department of Health and Human Services, Centers for Medicare and Medicaid Services "Health Care Financing Review, 2007 Statistical Supplement" (http://cms.hhs.gov/MedicareMedicaidStatSupp)
*Figures for calendar year 2006. Includes payments to aged and disabled enrollees. National rate does not include payments or enrollees in Puerto Rico and other outlying areas.

Medicare Program Payments per Enrollee in 2006

National Rate = $7,941*

ALPHA ORDER				RANK ORDER		
RANK	STATE	PER ENROLLEE		RANK	STATE	PER ENROLLEE
21	Alabama	$7,479		1	Maryland	$9,427
37	Alaska	6,625		2	Florida	9,273
29	Arizona	7,202		3	Louisiana	9,234
31	Arkansas	6,974		4	Texas	9,076
11	California	8,088		5	New Jersey	9,069
30	Colorado	7,135		6	New York	8,794
7	Connecticut	8,554		7	Connecticut	8,554
18	Delaware	7,548		8	Michigan	8,486
2	Florida	9,273		9	Massachusetts	8,474
25	Georgia	7,363		10	Illinois	8,193
50	Hawaii	4,953		11	California	8,088
46	Idaho	6,056		12	Mississippi	8,025
10	Illinois	8,193		13	Ohio	7,997
20	Indiana	7,481		14	Pennsylvania	7,898
39	Iowa	6,505		15	Oklahoma	7,795
27	Kansas	7,252		16	Tennessee	7,744
24	Kentucky	7,367		17	South Carolina	7,562
3	Louisiana	9,234		18	Delaware	7,548
44	Maine	6,187		19	Rhode Island	7,517
1	Maryland	9,427		20	Indiana	7,481
9	Massachusetts	8,474		21	Alabama	7,479
8	Michigan	8,486		22	Nevada	7,448
32	Minnesota	6,961		23	North Carolina	7,412
12	Mississippi	8,025		24	Kentucky	7,367
26	Missouri	7,348		25	Georgia	7,363
47	Montana	5,946		26	Missouri	7,348
35	Nebraska	6,792		27	Kansas	7,252
22	Nevada	7,448		28	West Virginia	7,204
33	New Hampshire	6,949		29	Arizona	7,202
5	New Jersey	9,069		30	Colorado	7,135
43	New Mexico	6,245		31	Arkansas	6,974
6	New York	8,794		32	Minnesota	6,961
23	North Carolina	7,412		33	New Hampshire	6,949
48	North Dakota	5,898		34	Wisconsin	6,829
13	Ohio	7,997		35	Nebraska	6,792
15	Oklahoma	7,795		36	Virginia	6,709
45	Oregon	6,125		37	Alaska	6,625
14	Pennsylvania	7,898		38	Vermont	6,564
19	Rhode Island	7,517		39	Iowa	6,505
17	South Carolina	7,562		40	Washington	6,485
49	South Dakota	5,840		41	Utah	6,477
16	Tennessee	7,744		42	Wyoming	6,276
4	Texas	9,076		43	New Mexico	6,245
41	Utah	6,477		44	Maine	6,187
38	Vermont	6,564		45	Oregon	6,125
36	Virginia	6,709		46	Idaho	6,056
40	Washington	6,485		47	Montana	5,946
28	West Virginia	7,204		48	North Dakota	5,898
34	Wisconsin	6,829		49	South Dakota	5,840
42	Wyoming	6,276		50	Hawaii	4,953
					District of Columbia	9,149

Source: U.S. Department of Health and Human Services, Centers for Medicare and Medicaid Services
   "Health Care Financing Review, 2007 Statistical Supplement" (http://cms.hhs.gov/MedicareMedicaidStatSupp)
*Figures for calendar year 2006. Includes payments to aged and disabled enrollees. National figure does not include enrollees in managed care plans in the denominator used to calculate average payments. National rate also does not include payments or enrollees in Puerto Rico and other outlying areas.

Medicaid Enrollment in 2006

National Total = 45,156,803 Enrollees*

ALPHA ORDER

RANK	STATE	ENROLLEES	% of USA
20	Alabama	738,971	1.6%
46	Alaska	103,671	0.2%
14	Arizona	970,967	2.2%
25	Arkansas	630,671	1.4%
1	California	6,435,557	14.3%
32	Colorado	390,520	0.9%
30	Connecticut	404,719	0.9%
43	Delaware	146,807	0.3%
4	Florida	2,206,524	4.9%
10	Georgia	1,271,472	2.8%
38	Hawaii	199,903	0.4%
42	Idaho	165,187	0.4%
5	Illinois	1,993,000	4.4%
19	Indiana	824,938	1.8%
33	Iowa	323,966	0.7%
35	Kansas	261,457	0.6%
21	Kentucky	708,837	1.6%
15	Louisiana	942,734	2.1%
36	Maine	251,060	0.6%
23	Maryland	692,437	1.5%
12	Massachusetts	1,091,128	2.4%
8	Michigan	1,475,917	3.3%
27	Minnesota	579,528	1.3%
28	Mississippi	555,881	1.2%
18	Missouri	825,378	1.8%
48	Montana	79,598	0.2%
37	Nebraska	208,836	0.5%
41	Nevada	166,471	0.4%
45	New Hampshire	110,117	0.2%
16	New Jersey	863,641	1.9%
29	New Mexico	426,118	0.9%
2	New York	4,024,784	8.9%
9	North Carolina	1,287,498	2.9%
50	North Dakota	51,447	0.1%
7	Ohio	1,729,515	3.8%
26	Oklahoma	581,308	1.3%
31	Oregon	402,371	0.9%
6	Pennsylvania	1,802,430	4.0%
40	Rhode Island	183,111	0.4%
24	South Carolina	667,581	1.5%
47	South Dakota	99,647	0.2%
11	Tennessee	1,179,335	2.6%
3	Texas	2,778,761	6.2%
39	Utah	198,243	0.4%
44	Vermont	130,608	0.3%
22	Virginia	701,193	1.6%
13	Washington	999,031	2.2%
34	West Virginia	293,056	0.6%
17	Wisconsin	844,962	1.9%
49	Wyoming	62,459	0.1%

RANK ORDER

RANK	STATE	ENROLLEES	% of USA
1	California	6,435,557	14.3%
2	New York	4,024,784	8.9%
3	Texas	2,778,761	6.2%
4	Florida	2,206,524	4.9%
5	Illinois	1,993,000	4.4%
6	Pennsylvania	1,802,430	4.0%
7	Ohio	1,729,515	3.8%
8	Michigan	1,475,917	3.3%
9	North Carolina	1,287,498	2.9%
10	Georgia	1,271,472	2.8%
11	Tennessee	1,179,335	2.6%
12	Massachusetts	1,091,128	2.4%
13	Washington	999,031	2.2%
14	Arizona	970,967	2.2%
15	Louisiana	942,734	2.1%
16	New Jersey	863,641	1.9%
17	Wisconsin	844,962	1.9%
18	Missouri	825,378	1.8%
19	Indiana	824,938	1.8%
20	Alabama	738,971	1.6%
21	Kentucky	708,837	1.6%
22	Virginia	701,193	1.6%
23	Maryland	692,437	1.5%
24	South Carolina	667,581	1.5%
25	Arkansas	630,671	1.4%
26	Oklahoma	581,308	1.3%
27	Minnesota	579,528	1.3%
28	Mississippi	555,881	1.2%
29	New Mexico	426,118	0.9%
30	Connecticut	404,719	0.9%
31	Oregon	402,371	0.9%
32	Colorado	390,520	0.9%
33	Iowa	323,966	0.7%
34	West Virginia	293,056	0.6%
35	Kansas	261,457	0.6%
36	Maine	251,060	0.6%
37	Nebraska	208,836	0.5%
38	Hawaii	199,903	0.4%
39	Utah	198,243	0.4%
40	Rhode Island	183,111	0.4%
41	Nevada	166,471	0.4%
42	Idaho	165,187	0.4%
43	Delaware	146,807	0.3%
44	Vermont	130,608	0.3%
45	New Hampshire	110,117	0.2%
46	Alaska	103,671	0.2%
47	South Dakota	99,647	0.2%
48	Montana	79,598	0.2%
49	Wyoming	62,459	0.1%
50	North Dakota	51,447	0.1%
	District of Columbia	146,014	0.3%

Source: U.S. Department of Health and Human Services, Centers for Medicare and Medicaid Services
"Medicaid Managed Care State Enrollment" (http://www.cms.hhs.gov/MedicaidDataSourcesGenInfo/)
*Unduplicated enrollment as of December 31, 2006. National total includes 947,438 Medicaid enrollees in Puerto Rico and the Virgin Islands.

Percent of Population Enrolled in Medicaid in 2006

National Percent = 14.8% of Population*

ALPHA ORDER

RANK	STATE	PERCENT
16	Alabama	16.1
22	Alaska	15.3
17	Arizona	15.7
1	Arkansas	22.5
9	California	17.8
47	Colorado	8.2
37	Connecticut	11.6
10	Delaware	17.2
33	Florida	12.2
29	Georgia	13.6
19	Hawaii	15.6
38	Idaho	11.3
19	Illinois	15.6
30	Indiana	13.1
40	Iowa	10.9
43	Kansas	9.5
13	Kentucky	16.9
2	Louisiana	22.2
8	Maine	19.1
32	Maryland	12.4
12	Massachusetts	17.0
25	Michigan	14.6
39	Minnesota	11.2
7	Mississippi	19.2
28	Missouri	14.1
45	Montana	8.4
36	Nebraska	11.8
50	Nevada	6.7
45	New Hampshire	8.4
42	New Jersey	10.0
3	New Mexico	21.9
5	New York	20.9
26	North Carolina	14.5
48	North Dakota	8.1
24	Ohio	15.1
14	Oklahoma	16.2
40	Oregon	10.9
26	Pennsylvania	14.5
10	Rhode Island	17.2
21	South Carolina	15.4
31	South Dakota	12.6
6	Tennessee	19.4
35	Texas	11.9
49	Utah	7.7
4	Vermont	21.0
44	Virginia	9.2
17	Washington	15.7
14	West Virginia	16.2
23	Wisconsin	15.2
33	Wyoming	12.2

RANK ORDER

RANK	STATE	PERCENT
1	Arkansas	22.5
2	Louisiana	22.2
3	New Mexico	21.9
4	Vermont	21.0
5	New York	20.9
6	Tennessee	19.4
7	Mississippi	19.2
8	Maine	19.1
9	California	17.8
10	Delaware	17.2
10	Rhode Island	17.2
12	Massachusetts	17.0
13	Kentucky	16.9
14	Oklahoma	16.2
14	West Virginia	16.2
16	Alabama	16.1
17	Arizona	15.7
17	Washington	15.7
19	Hawaii	15.6
19	Illinois	15.6
21	South Carolina	15.4
22	Alaska	15.3
23	Wisconsin	15.2
24	Ohio	15.1
25	Michigan	14.6
26	North Carolina	14.5
26	Pennsylvania	14.5
28	Missouri	14.1
29	Georgia	13.6
30	Indiana	13.1
31	South Dakota	12.6
32	Maryland	12.4
33	Florida	12.2
33	Wyoming	12.2
35	Texas	11.9
36	Nebraska	11.8
37	Connecticut	11.6
38	Idaho	11.3
39	Minnesota	11.2
40	Iowa	10.9
40	Oregon	10.9
42	New Jersey	10.0
43	Kansas	9.5
44	Virginia	9.2
45	Montana	8.4
45	New Hampshire	8.4
47	Colorado	8.2
48	North Dakota	8.1
49	Utah	7.7
50	Nevada	6.7

District of Columbia   24.9

Source: CQ Press using data from U.S. Department of Health and Human Services, Centers for Medicare and Medicaid Services
"Medicaid Managed Care State Enrollment" (http://www.cms.hhs.gov/MedicaidDataSourcesGenInfo/)
*Unduplicated enrollment as of December 31, 2006. National percent does not include recipients or population in U.S. territories.

Medicaid Managed Care Enrollment in 2006

National Total = 29,552,763 Enrollees*

<table>
<tr><td colspan="4">ALPHA ORDER</td><td colspan="4">RANK ORDER</td></tr>
<tr><td>RANK</td><td>STATE</td><td>ENROLLEES</td><td>% of USA</td><td>RANK</td><td>STATE</td><td>ENROLLEES</td><td>% of USA</td></tr>
<tr><td>22</td><td>Alabama</td><td>484,906</td><td>1.6%</td><td>1</td><td>California</td><td>3,253,572</td><td>11.0%</td></tr>
<tr><td>48</td><td>Alaska</td><td>0</td><td>0.0%</td><td>2</td><td>New York</td><td>2,543,355</td><td>8.6%</td></tr>
<tr><td>10</td><td>Arizona</td><td>870,225</td><td>2.9%</td><td>3</td><td>Texas</td><td>1,868,035</td><td>6.3%</td></tr>
<tr><td>19</td><td>Arkansas</td><td>523,088</td><td>1.8%</td><td>4</td><td>Pennsylvania</td><td>1,574,170</td><td>5.3%</td></tr>
<tr><td>1</td><td>California</td><td>3,253,572</td><td>11.0%</td><td>5</td><td>Florida</td><td>1,440,634</td><td>4.9%</td></tr>
<tr><td>25</td><td>Colorado</td><td>361,177</td><td>1.2%</td><td>6</td><td>Michigan</td><td>1,336,252</td><td>4.5%</td></tr>
<tr><td>28</td><td>Connecticut</td><td>309,431</td><td>1.0%</td><td>7</td><td>Tennessee</td><td>1,179,335</td><td>4.0%</td></tr>
<tr><td>42</td><td>Delaware</td><td>106,652</td><td>0.4%</td><td>8</td><td>Georgia</td><td>1,050,382</td><td>3.6%</td></tr>
<tr><td>5</td><td>Florida</td><td>1,440,634</td><td>4.9%</td><td>9</td><td>Ohio</td><td>957,443</td><td>3.2%</td></tr>
<tr><td>8</td><td>Georgia</td><td>1,050,382</td><td>3.6%</td><td>10</td><td>Arizona</td><td>870,225</td><td>2.9%</td></tr>
<tr><td>34</td><td>Hawaii</td><td>159,555</td><td>0.5%</td><td>11</td><td>North Carolina</td><td>843,480</td><td>2.9%</td></tr>
<tr><td>39</td><td>Idaho</td><td>134,588</td><td>0.5%</td><td>12</td><td>Washington</td><td>837,300</td><td>2.8%</td></tr>
<tr><td>41</td><td>Illinois</td><td>118,000</td><td>0.4%</td><td>13</td><td>Missouri</td><td>818,931</td><td>2.8%</td></tr>
<tr><td>18</td><td>Indiana</td><td>591,964</td><td>2.0%</td><td>14</td><td>Massachusetts</td><td>659,039</td><td>2.2%</td></tr>
<tr><td>29</td><td>Iowa</td><td>280,337</td><td>0.9%</td><td>15</td><td>Kentucky</td><td>653,256</td><td>2.2%</td></tr>
<tr><td>37</td><td>Kansas</td><td>144,157</td><td>0.5%</td><td>16</td><td>Louisiana</td><td>641,988</td><td>2.2%</td></tr>
<tr><td>15</td><td>Kentucky</td><td>653,256</td><td>2.2%</td><td>17</td><td>New Jersey</td><td>603,269</td><td>2.0%</td></tr>
<tr><td>16</td><td>Louisiana</td><td>641,988</td><td>2.2%</td><td>18</td><td>Indiana</td><td>591,964</td><td>2.0%</td></tr>
<tr><td>33</td><td>Maine</td><td>168,737</td><td>0.6%</td><td>19</td><td>Arkansas</td><td>523,088</td><td>1.8%</td></tr>
<tr><td>21</td><td>Maryland</td><td>503,266</td><td>1.7%</td><td>20</td><td>Oklahoma</td><td>516,446</td><td>1.7%</td></tr>
<tr><td>14</td><td>Massachusetts</td><td>659,039</td><td>2.2%</td><td>21</td><td>Maryland</td><td>503,266</td><td>1.7%</td></tr>
<tr><td>6</td><td>Michigan</td><td>1,336,252</td><td>4.5%</td><td>22</td><td>Alabama</td><td>484,906</td><td>1.6%</td></tr>
<tr><td>26</td><td>Minnesota</td><td>360,381</td><td>1.2%</td><td>23</td><td>Virginia</td><td>439,115</td><td>1.5%</td></tr>
<tr><td>48</td><td>Mississippi</td><td>0</td><td>0.0%</td><td>24</td><td>Oregon</td><td>368,554</td><td>1.2%</td></tr>
<tr><td>13</td><td>Missouri</td><td>818,931</td><td>2.8%</td><td>25</td><td>Colorado</td><td>361,177</td><td>1.2%</td></tr>
<tr><td>46</td><td>Montana</td><td>52,374</td><td>0.2%</td><td>26</td><td>Minnesota</td><td>360,381</td><td>1.2%</td></tr>
<tr><td>32</td><td>Nebraska</td><td>169,548</td><td>0.6%</td><td>27</td><td>Wisconsin</td><td>334,498</td><td>1.1%</td></tr>
<tr><td>38</td><td>Nevada</td><td>140,377</td><td>0.5%</td><td>28</td><td>Connecticut</td><td>309,431</td><td>1.0%</td></tr>
<tr><td>45</td><td>New Hampshire</td><td>82,201</td><td>0.3%</td><td>29</td><td>Iowa</td><td>280,337</td><td>0.9%</td></tr>
<tr><td>17</td><td>New Jersey</td><td>603,269</td><td>2.0%</td><td>30</td><td>New Mexico</td><td>276,992</td><td>0.9%</td></tr>
<tr><td>30</td><td>New Mexico</td><td>276,992</td><td>0.9%</td><td>31</td><td>Utah</td><td>171,524</td><td>0.6%</td></tr>
<tr><td>2</td><td>New York</td><td>2,543,355</td><td>8.6%</td><td>32</td><td>Nebraska</td><td>169,548</td><td>0.6%</td></tr>
<tr><td>11</td><td>North Carolina</td><td>843,480</td><td>2.9%</td><td>33</td><td>Maine</td><td>168,737</td><td>0.6%</td></tr>
<tr><td>47</td><td>North Dakota</td><td>27,741</td><td>0.1%</td><td>34</td><td>Hawaii</td><td>159,555</td><td>0.5%</td></tr>
<tr><td>9</td><td>Ohio</td><td>957,443</td><td>3.2%</td><td>35</td><td>West Virginia</td><td>159,322</td><td>0.5%</td></tr>
<tr><td>20</td><td>Oklahoma</td><td>516,446</td><td>1.7%</td><td>36</td><td>South Carolina</td><td>157,519</td><td>0.5%</td></tr>
<tr><td>24</td><td>Oregon</td><td>368,554</td><td>1.2%</td><td>37</td><td>Kansas</td><td>144,157</td><td>0.5%</td></tr>
<tr><td>4</td><td>Pennsylvania</td><td>1,574,170</td><td>5.3%</td><td>38</td><td>Nevada</td><td>140,377</td><td>0.5%</td></tr>
<tr><td>40</td><td>Rhode Island</td><td>118,434</td><td>0.4%</td><td>39</td><td>Idaho</td><td>134,588</td><td>0.5%</td></tr>
<tr><td>36</td><td>South Carolina</td><td>157,519</td><td>0.5%</td><td>40</td><td>Rhode Island</td><td>118,434</td><td>0.4%</td></tr>
<tr><td>43</td><td>South Dakota</td><td>98,225</td><td>0.3%</td><td>41</td><td>Illinois</td><td>118,000</td><td>0.4%</td></tr>
<tr><td>7</td><td>Tennessee</td><td>1,179,335</td><td>4.0%</td><td>42</td><td>Delaware</td><td>106,652</td><td>0.4%</td></tr>
<tr><td>3</td><td>Texas</td><td>1,868,035</td><td>6.3%</td><td>43</td><td>South Dakota</td><td>98,225</td><td>0.3%</td></tr>
<tr><td>31</td><td>Utah</td><td>171,524</td><td>0.6%</td><td>44</td><td>Vermont</td><td>84,790</td><td>0.3%</td></tr>
<tr><td>44</td><td>Vermont</td><td>84,790</td><td>0.3%</td><td>45</td><td>New Hampshire</td><td>82,201</td><td>0.3%</td></tr>
<tr><td>23</td><td>Virginia</td><td>439,115</td><td>1.5%</td><td>46</td><td>Montana</td><td>52,374</td><td>0.2%</td></tr>
<tr><td>12</td><td>Washington</td><td>837,300</td><td>2.8%</td><td>47</td><td>North Dakota</td><td>27,741</td><td>0.1%</td></tr>
<tr><td>35</td><td>West Virginia</td><td>159,322</td><td>0.5%</td><td>48</td><td>Alaska</td><td>0</td><td>0.0%</td></tr>
<tr><td>27</td><td>Wisconsin</td><td>334,498</td><td>1.1%</td><td>48</td><td>Mississippi</td><td>0</td><td>0.0%</td></tr>
<tr><td>48</td><td>Wyoming</td><td>0</td><td>0.0%</td><td>48</td><td>Wyoming</td><td>0</td><td>0.0%</td></tr>
<tr><td></td><td></td><td></td><td></td><td></td><td>District of Columbia</td><td>95,218</td><td>0.3%</td></tr>
</table>

Source: U.S. Department of Health and Human Services, Centers for Medicare and Medicaid Services
  "Medicaid Managed Care State Enrollment" (http://www.cms.hhs.gov/MedicaidDataSourcesGenInfo/)
*Unduplicated enrollment as of December 31, 2006. Enrollment in state health care reform programs that expand eligibility beyond traditional Medicaid standards. National total includes 882,980 Medicaid managed care enrollees in Puerto Rico.

Percent of Medicaid Enrollees in Managed Care in 2006

National Percent = 65.4% of Medicaid Enrollees*

ALPHA ORDER

RANK	STATE	PERCENT
30	Alabama	65.6
48	Alaska	0.0
8	Arizona	89.6
15	Arkansas	82.9
44	California	50.6
4	Colorado	92.5
20	Connecticut	76.5
22	Delaware	72.7
32	Florida	65.3
16	Georgia	82.6
19	Hawaii	79.8
17	Idaho	81.5
47	Illinois	5.9
24	Indiana	71.8
11	Iowa	86.5
41	Kansas	55.1
5	Kentucky	92.2
26	Louisiana	68.1
27	Maine	67.2
22	Maryland	72.7
39	Massachusetts	60.4
7	Michigan	90.5
38	Minnesota	62.2
48	Mississippi	0.0
2	Missouri	99.2
29	Montana	65.8
18	Nebraska	81.2
13	Nevada	84.3
21	New Hampshire	74.7
25	New Jersey	69.9
33	New Mexico	65.0
36	New York	63.2
31	North Carolina	65.5
43	North Dakota	53.9
40	Ohio	55.4
9	Oklahoma	88.8
6	Oregon	91.6
10	Pennsylvania	87.3
35	Rhode Island	64.7
46	South Carolina	23.6
3	South Dakota	98.6
1	Tennessee	100.0
27	Texas	67.2
11	Utah	86.5
34	Vermont	64.9
37	Virginia	62.6
14	Washington	83.8
42	West Virginia	54.4
45	Wisconsin	39.6
48	Wyoming	0.0

RANK ORDER

RANK	STATE	PERCENT
1	Tennessee	100.0
2	Missouri	99.2
3	South Dakota	98.6
4	Colorado	92.5
5	Kentucky	92.2
6	Oregon	91.6
7	Michigan	90.5
8	Arizona	89.6
9	Oklahoma	88.8
10	Pennsylvania	87.3
11	Iowa	86.5
11	Utah	86.5
13	Nevada	84.3
14	Washington	83.8
15	Arkansas	82.9
16	Georgia	82.6
17	Idaho	81.5
18	Nebraska	81.2
19	Hawaii	79.8
20	Connecticut	76.5
21	New Hampshire	74.7
22	Delaware	72.7
22	Maryland	72.7
24	Indiana	71.8
25	New Jersey	69.9
26	Louisiana	68.1
27	Maine	67.2
27	Texas	67.2
29	Montana	65.8
30	Alabama	65.6
31	North Carolina	65.5
32	Florida	65.3
33	New Mexico	65.0
34	Vermont	64.9
35	Rhode Island	64.7
36	New York	63.2
37	Virginia	62.6
38	Minnesota	62.2
39	Massachusetts	60.4
40	Ohio	55.4
41	Kansas	55.1
42	West Virginia	54.4
43	North Dakota	53.9
44	California	50.6
45	Wisconsin	39.6
46	South Carolina	23.6
47	Illinois	5.9
48	Alaska	0.0
48	Mississippi	0.0
48	Wyoming	0.0

District of Columbia	65.2

Source: U.S. Department of Health and Human Services, Centers for Medicare and Medicaid Services
    "Medicaid Managed Care State Enrollment" (http://www.cms.hhs.gov/MedicaidDataSourcesGenInfo/)
*Unduplicated enrollment as of December 31, 2006.   Enrollment in state health care reform programs that expand eligibility
beyond traditional Medicaid standards. National percent includes Medicaid enrollees in Puerto Rico and the Virgin Islands.

Estimated Medicaid Expenditures in 2007

National Total = $308,801,000,000*

ALPHA ORDER

RANK	STATE	EXPENDITURES	% of USA
24	Alabama	$4,497,000,000	1.5%
40	Alaska	1,218,000,000	0.4%
15	Arizona	6,508,000,000	2.1%
28	Arkansas	3,470,000,000	1.1%
1	California	35,488,000,000	11.5%
32	Colorado	2,651,000,000	0.9%
26	Connecticut	3,915,000,000	1.3%
45	Delaware	994,000,000	0.3%
5	Florida	14,574,000,000	4.7%
13	Georgia	7,219,000,000	2.3%
44	Hawaii	1,057,000,000	0.3%
42	Idaho	1,121,000,000	0.4%
7	Illinois	13,686,000,000	4.4%
22	Indiana	4,803,000,000	1.6%
33	Iowa	2,612,000,000	0.8%
35	Kansas	2,295,000,000	0.7%
25	Kentucky	4,381,000,000	1.4%
18	Louisiana	5,373,000,000	1.7%
34	Maine	2,334,000,000	0.8%
19	Maryland	5,348,000,000	1.7%
11	Massachusetts	7,583,000,000	2.5%
9	Michigan	9,233,000,000	3.0%
17	Minnesota	5,962,000,000	1.9%
27	Mississippi	3,747,000,000	1.2%
14	Missouri	6,576,000,000	2.1%
47	Montana	730,000,000	0.2%
37	Nebraska	1,646,000,000	0.5%
43	Nevada	1,079,000,000	0.3%
41	New Hampshire	1,150,000,000	0.4%
10	New Jersey	8,388,000,000	2.7%
31	New Mexico	2,767,000,000	0.9%
2	New York	32,388,000,000	10.5%
8	North Carolina	9,614,000,000	3.1%
49	North Dakota	513,000,000	0.2%
6	Ohio	14,137,000,000	4.6%
29	Oklahoma	3,321,000,000	1.1%
30	Oregon	3,144,000,000	1.0%
4	Pennsylvania	17,671,000,000	5.7%
38	Rhode Island	1,641,000,000	0.5%
21	South Carolina	4,908,000,000	1.6%
48	South Dakota	694,000,000	0.2%
12	Tennessee	7,475,000,000	2.4%
3	Texas	19,841,000,000	6.4%
39	Utah	1,560,000,000	0.5%
46	Vermont	809,000,000	0.3%
20	Virginia	5,042,000,000	1.6%
16	Washington	6,183,000,000	2.0%
36	West Virginia	2,214,000,000	0.7%
23	Wisconsin	4,787,000,000	1.6%
50	Wyoming	454,000,000	0.1%

RANK ORDER

RANK	STATE	EXPENDITURES	% of USA
1	California	$35,488,000,000	11.5%
2	New York	32,388,000,000	10.5%
3	Texas	19,841,000,000	6.4%
4	Pennsylvania	17,671,000,000	5.7%
5	Florida	14,574,000,000	4.7%
6	Ohio	14,137,000,000	4.6%
7	Illinois	13,686,000,000	4.4%
8	North Carolina	9,614,000,000	3.1%
9	Michigan	9,233,000,000	3.0%
10	New Jersey	8,388,000,000	2.7%
11	Massachusetts	7,583,000,000	2.5%
12	Tennessee	7,475,000,000	2.4%
13	Georgia	7,219,000,000	2.3%
14	Missouri	6,576,000,000	2.1%
15	Arizona	6,508,000,000	2.1%
16	Washington	6,183,000,000	2.0%
17	Minnesota	5,962,000,000	1.9%
18	Louisiana	5,373,000,000	1.7%
19	Maryland	5,348,000,000	1.7%
20	Virginia	5,042,000,000	1.6%
21	South Carolina	4,908,000,000	1.6%
22	Indiana	4,803,000,000	1.6%
23	Wisconsin	4,787,000,000	1.6%
24	Alabama	4,497,000,000	1.5%
25	Kentucky	4,381,000,000	1.4%
26	Connecticut	3,915,000,000	1.3%
27	Mississippi	3,747,000,000	1.2%
28	Arkansas	3,470,000,000	1.1%
29	Oklahoma	3,321,000,000	1.1%
30	Oregon	3,144,000,000	1.0%
31	New Mexico	2,767,000,000	0.9%
32	Colorado	2,651,000,000	0.9%
33	Iowa	2,612,000,000	0.8%
34	Maine	2,334,000,000	0.8%
35	Kansas	2,295,000,000	0.7%
36	West Virginia	2,214,000,000	0.7%
37	Nebraska	1,646,000,000	0.5%
38	Rhode Island	1,641,000,000	0.5%
39	Utah	1,560,000,000	0.5%
40	Alaska	1,218,000,000	0.4%
41	New Hampshire	1,150,000,000	0.4%
42	Idaho	1,121,000,000	0.4%
43	Nevada	1,079,000,000	0.3%
44	Hawaii	1,057,000,000	0.3%
45	Delaware	994,000,000	0.3%
46	Vermont	809,000,000	0.3%
47	Montana	730,000,000	0.2%
48	South Dakota	694,000,000	0.2%
49	North Dakota	513,000,000	0.2%
50	Wyoming	454,000,000	0.1%

District of Columbia **   NA   NA

Source: National Association of State Budget Officers
   "2006 State Expenditure Report" (http://www.nasbo.org)
*Estimates for fiscal year 2007.
**Not available.

Estimated Per Capita Medicaid Expenditures in 2007

National Per Capita = $1,054*

ALPHA ORDER			RANK ORDER		
RANK	STATE	PER CAPITA	RANK	STATE	PER CAPITA
24	Alabama	$972	1	Alaska	$1,782
1	Alaska	1,782	2	Maine	1,772
23	Arizona	1,027	3	New York	1,678
11	Arkansas	1,224	4	Rhode Island	1,551
25	California	971	5	Pennsylvania	1,421
49	Colorado	545	6	New Mexico	1,405
18	Connecticut	1,118	7	Vermont	1,302
15	Delaware	1,149	8	Mississippi	1,284
42	Florida	799	9	Louisiana	1,252
45	Georgia	756	10	Ohio	1,233
40	Hawaii	824	11	Arkansas	1,224
46	Idaho	748	12	West Virginia	1,222
20	Illinois	1,065	13	Tennessee	1,214
44	Indiana	757	14	Massachusetts	1,176
32	Iowa	874	15	Delaware	1,149
39	Kansas	827	16	Minnesota	1,147
22	Kentucky	1,033	17	Missouri	1,119
9	Louisiana	1,252	18	Connecticut	1,118
2	Maine	1,772	19	South Carolina	1,114
28	Maryland	952	20	Illinois	1,065
14	Massachusetts	1,176	21	North Carolina	1,061
31	Michigan	917	22	Kentucky	1,033
16	Minnesota	1,147	23	Arizona	1,027
8	Mississippi	1,284	24	Alabama	972
17	Missouri	1,119	25	California	971
43	Montana	762	26	New Jersey	966
29	Nebraska	928	27	Washington	956
50	Nevada	421	28	Maryland	952
32	New Hampshire	874	29	Nebraska	928
26	New Jersey	966	30	Oklahoma	918
6	New Mexico	1,405	31	Michigan	917
3	New York	1,678	32	Iowa	874
21	North Carolina	1,061	32	New Hampshire	874
41	North Dakota	802	34	South Dakota	872
10	Ohio	1,233	35	Wyoming	868
30	Oklahoma	918	36	Wisconsin	855
37	Oregon	839	37	Oregon	839
5	Pennsylvania	1,421	38	Texas	830
4	Rhode Island	1,551	39	Kansas	827
19	South Carolina	1,114	40	Hawaii	824
34	South Dakota	872	41	North Dakota	802
13	Tennessee	1,214	42	Florida	799
38	Texas	830	43	Montana	762
48	Utah	590	44	Indiana	757
7	Vermont	1,302	45	Georgia	756
47	Virginia	654	46	Idaho	748
27	Washington	956	47	Virginia	654
12	West Virginia	1,222	48	Utah	590
36	Wisconsin	855	49	Colorado	545
35	Wyoming	868	50	Nevada	421
			District of Columbia **		NA

Source: CQ Press using data from National Association of State Budget Officers
    "2006 State Expenditure Report" (http://www.nasbo.org)
*Estimates for fiscal year 2007.
**Not available.

Estimated Medicaid Expenditures as a Percent of Total Expenditures in 2007

National Percent = 21.1%*

ALPHA ORDER				RANK ORDER		
RANK	STATE	PERCENT		RANK	STATE	PERCENT
47	Alabama	11.6		1	Maine	31.4
48	Alaska	10.3		2	Pennsylvania	31.1
12	Arizona	23.7		3	Missouri	29.9
26	Arkansas	19.0		4	Tennessee	29.0
28	California	18.4		5	New York	28.7
36	Colorado	16.3		6	Illinois	28.4
36	Connecticut	16.3		7	Texas	26.4
31	Delaware	17.3		8	North Carolina	26.2
21	Florida	19.8		9	Ohio	25.9
20	Georgia	20.8		10	New Hampshire	25.5
49	Hawaii	9.4		11	South Carolina	25.0
23	Idaho	19.1		12	Arizona	23.7
6	Illinois	28.4		13	New Mexico	23.2
18	Indiana	21.4		14	Rhode Island	23.0
35	Iowa	16.7		15	South Dakota	21.9
27	Kansas	18.5		16	Mississippi	21.7
23	Kentucky	19.1		17	Minnesota	21.6
33	Louisiana	17.2		18	Indiana	21.4
1	Maine	31.4		18	Michigan	21.4
30	Maryland	18.0		20	Georgia	20.8
22	Massachusetts	19.3		21	Florida	19.8
18	Michigan	21.4		22	Massachusetts	19.3
17	Minnesota	21.6		23	Idaho	19.1
16	Mississippi	21.7		23	Kentucky	19.1
3	Missouri	29.9		23	Washington	19.1
42	Montana	14.4		26	Arkansas	19.0
34	Nebraska	17.0		27	Kansas	18.5
45	Nevada	13.3		28	California	18.4
10	New Hampshire	25.5		29	New Jersey	18.3
29	New Jersey	18.3		30	Maryland	18.0
13	New Mexico	23.2		31	Delaware	17.3
5	New York	28.7		31	Oklahoma	17.3
8	North Carolina	26.2		33	Louisiana	17.2
43	North Dakota	13.9		34	Nebraska	17.0
9	Ohio	25.9		35	Iowa	16.7
31	Oklahoma	17.3		36	Colorado	16.3
40	Oregon	15.1		36	Connecticut	16.3
2	Pennsylvania	31.1		38	Vermont	15.7
14	Rhode Island	23.0		39	Utah	15.3
11	South Carolina	25.0		40	Oregon	15.1
15	South Dakota	21.9		41	Virginia	14.5
4	Tennessee	29.0		42	Montana	14.4
7	Texas	26.4		43	North Dakota	13.9
39	Utah	15.3		43	Wisconsin	13.9
38	Vermont	15.7		45	Nevada	13.3
41	Virginia	14.5		46	West Virginia	11.9
23	Washington	19.1		47	Alabama	11.6
46	West Virginia	11.9		48	Alaska	10.3
43	Wisconsin	13.9		49	Hawaii	9.4
50	Wyoming	8.0		50	Wyoming	8.0
				District of Columbia **		NA

Source: National Association of State Budget Officers
    "2006 State Expenditure Report" (http://www.nasbo.org)
*Estimates for fiscal year 2007.
**Not available.

Percent Change in Medicaid Expenditures: 2006 to 2007

National Percent Change = 7.3% Increase*

ALPHA ORDER			RANK ORDER		
RANK	STATE	PERCENT	RANK	STATE	PERCENT
27	Alabama	6.3	1	South Carolina	26.6
3	Alaska	14.3	2	Illinois	20.1
23	Arizona	6.7	3	Alaska	14.3
10	Arkansas	10.4	4	California	13.8
4	California	13.8	5	Nebraska	13.4
40	Colorado	1.6	6	Mississippi	13.1
45	Connecticut	(0.2)	7	Louisiana	13.0
19	Delaware	7.7	8	Oklahoma	11.1
29	Florida	5.3	9	Wyoming	11.0
21	Georgia	7.2	10	Arkansas	10.4
15	Hawaii	8.4	11	Michigan	10.0
37	Idaho	2.3	12	Massachusetts	9.6
2	Illinois	20.1	13	New Mexico	8.8
39	Indiana	1.9	13	North Carolina	8.8
46	Iowa	(1.7)	15	Hawaii	8.4
28	Kansas	6.0	15	South Dakota	8.4
47	Kentucky	(2.4)	17	Tennessee	8.1
7	Louisiana	13.0	18	Texas	7.9
35	Maine	2.8	19	Delaware	7.7
24	Maryland	6.5	19	Minnesota	7.7
12	Massachusetts	9.6	21	Georgia	7.2
11	Michigan	10.0	21	New York	7.2
19	Minnesota	7.7	23	Arizona	6.7
6	Mississippi	13.1	24	Maryland	6.5
40	Missouri	1.6	24	Virginia	6.5
42	Montana	0.8	24	Wisconsin	6.5
5	Nebraska	13.4	27	Alabama	6.3
49	Nevada	(7.2)	28	Kansas	6.0
33	New Hampshire	4.4	29	Florida	5.3
48	New Jersey	(6.6)	30	Ohio	5.2
13	New Mexico	8.8	31	Rhode Island	5.1
21	New York	7.2	32	West Virginia	4.7
13	North Carolina	8.8	33	New Hampshire	4.4
42	North Dakota	0.8	34	Utah	3.0
30	Ohio	5.2	35	Maine	2.8
8	Oklahoma	11.1	36	Pennsylvania	2.6
44	Oregon	0.0	37	Idaho	2.3
36	Pennsylvania	2.6	38	Washington	2.0
31	Rhode Island	5.1	39	Indiana	1.9
1	South Carolina	26.6	40	Colorado	1.6
15	South Dakota	8.4	40	Missouri	1.6
17	Tennessee	8.1	42	Montana	0.8
18	Texas	7.9	42	North Dakota	0.8
34	Utah	3.0	44	Oregon	0.0
50	Vermont	(9.1)	45	Connecticut	(0.2)
24	Virginia	6.5	46	Iowa	(1.7)
38	Washington	2.0	47	Kentucky	(2.4)
32	West Virginia	4.7	48	New Jersey	(6.6)
24	Wisconsin	6.5	49	Nevada	(7.2)
9	Wyoming	11.0	50	Vermont	(9.1)
				District of Columbia **	NA

Source: National Association of State Budget Officers
    "2006 State Expenditure Report" (http://www.nasbo.org)
*Estimates for fiscal year 2007.
**Not available.

Medicaid Expenditures in 2006

National Total = $299,022,257,000*

ALPHA ORDER

RANK	STATE	EXPENDITURES	% of USA
26	Alabama	$3,860,047,000	1.3%
46	Alaska	945,092,000	0.3%
14	Arizona	6,189,139,000	2.1%
30	Arkansas	2,854,059,000	1.0%
2	California	33,840,049,000	11.3%
31	Colorado	2,850,465,000	1.0%
24	Connecticut	4,068,380,000	1.4%
45	Delaware	946,030,000	0.3%
5	Florida	12,620,833,000	4.2%
12	Georgia	6,480,304,000	2.2%
41	Hawaii	1,091,271,000	0.4%
43	Idaho	1,026,782,000	0.3%
7	Illinois	9,966,621,000	3.3%
16	Indiana	5,636,547,000	1.9%
32	Iowa	2,538,790,000	0.8%
35	Kansas	2,057,376,000	0.7%
23	Kentucky	4,328,810,000	1.4%
20	Louisiana	4,687,950,000	1.6%
36	Maine	1,896,516,000	0.6%
19	Maryland	4,915,508,000	1.6%
8	Massachusetts	9,561,334,000	3.2%
11	Michigan	8,236,839,000	2.8%
18	Minnesota	5,367,034,000	1.8%
27	Mississippi	3,239,823,000	1.1%
13	Missouri	6,382,377,000	2.1%
47	Montana	719,654,000	0.2%
38	Nebraska	1,499,164,000	0.5%
40	Nevada	1,175,450,000	0.4%
42	New Hampshire	1,086,240,000	0.4%
9	New Jersey	9,108,645,000	3.0%
33	New Mexico	2,444,448,000	0.8%
1	New York	43,553,527,000	14.6%
10	North Carolina	8,720,418,000	2.9%
49	North Dakota	498,703,000	0.2%
6	Ohio	11,768,240,000	3.9%
29	Oklahoma	2,871,056,000	1.0%
28	Oregon	2,899,767,000	1.0%
4	Pennsylvania	15,401,678,000	5.2%
37	Rhode Island	1,673,810,000	0.6%
25	South Carolina	3,934,440,000	1.3%
48	South Dakota	602,031,000	0.2%
15	Tennessee	6,013,806,000	2.0%
3	Texas	17,684,004,000	5.9%
39	Utah	1,449,762,000	0.5%
44	Vermont	946,931,000	0.3%
21	Virginia	4,608,205,000	1.5%
17	Washington	5,524,077,000	1.8%
34	West Virginia	2,076,405,000	0.7%
22	Wisconsin	4,582,776,000	1.5%
50	Wyoming	417,515,000	0.1%

RANK ORDER

RANK	STATE	EXPENDITURES	% of USA
1	New York	$43,553,527,000	14.6%
2	California	33,840,049,000	11.3%
3	Texas	17,684,004,000	5.9%
4	Pennsylvania	15,401,678,000	5.2%
5	Florida	12,620,833,000	4.2%
6	Ohio	11,768,240,000	3.9%
7	Illinois	9,966,621,000	3.3%
8	Massachusetts	9,561,334,000	3.2%
9	New Jersey	9,108,645,000	3.0%
10	North Carolina	8,720,418,000	2.9%
11	Michigan	8,236,839,000	2.8%
12	Georgia	6,480,304,000	2.2%
13	Missouri	6,382,377,000	2.1%
14	Arizona	6,189,139,000	2.1%
15	Tennessee	6,013,806,000	2.0%
16	Indiana	5,636,547,000	1.9%
17	Washington	5,524,077,000	1.8%
18	Minnesota	5,367,034,000	1.8%
19	Maryland	4,915,508,000	1.6%
20	Louisiana	4,687,950,000	1.6%
21	Virginia	4,608,205,000	1.5%
22	Wisconsin	4,582,776,000	1.5%
23	Kentucky	4,328,810,000	1.4%
24	Connecticut	4,068,380,000	1.4%
25	South Carolina	3,934,440,000	1.3%
26	Alabama	3,860,047,000	1.3%
27	Mississippi	3,239,823,000	1.1%
28	Oregon	2,899,767,000	1.0%
29	Oklahoma	2,871,056,000	1.0%
30	Arkansas	2,854,059,000	1.0%
31	Colorado	2,850,465,000	1.0%
32	Iowa	2,538,790,000	0.8%
33	New Mexico	2,444,448,000	0.8%
34	West Virginia	2,076,405,000	0.7%
35	Kansas	2,057,376,000	0.7%
36	Maine	1,896,516,000	0.6%
37	Rhode Island	1,673,810,000	0.6%
38	Nebraska	1,499,164,000	0.5%
39	Utah	1,449,762,000	0.5%
40	Nevada	1,175,450,000	0.4%
41	Hawaii	1,091,271,000	0.4%
42	New Hampshire	1,086,240,000	0.4%
43	Idaho	1,026,782,000	0.3%
44	Vermont	946,931,000	0.3%
45	Delaware	946,030,000	0.3%
46	Alaska	945,092,000	0.3%
47	Montana	719,654,000	0.2%
48	South Dakota	602,031,000	0.2%
49	North Dakota	498,703,000	0.2%
50	Wyoming	417,515,000	0.1%
	District of Columbia	1,284,858,000	0.4%

Source: U.S. Department of Health and Human Services, Centers for Medicare and Medicaid Services
   "2007 Data Compendium" (http://www.cms.hhs.gov/DataCompendium/)
*For fiscal year 2006. National total includes $888,669,000 in expenditures in U.S. territories. Net expenditures reported from
Form CMS-64. Excludes ADM, Medicaid SCHIP expansions and CMS adjustments.

Per Capita Medicaid Expenditures in 2006

National Per Capita = $998*

ALPHA ORDER				RANK ORDER		
RANK	STATE	PER CAPITA		RANK	STATE	PER CAPITA
31	Alabama	$841		1	New York	$2,259
6	Alaska	1,395		2	Rhode Island	1,577
20	Arizona	1,004		3	Vermont	1,525
19	Arkansas	1,016		4	Massachusetts	1,486
23	California	934		5	Maine	1,442
48	Colorado	598		6	Alaska	1,395
9	Connecticut	1,164		7	New Mexico	1,259
12	Delaware	1,109		8	Pennsylvania	1,242
45	Florida	699		9	Connecticut	1,164
46	Georgia	694		10	West Virginia	1,148
29	Hawaii	853		11	Mississippi	1,118
44	Idaho	701		12	Delaware	1,109
39	Illinois	780		13	Louisiana	1,105
25	Indiana	894		14	Missouri	1,093
28	Iowa	854		15	New Jersey	1,051
43	Kansas	747		16	Minnesota	1,041
17	Kentucky	1,030		17	Kentucky	1,030
13	Louisiana	1,105		18	Ohio	1,027
5	Maine	1,442		19	Arkansas	1,016
26	Maryland	877		20	Arizona	1,004
4	Massachusetts	1,486		21	Tennessee	990
34	Michigan	815		22	North Carolina	983
16	Minnesota	1,041		23	California	934
11	Mississippi	1,118		24	South Carolina	909
14	Missouri	1,093		25	Indiana	894
41	Montana	760		26	Maryland	877
30	Nebraska	850		27	Washington	867
50	Nevada	472		28	Iowa	854
32	New Hampshire	828		29	Hawaii	853
15	New Jersey	1,051		30	Nebraska	850
7	New Mexico	1,259		31	Alabama	841
1	New York	2,259		32	New Hampshire	828
22	North Carolina	983		33	Wisconsin	822
38	North Dakota	782		34	Michigan	815
18	Ohio	1,027		35	Wyoming	814
36	Oklahoma	803		36	Oklahoma	803
37	Oregon	786		37	Oregon	786
8	Pennsylvania	1,242		38	North Dakota	782
2	Rhode Island	1,577		39	Illinois	780
24	South Carolina	909		40	South Dakota	764
40	South Dakota	764		41	Montana	760
21	Tennessee	990		42	Texas	755
42	Texas	755		43	Kansas	747
49	Utah	562		44	Idaho	701
3	Vermont	1,525		45	Florida	699
47	Virginia	603		46	Georgia	694
27	Washington	867		47	Virginia	603
10	West Virginia	1,148		48	Colorado	598
33	Wisconsin	822		49	Utah	562
35	Wyoming	814		50	Nevada	472

District of Columbia   2,195

Source: CQ Press using data from U.S. Department of Health and Human Services, Centers for Medicare and Medicaid Services
    "2007 Data Compendium" (http://www.cms.hhs.gov/DataCompendium/)

*Figures for fiscal year 2006. National figure does not include expenditures or population in U.S. territories. Net expenditures reported from Form CMS-64. Excludes ADM, Medicaid SCHIP expansions and CMS adjustments.

Medicaid Expenditures per Beneficiary in 2006

National Rate = $6,744 per Beneficiary*

ALPHA ORDER

RANK	STATE	PER BENEFICIARY
44	Alabama	$5,224
8	Alaska	9,116
30	Arizona	6,374
50	Arkansas	4,525
43	California	5,258
17	Colorado	7,299
3	Connecticut	10,052
29	Delaware	6,444
38	Florida	5,720
46	Georgia	5,097
41	Hawaii	5,459
32	Idaho	6,216
47	Illinois	5,001
24	Indiana	6,833
13	Iowa	7,837
12	Kansas	7,869
33	Kentucky	6,107
48	Louisiana	4,973
15	Maine	7,554
21	Maryland	7,099
10	Massachusetts	8,763
39	Michigan	5,581
6	Minnesota	9,261
36	Mississippi	5,828
14	Missouri	7,733
9	Montana	9,041
20	Nebraska	7,179
23	Nevada	7,061
4	New Hampshire	9,864
2	New Jersey	10,547
37	New Mexico	5,737
1	New York	10,821
26	North Carolina	6,773
5	North Dakota	9,694
25	Ohio	6,804
49	Oklahoma	4,939
19	Oregon	7,207
11	Pennsylvania	8,545
7	Rhode Island	9,141
35	South Carolina	5,894
34	South Dakota	6,042
45	Tennessee	5,099
31	Texas	6,364
16	Utah	7,313
18	Vermont	7,250
28	Virginia	6,572
40	Washington	5,529
22	West Virginia	7,085
42	Wisconsin	5,424
27	Wyoming	6,685

RANK ORDER

RANK	STATE	PER BENEFICIARY
1	New York	$10,821
2	New Jersey	10,547
3	Connecticut	10,052
4	New Hampshire	9,864
5	North Dakota	9,694
6	Minnesota	9,261
7	Rhode Island	9,141
8	Alaska	9,116
9	Montana	9,041
10	Massachusetts	8,763
11	Pennsylvania	8,545
12	Kansas	7,869
13	Iowa	7,837
14	Missouri	7,733
15	Maine	7,554
16	Utah	7,313
17	Colorado	7,299
18	Vermont	7,250
19	Oregon	7,207
20	Nebraska	7,179
21	Maryland	7,099
22	West Virginia	7,085
23	Nevada	7,061
24	Indiana	6,833
25	Ohio	6,804
26	North Carolina	6,773
27	Wyoming	6,685
28	Virginia	6,572
29	Delaware	6,444
30	Arizona	6,374
31	Texas	6,364
32	Idaho	6,216
33	Kentucky	6,107
34	South Dakota	6,042
35	South Carolina	5,894
36	Mississippi	5,828
37	New Mexico	5,737
38	Florida	5,720
39	Michigan	5,581
40	Washington	5,529
41	Hawaii	5,459
42	Wisconsin	5,424
43	California	5,258
44	Alabama	5,224
45	Tennessee	5,099
46	Georgia	5,097
47	Illinois	5,001
48	Louisiana	4,973
49	Oklahoma	4,939
50	Arkansas	4,525

District of Columbia 8,800

Source: CQ Press using data from U.S. Department of Health and Human Services, Centers for Medicare and Medicaid Services
"2007 Data Compendium" (http://www.cms.hhs.gov/DataCompendium/)

*Figures for fiscal year 2006. National figure does not include expenditures or enrollees in U.S. territories. Net expenditures reported from Form CMS-64. Excludes ADM, Medicaid SCHIP expansions and CMS adjustments.

Federal Medicaid Matching Fund Rate for 2008

National Average = 71.91% of States' Funds Matched by Federal Government*

ALPHA ORDER

RANK	STATE	RATE
11	Alabama	77.33
36	Alaska	66.74
13	Arizona	76.34
3	Arkansas	81.06
38	California	65.00
38	Colorado	65.00
38	Connecticut	65.00
38	Delaware	65.00
31	Florida	69.78
18	Georgia	74.17
32	Hawaii	69.55
7	Idaho	78.91
38	Illinois	65.00
19	Indiana	73.88
21	Iowa	73.21
26	Kansas	71.60
8	Kentucky	78.85
4	Louisiana	80.73
17	Maine	74.32
38	Maryland	65.00
38	Massachusetts	65.00
28	Michigan	70.67
38	Minnesota	65.00
1	Mississippi	83.40
20	Missouri	73.69
10	Montana	77.97
29	Nebraska	70.61
34	Nevada	66.85
38	New Hampshire	65.00
38	New Jersey	65.00
6	New Mexico	79.73
38	New York	65.00
14	North Carolina	74.84
15	North Dakota	74.63
23	Ohio	72.55
12	Oklahoma	76.97
22	Oregon	72.60
33	Pennsylvania	67.86
35	Rhode Island	66.76
8	South Carolina	78.85
25	South Dakota	72.02
16	Tennessee	74.60
24	Texas	72.37
5	Utah	80.14
27	Vermont	71.32
38	Virginia	65.00
37	Washington	66.06
2	West Virginia	81.98
30	Wisconsin	70.33
38	Wyoming	65.00

RANK ORDER

RANK	STATE	RATE
1	Mississippi	83.40
2	West Virginia	81.98
3	Arkansas	81.06
4	Louisiana	80.73
5	Utah	80.14
6	New Mexico	79.73
7	Idaho	78.91
8	Kentucky	78.85
8	South Carolina	78.85
10	Montana	77.97
11	Alabama	77.33
12	Oklahoma	76.97
13	Arizona	76.34
14	North Carolina	74.84
15	North Dakota	74.63
16	Tennessee	74.60
17	Maine	74.32
18	Georgia	74.17
19	Indiana	73.88
20	Missouri	73.69
21	Iowa	73.21
22	Oregon	72.60
23	Ohio	72.55
24	Texas	72.37
25	South Dakota	72.02
26	Kansas	71.60
27	Vermont	71.32
28	Michigan	70.67
29	Nebraska	70.61
30	Wisconsin	70.33
31	Florida	69.78
32	Hawaii	69.55
33	Pennsylvania	67.86
34	Nevada	66.85
35	Rhode Island	66.76
36	Alaska	66.74
37	Washington	66.06
38	California	65.00
38	Colorado	65.00
38	Connecticut	65.00
38	Delaware	65.00
38	Illinois	65.00
38	Maryland	65.00
38	Massachusetts	65.00
38	Minnesota	65.00
38	New Hampshire	65.00
38	New Jersey	65.00
38	New York	65.00
38	Virginia	65.00
38	Wyoming	65.00
	District of Columbia	79.00

Source: U.S. Department of Health and Human Services, Centers for Medicare and Medicaid Services
"Enhanced Federal Medical Assistance Percentages" (http://aspe.hhs.gov/health/fmap08.htm)
*For fiscal year 2008. These are "enhanced" matching rates established by the Children's Health Insurance Program, signed into law in August 1997. Sixty-five percent is the minimum. National average is a simple average of the 51 individual rates and is not weighted for population or funds.

State and Local Government Expenditures for Hospitals in 2005

National Total = $103,313,970,000*

ALPHA ORDER

RANK	STATE	EXPENDITURES	% of USA
6	Alabama	$3,916,349,000	3.8%
42	Alaska	120,536,000	0.1%
29	Arizona	812,926,000	0.8%
30	Arkansas	783,128,000	0.8%
1	California	14,839,648,000	14.4%
23	Colorado	1,392,618,000	1.3%
25	Connecticut	1,126,934,000	1.1%
47	Delaware	57,976,000	0.1%
4	Florida	5,267,634,000	5.1%
7	Georgia	3,490,253,000	3.4%
40	Hawaii	377,934,000	0.4%
37	Idaho	590,163,000	0.6%
16	Illinois	2,291,810,000	2.2%
12	Indiana	2,845,177,000	2.8%
20	Iowa	1,835,827,000	1.8%
34	Kansas	650,970,000	0.6%
26	Kentucky	1,087,810,000	1.1%
10	Louisiana	3,154,519,000	3.1%
43	Maine	113,666,000	0.1%
39	Maryland	482,979,000	0.5%
24	Massachusetts	1,242,969,000	1.2%
13	Michigan	2,836,604,000	2.7%
22	Minnesota	1,407,137,000	1.4%
18	Mississippi	2,126,661,000	2.1%
17	Missouri	2,196,997,000	2.1%
45	Montana	89,258,000	0.1%
38	Nebraska	565,548,000	0.5%
32	Nevada	723,383,000	0.7%
48	New Hampshire	52,642,000	0.1%
21	New Jersey	1,699,297,000	1.6%
35	New Mexico	639,409,000	0.6%
2	New York	10,262,176,000	9.9%
5	North Carolina	4,030,437,000	3.9%
50	North Dakota	21,919,000	0.0%
9	Ohio	3,250,571,000	3.1%
31	Oklahoma	776,198,000	0.8%
28	Oregon	1,019,755,000	1.0%
19	Pennsylvania	2,012,795,000	1.9%
44	Rhode Island	108,080,000	0.1%
8	South Carolina	3,428,921,000	3.3%
46	South Dakota	88,286,000	0.1%
14	Tennessee	2,611,341,000	2.5%
3	Texas	8,623,088,000	8.3%
33	Utah	698,959,000	0.7%
49	Vermont	35,968,000	0.0%
15	Virginia	2,445,595,000	2.4%
11	Washington	2,908,607,000	2.8%
41	West Virginia	284,873,000	0.3%
27	Wisconsin	1,030,148,000	1.0%
36	Wyoming	595,856,000	0.6%

RANK ORDER

RANK	STATE	EXPENDITURES	% of USA
1	California	$14,839,648,000	14.4%
2	New York	10,262,176,000	9.9%
3	Texas	8,623,088,000	8.3%
4	Florida	5,267,634,000	5.1%
5	North Carolina	4,030,437,000	3.9%
6	Alabama	3,916,349,000	3.8%
7	Georgia	3,490,253,000	3.4%
8	South Carolina	3,428,921,000	3.3%
9	Ohio	3,250,571,000	3.1%
10	Louisiana	3,154,519,000	3.1%
11	Washington	2,908,607,000	2.8%
12	Indiana	2,845,177,000	2.8%
13	Michigan	2,836,604,000	2.7%
14	Tennessee	2,611,341,000	2.5%
15	Virginia	2,445,595,000	2.4%
16	Illinois	2,291,810,000	2.2%
17	Missouri	2,196,997,000	2.1%
18	Mississippi	2,126,661,000	2.1%
19	Pennsylvania	2,012,795,000	1.9%
20	Iowa	1,835,827,000	1.8%
21	New Jersey	1,699,297,000	1.6%
22	Minnesota	1,407,137,000	1.4%
23	Colorado	1,392,618,000	1.3%
24	Massachusetts	1,242,969,000	1.2%
25	Connecticut	1,126,934,000	1.1%
26	Kentucky	1,087,810,000	1.1%
27	Wisconsin	1,030,148,000	1.0%
28	Oregon	1,019,755,000	1.0%
29	Arizona	812,926,000	0.8%
30	Arkansas	783,128,000	0.8%
31	Oklahoma	776,198,000	0.8%
32	Nevada	723,383,000	0.7%
33	Utah	698,959,000	0.7%
34	Kansas	650,970,000	0.6%
35	New Mexico	639,409,000	0.6%
36	Wyoming	595,856,000	0.6%
37	Idaho	590,163,000	0.6%
38	Nebraska	565,548,000	0.5%
39	Maryland	482,979,000	0.5%
40	Hawaii	377,934,000	0.4%
41	West Virginia	284,873,000	0.3%
42	Alaska	120,536,000	0.1%
43	Maine	113,666,000	0.1%
44	Rhode Island	108,080,000	0.1%
45	Montana	89,258,000	0.1%
46	South Dakota	88,286,000	0.1%
47	Delaware	57,976,000	0.1%
48	New Hampshire	52,642,000	0.1%
49	Vermont	35,968,000	0.0%
50	North Dakota	21,919,000	0.0%
	District of Columbia	261,635,000	0.3%

Source: U.S. Bureau of the Census, Governments Division
   "State and Local Government Finances 2004-2005" (http://www.census.gov/govs/www/estimate05.html)
*Financing, construction, acquisition, maintenance or operation of hospital facilities, provision of hospital care, and support of public or private hospitals.

Per Capita State and Local Government Expenditures for Hospitals in 2005

National Per Capita = $349*

ALPHA ORDER

RANK	STATE	PER CAPITA
2	Alabama	$863
37	Alaska	180
41	Arizona	137
26	Arkansas	282
13	California	412
22	Colorado	298
19	Connecticut	323
47	Delaware	69
24	Florida	297
14	Georgia	383
22	Hawaii	298
12	Idaho	414
37	Illinois	180
10	Indiana	455
6	Iowa	621
32	Kansas	237
31	Kentucky	261
5	Louisiana	702
45	Maine	87
45	Maryland	87
35	Massachusetts	193
27	Michigan	281
30	Minnesota	275
4	Mississippi	733
15	Missouri	380
44	Montana	95
20	Nebraska	322
21	Nevada	300
49	New Hampshire	40
34	New Jersey	196
17	New Mexico	334
7	New York	533
8	North Carolina	464
50	North Dakota	34
25	Ohio	284
33	Oklahoma	220
27	Oregon	281
39	Pennsylvania	163
43	Rhode Island	101
3	South Carolina	806
42	South Dakota	113
11	Tennessee	436
16	Texas	377
29	Utah	279
48	Vermont	58
18	Virginia	324
8	Washington	464
40	West Virginia	158
36	Wisconsin	186
1	Wyoming	1,176

RANK ORDER

RANK	STATE	PER CAPITA
1	Wyoming	$1,176
2	Alabama	863
3	South Carolina	806
4	Mississippi	733
5	Louisiana	702
6	Iowa	621
7	New York	533
8	North Carolina	464
8	Washington	464
10	Indiana	455
11	Tennessee	436
12	Idaho	414
13	California	412
14	Georgia	383
15	Missouri	380
16	Texas	377
17	New Mexico	334
18	Virginia	324
19	Connecticut	323
20	Nebraska	322
21	Nevada	300
22	Colorado	298
22	Hawaii	298
24	Florida	297
25	Ohio	284
26	Arkansas	282
27	Michigan	281
27	Oregon	281
29	Utah	279
30	Minnesota	275
31	Kentucky	261
32	Kansas	237
33	Oklahoma	220
34	New Jersey	196
35	Massachusetts	193
36	Wisconsin	186
37	Alaska	180
37	Illinois	180
39	Pennsylvania	163
40	West Virginia	158
41	Arizona	137
42	South Dakota	113
43	Rhode Island	101
44	Montana	95
45	Maine	87
45	Maryland	87
47	Delaware	69
48	Vermont	58
49	New Hampshire	40
50	North Dakota	34
	District of Columbia	450

Source: CQ Press using data from U.S. Bureau of the Census, Governments Division
"State and Local Government Finances 2004-2005" (http://www.census.gov/govs/www/estimate05.html)
*Financing, construction, acquisition, maintenance or operation of hospital facilities, provision of hospital care, and support of public or private hospitals.

Percent of State and Local Government Expenditures
Used for Hospitals in 2005
National Percent = 5.1%*

ALPHA ORDER

RANK	STATE	PERCENT
1	Alabama	13.5
43	Alaska	1.4
38	Arizona	2.5
19	Arkansas	5.1
16	California	5.4
20	Colorado	4.8
26	Connecticut	4.3
47	Delaware	0.8
23	Florida	4.7
11	Georgia	6.9
30	Hawaii	4.1
10	Idaho	7.3
34	Illinois	2.8
9	Indiana	7.4
6	Iowa	9.4
32	Kansas	3.9
24	Kentucky	4.6
5	Louisiana	11.1
46	Maine	1.2
44	Maryland	1.3
38	Massachusetts	2.5
28	Michigan	4.2
33	Minnesota	3.7
3	Mississippi	11.9
12	Missouri	6.7
42	Montana	1.6
17	Nebraska	5.2
20	Nevada	4.8
49	New Hampshire	0.7
36	New Jersey	2.6
25	New Mexico	4.5
15	New York	5.6
7	North Carolina	7.7
50	North Dakota	0.5
28	Ohio	4.2
30	Oklahoma	4.1
26	Oregon	4.3
40	Pennsylvania	2.3
44	Rhode Island	1.3
2	South Carolina	12.2
41	South Dakota	2.0
7	Tennessee	7.7
13	Texas	6.6
20	Utah	4.8
47	Vermont	0.8
17	Virginia	5.2
13	Washington	6.6
36	West Virginia	2.6
35	Wisconsin	2.7
4	Wyoming	11.7

RANK ORDER

RANK	STATE	PERCENT
1	Alabama	13.5
2	South Carolina	12.2
3	Mississippi	11.9
4	Wyoming	11.7
5	Louisiana	11.1
6	Iowa	9.4
7	North Carolina	7.7
7	Tennessee	7.7
9	Indiana	7.4
10	Idaho	7.3
11	Georgia	6.9
12	Missouri	6.7
13	Texas	6.6
13	Washington	6.6
15	New York	5.6
16	California	5.4
17	Nebraska	5.2
17	Virginia	5.2
19	Arkansas	5.1
20	Colorado	4.8
20	Nevada	4.8
20	Utah	4.8
23	Florida	4.7
24	Kentucky	4.6
25	New Mexico	4.5
26	Connecticut	4.3
26	Oregon	4.3
28	Michigan	4.2
28	Ohio	4.2
30	Hawaii	4.1
30	Oklahoma	4.1
32	Kansas	3.9
33	Minnesota	3.7
34	Illinois	2.8
35	Wisconsin	2.7
36	New Jersey	2.6
36	West Virginia	2.6
38	Arizona	2.5
38	Massachusetts	2.5
40	Pennsylvania	2.3
41	South Dakota	2.0
42	Montana	1.6
43	Alaska	1.4
44	Maryland	1.3
44	Rhode Island	1.3
46	Maine	1.2
47	Delaware	0.8
47	Vermont	0.8
49	New Hampshire	0.7
50	North Dakota	0.5

| | District of Columbia | 3.6 |

Source: CQ Press using data from U.S. Bureau of the Census, Governments Division
   "State and Local Government Finances 2004-2005" (http://www.census.gov/govs/www/estimate05.html)
*As a percent of direct general expenditures. Financing, construction, acquisition, maintenance or operation of hospital facilities, provision of hospital care, and support of public or private hospitals.

State and Local Government Expenditures for Health Programs in 2005

National Total = $66,929,552,000*

ALPHA ORDER

RANK	STATE	EXPENDITURES	% of USA
17	Alabama	$1,184,433,000	1.8%
46	Alaska	177,765,000	0.3%
13	Arizona	1,437,531,000	2.1%
37	Arkansas	354,187,000	0.5%
1	California	11,098,272,000	16.6%
20	Colorado	991,101,000	1.5%
27	Connecticut	609,280,000	0.9%
41	Delaware	310,998,000	0.5%
4	Florida	3,713,536,000	5.5%
12	Georgia	1,488,828,000	2.2%
31	Hawaii	457,027,000	0.7%
43	Idaho	194,300,000	0.3%
7	Illinois	3,036,854,000	4.5%
25	Indiana	797,617,000	1.2%
33	Iowa	395,033,000	0.6%
35	Kansas	367,958,000	0.5%
28	Kentucky	558,581,000	0.8%
26	Louisiana	694,511,000	1.0%
30	Maine	511,065,000	0.8%
14	Maryland	1,377,287,000	2.1%
24	Massachusetts	808,628,000	1.2%
6	Michigan	3,475,471,000	5.2%
22	Minnesota	879,539,000	1.3%
36	Mississippi	355,384,000	0.5%
19	Missouri	1,016,541,000	1.5%
39	Montana	317,979,000	0.5%
44	Nebraska	192,041,000	0.3%
38	Nevada	347,916,000	0.5%
47	New Hampshire	127,263,000	0.2%
18	New Jersey	1,105,303,000	1.7%
34	New Mexico	369,639,000	0.6%
2	New York	4,838,209,000	7.2%
8	North Carolina	2,969,499,000	4.4%
50	North Dakota	76,608,000	0.1%
3	Ohio	3,781,187,000	5.6%
29	Oklahoma	520,670,000	0.8%
23	Oregon	869,012,000	1.3%
5	Pennsylvania	3,647,236,000	5.4%
45	Rhode Island	191,626,000	0.3%
21	South Carolina	958,215,000	1.4%
49	South Dakota	121,240,000	0.2%
16	Tennessee	1,273,430,000	1.9%
9	Texas	2,355,180,000	3.5%
32	Utah	426,043,000	0.6%
48	Vermont	126,949,000	0.2%
11	Virginia	1,639,214,000	2.4%
10	Washington	2,030,250,000	3.0%
40	West Virginia	311,567,000	0.5%
15	Wisconsin	1,350,229,000	2.0%
42	Wyoming	235,668,000	0.4%

RANK ORDER

RANK	STATE	EXPENDITURES	% of USA
1	California	$11,098,272,000	16.6%
2	New York	4,838,209,000	7.2%
3	Ohio	3,781,187,000	5.6%
4	Florida	3,713,536,000	5.5%
5	Pennsylvania	3,647,236,000	5.4%
6	Michigan	3,475,471,000	5.2%
7	Illinois	3,036,854,000	4.5%
8	North Carolina	2,969,499,000	4.4%
9	Texas	2,355,180,000	3.5%
10	Washington	2,030,250,000	3.0%
11	Virginia	1,639,214,000	2.4%
12	Georgia	1,488,828,000	2.2%
13	Arizona	1,437,531,000	2.1%
14	Maryland	1,377,287,000	2.1%
15	Wisconsin	1,350,229,000	2.0%
16	Tennessee	1,273,430,000	1.9%
17	Alabama	1,184,433,000	1.8%
18	New Jersey	1,105,303,000	1.7%
19	Missouri	1,016,541,000	1.5%
20	Colorado	991,101,000	1.5%
21	South Carolina	958,215,000	1.4%
22	Minnesota	879,539,000	1.3%
23	Oregon	869,012,000	1.3%
24	Massachusetts	808,628,000	1.2%
25	Indiana	797,617,000	1.2%
26	Louisiana	694,511,000	1.0%
27	Connecticut	609,280,000	0.9%
28	Kentucky	558,581,000	0.8%
29	Oklahoma	520,670,000	0.8%
30	Maine	511,065,000	0.8%
31	Hawaii	457,027,000	0.7%
32	Utah	426,043,000	0.6%
33	Iowa	395,033,000	0.6%
34	New Mexico	369,639,000	0.6%
35	Kansas	367,958,000	0.5%
36	Mississippi	355,384,000	0.5%
37	Arkansas	354,187,000	0.5%
38	Nevada	347,916,000	0.5%
39	Montana	317,979,000	0.5%
40	West Virginia	311,567,000	0.5%
41	Delaware	310,998,000	0.5%
42	Wyoming	235,668,000	0.4%
43	Idaho	194,300,000	0.3%
44	Nebraska	192,041,000	0.3%
45	Rhode Island	191,626,000	0.3%
46	Alaska	177,765,000	0.3%
47	New Hampshire	127,263,000	0.2%
48	Vermont	126,949,000	0.2%
49	South Dakota	121,240,000	0.2%
50	North Dakota	76,608,000	0.1%
	District of Columbia	455,652,000	0.7%

Source: U.S. Bureau of the Census, Governments Division
"State and Local Government Finances 2004-2005" (http://www.census.gov/govs/www/estimate05.html)
*Includes outpatient health services other than hospital care, research and education, categorical health programs, treatment and immunization clinics, nursing, and environmental health activities. Includes capital expenditures.

Per Capita State and Local Government Expenditures for Health Programs in 2005
National Per Capita = $226*

ALPHA ORDER

RANK	STATE	PER CAPITA
13	Alabama	$261
12	Alaska	266
17	Arizona	242
42	Arkansas	128
10	California	308
23	Colorado	212
29	Connecticut	175
3	Delaware	370
24	Florida	209
33	Georgia	163
4	Hawaii	361
38	Idaho	136
18	Illinois	239
44	Indiana	127
39	Iowa	134
39	Kansas	134
39	Kentucky	134
35	Louisiana	154
2	Maine	389
15	Maryland	247
45	Massachusetts	126
5	Michigan	344
31	Minnesota	172
46	Mississippi	123
28	Missouri	176
7	Montana	340
48	Nebraska	109
37	Nevada	144
50	New Hampshire	98
42	New Jersey	128
26	New Mexico	193
14	New York	251
6	North Carolina	342
47	North Dakota	120
8	Ohio	330
36	Oklahoma	147
18	Oregon	239
11	Pennsylvania	295
27	Rhode Island	180
20	South Carolina	225
34	South Dakota	155
22	Tennessee	213
49	Texas	103
32	Utah	170
25	Vermont	205
21	Virginia	217
9	Washington	324
30	West Virginia	173
16	Wisconsin	244
1	Wyoming	465

RANK ORDER

RANK	STATE	PER CAPITA
1	Wyoming	$465
2	Maine	389
3	Delaware	370
4	Hawaii	361
5	Michigan	344
6	North Carolina	342
7	Montana	340
8	Ohio	330
9	Washington	324
10	California	308
11	Pennsylvania	295
12	Alaska	266
13	Alabama	261
14	New York	251
15	Maryland	247
16	Wisconsin	244
17	Arizona	242
18	Illinois	239
18	Oregon	239
20	South Carolina	225
21	Virginia	217
22	Tennessee	213
23	Colorado	212
24	Florida	209
25	Vermont	205
26	New Mexico	193
27	Rhode Island	180
28	Missouri	176
29	Connecticut	175
30	West Virginia	173
31	Minnesota	172
32	Utah	170
33	Georgia	163
34	South Dakota	155
35	Louisiana	154
36	Oklahoma	147
37	Nevada	144
38	Idaho	136
39	Iowa	134
39	Kansas	134
39	Kentucky	134
42	Arkansas	128
42	New Jersey	128
44	Indiana	127
45	Massachusetts	126
46	Mississippi	123
47	North Dakota	120
48	Nebraska	109
49	Texas	103
50	New Hampshire	98

| | District of Columbia | 783 |

Source: CQ Press using data from U.S. Bureau of the Census, Governments Division
"State and Local Government Finances 2004-2005" (http://www.census.gov/govs/www/estimate05.html)
*Includes outpatient health services other than hospital care, research and education, categorical health programs, treatment and immunization clinics, nursing, and environmental health activities. Includes capital expenditures.

Percent of State and Local Government Expenditures
Used for Health Programs in 2005
National Percent = 3.3%*

RANK	STATE	PERCENT
12	Alabama	4.1
42	Alaska	2.0
10	Arizona	4.4
36	Arkansas	2.3
13	California	4.0
20	Colorado	3.4
36	Connecticut	2.3
7	Delaware	4.6
22	Florida	3.3
24	Georgia	2.9
5	Hawaii	4.9
32	Idaho	2.4
16	Illinois	3.7
41	Indiana	2.1
42	Iowa	2.0
40	Kansas	2.2
32	Kentucky	2.4
32	Louisiana	2.4
3	Maine	5.4
14	Maryland	3.8
49	Massachusetts	1.6
4	Michigan	5.2
36	Minnesota	2.3
42	Mississippi	2.0
23	Missouri	3.1
2	Montana	5.5
45	Nebraska	1.8
36	Nevada	2.3
49	New Hampshire	1.6
48	New Jersey	1.7
30	New Mexico	2.6
30	New York	2.6
1	North Carolina	5.6
45	North Dakota	1.8
5	Ohio	4.9
27	Oklahoma	2.7
16	Oregon	3.7
11	Pennsylvania	4.2
32	Rhode Island	2.4
20	South Carolina	3.4
27	South Dakota	2.7
14	Tennessee	3.8
45	Texas	1.8
24	Utah	2.9
27	Vermont	2.7
19	Virginia	3.5
7	Washington	4.6
26	West Virginia	2.8
18	Wisconsin	3.6
7	Wyoming	4.6

RANK	STATE	PERCENT
1	North Carolina	5.6
2	Montana	5.5
3	Maine	5.4
4	Michigan	5.2
5	Hawaii	4.9
5	Ohio	4.9
7	Delaware	4.6
7	Washington	4.6
7	Wyoming	4.6
10	Arizona	4.4
11	Pennsylvania	4.2
12	Alabama	4.1
13	California	4.0
14	Maryland	3.8
14	Tennessee	3.8
16	Illinois	3.7
16	Oregon	3.7
18	Wisconsin	3.6
19	Virginia	3.5
20	Colorado	3.4
20	South Carolina	3.4
22	Florida	3.3
23	Missouri	3.1
24	Georgia	2.9
24	Utah	2.9
26	West Virginia	2.8
27	Oklahoma	2.7
27	South Dakota	2.7
27	Vermont	2.7
30	New Mexico	2.6
30	New York	2.6
32	Idaho	2.4
32	Kentucky	2.4
32	Louisiana	2.4
32	Rhode Island	2.4
36	Arkansas	2.3
36	Connecticut	2.3
36	Minnesota	2.3
36	Nevada	2.3
40	Kansas	2.2
41	Indiana	2.1
42	Alaska	2.0
42	Iowa	2.0
42	Mississippi	2.0
45	Nebraska	1.8
45	North Dakota	1.8
45	Texas	1.8
48	New Jersey	1.7
49	Massachusetts	1.6
49	New Hampshire	1.6

	District of Columbia	6.3

Source: CQ Press using data from U.S. Bureau of the Census, Governments Division
"State and Local Government Finances 2004-2005" (http://www.census.gov/govs/www/estimate05.html)
*As a percent of direct general expenditures. Includes outpatient health services other than hospital care, research and education, categorical health programs, treatment and immunization clinics, nursing, and environmental health activities. Includes capital expenditures.

Estimated Tobacco Settlement Revenues in Fiscal Year 2008

National Total = $8,100,000,000*

ALPHA ORDER

RANK	STATE	REVENUE	% of USA
26	Alabama	$105,000,000	1.3%
45	Alaska	34,900,000	0.4%
24	Arizona	115,200,000	1.4%
35	Arkansas	56,800,000	0.7%
2	California	823,000,000	10.2%
27	Colorado	103,200,000	1.3%
21	Connecticut	140,700,000	1.7%
47	Delaware	30,400,000	0.4%
4	Florida	437,800,000	5.4%
16	Georgia	157,800,000	1.9%
36	Hawaii	56,200,000	0.7%
48	Idaho	28,400,000	0.4%
7	Illinois	306,900,000	3.8%
20	Indiana	146,500,000	1.8%
31	Iowa	75,500,000	0.9%
33	Kansas	66,200,000	0.8%
25	Kentucky	113,900,000	1.4%
14	Louisiana	159,500,000	2.0%
34	Maine	58,000,000	0.7%
13	Maryland	165,200,000	2.0%
9	Massachusetts	286,500,000	3.5%
8	Michigan	287,300,000	3.5%
11	Minnesota	180,400,000	2.2%
23	Mississippi	124,900,000	1.5%
18	Missouri	151,800,000	1.9%
46	Montana	34,600,000	0.4%
41	Nebraska	42,600,000	0.5%
39	Nevada	45,800,000	0.6%
38	New Hampshire	48,100,000	0.6%
10	New Jersey	259,800,000	3.2%
40	New Mexico	44,600,000	0.6%
1	New York	825,500,000	10.2%
15	North Carolina	158,600,000	2.0%
44	North Dakota	36,700,000	0.5%
6	Ohio	330,900,000	4.1%
29	Oklahoma	89,000,000	1.1%
28	Oregon	90,000,000	1.1%
5	Pennsylvania	378,200,000	4.7%
37	Rhode Island	53,000,000	0.7%
30	South Carolina	82,900,000	1.0%
49	South Dakota	27,500,000	0.3%
17	Tennessee	155,500,000	1.9%
3	Texas	517,000,000	6.4%
42	Utah	42,200,000	0.5%
43	Vermont	40,100,000	0.5%
22	Virginia	131,200,000	1.6%
12	Washington	172,900,000	2.1%
32	West Virginia	72,900,000	0.9%
19	Wisconsin	148,200,000	1.8%
50	Wyoming	21,400,000	0.3%

RANK ORDER

RANK	STATE	REVENUE	% of USA
1	New York	$825,500,000	10.2%
2	California	823,000,000	10.2%
3	Texas	517,000,000	6.4%
4	Florida	437,800,000	5.4%
5	Pennsylvania	378,200,000	4.7%
6	Ohio	330,900,000	4.1%
7	Illinois	306,900,000	3.8%
8	Michigan	287,300,000	3.5%
9	Massachusetts	286,500,000	3.5%
10	New Jersey	259,800,000	3.2%
11	Minnesota	180,400,000	2.2%
12	Washington	172,900,000	2.1%
13	Maryland	165,200,000	2.0%
14	Louisiana	159,500,000	2.0%
15	North Carolina	158,600,000	2.0%
16	Georgia	157,800,000	1.9%
17	Tennessee	155,500,000	1.9%
18	Missouri	151,800,000	1.9%
19	Wisconsin	148,200,000	1.8%
20	Indiana	146,500,000	1.8%
21	Connecticut	140,700,000	1.7%
22	Virginia	131,200,000	1.6%
23	Mississippi	124,900,000	1.5%
24	Arizona	115,200,000	1.4%
25	Kentucky	113,900,000	1.4%
26	Alabama	105,000,000	1.3%
27	Colorado	103,200,000	1.3%
28	Oregon	90,000,000	1.1%
29	Oklahoma	89,000,000	1.1%
30	South Carolina	82,900,000	1.0%
31	Iowa	75,500,000	0.9%
32	West Virginia	72,900,000	0.9%
33	Kansas	66,200,000	0.8%
34	Maine	58,000,000	0.7%
35	Arkansas	56,800,000	0.7%
36	Hawaii	56,200,000	0.7%
37	Rhode Island	53,000,000	0.7%
38	New Hampshire	48,100,000	0.6%
39	Nevada	45,800,000	0.6%
40	New Mexico	44,600,000	0.6%
41	Nebraska	42,600,000	0.5%
42	Utah	42,200,000	0.5%
43	Vermont	40,100,000	0.5%
44	North Dakota	36,700,000	0.5%
45	Alaska	34,900,000	0.4%
46	Montana	34,600,000	0.4%
47	Delaware	30,400,000	0.4%
48	Idaho	28,400,000	0.4%
49	South Dakota	27,500,000	0.3%
50	Wyoming	21,400,000	0.3%
	District of Columbia	43,300,000	0.5%

Source: Campaign for Tobacco-Free Kids
   "A Broken Promise to Our Children" (http://tobaccofreekids.org/reports/settlements/)
*For fiscal year 2008. Settlement originally reached in November 1998 and called for an estimated 25 years of payments.

Personal Health Care Expenditures in 2004

National Total = $1,551,255,000,000*

ALPHA ORDER

RANK	STATE	EXPENDITURES	% of USA
22	Alabama	$23,199,000,000	1.5%
46	Alaska	4,237,000,000	0.3%
21	Arizona	23,576,000,000	1.5%
33	Arkansas	13,357,000,000	0.9%
1	California	166,236,000,000	10.7%
26	Colorado	21,691,000,000	1.4%
25	Connecticut	22,167,000,000	1.4%
44	Delaware	5,226,000,000	0.3%
4	Florida	95,223,000,000	6.1%
12	Georgia	41,097,000,000	2.6%
42	Hawaii	6,222,000,000	0.4%
43	Idaho	6,197,000,000	0.4%
6	Illinois	67,292,000,000	4.3%
14	Indiana	32,951,000,000	2.1%
30	Iowa	15,892,000,000	1.0%
31	Kansas	14,736,000,000	0.9%
23	Kentucky	22,662,000,000	1.5%
24	Louisiana	22,658,000,000	1.5%
38	Maine	8,593,000,000	0.6%
19	Maryland	31,044,000,000	2.0%
11	Massachusetts	43,009,000,000	2.8%
8	Michigan	51,048,000,000	3.3%
20	Minnesota	29,524,000,000	1.9%
32	Mississippi	14,634,000,000	0.9%
17	Missouri	31,317,000,000	2.0%
45	Montana	4,706,000,000	0.3%
36	Nebraska	9,782,000,000	0.6%
35	Nevada	10,656,000,000	0.7%
40	New Hampshire	7,050,000,000	0.5%
9	New Jersey	50,384,000,000	3.2%
39	New Mexico	8,498,000,000	0.5%
2	New York	126,076,000,000	8.1%
10	North Carolina	44,281,000,000	2.9%
49	North Dakota	3,693,000,000	0.2%
7	Ohio	65,622,000,000	4.2%
29	Oklahoma	17,323,000,000	1.1%
28	Oregon	17,516,000,000	1.1%
5	Pennsylvania	73,441,000,000	4.7%
41	Rhode Island	6,682,000,000	0.4%
27	South Carolina	21,450,000,000	1.4%
47	South Dakota	4,103,000,000	0.3%
15	Tennessee	32,161,000,000	2.1%
3	Texas	103,600,000,000	6.7%
37	Utah	9,618,000,000	0.6%
48	Vermont	3,768,000,000	0.2%
13	Virginia	36,032,000,000	2.3%
16	Washington	31,600,000,000	2.0%
34	West Virginia	10,783,000,000	0.7%
18	Wisconsin	31,177,000,000	2.0%
50	Wyoming	2,662,000,000	0.2%

RANK ORDER

RANK	STATE	EXPENDITURES	% of USA
1	California	$166,236,000,000	10.7%
2	New York	126,076,000,000	8.1%
3	Texas	103,600,000,000	6.7%
4	Florida	95,223,000,000	6.1%
5	Pennsylvania	73,441,000,000	4.7%
6	Illinois	67,292,000,000	4.3%
7	Ohio	65,622,000,000	4.2%
8	Michigan	51,048,000,000	3.3%
9	New Jersey	50,384,000,000	3.2%
10	North Carolina	44,281,000,000	2.9%
11	Massachusetts	43,009,000,000	2.8%
12	Georgia	41,097,000,000	2.6%
13	Virginia	36,032,000,000	2.3%
14	Indiana	32,951,000,000	2.1%
15	Tennessee	32,161,000,000	2.1%
16	Washington	31,600,000,000	2.0%
17	Missouri	31,317,000,000	2.0%
18	Wisconsin	31,177,000,000	2.0%
19	Maryland	31,044,000,000	2.0%
20	Minnesota	29,524,000,000	1.9%
21	Arizona	23,576,000,000	1.5%
22	Alabama	23,199,000,000	1.5%
23	Kentucky	22,662,000,000	1.5%
24	Louisiana	22,658,000,000	1.5%
25	Connecticut	22,167,000,000	1.4%
26	Colorado	21,691,000,000	1.4%
27	South Carolina	21,450,000,000	1.4%
28	Oregon	17,516,000,000	1.1%
29	Oklahoma	17,323,000,000	1.1%
30	Iowa	15,892,000,000	1.0%
31	Kansas	14,736,000,000	0.9%
32	Mississippi	14,634,000,000	0.9%
33	Arkansas	13,357,000,000	0.9%
34	West Virginia	10,783,000,000	0.7%
35	Nevada	10,656,000,000	0.7%
36	Nebraska	9,782,000,000	0.6%
37	Utah	9,618,000,000	0.6%
38	Maine	8,593,000,000	0.6%
39	New Mexico	8,498,000,000	0.5%
40	New Hampshire	7,050,000,000	0.5%
41	Rhode Island	6,682,000,000	0.4%
42	Hawaii	6,222,000,000	0.4%
43	Idaho	6,197,000,000	0.4%
44	Delaware	5,226,000,000	0.3%
45	Montana	4,706,000,000	0.3%
46	Alaska	4,237,000,000	0.3%
47	South Dakota	4,103,000,000	0.3%
48	Vermont	3,768,000,000	0.2%
49	North Dakota	3,693,000,000	0.2%
50	Wyoming	2,662,000,000	0.2%
	District of Columbia	4,809,000,000	0.3%

Source: U.S. Department of Health and Human Services, Centers for Medicare and Medicaid Services
"State Health Care Expenditures" (http://www.cms.hhs.gov/NationalHealthExpendData/)
*By state of residence. Includes hospital care, physician services, dental services, home health care, drugs, vision products, nursing home care, and other personal health care services and products.

Health Care Expenditures as a Percent of Gross State Product in 2004

National Percent = 13.3% of Total Gross State Product*

ALPHA ORDER			RANK ORDER		
RANK	STATE	PERCENT	RANK	STATE	PERCENT
7	Alabama	16.2	1	West Virginia	20.3
44	Alaska	11.6	2	Maine	19.4
36	Arizona	12.5	3	Mississippi	18.1
16	Arkansas	15.4	4	North Dakota	17.6
46	California	11.0	5	Kentucky	16.9
45	Colorado	11.1	6	Montana	16.7
40	Connecticut	12.1	7	Alabama	16.2
49	Delaware	9.7	7	Rhode Island	16.2
13	Florida	15.6	7	Vermont	16.2
38	Georgia	12.2	10	Pennsylvania	16.1
36	Hawaii	12.5	11	Missouri	15.7
32	Idaho	13.0	11	South Carolina	15.7
38	Illinois	12.2	13	Florida	15.6
20	Indiana	14.4	13	Tennessee	15.6
27	Iowa	13.7	15	Ohio	15.5
20	Kansas	14.4	16	Arkansas	15.4
5	Kentucky	16.9	17	Oklahoma	14.8
23	Louisiana	14.2	17	Wisconsin	14.8
2	Maine	19.4	19	Nebraska	14.5
31	Maryland	13.3	20	Indiana	14.4
24	Massachusetts	14.1	20	Kansas	14.4
29	Michigan	13.5	20	South Dakota	14.4
27	Minnesota	13.7	23	Louisiana	14.2
3	Mississippi	18.1	24	Massachusetts	14.1
11	Missouri	15.7	25	New York	13.9
6	Montana	16.7	26	North Carolina	13.8
19	Nebraska	14.5	27	Iowa	13.7
46	Nevada	11.0	27	Minnesota	13.7
29	New Hampshire	13.5	29	Michigan	13.5
42	New Jersey	11.8	29	New Hampshire	13.5
34	New Mexico	12.6	31	Maryland	13.3
25	New York	13.9	32	Idaho	13.0
26	North Carolina	13.8	32	Oregon	13.0
4	North Dakota	17.6	34	New Mexico	12.6
15	Ohio	15.5	34	Washington	12.6
17	Oklahoma	14.8	36	Arizona	12.5
32	Oregon	13.0	36	Hawaii	12.5
10	Pennsylvania	16.1	38	Georgia	12.2
7	Rhode Island	16.2	38	Illinois	12.2
11	South Carolina	15.7	40	Connecticut	12.1
20	South Dakota	14.4	40	Utah	12.1
13	Tennessee	15.6	42	New Jersey	11.8
43	Texas	11.7	43	Texas	11.7
40	Utah	12.1	44	Alaska	11.6
7	Vermont	16.2	45	Colorado	11.1
48	Virginia	10.9	46	California	11.0
34	Washington	12.6	46	Nevada	11.0
1	West Virginia	20.3	48	Virginia	10.9
17	Wisconsin	14.8	49	Delaware	9.7
50	Wyoming	9.4	50	Wyoming	9.4
				District of Columbia	8.1

Source: U.S. Department of Health and Human Services, Centers for Medicare and Medicaid Services
   "State Health Care Expenditures" (http://www.cms.hhs.gov/NationalHealthExpendData/)
*By state of provider. Includes hospital care, physician services, dental services, home health care, drugs, vision products, nursing home care, and other personal health care services and products.

Per Capita Personal Health Care Expenditures in 2004

National Per Capita = $5,283*

ALPHA ORDER			RANK ORDER		
RANK	STATE	PER CAPITA	RANK	STATE	PER CAPITA
30	Alabama	$5,135	1	Massachusetts	$6,683
4	Alaska	6,450	2	Maine	6,540
49	Arizona	4,103	3	New York	6,535
40	Arkansas	4,863	4	Alaska	6,450
43	California	4,638	5	Connecticut	6,344
42	Colorado	4,717	6	Delaware	6,306
5	Connecticut	6,344	7	Rhode Island	6,193
6	Delaware	6,306	8	Vermont	6,069
18	Florida	5,483	9	West Virginia	5,954
45	Georgia	4,600	10	Pennsylvania	5,933
37	Hawaii	4,941	11	North Dakota	5,808
48	Idaho	4,444	12	New Jersey	5,807
27	Illinois	5,293	13	Minnesota	5,795
26	Indiana	5,295	14	Ohio	5,725
24	Iowa	5,380	15	Wisconsin	5,670
23	Kansas	5,382	16	Nebraska	5,599
19	Kentucky	5,473	17	Maryland	5,590
36	Louisiana	5,040	18	Florida	5,483
2	Maine	6,540	19	Kentucky	5,473
17	Maryland	5,590	20	Tennessee	5,464
1	Massachusetts	6,683	21	Missouri	5,444
35	Michigan	5,058	22	New Hampshire	5,432
13	Minnesota	5,795	23	Kansas	5,382
34	Mississippi	5,059	24	Iowa	5,380
21	Missouri	5,444	25	South Dakota	5,327
33	Montana	5,080	26	Indiana	5,295
16	Nebraska	5,599	27	Illinois	5,293
46	Nevada	4,569	28	Wyoming	5,265
22	New Hampshire	5,432	29	North Carolina	5,191
12	New Jersey	5,807	30	Alabama	5,135
47	New Mexico	4,471	31	South Carolina	5,114
3	New York	6,535	32	Washington	5,092
29	North Carolina	5,191	33	Montana	5,080
11	North Dakota	5,808	34	Mississippi	5,059
14	Ohio	5,725	35	Michigan	5,058
38	Oklahoma	4,917	36	Louisiana	5,040
39	Oregon	4,880	37	Hawaii	4,941
10	Pennsylvania	5,933	38	Oklahoma	4,917
7	Rhode Island	6,193	39	Oregon	4,880
31	South Carolina	5,114	40	Arkansas	4,863
25	South Dakota	5,327	41	Virginia	4,822
20	Tennessee	5,464	42	Colorado	4,717
44	Texas	4,601	43	California	4,638
50	Utah	3,972	44	Texas	4,601
8	Vermont	6,069	45	Georgia	4,600
41	Virginia	4,822	46	Nevada	4,569
32	Washington	5,092	47	New Mexico	4,471
9	West Virginia	5,954	48	Idaho	4,444
15	Wisconsin	5,670	49	Arizona	4,103
28	Wyoming	5,265	50	Utah	3,972
				District of Columbia	8,295

Source: U.S. Department of Health and Human Services, Centers for Medicare and Medicaid Services
   "State Health Care Expenditures" (http://www.cms.hhs.gov/NationalHealthExpendData/)
*By state of provider. Includes hospital care, physician services, dental services, home health care, drugs, vision products,
nursing home care, and other personal health care services and products.

Average Annual Growth in Personal Health Care Expenditures: 1991-2004

National Average = 6.7% Annual Growth*

ALPHA ORDER				RANK ORDER		
RANK	STATE	ANNUAL GROWTH		RANK	STATE	ANNUAL GROWTH
37	Alabama	6.4		1	Nevada	10.0
3	Alaska	8.4		2	North Carolina	8.6
10	Arizona	7.7		3	Alaska	8.4
30	Arkansas	6.9		3	Idaho	8.4
48	California	5.7		3	Vermont	8.4
10	Colorado	7.7		6	Maine	8.3
48	Connecticut	5.7		6	Utah	8.3
8	Delaware	8.0		8	Delaware	8.0
26	Florida	7.1		9	South Carolina	7.8
23	Georgia	7.2		10	Arizona	7.7
45	Hawaii	5.9		10	Colorado	7.7
3	Idaho	8.4		10	Oregon	7.7
44	Illinois	6.1		10	Wyoming	7.7
31	Indiana	6.8		14	Minnesota	7.6
37	Iowa	6.4		14	Mississippi	7.6
34	Kansas	6.6		14	Nebraska	7.6
18	Kentucky	7.5		14	New Hampshire	7.6
48	Louisiana	5.7		18	Kentucky	7.5
6	Maine	8.3		19	Tennessee	7.4
34	Maryland	6.6		19	Texas	7.4
40	Massachusetts	6.3		21	Montana	7.3
46	Michigan	5.8		21	Washington	7.3
14	Minnesota	7.6		23	Georgia	7.2
14	Mississippi	7.6		23	New Mexico	7.2
27	Missouri	7.0		23	Wisconsin	7.2
21	Montana	7.3		26	Florida	7.1
14	Nebraska	7.6		27	Missouri	7.0
1	Nevada	10.0		27	South Dakota	7.0
14	New Hampshire	7.6		27	Virginia	7.0
40	New Jersey	6.3		30	Arkansas	6.9
23	New Mexico	7.2		31	Indiana	6.8
40	New York	6.3		31	West Virginia	6.8
2	North Carolina	8.6		33	Oklahoma	6.7
40	North Dakota	6.3		34	Kansas	6.6
37	Ohio	6.4		34	Maryland	6.6
33	Oklahoma	6.7		34	Rhode Island	6.6
10	Oregon	7.7		37	Alabama	6.4
46	Pennsylvania	5.8		37	Iowa	6.4
34	Rhode Island	6.6		37	Ohio	6.4
9	South Carolina	7.8		40	Massachusetts	6.3
27	South Dakota	7.0		40	New Jersey	6.3
19	Tennessee	7.4		40	New York	6.3
19	Texas	7.4		40	North Dakota	6.3
6	Utah	8.3		44	Illinois	6.1
3	Vermont	8.4		45	Hawaii	5.9
27	Virginia	7.0		46	Michigan	5.8
21	Washington	7.3		46	Pennsylvania	5.8
31	West Virginia	6.8		48	California	5.7
23	Wisconsin	7.2		48	Connecticut	5.7
10	Wyoming	7.7		48	Louisiana	5.7
					District of Columbia	4.1

Source: U.S. Department of Health and Human Services, Centers for Medicare and Medicaid Services
    "State Health Care Expenditures" (http://www.cms.hhs.gov/NationalHealthExpendData/)
*By state of residence. Includes hospital care, physician services, dental services, home health care, drugs, vision products, nursing home care, and other personal health care services and products.

Expenditures for Hospital Care in 2004

National Total = $566,886,000,000*

ALPHA ORDER					RANK ORDER			
RANK	STATE	EXPENDITURES	% of USA		RANK	STATE	EXPENDITURES	% of USA
25	Alabama	$7,938,000,000	1.4%		1	California	$57,805,000,000	10.2%
47	Alaska	1,704,000,000	0.3%		2	New York	45,569,000,000	8.0%
22	Arizona	8,499,000,000	1.5%		3	Texas	38,910,000,000	6.9%
33	Arkansas	5,092,000,000	0.9%		4	Florida	31,494,000,000	5.6%
1	California	57,805,000,000	10.2%		5	Pennsylvania	26,715,000,000	4.7%
26	Colorado	7,624,000,000	1.3%		6	Illinois	25,801,000,000	4.6%
27	Connecticut	7,029,000,000	1.2%		7	Ohio	24,822,000,000	4.4%
45	Delaware	1,917,000,000	0.3%		8	Michigan	20,206,000,000	3.6%
4	Florida	31,494,000,000	5.6%		9	New Jersey	17,024,000,000	3.0%
12	Georgia	14,613,000,000	2.6%		10	Massachusetts	16,865,000,000	3.0%
42	Hawaii	2,310,000,000	0.4%		11	North Carolina	16,294,000,000	2.9%
43	Idaho	2,298,000,000	0.4%		12	Georgia	14,613,000,000	2.6%
6	Illinois	25,801,000,000	4.6%		13	Virginia	13,361,000,000	2.4%
15	Indiana	12,761,000,000	2.3%		14	Missouri	12,993,000,000	2.3%
29	Iowa	6,179,000,000	1.1%		15	Indiana	12,761,000,000	2.3%
32	Kansas	5,157,000,000	0.9%		16	Wisconsin	11,625,000,000	2.1%
24	Kentucky	8,283,000,000	1.5%		17	Maryland	11,559,000,000	2.0%
21	Louisiana	9,145,000,000	1.6%		18	Tennessee	10,744,000,000	1.9%
39	Maine	3,035,000,000	0.5%		19	Washington	10,702,000,000	1.9%
17	Maryland	11,559,000,000	2.0%		20	Minnesota	10,009,000,000	1.8%
10	Massachusetts	16,865,000,000	3.0%		21	Louisiana	9,145,000,000	1.6%
8	Michigan	20,206,000,000	3.6%		22	Arizona	8,499,000,000	1.5%
20	Minnesota	10,009,000,000	1.8%		23	South Carolina	8,316,000,000	1.5%
30	Mississippi	6,129,000,000	1.1%		24	Kentucky	8,283,000,000	1.5%
14	Missouri	12,993,000,000	2.3%		25	Alabama	7,938,000,000	1.4%
44	Montana	1,944,000,000	0.3%		26	Colorado	7,624,000,000	1.3%
35	Nebraska	3,938,000,000	0.7%		27	Connecticut	7,029,000,000	1.2%
37	Nevada	3,459,000,000	0.6%		28	Oklahoma	6,659,000,000	1.2%
40	New Hampshire	2,519,000,000	0.4%		29	Iowa	6,179,000,000	1.1%
9	New Jersey	17,024,000,000	3.0%		30	Mississippi	6,129,000,000	1.1%
38	New Mexico	3,315,000,000	0.6%		31	Oregon	5,998,000,000	1.1%
2	New York	45,569,000,000	8.0%		32	Kansas	5,157,000,000	0.9%
11	North Carolina	16,294,000,000	2.9%		33	Arkansas	5,092,000,000	0.9%
48	North Dakota	1,533,000,000	0.3%		34	West Virginia	4,432,000,000	0.8%
7	Ohio	24,822,000,000	4.4%		35	Nebraska	3,938,000,000	0.7%
28	Oklahoma	6,659,000,000	1.2%		36	Utah	3,468,000,000	0.6%
31	Oregon	5,998,000,000	1.1%		37	Nevada	3,459,000,000	0.6%
5	Pennsylvania	26,715,000,000	4.7%		38	New Mexico	3,315,000,000	0.6%
41	Rhode Island	2,437,000,000	0.4%		39	Maine	3,035,000,000	0.5%
23	South Carolina	8,316,000,000	1.5%		40	New Hampshire	2,519,000,000	0.4%
46	South Dakota	1,753,000,000	0.3%		41	Rhode Island	2,437,000,000	0.4%
18	Tennessee	10,744,000,000	1.9%		42	Hawaii	2,310,000,000	0.4%
3	Texas	38,910,000,000	6.9%		43	Idaho	2,298,000,000	0.4%
36	Utah	3,468,000,000	0.6%		44	Montana	1,944,000,000	0.3%
49	Vermont	1,446,000,000	0.3%		45	Delaware	1,917,000,000	0.3%
13	Virginia	13,361,000,000	2.4%		46	South Dakota	1,753,000,000	0.3%
19	Washington	10,702,000,000	1.9%		47	Alaska	1,704,000,000	0.3%
34	West Virginia	4,432,000,000	0.8%		48	North Dakota	1,533,000,000	0.3%
16	Wisconsin	11,625,000,000	2.1%		49	Vermont	1,446,000,000	0.3%
50	Wyoming	1,095,000,000	0.2%		50	Wyoming	1,095,000,000	0.2%
						District of Columbia	2,366,000,000	0.4%

Source: U.S. Department of Health and Human Services, Centers for Medicare and Medicaid Services
"State Health Care Expenditures" (http://www.cms.hhs.gov/NationalHealthExpendData/)
*By state of residence.

Percent of Total Personal Health Care Expenditures
Spent on Hospital Care in 2004
National Percent = 36.5%*

ALPHA ORDER

RANK	STATE	PERCENT
42	Alabama	34.2
10	Alaska	40.2
35	Arizona	36.0
20	Arkansas	38.1
41	California	34.8
39	Colorado	35.1
50	Connecticut	31.7
29	Delaware	36.7
48	Florida	33.1
37	Georgia	35.6
25	Hawaii	37.1
25	Idaho	37.1
19	Illinois	38.3
16	Indiana	38.7
14	Iowa	38.9
40	Kansas	35.0
30	Kentucky	36.6
8	Louisiana	40.4
38	Maine	35.3
24	Maryland	37.2
12	Massachusetts	39.2
11	Michigan	39.6
44	Minnesota	33.9
2	Mississippi	41.9
3	Missouri	41.5
5	Montana	41.3
9	Nebraska	40.3
49	Nevada	32.5
36	New Hampshire	35.7
46	New Jersey	33.8
13	New Mexico	39.0
33	New York	36.1
28	North Carolina	36.8
3	North Dakota	41.5
21	Ohio	37.8
17	Oklahoma	38.4
42	Oregon	34.2
32	Pennsylvania	36.4
31	Rhode Island	36.5
15	South Carolina	38.8
1	South Dakota	42.7
47	Tennessee	33.4
22	Texas	37.6
33	Utah	36.1
17	Vermont	38.4
25	Virginia	37.1
44	Washington	33.9
6	West Virginia	41.1
23	Wisconsin	37.3
6	Wyoming	41.1

RANK ORDER

RANK	STATE	PERCENT
1	South Dakota	42.7
2	Mississippi	41.9
3	Missouri	41.5
3	North Dakota	41.5
5	Montana	41.3
6	West Virginia	41.1
6	Wyoming	41.1
8	Louisiana	40.4
9	Nebraska	40.3
10	Alaska	40.2
11	Michigan	39.6
12	Massachusetts	39.2
13	New Mexico	39.0
14	Iowa	38.9
15	South Carolina	38.8
16	Indiana	38.7
17	Oklahoma	38.4
17	Vermont	38.4
19	Illinois	38.3
20	Arkansas	38.1
21	Ohio	37.8
22	Texas	37.6
23	Wisconsin	37.3
24	Maryland	37.2
25	Hawaii	37.1
25	Idaho	37.1
25	Virginia	37.1
28	North Carolina	36.8
29	Delaware	36.7
30	Kentucky	36.6
31	Rhode Island	36.5
32	Pennsylvania	36.4
33	New York	36.1
33	Utah	36.1
35	Arizona	36.0
36	New Hampshire	35.7
37	Georgia	35.6
38	Maine	35.3
39	Colorado	35.1
40	Kansas	35.0
41	California	34.8
42	Alabama	34.2
42	Oregon	34.2
44	Minnesota	33.9
44	Washington	33.9
46	New Jersey	33.8
47	Tennessee	33.4
48	Florida	33.1
49	Nevada	32.5
50	Connecticut	31.7

	District of Columbia	49.2

Source: CQ Press using data from U.S. Department of Health and Human Services, Centers for Medicare and Medicaid Services
"State Health Care Expenditures" (http://www.cms.hhs.gov/NationalHealthExpendData/)
*By state of residence.

Per Capita Expenditures for Hospital Care in 2004

National Per Capita = $1,931*

ALPHA ORDER

RANK	STATE	PER CAPITA
39	Alabama	$1,757
2	Alaska	2,594
49	Arizona	1,479
34	Arkansas	1,854
47	California	1,613
44	Colorado	1,658
24	Connecticut	2,012
7	Delaware	2,313
37	Florida	1,813
46	Georgia	1,635
35	Hawaii	1,834
45	Idaho	1,648
23	Illinois	2,029
21	Indiana	2,051
19	Iowa	2,092
33	Kansas	1,883
26	Kentucky	2,001
22	Louisiana	2,034
8	Maine	2,310
20	Maryland	2,081
1	Massachusetts	2,620
25	Michigan	2,002
28	Minnesota	1,965
16	Mississippi	2,119
10	Missouri	2,259
18	Montana	2,099
12	Nebraska	2,254
48	Nevada	1,483
30	New Hampshire	1,941
29	New Jersey	1,962
40	New Mexico	1,744
5	New York	2,362
31	North Carolina	1,910
4	North Dakota	2,411
13	Ohio	2,166
32	Oklahoma	1,890
43	Oregon	1,671
15	Pennsylvania	2,158
10	Rhode Island	2,259
27	South Carolina	1,982
9	South Dakota	2,276
36	Tennessee	1,826
41	Texas	1,728
50	Utah	1,432
6	Vermont	2,329
38	Virginia	1,788
42	Washington	1,725
3	West Virginia	2,447
17	Wisconsin	2,114
14	Wyoming	2,165

RANK ORDER

RANK	STATE	PER CAPITA
1	Massachusetts	$2,620
2	Alaska	2,594
3	West Virginia	2,447
4	North Dakota	2,411
5	New York	2,362
6	Vermont	2,329
7	Delaware	2,313
8	Maine	2,310
9	South Dakota	2,276
10	Missouri	2,259
10	Rhode Island	2,259
12	Nebraska	2,254
13	Ohio	2,166
14	Wyoming	2,165
15	Pennsylvania	2,158
16	Mississippi	2,119
17	Wisconsin	2,114
18	Montana	2,099
19	Iowa	2,092
20	Maryland	2,081
21	Indiana	2,051
22	Louisiana	2,034
23	Illinois	2,029
24	Connecticut	2,012
25	Michigan	2,002
26	Kentucky	2,001
27	South Carolina	1,982
28	Minnesota	1,965
29	New Jersey	1,962
30	New Hampshire	1,941
31	North Carolina	1,910
32	Oklahoma	1,890
33	Kansas	1,883
34	Arkansas	1,854
35	Hawaii	1,834
36	Tennessee	1,826
37	Florida	1,813
38	Virginia	1,788
39	Alabama	1,757
40	New Mexico	1,744
41	Texas	1,728
42	Washington	1,725
43	Oregon	1,671
44	Colorado	1,658
45	Idaho	1,648
46	Georgia	1,635
47	California	1,613
48	Nevada	1,483
49	Arizona	1,479
50	Utah	1,432
	District of Columbia	4,081

Source: U.S. Department of Health and Human Services, Centers for Medicare and Medicaid Services
"State Health Care Expenditures" (http://www.cms.hhs.gov/NationalHealthExpendData/)
*By state of residence.

Expenditures for Physician and Clinical Services in 2004

National Total = $393,713,000,000*

ALPHA ORDER

RANK	STATE	EXPENDITURES	% of USA
23	Alabama	$6,200,000,000	1.6%
45	Alaska	1,220,000,000	0.3%
21	Arizona	6,855,000,000	1.7%
33	Arkansas	3,316,000,000	0.8%
1	California	49,417,000,000	12.6%
22	Colorado	6,375,000,000	1.6%
27	Connecticut	5,155,000,000	1.3%
44	Delaware	1,228,000,000	0.3%
3	Florida	26,439,000,000	6.7%
10	Georgia	11,227,000,000	2.9%
41	Hawaii	1,587,000,000	0.4%
42	Idaho	1,466,000,000	0.4%
5	Illinois	16,984,000,000	4.3%
18	Indiana	7,869,000,000	2.0%
31	Iowa	3,719,000,000	0.9%
30	Kansas	4,144,000,000	1.1%
24	Kentucky	5,748,000,000	1.5%
26	Louisiana	5,271,000,000	1.3%
38	Maine	2,075,000,000	0.5%
17	Maryland	7,891,000,000	2.0%
13	Massachusetts	9,116,000,000	2.3%
9	Michigan	11,757,000,000	3.0%
19	Minnesota	7,757,000,000	2.0%
34	Mississippi	3,219,000,000	0.8%
20	Missouri	6,891,000,000	1.8%
46	Montana	1,157,000,000	0.3%
37	Nebraska	2,287,000,000	0.6%
32	Nevada	3,386,000,000	0.9%
40	New Hampshire	1,757,000,000	0.4%
8	New Jersey	12,265,000,000	3.1%
39	New Mexico	1,925,000,000	0.5%
4	New York	25,643,000,000	6.5%
11	North Carolina	10,248,000,000	2.6%
49	North Dakota	763,000,000	0.2%
7	Ohio	15,322,000,000	3.9%
29	Oklahoma	4,305,000,000	1.1%
28	Oregon	5,142,000,000	1.3%
6	Pennsylvania	16,942,000,000	4.3%
43	Rhode Island	1,325,000,000	0.3%
25	South Carolina	5,491,000,000	1.4%
47	South Dakota	920,000,000	0.2%
14	Tennessee	9,069,000,000	2.3%
2	Texas	28,769,000,000	7.3%
36	Utah	2,393,000,000	0.6%
48	Vermont	874,000,000	0.2%
12	Virginia	9,220,000,000	2.3%
15	Washington	9,004,000,000	2.3%
35	West Virginia	2,444,000,000	0.6%
16	Wisconsin	8,441,000,000	2.1%
50	Wyoming	670,000,000	0.2%

RANK ORDER

RANK	STATE	EXPENDITURES	% of USA
1	California	$49,417,000,000	12.6%
2	Texas	28,769,000,000	7.3%
3	Florida	26,439,000,000	6.7%
4	New York	25,643,000,000	6.5%
5	Illinois	16,984,000,000	4.3%
6	Pennsylvania	16,942,000,000	4.3%
7	Ohio	15,322,000,000	3.9%
8	New Jersey	12,265,000,000	3.1%
9	Michigan	11,757,000,000	3.0%
10	Georgia	11,227,000,000	2.9%
11	North Carolina	10,248,000,000	2.6%
12	Virginia	9,220,000,000	2.3%
13	Massachusetts	9,116,000,000	2.3%
14	Tennessee	9,069,000,000	2.3%
15	Washington	9,004,000,000	2.3%
16	Wisconsin	8,441,000,000	2.1%
17	Maryland	7,891,000,000	2.0%
18	Indiana	7,869,000,000	2.0%
19	Minnesota	7,757,000,000	2.0%
20	Missouri	6,891,000,000	1.8%
21	Arizona	6,855,000,000	1.7%
22	Colorado	6,375,000,000	1.6%
23	Alabama	6,200,000,000	1.6%
24	Kentucky	5,748,000,000	1.5%
25	South Carolina	5,491,000,000	1.4%
26	Louisiana	5,271,000,000	1.3%
27	Connecticut	5,155,000,000	1.3%
28	Oregon	5,142,000,000	1.3%
29	Oklahoma	4,305,000,000	1.1%
30	Kansas	4,144,000,000	1.1%
31	Iowa	3,719,000,000	0.9%
32	Nevada	3,386,000,000	0.9%
33	Arkansas	3,316,000,000	0.8%
34	Mississippi	3,219,000,000	0.8%
35	West Virginia	2,444,000,000	0.6%
36	Utah	2,393,000,000	0.6%
37	Nebraska	2,287,000,000	0.6%
38	Maine	2,075,000,000	0.5%
39	New Mexico	1,925,000,000	0.5%
40	New Hampshire	1,757,000,000	0.4%
41	Hawaii	1,587,000,000	0.4%
42	Idaho	1,466,000,000	0.4%
43	Rhode Island	1,325,000,000	0.3%
44	Delaware	1,228,000,000	0.3%
45	Alaska	1,220,000,000	0.3%
46	Montana	1,157,000,000	0.3%
47	South Dakota	920,000,000	0.2%
48	Vermont	874,000,000	0.2%
49	North Dakota	763,000,000	0.2%
50	Wyoming	670,000,000	0.2%
	District of Columbia	1,024,000,000	0.3%

Source: U.S. Department of Health and Human Services, Centers for Medicare and Medicaid Services
"State Health Care Expenditures" (http://www.cms.hhs.gov/NationalHealthExpendData/)
*By state of residence. Includes private physician offices and clinics, independently billing laboratories and clinics run by U.S. Department of Veteran Affairs and the U.S. Indian Health Service.

Percent of Total Personal Health Care Expenditures
Spent on Physician and Clinical Services in 2004
National Percent = 25.4%*

ALPHA ORDER

RANK	STATE	PERCENT
14	Alabama	26.7
6	Alaska	28.8
5	Arizona	29.1
26	Arkansas	24.8
2	California	29.7
3	Colorado	29.4
35	Connecticut	23.3
32	Delaware	23.5
10	Florida	27.8
12	Georgia	27.3
18	Hawaii	25.5
31	Idaho	23.7
21	Illinois	25.2
30	Indiana	23.9
33	Iowa	23.4
9	Kansas	28.1
19	Kentucky	25.4
35	Louisiana	23.3
29	Maine	24.1
19	Maryland	25.4
47	Massachusetts	21.2
41	Michigan	23.0
15	Minnesota	26.3
45	Mississippi	22.0
45	Missouri	22.0
27	Montana	24.6
33	Nebraska	23.4
1	Nevada	31.8
23	New Hampshire	24.9
28	New Jersey	24.3
42	New Mexico	22.7
49	New York	20.3
39	North Carolina	23.1
48	North Dakota	20.7
35	Ohio	23.3
23	Oklahoma	24.9
3	Oregon	29.4
39	Pennsylvania	23.1
50	Rhode Island	19.8
16	South Carolina	25.6
44	South Dakota	22.4
8	Tennessee	28.2
10	Texas	27.8
23	Utah	24.9
38	Vermont	23.2
16	Virginia	25.6
7	Washington	28.5
42	West Virginia	22.7
13	Wisconsin	27.1
21	Wyoming	25.2

RANK ORDER

RANK	STATE	PERCENT
1	Nevada	31.8
2	California	29.7
3	Colorado	29.4
3	Oregon	29.4
5	Arizona	29.1
6	Alaska	28.8
7	Washington	28.5
8	Tennessee	28.2
9	Kansas	28.1
10	Florida	27.8
10	Texas	27.8
12	Georgia	27.3
13	Wisconsin	27.1
14	Alabama	26.7
15	Minnesota	26.3
16	South Carolina	25.6
16	Virginia	25.6
18	Hawaii	25.5
19	Kentucky	25.4
19	Maryland	25.4
21	Illinois	25.2
21	Wyoming	25.2
23	New Hampshire	24.9
23	Oklahoma	24.9
23	Utah	24.9
26	Arkansas	24.8
27	Montana	24.6
28	New Jersey	24.3
29	Maine	24.1
30	Indiana	23.9
31	Idaho	23.7
32	Delaware	23.5
33	Iowa	23.4
33	Nebraska	23.4
35	Connecticut	23.3
35	Louisiana	23.3
35	Ohio	23.3
38	Vermont	23.2
39	North Carolina	23.1
39	Pennsylvania	23.1
41	Michigan	23.0
42	New Mexico	22.7
42	West Virginia	22.7
44	South Dakota	22.4
45	Mississippi	22.0
45	Missouri	22.0
47	Massachusetts	21.2
48	North Dakota	20.7
49	New York	20.3
50	Rhode Island	19.8
	District of Columbia	21.3

Source: CQ Press using data from U.S. Department of Health and Human Services, Centers for Medicare and Medicaid Services
"State Health Care Expenditures" (http://www.cms.hhs.gov/NationalHealthExpendData/)
*By state of residence. Includes private physician offices and clinics, independently billing laboratories and clinics run by U.S.
Department of Veteran Affairs and the U.S. Indian Health Service.

Per Capita Expenditures for Physician and Clinical Services in 2004

National Per Capita = $1,341*

ALPHA ORDER

RANK	STATE	PER CAPITA
20	Alabama	$1,372
1	Alaska	1,858
44	Arizona	1,193
39	Arkansas	1,207
19	California	1,379
18	Colorado	1,386
9	Connecticut	1,475
8	Delaware	1,482
6	Florida	1,522
34	Georgia	1,257
32	Hawaii	1,260
48	Idaho	1,051
25	Illinois	1,336
31	Indiana	1,264
33	Iowa	1,259
7	Kansas	1,513
17	Kentucky	1,388
45	Louisiana	1,173
2	Maine	1,579
13	Maryland	1,421
14	Massachusetts	1,416
46	Michigan	1,165
5	Minnesota	1,523
47	Mississippi	1,113
42	Missouri	1,198
35	Montana	1,249
28	Nebraska	1,309
10	Nevada	1,451
22	New Hampshire	1,354
15	New Jersey	1,414
49	New Mexico	1,013
26	New York	1,329
40	North Carolina	1,201
41	North Dakota	1,200
24	Ohio	1,337
38	Oklahoma	1,222
12	Oregon	1,433
21	Pennsylvania	1,369
37	Rhode Island	1,228
28	South Carolina	1,309
43	South Dakota	1,195
3	Tennessee	1,541
30	Texas	1,278
50	Utah	988
16	Vermont	1,408
36	Virginia	1,234
10	Washington	1,451
23	West Virginia	1,350
4	Wisconsin	1,535
27	Wyoming	1,326

RANK ORDER

RANK	STATE	PER CAPITA
1	Alaska	$1,858
2	Maine	1,579
3	Tennessee	1,541
4	Wisconsin	1,535
5	Minnesota	1,523
6	Florida	1,522
7	Kansas	1,513
8	Delaware	1,482
9	Connecticut	1,475
10	Nevada	1,451
10	Washington	1,451
12	Oregon	1,433
13	Maryland	1,421
14	Massachusetts	1,416
15	New Jersey	1,414
16	Vermont	1,408
17	Kentucky	1,388
18	Colorado	1,386
19	California	1,379
20	Alabama	1,372
21	Pennsylvania	1,369
22	New Hampshire	1,354
23	West Virginia	1,350
24	Ohio	1,337
25	Illinois	1,336
26	New York	1,329
27	Wyoming	1,326
28	Nebraska	1,309
28	South Carolina	1,309
30	Texas	1,278
31	Indiana	1,264
32	Hawaii	1,260
33	Iowa	1,259
34	Georgia	1,257
35	Montana	1,249
36	Virginia	1,234
37	Rhode Island	1,228
38	Oklahoma	1,222
39	Arkansas	1,207
40	North Carolina	1,201
41	North Dakota	1,200
42	Missouri	1,198
43	South Dakota	1,195
44	Arizona	1,193
45	Louisiana	1,173
46	Michigan	1,165
47	Mississippi	1,113
48	Idaho	1,051
49	New Mexico	1,013
50	Utah	988
	District of Columbia	1,767

Source: U.S. Department of Health and Human Services, Centers for Medicare and Medicaid Services
"State Health Care Expenditures" (http://www.cms.hhs.gov/NationalHealthExpendData/)
*By state of residence. Includes private physician offices and clinics, independently billing laboratories and clinics run by U.S. Department of Veteran Affairs and the U.S. Indian Health Service.

Expenditures for Dental Services in 2004

National Total = $81,476,000,000*

ALPHA ORDER					RANK ORDER			
RANK	STATE	EXPENDITURES	% of USA		RANK	STATE	EXPENDITURES	% of USA
26	Alabama	$977,000,000	1.2%		1	California	$11,625,000,000	14.3%
46	Alaska	241,000,000	0.3%		2	New York	5,445,000,000	6.7%
20	Arizona	1,457,000,000	1.8%		3	Texas	4,749,000,000	5.8%
34	Arkansas	601,000,000	0.7%		4	Florida	4,494,000,000	5.5%
1	California	11,625,000,000	14.3%		5	Illinois	3,488,000,000	4.3%
19	Colorado	1,537,000,000	1.9%		6	Pennsylvania	3,189,000,000	3.9%
22	Connecticut	1,336,000,000	1.6%		7	Michigan	3,147,000,000	3.9%
44	Delaware	279,000,000	0.3%		8	New Jersey	2,903,000,000	3.6%
4	Florida	4,494,000,000	5.5%		9	Ohio	2,901,000,000	3.6%
12	Georgia	2,257,000,000	2.8%		10	Washington	2,505,000,000	3.1%
41	Hawaii	382,000,000	0.5%		11	Massachusetts	2,276,000,000	2.8%
37	Idaho	468,000,000	0.6%		12	Georgia	2,257,000,000	2.8%
5	Illinois	3,488,000,000	4.3%		13	North Carolina	2,253,000,000	2.8%
17	Indiana	1,606,000,000	2.0%		14	Virginia	2,043,000,000	2.5%
30	Iowa	735,000,000	0.9%		15	Wisconsin	1,694,000,000	2.1%
31	Kansas	723,000,000	0.9%		16	Minnesota	1,678,000,000	2.1%
27	Kentucky	876,000,000	1.1%		17	Indiana	1,606,000,000	2.0%
29	Louisiana	781,000,000	1.0%		18	Maryland	1,553,000,000	1.9%
42	Maine	363,000,000	0.4%		19	Colorado	1,537,000,000	1.9%
18	Maryland	1,553,000,000	1.9%		20	Arizona	1,457,000,000	1.8%
11	Massachusetts	2,276,000,000	2.8%		21	Tennessee	1,428,000,000	1.8%
7	Michigan	3,147,000,000	3.9%		22	Connecticut	1,336,000,000	1.6%
16	Minnesota	1,678,000,000	2.1%		22	Missouri	1,336,000,000	1.6%
35	Mississippi	507,000,000	0.6%		24	Oregon	1,269,000,000	1.6%
22	Missouri	1,336,000,000	1.6%		25	South Carolina	1,003,000,000	1.2%
45	Montana	249,000,000	0.3%		26	Alabama	977,000,000	1.2%
39	Nebraska	423,000,000	0.5%		27	Kentucky	876,000,000	1.1%
33	Nevada	679,000,000	0.8%		28	Oklahoma	842,000,000	1.0%
36	New Hampshire	471,000,000	0.6%		29	Louisiana	781,000,000	1.0%
8	New Jersey	2,903,000,000	3.6%		30	Iowa	735,000,000	0.9%
38	New Mexico	425,000,000	0.5%		31	Kansas	723,000,000	0.9%
2	New York	5,445,000,000	6.7%		32	Utah	718,000,000	0.9%
13	North Carolina	2,253,000,000	2.8%		33	Nevada	679,000,000	0.8%
49	North Dakota	174,000,000	0.2%		34	Arkansas	601,000,000	0.7%
9	Ohio	2,901,000,000	3.6%		35	Mississippi	507,000,000	0.6%
28	Oklahoma	842,000,000	1.0%		36	New Hampshire	471,000,000	0.6%
24	Oregon	1,269,000,000	1.6%		37	Idaho	468,000,000	0.6%
6	Pennsylvania	3,189,000,000	3.9%		38	New Mexico	425,000,000	0.5%
43	Rhode Island	294,000,000	0.4%		39	Nebraska	423,000,000	0.5%
25	South Carolina	1,003,000,000	1.2%		40	West Virginia	384,000,000	0.5%
48	South Dakota	195,000,000	0.2%		41	Hawaii	382,000,000	0.5%
21	Tennessee	1,428,000,000	1.8%		42	Maine	363,000,000	0.4%
3	Texas	4,749,000,000	5.8%		43	Rhode Island	294,000,000	0.4%
32	Utah	718,000,000	0.9%		44	Delaware	279,000,000	0.3%
47	Vermont	198,000,000	0.2%		45	Montana	249,000,000	0.3%
14	Virginia	2,043,000,000	2.5%		46	Alaska	241,000,000	0.3%
10	Washington	2,505,000,000	3.1%		47	Vermont	198,000,000	0.2%
40	West Virginia	384,000,000	0.5%		48	South Dakota	195,000,000	0.2%
15	Wisconsin	1,694,000,000	2.1%		49	North Dakota	174,000,000	0.2%
50	Wyoming	134,000,000	0.2%		50	Wyoming	134,000,000	0.2%
						District of Columbia	183,000,000	0.2%

Source: U.S. Department of Health and Human Services, Centers for Medicare and Medicaid Services
"State Health Care Expenditures" (http://www.cms.hhs.gov/NationalHealthExpendData/)
*By state of residence.

Percent of Total Personal Health Care Expenditures
Spent on Dental Services in 2004
National Percent = 5.3%*

ALPHA ORDER

RANK	STATE	PERCENT
45	Alabama	4.2
14	Alaska	5.7
9	Arizona	6.2
37	Arkansas	4.5
6	California	7.0
5	Colorado	7.1
12	Connecticut	6.0
19	Delaware	5.3
32	Florida	4.7
17	Georgia	5.5
11	Hawaii	6.1
2	Idaho	7.6
23	Illinois	5.2
28	Indiana	4.9
35	Iowa	4.6
28	Kansas	4.9
47	Kentucky	3.9
50	Louisiana	3.4
45	Maine	4.2
25	Maryland	5.0
19	Massachusetts	5.3
9	Michigan	6.2
14	Minnesota	5.7
49	Mississippi	3.5
41	Missouri	4.3
19	Montana	5.3
41	Nebraska	4.3
8	Nevada	6.4
7	New Hampshire	6.7
13	New Jersey	5.8
25	New Mexico	5.0
41	New York	4.3
24	North Carolina	5.1
32	North Dakota	4.7
38	Ohio	4.4
28	Oklahoma	4.9
4	Oregon	7.2
41	Pennsylvania	4.3
38	Rhode Island	4.4
32	South Carolina	4.7
31	South Dakota	4.8
38	Tennessee	4.4
35	Texas	4.6
3	Utah	7.5
19	Vermont	5.3
14	Virginia	5.7
1	Washington	7.9
48	West Virginia	3.6
18	Wisconsin	5.4
25	Wyoming	5.0

RANK ORDER

RANK	STATE	PERCENT
1	Washington	7.9
2	Idaho	7.6
3	Utah	7.5
4	Oregon	7.2
5	Colorado	7.1
6	California	7.0
7	New Hampshire	6.7
8	Nevada	6.4
9	Arizona	6.2
9	Michigan	6.2
11	Hawaii	6.1
12	Connecticut	6.0
13	New Jersey	5.8
14	Alaska	5.7
14	Minnesota	5.7
14	Virginia	5.7
17	Georgia	5.5
18	Wisconsin	5.4
19	Delaware	5.3
19	Massachusetts	5.3
19	Montana	5.3
19	Vermont	5.3
23	Illinois	5.2
24	North Carolina	5.1
25	Maryland	5.0
25	New Mexico	5.0
25	Wyoming	5.0
28	Indiana	4.9
28	Kansas	4.9
28	Oklahoma	4.9
31	South Dakota	4.8
32	Florida	4.7
32	North Dakota	4.7
32	South Carolina	4.7
35	Iowa	4.6
35	Texas	4.6
37	Arkansas	4.5
38	Ohio	4.4
38	Rhode Island	4.4
38	Tennessee	4.4
41	Missouri	4.3
41	Nebraska	4.3
41	New York	4.3
41	Pennsylvania	4.3
45	Alabama	4.2
45	Maine	4.2
47	Kentucky	3.9
48	West Virginia	3.6
49	Mississippi	3.5
50	Louisiana	3.4

District of Columbia   3.8

Source: CQ Press using data from U.S. Department of Health and Human Services, Centers for Medicare and Medicaid Services
"State Health Care Expenditures" (http://www.cms.hhs.gov/NationalHealthExpendData/)
*By state of residence.

Per Capita Expenditures for Dental Care in 2004

National Per Capita = $277*

ALPHA ORDER

RANK	STATE	PER CAPITA
45	Alabama	$216
3	Alaska	366
33	Arizona	254
44	Arkansas	219
12	California	324
10	Colorado	334
2	Connecticut	382
7	Delaware	337
30	Florida	259
34	Georgia	253
16	Hawaii	303
8	Idaho	336
22	Illinois	274
31	Indiana	258
37	Iowa	249
28	Kansas	264
46	Kentucky	212
50	Louisiana	174
21	Maine	276
20	Maryland	280
5	Massachusetts	354
14	Michigan	312
11	Minnesota	329
49	Mississippi	175
42	Missouri	232
26	Montana	269
39	Nebraska	242
18	Nevada	291
4	New Hampshire	363
9	New Jersey	335
43	New Mexico	224
19	New York	282
28	North Carolina	264
22	North Dakota	274
34	Ohio	253
40	Oklahoma	239
5	Oregon	354
31	Pennsylvania	258
25	Rhode Island	272
40	South Carolina	239
34	South Dakota	253
38	Tennessee	243
48	Texas	211
17	Utah	297
13	Vermont	319
24	Virginia	273
1	Washington	404
46	West Virginia	212
15	Wisconsin	308
27	Wyoming	265

RANK ORDER

RANK	STATE	PER CAPITA
1	Washington	$404
2	Connecticut	382
3	Alaska	366
4	New Hampshire	363
5	Massachusetts	354
5	Oregon	354
7	Delaware	337
8	Idaho	336
9	New Jersey	335
10	Colorado	334
11	Minnesota	329
12	California	324
13	Vermont	319
14	Michigan	312
15	Wisconsin	308
16	Hawaii	303
17	Utah	297
18	Nevada	291
19	New York	282
20	Maryland	280
21	Maine	276
22	Illinois	274
22	North Dakota	274
24	Virginia	273
25	Rhode Island	272
26	Montana	269
27	Wyoming	265
28	Kansas	264
28	North Carolina	264
30	Florida	259
31	Indiana	258
31	Pennsylvania	258
33	Arizona	254
34	Georgia	253
34	Ohio	253
34	South Dakota	253
37	Iowa	249
38	Tennessee	243
39	Nebraska	242
40	Oklahoma	239
40	South Carolina	239
42	Missouri	232
43	New Mexico	224
44	Arkansas	219
45	Alabama	216
46	Kentucky	212
46	West Virginia	212
48	Texas	211
49	Mississippi	175
50	Louisiana	174

District of Columbia	315

Source: U.S. Department of Health and Human Services, Centers for Medicare and Medicaid Services
    "State Health Care Expenditures" (http://www.cms.hhs.gov/NationalHealthExpendData/)
*By state of residence.

Expenditures for Other Professional Health Care Services in 2004

National Total = $52,636,000,000*

ALPHA ORDER					RANK ORDER			
RANK	STATE	EXPENDITURES	% of USA		RANK	STATE	EXPENDITURES	% of USA
27	Alabama	$681,000,000	1.3%		1	California	$6,178,000,000	11.7%
46	Alaska	164,000,000	0.3%		2	New York	3,587,000,000	6.8%
22	Arizona	932,000,000	1.8%		3	Florida	3,529,000,000	6.7%
32	Arkansas	463,000,000	0.9%		4	Texas	3,177,000,000	6.0%
1	California	6,178,000,000	11.7%		5	Pennsylvania	2,613,000,000	5.0%
21	Colorado	939,000,000	1.8%		6	Illinois	2,365,000,000	4.5%
23	Connecticut	855,000,000	1.6%		7	Ohio	2,285,000,000	4.3%
43	Delaware	210,000,000	0.4%		8	New Jersey	1,919,000,000	3.6%
3	Florida	3,529,000,000	6.7%		9	Michigan	1,896,000,000	3.6%
13	Georgia	1,252,000,000	2.4%		10	Washington	1,363,000,000	2.6%
42	Hawaii	224,000,000	0.4%		11	North Carolina	1,336,000,000	2.5%
40	Idaho	303,000,000	0.6%		12	Massachusetts	1,289,000,000	2.4%
6	Illinois	2,365,000,000	4.5%		13	Georgia	1,252,000,000	2.4%
19	Indiana	1,002,000,000	1.9%		14	Virginia	1,123,000,000	2.1%
29	Iowa	557,000,000	1.1%		15	Tennessee	1,035,000,000	2.0%
31	Kansas	499,000,000	0.9%		16	Maryland	1,034,000,000	2.0%
24	Kentucky	796,000,000	1.5%		17	Wisconsin	1,031,000,000	2.0%
26	Louisiana	705,000,000	1.3%		18	Minnesota	1,005,000,000	1.9%
38	Maine	305,000,000	0.6%		19	Indiana	1,002,000,000	1.9%
16	Maryland	1,034,000,000	2.0%		20	Missouri	958,000,000	1.8%
12	Massachusetts	1,289,000,000	2.4%		21	Colorado	939,000,000	1.8%
9	Michigan	1,896,000,000	3.6%		22	Arizona	932,000,000	1.8%
18	Minnesota	1,005,000,000	1.9%		23	Connecticut	855,000,000	1.6%
35	Mississippi	351,000,000	0.7%		24	Kentucky	796,000,000	1.5%
20	Missouri	958,000,000	1.8%		25	Oregon	715,000,000	1.4%
45	Montana	172,000,000	0.3%		26	Louisiana	705,000,000	1.3%
39	Nebraska	304,000,000	0.6%		27	Alabama	681,000,000	1.3%
33	Nevada	370,000,000	0.7%		28	Oklahoma	561,000,000	1.1%
41	New Hampshire	229,000,000	0.4%		29	Iowa	557,000,000	1.1%
8	New Jersey	1,919,000,000	3.6%		30	South Carolina	534,000,000	1.0%
37	New Mexico	321,000,000	0.6%		31	Kansas	499,000,000	0.9%
2	New York	3,587,000,000	6.8%		32	Arkansas	463,000,000	0.9%
11	North Carolina	1,336,000,000	2.5%		33	Nevada	370,000,000	0.7%
50	North Dakota	103,000,000	0.2%		34	West Virginia	361,000,000	0.7%
7	Ohio	2,285,000,000	4.3%		35	Mississippi	351,000,000	0.7%
28	Oklahoma	561,000,000	1.1%		36	Utah	332,000,000	0.6%
25	Oregon	715,000,000	1.4%		37	New Mexico	321,000,000	0.6%
5	Pennsylvania	2,613,000,000	5.0%		38	Maine	305,000,000	0.6%
44	Rhode Island	193,000,000	0.4%		39	Nebraska	304,000,000	0.6%
30	South Carolina	534,000,000	1.0%		40	Idaho	303,000,000	0.6%
47	South Dakota	135,000,000	0.3%		41	New Hampshire	229,000,000	0.4%
15	Tennessee	1,035,000,000	2.0%		42	Hawaii	224,000,000	0.4%
4	Texas	3,177,000,000	6.0%		43	Delaware	210,000,000	0.4%
36	Utah	332,000,000	0.6%		44	Rhode Island	193,000,000	0.4%
48	Vermont	132,000,000	0.3%		45	Montana	172,000,000	0.3%
14	Virginia	1,123,000,000	2.1%		46	Alaska	164,000,000	0.3%
10	Washington	1,363,000,000	2.6%		47	South Dakota	135,000,000	0.3%
34	West Virginia	361,000,000	0.7%		48	Vermont	132,000,000	0.3%
17	Wisconsin	1,031,000,000	2.0%		49	Wyoming	117,000,000	0.2%
49	Wyoming	117,000,000	0.2%		50	North Dakota	103,000,000	0.2%
						District of Columbia	98,000,000	0.2%

Source: U.S. Department of Health and Human Services, Centers for Medicare and Medicaid Services
    "State Health Care Expenditures" (http://www.cms.hhs.gov/NationalHealthExpendData/)
*By state of residence. Includes services of licensed professionals such as chiropractors, optometrists, podiatrists, and
independently practicing nurses. Also includes Medicare ambulance services.

Percent of Total Personal Health Care Expenditures
Spent on Other Professional Health Care Services in 2004
National Percent = 3.4%*

ALPHA ORDER

RANK	STATE	PERCENT
45	Alabama	2.9
8	Alaska	3.9
6	Arizona	4.0
18	Arkansas	3.5
12	California	3.7
3	Colorado	4.3
8	Connecticut	3.9
6	Delaware	4.0
12	Florida	3.7
41	Georgia	3.0
16	Hawaii	3.6
1	Idaho	4.9
18	Illinois	3.5
41	Indiana	3.0
18	Iowa	3.5
27	Kansas	3.4
18	Kentucky	3.5
36	Louisiana	3.1
18	Maine	3.5
29	Maryland	3.3
41	Massachusetts	3.0
12	Michigan	3.7
27	Minnesota	3.4
50	Mississippi	2.4
36	Missouri	3.1
12	Montana	3.7
36	Nebraska	3.1
18	Nevada	3.5
33	New Hampshire	3.2
10	New Jersey	3.8
10	New Mexico	3.8
47	New York	2.8
41	North Carolina	3.0
47	North Dakota	2.8
18	Ohio	3.5
33	Oklahoma	3.2
5	Oregon	4.1
16	Pennsylvania	3.6
45	Rhode Island	2.9
49	South Carolina	2.5
29	South Dakota	3.3
33	Tennessee	3.2
36	Texas	3.1
18	Utah	3.5
18	Vermont	3.5
36	Virginia	3.1
3	Washington	4.3
29	West Virginia	3.3
29	Wisconsin	3.3
2	Wyoming	4.4

RANK ORDER

RANK	STATE	PERCENT
1	Idaho	4.9
2	Wyoming	4.4
3	Colorado	4.3
3	Washington	4.3
5	Oregon	4.1
6	Arizona	4.0
6	Delaware	4.0
8	Alaska	3.9
8	Connecticut	3.9
10	New Jersey	3.8
10	New Mexico	3.8
12	California	3.7
12	Florida	3.7
12	Michigan	3.7
12	Montana	3.7
16	Hawaii	3.6
16	Pennsylvania	3.6
18	Arkansas	3.5
18	Illinois	3.5
18	Iowa	3.5
18	Kentucky	3.5
18	Maine	3.5
18	Nevada	3.5
18	Ohio	3.5
18	Utah	3.5
18	Vermont	3.5
27	Kansas	3.4
27	Minnesota	3.4
29	Maryland	3.3
29	South Dakota	3.3
29	West Virginia	3.3
29	Wisconsin	3.3
33	New Hampshire	3.2
33	Oklahoma	3.2
33	Tennessee	3.2
36	Louisiana	3.1
36	Missouri	3.1
36	Nebraska	3.1
36	Texas	3.1
36	Virginia	3.1
41	Georgia	3.0
41	Indiana	3.0
41	Massachusetts	3.0
41	North Carolina	3.0
45	Alabama	2.9
45	Rhode Island	2.9
47	New York	2.8
47	North Dakota	2.8
49	South Carolina	2.5
50	Mississippi	2.4

District of Columbia 2.0

Source: CQ Press using data from U.S. Department of Health and Human Services, Centers for Medicare and Medicaid Services
   "State Health Care Expenditures" (http://www.cms.hhs.gov/NationalHealthExpendData/)
*By state of residence. Includes services of licensed professionals such as chiropractors, optometrists, podiatrists, and
independently practicing nurses. Also includes Medicare ambulance services.

Per Capita Expenditures for Other Professional Health Care Services in 2004

National Per Capita = $179*

<table>
<tr><td colspan="3">ALPHA ORDER</td><td colspan="3">RANK ORDER</td></tr>
<tr><th>RANK</th><th>STATE</th><th>PER CAPITA</th><th>RANK</th><th>STATE</th><th>PER CAPITA</th></tr>
<tr><td>44</td><td>Alabama</td><td>$151</td><td>1</td><td>Delaware</td><td>$253</td></tr>
<tr><td>2</td><td>Alaska</td><td>249</td><td>2</td><td>Alaska</td><td>249</td></tr>
<tr><td>37</td><td>Arizona</td><td>162</td><td>3</td><td>Connecticut</td><td>245</td></tr>
<tr><td>35</td><td>Arkansas</td><td>168</td><td>4</td><td>Maine</td><td>232</td></tr>
<tr><td>33</td><td>California</td><td>172</td><td>5</td><td>Wyoming</td><td>231</td></tr>
<tr><td>11</td><td>Colorado</td><td>204</td><td>6</td><td>New Jersey</td><td>221</td></tr>
<tr><td>3</td><td>Connecticut</td><td>245</td><td>7</td><td>Washington</td><td>220</td></tr>
<tr><td>1</td><td>Delaware</td><td>253</td><td>8</td><td>Idaho</td><td>217</td></tr>
<tr><td>12</td><td>Florida</td><td>203</td><td>9</td><td>Vermont</td><td>212</td></tr>
<tr><td>47</td><td>Georgia</td><td>140</td><td>10</td><td>Pennsylvania</td><td>211</td></tr>
<tr><td>27</td><td>Hawaii</td><td>178</td><td>11</td><td>Colorado</td><td>204</td></tr>
<tr><td>8</td><td>Idaho</td><td>217</td><td>12</td><td>Florida</td><td>203</td></tr>
<tr><td>22</td><td>Illinois</td><td>186</td><td>13</td><td>Massachusetts</td><td>200</td></tr>
<tr><td>39</td><td>Indiana</td><td>161</td><td>14</td><td>Ohio</td><td>199</td></tr>
<tr><td>19</td><td>Iowa</td><td>188</td><td>14</td><td>Oregon</td><td>199</td></tr>
<tr><td>26</td><td>Kansas</td><td>182</td><td>14</td><td>West Virginia</td><td>199</td></tr>
<tr><td>18</td><td>Kentucky</td><td>192</td><td>17</td><td>Minnesota</td><td>197</td></tr>
<tr><td>42</td><td>Louisiana</td><td>157</td><td>18</td><td>Kentucky</td><td>192</td></tr>
<tr><td>4</td><td>Maine</td><td>232</td><td>19</td><td>Iowa</td><td>188</td></tr>
<tr><td>22</td><td>Maryland</td><td>186</td><td>19</td><td>Michigan</td><td>188</td></tr>
<tr><td>13</td><td>Massachusetts</td><td>200</td><td>21</td><td>Wisconsin</td><td>187</td></tr>
<tr><td>19</td><td>Michigan</td><td>188</td><td>22</td><td>Illinois</td><td>186</td></tr>
<tr><td>17</td><td>Minnesota</td><td>197</td><td>22</td><td>Maryland</td><td>186</td></tr>
<tr><td>50</td><td>Mississippi</td><td>121</td><td>22</td><td>Montana</td><td>186</td></tr>
<tr><td>36</td><td>Missouri</td><td>167</td><td>22</td><td>New York</td><td>186</td></tr>
<tr><td>22</td><td>Montana</td><td>186</td><td>26</td><td>Kansas</td><td>182</td></tr>
<tr><td>32</td><td>Nebraska</td><td>174</td><td>27</td><td>Hawaii</td><td>178</td></tr>
<tr><td>40</td><td>Nevada</td><td>159</td><td>27</td><td>Rhode Island</td><td>178</td></tr>
<tr><td>29</td><td>New Hampshire</td><td>176</td><td>29</td><td>New Hampshire</td><td>176</td></tr>
<tr><td>6</td><td>New Jersey</td><td>221</td><td>29</td><td>South Dakota</td><td>176</td></tr>
<tr><td>34</td><td>New Mexico</td><td>169</td><td>29</td><td>Tennessee</td><td>176</td></tr>
<tr><td>22</td><td>New York</td><td>186</td><td>32</td><td>Nebraska</td><td>174</td></tr>
<tr><td>42</td><td>North Carolina</td><td>157</td><td>33</td><td>California</td><td>172</td></tr>
<tr><td>37</td><td>North Dakota</td><td>162</td><td>34</td><td>New Mexico</td><td>169</td></tr>
<tr><td>14</td><td>Ohio</td><td>199</td><td>35</td><td>Arkansas</td><td>168</td></tr>
<tr><td>40</td><td>Oklahoma</td><td>159</td><td>36</td><td>Missouri</td><td>167</td></tr>
<tr><td>14</td><td>Oregon</td><td>199</td><td>37</td><td>Arizona</td><td>162</td></tr>
<tr><td>10</td><td>Pennsylvania</td><td>211</td><td>37</td><td>North Dakota</td><td>162</td></tr>
<tr><td>27</td><td>Rhode Island</td><td>178</td><td>39</td><td>Indiana</td><td>161</td></tr>
<tr><td>49</td><td>South Carolina</td><td>127</td><td>40</td><td>Nevada</td><td>159</td></tr>
<tr><td>29</td><td>South Dakota</td><td>176</td><td>40</td><td>Oklahoma</td><td>159</td></tr>
<tr><td>29</td><td>Tennessee</td><td>176</td><td>42</td><td>Louisiana</td><td>157</td></tr>
<tr><td>46</td><td>Texas</td><td>141</td><td>42</td><td>North Carolina</td><td>157</td></tr>
<tr><td>48</td><td>Utah</td><td>137</td><td>44</td><td>Alabama</td><td>151</td></tr>
<tr><td>9</td><td>Vermont</td><td>212</td><td>45</td><td>Virginia</td><td>150</td></tr>
<tr><td>45</td><td>Virginia</td><td>150</td><td>46</td><td>Texas</td><td>141</td></tr>
<tr><td>7</td><td>Washington</td><td>220</td><td>47</td><td>Georgia</td><td>140</td></tr>
<tr><td>14</td><td>West Virginia</td><td>199</td><td>48</td><td>Utah</td><td>137</td></tr>
<tr><td>21</td><td>Wisconsin</td><td>187</td><td>49</td><td>South Carolina</td><td>127</td></tr>
<tr><td>5</td><td>Wyoming</td><td>231</td><td>50</td><td>Mississippi</td><td>121</td></tr>
<tr><td></td><td></td><td></td><td></td><td>District of Columbia</td><td>170</td></tr>
</table>

Source: U.S. Department of Health and Human Services, Centers for Medicare and Medicaid Services
   "State Health Care Expenditures" (http://www.cms.hhs.gov/NationalHealthExpendData/)
*By state of residence. Includes services of licensed professionals such as chiropractors, optometrists, podiatrists, and independently practicing nurses. Also includes Medicare ambulance services.

Expenditures for Nursing Home Care in 2004

National Total = $115,015,000,000*

ALPHA ORDER

RANK	STATE	EXPENDITURES	% of USA
25	Alabama	$1,475,000,000	1.3%
50	Alaska	80,000,000	0.1%
32	Arizona	1,023,000,000	0.9%
31	Arkansas	1,040,000,000	0.9%
2	California	8,424,000,000	7.3%
27	Colorado	1,178,000,000	1.0%
13	Connecticut	2,711,000,000	2.4%
40	Delaware	409,000,000	0.4%
5	Florida	6,503,000,000	5.7%
19	Georgia	2,272,000,000	2.0%
47	Hawaii	293,000,000	0.3%
44	Idaho	361,000,000	0.3%
7	Illinois	5,173,000,000	4.5%
12	Indiana	2,871,000,000	2.5%
22	Iowa	1,623,000,000	1.4%
29	Kansas	1,110,000,000	1.0%
24	Kentucky	1,526,000,000	1.3%
23	Louisiana	1,617,000,000	1.4%
36	Maine	630,000,000	0.5%
16	Maryland	2,419,000,000	2.1%
9	Massachusetts	4,124,000,000	3.6%
11	Michigan	3,193,000,000	2.8%
18	Minnesota	2,367,000,000	2.1%
30	Mississippi	1,094,000,000	1.0%
14	Missouri	2,479,000,000	2.2%
46	Montana	322,000,000	0.3%
34	Nebraska	860,000,000	0.7%
45	Nevada	341,000,000	0.3%
38	New Hampshire	548,000,000	0.5%
8	New Jersey	4,261,000,000	3.7%
43	New Mexico	372,000,000	0.3%
1	New York	13,364,000,000	11.6%
10	North Carolina	3,354,000,000	2.9%
42	North Dakota	387,000,000	0.3%
4	Ohio	6,834,000,000	5.9%
28	Oklahoma	1,157,000,000	1.0%
33	Oregon	897,000,000	0.8%
3	Pennsylvania	7,562,000,000	6.6%
37	Rhode Island	616,000,000	0.5%
26	South Carolina	1,236,000,000	1.1%
41	South Dakota	406,000,000	0.4%
20	Tennessee	2,211,000,000	1.9%
6	Texas	5,600,000,000	4.9%
39	Utah	428,000,000	0.4%
48	Vermont	235,000,000	0.2%
15	Virginia	2,448,000,000	2.1%
21	Washington	1,860,000,000	1.6%
35	West Virginia	716,000,000	0.6%
17	Wisconsin	2,405,000,000	2.1%
49	Wyoming	150,000,000	0.1%

RANK ORDER

RANK	STATE	EXPENDITURES	% of USA
1	New York	$13,364,000,000	11.6%
2	California	8,424,000,000	7.3%
3	Pennsylvania	7,562,000,000	6.6%
4	Ohio	6,834,000,000	5.9%
5	Florida	6,503,000,000	5.7%
6	Texas	5,600,000,000	4.9%
7	Illinois	5,173,000,000	4.5%
8	New Jersey	4,261,000,000	3.7%
9	Massachusetts	4,124,000,000	3.6%
10	North Carolina	3,354,000,000	2.9%
11	Michigan	3,193,000,000	2.8%
12	Indiana	2,871,000,000	2.5%
13	Connecticut	2,711,000,000	2.4%
14	Missouri	2,479,000,000	2.2%
15	Virginia	2,448,000,000	2.1%
16	Maryland	2,419,000,000	2.1%
17	Wisconsin	2,405,000,000	2.1%
18	Minnesota	2,367,000,000	2.1%
19	Georgia	2,272,000,000	2.0%
20	Tennessee	2,211,000,000	1.9%
21	Washington	1,860,000,000	1.6%
22	Iowa	1,623,000,000	1.4%
23	Louisiana	1,617,000,000	1.4%
24	Kentucky	1,526,000,000	1.3%
25	Alabama	1,475,000,000	1.3%
26	South Carolina	1,236,000,000	1.1%
27	Colorado	1,178,000,000	1.0%
28	Oklahoma	1,157,000,000	1.0%
29	Kansas	1,110,000,000	1.0%
30	Mississippi	1,094,000,000	1.0%
31	Arkansas	1,040,000,000	0.9%
32	Arizona	1,023,000,000	0.9%
33	Oregon	897,000,000	0.8%
34	Nebraska	860,000,000	0.7%
35	West Virginia	716,000,000	0.6%
36	Maine	630,000,000	0.5%
37	Rhode Island	616,000,000	0.5%
38	New Hampshire	548,000,000	0.5%
39	Utah	428,000,000	0.4%
40	Delaware	409,000,000	0.4%
41	South Dakota	406,000,000	0.4%
42	North Dakota	387,000,000	0.3%
43	New Mexico	372,000,000	0.3%
44	Idaho	361,000,000	0.3%
45	Nevada	341,000,000	0.3%
46	Montana	322,000,000	0.3%
47	Hawaii	293,000,000	0.3%
48	Vermont	235,000,000	0.2%
49	Wyoming	150,000,000	0.1%
50	Alaska	80,000,000	0.1%
	District of Columbia	452,000,000	0.4%

Source: U.S. Department of Health and Human Services, Centers for Medicare and Medicaid Services
"State Health Care Expenditures" (http://www.cms.hhs.gov/NationalHealthExpendData/)
*By state of residence. Includes all freestanding nursing homes. Does not include nursing home services provided in long-term care units of hospitals.

Percent of Total Personal Health Care Expenditures
Spent on Nursing Home Care in 2004
National Percent = 7.4%*

ALPHA ORDER

RANK ORDER

RANK	STATE	PERCENT		RANK	STATE	PERCENT
33	Alabama	6.4		1	Connecticut	12.2
50	Alaska	1.9		2	New York	10.6
48	Arizona	4.3		3	North Dakota	10.5
15	Arkansas	7.8		4	Ohio	10.4
43	California	5.1		5	Pennsylvania	10.3
41	Colorado	5.4		6	Iowa	10.2
1	Connecticut	12.2		7	South Dakota	9.9
15	Delaware	7.8		8	Massachusetts	9.6
27	Florida	6.8		9	Rhode Island	9.2
40	Georgia	5.5		10	Nebraska	8.8
45	Hawaii	4.7		11	Indiana	8.7
37	Idaho	5.8		12	New Jersey	8.5
19	Illinois	7.7		13	Minnesota	8.0
11	Indiana	8.7		14	Missouri	7.9
6	Iowa	10.2		15	Arkansas	7.8
22	Kansas	7.5		15	Delaware	7.8
30	Kentucky	6.7		15	Maryland	7.8
25	Louisiana	7.1		15	New Hampshire	7.8
24	Maine	7.3		19	Illinois	7.7
15	Maryland	7.8		19	Wisconsin	7.7
8	Massachusetts	9.6		21	North Carolina	7.6
34	Michigan	6.3		22	Kansas	7.5
13	Minnesota	8.0		22	Mississippi	7.5
22	Mississippi	7.5		24	Maine	7.3
14	Missouri	7.9		25	Louisiana	7.1
27	Montana	6.8		26	Tennessee	6.9
10	Nebraska	8.8		27	Florida	6.8
49	Nevada	3.2		27	Montana	6.8
15	New Hampshire	7.8		27	Virginia	6.8
12	New Jersey	8.5		30	Kentucky	6.7
46	New Mexico	4.4		30	Oklahoma	6.7
2	New York	10.6		32	West Virginia	6.6
21	North Carolina	7.6		33	Alabama	6.4
3	North Dakota	10.5		34	Michigan	6.3
4	Ohio	10.4		35	Vermont	6.2
30	Oklahoma	6.7		36	Washington	5.9
43	Oregon	5.1		37	Idaho	5.8
5	Pennsylvania	10.3		37	South Carolina	5.8
9	Rhode Island	9.2		39	Wyoming	5.6
37	South Carolina	5.8		40	Georgia	5.5
7	South Dakota	9.9		41	Colorado	5.4
26	Tennessee	6.9		41	Texas	5.4
41	Texas	5.4		43	California	5.1
46	Utah	4.4		43	Oregon	5.1
35	Vermont	6.2		45	Hawaii	4.7
27	Virginia	6.8		46	New Mexico	4.4
36	Washington	5.9		46	Utah	4.4
32	West Virginia	6.6		48	Arizona	4.3
19	Wisconsin	7.7		49	Nevada	3.2
39	Wyoming	5.6		50	Alaska	1.9

District of Columbia 9.4

Source: CQ Press using data from U.S. Department of Health and Human Services, Centers for Medicare and Medicaid Services
"State Health Care Expenditures" (http://www.cms.hhs.gov/NationalHealthExpendData/)
*By state of residence. Includes all freestanding nursing homes. Does not include nursing home services provided in long-term care units of hospitals.

Per Capita Expenditures for Nursing Home Care in 2004

National Per Capita = $392*

ALPHA ORDER

RANK ORDER

RANK	STATE	PER CAPITA		RANK	STATE	PER CAPITA
34	Alabama	$326		1	Connecticut	$776
50	Alaska	122		2	New York	693
47	Arizona	178		3	Massachusetts	641
24	Arkansas	378		4	Pennsylvania	611
44	California	235		5	North Dakota	608
40	Colorado	256		6	Ohio	596
1	Connecticut	776		7	Rhode Island	570
10	Delaware	493		8	Iowa	549
28	Florida	374		9	South Dakota	527
41	Georgia	254		10	Delaware	493
45	Hawaii	233		11	Nebraska	492
39	Idaho	259		12	New Jersey	491
20	Illinois	407		13	Maine	480
15	Indiana	461		14	Minnesota	465
8	Iowa	549		15	Indiana	461
21	Kansas	406		16	Wisconsin	437
29	Kentucky	369		17	Maryland	436
30	Louisiana	360		18	Missouri	431
13	Maine	480		19	New Hampshire	422
17	Maryland	436		20	Illinois	407
3	Massachusetts	641		21	Kansas	406
35	Michigan	316		22	West Virginia	395
14	Minnesota	465		23	North Carolina	393
24	Mississippi	378		24	Arkansas	378
18	Missouri	431		24	Mississippi	378
31	Montana	348		24	Vermont	378
11	Nebraska	492		27	Tennessee	376
49	Nevada	146		28	Florida	374
19	New Hampshire	422		29	Kentucky	369
12	New Jersey	491		30	Louisiana	360
46	New Mexico	196		31	Montana	348
2	New York	693		32	Oklahoma	329
23	North Carolina	393		33	Virginia	328
5	North Dakota	608		34	Alabama	326
6	Ohio	596		35	Michigan	316
32	Oklahoma	329		36	Washington	300
42	Oregon	250		37	Wyoming	297
4	Pennsylvania	611		38	South Carolina	295
7	Rhode Island	570		39	Idaho	259
38	South Carolina	295		40	Colorado	256
9	South Dakota	527		41	Georgia	254
27	Tennessee	376		42	Oregon	250
43	Texas	249		43	Texas	249
48	Utah	177		44	California	235
24	Vermont	378		45	Hawaii	233
33	Virginia	328		46	New Mexico	196
36	Washington	300		47	Arizona	178
22	West Virginia	395		48	Utah	177
16	Wisconsin	437		49	Nevada	146
37	Wyoming	297		50	Alaska	122

District of Columbia   780

Source: U.S. Department of Health and Human Services, Centers for Medicare and Medicaid Services
   "State Health Care Expenditures" (http://www.cms.hhs.gov/NationalHealthExpendData/)
*By state of residence. Includes all freestanding nursing homes. Does not include nursing home services provided in long-term care units of hospitals.

Expenditures for Home Health Care in 2004

National Total = $42,710,000,000*

ALPHA ORDER

RANK	STATE	EXPENDITURES	% of USA
18	Alabama	$661,000,000	1.5%
47	Alaska	64,000,000	0.1%
19	Arizona	656,000,000	1.5%
31	Arkansas	325,000,000	0.8%
2	California	5,537,000,000	13.0%
30	Colorado	367,000,000	0.9%
15	Connecticut	708,000,000	1.7%
43	Delaware	94,000,000	0.2%
4	Florida	2,876,000,000	6.7%
12	Georgia	876,000,000	2.1%
42	Hawaii	105,000,000	0.2%
41	Idaho	115,000,000	0.3%
11	Illinois	1,269,000,000	3.0%
25	Indiana	509,000,000	1.2%
32	Iowa	310,000,000	0.7%
34	Kansas	241,000,000	0.6%
23	Kentucky	531,000,000	1.2%
21	Louisiana	624,000,000	1.5%
38	Maine	173,000,000	0.4%
24	Maryland	511,000,000	1.2%
5	Massachusetts	1,743,000,000	4.1%
10	Michigan	1,326,000,000	3.1%
17	Minnesota	679,000,000	1.6%
26	Mississippi	484,000,000	1.1%
15	Missouri	708,000,000	1.7%
45	Montana	89,000,000	0.2%
46	Nebraska	79,000,000	0.2%
35	Nevada	231,000,000	0.5%
39	New Hampshire	168,000,000	0.4%
8	New Jersey	1,427,000,000	3.3%
28	New Mexico	451,000,000	1.1%
1	New York	6,021,000,000	14.1%
9	North Carolina	1,413,000,000	3.3%
50	North Dakota	18,000,000	0.0%
7	Ohio	1,519,000,000	3.6%
27	Oklahoma	464,000,000	1.1%
36	Oregon	201,000,000	0.5%
6	Pennsylvania	1,527,000,000	3.6%
40	Rhode Island	116,000,000	0.3%
29	South Carolina	422,000,000	1.0%
49	South Dakota	20,000,000	0.0%
14	Tennessee	738,000,000	1.7%
3	Texas	3,604,000,000	8.4%
33	Utah	245,000,000	0.6%
43	Vermont	94,000,000	0.2%
22	Virginia	605,000,000	1.4%
13	Washington	823,000,000	1.9%
37	West Virginia	197,000,000	0.5%
20	Wisconsin	642,000,000	1.5%
48	Wyoming	28,000,000	0.1%

RANK ORDER

RANK	STATE	EXPENDITURES	% of USA
1	New York	$6,021,000,000	14.1%
2	California	5,537,000,000	13.0%
3	Texas	3,604,000,000	8.4%
4	Florida	2,876,000,000	6.7%
5	Massachusetts	1,743,000,000	4.1%
6	Pennsylvania	1,527,000,000	3.6%
7	Ohio	1,519,000,000	3.6%
8	New Jersey	1,427,000,000	3.3%
9	North Carolina	1,413,000,000	3.3%
10	Michigan	1,326,000,000	3.1%
11	Illinois	1,269,000,000	3.0%
12	Georgia	876,000,000	2.1%
13	Washington	823,000,000	1.9%
14	Tennessee	738,000,000	1.7%
15	Connecticut	708,000,000	1.7%
15	Missouri	708,000,000	1.7%
17	Minnesota	679,000,000	1.6%
18	Alabama	661,000,000	1.5%
19	Arizona	656,000,000	1.5%
20	Wisconsin	642,000,000	1.5%
21	Louisiana	624,000,000	1.5%
22	Virginia	605,000,000	1.4%
23	Kentucky	531,000,000	1.2%
24	Maryland	511,000,000	1.2%
25	Indiana	509,000,000	1.2%
26	Mississippi	484,000,000	1.1%
27	Oklahoma	464,000,000	1.1%
28	New Mexico	451,000,000	1.1%
29	South Carolina	422,000,000	1.0%
30	Colorado	367,000,000	0.9%
31	Arkansas	325,000,000	0.8%
32	Iowa	310,000,000	0.7%
33	Utah	245,000,000	0.6%
34	Kansas	241,000,000	0.6%
35	Nevada	231,000,000	0.5%
36	Oregon	201,000,000	0.5%
37	West Virginia	197,000,000	0.5%
38	Maine	173,000,000	0.4%
39	New Hampshire	168,000,000	0.4%
40	Rhode Island	116,000,000	0.3%
41	Idaho	115,000,000	0.3%
42	Hawaii	105,000,000	0.2%
43	Delaware	94,000,000	0.2%
43	Vermont	94,000,000	0.2%
45	Montana	89,000,000	0.2%
46	Nebraska	79,000,000	0.2%
47	Alaska	64,000,000	0.1%
48	Wyoming	28,000,000	0.1%
49	South Dakota	20,000,000	0.0%
50	North Dakota	18,000,000	0.0%
	District of Columbia	78,000,000	0.2%

Source: U.S. Department of Health and Human Services, Centers for Medicare and Medicaid Services
"State Health Care Expenditures" (http://www.cms.hhs.gov/NationalHealthExpendData/)
*By state of residence. Includes spending for services and products by public and private freestanding home health agencies.
Excludes home health care services provided by hospital-based agencies which are included in hospital expenditures.

Percent of Total Personal Health Care Expenditures
Spent on Home Health Care in 2004
National Percent = 2.8%*

RANK	STATE	PERCENT
10	Alabama	2.8
44	Alaska	1.5
10	Arizona	2.8
19	Arkansas	2.4
5	California	3.3
38	Colorado	1.7
7	Connecticut	3.2
36	Delaware	1.8
9	Florida	3.0
27	Georgia	2.1
38	Hawaii	1.7
33	Idaho	1.9
33	Illinois	1.9
44	Indiana	1.5
30	Iowa	2.0
42	Kansas	1.6
21	Kentucky	2.3
10	Louisiana	2.8
30	Maine	2.0
42	Maryland	1.6
3	Massachusetts	4.1
15	Michigan	2.6
21	Minnesota	2.3
5	Mississippi	3.3
21	Missouri	2.3
33	Montana	1.9
48	Nebraska	0.8
26	Nevada	2.2
19	New Hampshire	2.4
10	New Jersey	2.8
1	New Mexico	5.3
2	New York	4.8
7	North Carolina	3.2
49	North Dakota	0.5
21	Ohio	2.3
14	Oklahoma	2.7
46	Oregon	1.1
27	Pennsylvania	2.1
38	Rhode Island	1.7
30	South Carolina	2.0
49	South Dakota	0.5
21	Tennessee	2.3
4	Texas	3.5
17	Utah	2.5
17	Vermont	2.5
38	Virginia	1.7
15	Washington	2.6
36	West Virginia	1.8
27	Wisconsin	2.1
46	Wyoming	1.1

RANK	STATE	PERCENT
1	New Mexico	5.3
2	New York	4.8
3	Massachusetts	4.1
4	Texas	3.5
5	California	3.3
5	Mississippi	3.3
7	Connecticut	3.2
7	North Carolina	3.2
9	Florida	3.0
10	Alabama	2.8
10	Arizona	2.8
10	Louisiana	2.8
10	New Jersey	2.8
14	Oklahoma	2.7
15	Michigan	2.6
15	Washington	2.6
17	Utah	2.5
17	Vermont	2.5
19	Arkansas	2.4
19	New Hampshire	2.4
21	Kentucky	2.3
21	Minnesota	2.3
21	Missouri	2.3
21	Ohio	2.3
21	Tennessee	2.3
26	Nevada	2.2
27	Georgia	2.1
27	Pennsylvania	2.1
27	Wisconsin	2.1
30	Iowa	2.0
30	Maine	2.0
30	South Carolina	2.0
33	Idaho	1.9
33	Illinois	1.9
33	Montana	1.9
36	Delaware	1.8
36	West Virginia	1.8
38	Colorado	1.7
38	Hawaii	1.7
38	Rhode Island	1.7
38	Virginia	1.7
42	Kansas	1.6
42	Maryland	1.6
44	Alaska	1.5
44	Indiana	1.5
46	Oregon	1.1
46	Wyoming	1.1
48	Nebraska	0.8
49	North Dakota	0.5
49	South Dakota	0.5

| | District of Columbia | 1.6 |

Source: CQ Press using data from U.S. Department of Health and Human Services, Centers for Medicare and Medicaid Services
"State Health Care Expenditures" (http://www.cms.hhs.gov/NationalHealthExpendData/)
*By state of residence. Includes spending for services and products by public and private freestanding home health agencies.
Excludes home health care services provided by hospital-based agencies which are included in hospital expenditures.

Per Capita Expenditures for Home Health Care in 2004

National Per Capita = $145*

<table>
<tr><td colspan="3">ALPHA ORDER</td><td colspan="3">RANK ORDER</td></tr>
<tr><td>RANK</td><td>STATE</td><td>PER CAPITA</td><td>RANK</td><td>STATE</td><td>PER CAPITA</td></tr>
<tr><td>12</td><td>Alabama</td><td>$146</td><td>1</td><td>New York</td><td>$312</td></tr>
<tr><td>36</td><td>Alaska</td><td>98</td><td>2</td><td>Massachusetts</td><td>271</td></tr>
<tr><td>27</td><td>Arizona</td><td>114</td><td>3</td><td>New Mexico</td><td>237</td></tr>
<tr><td>25</td><td>Arkansas</td><td>118</td><td>4</td><td>Connecticut</td><td>203</td></tr>
<tr><td>10</td><td>California</td><td>154</td><td>5</td><td>Mississippi</td><td>167</td></tr>
<tr><td>45</td><td>Colorado</td><td>80</td><td>6</td><td>Florida</td><td>166</td></tr>
<tr><td>4</td><td>Connecticut</td><td>203</td><td>6</td><td>North Carolina</td><td>166</td></tr>
<tr><td>28</td><td>Delaware</td><td>113</td><td>8</td><td>New Jersey</td><td>164</td></tr>
<tr><td>6</td><td>Florida</td><td>166</td><td>9</td><td>Texas</td><td>160</td></tr>
<tr><td>36</td><td>Georgia</td><td>98</td><td>10</td><td>California</td><td>154</td></tr>
<tr><td>41</td><td>Hawaii</td><td>84</td><td>11</td><td>Vermont</td><td>152</td></tr>
<tr><td>42</td><td>Idaho</td><td>82</td><td>12</td><td>Alabama</td><td>146</td></tr>
<tr><td>34</td><td>Illinois</td><td>100</td><td>13</td><td>Louisiana</td><td>139</td></tr>
<tr><td>42</td><td>Indiana</td><td>82</td><td>14</td><td>Minnesota</td><td>133</td></tr>
<tr><td>31</td><td>Iowa</td><td>105</td><td>14</td><td>Ohio</td><td>133</td></tr>
<tr><td>40</td><td>Kansas</td><td>88</td><td>14</td><td>Washington</td><td>133</td></tr>
<tr><td>21</td><td>Kentucky</td><td>128</td><td>17</td><td>Maine</td><td>132</td></tr>
<tr><td>13</td><td>Louisiana</td><td>139</td><td>17</td><td>Oklahoma</td><td>132</td></tr>
<tr><td>17</td><td>Maine</td><td>132</td><td>19</td><td>Michigan</td><td>131</td></tr>
<tr><td>39</td><td>Maryland</td><td>92</td><td>20</td><td>New Hampshire</td><td>130</td></tr>
<tr><td>2</td><td>Massachusetts</td><td>271</td><td>21</td><td>Kentucky</td><td>128</td></tr>
<tr><td>19</td><td>Michigan</td><td>131</td><td>22</td><td>Tennessee</td><td>125</td></tr>
<tr><td>14</td><td>Minnesota</td><td>133</td><td>23</td><td>Missouri</td><td>123</td></tr>
<tr><td>5</td><td>Mississippi</td><td>167</td><td>23</td><td>Pennsylvania</td><td>123</td></tr>
<tr><td>23</td><td>Missouri</td><td>123</td><td>25</td><td>Arkansas</td><td>118</td></tr>
<tr><td>38</td><td>Montana</td><td>96</td><td>26</td><td>Wisconsin</td><td>117</td></tr>
<tr><td>48</td><td>Nebraska</td><td>45</td><td>27</td><td>Arizona</td><td>114</td></tr>
<tr><td>35</td><td>Nevada</td><td>99</td><td>28</td><td>Delaware</td><td>113</td></tr>
<tr><td>20</td><td>New Hampshire</td><td>130</td><td>29</td><td>West Virginia</td><td>109</td></tr>
<tr><td>8</td><td>New Jersey</td><td>164</td><td>30</td><td>Rhode Island</td><td>107</td></tr>
<tr><td>3</td><td>New Mexico</td><td>237</td><td>31</td><td>Iowa</td><td>105</td></tr>
<tr><td>1</td><td>New York</td><td>312</td><td>32</td><td>South Carolina</td><td>101</td></tr>
<tr><td>6</td><td>North Carolina</td><td>166</td><td>32</td><td>Utah</td><td>101</td></tr>
<tr><td>49</td><td>North Dakota</td><td>28</td><td>34</td><td>Illinois</td><td>100</td></tr>
<tr><td>14</td><td>Ohio</td><td>133</td><td>35</td><td>Nevada</td><td>99</td></tr>
<tr><td>17</td><td>Oklahoma</td><td>132</td><td>36</td><td>Alaska</td><td>98</td></tr>
<tr><td>46</td><td>Oregon</td><td>56</td><td>36</td><td>Georgia</td><td>98</td></tr>
<tr><td>23</td><td>Pennsylvania</td><td>123</td><td>38</td><td>Montana</td><td>96</td></tr>
<tr><td>30</td><td>Rhode Island</td><td>107</td><td>39</td><td>Maryland</td><td>92</td></tr>
<tr><td>32</td><td>South Carolina</td><td>101</td><td>40</td><td>Kansas</td><td>88</td></tr>
<tr><td>50</td><td>South Dakota</td><td>26</td><td>41</td><td>Hawaii</td><td>84</td></tr>
<tr><td>22</td><td>Tennessee</td><td>125</td><td>42</td><td>Idaho</td><td>82</td></tr>
<tr><td>9</td><td>Texas</td><td>160</td><td>42</td><td>Indiana</td><td>82</td></tr>
<tr><td>32</td><td>Utah</td><td>101</td><td>44</td><td>Virginia</td><td>81</td></tr>
<tr><td>11</td><td>Vermont</td><td>152</td><td>45</td><td>Colorado</td><td>80</td></tr>
<tr><td>44</td><td>Virginia</td><td>81</td><td>46</td><td>Oregon</td><td>56</td></tr>
<tr><td>14</td><td>Washington</td><td>133</td><td>47</td><td>Wyoming</td><td>55</td></tr>
<tr><td>29</td><td>West Virginia</td><td>109</td><td>48</td><td>Nebraska</td><td>45</td></tr>
<tr><td>26</td><td>Wisconsin</td><td>117</td><td>49</td><td>North Dakota</td><td>28</td></tr>
<tr><td>47</td><td>Wyoming</td><td>55</td><td>50</td><td>South Dakota</td><td>26</td></tr>
<tr><td></td><td></td><td></td><td></td><td>District of Columbia</td><td>134</td></tr>
</table>

Source: U.S. Department of Health and Human Services, Centers for Medicare and Medicaid Services
"State Health Care Expenditures" (http://www.cms.hhs.gov/NationalHealthExpendData/)
*By state of residence. Includes spending for services and products by public and private freestanding home health agencies.
Excludes home health care services provided by hospital-based agencies which are included in hospital expenditures.

Expenditures for Drugs and Other Medical Nondurables in 2004

National Total = $222,412,000,000*

ALPHA ORDER					RANK ORDER			

RANK	STATE	EXPENDITURES	% of USA		RANK	STATE	EXPENDITURES	% of USA
18	Alabama	$4,241,000,000	1.9%		1	California	$20,799,000,000	9.4%
49	Alaska	418,000,000	0.2%		2	New York	17,722,000,000	8.0%
24	Arizona	3,378,000,000	1.5%		3	Florida	15,545,000,000	7.0%
32	Arkansas	1,938,000,000	0.9%		4	Texas	13,870,000,000	6.2%
1	California	20,799,000,000	9.4%		5	Pennsylvania	11,086,000,000	5.0%
28	Colorado	2,346,000,000	1.1%		6	Ohio	9,205,000,000	4.1%
26	Connecticut	3,246,000,000	1.5%		7	Illinois	9,098,000,000	4.1%
44	Delaware	769,000,000	0.3%		8	New Jersey	8,317,000,000	3.7%
3	Florida	15,545,000,000	7.0%		9	Michigan	7,790,000,000	3.5%
11	Georgia	6,493,000,000	2.9%		10	North Carolina	7,445,000,000	3.3%
42	Hawaii	925,000,000	0.4%		11	Georgia	6,493,000,000	2.9%
43	Idaho	834,000,000	0.4%		12	Tennessee	5,785,000,000	2.6%
7	Illinois	9,098,000,000	4.1%		13	Virginia	5,651,000,000	2.5%
15	Indiana	4,951,000,000	2.2%		14	Massachusetts	5,462,000,000	2.5%
31	Iowa	2,021,000,000	0.9%		15	Indiana	4,951,000,000	2.2%
33	Kansas	1,897,000,000	0.9%		16	Missouri	4,664,000,000	2.1%
19	Kentucky	3,917,000,000	1.8%		17	Maryland	4,595,000,000	2.1%
23	Louisiana	3,586,000,000	1.6%		18	Alabama	4,241,000,000	1.9%
40	Maine	1,052,000,000	0.5%		19	Kentucky	3,917,000,000	1.8%
17	Maryland	4,595,000,000	2.1%		20	Wisconsin	3,831,000,000	1.7%
14	Massachusetts	5,462,000,000	2.5%		21	Washington	3,792,000,000	1.7%
9	Michigan	7,790,000,000	3.5%		22	Minnesota	3,639,000,000	1.6%
22	Minnesota	3,639,000,000	1.6%		23	Louisiana	3,586,000,000	1.6%
29	Mississippi	2,208,000,000	1.0%		24	Arizona	3,378,000,000	1.5%
16	Missouri	4,664,000,000	2.1%		25	South Carolina	3,369,000,000	1.5%
46	Montana	499,000,000	0.2%		26	Connecticut	3,246,000,000	1.5%
37	Nebraska	1,288,000,000	0.6%		27	Oklahoma	2,472,000,000	1.1%
34	Nevada	1,786,000,000	0.8%		28	Colorado	2,346,000,000	1.1%
41	New Hampshire	962,000,000	0.4%		29	Mississippi	2,208,000,000	1.0%
8	New Jersey	8,317,000,000	3.7%		30	Oregon	2,042,000,000	0.9%
38	New Mexico	1,127,000,000	0.5%		31	Iowa	2,021,000,000	0.9%
2	New York	17,722,000,000	8.0%		32	Arkansas	1,938,000,000	0.9%
10	North Carolina	7,445,000,000	3.3%		33	Kansas	1,897,000,000	0.9%
45	North Dakota	537,000,000	0.2%		34	Nevada	1,786,000,000	0.8%
6	Ohio	9,205,000,000	4.1%		35	West Virginia	1,627,000,000	0.7%
27	Oklahoma	2,472,000,000	1.1%		36	Utah	1,592,000,000	0.7%
30	Oregon	2,042,000,000	0.9%		37	Nebraska	1,288,000,000	0.6%
5	Pennsylvania	11,086,000,000	5.0%		38	New Mexico	1,127,000,000	0.5%
39	Rhode Island	1,066,000,000	0.5%		39	Rhode Island	1,066,000,000	0.5%
25	South Carolina	3,369,000,000	1.5%		40	Maine	1,052,000,000	0.5%
48	South Dakota	440,000,000	0.2%		41	New Hampshire	962,000,000	0.4%
12	Tennessee	5,785,000,000	2.6%		42	Hawaii	925,000,000	0.4%
4	Texas	13,870,000,000	6.2%		43	Idaho	834,000,000	0.4%
36	Utah	1,592,000,000	0.7%		44	Delaware	769,000,000	0.3%
47	Vermont	444,000,000	0.2%		45	North Dakota	537,000,000	0.2%
13	Virginia	5,651,000,000	2.5%		46	Montana	499,000,000	0.2%
21	Washington	3,792,000,000	1.7%		47	Vermont	444,000,000	0.2%
35	West Virginia	1,627,000,000	0.7%		48	South Dakota	440,000,000	0.2%
20	Wisconsin	3,831,000,000	1.7%		49	Alaska	418,000,000	0.2%
50	Wyoming	302,000,000	0.1%		50	Wyoming	302,000,000	0.1%
						District of Columbia	345,000,000	0.2%

Source: U.S. Department of Health and Human Services, Centers for Medicare and Medicaid Services
"State Health Care Expenditures" (http://www.cms.hhs.gov/NationalHealthExpendData/)
*Purchases in retail outlets. By state of residence. Includes prescription drugs, over-the-counter drugs, and sundries.

Percent of Total Personal Health Care Expenditures
Spent on Drugs and Other Medical Nondurables in 2004
National Percent = 14.3%*

ALPHA ORDER

RANK	STATE	PERCENT
1	Alabama	18.3
50	Alaska	9.9
26	Arizona	14.3
24	Arkansas	14.5
39	California	12.5
47	Colorado	10.8
23	Connecticut	14.6
22	Delaware	14.7
8	Florida	16.3
10	Georgia	15.8
19	Hawaii	14.9
31	Idaho	13.5
31	Illinois	13.5
18	Indiana	15.0
37	Iowa	12.7
36	Kansas	12.9
3	Kentucky	17.3
10	Louisiana	15.8
42	Maine	12.2
21	Maryland	14.8
37	Massachusetts	12.7
14	Michigan	15.3
40	Minnesota	12.3
15	Mississippi	15.1
19	Missouri	14.9
49	Montana	10.6
35	Nebraska	13.2
4	Nevada	16.8
30	New Hampshire	13.6
7	New Jersey	16.5
34	New Mexico	13.3
28	New York	14.1
4	North Carolina	16.8
24	North Dakota	14.5
29	Ohio	14.0
26	Oklahoma	14.3
45	Oregon	11.7
15	Pennsylvania	15.1
9	Rhode Island	16.0
12	South Carolina	15.7
48	South Dakota	10.7
2	Tennessee	18.0
33	Texas	13.4
6	Utah	16.6
44	Vermont	11.8
12	Virginia	15.7
43	Washington	12.0
15	West Virginia	15.1
40	Wisconsin	12.3
46	Wyoming	11.3

RANK ORDER

RANK	STATE	PERCENT
1	Alabama	18.3
2	Tennessee	18.0
3	Kentucky	17.3
4	Nevada	16.8
4	North Carolina	16.8
6	Utah	16.6
7	New Jersey	16.5
8	Florida	16.3
9	Rhode Island	16.0
10	Georgia	15.8
10	Louisiana	15.8
12	South Carolina	15.7
12	Virginia	15.7
14	Michigan	15.3
15	Mississippi	15.1
15	Pennsylvania	15.1
15	West Virginia	15.1
18	Indiana	15.0
19	Hawaii	14.9
19	Missouri	14.9
21	Maryland	14.8
22	Delaware	14.7
23	Connecticut	14.6
24	Arkansas	14.5
24	North Dakota	14.5
26	Arizona	14.3
26	Oklahoma	14.3
28	New York	14.1
29	Ohio	14.0
30	New Hampshire	13.6
31	Idaho	13.5
31	Illinois	13.5
33	Texas	13.4
34	New Mexico	13.3
35	Nebraska	13.2
36	Kansas	12.9
37	Iowa	12.7
37	Massachusetts	12.7
39	California	12.5
40	Minnesota	12.3
40	Wisconsin	12.3
42	Maine	12.2
43	Washington	12.0
44	Vermont	11.8
45	Oregon	11.7
46	Wyoming	11.3
47	Colorado	10.8
48	South Dakota	10.7
49	Montana	10.6
50	Alaska	9.9

| District of Columbia | | 7.2 |

Source: CQ Press using data from U.S. Department of Health and Human Services, Centers for Medicare and Medicaid Services
"State Health Care Expenditures" (http://www.cms.hhs.gov/NationalHealthExpendData/)
*Purchases in retail outlets. By state of residence. Includes prescription drugs, over-the-counter drugs, and sundries.

Per Capita Expenditures for Drugs and Other Medical Nondurables in 2004

National Per Capita = $757*

ALPHA ORDER

RANK	STATE	PER CAPITA
5	Alabama	$939
39	Alaska	636
45	Arizona	588
33	Arkansas	705
46	California	580
50	Colorado	510
6	Connecticut	929
7	Delaware	928
11	Florida	895
29	Georgia	727
28	Hawaii	734
42	Idaho	598
30	Illinois	716
21	Indiana	796
37	Iowa	684
36	Kansas	693
4	Kentucky	946
20	Louisiana	798
19	Maine	800
15	Maryland	827
13	Massachusetts	849
22	Michigan	772
32	Minnesota	714
24	Mississippi	763
16	Missouri	811
49	Montana	539
27	Nebraska	737
23	Nevada	766
26	New Hampshire	741
3	New Jersey	959
44	New Mexico	593
8	New York	919
12	North Carolina	873
14	North Dakota	845
17	Ohio	803
34	Oklahoma	702
48	Oregon	569
10	Pennsylvania	896
1	Rhode Island	988
17	South Carolina	803
47	South Dakota	572
2	Tennessee	983
40	Texas	616
38	Utah	658
31	Vermont	715
25	Virginia	756
41	Washington	611
9	West Virginia	898
35	Wisconsin	697
43	Wyoming	597

RANK ORDER

RANK	STATE	PER CAPITA
1	Rhode Island	$988
2	Tennessee	983
3	New Jersey	959
4	Kentucky	946
5	Alabama	939
6	Connecticut	929
7	Delaware	928
8	New York	919
9	West Virginia	898
10	Pennsylvania	896
11	Florida	895
12	North Carolina	873
13	Massachusetts	849
14	North Dakota	845
15	Maryland	827
16	Missouri	811
17	Ohio	803
17	South Carolina	803
19	Maine	800
20	Louisiana	798
21	Indiana	796
22	Michigan	772
23	Nevada	766
24	Mississippi	763
25	Virginia	756
26	New Hampshire	741
27	Nebraska	737
28	Hawaii	734
29	Georgia	727
30	Illinois	716
31	Vermont	715
32	Minnesota	714
33	Arkansas	705
34	Oklahoma	702
35	Wisconsin	697
36	Kansas	693
37	Iowa	684
38	Utah	658
39	Alaska	636
40	Texas	616
41	Washington	611
42	Idaho	598
43	Wyoming	597
44	New Mexico	593
45	Arizona	588
46	California	580
47	South Dakota	572
48	Oregon	569
49	Montana	539
50	Colorado	510
	District of Columbia	594

Source: U.S. Department of Health and Human Services, Centers for Medicare and Medicaid Services
"State Health Care Expenditures" (http://www.cms.hhs.gov/NationalHealthExpendData/)
*Purchases in retail outlets. By state of residence. Includes prescription drugs, over-the-counter drugs, and sundries.

Expenditures for Durable Medical Products in 2004

National Total = $23,128,000,000*

ALPHA ORDER

RANK	STATE	EXPENDITURES	% of USA
24	Alabama	$316,000,000	1.4%
46	Alaska	61,000,000	0.3%
21	Arizona	422,000,000	1.8%
36	Arkansas	164,000,000	0.7%
1	California	2,552,000,000	11.0%
18	Colorado	440,000,000	1.9%
23	Connecticut	317,000,000	1.4%
44	Delaware	78,000,000	0.3%
4	Florida	1,574,000,000	6.8%
11	Georgia	619,000,000	2.7%
39	Hawaii	118,000,000	0.5%
41	Idaho	101,000,000	0.4%
6	Illinois	987,000,000	4.3%
16	Indiana	470,000,000	2.0%
29	Iowa	261,000,000	1.1%
32	Kansas	215,000,000	0.9%
25	Kentucky	281,000,000	1.2%
28	Louisiana	272,000,000	1.2%
42	Maine	92,000,000	0.4%
13	Maryland	503,000,000	2.2%
14	Massachusetts	501,000,000	2.2%
9	Michigan	779,000,000	3.4%
17	Minnesota	456,000,000	2.0%
34	Mississippi	172,000,000	0.7%
20	Missouri	424,000,000	1.8%
43	Montana	85,000,000	0.4%
29	Nebraska	261,000,000	1.1%
33	Nevada	211,000,000	0.9%
40	New Hampshire	116,000,000	0.5%
7	New Jersey	964,000,000	4.2%
37	New Mexico	141,000,000	0.6%
2	New York	1,685,000,000	7.3%
12	North Carolina	524,000,000	2.3%
48	North Dakota	55,000,000	0.2%
8	Ohio	880,000,000	3.8%
31	Oklahoma	239,000,000	1.0%
26	Oregon	279,000,000	1.2%
5	Pennsylvania	1,026,000,000	4.4%
45	Rhode Island	62,000,000	0.3%
27	South Carolina	275,000,000	1.2%
47	South Dakota	60,000,000	0.3%
19	Tennessee	431,000,000	1.9%
3	Texas	1,678,000,000	7.3%
35	Utah	171,000,000	0.7%
50	Vermont	44,000,000	0.2%
10	Virginia	630,000,000	2.7%
15	Washington	485,000,000	2.1%
38	West Virginia	129,000,000	0.6%
22	Wisconsin	419,000,000	1.8%
49	Wyoming	47,000,000	0.2%

RANK ORDER

RANK	STATE	EXPENDITURES	% of USA
1	California	$2,552,000,000	11.0%
2	New York	1,685,000,000	7.3%
3	Texas	1,678,000,000	7.3%
4	Florida	1,574,000,000	6.8%
5	Pennsylvania	1,026,000,000	4.4%
6	Illinois	987,000,000	4.3%
7	New Jersey	964,000,000	4.2%
8	Ohio	880,000,000	3.8%
9	Michigan	779,000,000	3.4%
10	Virginia	630,000,000	2.7%
11	Georgia	619,000,000	2.7%
12	North Carolina	524,000,000	2.3%
13	Maryland	503,000,000	2.2%
14	Massachusetts	501,000,000	2.2%
15	Washington	485,000,000	2.1%
16	Indiana	470,000,000	2.0%
17	Minnesota	456,000,000	2.0%
18	Colorado	440,000,000	1.9%
19	Tennessee	431,000,000	1.9%
20	Missouri	424,000,000	1.8%
21	Arizona	422,000,000	1.8%
22	Wisconsin	419,000,000	1.8%
23	Connecticut	317,000,000	1.4%
24	Alabama	316,000,000	1.4%
25	Kentucky	281,000,000	1.2%
26	Oregon	279,000,000	1.2%
27	South Carolina	275,000,000	1.2%
28	Louisiana	272,000,000	1.2%
29	Iowa	261,000,000	1.1%
29	Nebraska	261,000,000	1.1%
31	Oklahoma	239,000,000	1.0%
32	Kansas	215,000,000	0.9%
33	Nevada	211,000,000	0.9%
34	Mississippi	172,000,000	0.7%
35	Utah	171,000,000	0.7%
36	Arkansas	164,000,000	0.7%
37	New Mexico	141,000,000	0.6%
38	West Virginia	129,000,000	0.6%
39	Hawaii	118,000,000	0.5%
40	New Hampshire	116,000,000	0.5%
41	Idaho	101,000,000	0.4%
42	Maine	92,000,000	0.4%
43	Montana	85,000,000	0.4%
44	Delaware	78,000,000	0.3%
45	Rhode Island	62,000,000	0.3%
46	Alaska	61,000,000	0.3%
47	South Dakota	60,000,000	0.3%
48	North Dakota	55,000,000	0.2%
49	Wyoming	47,000,000	0.2%
50	Vermont	44,000,000	0.2%
	District of Columbia	59,000,000	0.3%

Source: U.S. Department of Health and Human Services, Centers for Medicare and Medicaid Services
"State Health Care Expenditures" (http://www.cms.hhs.gov/NationalHealthExpendData/)
*By state of residence. Includes eyeglasses, hearing aids, surgical appliances and supplies, bulk and cylinder oxygen, and medical equipment rentals.

Percent of Total Personal Health Care Expenditures Spent on Durable Medical Products in 2004
National Percent = 1.5%*

<table>
<tr><td colspan="3">ALPHA ORDER</td><td colspan="3">RANK ORDER</td></tr>
<tr><td>RANK</td><td>STATE</td><td>PERCENT</td><td>RANK</td><td>STATE</td><td>PERCENT</td></tr>
<tr><td>29</td><td>Alabama</td><td>1.4</td><td>1</td><td>Nebraska</td><td>2.7</td></tr>
<tr><td>29</td><td>Alaska</td><td>1.4</td><td>2</td><td>Colorado</td><td>2.0</td></tr>
<tr><td>6</td><td>Arizona</td><td>1.8</td><td>2</td><td>Nevada</td><td>2.0</td></tr>
<tr><td>41</td><td>Arkansas</td><td>1.2</td><td>4</td><td>Hawaii</td><td>1.9</td></tr>
<tr><td>19</td><td>California</td><td>1.5</td><td>4</td><td>New Jersey</td><td>1.9</td></tr>
<tr><td>2</td><td>Colorado</td><td>2.0</td><td>6</td><td>Arizona</td><td>1.8</td></tr>
<tr><td>29</td><td>Connecticut</td><td>1.4</td><td>6</td><td>Montana</td><td>1.8</td></tr>
<tr><td>19</td><td>Delaware</td><td>1.5</td><td>6</td><td>Utah</td><td>1.8</td></tr>
<tr><td>10</td><td>Florida</td><td>1.7</td><td>6</td><td>Wyoming</td><td>1.8</td></tr>
<tr><td>19</td><td>Georgia</td><td>1.5</td><td>10</td><td>Florida</td><td>1.7</td></tr>
<tr><td>4</td><td>Hawaii</td><td>1.9</td><td>10</td><td>New Mexico</td><td>1.7</td></tr>
<tr><td>13</td><td>Idaho</td><td>1.6</td><td>10</td><td>Virginia</td><td>1.7</td></tr>
<tr><td>19</td><td>Illinois</td><td>1.5</td><td>13</td><td>Idaho</td><td>1.6</td></tr>
<tr><td>29</td><td>Indiana</td><td>1.4</td><td>13</td><td>Iowa</td><td>1.6</td></tr>
<tr><td>13</td><td>Iowa</td><td>1.6</td><td>13</td><td>Maryland</td><td>1.6</td></tr>
<tr><td>19</td><td>Kansas</td><td>1.5</td><td>13</td><td>New Hampshire</td><td>1.6</td></tr>
<tr><td>41</td><td>Kentucky</td><td>1.2</td><td>13</td><td>Oregon</td><td>1.6</td></tr>
<tr><td>41</td><td>Louisiana</td><td>1.2</td><td>13</td><td>Texas</td><td>1.6</td></tr>
<tr><td>49</td><td>Maine</td><td>1.1</td><td>19</td><td>California</td><td>1.5</td></tr>
<tr><td>13</td><td>Maryland</td><td>1.6</td><td>19</td><td>Delaware</td><td>1.5</td></tr>
<tr><td>41</td><td>Massachusetts</td><td>1.2</td><td>19</td><td>Georgia</td><td>1.5</td></tr>
<tr><td>19</td><td>Michigan</td><td>1.5</td><td>19</td><td>Illinois</td><td>1.5</td></tr>
<tr><td>19</td><td>Minnesota</td><td>1.5</td><td>19</td><td>Kansas</td><td>1.5</td></tr>
<tr><td>41</td><td>Mississippi</td><td>1.2</td><td>19</td><td>Michigan</td><td>1.5</td></tr>
<tr><td>29</td><td>Missouri</td><td>1.4</td><td>19</td><td>Minnesota</td><td>1.5</td></tr>
<tr><td>6</td><td>Montana</td><td>1.8</td><td>19</td><td>North Dakota</td><td>1.5</td></tr>
<tr><td>1</td><td>Nebraska</td><td>2.7</td><td>19</td><td>South Dakota</td><td>1.5</td></tr>
<tr><td>2</td><td>Nevada</td><td>2.0</td><td>19</td><td>Washington</td><td>1.5</td></tr>
<tr><td>13</td><td>New Hampshire</td><td>1.6</td><td>29</td><td>Alabama</td><td>1.4</td></tr>
<tr><td>4</td><td>New Jersey</td><td>1.9</td><td>29</td><td>Alaska</td><td>1.4</td></tr>
<tr><td>10</td><td>New Mexico</td><td>1.7</td><td>29</td><td>Connecticut</td><td>1.4</td></tr>
<tr><td>36</td><td>New York</td><td>1.3</td><td>29</td><td>Indiana</td><td>1.4</td></tr>
<tr><td>41</td><td>North Carolina</td><td>1.2</td><td>29</td><td>Missouri</td><td>1.4</td></tr>
<tr><td>19</td><td>North Dakota</td><td>1.5</td><td>29</td><td>Oklahoma</td><td>1.4</td></tr>
<tr><td>36</td><td>Ohio</td><td>1.3</td><td>29</td><td>Pennsylvania</td><td>1.4</td></tr>
<tr><td>29</td><td>Oklahoma</td><td>1.4</td><td>36</td><td>New York</td><td>1.3</td></tr>
<tr><td>13</td><td>Oregon</td><td>1.6</td><td>36</td><td>Ohio</td><td>1.3</td></tr>
<tr><td>29</td><td>Pennsylvania</td><td>1.4</td><td>36</td><td>South Carolina</td><td>1.3</td></tr>
<tr><td>50</td><td>Rhode Island</td><td>0.9</td><td>36</td><td>Tennessee</td><td>1.3</td></tr>
<tr><td>36</td><td>South Carolina</td><td>1.3</td><td>36</td><td>Wisconsin</td><td>1.3</td></tr>
<tr><td>19</td><td>South Dakota</td><td>1.5</td><td>41</td><td>Arkansas</td><td>1.2</td></tr>
<tr><td>36</td><td>Tennessee</td><td>1.3</td><td>41</td><td>Kentucky</td><td>1.2</td></tr>
<tr><td>13</td><td>Texas</td><td>1.6</td><td>41</td><td>Louisiana</td><td>1.2</td></tr>
<tr><td>6</td><td>Utah</td><td>1.8</td><td>41</td><td>Massachusetts</td><td>1.2</td></tr>
<tr><td>41</td><td>Vermont</td><td>1.2</td><td>41</td><td>Mississippi</td><td>1.2</td></tr>
<tr><td>10</td><td>Virginia</td><td>1.7</td><td>41</td><td>North Carolina</td><td>1.2</td></tr>
<tr><td>19</td><td>Washington</td><td>1.5</td><td>41</td><td>Vermont</td><td>1.2</td></tr>
<tr><td>41</td><td>West Virginia</td><td>1.2</td><td>41</td><td>West Virginia</td><td>1.2</td></tr>
<tr><td>36</td><td>Wisconsin</td><td>1.3</td><td>49</td><td>Maine</td><td>1.1</td></tr>
<tr><td>6</td><td>Wyoming</td><td>1.8</td><td>50</td><td>Rhode Island</td><td>0.9</td></tr>
<tr><td></td><td></td><td></td><td></td><td>District of Columbia</td><td>1.2</td></tr>
</table>

Source: CQ Press using data from U.S. Department of Health and Human Services, Centers for Medicare and Medicaid Services "State Health Care Expenditures" (http://www.cms.hhs.gov/NationalHealthExpendData/)
*By state of residence. Includes eyeglasses, hearing aids, surgical appliances and supplies, bulk and cylinder oxygen, and medical equipment rentals.

Per Capita Expenditures for Durable Medical Products in 2004

National Per Capita = $79*

<table>
<tr><th colspan="3">ALPHA ORDER</th><th colspan="3">RANK ORDER</th></tr>
<tr><th>RANK</th><th>STATE</th><th>PER CAPITA</th><th>RANK</th><th>STATE</th><th>PER CAPITA</th></tr>
<tr><td>40</td><td>Alabama</td><td>$70</td><td>1</td><td>Nebraska</td><td>$149</td></tr>
<tr><td>6</td><td>Alaska</td><td>93</td><td>2</td><td>New Jersey</td><td>111</td></tr>
<tr><td>30</td><td>Arizona</td><td>74</td><td>3</td><td>Colorado</td><td>96</td></tr>
<tr><td>47</td><td>Arkansas</td><td>60</td><td>4</td><td>Delaware</td><td>95</td></tr>
<tr><td>37</td><td>California</td><td>71</td><td>5</td><td>Hawaii</td><td>94</td></tr>
<tr><td>3</td><td>Colorado</td><td>96</td><td>6</td><td>Alaska</td><td>93</td></tr>
<tr><td>9</td><td>Connecticut</td><td>91</td><td>7</td><td>Montana</td><td>92</td></tr>
<tr><td>4</td><td>Delaware</td><td>95</td><td>7</td><td>Wyoming</td><td>92</td></tr>
<tr><td>9</td><td>Florida</td><td>91</td><td>9</td><td>Connecticut</td><td>91</td></tr>
<tr><td>42</td><td>Georgia</td><td>69</td><td>9</td><td>Florida</td><td>91</td></tr>
<tr><td>5</td><td>Hawaii</td><td>94</td><td>9</td><td>Maryland</td><td>91</td></tr>
<tr><td>35</td><td>Idaho</td><td>72</td><td>12</td><td>Nevada</td><td>90</td></tr>
<tr><td>20</td><td>Illinois</td><td>78</td><td>12</td><td>New Hampshire</td><td>90</td></tr>
<tr><td>28</td><td>Indiana</td><td>76</td><td>14</td><td>Minnesota</td><td>89</td></tr>
<tr><td>15</td><td>Iowa</td><td>88</td><td>15</td><td>Iowa</td><td>88</td></tr>
<tr><td>20</td><td>Kansas</td><td>78</td><td>16</td><td>New York</td><td>87</td></tr>
<tr><td>43</td><td>Kentucky</td><td>68</td><td>17</td><td>North Dakota</td><td>86</td></tr>
<tr><td>47</td><td>Louisiana</td><td>60</td><td>18</td><td>Virginia</td><td>84</td></tr>
<tr><td>40</td><td>Maine</td><td>70</td><td>19</td><td>Pennsylvania</td><td>83</td></tr>
<tr><td>9</td><td>Maryland</td><td>91</td><td>20</td><td>Illinois</td><td>78</td></tr>
<tr><td>20</td><td>Massachusetts</td><td>78</td><td>20</td><td>Kansas</td><td>78</td></tr>
<tr><td>25</td><td>Michigan</td><td>77</td><td>20</td><td>Massachusetts</td><td>78</td></tr>
<tr><td>14</td><td>Minnesota</td><td>89</td><td>20</td><td>Oregon</td><td>78</td></tr>
<tr><td>47</td><td>Mississippi</td><td>60</td><td>20</td><td>Washington</td><td>78</td></tr>
<tr><td>30</td><td>Missouri</td><td>74</td><td>25</td><td>Michigan</td><td>77</td></tr>
<tr><td>7</td><td>Montana</td><td>92</td><td>25</td><td>Ohio</td><td>77</td></tr>
<tr><td>1</td><td>Nebraska</td><td>149</td><td>25</td><td>South Dakota</td><td>77</td></tr>
<tr><td>12</td><td>Nevada</td><td>90</td><td>28</td><td>Indiana</td><td>76</td></tr>
<tr><td>12</td><td>New Hampshire</td><td>90</td><td>28</td><td>Wisconsin</td><td>76</td></tr>
<tr><td>2</td><td>New Jersey</td><td>111</td><td>30</td><td>Arizona</td><td>74</td></tr>
<tr><td>30</td><td>New Mexico</td><td>74</td><td>30</td><td>Missouri</td><td>74</td></tr>
<tr><td>16</td><td>New York</td><td>87</td><td>30</td><td>New Mexico</td><td>74</td></tr>
<tr><td>46</td><td>North Carolina</td><td>61</td><td>30</td><td>Texas</td><td>74</td></tr>
<tr><td>17</td><td>North Dakota</td><td>86</td><td>34</td><td>Tennessee</td><td>73</td></tr>
<tr><td>25</td><td>Ohio</td><td>77</td><td>35</td><td>Idaho</td><td>72</td></tr>
<tr><td>43</td><td>Oklahoma</td><td>68</td><td>35</td><td>Vermont</td><td>72</td></tr>
<tr><td>20</td><td>Oregon</td><td>78</td><td>37</td><td>California</td><td>71</td></tr>
<tr><td>19</td><td>Pennsylvania</td><td>83</td><td>37</td><td>Utah</td><td>71</td></tr>
<tr><td>50</td><td>Rhode Island</td><td>57</td><td>37</td><td>West Virginia</td><td>71</td></tr>
<tr><td>45</td><td>South Carolina</td><td>66</td><td>40</td><td>Alabama</td><td>70</td></tr>
<tr><td>25</td><td>South Dakota</td><td>77</td><td>40</td><td>Maine</td><td>70</td></tr>
<tr><td>34</td><td>Tennessee</td><td>73</td><td>42</td><td>Georgia</td><td>69</td></tr>
<tr><td>30</td><td>Texas</td><td>74</td><td>43</td><td>Kentucky</td><td>68</td></tr>
<tr><td>37</td><td>Utah</td><td>71</td><td>43</td><td>Oklahoma</td><td>68</td></tr>
<tr><td>35</td><td>Vermont</td><td>72</td><td>45</td><td>South Carolina</td><td>66</td></tr>
<tr><td>18</td><td>Virginia</td><td>84</td><td>46</td><td>North Carolina</td><td>61</td></tr>
<tr><td>20</td><td>Washington</td><td>78</td><td>47</td><td>Arkansas</td><td>60</td></tr>
<tr><td>37</td><td>West Virginia</td><td>71</td><td>47</td><td>Louisiana</td><td>60</td></tr>
<tr><td>28</td><td>Wisconsin</td><td>76</td><td>47</td><td>Mississippi</td><td>60</td></tr>
<tr><td>7</td><td>Wyoming</td><td>92</td><td>50</td><td>Rhode Island</td><td>57</td></tr>
<tr><td></td><td></td><td></td><td></td><td>District of Columbia</td><td>102</td></tr>
</table>

Source: U.S. Department of Health and Human Services, Centers for Medicare and Medicaid Services
"State Health Care Expenditures" (http://www.cms.hhs.gov/NationalHealthExpendData/)
*By state of residence. Includes eyeglasses, hearing aids, surgical appliances and supplies, bulk and cylinder oxygen, and medical equipment rentals.

Projected National Health Care Expenditures in 2008

Total Health Care Expenditures = $2,420,000,000,000*

The 2004 health care expenditures broken down to the state level and shown on pages 305 to 332 were released in February of 2007 and are the most recent state health expenditure data available from the Centers for Medicare and Medicaid Services (CMS).

Given the high level of interest in health care finance data, we have assembled a table showing the most recent national level health care expenditure projections.

	PROJECTED EXPENDITURES IN 2008	PROJECTED PERCENT CHANGE: 2007 TO 2008
Total Health Care Expenditures	$2,420,000,000,000	7.0
Per Capita Total Health Care Expenditures	$8,023	
Personal Health Care Expenditures	$2,016,600,000,000	7.0
Per Capita Personal Health Care Expenditures	$6,686	
Hospital Care Expenditures	$747,200,000,000	7.1
Per Capita Hospital Care Expenditures	$2,477	
Physician Services Expenditures	$506,200,000,000	6.7
Per Capita Physician Services Expenditures	$1,678	
Dental Services Expenditures	$104,900,000,000	6.4
Per Capita Dental Services Expenditures	$348	
Other Professional Services	$69,100,000,000	6.5
Per Capita Other Professional Services	$229	
Home Health Care Expenditures	$62,700,000,000	8.3
Per Capita Home Health Care Expenditures	$208	
Prescription Drugs	$247,600,000,000	7.9
Per Capita Prescription Drugs	$821	
Nursing Home Care	$138,800,000,000	5.1
Per Capita Nursing Home Care	$460	
Other Personal Care Expenditures	$73,000,000,000	10.3
Per Capita Other Personal Care Expenditures	$242	

Source: U.S. Department of Health and Human Services, Centers for Medicare and Medicaid Services
"National Health Care Expenditures Projections: 2001-2016"
http://www.cms.hhs.gov/NationalHealthExpendData/downloads/proj2006.pdf
*Per Capita and percent change figures calculated by CQ Press using 2007 Census population estimates. For definitions see the corresponding 2004 state tables in this chapter.

V. Incidence of Disease

Estimated New Cancer Cases in 2007 336
Estimated Rate of New Cancer Cases in 2007 337
Age-Adjusted Cancer Incidence Rates for Males
in 2003 338
Age-Adjusted Cancer Incidence Rates for Females
in 2003 339
Estimated New Cases of Bladder Cancer in 2007 340
Estimated Rate of New Bladder Cancer Cases in 2007 ... 341
Estimated New Female Breast Cancer Cases in 2007 342
Age-Adjusted Incidence Rate of Female Breast Cancer
Cases in 2003 343
Percent of Women 40 and Older Who Have Had a
Mammogram in the Past Two Years: 2006 344
Estimated New Colon and Rectum Cancer Cases
in 2007 345
Estimated Rate of New Colon and Rectum Cancer Cases
in 2007 346
Percent of Adults Who Have Ever Had a Sigmoidoscopy
or Colonoscopy Exam: 2006 347
Estimated New Leukemia Cases in 2007 348
Estimated Rate of New Leukemia Cases in 2007 349
Estimated New Lung Cancer Cases in 2007 350
Estimated Rate of New Lung Cancer Cases in 2007 351
Estimated New Non-Hodgkin's Lymphoma Cases
in 2007 352
Estimated Rate of New Non-Hodgkin's Lymphoma
Cases in 2007 353
Estimated New Prostate Cancer Cases in 2007 354
Age-Adjusted Incidence Rate of Prostate Cancer Cases
in 2003 355
Percent of Males Receiving PSA Test for Prostate Cancer:
2006 356
Estimated New Skin Melanoma Cases in 2007 357
Estimated Rate of New Skin Melanoma Cases in 2007 .. 358
Estimated New Cervical Cancer Cases in 2007 359
Estimated Rate of New Cervical Cancer Cases in 2007 .. 360
Percent of Women 18 Years Old and Older Who Had a
Pap Smear within the Past Three Years: 2006 361
Estimated New Uterine Cancer Cases in 2007 362

Estimated Rate of New Uterine Cancer Cases in 2007 ... 363
AIDS Cases Reported in 2005 364
AIDS Rate in 2005 365
AIDS Cases Reported through December 2005 366
AIDS Cases in Children 12 Years and Younger through
December 2005 367
Chickenpox (Varicella) Cases Reported in 2007 368
Chickenpox (Varicella) Rate in 2007 369
E. Coli Cases Reported in 2007 370
E. Coli Rate in 2007 371
Hepatitis A and B Cases Reported in 2007 372
Hepatitis A and B Rate in 2007 373
Legionellosis Cases Reported in 2007 374
Legionellosis Rate in 2007 375
Lyme Disease Cases in 2007 376
Lyme Disease Rate in 2007 377
Malaria Cases Reported in 2007 378
Malaria Rate in 2007 379
Meningococcal Infections Reported in 2007 380
Meningococcal Infection Rate in 2007 381
Rabies (Animal) Cases Reported in 2007 382
Rabies (Animal) Rate in 2007 383
Rocky Mountain Spotted Fever Cases Reported
in 2007 384
Rocky Mountain Spotted Fever Rate in 2007 385
Salmonellosis Cases Reported in 2007 386
Salmonellosis Rate in 2007 387
Shigellosis Cases Reported in 2007 388
Shigellosis Rate in 2007 389
West Nile Virus Disease Cases Reported in 2007 390
West Nile Disease Rate in 2007 391
Whooping Cough (Pertussis) Cases Reported in 2007 ... 392
Whooping Cough (Pertussis) Rate in 2007 393
Percent of Children Aged 19 to 35 Months Fully
Immunized in 2006 394
Percent of Adults Aged 65 Years and Older Who
Received Flu Shots in 2006 395
Percent of Adults Aged 65 Years and Older Who Have
Had a Pneumonia Vaccine: 2006 396

Sexually Transmitted Diseases in 2006 397
Sexually Transmitted Disease Rate in 2006 398
Chlamydia Cases Reported in 2006 399
Chlamydia Rate in 2006 400
Gonorrhea Cases Reported in 2006 401
Gonorrhea Rate in 2006 402
Syphilis Cases Reported in 2006 403
Syphilis Rate in 2006 404

Percent of Adults Who Have Asthma: 2006 405
Percent of Adults Who Have Been Told They Have
    Arthritis: 2005 406
Percent of Adults Who Have Been Told They Have
    Diabetes: 2006 407
Percent of Adults Reporting Serious Psychological
    Distress: 2005 408

Estimated New Cancer Cases in 2007

National Estimated Total = 1,444,920 New Cases*

ALPHA ORDER					RANK ORDER			
RANK	STATE	CASES	% of USA		RANK	STATE	CASES	% of USA
25	Alabama	20,590	1.4%		1	California	151,250	10.5%
49	Alaska	2,500	0.2%		2	Florida	106,560	7.4%
20	Arizona	26,270	1.8%		3	New York	100,960	7.0%
31	Arkansas	14,130	1.0%		4	Texas	91,020	6.3%
1	California	151,250	10.5%		5	Pennsylvania	75,130	5.2%
27	Colorado	19,190	1.3%		6	Illinois	62,010	4.3%
26	Connecticut	19,780	1.4%		7	Ohio	59,220	4.1%
45	Delaware	4,530	0.3%		8	Michigan	54,410	3.8%
2	Florida	106,560	7.4%		9	New Jersey	49,370	3.4%
11	Georgia	35,440	2.5%		10	North Carolina	38,210	2.6%
43	Hawaii	6,020	0.4%		11	Georgia	35,440	2.5%
42	Idaho	6,140	0.4%		12	Virginia	35,090	2.4%
6	Illinois	62,010	4.3%		13	Massachusetts	34,920	2.4%
15	Indiana	30,040	2.1%		14	Washington	31,080	2.2%
30	Iowa	16,540	1.1%		15	Indiana	30,040	2.1%
32	Kansas	12,760	0.9%		16	Missouri	29,930	2.1%
22	Kentucky	22,850	1.6%		17	Tennessee	28,440	2.0%
23	Louisiana	22,540	1.6%		18	Wisconsin	28,130	1.9%
37	Maine	8,340	0.6%		19	Maryland	26,390	1.8%
19	Maryland	26,390	1.8%		20	Arizona	26,270	1.8%
13	Massachusetts	34,920	2.4%		21	Minnesota	25,420	1.8%
8	Michigan	54,410	3.8%		22	Kentucky	22,850	1.6%
21	Minnesota	25,420	1.8%		23	Louisiana	22,540	1.6%
33	Mississippi	12,470	0.9%		24	South Carolina	21,370	1.5%
16	Missouri	29,930	2.1%		25	Alabama	20,590	1.4%
44	Montana	4,920	0.3%		26	Connecticut	19,780	1.4%
36	Nebraska	8,720	0.6%		27	Colorado	19,190	1.3%
34	Nevada	11,030	0.8%		28	Oregon	18,630	1.3%
40	New Hampshire	7,140	0.5%		29	Oklahoma	17,170	1.2%
9	New Jersey	49,370	3.4%		30	Iowa	16,540	1.1%
38	New Mexico	8,030	0.6%		31	Arkansas	14,130	1.0%
3	New York	100,960	7.0%		32	Kansas	12,760	0.9%
10	North Carolina	38,210	2.6%		33	Mississippi	12,470	0.9%
48	North Dakota	3,340	0.2%		34	Nevada	11,030	0.8%
7	Ohio	59,220	4.1%		35	West Virginia	10,490	0.7%
29	Oklahoma	17,170	1.2%		36	Nebraska	8,720	0.6%
28	Oregon	18,630	1.3%		37	Maine	8,340	0.6%
5	Pennsylvania	75,130	5.2%		38	New Mexico	8,030	0.6%
41	Rhode Island	6,360	0.4%		39	Utah	7,660	0.5%
24	South Carolina	21,370	1.5%		40	New Hampshire	7,140	0.5%
46	South Dakota	3,990	0.3%		41	Rhode Island	6,360	0.4%
17	Tennessee	28,440	2.0%		42	Idaho	6,140	0.4%
4	Texas	91,020	6.3%		43	Hawaii	6,020	0.4%
39	Utah	7,660	0.5%		44	Montana	4,920	0.3%
47	Vermont	3,500	0.2%		45	Delaware	4,530	0.3%
12	Virginia	35,090	2.4%		46	South Dakota	3,990	0.3%
14	Washington	31,080	2.2%		47	Vermont	3,500	0.2%
35	West Virginia	10,490	0.7%		48	North Dakota	3,340	0.2%
18	Wisconsin	28,130	1.9%		49	Alaska	2,500	0.2%
50	Wyoming	2,340	0.2%		50	Wyoming	2,340	0.2%
						District of Columbia	2,540	0.2%

Source: American Cancer Society
    "Cancer Facts & Figures 2007" (Copyright 2007, American Cancer Society)
*These estimates are offered as a rough guide and should not be regarded as definitive. They are calculated according to the distribution of estimated 2007 cancer deaths by state. Totals do not include basal and squamous cell skin cancers or in situ carcinomas except urinary bladder.

Estimated Rate of New Cancer Cases in 2007

National Estimated Rate = 482.6 New Cases per 100,000 Population*

ALPHA ORDER

RANK	STATE	RATE
38	Alabama	447.7
49	Alaska	373.1
42	Arizona	426.0
24	Arkansas	502.7
44	California	414.9
46	Colorado	403.7
7	Connecticut	564.4
14	Delaware	530.8
4	Florida	589.1
48	Georgia	378.5
34	Hawaii	468.3
43	Idaho	418.7
29	Illinois	483.2
31	Indiana	475.8
9	Iowa	554.6
35	Kansas	461.6
10	Kentucky	543.3
15	Louisiana	525.7
1	Maine	631.1
33	Maryland	469.9
12	Massachusetts	542.5
13	Michigan	538.9
27	Minnesota	492.0
41	Mississippi	428.4
20	Missouri	512.3
18	Montana	520.8
26	Nebraska	493.1
39	Nevada	442.0
11	New Hampshire	543.0
6	New Jersey	565.9
45	New Mexico	410.8
17	New York	522.9
40	North Carolina	431.4
16	North Dakota	525.3
19	Ohio	515.9
30	Oklahoma	479.7
23	Oregon	503.4
2	Pennsylvania	603.9
3	Rhode Island	595.7
25	South Carolina	494.5
21	South Dakota	510.3
32	Tennessee	471.0
47	Texas	387.2
50	Utah	300.4
8	Vermont	561.0
36	Virginia	459.1
28	Washington	485.9
5	West Virginia	576.9
22	Wisconsin	506.3
37	Wyoming	454.4

RANK ORDER

RANK	STATE	RATE
1	Maine	631.1
2	Pennsylvania	603.9
3	Rhode Island	595.7
4	Florida	589.1
5	West Virginia	576.9
6	New Jersey	565.9
7	Connecticut	564.4
8	Vermont	561.0
9	Iowa	554.6
10	Kentucky	543.3
11	New Hampshire	543.0
12	Massachusetts	542.5
13	Michigan	538.9
14	Delaware	530.8
15	Louisiana	525.7
16	North Dakota	525.3
17	New York	522.9
18	Montana	520.8
19	Ohio	515.9
20	Missouri	512.3
21	South Dakota	510.3
22	Wisconsin	506.3
23	Oregon	503.4
24	Arkansas	502.7
25	South Carolina	494.5
26	Nebraska	493.1
27	Minnesota	492.0
28	Washington	485.9
29	Illinois	483.2
30	Oklahoma	479.7
31	Indiana	475.8
32	Tennessee	471.0
33	Maryland	469.9
34	Hawaii	468.3
35	Kansas	461.6
36	Virginia	459.1
37	Wyoming	454.4
38	Alabama	447.7
39	Nevada	442.0
40	North Carolina	431.4
41	Mississippi	428.4
42	Arizona	426.0
43	Idaho	418.7
44	California	414.9
45	New Mexico	410.8
46	Colorado	403.7
47	Texas	387.2
48	Georgia	378.5
49	Alaska	373.1
50	Utah	300.4

District of Columbia   436.8

Source: CQ Press using data from American Cancer Society
    "Cancer Facts & Figures 2007" (Copyright 2007, American Cancer Society)
*These estimates are offered as a rough guide and should not be regarded as definitive. They are calculated according to the distribution of estimated 2007 cancer deaths by state. Totals do not include basal and squamous cell skin cancers or in situ carcinomas except urinary bladder. Rates calculated using 2006 Census resident population estimates.

Age-Adjusted Cancer Incidence Rates for Males in 2003

National Rate = 562.1 New Cases per 100,000 Male Population*

ALPHA ORDER

RANK	STATE	RATE
36	Alabama	526.5
25	Alaska	556.8
46	Arizona	462.4
31	Arkansas	544.1
38	California	520.9
41	Colorado	516.2
7	Connecticut	597.3
11	Delaware	586.8
20	Florida	562.2
17	Georgia	565.8
45	Hawaii	481.8
35	Idaho	530.0
13	Illinois	580.9
29	Indiana	545.7
24	Iowa	557.1
NA	Kansas**	NA
3	Kentucky	616.9
4	Louisiana	613.8
5	Maine	609.9
12	Maryland	581.6
9	Massachusetts	591.6
6	Michigan	608.6
22	Minnesota	559.4
NA	Mississippi**	NA
33	Missouri	537.4
23	Montana	558.8
27	Nebraska	551.0
32	Nevada	541.3
16	New Hampshire	571.7
2	New Jersey	623.9
44	New Mexico	485.0
18	New York	565.4
39	North Carolina	519.2
40	North Dakota	518.0
26	Ohio	551.9
28	Oklahoma	547.0
30	Oregon	545.4
8	Pennsylvania	594.4
1	Rhode Island	627.2
10	South Carolina	590.1
19	South Dakota	564.1
47	Tennessee	442.0
34	Texas	530.7
43	Utah	490.2
NA	Vermont**	NA
42	Virginia	510.5
15	Washington	573.7
14	West Virginia	574.6
21	Wisconsin	562.0
37	Wyoming	524.9

RANK ORDER

RANK	STATE	RATE
1	Rhode Island	627.2
2	New Jersey	623.9
3	Kentucky	616.9
4	Louisiana	613.8
5	Maine	609.9
6	Michigan	608.6
7	Connecticut	597.3
8	Pennsylvania	594.4
9	Massachusetts	591.6
10	South Carolina	590.1
11	Delaware	586.8
12	Maryland	581.6
13	Illinois	580.9
14	West Virginia	574.6
15	Washington	573.7
16	New Hampshire	571.7
17	Georgia	565.8
18	New York	565.4
19	South Dakota	564.1
20	Florida	562.2
21	Wisconsin	562.0
22	Minnesota	559.4
23	Montana	558.8
24	Iowa	557.1
25	Alaska	556.8
26	Ohio	551.9
27	Nebraska	551.0
28	Oklahoma	547.0
29	Indiana	545.7
30	Oregon	545.4
31	Arkansas	544.1
32	Nevada	541.3
33	Missouri	537.4
34	Texas	530.7
35	Idaho	530.0
36	Alabama	526.5
37	Wyoming	524.9
38	California	520.9
39	North Carolina	519.2
40	North Dakota	518.0
41	Colorado	516.2
42	Virginia	510.5
43	Utah	490.2
44	New Mexico	485.0
45	Hawaii	481.8
46	Arizona	462.4
47	Tennessee	442.0
NA	Kansas**	NA
NA	Mississippi**	NA
NA	Vermont**	NA

| | District of Columbia | 635.6 |

Source: American Cancer Society
    "Cancer Facts & Figures 2007" (Copyright 2007, American Cancer Society)
*For 1999 to 2003. Age-adjusted to the 2000 U.S. standard population.
**Not available.

Age-Adjusted Cancer Incidence Rates for Females in 2003

National Rate = 415.3 New Cases per 100,000 Female Population*

ALPHA ORDER

RANK	STATE	RATE
43	Alabama	365.2
19	Alaska	421.2
44	Arizona	364.1
38	Arkansas	377.1
31	California	398.5
29	Colorado	400.3
4	Connecticut	448.3
11	Delaware	433.4
20	Florida	415.6
34	Georgia	391.5
39	Hawaii	375.2
32	Idaho	396.0
15	Illinois	425.5
21	Indiana	414.4
18	Iowa	424.2
NA	Kansas**	NA
7	Kentucky	440.5
28	Louisiana	402.3
6	Maine	447.6
13	Maryland	428.3
1	Massachusetts	451.8
12	Michigan	429.9
25	Minnesota	412.3
NA	Mississippi**	NA
27	Missouri	408.8
26	Montana	412.0
23	Nebraska	413.4
22	Nevada	414.2
8	New Hampshire	436.6
2	New Jersey	448.7
45	New Mexico	357.3
16	New York	424.8
40	North Carolina	372.6
42	North Dakota	366.9
24	Ohio	412.6
30	Oklahoma	399.6
9	Oregon	436.5
9	Pennsylvania	436.5
3	Rhode Island	448.6
36	South Carolina	389.4
33	South Dakota	395.7
46	Tennessee	351.2
37	Texas	383.4
47	Utah	346.3
NA	Vermont**	NA
41	Virginia	367.6
5	Washington	448.0
14	West Virginia	427.8
17	Wisconsin	424.4
35	Wyoming	390.3

RANK ORDER

RANK	STATE	RATE
1	Massachusetts	451.8
2	New Jersey	448.7
3	Rhode Island	448.6
4	Connecticut	448.3
5	Washington	448.0
6	Maine	447.6
7	Kentucky	440.5
8	New Hampshire	436.6
9	Oregon	436.5
9	Pennsylvania	436.5
11	Delaware	433.4
12	Michigan	429.9
13	Maryland	428.3
14	West Virginia	427.8
15	Illinois	425.5
16	New York	424.8
17	Wisconsin	424.4
18	Iowa	424.2
19	Alaska	421.2
20	Florida	415.6
21	Indiana	414.4
22	Nevada	414.2
23	Nebraska	413.4
24	Ohio	412.6
25	Minnesota	412.3
26	Montana	412.0
27	Missouri	408.8
28	Louisiana	402.3
29	Colorado	400.3
30	Oklahoma	399.6
31	California	398.5
32	Idaho	396.0
33	South Dakota	395.7
34	Georgia	391.5
35	Wyoming	390.3
36	South Carolina	389.4
37	Texas	383.4
38	Arkansas	377.1
39	Hawaii	375.2
40	North Carolina	372.6
41	Virginia	367.6
42	North Dakota	366.9
43	Alabama	365.2
44	Arizona	364.1
45	New Mexico	357.3
46	Tennessee	351.2
47	Utah	346.3
NA	Kansas**	NA
NA	Mississippi**	NA
NA	Vermont**	NA
	District of Columbia	422.6

Source: American Cancer Society
   "Cancer Facts & Figures 2007" (Copyright 2007, American Cancer Society)
*For 1999 to 2003. Age-adjusted to the 2000 U.S. standard population.
**Not available.

Estimated New Cases of Bladder Cancer in 2007

National Estimated Total = 67,160 New Cases*

ALPHA ORDER

RANK	STATE	CASES	% of USA
26	Alabama	850	1.3%
49	Alaska	110	0.2%
15	Arizona	1,360	2.0%
33	Arkansas	560	0.8%
1	California	6,590	9.8%
25	Colorado	880	1.3%
22	Connecticut	1,090	1.6%
44	Delaware	220	0.3%
2	Florida	5,460	8.1%
15	Georgia	1,360	2.0%
46	Hawaii	200	0.3%
42	Idaho	310	0.5%
7	Illinois	2,880	4.3%
13	Indiana	1,390	2.1%
29	Iowa	820	1.2%
31	Kansas	570	0.8%
23	Kentucky	970	1.4%
26	Louisiana	850	1.3%
36	Maine	470	0.7%
21	Maryland	1,150	1.7%
10	Massachusetts	1,950	2.9%
8	Michigan	2,700	4.0%
19	Minnesota	1,250	1.9%
35	Mississippi	480	0.7%
17	Missouri	1,350	2.0%
43	Montana	260	0.4%
37	Nebraska	430	0.6%
31	Nevada	570	0.8%
38	New Hampshire	390	0.6%
9	New Jersey	2,450	3.6%
40	New Mexico	350	0.5%
3	New York	4,980	7.4%
11	North Carolina	1,690	2.5%
46	North Dakota	200	0.3%
6	Ohio	2,940	4.4%
30	Oklahoma	710	1.1%
23	Oregon	970	1.4%
4	Pennsylvania	4,030	6.0%
39	Rhode Island	370	0.6%
28	South Carolina	840	1.3%
44	South Dakota	220	0.3%
20	Tennessee	1,230	1.8%
5	Texas	3,300	4.9%
41	Utah	340	0.5%
48	Vermont	170	0.3%
14	Virginia	1,380	2.1%
12	Washington	1,490	2.2%
34	West Virginia	500	0.7%
17	Wisconsin	1,350	2.0%
49	Wyoming	110	0.2%

RANK ORDER

RANK	STATE	CASES	% of USA
1	California	6,590	9.8%
2	Florida	5,460	8.1%
3	New York	4,980	7.4%
4	Pennsylvania	4,030	6.0%
5	Texas	3,300	4.9%
6	Ohio	2,940	4.4%
7	Illinois	2,880	4.3%
8	Michigan	2,700	4.0%
9	New Jersey	2,450	3.6%
10	Massachusetts	1,950	2.9%
11	North Carolina	1,690	2.5%
12	Washington	1,490	2.2%
13	Indiana	1,390	2.1%
14	Virginia	1,380	2.1%
15	Arizona	1,360	2.0%
15	Georgia	1,360	2.0%
17	Missouri	1,350	2.0%
17	Wisconsin	1,350	2.0%
19	Minnesota	1,250	1.9%
20	Tennessee	1,230	1.8%
21	Maryland	1,150	1.7%
22	Connecticut	1,090	1.6%
23	Kentucky	970	1.4%
23	Oregon	970	1.4%
25	Colorado	880	1.3%
26	Alabama	850	1.3%
26	Louisiana	850	1.3%
28	South Carolina	840	1.3%
29	Iowa	820	1.2%
30	Oklahoma	710	1.1%
31	Kansas	570	0.8%
31	Nevada	570	0.8%
33	Arkansas	560	0.8%
34	West Virginia	500	0.7%
35	Mississippi	480	0.7%
36	Maine	470	0.7%
37	Nebraska	430	0.6%
38	New Hampshire	390	0.6%
39	Rhode Island	370	0.6%
40	New Mexico	350	0.5%
41	Utah	340	0.5%
42	Idaho	310	0.5%
43	Montana	260	0.4%
44	Delaware	220	0.3%
44	South Dakota	220	0.3%
46	Hawaii	200	0.3%
46	North Dakota	200	0.3%
48	Vermont	170	0.3%
49	Alaska	110	0.2%
49	Wyoming	110	0.2%
	District of Columbia	90	0.1%

Source: American Cancer Society
    "Cancer Facts & Figures 2007" (Copyright 2007, American Cancer Society)
*These estimates are offered as a rough guide and should be interpreted with caution. They are calculated according to the distribution of estimated 2007 cancer deaths by state.

Estimated Rate of New Bladder Cancer Cases in 2007

National Estimated Rate = 22.4 New Cases per 100,000 Population*

ALPHA ORDER				RANK ORDER		
RANK	STATE	RATE		RANK	STATE	RATE
40	Alabama	18.5		1	Maine	35.6
46	Alaska	16.4		2	Rhode Island	34.7
28	Arizona	22.1		3	Pennsylvania	32.4
35	Arkansas	19.9		4	North Dakota	31.5
42	California	18.1		5	Connecticut	31.1
40	Colorado	18.5		6	Massachusetts	30.3
5	Connecticut	31.1		7	Florida	30.2
17	Delaware	25.8		8	New Hampshire	29.7
7	Florida	30.2		9	New Jersey	28.1
48	Georgia	14.5		9	South Dakota	28.1
47	Hawaii	15.6		11	Iowa	27.5
31	Idaho	21.1		11	Montana	27.5
27	Illinois	22.4		11	West Virginia	27.5
29	Indiana	22.0		14	Vermont	27.2
11	Iowa	27.5		15	Michigan	26.7
32	Kansas	20.6		16	Oregon	26.2
24	Kentucky	23.1		17	Delaware	25.8
36	Louisiana	19.8		17	New York	25.8
1	Maine	35.6		19	Ohio	25.6
33	Maryland	20.5		20	Nebraska	24.3
6	Massachusetts	30.3		20	Wisconsin	24.3
15	Michigan	26.7		22	Minnesota	24.2
22	Minnesota	24.2		23	Washington	23.3
45	Mississippi	16.5		24	Kentucky	23.1
24	Missouri	23.1		24	Missouri	23.1
11	Montana	27.5		26	Nevada	22.8
20	Nebraska	24.3		27	Illinois	22.4
26	Nevada	22.8		28	Arizona	22.1
8	New Hampshire	29.7		29	Indiana	22.0
9	New Jersey	28.1		30	Wyoming	21.4
44	New Mexico	17.9		31	Idaho	21.1
17	New York	25.8		32	Kansas	20.6
39	North Carolina	19.1		33	Maryland	20.5
4	North Dakota	31.5		34	Tennessee	20.4
19	Ohio	25.6		35	Arkansas	19.9
36	Oklahoma	19.8		36	Louisiana	19.8
16	Oregon	26.2		36	Oklahoma	19.8
3	Pennsylvania	32.4		38	South Carolina	19.4
2	Rhode Island	34.7		39	North Carolina	19.1
38	South Carolina	19.4		40	Alabama	18.5
9	South Dakota	28.1		40	Colorado	18.5
34	Tennessee	20.4		42	California	18.1
49	Texas	14.0		42	Virginia	18.1
50	Utah	13.3		44	New Mexico	17.9
14	Vermont	27.2		45	Mississippi	16.5
42	Virginia	18.1		46	Alaska	16.4
23	Washington	23.3		47	Hawaii	15.6
11	West Virginia	27.5		48	Georgia	14.5
20	Wisconsin	24.3		49	Texas	14.0
30	Wyoming	21.4		50	Utah	13.3
					District of Columbia	15.5

Source: CQ Press using data from American Cancer Society
  "Cancer Facts & Figures 2007" (Copyright 2007, American Cancer Society)
*These estimates are offered as a rough guide and should be interpreted with caution. They are calculated according to the distribution of estimated 2007 cancer deaths by state. Rates calculated using 2006 Census resident population estimates.

Estimated New Female Breast Cancer Cases in 2007

National Estimated Total = 178,480 New Cases*

ALPHA ORDER

RANK	STATE	CASES	% of USA
23	Alabama	2,750	1.5%
49	Alaska	340	0.2%
21	Arizona	3,220	1.8%
31	Arkansas	1,830	1.0%
1	California	19,790	11.1%
24	Colorado	2,660	1.5%
27	Connecticut	2,510	1.4%
45	Delaware	560	0.3%
4	Florida	11,710	6.6%
12	Georgia	4,520	2.5%
41	Hawaii	820	0.5%
42	Idaho	780	0.4%
6	Illinois	7,030	3.9%
17	Indiana	3,560	2.0%
30	Iowa	2,000	1.1%
32	Kansas	1,750	1.0%
26	Kentucky	2,590	1.5%
22	Louisiana	2,820	1.6%
38	Maine	980	0.5%
17	Maryland	3,560	2.0%
13	Massachusetts	4,260	2.4%
9	Michigan	5,900	3.3%
20	Minnesota	3,240	1.8%
33	Mississippi	1,620	0.9%
15	Missouri	3,730	2.1%
44	Montana	630	0.4%
36	Nebraska	1,160	0.6%
34	Nevada	1,180	0.7%
40	New Hampshire	890	0.5%
8	New Jersey	6,080	3.4%
37	New Mexico	1,080	0.6%
2	New York	12,580	7.0%
10	North Carolina	4,870	2.7%
47	North Dakota	440	0.2%
7	Ohio	6,710	3.8%
29	Oklahoma	2,200	1.2%
28	Oregon	2,460	1.4%
5	Pennsylvania	8,860	5.0%
43	Rhode Island	730	0.4%
25	South Carolina	2,600	1.5%
46	South Dakota	510	0.3%
16	Tennessee	3,690	2.1%
3	Texas	12,120	6.8%
39	Utah	920	0.5%
48	Vermont	420	0.2%
11	Virginia	4,570	2.6%
14	Washington	4,090	2.3%
34	West Virginia	1,180	0.7%
19	Wisconsin	3,340	1.9%
50	Wyoming	310	0.2%

RANK ORDER

RANK	STATE	CASES	% of USA
1	California	19,790	11.1%
2	New York	12,580	7.0%
3	Texas	12,120	6.8%
4	Florida	11,710	6.6%
5	Pennsylvania	8,860	5.0%
6	Illinois	7,030	3.9%
7	Ohio	6,710	3.8%
8	New Jersey	6,080	3.4%
9	Michigan	5,900	3.3%
10	North Carolina	4,870	2.7%
11	Virginia	4,570	2.6%
12	Georgia	4,520	2.5%
13	Massachusetts	4,260	2.4%
14	Washington	4,090	2.3%
15	Missouri	3,730	2.1%
16	Tennessee	3,690	2.1%
17	Indiana	3,560	2.0%
17	Maryland	3,560	2.0%
19	Wisconsin	3,340	1.9%
20	Minnesota	3,240	1.8%
21	Arizona	3,220	1.8%
22	Louisiana	2,820	1.6%
23	Alabama	2,750	1.5%
24	Colorado	2,660	1.5%
25	South Carolina	2,600	1.5%
26	Kentucky	2,590	1.5%
27	Connecticut	2,510	1.4%
28	Oregon	2,460	1.4%
29	Oklahoma	2,200	1.2%
30	Iowa	2,000	1.1%
31	Arkansas	1,830	1.0%
32	Kansas	1,750	1.0%
33	Mississippi	1,620	0.9%
34	Nevada	1,180	0.7%
34	West Virginia	1,180	0.7%
36	Nebraska	1,160	0.6%
37	New Mexico	1,080	0.6%
38	Maine	980	0.5%
39	Utah	920	0.5%
40	New Hampshire	890	0.5%
41	Hawaii	820	0.5%
42	Idaho	780	0.4%
43	Rhode Island	730	0.4%
44	Montana	630	0.4%
45	Delaware	560	0.3%
46	South Dakota	510	0.3%
47	North Dakota	440	0.2%
48	Vermont	420	0.2%
49	Alaska	340	0.2%
50	Wyoming	310	0.2%
	District of Columbia	320	0.2%

Source: American Cancer Society
    "Cancer Facts & Figures 2007" (Copyright 2007, American Cancer Society)
*These estimates are offered as a rough guide and should be interpreted with caution. They are calculated according to the distribution of estimated 2007 cancer deaths by state.

Age-Adjusted Incidence Rate of Female Breast Cancer Cases in 2003

National Rate = 128.2 New Cases per 100,000 Female Population*

ALPHA ORDER

RANK	STATE	RATE
45	Alabama	115.3
7	Alaska	134.2
44	Arizona	116.7
39	Arkansas	121.0
15	California	129.8
7	Colorado	134.2
3	Connecticut	140.4
19	Delaware	128.8
35	Florida	123.0
32	Georgia	124.0
25	Hawaii	127.3
24	Idaho	128.2
16	Illinois	129.7
30	Indiana	124.8
20	Iowa	128.7
NA	Kansas**	NA
30	Kentucky	124.8
36	Louisiana	122.8
12	Maine	131.4
11	Maryland	131.9
4	Massachusetts	138.8
17	Michigan	129.4
5	Minnesota	135.9
NA	Mississippi**	NA
28	Missouri	125.4
22	Montana	128.4
12	Nebraska	131.4
40	Nevada	120.8
6	New Hampshire	135.2
9	New Jersey	133.9
46	New Mexico	115.0
26	New York	126.7
38	North Carolina	121.5
34	North Dakota	123.1
27	Ohio	126.6
23	Oklahoma	128.3
2	Oregon	142.6
17	Pennsylvania	129.4
14	Rhode Island	130.7
33	South Carolina	123.5
21	South Dakota	128.6
47	Tennessee	113.7
41	Texas	118.6
42	Utah	117.1
NA	Vermont**	NA
37	Virginia	122.2
1	Washington	146.7
43	West Virginia	116.9
9	Wisconsin	133.9
29	Wyoming	125.2

RANK ORDER

RANK	STATE	RATE
1	Washington	146.7
2	Oregon	142.6
3	Connecticut	140.4
4	Massachusetts	138.8
5	Minnesota	135.9
6	New Hampshire	135.2
7	Alaska	134.2
7	Colorado	134.2
9	New Jersey	133.9
9	Wisconsin	133.9
11	Maryland	131.9
12	Maine	131.4
12	Nebraska	131.4
14	Rhode Island	130.7
15	California	129.8
16	Illinois	129.7
17	Michigan	129.4
17	Pennsylvania	129.4
19	Delaware	128.8
20	Iowa	128.7
21	South Dakota	128.6
22	Montana	128.4
23	Oklahoma	128.3
24	Idaho	128.2
25	Hawaii	127.3
26	New York	126.7
27	Ohio	126.6
28	Missouri	125.4
29	Wyoming	125.2
30	Indiana	124.8
30	Kentucky	124.8
32	Georgia	124.0
33	South Carolina	123.5
34	North Dakota	123.1
35	Florida	123.0
36	Louisiana	122.8
37	Virginia	122.2
38	North Carolina	121.5
39	Arkansas	121.0
40	Nevada	120.8
41	Texas	118.6
42	Utah	117.1
43	West Virginia	116.9
44	Arizona	116.7
45	Alabama	115.3
46	New Mexico	115.0
47	Tennessee	113.7
NA	Kansas**	NA
NA	Mississippi**	NA
NA	Vermont**	NA
	District of Columbia	135.3

Source: American Cancer Society
    "Cancer Facts & Figures 2007" (Copyright 2007, American Cancer Society)
*For 1999 to 2003. Age-adjusted to the 2000 U.S. standard population.
**Not available.

Percent of Women 40 and Older Who Have Had a Mammogram in the Past Two Years: 2006
National Median = 76.5% of Women*

ALPHA ORDER

RANK	STATE	PERCENT
22	Alabama	77.2
36	Alaska	73.4
20	Arizona	77.4
44	Arkansas	70.0
15	California	78.5
39	Colorado	72.0
4	Connecticut	82.0
3	Delaware	83.7
16	Florida	78.0
14	Georgia	78.6
21	Hawaii	77.3
50	Idaho	67.3
31	Illinois	74.6
40	Indiana	71.6
19	Iowa	77.5
31	Kansas	74.6
30	Kentucky	75.1
28	Louisiana	75.8
5	Maine	81.8
8	Maryland	79.8
1	Massachusetts	84.8
7	Michigan	79.9
6	Minnesota	81.4
48	Mississippi	67.8
41	Missouri	71.1
38	Montana	72.2
37	Nebraska	73.3
43	Nevada	70.7
13	New Hampshire	79.0
17	New Jersey	77.9
44	New Mexico	70.0
10	New York	79.3
12	North Carolina	79.2
22	North Dakota	77.2
24	Ohio	76.7
49	Oklahoma	67.7
25	Oregon	76.5
29	Pennsylvania	75.7
2	Rhode Island	84.5
33	South Carolina	74.5
35	South Dakota	74.2
9	Tennessee	79.4
42	Texas	71.0
47	Utah	68.2
10	Vermont	79.3
25	Virginia	76.5
27	Washington	76.0
33	West Virginia	74.5
17	Wisconsin	77.9
46	Wyoming	68.6

RANK ORDER

RANK	STATE	PERCENT
1	Massachusetts	84.8
2	Rhode Island	84.5
3	Delaware	83.7
4	Connecticut	82.0
5	Maine	81.8
6	Minnesota	81.4
7	Michigan	79.9
8	Maryland	79.8
9	Tennessee	79.4
10	New York	79.3
10	Vermont	79.3
12	North Carolina	79.2
13	New Hampshire	79.0
14	Georgia	78.6
15	California	78.5
16	Florida	78.0
17	New Jersey	77.9
17	Wisconsin	77.9
19	Iowa	77.5
20	Arizona	77.4
21	Hawaii	77.3
22	Alabama	77.2
22	North Dakota	77.2
24	Ohio	76.7
25	Oregon	76.5
25	Virginia	76.5
27	Washington	76.0
28	Louisiana	75.8
29	Pennsylvania	75.7
30	Kentucky	75.1
31	Illinois	74.6
31	Kansas	74.6
33	South Carolina	74.5
33	West Virginia	74.5
35	South Dakota	74.2
36	Alaska	73.4
37	Nebraska	73.3
38	Montana	72.2
39	Colorado	72.0
40	Indiana	71.6
41	Missouri	71.1
42	Texas	71.0
43	Nevada	70.7
44	Arkansas	70.0
44	New Mexico	70.0
46	Wyoming	68.6
47	Utah	68.2
48	Mississippi	67.8
49	Oklahoma	67.7
50	Idaho	67.3

| | District of Columbia | 81.8 |

Source: U.S. Department of Health and Human Services, Centers for Disease Control and Prevention
  "2006 Behavioral Risk Factor Surveillance Summary Prevalence Data" (http://apps.nccd.cdc.gov/brfss/)
*Percent of women 40 years and older.

Estimated New Colon and Rectum Cancer Cases in 2007

National Estimated Total = 153,760 New Cases*

<table>
<tr><td colspan="4">ALPHA ORDER</td><td colspan="4">RANK ORDER</td></tr>
<tr><td>RANK</td><td>STATE</td><td>CASES</td><td>% of USA</td><td>RANK</td><td>STATE</td><td>CASES</td><td>% of USA</td></tr>
<tr><td>24</td><td>Alabama</td><td>2,350</td><td>1.5%</td><td>1</td><td>California</td><td>15,000</td><td>9.8%</td></tr>
<tr><td>49</td><td>Alaska</td><td>270</td><td>0.2%</td><td>2</td><td>Florida</td><td>11,420</td><td>7.4%</td></tr>
<tr><td>20</td><td>Arizona</td><td>2,750</td><td>1.8%</td><td>3</td><td>New York</td><td>10,710</td><td>7.0%</td></tr>
<tr><td>31</td><td>Arkansas</td><td>1,640</td><td>1.1%</td><td>4</td><td>Texas</td><td>9,510</td><td>6.2%</td></tr>
<tr><td>1</td><td>California</td><td>15,000</td><td>9.8%</td><td>5</td><td>Pennsylvania</td><td>8,220</td><td>5.3%</td></tr>
<tr><td>30</td><td>Colorado</td><td>1,790</td><td>1.2%</td><td>6</td><td>Illinois</td><td>6,890</td><td>4.5%</td></tr>
<tr><td>26</td><td>Connecticut</td><td>2,190</td><td>1.4%</td><td>7</td><td>Ohio</td><td>6,410</td><td>4.2%</td></tr>
<tr><td>45</td><td>Delaware</td><td>480</td><td>0.3%</td><td>8</td><td>Michigan</td><td>5,570</td><td>3.6%</td></tr>
<tr><td>2</td><td>Florida</td><td>11,420</td><td>7.4%</td><td>9</td><td>New Jersey</td><td>5,160</td><td>3.4%</td></tr>
<tr><td>12</td><td>Georgia</td><td>3,690</td><td>2.4%</td><td>10</td><td>North Carolina</td><td>4,290</td><td>2.8%</td></tr>
<tr><td>39</td><td>Hawaii</td><td>790</td><td>0.5%</td><td>11</td><td>Massachusetts</td><td>3,850</td><td>2.5%</td></tr>
<tr><td>43</td><td>Idaho</td><td>600</td><td>0.4%</td><td>12</td><td>Georgia</td><td>3,690</td><td>2.4%</td></tr>
<tr><td>6</td><td>Illinois</td><td>6,890</td><td>4.5%</td><td>13</td><td>Virginia</td><td>3,530</td><td>2.3%</td></tr>
<tr><td>14</td><td>Indiana</td><td>3,390</td><td>2.2%</td><td>14</td><td>Indiana</td><td>3,390</td><td>2.2%</td></tr>
<tr><td>27</td><td>Iowa</td><td>1,930</td><td>1.3%</td><td>15</td><td>Missouri</td><td>3,380</td><td>2.2%</td></tr>
<tr><td>33</td><td>Kansas</td><td>1,360</td><td>0.9%</td><td>16</td><td>Tennessee</td><td>3,100</td><td>2.0%</td></tr>
<tr><td>22</td><td>Kentucky</td><td>2,570</td><td>1.7%</td><td>17</td><td>Wisconsin</td><td>3,090</td><td>2.0%</td></tr>
<tr><td>23</td><td>Louisiana</td><td>2,520</td><td>1.6%</td><td>18</td><td>Washington</td><td>2,920</td><td>1.9%</td></tr>
<tr><td>37</td><td>Maine</td><td>880</td><td>0.6%</td><td>19</td><td>Maryland</td><td>2,870</td><td>1.9%</td></tr>
<tr><td>19</td><td>Maryland</td><td>2,870</td><td>1.9%</td><td>20</td><td>Arizona</td><td>2,750</td><td>1.8%</td></tr>
<tr><td>11</td><td>Massachusetts</td><td>3,850</td><td>2.5%</td><td>21</td><td>Minnesota</td><td>2,650</td><td>1.7%</td></tr>
<tr><td>8</td><td>Michigan</td><td>5,570</td><td>3.6%</td><td>22</td><td>Kentucky</td><td>2,570</td><td>1.7%</td></tr>
<tr><td>21</td><td>Minnesota</td><td>2,650</td><td>1.7%</td><td>23</td><td>Louisiana</td><td>2,520</td><td>1.6%</td></tr>
<tr><td>32</td><td>Mississippi</td><td>1,440</td><td>0.9%</td><td>24</td><td>Alabama</td><td>2,350</td><td>1.5%</td></tr>
<tr><td>15</td><td>Missouri</td><td>3,380</td><td>2.2%</td><td>25</td><td>South Carolina</td><td>2,230</td><td>1.5%</td></tr>
<tr><td>44</td><td>Montana</td><td>520</td><td>0.3%</td><td>26</td><td>Connecticut</td><td>2,190</td><td>1.4%</td></tr>
<tr><td>36</td><td>Nebraska</td><td>920</td><td>0.6%</td><td>27</td><td>Iowa</td><td>1,930</td><td>1.3%</td></tr>
<tr><td>35</td><td>Nevada</td><td>1,120</td><td>0.7%</td><td>28</td><td>Oklahoma</td><td>1,880</td><td>1.2%</td></tr>
<tr><td>38</td><td>New Hampshire</td><td>800</td><td>0.5%</td><td>29</td><td>Oregon</td><td>1,830</td><td>1.2%</td></tr>
<tr><td>9</td><td>New Jersey</td><td>5,160</td><td>3.4%</td><td>30</td><td>Colorado</td><td>1,790</td><td>1.2%</td></tr>
<tr><td>39</td><td>New Mexico</td><td>790</td><td>0.5%</td><td>31</td><td>Arkansas</td><td>1,640</td><td>1.1%</td></tr>
<tr><td>3</td><td>New York</td><td>10,710</td><td>7.0%</td><td>32</td><td>Mississippi</td><td>1,440</td><td>0.9%</td></tr>
<tr><td>10</td><td>North Carolina</td><td>4,290</td><td>2.8%</td><td>33</td><td>Kansas</td><td>1,360</td><td>0.9%</td></tr>
<tr><td>47</td><td>North Dakota</td><td>410</td><td>0.3%</td><td>34</td><td>West Virginia</td><td>1,210</td><td>0.8%</td></tr>
<tr><td>7</td><td>Ohio</td><td>6,410</td><td>4.2%</td><td>35</td><td>Nevada</td><td>1,120</td><td>0.7%</td></tr>
<tr><td>28</td><td>Oklahoma</td><td>1,880</td><td>1.2%</td><td>36</td><td>Nebraska</td><td>920</td><td>0.6%</td></tr>
<tr><td>29</td><td>Oregon</td><td>1,830</td><td>1.2%</td><td>37</td><td>Maine</td><td>880</td><td>0.6%</td></tr>
<tr><td>5</td><td>Pennsylvania</td><td>8,220</td><td>5.3%</td><td>38</td><td>New Hampshire</td><td>800</td><td>0.5%</td></tr>
<tr><td>42</td><td>Rhode Island</td><td>690</td><td>0.4%</td><td>39</td><td>Hawaii</td><td>790</td><td>0.5%</td></tr>
<tr><td>25</td><td>South Carolina</td><td>2,230</td><td>1.5%</td><td>39</td><td>New Mexico</td><td>790</td><td>0.5%</td></tr>
<tr><td>46</td><td>South Dakota</td><td>470</td><td>0.3%</td><td>41</td><td>Utah</td><td>740</td><td>0.5%</td></tr>
<tr><td>16</td><td>Tennessee</td><td>3,100</td><td>2.0%</td><td>42</td><td>Rhode Island</td><td>690</td><td>0.4%</td></tr>
<tr><td>4</td><td>Texas</td><td>9,510</td><td>6.2%</td><td>43</td><td>Idaho</td><td>600</td><td>0.4%</td></tr>
<tr><td>41</td><td>Utah</td><td>740</td><td>0.5%</td><td>44</td><td>Montana</td><td>520</td><td>0.3%</td></tr>
<tr><td>48</td><td>Vermont</td><td>390</td><td>0.3%</td><td>45</td><td>Delaware</td><td>480</td><td>0.3%</td></tr>
<tr><td>13</td><td>Virginia</td><td>3,530</td><td>2.3%</td><td>46</td><td>South Dakota</td><td>470</td><td>0.3%</td></tr>
<tr><td>18</td><td>Washington</td><td>2,920</td><td>1.9%</td><td>47</td><td>North Dakota</td><td>410</td><td>0.3%</td></tr>
<tr><td>34</td><td>West Virginia</td><td>1,210</td><td>0.8%</td><td>48</td><td>Vermont</td><td>390</td><td>0.3%</td></tr>
<tr><td>17</td><td>Wisconsin</td><td>3,090</td><td>2.0%</td><td>49</td><td>Alaska</td><td>270</td><td>0.2%</td></tr>
<tr><td>50</td><td>Wyoming</td><td>260</td><td>0.2%</td><td>50</td><td>Wyoming</td><td>260</td><td>0.2%</td></tr>
<tr><td></td><td></td><td></td><td></td><td></td><td>District of Columbia</td><td>270</td><td>0.2%</td></tr>
</table>

Source: American Cancer Society
    "Cancer Facts & Figures 2007" (Copyright 2007, American Cancer Society)
*These estimates are offered as a rough guide and should be interpreted with caution. They are calculated according to the distribution of estimated 2007 cancer deaths by state.

Estimated Rate of New Colon and Rectum Cancer Cases in 2007

National Estimated Rate = 51.4 New Cases per 100,000 Population*

ALPHA ORDER

RANK	STATE	RATE
32	Alabama	51.1
47	Alaska	40.3
42	Arizona	44.6
17	Arkansas	58.3
43	California	41.1
49	Colorado	37.7
8	Connecticut	62.5
19	Delaware	56.2
7	Florida	63.1
48	Georgia	39.4
10	Hawaii	61.5
44	Idaho	40.9
25	Illinois	53.7
25	Indiana	53.7
4	Iowa	64.7
37	Kansas	49.2
11	Kentucky	61.1
16	Louisiana	58.8
1	Maine	66.6
32	Maryland	51.1
14	Massachusetts	59.8
23	Michigan	55.2
30	Minnesota	51.3
35	Mississippi	49.5
18	Missouri	57.8
24	Montana	55.0
28	Nebraska	52.0
41	Nevada	44.9
12	New Hampshire	60.8
15	New Jersey	59.1
46	New Mexico	40.4
22	New York	55.5
38	North Carolina	48.4
6	North Dakota	64.5
20	Ohio	55.8
27	Oklahoma	52.5
36	Oregon	49.4
3	Pennsylvania	66.1
5	Rhode Island	64.6
29	South Carolina	51.6
13	South Dakota	60.1
30	Tennessee	51.3
45	Texas	40.5
50	Utah	29.0
8	Vermont	62.5
39	Virginia	46.2
40	Washington	45.7
2	West Virginia	66.5
21	Wisconsin	55.6
34	Wyoming	50.5

RANK ORDER

RANK	STATE	RATE
1	Maine	66.6
2	West Virginia	66.5
3	Pennsylvania	66.1
4	Iowa	64.7
5	Rhode Island	64.6
6	North Dakota	64.5
7	Florida	63.1
8	Connecticut	62.5
8	Vermont	62.5
10	Hawaii	61.5
11	Kentucky	61.1
12	New Hampshire	60.8
13	South Dakota	60.1
14	Massachusetts	59.8
15	New Jersey	59.1
16	Louisiana	58.8
17	Arkansas	58.3
18	Missouri	57.8
19	Delaware	56.2
20	Ohio	55.8
21	Wisconsin	55.6
22	New York	55.5
23	Michigan	55.2
24	Montana	55.0
25	Illinois	53.7
25	Indiana	53.7
27	Oklahoma	52.5
28	Nebraska	52.0
29	South Carolina	51.6
30	Minnesota	51.3
30	Tennessee	51.3
32	Alabama	51.1
32	Maryland	51.1
34	Wyoming	50.5
35	Mississippi	49.5
36	Oregon	49.4
37	Kansas	49.2
38	North Carolina	48.4
39	Virginia	46.2
40	Washington	45.7
41	Nevada	44.9
42	Arizona	44.6
43	California	41.1
44	Idaho	40.9
45	Texas	40.5
46	New Mexico	40.4
47	Alaska	40.3
48	Georgia	39.4
49	Colorado	37.7
50	Utah	29.0

District of Columbia   46.4

Source: CQ Press using data from American Cancer Society
"Cancer Facts & Figures 2007" (Copyright 2007, American Cancer Society)
*These estimates are offered as a rough guide and should be interpreted with caution. They are calculated according to the distribution of estimated 2007 cancer deaths by state. Rates calculated using 2006 Census resident population estimates.

Percent of Adults Who Have Ever Had a Sigmoidoscopy or Colonoscopy Exam: 2006
National Median = 57.1% of Adults*

ALPHA ORDER				RANK ORDER		
RANK	STATE	PERCENT		RANK	STATE	PERCENT
42	Alabama	53.3		1	Rhode Island	69.2
37	Alaska	55.2		2	Connecticut	68.7
28	Arizona	56.6		3	Delaware	68.4
45	Arkansas	52.6		4	Minnesota	68.2
25	California	57.1		5	Maryland	66.7
24	Colorado	57.2		6	Massachusetts	66.3
2	Connecticut	68.7		7	Michigan	66.1
3	Delaware	68.4		8	Virginia	65.3
19	Florida	58.9		9	Vermont	64.8
27	Georgia	57.0		10	Maine	64.2
40	Hawaii	54.1		11	Wisconsin	64.0
39	Idaho	54.2		12	New York	63.9
36	Illinois	55.6		13	Washington	63.7
31	Indiana	56.4		14	New Hampshire	63.6
35	Iowa	55.8		15	Utah	62.7
29	Kansas	56.5		16	North Carolina	61.8
21	Kentucky	58.6		17	Oregon	60.7
50	Louisiana	49.8		18	South Carolina	59.5
10	Maine	64.2		19	Florida	58.9
5	Maryland	66.7		20	Pennsylvania	58.8
6	Massachusetts	66.3		21	Kentucky	58.6
7	Michigan	66.1		22	New Jersey	58.3
4	Minnesota	68.2		23	Missouri	57.8
49	Mississippi	50.4		24	Colorado	57.2
23	Missouri	57.8		25	California	57.1
43	Montana	52.9		25	Ohio	57.1
48	Nebraska	51.4		27	Georgia	57.0
37	Nevada	55.2		28	Arizona	56.6
14	New Hampshire	63.6		29	Kansas	56.5
22	New Jersey	58.3		29	North Dakota	56.5
43	New Mexico	52.9		31	Indiana	56.4
12	New York	63.9		32	Texas	56.3
16	North Carolina	61.8		33	Tennessee	56.2
29	North Dakota	56.5		34	South Dakota	55.9
25	Ohio	57.1		35	Iowa	55.8
47	Oklahoma	51.7		36	Illinois	55.6
17	Oregon	60.7		37	Alaska	55.2
20	Pennsylvania	58.8		37	Nevada	55.2
1	Rhode Island	69.2		39	Idaho	54.2
18	South Carolina	59.5		40	Hawaii	54.1
34	South Dakota	55.9		41	West Virginia	53.4
33	Tennessee	56.2		42	Alabama	53.3
32	Texas	56.3		43	Montana	52.9
15	Utah	62.7		43	New Mexico	52.9
9	Vermont	64.8		45	Arkansas	52.6
8	Virginia	65.3		45	Wyoming	52.6
13	Washington	63.7		47	Oklahoma	51.7
41	West Virginia	53.4		48	Nebraska	51.4
11	Wisconsin	64.0		49	Mississippi	50.4
45	Wyoming	52.6		50	Louisiana	49.8
					District of Columbia	64.7

Source: U.S. Department of Health and Human Services, Centers for Disease Control and Prevention
   "2006 Behavioral Risk Factor Surveillance Summary Prevalence Data" (http://apps.nccd.cdc.gov/brfss/)
*Persons 50 and older.

Estimated New Leukemia Cases in 2007

National Estimated Total = 44,240 New Cases*

ALPHA ORDER

RANK	STATE	CASES	% of USA
28	Alabama	550	1.2%
49	Alaska	70	0.2%
20	Arizona	740	1.7%
30	Arkansas	510	1.2%
1	California	4,610	10.4%
23	Colorado	670	1.5%
26	Connecticut	610	1.4%
46	Delaware	110	0.2%
2	Florida	3,360	7.6%
13	Georgia	960	2.2%
42	Hawaii	170	0.4%
40	Idaho	220	0.5%
6	Illinois	2,030	4.6%
16	Indiana	910	2.1%
25	Iowa	620	1.4%
32	Kansas	420	0.9%
21	Kentucky	680	1.5%
21	Louisiana	680	1.5%
39	Maine	250	0.6%
24	Maryland	630	1.4%
12	Massachusetts	1,010	2.3%
8	Michigan	1,680	3.8%
15	Minnesota	920	2.1%
33	Mississippi	340	0.8%
18	Missouri	890	2.0%
42	Montana	170	0.4%
38	Nebraska	290	0.7%
34	Nevada	330	0.7%
41	New Hampshire	190	0.4%
9	New Jersey	1,520	3.4%
35	New Mexico	310	0.7%
4	New York	3,080	7.0%
10	North Carolina	1,070	2.4%
46	North Dakota	110	0.2%
7	Ohio	1,710	3.9%
27	Oklahoma	570	1.3%
31	Oregon	500	1.1%
5	Pennsylvania	2,240	5.1%
42	Rhode Island	170	0.4%
28	South Carolina	550	1.2%
45	South Dakota	130	0.3%
19	Tennessee	800	1.8%
3	Texas	3,130	7.1%
36	Utah	300	0.7%
48	Vermont	80	0.2%
17	Virginia	900	2.0%
13	Washington	960	2.2%
36	West Virginia	300	0.7%
11	Wisconsin	1,040	2.4%
49	Wyoming	70	0.2%

RANK ORDER

RANK	STATE	CASES	% of USA
1	California	4,610	10.4%
2	Florida	3,360	7.6%
3	Texas	3,130	7.1%
4	New York	3,080	7.0%
5	Pennsylvania	2,240	5.1%
6	Illinois	2,030	4.6%
7	Ohio	1,710	3.9%
8	Michigan	1,680	3.8%
9	New Jersey	1,520	3.4%
10	North Carolina	1,070	2.4%
11	Wisconsin	1,040	2.4%
12	Massachusetts	1,010	2.3%
13	Georgia	960	2.2%
13	Washington	960	2.2%
15	Minnesota	920	2.1%
16	Indiana	910	2.1%
17	Virginia	900	2.0%
18	Missouri	890	2.0%
19	Tennessee	800	1.8%
20	Arizona	740	1.7%
21	Kentucky	680	1.5%
21	Louisiana	680	1.5%
23	Colorado	670	1.5%
24	Maryland	630	1.4%
25	Iowa	620	1.4%
26	Connecticut	610	1.4%
27	Oklahoma	570	1.3%
28	Alabama	550	1.2%
28	South Carolina	550	1.2%
30	Arkansas	510	1.2%
31	Oregon	500	1.1%
32	Kansas	420	0.9%
33	Mississippi	340	0.8%
34	Nevada	330	0.7%
35	New Mexico	310	0.7%
36	Utah	300	0.7%
36	West Virginia	300	0.7%
38	Nebraska	290	0.7%
39	Maine	250	0.6%
40	Idaho	220	0.5%
41	New Hampshire	190	0.4%
42	Hawaii	170	0.4%
42	Montana	170	0.4%
42	Rhode Island	170	0.4%
45	South Dakota	130	0.3%
46	Delaware	110	0.2%
46	North Dakota	110	0.2%
48	Vermont	80	0.2%
49	Alaska	70	0.2%
49	Wyoming	70	0.2%
	District of Columbia	60	0.1%

Source: American Cancer Society
    "Cancer Facts & Figures 2007" (Copyright 2007, American Cancer Society)
*These estimates are offered as a rough guide and should be interpreted with caution. They are calculated according to the distribution of estimated 2007 cancer deaths by state.

Estimated Rate of New Leukemia Cases in 2007

National Estimated Rate = 14.8 New Cases per 100,000 Population*

ALPHA ORDER				RANK ORDER		
RANK	STATE	RATE		RANK	STATE	RATE
43	Alabama	12.0		1	Iowa	20.8
49	Alaska	10.4		2	Maine	18.9
43	Arizona	12.0		3	Wisconsin	18.7
5	Arkansas	18.1		4	Florida	18.6
41	California	12.6		5	Arkansas	18.1
31	Colorado	14.1		6	Montana	18.0
9	Connecticut	17.4		6	Pennsylvania	18.0
38	Delaware	12.9		8	Minnesota	17.8
4	Florida	18.6		9	Connecticut	17.4
50	Georgia	10.3		9	New Jersey	17.4
35	Hawaii	13.2		11	North Dakota	17.3
26	Idaho	15.0		12	Michigan	16.6
22	Illinois	15.8		12	South Dakota	16.6
29	Indiana	14.4		14	West Virginia	16.5
1	Iowa	20.8		15	Nebraska	16.4
24	Kansas	15.2		16	Kentucky	16.2
16	Kentucky	16.2		17	New York	16.0
18	Louisiana	15.9		18	Louisiana	15.9
2	Maine	18.9		18	New Mexico	15.9
48	Maryland	11.2		18	Oklahoma	15.9
23	Massachusetts	15.7		18	Rhode Island	15.9
12	Michigan	16.6		22	Illinois	15.8
8	Minnesota	17.8		23	Massachusetts	15.7
47	Mississippi	11.7		24	Kansas	15.2
24	Missouri	15.2		24	Missouri	15.2
6	Montana	18.0		26	Idaho	15.0
15	Nebraska	16.4		26	Washington	15.0
35	Nevada	13.2		28	Ohio	14.9
29	New Hampshire	14.4		29	Indiana	14.4
9	New Jersey	17.4		29	New Hampshire	14.4
18	New Mexico	15.9		31	Colorado	14.1
17	New York	16.0		32	Wyoming	13.6
42	North Carolina	12.1		33	Oregon	13.5
11	North Dakota	17.3		34	Texas	13.3
28	Ohio	14.9		35	Hawaii	13.2
18	Oklahoma	15.9		35	Nevada	13.2
33	Oregon	13.5		35	Tennessee	13.2
6	Pennsylvania	18.0		38	Delaware	12.9
18	Rhode Island	15.9		39	Vermont	12.8
40	South Carolina	12.7		40	South Carolina	12.7
12	South Dakota	16.6		41	California	12.6
35	Tennessee	13.2		42	North Carolina	12.1
34	Texas	13.3		43	Alabama	12.0
45	Utah	11.8		43	Arizona	12.0
39	Vermont	12.8		45	Utah	11.8
45	Virginia	11.8		45	Virginia	11.8
26	Washington	15.0		47	Mississippi	11.7
14	West Virginia	16.5		48	Maryland	11.2
3	Wisconsin	18.7		49	Alaska	10.4
32	Wyoming	13.6		50	Georgia	10.3
					District of Columbia	10.3

Source: CQ Press using data from American Cancer Society
   "Cancer Facts & Figures 2007" (Copyright 2007, American Cancer Society)
*These estimates are offered as a rough guide and should be interpreted with caution. They are calculated according to the distribution of estimated 2007 cancer deaths by state. Rates calculated using 2006 Census resident population estimates.

Estimated New Lung Cancer Cases in 2007

National Estimated Total = 213,380 New Cases*

ALPHA ORDER

RANK	STATE	CASES	% of USA
21	Alabama	3,850	1.8%
49	Alaska	330	0.2%
22	Arizona	3,740	1.8%
29	Arkansas	2,420	1.1%
1	California	17,920	8.4%
33	Colorado	2,100	1.0%
27	Connecticut	2,720	1.3%
41	Delaware	770	0.4%
2	Florida	17,490	8.2%
11	Georgia	5,780	2.7%
43	Hawaii	690	0.3%
42	Idaho	760	0.4%
7	Illinois	9,550	4.5%
14	Indiana	5,210	2.4%
30	Iowa	2,290	1.1%
34	Kansas	1,870	0.9%
17	Kentucky	4,450	2.1%
23	Louisiana	3,510	1.6%
36	Maine	1,360	0.6%
18	Maryland	4,130	1.9%
16	Massachusetts	5,060	2.4%
8	Michigan	8,210	3.8%
26	Minnesota	3,160	1.5%
31	Mississippi	2,190	1.0%
13	Missouri	5,350	2.5%
43	Montana	690	0.3%
37	Nebraska	1,190	0.6%
35	Nevada	1,750	0.8%
38	New Hampshire	1,010	0.5%
9	New Jersey	6,310	3.0%
39	New Mexico	940	0.4%
4	New York	13,390	6.3%
10	North Carolina	6,290	2.9%
48	North Dakota	390	0.2%
6	Ohio	9,790	4.6%
25	Oklahoma	3,180	1.5%
28	Oregon	2,520	1.2%
5	Pennsylvania	10,500	4.9%
40	Rhode Island	920	0.4%
24	South Carolina	3,460	1.6%
46	South Dakota	490	0.2%
15	Tennessee	5,110	2.4%
3	Texas	13,520	6.3%
45	Utah	600	0.3%
47	Vermont	440	0.2%
12	Virginia	5,360	2.5%
19	Washington	3,970	1.9%
32	West Virginia	2,110	1.0%
20	Wisconsin	3,930	1.8%
50	Wyoming	290	0.1%

RANK ORDER

RANK	STATE	CASES	% of USA
1	California	17,920	8.4%
2	Florida	17,490	8.2%
3	Texas	13,520	6.3%
4	New York	13,390	6.3%
5	Pennsylvania	10,500	4.9%
6	Ohio	9,790	4.6%
7	Illinois	9,550	4.5%
8	Michigan	8,210	3.8%
9	New Jersey	6,310	3.0%
10	North Carolina	6,290	2.9%
11	Georgia	5,780	2.7%
12	Virginia	5,360	2.5%
13	Missouri	5,350	2.5%
14	Indiana	5,210	2.4%
15	Tennessee	5,110	2.4%
16	Massachusetts	5,060	2.4%
17	Kentucky	4,450	2.1%
18	Maryland	4,130	1.9%
19	Washington	3,970	1.9%
20	Wisconsin	3,930	1.8%
21	Alabama	3,850	1.8%
22	Arizona	3,740	1.8%
23	Louisiana	3,510	1.6%
24	South Carolina	3,460	1.6%
25	Oklahoma	3,180	1.5%
26	Minnesota	3,160	1.5%
27	Connecticut	2,720	1.3%
28	Oregon	2,520	1.2%
29	Arkansas	2,420	1.1%
30	Iowa	2,290	1.1%
31	Mississippi	2,190	1.0%
32	West Virginia	2,110	1.0%
33	Colorado	2,100	1.0%
34	Kansas	1,870	0.9%
35	Nevada	1,750	0.8%
36	Maine	1,360	0.6%
37	Nebraska	1,190	0.6%
38	New Hampshire	1,010	0.5%
39	New Mexico	940	0.4%
40	Rhode Island	920	0.4%
41	Delaware	770	0.4%
42	Idaho	760	0.4%
43	Hawaii	690	0.3%
43	Montana	690	0.3%
45	Utah	600	0.3%
46	South Dakota	490	0.2%
47	Vermont	440	0.2%
48	North Dakota	390	0.2%
49	Alaska	330	0.2%
50	Wyoming	290	0.1%
	District of Columbia	380	0.2%

Source: American Cancer Society
"Cancer Facts & Figures 2007" (Copyright 2007, American Cancer Society)
*These estimates are offered as a rough guide and should be interpreted with caution. They are calculated according to the distribution of estimated 2007 cancer deaths by state.

Estimated Rate of New Lung Cancer Cases in 2007

National Estimated Rate = 71.3 New Cases per 100,000 Population*

ALPHA ORDER

RANK	STATE	RATE
13	Alabama	83.7
46	Alaska	49.2
41	Arizona	60.7
9	Arkansas	86.1
46	California	49.2
49	Colorado	44.2
19	Connecticut	77.6
6	Delaware	90.2
4	Florida	96.7
38	Georgia	61.7
44	Hawaii	53.7
45	Idaho	51.8
23	Illinois	74.4
14	Indiana	82.5
20	Iowa	76.8
34	Kansas	67.7
2	Kentucky	105.8
15	Louisiana	81.9
3	Maine	102.9
24	Maryland	73.5
18	Massachusetts	78.6
16	Michigan	81.3
40	Minnesota	61.2
22	Mississippi	75.2
5	Missouri	91.6
25	Montana	73.0
35	Nebraska	67.3
30	Nevada	70.1
20	New Hampshire	76.8
26	New Jersey	72.3
48	New Mexico	48.1
32	New York	69.4
27	North Carolina	71.0
39	North Dakota	61.3
10	Ohio	85.3
7	Oklahoma	88.8
33	Oregon	68.1
12	Pennsylvania	84.4
8	Rhode Island	86.2
17	South Carolina	80.1
36	South Dakota	62.7
11	Tennessee	84.6
42	Texas	57.5
50	Utah	23.5
29	Vermont	70.5
30	Virginia	70.1
37	Washington	62.1
1	West Virginia	116.0
28	Wisconsin	70.7
43	Wyoming	56.3

RANK ORDER

RANK	STATE	RATE
1	West Virginia	116.0
2	Kentucky	105.8
3	Maine	102.9
4	Florida	96.7
5	Missouri	91.6
6	Delaware	90.2
7	Oklahoma	88.8
8	Rhode Island	86.2
9	Arkansas	86.1
10	Ohio	85.3
11	Tennessee	84.6
12	Pennsylvania	84.4
13	Alabama	83.7
14	Indiana	82.5
15	Louisiana	81.9
16	Michigan	81.3
17	South Carolina	80.1
18	Massachusetts	78.6
19	Connecticut	77.6
20	Iowa	76.8
20	New Hampshire	76.8
22	Mississippi	75.2
23	Illinois	74.4
24	Maryland	73.5
25	Montana	73.0
26	New Jersey	72.3
27	North Carolina	71.0
28	Wisconsin	70.7
29	Vermont	70.5
30	Nevada	70.1
30	Virginia	70.1
32	New York	69.4
33	Oregon	68.1
34	Kansas	67.7
35	Nebraska	67.3
36	South Dakota	62.7
37	Washington	62.1
38	Georgia	61.7
39	North Dakota	61.3
40	Minnesota	61.2
41	Arizona	60.7
42	Texas	57.5
43	Wyoming	56.3
44	Hawaii	53.7
45	Idaho	51.8
46	Alaska	49.2
46	California	49.2
48	New Mexico	48.1
49	Colorado	44.2
50	Utah	23.5

District of Columbia 65.3

Source: CQ Press using data from American Cancer Society
    "Cancer Facts & Figures 2007" (Copyright 2007, American Cancer Society)
*These estimates are offered as a rough guide and should be interpreted with caution. They are calculated according to the distribution of estimated 2007 cancer deaths by state. Rates calculated using 2006 Census resident population estimates.

Estimated New Non-Hodgkin's Lymphoma Cases in 2007

National Estimated Total = 63,190 New Cases*

ALPHA ORDER					RANK ORDER			
RANK	STATE	CASES	% of USA		RANK	STATE	CASES	% of USA
27	Alabama	860	1.4%		1	California	7,190	11.4%
49	Alaska	110	0.2%		2	New York	4,540	7.2%
21	Arizona	1,080	1.7%		3	Florida	4,530	7.2%
31	Arkansas	600	0.9%		4	Texas	4,140	6.6%
1	California	7,190	11.4%		5	Pennsylvania	3,330	5.3%
25	Colorado	880	1.4%		6	Illinois	2,670	4.2%
26	Connecticut	870	1.4%		7	Ohio	2,560	4.1%
46	Delaware	170	0.3%		8	Michigan	2,250	3.6%
3	Florida	4,530	7.2%		9	New Jersey	2,200	3.5%
14	Georgia	1,370	2.2%		10	North Carolina	1,610	2.5%
43	Hawaii	250	0.4%		11	Massachusetts	1,550	2.5%
41	Idaho	280	0.4%		12	Washington	1,500	2.4%
6	Illinois	2,670	4.2%		13	Virginia	1,390	2.2%
15	Indiana	1,310	2.1%		14	Georgia	1,370	2.2%
28	Iowa	800	1.3%		15	Indiana	1,310	2.1%
31	Kansas	600	0.9%		16	Wisconsin	1,300	2.1%
23	Kentucky	900	1.4%		17	Missouri	1,260	2.0%
22	Louisiana	920	1.5%		18	Tennessee	1,180	1.9%
39	Maine	330	0.5%		19	Minnesota	1,170	1.9%
20	Maryland	1,160	1.8%		20	Maryland	1,160	1.8%
11	Massachusetts	1,550	2.5%		21	Arizona	1,080	1.7%
8	Michigan	2,250	3.6%		22	Louisiana	920	1.5%
19	Minnesota	1,170	1.9%		23	Kentucky	900	1.4%
33	Mississippi	480	0.8%		24	Oregon	890	1.4%
17	Missouri	1,260	2.0%		25	Colorado	880	1.4%
44	Montana	220	0.3%		26	Connecticut	870	1.4%
36	Nebraska	400	0.6%		27	Alabama	860	1.4%
35	Nevada	420	0.7%		28	Iowa	800	1.3%
40	New Hampshire	290	0.5%		29	South Carolina	780	1.2%
9	New Jersey	2,200	3.5%		30	Oklahoma	770	1.2%
38	New Mexico	350	0.6%		31	Arkansas	600	0.9%
2	New York	4,540	7.2%		31	Kansas	600	0.9%
10	North Carolina	1,610	2.5%		33	Mississippi	480	0.8%
47	North Dakota	150	0.2%		34	West Virginia	430	0.7%
7	Ohio	2,560	4.1%		35	Nevada	420	0.7%
30	Oklahoma	770	1.2%		36	Nebraska	400	0.6%
24	Oregon	890	1.4%		37	Utah	380	0.6%
5	Pennsylvania	3,330	5.3%		38	New Mexico	350	0.6%
42	Rhode Island	260	0.4%		39	Maine	330	0.5%
29	South Carolina	780	1.2%		40	New Hampshire	290	0.5%
45	South Dakota	180	0.3%		41	Idaho	280	0.4%
18	Tennessee	1,180	1.9%		42	Rhode Island	260	0.4%
4	Texas	4,140	6.6%		43	Hawaii	250	0.4%
37	Utah	380	0.6%		44	Montana	220	0.3%
48	Vermont	140	0.2%		45	South Dakota	180	0.3%
13	Virginia	1,390	2.2%		46	Delaware	170	0.3%
12	Washington	1,500	2.4%		47	North Dakota	150	0.2%
34	West Virginia	430	0.7%		48	Vermont	140	0.2%
16	Wisconsin	1,300	2.1%		49	Alaska	110	0.2%
49	Wyoming	110	0.2%		49	Wyoming	110	0.2%
					District of Columbia		100	0.2%

Source: American Cancer Society
     "Cancer Facts & Figures 2007" (Copyright 2007, American Cancer Society)
*These estimates are offered as a rough guide and should be interpreted with caution. They are calculated according to the distribution of estimated 2007 cancer deaths by state.

Estimated Rate of New Non-Hodgkin's Lymphoma Cases in 2007

National Estimated Rate = 21.1 New Cases per 100,000 Population*

ALPHA ORDER

RANK	STATE	RATE
38	Alabama	18.7
48	Alaska	16.4
45	Arizona	17.5
29	Arkansas	21.3
34	California	19.7
39	Colorado	18.5
6	Connecticut	24.8
33	Delaware	19.9
4	Florida	25.0
50	Georgia	14.6
36	Hawaii	19.4
37	Idaho	19.1
30	Illinois	20.8
31	Indiana	20.7
1	Iowa	26.8
23	Kansas	21.7
27	Kentucky	21.4
25	Louisiana	21.5
4	Maine	25.0
31	Maryland	20.7
8	Massachusetts	24.1
20	Michigan	22.3
17	Minnesota	22.6
47	Mississippi	16.5
24	Missouri	21.6
15	Montana	23.3
17	Nebraska	22.6
46	Nevada	16.8
22	New Hampshire	22.1
3	New Jersey	25.2
43	New Mexico	17.9
12	New York	23.5
40	North Carolina	18.2
10	North Dakota	23.6
20	Ohio	22.3
25	Oklahoma	21.5
9	Oregon	24.0
1	Pennsylvania	26.8
7	Rhode Island	24.4
42	South Carolina	18.1
16	South Dakota	23.0
35	Tennessee	19.5
44	Texas	17.6
49	Utah	14.9
19	Vermont	22.4
40	Virginia	18.2
12	Washington	23.5
10	West Virginia	23.6
14	Wisconsin	23.4
27	Wyoming	21.4

RANK ORDER

RANK	STATE	RATE
1	Iowa	26.8
1	Pennsylvania	26.8
3	New Jersey	25.2
4	Florida	25.0
4	Maine	25.0
6	Connecticut	24.8
7	Rhode Island	24.4
8	Massachusetts	24.1
9	Oregon	24.0
10	North Dakota	23.6
10	West Virginia	23.6
12	New York	23.5
12	Washington	23.5
14	Wisconsin	23.4
15	Montana	23.3
16	South Dakota	23.0
17	Minnesota	22.6
17	Nebraska	22.6
19	Vermont	22.4
20	Michigan	22.3
20	Ohio	22.3
22	New Hampshire	22.1
23	Kansas	21.7
24	Missouri	21.6
25	Louisiana	21.5
25	Oklahoma	21.5
27	Kentucky	21.4
27	Wyoming	21.4
29	Arkansas	21.3
30	Illinois	20.8
31	Indiana	20.7
31	Maryland	20.7
33	Delaware	19.9
34	California	19.7
35	Tennessee	19.5
36	Hawaii	19.4
37	Idaho	19.1
38	Alabama	18.7
39	Colorado	18.5
40	North Carolina	18.2
40	Virginia	18.2
42	South Carolina	18.1
43	New Mexico	17.9
44	Texas	17.6
45	Arizona	17.5
46	Nevada	16.8
47	Mississippi	16.5
48	Alaska	16.4
49	Utah	14.9
50	Georgia	14.6
	District of Columbia	17.2

Source: CQ Press using data from American Cancer Society
    "Cancer Facts & Figures 2007" (Copyright 2007, American Cancer Society)
*These estimates are offered as a rough guide and should be interpreted with caution. They are calculated according to the distribution of estimated 2007 cancer deaths by state. Rates calculated using 2006 Census resident population estimates.

Estimated New Prostate Cancer Cases in 2007

National Estimated Total = 218,890 New Cases*

ALPHA ORDER

RANK	STATE	CASES	% of USA
24	Alabama	3,010	1.4%
49	Alaska	420	0.2%
21	Arizona	3,400	1.6%
32	Arkansas	1,960	0.9%
1	California	24,590	11.2%
23	Colorado	3,160	1.4%
26	Connecticut	2,890	1.3%
44	Delaware	800	0.4%
3	Florida	15,710	7.2%
11	Georgia	5,850	2.7%
45	Hawaii	780	0.4%
40	Idaho	1,080	0.5%
9	Illinois	8,060	3.7%
19	Indiana	3,710	1.7%
30	Iowa	2,140	1.0%
35	Kansas	1,490	0.7%
27	Kentucky	2,880	1.3%
20	Louisiana	3,640	1.7%
39	Maine	1,210	0.6%
17	Maryland	4,690	2.1%
13	Massachusetts	5,180	2.4%
7	Michigan	8,200	3.7%
15	Minnesota	4,800	2.2%
31	Mississippi	2,010	0.9%
18	Missouri	3,910	1.8%
42	Montana	940	0.4%
38	Nebraska	1,260	0.6%
33	Nevada	1,550	0.7%
41	New Hampshire	1,050	0.5%
8	New Jersey	8,070	3.7%
37	New Mexico	1,410	0.6%
2	New York	15,770	7.2%
10	North Carolina	6,040	2.8%
48	North Dakota	520	0.2%
6	Ohio	8,260	3.8%
29	Oklahoma	2,510	1.1%
28	Oregon	2,870	1.3%
5	Pennsylvania	12,230	5.6%
43	Rhode Island	920	0.4%
22	South Carolina	3,380	1.5%
46	South Dakota	710	0.3%
25	Tennessee	3,000	1.4%
4	Texas	13,280	6.1%
34	Utah	1,510	0.7%
47	Vermont	550	0.3%
12	Virginia	5,330	2.4%
14	Washington	5,000	2.3%
36	West Virginia	1,430	0.7%
16	Wisconsin	4,770	2.2%
50	Wyoming	410	0.2%

RANK ORDER

RANK	STATE	CASES	% of USA
1	California	24,590	11.2%
2	New York	15,770	7.2%
3	Florida	15,710	7.2%
4	Texas	13,280	6.1%
5	Pennsylvania	12,230	5.6%
6	Ohio	8,260	3.8%
7	Michigan	8,200	3.7%
8	New Jersey	8,070	3.7%
9	Illinois	8,060	3.7%
10	North Carolina	6,040	2.8%
11	Georgia	5,850	2.7%
12	Virginia	5,330	2.4%
13	Massachusetts	5,180	2.4%
14	Washington	5,000	2.3%
15	Minnesota	4,800	2.2%
16	Wisconsin	4,770	2.2%
17	Maryland	4,690	2.1%
18	Missouri	3,910	1.8%
19	Indiana	3,710	1.7%
20	Louisiana	3,640	1.7%
21	Arizona	3,400	1.6%
22	South Carolina	3,380	1.5%
23	Colorado	3,160	1.4%
24	Alabama	3,010	1.4%
25	Tennessee	3,000	1.4%
26	Connecticut	2,890	1.3%
27	Kentucky	2,880	1.3%
28	Oregon	2,870	1.3%
29	Oklahoma	2,510	1.1%
30	Iowa	2,140	1.0%
31	Mississippi	2,010	0.9%
32	Arkansas	1,960	0.9%
33	Nevada	1,550	0.7%
34	Utah	1,510	0.7%
35	Kansas	1,490	0.7%
36	West Virginia	1,430	0.7%
37	New Mexico	1,410	0.6%
38	Nebraska	1,260	0.6%
39	Maine	1,210	0.6%
40	Idaho	1,080	0.5%
41	New Hampshire	1,050	0.5%
42	Montana	940	0.4%
43	Rhode Island	920	0.4%
44	Delaware	800	0.4%
45	Hawaii	780	0.4%
46	South Dakota	710	0.3%
47	Vermont	550	0.3%
48	North Dakota	520	0.2%
49	Alaska	420	0.2%
50	Wyoming	410	0.2%
	District of Columbia	540	0.2%

Source: American Cancer Society
"Cancer Facts & Figures 2007" (Copyright 2007, American Cancer Society)
*These estimates are offered as a rough guide and should be interpreted with caution. They are calculated according to the distribution of estimated 2007 cancer deaths by state.

Age-Adjusted Incidence Rate of Prostate Cancer Cases in 2003

National Rate = 165.0 New Cases per 100,000 Male Population*

ALPHA ORDER

RANK	STATE	RATE
42	Alabama	140.4
22	Alaska	167.7
46	Arizona	118.2
32	Arkansas	154.2
30	California	158.3
27	Colorado	164.8
10	Connecticut	179.8
16	Delaware	176.1
35	Florida	152.7
23	Georgia	166.2
45	Hawaii	132.3
18	Idaho	171.9
25	Illinois	165.6
43	Indiana	138.6
32	Iowa	154.2
NA	Kansas**	NA
31	Kentucky	155.1
11	Louisiana	179.5
19	Maine	171.3
6	Maryland	185.2
12	Massachusetts	178.2
2	Michigan	199.1
4	Minnesota	188.6
NA	Mississippi**	NA
44	Missouri	136.8
7	Montana	183.6
24	Nebraska	165.7
38	Nevada	150.6
26	New Hampshire	165.3
1	New Jersey	200.3
37	New Mexico	152.2
21	New York	168.1
36	North Carolina	152.4
9	North Dakota	181.8
34	Ohio	154.1
39	Oklahoma	148.8
28	Oregon	164.1
17	Pennsylvania	172.3
13	Rhode Island	177.9
15	South Carolina	176.9
3	South Dakota	190.1
47	Tennessee	108.7
40	Texas	148.3
5	Utah	186.5
NA	Vermont**	NA
29	Virginia	161.4
14	Washington	177.1
41	West Virginia	148.2
20	Wisconsin	169.1
8	Wyoming	182.2

RANK ORDER

RANK	STATE	RATE
1	New Jersey	200.3
2	Michigan	199.1
3	South Dakota	190.1
4	Minnesota	188.6
5	Utah	186.5
6	Maryland	185.2
7	Montana	183.6
8	Wyoming	182.2
9	North Dakota	181.8
10	Connecticut	179.8
11	Louisiana	179.5
12	Massachusetts	178.2
13	Rhode Island	177.9
14	Washington	177.1
15	South Carolina	176.9
16	Delaware	176.1
17	Pennsylvania	172.3
18	Idaho	171.9
19	Maine	171.3
20	Wisconsin	169.1
21	New York	168.1
22	Alaska	167.7
23	Georgia	166.2
24	Nebraska	165.7
25	Illinois	165.6
26	New Hampshire	165.3
27	Colorado	164.8
28	Oregon	164.1
29	Virginia	161.4
30	California	158.3
31	Kentucky	155.1
32	Arkansas	154.2
32	Iowa	154.2
34	Ohio	154.1
35	Florida	152.7
36	North Carolina	152.4
37	New Mexico	152.2
38	Nevada	150.6
39	Oklahoma	148.8
40	Texas	148.3
41	West Virginia	148.2
42	Alabama	140.4
43	Indiana	138.6
44	Missouri	136.8
45	Hawaii	132.3
46	Arizona	118.2
47	Tennessee	108.7
NA	Kansas**	NA
NA	Mississippi**	NA
NA	Vermont**	NA

District of Columbia   227.1

Source: American Cancer Society
    "Cancer Facts & Figures 2007" (Copyright 2007, American Cancer Society)
*For 1999 to 2003. Age-adjusted to the 2000 U.S. standard population.
**Not available.

Percent of Males Receiving PSA Test for Prostate Cancer: 2006

National Median = 53.5% of Men*

<table>
<tr><td colspan="3">ALPHA ORDER</td><td colspan="3">RANK ORDER</td></tr>
<tr><td>RANK</td><td>STATE</td><td>PERCENT</td><td>RANK</td><td>STATE</td><td>PERCENT</td></tr>
<tr><td>7</td><td>Alabama</td><td>56.6</td><td>1</td><td>Wyoming</td><td>63.0</td></tr>
<tr><td>49</td><td>Alaska</td><td>45.9</td><td>2</td><td>Rhode Island</td><td>61.0</td></tr>
<tr><td>10</td><td>Arizona</td><td>56.1</td><td>3</td><td>Florida</td><td>60.1</td></tr>
<tr><td>28</td><td>Arkansas</td><td>52.8</td><td>4</td><td>Georgia</td><td>57.2</td></tr>
<tr><td>39</td><td>California</td><td>49.3</td><td>5</td><td>Delaware</td><td>56.9</td></tr>
<tr><td>24</td><td>Colorado</td><td>53.8</td><td>5</td><td>Michigan</td><td>56.9</td></tr>
<tr><td>18</td><td>Connecticut</td><td>54.7</td><td>7</td><td>Alabama</td><td>56.6</td></tr>
<tr><td>5</td><td>Delaware</td><td>56.9</td><td>8</td><td>Montana</td><td>56.3</td></tr>
<tr><td>3</td><td>Florida</td><td>60.1</td><td>8</td><td>South Carolina</td><td>56.3</td></tr>
<tr><td>4</td><td>Georgia</td><td>57.2</td><td>10</td><td>Arizona</td><td>56.1</td></tr>
<tr><td>50</td><td>Hawaii</td><td>40.0</td><td>10</td><td>Massachusetts</td><td>56.1</td></tr>
<tr><td>35</td><td>Idaho</td><td>51.3</td><td>10</td><td>Ohio</td><td>56.1</td></tr>
<tr><td>46</td><td>Illinois</td><td>47.9</td><td>13</td><td>Louisiana</td><td>55.8</td></tr>
<tr><td>38</td><td>Indiana</td><td>49.6</td><td>14</td><td>Maryland</td><td>55.7</td></tr>
<tr><td>29</td><td>Iowa</td><td>52.7</td><td>14</td><td>North Carolina</td><td>55.7</td></tr>
<tr><td>17</td><td>Kansas</td><td>54.8</td><td>16</td><td>New Jersey</td><td>55.4</td></tr>
<tr><td>26</td><td>Kentucky</td><td>53.0</td><td>17</td><td>Kansas</td><td>54.8</td></tr>
<tr><td>13</td><td>Louisiana</td><td>55.8</td><td>18</td><td>Connecticut</td><td>54.7</td></tr>
<tr><td>44</td><td>Maine</td><td>48.0</td><td>18</td><td>Mississippi</td><td>54.7</td></tr>
<tr><td>14</td><td>Maryland</td><td>55.7</td><td>20</td><td>New York</td><td>54.5</td></tr>
<tr><td>10</td><td>Massachusetts</td><td>56.1</td><td>21</td><td>South Dakota</td><td>54.4</td></tr>
<tr><td>5</td><td>Michigan</td><td>56.9</td><td>22</td><td>Tennessee</td><td>54.3</td></tr>
<tr><td>41</td><td>Minnesota</td><td>48.8</td><td>23</td><td>West Virginia</td><td>54.1</td></tr>
<tr><td>18</td><td>Mississippi</td><td>54.7</td><td>24</td><td>Colorado</td><td>53.8</td></tr>
<tr><td>33</td><td>Missouri</td><td>51.7</td><td>25</td><td>Virginia</td><td>53.5</td></tr>
<tr><td>8</td><td>Montana</td><td>56.3</td><td>26</td><td>Kentucky</td><td>53.0</td></tr>
<tr><td>32</td><td>Nebraska</td><td>51.9</td><td>26</td><td>Pennsylvania</td><td>53.0</td></tr>
<tr><td>29</td><td>Nevada</td><td>52.7</td><td>28</td><td>Arkansas</td><td>52.8</td></tr>
<tr><td>36</td><td>New Hampshire</td><td>50.2</td><td>29</td><td>Iowa</td><td>52.7</td></tr>
<tr><td>16</td><td>New Jersey</td><td>55.4</td><td>29</td><td>Nevada</td><td>52.7</td></tr>
<tr><td>40</td><td>New Mexico</td><td>49.0</td><td>31</td><td>North Dakota</td><td>52.2</td></tr>
<tr><td>20</td><td>New York</td><td>54.5</td><td>32</td><td>Nebraska</td><td>51.9</td></tr>
<tr><td>14</td><td>North Carolina</td><td>55.7</td><td>33</td><td>Missouri</td><td>51.7</td></tr>
<tr><td>31</td><td>North Dakota</td><td>52.2</td><td>33</td><td>Oklahoma</td><td>51.7</td></tr>
<tr><td>10</td><td>Ohio</td><td>56.1</td><td>35</td><td>Idaho</td><td>51.3</td></tr>
<tr><td>33</td><td>Oklahoma</td><td>51.7</td><td>36</td><td>New Hampshire</td><td>50.2</td></tr>
<tr><td>37</td><td>Oregon</td><td>50.0</td><td>37</td><td>Oregon</td><td>50.0</td></tr>
<tr><td>26</td><td>Pennsylvania</td><td>53.0</td><td>38</td><td>Indiana</td><td>49.6</td></tr>
<tr><td>2</td><td>Rhode Island</td><td>61.0</td><td>39</td><td>California</td><td>49.3</td></tr>
<tr><td>8</td><td>South Carolina</td><td>56.3</td><td>40</td><td>New Mexico</td><td>49.0</td></tr>
<tr><td>21</td><td>South Dakota</td><td>54.4</td><td>41</td><td>Minnesota</td><td>48.8</td></tr>
<tr><td>22</td><td>Tennessee</td><td>54.3</td><td>42</td><td>Texas</td><td>48.4</td></tr>
<tr><td>42</td><td>Texas</td><td>48.4</td><td>42</td><td>Wisconsin</td><td>48.4</td></tr>
<tr><td>48</td><td>Utah</td><td>46.6</td><td>44</td><td>Maine</td><td>48.0</td></tr>
<tr><td>47</td><td>Vermont</td><td>47.7</td><td>44</td><td>Washington</td><td>48.0</td></tr>
<tr><td>25</td><td>Virginia</td><td>53.5</td><td>46</td><td>Illinois</td><td>47.9</td></tr>
<tr><td>44</td><td>Washington</td><td>48.0</td><td>47</td><td>Vermont</td><td>47.7</td></tr>
<tr><td>23</td><td>West Virginia</td><td>54.1</td><td>48</td><td>Utah</td><td>46.6</td></tr>
<tr><td>42</td><td>Wisconsin</td><td>48.4</td><td>49</td><td>Alaska</td><td>45.9</td></tr>
<tr><td>1</td><td>Wyoming</td><td>63.0</td><td>50</td><td>Hawaii</td><td>40.0</td></tr>
<tr><td></td><td></td><td></td><td></td><td>District of Columbia</td><td>58.8</td></tr>
</table>

Source: U.S. Department of Health and Human Services, Centers for Disease Control and Prevention
    "2006 Behavioral Risk Factor Surveillance Summary Prevalence Data" (http://apps.nccd.cdc.gov/brfss/)
*Men 40 and older receiving prostate-specific antigen (PSA) test within the past two years.

Estimated New Skin Melanoma Cases in 2007

National Estimated Total = 59,940 New Cases*

ALPHA ORDER

RANK	STATE	CASES	% of USA
27	Alabama	740	1.2%
50	Alaska	80	0.1%
15	Arizona	1,300	2.2%
31	Arkansas	550	0.9%
1	California	6,860	11.4%
17	Colorado	1,210	2.0%
20	Connecticut	1,120	1.9%
44	Delaware	190	0.3%
2	Florida	4,380	7.3%
14	Georgia	1,460	2.4%
43	Hawaii	270	0.5%
39	Idaho	350	0.6%
9	Illinois	2,050	3.4%
16	Indiana	1,220	2.0%
29	Iowa	690	1.2%
33	Kansas	430	0.7%
22	Kentucky	1,050	1.8%
30	Louisiana	670	1.1%
35	Maine	410	0.7%
18	Maryland	1,150	1.9%
10	Massachusetts	1,820	3.0%
8	Michigan	2,080	3.5%
19	Minnesota	1,130	1.9%
41	Mississippi	320	0.5%
25	Missouri	870	1.5%
44	Montana	190	0.3%
40	Nebraska	340	0.6%
37	Nevada	390	0.7%
38	New Hampshire	370	0.6%
7	New Jersey	2,210	3.7%
34	New Mexico	420	0.7%
5	New York	3,070	5.1%
11	North Carolina	1,630	2.7%
48	North Dakota	120	0.2%
6	Ohio	2,390	4.0%
28	Oklahoma	720	1.2%
23	Oregon	990	1.7%
4	Pennsylvania	3,120	5.2%
42	Rhode Island	300	0.5%
25	South Carolina	870	1.5%
46	South Dakota	160	0.3%
24	Tennessee	980	1.6%
3	Texas	3,860	6.4%
32	Utah	500	0.8%
47	Vermont	150	0.3%
13	Virginia	1,510	2.5%
11	Washington	1,630	2.7%
35	West Virginia	410	0.7%
21	Wisconsin	1,070	1.8%
49	Wyoming	100	0.2%

RANK ORDER

RANK	STATE	CASES	% of USA
1	California	6,860	11.4%
2	Florida	4,380	7.3%
3	Texas	3,860	6.4%
4	Pennsylvania	3,120	5.2%
5	New York	3,070	5.1%
6	Ohio	2,390	4.0%
7	New Jersey	2,210	3.7%
8	Michigan	2,080	3.5%
9	Illinois	2,050	3.4%
10	Massachusetts	1,820	3.0%
11	North Carolina	1,630	2.7%
11	Washington	1,630	2.7%
13	Virginia	1,510	2.5%
14	Georgia	1,460	2.4%
15	Arizona	1,300	2.2%
16	Indiana	1,220	2.0%
17	Colorado	1,210	2.0%
18	Maryland	1,150	1.9%
19	Minnesota	1,130	1.9%
20	Connecticut	1,120	1.9%
21	Wisconsin	1,070	1.8%
22	Kentucky	1,050	1.8%
23	Oregon	990	1.7%
24	Tennessee	980	1.6%
25	Missouri	870	1.5%
25	South Carolina	870	1.5%
27	Alabama	740	1.2%
28	Oklahoma	720	1.2%
29	Iowa	690	1.2%
30	Louisiana	670	1.1%
31	Arkansas	550	0.9%
32	Utah	500	0.8%
33	Kansas	430	0.7%
34	New Mexico	420	0.7%
35	Maine	410	0.7%
35	West Virginia	410	0.7%
37	Nevada	390	0.7%
38	New Hampshire	370	0.6%
39	Idaho	350	0.6%
40	Nebraska	340	0.6%
41	Mississippi	320	0.5%
42	Rhode Island	300	0.5%
43	Hawaii	270	0.5%
44	Delaware	190	0.3%
44	Montana	190	0.3%
46	South Dakota	160	0.3%
47	Vermont	150	0.3%
48	North Dakota	120	0.2%
49	Wyoming	100	0.2%
50	Alaska	80	0.1%
	District of Columbia	60	0.1%

Source: American Cancer Society
    "Cancer Facts & Figures 2007" (Copyright 2007, American Cancer Society)
*These estimates are offered as a rough guide and should be interpreted with caution. They are calculated according to the distribution of estimated 2007 cancer deaths by state.

Estimated Rate of New Skin Melanoma Cases in 2007

National Estimated Rate = 20.0 New Cases per 100,000 Population*

ALPHA ORDER

RANK	STATE	CASES
41	Alabama	16.1
49	Alaska	11.9
20	Arizona	21.1
30	Arkansas	19.6
37	California	18.8
7	Colorado	25.5
1	Connecticut	32.0
17	Delaware	22.3
12	Florida	24.2
44	Georgia	15.6
21	Hawaii	21.0
14	Idaho	23.9
42	Illinois	16.0
33	Indiana	19.3
15	Iowa	23.1
44	Kansas	15.6
11	Kentucky	25.0
44	Louisiana	15.6
2	Maine	31.0
24	Maryland	20.5
3	Massachusetts	28.3
23	Michigan	20.6
18	Minnesota	21.9
50	Mississippi	11.0
48	Missouri	14.9
26	Montana	20.1
35	Nebraska	19.2
44	Nevada	15.6
4	New Hampshire	28.1
9	New Jersey	25.3
19	New Mexico	21.5
43	New York	15.9
38	North Carolina	18.4
36	North Dakota	18.9
22	Ohio	20.8
26	Oklahoma	20.1
6	Oregon	26.8
10	Pennsylvania	25.1
4	Rhode Island	28.1
26	South Carolina	20.1
24	South Dakota	20.5
40	Tennessee	16.2
39	Texas	16.4
30	Utah	19.6
13	Vermont	24.0
29	Virginia	19.8
7	Washington	25.5
16	West Virginia	22.5
33	Wisconsin	19.3
32	Wyoming	19.4

RANK ORDER

RANK	STATE	CASES
1	Connecticut	32.0
2	Maine	31.0
3	Massachusetts	28.3
4	New Hampshire	28.1
4	Rhode Island	28.1
6	Oregon	26.8
7	Colorado	25.5
7	Washington	25.5
9	New Jersey	25.3
10	Pennsylvania	25.1
11	Kentucky	25.0
12	Florida	24.2
13	Vermont	24.0
14	Idaho	23.9
15	Iowa	23.1
16	West Virginia	22.5
17	Delaware	22.3
18	Minnesota	21.9
19	New Mexico	21.5
20	Arizona	21.1
21	Hawaii	21.0
22	Ohio	20.8
23	Michigan	20.6
24	Maryland	20.5
24	South Dakota	20.5
26	Montana	20.1
26	Oklahoma	20.1
26	South Carolina	20.1
29	Virginia	19.8
30	Arkansas	19.6
30	Utah	19.6
32	Wyoming	19.4
33	Indiana	19.3
33	Wisconsin	19.3
35	Nebraska	19.2
36	North Dakota	18.9
37	California	18.8
38	North Carolina	18.4
39	Texas	16.4
40	Tennessee	16.2
41	Alabama	16.1
42	Illinois	16.0
43	New York	15.9
44	Georgia	15.6
44	Kansas	15.6
44	Louisiana	15.6
44	Nevada	15.6
48	Missouri	14.9
49	Alaska	11.9
50	Mississippi	11.0
	District of Columbia	10.3

Source: CQ Press using data from American Cancer Society
"Cancer Facts & Figures 2007" (Copyright 2007, American Cancer Society)
*These estimates are offered as a rough guide and should be interpreted with caution. They are calculated according to the distribution of estimated 2007 cancer deaths by state. Rates calculated using 2006 Census resident population estimates.

Estimated New Cervical Cancer Cases in 2007

National Estimated Total = 11,150 New Cases*

ALPHA ORDER | | | | RANK ORDER | | |

RANK	STATE	CASES	% of USA	RANK	STATE	CASES	% of USA
22	Alabama	170	1.5%	1	California	1,350	12.1%
NA	Alaska**	NA	NA	2	Texas	940	8.4%
18	Arizona	190	1.7%	3	Florida	850	7.6%
28	Arkansas	130	1.2%	4	New York	790	7.1%
1	California	1,350	12.1%	5	Illinois	530	4.8%
25	Colorado	150	1.3%	6	Pennsylvania	420	3.8%
31	Connecticut	100	0.9%	7	Ohio	390	3.5%
NA	Delaware**	NA	NA	8	Michigan	370	3.3%
3	Florida	850	7.6%	9	New Jersey	350	3.1%
10	Georgia	330	3.0%	10	Georgia	330	3.0%
38	Hawaii	50	0.4%	11	North Carolina	280	2.5%
NA	Idaho**	NA	NA	11	Virginia	280	2.5%
5	Illinois	530	4.8%	13	Tennessee	250	2.2%
14	Indiana	240	2.2%	14	Indiana	240	2.2%
31	Iowa	100	0.9%	14	Missouri	240	2.2%
31	Kansas	100	0.9%	16	Kentucky	200	1.8%
16	Kentucky	200	1.8%	16	Louisiana	200	1.8%
16	Louisiana	200	1.8%	18	Arizona	190	1.7%
NA	Maine**	NA	NA	18	Maryland	190	1.7%
18	Maryland	190	1.7%	18	South Carolina	190	1.7%
21	Massachusetts	180	1.6%	21	Massachusetts	180	1.6%
8	Michigan	370	3.3%	22	Alabama	170	1.5%
25	Minnesota	150	1.3%	22	Wisconsin	170	1.5%
29	Mississippi	120	1.1%	24	Oklahoma	160	1.4%
14	Missouri	240	2.2%	25	Colorado	150	1.3%
NA	Montana**	NA	NA	25	Minnesota	150	1.3%
37	Nebraska	60	0.5%	25	Washington	150	1.3%
34	Nevada	80	0.7%	28	Arkansas	130	1.2%
NA	New Hampshire**	NA	NA	29	Mississippi	120	1.1%
9	New Jersey	350	3.1%	30	Oregon	110	1.0%
36	New Mexico	70	0.6%	31	Connecticut	100	0.9%
4	New York	790	7.1%	31	Iowa	100	0.9%
11	North Carolina	280	2.5%	31	Kansas	100	0.9%
NA	North Dakota**	NA	NA	34	Nevada	80	0.7%
7	Ohio	390	3.5%	34	West Virginia	80	0.7%
24	Oklahoma	160	1.4%	36	New Mexico	70	0.6%
30	Oregon	110	1.0%	37	Nebraska	60	0.5%
6	Pennsylvania	420	3.8%	38	Hawaii	50	0.4%
NA	Rhode Island**	NA	NA	38	Utah	50	0.4%
18	South Carolina	190	1.7%	NA	Alaska**	NA	NA
NA	South Dakota**	NA	NA	NA	Delaware**	NA	NA
13	Tennessee	250	2.2%	NA	Idaho**	NA	NA
2	Texas	940	8.4%	NA	Maine**	NA	NA
38	Utah	50	0.4%	NA	Montana**	NA	NA
NA	Vermont**	NA	NA	NA	New Hampshire**	NA	NA
11	Virginia	280	2.5%	NA	North Dakota**	NA	NA
25	Washington	150	1.3%	NA	Rhode Island**	NA	NA
34	West Virginia	80	0.7%	NA	South Dakota**	NA	NA
22	Wisconsin	170	1.5%	NA	Vermont**	NA	NA
NA	Wyoming**	NA	NA	NA	Wyoming**	NA	NA
					District of Columbia**	NA	NA

Source: American Cancer Society
    "Cancer Facts & Figures 2007" (Copyright 2007, American Cancer Society)
*These estimates are offered as a rough guide and should be interpreted with caution. They are calculated according to the distribution of estimated 2007 cancer deaths by state.
**Not available.

Estimated Rate of New Cervical Cancer Cases in 2007

National Estimated Rate = 7.4 New Cases per 100,000 Female Population*

ALPHA ORDER

RANK	STATE	RATE
19	Alabama	7.2
NA	Alaska**	NA
31	Arizona	6.4
3	Arkansas	9.2
16	California	7.5
30	Colorado	6.5
36	Connecticut	5.5
NA	Delaware**	NA
1	Florida	9.4
19	Georgia	7.2
14	Hawaii	7.8
NA	Idaho**	NA
8	Illinois	8.2
16	Indiana	7.5
26	Iowa	6.6
19	Kansas	7.2
1	Kentucky	9.4
6	Louisiana	8.6
NA	Maine**	NA
26	Maryland	6.6
36	Massachusetts	5.5
19	Michigan	7.2
35	Minnesota	5.8
12	Mississippi	8.0
11	Missouri	8.1
NA	Montana**	NA
24	Nebraska	6.7
24	Nevada	6.7
NA	New Hampshire**	NA
14	New Jersey	7.8
23	New Mexico	7.1
12	New York	8.0
32	North Carolina	6.3
NA	North Dakota**	NA
26	Ohio	6.6
4	Oklahoma	8.9
34	Oregon	6.0
26	Pennsylvania	6.6
NA	Rhode Island**	NA
5	South Carolina	8.7
NA	South Dakota**	NA
8	Tennessee	8.2
8	Texas	8.2
39	Utah	4.1
NA	Vermont**	NA
18	Virginia	7.3
38	Washington	4.8
6	West Virginia	8.6
33	Wisconsin	6.1
NA	Wyoming**	NA

RANK ORDER

RANK	STATE	RATE
1	Florida	9.4
1	Kentucky	9.4
3	Arkansas	9.2
4	Oklahoma	8.9
5	South Carolina	8.7
6	Louisiana	8.6
6	West Virginia	8.6
8	Illinois	8.2
8	Tennessee	8.2
8	Texas	8.2
11	Missouri	8.1
12	Mississippi	8.0
12	New York	8.0
14	Hawaii	7.8
14	New Jersey	7.8
16	California	7.5
16	Indiana	7.5
18	Virginia	7.3
19	Alabama	7.2
19	Georgia	7.2
19	Kansas	7.2
19	Michigan	7.2
23	New Mexico	7.1
24	Nebraska	6.7
24	Nevada	6.7
26	Iowa	6.6
26	Maryland	6.6
26	Ohio	6.6
26	Pennsylvania	6.6
30	Colorado	6.5
31	Arizona	6.4
32	North Carolina	6.3
33	Wisconsin	6.1
34	Oregon	6.0
35	Minnesota	5.8
36	Connecticut	5.5
36	Massachusetts	5.5
38	Washington	4.8
39	Utah	4.1
NA	Alaska**	NA
NA	Delaware**	NA
NA	Idaho**	NA
NA	Maine**	NA
NA	Montana**	NA
NA	New Hampshire**	NA
NA	North Dakota**	NA
NA	Rhode Island**	NA
NA	South Dakota**	NA
NA	Vermont**	NA
NA	Wyoming**	NA
	District of Columbia**	NA

Source: CQ Press using data from American Cancer Society
"Cancer Facts & Figures 2007" (Copyright 2007, American Cancer Society)
*These estimates are offered as a rough guide and should be interpreted with caution. They are calculated according to the distribution of estimated 2007 cancer deaths by state. Rates calculated using 2005 Census female population estimates.
**Not available.

Percent of Women 18 Years Old and Older
Who Had a Pap Smear within the Past Three Years: 2006
National Median = 84.0% of Women 18 Years and Older*

ALPHA ORDER

RANK	STATE	PERCENT
32	Alabama	83.4
9	Alaska	87.0
24	Arizona	84.1
45	Arkansas	80.5
25	California	84.0
19	Colorado	85.3
10	Connecticut	86.8
2	Delaware	89.0
37	Florida	82.8
7	Georgia	87.4
41	Hawaii	82.0
49	Idaho	77.6
30	Illinois	83.6
43	Indiana	81.0
14	Iowa	86.1
30	Kansas	83.6
35	Kentucky	83.1
22	Louisiana	84.5
1	Maine	89.1
4	Maryland	87.8
6	Massachusetts	87.7
17	Michigan	85.8
13	Minnesota	86.2
25	Mississippi	84.0
47	Missouri	79.9
39	Montana	82.1
42	Nebraska	81.6
39	Nevada	82.1
3	New Hampshire	88.0
25	New Jersey	84.0
35	New Mexico	83.1
20	New York	85.1
10	North Carolina	86.8
22	North Dakota	84.5
32	Ohio	83.4
48	Oklahoma	79.4
32	Oregon	83.4
37	Pennsylvania	82.8
4	Rhode Island	87.8
10	South Carolina	86.8
20	South Dakota	85.1
16	Tennessee	85.9
46	Texas	80.2
50	Utah	74.3
8	Vermont	87.1
18	Virginia	85.6
25	Washington	84.0
29	West Virginia	83.8
15	Wisconsin	86.0
44	Wyoming	80.9

RANK ORDER

RANK	STATE	PERCENT
1	Maine	89.1
2	Delaware	89.0
3	New Hampshire	88.0
4	Maryland	87.8
4	Rhode Island	87.8
6	Massachusetts	87.7
7	Georgia	87.4
8	Vermont	87.1
9	Alaska	87.0
10	Connecticut	86.8
10	North Carolina	86.8
10	South Carolina	86.8
13	Minnesota	86.2
14	Iowa	86.1
15	Wisconsin	86.0
16	Tennessee	85.9
17	Michigan	85.8
18	Virginia	85.6
19	Colorado	85.3
20	New York	85.1
20	South Dakota	85.1
22	Louisiana	84.5
22	North Dakota	84.5
24	Arizona	84.1
25	California	84.0
25	Mississippi	84.0
25	New Jersey	84.0
25	Washington	84.0
29	West Virginia	83.8
30	Illinois	83.6
30	Kansas	83.6
32	Alabama	83.4
32	Ohio	83.4
32	Oregon	83.4
35	Kentucky	83.1
35	New Mexico	83.1
37	Florida	82.8
37	Pennsylvania	82.8
39	Montana	82.1
39	Nevada	82.1
41	Hawaii	82.0
42	Nebraska	81.6
43	Indiana	81.0
44	Wyoming	80.9
45	Arkansas	80.5
46	Texas	80.2
47	Missouri	79.9
48	Oklahoma	79.4
49	Idaho	77.6
50	Utah	74.3

| | District of Columbia | 89.4 |

Source: U.S. Department of Health and Human Services, Centers for Disease Control and Prevention
   "2006 Behavioral Risk Factor Surveillance Summary Prevalence Data" (http://apps.nccd.cdc.gov/brfss/)
*A Pap test is a test for cancer, especially of the female genital tract such as cancer of the cervix. Named after George Papanicolaou (1883-1962), American anatomist.

Estimated New Uterine Cancer Cases in 2007

National Estimated Total = 39,080 New Cases*

ALPHA ORDER

RANK	STATE	CASES	% of USA
28	Alabama	460	1.2%
49	Alaska	60	0.2%
23	Arizona	550	1.4%
32	Arkansas	320	0.8%
1	California	3,870	9.9%
25	Colorado	490	1.3%
21	Connecticut	650	1.7%
44	Delaware	130	0.3%
3	Florida	2,490	6.4%
16	Georgia	810	2.1%
42	Hawaii	170	0.4%
43	Idaho	150	0.4%
7	Illinois	1,730	4.4%
13	Indiana	880	2.3%
24	Iowa	500	1.3%
31	Kansas	360	0.9%
22	Kentucky	560	1.4%
29	Louisiana	420	1.1%
34	Maine	270	0.7%
16	Maryland	810	2.1%
10	Massachusetts	1,110	2.8%
8	Michigan	1,610	4.1%
19	Minnesota	750	1.9%
36	Mississippi	230	0.6%
15	Missouri	830	2.1%
45	Montana	120	0.3%
35	Nebraska	260	0.7%
36	Nevada	230	0.6%
36	New Hampshire	230	0.6%
9	New Jersey	1,550	4.0%
40	New Mexico	200	0.5%
2	New York	3,240	8.3%
11	North Carolina	1,020	2.6%
48	North Dakota	100	0.3%
6	Ohio	1,800	4.6%
30	Oklahoma	400	1.0%
27	Oregon	470	1.2%
4	Pennsylvania	2,400	6.1%
41	Rhode Island	190	0.5%
26	South Carolina	480	1.2%
45	South Dakota	120	0.3%
20	Tennessee	660	1.7%
5	Texas	2,040	5.2%
39	Utah	220	0.6%
47	Vermont	110	0.3%
12	Virginia	970	2.5%
18	Washington	800	2.0%
33	West Virginia	310	0.8%
14	Wisconsin	860	2.2%
49	Wyoming	60	0.2%

RANK ORDER

RANK	STATE	CASES	% of USA
1	California	3,870	9.9%
2	New York	3,240	8.3%
3	Florida	2,490	6.4%
4	Pennsylvania	2,400	6.1%
5	Texas	2,040	5.2%
6	Ohio	1,800	4.6%
7	Illinois	1,730	4.4%
8	Michigan	1,610	4.1%
9	New Jersey	1,550	4.0%
10	Massachusetts	1,110	2.8%
11	North Carolina	1,020	2.6%
12	Virginia	970	2.5%
13	Indiana	880	2.3%
14	Wisconsin	860	2.2%
15	Missouri	830	2.1%
16	Georgia	810	2.1%
16	Maryland	810	2.1%
18	Washington	800	2.0%
19	Minnesota	750	1.9%
20	Tennessee	660	1.7%
21	Connecticut	650	1.7%
22	Kentucky	560	1.4%
23	Arizona	550	1.4%
24	Iowa	500	1.3%
25	Colorado	490	1.3%
26	South Carolina	480	1.2%
27	Oregon	470	1.2%
28	Alabama	460	1.2%
29	Louisiana	420	1.1%
30	Oklahoma	400	1.0%
31	Kansas	360	0.9%
32	Arkansas	320	0.8%
33	West Virginia	310	0.8%
34	Maine	270	0.7%
35	Nebraska	260	0.7%
36	Mississippi	230	0.6%
36	Nevada	230	0.6%
36	New Hampshire	230	0.6%
39	Utah	220	0.6%
40	New Mexico	200	0.5%
41	Rhode Island	190	0.5%
42	Hawaii	170	0.4%
43	Idaho	150	0.4%
44	Delaware	130	0.3%
45	Montana	120	0.3%
45	South Dakota	120	0.3%
47	Vermont	110	0.3%
48	North Dakota	100	0.3%
49	Alaska	60	0.2%
49	Wyoming	60	0.2%
	District of Columbia	70	0.2%

Source: American Cancer Society
    "Cancer Facts & Figures 2007" (Copyright 2007, American Cancer Society)
*These estimates are offered as a rough guide and should be interpreted with caution. They are calculated according to the distribution of estimated 2007 cancer deaths by state.

Estimated Rate of New Uterine Cancer Cases in 2007

National Estimated Rate = 26.0 New Cases per 100,000 Female Population*

ALPHA ORDER

RANK	STATE	RATE
42	Alabama	19.6
44	Alaska	18.7
45	Arizona	18.5
34	Arkansas	22.6
38	California	21.4
39	Colorado	21.2
3	Connecticut	36.0
17	Delaware	30.1
23	Florida	27.5
49	Georgia	17.7
24	Hawaii	26.6
40	Idaho	21.1
24	Illinois	26.6
22	Indiana	27.6
10	Iowa	33.2
27	Kansas	26.1
26	Kentucky	26.4
46	Louisiana	18.1
1	Maine	39.9
20	Maryland	28.1
8	Massachusetts	33.7
13	Michigan	31.3
19	Minnesota	29.0
50	Mississippi	15.3
21	Missouri	28.0
29	Montana	25.6
18	Nebraska	29.2
43	Nevada	19.4
6	New Hampshire	34.6
5	New Jersey	34.7
41	New Mexico	20.4
11	New York	32.6
33	North Carolina	23.1
12	North Dakota	31.4
16	Ohio	30.6
35	Oklahoma	22.3
28	Oregon	25.7
2	Pennsylvania	37.5
7	Rhode Island	34.2
36	South Carolina	22.0
15	South Dakota	30.7
37	Tennessee	21.7
48	Texas	17.8
47	Utah	17.9
4	Vermont	34.8
31	Virginia	25.2
30	Washington	25.4
9	West Virginia	33.4
14	Wisconsin	30.8
32	Wyoming	23.8

RANK ORDER

RANK	STATE	RATE
1	Maine	39.9
2	Pennsylvania	37.5
3	Connecticut	36.0
4	Vermont	34.8
5	New Jersey	34.7
6	New Hampshire	34.6
7	Rhode Island	34.2
8	Massachusetts	33.7
9	West Virginia	33.4
10	Iowa	33.2
11	New York	32.6
12	North Dakota	31.4
13	Michigan	31.3
14	Wisconsin	30.8
15	South Dakota	30.7
16	Ohio	30.6
17	Delaware	30.1
18	Nebraska	29.2
19	Minnesota	29.0
20	Maryland	28.1
21	Missouri	28.0
22	Indiana	27.6
23	Florida	27.5
24	Hawaii	26.6
24	Illinois	26.6
26	Kentucky	26.4
27	Kansas	26.1
28	Oregon	25.7
29	Montana	25.6
30	Washington	25.4
31	Virginia	25.2
32	Wyoming	23.8
33	North Carolina	23.1
34	Arkansas	22.6
35	Oklahoma	22.3
36	South Carolina	22.0
37	Tennessee	21.7
38	California	21.4
39	Colorado	21.2
40	Idaho	21.1
41	New Mexico	20.4
42	Alabama	19.6
43	Nevada	19.4
44	Alaska	18.7
45	Arizona	18.5
46	Louisiana	18.1
47	Utah	17.9
48	Texas	17.8
49	Georgia	17.7
50	Mississippi	15.3

District of Columbia   24.2

Source: CQ Press using data from American Cancer Society
    "Cancer Facts & Figures 2007" (Copyright 2007, American Cancer Society)
*These estimates are offered as a rough guide and should be interpreted with caution. They are calculated according to the
distribution of estimated 2007 cancer deaths by state. Rates calculated using 2005 Census female population estimates.

AIDS Cases Reported in 2005

National Total = 40,733 New AIDS Cases*

ALPHA ORDER					RANK ORDER			
RANK	STATE		CASES	% of USA	RANK	STATE	CASES	% of USA
20	Alabama		518	1.3%	1	New York	6,299	15.5%
43	Alaska		26	0.1%	2	Florida	4,960	12.2%
19	Arizona		642	1.6%	3	California	4,088	10.0%
29	Arkansas		242	0.6%	4	Texas	3,113	7.6%
3	California		4,088	10.0%	5	Georgia	2,333	5.7%
25	Colorado		359	0.9%	6	Illinois	1,922	4.7%
17	Connecticut		666	1.6%	7	Maryland	1,595	3.9%
32	Delaware		176	0.4%	8	Pennsylvania	1,510	3.7%
2	Florida		4,960	12.2%	9	New Jersey	1,278	3.1%
5	Georgia		2,333	5.7%	10	Louisiana	961	2.4%
35	Hawaii		109	0.3%	11	North Carolina	945	2.3%
44	Idaho		25	0.1%	12	Tennessee	841	2.1%
6	Illinois		1,922	4.7%	13	Michigan	822	2.0%
22	Indiana		409	1.0%	14	Ohio	784	1.9%
37	Iowa		95	0.2%	15	Massachusetts	692	1.7%
36	Kansas		107	0.3%	16	South Carolina	668	1.6%
28	Kentucky		257	0.6%	17	Connecticut	666	1.6%
10	Louisiana		961	2.4%	18	Virginia	646	1.6%
45	Maine		21	0.1%	19	Arizona	642	1.6%
7	Maryland		1,595	3.9%	20	Alabama	518	1.3%
15	Massachusetts		692	1.7%	21	Washington	486	1.2%
13	Michigan		822	2.0%	22	Indiana	409	1.0%
30	Minnesota		225	0.6%	23	Mississippi	387	1.0%
23	Mississippi		387	1.0%	24	Missouri	386	0.9%
24	Missouri		386	0.9%	25	Colorado	359	0.9%
46	Montana		20	0.0%	26	Nevada	296	0.7%
41	Nebraska		53	0.1%	27	Oklahoma	282	0.7%
26	Nevada		296	0.7%	28	Kentucky	257	0.6%
42	New Hampshire		34	0.1%	29	Arkansas	242	0.6%
9	New Jersey		1,278	3.1%	30	Minnesota	225	0.6%
33	New Mexico		136	0.3%	31	Oregon	220	0.5%
1	New York		6,299	15.5%	32	Delaware	176	0.4%
11	North Carolina		945	2.3%	33	New Mexico	136	0.3%
48	North Dakota		10	0.0%	34	Wisconsin	123	0.3%
14	Ohio		784	1.9%	35	Hawaii	109	0.3%
27	Oklahoma		282	0.7%	36	Kansas	107	0.3%
31	Oregon		220	0.5%	37	Iowa	95	0.2%
8	Pennsylvania		1,510	3.7%	38	Rhode Island	89	0.2%
38	Rhode Island		89	0.2%	39	West Virginia	74	0.2%
16	South Carolina		668	1.6%	40	Utah	65	0.2%
47	South Dakota		19	0.0%	41	Nebraska	53	0.1%
12	Tennessee		841	2.1%	42	New Hampshire	34	0.1%
4	Texas		3,113	7.6%	43	Alaska	26	0.1%
40	Utah		65	0.2%	44	Idaho	25	0.1%
49	Vermont		6	0.0%	45	Maine	21	0.1%
18	Virginia		646	1.6%	46	Montana	20	0.0%
21	Washington		486	1.2%	47	South Dakota	19	0.0%
39	West Virginia		74	0.2%	48	North Dakota	10	0.0%
34	Wisconsin		123	0.3%	49	Vermont	6	0.0%
49	Wyoming		6	0.0%	49	Wyoming	6	0.0%
						District of Columbia	707	1.7%

Source: U.S. Department of Health and Human Services, Centers for Disease Control and Prevention
    "HIV/AIDS Surveillance Report, 2005" (Vol. 17)
*AIDS is Acquired Immunodeficiency Syndrome. It is a specific group of diseases or conditions which are indicative of severe immunosuppression related to infection with the Human Immunodeficiency Virus (HIV). National total does not include 1,033 new cases in Puerto Rico, 17 in the Virgin Islands and one in Guam.

AIDS Rate in 2005

National Rate = 13.7 New AIDS Cases Reported per 100,000 Population*

ALPHA ORDER

RANK	STATE	RATE
16	Alabama	11.4
37	Alaska	3.9
19	Arizona	10.8
21	Arkansas	8.7
17	California	11.3
27	Colorado	7.7
7	Connecticut	19.0
6	Delaware	20.9
3	Florida	27.9
4	Georgia	25.7
22	Hawaii	8.5
46	Idaho	1.7
9	Illinois	15.1
32	Indiana	6.5
39	Iowa	3.2
37	Kansas	3.9
33	Kentucky	6.2
5	Louisiana	21.2
47	Maine	1.6
2	Maryland	28.5
19	Massachusetts	10.8
25	Michigan	8.1
35	Minnesota	4.4
13	Mississippi	13.2
31	Missouri	6.7
45	Montana	2.1
40	Nebraska	3.0
14	Nevada	12.3
41	New Hampshire	2.6
10	New Jersey	14.7
29	New Mexico	7.1
1	New York	32.7
18	North Carolina	10.9
47	North Dakota	1.6
30	Ohio	6.8
26	Oklahoma	7.9
34	Oregon	6.0
15	Pennsylvania	12.1
24	Rhode Island	8.3
8	South Carolina	15.7
43	South Dakota	2.4
11	Tennessee	14.1
12	Texas	13.6
41	Utah	2.6
50	Vermont	1.0
22	Virginia	8.5
27	Washington	7.7
36	West Virginia	4.1
44	Wisconsin	2.2
49	Wyoming	1.2

RANK ORDER

RANK	STATE	RATE
1	New York	32.7
2	Maryland	28.5
3	Florida	27.9
4	Georgia	25.7
5	Louisiana	21.2
6	Delaware	20.9
7	Connecticut	19.0
8	South Carolina	15.7
9	Illinois	15.1
10	New Jersey	14.7
11	Tennessee	14.1
12	Texas	13.6
13	Mississippi	13.2
14	Nevada	12.3
15	Pennsylvania	12.1
16	Alabama	11.4
17	California	11.3
18	North Carolina	10.9
19	Arizona	10.8
19	Massachusetts	10.8
21	Arkansas	8.7
22	Hawaii	8.5
22	Virginia	8.5
24	Rhode Island	8.3
25	Michigan	8.1
26	Oklahoma	7.9
27	Colorado	7.7
27	Washington	7.7
29	New Mexico	7.1
30	Ohio	6.8
31	Missouri	6.7
32	Indiana	6.5
33	Kentucky	6.2
34	Oregon	6.0
35	Minnesota	4.4
36	West Virginia	4.1
37	Alaska	3.9
37	Kansas	3.9
39	Iowa	3.2
40	Nebraska	3.0
41	New Hampshire	2.6
41	Utah	2.6
43	South Dakota	2.4
44	Wisconsin	2.2
45	Montana	2.1
46	Idaho	1.7
47	Maine	1.6
47	North Dakota	1.6
49	Wyoming	1.2
50	Vermont	1.0

	District of Columbia	128.4

Source: U.S. Department of Health and Human Services, Centers for Disease Control and Prevention
"HIV/AIDS Surveillance Report, 2005" (Vol. 17)

*AIDS is Acquired Immunodeficiency Syndrome. It is a specific group of diseases or conditions which are indicative of severe immunosuppression related to infection with the Human Immunodeficiency Virus (HIV). National rate does not include cases or population in U.S. territories.

AIDS Cases Reported through December 2005

National Total = 925,452 Reported AIDS Cases*

ALPHA ORDER

RANK	STATE	CASES	% of USA
23	Alabama	8,252	0.9%
44	Alaska	621	0.1%
21	Arizona	9,952	1.1%
32	Arkansas	3,703	0.4%
2	California	139,019	15.0%
22	Colorado	8,480	0.9%
14	Connecticut	14,487	1.6%
33	Delaware	3,458	0.4%
3	Florida	100,809	10.9%
8	Georgia	30,405	3.3%
34	Hawaii	2,857	0.3%
45	Idaho	578	0.1%
6	Illinois	32,595	3.5%
24	Indiana	7,963	0.9%
39	Iowa	1,656	0.2%
35	Kansas	2,680	0.3%
30	Kentucky	4,453	0.5%
11	Louisiana	16,952	1.8%
42	Maine	1,053	0.1%
9	Maryland	29,116	3.1%
10	Massachusetts	18,896	2.0%
15	Michigan	14,386	1.6%
29	Minnesota	4,632	0.5%
25	Mississippi	6,376	0.7%
20	Missouri	10,630	1.1%
47	Montana	372	0.0%
41	Nebraska	1,377	0.1%
27	Nevada	5,481	0.6%
43	New Hampshire	1,032	0.1%
5	New Jersey	48,431	5.2%
36	New Mexico	2,526	0.3%
1	New York	172,377	18.6%
13	North Carolina	14,915	1.6%
50	North Dakota	140	0.0%
16	Ohio	14,381	1.6%
28	Oklahoma	4,651	0.5%
26	Oregon	5,740	0.6%
7	Pennsylvania	31,977	3.5%
37	Rhode Island	2,503	0.3%
17	South Carolina	12,715	1.4%
48	South Dakota	244	0.0%
18	Tennessee	11,867	1.3%
4	Texas	67,227	7.3%
38	Utah	2,261	0.2%
46	Vermont	447	0.0%
12	Virginia	16,378	1.8%
19	Washington	11,438	1.2%
40	West Virginia	1,444	0.2%
31	Wisconsin	4,332	0.5%
49	Wyoming	225	0.0%

RANK ORDER

RANK	STATE	CASES	% of USA
1	New York	172,377	18.6%
2	California	139,019	15.0%
3	Florida	100,809	10.9%
4	Texas	67,227	7.3%
5	New Jersey	48,431	5.2%
6	Illinois	32,595	3.5%
7	Pennsylvania	31,977	3.5%
8	Georgia	30,405	3.3%
9	Maryland	29,116	3.1%
10	Massachusetts	18,896	2.0%
11	Louisiana	16,952	1.8%
12	Virginia	16,378	1.8%
13	North Carolina	14,915	1.6%
14	Connecticut	14,487	1.6%
15	Michigan	14,386	1.6%
16	Ohio	14,381	1.6%
17	South Carolina	12,715	1.4%
18	Tennessee	11,867	1.3%
19	Washington	11,438	1.2%
20	Missouri	10,630	1.1%
21	Arizona	9,952	1.1%
22	Colorado	8,480	0.9%
23	Alabama	8,252	0.9%
24	Indiana	7,963	0.9%
25	Mississippi	6,376	0.7%
26	Oregon	5,740	0.6%
27	Nevada	5,481	0.6%
28	Oklahoma	4,651	0.5%
29	Minnesota	4,632	0.5%
30	Kentucky	4,453	0.5%
31	Wisconsin	4,332	0.5%
32	Arkansas	3,703	0.4%
33	Delaware	3,458	0.4%
34	Hawaii	2,857	0.3%
35	Kansas	2,680	0.3%
36	New Mexico	2,526	0.3%
37	Rhode Island	2,503	0.3%
38	Utah	2,261	0.2%
39	Iowa	1,656	0.2%
40	West Virginia	1,444	0.2%
41	Nebraska	1,377	0.1%
42	Maine	1,053	0.1%
43	New Hampshire	1,032	0.1%
44	Alaska	621	0.1%
45	Idaho	578	0.1%
46	Vermont	447	0.0%
47	Montana	372	0.0%
48	South Dakota	244	0.0%
49	Wyoming	225	0.0%
50	North Dakota	140	0.0%
	District of Columbia	16,962	1.8%

Source: U.S. Department of Health and Human Services, Centers for Disease Control and Prevention
"HIV/AIDS Surveillance Report, 2005" (Vol. 17)

*Cumulative through December 2005. AIDS is Acquired Immunodeficiency Syndrome. It is a specific group of diseases or conditions which are indicative of severe immunosuppression related to infection with the Human Immunodeficiency Virus (HIV). National total does not include 29,092 cases in Puerto Rico, 618 cases in the Virgin Islands and 75 cases in other U.S. territories.

AIDS Cases in Children 12 Years and Younger through December 2005

National Total = 9,017 Juvenile AIDS Cases*

ALPHA ORDER					RANK ORDER				
RANK	STATE		CASES	% of USA	RANK	STATE		CASES	% of USA
18	Alabama		76	0.8%	1	New York		2,342	26.0%
44	Alaska		7	0.1%	2	Florida		1,519	16.8%
23	Arizona		45	0.5%	3	New Jersey		772	8.6%
24	Arkansas		36	0.4%	4	California		658	7.3%
4	California		658	7.3%	5	Texas		391	4.3%
27	Colorado		31	0.3%	6	Pennsylvania		358	4.0%
11	Connecticut		183	2.0%	7	Maryland		312	3.5%
32	Delaware		25	0.3%	8	Illinois		281	3.1%
2	Florida		1,519	16.8%	9	Georgia		226	2.5%
9	Georgia		226	2.5%	10	Massachusetts		213	2.4%
36	Hawaii		17	0.2%	11	Connecticut		183	2.0%
48	Idaho		2	0.0%	12	Virginia		176	2.0%
8	Illinois		281	3.1%	13	Ohio		135	1.5%
22	Indiana		55	0.6%	14	Louisiana		131	1.5%
37	Iowa		14	0.2%	15	North Carolina		118	1.3%
37	Kansas		14	0.2%	16	Michigan		112	1.2%
28	Kentucky		29	0.3%	17	South Carolina		101	1.1%
14	Louisiana		131	1.5%	18	Alabama		76	0.8%
42	Maine		8	0.1%	19	Missouri		61	0.7%
7	Maryland		312	3.5%	20	Mississippi		57	0.6%
10	Massachusetts		213	2.4%	20	Tennessee		57	0.6%
16	Michigan		112	1.2%	22	Indiana		55	0.6%
30	Minnesota		27	0.3%	23	Arizona		45	0.5%
20	Mississippi		57	0.6%	24	Arkansas		36	0.4%
19	Missouri		61	0.7%	25	Washington		34	0.4%
47	Montana		3	0.0%	26	Wisconsin		32	0.4%
39	Nebraska		11	0.1%	27	Colorado		31	0.3%
28	Nevada		29	0.3%	28	Kentucky		29	0.3%
41	New Hampshire		10	0.1%	28	Nevada		29	0.3%
3	New Jersey		772	8.6%	30	Minnesota		27	0.3%
42	New Mexico		8	0.1%	30	Rhode Island		27	0.3%
1	New York		2,342	26.0%	32	Delaware		25	0.3%
15	North Carolina		118	1.3%	32	Oklahoma		25	0.3%
50	North Dakota		1	0.0%	34	Utah		20	0.2%
13	Ohio		135	1.5%	35	Oregon		19	0.2%
32	Oklahoma		25	0.3%	36	Hawaii		17	0.2%
35	Oregon		19	0.2%	37	Iowa		14	0.2%
6	Pennsylvania		358	4.0%	37	Kansas		14	0.2%
30	Rhode Island		27	0.3%	39	Nebraska		11	0.1%
17	South Carolina		101	1.1%	39	West Virginia		11	0.1%
46	South Dakota		5	0.1%	41	New Hampshire		10	0.1%
20	Tennessee		57	0.6%	42	Maine		8	0.1%
5	Texas		391	4.3%	42	New Mexico		8	0.1%
34	Utah		20	0.2%	44	Alaska		7	0.1%
45	Vermont		6	0.1%	45	Vermont		6	0.1%
12	Virginia		176	2.0%	46	South Dakota		5	0.1%
25	Washington		34	0.4%	47	Montana		3	0.0%
39	West Virginia		11	0.1%	48	Idaho		2	0.0%
26	Wisconsin		32	0.4%	48	Wyoming		2	0.0%
48	Wyoming		2	0.0%	50	North Dakota		1	0.0%
						District of Columbia		185	2.1%

Source: U.S. Department of Health and Human Services, Centers for Disease Control and Prevention
   "HIV/AIDS Surveillance Report, 2005" (Vol. 17)

*Cumulative through December 2005. AIDS is Acquired Immunodeficiency Syndrome. It is a specific group of diseases or conditions which are indicative of severe immunosuppression related to infection with the Human Immunodeficiency Virus (HIV). National total does not include 399 cases in Puerto Rico, 17 cases in the Virgin Islands and one case in Guam.

Chickenpox (Varicella) Cases Reported in 2007

National Total = 34,507 Cases*

ALPHA ORDER					RANK ORDER			
RANK	STATE		CASES	% of USA	RANK	STATE	CASES	% of USA
14	Alabama		654	1.9%	1	Texas	9,046	26.2%
25	Alaska		41	0.1%	2	Ohio	4,550	13.2%
30	Arizona		0	0.0%	3	Pennsylvania	4,426	12.8%
13	Arkansas		659	1.9%	4	Michigan	4,048	11.7%
30	California		0	0.0%	5	Florida	1,308	3.8%
8	Colorado		1,085	3.1%	6	Virginia	1,306	3.8%
28	Connecticut		2	0.0%	7	West Virginia	1,162	3.4%
24	Delaware		45	0.1%	8	Colorado	1,085	3.1%
5	Florida		1,308	3.8%	9	South Carolina	1,067	3.1%
NA	Georgia**		NA	NA	10	Wisconsin	940	2.7%
NA	Hawaii**		NA	NA	11	Missouri	923	2.7%
NA	Idaho**		NA	NA	12	Utah	724	2.1%
20	Illinois		173	0.5%	13	Arkansas	659	1.9%
NA	Indiana**		NA	NA	14	Alabama	654	1.9%
NA	Iowa**		NA	NA	15	Kansas	521	1.5%
15	Kansas		521	1.5%	16	Montana	420	1.2%
NA	Kentucky**		NA	NA	17	Vermont	380	1.1%
21	Louisiana		110	0.3%	18	New Mexico	374	1.1%
30	Maine		0	0.0%	19	New Hampshire	341	1.0%
NA	Maryland**		NA	NA	20	Illinois	173	0.5%
30	Massachusetts		0	0.0%	21	Louisiana	110	0.3%
4	Michigan		4,048	11.7%	22	North Dakota	84	0.2%
30	Minnesota		0	0.0%	23	South Dakota	65	0.2%
27	Mississippi		3	0.0%	24	Delaware	45	0.1%
11	Missouri		923	2.7%	25	Alaska	41	0.1%
16	Montana		420	1.2%	26	Wyoming	34	0.1%
NA	Nebraska**		NA	NA	27	Mississippi	3	0.0%
28	Nevada		2	0.0%	28	Connecticut	2	0.0%
19	New Hampshire		341	1.0%	28	Nevada	2	0.0%
NA	New Jersey**		NA	NA	30	Arizona	0	0.0%
18	New Mexico		374	1.1%	30	California	0	0.0%
NA	New York**		NA	NA	30	Maine	0	0.0%
30	North Carolina		0	0.0%	30	Massachusetts	0	0.0%
22	North Dakota		84	0.2%	30	Minnesota	0	0.0%
2	Ohio		4,550	13.2%	30	North Carolina	0	0.0%
30	Oklahoma		0	0.0%	30	Oklahoma	0	0.0%
NA	Oregon**		NA	NA	30	Rhode Island	0	0.0%
3	Pennsylvania		4,426	12.8%	NA	Georgia**	NA	NA
30	Rhode Island		0	0.0%	NA	Hawaii**	NA	NA
9	South Carolina		1,067	3.1%	NA	Idaho**	NA	NA
23	South Dakota		65	0.2%	NA	Indiana**	NA	NA
NA	Tennessee**		NA	NA	NA	Iowa**	NA	NA
1	Texas		9,046	26.2%	NA	Kentucky**	NA	NA
12	Utah		724	2.1%	NA	Maryland**	NA	NA
17	Vermont		380	1.1%	NA	Nebraska**	NA	NA
6	Virginia		1,306	3.8%	NA	New Jersey**	NA	NA
NA	Washington**		NA	NA	NA	New York**	NA	NA
7	West Virginia		1,162	3.4%	NA	Oregon**	NA	NA
10	Wisconsin		940	2.7%	NA	Tennessee**	NA	NA
26	Wyoming		34	0.1%	NA	Washington**	NA	NA
						District of Columbia	14	0.0%

Source: U.S. Department of Health and Human Services, National Center for Health Statistics
   "Morbidity and Mortality Weekly Report" (January 4, 2008, Vol. 56, Nos. 51 & 52)
*Provisional data. An illness with acute onset of generalized maculo-papulovesicular rash without other apparent cause.
**Not notifiable.

Chickenpox (Varicella) Rate in 2007

National Rate = 11.4 Cases per 100,000 Population*

ALPHA ORDER

RANK	STATE	RATE
18	Alabama	14.1
23	Alaska	6.0
30	Arizona	0.0
11	Arkansas	23.2
30	California	0.0
12	Colorado	22.3
27	Connecticut	0.1
24	Delaware	5.2
21	Florida	7.2
NA	Georgia**	NA
NA	Hawaii**	NA
NA	Idaho**	NA
26	Illinois	1.3
NA	Indiana**	NA
NA	Iowa**	NA
14	Kansas	18.8
NA	Kentucky**	NA
25	Louisiana	2.6
30	Maine	0.0
NA	Maryland**	NA
30	Massachusetts	0.0
4	Michigan	40.2
30	Minnesota	0.0
27	Mississippi	0.1
17	Missouri	15.7
3	Montana	43.8
NA	Nebraska**	NA
27	Nevada	0.1
9	New Hampshire	25.9
NA	New Jersey**	NA
13	New Mexico	19.0
NA	New York**	NA
30	North Carolina	0.0
19	North Dakota	13.1
5	Ohio	39.7
30	Oklahoma	0.0
NA	Oregon**	NA
7	Pennsylvania	35.6
30	Rhode Island	0.0
10	South Carolina	24.2
20	South Dakota	8.2
NA	Tennessee**	NA
6	Texas	37.8
8	Utah	27.4
2	Vermont	61.2
15	Virginia	16.9
NA	Washington**	NA
1	West Virginia	64.1
16	Wisconsin	16.8
22	Wyoming	6.5

RANK ORDER

RANK	STATE	RATE
1	West Virginia	64.1
2	Vermont	61.2
3	Montana	43.8
4	Michigan	40.2
5	Ohio	39.7
6	Texas	37.8
7	Pennsylvania	35.6
8	Utah	27.4
9	New Hampshire	25.9
10	South Carolina	24.2
11	Arkansas	23.2
12	Colorado	22.3
13	New Mexico	19.0
14	Kansas	18.8
15	Virginia	16.9
16	Wisconsin	16.8
17	Missouri	15.7
18	Alabama	14.1
19	North Dakota	13.1
20	South Dakota	8.2
21	Florida	7.2
22	Wyoming	6.5
23	Alaska	6.0
24	Delaware	5.2
25	Louisiana	2.6
26	Illinois	1.3
27	Connecticut	0.1
27	Mississippi	0.1
27	Nevada	0.1
30	Arizona	0.0
30	California	0.0
30	Maine	0.0
30	Massachusetts	0.0
30	Minnesota	0.0
30	North Carolina	0.0
30	Oklahoma	0.0
30	Rhode Island	0.0
NA	Georgia**	NA
NA	Hawaii**	NA
NA	Idaho**	NA
NA	Indiana**	NA
NA	Iowa**	NA
NA	Kentucky**	NA
NA	Maryland**	NA
NA	Nebraska**	NA
NA	New Jersey**	NA
NA	New York**	NA
NA	Oregon**	NA
NA	Tennessee**	NA
NA	Washington**	NA

District of Columbia 2.4

Source: CQ Press using data from U.S. Department of Health and Human Services, National Center for Health Statistics
"Morbidity and Mortality Weekly Report" (January 4, 2008, Vol. 56, Nos. 51 & 52)
*Provisional data. An illness with acute onset of generalized maculo-papulovesicular rash without other apparent cause.
**Not notifiable.

E. Coli Cases Reported in 2007

National Total = 4,397 Cases*

ALPHA ORDER

RANK	STATE	CASES	% of USA
29	Alabama	64	1.5%
NA	Alaska**	NA	NA
18	Arizona	113	2.6%
35	Arkansas	34	0.8%
1	California	263	6.0%
12	Colorado	146	3.3%
28	Connecticut	73	1.7%
41	Delaware	16	0.4%
6	Florida	171	3.9%
25	Georgia	92	2.1%
43	Hawaii	8	0.2%
15	Idaho	131	3.0%
20	Illinois	108	2.5%
21	Indiana	104	2.4%
5	Iowa	173	3.9%
30	Kansas	54	1.2%
16	Kentucky	122	2.8%
47	Louisiana	3	0.1%
33	Maine	40	0.9%
23	Maryland	97	2.2%
14	Massachusetts	133	3.0%
22	Michigan	102	2.3%
3	Minnesota	244	5.5%
45	Mississippi	5	0.1%
8	Missouri	150	3.4%
48	Montana	0	0.0%
26	Nebraska	91	2.1%
36	Nevada	29	0.7%
37	New Hampshire	27	0.6%
31	New Jersey	51	1.2%
34	New Mexico	37	0.8%
2	New York	249	5.7%
8	North Carolina	150	3.4%
46	North Dakota	4	0.1%
7	Ohio	155	3.5%
39	Oklahoma	20	0.5%
27	Oregon	84	1.9%
11	Pennsylvania	149	3.4%
44	Rhode Island	6	0.1%
38	South Carolina	24	0.5%
32	South Dakota	47	1.1%
17	Tennessee	119	2.7%
18	Texas	113	2.6%
24	Utah	96	2.2%
42	Vermont	15	0.3%
8	Virginia	150	3.4%
13	Washington	135	3.1%
40	West Virginia	19	0.4%
4	Wisconsin	180	4.1%
48	Wyoming	0	0.0%

RANK ORDER

RANK	STATE	CASES	% of USA
1	California	263	6.0%
2	New York	249	5.7%
3	Minnesota	244	5.5%
4	Wisconsin	180	4.1%
5	Iowa	173	3.9%
6	Florida	171	3.9%
7	Ohio	155	3.5%
8	Missouri	150	3.4%
8	North Carolina	150	3.4%
8	Virginia	150	3.4%
11	Pennsylvania	149	3.4%
12	Colorado	146	3.3%
13	Washington	135	3.1%
14	Massachusetts	133	3.0%
15	Idaho	131	3.0%
16	Kentucky	122	2.8%
17	Tennessee	119	2.7%
18	Arizona	113	2.6%
18	Texas	113	2.6%
20	Illinois	108	2.5%
21	Indiana	104	2.4%
22	Michigan	102	2.3%
23	Maryland	97	2.2%
24	Utah	96	2.2%
25	Georgia	92	2.1%
26	Nebraska	91	2.1%
27	Oregon	84	1.9%
28	Connecticut	73	1.7%
29	Alabama	64	1.5%
30	Kansas	54	1.2%
31	New Jersey	51	1.2%
32	South Dakota	47	1.1%
33	Maine	40	0.9%
34	New Mexico	37	0.8%
35	Arkansas	34	0.8%
36	Nevada	29	0.7%
37	New Hampshire	27	0.6%
38	South Carolina	24	0.5%
39	Oklahoma	20	0.5%
40	West Virginia	19	0.4%
41	Delaware	16	0.4%
42	Vermont	15	0.3%
43	Hawaii	8	0.2%
44	Rhode Island	6	0.1%
45	Mississippi	5	0.1%
46	North Dakota	4	0.1%
47	Louisiana	3	0.1%
48	Montana	0	0.0%
48	Wyoming	0	0.0%
NA	Alaska**	NA	NA
	District of Columbia	1	0.0%

Source: U.S. Department of Health and Human Services, National Center for Health Statistics
"Morbidity and Mortality Weekly Report" (January 4, 2008, Vol. 56, Nos. 51 & 52)
*Escherichia Coli is a common bacterium that normally inhabits the intestinal tracts of humans and animals but can cause infection in other parts of the body, especially the urinary tract. One strain, sometimes transmitted in hamburger meat, can cause serious infection resulting in sickness and death.
**Not notifiable.

E. Coli Rate in 2007

National Rate = 1.5 Cases per 100,000 Population*

ALPHA ORDER

RANK	STATE	RATE
27	Alabama	1.4
NA	Alaska**	NA
23	Arizona	1.8
30	Arkansas	1.2
38	California	0.7
8	Colorado	3.0
14	Connecticut	2.1
18	Delaware	1.9
36	Florida	0.9
33	Georgia	1.0
39	Hawaii	0.6
1	Idaho	8.7
37	Illinois	0.8
26	Indiana	1.6
3	Iowa	5.8
18	Kansas	1.9
10	Kentucky	2.9
47	Louisiana	0.1
8	Maine	3.0
24	Maryland	1.7
14	Massachusetts	2.1
33	Michigan	1.0
5	Minnesota	4.7
46	Mississippi	0.2
11	Missouri	2.6
48	Montana	0.0
4	Nebraska	5.1
32	Nevada	1.1
14	New Hampshire	2.1
39	New Jersey	0.6
18	New Mexico	1.9
29	New York	1.3
24	North Carolina	1.7
39	North Dakota	0.6
27	Ohio	1.4
39	Oklahoma	0.6
13	Oregon	2.2
30	Pennsylvania	1.2
39	Rhode Island	0.6
44	South Carolina	0.5
2	South Dakota	5.9
18	Tennessee	1.9
44	Texas	0.5
6	Utah	3.6
12	Vermont	2.4
18	Virginia	1.9
14	Washington	2.1
33	West Virginia	1.0
7	Wisconsin	3.2
48	Wyoming	0.0

RANK ORDER

RANK	STATE	RATE
1	Idaho	8.7
2	South Dakota	5.9
3	Iowa	5.8
4	Nebraska	5.1
5	Minnesota	4.7
6	Utah	3.6
7	Wisconsin	3.2
8	Colorado	3.0
8	Maine	3.0
10	Kentucky	2.9
11	Missouri	2.6
12	Vermont	2.4
13	Oregon	2.2
14	Connecticut	2.1
14	Massachusetts	2.1
14	New Hampshire	2.1
14	Washington	2.1
18	Delaware	1.9
18	Kansas	1.9
18	New Mexico	1.9
18	Tennessee	1.9
18	Virginia	1.9
23	Arizona	1.8
24	Maryland	1.7
24	North Carolina	1.7
26	Indiana	1.6
27	Alabama	1.4
27	Ohio	1.4
29	New York	1.3
30	Arkansas	1.2
30	Pennsylvania	1.2
32	Nevada	1.1
33	Georgia	1.0
33	Michigan	1.0
33	West Virginia	1.0
36	Florida	0.9
37	Illinois	0.8
38	California	0.7
39	Hawaii	0.6
39	New Jersey	0.6
39	North Dakota	0.6
39	Oklahoma	0.6
39	Rhode Island	0.6
44	South Carolina	0.5
44	Texas	0.5
46	Mississippi	0.2
47	Louisiana	0.1
48	Montana	0.0
48	Wyoming	0.0
NA	Alaska**	NA

District of Columbia   0.2

Source: CQ Press using data from U.S. Department of Health and Human Services, National Center for Health Statistics
    "Morbidity and Mortality Weekly Report" (January 4, 2008, Vol. 56, Nos. 51 & 52)
*Escherichia Coli is a common bacterium that normally inhabits the intestinal tracts of humans and animals but can cause
infection in other parts of the body, especially the urinary tract. One strain, sometimes transmitted in hamburger meat, can
cause serious infection resulting in sickness and death.
**Not notifiable.

Hepatitis A and B Cases Reported in 2007

National Total = 6,644 Cases*

ALPHA ORDER

RANK	STATE	CASES	% of USA
17	Alabama	143	2.2%
44	Alaska	13	0.2%
6	Arizona	226	3.4%
26	Arkansas	77	1.2%
1	California	920	13.8%
29	Colorado	55	0.8%
29	Connecticut	55	0.8%
38	Delaware	23	0.3%
3	Florida	495	7.5%
12	Georgia	192	2.9%
48	Hawaii	6	0.1%
40	Idaho	21	0.3%
7	Illinois	211	3.2%
24	Indiana	85	1.3%
27	Iowa	70	1.1%
42	Kansas	19	0.3%
20	Kentucky	94	1.4%
19	Louisiana	106	1.6%
40	Maine	21	0.3%
15	Maryland	181	2.7%
31	Massachusetts	53	0.8%
10	Michigan	194	2.9%
23	Minnesota	90	1.4%
33	Mississippi	35	0.5%
21	Missouri	92	1.4%
47	Montana	9	0.1%
35	Nebraska	28	0.4%
32	Nevada	51	0.8%
43	New Hampshire	17	0.3%
14	New Jersey	183	2.8%
39	New Mexico	22	0.3%
4	New York	405	6.1%
11	North Carolina	193	2.9%
50	North Dakota	1	0.0%
9	Ohio	196	3.0%
16	Oklahoma	148	2.2%
21	Oregon	92	1.4%
5	Pennsylvania	265	4.0%
35	Rhode Island	28	0.4%
25	South Carolina	78	1.2%
46	South Dakota	12	0.2%
13	Tennessee	187	2.8%
2	Texas	776	11.7%
35	Utah	28	0.4%
44	Vermont	13	0.2%
8	Virginia	209	3.1%
18	Washington	114	1.7%
28	West Virginia	61	0.9%
34	Wisconsin	30	0.5%
48	Wyoming	6	0.1%

RANK ORDER

RANK	STATE	CASES	% of USA
1	California	920	13.8%
2	Texas	776	11.7%
3	Florida	495	7.5%
4	New York	405	6.1%
5	Pennsylvania	265	4.0%
6	Arizona	226	3.4%
7	Illinois	211	3.2%
8	Virginia	209	3.1%
9	Ohio	196	3.0%
10	Michigan	194	2.9%
11	North Carolina	193	2.9%
12	Georgia	192	2.9%
13	Tennessee	187	2.8%
14	New Jersey	183	2.8%
15	Maryland	181	2.7%
16	Oklahoma	148	2.2%
17	Alabama	143	2.2%
18	Washington	114	1.7%
19	Louisiana	106	1.6%
20	Kentucky	94	1.4%
21	Missouri	92	1.4%
21	Oregon	92	1.4%
23	Minnesota	90	1.4%
24	Indiana	85	1.3%
25	South Carolina	78	1.2%
26	Arkansas	77	1.2%
27	Iowa	70	1.1%
28	West Virginia	61	0.9%
29	Colorado	55	0.8%
29	Connecticut	55	0.8%
31	Massachusetts	53	0.8%
32	Nevada	51	0.8%
33	Mississippi	35	0.5%
34	Wisconsin	30	0.5%
35	Nebraska	28	0.4%
35	Rhode Island	28	0.4%
35	Utah	28	0.4%
38	Delaware	23	0.3%
39	New Mexico	22	0.3%
40	Idaho	21	0.3%
40	Maine	21	0.3%
42	Kansas	19	0.3%
43	New Hampshire	17	0.3%
44	Alaska	13	0.2%
44	Vermont	13	0.2%
46	South Dakota	12	0.2%
47	Montana	9	0.1%
48	Hawaii	6	0.1%
48	Wyoming	6	0.1%
50	North Dakota	1	0.0%
	District of Columbia	15	0.2%

Source: U.S. Department of Health and Human Services, National Center for Health Statistics
"Morbidity and Mortality Weekly Report" (January 4, 2008, Vol. 56, Nos. 51 & 52)
*Provisional data. An inflammation of the liver.

Hepatitis A and B Rate in 2007

National Rate = 2.2 Cases per 100,000 Population*

ALPHA ORDER

RANK	STATE	RATE
6	Alabama	3.1
25	Alaska	1.9
2	Arizona	3.6
8	Arkansas	2.7
13	California	2.5
41	Colorado	1.1
31	Connecticut	1.6
8	Delaware	2.7
8	Florida	2.7
23	Georgia	2.0
48	Hawaii	0.5
37	Idaho	1.4
31	Illinois	1.6
38	Indiana	1.3
16	Iowa	2.3
47	Kansas	0.7
17	Kentucky	2.2
13	Louisiana	2.5
31	Maine	1.6
4	Maryland	3.2
46	Massachusetts	0.8
25	Michigan	1.9
29	Minnesota	1.7
40	Mississippi	1.2
31	Missouri	1.6
45	Montana	0.9
31	Nebraska	1.6
23	Nevada	2.0
38	New Hampshire	1.3
18	New Jersey	2.1
41	New Mexico	1.1
18	New York	2.1
18	North Carolina	2.1
50	North Dakota	0.2
29	Ohio	1.7
1	Oklahoma	4.1
13	Oregon	2.5
18	Pennsylvania	2.1
12	Rhode Island	2.6
27	South Carolina	1.8
36	South Dakota	1.5
7	Tennessee	3.0
4	Texas	3.2
41	Utah	1.1
18	Vermont	2.1
8	Virginia	2.7
27	Washington	1.8
3	West Virginia	3.4
48	Wisconsin	0.5
41	Wyoming	1.1

RANK ORDER

RANK	STATE	RATE
1	Oklahoma	4.1
2	Arizona	3.6
3	West Virginia	3.4
4	Maryland	3.2
4	Texas	3.2
6	Alabama	3.1
7	Tennessee	3.0
8	Arkansas	2.7
8	Delaware	2.7
8	Florida	2.7
8	Virginia	2.7
12	Rhode Island	2.6
13	California	2.5
13	Louisiana	2.5
13	Oregon	2.5
16	Iowa	2.3
17	Kentucky	2.2
18	New Jersey	2.1
18	New York	2.1
18	North Carolina	2.1
18	Pennsylvania	2.1
18	Vermont	2.1
23	Georgia	2.0
23	Nevada	2.0
25	Alaska	1.9
25	Michigan	1.9
27	South Carolina	1.8
27	Washington	1.8
29	Minnesota	1.7
29	Ohio	1.7
31	Connecticut	1.6
31	Illinois	1.6
31	Maine	1.6
31	Missouri	1.6
31	Nebraska	1.6
36	South Dakota	1.5
37	Idaho	1.4
38	Indiana	1.3
38	New Hampshire	1.3
40	Mississippi	1.2
41	Colorado	1.1
41	New Mexico	1.1
41	Utah	1.1
41	Wyoming	1.1
45	Montana	0.9
46	Massachusetts	0.8
47	Kansas	0.7
48	Hawaii	0.5
48	Wisconsin	0.5
50	North Dakota	0.2

District of Columbia 2.5

Source: CQ Press using data from U.S. Department of Health and Human Services, National Center for Health Statistics
"Morbidity and Mortality Weekly Report" (January 4, 2008, Vol. 56, Nos. 51 & 52)
*Provisional data. An inflammation of the liver.

Legionellosis Cases Reported in 2007

National Total = 2,371 Cases*

ALPHA ORDER

RANK	STATE	CASES	% of USA
30	Alabama	11	0.5%
47	Alaska	0	0.0%
18	Arizona	35	1.5%
34	Arkansas	9	0.4%
6	California	102	4.3%
24	Colorado	21	0.9%
15	Connecticut	44	1.9%
38	Delaware	8	0.3%
4	Florida	158	6.7%
20	Georgia	31	1.3%
47	Hawaii	0	0.0%
40	Idaho	6	0.3%
8	Illinois	87	3.7%
11	Indiana	53	2.2%
30	Iowa	11	0.5%
44	Kansas	3	0.1%
13	Kentucky	48	2.0%
42	Louisiana	4	0.2%
34	Maine	9	0.4%
10	Maryland	85	3.6%
22	Massachusetts	26	1.1%
5	Michigan	151	6.4%
21	Minnesota	28	1.2%
47	Mississippi	0	0.0%
15	Missouri	44	1.9%
44	Montana	3	0.1%
28	Nebraska	14	0.6%
34	Nevada	9	0.4%
38	New Hampshire	8	0.3%
9	New Jersey	86	3.6%
32	New Mexico	10	0.4%
1	New York	357	15.1%
14	North Carolina	47	2.0%
47	North Dakota	0	0.0%
3	Ohio	215	9.1%
40	Oklahoma	6	0.3%
29	Oregon	12	0.5%
2	Pennsylvania	304	12.8%
18	Rhode Island	35	1.5%
27	South Carolina	17	0.7%
42	South Dakota	4	0.2%
17	Tennessee	39	1.6%
7	Texas	97	4.1%
25	Utah	19	0.8%
34	Vermont	9	0.4%
12	Virginia	51	2.2%
23	Washington	22	0.9%
25	West Virginia	19	0.8%
32	Wisconsin	10	0.4%
44	Wyoming	3	0.1%

RANK ORDER

RANK	STATE	CASES	% of USA
1	New York	357	15.1%
2	Pennsylvania	304	12.8%
3	Ohio	215	9.1%
4	Florida	158	6.7%
5	Michigan	151	6.4%
6	California	102	4.3%
7	Texas	97	4.1%
8	Illinois	87	3.7%
9	New Jersey	86	3.6%
10	Maryland	85	3.6%
11	Indiana	53	2.2%
12	Virginia	51	2.2%
13	Kentucky	48	2.0%
14	North Carolina	47	2.0%
15	Connecticut	44	1.9%
15	Missouri	44	1.9%
17	Tennessee	39	1.6%
18	Arizona	35	1.5%
18	Rhode Island	35	1.5%
20	Georgia	31	1.3%
21	Minnesota	28	1.2%
22	Massachusetts	26	1.1%
23	Washington	22	0.9%
24	Colorado	21	0.9%
25	Utah	19	0.8%
25	West Virginia	19	0.8%
27	South Carolina	17	0.7%
28	Nebraska	14	0.6%
29	Oregon	12	0.5%
30	Alabama	11	0.5%
30	Iowa	11	0.5%
32	New Mexico	10	0.4%
32	Wisconsin	10	0.4%
34	Arkansas	9	0.4%
34	Maine	9	0.4%
34	Nevada	9	0.4%
34	Vermont	9	0.4%
38	Delaware	8	0.3%
38	New Hampshire	8	0.3%
40	Idaho	6	0.3%
40	Oklahoma	6	0.3%
42	Louisiana	4	0.2%
42	South Dakota	4	0.2%
44	Kansas	3	0.1%
44	Montana	3	0.1%
44	Wyoming	3	0.1%
47	Alaska	0	0.0%
47	Hawaii	0	0.0%
47	Mississippi	0	0.0%
47	North Dakota	0	0.0%
	District of Columbia	1	0.0%

Source: U.S. Department of Health and Human Services, National Center for Health Statistics
"Morbidity and Mortality Weekly Report" (January 4, 2008, Vol. 56, Nos. 51 & 52)
*Provisional data. A pneumonia-like disease (Legionnaire's Disease).

Legionellosis Rate in 2007

National Rate = 0.8 Cases per 100,000 Population*

<table>
<tr><td colspan="3">ALPHA ORDER</td><td colspan="3">RANK ORDER</td></tr>
<tr><td>RANK</td><td>STATE</td><td>RATE</td><td>RANK</td><td>STATE</td><td>RATE</td></tr>
<tr><td>42</td><td>Alabama</td><td>0.2</td><td>1</td><td>Rhode Island</td><td>3.3</td></tr>
<tr><td>47</td><td>Alaska</td><td>0.0</td><td>2</td><td>Pennsylvania</td><td>2.4</td></tr>
<tr><td>21</td><td>Arizona</td><td>0.6</td><td>3</td><td>Ohio</td><td>1.9</td></tr>
<tr><td>36</td><td>Arkansas</td><td>0.3</td><td>4</td><td>New York</td><td>1.8</td></tr>
<tr><td>36</td><td>California</td><td>0.3</td><td>5</td><td>Maryland</td><td>1.5</td></tr>
<tr><td>29</td><td>Colorado</td><td>0.4</td><td>5</td><td>Michigan</td><td>1.5</td></tr>
<tr><td>8</td><td>Connecticut</td><td>1.3</td><td>7</td><td>Vermont</td><td>1.4</td></tr>
<tr><td>12</td><td>Delaware</td><td>0.9</td><td>8</td><td>Connecticut</td><td>1.3</td></tr>
<tr><td>12</td><td>Florida</td><td>0.9</td><td>9</td><td>Kentucky</td><td>1.1</td></tr>
<tr><td>36</td><td>Georgia</td><td>0.3</td><td>10</td><td>New Jersey</td><td>1.0</td></tr>
<tr><td>47</td><td>Hawaii</td><td>0.0</td><td>10</td><td>West Virginia</td><td>1.0</td></tr>
<tr><td>29</td><td>Idaho</td><td>0.4</td><td>12</td><td>Delaware</td><td>0.9</td></tr>
<tr><td>16</td><td>Illinois</td><td>0.7</td><td>12</td><td>Florida</td><td>0.9</td></tr>
<tr><td>14</td><td>Indiana</td><td>0.8</td><td>14</td><td>Indiana</td><td>0.8</td></tr>
<tr><td>29</td><td>Iowa</td><td>0.4</td><td>14</td><td>Nebraska</td><td>0.8</td></tr>
<tr><td>45</td><td>Kansas</td><td>0.1</td><td>16</td><td>Illinois</td><td>0.7</td></tr>
<tr><td>9</td><td>Kentucky</td><td>1.1</td><td>16</td><td>Maine</td><td>0.7</td></tr>
<tr><td>45</td><td>Louisiana</td><td>0.1</td><td>16</td><td>Missouri</td><td>0.7</td></tr>
<tr><td>16</td><td>Maine</td><td>0.7</td><td>16</td><td>Utah</td><td>0.7</td></tr>
<tr><td>5</td><td>Maryland</td><td>1.5</td><td>16</td><td>Virginia</td><td>0.7</td></tr>
<tr><td>29</td><td>Massachusetts</td><td>0.4</td><td>21</td><td>Arizona</td><td>0.6</td></tr>
<tr><td>5</td><td>Michigan</td><td>1.5</td><td>21</td><td>New Hampshire</td><td>0.6</td></tr>
<tr><td>25</td><td>Minnesota</td><td>0.5</td><td>21</td><td>Tennessee</td><td>0.6</td></tr>
<tr><td>47</td><td>Mississippi</td><td>0.0</td><td>21</td><td>Wyoming</td><td>0.6</td></tr>
<tr><td>16</td><td>Missouri</td><td>0.7</td><td>25</td><td>Minnesota</td><td>0.5</td></tr>
<tr><td>36</td><td>Montana</td><td>0.3</td><td>25</td><td>New Mexico</td><td>0.5</td></tr>
<tr><td>14</td><td>Nebraska</td><td>0.8</td><td>25</td><td>North Carolina</td><td>0.5</td></tr>
<tr><td>29</td><td>Nevada</td><td>0.4</td><td>25</td><td>South Dakota</td><td>0.5</td></tr>
<tr><td>21</td><td>New Hampshire</td><td>0.6</td><td>29</td><td>Colorado</td><td>0.4</td></tr>
<tr><td>10</td><td>New Jersey</td><td>1.0</td><td>29</td><td>Idaho</td><td>0.4</td></tr>
<tr><td>25</td><td>New Mexico</td><td>0.5</td><td>29</td><td>Iowa</td><td>0.4</td></tr>
<tr><td>4</td><td>New York</td><td>1.8</td><td>29</td><td>Massachusetts</td><td>0.4</td></tr>
<tr><td>25</td><td>North Carolina</td><td>0.5</td><td>29</td><td>Nevada</td><td>0.4</td></tr>
<tr><td>47</td><td>North Dakota</td><td>0.0</td><td>29</td><td>South Carolina</td><td>0.4</td></tr>
<tr><td>3</td><td>Ohio</td><td>1.9</td><td>29</td><td>Texas</td><td>0.4</td></tr>
<tr><td>42</td><td>Oklahoma</td><td>0.2</td><td>36</td><td>Arkansas</td><td>0.3</td></tr>
<tr><td>36</td><td>Oregon</td><td>0.3</td><td>36</td><td>California</td><td>0.3</td></tr>
<tr><td>2</td><td>Pennsylvania</td><td>2.4</td><td>36</td><td>Georgia</td><td>0.3</td></tr>
<tr><td>1</td><td>Rhode Island</td><td>3.3</td><td>36</td><td>Montana</td><td>0.3</td></tr>
<tr><td>29</td><td>South Carolina</td><td>0.4</td><td>36</td><td>Oregon</td><td>0.3</td></tr>
<tr><td>25</td><td>South Dakota</td><td>0.5</td><td>36</td><td>Washington</td><td>0.3</td></tr>
<tr><td>21</td><td>Tennessee</td><td>0.6</td><td>42</td><td>Alabama</td><td>0.2</td></tr>
<tr><td>29</td><td>Texas</td><td>0.4</td><td>42</td><td>Oklahoma</td><td>0.2</td></tr>
<tr><td>16</td><td>Utah</td><td>0.7</td><td>42</td><td>Wisconsin</td><td>0.2</td></tr>
<tr><td>7</td><td>Vermont</td><td>1.4</td><td>45</td><td>Kansas</td><td>0.1</td></tr>
<tr><td>16</td><td>Virginia</td><td>0.7</td><td>45</td><td>Louisiana</td><td>0.1</td></tr>
<tr><td>36</td><td>Washington</td><td>0.3</td><td>47</td><td>Alaska</td><td>0.0</td></tr>
<tr><td>10</td><td>West Virginia</td><td>1.0</td><td>47</td><td>Hawaii</td><td>0.0</td></tr>
<tr><td>42</td><td>Wisconsin</td><td>0.2</td><td>47</td><td>Mississippi</td><td>0.0</td></tr>
<tr><td>21</td><td>Wyoming</td><td>0.6</td><td>47</td><td>North Dakota</td><td>0.0</td></tr>
<tr><td></td><td></td><td></td><td></td><td>District of Columbia</td><td>0.2</td></tr>
</table>

Source: CQ Press using data from U.S. Department of Health and Human Services, National Center for Health Statistics
"Morbidity and Mortality Weekly Report" (January 4, 2008, Vol. 56, Nos. 51 & 52)
*Provisional data. A pneumonia-like disease (Legionnaire's Disease).

Lyme Disease Cases in 2007

National Total = 20,599 Cases*

ALPHA ORDER

RANK	STATE	CASES	% of USA
28	Alabama	13	0.1%
31	Alaska	9	0.0%
43	Arizona	2	0.0%
46	Arkansas	1	0.0%
17	California	104	0.5%
43	Colorado	2	0.0%
5	Connecticut	1,660	8.1%
9	Delaware	697	3.4%
18	Florida	90	0.4%
31	Georgia	9	0.0%
NA	Hawaii**	NA	NA
31	Idaho	9	0.0%
15	Illinois	135	0.7%
23	Indiana	44	0.2%
16	Iowa	118	0.6%
31	Kansas	9	0.0%
37	Kentucky	6	0.0%
43	Louisiana	2	0.0%
11	Maine	492	2.4%
3	Maryland	2,298	11.2%
12	Massachusetts	266	1.3%
21	Michigan	50	0.2%
10	Minnesota	512	2.5%
46	Mississippi	1	0.0%
26	Missouri	21	0.1%
38	Montana	4	0.0%
35	Nebraska	8	0.0%
29	Nevada	12	0.1%
8	New Hampshire	833	4.0%
4	New Jersey	2,253	10.9%
38	New Mexico	4	0.0%
2	New York	3,530	17.1%
21	North Carolina	50	0.2%
41	North Dakota	3	0.0%
27	Ohio	19	0.1%
48	Oklahoma	0	0.0%
38	Oregon	4	0.0%
1	Pennsylvania	4,666	22.7%
13	Rhode Island	162	0.8%
25	South Carolina	28	0.1%
48	South Dakota	0	0.0%
24	Tennessee	32	0.2%
20	Texas	66	0.3%
35	Utah	8	0.0%
14	Vermont	138	0.7%
7	Virginia	850	4.1%
30	Washington	10	0.0%
19	West Virginia	79	0.4%
6	Wisconsin	1,274	6.2%
41	Wyoming	3	0.0%

RANK ORDER

RANK	STATE	CASES	% of USA
1	Pennsylvania	4,666	22.7%
2	New York	3,530	17.1%
3	Maryland	2,298	11.2%
4	New Jersey	2,253	10.9%
5	Connecticut	1,660	8.1%
6	Wisconsin	1,274	6.2%
7	Virginia	850	4.1%
8	New Hampshire	833	4.0%
9	Delaware	697	3.4%
10	Minnesota	512	2.5%
11	Maine	492	2.4%
12	Massachusetts	266	1.3%
13	Rhode Island	162	0.8%
14	Vermont	138	0.7%
15	Illinois	135	0.7%
16	Iowa	118	0.6%
17	California	104	0.5%
18	Florida	90	0.4%
19	West Virginia	79	0.4%
20	Texas	66	0.3%
21	Michigan	50	0.2%
21	North Carolina	50	0.2%
23	Indiana	44	0.2%
24	Tennessee	32	0.2%
25	South Carolina	28	0.1%
26	Missouri	21	0.1%
27	Ohio	19	0.1%
28	Alabama	13	0.1%
29	Nevada	12	0.1%
30	Washington	10	0.0%
31	Alaska	9	0.0%
31	Georgia	9	0.0%
31	Idaho	9	0.0%
31	Kansas	9	0.0%
35	Nebraska	8	0.0%
35	Utah	8	0.0%
37	Kentucky	6	0.0%
38	Montana	4	0.0%
38	New Mexico	4	0.0%
38	Oregon	4	0.0%
41	North Dakota	3	0.0%
41	Wyoming	3	0.0%
43	Arizona	2	0.0%
43	Colorado	2	0.0%
43	Louisiana	2	0.0%
46	Arkansas	1	0.0%
46	Mississippi	1	0.0%
48	Oklahoma	0	0.0%
48	South Dakota	0	0.0%
NA	Hawaii**	NA	NA
	District of Columbia	13	0.1%

Source: U.S. Department of Health and Human Services, National Center for Health Statistics
  "Morbidity and Mortality Weekly Report" (January 4, 2008, Vol. 56, Nos. 51 & 52)
*Provisional data. Caused by ticks-lesions, followed by arthritis of large joints, myalgia, malaise and neurologic and cardiac manifestations. Named after Old Lyme, CT, where the disease was first reported.
**Not notifiable.

Lyme Disease Rate in 2007

National Rate = 6.8 Cases per 100,000 Population*

ALPHA ORDER

RANK	STATE	RATE
32	Alabama	0.3
17	Alaska	1.3
43	Arizona	0.0
43	Arkansas	0.0
32	California	0.3
43	Colorado	0.0
3	Connecticut	47.4
1	Delaware	80.6
24	Florida	0.5
40	Georgia	0.1
NA	Hawaii**	NA
20	Idaho	0.6
18	Illinois	1.1
19	Indiana	0.7
16	Iowa	3.9
32	Kansas	0.3
40	Kentucky	0.1
43	Louisiana	0.0
6	Maine	37.4
4	Maryland	40.9
15	Massachusetts	4.1
24	Michigan	0.5
13	Minnesota	9.9
43	Mississippi	0.0
30	Missouri	0.4
30	Montana	0.4
24	Nebraska	0.5
24	Nevada	0.5
2	New Hampshire	63.3
7	New Jersey	25.9
37	New Mexico	0.2
10	New York	18.3
20	North Carolina	0.6
24	North Dakota	0.5
37	Ohio	0.2
43	Oklahoma	0.0
40	Oregon	0.1
5	Pennsylvania	37.5
11	Rhode Island	15.3
20	South Carolina	0.6
43	South Dakota	0.0
24	Tennessee	0.5
32	Texas	0.3
32	Utah	0.3
9	Vermont	22.2
12	Virginia	11.0
37	Washington	0.2
14	West Virginia	4.4
8	Wisconsin	22.7
20	Wyoming	0.6

RANK ORDER

RANK	STATE	RATE
1	Delaware	80.6
2	New Hampshire	63.3
3	Connecticut	47.4
4	Maryland	40.9
5	Pennsylvania	37.5
6	Maine	37.4
7	New Jersey	25.9
8	Wisconsin	22.7
9	Vermont	22.2
10	New York	18.3
11	Rhode Island	15.3
12	Virginia	11.0
13	Minnesota	9.9
14	West Virginia	4.4
15	Massachusetts	4.1
16	Iowa	3.9
17	Alaska	1.3
18	Illinois	1.1
19	Indiana	0.7
20	Idaho	0.6
20	North Carolina	0.6
20	South Carolina	0.6
20	Wyoming	0.6
24	Florida	0.5
24	Michigan	0.5
24	Nebraska	0.5
24	Nevada	0.5
24	North Dakota	0.5
24	Tennessee	0.5
30	Missouri	0.4
30	Montana	0.4
32	Alabama	0.3
32	California	0.3
32	Kansas	0.3
32	Texas	0.3
32	Utah	0.3
37	New Mexico	0.2
37	Ohio	0.2
37	Washington	0.2
40	Georgia	0.1
40	Kentucky	0.1
40	Oregon	0.1
43	Arizona	0.0
43	Arkansas	0.0
43	Colorado	0.0
43	Louisiana	0.0
43	Mississippi	0.0
43	Oklahoma	0.0
43	South Dakota	0.0
NA	Hawaii**	NA

District of Columbia 2.2

Source: CQ Press using data from U.S. Department of Health and Human Services, National Center for Health Statistics
"Morbidity and Mortality Weekly Report" (January 4, 2008, Vol. 56, Nos. 51 & 52)
*Provisional data. Caused by ticks-lesions, followed by arthritis of large joints, myalgia, malaise and neurologic and cardiac manifestations. Named after Old Lyme, CT, where the disease was first reported.
**Not notifiable.

Malaria Cases Reported in 2007

National Total = 1,085 Cases*

ALPHA ORDER

RANK	STATE	CASES	% of USA
28	Alabama	7	0.6%
40	Alaska	2	0.2%
20	Arizona	13	1.2%
40	Arkansas	2	0.2%
2	California	113	10.4%
14	Colorado	23	2.1%
40	Connecticut	2	0.2%
35	Delaware	4	0.4%
6	Florida	57	5.3%
9	Georgia	35	3.2%
47	Hawaii	0	0.0%
32	Idaho	5	0.5%
7	Illinois	44	4.1%
22	Indiana	10	0.9%
36	Iowa	3	0.3%
36	Kansas	3	0.3%
23	Kentucky	9	0.8%
19	Louisiana	14	1.3%
25	Maine	8	0.7%
3	Maryland	63	5.8%
10	Massachusetts	30	2.8%
17	Michigan	18	1.7%
11	Minnesota	29	2.7%
40	Mississippi	2	0.2%
25	Missouri	8	0.7%
36	Montana	3	0.3%
28	Nebraska	7	0.6%
36	Nevada	3	0.3%
25	New Hampshire	8	0.7%
47	New Jersey	0	0.0%
32	New Mexico	5	0.5%
1	New York	236	21.8%
15	North Carolina	21	1.9%
40	North Dakota	2	0.2%
12	Ohio	28	2.6%
31	Oklahoma	6	0.6%
18	Oregon	17	1.6%
8	Pennsylvania	42	3.9%
47	Rhode Island	0	0.0%
28	South Carolina	7	0.6%
46	South Dakota	1	0.1%
16	Tennessee	20	1.8%
5	Texas	58	5.3%
21	Utah	11	1.0%
32	Vermont	5	0.5%
4	Virginia	59	5.4%
12	Washington	28	2.6%
40	West Virginia	2	0.2%
23	Wisconsin	9	0.8%
47	Wyoming	0	0.0%

RANK ORDER

RANK	STATE	CASES	% of USA
1	New York	236	21.8%
2	California	113	10.4%
3	Maryland	63	5.8%
4	Virginia	59	5.4%
5	Texas	58	5.3%
6	Florida	57	5.3%
7	Illinois	44	4.1%
8	Pennsylvania	42	3.9%
9	Georgia	35	3.2%
10	Massachusetts	30	2.8%
11	Minnesota	29	2.7%
12	Ohio	28	2.6%
12	Washington	28	2.6%
14	Colorado	23	2.1%
15	North Carolina	21	1.9%
16	Tennessee	20	1.8%
17	Michigan	18	1.7%
18	Oregon	17	1.6%
19	Louisiana	14	1.3%
20	Arizona	13	1.2%
21	Utah	11	1.0%
22	Indiana	10	0.9%
23	Kentucky	9	0.8%
23	Wisconsin	9	0.8%
25	Maine	8	0.7%
25	Missouri	8	0.7%
25	New Hampshire	8	0.7%
28	Alabama	7	0.6%
28	Nebraska	7	0.6%
28	South Carolina	7	0.6%
31	Oklahoma	6	0.6%
32	Idaho	5	0.5%
32	New Mexico	5	0.5%
32	Vermont	5	0.5%
35	Delaware	4	0.4%
36	Iowa	3	0.3%
36	Kansas	3	0.3%
36	Montana	3	0.3%
36	Nevada	3	0.3%
40	Alaska	2	0.2%
40	Arkansas	2	0.2%
40	Connecticut	2	0.2%
40	Mississippi	2	0.2%
40	North Dakota	2	0.2%
40	West Virginia	2	0.2%
46	South Dakota	1	0.1%
47	Hawaii	0	0.0%
47	New Jersey	0	0.0%
47	Rhode Island	0	0.0%
47	Wyoming	0	0.0%
	District of Columbia	3	0.3%

Source: U.S. Department of Health and Human Services, National Center for Health Statistics
    "Morbidity and Mortality Weekly Report" (January 4, 2008, Vol. 56, Nos. 51 & 52)
*Provisional data. Infectious disease usually transmitted by bites of infected mosquitoes. Symptoms include high fever, shaking chills, sweating, and anemia.

Malaria Rate in 2007

National Rate = 0.4 Cases per 100,000 Population*

ALPHA ORDER

RANK	STATE	RATE
27	Alabama	0.2
16	Alaska	0.3
27	Arizona	0.2
38	Arkansas	0.1
16	California	0.3
8	Colorado	0.5
38	Connecticut	0.1
8	Delaware	0.5
16	Florida	0.3
12	Georgia	0.4
47	Hawaii	0.0
16	Idaho	0.3
16	Illinois	0.3
27	Indiana	0.2
38	Iowa	0.1
38	Kansas	0.1
27	Kentucky	0.2
16	Louisiana	0.3
5	Maine	0.6
2	Maryland	1.1
8	Massachusetts	0.5
27	Michigan	0.2
5	Minnesota	0.6
38	Mississippi	0.1
38	Missouri	0.1
16	Montana	0.3
12	Nebraska	0.4
38	Nevada	0.1
5	New Hampshire	0.6
47	New Jersey	0.0
16	New Mexico	0.3
1	New York	1.2
27	North Carolina	0.2
16	North Dakota	0.3
27	Ohio	0.2
27	Oklahoma	0.2
8	Oregon	0.5
16	Pennsylvania	0.3
47	Rhode Island	0.0
27	South Carolina	0.2
38	South Dakota	0.1
16	Tennessee	0.3
27	Texas	0.2
12	Utah	0.4
3	Vermont	0.8
3	Virginia	0.8
12	Washington	0.4
38	West Virginia	0.1
27	Wisconsin	0.2
47	Wyoming	0.0

RANK ORDER

RANK	STATE	RATE
1	New York	1.2
2	Maryland	1.1
3	Vermont	0.8
3	Virginia	0.8
5	Maine	0.6
5	Minnesota	0.6
5	New Hampshire	0.6
8	Colorado	0.5
8	Delaware	0.5
8	Massachusetts	0.5
8	Oregon	0.5
12	Georgia	0.4
12	Nebraska	0.4
12	Utah	0.4
12	Washington	0.4
16	Alaska	0.3
16	California	0.3
16	Florida	0.3
16	Idaho	0.3
16	Illinois	0.3
16	Louisiana	0.3
16	Montana	0.3
16	New Mexico	0.3
16	North Dakota	0.3
16	Pennsylvania	0.3
16	Tennessee	0.3
27	Alabama	0.2
27	Arizona	0.2
27	Indiana	0.2
27	Kentucky	0.2
27	Michigan	0.2
27	North Carolina	0.2
27	Ohio	0.2
27	Oklahoma	0.2
27	South Carolina	0.2
27	Texas	0.2
27	Wisconsin	0.2
38	Arkansas	0.1
38	Connecticut	0.1
38	Iowa	0.1
38	Kansas	0.1
38	Mississippi	0.1
38	Missouri	0.1
38	Nevada	0.1
38	South Dakota	0.1
38	West Virginia	0.1
47	Hawaii	0.0
47	New Jersey	0.0
47	Rhode Island	0.0
47	Wyoming	0.0

District of Columbia   0.5

Source: CQ Press using data from U.S. Department of Health and Human Services, National Center for Health Statistics
"Morbidity and Mortality Weekly Report" (January 4, 2008, Vol. 56, Nos. 51 & 52)
*Provisional data. Infectious disease usually transmitted by bites of infected mosquitoes. Symptoms include high fever,
shaking chills, sweating, and anemia.

Meningococcal Infections Reported in 2007

National Total = 974 Cases*

ALPHA ORDER

RANK	STATE	CASES	% of USA
30	Alabama	9	0.9%
47	Alaska	1	0.1%
25	Arizona	14	1.4%
30	Arkansas	9	0.9%
1	California	160	16.4%
17	Colorado	21	2.2%
35	Connecticut	6	0.6%
47	Delaware	1	0.1%
2	Florida	67	6.9%
12	Georgia	24	2.5%
47	Hawaii	1	0.1%
33	Idaho	7	0.7%
5	Illinois	45	4.6%
9	Indiana	28	2.9%
22	Iowa	16	1.6%
36	Kansas	5	0.5%
27	Kentucky	13	1.3%
10	Louisiana	27	2.8%
33	Maine	7	0.7%
15	Maryland	22	2.3%
18	Massachusetts	19	2.0%
11	Michigan	26	2.7%
13	Minnesota	23	2.4%
29	Mississippi	10	1.0%
19	Missouri	18	1.8%
41	Montana	2	0.2%
36	Nebraska	5	0.5%
36	Nevada	5	0.5%
47	New Hampshire	1	0.1%
19	New Jersey	18	1.8%
41	New Mexico	2	0.2%
3	New York	62	6.4%
15	North Carolina	22	2.3%
41	North Dakota	2	0.2%
7	Ohio	34	3.5%
21	Oklahoma	17	1.7%
8	Oregon	32	3.3%
4	Pennsylvania	50	5.1%
41	Rhode Island	2	0.2%
24	South Carolina	15	1.5%
40	South Dakota	3	0.3%
22	Tennessee	16	1.6%
6	Texas	41	4.2%
28	Utah	12	1.2%
39	Vermont	4	0.4%
25	Virginia	14	1.4%
13	Washington	23	2.4%
41	West Virginia	2	0.2%
30	Wisconsin	9	0.9%
41	Wyoming	2	0.2%

RANK ORDER

RANK	STATE	CASES	% of USA
1	California	160	16.4%
2	Florida	67	6.9%
3	New York	62	6.4%
4	Pennsylvania	50	5.1%
5	Illinois	45	4.6%
6	Texas	41	4.2%
7	Ohio	34	3.5%
8	Oregon	32	3.3%
9	Indiana	28	2.9%
10	Louisiana	27	2.8%
11	Michigan	26	2.7%
12	Georgia	24	2.5%
13	Minnesota	23	2.4%
13	Washington	23	2.4%
15	Maryland	22	2.3%
15	North Carolina	22	2.3%
17	Colorado	21	2.2%
18	Massachusetts	19	2.0%
19	Missouri	18	1.8%
19	New Jersey	18	1.8%
21	Oklahoma	17	1.7%
22	Iowa	16	1.6%
22	Tennessee	16	1.6%
24	South Carolina	15	1.5%
25	Arizona	14	1.4%
25	Virginia	14	1.4%
27	Kentucky	13	1.3%
28	Utah	12	1.2%
29	Mississippi	10	1.0%
30	Alabama	9	0.9%
30	Arkansas	9	0.9%
30	Wisconsin	9	0.9%
33	Idaho	7	0.7%
33	Maine	7	0.7%
35	Connecticut	6	0.6%
36	Kansas	5	0.5%
36	Nebraska	5	0.5%
36	Nevada	5	0.5%
39	Vermont	4	0.4%
40	South Dakota	3	0.3%
41	Montana	2	0.2%
41	New Mexico	2	0.2%
41	North Dakota	2	0.2%
41	Rhode Island	2	0.2%
41	West Virginia	2	0.2%
41	Wyoming	2	0.2%
47	Alaska	1	0.1%
47	Delaware	1	0.1%
47	Hawaii	1	0.1%
47	New Hampshire	1	0.1%
	District of Columbia	0	0.0%

Source: U.S. Department of Health and Human Services, National Center for Health Statistics
   "Morbidity and Mortality Weekly Report" (January 4, 2008, Vol. 56, Nos. 51 & 52)
*Provisional data. A bacterium (Neisseria meningitidis) that causes cerebrospinal meningitis.

Meningococcal Infection Rate in 2007

National Rate = 0.3 Cases per 100,000 Population*

ALPHA ORDER

RANK	STATE	RATE
33	Alabama	0.2
45	Alaska	0.1
33	Arizona	0.2
20	Arkansas	0.3
9	California	0.4
9	Colorado	0.4
33	Connecticut	0.2
45	Delaware	0.1
9	Florida	0.4
20	Georgia	0.3
45	Hawaii	0.1
4	Idaho	0.5
9	Illinois	0.4
9	Indiana	0.4
4	Iowa	0.5
33	Kansas	0.2
20	Kentucky	0.3
2	Louisiana	0.6
4	Maine	0.5
9	Maryland	0.4
20	Massachusetts	0.3
20	Michigan	0.3
9	Minnesota	0.4
20	Mississippi	0.3
20	Missouri	0.3
33	Montana	0.2
20	Nebraska	0.3
33	Nevada	0.2
45	New Hampshire	0.1
33	New Jersey	0.2
45	New Mexico	0.1
20	New York	0.3
33	North Carolina	0.2
20	North Dakota	0.3
20	Ohio	0.3
4	Oklahoma	0.5
1	Oregon	0.9
9	Pennsylvania	0.4
33	Rhode Island	0.2
20	South Carolina	0.3
9	South Dakota	0.4
20	Tennessee	0.3
33	Texas	0.2
4	Utah	0.5
2	Vermont	0.6
33	Virginia	0.2
9	Washington	0.4
45	West Virginia	0.1
33	Wisconsin	0.2
9	Wyoming	0.4

RANK ORDER

RANK	STATE	RATE
1	Oregon	0.9
2	Louisiana	0.6
2	Vermont	0.6
4	Idaho	0.5
4	Iowa	0.5
4	Maine	0.5
4	Oklahoma	0.5
4	Utah	0.5
9	California	0.4
9	Colorado	0.4
9	Florida	0.4
9	Illinois	0.4
9	Indiana	0.4
9	Maryland	0.4
9	Minnesota	0.4
9	Pennsylvania	0.4
9	South Dakota	0.4
9	Washington	0.4
9	Wyoming	0.4
20	Arkansas	0.3
20	Georgia	0.3
20	Kentucky	0.3
20	Massachusetts	0.3
20	Michigan	0.3
20	Mississippi	0.3
20	Missouri	0.3
20	Nebraska	0.3
20	New York	0.3
20	North Dakota	0.3
20	Ohio	0.3
20	South Carolina	0.3
20	Tennessee	0.3
33	Alabama	0.2
33	Arizona	0.2
33	Connecticut	0.2
33	Kansas	0.2
33	Montana	0.2
33	Nevada	0.2
33	New Jersey	0.2
33	North Carolina	0.2
33	Rhode Island	0.2
33	Texas	0.2
33	Virginia	0.2
33	Wisconsin	0.2
45	Alaska	0.1
45	Delaware	0.1
45	Hawaii	0.1
45	New Hampshire	0.1
45	New Mexico	0.1
45	West Virginia	0.1

District of Columbia 0.0

Source: CQ Press using data from U.S. Department of Health and Human Services, National Center for Health Statistics
"Morbidity and Mortality Weekly Report" (January 4, 2008, Vol. 56, Nos. 51 & 52)
*Provisional data. A bacterium (Neisseria meningitidis) that causes cerebrospinal meningitis.

Rabies (Animal) Cases Reported in 2007

National Total = 5,316 Cases*

ALPHA ORDER

RANK	STATE	CASES	% of USA
39	Alabama	0	0.0%
22	Alaska	42	0.8%
11	Arizona	151	2.8%
26	Arkansas	33	0.6%
10	California	163	3.1%
39	Colorado	0	0.0%
7	Connecticut	213	4.0%
39	Delaware	0	0.0%
13	Florida	120	2.3%
6	Georgia	274	5.2%
NA	Hawaii**	NA	NA
39	Idaho	0	0.0%
14	Illinois	113	2.1%
35	Indiana	12	0.2%
27	Iowa	30	0.6%
15	Kansas	101	1.9%
30	Kentucky	21	0.4%
39	Louisiana	0	0.0%
17	Maine	82	1.5%
5	Maryland	389	7.3%
39	Massachusetts	0	0.0%
8	Michigan	185	3.5%
24	Minnesota	39	0.7%
38	Mississippi	1	0.0%
25	Missouri	38	0.7%
31	Montana	20	0.4%
39	Nebraska	0	0.0%
37	Nevada	8	0.2%
19	New Hampshire	53	1.0%
NA	New Jersey**	NA	NA
34	New Mexico	14	0.3%
3	New York	558	10.5%
4	North Carolina	474	8.9%
29	North Dakota	22	0.4%
16	Ohio	84	1.6%
20	Oklahoma	46	0.9%
35	Oregon	12	0.2%
1	Pennsylvania	797	15.0%
23	Rhode Island	40	0.8%
20	South Carolina	46	0.9%
28	South Dakota	23	0.4%
12	Tennessee	124	2.3%
39	Texas	0	0.0%
33	Utah	16	0.3%
9	Vermont	164	3.1%
2	Virginia	711	13.4%
39	Washington	0	0.0%
18	West Virginia	77	1.4%
NA	Wisconsin**	NA	NA
31	Wyoming	20	0.4%

RANK ORDER

RANK	STATE	CASES	% of USA
1	Pennsylvania	797	15.0%
2	Virginia	711	13.4%
3	New York	558	10.5%
4	North Carolina	474	8.9%
5	Maryland	389	7.3%
6	Georgia	274	5.2%
7	Connecticut	213	4.0%
8	Michigan	185	3.5%
9	Vermont	164	3.1%
10	California	163	3.1%
11	Arizona	151	2.8%
12	Tennessee	124	2.3%
13	Florida	120	2.3%
14	Illinois	113	2.1%
15	Kansas	101	1.9%
16	Ohio	84	1.6%
17	Maine	82	1.5%
18	West Virginia	77	1.4%
19	New Hampshire	53	1.0%
20	Oklahoma	46	0.9%
20	South Carolina	46	0.9%
22	Alaska	42	0.8%
23	Rhode Island	40	0.8%
24	Minnesota	39	0.7%
25	Missouri	38	0.7%
26	Arkansas	33	0.6%
27	Iowa	30	0.6%
28	South Dakota	23	0.4%
29	North Dakota	22	0.4%
30	Kentucky	21	0.4%
31	Montana	20	0.4%
31	Wyoming	20	0.4%
33	Utah	16	0.3%
34	New Mexico	14	0.3%
35	Indiana	12	0.2%
35	Oregon	12	0.2%
37	Nevada	8	0.2%
38	Mississippi	1	0.0%
39	Alabama	0	0.0%
39	Colorado	0	0.0%
39	Delaware	0	0.0%
39	Idaho	0	0.0%
39	Louisiana	0	0.0%
39	Massachusetts	0	0.0%
39	Nebraska	0	0.0%
39	Texas	0	0.0%
39	Washington	0	0.0%
NA	Hawaii**	NA	NA
NA	New Jersey**	NA	NA
NA	Wisconsin**	NA	NA
	District of Columbia	0	0.0%

Source: U.S. Department of Health and Human Services, National Center for Health Statistics
"Morbidity and Mortality Weekly Report" (January 4, 2008, Vol. 56, Nos. 51 & 52)
*Provisional data. An acute, infectious, often fatal viral disease of most warm-blooded animals, especially wolves, cats, and dogs, that attacks the central nervous system and is transmitted by the bite of infected animals.
**Not notifiable.

Rabies (Animal) Rate in 2007

National Rate = 1.8 Cases per 100,000 Human Population*

ALPHA ORDER

RANK	STATE	RATE
38	Alabama	0.0
6	Alaska	6.1
18	Arizona	2.4
23	Arkansas	1.2
34	California	0.4
38	Colorado	0.0
6	Connecticut	6.1
38	Delaware	0.0
28	Florida	0.7
15	Georgia	2.9
NA	Hawaii**	NA
38	Idaho	0.0
26	Illinois	0.9
37	Indiana	0.2
24	Iowa	1.0
13	Kansas	3.6
33	Kentucky	0.5
38	Louisiana	0.0
5	Maine	6.2
3	Maryland	6.9
38	Massachusetts	0.0
21	Michigan	1.8
27	Minnesota	0.8
38	Mississippi	0.0
31	Missouri	0.6
19	Montana	2.1
38	Nebraska	0.0
35	Nevada	0.3
10	New Hampshire	4.0
NA	New Jersey**	NA
28	New Mexico	0.7
15	New York	2.9
8	North Carolina	5.2
14	North Dakota	3.4
28	Ohio	0.7
22	Oklahoma	1.3
35	Oregon	0.3
4	Pennsylvania	6.4
11	Rhode Island	3.8
24	South Carolina	1.0
15	South Dakota	2.9
20	Tennessee	2.0
38	Texas	0.0
31	Utah	0.6
1	Vermont	26.4
38	Washington	0.0
9	West Virginia	4.2
NA	Wisconsin**	NA
11	Wyoming	3.8

RANK ORDER

RANK	STATE	RATE
1	Vermont	26.4
2	Virginia	9.2
3	Maryland	6.9
4	Pennsylvania	6.4
5	Maine	6.2
6	Alaska	6.1
6	Connecticut	6.1
8	North Carolina	5.2
9	West Virginia	4.2
10	New Hampshire	4.0
11	Rhode Island	3.8
11	Wyoming	3.8
13	Kansas	3.6
14	North Dakota	3.4
15	Georgia	2.9
15	New York	2.9
15	South Dakota	2.9
18	Arizona	2.4
19	Montana	2.1
20	Tennessee	2.0
21	Michigan	1.8
22	Oklahoma	1.3
23	Arkansas	1.2
24	Iowa	1.0
24	South Carolina	1.0
26	Illinois	0.9
27	Minnesota	0.8
28	Florida	0.7
28	New Mexico	0.7
28	Ohio	0.7
31	Missouri	0.6
31	Utah	0.6
33	Kentucky	0.5
34	California	0.4
35	Nevada	0.3
35	Oregon	0.3
37	Indiana	0.2
38	Alabama	0.0
38	Colorado	0.0
38	Delaware	0.0
38	Idaho	0.0
38	Louisiana	0.0
38	Massachusetts	0.0
38	Mississippi	0.0
38	Nebraska	0.0
38	Texas	0.0
38	Washington	0.0
NA	Hawaii**	NA
NA	New Jersey**	NA
NA	Wisconsin**	NA

District of Columbia   0.0

Source: CQ Press using data from U.S. Department of Health and Human Services, National Center for Health Statistics
    "Morbidity and Mortality Weekly Report" (January 4, 2008, Vol. 56, Nos. 51 & 52)
*Provisional data. An acute, infectious, often fatal viral disease of most warm-blooded animals, especially wolves, cats, and dogs, that attacks the central nervous system and is transmitted by the bite of infected animals.
**Not notifiable.

Rocky Mountain Spotted Fever Cases Reported in 2007

National Total = 2,106 Cases*

ALPHA ORDER

RANK	STATE	CASES	% of USA
6	Alabama	92	4.4%
NA	Alaska**	NA	NA
23	Arizona	11	0.5%
5	Arkansas	101	4.8%
34	California	3	0.1%
27	Colorado	4	0.2%
42	Connecticut	0	0.0%
18	Delaware	15	0.7%
15	Florida	25	1.2%
10	Georgia	51	2.4%
NA	Hawaii**	NA	NA
27	Idaho	4	0.2%
12	Illinois	33	1.6%
27	Indiana	4	0.2%
17	Iowa	16	0.8%
21	Kansas	13	0.6%
25	Kentucky	5	0.2%
34	Louisiana	3	0.1%
38	Maine	1	0.0%
7	Maryland	65	3.1%
27	Massachusetts	4	0.2%
27	Michigan	4	0.2%
36	Minnesota	2	0.1%
19	Mississippi	14	0.7%
2	Missouri	403	19.1%
38	Montana	1	0.0%
19	Nebraska	14	0.7%
42	Nevada	0	0.0%
38	New Hampshire	1	0.0%
16	New Jersey	23	1.1%
27	New Mexico	4	0.2%
13	New York	32	1.5%
1	North Carolina	646	30.7%
42	North Dakota	0	0.0%
24	Ohio	10	0.5%
9	Oklahoma	57	2.7%
36	Oregon	2	0.1%
14	Pennsylvania	31	1.5%
42	Rhode Island	0	0.0%
8	South Carolina	63	3.0%
27	South Dakota	4	0.2%
3	Tennessee	147	7.0%
11	Texas	39	1.9%
38	Utah	1	0.0%
42	Vermont	0	0.0%
4	Virginia	140	6.6%
NA	Washington**	NA	NA
25	West Virginia	5	0.2%
42	Wisconsin	0	0.0%
22	Wyoming	12	0.6%

RANK ORDER

RANK	STATE	CASES	% of USA
1	North Carolina	646	30.7%
2	Missouri	403	19.1%
3	Tennessee	147	7.0%
4	Virginia	140	6.6%
5	Arkansas	101	4.8%
6	Alabama	92	4.4%
7	Maryland	65	3.1%
8	South Carolina	63	3.0%
9	Oklahoma	57	2.7%
10	Georgia	51	2.4%
11	Texas	39	1.9%
12	Illinois	33	1.6%
13	New York	32	1.5%
14	Pennsylvania	31	1.5%
15	Florida	25	1.2%
16	New Jersey	23	1.1%
17	Iowa	16	0.8%
18	Delaware	15	0.7%
19	Mississippi	14	0.7%
19	Nebraska	14	0.7%
21	Kansas	13	0.6%
22	Wyoming	12	0.6%
23	Arizona	11	0.5%
24	Ohio	10	0.5%
25	Kentucky	5	0.2%
25	West Virginia	5	0.2%
27	Colorado	4	0.2%
27	Idaho	4	0.2%
27	Indiana	4	0.2%
27	Massachusetts	4	0.2%
27	Michigan	4	0.2%
27	New Mexico	4	0.2%
27	South Dakota	4	0.2%
34	California	3	0.1%
34	Louisiana	3	0.1%
36	Minnesota	2	0.1%
36	Oregon	2	0.1%
38	Maine	1	0.0%
38	Montana	1	0.0%
38	New Hampshire	1	0.0%
38	Utah	1	0.0%
42	Connecticut	0	0.0%
42	Nevada	0	0.0%
42	North Dakota	0	0.0%
42	Rhode Island	0	0.0%
42	Vermont	0	0.0%
42	Wisconsin	0	0.0%
NA	Alaska**	NA	NA
NA	Hawaii**	NA	NA
NA	Washington**	NA	NA
	District of Columbia	1	0.0%

Source: U.S. Department of Health and Human Services, National Center for Health Statistics
    "Morbidity and Mortality Weekly Report" (January 4, 2008, Vol. 56, Nos. 51 & 52)

*Provisional data. An illness caused by Rickettsia rickettsii, a bacterial pathogen transmitted to humans through contact with ticks. Characterized by acute onset of fever, and may be accompanied by headache, malaise, myalgia, nausea/vomiting, or neurologic signs. A rash is often present on the palms and soles.
**Not notifiable.

Rocky Mountain Spotted Fever Rate in 2007

National Rate = 0.7 Cases per 100,000 Population*

ALPHA ORDER

RANK	STATE	RATE
6	Alabama	2.0
NA	Alaska**	NA
22	Arizona	0.2
3	Arkansas	3.6
38	California	0.0
27	Colorado	0.1
38	Connecticut	0.0
8	Delaware	1.7
27	Florida	0.1
13	Georgia	0.5
NA	Hawaii**	NA
18	Idaho	0.3
18	Illinois	0.3
27	Indiana	0.1
13	Iowa	0.5
13	Kansas	0.5
27	Kentucky	0.1
27	Louisiana	0.1
27	Maine	0.1
11	Maryland	1.2
27	Massachusetts	0.1
38	Michigan	0.0
38	Minnesota	0.0
13	Mississippi	0.5
2	Missouri	6.9
27	Montana	0.1
12	Nebraska	0.8
38	Nevada	0.0
27	New Hampshire	0.1
18	New Jersey	0.3
22	New Mexico	0.2
22	New York	0.2
1	North Carolina	7.1
38	North Dakota	0.0
27	Ohio	0.1
9	Oklahoma	1.6
27	Oregon	0.1
22	Pennsylvania	0.2
38	Rhode Island	0.0
10	South Carolina	1.4
13	South Dakota	0.5
4	Tennessee	2.4
22	Texas	0.2
38	Utah	0.0
38	Vermont	0.0
7	Virginia	1.8
NA	Washington**	NA
18	West Virginia	0.3
38	Wisconsin	0.0
5	Wyoming	2.3

RANK ORDER

RANK	STATE	RATE
1	North Carolina	7.1
2	Missouri	6.9
3	Arkansas	3.6
4	Tennessee	2.4
5	Wyoming	2.3
6	Alabama	2.0
7	Virginia	1.8
8	Delaware	1.7
9	Oklahoma	1.6
10	South Carolina	1.4
11	Maryland	1.2
12	Nebraska	0.8
13	Georgia	0.5
13	Iowa	0.5
13	Kansas	0.5
13	Mississippi	0.5
13	South Dakota	0.5
18	Idaho	0.3
18	Illinois	0.3
18	New Jersey	0.3
18	West Virginia	0.3
22	Arizona	0.2
22	New Mexico	0.2
22	New York	0.2
22	Pennsylvania	0.2
22	Texas	0.2
27	Colorado	0.1
27	Florida	0.1
27	Indiana	0.1
27	Kentucky	0.1
27	Louisiana	0.1
27	Maine	0.1
27	Massachusetts	0.1
27	Montana	0.1
27	New Hampshire	0.1
27	Ohio	0.1
27	Oregon	0.1
38	California	0.0
38	Connecticut	0.0
38	Michigan	0.0
38	Minnesota	0.0
38	Nevada	0.0
38	North Dakota	0.0
38	Rhode Island	0.0
38	Utah	0.0
38	Vermont	0.0
38	Wisconsin	0.0
NA	Alaska**	NA
NA	Hawaii**	NA
NA	Washington**	NA

District of Columbia 0.2

Source: CQ Press using data from U.S. Department of Health and Human Services, National Center for Health Statistics
"Morbidity and Mortality Weekly Report" (January 4, 2008, Vol. 56, Nos. 51 & 52)

*Provisional data. An illness caused by Rickettsia rickettsii, a bacterial pathogen transmitted to humans through contact with ticks. Characterized by acute onset of fever, and may be accompanied by headache, malaise, myalgia, nausea/vomiting, or neurologic signs. A rash is often present on the palms and soles.

**Not notifiable.

Salmonellosis Cases Reported in 2007

National Total = 43,748 Cases*

ALPHA ORDER

RANK	STATE	CASES	% of USA
14	Alabama	938	2.1%
48	Alaska	77	0.2%
13	Arizona	1,021	2.3%
20	Arkansas	831	1.9%
2	California	4,236	9.7%
29	Colorado	563	1.3%
31	Connecticut	415	0.9%
42	Delaware	136	0.3%
1	Florida	5,030	11.5%
5	Georgia	1,944	4.4%
46	Hawaii	97	0.2%
41	Idaho	152	0.3%
8	Illinois	1,745	4.0%
24	Indiana	691	1.6%
30	Iowa	464	1.1%
32	Kansas	389	0.9%
28	Kentucky	569	1.3%
15	Louisiana	923	2.1%
42	Maine	136	0.3%
18	Maryland	877	2.0%
10	Massachusetts	1,212	2.8%
16	Michigan	920	2.1%
26	Minnesota	679	1.6%
17	Mississippi	885	2.0%
23	Missouri	763	1.7%
44	Montana	112	0.3%
35	Nebraska	273	0.6%
37	Nevada	229	0.5%
40	New Hampshire	158	0.4%
21	New Jersey	824	1.9%
36	New Mexico	269	0.6%
3	New York	2,772	6.3%
7	North Carolina	1,805	4.1%
50	North Dakota	44	0.1%
9	Ohio	1,323	3.0%
27	Oklahoma	650	1.5%
33	Oregon	323	0.7%
6	Pennsylvania	1,875	4.3%
45	Rhode Island	102	0.2%
11	South Carolina	1,109	2.5%
39	South Dakota	161	0.4%
19	Tennessee	852	1.9%
4	Texas	1,955	4.5%
34	Utah	280	0.6%
47	Vermont	80	0.2%
12	Virginia	1,062	2.4%
25	Washington	685	1.6%
38	West Virginia	206	0.5%
22	Wisconsin	817	1.9%
49	Wyoming	73	0.2%

RANK ORDER

RANK	STATE	CASES	% of USA
1	Florida	5,030	11.5%
2	California	4,236	9.7%
3	New York	2,772	6.3%
4	Texas	1,955	4.5%
5	Georgia	1,944	4.4%
6	Pennsylvania	1,875	4.3%
7	North Carolina	1,805	4.1%
8	Illinois	1,745	4.0%
9	Ohio	1,323	3.0%
10	Massachusetts	1,212	2.8%
11	South Carolina	1,109	2.5%
12	Virginia	1,062	2.4%
13	Arizona	1,021	2.3%
14	Alabama	938	2.1%
15	Louisiana	923	2.1%
16	Michigan	920	2.1%
17	Mississippi	885	2.0%
18	Maryland	877	2.0%
19	Tennessee	852	1.9%
20	Arkansas	831	1.9%
21	New Jersey	824	1.9%
22	Wisconsin	817	1.9%
23	Missouri	763	1.7%
24	Indiana	691	1.6%
25	Washington	685	1.6%
26	Minnesota	679	1.6%
27	Oklahoma	650	1.5%
28	Kentucky	569	1.3%
29	Colorado	563	1.3%
30	Iowa	464	1.1%
31	Connecticut	415	0.9%
32	Kansas	389	0.9%
33	Oregon	323	0.7%
34	Utah	280	0.6%
35	Nebraska	273	0.6%
36	New Mexico	269	0.6%
37	Nevada	229	0.5%
38	West Virginia	206	0.5%
39	South Dakota	161	0.4%
40	New Hampshire	158	0.4%
41	Idaho	152	0.3%
42	Delaware	136	0.3%
42	Maine	136	0.3%
44	Montana	112	0.3%
45	Rhode Island	102	0.2%
46	Hawaii	97	0.2%
47	Vermont	80	0.2%
48	Alaska	77	0.2%
49	Wyoming	73	0.2%
50	North Dakota	44	0.1%
	District of Columbia	16	0.0%

Source: U.S. Department of Health and Human Services, National Center for Health Statistics
   "Morbidity and Mortality Weekly Report" (January 4, 2008, Vol. 56, Nos. 51 & 52)
*Provisional data. Any disease caused by a salmonella infection, which may be manifested as food poisoning with acute gastroenteritis, vomiting, and diarrhea.

Salmonellosis Rate in 2007

National Rate = 14.5 Cases per 100,000 Population*

ALPHA ORDER				RANK ORDER		
RANK	STATE	RATE		RANK	STATE	RATE
7	Alabama	20.3		1	Mississippi	30.3
37	Alaska	11.3		2	Arkansas	29.3
12	Arizona	16.1		3	Florida	27.6
2	Arkansas	29.3		4	South Carolina	25.2
33	California	11.6		5	Louisiana	21.5
33	Colorado	11.6		6	Georgia	20.4
31	Connecticut	11.8		7	Alabama	20.3
13	Delaware	15.7		8	South Dakota	20.2
3	Florida	27.6		9	North Carolina	19.9
6	Georgia	20.4		10	Massachusetts	18.8
49	Hawaii	7.6		11	Oklahoma	18.0
42	Idaho	10.1		12	Arizona	16.1
25	Illinois	13.6		13	Delaware	15.7
38	Indiana	10.9		14	Maryland	15.6
15	Iowa	15.5		15	Iowa	15.5
20	Kansas	14.0		16	Nebraska	15.4
26	Kentucky	13.4		17	Pennsylvania	15.1
5	Louisiana	21.5		18	Wisconsin	14.6
41	Maine	10.3		19	New York	14.4
14	Maryland	15.6		20	Kansas	14.0
10	Massachusetts	18.8		20	Wyoming	14.0
45	Michigan	9.1		22	Tennessee	13.8
27	Minnesota	13.1		22	Virginia	13.8
1	Mississippi	30.3		24	New Mexico	13.7
28	Missouri	13.0		25	Illinois	13.6
32	Montana	11.7		26	Kentucky	13.4
16	Nebraska	15.4		27	Minnesota	13.1
46	Nevada	8.9		28	Missouri	13.0
30	New Hampshire	12.0		29	Vermont	12.9
44	New Jersey	9.5		30	New Hampshire	12.0
24	New Mexico	13.7		31	Connecticut	11.8
19	New York	14.4		32	Montana	11.7
9	North Carolina	19.9		33	California	11.6
50	North Dakota	6.9		33	Colorado	11.6
35	Ohio	11.5		35	Ohio	11.5
11	Oklahoma	18.0		36	West Virginia	11.4
47	Oregon	8.6		37	Alaska	11.3
17	Pennsylvania	15.1		38	Indiana	10.9
43	Rhode Island	9.6		39	Utah	10.6
4	South Carolina	25.2		39	Washington	10.6
8	South Dakota	20.2		41	Maine	10.3
22	Tennessee	13.8		42	Idaho	10.1
48	Texas	8.2		43	Rhode Island	9.6
39	Utah	10.6		44	New Jersey	9.5
29	Vermont	12.9		45	Michigan	9.1
22	Virginia	13.8		46	Nevada	8.9
39	Washington	10.6		47	Oregon	8.6
36	West Virginia	11.4		48	Texas	8.2
18	Wisconsin	14.6		49	Hawaii	7.6
20	Wyoming	14.0		50	North Dakota	6.9
					District of Columbia	2.7

Source: CQ Press using data from U.S. Department of Health and Human Services, National Center for Health Statistics
"Morbidity and Mortality Weekly Report" (January 4, 2008, Vol. 56, Nos. 51 & 52)
*Provisional data. Any disease caused by a salmonella infection, which may be manifested as food poisoning with acute gastroenteritis, vomiting, and diarrhea.

Shigellosis Cases Reported in 2007

National Total = 17,193 Cases*

ALPHA ORDER

RANK	STATE	CASES	% of USA
8	Alabama	702	4.1%
48	Alaska	7	0.0%
10	Arizona	572	3.3%
32	Arkansas	96	0.6%
7	California	1,231	7.2%
25	Colorado	123	0.7%
36	Connecticut	44	0.3%
45	Delaware	11	0.1%
1	Florida	2,289	13.3%
2	Georgia	1,586	9.2%
46	Hawaii	10	0.1%
44	Idaho	12	0.1%
9	Illinois	597	3.5%
17	Indiana	217	1.3%
30	Iowa	104	0.6%
40	Kansas	25	0.1%
11	Kentucky	499	2.9%
12	Louisiana	468	2.7%
43	Maine	14	0.1%
27	Maryland	114	0.7%
22	Massachusetts	144	0.8%
34	Michigan	73	0.4%
15	Minnesota	231	1.3%
4	Mississippi	1,328	7.7%
5	Missouri	1,279	7.4%
40	Montana	25	0.1%
39	Nebraska	27	0.2%
35	Nevada	70	0.4%
49	New Hampshire	5	0.0%
23	New Jersey	134	0.8%
30	New Mexico	104	0.6%
13	New York	453	2.6%
29	North Carolina	105	0.6%
47	North Dakota	9	0.1%
6	Ohio	1,260	7.3%
24	Oklahoma	129	0.8%
33	Oregon	79	0.5%
19	Pennsylvania	185	1.1%
42	Rhode Island	22	0.1%
18	South Carolina	201	1.2%
26	South Dakota	116	0.7%
14	Tennessee	341	2.0%
3	Texas	1,413	8.2%
37	Utah	38	0.2%
50	Vermont	4	0.0%
20	Virginia	175	1.0%
21	Washington	147	0.9%
28	West Virginia	111	0.6%
16	Wisconsin	227	1.3%
38	Wyoming	33	0.2%

RANK ORDER

RANK	STATE	CASES	% of USA
1	Florida	2,289	13.3%
2	Georgia	1,586	9.2%
3	Texas	1,413	8.2%
4	Mississippi	1,328	7.7%
5	Missouri	1,279	7.4%
6	Ohio	1,260	7.3%
7	California	1,231	7.2%
8	Alabama	702	4.1%
9	Illinois	597	3.5%
10	Arizona	572	3.3%
11	Kentucky	499	2.9%
12	Louisiana	468	2.7%
13	New York	453	2.6%
14	Tennessee	341	2.0%
15	Minnesota	231	1.3%
16	Wisconsin	227	1.3%
17	Indiana	217	1.3%
18	South Carolina	201	1.2%
19	Pennsylvania	185	1.1%
20	Virginia	175	1.0%
21	Washington	147	0.9%
22	Massachusetts	144	0.8%
23	New Jersey	134	0.8%
24	Oklahoma	129	0.8%
25	Colorado	123	0.7%
26	South Dakota	116	0.7%
27	Maryland	114	0.7%
28	West Virginia	111	0.6%
29	North Carolina	105	0.6%
30	Iowa	104	0.6%
30	New Mexico	104	0.6%
32	Arkansas	96	0.6%
33	Oregon	79	0.5%
34	Michigan	73	0.4%
35	Nevada	70	0.4%
36	Connecticut	44	0.3%
37	Utah	38	0.2%
38	Wyoming	33	0.2%
39	Nebraska	27	0.2%
40	Kansas	25	0.1%
40	Montana	25	0.1%
42	Rhode Island	22	0.1%
43	Maine	14	0.1%
44	Idaho	12	0.1%
45	Delaware	11	0.1%
46	Hawaii	10	0.1%
47	North Dakota	9	0.1%
48	Alaska	7	0.0%
49	New Hampshire	5	0.0%
50	Vermont	4	0.0%
	District of Columbia	4	0.0%

Source: U.S. Department of Health and Human Services, National Center for Health Statistics
    "Morbidity and Mortality Weekly Report" (January 4, 2008, Vol. 56, Nos. 51 & 52)
*Provisional data. Dysentery caused by any of various species of shigellae, occurring most frequently in areas where poor sanitation and malnutrition are prevalent and commonly affecting children and infants.

Shigellosis Rate in 2007

National Rate = 5.7 Cases per 100,000 Population*

ALPHA ORDER

RANK	STATE	RATE
4	Alabama	15.2
44	Alaska	1.0
10	Arizona	9.0
22	Arkansas	3.4
22	California	3.4
27	Colorado	2.5
40	Connecticut	1.3
40	Delaware	1.3
6	Florida	12.5
3	Georgia	16.6
46	Hawaii	0.8
46	Idaho	0.8
16	Illinois	4.6
22	Indiana	3.4
21	Iowa	3.5
45	Kansas	0.9
7	Kentucky	11.8
9	Louisiana	10.9
43	Maine	1.1
34	Maryland	2.0
31	Massachusetts	2.2
48	Michigan	0.7
18	Minnesota	4.4
1	Mississippi	45.5
2	Missouri	21.8
26	Montana	2.6
35	Nebraska	1.5
25	Nevada	2.7
50	New Hampshire	0.4
35	New Jersey	1.5
15	New Mexico	5.3
28	New York	2.3
42	North Carolina	1.2
38	North Dakota	1.4
8	Ohio	11.0
20	Oklahoma	3.6
32	Oregon	2.1
35	Pennsylvania	1.5
32	Rhode Island	2.1
16	South Carolina	4.6
5	South Dakota	14.6
14	Tennessee	5.5
13	Texas	5.9
38	Utah	1.4
49	Vermont	0.6
28	Virginia	2.3
28	Washington	2.3
12	West Virginia	6.1
19	Wisconsin	4.1
11	Wyoming	6.3

RANK ORDER

RANK	STATE	RATE
1	Mississippi	45.5
2	Missouri	21.8
3	Georgia	16.6
4	Alabama	15.2
5	South Dakota	14.6
6	Florida	12.5
7	Kentucky	11.8
8	Ohio	11.0
9	Louisiana	10.9
10	Arizona	9.0
11	Wyoming	6.3
12	West Virginia	6.1
13	Texas	5.9
14	Tennessee	5.5
15	New Mexico	5.3
16	Illinois	4.6
16	South Carolina	4.6
18	Minnesota	4.4
19	Wisconsin	4.1
20	Oklahoma	3.6
21	Iowa	3.5
22	Arkansas	3.4
22	California	3.4
22	Indiana	3.4
25	Nevada	2.7
26	Montana	2.6
27	Colorado	2.5
28	New York	2.3
28	Virginia	2.3
28	Washington	2.3
31	Massachusetts	2.2
32	Oregon	2.1
32	Rhode Island	2.1
34	Maryland	2.0
35	Nebraska	1.5
35	New Jersey	1.5
35	Pennsylvania	1.5
38	North Dakota	1.4
38	Utah	1.4
40	Connecticut	1.3
40	Delaware	1.3
42	North Carolina	1.2
43	Maine	1.1
44	Alaska	1.0
45	Kansas	0.9
46	Hawaii	0.8
46	Idaho	0.8
48	Michigan	0.7
49	Vermont	0.6
50	New Hampshire	0.4
	District of Columbia	0.7

Source: CQ Press using data from U.S. Department of Health and Human Services, National Center for Health Statistics
   "Morbidity and Mortality Weekly Report" (January 4, 2008, Vol. 56, Nos. 51 & 52)
*Provisional data. Dysentery caused by any of various species of shigellae, occurring most frequently in areas where poor
sanitation and malnutrition are prevalent and commonly affecting children and infants.

West Nile Virus Disease Cases Reported in 2007

National Total = 3,506 Cases*

ALPHA ORDER

RANK	STATE	CASES	% of USA
23	Alabama	24	0.7%
44	Alaska	0	0.0%
14	Arizona	94	2.7%
27	Arkansas	20	0.6%
2	California	379	10.8%
1	Colorado	555	15.8%
36	Connecticut	5	0.1%
41	Delaware	1	0.0%
39	Florida	3	0.1%
18	Georgia	49	1.4%
44	Hawaii	0	0.0%
9	Idaho	131	3.7%
13	Illinois	98	2.8%
23	Indiana	24	0.7%
21	Iowa	30	0.9%
20	Kansas	39	1.1%
38	Kentucky	4	0.1%
19	Louisiana	40	1.1%
44	Maine	0	0.0%
31	Maryland	10	0.3%
34	Massachusetts	6	0.2%
28	Michigan	13	0.4%
11	Minnesota	101	2.9%
10	Mississippi	129	3.7%
15	Missouri	75	2.1%
6	Montana	201	5.7%
8	Nebraska	144	4.1%
29	Nevada	11	0.3%
44	New Hampshire	0	0.0%
41	New Jersey	1	0.0%
17	New Mexico	60	1.7%
26	New York	21	0.6%
34	North Carolina	6	0.2%
3	North Dakota	369	10.5%
25	Ohio	23	0.7%
11	Oklahoma	101	2.9%
22	Oregon	26	0.7%
33	Pennsylvania	9	0.3%
41	Rhode Island	1	0.0%
36	South Carolina	5	0.1%
5	South Dakota	207	5.9%
31	Tennessee	10	0.3%
4	Texas	219	6.2%
16	Utah	68	1.9%
44	Vermont	0	0.0%
39	Virginia	3	0.1%
44	Washington	0	0.0%
44	West Virginia	0	0.0%
29	Wisconsin	11	0.3%
7	Wyoming	180	5.1%

RANK ORDER

RANK	STATE	CASES	% of USA
1	Colorado	555	15.8%
2	California	379	10.8%
3	North Dakota	369	10.5%
4	Texas	219	6.2%
5	South Dakota	207	5.9%
6	Montana	201	5.7%
7	Wyoming	180	5.1%
8	Nebraska	144	4.1%
9	Idaho	131	3.7%
10	Mississippi	129	3.7%
11	Minnesota	101	2.9%
11	Oklahoma	101	2.9%
13	Illinois	98	2.8%
14	Arizona	94	2.7%
15	Missouri	75	2.1%
16	Utah	68	1.9%
17	New Mexico	60	1.7%
18	Georgia	49	1.4%
19	Louisiana	40	1.1%
20	Kansas	39	1.1%
21	Iowa	30	0.9%
22	Oregon	26	0.7%
23	Alabama	24	0.7%
23	Indiana	24	0.7%
25	Ohio	23	0.7%
26	New York	21	0.6%
27	Arkansas	20	0.6%
28	Michigan	13	0.4%
29	Nevada	11	0.3%
29	Wisconsin	11	0.3%
31	Maryland	10	0.3%
31	Tennessee	10	0.3%
33	Pennsylvania	9	0.3%
34	Massachusetts	6	0.2%
34	North Carolina	6	0.2%
36	Connecticut	5	0.1%
36	South Carolina	5	0.1%
38	Kentucky	4	0.1%
39	Florida	3	0.1%
39	Virginia	3	0.1%
41	Delaware	1	0.0%
41	New Jersey	1	0.0%
41	Rhode Island	1	0.0%
44	Alaska	0	0.0%
44	Hawaii	0	0.0%
44	Maine	0	0.0%
44	New Hampshire	0	0.0%
44	Vermont	0	0.0%
44	Washington	0	0.0%
44	West Virginia	0	0.0%
	District of Columbia	0	0.0%

Source: U.S. Department of Health and Human Services, National Center for Health Statistics
"Morbidity and Mortality Weekly Report" (January 4, 2008, Vol. 56, Nos. 51 & 52)
*Provisional data. A flavivirus typically carried by mosquitoes.

West Nile Disease Rate in 2007

National Rate = 1.2 Cases per 100,000 Population

ALPHA ORDER

RANK	STATE	RATE
23	Alabama	0.5
41	Alaska	0.0
13	Arizona	1.5
21	Arkansas	0.7
16	California	1.0
5	Colorado	11.4
31	Connecticut	0.1
31	Delaware	0.1
41	Florida	0.0
23	Georgia	0.5
41	Hawaii	0.0
6	Idaho	8.7
20	Illinois	0.8
25	Indiana	0.4
16	Iowa	1.0
14	Kansas	1.4
31	Kentucky	0.1
18	Louisiana	0.9
41	Maine	0.0
27	Maryland	0.2
31	Massachusetts	0.1
31	Michigan	0.1
12	Minnesota	1.9
8	Mississippi	4.4
15	Missouri	1.3
4	Montana	21.0
7	Nebraska	8.1
25	Nevada	0.4
41	New Hampshire	0.0
41	New Jersey	0.0
9	New Mexico	3.0
31	New York	0.1
31	North Carolina	0.1
1	North Dakota	57.7
27	Ohio	0.2
10	Oklahoma	2.8
21	Oregon	0.7
31	Pennsylvania	0.1
31	Rhode Island	0.1
31	South Carolina	0.1
3	South Dakota	26.0
27	Tennessee	0.2
18	Texas	0.9
11	Utah	2.6
41	Vermont	0.0
41	Virginia	0.0
41	Washington	0.0
41	West Virginia	0.0
27	Wisconsin	0.2
2	Wyoming	34.4

RANK ORDER

RANK	STATE	RATE
1	North Dakota	57.7
2	Wyoming	34.4
3	South Dakota	26.0
4	Montana	21.0
5	Colorado	11.4
6	Idaho	8.7
7	Nebraska	8.1
8	Mississippi	4.4
9	New Mexico	3.0
10	Oklahoma	2.8
11	Utah	2.6
12	Minnesota	1.9
13	Arizona	1.5
14	Kansas	1.4
15	Missouri	1.3
16	California	1.0
16	Iowa	1.0
18	Louisiana	0.9
18	Texas	0.9
20	Illinois	0.8
21	Arkansas	0.7
21	Oregon	0.7
23	Alabama	0.5
23	Georgia	0.5
25	Indiana	0.4
25	Nevada	0.4
27	Maryland	0.2
27	Ohio	0.2
27	Tennessee	0.2
27	Wisconsin	0.2
31	Connecticut	0.1
31	Delaware	0.1
31	Kentucky	0.1
31	Massachusetts	0.1
31	Michigan	0.1
31	New York	0.1
31	North Carolina	0.1
31	Pennsylvania	0.1
31	Rhode Island	0.1
31	South Carolina	0.1
41	Alaska	0.0
41	Florida	0.0
41	Hawaii	0.0
41	Maine	0.0
41	New Hampshire	0.0
41	New Jersey	0.0
41	Vermont	0.0
41	Virginia	0.0
41	Washington	0.0
41	West Virginia	0.0
	District of Columbia	0.0

Source: CQ Press using data from U.S. Department of Health and Human Services, National Center for Health Statistics
    "Morbidity and Mortality Weekly Report" (January 4, 2008, Vol. 56, Nos. 51 & 52)
*Provisional data. A flavivirus typically carried by mosquitoes.

Whooping Cough (Pertussis) Cases Reported in 2007

National Total = 8,739 Cases*

ALPHA ORDER

RANK	STATE	CASES	% of USA
26	Alabama	82	0.9%
37	Alaska	52	0.6%
15	Arizona	201	2.3%
20	Arkansas	137	1.6%
11	California	272	3.1%
9	Colorado	306	3.5%
34	Connecticut	59	0.7%
48	Delaware	11	0.1%
14	Florida	213	2.4%
41	Georgia	32	0.4%
50	Hawaii	4	0.0%
40	Idaho	42	0.5%
17	Illinois	166	1.9%
36	Indiana	55	0.6%
18	Iowa	139	1.6%
21	Kansas	133	1.5%
44	Kentucky	27	0.3%
46	Louisiana	19	0.2%
28	Maine	77	0.9%
23	Maryland	113	1.3%
1	Massachusetts	956	10.9%
10	Michigan	279	3.2%
12	Minnesota	262	3.0%
13	Mississippi	221	2.5%
25	Missouri	103	1.2%
39	Montana	46	0.5%
31	Nebraska	69	0.8%
47	Nevada	14	0.2%
32	New Hampshire	61	0.7%
18	New Jersey	139	1.6%
30	New Mexico	71	0.8%
3	New York	663	7.6%
7	North Carolina	326	3.7%
49	North Dakota	10	0.1%
4	Ohio	610	7.0%
38	Oklahoma	50	0.6%
24	Oregon	112	1.3%
6	Pennsylvania	388	4.4%
41	Rhode Island	32	0.4%
29	South Carolina	72	0.8%
35	South Dakota	57	0.7%
27	Tennessee	80	0.9%
2	Texas	825	9.4%
5	Utah	402	4.6%
32	Vermont	61	0.7%
22	Virginia	123	1.4%
8	Washington	313	3.6%
43	West Virginia	30	0.3%
16	Wisconsin	199	2.3%
45	Wyoming	23	0.3%

RANK ORDER

RANK	STATE	CASES	% of USA
1	Massachusetts	956	10.9%
2	Texas	825	9.4%
3	New York	663	7.6%
4	Ohio	610	7.0%
5	Utah	402	4.6%
6	Pennsylvania	388	4.4%
7	North Carolina	326	3.7%
8	Washington	313	3.6%
9	Colorado	306	3.5%
10	Michigan	279	3.2%
11	California	272	3.1%
12	Minnesota	262	3.0%
13	Mississippi	221	2.5%
14	Florida	213	2.4%
15	Arizona	201	2.3%
16	Wisconsin	199	2.3%
17	Illinois	166	1.9%
18	Iowa	139	1.6%
18	New Jersey	139	1.6%
20	Arkansas	137	1.6%
21	Kansas	133	1.5%
22	Virginia	123	1.4%
23	Maryland	113	1.3%
24	Oregon	112	1.3%
25	Missouri	103	1.2%
26	Alabama	82	0.9%
27	Tennessee	80	0.9%
28	Maine	77	0.9%
29	South Carolina	72	0.8%
30	New Mexico	71	0.8%
31	Nebraska	69	0.8%
32	New Hampshire	61	0.7%
32	Vermont	61	0.7%
34	Connecticut	59	0.7%
35	South Dakota	57	0.7%
36	Indiana	55	0.6%
37	Alaska	52	0.6%
38	Oklahoma	50	0.6%
39	Montana	46	0.5%
40	Idaho	42	0.5%
41	Georgia	32	0.4%
41	Rhode Island	32	0.4%
43	West Virginia	30	0.3%
44	Kentucky	27	0.3%
45	Wyoming	23	0.3%
46	Louisiana	19	0.2%
47	Nevada	14	0.2%
48	Delaware	11	0.1%
49	North Dakota	10	0.1%
50	Hawaii	4	0.0%
	District of Columbia	2	0.0%

Source: U.S. Department of Health and Human Services, National Center for Health Statistics
"Morbidity and Mortality Weekly Report" (January 4, 2008, Vol. 56, Nos. 51 & 52)
*Provisional data. Acute, highly contagious infection of respiratory tract.

Whooping Cough (Pertussis) Rate in 2007

National Rate = 2.9 Cases per 100,000 Population*

ALPHA ORDER

RANK	STATE	RATE
31	Alabama	1.8
4	Alaska	7.6
24	Arizona	3.2
11	Arkansas	4.8
45	California	0.7
7	Colorado	6.3
33	Connecticut	1.7
40	Delaware	1.3
43	Florida	1.2
49	Georgia	0.3
49	Hawaii	0.3
28	Idaho	2.8
40	Illinois	1.3
44	Indiana	0.9
15	Iowa	4.7
11	Kansas	4.8
46	Kentucky	0.6
48	Louisiana	0.4
8	Maine	5.8
30	Maryland	2.0
2	Massachusetts	14.8
28	Michigan	2.8
10	Minnesota	5.0
4	Mississippi	7.6
31	Missouri	1.8
11	Montana	4.8
18	Nebraska	3.9
47	Nevada	0.5
16	New Hampshire	4.6
35	New Jersey	1.6
19	New Mexico	3.6
23	New York	3.4
19	North Carolina	3.6
35	North Dakota	1.6
9	Ohio	5.3
39	Oklahoma	1.4
26	Oregon	3.0
25	Pennsylvania	3.1
26	Rhode Island	3.0
35	South Carolina	1.6
6	South Dakota	7.2
40	Tennessee	1.3
22	Texas	3.5
1	Utah	15.2
3	Vermont	9.8
35	Virginia	1.6
11	Washington	4.8
33	West Virginia	1.7
19	Wisconsin	3.6
17	Wyoming	4.4

RANK ORDER

RANK	STATE	RATE
1	Utah	15.2
2	Massachusetts	14.8
3	Vermont	9.8
4	Alaska	7.6
4	Mississippi	7.6
6	South Dakota	7.2
7	Colorado	6.3
8	Maine	5.8
9	Ohio	5.3
10	Minnesota	5.0
11	Arkansas	4.8
11	Kansas	4.8
11	Montana	4.8
11	Washington	4.8
15	Iowa	4.7
16	New Hampshire	4.6
17	Wyoming	4.4
18	Nebraska	3.9
19	New Mexico	3.6
19	North Carolina	3.6
19	Wisconsin	3.6
22	Texas	3.5
23	New York	3.4
24	Arizona	3.2
25	Pennsylvania	3.1
26	Oregon	3.0
26	Rhode Island	3.0
28	Idaho	2.8
28	Michigan	2.8
30	Maryland	2.0
31	Alabama	1.8
31	Missouri	1.8
33	Connecticut	1.7
33	West Virginia	1.7
35	New Jersey	1.6
35	North Dakota	1.6
35	South Carolina	1.6
35	Virginia	1.6
39	Oklahoma	1.4
40	Delaware	1.3
40	Illinois	1.3
40	Tennessee	1.3
43	Florida	1.2
44	Indiana	0.9
45	California	0.7
46	Kentucky	0.6
47	Nevada	0.5
48	Louisiana	0.4
49	Georgia	0.3
49	Hawaii	0.3
	District of Columbia	0.3

Source: CQ Press using data from U.S. Department of Health and Human Services, National Center for Health Statistics
"Morbidity and Mortality Weekly Report" (January 4, 2008, Vol. 56, Nos. 51 & 52)
*Provisional data. Acute, highly contagious infection of respiratory tract.

Percent of Children Aged 19 to 35 Months Fully Immunized in 2006

National Percent = 77.0%*

ALPHA ORDER				RANK ORDER		
RANK	STATE	PERCENT		RANK	STATE	PERCENT
13	Alabama	79.1		1	Massachusetts	83.6
47	Alaska	67.3		2	Connecticut	82.0
42	Arizona	70.6		3	North Carolina	81.5
39	Arkansas	72.9		4	Georgia	81.4
18	California	78.6		5	Pennsylvania	80.8
28	Colorado	75.9		6	Missouri	80.7
2	Connecticut	82.0		7	Rhode Island	80.6
9	Delaware	80.3		8	Wisconsin	80.5
10	Florida	80.2		9	Delaware	80.3
4	Georgia	81.4		10	Florida	80.2
16	Hawaii	78.8		11	North Dakota	80.1
45	Idaho	68.8		12	South Carolina	79.6
36	Illinois	74.1		13	Alabama	79.1
28	Indiana	75.9		14	Iowa	79.0
14	Iowa	79.0		14	Kentucky	79.0
43	Kansas	70.1		16	Hawaii	78.8
14	Kentucky	79.0		17	New York	78.7
44	Louisiana	69.6		18	California	78.6
30	Maine	75.7		19	Maryland	78.3
19	Maryland	78.3		20	Utah	78.0
1	Massachusetts	83.6		21	Michigan	77.9
21	Michigan	77.9		22	Minnesota	77.6
22	Minnesota	77.6		22	Oklahoma	77.6
37	Mississippi	73.3		24	Virginia	77.4
6	Missouri	80.7		25	Tennessee	76.8
48	Montana	65.6		26	New Hampshire	76.3
33	Nebraska	74.9		27	New Jersey	76.1
50	Nevada	59.5		28	Colorado	75.9
26	New Hampshire	76.3		28	Indiana	75.9
27	New Jersey	76.1		30	Maine	75.7
40	New Mexico	71.6		31	Vermont	75.2
17	New York	78.7		32	Ohio	75.0
3	North Carolina	81.5		33	Nebraska	74.9
11	North Dakota	80.1		34	Texas	74.7
32	Ohio	75.0		35	South Dakota	74.4
22	Oklahoma	77.6		36	Illinois	74.1
38	Oregon	73.2		37	Mississippi	73.3
5	Pennsylvania	80.8		38	Oregon	73.2
7	Rhode Island	80.6		39	Arkansas	72.9
12	South Carolina	79.6		40	New Mexico	71.6
35	South Dakota	74.4		41	Washington	71.4
25	Tennessee	76.8		42	Arizona	70.6
34	Texas	74.7		43	Kansas	70.1
20	Utah	78.0		44	Louisiana	69.6
31	Vermont	75.2		45	Idaho	68.8
24	Virginia	77.4		46	West Virginia	68.4
41	Washington	71.4		47	Alaska	67.3
46	West Virginia	68.4		48	Montana	65.6
8	Wisconsin	80.5		49	Wyoming	63.5
49	Wyoming	63.5		50	Nevada	59.5

District of Columbia   78.4

Source: U.S. Department of Health and Human Services, Centers for Disease Control and Prevention
    "State Vaccination Coverage Levels" (Morbidity and Mortality Weekly Report, Vol. 56, No. 34, August 31, 2007)
*Fully immunized (4:3:1:3:3:1 series) children received four doses of DTP/DT/DTaP (Diphtheria, Tetanus, Pertussis (Whooping Cough), Acellular Pertussis), three doses of OPV (Oral Poliovirus Vaccine), one dose of MCV (Measles-Containing Vaccine), three doses of Hib (Haemophilus influenzae type b), three doses of Hepatitis B vaccine and one dose of Varicella (chickenpox) vaccine. This differs from previous "fully" immunized tables.

Percent of Adults Aged 65 Years and Older Who Received Flu Shots in 2006

National Median = 69.6%*

ALPHA ORDER

RANK	STATE	PERCENT		RANK	STATE	PERCENT
48	Alabama	62.0		1	Colorado	75.9
47	Alaska	62.5		2	Hawaii	75.7
39	Arizona	65.4		3	Rhode Island	74.7
28	Arkansas	68.6		4	South Dakota	74.1
32	California	66.9		5	Minnesota	73.8
1	Colorado	75.9		6	Iowa	73.6
20	Connecticut	71.1		7	Nebraska	73.3
25	Delaware	70.3		8	Massachusetts	73.1
49	Florida	61.5		9	Vermont	72.8
43	Georgia	64.8		10	Montana	72.6
2	Hawaii	75.7		11	Kansas	72.5
42	Idaho	65.2		12	Missouri	72.2
33	Illinois	66.4		13	Utah	72.1
41	Indiana	65.3		14	Maine	72.0
6	Iowa	73.6		14	Wisconsin	72.0
11	Kansas	72.5		16	New Hampshire	71.9
38	Kentucky	66.0		17	North Dakota	71.4
45	Louisiana	64.4		18	Michigan	71.3
14	Maine	72.0		18	Oregon	71.3
37	Maryland	66.1		20	Connecticut	71.1
8	Massachusetts	73.1		21	Wyoming	70.8
18	Michigan	71.3		22	Oklahoma	70.6
5	Minnesota	73.8		22	Washington	70.6
39	Mississippi	65.4		24	Tennessee	70.4
12	Missouri	72.2		25	Delaware	70.3
10	Montana	72.6		26	North Carolina	69.6
7	Nebraska	73.3		27	Virginia	69.1
50	Nevada	57.7		28	Arkansas	68.6
16	New Hampshire	71.9		29	Pennsylvania	68.3
36	New Jersey	66.3		30	Ohio	68.2
31	New Mexico	67.6		31	New Mexico	67.6
44	New York	64.7		32	California	66.9
26	North Carolina	69.6		33	Illinois	66.4
17	North Dakota	71.4		33	Texas	66.4
30	Ohio	68.2		33	West Virginia	66.4
22	Oklahoma	70.6		36	New Jersey	66.3
18	Oregon	71.3		37	Maryland	66.1
29	Pennsylvania	68.3		38	Kentucky	66.0
3	Rhode Island	74.7		39	Arizona	65.4
46	South Carolina	62.9		39	Mississippi	65.4
4	South Dakota	74.1		41	Indiana	65.3
24	Tennessee	70.4		42	Idaho	65.2
33	Texas	66.4		43	Georgia	64.8
13	Utah	72.1		44	New York	64.7
9	Vermont	72.8		45	Louisiana	64.4
27	Virginia	69.1		46	South Carolina	62.9
22	Washington	70.6		47	Alaska	62.5
33	West Virginia	66.4		48	Alabama	62.0
14	Wisconsin	72.0		49	Florida	61.5
21	Wyoming	70.8		50	Nevada	57.7

RANK ORDER

	District of Columbia	61.2

Source: U.S. Department of Health and Human Services, Centers for Disease Control and Prevention
"2006 Behavioral Risk Factor Surveillance Summary Prevalence Data" (http://apps.nccd.cdc.gov/brfss/)
*Percent of adults 65 years old and older who reported receiving influenza vaccine during the preceding 12 months.

Percent of Adults Aged 65 Years and Older
Who Have Had a Pneumonia Vaccine: 2006
National Median = 66.9%*

ALPHA ORDER

RANK ORDER

RANK	STATE	PERCENT	RANK	STATE	PERCENT
50	Alabama	59.7	1	Oregon	74.7
49	Alaska	59.9	2	Colorado	72.9
28	Arizona	66.5	3	Rhode Island	72.5
39	Arkansas	64.4	4	Wisconsin	71.9
47	California	60.0	5	Montana	71.5
2	Colorado	72.9	6	Iowa	71.1
22	Connecticut	68.1	6	Minnesota	71.1
34	Delaware	65.6	8	Massachusetts	70.8
43	Florida	62.9	9	Oklahoma	70.2
42	Georgia	63.1	10	Wyoming	69.7
15	Hawaii	68.8	11	Washington	69.6
44	Idaho	62.8	12	Kansas	69.5
47	Illinois	60.0	13	North Dakota	69.4
40	Indiana	63.8	14	Nevada	69.1
6	Iowa	71.1	15	Hawaii	68.8
12	Kansas	69.5	15	Pennsylvania	68.8
37	Kentucky	64.6	17	Mississippi	68.7
30	Louisiana	66.4	18	North Carolina	68.5
23	Maine	67.9	18	Ohio	68.5
32	Maryland	66.0	20	New Hampshire	68.4
8	Massachusetts	70.8	21	Nebraska	68.3
25	Michigan	67.6	22	Connecticut	68.1
6	Minnesota	71.1	23	Maine	67.9
17	Mississippi	68.7	24	Missouri	67.8
24	Missouri	67.8	25	Michigan	67.6
5	Montana	71.5	26	Vermont	66.9
21	Nebraska	68.3	27	Virginia	66.8
14	Nevada	69.1	28	Arizona	66.5
20	New Hampshire	68.4	28	Tennessee	66.5
30	New Jersey	66.4	30	Louisiana	66.4
38	New Mexico	64.5	30	New Jersey	66.4
46	New York	61.0	32	Maryland	66.0
18	North Carolina	68.5	33	Utah	65.9
13	North Dakota	69.4	34	Delaware	65.6
18	Ohio	68.5	35	West Virginia	65.4
9	Oklahoma	70.2	36	South Dakota	65.0
1	Oregon	74.7	37	Kentucky	64.6
15	Pennsylvania	68.8	38	New Mexico	64.5
3	Rhode Island	72.5	39	Arkansas	64.4
45	South Carolina	61.5	40	Indiana	63.8
36	South Dakota	65.0	41	Texas	63.7
28	Tennessee	66.5	42	Georgia	63.1
41	Texas	63.7	43	Florida	62.9
33	Utah	65.9	44	Idaho	62.8
26	Vermont	66.9	45	South Carolina	61.5
27	Virginia	66.8	46	New York	61.0
11	Washington	69.6	47	California	60.0
35	West Virginia	65.4	47	Illinois	60.0
4	Wisconsin	71.9	49	Alaska	59.9
10	Wyoming	69.7	50	Alabama	59.7
				District of Columbia	52.0

Source: U.S. Department of Health and Human Services, Centers for Disease Control and Prevention
    "2006 Behavioral Risk Factor Surveillance Summary Prevalence Data" (http://apps.nccd.cdc.gov/brfss/)
*Percent of adults 65 years old and older who reported ever receiving a pneumonia vaccine.

Sexually Transmitted Diseases in 2006

National Total = 1,399,066 Cases*

<table>
<tr><td colspan="4">ALPHA ORDER</td><td colspan="4">RANK ORDER</td></tr>
<tr><th>RANK</th><th>STATE</th><th>CASES</th><th>% of USA</th><th>RANK</th><th>STATE</th><th>CASES</th><th>% of USA</th></tr>
<tr><td>12</td><td>Alabama</td><td>33,899</td><td>2.4%</td><td>1</td><td>California</td><td>171,402</td><td>12.3%</td></tr>
<tr><td>39</td><td>Alaska</td><td>5,166</td><td>0.4%</td><td>2</td><td>Texas</td><td>107,061</td><td>7.7%</td></tr>
<tr><td>16</td><td>Arizona</td><td>30,242</td><td>2.2%</td><td>3</td><td>New York</td><td>86,920</td><td>6.2%</td></tr>
<tr><td>29</td><td>Arkansas</td><td>12,642</td><td>0.9%</td><td>4</td><td>Illinois</td><td>74,203</td><td>5.3%</td></tr>
<tr><td>1</td><td>California</td><td>171,402</td><td>12.3%</td><td>5</td><td>Florida</td><td>73,651</td><td>5.3%</td></tr>
<tr><td>24</td><td>Colorado</td><td>20,077</td><td>1.4%</td><td>6</td><td>Ohio</td><td>59,480</td><td>4.3%</td></tr>
<tr><td>28</td><td>Connecticut</td><td>13,620</td><td>1.0%</td><td>7</td><td>Georgia</td><td>59,222</td><td>4.2%</td></tr>
<tr><td>40</td><td>Delaware</td><td>5,120</td><td>0.4%</td><td>8</td><td>Michigan</td><td>52,549</td><td>3.8%</td></tr>
<tr><td>5</td><td>Florida</td><td>73,651</td><td>5.3%</td><td>9</td><td>North Carolina</td><td>51,241</td><td>3.7%</td></tr>
<tr><td>7</td><td>Georgia</td><td>59,222</td><td>4.2%</td><td>10</td><td>Pennsylvania</td><td>51,217</td><td>3.7%</td></tr>
<tr><td>37</td><td>Hawaii</td><td>6,451</td><td>0.5%</td><td>11</td><td>Tennessee</td><td>35,263</td><td>2.5%</td></tr>
<tr><td>43</td><td>Idaho</td><td>3,554</td><td>0.3%</td><td>12</td><td>Alabama</td><td>33,899</td><td>2.4%</td></tr>
<tr><td>4</td><td>Illinois</td><td>74,203</td><td>5.3%</td><td>13</td><td>Missouri</td><td>33,354</td><td>2.4%</td></tr>
<tr><td>19</td><td>Indiana</td><td>28,684</td><td>2.1%</td><td>14</td><td>South Carolina</td><td>32,751</td><td>2.3%</td></tr>
<tr><td>34</td><td>Iowa</td><td>10,375</td><td>0.7%</td><td>15</td><td>Virginia</td><td>30,754</td><td>2.2%</td></tr>
<tr><td>35</td><td>Kansas</td><td>10,066</td><td>0.7%</td><td>16</td><td>Arizona</td><td>30,242</td><td>2.2%</td></tr>
<tr><td>30</td><td>Kentucky</td><td>12,290</td><td>0.9%</td><td>17</td><td>Maryland</td><td>29,487</td><td>2.1%</td></tr>
<tr><td>18</td><td>Louisiana</td><td>29,111</td><td>2.1%</td><td>18</td><td>Louisiana</td><td>29,111</td><td>2.1%</td></tr>
<tr><td>46</td><td>Maine</td><td>2,452</td><td>0.2%</td><td>19</td><td>Indiana</td><td>28,684</td><td>2.1%</td></tr>
<tr><td>17</td><td>Maryland</td><td>29,487</td><td>2.1%</td><td>20</td><td>Wisconsin</td><td>27,185</td><td>1.9%</td></tr>
<tr><td>26</td><td>Massachusetts</td><td>17,947</td><td>1.3%</td><td>21</td><td>Mississippi</td><td>26,599</td><td>1.9%</td></tr>
<tr><td>8</td><td>Michigan</td><td>52,549</td><td>3.8%</td><td>22</td><td>New Jersey</td><td>25,859</td><td>1.8%</td></tr>
<tr><td>27</td><td>Minnesota</td><td>16,285</td><td>1.2%</td><td>23</td><td>Washington</td><td>22,232</td><td>1.6%</td></tr>
<tr><td>21</td><td>Mississippi</td><td>26,599</td><td>1.9%</td><td>24</td><td>Colorado</td><td>20,077</td><td>1.4%</td></tr>
<tr><td>13</td><td>Missouri</td><td>33,354</td><td>2.4%</td><td>25</td><td>Oklahoma</td><td>18,013</td><td>1.3%</td></tr>
<tr><td>45</td><td>Montana</td><td>2,845</td><td>0.2%</td><td>26</td><td>Massachusetts</td><td>17,947</td><td>1.3%</td></tr>
<tr><td>36</td><td>Nebraska</td><td>6,868</td><td>0.5%</td><td>27</td><td>Minnesota</td><td>16,285</td><td>1.2%</td></tr>
<tr><td>32</td><td>Nevada</td><td>11,326</td><td>0.8%</td><td>28</td><td>Connecticut</td><td>13,620</td><td>1.0%</td></tr>
<tr><td>47</td><td>New Hampshire</td><td>2,190</td><td>0.2%</td><td>29</td><td>Arkansas</td><td>12,642</td><td>0.9%</td></tr>
<tr><td>22</td><td>New Jersey</td><td>25,859</td><td>1.8%</td><td>30</td><td>Kentucky</td><td>12,290</td><td>0.9%</td></tr>
<tr><td>31</td><td>New Mexico</td><td>11,641</td><td>0.8%</td><td>31</td><td>New Mexico</td><td>11,641</td><td>0.8%</td></tr>
<tr><td>3</td><td>New York</td><td>86,920</td><td>6.2%</td><td>32</td><td>Nevada</td><td>11,326</td><td>0.8%</td></tr>
<tr><td>9</td><td>North Carolina</td><td>51,241</td><td>3.7%</td><td>33</td><td>Oregon</td><td>11,067</td><td>0.8%</td></tr>
<tr><td>48</td><td>North Dakota</td><td>1,974</td><td>0.1%</td><td>34</td><td>Iowa</td><td>10,375</td><td>0.7%</td></tr>
<tr><td>6</td><td>Ohio</td><td>59,480</td><td>4.3%</td><td>35</td><td>Kansas</td><td>10,066</td><td>0.7%</td></tr>
<tr><td>25</td><td>Oklahoma</td><td>18,013</td><td>1.3%</td><td>36</td><td>Nebraska</td><td>6,868</td><td>0.5%</td></tr>
<tr><td>33</td><td>Oregon</td><td>11,067</td><td>0.8%</td><td>37</td><td>Hawaii</td><td>6,451</td><td>0.5%</td></tr>
<tr><td>10</td><td>Pennsylvania</td><td>51,217</td><td>3.7%</td><td>38</td><td>Utah</td><td>6,001</td><td>0.4%</td></tr>
<tr><td>42</td><td>Rhode Island</td><td>3,664</td><td>0.3%</td><td>39</td><td>Alaska</td><td>5,166</td><td>0.4%</td></tr>
<tr><td>14</td><td>South Carolina</td><td>32,751</td><td>2.3%</td><td>40</td><td>Delaware</td><td>5,120</td><td>0.4%</td></tr>
<tr><td>44</td><td>South Dakota</td><td>3,013</td><td>0.2%</td><td>41</td><td>West Virginia</td><td>3,874</td><td>0.3%</td></tr>
<tr><td>11</td><td>Tennessee</td><td>35,263</td><td>2.5%</td><td>42</td><td>Rhode Island</td><td>3,664</td><td>0.3%</td></tr>
<tr><td>2</td><td>Texas</td><td>107,061</td><td>7.7%</td><td>43</td><td>Idaho</td><td>3,554</td><td>0.3%</td></tr>
<tr><td>38</td><td>Utah</td><td>6,001</td><td>0.4%</td><td>44</td><td>South Dakota</td><td>3,013</td><td>0.2%</td></tr>
<tr><td>50</td><td>Vermont</td><td>1,266</td><td>0.1%</td><td>45</td><td>Montana</td><td>2,845</td><td>0.2%</td></tr>
<tr><td>15</td><td>Virginia</td><td>30,754</td><td>2.2%</td><td>46</td><td>Maine</td><td>2,452</td><td>0.2%</td></tr>
<tr><td>23</td><td>Washington</td><td>22,232</td><td>1.6%</td><td>47</td><td>New Hampshire</td><td>2,190</td><td>0.2%</td></tr>
<tr><td>41</td><td>West Virginia</td><td>3,874</td><td>0.3%</td><td>48</td><td>North Dakota</td><td>1,974</td><td>0.1%</td></tr>
<tr><td>20</td><td>Wisconsin</td><td>27,185</td><td>1.9%</td><td>49</td><td>Wyoming</td><td>1,542</td><td>0.1%</td></tr>
<tr><td>49</td><td>Wyoming</td><td>1,542</td><td>0.1%</td><td>50</td><td>Vermont</td><td>1,266</td><td>0.1%</td></tr>
<tr><td></td><td></td><td></td><td></td><td></td><td>District of Columbia</td><td>5,371</td><td>0.4%</td></tr>
</table>

Source: CQ Press using data from U.S. Dept. of Health and Human Services, Nat'l Center for Health Statistics
"Sexually Transmitted Disease Surveillance 2006" (http://www.cdc.gov/std/stats/TOC2006.htm)
*Includes chancroid, chlamydia, gonorrhea, and primary and secondary syphilis.

Sexually Transmitted Disease Rate in 2006

National Rate = 472.0 Cases per 100,000 Population*

ALPHA ORDER

RANK ORDER

RANK	STATE	RATE	RANK	STATE	RATE
4	Alabama	743.8	1	Mississippi	910.5
2	Alaska	778.4	2	Alaska	778.4
16	Arizona	509.2	3	South Carolina	769.7
24	Arkansas	454.9	4	Alabama	743.8
20	California	474.4	5	Georgia	652.8
26	Colorado	430.4	6	Louisiana	643.6
32	Connecticut	388.0	7	Delaware	607.0
7	Delaware	607.0	8	New Mexico	603.7
27	Florida	414.0	9	Tennessee	591.4
5	Georgia	652.8	10	North Carolina	590.2
18	Hawaii	505.9	11	Illinois	581.4
45	Idaho	248.7	12	Missouri	575.0
11	Illinois	581.4	13	Maryland	526.5
23	Indiana	457.3	14	Michigan	519.2
35	Iowa	349.7	15	Ohio	518.8
33	Kansas	366.7	16	Arizona	509.2
43	Kentucky	294.4	17	Oklahoma	507.7
6	Louisiana	643.6	18	Hawaii	505.9
49	Maine	185.6	19	Wisconsin	491.0
13	Maryland	526.5	20	California	474.4
44	Massachusetts	280.5	21	Nevada	469.1
14	Michigan	519.2	22	Texas	468.4
37	Minnesota	317.3	23	Indiana	457.3
1	Mississippi	910.5	24	Arkansas	454.9
12	Missouri	575.0	25	New York	451.4
39	Montana	304.0	26	Colorado	430.4
30	Nebraska	390.5	27	Florida	414.0
21	Nevada	469.1	28	Pennsylvania	412.0
50	New Hampshire	167.1	29	Virginia	406.4
42	New Jersey	296.6	30	Nebraska	390.5
8	New Mexico	603.7	31	South Dakota	388.3
25	New York	451.4	32	Connecticut	388.0
10	North Carolina	590.2	33	Kansas	366.7
38	North Dakota	310.1	34	Washington	353.6
15	Ohio	518.8	35	Iowa	349.7
17	Oklahoma	507.7	36	Rhode Island	340.5
40	Oregon	303.9	37	Minnesota	317.3
28	Pennsylvania	412.0	38	North Dakota	310.1
36	Rhode Island	340.5	39	Montana	304.0
3	South Carolina	769.7	40	Oregon	303.9
31	South Dakota	388.3	41	Wyoming	302.8
9	Tennessee	591.4	42	New Jersey	296.6
22	Texas	468.4	43	Kentucky	294.4
46	Utah	243.1	44	Massachusetts	280.5
48	Vermont	203.3	45	Idaho	248.7
29	Virginia	406.4	46	Utah	243.1
34	Washington	353.6	47	West Virginia	213.3
47	West Virginia	213.3	48	Vermont	203.3
19	Wisconsin	491.0	49	Maine	185.6
41	Wyoming	302.8	50	New Hampshire	167.1
				District of Columbia	975.7

Source: CQ Press using data from U.S. Dept. of Health and Human Services, Nat'l Center for Health Statistics
"Sexually Transmitted Disease Surveillance 2006" (http://www.cdc.gov/std/stats/TOC2006.htm)
*Includes chancroid, chlamydia, gonorrhea, and primary and secondary syphilis.

Chlamydia Cases Reported in 2006

National Total = 1,030,911 Cases*

ALPHA ORDER

RANK	STATE	CASES	% of USA
15	Alabama	22,915	2.2%
39	Alaska	4,525	0.4%
12	Arizona	24,090	2.3%
34	Arkansas	8,259	0.8%
1	California	135,827	13.2%
24	Colorado	16,313	1.6%
28	Connecticut	10,946	1.1%
40	Delaware	3,615	0.4%
5	Florida	48,955	4.7%
8	Georgia	38,972	3.8%
36	Hawaii	5,548	0.5%
41	Idaho	3,345	0.3%
4	Illinois	53,586	5.2%
20	Indiana	19,859	1.9%
33	Iowa	8,390	0.8%
35	Kansas	7,829	0.8%
31	Kentucky	8,940	0.9%
22	Louisiana	17,885	1.7%
46	Maine	2,306	0.2%
17	Maryland	21,859	2.1%
25	Massachusetts	15,394	1.5%
9	Michigan	36,753	3.6%
27	Minnesota	12,935	1.3%
21	Mississippi	19,002	1.8%
14	Missouri	22,982	2.2%
44	Montana	2,650	0.3%
37	Nebraska	5,428	0.5%
32	Nevada	8,398	0.8%
47	New Hampshire	1,997	0.2%
18	New Jersey	20,194	2.0%
29	New Mexico	9,829	1.0%
3	New York	68,720	6.7%
10	North Carolina	33,615	3.3%
48	North Dakota	1,820	0.2%
6	Ohio	40,106	3.9%
26	Oklahoma	12,992	1.3%
30	Oregon	9,577	0.9%
7	Pennsylvania	39,487	3.8%
42	Rhode Island	3,142	0.3%
16	South Carolina	22,351	2.2%
45	South Dakota	2,633	0.3%
11	Tennessee	25,320	2.5%
2	Texas	75,543	7.3%
38	Utah	5,092	0.5%
50	Vermont	1,191	0.1%
13	Virginia	24,087	2.3%
23	Washington	17,819	1.7%
43	West Virginia	2,910	0.3%
19	Wisconsin	20,190	2.0%
49	Wyoming	1,422	0.1%

RANK ORDER

RANK	STATE	CASES	% of USA
1	California	135,827	13.2%
2	Texas	75,543	7.3%
3	New York	68,720	6.7%
4	Illinois	53,586	5.2%
5	Florida	48,955	4.7%
6	Ohio	40,106	3.9%
7	Pennsylvania	39,487	3.8%
8	Georgia	38,972	3.8%
9	Michigan	36,753	3.6%
10	North Carolina	33,615	3.3%
11	Tennessee	25,320	2.5%
12	Arizona	24,090	2.3%
13	Virginia	24,087	2.3%
14	Missouri	22,982	2.2%
15	Alabama	22,915	2.2%
16	South Carolina	22,351	2.2%
17	Maryland	21,859	2.1%
18	New Jersey	20,194	2.0%
19	Wisconsin	20,190	2.0%
20	Indiana	19,859	1.9%
21	Mississippi	19,002	1.8%
22	Louisiana	17,885	1.7%
23	Washington	17,819	1.7%
24	Colorado	16,313	1.6%
25	Massachusetts	15,394	1.5%
26	Oklahoma	12,992	1.3%
27	Minnesota	12,935	1.3%
28	Connecticut	10,946	1.1%
29	New Mexico	9,829	1.0%
30	Oregon	9,577	0.9%
31	Kentucky	8,940	0.9%
32	Nevada	8,398	0.8%
33	Iowa	8,390	0.8%
34	Arkansas	8,259	0.8%
35	Kansas	7,829	0.8%
36	Hawaii	5,548	0.5%
37	Nebraska	5,428	0.5%
38	Utah	5,092	0.5%
39	Alaska	4,525	0.4%
40	Delaware	3,615	0.4%
41	Idaho	3,345	0.3%
42	Rhode Island	3,142	0.3%
43	West Virginia	2,910	0.3%
44	Montana	2,650	0.3%
45	South Dakota	2,633	0.3%
46	Maine	2,306	0.2%
47	New Hampshire	1,997	0.2%
48	North Dakota	1,820	0.2%
49	Wyoming	1,422	0.1%
50	Vermont	1,191	0.1%
	District of Columbia	3,368	0.3%

Source: U.S. Department of Health and Human Services, National Center for Health Statistics
    "Sexually Transmitted Disease Surveillance 2006" (http://www.cdc.gov/std/stats/TOC2006.htm)
*Any of several common, often asymptomatic, sexually transmitted diseases caused by the microorganism Chlamydia trachomatis, including nonspecific urethritis in men.

Chlamydia Rate in 2006

National Rate = 347.8 Cases per 100,000 Population*

ALPHA ORDER				RANK ORDER		
RANK	STATE	RATE		RANK	STATE	RATE
5	Alabama	502.8		1	Alaska	681.8
1	Alaska	681.8		2	Mississippi	650.5
11	Arizona	405.6		3	South Carolina	525.3
31	Arkansas	297.2		4	New Mexico	509.7
16	California	375.9		5	Alabama	502.8
22	Colorado	349.7		6	Hawaii	435.1
29	Connecticut	311.8		7	Georgia	429.6
8	Delaware	428.6		8	Delaware	428.6
39	Florida	275.2		9	Tennessee	424.6
7	Georgia	429.6		10	Illinois	419.8
6	Hawaii	435.1		11	Arizona	405.6
43	Idaho	234.1		12	Missouri	396.2
10	Illinois	419.8		13	Louisiana	395.4
28	Indiana	316.6		14	Maryland	390.3
37	Iowa	282.8		15	North Carolina	387.1
34	Kansas	285.2		16	California	375.9
45	Kentucky	214.2		17	Oklahoma	366.2
13	Louisiana	395.4		18	Wisconsin	364.7
48	Maine	174.5		19	Michigan	363.1
14	Maryland	390.3		20	New York	356.9
42	Massachusetts	240.6		21	Ohio	349.8
19	Michigan	363.1		22	Colorado	349.7
41	Minnesota	252.0		23	Nevada	347.8
2	Mississippi	650.5		24	South Dakota	339.3
12	Missouri	396.2		25	Texas	330.5
36	Montana	283.2		26	Virginia	318.3
30	Nebraska	308.6		27	Pennsylvania	317.7
23	Nevada	347.8		28	Indiana	316.6
50	New Hampshire	152.4		29	Connecticut	311.8
44	New Jersey	231.6		30	Nebraska	308.6
4	New Mexico	509.7		31	Arkansas	297.2
20	New York	356.9		32	Rhode Island	292.0
15	North Carolina	387.1		33	North Dakota	285.9
33	North Dakota	285.9		34	Kansas	285.2
21	Ohio	349.8		35	Washington	283.4
17	Oklahoma	366.2		36	Montana	283.2
40	Oregon	263.0		37	Iowa	282.8
27	Pennsylvania	317.7		38	Wyoming	279.2
32	Rhode Island	292.0		39	Florida	275.2
3	South Carolina	525.3		40	Oregon	263.0
24	South Dakota	339.3		41	Minnesota	252.0
9	Tennessee	424.6		42	Massachusetts	240.6
25	Texas	330.5		43	Idaho	234.1
46	Utah	206.2		44	New Jersey	231.6
47	Vermont	191.2		45	Kentucky	214.2
26	Virginia	318.3		46	Utah	206.2
35	Washington	283.4		47	Vermont	191.2
49	West Virginia	160.2		48	Maine	174.5
18	Wisconsin	364.7		49	West Virginia	160.2
38	Wyoming	279.2		50	New Hampshire	152.4
					District of Columbia	611.8

Source: U.S. Department of Health and Human Services, National Center for Health Statistics
"Sexually Transmitted Disease Surveillance 2006" (http://www.cdc.gov/std/stats/TOC2006.htm)
*Any of several common, often asymptomatic, sexually transmitted diseases caused by the microorganism Chlamydia trachomatis, including nonspecific urethritis in men.

Gonorrhea Cases Reported in 2006

National Total = 358,366 Cases*

ALPHA ORDER					RANK ORDER			
RANK	STATE	CASES	% of USA		RANK	STATE	CASES	% of USA
12	Alabama	10,665	3.0%		1	California	33,740	9.4%
41	Alaska	630	0.2%		2	Texas	30,449	8.5%
21	Arizona	5,949	1.7%		3	Florida	23,976	6.7%
24	Arkansas	4,306	1.2%		4	Illinois	20,186	5.6%
1	California	33,740	9.4%		5	Georgia	19,669	5.5%
26	Colorado	3,695	1.0%		6	Ohio	19,190	5.4%
30	Connecticut	2,610	0.7%		7	New York	17,459	4.9%
35	Delaware	1,485	0.4%		8	North Carolina	17,312	4.8%
3	Florida	23,976	6.7%		9	Michigan	15,677	4.4%
5	Georgia	19,669	5.5%		10	Pennsylvania	11,466	3.2%
40	Hawaii	885	0.2%		11	Louisiana	10,883	3.0%
44	Idaho	206	0.1%		12	Alabama	10,665	3.0%
4	Illinois	20,186	5.6%		13	South Carolina	10,320	2.9%
16	Indiana	8,732	2.4%		14	Missouri	10,204	2.8%
33	Iowa	1,966	0.5%		15	Tennessee	9,694	2.7%
32	Kansas	2,210	0.6%		16	Indiana	8,732	2.4%
28	Kentucky	3,277	0.9%		17	Mississippi	7,511	2.1%
11	Louisiana	10,883	3.0%		18	Maryland	7,328	2.0%
48	Maine	137	0.0%		19	Wisconsin	6,927	1.9%
18	Maryland	7,328	2.0%		20	Virginia	6,476	1.8%
31	Massachusetts	2,429	0.7%		21	Arizona	5,949	1.7%
9	Michigan	15,677	4.4%		22	New Jersey	5,492	1.5%
27	Minnesota	3,303	0.9%		23	Oklahoma	4,951	1.4%
17	Mississippi	7,511	2.1%		24	Arkansas	4,306	1.2%
14	Missouri	10,204	2.8%		25	Washington	4,231	1.2%
45	Montana	194	0.1%		26	Colorado	3,695	1.0%
37	Nebraska	1,433	0.4%		27	Minnesota	3,303	0.9%
29	Nevada	2,791	0.8%		28	Kentucky	3,277	0.9%
46	New Hampshire	180	0.1%		29	Nevada	2,791	0.8%
22	New Jersey	5,492	1.5%		30	Connecticut	2,610	0.7%
34	New Mexico	1,733	0.5%		31	Massachusetts	2,429	0.7%
7	New York	17,459	4.9%		32	Kansas	2,210	0.6%
8	North Carolina	17,312	4.8%		33	Iowa	1,966	0.5%
47	North Dakota	153	0.0%		34	New Mexico	1,733	0.5%
6	Ohio	19,190	5.4%		35	Delaware	1,485	0.4%
23	Oklahoma	4,951	1.4%		36	Oregon	1,461	0.4%
36	Oregon	1,461	0.4%		37	Nebraska	1,433	0.4%
10	Pennsylvania	11,466	3.2%		38	West Virginia	953	0.3%
42	Rhode Island	508	0.1%		39	Utah	888	0.2%
13	South Carolina	10,320	2.9%		40	Hawaii	885	0.2%
43	South Dakota	367	0.1%		41	Alaska	630	0.2%
15	Tennessee	9,694	2.7%		42	Rhode Island	508	0.1%
2	Texas	30,449	8.5%		43	South Dakota	367	0.1%
39	Utah	888	0.2%		44	Idaho	206	0.1%
50	Vermont	72	0.0%		45	Montana	194	0.1%
20	Virginia	6,476	1.8%		46	New Hampshire	180	0.1%
25	Washington	4,231	1.2%		47	North Dakota	153	0.0%
38	West Virginia	953	0.3%		48	Maine	137	0.0%
19	Wisconsin	6,927	1.9%		49	Wyoming	120	0.0%
49	Wyoming	120	0.0%		50	Vermont	72	0.0%
						District of Columbia	1,887	0.5%

Source: U.S. Department of Health and Human Services, National Center for Health Statistics
    "Sexually Transmitted Disease Surveillance 2006" (http://www.cdc.gov/std/stats/TOC2006.htm)
*Gonorrhea is a sexually transmitted disease caused by gonococcal bacteria that affects the mucous membrane chiefly of the genital and urinary tracts and is characterized by an acute purulent discharge and painful or difficult urination, though women often have no symptoms.

Gonorrhea Rate in 2006

National Rate = 120.9 Cases per 100,000 Population*

<table>
<tr><td colspan="3">ALPHA ORDER</td><td colspan="3">RANK ORDER</td></tr>
<tr><td>RANK</td><td>STATE</td><td>RATE</td><td>RANK</td><td>STATE</td><td>RATE</td></tr>
<tr><td>4</td><td>Alabama</td><td>234.0</td><td>1</td><td>Mississippi</td><td>257.1</td></tr>
<tr><td>22</td><td>Alaska</td><td>94.9</td><td>2</td><td>South Carolina</td><td>242.5</td></tr>
<tr><td>21</td><td>Arizona</td><td>100.2</td><td>3</td><td>Louisiana</td><td>240.6</td></tr>
<tr><td>12</td><td>Arkansas</td><td>154.9</td><td>4</td><td>Alabama</td><td>234.0</td></tr>
<tr><td>23</td><td>California</td><td>93.4</td><td>5</td><td>Georgia</td><td>216.8</td></tr>
<tr><td>30</td><td>Colorado</td><td>79.2</td><td>6</td><td>North Carolina</td><td>199.4</td></tr>
<tr><td>32</td><td>Connecticut</td><td>74.4</td><td>7</td><td>Delaware</td><td>176.0</td></tr>
<tr><td>7</td><td>Delaware</td><td>176.0</td><td>8</td><td>Missouri</td><td>175.9</td></tr>
<tr><td>16</td><td>Florida</td><td>134.8</td><td>9</td><td>Ohio</td><td>167.4</td></tr>
<tr><td>5</td><td>Georgia</td><td>216.8</td><td>10</td><td>Tennessee</td><td>162.6</td></tr>
<tr><td>33</td><td>Hawaii</td><td>69.4</td><td>11</td><td>Illinois</td><td>158.2</td></tr>
<tr><td>47</td><td>Idaho</td><td>14.4</td><td>12</td><td>Arkansas</td><td>154.9</td></tr>
<tr><td>11</td><td>Illinois</td><td>158.2</td><td>12</td><td>Michigan</td><td>154.9</td></tr>
<tr><td>15</td><td>Indiana</td><td>139.2</td><td>14</td><td>Oklahoma</td><td>139.5</td></tr>
<tr><td>35</td><td>Iowa</td><td>66.3</td><td>15</td><td>Indiana</td><td>139.2</td></tr>
<tr><td>29</td><td>Kansas</td><td>80.5</td><td>16</td><td>Florida</td><td>134.8</td></tr>
<tr><td>31</td><td>Kentucky</td><td>78.5</td><td>17</td><td>Texas</td><td>133.2</td></tr>
<tr><td>3</td><td>Louisiana</td><td>240.6</td><td>18</td><td>Maryland</td><td>130.8</td></tr>
<tr><td>50</td><td>Maine</td><td>10.4</td><td>19</td><td>Wisconsin</td><td>125.1</td></tr>
<tr><td>18</td><td>Maryland</td><td>130.8</td><td>20</td><td>Nevada</td><td>115.6</td></tr>
<tr><td>42</td><td>Massachusetts</td><td>38.0</td><td>21</td><td>Arizona</td><td>100.2</td></tr>
<tr><td>12</td><td>Michigan</td><td>154.9</td><td>22</td><td>Alaska</td><td>94.9</td></tr>
<tr><td>36</td><td>Minnesota</td><td>64.4</td><td>23</td><td>California</td><td>93.4</td></tr>
<tr><td>1</td><td>Mississippi</td><td>257.1</td><td>24</td><td>Pennsylvania</td><td>92.2</td></tr>
<tr><td>8</td><td>Missouri</td><td>175.9</td><td>25</td><td>New York</td><td>90.7</td></tr>
<tr><td>46</td><td>Montana</td><td>20.7</td><td>26</td><td>New Mexico</td><td>89.9</td></tr>
<tr><td>28</td><td>Nebraska</td><td>81.5</td><td>27</td><td>Virginia</td><td>85.6</td></tr>
<tr><td>20</td><td>Nevada</td><td>115.6</td><td>28</td><td>Nebraska</td><td>81.5</td></tr>
<tr><td>48</td><td>New Hampshire</td><td>13.7</td><td>29</td><td>Kansas</td><td>80.5</td></tr>
<tr><td>37</td><td>New Jersey</td><td>63.0</td><td>30</td><td>Colorado</td><td>79.2</td></tr>
<tr><td>26</td><td>New Mexico</td><td>89.9</td><td>31</td><td>Kentucky</td><td>78.5</td></tr>
<tr><td>25</td><td>New York</td><td>90.7</td><td>32</td><td>Connecticut</td><td>74.4</td></tr>
<tr><td>6</td><td>North Carolina</td><td>199.4</td><td>33</td><td>Hawaii</td><td>69.4</td></tr>
<tr><td>44</td><td>North Dakota</td><td>24.0</td><td>34</td><td>Washington</td><td>67.3</td></tr>
<tr><td>9</td><td>Ohio</td><td>167.4</td><td>35</td><td>Iowa</td><td>66.3</td></tr>
<tr><td>14</td><td>Oklahoma</td><td>139.5</td><td>36</td><td>Minnesota</td><td>64.4</td></tr>
<tr><td>41</td><td>Oregon</td><td>40.1</td><td>37</td><td>New Jersey</td><td>63.0</td></tr>
<tr><td>24</td><td>Pennsylvania</td><td>92.2</td><td>38</td><td>West Virginia</td><td>52.5</td></tr>
<tr><td>40</td><td>Rhode Island</td><td>47.2</td><td>39</td><td>South Dakota</td><td>47.3</td></tr>
<tr><td>2</td><td>South Carolina</td><td>242.5</td><td>40</td><td>Rhode Island</td><td>47.2</td></tr>
<tr><td>39</td><td>South Dakota</td><td>47.3</td><td>41</td><td>Oregon</td><td>40.1</td></tr>
<tr><td>10</td><td>Tennessee</td><td>162.6</td><td>42</td><td>Massachusetts</td><td>38.0</td></tr>
<tr><td>17</td><td>Texas</td><td>133.2</td><td>43</td><td>Utah</td><td>36.0</td></tr>
<tr><td>43</td><td>Utah</td><td>36.0</td><td>44</td><td>North Dakota</td><td>24.0</td></tr>
<tr><td>49</td><td>Vermont</td><td>11.6</td><td>45</td><td>Wyoming</td><td>23.6</td></tr>
<tr><td>27</td><td>Virginia</td><td>85.6</td><td>46</td><td>Montana</td><td>20.7</td></tr>
<tr><td>34</td><td>Washington</td><td>67.3</td><td>47</td><td>Idaho</td><td>14.4</td></tr>
<tr><td>38</td><td>West Virginia</td><td>52.5</td><td>48</td><td>New Hampshire</td><td>13.7</td></tr>
<tr><td>19</td><td>Wisconsin</td><td>125.1</td><td>49</td><td>Vermont</td><td>11.6</td></tr>
<tr><td>45</td><td>Wyoming</td><td>23.6</td><td>50</td><td>Maine</td><td>10.4</td></tr>
<tr><td></td><td></td><td></td><td></td><td>District of Columbia</td><td>342.8</td></tr>
</table>

Source: U.S. Department of Health and Human Services, National Center for Health Statistics
"Sexually Transmitted Disease Surveillance 2006" (http://www.cdc.gov/std/stats/TOC2006.htm)
*Gonorrhea is a sexually transmitted disease caused by gonococcal bacteria that affects the mucous membrane chiefly of the genital and urinary tracts and is characterized by an acute purulent discharge and painful or difficult urination, though women often have no symptoms.

Syphilis Cases Reported in 2006

National Total = 9,756 Cases*

ALPHA ORDER

RANK	STATE	CASES	% of USA
8	Alabama	319	3.3%
42	Alaska	11	0.1%
13	Arizona	203	2.1%
25	Arkansas	77	0.8%
1	California	1,835	18.8%
28	Colorado	69	0.7%
31	Connecticut	64	0.7%
36	Delaware	20	0.2%
4	Florida	719	7.4%
5	Georgia	581	6.0%
38	Hawaii	18	0.2%
46	Idaho	3	0.0%
6	Illinois	431	4.4%
22	Indiana	93	1.0%
37	Iowa	19	0.2%
34	Kansas	27	0.3%
26	Kentucky	73	0.7%
7	Louisiana	342	3.5%
44	Maine	9	0.1%
10	Maryland	300	3.1%
20	Massachusetts	124	1.3%
21	Michigan	118	1.2%
32	Minnesota	47	0.5%
23	Mississippi	86	0.9%
18	Missouri	168	1.7%
48	Montana	1	0.0%
45	Nebraska	7	0.1%
19	Nevada	137	1.4%
40	New Hampshire	13	0.1%
17	New Jersey	173	1.8%
24	New Mexico	79	0.8%
3	New York	736	7.5%
9	North Carolina	309	3.2%
48	North Dakota	1	0.0%
15	Ohio	184	1.9%
27	Oklahoma	70	0.7%
33	Oregon	29	0.3%
11	Pennsylvania	264	2.7%
39	Rhode Island	14	0.1%
30	South Carolina	66	0.7%
40	South Dakota	13	0.1%
12	Tennessee	249	2.6%
2	Texas	1,064	10.9%
35	Utah	21	0.2%
46	Vermont	3	0.0%
14	Virginia	190	1.9%
16	Washington	182	1.9%
42	West Virginia	11	0.1%
29	Wisconsin	68	0.7%
50	Wyoming	0	0.0%

RANK ORDER

RANK	STATE	CASES	% of USA
1	California	1,835	18.8%
2	Texas	1,064	10.9%
3	New York	736	7.5%
4	Florida	719	7.4%
5	Georgia	581	6.0%
6	Illinois	431	4.4%
7	Louisiana	342	3.5%
8	Alabama	319	3.3%
9	North Carolina	309	3.2%
10	Maryland	300	3.1%
11	Pennsylvania	264	2.7%
12	Tennessee	249	2.6%
13	Arizona	203	2.1%
14	Virginia	190	1.9%
15	Ohio	184	1.9%
16	Washington	182	1.9%
17	New Jersey	173	1.8%
18	Missouri	168	1.7%
19	Nevada	137	1.4%
20	Massachusetts	124	1.3%
21	Michigan	118	1.2%
22	Indiana	93	1.0%
23	Mississippi	86	0.9%
24	New Mexico	79	0.8%
25	Arkansas	77	0.8%
26	Kentucky	73	0.7%
27	Oklahoma	70	0.7%
28	Colorado	69	0.7%
29	Wisconsin	68	0.7%
30	South Carolina	66	0.7%
31	Connecticut	64	0.7%
32	Minnesota	47	0.5%
33	Oregon	29	0.3%
34	Kansas	27	0.3%
35	Utah	21	0.2%
36	Delaware	20	0.2%
37	Iowa	19	0.2%
38	Hawaii	18	0.2%
39	Rhode Island	14	0.1%
40	New Hampshire	13	0.1%
40	South Dakota	13	0.1%
42	Alaska	11	0.1%
42	West Virginia	11	0.1%
44	Maine	9	0.1%
45	Nebraska	7	0.1%
46	Idaho	3	0.0%
46	Vermont	3	0.0%
48	Montana	1	0.0%
48	North Dakota	1	0.0%
50	Wyoming	0	0.0%
	District of Columbia	116	1.2%

Source: U.S. Department of Health and Human Services, National Center for Health Statistics
"Sexually Transmitted Disease Surveillance 2006" (http://www.cdc.gov/std/stats/TOC2006.htm)
*Includes only primary and secondary cases. Does not include 27,159 cases in other stages. A chronic infectious disease caused by a spirochete (Treponema pallidum), either transmitted by direct contact, usually in sexual intercourse, or passed from mother to child in utero, and progressing through three stages characterized respectively by local formation of chancres, ulcerous skin eruptions, and systemic infection leading to general paresis.

Syphilis Rate in 2006

National Rate = 3.3 Cases per 100,000 Population*

ALPHA ORDER

RANK	STATE	RATE
2	Alabama	7.0
26	Alaska	1.7
13	Arizona	3.4
18	Arkansas	2.8
6	California	5.1
31	Colorado	1.5
25	Connecticut	1.8
20	Delaware	2.4
10	Florida	4.0
3	Georgia	6.4
33	Hawaii	1.4
47	Idaho	0.2
13	Illinois	3.4
31	Indiana	1.5
43	Iowa	0.6
37	Kansas	1.0
26	Kentucky	1.7
1	Louisiana	7.6
42	Maine	0.7
5	Maryland	5.4
24	Massachusetts	1.9
35	Michigan	1.2
39	Minnesota	0.9
15	Mississippi	2.9
15	Missouri	2.9
49	Montana	0.1
46	Nebraska	0.4
4	Nevada	5.7
37	New Hampshire	1.0
22	New Jersey	2.0
9	New Mexico	4.1
11	New York	3.8
12	North Carolina	3.6
47	North Dakota	0.2
29	Ohio	1.6
22	Oklahoma	2.0
41	Oregon	0.8
21	Pennsylvania	2.1
34	Rhode Island	1.3
29	South Carolina	1.6
26	South Dakota	1.7
8	Tennessee	4.2
7	Texas	4.7
39	Utah	0.9
45	Vermont	0.5
19	Virginia	2.5
15	Washington	2.9
43	West Virginia	0.6
35	Wisconsin	1.2
50	Wyoming	0.0

RANK ORDER

RANK	STATE	RATE
1	Louisiana	7.6
2	Alabama	7.0
3	Georgia	6.4
4	Nevada	5.7
5	Maryland	5.4
6	California	5.1
7	Texas	4.7
8	Tennessee	4.2
9	New Mexico	4.1
10	Florida	4.0
11	New York	3.8
12	North Carolina	3.6
13	Arizona	3.4
13	Illinois	3.4
15	Mississippi	2.9
15	Missouri	2.9
15	Washington	2.9
18	Arkansas	2.8
19	Virginia	2.5
20	Delaware	2.4
21	Pennsylvania	2.1
22	New Jersey	2.0
22	Oklahoma	2.0
24	Massachusetts	1.9
25	Connecticut	1.8
26	Alaska	1.7
26	Kentucky	1.7
26	South Dakota	1.7
29	Ohio	1.6
29	South Carolina	1.6
31	Colorado	1.5
31	Indiana	1.5
33	Hawaii	1.4
34	Rhode Island	1.3
35	Michigan	1.2
35	Wisconsin	1.2
37	Kansas	1.0
37	New Hampshire	1.0
39	Minnesota	0.9
39	Utah	0.9
41	Oregon	0.8
42	Maine	0.7
43	Iowa	0.6
43	West Virginia	0.6
45	Vermont	0.5
46	Nebraska	0.4
47	Idaho	0.2
47	North Dakota	0.2
49	Montana	0.1
50	Wyoming	0.0
	District of Columbia	21.1

Source: U.S. Department of Health and Human Services, National Center for Health Statistics
   "Sexually Transmitted Disease Surveillance 2006" (http://www.cdc.gov/std/stats/TOC2006.htm)
*Includes only primary and secondary cases. Does not include 27,159 cases in other stages. A chronic infectious disease
caused by a spirochete (Treponema pallidum), either transmitted by direct contact, usually in sexual intercourse, or passed from
mother to child in utero, and progressing through three stages characterized respectively by local formation of chancres, ulcerous
skin eruptions, and systemic infection leading to general paresis.

Percent of Adults Who Have Asthma: 2006

National Median = 8.5% of Adults*

ALPHA ORDER

RANK	STATE	PERCENT
13	Alabama	8.9
9	Alaska	9.5
13	Arizona	8.9
40	Arkansas	7.6
40	California	7.6
35	Colorado	7.9
10	Connecticut	9.3
7	Delaware	9.6
45	Florida	7.2
34	Georgia	8.0
33	Hawaii	8.1
12	Idaho	9.2
29	Illinois	8.3
26	Indiana	8.4
49	Iowa	6.5
29	Kansas	8.3
32	Kentucky	8.2
50	Louisiana	5.9
5	Maine	9.7
13	Maryland	8.9
2	Massachusetts	9.9
7	Michigan	9.6
36	Minnesota	7.8
47	Mississippi	6.9
21	Missouri	8.6
29	Montana	8.3
43	Nebraska	7.5
37	Nevada	7.7
5	New Hampshire	9.7
40	New Jersey	7.6
23	New Mexico	8.5
23	New York	8.5
48	North Carolina	6.8
46	North Dakota	7.1
3	Ohio	9.8
13	Oklahoma	8.9
3	Oregon	9.8
18	Pennsylvania	8.8
1	Rhode Island	10.5
37	South Carolina	7.7
37	South Dakota	7.7
23	Tennessee	8.5
44	Texas	7.3
26	Utah	8.4
10	Vermont	9.3
26	Virginia	8.4
13	Washington	8.9
21	West Virginia	8.6
18	Wisconsin	8.8
20	Wyoming	8.7

RANK ORDER

RANK	STATE	PERCENT
1	Rhode Island	10.5
2	Massachusetts	9.9
3	Ohio	9.8
3	Oregon	9.8
5	Maine	9.7
5	New Hampshire	9.7
7	Delaware	9.6
7	Michigan	9.6
9	Alaska	9.5
10	Connecticut	9.3
10	Vermont	9.3
12	Idaho	9.2
13	Alabama	8.9
13	Arizona	8.9
13	Maryland	8.9
13	Oklahoma	8.9
13	Washington	8.9
18	Pennsylvania	8.8
18	Wisconsin	8.8
20	Wyoming	8.7
21	Missouri	8.6
21	West Virginia	8.6
23	New Mexico	8.5
23	New York	8.5
23	Tennessee	8.5
26	Indiana	8.4
26	Utah	8.4
26	Virginia	8.4
29	Illinois	8.3
29	Kansas	8.3
29	Montana	8.3
32	Kentucky	8.2
33	Hawaii	8.1
34	Georgia	8.0
35	Colorado	7.9
36	Minnesota	7.8
37	Nevada	7.7
37	South Carolina	7.7
37	South Dakota	7.7
40	Arkansas	7.6
40	California	7.6
40	New Jersey	7.6
43	Nebraska	7.5
44	Texas	7.3
45	Florida	7.2
46	North Dakota	7.1
47	Mississippi	6.9
48	North Carolina	6.8
49	Iowa	6.5
50	Louisiana	5.9
	District of Columbia	10.0

Source: U.S. Department of Health and Human Services, Centers for Disease Control and Prevention
   "2006 Behavioral Risk Factor Surveillance Summary Prevalence Data" (http://apps.nccd.cdc.gov/brfss/)
*Percent of adults who answered yes to the questions "Have you ever been told by a doctor, nurse or other health professional that you had asthma?" and "Do you still have asthma?"

Percent of Adults Who Have Been Told They Have Arthritis: 2005

National Median = 27.0%*

ALPHA ORDER				RANK ORDER		
RANK	STATE	PERCENT		RANK	STATE	PERCENT
2	Alabama	32.9		1	West Virginia	34.9
46	Alaska	23.2		2	Alabama	32.9
32	Arizona	26.1		3	Mississippi	32.1
8	Arkansas	30.7		3	Missouri	32.1
48	California	22.3		5	Pennsylvania	31.7
45	Colorado	23.3		6	Michigan	30.8
38	Connecticut	25.5		6	South Carolina	30.8
14	Delaware	29.2		8	Arkansas	30.7
21	Florida	27.4		9	Maine	30.5
37	Georgia	25.8		10	Oklahoma	30.3
50	Hawaii	22.1		11	Ohio	30.1
38	Idaho	25.5		12	Tennessee	29.7
42	Illinois	24.8		13	Indiana	29.3
13	Indiana	29.3		14	Delaware	29.2
21	Iowa	27.4		15	Kentucky	28.8
27	Kansas	26.9		16	Rhode Island	28.2
15	Kentucky	28.8		17	South Dakota	27.9
29	Louisiana	26.7		18	Wisconsin	27.7
9	Maine	30.5		19	Virginia	27.6
20	Maryland	27.5		20	Maryland	27.5
36	Massachusetts	25.9		21	Florida	27.4
6	Michigan	30.8		21	Iowa	27.4
38	Minnesota	25.5		21	Vermont	27.4
3	Mississippi	32.1		21	Wyoming	27.4
3	Missouri	32.1		25	North Carolina	27.3
30	Montana	26.4		26	Oregon	27.0
32	Nebraska	26.1		27	Kansas	26.9
41	Nevada	25.1		27	New Hampshire	26.9
27	New Hampshire	26.9		29	Louisiana	26.7
43	New Jersey	24.4		30	Montana	26.4
43	New Mexico	24.4		31	Washington	26.2
32	New York	26.1		32	Arizona	26.1
25	North Carolina	27.3		32	Nebraska	26.1
35	North Dakota	26.0		32	New York	26.1
11	Ohio	30.1		35	North Dakota	26.0
10	Oklahoma	30.3		36	Massachusetts	25.9
26	Oregon	27.0		37	Georgia	25.8
5	Pennsylvania	31.7		38	Connecticut	25.5
16	Rhode Island	28.2		38	Idaho	25.5
6	South Carolina	30.8		38	Minnesota	25.5
17	South Dakota	27.9		41	Nevada	25.1
12	Tennessee	29.7		42	Illinois	24.8
48	Texas	22.3		43	New Jersey	24.4
47	Utah	22.7		43	New Mexico	24.4
21	Vermont	27.4		45	Colorado	23.3
19	Virginia	27.6		46	Alaska	23.2
31	Washington	26.2		47	Utah	22.7
1	West Virginia	34.9		48	California	22.3
18	Wisconsin	27.7		48	Texas	22.3
21	Wyoming	27.4		50	Hawaii	22.1
					District of Columbia	22.4

Source: U.S. Department of Health and Human Services, Centers for Disease Control and Prevention
   "2005 Behavioral Risk Factor Surveillance Summary Prevalence Data" (http://apps.nccd.cdc.gov/brfss/)
*Of population 18 years old and older.

Percent of Adults Who Have Been Told They Have Diabetes: 2006

National Median = 7.5% of Adults*

ALPHA ORDER

RANK	STATE	PERCENT
4	Alabama	10.0
46	Alaska	5.9
12	Arizona	8.5
17	Arkansas	8.1
15	California	8.2
50	Colorado	5.3
41	Connecticut	6.4
17	Delaware	8.1
12	Florida	8.5
9	Georgia	9.1
15	Hawaii	8.2
36	Idaho	6.8
17	Illinois	8.1
17	Indiana	8.1
31	Iowa	7.3
31	Kansas	7.3
6	Kentucky	9.9
8	Louisiana	9.2
35	Maine	6.9
22	Maryland	7.9
41	Massachusetts	6.4
11	Michigan	9.0
48	Minnesota	5.7
2	Mississippi	10.9
26	Missouri	7.4
41	Montana	6.4
26	Nebraska	7.4
24	Nevada	7.5
26	New Hampshire	7.4
24	New Jersey	7.5
31	New Mexico	7.3
23	New York	7.6
9	North Carolina	9.1
37	North Dakota	6.7
37	Ohio	6.7
4	Oklahoma	10.0
37	Oregon	6.7
12	Pennsylvania	8.5
26	Rhode Island	7.4
7	South Carolina	9.6
40	South Dakota	6.5
3	Tennessee	10.7
21	Texas	8.0
48	Utah	5.7
46	Vermont	5.9
26	Virginia	7.4
34	Washington	7.1
1	West Virginia	12.1
45	Wisconsin	6.2
41	Wyoming	6.4

RANK ORDER

RANK	STATE	PERCENT
1	West Virginia	12.1
2	Mississippi	10.9
3	Tennessee	10.7
4	Alabama	10.0
4	Oklahoma	10.0
6	Kentucky	9.9
7	South Carolina	9.6
8	Louisiana	9.2
9	Georgia	9.1
9	North Carolina	9.1
11	Michigan	9.0
12	Arizona	8.5
12	Florida	8.5
12	Pennsylvania	8.5
15	California	8.2
15	Hawaii	8.2
17	Arkansas	8.1
17	Delaware	8.1
17	Illinois	8.1
17	Indiana	8.1
21	Texas	8.0
22	Maryland	7.9
23	New York	7.6
24	Nevada	7.5
24	New Jersey	7.5
26	Missouri	7.4
26	Nebraska	7.4
26	New Hampshire	7.4
26	Rhode Island	7.4
26	Virginia	7.4
31	Iowa	7.3
31	Kansas	7.3
31	New Mexico	7.3
34	Washington	7.1
35	Maine	6.9
36	Idaho	6.8
37	North Dakota	6.7
37	Ohio	6.7
37	Oregon	6.7
40	South Dakota	6.5
41	Connecticut	6.4
41	Massachusetts	6.4
41	Montana	6.4
41	Wyoming	6.4
45	Wisconsin	6.2
46	Alaska	5.9
46	Vermont	5.9
48	Minnesota	5.7
48	Utah	5.7
50	Colorado	5.3

	District of Columbia	8.1

Source: U.S. Department of Health and Human Services, Centers for Disease Control and Prevention
    "2006 Behavioral Risk Factor Surveillance Summary Prevalence Data" (http://apps.nccd.cdc.gov/brfss/)
*Of population 18 years old and older. Does not include pregnancy-related diabetes.

Percent of Adults Reporting Serious Psychological Distress: 2005

National Percent = 11.6% of Population*

ALPHA ORDER			RANK ORDER		
RANK	STATE	PERCENT	RANK	STATE	PERCENT
47	Alabama	10.6	1	West Virginia	15.3
22	Alaska	11.9	2	Kentucky	14.7
28	Arizona	11.7	3	Utah	14.6
10	Arkansas	12.8	4	Rhode Island	14.2
46	California	10.7	5	Missouri	14.1
35	Colorado	11.4	6	Kansas	13.6
31	Connecticut	11.5	7	Oklahoma	13.3
29	Delaware	11.6	7	Wyoming	13.3
41	Florida	11.1	9	South Carolina	12.9
31	Georgia	11.5	10	Arkansas	12.8
50	Hawaii	9.8	10	New Mexico	12.8
19	Idaho	12.0	10	Ohio	12.8
43	Illinois	11.0	13	Washington	12.6
14	Indiana	12.5	14	Indiana	12.5
24	Iowa	11.8	14	Montana	12.5
6	Kansas	13.6	16	Tennessee	12.4
2	Kentucky	14.7	17	Oregon	12.3
18	Louisiana	12.2	18	Louisiana	12.2
24	Maine	11.8	19	Idaho	12.0
48	Maryland	10.4	19	Mississippi	12.0
44	Massachusetts	10.9	19	Nevada	12.0
41	Michigan	11.1	22	Alaska	11.9
35	Minnesota	11.4	22	North Carolina	11.9
19	Mississippi	12.0	24	Iowa	11.8
5	Missouri	14.1	24	Maine	11.8
14	Montana	12.5	24	North Dakota	11.8
38	Nebraska	11.2	24	Wisconsin	11.8
19	Nevada	12.0	28	Arizona	11.7
29	New Hampshire	11.6	29	Delaware	11.6
49	New Jersey	10.3	29	New Hampshire	11.6
10	New Mexico	12.8	31	Connecticut	11.5
31	New York	11.5	31	Georgia	11.5
22	North Carolina	11.9	31	New York	11.5
24	North Dakota	11.8	31	Vermont	11.5
10	Ohio	12.8	35	Colorado	11.4
7	Oklahoma	13.3	35	Minnesota	11.4
17	Oregon	12.3	35	Texas	11.4
38	Pennsylvania	11.2	38	Nebraska	11.2
4	Rhode Island	14.2	38	Pennsylvania	11.2
9	South Carolina	12.9	38	South Dakota	11.2
38	South Dakota	11.2	41	Florida	11.1
16	Tennessee	12.4	41	Michigan	11.1
35	Texas	11.4	43	Illinois	11.0
3	Utah	14.6	44	Massachusetts	10.9
31	Vermont	11.5	45	Virginia	10.8
45	Virginia	10.8	46	California	10.7
13	Washington	12.6	47	Alabama	10.6
1	West Virginia	15.3	48	Maryland	10.4
24	Wisconsin	11.8	49	New Jersey	10.3
7	Wyoming	13.3	50	Hawaii	9.8

	District of Columbia	12.1

Source: U.S. Department of Health and Human Services, Substance Abuse and Mental Health Services Administration
"2004-2005 National Surveys on Drug Use and Health" (February 2007)

*Population 18 years and older. Serious psychological distress was previously referred to as serious mental illness. It is defined as having a diagnosable mental, behavioral or emotional disorder that resulted in functional impairment that substantially interfered with or limited one or more major life activities.

VI. Providers

Health Care Practitioners and Technicians in 2006 411

Rate of Health Care Practitioners and Technicians
in 2006 412

Average Annual Wages of Health Care Practitioners and
Technicians in 2006 413

Physicians in 2006 414

Rate of Physicians in 2006 415

Percent of Physicians Who Are Female: 2006 416

Percent of Physicians Under 35 Years Old in 2006 417

Percent of Physicians 65 Years Old and Older in 2006 . . . 418

Physicians in Patient Care in 2006 419

Rate of Physicians in Patient Care in 2006 420

Physicians in Primary Care in 2006 421

Rate of Physicians in Primary Care in 2006 422

Percent of Physicians in Primary Care in 2006 423

Percent of Population Lacking Access to Primary Care
in 2007 424

Physicians in General/Family Practice in 2006 425

Rate of Physicians in General/Family Practice in 2006 . . . 426

Average Annual Wages of Family and General
Practitioners in 2006 427

Percent of Physicians Who Are Specialists in 2006 428

Physicians in Medical Specialties in 2006 429

Rate of Nonfederal Physicians in Medical Specialties
in 2006 430

Physicians in Internal Medicine in 2006 431

Rate of Physicians in Internal Medicine in 2006 432

Physicians in Pediatrics in 2006 433

Rate of Physicians in Pediatrics in 2006 434

Physicians in Surgical Specialties in 2006 435

Rate of Physicians in Surgical Specialties in 2006 436

Average Annual Wages of Surgeons in 2006 437

Physicians in General Surgery in 2006 438

Rate of Physicians in General Surgery in 2006 439

Physicians in Obstetrics and Gynecology in 2006 440

Rate of Physicians in Obstetrics and Gynecology
in 2006 441

Physicians in Ophthalmology in 2006 442

Rate of Physicians in Ophthalmology in 2006 443

Physicians in Orthopedic Surgery in 2006 444

Rate of Physicians in Orthopedic Surgery in 2006 445

Physicians in Plastic Surgery in 2006 446

Rate of Physicians in Plastic Surgery in 2006 447

Physicians in Other Specialties in 2006 448

Rate of Physicians in Other Specialties in 2006 449

Physicians in Anesthesiology in 2006 450

Rate of Physicians in Anesthesiology in 2006 451

Physicians in Psychiatry in 2006 452

Rate of Physicians in Psychiatry in 2006 453

Percent of Population Lacking Access to Mental
Health Care in 2007 454

International Medical School Graduates in 2006 455

International Medical School Graduates as a Percent of
Physicians in 2006 456

Osteopathic Physicians in 2007 457

Rate of Osteopathic Physicians in 2007 458

Podiatrists in 2006 459

Rate of Podiatrists in 2006 460

Average Annual Wages of Podiatrists in 2006 461

Doctors of Chiropractic in 2006 462

Rate of Doctors of Chiropractic in 2006 463

Average Annual Wages of Chiropractors in 2006 464

Physician Assistants in Clinical Practice in 2008 465

Rate of Physician Assistants in Clinical Practice
in 2007 466

Average Annual Wages of Physician Assistants
in 2006 467

Registered Nurses in 2006 468

Rate of Registered Nurses in 2006 469

Average Annual Wages of Registered Nurses in 2006 470

Licensed Practical and Licensed Vocational Nurses
in 2006 471

Rate of Licensed Practical and Licensed Vocational
Nurses in 2006 472

Average Annual Wages of Licensed Practical and
Licensed Vocational Nurses in 2006 473

Physical Therapists in 2006 474

Rate of Physical Therapists in 2006 475

Average Annual Wages of Physical Therapists in 2006 . . . 476
Dentists in 2005 477
Rate of Dentists in 2005 478
Average Annual Wages of Dentists in 2006 479
Percent of Population Lacking Access to Dental Care
    in 2007 480
Pharmacists in 2006 481
Rate of Pharmacists in 2006 482
Average Annual Wages of Pharmacists in 2006 483
Optometrists in 2006 484
Rate of Optometrists in 2006 485
Average Annual Wages of Optometrists in 2006 486

Emergency Medical Technicians and Paramedics
    in 2006 487
Rate of Emergency Medical Technicians and
    Paramedics in 2006 488
Average Annual Wages of Emergency Medical
    Technicians and Paramedics in 2006 489
Employment in Health Care Support Industries in 2006 . . 490
Rate of Employees in Health Care Support Industries
    in 2006 491
Average Annual Wages of Employees in Health Care
    Support Industries in 2006 492

Health Care Practitioners and Technicians in 2006

National Total = 6,594,330 Practitioners and Technicians*

ALPHA ORDER

RANK ORDER

RANK	STATE	PRACTITIONERS	% of USA		RANK	STATE	PRACTITIONERS	% of USA
21	Alabama	107,040	1.6%		1	California	603,350	9.1%
49	Alaska	12,870	0.2%		2	Texas	453,850	6.9%
22	Arizona	104,160	1.6%		3	New York	438,770	6.7%
32	Arkansas	64,330	1.0%		4	Florida	404,900	6.1%
1	California	603,350	9.1%		5	Pennsylvania	336,780	5.1%
25	Colorado	96,490	1.5%		6	Ohio	296,300	4.5%
27	Connecticut	88,270	1.3%		7	Illinois	292,740	4.4%
45	Delaware	21,530	0.3%		8	Michigan	230,340	3.5%
4	Florida	404,900	6.1%		9	New Jersey	198,190	3.0%
12	Georgia	181,000	2.7%		10	North Carolina	194,670	3.0%
43	Hawaii	24,200	0.4%		11	Massachusetts	194,320	2.9%
42	Idaho	27,300	0.4%		12	Georgia	181,000	2.7%
7	Illinois	292,740	4.4%		13	Missouri	157,740	2.4%
16	Indiana	152,680	2.3%		14	Virginia	156,450	2.4%
29	Iowa	72,680	1.1%		15	Tennessee	153,410	2.3%
33	Kansas	63,920	1.0%		16	Indiana	152,680	2.3%
24	Kentucky	99,740	1.5%		17	Minnesota	139,260	2.1%
23	Louisiana	103,390	1.6%		18	Wisconsin	133,770	2.0%
39	Maine	34,320	0.5%		19	Maryland	130,420	2.0%
19	Maryland	130,420	2.0%		20	Washington	126,330	1.9%
11	Massachusetts	194,320	2.9%		21	Alabama	107,040	1.6%
8	Michigan	230,340	3.5%		22	Arizona	104,160	1.6%
17	Minnesota	139,260	2.1%		23	Louisiana	103,390	1.6%
31	Mississippi	64,590	1.0%		24	Kentucky	99,740	1.5%
13	Missouri	157,740	2.4%		25	Colorado	96,490	1.5%
46	Montana	21,220	0.3%		26	South Carolina	89,810	1.4%
35	Nebraska	47,830	0.7%		27	Connecticut	88,270	1.3%
37	Nevada	38,570	0.6%		28	Oklahoma	81,410	1.2%
40	New Hampshire	30,950	0.5%		29	Iowa	72,680	1.1%
9	New Jersey	198,190	3.0%		30	Oregon	70,170	1.1%
38	New Mexico	38,310	0.6%		31	Mississippi	64,590	1.0%
3	New York	438,770	6.7%		32	Arkansas	64,330	1.0%
10	North Carolina	194,670	3.0%		33	Kansas	63,920	1.0%
47	North Dakota	18,920	0.3%		34	Utah	48,800	0.7%
6	Ohio	296,300	4.5%		35	Nebraska	47,830	0.7%
28	Oklahoma	81,410	1.2%		36	West Virginia	45,610	0.7%
30	Oregon	70,170	1.1%		37	Nevada	38,570	0.6%
5	Pennsylvania	336,780	5.1%		38	New Mexico	38,310	0.6%
41	Rhode Island	28,380	0.4%		39	Maine	34,320	0.5%
26	South Carolina	89,810	1.4%		40	New Hampshire	30,950	0.5%
44	South Dakota	22,870	0.3%		41	Rhode Island	28,380	0.4%
15	Tennessee	153,410	2.3%		42	Idaho	27,300	0.4%
2	Texas	453,850	6.9%		43	Hawaii	24,200	0.4%
34	Utah	48,800	0.7%		44	South Dakota	22,870	0.3%
48	Vermont	15,930	0.2%		45	Delaware	21,530	0.3%
14	Virginia	156,450	2.4%		46	Montana	21,220	0.3%
20	Washington	126,330	1.9%		47	North Dakota	18,920	0.3%
36	West Virginia	45,610	0.7%		48	Vermont	15,930	0.2%
18	Wisconsin	133,770	2.0%		49	Alaska	12,870	0.2%
50	Wyoming	10,580	0.2%		50	Wyoming	10,580	0.2%
						District of Columbia	24,980	0.4%

Source: U.S. Department of Labor, Bureau of Labor Statistics
    "Occupational Employment and Wages, 2006" (http://www.bls.gov/oes/)
*Does not include self-employed. Includes various doctors, dentists, nurses, therapists, optometrists, paramedics, and technicians. Does not include assistants and aides listed under health care support occupations. Veterinarians and veterinarian technicians have been subtracted from the totals.

Rate of Health Care Practitioners and Technicians in 2006

National Rate = 2,207 Practitioners and Technicians per 100,000 Population*

ALPHA ORDER

RANK	STATE	RATE
22	Alabama	2,332
44	Alaska	1,900
48	Arizona	1,689
26	Arkansas	2,290
49	California	1,664
38	Colorado	2,024
12	Connecticut	2,525
12	Delaware	2,525
31	Florida	2,242
42	Georgia	1,937
45	Hawaii	1,893
47	Idaho	1,865
25	Illinois	2,291
18	Indiana	2,422
16	Iowa	2,445
24	Kansas	2,319
20	Kentucky	2,372
17	Louisiana	2,437
9	Maine	2,610
23	Maryland	2,328
1	Massachusetts	3,020
28	Michigan	2,280
6	Minnesota	2,702
33	Mississippi	2,228
6	Missouri	2,702
32	Montana	2,241
5	Nebraska	2,712
50	Nevada	1,547
21	New Hampshire	2,359
27	New Jersey	2,287
40	New Mexico	1,972
29	New York	2,276
34	North Carolina	2,195
2	North Dakota	2,968
10	Ohio	2,585
29	Oklahoma	2,276
43	Oregon	1,901
4	Pennsylvania	2,715
8	Rhode Island	2,673
35	South Carolina	2,074
3	South Dakota	2,901
12	Tennessee	2,525
41	Texas	1,939
46	Utah	1,892
11	Vermont	2,566
37	Virginia	2,048
39	Washington	1,982
15	West Virginia	2,522
19	Wisconsin	2,400
36	Wyoming	2,063

RANK ORDER

RANK	STATE	RATE
1	Massachusetts	3,020
2	North Dakota	2,968
3	South Dakota	2,901
4	Pennsylvania	2,715
5	Nebraska	2,712
6	Minnesota	2,702
6	Missouri	2,702
8	Rhode Island	2,673
9	Maine	2,610
10	Ohio	2,585
11	Vermont	2,566
12	Connecticut	2,525
12	Delaware	2,525
12	Tennessee	2,525
15	West Virginia	2,522
16	Iowa	2,445
17	Louisiana	2,437
18	Indiana	2,422
19	Wisconsin	2,400
20	Kentucky	2,372
21	New Hampshire	2,359
22	Alabama	2,332
23	Maryland	2,328
24	Kansas	2,319
25	Illinois	2,291
26	Arkansas	2,290
27	New Jersey	2,287
28	Michigan	2,280
29	New York	2,276
29	Oklahoma	2,276
31	Florida	2,242
32	Montana	2,241
33	Mississippi	2,228
34	North Carolina	2,195
35	South Carolina	2,074
36	Wyoming	2,063
37	Virginia	2,048
38	Colorado	2,024
39	Washington	1,982
40	New Mexico	1,972
41	Texas	1,939
42	Georgia	1,937
43	Oregon	1,901
44	Alaska	1,900
45	Hawaii	1,893
46	Utah	1,892
47	Idaho	1,865
48	Arizona	1,689
49	California	1,664
50	Nevada	1,547
	District of Columbia	4,267

Source: CQ Press using data from U.S. Department of Labor, Bureau of Labor Statistics
"Occupational Employment and Wages, 2006" (http://www.bls.gov/oes/)
*Does not include self-employed. Includes various doctors, dentists, nurses, therapists, optometrists, paramedics, and technicians. Does not include assistants and aides listed under health care support occupations. Veterinarians and veterinarian technicians have been subtracted from the totals.

Average Annual Wages of Health Care Practitioners and Technicians in 2006

National Average = $62,030*

ALPHA ORDER			RANK ORDER		
RANK	STATE	WAGES	RANK	STATE	WAGES
47	Alabama	$51,540	1	California	$73,240
3	Alaska	72,050	2	New Jersey	72,510
21	Arizona	60,900	3	Alaska	72,050
49	Arkansas	51,030	4	Maryland	71,420
1	California	73,240	5	Oregon	69,050
16	Colorado	63,580	6	New York	68,990
9	Connecticut	67,890	7	Massachusetts	68,470
14	Delaware	64,380	8	Hawaii	68,220
23	Florida	59,780	9	Connecticut	67,890
26	Georgia	59,390	10	Washington	67,540
8	Hawaii	68,220	11	Minnesota	67,370
32	Idaho	57,140	12	Nevada	66,580
31	Illinois	58,010	13	Rhode Island	66,510
36	Indiana	55,450	14	Delaware	64,380
43	Iowa	52,670	15	Michigan	64,220
37	Kansas	55,320	16	Colorado	63,580
41	Kentucky	53,700	17	New Hampshire	62,570
45	Louisiana	52,120	18	Maine	62,530
18	Maine	62,530	19	Wisconsin	61,770
4	Maryland	71,420	20	Virginia	61,130
7	Massachusetts	68,470	21	Arizona	60,900
15	Michigan	64,220	22	Ohio	60,570
11	Minnesota	67,370	23	Florida	59,780
46	Mississippi	51,960	24	Utah	59,710
35	Missouri	55,550	25	North Carolina	59,420
44	Montana	52,500	26	Georgia	59,390
38	Nebraska	55,270	27	Texas	58,730
12	Nevada	66,580	28	Pennsylvania	58,610
17	New Hampshire	62,570	29	Vermont	58,470
2	New Jersey	72,510	30	New Mexico	58,060
30	New Mexico	58,060	31	Illinois	58,010
6	New York	68,990	32	Idaho	57,140
25	North Carolina	59,420	33	Wyoming	56,930
50	North Dakota	50,650	34	South Carolina	56,350
22	Ohio	60,570	35	Missouri	55,550
48	Oklahoma	51,180	36	Indiana	55,450
5	Oregon	69,050	37	Kansas	55,320
28	Pennsylvania	58,610	38	Nebraska	55,270
13	Rhode Island	66,510	39	West Virginia	54,690
34	South Carolina	56,350	40	Tennessee	54,660
42	South Dakota	53,230	41	Kentucky	53,700
40	Tennessee	54,660	42	South Dakota	53,230
27	Texas	58,730	43	Iowa	52,670
24	Utah	59,710	44	Montana	52,500
29	Vermont	58,470	45	Louisiana	52,120
20	Virginia	61,130	46	Mississippi	51,960
10	Washington	67,540	47	Alabama	51,540
39	West Virginia	54,690	48	Oklahoma	51,180
19	Wisconsin	61,770	49	Arkansas	51,030
33	Wyoming	56,930	50	North Dakota	50,650
				District of Columbia	64,290

Source: U.S. Department of Labor, Bureau of Labor Statistics
   "Occupational Employment and Wages, 2006" (http://www.bls.gov/oes/)
*Does not include self-employed. Includes various doctors, dentists, nurses, therapists, optometrists, paramedics and, technicians. Does not include assistants and aides listed under health care support occupations.

Physicians in 2006

National Total = 908,065 Physicians*

ALPHA ORDER

RANK	STATE	PHYSICIANS	% of USA
27	Alabama	10,994	1.2%
49	Alaska	1,697	0.2%
21	Arizona	15,127	1.7%
31	Arkansas	6,464	0.7%
1	California	110,406	12.2%
23	Colorado	14,175	1.6%
22	Connecticut	14,488	1.6%
46	Delaware	2,414	0.3%
4	Florida	53,566	5.9%
14	Georgia	22,805	2.5%
39	Hawaii	4,599	0.5%
43	Idaho	2,934	0.3%
6	Illinois	39,240	4.3%
20	Indiana	15,229	1.7%
32	Iowa	6,428	0.7%
30	Kansas	7,079	0.8%
28	Kentucky	10,828	1.2%
24	Louisiana	12,643	1.4%
41	Maine	4,197	0.5%
11	Maryland	25,969	2.9%
8	Massachusetts	32,575	3.6%
10	Michigan	27,877	3.1%
17	Minnesota	16,756	1.8%
34	Mississippi	5,890	0.6%
19	Missouri	15,586	1.7%
45	Montana	2,548	0.3%
37	Nebraska	4,852	0.5%
36	Nevada	5,384	0.6%
42	New Hampshire	4,079	0.4%
9	New Jersey	30,183	3.3%
35	New Mexico	5,424	0.6%
2	New York	83,826	9.2%
12	North Carolina	25,385	2.8%
48	North Dakota	1,745	0.2%
7	Ohio	34,091	3.8%
29	Oklahoma	7,111	0.8%
25	Oregon	11,741	1.3%
5	Pennsylvania	42,204	4.6%
40	Rhode Island	4,368	0.5%
26	South Carolina	11,241	1.2%
47	South Dakota	1,975	0.2%
16	Tennessee	17,791	2.0%
3	Texas	54,971	6.1%
33	Utah	6,093	0.7%
44	Vermont	2,659	0.3%
13	Virginia	23,545	2.6%
15	Washington	19,864	2.2%
38	West Virginia	4,710	0.5%
18	Wisconsin	16,154	1.8%
50	Wyoming	1,132	0.1%

RANK ORDER

RANK	STATE	PHYSICIANS	% of USA
1	California	110,406	12.2%
2	New York	83,826	9.2%
3	Texas	54,971	6.1%
4	Florida	53,566	5.9%
5	Pennsylvania	42,204	4.6%
6	Illinois	39,240	4.3%
7	Ohio	34,091	3.8%
8	Massachusetts	32,575	3.6%
9	New Jersey	30,183	3.3%
10	Michigan	27,877	3.1%
11	Maryland	25,969	2.9%
12	North Carolina	25,385	2.8%
13	Virginia	23,545	2.6%
14	Georgia	22,805	2.5%
15	Washington	19,864	2.2%
16	Tennessee	17,791	2.0%
17	Minnesota	16,756	1.8%
18	Wisconsin	16,154	1.8%
19	Missouri	15,586	1.7%
20	Indiana	15,229	1.7%
21	Arizona	15,127	1.7%
22	Connecticut	14,488	1.6%
23	Colorado	14,175	1.6%
24	Louisiana	12,643	1.4%
25	Oregon	11,741	1.3%
26	South Carolina	11,241	1.2%
27	Alabama	10,994	1.2%
28	Kentucky	10,828	1.2%
29	Oklahoma	7,111	0.8%
30	Kansas	7,079	0.8%
31	Arkansas	6,464	0.7%
32	Iowa	6,428	0.7%
33	Utah	6,093	0.7%
34	Mississippi	5,890	0.6%
35	New Mexico	5,424	0.6%
36	Nevada	5,384	0.6%
37	Nebraska	4,852	0.5%
38	West Virginia	4,710	0.5%
39	Hawaii	4,599	0.5%
40	Rhode Island	4,368	0.5%
41	Maine	4,197	0.5%
42	New Hampshire	4,079	0.4%
43	Idaho	2,934	0.3%
44	Vermont	2,659	0.3%
45	Montana	2,548	0.3%
46	Delaware	2,414	0.3%
47	South Dakota	1,975	0.2%
48	North Dakota	1,745	0.2%
49	Alaska	1,697	0.2%
50	Wyoming	1,132	0.1%
	District of Columbia	5,023	0.6%

Source: American Medical Association (Chicago, Illinois)
   "Physician Characteristics and Distribution in the U.S." (2008 Edition)
*As of December 31, 2006. Total does not include 13,839 physicians in the U.S. territories and possessions, at APO's and FPO's or whose addresses are unknown.

Rate of Physicians in 2006

National Rate = 304 Physicians per 100,000 Population*

ALPHA ORDER

RANK	STATE	RATE
41	Alabama	240
36	Alaska	250
38	Arizona	245
44	Arkansas	230
17	California	305
19	Colorado	297
5	Connecticut	414
25	Delaware	283
19	Florida	297
39	Georgia	244
7	Hawaii	360
49	Idaho	200
16	Illinois	307
40	Indiana	242
46	Iowa	216
35	Kansas	257
34	Kentucky	258
18	Louisiana	298
11	Maine	319
2	Maryland	464
1	Massachusetts	506
27	Michigan	276
10	Minnesota	325
48	Mississippi	203
31	Missouri	267
30	Montana	269
28	Nebraska	275
46	Nevada	216
14	New Hampshire	311
8	New Jersey	348
26	New Mexico	279
3	New York	435
24	North Carolina	286
29	North Dakota	274
19	Ohio	297
50	Oklahoma	199
12	Oregon	318
9	Pennsylvania	340
6	Rhode Island	411
32	South Carolina	260
36	South Dakota	250
22	Tennessee	293
43	Texas	235
42	Utah	236
4	Vermont	428
15	Virginia	308
13	Washington	312
32	West Virginia	260
23	Wisconsin	290
45	Wyoming	221

RANK ORDER

RANK	STATE	RATE
1	Massachusetts	506
2	Maryland	464
3	New York	435
4	Vermont	428
5	Connecticut	414
6	Rhode Island	411
7	Hawaii	360
8	New Jersey	348
9	Pennsylvania	340
10	Minnesota	325
11	Maine	319
12	Oregon	318
13	Washington	312
14	New Hampshire	311
15	Virginia	308
16	Illinois	307
17	California	305
18	Louisiana	298
19	Colorado	297
19	Florida	297
19	Ohio	297
22	Tennessee	293
23	Wisconsin	290
24	North Carolina	286
25	Delaware	283
26	New Mexico	279
27	Michigan	276
28	Nebraska	275
29	North Dakota	274
30	Montana	269
31	Missouri	267
32	South Carolina	260
32	West Virginia	260
34	Kentucky	258
35	Kansas	257
36	Alaska	250
36	South Dakota	250
38	Arizona	245
39	Georgia	244
40	Indiana	242
41	Alabama	240
42	Utah	236
43	Texas	235
44	Arkansas	230
45	Wyoming	221
46	Iowa	216
46	Nevada	216
48	Mississippi	203
49	Idaho	200
50	Oklahoma	199

	District of Columbia	858

Source: CQ Press using data from American Medical Association (Chicago, Illinois)
   "Physician Characteristics and Distribution in the U.S." (2008 Edition)
*As of December 31, 2006. National rate does not include physicians in the U.S. territories and possessions, at APO's and FPO's or whose addresses are unknown.

Percent of Physicians Who Are Female: 2006

National Percent = 27.7% of Physicians*

ALPHA ORDER

ALPHA ORDER

RANK	STATE	RATE
41	Alabama	22.1
9	Alaska	30.1
29	Arizona	25.1
44	Arkansas	21.5
16	California	28.2
13	Colorado	28.9
11	Connecticut	29.2
10	Delaware	30.0
42	Florida	21.7
23	Georgia	26.8
21	Hawaii	27.4
50	Idaho	18.6
4	Illinois	31.9
30	Indiana	25.0
36	Iowa	22.9
31	Kansas	24.9
32	Kentucky	24.8
34	Louisiana	24.2
22	Maine	26.9
2	Maryland	32.3
1	Massachusetts	33.9
12	Michigan	29.0
15	Minnesota	28.4
48	Mississippi	19.7
24	Missouri	26.7
46	Montana	20.8
33	Nebraska	24.6
38	Nevada	22.4
27	New Hampshire	26.2
6	New Jersey	31.3
7	New Mexico	31.0
4	New York	31.9
24	North Carolina	26.7
45	North Dakota	21.0
20	Ohio	27.6
39	Oklahoma	22.3
19	Oregon	27.9
17	Pennsylvania	28.1
3	Rhode Island	32.1
36	South Carolina	22.9
42	South Dakota	21.7
35	Tennessee	23.2
24	Texas	26.7
47	Utah	20.1
8	Vermont	30.2
14	Virginia	28.8
17	Washington	28.1
39	West Virginia	22.3
27	Wisconsin	26.2
49	Wyoming	19.2

RANK ORDER

RANK	STATE	RATE
1	Massachusetts	33.9
2	Maryland	32.3
3	Rhode Island	32.1
4	Illinois	31.9
4	New York	31.9
6	New Jersey	31.3
7	New Mexico	31.0
8	Vermont	30.2
9	Alaska	30.1
10	Delaware	30.0
11	Connecticut	29.2
12	Michigan	29.0
13	Colorado	28.9
14	Virginia	28.8
15	Minnesota	28.4
16	California	28.2
17	Pennsylvania	28.1
17	Washington	28.1
19	Oregon	27.9
20	Ohio	27.6
21	Hawaii	27.4
22	Maine	26.9
23	Georgia	26.8
24	Missouri	26.7
24	North Carolina	26.7
24	Texas	26.7
27	New Hampshire	26.2
27	Wisconsin	26.2
29	Arizona	25.1
30	Indiana	25.0
31	Kansas	24.9
32	Kentucky	24.8
33	Nebraska	24.6
34	Louisiana	24.2
35	Tennessee	23.2
36	Iowa	22.9
36	South Carolina	22.9
38	Nevada	22.4
39	Oklahoma	22.3
39	West Virginia	22.3
41	Alabama	22.1
42	Florida	21.7
42	South Dakota	21.7
44	Arkansas	21.5
45	North Dakota	21.0
46	Montana	20.8
47	Utah	20.1
48	Mississippi	19.7
49	Wyoming	19.2
50	Idaho	18.6

District of Columbia — 36.8

Source: CQ Press using data from American Medical Association (Chicago, Illinois)
   "Physician Characteristics and Distribution in the U.S." (2008 Edition)
*As of December 31, 2006. National percent does not include physicians in the U.S. territories and possessions, at APO's and FPO's or whose addresses are unknown.

Percent of Physicians Under 35 Years Old in 2006

National Percent = 15.3% of Physicians*

ALPHA ORDER				RANK ORDER		
RANK	STATE	RATE		RANK	STATE	RATE
15	Alabama	15.5		1	Rhode Island	20.1
47	Alaska	8.0		2	Illinois	20.0
38	Arizona	11.5		3	Missouri	19.5
25	Arkansas	14.6		4	Massachusetts	19.4
32	California	13.2		5	New York	19.3
34	Colorado	12.5		6	Ohio	18.9
13	Connecticut	15.8		7	Michigan	18.7
19	Delaware	15.2		8	Nebraska	18.0
45	Florida	9.2		9	Pennsylvania	17.8
28	Georgia	14.0		10	Louisiana	17.1
37	Hawaii	11.7		11	Minnesota	16.7
48	Idaho	6.7		12	Texas	16.4
2	Illinois	20.0		13	Connecticut	15.8
27	Indiana	14.1		14	North Carolina	15.7
18	Iowa	15.3		15	Alabama	15.5
26	Kansas	14.3		15	West Virginia	15.5
23	Kentucky	14.8		17	South Carolina	15.4
10	Louisiana	17.1		18	Iowa	15.3
46	Maine	8.5		19	Delaware	15.2
19	Maryland	15.2		19	Maryland	15.2
4	Massachusetts	19.4		21	Tennessee	15.1
7	Michigan	18.7		22	Utah	15.0
11	Minnesota	16.7		23	Kentucky	14.8
35	Mississippi	12.2		23	Virginia	14.8
3	Missouri	19.5		25	Arkansas	14.6
50	Montana	4.6		26	Kansas	14.3
8	Nebraska	18.0		27	Indiana	14.1
44	Nevada	9.5		28	Georgia	14.0
43	New Hampshire	9.9		28	Vermont	14.0
33	New Jersey	12.9		30	Wisconsin	13.9
36	New Mexico	12.0		31	Oklahoma	13.7
5	New York	19.3		32	California	13.2
14	North Carolina	15.7		33	New Jersey	12.9
41	North Dakota	10.7		34	Colorado	12.5
6	Ohio	18.9		35	Mississippi	12.2
31	Oklahoma	13.7		36	New Mexico	12.0
40	Oregon	10.8		37	Hawaii	11.7
9	Pennsylvania	17.8		38	Arizona	11.5
1	Rhode Island	20.1		39	Washington	10.9
17	South Carolina	15.4		40	Oregon	10.8
42	South Dakota	10.1		41	North Dakota	10.7
21	Tennessee	15.1		42	South Dakota	10.1
12	Texas	16.4		43	New Hampshire	9.9
22	Utah	15.0		44	Nevada	9.5
28	Vermont	14.0		45	Florida	9.2
23	Virginia	14.8		46	Maine	8.5
39	Washington	10.9		47	Alaska	8.0
15	West Virginia	15.5		48	Idaho	6.7
30	Wisconsin	13.9		49	Wyoming	5.6
49	Wyoming	5.6		50	Montana	4.6
					District of Columbia	24.9

Source: CQ Press using data from American Medical Association (Chicago, Illinois)
"Physician Characteristics and Distribution in the U.S." (2008 Edition)

*As of December 31, 2006. National percent does not include physicians in the U.S. territories and possessions, at APO's and FPO's or whose addresses are unknown.

Percent of Physicians 65 Years Old and Older in 2006

National Percent = 19.2% of Physicians*

ALPHA ORDER				RANK ORDER		
RANK	STATE	PERCENT		RANK	STATE	PERCENT
47	Alabama	16.2		1	Florida	26.4
50	Alaska	14.9		2	Montana	23.5
6	Arizona	21.4		3	Wyoming	23.2
30	Arkansas	17.8		4	California	22.6
4	California	22.6		5	Maine	22.5
26	Colorado	18.7		6	Arizona	21.4
19	Connecticut	19.4		7	Idaho	20.9
15	Delaware	19.9		7	Nevada	20.9
1	Florida	26.4		9	New Hampshire	20.7
46	Georgia	16.3		9	Vermont	20.7
11	Hawaii	20.6		11	Hawaii	20.6
7	Idaho	20.9		12	Oregon	20.3
37	Illinois	16.7		13	Kansas	20.1
40	Indiana	16.6		14	Washington	20.0
31	Iowa	17.7		15	Delaware	19.9
13	Kansas	20.1		16	New York	19.8
43	Kentucky	16.4		16	Oklahoma	19.8
33	Louisiana	17.5		16	West Virginia	19.8
5	Maine	22.5		19	Connecticut	19.4
22	Maryland	19.1		20	New Jersey	19.3
37	Massachusetts	16.7		20	New Mexico	19.3
28	Michigan	18.1		22	Maryland	19.1
49	Minnesota	16.0		23	Pennsylvania	19.0
26	Mississippi	18.7		23	Virginia	19.0
48	Missouri	16.1		25	Rhode Island	18.8
2	Montana	23.5		26	Colorado	18.7
37	Nebraska	16.7		26	Mississippi	18.7
7	Nevada	20.9		28	Michigan	18.1
9	New Hampshire	20.7		28	South Carolina	18.1
20	New Jersey	19.3		30	Arkansas	17.8
20	New Mexico	19.3		31	Iowa	17.7
16	New York	19.8		32	Ohio	17.6
40	North Carolina	16.6		33	Louisiana	17.5
34	North Dakota	17.2		34	North Dakota	17.2
32	Ohio	17.6		35	Wisconsin	16.9
16	Oklahoma	19.8		36	South Dakota	16.8
12	Oregon	20.3		37	Illinois	16.7
23	Pennsylvania	19.0		37	Massachusetts	16.7
25	Rhode Island	18.8		37	Nebraska	16.7
28	South Carolina	18.1		40	Indiana	16.6
36	South Dakota	16.8		40	North Carolina	16.6
43	Tennessee	16.4		42	Texas	16.5
42	Texas	16.5		43	Kentucky	16.4
43	Utah	16.4		43	Tennessee	16.4
9	Vermont	20.7		43	Utah	16.4
23	Virginia	19.0		46	Georgia	16.3
14	Washington	20.0		47	Alabama	16.2
16	West Virginia	19.8		48	Missouri	16.1
35	Wisconsin	16.9		49	Minnesota	16.0
3	Wyoming	23.2		50	Alaska	14.9
					District of Columbia	19.6

Source: CQ Press using data from American Medical Association (Chicago, Illinois)
"Physician Characteristics and Distribution in the U.S." (2008 Edition)
*As of December 31, 2006. National percent does not include physicians in the U.S. territories and possessions, at APO's and FPO's or whose addresses are unknown.

Physicians in Patient Care in 2006

National Total = 712,687 Physicians*

ALPHA ORDER

RANK	STATE	PHYSICIANS	% of USA
26	Alabama	9,091	1.3%
48	Alaska	1,437	0.2%
21	Arizona	11,622	1.6%
31	Arkansas	5,316	0.7%
1	California	84,907	11.9%
23	Colorado	11,180	1.6%
22	Connecticut	11,224	1.6%
46	Delaware	1,927	0.3%
4	Florida	40,211	5.6%
14	Georgia	18,418	2.6%
39	Hawaii	3,628	0.5%
43	Idaho	2,373	0.3%
6	Illinois	31,367	4.4%
20	Indiana	12,560	1.8%
32	Iowa	4,957	0.7%
30	Kansas	5,602	0.8%
28	Kentucky	8,825	1.2%
24	Louisiana	10,393	1.5%
41	Maine	3,250	0.5%
12	Maryland	19,205	2.7%
8	Massachusetts	24,657	3.5%
10	Michigan	22,003	3.1%
17	Minnesota	13,318	1.9%
34	Mississippi	4,782	0.7%
19	Missouri	12,590	1.8%
44	Montana	1,991	0.3%
37	Nebraska	3,874	0.5%
35	Nevada	4,307	0.6%
42	New Hampshire	3,176	0.4%
9	New Jersey	24,128	3.4%
36	New Mexico	4,162	0.6%
2	New York	65,224	9.2%
11	North Carolina	20,015	2.8%
48	North Dakota	1,437	0.2%
7	Ohio	26,844	3.8%
29	Oklahoma	5,667	0.8%
27	Oregon	9,036	1.3%
5	Pennsylvania	32,324	4.5%
40	Rhode Island	3,458	0.5%
25	South Carolina	9,155	1.3%
47	South Dakota	1,627	0.2%
16	Tennessee	14,557	2.0%
3	Texas	44,813	6.3%
33	Utah	4,862	0.7%
45	Vermont	1,980	0.3%
13	Virginia	18,538	2.6%
15	Washington	15,168	2.1%
38	West Virginia	3,762	0.5%
18	Wisconsin	13,126	1.8%
50	Wyoming	903	0.1%

RANK ORDER

RANK	STATE	PHYSICIANS	% of USA
1	California	84,907	11.9%
2	New York	65,224	9.2%
3	Texas	44,813	6.3%
4	Florida	40,211	5.6%
5	Pennsylvania	32,324	4.5%
6	Illinois	31,367	4.4%
7	Ohio	26,844	3.8%
8	Massachusetts	24,657	3.5%
9	New Jersey	24,128	3.4%
10	Michigan	22,003	3.1%
11	North Carolina	20,015	2.8%
12	Maryland	19,205	2.7%
13	Virginia	18,538	2.6%
14	Georgia	18,418	2.6%
15	Washington	15,168	2.1%
16	Tennessee	14,557	2.0%
17	Minnesota	13,318	1.9%
18	Wisconsin	13,126	1.8%
19	Missouri	12,590	1.8%
20	Indiana	12,560	1.8%
21	Arizona	11,622	1.6%
22	Connecticut	11,224	1.6%
23	Colorado	11,180	1.6%
24	Louisiana	10,393	1.5%
25	South Carolina	9,155	1.3%
26	Alabama	9,091	1.3%
27	Oregon	9,036	1.3%
28	Kentucky	8,825	1.2%
29	Oklahoma	5,667	0.8%
30	Kansas	5,602	0.8%
31	Arkansas	5,316	0.7%
32	Iowa	4,957	0.7%
33	Utah	4,862	0.7%
34	Mississippi	4,782	0.7%
35	Nevada	4,307	0.6%
36	New Mexico	4,162	0.6%
37	Nebraska	3,874	0.5%
38	West Virginia	3,762	0.5%
39	Hawaii	3,628	0.5%
40	Rhode Island	3,458	0.5%
41	Maine	3,250	0.5%
42	New Hampshire	3,176	0.4%
43	Idaho	2,373	0.3%
44	Montana	1,991	0.3%
45	Vermont	1,980	0.3%
46	Delaware	1,927	0.3%
47	South Dakota	1,627	0.2%
48	Alaska	1,437	0.2%
48	North Dakota	1,437	0.2%
50	Wyoming	903	0.1%
	District of Columbia	3,710	0.5%

Source: American Medical Association (Chicago, Illinois)
"Physician Characteristics and Distribution in the U.S." (2008 Edition)
*As of December 31, 2006. Total does not include 10,431 physicians in U.S. territories and possessions.

Rate of Physicians in Patient Care in 2006

National Rate = 239 Physicians per 100,000 Population*

ALPHA ORDER				RANK ORDER		
RANK	STATE	RATE		RANK	STATE	RATE
39	Alabama	198		1	Massachusetts	383
31	Alaska	212		2	Maryland	343
43	Arizona	188		3	New York	338
42	Arkansas	189		4	Rhode Island	326
21	California	234		5	Connecticut	321
20	Colorado	235		6	Vermont	319
5	Connecticut	321		7	Hawaii	284
23	Delaware	226		8	New Jersey	278
26	Florida	223		9	Pennsylvania	261
40	Georgia	197		10	Minnesota	258
7	Hawaii	284		11	Maine	247
49	Idaho	162		12	Illinois	245
12	Illinois	245		12	Louisiana	245
38	Indiana	199		12	Oregon	245
47	Iowa	167		15	Virginia	243
37	Kansas	203		16	New Hampshire	242
33	Kentucky	210		17	Tennessee	240
12	Louisiana	245		18	Washington	238
11	Maine	247		19	Wisconsin	236
2	Maryland	343		20	Colorado	235
1	Massachusetts	383		21	California	234
28	Michigan	218		21	Ohio	234
10	Minnesota	258		23	Delaware	226
48	Mississippi	165		23	North Carolina	226
29	Missouri	216		25	North Dakota	225
33	Montana	210		26	Florida	223
27	Nebraska	220		27	Nebraska	220
46	Nevada	173		28	Michigan	218
16	New Hampshire	242		29	Missouri	216
8	New Jersey	278		30	New Mexico	214
30	New Mexico	214		31	Alaska	212
3	New York	338		32	South Carolina	211
23	North Carolina	226		33	Kentucky	210
25	North Dakota	225		33	Montana	210
21	Ohio	234		35	West Virginia	208
50	Oklahoma	158		36	South Dakota	206
12	Oregon	245		37	Kansas	203
9	Pennsylvania	261		38	Indiana	199
4	Rhode Island	326		39	Alabama	198
32	South Carolina	211		40	Georgia	197
36	South Dakota	206		41	Texas	191
17	Tennessee	240		42	Arkansas	189
41	Texas	191		43	Arizona	188
43	Utah	188		43	Utah	188
6	Vermont	319		45	Wyoming	176
15	Virginia	243		46	Nevada	173
18	Washington	238		47	Iowa	167
35	West Virginia	208		48	Mississippi	165
19	Wisconsin	236		49	Idaho	162
45	Wyoming	176		50	Oklahoma	158
					District of Columbia	634

Source: CQ Press using data from American Medical Association (Chicago, Illinois)
"Physician Characteristics and Distribution in the U.S." (2008 Edition)
*As of December 31, 2006. National rate does not include physicians in the U.S. territories and possessions.

Physicians in Primary Care in 2006

National Total = 295,488 Physicians*

<table>
<tr><td colspan="4">ALPHA ORDER</td><td colspan="4">RANK ORDER</td></tr>
<tr><td>RANK</td><td>STATE</td><td>PHYSICIANS</td><td>% of USA</td><td>RANK</td><td>STATE</td><td>PHYSICIANS</td><td>% of USA</td></tr>
<tr><td>27</td><td>Alabama</td><td>3,855</td><td>1.3%</td><td>1</td><td>California</td><td>35,917</td><td>12.2%</td></tr>
<tr><td>48</td><td>Alaska</td><td>707</td><td>0.2%</td><td>2</td><td>New York</td><td>26,580</td><td>9.0%</td></tr>
<tr><td>21</td><td>Arizona</td><td>4,687</td><td>1.6%</td><td>3</td><td>Texas</td><td>18,178</td><td>6.2%</td></tr>
<tr><td>31</td><td>Arkansas</td><td>2,315</td><td>0.8%</td><td>4</td><td>Florida</td><td>15,618</td><td>5.3%</td></tr>
<tr><td>1</td><td>California</td><td>35,917</td><td>12.2%</td><td>5</td><td>Illinois</td><td>13,738</td><td>4.6%</td></tr>
<tr><td>22</td><td>Colorado</td><td>4,589</td><td>1.6%</td><td>6</td><td>Pennsylvania</td><td>12,435</td><td>4.2%</td></tr>
<tr><td>23</td><td>Connecticut</td><td>4,477</td><td>1.5%</td><td>7</td><td>Ohio</td><td>11,018</td><td>3.7%</td></tr>
<tr><td>46</td><td>Delaware</td><td>747</td><td>0.3%</td><td>8</td><td>New Jersey</td><td>10,062</td><td>3.4%</td></tr>
<tr><td>4</td><td>Florida</td><td>15,618</td><td>5.3%</td><td>9</td><td>Michigan</td><td>9,419</td><td>3.2%</td></tr>
<tr><td>12</td><td>Georgia</td><td>8,030</td><td>2.7%</td><td>10</td><td>Massachusetts</td><td>9,344</td><td>3.2%</td></tr>
<tr><td>39</td><td>Hawaii</td><td>1,601</td><td>0.5%</td><td>11</td><td>North Carolina</td><td>8,311</td><td>2.8%</td></tr>
<tr><td>43</td><td>Idaho</td><td>1,018</td><td>0.3%</td><td>12</td><td>Georgia</td><td>8,030</td><td>2.7%</td></tr>
<tr><td>5</td><td>Illinois</td><td>13,738</td><td>4.6%</td><td>13</td><td>Virginia</td><td>7,986</td><td>2.7%</td></tr>
<tr><td>19</td><td>Indiana</td><td>5,292</td><td>1.8%</td><td>14</td><td>Maryland</td><td>7,690</td><td>2.6%</td></tr>
<tr><td>32</td><td>Iowa</td><td>2,107</td><td>0.7%</td><td>15</td><td>Washington</td><td>6,687</td><td>2.3%</td></tr>
<tr><td>30</td><td>Kansas</td><td>2,366</td><td>0.8%</td><td>16</td><td>Tennessee</td><td>5,996</td><td>2.0%</td></tr>
<tr><td>28</td><td>Kentucky</td><td>3,630</td><td>1.2%</td><td>17</td><td>Minnesota</td><td>5,840</td><td>2.0%</td></tr>
<tr><td>24</td><td>Louisiana</td><td>4,186</td><td>1.4%</td><td>18</td><td>Wisconsin</td><td>5,640</td><td>1.9%</td></tr>
<tr><td>40</td><td>Maine</td><td>1,429</td><td>0.5%</td><td>19</td><td>Indiana</td><td>5,292</td><td>1.8%</td></tr>
<tr><td>14</td><td>Maryland</td><td>7,690</td><td>2.6%</td><td>20</td><td>Missouri</td><td>4,901</td><td>1.7%</td></tr>
<tr><td>10</td><td>Massachusetts</td><td>9,344</td><td>3.2%</td><td>21</td><td>Arizona</td><td>4,687</td><td>1.6%</td></tr>
<tr><td>9</td><td>Michigan</td><td>9,419</td><td>3.2%</td><td>22</td><td>Colorado</td><td>4,589</td><td>1.6%</td></tr>
<tr><td>17</td><td>Minnesota</td><td>5,840</td><td>2.0%</td><td>23</td><td>Connecticut</td><td>4,477</td><td>1.5%</td></tr>
<tr><td>33</td><td>Mississippi</td><td>2,011</td><td>0.7%</td><td>24</td><td>Louisiana</td><td>4,186</td><td>1.4%</td></tr>
<tr><td>20</td><td>Missouri</td><td>4,901</td><td>1.7%</td><td>25</td><td>Oregon</td><td>3,949</td><td>1.3%</td></tr>
<tr><td>45</td><td>Montana</td><td>865</td><td>0.3%</td><td>26</td><td>South Carolina</td><td>3,897</td><td>1.3%</td></tr>
<tr><td>37</td><td>Nebraska</td><td>1,737</td><td>0.6%</td><td>27</td><td>Alabama</td><td>3,855</td><td>1.3%</td></tr>
<tr><td>36</td><td>Nevada</td><td>1,816</td><td>0.6%</td><td>28</td><td>Kentucky</td><td>3,630</td><td>1.2%</td></tr>
<tr><td>42</td><td>New Hampshire</td><td>1,363</td><td>0.5%</td><td>29</td><td>Oklahoma</td><td>2,418</td><td>0.8%</td></tr>
<tr><td>8</td><td>New Jersey</td><td>10,062</td><td>3.4%</td><td>30</td><td>Kansas</td><td>2,366</td><td>0.8%</td></tr>
<tr><td>35</td><td>New Mexico</td><td>1,891</td><td>0.6%</td><td>31</td><td>Arkansas</td><td>2,315</td><td>0.8%</td></tr>
<tr><td>2</td><td>New York</td><td>26,580</td><td>9.0%</td><td>32</td><td>Iowa</td><td>2,107</td><td>0.7%</td></tr>
<tr><td>11</td><td>North Carolina</td><td>8,311</td><td>2.8%</td><td>33</td><td>Mississippi</td><td>2,011</td><td>0.7%</td></tr>
<tr><td>49</td><td>North Dakota</td><td>675</td><td>0.2%</td><td>34</td><td>Utah</td><td>1,951</td><td>0.7%</td></tr>
<tr><td>7</td><td>Ohio</td><td>11,018</td><td>3.7%</td><td>35</td><td>New Mexico</td><td>1,891</td><td>0.6%</td></tr>
<tr><td>29</td><td>Oklahoma</td><td>2,418</td><td>0.8%</td><td>36</td><td>Nevada</td><td>1,816</td><td>0.6%</td></tr>
<tr><td>25</td><td>Oregon</td><td>3,949</td><td>1.3%</td><td>37</td><td>Nebraska</td><td>1,737</td><td>0.6%</td></tr>
<tr><td>6</td><td>Pennsylvania</td><td>12,435</td><td>4.2%</td><td>38</td><td>West Virginia</td><td>1,623</td><td>0.5%</td></tr>
<tr><td>41</td><td>Rhode Island</td><td>1,426</td><td>0.5%</td><td>39</td><td>Hawaii</td><td>1,601</td><td>0.5%</td></tr>
<tr><td>26</td><td>South Carolina</td><td>3,897</td><td>1.3%</td><td>40</td><td>Maine</td><td>1,429</td><td>0.5%</td></tr>
<tr><td>47</td><td>South Dakota</td><td>735</td><td>0.2%</td><td>41</td><td>Rhode Island</td><td>1,426</td><td>0.5%</td></tr>
<tr><td>16</td><td>Tennessee</td><td>5,996</td><td>2.0%</td><td>42</td><td>New Hampshire</td><td>1,363</td><td>0.5%</td></tr>
<tr><td>3</td><td>Texas</td><td>18,178</td><td>6.2%</td><td>43</td><td>Idaho</td><td>1,018</td><td>0.3%</td></tr>
<tr><td>34</td><td>Utah</td><td>1,951</td><td>0.7%</td><td>44</td><td>Vermont</td><td>884</td><td>0.3%</td></tr>
<tr><td>44</td><td>Vermont</td><td>884</td><td>0.3%</td><td>45</td><td>Montana</td><td>865</td><td>0.3%</td></tr>
<tr><td>13</td><td>Virginia</td><td>7,986</td><td>2.7%</td><td>46</td><td>Delaware</td><td>747</td><td>0.3%</td></tr>
<tr><td>15</td><td>Washington</td><td>6,687</td><td>2.3%</td><td>47</td><td>South Dakota</td><td>735</td><td>0.2%</td></tr>
<tr><td>38</td><td>West Virginia</td><td>1,623</td><td>0.5%</td><td>48</td><td>Alaska</td><td>707</td><td>0.2%</td></tr>
<tr><td>18</td><td>Wisconsin</td><td>5,640</td><td>1.9%</td><td>49</td><td>North Dakota</td><td>675</td><td>0.2%</td></tr>
<tr><td>50</td><td>Wyoming</td><td>430</td><td>0.1%</td><td>50</td><td>Wyoming</td><td>430</td><td>0.1%</td></tr>
<tr><td></td><td></td><td></td><td></td><td></td><td>District of Columbia</td><td>1,421</td><td>0.5%</td></tr>
</table>

Source: American Medical Association (Chicago, Illinois)
   "Physician Characteristics and Distribution in the U.S." (2008 Edition)
*As of December 31, 2006. National total does not include 5,419 physicians in U.S. territories and possessions. Primary Care Specialties include Family Practice, General Practice, Internal Medicine, Obstetrics/Gynecology, and Pediatrics excluding subspecialties within each category.

Rate of Physicians in Primary Care in 2006

National Rate = 99 Physicians per 100,000 Population*

ALPHA ORDER

RANK	STATE	RATE
38	Alabama	84
16	Alaska	104
44	Arizona	76
42	Arkansas	82
20	California	99
25	Colorado	96
6	Connecticut	128
33	Delaware	88
34	Florida	86
34	Georgia	86
7	Hawaii	125
48	Idaho	70
11	Illinois	108
38	Indiana	84
47	Iowa	71
34	Kansas	86
34	Kentucky	86
20	Louisiana	99
10	Maine	109
4	Maryland	137
1	Massachusetts	145
28	Michigan	93
9	Minnesota	113
49	Mississippi	69
38	Missouri	84
30	Montana	91
23	Nebraska	98
46	Nevada	73
16	New Hampshire	104
8	New Jersey	116
24	New Mexico	97
3	New York	138
27	North Carolina	94
13	North Dakota	106
25	Ohio	96
50	Oklahoma	68
12	Oregon	107
19	Pennsylvania	100
5	Rhode Island	134
31	South Carolina	90
28	South Dakota	93
20	Tennessee	99
43	Texas	78
44	Utah	76
2	Vermont	142
14	Virginia	105
14	Washington	105
31	West Virginia	90
18	Wisconsin	101
38	Wyoming	84

RANK ORDER

RANK	STATE	RATE
1	Massachusetts	145
2	Vermont	142
3	New York	138
4	Maryland	137
5	Rhode Island	134
6	Connecticut	128
7	Hawaii	125
8	New Jersey	116
9	Minnesota	113
10	Maine	109
11	Illinois	108
12	Oregon	107
13	North Dakota	106
14	Virginia	105
14	Washington	105
16	Alaska	104
16	New Hampshire	104
18	Wisconsin	101
19	Pennsylvania	100
20	California	99
20	Louisiana	99
20	Tennessee	99
23	Nebraska	98
24	New Mexico	97
25	Colorado	96
25	Ohio	96
27	North Carolina	94
28	Michigan	93
28	South Dakota	93
30	Montana	91
31	South Carolina	90
31	West Virginia	90
33	Delaware	88
34	Florida	86
34	Georgia	86
34	Kansas	86
34	Kentucky	86
38	Alabama	84
38	Indiana	84
38	Missouri	84
38	Wyoming	84
42	Arkansas	82
43	Texas	78
44	Arizona	76
44	Utah	76
46	Nevada	73
47	Iowa	71
48	Idaho	70
49	Mississippi	69
50	Oklahoma	68

District of Columbia	243

Source: CQ Press using data from American Medical Association (Chicago, Illinois)
"Physician Characteristics and Distribution in the U.S." (2008 Edition)

*As of December 31, 2006. National rate does not include physicians in U.S. territories and possessions. Primary Care Specialties include Family Practice, General Practice, Internal Medicine, Obstetrics/Gynecology, and Pediatrics excluding subspecialties within each category.

Percent of Physicians in Primary Care in 2006

National Percent = 32.5% of Physicians*

ALPHA ORDER

RANK	STATE	PERCENT
8	Alabama	35.1
1	Alaska	41.7
44	Arizona	31.0
5	Arkansas	35.8
38	California	32.5
39	Colorado	32.4
45	Connecticut	30.9
45	Delaware	30.9
49	Florida	29.2
7	Georgia	35.2
13	Hawaii	34.8
14	Idaho	34.7
9	Illinois	35.0
14	Indiana	34.7
35	Iowa	32.8
29	Kansas	33.4
28	Kentucky	33.5
33	Louisiana	33.1
19	Maine	34.0
47	Maryland	29.6
50	Massachusetts	28.7
23	Michigan	33.8
10	Minnesota	34.9
18	Mississippi	34.1
43	Missouri	31.4
21	Montana	33.9
5	Nebraska	35.8
24	Nevada	33.7
29	New Hampshire	33.4
31	New Jersey	33.3
10	New Mexico	34.9
42	New York	31.7
36	North Carolina	32.7
2	North Dakota	38.7
40	Ohio	32.3
19	Oklahoma	34.0
27	Oregon	33.6
48	Pennsylvania	29.5
37	Rhode Island	32.6
14	South Carolina	34.7
4	South Dakota	37.2
24	Tennessee	33.7
33	Texas	33.1
41	Utah	32.0
32	Vermont	33.2
21	Virginia	33.9
24	Washington	33.7
17	West Virginia	34.5
10	Wisconsin	34.9
3	Wyoming	38.0

RANK ORDER

RANK	STATE	PERCENT
1	Alaska	41.7
2	North Dakota	38.7
3	Wyoming	38.0
4	South Dakota	37.2
5	Arkansas	35.8
5	Nebraska	35.8
7	Georgia	35.2
8	Alabama	35.1
9	Illinois	35.0
10	Minnesota	34.9
10	New Mexico	34.9
10	Wisconsin	34.9
13	Hawaii	34.8
14	Idaho	34.7
14	Indiana	34.7
14	South Carolina	34.7
17	West Virginia	34.5
18	Mississippi	34.1
19	Maine	34.0
19	Oklahoma	34.0
21	Montana	33.9
21	Virginia	33.9
23	Michigan	33.8
24	Nevada	33.7
24	Tennessee	33.7
24	Washington	33.7
27	Oregon	33.6
28	Kentucky	33.5
29	Kansas	33.4
29	New Hampshire	33.4
31	New Jersey	33.3
32	Vermont	33.2
33	Louisiana	33.1
33	Texas	33.1
35	Iowa	32.8
36	North Carolina	32.7
37	Rhode Island	32.6
38	California	32.5
39	Colorado	32.4
40	Ohio	32.3
41	Utah	32.0
42	New York	31.7
43	Missouri	31.4
44	Arizona	31.0
45	Connecticut	30.9
45	Delaware	30.9
47	Maryland	29.6
48	Pennsylvania	29.5
49	Florida	29.2
50	Massachusetts	28.7

District of Columbia 28.3

Source: CQ Press using data from American Medical Association (Chicago, Illinois)
"Physician Characteristics and Distribution in the U.S." (2008 Edition)

*As of December 31, 2006. National percent does not include physicians in U.S. territories and possessions. Primary Care Specialties include Family Practice, General Practice, Internal Medicine, Obstetrics/Gynecology, and Pediatrics excluding subspecialties within each category.

Percent of Population Lacking Access to Primary Care in 2007

National Percent = 11.1% of Population*

<table>
<tr><td colspan="3">ALPHA ORDER</td><td colspan="3">RANK ORDER</td></tr>
<tr><td>RANK</td><td>STATE</td><td>PERCENT</td><td>RANK</td><td>STATE</td><td>PERCENT</td></tr>
<tr><td>5</td><td>Alabama</td><td>22.0</td><td>1</td><td>Louisiana</td><td>35.8</td></tr>
<tr><td>25</td><td>Alaska</td><td>10.6</td><td>2</td><td>Mississippi</td><td>31.7</td></tr>
<tr><td>18</td><td>Arizona</td><td>13.1</td><td>3</td><td>New Mexico</td><td>30.0</td></tr>
<tr><td>28</td><td>Arkansas</td><td>9.8</td><td>4</td><td>South Dakota</td><td>24.5</td></tr>
<tr><td>32</td><td>California</td><td>8.9</td><td>5</td><td>Alabama</td><td>22.0</td></tr>
<tr><td>30</td><td>Colorado</td><td>9.4</td><td>6</td><td>North Dakota</td><td>20.9</td></tr>
<tr><td>34</td><td>Connecticut</td><td>8.5</td><td>7</td><td>Wyoming</td><td>20.5</td></tr>
<tr><td>17</td><td>Delaware</td><td>13.2</td><td>8</td><td>Montana</td><td>20.2</td></tr>
<tr><td>12</td><td>Florida</td><td>14.9</td><td>9</td><td>Missouri</td><td>19.6</td></tr>
<tr><td>14</td><td>Georgia</td><td>14.4</td><td>10</td><td>Idaho</td><td>16.9</td></tr>
<tr><td>48</td><td>Hawaii</td><td>3.6</td><td>11</td><td>Illinois</td><td>15.7</td></tr>
<tr><td>10</td><td>Idaho</td><td>16.9</td><td>12</td><td>Florida</td><td>14.9</td></tr>
<tr><td>11</td><td>Illinois</td><td>15.7</td><td>13</td><td>Oklahoma</td><td>14.7</td></tr>
<tr><td>35</td><td>Indiana</td><td>8.1</td><td>14</td><td>Georgia</td><td>14.4</td></tr>
<tr><td>36</td><td>Iowa</td><td>7.7</td><td>15</td><td>Nevada</td><td>14.3</td></tr>
<tr><td>26</td><td>Kansas</td><td>10.3</td><td>15</td><td>South Carolina</td><td>14.3</td></tr>
<tr><td>22</td><td>Kentucky</td><td>11.3</td><td>17</td><td>Delaware</td><td>13.2</td></tr>
<tr><td>1</td><td>Louisiana</td><td>35.8</td><td>18</td><td>Arizona</td><td>13.1</td></tr>
<tr><td>41</td><td>Maine</td><td>5.9</td><td>19</td><td>Tennessee</td><td>12.1</td></tr>
<tr><td>47</td><td>Maryland</td><td>4.8</td><td>19</td><td>Texas</td><td>12.1</td></tr>
<tr><td>39</td><td>Massachusetts</td><td>6.3</td><td>21</td><td>Utah</td><td>11.4</td></tr>
<tr><td>23</td><td>Michigan</td><td>11.0</td><td>22</td><td>Kentucky</td><td>11.3</td></tr>
<tr><td>43</td><td>Minnesota</td><td>5.5</td><td>23</td><td>Michigan</td><td>11.0</td></tr>
<tr><td>2</td><td>Mississippi</td><td>31.7</td><td>24</td><td>New York</td><td>10.9</td></tr>
<tr><td>9</td><td>Missouri</td><td>19.6</td><td>25</td><td>Alaska</td><td>10.6</td></tr>
<tr><td>8</td><td>Montana</td><td>20.2</td><td>26</td><td>Kansas</td><td>10.3</td></tr>
<tr><td>46</td><td>Nebraska</td><td>5.1</td><td>27</td><td>West Virginia</td><td>10.1</td></tr>
<tr><td>15</td><td>Nevada</td><td>14.3</td><td>28</td><td>Arkansas</td><td>9.8</td></tr>
<tr><td>45</td><td>New Hampshire</td><td>5.3</td><td>29</td><td>Wisconsin</td><td>9.6</td></tr>
<tr><td>50</td><td>New Jersey</td><td>2.2</td><td>30</td><td>Colorado</td><td>9.4</td></tr>
<tr><td>3</td><td>New Mexico</td><td>30.0</td><td>31</td><td>Washington</td><td>9.1</td></tr>
<tr><td>24</td><td>New York</td><td>10.9</td><td>32</td><td>California</td><td>8.9</td></tr>
<tr><td>43</td><td>North Carolina</td><td>5.5</td><td>33</td><td>Virginia</td><td>8.6</td></tr>
<tr><td>6</td><td>North Dakota</td><td>20.9</td><td>34</td><td>Connecticut</td><td>8.5</td></tr>
<tr><td>37</td><td>Ohio</td><td>6.7</td><td>35</td><td>Indiana</td><td>8.1</td></tr>
<tr><td>13</td><td>Oklahoma</td><td>14.7</td><td>36</td><td>Iowa</td><td>7.7</td></tr>
<tr><td>38</td><td>Oregon</td><td>6.4</td><td>37</td><td>Ohio</td><td>6.7</td></tr>
<tr><td>42</td><td>Pennsylvania</td><td>5.8</td><td>38</td><td>Oregon</td><td>6.4</td></tr>
<tr><td>39</td><td>Rhode Island</td><td>6.3</td><td>39</td><td>Massachusetts</td><td>6.3</td></tr>
<tr><td>15</td><td>South Carolina</td><td>14.3</td><td>39</td><td>Rhode Island</td><td>6.3</td></tr>
<tr><td>4</td><td>South Dakota</td><td>24.5</td><td>41</td><td>Maine</td><td>5.9</td></tr>
<tr><td>19</td><td>Tennessee</td><td>12.1</td><td>42</td><td>Pennsylvania</td><td>5.8</td></tr>
<tr><td>19</td><td>Texas</td><td>12.1</td><td>43</td><td>Minnesota</td><td>5.5</td></tr>
<tr><td>21</td><td>Utah</td><td>11.4</td><td>43</td><td>North Carolina</td><td>5.5</td></tr>
<tr><td>49</td><td>Vermont</td><td>2.7</td><td>45</td><td>New Hampshire</td><td>5.3</td></tr>
<tr><td>33</td><td>Virginia</td><td>8.6</td><td>46</td><td>Nebraska</td><td>5.1</td></tr>
<tr><td>31</td><td>Washington</td><td>9.1</td><td>47</td><td>Maryland</td><td>4.8</td></tr>
<tr><td>27</td><td>West Virginia</td><td>10.1</td><td>48</td><td>Hawaii</td><td>3.6</td></tr>
<tr><td>29</td><td>Wisconsin</td><td>9.6</td><td>49</td><td>Vermont</td><td>2.7</td></tr>
<tr><td>7</td><td>Wyoming</td><td>20.5</td><td>50</td><td>New Jersey</td><td>2.2</td></tr>
<tr><td></td><td></td><td></td><td></td><td>District of Columbia</td><td>25.7</td></tr>
</table>

Source: CQ Press using data from U.S. Dept. of Health and Human Services, Div. of Shortage Designation
   "Selected Statistics on Health Professional Shortage Areas" (as of June 30, 2007)
*Percent of population considered under-served by primary medical practitioners (Family & General Practice doctors, Internists, Ob/Gyns, and Pediatricians). An under-served population does not have primary medical care within reasonable economic and geographic bounds.

Physicians in General/Family Practice in 2006

National Total = 90,922 Physicians*

ALPHA ORDER					RANK ORDER			

RANK	STATE	PHYSICIANS	% of USA		RANK	STATE	PHYSICIANS	% of USA
25	Alabama	1,335	1.5%		1	California	10,873	12.0%
44	Alaska	394	0.4%		2	Texas	6,361	7.0%
20	Arizona	1,525	1.7%		3	Florida	4,911	5.4%
28	Arkansas	1,237	1.4%		4	Illinois	3,875	4.3%
1	California	10,873	12.0%		5	New York	3,866	4.3%
17	Colorado	1,796	2.0%		6	Pennsylvania	3,741	4.1%
38	Connecticut	602	0.7%		7	Ohio	3,491	3.8%
49	Delaware	250	0.3%		8	Washington	2,970	3.3%
3	Florida	4,911	5.4%		9	North Carolina	2,880	3.2%
15	Georgia	2,344	2.6%		10	Michigan	2,815	3.1%
43	Hawaii	417	0.5%		11	Minnesota	2,799	3.1%
39	Idaho	566	0.6%		12	Virginia	2,690	3.0%
4	Illinois	3,875	4.3%		13	Indiana	2,428	2.7%
13	Indiana	2,428	2.7%		14	Wisconsin	2,421	2.7%
29	Iowa	1,152	1.3%		15	Georgia	2,344	2.6%
30	Kansas	1,112	1.2%		16	Tennessee	1,946	2.1%
24	Kentucky	1,346	1.5%		17	Colorado	1,796	2.0%
26	Louisiana	1,325	1.5%		18	New Jersey	1,609	1.8%
37	Maine	603	0.7%		19	South Carolina	1,575	1.7%
23	Maryland	1,359	1.5%		20	Arizona	1,525	1.7%
27	Massachusetts	1,320	1.5%		21	Oregon	1,399	1.5%
10	Michigan	2,815	3.1%		22	Missouri	1,369	1.5%
11	Minnesota	2,799	3.1%		23	Maryland	1,359	1.5%
33	Mississippi	806	0.9%		24	Kentucky	1,346	1.5%
22	Missouri	1,369	1.5%		25	Alabama	1,335	1.5%
42	Montana	445	0.5%		26	Louisiana	1,325	1.5%
32	Nebraska	881	1.0%		27	Massachusetts	1,320	1.5%
40	Nevada	563	0.6%		28	Arkansas	1,237	1.4%
41	New Hampshire	484	0.5%		29	Iowa	1,152	1.3%
18	New Jersey	1,609	1.8%		30	Kansas	1,112	1.2%
34	New Mexico	791	0.9%		31	Oklahoma	1,064	1.2%
5	New York	3,866	4.3%		32	Nebraska	881	1.0%
9	North Carolina	2,880	3.2%		33	Mississippi	806	0.9%
46	North Dakota	372	0.4%		34	New Mexico	791	0.9%
7	Ohio	3,491	3.8%		35	Utah	742	0.8%
31	Oklahoma	1,064	1.2%		36	West Virginia	672	0.7%
21	Oregon	1,399	1.5%		37	Maine	603	0.7%
6	Pennsylvania	3,741	4.1%		38	Connecticut	602	0.7%
50	Rhode Island	229	0.3%		39	Idaho	566	0.6%
19	South Carolina	1,575	1.7%		40	Nevada	563	0.6%
45	South Dakota	387	0.4%		41	New Hampshire	484	0.5%
16	Tennessee	1,946	2.1%		42	Montana	445	0.5%
2	Texas	6,361	7.0%		43	Hawaii	417	0.5%
35	Utah	742	0.8%		44	Alaska	394	0.4%
47	Vermont	317	0.3%		45	South Dakota	387	0.4%
12	Virginia	2,690	3.0%		46	North Dakota	372	0.4%
8	Washington	2,970	3.3%		47	Vermont	317	0.3%
36	West Virginia	672	0.7%		48	Wyoming	251	0.3%
14	Wisconsin	2,421	2.7%		49	Delaware	250	0.3%
48	Wyoming	251	0.3%		50	Rhode Island	229	0.3%
						District of Columbia	216	0.2%

Source: American Medical Association (Chicago, Illinois)
"Physician Characteristics and Distribution in the U.S." (2008 Edition)
*As of December 31, 2006. Total does not include 2,437 physicians in U.S. territories and possessions.

Rate of Physicians in General/Family Practice in 2006

National Rate = 30 Physicians per 100,000 Population*

ALPHA ORDER

RANK ORDER

RANK	STATE	RATE
34	Alabama	29
1	Alaska	58
41	Arizona	25
11	Arkansas	44
29	California	30
18	Colorado	38
50	Connecticut	17
34	Delaware	29
39	Florida	27
41	Georgia	25
24	Hawaii	33
15	Idaho	39
29	Illinois	30
15	Indiana	39
15	Iowa	39
14	Kansas	40
25	Kentucky	32
28	Louisiana	31
10	Maine	46
43	Maryland	24
47	Massachusetts	21
37	Michigan	28
3	Minnesota	54
37	Mississippi	28
44	Missouri	23
8	Montana	47
5	Nebraska	50
44	Nevada	23
20	New Hampshire	37
49	New Jersey	19
13	New Mexico	41
48	New York	20
25	North Carolina	32
1	North Dakota	58
29	Ohio	30
29	Oklahoma	30
18	Oregon	38
29	Pennsylvania	30
46	Rhode Island	22
22	South Carolina	36
6	South Dakota	49
25	Tennessee	32
39	Texas	27
34	Utah	29
4	Vermont	51
23	Virginia	35
8	Washington	47
20	West Virginia	37
12	Wisconsin	43
6	Wyoming	49

RANK	STATE	RATE
1	Alaska	58
1	North Dakota	58
3	Minnesota	54
4	Vermont	51
5	Nebraska	50
6	South Dakota	49
6	Wyoming	49
8	Montana	47
8	Washington	47
10	Maine	46
11	Arkansas	44
12	Wisconsin	43
13	New Mexico	41
14	Kansas	40
15	Idaho	39
15	Indiana	39
15	Iowa	39
18	Colorado	38
18	Oregon	38
20	New Hampshire	37
20	West Virginia	37
22	South Carolina	36
23	Virginia	35
24	Hawaii	33
25	Kentucky	32
25	North Carolina	32
25	Tennessee	32
28	Louisiana	31
29	California	30
29	Illinois	30
29	Ohio	30
29	Oklahoma	30
29	Pennsylvania	30
34	Alabama	29
34	Delaware	29
34	Utah	29
37	Michigan	28
37	Mississippi	28
39	Florida	27
39	Texas	27
41	Arizona	25
41	Georgia	25
43	Maryland	24
44	Missouri	23
44	Nevada	23
46	Rhode Island	22
47	Massachusetts	21
48	New York	20
49	New Jersey	19
50	Connecticut	17

District of Columbia	37

Source: CQ Press using data from American Medical Association (Chicago, Illinois)
   "Physician Characteristics and Distribution in the U.S." (2008 Edition)
*As of December 31, 2006. National rate does not include physicians in the U.S. territories and possessions.

Average Annual Wages of Family and General Practitioners in 2006

National Average = $149,850*

ALPHA ORDER

RANK	STATE	WAGES
19	Alabama	$155,190
39	Alaska	143,810
41	Arizona	141,270
6	Arkansas	168,530
47	California	136,290
48	Colorado	134,690
32	Connecticut	148,810
36	Delaware	145,960
20	Florida	154,770
22	Georgia	154,160
23	Hawaii	154,130
28	Idaho	152,150
43	Illinois	139,700
24	Indiana	152,680
16	Iowa	156,220
1	Kansas	177,930
26	Kentucky	152,450
3	Louisiana	169,830
45	Maine	137,730
7	Maryland	167,290
13	Massachusetts	157,510
25	Michigan	152,530
29	Minnesota	152,030
5	Mississippi	169,240
14	Missouri	157,330
50	Montana	123,140
4	Nebraska	169,260
12	Nevada	158,080
40	New Hampshire	141,380
33	New Jersey	147,320
31	New Mexico	151,010
11	New York	158,800
9	North Carolina	163,800
17	North Dakota	155,870
15	Ohio	156,720
34	Oklahoma	147,240
37	Oregon	145,770
44	Pennsylvania	138,610
2	Rhode Island	170,600
18	South Carolina	155,750
35	South Dakota	147,100
42	Tennessee	140,410
46	Texas	137,000
30	Utah	151,590
49	Vermont	128,030
21	Virginia	154,580
38	Washington	145,690
10	West Virginia	163,020
8	Wisconsin	167,140
27	Wyoming	152,290

RANK ORDER

RANK	STATE	WAGES
1	Kansas	$177,930
2	Rhode Island	170,600
3	Louisiana	169,830
4	Nebraska	169,260
5	Mississippi	169,240
6	Arkansas	168,530
7	Maryland	167,290
8	Wisconsin	167,140
9	North Carolina	163,800
10	West Virginia	163,020
11	New York	158,800
12	Nevada	158,080
13	Massachusetts	157,510
14	Missouri	157,330
15	Ohio	156,720
16	Iowa	156,220
17	North Dakota	155,870
18	South Carolina	155,750
19	Alabama	155,190
20	Florida	154,770
21	Virginia	154,580
22	Georgia	154,160
23	Hawaii	154,130
24	Indiana	152,680
25	Michigan	152,530
26	Kentucky	152,450
27	Wyoming	152,290
28	Idaho	152,150
29	Minnesota	152,030
30	Utah	151,590
31	New Mexico	151,010
32	Connecticut	148,810
33	New Jersey	147,320
34	Oklahoma	147,240
35	South Dakota	147,100
36	Delaware	145,960
37	Oregon	145,770
38	Washington	145,690
39	Alaska	143,810
40	New Hampshire	141,380
41	Arizona	141,270
42	Tennessee	140,410
43	Illinois	139,700
44	Pennsylvania	138,610
45	Maine	137,730
46	Texas	137,000
47	California	136,290
48	Colorado	134,690
49	Vermont	128,030
50	Montana	123,140

District of Columbia**   NA

Source: U.S. Department of Labor, Bureau of Labor Statistics
    "Occupational Employment and Wages, 2006" (http://www.bls.gov/oes/)
*Does not include self-employed.
**Not available.

Percent of Physicians Who Are Specialists in 2006

National Percent = 73.2% of Physicians*

ALPHA ORDER			RANK ORDER		
RANK	STATE	PERCENT	RANK	STATE	PERCENT
13	Alabama	74.2	1	New Jersey	79.6
44	Alaska	65.8	2	Connecticut	79.5
28	Arizona	70.6	3	Massachusetts	78.8
42	Arkansas	66.6	4	Rhode Island	78.7
23	California	71.8	5	New York	78.6
25	Colorado	71.0	6	Maryland	78.2
2	Connecticut	79.5	7	Missouri	76.8
15	Delaware	73.4	8	Louisiana	75.4
34	Florida	69.3	9	Georgia	75.1
9	Georgia	75.1	10	Tennessee	75.0
11	Hawaii	74.5	11	Hawaii	74.5
48	Idaho	63.9	12	Illinois	74.4
12	Illinois	74.4	13	Alabama	74.2
30	Indiana	70.3	14	Texas	74.0
47	Iowa	64.0	15	Delaware	73.4
40	Kansas	67.1	16	Michigan	73.3
19	Kentucky	72.5	16	Pennsylvania	73.3
8	Louisiana	75.4	18	Ohio	72.6
37	Maine	67.9	19	Kentucky	72.5
6	Maryland	78.2	20	North Carolina	72.4
3	Massachusetts	78.8	21	Utah	72.3
16	Michigan	73.3	22	Nevada	72.0
38	Minnesota	67.3	23	California	71.8
27	Mississippi	70.7	24	Virginia	71.6
7	Missouri	76.8	25	Colorado	71.0
49	Montana	63.3	25	South Carolina	71.0
43	Nebraska	66.0	27	Mississippi	70.7
22	Nevada	72.0	28	Arizona	70.6
31	New Hampshire	69.9	29	Wisconsin	70.5
1	New Jersey	79.6	30	Indiana	70.3
38	New Mexico	67.3	31	New Hampshire	69.9
5	New York	78.6	32	West Virginia	69.6
20	North Carolina	72.4	33	Oregon	69.4
46	North Dakota	64.6	34	Florida	69.3
18	Ohio	72.6	35	Oklahoma	68.6
35	Oklahoma	68.6	36	Vermont	68.4
33	Oregon	69.4	37	Maine	67.9
16	Pennsylvania	73.3	38	Minnesota	67.3
4	Rhode Island	78.7	38	New Mexico	67.3
25	South Carolina	71.0	40	Kansas	67.1
45	South Dakota	65.5	41	Washington	66.8
10	Tennessee	75.0	42	Arkansas	66.6
14	Texas	74.0	43	Nebraska	66.0
21	Utah	72.3	44	Alaska	65.8
36	Vermont	68.4	45	South Dakota	65.5
24	Virginia	71.6	46	North Dakota	64.6
41	Washington	66.8	47	Iowa	64.0
32	West Virginia	69.6	48	Idaho	63.9
29	Wisconsin	70.5	49	Montana	63.3
50	Wyoming	61.0	50	Wyoming	61.0
				District of Columbia	79.8

Source: CQ Press using data from American Medical Association (Chicago, Illinois)
"Physician Characteristics and Distribution in the U.S." (2008 Edition)
*As of December 31, 2006. National percent does not include physicians in the U.S. territories and possessions. Includes physicians in medical, surgical, and other specialties.

Physicians in Medical Specialties in 2006

National Total = 287,149 Physicians*

ALPHA ORDER

ALPHA ORDER   RANK ORDER

RANK	STATE	PHYSICIANS	% of USA		RANK	STATE	PHYSICIANS	% of USA
25	Alabama	3,449	1.2%		1	California	33,679	11.7%
49	Alaska	356	0.1%		2	New York	31,013	10.8%
21	Arizona	4,442	1.5%		3	Texas	16,751	5.8%
31	Arkansas	1,678	0.6%		4	Florida	16,108	5.6%
1	California	33,679	11.7%		5	Pennsylvania	13,341	4.6%
24	Colorado	3,930	1.4%		6	Illinois	13,268	4.6%
16	Connecticut	5,370	1.9%		7	Massachusetts	12,093	4.2%
43	Delaware	770	0.3%		8	New Jersey	11,648	4.1%
4	Florida	16,108	5.6%		9	Ohio	10,808	3.8%
13	Georgia	7,271	2.5%		10	Maryland	9,314	3.2%
38	Hawaii	1,439	0.5%		11	Michigan	8,904	3.1%
45	Idaho	619	0.2%		12	North Carolina	7,777	2.7%
6	Illinois	13,268	4.6%		13	Georgia	7,271	2.5%
22	Indiana	4,287	1.5%		14	Virginia	7,028	2.4%
36	Iowa	1,516	0.5%		15	Tennessee	5,799	2.0%
30	Kansas	1,805	0.6%		16	Connecticut	5,370	1.9%
27	Kentucky	3,186	1.1%		17	Washington	5,306	1.8%
23	Louisiana	3,988	1.4%		18	Missouri	5,281	1.8%
42	Maine	1,109	0.4%		19	Minnesota	4,810	1.7%
10	Maryland	9,314	3.2%		20	Wisconsin	4,593	1.6%
7	Massachusetts	12,093	4.2%		21	Arizona	4,442	1.5%
11	Michigan	8,904	3.1%		22	Indiana	4,287	1.5%
19	Minnesota	4,810	1.7%		23	Louisiana	3,988	1.4%
35	Mississippi	1,625	0.6%		24	Colorado	3,930	1.4%
18	Missouri	5,281	1.8%		25	Alabama	3,449	1.2%
46	Montana	554	0.2%		26	Oregon	3,261	1.1%
40	Nebraska	1,247	0.4%		27	Kentucky	3,186	1.1%
34	Nevada	1,637	0.6%		28	South Carolina	3,143	1.1%
41	New Hampshire	1,176	0.4%		29	Oklahoma	1,927	0.7%
8	New Jersey	11,648	4.1%		30	Kansas	1,805	0.6%
37	New Mexico	1,491	0.5%		31	Arkansas	1,678	0.6%
2	New York	31,013	10.8%		32	Rhode Island	1,672	0.6%
12	North Carolina	7,777	2.7%		33	Utah	1,670	0.6%
48	North Dakota	438	0.2%		34	Nevada	1,637	0.6%
9	Ohio	10,808	3.8%		35	Mississippi	1,625	0.6%
29	Oklahoma	1,927	0.7%		36	Iowa	1,516	0.5%
26	Oregon	3,261	1.1%		37	New Mexico	1,491	0.5%
5	Pennsylvania	13,341	4.6%		38	Hawaii	1,439	0.5%
32	Rhode Island	1,672	0.6%		39	West Virginia	1,338	0.5%
28	South Carolina	3,143	1.1%		40	Nebraska	1,247	0.4%
47	South Dakota	489	0.2%		41	New Hampshire	1,176	0.4%
15	Tennessee	5,799	2.0%		42	Maine	1,109	0.4%
3	Texas	16,751	5.8%		43	Delaware	770	0.3%
33	Utah	1,670	0.6%		44	Vermont	734	0.3%
44	Vermont	734	0.3%		45	Idaho	619	0.2%
14	Virginia	7,028	2.4%		46	Montana	554	0.2%
17	Washington	5,306	1.8%		47	South Dakota	489	0.2%
39	West Virginia	1,338	0.5%		48	North Dakota	438	0.2%
20	Wisconsin	4,593	1.6%		49	Alaska	356	0.1%
50	Wyoming	200	0.1%		50	Wyoming	200	0.1%
						District of Columbia	1,805	0.6%

Source: American Medical Association (Chicago, Illinois)
   "Physician Characteristics and Distribution in the U.S." (2008 Edition)
*As of December 31, 2006. Total does not include 3,507 physicians in U.S. territories and possessions. Medical Specialties are Allergy/Immunology, Cardiovascular Diseases, Dermatology, Gastroenterology, Internal Medicine, Pediatrics, Pediatric Cardiology, and Pulmonary Diseases.

Rate of Nonfederal Physicians in Medical Specialties in 2006

National Rate = 96 Physicians per 100,000 Population*

<table>
<tr><td colspan="3"><u>ALPHA ORDER</u></td><td colspan="3"><u>RANK ORDER</u></td></tr>
<tr><td>RANK</td><td>STATE</td><td>RATE</td><td>RANK</td><td>STATE</td><td>RATE</td></tr>
<tr><td>31</td><td>Alabama</td><td>75</td><td>1</td><td>Massachusetts</td><td>188</td></tr>
<tr><td>47</td><td>Alaska</td><td>53</td><td>2</td><td>Maryland</td><td>166</td></tr>
<tr><td>34</td><td>Arizona</td><td>72</td><td>3</td><td>New York</td><td>161</td></tr>
<tr><td>43</td><td>Arkansas</td><td>60</td><td>4</td><td>Rhode Island</td><td>157</td></tr>
<tr><td>14</td><td>California</td><td>93</td><td>5</td><td>Connecticut</td><td>154</td></tr>
<tr><td>26</td><td>Colorado</td><td>82</td><td>6</td><td>New Jersey</td><td>134</td></tr>
<tr><td>5</td><td>Connecticut</td><td>154</td><td>7</td><td>Vermont</td><td>118</td></tr>
<tr><td>17</td><td>Delaware</td><td>90</td><td>8</td><td>Hawaii</td><td>113</td></tr>
<tr><td>20</td><td>Florida</td><td>89</td><td>9</td><td>Pennsylvania</td><td>108</td></tr>
<tr><td>28</td><td>Georgia</td><td>78</td><td>10</td><td>Illinois</td><td>104</td></tr>
<tr><td>8</td><td>Hawaii</td><td>113</td><td>11</td><td>Tennessee</td><td>95</td></tr>
<tr><td>49</td><td>Idaho</td><td>42</td><td>12</td><td>Louisiana</td><td>94</td></tr>
<tr><td>10</td><td>Illinois</td><td>104</td><td>12</td><td>Ohio</td><td>94</td></tr>
<tr><td>38</td><td>Indiana</td><td>68</td><td>14</td><td>California</td><td>93</td></tr>
<tr><td>48</td><td>Iowa</td><td>51</td><td>14</td><td>Minnesota</td><td>93</td></tr>
<tr><td>40</td><td>Kansas</td><td>65</td><td>16</td><td>Virginia</td><td>92</td></tr>
<tr><td>30</td><td>Kentucky</td><td>76</td><td>17</td><td>Delaware</td><td>90</td></tr>
<tr><td>12</td><td>Louisiana</td><td>94</td><td>17</td><td>Missouri</td><td>90</td></tr>
<tr><td>24</td><td>Maine</td><td>84</td><td>17</td><td>New Hampshire</td><td>90</td></tr>
<tr><td>2</td><td>Maryland</td><td>166</td><td>20</td><td>Florida</td><td>89</td></tr>
<tr><td>1</td><td>Massachusetts</td><td>188</td><td>21</td><td>Michigan</td><td>88</td></tr>
<tr><td>21</td><td>Michigan</td><td>88</td><td>21</td><td>North Carolina</td><td>88</td></tr>
<tr><td>14</td><td>Minnesota</td><td>93</td><td>21</td><td>Oregon</td><td>88</td></tr>
<tr><td>45</td><td>Mississippi</td><td>56</td><td>24</td><td>Maine</td><td>84</td></tr>
<tr><td>17</td><td>Missouri</td><td>90</td><td>25</td><td>Washington</td><td>83</td></tr>
<tr><td>44</td><td>Montana</td><td>59</td><td>26</td><td>Colorado</td><td>82</td></tr>
<tr><td>36</td><td>Nebraska</td><td>71</td><td>26</td><td>Wisconsin</td><td>82</td></tr>
<tr><td>39</td><td>Nevada</td><td>66</td><td>28</td><td>Georgia</td><td>78</td></tr>
<tr><td>17</td><td>New Hampshire</td><td>90</td><td>29</td><td>New Mexico</td><td>77</td></tr>
<tr><td>6</td><td>New Jersey</td><td>134</td><td>30</td><td>Kentucky</td><td>76</td></tr>
<tr><td>29</td><td>New Mexico</td><td>77</td><td>31</td><td>Alabama</td><td>75</td></tr>
<tr><td>3</td><td>New York</td><td>161</td><td>32</td><td>West Virginia</td><td>74</td></tr>
<tr><td>21</td><td>North Carolina</td><td>88</td><td>33</td><td>South Carolina</td><td>73</td></tr>
<tr><td>37</td><td>North Dakota</td><td>69</td><td>34</td><td>Arizona</td><td>72</td></tr>
<tr><td>12</td><td>Ohio</td><td>94</td><td>34</td><td>Texas</td><td>72</td></tr>
<tr><td>46</td><td>Oklahoma</td><td>54</td><td>36</td><td>Nebraska</td><td>71</td></tr>
<tr><td>21</td><td>Oregon</td><td>88</td><td>37</td><td>North Dakota</td><td>69</td></tr>
<tr><td>9</td><td>Pennsylvania</td><td>108</td><td>38</td><td>Indiana</td><td>68</td></tr>
<tr><td>4</td><td>Rhode Island</td><td>157</td><td>39</td><td>Nevada</td><td>66</td></tr>
<tr><td>33</td><td>South Carolina</td><td>73</td><td>40</td><td>Kansas</td><td>65</td></tr>
<tr><td>42</td><td>South Dakota</td><td>62</td><td>40</td><td>Utah</td><td>65</td></tr>
<tr><td>11</td><td>Tennessee</td><td>95</td><td>42</td><td>South Dakota</td><td>62</td></tr>
<tr><td>34</td><td>Texas</td><td>72</td><td>43</td><td>Arkansas</td><td>60</td></tr>
<tr><td>40</td><td>Utah</td><td>65</td><td>44</td><td>Montana</td><td>59</td></tr>
<tr><td>7</td><td>Vermont</td><td>118</td><td>45</td><td>Mississippi</td><td>56</td></tr>
<tr><td>16</td><td>Virginia</td><td>92</td><td>46</td><td>Oklahoma</td><td>54</td></tr>
<tr><td>25</td><td>Washington</td><td>83</td><td>47</td><td>Alaska</td><td>53</td></tr>
<tr><td>32</td><td>West Virginia</td><td>74</td><td>48</td><td>Iowa</td><td>51</td></tr>
<tr><td>26</td><td>Wisconsin</td><td>82</td><td>49</td><td>Idaho</td><td>42</td></tr>
<tr><td>50</td><td>Wyoming</td><td>39</td><td>50</td><td>Wyoming</td><td>39</td></tr>
<tr><td></td><td></td><td></td><td></td><td>District of Columbia</td><td>308</td></tr>
</table>

Source: CQ Press using data from American Medical Association (Chicago, Illinois)
"Physician Characteristics and Distribution in the U.S." (2008 Edition)
*As of December 31, 2006. National rate does not include physicians in U.S. territories and possessions. Medical Specialties are Allergy/Immunology, Cardiovascular Diseases, Dermatology, Gastroenterology, Internal Medicine, Pediatrics, Pediatric Cardiology, and Pulmonary Diseases.

Physicians in Internal Medicine in 2006

National Total = 153,969 Physicians*

ALPHA ORDER

RANK	STATE	PHYSICIANS	% of USA
26	Alabama	1,857	1.2%
49	Alaska	173	0.1%
21	Arizona	2,282	1.5%
36	Arkansas	766	0.5%
1	California	17,928	11.6%
23	Colorado	2,018	1.3%
15	Connecticut	3,131	2.0%
44	Delaware	362	0.2%
3	Florida	8,157	5.3%
13	Georgia	3,841	2.5%
35	Hawaii	799	0.5%
45	Idaho	316	0.2%
5	Illinois	7,601	4.9%
22	Indiana	2,157	1.4%
38	Iowa	721	0.5%
32	Kansas	897	0.6%
27	Kentucky	1,601	1.0%
24	Louisiana	1,970	1.3%
42	Maine	612	0.4%
10	Maryland	5,247	3.4%
7	Massachusetts	7,012	4.6%
11	Michigan	5,036	3.3%
19	Minnesota	2,577	1.7%
33	Mississippi	833	0.5%
18	Missouri	2,793	1.8%
46	Montana	307	0.2%
41	Nebraska	636	0.4%
30	Nevada	945	0.6%
40	New Hampshire	640	0.4%
8	New Jersey	6,234	4.0%
34	New Mexico	814	0.5%
2	New York	17,820	11.6%
12	North Carolina	4,021	2.6%
48	North Dakota	269	0.2%
9	Ohio	5,540	3.6%
29	Oklahoma	990	0.6%
25	Oregon	1,955	1.3%
6	Pennsylvania	7,245	4.7%
31	Rhode Island	936	0.6%
28	South Carolina	1,550	1.0%
47	South Dakota	279	0.2%
16	Tennessee	3,008	2.0%
4	Texas	8,148	5.3%
37	Utah	736	0.5%
43	Vermont	417	0.3%
14	Virginia	3,660	2.4%
17	Washington	2,841	1.8%
39	West Virginia	705	0.5%
20	Wisconsin	2,478	1.6%
50	Wyoming	113	0.1%

RANK ORDER

RANK	STATE	PHYSICIANS	% of USA
1	California	17,928	11.6%
2	New York	17,820	11.6%
3	Florida	8,157	5.3%
4	Texas	8,148	5.3%
5	Illinois	7,601	4.9%
6	Pennsylvania	7,245	4.7%
7	Massachusetts	7,012	4.6%
8	New Jersey	6,234	4.0%
9	Ohio	5,540	3.6%
10	Maryland	5,247	3.4%
11	Michigan	5,036	3.3%
12	North Carolina	4,021	2.6%
13	Georgia	3,841	2.5%
14	Virginia	3,660	2.4%
15	Connecticut	3,131	2.0%
16	Tennessee	3,008	2.0%
17	Washington	2,841	1.8%
18	Missouri	2,793	1.8%
19	Minnesota	2,577	1.7%
20	Wisconsin	2,478	1.6%
21	Arizona	2,282	1.5%
22	Indiana	2,157	1.4%
23	Colorado	2,018	1.3%
24	Louisiana	1,970	1.3%
25	Oregon	1,955	1.3%
26	Alabama	1,857	1.2%
27	Kentucky	1,601	1.0%
28	South Carolina	1,550	1.0%
29	Oklahoma	990	0.6%
30	Nevada	945	0.6%
31	Rhode Island	936	0.6%
32	Kansas	897	0.6%
33	Mississippi	833	0.5%
34	New Mexico	814	0.5%
35	Hawaii	799	0.5%
36	Arkansas	766	0.5%
37	Utah	736	0.5%
38	Iowa	721	0.5%
39	West Virginia	705	0.5%
40	New Hampshire	640	0.4%
41	Nebraska	636	0.4%
42	Maine	612	0.4%
43	Vermont	417	0.3%
44	Delaware	362	0.2%
45	Idaho	316	0.2%
46	Montana	307	0.2%
47	South Dakota	279	0.2%
48	North Dakota	269	0.2%
49	Alaska	173	0.1%
50	Wyoming	113	0.1%
	District of Columbia	995	0.6%

Source: American Medical Association (Chicago, Illinois)
"Physician Characteristics and Distribution in the U.S." (2008 Edition)

*As of December 31, 2006. Total does not include 1,736 physicians in U.S. territories and possessions. Internal Medicine includes Diabetes, Endocrinology, Geriatrics, Hematology, Infectious Diseases, Nephrology, Nutrition, Medical Oncology, and Rheumatology.

Rate of Physicians in Internal Medicine in 2006

National Rate = 52 Physicians per 100,000 Population*

ALPHA ORDER

RANK ORDER

RANK	STATE	RATE		RANK	STATE	RATE
31	Alabama	40		1	Massachusetts	109
47	Alaska	26		2	Maryland	94
35	Arizona	37		3	New York	92
46	Arkansas	27		4	Connecticut	90
15	California	49		5	Rhode Island	88
26	Colorado	42		6	New Jersey	72
4	Connecticut	90		7	Vermont	67
26	Delaware	42		8	Hawaii	62
22	Florida	45		9	Illinois	59
30	Georgia	41		10	Pennsylvania	58
8	Hawaii	62		11	Oregon	53
49	Idaho	22		12	Michigan	50
9	Illinois	59		12	Minnesota	50
40	Indiana	34		12	Tennessee	50
48	Iowa	24		15	California	49
41	Kansas	33		15	New Hampshire	49
33	Kentucky	38		17	Missouri	48
21	Louisiana	46		17	Ohio	48
20	Maine	47		17	Virginia	48
2	Maryland	94		20	Maine	47
1	Massachusetts	109		21	Louisiana	46
12	Michigan	50		22	Florida	45
12	Minnesota	50		22	North Carolina	45
43	Mississippi	29		22	Washington	45
17	Missouri	48		25	Wisconsin	44
42	Montana	32		26	Colorado	42
36	Nebraska	36		26	Delaware	42
33	Nevada	38		26	New Mexico	42
15	New Hampshire	49		26	North Dakota	42
6	New Jersey	72		30	Georgia	41
26	New Mexico	42		31	Alabama	40
3	New York	92		32	West Virginia	39
22	North Carolina	45		33	Kentucky	38
26	North Dakota	42		33	Nevada	38
17	Ohio	48		35	Arizona	37
45	Oklahoma	28		36	Nebraska	36
11	Oregon	53		36	South Carolina	36
10	Pennsylvania	58		38	South Dakota	35
5	Rhode Island	88		38	Texas	35
36	South Carolina	36		40	Indiana	34
38	South Dakota	35		41	Kansas	33
12	Tennessee	50		42	Montana	32
38	Texas	35		43	Mississippi	29
43	Utah	29		43	Utah	29
7	Vermont	67		45	Oklahoma	28
17	Virginia	48		46	Arkansas	27
22	Washington	45		47	Alaska	26
32	West Virginia	39		48	Iowa	24
25	Wisconsin	44		49	Idaho	22
49	Wyoming	22		49	Wyoming	22
					District of Columbia	170

Source: CQ Press using data from American Medical Association (Chicago, Illinois)
    "Physician Characteristics and Distribution in the U.S." (2008 Edition)
*As of December 31, 2006. National rate does not include physicians in U.S. territories and possessions. Internal Medicine includes Diabetes, Endocrinology, Geriatrics, Hematology, Infectious Diseases, Nephrology, Nutrition, Medical Oncology, and Rheumatology.

Physicians in Pediatrics in 2006

National Total = 72,014 Physicians*

ALPHA ORDER					RANK ORDER			
RANK	STATE		PHYSICIANS	% of USA	RANK	STATE	PHYSICIANS	% of USA
27	Alabama		820	1.1%	1	California	8,723	12.1%
46	Alaska		122	0.2%	2	New York	7,378	10.2%
22	Arizona		1,116	1.5%	3	Texas	4,754	6.6%
30	Arkansas		496	0.7%	4	Florida	3,820	5.3%
1	California		8,723	12.1%	5	Illinois	3,131	4.3%
24	Colorado		1,027	1.4%	6	Ohio	3,022	4.2%
18	Connecticut		1,137	1.6%	7	New Jersey	3,008	4.2%
43	Delaware		256	0.4%	8	Pennsylvania	2,953	4.1%
4	Florida		3,820	5.3%	9	Massachusetts	2,698	3.7%
13	Georgia		1,940	2.7%	10	Maryland	2,267	3.1%
33	Hawaii		415	0.6%	11	Michigan	2,190	3.0%
45	Idaho		131	0.2%	12	North Carolina	2,017	2.8%
5	Illinois		3,131	4.3%	13	Georgia	1,940	2.7%
19	Indiana		1,136	1.6%	14	Virginia	1,913	2.7%
36	Iowa		378	0.5%	15	Tennessee	1,542	2.1%
32	Kansas		471	0.7%	16	Washington	1,325	1.8%
25	Kentucky		873	1.2%	17	Missouri	1,311	1.8%
23	Louisiana		1,078	1.5%	18	Connecticut	1,137	1.6%
42	Maine		266	0.4%	19	Indiana	1,136	1.6%
10	Maryland		2,267	3.1%	20	Wisconsin	1,131	1.6%
9	Massachusetts		2,698	3.7%	21	Minnesota	1,119	1.6%
11	Michigan		2,190	3.0%	22	Arizona	1,116	1.5%
21	Minnesota		1,119	1.6%	23	Louisiana	1,078	1.5%
35	Mississippi		391	0.5%	24	Colorado	1,027	1.4%
17	Missouri		1,311	1.8%	25	Kentucky	873	1.2%
47	Montana		115	0.2%	26	South Carolina	850	1.2%
40	Nebraska		328	0.5%	27	Alabama	820	1.1%
38	Nevada		360	0.5%	28	Oregon	697	1.0%
41	New Hampshire		295	0.4%	29	Utah	542	0.8%
7	New Jersey		3,008	4.2%	30	Arkansas	496	0.7%
36	New Mexico		378	0.5%	31	Oklahoma	472	0.7%
2	New York		7,378	10.2%	32	Kansas	471	0.7%
12	North Carolina		2,017	2.8%	33	Hawaii	415	0.6%
49	North Dakota		83	0.1%	34	Rhode Island	411	0.6%
6	Ohio		3,022	4.2%	35	Mississippi	391	0.5%
31	Oklahoma		472	0.7%	36	Iowa	378	0.5%
28	Oregon		697	1.0%	36	New Mexico	378	0.5%
8	Pennsylvania		2,953	4.1%	38	Nevada	360	0.5%
34	Rhode Island		411	0.6%	39	West Virginia	334	0.5%
26	South Carolina		850	1.2%	40	Nebraska	328	0.5%
48	South Dakota		101	0.1%	41	New Hampshire	295	0.4%
15	Tennessee		1,542	2.1%	42	Maine	266	0.4%
3	Texas		4,754	6.6%	43	Delaware	256	0.4%
29	Utah		542	0.8%	44	Vermont	179	0.2%
44	Vermont		179	0.2%	45	Idaho	131	0.2%
14	Virginia		1,913	2.7%	46	Alaska	122	0.2%
16	Washington		1,325	1.8%	47	Montana	115	0.2%
39	West Virginia		334	0.5%	48	South Dakota	101	0.1%
20	Wisconsin		1,131	1.6%	49	North Dakota	83	0.1%
50	Wyoming		47	0.1%	50	Wyoming	47	0.1%
						District of Columbia	461	0.6%

Source: American Medical Association (Chicago, Illinois)
    "Physician Characteristics and Distribution in the U.S." (2008 Edition)
*As of December 31, 2006. Total does not include 1,194 physicians in U.S. territories and possessions. Pediatrics includes
Adolescent Medicine, Neonatal-Perinatal, Pediatric Allergy, Pediatric Endocrinology, Pediatric Pulmonology, Pediatric
Hematology-Oncology, and Pediatric Nephrology.

Rate of Physicians in Pediatrics in 2006

National Rate = 98 Physicians per 100,000 Population 17 Years and Younger*

ALPHA ORDER

ALPHA ORDER

RANK	STATE	RATE
32	Alabama	74
41	Alaska	67
38	Arizona	69
36	Arkansas	72
21	California	92
23	Colorado	88
6	Connecticut	139
9	Delaware	126
17	Florida	95
31	Georgia	79
6	Hawaii	139
50	Idaho	33
16	Illinois	97
36	Indiana	72
44	Iowa	53
40	Kansas	68
25	Kentucky	87
14	Louisiana	99
17	Maine	95
3	Maryland	167
1	Massachusetts	186
23	Michigan	88
22	Minnesota	89
48	Mississippi	51
20	Missouri	93
44	Montana	53
32	Nebraska	74
42	Nevada	57
14	New Hampshire	99
5	New Jersey	144
32	New Mexico	74
4	New York	163
19	North Carolina	94
42	North Dakota	57
10	Ohio	109
44	Oklahoma	53
30	Oregon	81
13	Pennsylvania	105
2	Rhode Island	173
29	South Carolina	82
47	South Dakota	52
11	Tennessee	107
35	Texas	73
38	Utah	69
8	Vermont	134
12	Virginia	106
25	Washington	87
27	West Virginia	86
27	Wisconsin	86
49	Wyoming	39

RANK ORDER

RANK	STATE	RATE
1	Massachusetts	186
2	Rhode Island	173
3	Maryland	167
4	New York	163
5	New Jersey	144
6	Connecticut	139
6	Hawaii	139
8	Vermont	134
9	Delaware	126
10	Ohio	109
11	Tennessee	107
12	Virginia	106
13	Pennsylvania	105
14	Louisiana	99
14	New Hampshire	99
16	Illinois	97
17	Florida	95
17	Maine	95
19	North Carolina	94
20	Missouri	93
21	California	92
22	Minnesota	89
23	Colorado	88
23	Michigan	88
25	Kentucky	87
25	Washington	87
27	West Virginia	86
27	Wisconsin	86
29	South Carolina	82
30	Oregon	81
31	Georgia	79
32	Alabama	74
32	Nebraska	74
32	New Mexico	74
35	Texas	73
36	Arkansas	72
36	Indiana	72
38	Arizona	69
38	Utah	69
40	Kansas	68
41	Alaska	67
42	Nevada	57
42	North Dakota	57
44	Iowa	53
44	Montana	53
44	Oklahoma	53
47	South Dakota	52
48	Mississippi	51
49	Wyoming	39
50	Idaho	33

| | District of Columbia | 401 |

Source: CQ Press using data from American Medical Association (Chicago, Illinois)
"Physician Characteristics and Distribution in the U.S." (2008 Edition)

*As of December 31, 2006. National rate does not include physicians in U.S. territories and possessions. Pediatrics includes Adolescent Medicine, Neonatal-Perinatal, Pediatric Allergy, Pediatric Endocrinology, Pediatric Pulmonology, Pediatric Hematology-Oncology, and Pediatric Nephrology.

Physicians in Surgical Specialties in 2006

National Total = 159,597 Physicians*

ALPHA ORDER

ALPHA ORDER

RANK	STATE	PHYSICIANS	% of USA
25	Alabama	2,275	1.4%
48	Alaska	340	0.2%
22	Arizona	2,559	1.6%
33	Arkansas	1,170	0.7%
1	California	18,664	11.7%
23	Colorado	2,544	1.6%
24	Connecticut	2,512	1.6%
45	Delaware	439	0.3%
4	Florida	9,178	5.8%
12	Georgia	4,437	2.8%
39	Hawaii	809	0.5%
43	Idaho	592	0.4%
6	Illinois	6,561	4.1%
19	Indiana	2,714	1.7%
34	Iowa	1,167	0.7%
30	Kansas	1,289	0.8%
27	Kentucky	2,061	1.3%
20	Louisiana	2,707	1.7%
42	Maine	705	0.4%
13	Maryland	4,212	2.6%
10	Massachusetts	4,702	2.9%
9	Michigan	4,909	3.1%
21	Minnesota	2,687	1.7%
31	Mississippi	1,267	0.8%
17	Missouri	2,909	1.8%
44	Montana	495	0.3%
36	Nebraska	899	0.6%
35	Nevada	925	0.6%
41	New Hampshire	724	0.5%
8	New Jersey	5,305	3.3%
38	New Mexico	825	0.5%
2	New York	13,996	8.8%
11	North Carolina	4,684	2.9%
49	North Dakota	297	0.2%
7	Ohio	6,034	3.8%
29	Oklahoma	1,358	0.9%
28	Oregon	2,048	1.3%
5	Pennsylvania	7,276	4.6%
40	Rhode Island	735	0.5%
26	South Carolina	2,233	1.4%
47	South Dakota	392	0.2%
15	Tennessee	3,583	2.2%
3	Texas	10,636	6.7%
32	Utah	1,174	0.7%
46	Vermont	424	0.3%
14	Virginia	4,206	2.6%
16	Washington	3,140	2.0%
37	West Virginia	887	0.6%
18	Wisconsin	2,798	1.8%
50	Wyoming	230	0.1%

RANK ORDER

RANK	STATE	PHYSICIANS	% of USA
1	California	18,664	11.7%
2	New York	13,996	8.8%
3	Texas	10,636	6.7%
4	Florida	9,178	5.8%
5	Pennsylvania	7,276	4.6%
6	Illinois	6,561	4.1%
7	Ohio	6,034	3.8%
8	New Jersey	5,305	3.3%
9	Michigan	4,909	3.1%
10	Massachusetts	4,702	2.9%
11	North Carolina	4,684	2.9%
12	Georgia	4,437	2.8%
13	Maryland	4,212	2.6%
14	Virginia	4,206	2.6%
15	Tennessee	3,583	2.2%
16	Washington	3,140	2.0%
17	Missouri	2,909	1.8%
18	Wisconsin	2,798	1.8%
19	Indiana	2,714	1.7%
20	Louisiana	2,707	1.7%
21	Minnesota	2,687	1.7%
22	Arizona	2,559	1.6%
23	Colorado	2,544	1.6%
24	Connecticut	2,512	1.6%
25	Alabama	2,275	1.4%
26	South Carolina	2,233	1.4%
27	Kentucky	2,061	1.3%
28	Oregon	2,048	1.3%
29	Oklahoma	1,358	0.9%
30	Kansas	1,289	0.8%
31	Mississippi	1,267	0.8%
32	Utah	1,174	0.7%
33	Arkansas	1,170	0.7%
34	Iowa	1,167	0.7%
35	Nevada	925	0.6%
36	Nebraska	899	0.6%
37	West Virginia	887	0.6%
38	New Mexico	825	0.5%
39	Hawaii	809	0.5%
40	Rhode Island	735	0.5%
41	New Hampshire	724	0.5%
42	Maine	705	0.4%
43	Idaho	592	0.4%
44	Montana	495	0.3%
45	Delaware	439	0.3%
46	Vermont	424	0.3%
47	South Dakota	392	0.2%
48	Alaska	340	0.2%
49	North Dakota	297	0.2%
50	Wyoming	230	0.1%
	District of Columbia	890	0.6%

Source: American Medical Association (Chicago, Illinois)
   "Physician Characteristics and Distribution in the U.S." (2008 Edition)

*As of December 31, 2006. Total does not include 1,773 physicians in U.S. territories and possessions. Surgical Specialties include Colon and Rectal, General, Neurological, Obstetrics & Gynecology, Ophthalmology, Orthopedic, Otolaryngology, Plastic, Thoracic, and Urological Surgeries.

Rate of Physicians in Surgical Specialties in 2006

National Rate = 53 Physicians per 100,000 Population*

<table>
<tr><td colspan="3">ALPHA ORDER</td><td colspan="3">RANK ORDER</td></tr>
<tr><th>RANK</th><th>STATE</th><th>RATE</th><th>RANK</th><th>STATE</th><th>RATE</th></tr>
<tr><td>27</td><td>Alabama</td><td>50</td><td>1</td><td>Maryland</td><td>75</td></tr>
<tr><td>27</td><td>Alaska</td><td>50</td><td>2</td><td>Massachusetts</td><td>73</td></tr>
<tr><td>44</td><td>Arizona</td><td>42</td><td>2</td><td>New York</td><td>73</td></tr>
<tr><td>44</td><td>Arkansas</td><td>42</td><td>4</td><td>Connecticut</td><td>72</td></tr>
<tr><td>22</td><td>California</td><td>51</td><td>5</td><td>Rhode Island</td><td>69</td></tr>
<tr><td>16</td><td>Colorado</td><td>53</td><td>6</td><td>Vermont</td><td>68</td></tr>
<tr><td>4</td><td>Connecticut</td><td>72</td><td>7</td><td>Louisiana</td><td>64</td></tr>
<tr><td>22</td><td>Delaware</td><td>51</td><td>8</td><td>Hawaii</td><td>63</td></tr>
<tr><td>22</td><td>Florida</td><td>51</td><td>9</td><td>New Jersey</td><td>61</td></tr>
<tr><td>36</td><td>Georgia</td><td>47</td><td>10</td><td>Pennsylvania</td><td>59</td></tr>
<tr><td>8</td><td>Hawaii</td><td>63</td><td>10</td><td>Tennessee</td><td>59</td></tr>
<tr><td>47</td><td>Idaho</td><td>40</td><td>12</td><td>New Hampshire</td><td>55</td></tr>
<tr><td>22</td><td>Illinois</td><td>51</td><td>12</td><td>Oregon</td><td>55</td></tr>
<tr><td>43</td><td>Indiana</td><td>43</td><td>12</td><td>Virginia</td><td>55</td></tr>
<tr><td>48</td><td>Iowa</td><td>39</td><td>15</td><td>Maine</td><td>54</td></tr>
<tr><td>36</td><td>Kansas</td><td>47</td><td>16</td><td>Colorado</td><td>53</td></tr>
<tr><td>32</td><td>Kentucky</td><td>49</td><td>16</td><td>North Carolina</td><td>53</td></tr>
<tr><td>7</td><td>Louisiana</td><td>64</td><td>16</td><td>Ohio</td><td>53</td></tr>
<tr><td>15</td><td>Maine</td><td>54</td><td>19</td><td>Minnesota</td><td>52</td></tr>
<tr><td>1</td><td>Maryland</td><td>75</td><td>19</td><td>Montana</td><td>52</td></tr>
<tr><td>2</td><td>Massachusetts</td><td>73</td><td>19</td><td>South Carolina</td><td>52</td></tr>
<tr><td>32</td><td>Michigan</td><td>49</td><td>22</td><td>California</td><td>51</td></tr>
<tr><td>19</td><td>Minnesota</td><td>52</td><td>22</td><td>Delaware</td><td>51</td></tr>
<tr><td>42</td><td>Mississippi</td><td>44</td><td>22</td><td>Florida</td><td>51</td></tr>
<tr><td>27</td><td>Missouri</td><td>50</td><td>22</td><td>Illinois</td><td>51</td></tr>
<tr><td>19</td><td>Montana</td><td>52</td><td>22</td><td>Nebraska</td><td>51</td></tr>
<tr><td>22</td><td>Nebraska</td><td>51</td><td>27</td><td>Alabama</td><td>50</td></tr>
<tr><td>50</td><td>Nevada</td><td>37</td><td>27</td><td>Alaska</td><td>50</td></tr>
<tr><td>12</td><td>New Hampshire</td><td>55</td><td>27</td><td>Missouri</td><td>50</td></tr>
<tr><td>9</td><td>New Jersey</td><td>61</td><td>27</td><td>South Dakota</td><td>50</td></tr>
<tr><td>44</td><td>New Mexico</td><td>42</td><td>27</td><td>Wisconsin</td><td>50</td></tr>
<tr><td>2</td><td>New York</td><td>73</td><td>32</td><td>Kentucky</td><td>49</td></tr>
<tr><td>16</td><td>North Carolina</td><td>53</td><td>32</td><td>Michigan</td><td>49</td></tr>
<tr><td>36</td><td>North Dakota</td><td>47</td><td>32</td><td>Washington</td><td>49</td></tr>
<tr><td>16</td><td>Ohio</td><td>53</td><td>32</td><td>West Virginia</td><td>49</td></tr>
<tr><td>49</td><td>Oklahoma</td><td>38</td><td>36</td><td>Georgia</td><td>47</td></tr>
<tr><td>12</td><td>Oregon</td><td>55</td><td>36</td><td>Kansas</td><td>47</td></tr>
<tr><td>10</td><td>Pennsylvania</td><td>59</td><td>36</td><td>North Dakota</td><td>47</td></tr>
<tr><td>5</td><td>Rhode Island</td><td>69</td><td>39</td><td>Utah</td><td>46</td></tr>
<tr><td>19</td><td>South Carolina</td><td>52</td><td>40</td><td>Texas</td><td>45</td></tr>
<tr><td>27</td><td>South Dakota</td><td>50</td><td>40</td><td>Wyoming</td><td>45</td></tr>
<tr><td>10</td><td>Tennessee</td><td>59</td><td>42</td><td>Mississippi</td><td>44</td></tr>
<tr><td>40</td><td>Texas</td><td>45</td><td>43</td><td>Indiana</td><td>43</td></tr>
<tr><td>39</td><td>Utah</td><td>46</td><td>44</td><td>Arizona</td><td>42</td></tr>
<tr><td>6</td><td>Vermont</td><td>68</td><td>44</td><td>Arkansas</td><td>42</td></tr>
<tr><td>12</td><td>Virginia</td><td>55</td><td>44</td><td>New Mexico</td><td>42</td></tr>
<tr><td>32</td><td>Washington</td><td>49</td><td>47</td><td>Idaho</td><td>40</td></tr>
<tr><td>32</td><td>West Virginia</td><td>49</td><td>48</td><td>Iowa</td><td>39</td></tr>
<tr><td>27</td><td>Wisconsin</td><td>50</td><td>49</td><td>Oklahoma</td><td>38</td></tr>
<tr><td>40</td><td>Wyoming</td><td>45</td><td>50</td><td>Nevada</td><td>37</td></tr>
<tr><td colspan="3"></td><td colspan="2">District of Columbia</td><td>152</td></tr>
</table>

Source: CQ Press using data from American Medical Association (Chicago, Illinois)
   "Physician Characteristics and Distribution in the U.S." (2008 Edition)
*As of December 31, 2006. National rate does not include physicians in U.S. territories and possessions. Surgical Specialties include Colon and Rectal, General, Neurological, Obstetrics & Gynecology, Ophthalmology, Orthopedic, Otolaryngology, Plastic, Thoracic, and Urological Surgeries.

Average Annual Wages of Surgeons in 2006

National Average = $184,150*

ALPHA ORDER				RANK ORDER		
RANK	STATE	WAGES		RANK	STATE	WAGES
21	Alabama	$183,530		1	Massachusetts	$197,940
NA	Alaska**	NA		2	Georgia	196,640
6	Arizona	193,540		3	Wisconsin	195,440
12	Arkansas	190,330		4	South Carolina	194,290
30	California	165,570		5	South Dakota	194,140
14	Colorado	187,810		6	Arizona	193,540
19	Connecticut	185,090		7	Washington	193,380
27	Delaware	174,010		8	Missouri	193,180
29	Florida	165,650		9	Tennessee	192,470
2	Georgia	196,640		10	Michigan	192,280
NA	Hawaii**	NA		11	North Carolina	191,460
NA	Idaho**	NA		12	Arkansas	190,330
26	Illinois	177,200		13	Ohio	188,210
NA	Indiana**	NA		14	Colorado	187,810
23	Iowa	180,050		15	Maryland	187,800
NA	Kansas**	NA		16	Texas	187,720
NA	Kentucky**	NA		17	Nevada	187,630
24	Louisiana	179,670		18	New Mexico	186,460
NA	Maine**	NA		19	Connecticut	185,090
15	Maryland	187,800		20	Oregon	184,510
1	Massachusetts	197,940		21	Alabama	183,530
10	Michigan	192,280		22	West Virginia	180,420
NA	Minnesota**	NA		23	Iowa	180,050
NA	Mississippi**	NA		24	Louisiana	179,670
8	Missouri	193,180		25	New York	179,630
NA	Montana**	NA		26	Illinois	177,200
31	Nebraska	149,180		27	Delaware	174,010
17	Nevada	187,630		28	Pennsylvania	169,940
NA	New Hampshire**	NA		29	Florida	165,650
NA	New Jersey**	NA		30	California	165,570
18	New Mexico	186,460		31	Nebraska	149,180
25	New York	179,630		32	North Dakota	132,690
11	North Carolina	191,460		NA	Alaska**	NA
32	North Dakota	132,690		NA	Hawaii**	NA
13	Ohio	188,210		NA	Idaho**	NA
NA	Oklahoma**	NA		NA	Indiana**	NA
20	Oregon	184,510		NA	Kansas**	NA
28	Pennsylvania	169,940		NA	Kentucky**	NA
NA	Rhode Island**	NA		NA	Maine**	NA
4	South Carolina	194,290		NA	Minnesota**	NA
5	South Dakota	194,140		NA	Mississippi**	NA
9	Tennessee	192,470		NA	Montana**	NA
16	Texas	187,720		NA	New Hampshire**	NA
NA	Utah**	NA		NA	New Jersey**	NA
NA	Vermont**	NA		NA	Oklahoma**	NA
NA	Virginia**	NA		NA	Rhode Island**	NA
7	Washington	193,380		NA	Utah**	NA
22	West Virginia	180,420		NA	Vermont**	NA
3	Wisconsin	195,440		NA	Virginia**	NA
NA	Wyoming**	NA		NA	Wyoming**	NA
					District of Columbia**	NA

Source: U.S. Department of Labor, Bureau of Labor Statistics
"Occupational Employment and Wages, 2006" (http://www.bls.gov/oes/)
*Does not include self-employed.
**Not available.

Physicians in General Surgery in 2006

National Total = 37,096 Physicians*

ALPHA ORDER

RANK ORDER

RANK	STATE	PHYSICIANS	% of USA
25	Alabama	539	1.5%
49	Alaska	77	0.2%
20	Arizona	607	1.6%
32	Arkansas	279	0.8%
1	California	4,013	10.8%
23	Colorado	580	1.6%
24	Connecticut	568	1.5%
45	Delaware	114	0.3%
5	Florida	1,848	5.0%
12	Georgia	1,024	2.8%
41	Hawaii	174	0.5%
43	Idaho	137	0.4%
6	Illinois	1,521	4.1%
22	Indiana	588	1.6%
31	Iowa	305	0.8%
30	Kansas	314	0.8%
27	Kentucky	516	1.4%
20	Louisiana	607	1.6%
39	Maine	194	0.5%
13	Maryland	945	2.5%
9	Massachusetts	1,211	3.3%
8	Michigan	1,267	3.4%
19	Minnesota	633	1.7%
33	Mississippi	277	0.7%
17	Missouri	646	1.7%
46	Montana	109	0.3%
35	Nebraska	239	0.6%
37	Nevada	209	0.6%
40	New Hampshire	175	0.5%
10	New Jersey	1,204	3.2%
38	New Mexico	202	0.5%
2	New York	3,389	9.1%
11	North Carolina	1,094	2.9%
48	North Dakota	85	0.2%
7	Ohio	1,515	4.1%
29	Oklahoma	317	0.9%
28	Oregon	486	1.3%
4	Pennsylvania	1,892	5.1%
41	Rhode Island	174	0.5%
26	South Carolina	536	1.4%
47	South Dakota	107	0.3%
15	Tennessee	909	2.5%
3	Texas	2,308	6.2%
36	Utah	225	0.6%
44	Vermont	121	0.3%
14	Virginia	919	2.5%
16	Washington	714	1.9%
34	West Virginia	243	0.7%
18	Wisconsin	645	1.7%
50	Wyoming	55	0.1%

RANK	STATE	PHYSICIANS	% of USA
1	California	4,013	10.8%
2	New York	3,389	9.1%
3	Texas	2,308	6.2%
4	Pennsylvania	1,892	5.1%
5	Florida	1,848	5.0%
6	Illinois	1,521	4.1%
7	Ohio	1,515	4.1%
8	Michigan	1,267	3.4%
9	Massachusetts	1,211	3.3%
10	New Jersey	1,204	3.2%
11	North Carolina	1,094	2.9%
12	Georgia	1,024	2.8%
13	Maryland	945	2.5%
14	Virginia	919	2.5%
15	Tennessee	909	2.5%
16	Washington	714	1.9%
17	Missouri	646	1.7%
18	Wisconsin	645	1.7%
19	Minnesota	633	1.7%
20	Arizona	607	1.6%
20	Louisiana	607	1.6%
22	Indiana	588	1.6%
23	Colorado	580	1.6%
24	Connecticut	568	1.5%
25	Alabama	539	1.5%
26	South Carolina	536	1.4%
27	Kentucky	516	1.4%
28	Oregon	486	1.3%
29	Oklahoma	317	0.9%
30	Kansas	314	0.8%
31	Iowa	305	0.8%
32	Arkansas	279	0.8%
33	Mississippi	277	0.7%
34	West Virginia	243	0.7%
35	Nebraska	239	0.6%
36	Utah	225	0.6%
37	Nevada	209	0.6%
38	New Mexico	202	0.5%
39	Maine	194	0.5%
40	New Hampshire	175	0.5%
41	Hawaii	174	0.5%
41	Rhode Island	174	0.5%
43	Idaho	137	0.4%
44	Vermont	121	0.3%
45	Delaware	114	0.3%
46	Montana	109	0.3%
47	South Dakota	107	0.3%
48	North Dakota	85	0.2%
49	Alaska	77	0.2%
50	Wyoming	55	0.1%
	District of Columbia	240	0.6%

Source: American Medical Association (Chicago, Illinois)
   "Physician Characteristics and Distribution in the U.S." (2008 Edition)
*As of December 31, 2006. Total does not include 460 physicians in U.S. territories and possessions. General Surgery includes Abdominal, Cardiovascular, Hand, Head and Neck, Pediatric, Traumatic, and Vascular Surgeries.

Rate of Physicians in General Surgery in 2006

National Rate = 12 Physicians per 100,000 Population*

ALPHA ORDER			RANK ORDER		
RANK	STATE	RATE	RANK	STATE	RATE
22	Alabama	12	1	Massachusetts	19
32	Alaska	11	1	Vermont	19
39	Arizona	10	3	New York	18
39	Arkansas	10	4	Maryland	17
32	California	11	5	Connecticut	16
22	Colorado	12	5	Rhode Island	16
5	Connecticut	16	7	Maine	15
15	Delaware	13	7	Pennsylvania	15
39	Florida	10	7	Tennessee	15
32	Georgia	11	10	Hawaii	14
10	Hawaii	14	10	Louisiana	14
46	Idaho	9	10	Nebraska	14
22	Illinois	12	10	New Jersey	14
46	Indiana	9	10	South Dakota	14
39	Iowa	10	15	Delaware	13
32	Kansas	11	15	Michigan	13
22	Kentucky	12	15	New Hampshire	13
10	Louisiana	14	15	North Dakota	13
7	Maine	15	15	Ohio	13
4	Maryland	17	15	Oregon	13
1	Massachusetts	19	15	West Virginia	13
15	Michigan	13	22	Alabama	12
22	Minnesota	12	22	Colorado	12
39	Mississippi	10	22	Illinois	12
32	Missouri	11	22	Kentucky	12
22	Montana	12	22	Minnesota	12
10	Nebraska	14	22	Montana	12
50	Nevada	8	22	North Carolina	12
15	New Hampshire	13	22	South Carolina	12
10	New Jersey	14	22	Virginia	12
39	New Mexico	10	22	Wisconsin	12
3	New York	18	32	Alaska	11
22	North Carolina	12	32	California	11
15	North Dakota	13	32	Georgia	11
15	Ohio	13	32	Kansas	11
46	Oklahoma	9	32	Missouri	11
15	Oregon	13	32	Washington	11
7	Pennsylvania	15	32	Wyoming	11
5	Rhode Island	16	39	Arizona	10
22	South Carolina	12	39	Arkansas	10
10	South Dakota	14	39	Florida	10
7	Tennessee	15	39	Iowa	10
39	Texas	10	39	Mississippi	10
46	Utah	9	39	New Mexico	10
1	Vermont	19	39	Texas	10
22	Virginia	12	46	Idaho	9
32	Washington	11	46	Indiana	9
15	West Virginia	13	46	Oklahoma	9
22	Wisconsin	12	46	Utah	9
32	Wyoming	11	50	Nevada	8

District of Columbia   41

Source: CQ Press using data from American Medical Association (Chicago, Illinois)
"Physician Characteristics and Distribution in the U.S." (2008 Edition)
*As of December 31, 2006. National rate does not include physicians in U.S. territories and possessions. General Surgery includes Abdominal, Cardiovascular, Hand, Head and Neck, Pediatric, Traumatic, and Vascular Surgeries.

Physicians in Obstetrics and Gynecology in 2006

National Total = 41,700 Physicians*

ALPHA ORDER						RANK ORDER			

RANK	STATE	PHYSICIANS	% of USA	RANK	STATE	PHYSICIANS	% of USA
26	Alabama	563	1.4%	1	California	4,977	11.9%
47	Alaska	84	0.2%	2	New York	3,778	9.1%
21	Arizona	681	1.6%	3	Texas	2,968	7.1%
33	Arkansas	267	0.6%	4	Florida	2,238	5.4%
1	California	4,977	11.9%	5	Illinois	1,859	4.5%
22	Colorado	660	1.6%	6	Pennsylvania	1,678	4.0%
18	Connecticut	710	1.7%	7	New Jersey	1,531	3.7%
46	Delaware	102	0.2%	8	Ohio	1,501	3.6%
4	Florida	2,238	5.4%	9	Georgia	1,382	3.3%
9	Georgia	1,382	3.3%	10	Michigan	1,367	3.3%
35	Hawaii	247	0.6%	11	North Carolina	1,286	3.1%
43	Idaho	142	0.3%	12	Virginia	1,211	2.9%
5	Illinois	1,859	4.5%	13	Massachusetts	1,140	2.7%
19	Indiana	702	1.7%	14	Maryland	1,132	2.7%
37	Iowa	216	0.5%	15	Tennessee	894	2.1%
32	Kansas	289	0.7%	16	Washington	767	1.8%
28	Kentucky	520	1.2%	17	Missouri	729	1.7%
20	Louisiana	695	1.7%	18	Connecticut	710	1.7%
42	Maine	166	0.4%	19	Indiana	702	1.7%
14	Maryland	1,132	2.7%	20	Louisiana	695	1.7%
13	Massachusetts	1,140	2.7%	21	Arizona	681	1.6%
10	Michigan	1,367	3.3%	22	Colorado	660	1.6%
24	Minnesota	605	1.5%	23	Wisconsin	628	1.5%
29	Mississippi	333	0.8%	24	Minnesota	605	1.5%
17	Missouri	729	1.7%	25	South Carolina	594	1.4%
44	Montana	113	0.3%	26	Alabama	563	1.4%
41	Nebraska	190	0.5%	27	Oregon	525	1.3%
34	Nevada	258	0.6%	28	Kentucky	520	1.2%
40	New Hampshire	197	0.5%	29	Mississippi	333	0.8%
7	New Jersey	1,531	3.7%	30	Oklahoma	331	0.8%
36	New Mexico	219	0.5%	31	Utah	290	0.7%
2	New York	3,778	9.1%	32	Kansas	289	0.7%
11	North Carolina	1,286	3.1%	33	Arkansas	267	0.6%
50	North Dakota	50	0.1%	34	Nevada	258	0.6%
8	Ohio	1,501	3.6%	35	Hawaii	247	0.6%
30	Oklahoma	331	0.8%	36	New Mexico	219	0.5%
27	Oregon	525	1.3%	37	Iowa	216	0.5%
6	Pennsylvania	1,678	4.0%	38	West Virginia	210	0.5%
39	Rhode Island	203	0.5%	39	Rhode Island	203	0.5%
25	South Carolina	594	1.4%	40	New Hampshire	197	0.5%
48	South Dakota	78	0.2%	41	Nebraska	190	0.5%
15	Tennessee	894	2.1%	42	Maine	166	0.4%
3	Texas	2,968	7.1%	43	Idaho	142	0.3%
31	Utah	290	0.7%	44	Montana	113	0.3%
45	Vermont	112	0.3%	45	Vermont	112	0.3%
12	Virginia	1,211	2.9%	46	Delaware	102	0.2%
16	Washington	767	1.8%	47	Alaska	84	0.2%
38	West Virginia	210	0.5%	48	South Dakota	78	0.2%
23	Wisconsin	628	1.5%	49	Wyoming	51	0.1%
49	Wyoming	51	0.1%	50	North Dakota	50	0.1%
					District of Columbia	231	0.6%

Source: American Medical Association (Chicago, Illinois)
"Physician Characteristics and Distribution in the U.S." (2008 Edition)
*As of December 31, 2006. Total does not include 633 physicians in U.S. territories and possessions. Obstetrics and Gynecology includes Gynecology and Oncology, Maternal and Fetal Medicine, and Reproductive Endocrinology.

Rate of Physicians in Obstetrics and Gynecology in 2006

National Rate = 27 Physicians per 100,000 Female Population*

ALPHA ORDER

RANK	STATE	RATE
26	Alabama	24
21	Alaska	26
36	Arizona	22
47	Arkansas	19
18	California	27
15	Colorado	28
1	Connecticut	39
32	Delaware	23
26	Florida	24
12	Georgia	29
3	Hawaii	38
44	Idaho	20
12	Illinois	29
36	Indiana	22
50	Iowa	14
41	Kansas	21
26	Kentucky	24
9	Louisiana	32
24	Maine	25
1	Maryland	39
7	Massachusetts	34
18	Michigan	27
32	Minnesota	23
36	Mississippi	22
26	Missouri	24
26	Montana	24
41	Nebraska	21
41	Nevada	21
11	New Hampshire	30
7	New Jersey	34
36	New Mexico	22
3	New York	38
15	North Carolina	28
49	North Dakota	16
21	Ohio	26
48	Oklahoma	18
15	Oregon	28
21	Pennsylvania	26
5	Rhode Island	37
18	South Carolina	27
44	South Dakota	20
12	Tennessee	29
24	Texas	25
32	Utah	23
6	Vermont	35
10	Virginia	31
26	Washington	24
32	West Virginia	23
36	Wisconsin	22
44	Wyoming	20

RANK ORDER

RANK	STATE	RATE
1	Connecticut	39
1	Maryland	39
3	Hawaii	38
3	New York	38
5	Rhode Island	37
6	Vermont	35
7	Massachusetts	34
7	New Jersey	34
9	Louisiana	32
10	Virginia	31
11	New Hampshire	30
12	Georgia	29
12	Illinois	29
12	Tennessee	29
15	Colorado	28
15	North Carolina	28
15	Oregon	28
18	California	27
18	Michigan	27
18	South Carolina	27
21	Alaska	26
21	Ohio	26
21	Pennsylvania	26
24	Maine	25
24	Texas	25
26	Alabama	24
26	Florida	24
26	Kentucky	24
26	Missouri	24
26	Montana	24
26	Washington	24
32	Delaware	23
32	Minnesota	23
32	Utah	23
32	West Virginia	23
36	Arizona	22
36	Indiana	22
36	Mississippi	22
36	New Mexico	22
36	Wisconsin	22
41	Kansas	21
41	Nebraska	21
41	Nevada	21
44	Idaho	20
44	South Dakota	20
44	Wyoming	20
47	Arkansas	19
48	Oklahoma	18
49	North Dakota	16
50	Iowa	14

District of Columbia	75

Source: CQ Press using data from American Medical Association (Chicago, Illinois)
"Physician Characteristics and Distribution in the U.S." (2008 Edition)
*As of December 31, 2006. National rate does not include physicians in U.S. territories and possessions. Obstetrics and Gynecology includes Gynecology and Oncology, Maternal and Fetal Medicine, and Reproductive Endocrinology.

Physicians in Ophthalmology in 2006

National Total = 17,875 Physicians*

ALPHA ORDER

RANK	STATE	PHYSICIANS	% of USA
27	Alabama	218	1.2%
49	Alaska	29	0.2%
23	Arizona	276	1.5%
34	Arkansas	134	0.7%
1	California	2,177	12.2%
24	Colorado	272	1.5%
19	Connecticut	306	1.7%
45	Delaware	43	0.2%
3	Florida	1,158	6.5%
14	Georgia	419	2.3%
35	Hawaii	96	0.5%
43	Idaho	55	0.3%
6	Illinois	736	4.1%
22	Indiana	280	1.6%
29	Iowa	158	0.9%
30	Kansas	154	0.9%
28	Kentucky	188	1.1%
21	Louisiana	294	1.6%
41	Maine	70	0.4%
10	Maryland	537	3.0%
11	Massachusetts	516	2.9%
9	Michigan	556	3.1%
20	Minnesota	304	1.7%
32	Mississippi	138	0.8%
18	Missouri	318	1.8%
44	Montana	47	0.3%
37	Nebraska	94	0.5%
38	Nevada	92	0.5%
42	New Hampshire	68	0.4%
8	New Jersey	617	3.5%
40	New Mexico	74	0.4%
2	New York	1,756	9.8%
12	North Carolina	461	2.6%
48	North Dakota	34	0.2%
7	Ohio	631	3.5%
31	Oklahoma	145	0.8%
26	Oregon	224	1.3%
5	Pennsylvania	864	4.8%
39	Rhode Island	78	0.4%
25	South Carolina	241	1.3%
46	South Dakota	42	0.2%
15	Tennessee	349	2.0%
4	Texas	1,105	6.2%
33	Utah	137	0.8%
47	Vermont	36	0.2%
12	Virginia	461	2.6%
16	Washington	339	1.9%
36	West Virginia	95	0.5%
17	Wisconsin	330	1.8%
50	Wyoming	16	0.1%

RANK ORDER

RANK	STATE	PHYSICIANS	% of USA
1	California	2,177	12.2%
2	New York	1,756	9.8%
3	Florida	1,158	6.5%
4	Texas	1,105	6.2%
5	Pennsylvania	864	4.8%
6	Illinois	736	4.1%
7	Ohio	631	3.5%
8	New Jersey	617	3.5%
9	Michigan	556	3.1%
10	Maryland	537	3.0%
11	Massachusetts	516	2.9%
12	North Carolina	461	2.6%
12	Virginia	461	2.6%
14	Georgia	419	2.3%
15	Tennessee	349	2.0%
16	Washington	339	1.9%
17	Wisconsin	330	1.8%
18	Missouri	318	1.8%
19	Connecticut	306	1.7%
20	Minnesota	304	1.7%
21	Louisiana	294	1.6%
22	Indiana	280	1.6%
23	Arizona	276	1.5%
24	Colorado	272	1.5%
25	South Carolina	241	1.3%
26	Oregon	224	1.3%
27	Alabama	218	1.2%
28	Kentucky	188	1.1%
29	Iowa	158	0.9%
30	Kansas	154	0.9%
31	Oklahoma	145	0.8%
32	Mississippi	138	0.8%
33	Utah	137	0.8%
34	Arkansas	134	0.7%
35	Hawaii	96	0.5%
36	West Virginia	95	0.5%
37	Nebraska	94	0.5%
38	Nevada	92	0.5%
39	Rhode Island	78	0.4%
40	New Mexico	74	0.4%
41	Maine	70	0.4%
42	New Hampshire	68	0.4%
43	Idaho	55	0.3%
44	Montana	47	0.3%
45	Delaware	43	0.2%
46	South Dakota	42	0.2%
47	Vermont	36	0.2%
48	North Dakota	34	0.2%
49	Alaska	29	0.2%
50	Wyoming	16	0.1%
	District of Columbia	107	0.6%

Source: American Medical Association (Chicago, Illinois)
"Physician Characteristics and Distribution in the U.S." (2008 Edition)
*As of December 31, 2006. Total does not include 183 physicians in U.S. territories and possessions. Ophthalmology is the branch of medicine dealing with the anatomy, functions, and diseases of the eye.

Rate of Physicians in Ophthalmology in 2006

National Rate = 6 Physicians per 100,000 Population*

ALPHA ORDER

RANK	STATE	RATE
24	Alabama	5
41	Alaska	4
41	Arizona	4
24	Arkansas	5
10	California	6
10	Colorado	6
2	Connecticut	9
24	Delaware	5
10	Florida	6
41	Georgia	4
4	Hawaii	8
41	Idaho	4
10	Illinois	6
41	Indiana	4
24	Iowa	5
10	Kansas	6
41	Kentucky	4
6	Louisiana	7
24	Maine	5
1	Maryland	10
4	Massachusetts	8
10	Michigan	6
10	Minnesota	6
24	Mississippi	5
24	Missouri	5
24	Montana	5
24	Nebraska	5
41	Nevada	4
24	New Hampshire	5
6	New Jersey	7
41	New Mexico	4
2	New York	9
24	North Carolina	5
24	North Dakota	5
10	Ohio	6
41	Oklahoma	4
10	Oregon	6
6	Pennsylvania	7
6	Rhode Island	7
10	South Carolina	6
24	South Dakota	5
10	Tennessee	6
24	Texas	5
24	Utah	5
10	Vermont	6
10	Virginia	6
24	Washington	5
24	West Virginia	5
10	Wisconsin	6
50	Wyoming	3

RANK ORDER

RANK	STATE	RATE
1	Maryland	10
2	Connecticut	9
2	New York	9
4	Hawaii	8
4	Massachusetts	8
6	Louisiana	7
6	New Jersey	7
6	Pennsylvania	7
6	Rhode Island	7
10	California	6
10	Colorado	6
10	Florida	6
10	Illinois	6
10	Kansas	6
10	Michigan	6
10	Minnesota	6
10	Ohio	6
10	Oregon	6
10	South Carolina	6
10	Tennessee	6
10	Vermont	6
10	Virginia	6
10	Wisconsin	6
24	Alabama	5
24	Arkansas	5
24	Delaware	5
24	Iowa	5
24	Maine	5
24	Mississippi	5
24	Missouri	5
24	Montana	5
24	Nebraska	5
24	New Hampshire	5
24	North Carolina	5
24	North Dakota	5
24	South Dakota	5
24	Texas	5
24	Utah	5
24	Washington	5
24	West Virginia	5
41	Alaska	4
41	Arizona	4
41	Georgia	4
41	Idaho	4
41	Indiana	4
41	Kentucky	4
41	Nevada	4
41	New Mexico	4
41	Oklahoma	4
50	Wyoming	3

District of Columbia — 18

Source: CQ Press using data from American Medical Association (Chicago, Illinois)
   "Physician Characteristics and Distribution in the U.S." (2008 Edition)
*As of December 31, 2006. National rate does not include physicians in U.S. territories and possessions. Ophthalmology is the branch of medicine dealing with the anatomy, functions, and diseases of the eye.

Physicians in Orthopedic Surgery in 2006

National Total = 24,125 Physicians*

ALPHA ORDER

RANK	STATE	PHYSICIANS	% of USA
25	Alabama	367	1.5%
45	Alaska	77	0.3%
24	Arizona	370	1.5%
33	Arkansas	185	0.8%
1	California	2,918	12.1%
19	Colorado	451	1.9%
23	Connecticut	372	1.5%
48	Delaware	70	0.3%
4	Florida	1,312	5.4%
14	Georgia	596	2.5%
41	Hawaii	121	0.5%
40	Idaho	126	0.5%
6	Illinois	925	3.8%
19	Indiana	451	1.9%
32	Iowa	198	0.8%
29	Kansas	231	1.0%
28	Kentucky	310	1.3%
22	Louisiana	398	1.6%
38	Maine	130	0.5%
13	Maryland	605	2.5%
8	Massachusetts	751	3.1%
12	Michigan	614	2.5%
18	Minnesota	500	2.1%
34	Mississippi	178	0.7%
21	Missouri	444	1.8%
44	Montana	109	0.5%
35	Nebraska	161	0.7%
37	Nevada	138	0.6%
38	New Hampshire	130	0.5%
9	New Jersey	722	3.0%
36	New Mexico	147	0.6%
2	New York	1,838	7.6%
10	North Carolina	721	3.0%
50	North Dakota	51	0.2%
7	Ohio	883	3.7%
30	Oklahoma	227	0.9%
27	Oregon	326	1.4%
5	Pennsylvania	1,078	4.5%
42	Rhode Island	114	0.5%
26	South Carolina	365	1.5%
47	South Dakota	72	0.3%
15	Tennessee	548	2.3%
3	Texas	1,566	6.5%
31	Utah	206	0.9%
46	Vermont	76	0.3%
11	Virginia	621	2.6%
16	Washington	543	2.3%
43	West Virginia	112	0.5%
17	Wisconsin	502	2.1%
49	Wyoming	63	0.3%

RANK ORDER

RANK	STATE	PHYSICIANS	% of USA
1	California	2,918	12.1%
2	New York	1,838	7.6%
3	Texas	1,566	6.5%
4	Florida	1,312	5.4%
5	Pennsylvania	1,078	4.5%
6	Illinois	925	3.8%
7	Ohio	883	3.7%
8	Massachusetts	751	3.1%
9	New Jersey	722	3.0%
10	North Carolina	721	3.0%
11	Virginia	621	2.6%
12	Michigan	614	2.5%
13	Maryland	605	2.5%
14	Georgia	596	2.5%
15	Tennessee	548	2.3%
16	Washington	543	2.3%
17	Wisconsin	502	2.1%
18	Minnesota	500	2.1%
19	Colorado	451	1.9%
19	Indiana	451	1.9%
21	Missouri	444	1.8%
22	Louisiana	398	1.6%
23	Connecticut	372	1.5%
24	Arizona	370	1.5%
25	Alabama	367	1.5%
26	South Carolina	365	1.5%
27	Oregon	326	1.4%
28	Kentucky	310	1.3%
29	Kansas	231	1.0%
30	Oklahoma	227	0.9%
31	Utah	206	0.9%
32	Iowa	198	0.8%
33	Arkansas	185	0.8%
34	Mississippi	178	0.7%
35	Nebraska	161	0.7%
36	New Mexico	147	0.6%
37	Nevada	138	0.6%
38	Maine	130	0.5%
38	New Hampshire	130	0.5%
40	Idaho	126	0.5%
41	Hawaii	121	0.5%
42	Rhode Island	114	0.5%
43	West Virginia	112	0.5%
44	Montana	109	0.5%
45	Alaska	77	0.3%
46	Vermont	76	0.3%
47	South Dakota	72	0.3%
48	Delaware	70	0.3%
49	Wyoming	63	0.3%
50	North Dakota	51	0.2%
	District of Columbia	106	0.4%

Source: American Medical Association (Chicago, Illinois)
   "Physician Characteristics and Distribution in the U.S." (2008 Edition)
*As of December 31, 2006. Total does not include 171 physicians in U.S. territories and possessions. Orthopedics is the branch of medicine dealing with the skeletal system.

Rate of Physicians in Orthopedic Surgery in 2006

National Rate = 8 Physicians per 100,000 Population*

ALPHA ORDER

RANK	STATE	RATE
24	Alabama	8
5	Alaska	11
44	Arizona	6
37	Arkansas	7
24	California	8
13	Colorado	9
5	Connecticut	11
24	Delaware	8
37	Florida	7
44	Georgia	6
13	Hawaii	9
13	Idaho	9
37	Illinois	7
37	Indiana	7
37	Iowa	7
24	Kansas	8
37	Kentucky	7
13	Louisiana	9
9	Maine	10
5	Maryland	11
1	Massachusetts	12
44	Michigan	6
9	Minnesota	10
44	Mississippi	6
24	Missouri	8
1	Montana	12
13	Nebraska	9
44	Nevada	6
9	New Hampshire	10
24	New Jersey	8
24	New Mexico	8
9	New York	10
24	North Carolina	8
24	North Dakota	8
24	Ohio	8
44	Oklahoma	6
13	Oregon	9
13	Pennsylvania	9
5	Rhode Island	11
24	South Carolina	8
13	South Dakota	9
13	Tennessee	9
37	Texas	7
24	Utah	8
1	Vermont	12
24	Virginia	8
13	Washington	9
44	West Virginia	6
13	Wisconsin	9
1	Wyoming	12

RANK ORDER

RANK	STATE	RATE
1	Massachusetts	12
1	Montana	12
1	Vermont	12
1	Wyoming	12
5	Alaska	11
5	Connecticut	11
5	Maryland	11
5	Rhode Island	11
9	Maine	10
9	Minnesota	10
9	New Hampshire	10
9	New York	10
13	Colorado	9
13	Hawaii	9
13	Idaho	9
13	Louisiana	9
13	Nebraska	9
13	Oregon	9
13	Pennsylvania	9
13	South Dakota	9
13	Tennessee	9
13	Washington	9
13	Wisconsin	9
24	Alabama	8
24	California	8
24	Delaware	8
24	Kansas	8
24	Missouri	8
24	New Jersey	8
24	New Mexico	8
24	North Carolina	8
24	North Dakota	8
24	Ohio	8
24	South Carolina	8
24	Utah	8
24	Virginia	8
37	Arkansas	7
37	Florida	7
37	Illinois	7
37	Indiana	7
37	Iowa	7
37	Kentucky	7
37	Texas	7
44	Arizona	6
44	Georgia	6
44	Michigan	6
44	Mississippi	6
44	Nevada	6
44	Oklahoma	6
44	West Virginia	6

District of Columbia	18

Source: CQ Press using data from American Medical Association (Chicago, Illinois)
   "Physician Characteristics and Distribution in the U.S." (2008 Edition)
*As of December 31, 2006. National rate does not include physicians in U.S. territories and possessions. Orthopedics is the branch of medicine dealing with the skeletal system.

Physicians in Plastic Surgery in 2006

National Total = 7,022 Physicians*

ALPHA ORDER					RANK ORDER			
RANK	STATE	PHYSICIANS	% of USA		RANK	STATE	PHYSICIANS	% of USA
27	Alabama	81	1.2%		1	California	1,085	15.4%
49	Alaska	7	0.1%		2	New York	624	8.9%
17	Arizona	136	1.9%		3	Florida	577	8.2%
34	Arkansas	34	0.5%		4	Texas	549	7.8%
1	California	1,085	15.4%		5	Pennsylvania	268	3.8%
19	Colorado	109	1.6%		6	Illinois	255	3.6%
22	Connecticut	94	1.3%		7	New Jersey	230	3.3%
41	Delaware	24	0.3%		8	Ohio	207	2.9%
3	Florida	577	8.2%		9	Michigan	203	2.9%
11	Georgia	187	2.7%		10	Massachusetts	197	2.8%
36	Hawaii	31	0.4%		11	Georgia	187	2.7%
43	Idaho	18	0.3%		12	Maryland	184	2.6%
6	Illinois	255	3.6%		13	North Carolina	177	2.5%
21	Indiana	96	1.4%		14	Virginia	171	2.4%
35	Iowa	32	0.5%		15	Tennessee	148	2.1%
30	Kansas	61	0.9%		16	Missouri	140	2.0%
22	Kentucky	94	1.3%		17	Arizona	136	1.9%
25	Louisiana	88	1.3%		18	Washington	130	1.8%
44	Maine	15	0.2%		19	Colorado	109	1.6%
12	Maryland	184	2.6%		20	Wisconsin	97	1.4%
10	Massachusetts	197	2.8%		21	Indiana	96	1.4%
9	Michigan	203	2.9%		22	Connecticut	94	1.3%
24	Minnesota	93	1.3%		22	Kentucky	94	1.3%
32	Mississippi	44	0.6%		24	Minnesota	93	1.3%
16	Missouri	140	2.0%		25	Louisiana	88	1.3%
44	Montana	15	0.2%		26	South Carolina	82	1.2%
36	Nebraska	31	0.4%		27	Alabama	81	1.2%
31	Nevada	47	0.7%		28	Utah	77	1.1%
42	New Hampshire	22	0.3%		29	Oregon	65	0.9%
7	New Jersey	230	3.3%		30	Kansas	61	0.9%
36	New Mexico	31	0.4%		31	Nevada	47	0.7%
2	New York	624	8.9%		32	Mississippi	44	0.6%
13	North Carolina	177	2.5%		33	Oklahoma	41	0.6%
47	North Dakota	11	0.2%		34	Arkansas	34	0.5%
8	Ohio	207	2.9%		35	Iowa	32	0.5%
33	Oklahoma	41	0.6%		36	Hawaii	31	0.4%
29	Oregon	65	0.9%		36	Nebraska	31	0.4%
5	Pennsylvania	268	3.8%		36	New Mexico	31	0.4%
40	Rhode Island	29	0.4%		39	West Virginia	30	0.4%
26	South Carolina	82	1.2%		40	Rhode Island	29	0.4%
46	South Dakota	13	0.2%		41	Delaware	24	0.3%
15	Tennessee	148	2.1%		42	New Hampshire	22	0.3%
4	Texas	549	7.8%		43	Idaho	18	0.3%
28	Utah	77	1.1%		44	Maine	15	0.2%
48	Vermont	8	0.1%		44	Montana	15	0.2%
14	Virginia	171	2.4%		46	South Dakota	13	0.2%
18	Washington	130	1.8%		47	North Dakota	11	0.2%
39	West Virginia	30	0.4%		48	Vermont	8	0.1%
20	Wisconsin	97	1.4%		49	Alaska	7	0.1%
50	Wyoming	2	0.0%		50	Wyoming	2	0.0%
						District of Columbia	38	0.5%

Source: American Medical Association (Chicago, Illinois)
    "Physician Characteristics and Distribution in the U.S." (2008 Edition)
*As of December 31, 2006. Total does not include 41 physicians in U.S. territories and possessions.

Rate of Physicians in Plastic Surgery in 2006

National Rate = 2 Physicians per 100,000 Population*

ALPHA ORDER

RANK	STATE	RATE
11	Alabama	2
43	Alaska	1
11	Arizona	2
43	Arkansas	1
1	California	3
11	Colorado	2
1	Connecticut	3
1	Delaware	3
1	Florida	3
11	Georgia	2
11	Hawaii	2
43	Idaho	1
11	Illinois	2
11	Indiana	2
43	Iowa	1
11	Kansas	2
11	Kentucky	2
11	Louisiana	2
43	Maine	1
1	Maryland	3
1	Massachusetts	3
11	Michigan	2
11	Minnesota	2
11	Mississippi	2
11	Missouri	2
11	Montana	2
11	Nebraska	2
11	Nevada	2
11	New Hampshire	2
1	New Jersey	3
11	New Mexico	2
1	New York	3
11	North Carolina	2
11	North Dakota	2
11	Ohio	2
43	Oklahoma	1
11	Oregon	2
11	Pennsylvania	2
1	Rhode Island	3
11	South Carolina	2
11	South Dakota	2
11	Tennessee	2
11	Texas	2
1	Utah	3
43	Vermont	1
11	Virginia	2
11	Washington	2
11	West Virginia	2
11	Wisconsin	2
50	Wyoming	0

RANK ORDER

RANK	STATE	RATE
1	California	3
1	Connecticut	3
1	Delaware	3
1	Florida	3
1	Maryland	3
1	Massachusetts	3
1	New Jersey	3
1	New York	3
1	Rhode Island	3
1	Utah	3
11	Alabama	2
11	Arizona	2
11	Colorado	2
11	Georgia	2
11	Hawaii	2
11	Illinois	2
11	Indiana	2
11	Kansas	2
11	Kentucky	2
11	Louisiana	2
11	Michigan	2
11	Minnesota	2
11	Mississippi	2
11	Missouri	2
11	Montana	2
11	Nebraska	2
11	Nevada	2
11	New Hampshire	2
11	New Mexico	2
11	North Carolina	2
11	North Dakota	2
11	Ohio	2
11	Oregon	2
11	Pennsylvania	2
11	South Carolina	2
11	South Dakota	2
11	Tennessee	2
11	Texas	2
11	Virginia	2
11	Washington	2
11	West Virginia	2
11	Wisconsin	2
43	Alaska	1
43	Arkansas	1
43	Idaho	1
43	Iowa	1
43	Maine	1
43	Oklahoma	1
43	Vermont	1
50	Wyoming	0

District of Columbia   6

Source: CQ Press using data from American Medical Association (Chicago, Illinois)
   "Physician Characteristics and Distribution in the U.S." (2008 Edition)
*As of December 31, 2006. National rate does not include physicians in U.S. territories and possessions.

Physicians in Other Specialties in 2006

National Total = 218,244 Physicians*

ALPHA ORDER

ALPHA ORDER

RANK	STATE	PHYSICIANS	% of USA
28	Alabama	2,429	1.1%
47	Alaska	420	0.2%
21	Arizona	3,676	1.7%
32	Arkansas	1,455	0.7%
1	California	26,972	12.4%
23	Colorado	3,590	1.6%
22	Connecticut	3,634	1.7%
45	Delaware	563	0.3%
4	Florida	11,822	5.4%
14	Georgia	5,421	2.5%
37	Hawaii	1,179	0.5%
43	Idaho	664	0.3%
6	Illinois	9,362	4.3%
20	Indiana	3,711	1.7%
33	Iowa	1,431	0.7%
29	Kansas	1,655	0.8%
26	Kentucky	2,605	1.2%
25	Louisiana	2,832	1.3%
40	Maine	1,036	0.5%
10	Maryland	6,778	3.1%
7	Massachusetts	8,861	4.1%
11	Michigan	6,610	3.0%
19	Minnesota	3,772	1.7%
36	Mississippi	1,275	0.6%
18	Missouri	3,776	1.7%
45	Montana	563	0.3%
38	Nebraska	1,056	0.5%
35	Nevada	1,313	0.6%
42	New Hampshire	953	0.4%
9	New Jersey	7,086	3.2%
34	New Mexico	1,335	0.6%
2	New York	20,856	9.6%
12	North Carolina	5,930	2.7%
49	North Dakota	392	0.2%
8	Ohio	7,903	3.6%
30	Oklahoma	1,590	0.7%
24	Oregon	2,838	1.3%
5	Pennsylvania	10,309	4.7%
41	Rhode Island	1,031	0.5%
26	South Carolina	2,605	1.2%
48	South Dakota	412	0.2%
17	Tennessee	3,959	1.8%
3	Texas	13,294	6.1%
31	Utah	1,562	0.7%
44	Vermont	660	0.3%
13	Virginia	5,633	2.6%
15	Washington	4,818	2.2%
39	West Virginia	1,054	0.5%
16	Wisconsin	3,991	1.8%
50	Wyoming	260	0.1%

RANK ORDER

RANK	STATE	PHYSICIANS	% of USA
1	California	26,972	12.4%
2	New York	20,856	9.6%
3	Texas	13,294	6.1%
4	Florida	11,822	5.4%
5	Pennsylvania	10,309	4.7%
6	Illinois	9,362	4.3%
7	Massachusetts	8,861	4.1%
8	Ohio	7,903	3.6%
9	New Jersey	7,086	3.2%
10	Maryland	6,778	3.1%
11	Michigan	6,610	3.0%
12	North Carolina	5,930	2.7%
13	Virginia	5,633	2.6%
14	Georgia	5,421	2.5%
15	Washington	4,818	2.2%
16	Wisconsin	3,991	1.8%
17	Tennessee	3,959	1.8%
18	Missouri	3,776	1.7%
19	Minnesota	3,772	1.7%
20	Indiana	3,711	1.7%
21	Arizona	3,676	1.7%
22	Connecticut	3,634	1.7%
23	Colorado	3,590	1.6%
24	Oregon	2,838	1.3%
25	Louisiana	2,832	1.3%
26	Kentucky	2,605	1.2%
26	South Carolina	2,605	1.2%
28	Alabama	2,429	1.1%
29	Kansas	1,655	0.8%
30	Oklahoma	1,590	0.7%
31	Utah	1,562	0.7%
32	Arkansas	1,455	0.7%
33	Iowa	1,431	0.7%
34	New Mexico	1,335	0.6%
35	Nevada	1,313	0.6%
36	Mississippi	1,275	0.6%
37	Hawaii	1,179	0.5%
38	Nebraska	1,056	0.5%
39	West Virginia	1,054	0.5%
40	Maine	1,036	0.5%
41	Rhode Island	1,031	0.5%
42	New Hampshire	953	0.4%
43	Idaho	664	0.3%
44	Vermont	660	0.3%
45	Delaware	563	0.3%
45	Montana	563	0.3%
47	Alaska	420	0.2%
48	South Dakota	412	0.2%
49	North Dakota	392	0.2%
50	Wyoming	260	0.1%
	District of Columbia	1,312	0.6%

Source: American Medical Association (Chicago, Illinois)
"Physician Characteristics and Distribution in the U.S." (2008 Edition)
*As of December 31, 2006. Total does not include 3,207 physicians in U.S. territories and possessions. Other Specialties include Aerospace Medicine, Anesthesiology, Child Psychiatry, Diagnostic Radiology, Emergency Medicine, Forensic Pathology, Nuclear Medicine, Occupational Medicine, Neurology, Psychiatry, Public Health, Anatomic/Clinical Pathology, Radiology, Radiation Oncology, and other specialties.

Rate of Physicians in Other Specialties in 2006

National Rate = 73 Physicians per 100,000 Population*

ALPHA ORDER				RANK ORDER		
RANK	STATE	RATE		RANK	STATE	RATE
42	Alabama	53		1	Massachusetts	138
29	Alaska	62		2	Maryland	121
33	Arizona	60		3	New York	108
44	Arkansas	52		4	Vermont	106
14	California	74		5	Connecticut	104
13	Colorado	75		6	Rhode Island	97
5	Connecticut	104		7	Hawaii	92
24	Delaware	66		8	Pennsylvania	83
25	Florida	65		9	New Jersey	82
39	Georgia	58		10	Maine	79
7	Hawaii	92		11	Oregon	77
48	Idaho	45		12	Washington	76
16	Illinois	73		13	Colorado	75
37	Indiana	59		14	California	74
47	Iowa	48		14	Virginia	74
33	Kansas	60		16	Illinois	73
29	Kentucky	62		16	Minnesota	73
22	Louisiana	67		16	New Hampshire	73
10	Maine	79		19	Wisconsin	72
2	Maryland	121		20	New Mexico	69
1	Massachusetts	138		20	Ohio	69
25	Michigan	65		22	Louisiana	67
16	Minnesota	73		22	North Carolina	67
49	Mississippi	44		24	Delaware	66
25	Missouri	65		25	Florida	65
37	Montana	59		25	Michigan	65
33	Nebraska	60		25	Missouri	65
42	Nevada	53		25	Tennessee	65
16	New Hampshire	73		29	Alaska	62
9	New Jersey	82		29	Kentucky	62
20	New Mexico	69		31	North Dakota	61
3	New York	108		31	Utah	61
22	North Carolina	67		33	Arizona	60
31	North Dakota	61		33	Kansas	60
20	Ohio	69		33	Nebraska	60
49	Oklahoma	44		33	South Carolina	60
11	Oregon	77		37	Indiana	59
8	Pennsylvania	83		37	Montana	59
6	Rhode Island	97		39	Georgia	58
33	South Carolina	60		39	West Virginia	58
44	South Dakota	52		41	Texas	57
25	Tennessee	65		42	Alabama	53
41	Texas	57		42	Nevada	53
31	Utah	61		44	Arkansas	52
4	Vermont	106		44	South Dakota	52
14	Virginia	74		46	Wyoming	51
12	Washington	76		47	Iowa	48
39	West Virginia	58		48	Idaho	45
19	Wisconsin	72		49	Mississippi	44
46	Wyoming	51		49	Oklahoma	44
					District of Columbia	224

Source: CQ Press using data from American Medical Association (Chicago, Illinois)
   "Physician Characteristics and Distribution in the U.S." (2008 Edition)
*As of December 31, 2006. National rate does not include physicians in U.S. territories and possessions. Other Specialties include Aerospace Medicine, Anesthesiology, Child Psychiatry, Diagnostic Radiology, Emergency Medicine, Forensic Pathology, Nuclear Medicine, Occupational Medicine, Neurology, Psychiatry, Public Health, Anatomic/Clinical Pathology, Radiology, Radiation Oncology, and other specialties.

Physicians in Anesthesiology in 2006

National Total = 40,952 Physicians*

ALPHA ORDER

RANK	STATE	PHYSICIANS	% of USA
27	Alabama	474	1.2%
47	Alaska	85	0.2%
17	Arizona	865	2.1%
34	Arkansas	300	0.7%
1	California	5,114	12.5%
20	Colorado	728	1.8%
22	Connecticut	568	1.4%
46	Delaware	90	0.2%
4	Florida	2,577	6.3%
15	Georgia	941	2.3%
40	Hawaii	165	0.4%
44	Idaho	115	0.3%
5	Illinois	1,867	4.6%
16	Indiana	925	2.3%
33	Iowa	318	0.8%
32	Kansas	332	0.8%
25	Kentucky	555	1.4%
26	Louisiana	517	1.3%
39	Maine	171	0.4%
10	Maryland	1,062	2.6%
9	Massachusetts	1,400	3.4%
12	Michigan	973	2.4%
24	Minnesota	561	1.4%
35	Mississippi	250	0.6%
21	Missouri	712	1.7%
42	Montana	122	0.3%
36	Nebraska	233	0.6%
30	Nevada	361	0.9%
38	New Hampshire	174	0.4%
7	New Jersey	1,516	3.7%
37	New Mexico	218	0.5%
2	New York	3,433	8.4%
14	North Carolina	959	2.3%
48	North Dakota	64	0.2%
8	Ohio	1,501	3.7%
31	Oklahoma	358	0.9%
23	Oregon	564	1.4%
6	Pennsylvania	1,671	4.1%
43	Rhode Island	118	0.3%
28	South Carolina	462	1.1%
48	South Dakota	64	0.2%
19	Tennessee	786	1.9%
3	Texas	3,071	7.5%
29	Utah	364	0.9%
45	Vermont	108	0.3%
11	Virginia	990	2.4%
13	Washington	967	2.4%
41	West Virginia	157	0.4%
18	Wisconsin	836	2.0%
50	Wyoming	52	0.1%

RANK ORDER

RANK	STATE	PHYSICIANS	% of USA
1	California	5,114	12.5%
2	New York	3,433	8.4%
3	Texas	3,071	7.5%
4	Florida	2,577	6.3%
5	Illinois	1,867	4.6%
6	Pennsylvania	1,671	4.1%
7	New Jersey	1,516	3.7%
8	Ohio	1,501	3.7%
9	Massachusetts	1,400	3.4%
10	Maryland	1,062	2.6%
11	Virginia	990	2.4%
12	Michigan	973	2.4%
13	Washington	967	2.4%
14	North Carolina	959	2.3%
15	Georgia	941	2.3%
16	Indiana	925	2.3%
17	Arizona	865	2.1%
18	Wisconsin	836	2.0%
19	Tennessee	786	1.9%
20	Colorado	728	1.8%
21	Missouri	712	1.7%
22	Connecticut	568	1.4%
23	Oregon	564	1.4%
24	Minnesota	561	1.4%
25	Kentucky	555	1.4%
26	Louisiana	517	1.3%
27	Alabama	474	1.2%
28	South Carolina	462	1.1%
29	Utah	364	0.9%
30	Nevada	361	0.9%
31	Oklahoma	358	0.9%
32	Kansas	332	0.8%
33	Iowa	318	0.8%
34	Arkansas	300	0.7%
35	Mississippi	250	0.6%
36	Nebraska	233	0.6%
37	New Mexico	218	0.5%
38	New Hampshire	174	0.4%
39	Maine	171	0.4%
40	Hawaii	165	0.4%
41	West Virginia	157	0.4%
42	Montana	122	0.3%
43	Rhode Island	118	0.3%
44	Idaho	115	0.3%
45	Vermont	108	0.3%
46	Delaware	90	0.2%
47	Alaska	85	0.2%
48	North Dakota	64	0.2%
48	South Dakota	64	0.2%
50	Wyoming	52	0.1%
	District of Columbia	138	0.3%

Source: American Medical Association (Chicago, Illinois)
"Physician Characteristics and Distribution in the U.S." (2008 Edition)
*As of December 31, 2006. Total does not include 241 physicians in U.S. territories and possessions.

Rate of Physicians in Anesthesiology in 2006

National Rate = 14 Physicians per 100,000 Population*

ALPHA ORDER

ALPHA ORDER

RANK	STATE	RATE
41	Alabama	10
18	Alaska	13
13	Arizona	14
33	Arkansas	11
13	California	14
7	Colorado	15
6	Connecticut	16
33	Delaware	11
13	Florida	14
41	Georgia	10
18	Hawaii	13
49	Idaho	8
7	Illinois	15
7	Indiana	15
33	Iowa	11
30	Kansas	12
18	Kentucky	13
30	Louisiana	12
18	Maine	13
2	Maryland	19
1	Massachusetts	22
41	Michigan	10
33	Minnesota	11
47	Mississippi	9
30	Missouri	12
18	Montana	13
18	Nebraska	13
13	Nevada	14
18	New Hampshire	13
4	New Jersey	17
33	New Mexico	11
3	New York	18
33	North Carolina	11
41	North Dakota	10
18	Ohio	13
41	Oklahoma	10
7	Oregon	15
18	Pennsylvania	13
33	Rhode Island	11
33	South Carolina	11
49	South Dakota	8
18	Tennessee	13
18	Texas	13
13	Utah	14
4	Vermont	17
18	Virginia	13
7	Washington	15
47	West Virginia	9
7	Wisconsin	15
41	Wyoming	10

RANK ORDER

RANK	STATE	RATE
1	Massachusetts	22
2	Maryland	19
3	New York	18
4	New Jersey	17
4	Vermont	17
6	Connecticut	16
7	Colorado	15
7	Illinois	15
7	Indiana	15
7	Oregon	15
7	Washington	15
7	Wisconsin	15
13	Arizona	14
13	California	14
13	Florida	14
13	Nevada	14
13	Utah	14
18	Alaska	13
18	Hawaii	13
18	Kentucky	13
18	Maine	13
18	Montana	13
18	Nebraska	13
18	New Hampshire	13
18	Ohio	13
18	Pennsylvania	13
18	Tennessee	13
18	Texas	13
18	Virginia	13
30	Kansas	12
30	Louisiana	12
30	Missouri	12
33	Arkansas	11
33	Delaware	11
33	Iowa	11
33	Minnesota	11
33	New Mexico	11
33	North Carolina	11
33	Rhode Island	11
33	South Carolina	11
41	Alabama	10
41	Georgia	10
41	Michigan	10
41	North Dakota	10
41	Oklahoma	10
41	Wyoming	10
47	Mississippi	9
47	West Virginia	9
49	Idaho	8
49	South Dakota	8

District of Columbia	24

Source: CQ Press using data from American Medical Association (Chicago, Illinois)
"Physician Characteristics and Distribution in the U.S." (2008 Edition)
*As of December 31, 2006. National rate does not include physicians in U.S. territories and possessions.

Physicians in Psychiatry in 2006

National Total = 40,880 Physicians*

ALPHA ORDER

RANK	STATE	PHYSICIANS	% of USA
28	Alabama	350	0.9%
46	Alaska	83	0.2%
21	Arizona	574	1.4%
35	Arkansas	227	0.6%
2	California	5,626	13.8%
19	Colorado	599	1.5%
14	Connecticut	937	2.3%
44	Delaware	92	0.2%
6	Florida	1,761	4.3%
15	Georgia	906	2.2%
32	Hawaii	263	0.6%
47	Idaho	77	0.2%
7	Illinois	1,572	3.8%
26	Indiana	462	1.1%
36	Iowa	206	0.5%
30	Kansas	288	0.7%
27	Kentucky	403	1.0%
25	Louisiana	470	1.1%
34	Maine	236	0.6%
9	Maryland	1,398	3.4%
3	Massachusetts	2,163	5.3%
11	Michigan	1,081	2.6%
22	Minnesota	554	1.4%
37	Mississippi	204	0.5%
20	Missouri	596	1.5%
45	Montana	85	0.2%
41	Nebraska	171	0.4%
40	Nevada	173	0.4%
39	New Hampshire	185	0.5%
8	New Jersey	1,448	3.5%
31	New Mexico	280	0.7%
1	New York	5,650	13.8%
13	North Carolina	1,051	2.6%
47	North Dakota	77	0.2%
10	Ohio	1,208	3.0%
29	Oklahoma	292	0.7%
23	Oregon	477	1.2%
4	Pennsylvania	1,994	4.9%
33	Rhode Island	254	0.6%
24	South Carolina	475	1.2%
49	South Dakota	68	0.2%
18	Tennessee	601	1.5%
5	Texas	1,858	4.5%
38	Utah	199	0.5%
43	Vermont	165	0.4%
11	Virginia	1,081	2.6%
16	Washington	810	2.0%
42	West Virginia	167	0.4%
17	Wisconsin	603	1.5%
50	Wyoming	40	0.1%

RANK ORDER

RANK	STATE	PHYSICIANS	% of USA
1	New York	5,650	13.8%
2	California	5,626	13.8%
3	Massachusetts	2,163	5.3%
4	Pennsylvania	1,994	4.9%
5	Texas	1,858	4.5%
6	Florida	1,761	4.3%
7	Illinois	1,572	3.8%
8	New Jersey	1,448	3.5%
9	Maryland	1,398	3.4%
10	Ohio	1,208	3.0%
11	Michigan	1,081	2.6%
11	Virginia	1,081	2.6%
13	North Carolina	1,051	2.6%
14	Connecticut	937	2.3%
15	Georgia	906	2.2%
16	Washington	810	2.0%
17	Wisconsin	603	1.5%
18	Tennessee	601	1.5%
19	Colorado	599	1.5%
20	Missouri	596	1.5%
21	Arizona	574	1.4%
22	Minnesota	554	1.4%
23	Oregon	477	1.2%
24	South Carolina	475	1.2%
25	Louisiana	470	1.1%
26	Indiana	462	1.1%
27	Kentucky	403	1.0%
28	Alabama	350	0.9%
29	Oklahoma	292	0.7%
30	Kansas	288	0.7%
31	New Mexico	280	0.7%
32	Hawaii	263	0.6%
33	Rhode Island	254	0.6%
34	Maine	236	0.6%
35	Arkansas	227	0.6%
36	Iowa	206	0.5%
37	Mississippi	204	0.5%
38	Utah	199	0.5%
39	New Hampshire	185	0.5%
40	Nevada	173	0.4%
41	Nebraska	171	0.4%
42	West Virginia	167	0.4%
43	Vermont	165	0.4%
44	Delaware	92	0.2%
45	Montana	85	0.2%
46	Alaska	83	0.2%
47	Idaho	77	0.2%
47	North Dakota	77	0.2%
49	South Dakota	68	0.2%
50	Wyoming	40	0.1%
	District of Columbia	340	0.8%

Source: American Medical Association (Chicago, Illinois)
    "Physician Characteristics and Distribution in the U.S." (2008 Edition)
*As of December 31, 2006. Total does not include 505 physicians in U.S. territories and possessions. Psychiatry includes psychoanalysis.

Rate of Physicians in Psychiatry in 2006

National Rate = 14 Physicians per 100,000 Population*

<table>
<tr><td colspan="3">ALPHA ORDER</td><td colspan="3">RANK ORDER</td></tr>
<tr><td>RANK</td><td>STATE</td><td>RATE</td><td>RANK</td><td>STATE</td><td>RATE</td></tr>
<tr><td>40</td><td>Alabama</td><td>8</td><td>1</td><td>Massachusetts</td><td>34</td></tr>
<tr><td>18</td><td>Alaska</td><td>12</td><td>2</td><td>New York</td><td>29</td></tr>
<tr><td>36</td><td>Arizona</td><td>9</td><td>3</td><td>Connecticut</td><td>27</td></tr>
<tr><td>40</td><td>Arkansas</td><td>8</td><td>3</td><td>Vermont</td><td>27</td></tr>
<tr><td>10</td><td>California</td><td>16</td><td>5</td><td>Maryland</td><td>25</td></tr>
<tr><td>15</td><td>Colorado</td><td>13</td><td>6</td><td>Rhode Island</td><td>24</td></tr>
<tr><td>3</td><td>Connecticut</td><td>27</td><td>7</td><td>Hawaii</td><td>21</td></tr>
<tr><td>22</td><td>Delaware</td><td>11</td><td>8</td><td>Maine</td><td>18</td></tr>
<tr><td>29</td><td>Florida</td><td>10</td><td>9</td><td>New Jersey</td><td>17</td></tr>
<tr><td>29</td><td>Georgia</td><td>10</td><td>10</td><td>California</td><td>16</td></tr>
<tr><td>7</td><td>Hawaii</td><td>21</td><td>10</td><td>Pennsylvania</td><td>16</td></tr>
<tr><td>50</td><td>Idaho</td><td>5</td><td>12</td><td>New Hampshire</td><td>14</td></tr>
<tr><td>18</td><td>Illinois</td><td>12</td><td>12</td><td>New Mexico</td><td>14</td></tr>
<tr><td>46</td><td>Indiana</td><td>7</td><td>12</td><td>Virginia</td><td>14</td></tr>
<tr><td>46</td><td>Iowa</td><td>7</td><td>15</td><td>Colorado</td><td>13</td></tr>
<tr><td>29</td><td>Kansas</td><td>10</td><td>15</td><td>Oregon</td><td>13</td></tr>
<tr><td>29</td><td>Kentucky</td><td>10</td><td>15</td><td>Washington</td><td>13</td></tr>
<tr><td>22</td><td>Louisiana</td><td>11</td><td>18</td><td>Alaska</td><td>12</td></tr>
<tr><td>8</td><td>Maine</td><td>18</td><td>18</td><td>Illinois</td><td>12</td></tr>
<tr><td>5</td><td>Maryland</td><td>25</td><td>18</td><td>North Carolina</td><td>12</td></tr>
<tr><td>1</td><td>Massachusetts</td><td>34</td><td>18</td><td>North Dakota</td><td>12</td></tr>
<tr><td>22</td><td>Michigan</td><td>11</td><td>22</td><td>Delaware</td><td>11</td></tr>
<tr><td>22</td><td>Minnesota</td><td>11</td><td>22</td><td>Louisiana</td><td>11</td></tr>
<tr><td>46</td><td>Mississippi</td><td>7</td><td>22</td><td>Michigan</td><td>11</td></tr>
<tr><td>29</td><td>Missouri</td><td>10</td><td>22</td><td>Minnesota</td><td>11</td></tr>
<tr><td>36</td><td>Montana</td><td>9</td><td>22</td><td>Ohio</td><td>11</td></tr>
<tr><td>29</td><td>Nebraska</td><td>10</td><td>22</td><td>South Carolina</td><td>11</td></tr>
<tr><td>46</td><td>Nevada</td><td>7</td><td>22</td><td>Wisconsin</td><td>11</td></tr>
<tr><td>12</td><td>New Hampshire</td><td>14</td><td>29</td><td>Florida</td><td>10</td></tr>
<tr><td>9</td><td>New Jersey</td><td>17</td><td>29</td><td>Georgia</td><td>10</td></tr>
<tr><td>12</td><td>New Mexico</td><td>14</td><td>29</td><td>Kansas</td><td>10</td></tr>
<tr><td>2</td><td>New York</td><td>29</td><td>29</td><td>Kentucky</td><td>10</td></tr>
<tr><td>18</td><td>North Carolina</td><td>12</td><td>29</td><td>Missouri</td><td>10</td></tr>
<tr><td>18</td><td>North Dakota</td><td>12</td><td>29</td><td>Nebraska</td><td>10</td></tr>
<tr><td>22</td><td>Ohio</td><td>11</td><td>29</td><td>Tennessee</td><td>10</td></tr>
<tr><td>40</td><td>Oklahoma</td><td>8</td><td>36</td><td>Arizona</td><td>9</td></tr>
<tr><td>15</td><td>Oregon</td><td>13</td><td>36</td><td>Montana</td><td>9</td></tr>
<tr><td>10</td><td>Pennsylvania</td><td>16</td><td>36</td><td>South Dakota</td><td>9</td></tr>
<tr><td>6</td><td>Rhode Island</td><td>24</td><td>36</td><td>West Virginia</td><td>9</td></tr>
<tr><td>22</td><td>South Carolina</td><td>11</td><td>40</td><td>Alabama</td><td>8</td></tr>
<tr><td>36</td><td>South Dakota</td><td>9</td><td>40</td><td>Arkansas</td><td>8</td></tr>
<tr><td>29</td><td>Tennessee</td><td>10</td><td>40</td><td>Oklahoma</td><td>8</td></tr>
<tr><td>40</td><td>Texas</td><td>8</td><td>40</td><td>Texas</td><td>8</td></tr>
<tr><td>40</td><td>Utah</td><td>8</td><td>40</td><td>Utah</td><td>8</td></tr>
<tr><td>3</td><td>Vermont</td><td>27</td><td>40</td><td>Wyoming</td><td>8</td></tr>
<tr><td>12</td><td>Virginia</td><td>14</td><td>46</td><td>Indiana</td><td>7</td></tr>
<tr><td>15</td><td>Washington</td><td>13</td><td>46</td><td>Iowa</td><td>7</td></tr>
<tr><td>36</td><td>West Virginia</td><td>9</td><td>46</td><td>Mississippi</td><td>7</td></tr>
<tr><td>22</td><td>Wisconsin</td><td>11</td><td>46</td><td>Nevada</td><td>7</td></tr>
<tr><td>40</td><td>Wyoming</td><td>8</td><td>50</td><td>Idaho</td><td>5</td></tr>
<tr><td></td><td></td><td></td><td></td><td>District of Columbia</td><td>58</td></tr>
</table>

Source: CQ Press using data from American Medical Association (Chicago, Illinois)
"Physician Characteristics and Distribution in the U.S." (2008 Edition)
*As of December 31, 2006. National rate does not include physicians in U.S. territories and possessions. Psychiatry includes psychoanalysis.

Percent of Population Lacking Access to Mental Health Care in 2007

National Percent = 17.8% of Population*

<table>
<tr><td colspan="3">ALPHA ORDER</td><td colspan="3">RANK ORDER</td></tr>
<tr><td>RANK</td><td>STATE</td><td>PERCENT</td><td>RANK</td><td>STATE</td><td>PERCENT</td></tr>
<tr><td>5</td><td>Alabama</td><td>48.3</td><td>1</td><td>Wyoming</td><td>75.7</td></tr>
<tr><td>34</td><td>Alaska</td><td>11.9</td><td>2</td><td>Idaho</td><td>61.6</td></tr>
<tr><td>31</td><td>Arizona</td><td>14.5</td><td>3</td><td>South Dakota</td><td>49.6</td></tr>
<tr><td>7</td><td>Arkansas</td><td>41.9</td><td>4</td><td>Louisiana</td><td>49.2</td></tr>
<tr><td>38</td><td>California</td><td>8.2</td><td>5</td><td>Alabama</td><td>48.3</td></tr>
<tr><td>37</td><td>Colorado</td><td>9.3</td><td>6</td><td>New Mexico</td><td>45.8</td></tr>
<tr><td>48</td><td>Connecticut</td><td>1.6</td><td>7</td><td>Arkansas</td><td>41.9</td></tr>
<tr><td>50</td><td>Delaware</td><td>0.0</td><td>8</td><td>Kentucky</td><td>41.7</td></tr>
<tr><td>39</td><td>Florida</td><td>7.9</td><td>9</td><td>Nebraska</td><td>41.2</td></tr>
<tr><td>22</td><td>Georgia</td><td>25.7</td><td>10</td><td>Mississippi</td><td>40.5</td></tr>
<tr><td>40</td><td>Hawaii</td><td>7.6</td><td>11</td><td>Montana</td><td>39.5</td></tr>
<tr><td>2</td><td>Idaho</td><td>61.6</td><td>12</td><td>Kansas</td><td>35.9</td></tr>
<tr><td>28</td><td>Illinois</td><td>17.7</td><td>13</td><td>Iowa</td><td>35.3</td></tr>
<tr><td>30</td><td>Indiana</td><td>14.8</td><td>14</td><td>Oklahoma</td><td>35.0</td></tr>
<tr><td>13</td><td>Iowa</td><td>35.3</td><td>15</td><td>North Dakota</td><td>34.3</td></tr>
<tr><td>12</td><td>Kansas</td><td>35.9</td><td>16</td><td>South Carolina</td><td>33.9</td></tr>
<tr><td>8</td><td>Kentucky</td><td>41.7</td><td>17</td><td>Tennessee</td><td>32.6</td></tr>
<tr><td>4</td><td>Louisiana</td><td>49.2</td><td>18</td><td>Utah</td><td>31.7</td></tr>
<tr><td>35</td><td>Maine</td><td>11.7</td><td>19</td><td>Missouri</td><td>30.9</td></tr>
<tr><td>43</td><td>Maryland</td><td>6.2</td><td>20</td><td>Minnesota</td><td>26.2</td></tr>
<tr><td>49</td><td>Massachusetts</td><td>0.7</td><td>21</td><td>Texas</td><td>26.1</td></tr>
<tr><td>33</td><td>Michigan</td><td>12.7</td><td>22</td><td>Georgia</td><td>25.7</td></tr>
<tr><td>20</td><td>Minnesota</td><td>26.2</td><td>23</td><td>West Virginia</td><td>25.0</td></tr>
<tr><td>10</td><td>Mississippi</td><td>40.5</td><td>24</td><td>Wisconsin</td><td>24.4</td></tr>
<tr><td>19</td><td>Missouri</td><td>30.9</td><td>25</td><td>Rhode Island</td><td>23.3</td></tr>
<tr><td>11</td><td>Montana</td><td>39.5</td><td>26</td><td>Washington</td><td>20.9</td></tr>
<tr><td>9</td><td>Nebraska</td><td>41.2</td><td>27</td><td>Oregon</td><td>19.5</td></tr>
<tr><td>43</td><td>Nevada</td><td>6.2</td><td>28</td><td>Illinois</td><td>17.7</td></tr>
<tr><td>46</td><td>New Hampshire</td><td>5.2</td><td>29</td><td>Virginia</td><td>14.9</td></tr>
<tr><td>47</td><td>New Jersey</td><td>4.3</td><td>30</td><td>Indiana</td><td>14.8</td></tr>
<tr><td>6</td><td>New Mexico</td><td>45.8</td><td>31</td><td>Arizona</td><td>14.5</td></tr>
<tr><td>41</td><td>New York</td><td>7.5</td><td>32</td><td>Ohio</td><td>13.1</td></tr>
<tr><td>45</td><td>North Carolina</td><td>5.8</td><td>33</td><td>Michigan</td><td>12.7</td></tr>
<tr><td>15</td><td>North Dakota</td><td>34.3</td><td>34</td><td>Alaska</td><td>11.9</td></tr>
<tr><td>32</td><td>Ohio</td><td>13.1</td><td>35</td><td>Maine</td><td>11.7</td></tr>
<tr><td>14</td><td>Oklahoma</td><td>35.0</td><td>36</td><td>Pennsylvania</td><td>10.1</td></tr>
<tr><td>27</td><td>Oregon</td><td>19.5</td><td>37</td><td>Colorado</td><td>9.3</td></tr>
<tr><td>36</td><td>Pennsylvania</td><td>10.1</td><td>38</td><td>California</td><td>8.2</td></tr>
<tr><td>25</td><td>Rhode Island</td><td>23.3</td><td>39</td><td>Florida</td><td>7.9</td></tr>
<tr><td>16</td><td>South Carolina</td><td>33.9</td><td>40</td><td>Hawaii</td><td>7.6</td></tr>
<tr><td>3</td><td>South Dakota</td><td>49.6</td><td>41</td><td>New York</td><td>7.5</td></tr>
<tr><td>17</td><td>Tennessee</td><td>32.6</td><td>42</td><td>Vermont</td><td>7.4</td></tr>
<tr><td>21</td><td>Texas</td><td>26.1</td><td>43</td><td>Maryland</td><td>6.2</td></tr>
<tr><td>18</td><td>Utah</td><td>31.7</td><td>43</td><td>Nevada</td><td>6.2</td></tr>
<tr><td>42</td><td>Vermont</td><td>7.4</td><td>45</td><td>North Carolina</td><td>5.8</td></tr>
<tr><td>29</td><td>Virginia</td><td>14.9</td><td>46</td><td>New Hampshire</td><td>5.2</td></tr>
<tr><td>26</td><td>Washington</td><td>20.9</td><td>47</td><td>New Jersey</td><td>4.3</td></tr>
<tr><td>23</td><td>West Virginia</td><td>25.0</td><td>48</td><td>Connecticut</td><td>1.6</td></tr>
<tr><td>24</td><td>Wisconsin</td><td>24.4</td><td>49</td><td>Massachusetts</td><td>0.7</td></tr>
<tr><td>1</td><td>Wyoming</td><td>75.7</td><td>50</td><td>Delaware</td><td>0.0</td></tr>
</table>

District of Columbia   13.3

Source: CQ Press using data from U.S. Dept. of Health and Human Services, Div. of Shortage Designation
"Selected Statistics on Health Professional Shortage Areas" (as of June 30, 2007)
*Percent of population considered under-served by mental health practitioners. An under-served population does not have primary medical care within reasonable economic and geographic bounds.

International Medical School Graduates in 2006

National Total = 229,632 Nonfederal Physicians*

ALPHA ORDER

RANK	STATE	PHYSICIANS	% of USA
25	Alabama	1,754	0.8%
47	Alaska	118	0.1%
17	Arizona	3,215	1.4%
35	Arkansas	1,017	0.4%
2	California	25,408	11.1%
33	Colorado	1,053	0.5%
14	Connecticut	4,192	1.8%
38	Delaware	753	0.3%
3	Florida	19,536	8.5%
13	Georgia	4,438	1.9%
39	Hawaii	708	0.3%
50	Idaho	105	0.0%
5	Illinois	13,439	5.9%
18	Indiana	3,157	1.4%
31	Iowa	1,252	0.5%
30	Kansas	1,314	0.6%
24	Kentucky	2,272	1.0%
23	Louisiana	2,285	1.0%
41	Maine	592	0.3%
10	Maryland	7,106	3.1%
10	Massachusetts	7,106	3.1%
9	Michigan	9,459	4.1%
21	Minnesota	2,482	1.1%
37	Mississippi	780	0.3%
15	Missouri	3,431	1.5%
48	Montana	116	0.1%
40	Nebraska	678	0.3%
27	Nevada	1,580	0.7%
42	New Hampshire	577	0.3%
4	New Jersey	13,617	5.9%
36	New Mexico	936	0.4%
1	New York	35,180	15.3%
16	North Carolina	3,221	1.4%
44	North Dakota	459	0.2%
8	Ohio	9,911	4.3%
29	Oklahoma	1,351	0.6%
34	Oregon	1,034	0.5%
7	Pennsylvania	10,920	4.8%
32	Rhode Island	1,177	0.5%
28	South Carolina	1,427	0.6%
45	South Dakota	270	0.1%
20	Tennessee	2,930	1.3%
6	Texas	13,250	5.8%
43	Utah	510	0.2%
46	Vermont	244	0.1%
12	Virginia	4,981	2.2%
22	Washington	2,448	1.1%
26	West Virginia	1,711	0.7%
19	Wisconsin	2,948	1.3%
49	Wyoming	109	0.0%

RANK ORDER

RANK	STATE	PHYSICIANS	% of USA
1	New York	35,180	15.3%
2	California	25,408	11.1%
3	Florida	19,536	8.5%
4	New Jersey	13,617	5.9%
5	Illinois	13,439	5.9%
6	Texas	13,250	5.8%
7	Pennsylvania	10,920	4.8%
8	Ohio	9,911	4.3%
9	Michigan	9,459	4.1%
10	Maryland	7,106	3.1%
10	Massachusetts	7,106	3.1%
12	Virginia	4,981	2.2%
13	Georgia	4,438	1.9%
14	Connecticut	4,192	1.8%
15	Missouri	3,431	1.5%
16	North Carolina	3,221	1.4%
17	Arizona	3,215	1.4%
18	Indiana	3,157	1.4%
19	Wisconsin	2,948	1.3%
20	Tennessee	2,930	1.3%
21	Minnesota	2,482	1.1%
22	Washington	2,448	1.1%
23	Louisiana	2,285	1.0%
24	Kentucky	2,272	1.0%
25	Alabama	1,754	0.8%
26	West Virginia	1,711	0.7%
27	Nevada	1,580	0.7%
28	South Carolina	1,427	0.6%
29	Oklahoma	1,351	0.6%
30	Kansas	1,314	0.6%
31	Iowa	1,252	0.5%
32	Rhode Island	1,177	0.5%
33	Colorado	1,053	0.5%
34	Oregon	1,034	0.5%
35	Arkansas	1,017	0.4%
36	New Mexico	936	0.4%
37	Mississippi	780	0.3%
38	Delaware	753	0.3%
39	Hawaii	708	0.3%
40	Nebraska	678	0.3%
41	Maine	592	0.3%
42	New Hampshire	577	0.3%
43	Utah	510	0.2%
44	North Dakota	459	0.2%
45	South Dakota	270	0.1%
46	Vermont	244	0.1%
47	Alaska	118	0.1%
48	Montana	116	0.1%
49	Wyoming	109	0.0%
50	Idaho	105	0.0%
	District of Columbia	1,075	0.5%

Source: American Medical Association (Chicago, Illinois)
   "Physician Characteristics and Distribution in the U.S." (2008 Edition)
*As of December 31, 2006. Total does not include 7,037 physicians in U.S. territories and possessions.

International Medical School Graduates as a Percent of Physicians in 2006

National Percent = 25.3% of Physicians*

ALPHA ORDER				RANK ORDER		
RANK	STATE	PERCENT		RANK	STATE	PERCENT
31	Alabama	16.0		1	New Jersey	45.1
48	Alaska	7.0		2	New York	42.0
19	Arizona	21.3		3	Florida	36.5
32	Arkansas	15.7		4	West Virginia	36.3
16	California	23.0		5	Illinois	34.2
47	Colorado	7.4		6	Michigan	33.9
10	Connecticut	28.9		7	Delaware	31.2
7	Delaware	31.2		8	Nevada	29.3
3	Florida	36.5		9	Ohio	29.1
23	Georgia	19.5		10	Connecticut	28.9
33	Hawaii	15.4		11	Maryland	27.4
50	Idaho	3.6		12	Rhode Island	26.9
5	Illinois	34.2		13	North Dakota	26.3
22	Indiana	20.7		14	Pennsylvania	25.9
23	Iowa	19.5		15	Texas	24.1
26	Kansas	18.6		16	California	23.0
21	Kentucky	21.0		17	Missouri	22.0
28	Louisiana	18.1		18	Massachusetts	21.8
35	Maine	14.1		19	Arizona	21.3
11	Maryland	27.4		20	Virginia	21.2
18	Massachusetts	21.8		21	Kentucky	21.0
6	Michigan	33.9		22	Indiana	20.7
34	Minnesota	14.8		23	Georgia	19.5
39	Mississippi	13.2		23	Iowa	19.5
17	Missouri	22.0		25	Oklahoma	19.0
49	Montana	4.6		26	Kansas	18.6
37	Nebraska	14.0		27	Wisconsin	18.2
8	Nevada	29.3		28	Louisiana	18.1
35	New Hampshire	14.1		29	New Mexico	17.3
1	New Jersey	45.1		30	Tennessee	16.5
29	New Mexico	17.3		31	Alabama	16.0
2	New York	42.0		32	Arkansas	15.7
40	North Carolina	12.7		33	Hawaii	15.4
13	North Dakota	26.3		34	Minnesota	14.8
9	Ohio	29.1		35	Maine	14.1
25	Oklahoma	19.0		35	New Hampshire	14.1
45	Oregon	8.8		37	Nebraska	14.0
14	Pennsylvania	25.9		38	South Dakota	13.7
12	Rhode Island	26.9		39	Mississippi	13.2
40	South Carolina	12.7		40	North Carolina	12.7
38	South Dakota	13.7		40	South Carolina	12.7
30	Tennessee	16.5		42	Washington	12.3
15	Texas	24.1		43	Wyoming	9.6
46	Utah	8.4		44	Vermont	9.2
44	Vermont	9.2		45	Oregon	8.8
20	Virginia	21.2		46	Utah	8.4
42	Washington	12.3		47	Colorado	7.4
4	West Virginia	36.3		48	Alaska	7.0
27	Wisconsin	18.2		49	Montana	4.6
43	Wyoming	9.6		50	Idaho	3.6

District of Columbia 21.4

Source: CQ Press using data from American Medical Association (Chicago, Illinois)
    "Physician Characteristics and Distribution in the U.S." (2008 Edition)
*As of December 31, 2006. National rate does not include physicians in the U.S. territories and possessions.

Osteopathic Physicians in 2007

National Total = 54,481 Osteopathic Physicians*

ALPHA ORDER

RANK	STATE	OSTEOPATHS	% of USA
32	Alabama	373	0.7%
44	Alaska	135	0.2%
11	Arizona	1,517	2.8%
36	Arkansas	232	0.4%
4	California	3,713	6.8%
14	Colorado	898	1.6%
30	Connecticut	407	0.7%
37	Delaware	224	0.4%
6	Florida	3,640	6.7%
18	Georgia	728	1.3%
42	Hawaii	180	0.3%
38	Idaho	215	0.4%
9	Illinois	2,341	4.3%
16	Indiana	785	1.4%
13	Iowa	1,100	2.0%
22	Kansas	646	1.2%
29	Kentucky	423	0.8%
46	Louisiana	112	0.2%
23	Maine	621	1.1%
21	Maryland	654	1.2%
24	Massachusetts	618	1.1%
2	Michigan	4,875	8.9%
28	Minnesota	430	0.8%
34	Mississippi	295	0.5%
10	Missouri	1,861	3.4%
45	Montana	123	0.2%
43	Nebraska	155	0.3%
27	Nevada	436	0.8%
39	New Hampshire	210	0.4%
8	New Jersey	2,920	5.4%
40	New Mexico	201	0.4%
5	New York	3,671	6.7%
31	North Carolina	379	0.7%
49	North Dakota	57	0.1%
3	Ohio	3,721	6.8%
12	Oklahoma	1,475	2.7%
25	Oregon	526	1.0%
1	Pennsylvania	5,541	10.2%
40	Rhode Island	201	0.4%
33	South Carolina	349	0.6%
47	South Dakota	97	0.2%
26	Tennessee	509	0.9%
7	Texas	3,217	5.9%
35	Utah	270	0.5%
50	Vermont	54	0.1%
15	Virginia	831	1.5%
17	Washington	738	1.4%
20	West Virginia	656	1.2%
19	Wisconsin	683	1.3%
48	Wyoming	74	0.1%

RANK ORDER

RANK	STATE	OSTEOPATHS	% of USA
1	Pennsylvania	5,541	10.2%
2	Michigan	4,875	8.9%
3	Ohio	3,721	6.8%
4	California	3,713	6.8%
5	New York	3,671	6.7%
6	Florida	3,640	6.7%
7	Texas	3,217	5.9%
8	New Jersey	2,920	5.4%
9	Illinois	2,341	4.3%
10	Missouri	1,861	3.4%
11	Arizona	1,517	2.8%
12	Oklahoma	1,475	2.7%
13	Iowa	1,100	2.0%
14	Colorado	898	1.6%
15	Virginia	831	1.5%
16	Indiana	785	1.4%
17	Washington	738	1.4%
18	Georgia	728	1.3%
19	Wisconsin	683	1.3%
20	West Virginia	656	1.2%
21	Maryland	654	1.2%
22	Kansas	646	1.2%
23	Maine	621	1.1%
24	Massachusetts	618	1.1%
25	Oregon	526	1.0%
26	Tennessee	509	0.9%
27	Nevada	436	0.8%
28	Minnesota	430	0.8%
29	Kentucky	423	0.8%
30	Connecticut	407	0.7%
31	North Carolina	379	0.7%
32	Alabama	373	0.7%
33	South Carolina	349	0.6%
34	Mississippi	295	0.5%
35	Utah	270	0.5%
36	Arkansas	232	0.4%
37	Delaware	224	0.4%
38	Idaho	215	0.4%
39	New Hampshire	210	0.4%
40	New Mexico	201	0.4%
40	Rhode Island	201	0.4%
42	Hawaii	180	0.3%
43	Nebraska	155	0.3%
44	Alaska	135	0.2%
45	Montana	123	0.2%
46	Louisiana	112	0.2%
47	South Dakota	97	0.2%
48	Wyoming	74	0.1%
49	North Dakota	57	0.1%
50	Vermont	54	0.1%
	District of Columbia	64	0.1%

Source: American Osteopathic Association
"Fact Sheet 2007" (https://www.do-online.org/index.cfm?PageID=aoa_ompreport_us)
*Active osteopaths under age 65 as of May 31, 2007. National total does not include 226 osteopaths not shown by state.
Osteopaths practice a system of medicine based on the theory that disturbances in the musculoskeletal system affect other
body parts, causing many disorders that can be corrected by various manipulative techniques in conjunction with conventional
medical, surgical, pharmacological, and other therapeutic procedures.

Rate of Osteopathic Physicians in 2007

National Rate = 18 Osteopaths per 100,000 Population*

ALPHA ORDER				RANK ORDER		
RANK	STATE	RATE		RANK	STATE	RATE
43	Alabama	8		1	Michigan	48
13	Alaska	20		2	Maine	47
11	Arizona	24		3	Pennsylvania	45
43	Arkansas	8		4	Oklahoma	41
34	California	10		5	Iowa	37
17	Colorado	18		6	West Virginia	36
27	Connecticut	12		7	New Jersey	34
10	Delaware	26		8	Missouri	32
13	Florida	20		8	Ohio	32
43	Georgia	8		10	Delaware	26
21	Hawaii	14		11	Arizona	24
21	Idaho	14		12	Kansas	23
17	Illinois	18		13	Alaska	20
27	Indiana	12		13	Florida	20
5	Iowa	37		15	New York	19
12	Kansas	23		15	Rhode Island	19
34	Kentucky	10		17	Colorado	18
50	Louisiana	3		17	Illinois	18
2	Maine	47		19	Nevada	17
27	Maryland	12		20	New Hampshire	16
34	Massachusetts	10		21	Hawaii	14
1	Michigan	48		21	Idaho	14
43	Minnesota	8		21	Oregon	14
34	Mississippi	10		21	Wyoming	14
8	Missouri	32		25	Montana	13
25	Montana	13		25	Texas	13
40	Nebraska	9		27	Connecticut	12
19	Nevada	17		27	Indiana	12
20	New Hampshire	16		27	Maryland	12
7	New Jersey	34		27	South Dakota	12
34	New Mexico	10		27	Wisconsin	12
15	New York	19		32	Virginia	11
49	North Carolina	4		32	Washington	11
40	North Dakota	9		34	California	10
8	Ohio	32		34	Kentucky	10
4	Oklahoma	41		34	Massachusetts	10
21	Oregon	14		34	Mississippi	10
3	Pennsylvania	45		34	New Mexico	10
15	Rhode Island	19		34	Utah	10
43	South Carolina	8		40	Nebraska	9
27	South Dakota	12		40	North Dakota	9
43	Tennessee	8		40	Vermont	9
25	Texas	13		43	Alabama	8
34	Utah	10		43	Arkansas	8
40	Vermont	9		43	Georgia	8
32	Virginia	11		43	Minnesota	8
32	Washington	11		43	South Carolina	8
6	West Virginia	36		43	Tennessee	8
27	Wisconsin	12		49	North Carolina	4
21	Wyoming	14		50	Louisiana	3
					District of Columbia	11

Source: CQ Press using data from American Osteopathic Association
   "Fact Sheet 2007" (https://www.do-online.org/index.cfm?PageID=aoa_ompreport_us)
*Active osteopaths under age 65 as of May 31, 2007. National rate does not include osteopaths not shown by state.
Osteopaths practice a system of medicine based on the theory that disturbances in the musculoskeletal system affect other body parts, causing many disorders that can be corrected by various manipulative techniques in conjunction with conventional medical, surgical, pharmacological, and other therapeutic procedures.

Podiatrists in 2006

National Total = 9,020 Podiatrists*

ALPHA ORDER

RANK	STATE	PODIATRISTS	% of USA
27	Alabama	60	0.7%
NA	Alaska**	NA	NA
11	Arizona	240	2.7%
NA	Arkansas**	NA	NA
1	California	1,000	11.1%
NA	Colorado**	NA	NA
16	Connecticut	150	1.7%
26	Delaware	70	0.8%
3	Florida	650	7.2%
10	Georgia	270	3.0%
NA	Hawaii**	NA	NA
NA	Idaho**	NA	NA
7	Illinois	390	4.3%
20	Indiana	100	1.1%
25	Iowa	90	1.0%
32	Kansas	40	0.4%
27	Kentucky	60	0.7%
30	Louisiana	50	0.6%
32	Maine	40	0.4%
12	Maryland	230	2.5%
20	Massachusetts	100	1.1%
7	Michigan	390	4.3%
18	Minnesota	120	1.3%
NA	Mississippi**	NA	NA
14	Missouri	160	1.8%
NA	Montana**	NA	NA
30	Nebraska	50	0.6%
27	Nevada	60	0.7%
32	New Hampshire	40	0.4%
5	New Jersey	570	6.3%
18	New Mexico	120	1.3%
2	New York	920	10.2%
14	North Carolina	160	1.8%
NA	North Dakota**	NA	NA
6	Ohio	510	5.7%
NA	Oklahoma**	NA	NA
NA	Oregon**	NA	NA
4	Pennsylvania	630	7.0%
NA	Rhode Island**	NA	NA
20	South Carolina	100	1.1%
NA	South Dakota**	NA	NA
17	Tennessee	140	1.6%
7	Texas	390	4.3%
NA	Utah**	NA	NA
NA	Vermont**	NA	NA
13	Virginia	170	1.9%
20	Washington	100	1.1%
NA	West Virginia**	NA	NA
20	Wisconsin	100	1.1%
NA	Wyoming**	NA	NA

RANK ORDER

RANK	STATE	PODIATRISTS	% of USA
1	California	1,000	11.1%
2	New York	920	10.2%
3	Florida	650	7.2%
4	Pennsylvania	630	7.0%
5	New Jersey	570	6.3%
6	Ohio	510	5.7%
7	Illinois	390	4.3%
7	Michigan	390	4.3%
7	Texas	390	4.3%
10	Georgia	270	3.0%
11	Arizona	240	2.7%
12	Maryland	230	2.5%
13	Virginia	170	1.9%
14	Missouri	160	1.8%
14	North Carolina	160	1.8%
16	Connecticut	150	1.7%
17	Tennessee	140	1.6%
18	Minnesota	120	1.3%
18	New Mexico	120	1.3%
20	Indiana	100	1.1%
20	Massachusetts	100	1.1%
20	South Carolina	100	1.1%
20	Washington	100	1.1%
20	Wisconsin	100	1.1%
25	Iowa	90	1.0%
26	Delaware	70	0.8%
27	Alabama	60	0.7%
27	Kentucky	60	0.7%
27	Nevada	60	0.7%
30	Louisiana	50	0.6%
30	Nebraska	50	0.6%
32	Kansas	40	0.4%
32	Maine	40	0.4%
32	New Hampshire	40	0.4%
NA	Alaska**	NA	NA
NA	Arkansas**	NA	NA
NA	Colorado**	NA	NA
NA	Hawaii**	NA	NA
NA	Idaho**	NA	NA
NA	Mississippi**	NA	NA
NA	Montana**	NA	NA
NA	North Dakota**	NA	NA
NA	Oklahoma**	NA	NA
NA	Oregon**	NA	NA
NA	Rhode Island**	NA	NA
NA	South Dakota**	NA	NA
NA	Utah**	NA	NA
NA	Vermont**	NA	NA
NA	West Virginia**	NA	NA
NA	Wyoming**	NA	NA
	District of Columbia**	NA	NA

Source: U.S. Department of Labor, Bureau of Labor Statistics
"Occupational Employment and Wages, 2006" (http://www.bls.gov/oes/)
*Does not include self-employed.
**Not available.

Rate of Podiatrists in 2006

National Rate = 3 Podiatrists per 100,000 Population*

ALPHA ORDER

RANK	STATE	RATE
31	Alabama	1
NA	Alaska**	NA
6	Arizona	4
NA	Arkansas**	NA
12	California	3
NA	Colorado**	NA
6	Connecticut	4
1	Delaware	8
6	Florida	4
12	Georgia	3
NA	Hawaii**	NA
NA	Idaho**	NA
12	Illinois	3
20	Indiana	2
12	Iowa	3
31	Kansas	1
31	Kentucky	1
31	Louisiana	1
12	Maine	3
6	Maryland	4
20	Massachusetts	2
6	Michigan	4
20	Minnesota	2
NA	Mississippi**	NA
12	Missouri	3
NA	Montana**	NA
12	Nebraska	3
20	Nevada	2
12	New Hampshire	3
2	New Jersey	7
3	New Mexico	6
4	New York	5
20	North Carolina	2
NA	North Dakota**	NA
6	Ohio	4
NA	Oklahoma**	NA
NA	Oregon**	NA
4	Pennsylvania	5
NA	Rhode Island**	NA
20	South Carolina	2
NA	South Dakota**	NA
20	Tennessee	2
20	Texas	2
NA	Utah**	NA
NA	Vermont**	NA
20	Virginia	2
20	Washington	2
NA	West Virginia**	NA
20	Wisconsin	2
NA	Wyoming**	NA

RANK ORDER

RANK	STATE	RATE
1	Delaware	8
2	New Jersey	7
3	New Mexico	6
4	New York	5
4	Pennsylvania	5
6	Arizona	4
6	Connecticut	4
6	Florida	4
6	Maryland	4
6	Michigan	4
6	Ohio	4
12	California	3
12	Georgia	3
12	Illinois	3
12	Iowa	3
12	Maine	3
12	Missouri	3
12	Nebraska	3
12	New Hampshire	3
20	Indiana	2
20	Massachusetts	2
20	Minnesota	2
20	Nevada	2
20	North Carolina	2
20	South Carolina	2
20	Tennessee	2
20	Texas	2
20	Virginia	2
20	Washington	2
20	Wisconsin	2
31	Alabama	1
31	Kansas	1
31	Kentucky	1
31	Louisiana	1
NA	Alaska**	NA
NA	Arkansas**	NA
NA	Colorado**	NA
NA	Hawaii**	NA
NA	Idaho**	NA
NA	Mississippi**	NA
NA	Montana**	NA
NA	North Dakota**	NA
NA	Oklahoma**	NA
NA	Oregon**	NA
NA	Rhode Island**	NA
NA	South Dakota**	NA
NA	Utah**	NA
NA	Vermont**	NA
NA	West Virginia**	NA
NA	Wyoming**	NA
	District of Columbia**	NA

Source: CQ Press using data from U.S. Department of Labor, Bureau of Labor Statistics
"Occupational Employment and Wages, 2006" (http://www.bls.gov/oes/)
*Does not include self-employed.
**Not available.

Average Annual Wages of Podiatrists in 2006

National Average = $118,500*

ALPHA ORDER			RANK ORDER		
RANK	STATE	WAGES	RANK	STATE	WAGES
30	Alabama	$104,320	1	Oregon	$176,740
NA	Alaska**	NA	2	Georgia	167,230
28	Arizona	105,850	3	Kentucky	165,440
NA	Arkansas**	NA	4	Oklahoma	162,610
33	California	94,560	5	North Carolina	157,530
22	Colorado	116,520	6	Kansas	156,280
27	Connecticut	112,150	7	New Hampshire	155,230
29	Delaware	104,470	8	Minnesota	147,160
24	Florida	115,830	9	Washington	145,920
2	Georgia	167,230	10	Missouri	141,540
NA	Hawaii**	NA	11	Tennessee	139,930
NA	Idaho**	NA	12	Virginia	134,160
16	Illinois	122,200	13	Indiana	128,850
13	Indiana	128,850	14	New York	126,330
25	Iowa	114,740	15	Wisconsin	123,720
6	Kansas	156,280	16	Illinois	122,200
3	Kentucky	165,440	17	Nebraska	120,790
NA	Louisiana**	NA	18	Massachusetts	120,770
34	Maine	93,360	19	Texas	118,700
20	Maryland	118,440	20	Maryland	118,440
18	Massachusetts	120,770	21	Nevada	118,150
NA	Michigan**	NA	22	Colorado	116,520
8	Minnesota	147,160	23	Pennsylvania	115,840
NA	Mississippi**	NA	24	Florida	115,830
10	Missouri	141,540	25	Iowa	114,740
NA	Montana**	NA	26	South Carolina	114,290
17	Nebraska	120,790	27	Connecticut	112,150
21	Nevada	118,150	28	Arizona	105,850
7	New Hampshire	155,230	29	Delaware	104,470
31	New Jersey	104,040	30	Alabama	104,320
NA	New Mexico**	NA	31	New Jersey	104,040
14	New York	126,330	32	Ohio	103,690
5	North Carolina	157,530	33	California	94,560
NA	North Dakota**	NA	34	Maine	93,360
32	Ohio	103,690	35	Utah	58,550
4	Oklahoma	162,610	NA	Alaska**	NA
1	Oregon	176,740	NA	Arkansas**	NA
23	Pennsylvania	115,840	NA	Hawaii**	NA
NA	Rhode Island**	NA	NA	Idaho**	NA
26	South Carolina	114,290	NA	Louisiana**	NA
NA	South Dakota**	NA	NA	Michigan**	NA
11	Tennessee	139,930	NA	Mississippi**	NA
19	Texas	118,700	NA	Montana**	NA
35	Utah	58,550	NA	New Mexico**	NA
NA	Vermont**	NA	NA	North Dakota**	NA
12	Virginia	134,160	NA	Rhode Island**	NA
9	Washington	145,920	NA	South Dakota**	NA
NA	West Virginia**	NA	NA	Vermont**	NA
15	Wisconsin	123,720	NA	West Virginia**	NA
NA	Wyoming**	NA	NA	Wyoming**	NA
				District of Columbia**	NA

Source: U.S. Department of Labor, Bureau of Labor Statistics
    "Occupational Employment and Wages, 2006" (http://www.bls.gov/oes/)
*Does not include self-employed.
**Not available.

Doctors of Chiropractic in 2006

National Total = 87,237 Chiropractors*

ALPHA ORDER				RANK ORDER			
RANK	STATE	CHIROPRACTORS	% of USA	RANK	STATE	CHIROPRACTORS	% of USA
29	Alabama	786	0.9%	1	California	13,786	15.8%
49	Alaska	219	0.3%	2	New York	5,830	6.7%
10	Arizona	2,722	3.1%	3	Florida	4,721	5.4%
34	Arkansas	580	0.7%	4	Texas	4,437	5.1%
1	California	13,786	15.8%	5	Pennsylvania	4,000	4.6%
11	Colorado	2,495	2.9%	6	Illinois	3,902	4.5%
24	Connecticut	994	1.1%	7	New Jersey	3,392	3.9%
45	Delaware	305	0.3%	8	Georgia	3,203	3.7%
3	Florida	4,721	5.4%	9	Michigan	2,846	3.3%
8	Georgia	3,203	3.7%	10	Arizona	2,722	3.1%
37	Hawaii	486	0.6%	11	Colorado	2,495	2.9%
36	Idaho	501	0.6%	12	Minnesota	2,323	2.7%
6	Illinois	3,902	4.5%	13	Washington	2,254	2.6%
23	Indiana	1,042	1.2%	14	Ohio	2,228	2.6%
21	Iowa	1,430	1.6%	15	Massachusetts	2,203	2.5%
26	Kansas	880	1.0%	16	Missouri	2,130	2.4%
28	Kentucky	790	0.9%	17	Wisconsin	1,881	2.2%
35	Louisiana	542	0.6%	18	North Carolina	1,826	2.1%
40	Maine	381	0.4%	19	Virginia	1,547	1.8%
31	Maryland	761	0.9%	20	South Carolina	1,457	1.7%
15	Massachusetts	2,203	2.5%	21	Iowa	1,430	1.6%
9	Michigan	2,846	3.3%	22	Oregon	1,274	1.5%
12	Minnesota	2,323	2.7%	23	Indiana	1,042	1.2%
43	Mississippi	328	0.4%	24	Connecticut	994	1.1%
16	Missouri	2,130	2.4%	25	Tennessee	975	1.1%
41	Montana	356	0.4%	26	Kansas	880	1.0%
38	Nebraska	447	0.5%	27	Utah	809	0.9%
33	Nevada	621	0.7%	28	Kentucky	790	0.9%
39	New Hampshire	442	0.5%	29	Alabama	786	0.9%
7	New Jersey	3,392	3.9%	30	Oklahoma	785	0.9%
32	New Mexico	627	0.7%	31	Maryland	761	0.9%
2	New York	5,830	6.7%	32	New Mexico	627	0.7%
18	North Carolina	1,826	2.1%	33	Nevada	621	0.7%
47	North Dakota	262	0.3%	34	Arkansas	580	0.7%
14	Ohio	2,228	2.6%	35	Louisiana	542	0.6%
30	Oklahoma	785	0.9%	36	Idaho	501	0.6%
22	Oregon	1,274	1.5%	37	Hawaii	486	0.6%
5	Pennsylvania	4,000	4.6%	38	Nebraska	447	0.5%
46	Rhode Island	272	0.3%	39	New Hampshire	442	0.5%
20	South Carolina	1,457	1.7%	40	Maine	381	0.4%
44	South Dakota	323	0.4%	41	Montana	356	0.4%
25	Tennessee	975	1.1%	42	West Virginia	338	0.4%
4	Texas	4,437	5.1%	43	Mississippi	328	0.4%
27	Utah	809	0.9%	44	South Dakota	323	0.4%
48	Vermont	226	0.3%	45	Delaware	305	0.3%
19	Virginia	1,547	1.8%	46	Rhode Island	272	0.3%
13	Washington	2,254	2.6%	47	North Dakota	262	0.3%
42	West Virginia	338	0.4%	48	Vermont	226	0.3%
17	Wisconsin	1,881	2.2%	49	Alaska	219	0.3%
50	Wyoming	202	0.2%	50	Wyoming	202	0.2%
					District of Columbia	70	0.1%

Source: Federation of Chiropractic Licensing Boards
  "Official Directory" (http://www.fclb.org/directory/index.htm)
*As of December 2006. Licensed active doctors. There is some duplication as some doctors are licensed in more than one state.

Rate of Doctors of Chiropractic in 2006

National Rate = 29 Chiropractors per 100,000 Population*

RANK	STATE	RATE
45	Alabama	17
23	Alaska	32
4	Arizona	44
38	Arkansas	21
9	California	38
1	Colorado	52
31	Connecticut	28
12	Delaware	36
33	Florida	26
17	Georgia	34
9	Hawaii	38
17	Idaho	34
27	Illinois	31
45	Indiana	17
2	Iowa	48
23	Kansas	32
41	Kentucky	19
49	Louisiana	13
30	Maine	29
48	Maryland	14
17	Massachusetts	34
31	Michigan	28
3	Minnesota	45
50	Mississippi	11
12	Missouri	36
9	Montana	38
35	Nebraska	25
35	Nevada	25
17	New Hampshire	34
7	New Jersey	39
23	New Mexico	32
29	New York	30
38	North Carolina	21
5	North Dakota	41
41	Ohio	19
37	Oklahoma	22
15	Oregon	35
23	Pennsylvania	32
33	Rhode Island	26
17	South Carolina	34
5	South Dakota	41
47	Tennessee	16
41	Texas	19
27	Utah	31
12	Vermont	36
40	Virginia	20
15	Washington	35
41	West Virginia	19
17	Wisconsin	34
7	Wyoming	39

RANK	STATE	RATE
1	Colorado	52
2	Iowa	48
3	Minnesota	45
4	Arizona	44
5	North Dakota	41
5	South Dakota	41
7	New Jersey	39
7	Wyoming	39
9	California	38
9	Hawaii	38
9	Montana	38
12	Delaware	36
12	Missouri	36
12	Vermont	36
15	Oregon	35
15	Washington	35
17	Georgia	34
17	Idaho	34
17	Massachusetts	34
17	New Hampshire	34
17	South Carolina	34
17	Wisconsin	34
23	Alaska	32
23	Kansas	32
23	New Mexico	32
23	Pennsylvania	32
27	Illinois	31
27	Utah	31
29	New York	30
30	Maine	29
31	Connecticut	28
31	Michigan	28
33	Florida	26
33	Rhode Island	26
35	Nebraska	25
35	Nevada	25
37	Oklahoma	22
38	Arkansas	21
38	North Carolina	21
40	Virginia	20
41	Kentucky	19
41	Ohio	19
41	Texas	19
41	West Virginia	19
45	Alabama	17
45	Indiana	17
47	Tennessee	16
48	Maryland	14
49	Louisiana	13
50	Mississippi	11

District of Columbia — 12

Source: CQ Press using data from Federation of Chiropractic Licensing Boards
"Official Directory" (http://www.fclb.org/directory/index.htm)
*As of December 2006. Licensed active doctors. There is some duplication as some doctors are licensed in more than one state.

Average Annual Wages of Chiropractors in 2006

National Average = $81,070*

ALPHA ORDER				RANK ORDER		
RANK	STATE	WAGES		RANK	STATE	WAGES
1	Alabama	$139,960		1	Alabama	$139,960
NA	Alaska**	NA		2	Maryland	119,810
27	Arizona	79,060		3	Nevada	116,490
29	Arkansas	76,910		4	Washington	109,120
38	California	68,590		5	North Carolina	104,510
NA	Colorado**	NA		6	Ohio	101,910
8	Connecticut	96,740		7	Wisconsin	101,250
14	Delaware	87,890		8	Connecticut	96,740
34	Florida	70,520		9	Tennessee	95,720
42	Georgia	61,740		10	Illinois	91,870
46	Hawaii	54,070		11	Kentucky	90,760
25	Idaho	79,630		12	New Hampshire	89,110
10	Illinois	91,870		13	Kansas	88,110
16	Indiana	85,920		14	Delaware	87,890
24	Iowa	80,810		15	Oklahoma	87,390
13	Kansas	88,110		16	Indiana	85,920
11	Kentucky	90,760		17	Michigan	84,690
20	Louisiana	82,420		18	South Dakota	84,290
40	Maine	67,300		19	Nebraska	82,880
2	Maryland	119,810		20	Louisiana	82,420
21	Massachusetts	81,550		21	Massachusetts	81,550
17	Michigan	84,690		22	Virginia	81,060
31	Minnesota	72,990		23	Rhode Island	80,970
41	Mississippi	67,170		24	Iowa	80,810
39	Missouri	68,290		25	Idaho	79,630
47	Montana	53,500		26	New Jersey	79,380
19	Nebraska	82,880		27	Arizona	79,060
3	Nevada	116,490		28	New York	77,720
12	New Hampshire	89,110		29	Arkansas	76,910
26	New Jersey	79,380		30	South Carolina	75,060
45	New Mexico	54,930		31	Minnesota	72,990
28	New York	77,720		32	Pennsylvania	72,520
5	North Carolina	104,510		33	Wyoming	70,680
44	North Dakota	58,820		34	Florida	70,520
6	Ohio	101,910		35	Utah	70,500
15	Oklahoma	87,390		36	Texas	69,570
48	Oregon	50,540		37	West Virginia	69,060
32	Pennsylvania	72,520		38	California	68,590
23	Rhode Island	80,970		39	Missouri	68,290
30	South Carolina	75,060		40	Maine	67,300
18	South Dakota	84,290		41	Mississippi	67,170
9	Tennessee	95,720		42	Georgia	61,740
36	Texas	69,570		43	Vermont	60,970
35	Utah	70,500		44	North Dakota	58,820
43	Vermont	60,970		45	New Mexico	54,930
22	Virginia	81,060		46	Hawaii	54,070
4	Washington	109,120		47	Montana	53,500
37	West Virginia	69,060		48	Oregon	50,540
7	Wisconsin	101,250		NA	Alaska**	NA
33	Wyoming	70,680		NA	Colorado**	NA
					District of Columbia**	NA

Source: U.S. Department of Labor, Bureau of Labor Statistics
   "Occupational Employment and Wages, 2006" (http://www.bls.gov/oes/)
*Does not include self-employed.
**Not available.

Physician Assistants in Clinical Practice in 2008

National Total = 67,765 Physician Assistants*

RANK	STATE	PAs	% of USA
38	Alabama	433	0.6%
41	Alaska	353	0.5%
14	Arizona	1,595	2.4%
49	Arkansas	121	0.2%
2	California	6,414	9.5%
13	Colorado	1,625	2.4%
19	Connecticut	1,269	1.9%
46	Delaware	206	0.3%
4	Florida	4,090	6.0%
8	Georgia	2,242	3.3%
48	Hawaii	164	0.2%
35	Idaho	475	0.7%
11	Illinois	1,810	2.7%
31	Indiana	593	0.9%
26	Iowa	729	1.1%
25	Kansas	739	1.1%
23	Kentucky	770	1.1%
36	Louisiana	468	0.7%
32	Maine	561	0.8%
10	Maryland	1,829	2.7%
15	Massachusetts	1,558	2.3%
7	Michigan	2,837	4.2%
20	Minnesota	1,113	1.6%
50	Mississippi	79	0.1%
33	Missouri	557	0.8%
42	Montana	339	0.5%
28	Nebraska	675	1.0%
37	Nevada	446	0.7%
39	New Hampshire	373	0.6%
18	New Jersey	1,304	1.9%
34	New Mexico	506	0.7%
1	New York	7,359	10.9%
6	North Carolina	3,282	4.8%
44	North Dakota	225	0.3%
9	Ohio	1,852	2.7%
21	Oklahoma	965	1.4%
24	Oregon	740	1.1%
5	Pennsylvania	4,023	5.9%
43	Rhode Island	229	0.3%
29	South Carolina	674	1.0%
40	South Dakota	371	0.5%
22	Tennessee	885	1.3%
3	Texas	4,259	6.3%
30	Utah	631	0.9%
45	Vermont	212	0.3%
16	Virginia	1,492	2.2%
12	Washington	1,800	2.7%
27	West Virginia	701	1.0%
17	Wisconsin	1,432	2.1%
47	Wyoming	173	0.3%

RANK	STATE	PAs	% of USA
1	New York	7,359	10.9%
2	California	6,414	9.5%
3	Texas	4,259	6.3%
4	Florida	4,090	6.0%
5	Pennsylvania	4,023	5.9%
6	North Carolina	3,282	4.8%
7	Michigan	2,837	4.2%
8	Georgia	2,242	3.3%
9	Ohio	1,852	2.7%
10	Maryland	1,829	2.7%
11	Illinois	1,810	2.7%
12	Washington	1,800	2.7%
13	Colorado	1,625	2.4%
14	Arizona	1,595	2.4%
15	Massachusetts	1,558	2.3%
16	Virginia	1,492	2.2%
17	Wisconsin	1,432	2.1%
18	New Jersey	1,304	1.9%
19	Connecticut	1,269	1.9%
20	Minnesota	1,113	1.6%
21	Oklahoma	965	1.4%
22	Tennessee	885	1.3%
23	Kentucky	770	1.1%
24	Oregon	740	1.1%
25	Kansas	739	1.1%
26	Iowa	729	1.1%
27	West Virginia	701	1.0%
28	Nebraska	675	1.0%
29	South Carolina	674	1.0%
30	Utah	631	0.9%
31	Indiana	593	0.9%
32	Maine	561	0.8%
33	Missouri	557	0.8%
34	New Mexico	506	0.7%
35	Idaho	475	0.7%
36	Louisiana	468	0.7%
37	Nevada	446	0.7%
38	Alabama	433	0.6%
39	New Hampshire	373	0.6%
40	South Dakota	371	0.5%
41	Alaska	353	0.5%
42	Montana	339	0.5%
43	Rhode Island	229	0.3%
44	North Dakota	225	0.3%
45	Vermont	212	0.3%
46	Delaware	206	0.3%
47	Wyoming	173	0.3%
48	Hawaii	164	0.2%
49	Arkansas	121	0.2%
50	Mississippi	79	0.1%
	District of Columbia	187	0.3%

Source: The American Academy of Physician Assistants

   "Projected Number of People in Clinical Practice as PAs as of January 1, 2008" (http://www.aapa.org/research/)

*Projected. National total does not include 329 physician assistants who work outside the United States or whose location is unknown.

Rate of Physician Assistants in Clinical Practice in 2007

National Rate = 22 PAs per 100,000 Population*

ALPHA ORDER

RANK	STATE	RATE
46	Alabama	9
1	Alaska	52
24	Arizona	25
49	Arkansas	4
35	California	18
12	Colorado	33
7	Connecticut	36
25	Delaware	24
30	Florida	22
29	Georgia	23
44	Hawaii	13
15	Idaho	32
42	Illinois	14
46	Indiana	9
25	Iowa	24
20	Kansas	27
35	Kentucky	18
45	Louisiana	11
3	Maine	43
12	Maryland	33
25	Massachusetts	24
17	Michigan	28
32	Minnesota	21
50	Mississippi	3
46	Missouri	9
9	Montana	35
5	Nebraska	38
38	Nevada	17
17	New Hampshire	28
40	New Jersey	15
22	New Mexico	26
5	New York	38
7	North Carolina	36
9	North Dakota	35
39	Ohio	16
20	Oklahoma	27
33	Oregon	20
15	Pennsylvania	32
30	Rhode Island	22
40	South Carolina	15
2	South Dakota	47
42	Tennessee	14
35	Texas	18
25	Utah	24
11	Vermont	34
34	Virginia	19
17	Washington	28
4	West Virginia	39
22	Wisconsin	26
12	Wyoming	33

RANK ORDER

RANK	STATE	RATE
1	Alaska	52
2	South Dakota	47
3	Maine	43
4	West Virginia	39
5	Nebraska	38
5	New York	38
7	Connecticut	36
7	North Carolina	36
9	Montana	35
9	North Dakota	35
11	Vermont	34
12	Colorado	33
12	Maryland	33
12	Wyoming	33
15	Idaho	32
15	Pennsylvania	32
17	Michigan	28
17	New Hampshire	28
17	Washington	28
20	Kansas	27
20	Oklahoma	27
22	New Mexico	26
22	Wisconsin	26
24	Arizona	25
25	Delaware	24
25	Iowa	24
25	Massachusetts	24
25	Utah	24
29	Georgia	23
30	Florida	22
30	Rhode Island	22
32	Minnesota	21
33	Oregon	20
34	Virginia	19
35	California	18
35	Kentucky	18
35	Texas	18
38	Nevada	17
39	Ohio	16
40	New Jersey	15
40	South Carolina	15
42	Illinois	14
42	Tennessee	14
44	Hawaii	13
45	Louisiana	11
46	Alabama	9
46	Indiana	9
46	Missouri	9
49	Arkansas	4
50	Mississippi	3
	District of Columbia	32

Source: CQ Press using data from The American Academy of Physician Assistants
"Projected Number of People in Clinical Practice as PAs as of January 1, 2008" (http://www.aapa.org/research/)
*Projected. Rates calculated using 2007 Census population figures.

Average Annual Wages of Physician Assistants in 2006

National Average = $74,270*

<table>
<tr><td colspan="3">ALPHA ORDER</td><td colspan="3">RANK ORDER</td></tr>
<tr><td>RANK</td><td>STATE</td><td>WAGES</td><td>RANK</td><td>STATE</td><td>WAGES</td></tr>
<tr><td>46</td><td>Alabama</td><td>$52,620</td><td>1</td><td>Alaska</td><td>$86,460</td></tr>
<tr><td>1</td><td>Alaska</td><td>86,460</td><td>2</td><td>Utah</td><td>85,460</td></tr>
<tr><td>38</td><td>Arizona</td><td>66,130</td><td>3</td><td>Maryland</td><td>85,140</td></tr>
<tr><td>39</td><td>Arkansas</td><td>65,150</td><td>4</td><td>Texas</td><td>81,330</td></tr>
<tr><td>5</td><td>California</td><td>80,960</td><td>5</td><td>California</td><td>80,960</td></tr>
<tr><td>30</td><td>Colorado</td><td>71,220</td><td>6</td><td>Connecticut</td><td>80,770</td></tr>
<tr><td>6</td><td>Connecticut</td><td>80,770</td><td>7</td><td>Maine</td><td>80,520</td></tr>
<tr><td>24</td><td>Delaware</td><td>74,640</td><td>8</td><td>Washington</td><td>79,880</td></tr>
<tr><td>12</td><td>Florida</td><td>78,330</td><td>9</td><td>New York</td><td>79,060</td></tr>
<tr><td>32</td><td>Georgia</td><td>69,650</td><td>10</td><td>Vermont</td><td>78,560</td></tr>
<tr><td>43</td><td>Hawaii</td><td>61,140</td><td>11</td><td>Wisconsin</td><td>78,370</td></tr>
<tr><td>31</td><td>Idaho</td><td>70,870</td><td>12</td><td>Florida</td><td>78,330</td></tr>
<tr><td>35</td><td>Illinois</td><td>67,330</td><td>13</td><td>Minnesota</td><td>77,980</td></tr>
<tr><td>34</td><td>Indiana</td><td>69,010</td><td>14</td><td>Massachusetts</td><td>77,800</td></tr>
<tr><td>29</td><td>Iowa</td><td>71,990</td><td>15</td><td>Nebraska</td><td>77,610</td></tr>
<tr><td>27</td><td>Kansas</td><td>73,420</td><td>16</td><td>Oregon</td><td>76,700</td></tr>
<tr><td>33</td><td>Kentucky</td><td>69,580</td><td>17</td><td>Oklahoma</td><td>76,390</td></tr>
<tr><td>47</td><td>Louisiana</td><td>49,960</td><td>18</td><td>New Hampshire</td><td>76,150</td></tr>
<tr><td>7</td><td>Maine</td><td>80,520</td><td>19</td><td>South Carolina</td><td>75,980</td></tr>
<tr><td>3</td><td>Maryland</td><td>85,140</td><td>20</td><td>South Dakota</td><td>75,720</td></tr>
<tr><td>14</td><td>Massachusetts</td><td>77,800</td><td>21</td><td>New Jersey</td><td>75,610</td></tr>
<tr><td>23</td><td>Michigan</td><td>74,930</td><td>22</td><td>North Carolina</td><td>74,970</td></tr>
<tr><td>13</td><td>Minnesota</td><td>77,980</td><td>23</td><td>Michigan</td><td>74,930</td></tr>
<tr><td>49</td><td>Mississippi</td><td>44,030</td><td>24</td><td>Delaware</td><td>74,640</td></tr>
<tr><td>41</td><td>Missouri</td><td>62,360</td><td>25</td><td>Ohio</td><td>74,230</td></tr>
<tr><td>NA</td><td>Montana**</td><td>NA</td><td>25</td><td>Rhode Island</td><td>74,230</td></tr>
<tr><td>15</td><td>Nebraska</td><td>77,610</td><td>27</td><td>Kansas</td><td>73,420</td></tr>
<tr><td>40</td><td>Nevada</td><td>64,720</td><td>28</td><td>West Virginia</td><td>72,420</td></tr>
<tr><td>18</td><td>New Hampshire</td><td>76,150</td><td>29</td><td>Iowa</td><td>71,990</td></tr>
<tr><td>21</td><td>New Jersey</td><td>75,610</td><td>30</td><td>Colorado</td><td>71,220</td></tr>
<tr><td>48</td><td>New Mexico</td><td>46,370</td><td>31</td><td>Idaho</td><td>70,870</td></tr>
<tr><td>9</td><td>New York</td><td>79,060</td><td>32</td><td>Georgia</td><td>69,650</td></tr>
<tr><td>22</td><td>North Carolina</td><td>74,970</td><td>33</td><td>Kentucky</td><td>69,580</td></tr>
<tr><td>36</td><td>North Dakota</td><td>66,620</td><td>34</td><td>Indiana</td><td>69,010</td></tr>
<tr><td>25</td><td>Ohio</td><td>74,230</td><td>35</td><td>Illinois</td><td>67,330</td></tr>
<tr><td>17</td><td>Oklahoma</td><td>76,390</td><td>36</td><td>North Dakota</td><td>66,620</td></tr>
<tr><td>16</td><td>Oregon</td><td>76,700</td><td>37</td><td>Tennessee</td><td>66,310</td></tr>
<tr><td>42</td><td>Pennsylvania</td><td>62,310</td><td>38</td><td>Arizona</td><td>66,130</td></tr>
<tr><td>25</td><td>Rhode Island</td><td>74,230</td><td>39</td><td>Arkansas</td><td>65,150</td></tr>
<tr><td>19</td><td>South Carolina</td><td>75,980</td><td>40</td><td>Nevada</td><td>64,720</td></tr>
<tr><td>20</td><td>South Dakota</td><td>75,720</td><td>41</td><td>Missouri</td><td>62,360</td></tr>
<tr><td>37</td><td>Tennessee</td><td>66,310</td><td>42</td><td>Pennsylvania</td><td>62,310</td></tr>
<tr><td>4</td><td>Texas</td><td>81,330</td><td>43</td><td>Hawaii</td><td>61,140</td></tr>
<tr><td>2</td><td>Utah</td><td>85,460</td><td>44</td><td>Wyoming</td><td>58,870</td></tr>
<tr><td>10</td><td>Vermont</td><td>78,560</td><td>45</td><td>Virginia</td><td>58,390</td></tr>
<tr><td>45</td><td>Virginia</td><td>58,390</td><td>46</td><td>Alabama</td><td>52,620</td></tr>
<tr><td>8</td><td>Washington</td><td>79,880</td><td>47</td><td>Louisiana</td><td>49,960</td></tr>
<tr><td>28</td><td>West Virginia</td><td>72,420</td><td>48</td><td>New Mexico</td><td>46,370</td></tr>
<tr><td>11</td><td>Wisconsin</td><td>78,370</td><td>49</td><td>Mississippi</td><td>44,030</td></tr>
<tr><td>44</td><td>Wyoming</td><td>58,870</td><td>NA</td><td>Montana**</td><td>NA</td></tr>
<tr><td></td><td></td><td></td><td colspan="2">District of Columbia</td><td>65,850</td></tr>
</table>

Source: U.S. Department of Labor, Bureau of Labor Statistics
   "Occupational Employment and Wages, 2006" (http://www.bls.gov/oes/)
*Does not include self-employed.
**Not available.

Registered Nurses in 2006

National Total = 2,417,150 Registered Nurses*

<table>
<tr><td colspan="4">ALPHA ORDER</td><td colspan="4">RANK ORDER</td></tr>
<tr><td>RANK</td><td>STATE</td><td>NURSES</td><td>% of USA</td><td>RANK</td><td>STATE</td><td>NURSES</td><td>% of USA</td></tr>
<tr><td>21</td><td>Alabama</td><td>40,010</td><td>1.7%</td><td>1</td><td>California</td><td>234,260</td><td>9.7%</td></tr>
<tr><td>49</td><td>Alaska</td><td>5,260</td><td>0.2%</td><td>2</td><td>New York</td><td>164,970</td><td>6.8%</td></tr>
<tr><td>26</td><td>Arizona</td><td>31,890</td><td>1.3%</td><td>3</td><td>Texas</td><td>156,590</td><td>6.5%</td></tr>
<tr><td>33</td><td>Arkansas</td><td>21,020</td><td>0.9%</td><td>4</td><td>Florida</td><td>146,290</td><td>6.1%</td></tr>
<tr><td>1</td><td>California</td><td>234,260</td><td>9.7%</td><td>5</td><td>Pennsylvania</td><td>126,120</td><td>5.2%</td></tr>
<tr><td>25</td><td>Colorado</td><td>34,520</td><td>1.4%</td><td>6</td><td>Ohio</td><td>111,840</td><td>4.6%</td></tr>
<tr><td>24</td><td>Connecticut</td><td>34,710</td><td>1.4%</td><td>7</td><td>Illinois</td><td>103,100</td><td>4.3%</td></tr>
<tr><td>45</td><td>Delaware</td><td>7,830</td><td>0.3%</td><td>8</td><td>Michigan</td><td>84,880</td><td>3.5%</td></tr>
<tr><td>4</td><td>Florida</td><td>146,290</td><td>6.1%</td><td>9</td><td>New Jersey</td><td>80,330</td><td>3.3%</td></tr>
<tr><td>12</td><td>Georgia</td><td>60,850</td><td>2.5%</td><td>10</td><td>Massachusetts</td><td>76,350</td><td>3.2%</td></tr>
<tr><td>42</td><td>Hawaii</td><td>9,610</td><td>0.4%</td><td>11</td><td>North Carolina</td><td>74,400</td><td>3.1%</td></tr>
<tr><td>44</td><td>Idaho</td><td>9,100</td><td>0.4%</td><td>12</td><td>Georgia</td><td>60,850</td><td>2.5%</td></tr>
<tr><td>7</td><td>Illinois</td><td>103,100</td><td>4.3%</td><td>13</td><td>Missouri</td><td>55,470</td><td>2.3%</td></tr>
<tr><td>15</td><td>Indiana</td><td>52,910</td><td>2.2%</td><td>14</td><td>Virginia</td><td>55,300</td><td>2.3%</td></tr>
<tr><td>28</td><td>Iowa</td><td>31,040</td><td>1.3%</td><td>15</td><td>Indiana</td><td>52,910</td><td>2.2%</td></tr>
<tr><td>32</td><td>Kansas</td><td>23,590</td><td>1.0%</td><td>16</td><td>Tennessee</td><td>52,780</td><td>2.2%</td></tr>
<tr><td>22</td><td>Kentucky</td><td>38,120</td><td>1.6%</td><td>17</td><td>Minnesota</td><td>49,580</td><td>2.1%</td></tr>
<tr><td>23</td><td>Louisiana</td><td>37,940</td><td>1.6%</td><td>18</td><td>Wisconsin</td><td>48,460</td><td>2.0%</td></tr>
<tr><td>38</td><td>Maine</td><td>13,690</td><td>0.6%</td><td>19</td><td>Washington</td><td>48,190</td><td>2.0%</td></tr>
<tr><td>20</td><td>Maryland</td><td>47,560</td><td>2.0%</td><td>20</td><td>Maryland</td><td>47,560</td><td>2.0%</td></tr>
<tr><td>10</td><td>Massachusetts</td><td>76,350</td><td>3.2%</td><td>21</td><td>Alabama</td><td>40,010</td><td>1.7%</td></tr>
<tr><td>8</td><td>Michigan</td><td>84,880</td><td>3.5%</td><td>22</td><td>Kentucky</td><td>38,120</td><td>1.6%</td></tr>
<tr><td>17</td><td>Minnesota</td><td>49,580</td><td>2.1%</td><td>23</td><td>Louisiana</td><td>37,940</td><td>1.6%</td></tr>
<tr><td>30</td><td>Mississippi</td><td>25,100</td><td>1.0%</td><td>24</td><td>Connecticut</td><td>34,710</td><td>1.4%</td></tr>
<tr><td>13</td><td>Missouri</td><td>55,470</td><td>2.3%</td><td>25</td><td>Colorado</td><td>34,520</td><td>1.4%</td></tr>
<tr><td>46</td><td>Montana</td><td>7,290</td><td>0.3%</td><td>26</td><td>Arizona</td><td>31,890</td><td>1.3%</td></tr>
<tr><td>34</td><td>Nebraska</td><td>16,840</td><td>0.7%</td><td>27</td><td>South Carolina</td><td>31,810</td><td>1.3%</td></tr>
<tr><td>37</td><td>Nevada</td><td>14,050</td><td>0.6%</td><td>28</td><td>Iowa</td><td>31,040</td><td>1.3%</td></tr>
<tr><td>39</td><td>New Hampshire</td><td>12,440</td><td>0.5%</td><td>29</td><td>Oregon</td><td>28,090</td><td>1.2%</td></tr>
<tr><td>9</td><td>New Jersey</td><td>80,330</td><td>3.3%</td><td>30</td><td>Mississippi</td><td>25,100</td><td>1.0%</td></tr>
<tr><td>40</td><td>New Mexico</td><td>11,680</td><td>0.5%</td><td>31</td><td>Oklahoma</td><td>24,720</td><td>1.0%</td></tr>
<tr><td>2</td><td>New York</td><td>164,970</td><td>6.8%</td><td>32</td><td>Kansas</td><td>23,590</td><td>1.0%</td></tr>
<tr><td>11</td><td>North Carolina</td><td>74,400</td><td>3.1%</td><td>33</td><td>Arkansas</td><td>21,020</td><td>0.9%</td></tr>
<tr><td>47</td><td>North Dakota</td><td>6,900</td><td>0.3%</td><td>34</td><td>Nebraska</td><td>16,840</td><td>0.7%</td></tr>
<tr><td>6</td><td>Ohio</td><td>111,840</td><td>4.6%</td><td>35</td><td>Utah</td><td>16,510</td><td>0.7%</td></tr>
<tr><td>31</td><td>Oklahoma</td><td>24,720</td><td>1.0%</td><td>36</td><td>West Virginia</td><td>15,380</td><td>0.6%</td></tr>
<tr><td>29</td><td>Oregon</td><td>28,090</td><td>1.2%</td><td>37</td><td>Nevada</td><td>14,050</td><td>0.6%</td></tr>
<tr><td>5</td><td>Pennsylvania</td><td>126,120</td><td>5.2%</td><td>38</td><td>Maine</td><td>13,690</td><td>0.6%</td></tr>
<tr><td>41</td><td>Rhode Island</td><td>10,550</td><td>0.4%</td><td>39</td><td>New Hampshire</td><td>12,440</td><td>0.5%</td></tr>
<tr><td>27</td><td>South Carolina</td><td>31,810</td><td>1.3%</td><td>40</td><td>New Mexico</td><td>11,680</td><td>0.5%</td></tr>
<tr><td>43</td><td>South Dakota</td><td>9,420</td><td>0.4%</td><td>41</td><td>Rhode Island</td><td>10,550</td><td>0.4%</td></tr>
<tr><td>16</td><td>Tennessee</td><td>52,780</td><td>2.2%</td><td>42</td><td>Hawaii</td><td>9,610</td><td>0.4%</td></tr>
<tr><td>3</td><td>Texas</td><td>156,590</td><td>6.5%</td><td>43</td><td>South Dakota</td><td>9,420</td><td>0.4%</td></tr>
<tr><td>35</td><td>Utah</td><td>16,510</td><td>0.7%</td><td>44</td><td>Idaho</td><td>9,100</td><td>0.4%</td></tr>
<tr><td>48</td><td>Vermont</td><td>5,870</td><td>0.2%</td><td>45</td><td>Delaware</td><td>7,830</td><td>0.3%</td></tr>
<tr><td>14</td><td>Virginia</td><td>55,300</td><td>2.3%</td><td>46</td><td>Montana</td><td>7,290</td><td>0.3%</td></tr>
<tr><td>19</td><td>Washington</td><td>48,190</td><td>2.0%</td><td>47</td><td>North Dakota</td><td>6,900</td><td>0.3%</td></tr>
<tr><td>36</td><td>West Virginia</td><td>15,380</td><td>0.6%</td><td>48</td><td>Vermont</td><td>5,870</td><td>0.2%</td></tr>
<tr><td>18</td><td>Wisconsin</td><td>48,460</td><td>2.0%</td><td>49</td><td>Alaska</td><td>5,260</td><td>0.2%</td></tr>
<tr><td>50</td><td>Wyoming</td><td>4,010</td><td>0.2%</td><td>50</td><td>Wyoming</td><td>4,010</td><td>0.2%</td></tr>
<tr><td></td><td></td><td></td><td></td><td></td><td>District of Columbia</td><td>7,930</td><td>0.3%</td></tr>
</table>

Source: U.S. Department of Labor, Bureau of Labor Statistics
"Occupational Employment and Wages, 2006" (http://www.bls.gov/oes/)
*Does not include self-employed.

Rate of Registered Nurses in 2006

National Rate = 809 Nurses per 100,000 Population*

<table>
<tr><td colspan="3">ALPHA ORDER</td><td colspan="3">RANK ORDER</td></tr>
<tr><th>RANK</th><th>STATE</th><th>RATE</th><th>RANK</th><th>STATE</th><th>RATE</th></tr>
<tr><td>19</td><td>Alabama</td><td>872</td><td>1</td><td>South Dakota</td><td>1,195</td></tr>
<tr><td>33</td><td>Alaska</td><td>776</td><td>2</td><td>Massachusetts</td><td>1,187</td></tr>
<tr><td>50</td><td>Arizona</td><td>517</td><td>3</td><td>North Dakota</td><td>1,082</td></tr>
<tr><td>38</td><td>Arkansas</td><td>748</td><td>4</td><td>Iowa</td><td>1,044</td></tr>
<tr><td>45</td><td>California</td><td>646</td><td>5</td><td>Maine</td><td>1,041</td></tr>
<tr><td>40</td><td>Colorado</td><td>724</td><td>6</td><td>Pennsylvania</td><td>1,017</td></tr>
<tr><td>8</td><td>Connecticut</td><td>993</td><td>7</td><td>Rhode Island</td><td>994</td></tr>
<tr><td>16</td><td>Delaware</td><td>918</td><td>8</td><td>Connecticut</td><td>993</td></tr>
<tr><td>30</td><td>Florida</td><td>810</td><td>9</td><td>Ohio</td><td>976</td></tr>
<tr><td>44</td><td>Georgia</td><td>651</td><td>10</td><td>Minnesota</td><td>962</td></tr>
<tr><td>37</td><td>Hawaii</td><td>752</td><td>11</td><td>Nebraska</td><td>955</td></tr>
<tr><td>47</td><td>Idaho</td><td>622</td><td>12</td><td>Missouri</td><td>950</td></tr>
<tr><td>31</td><td>Illinois</td><td>807</td><td>13</td><td>New Hampshire</td><td>948</td></tr>
<tr><td>28</td><td>Indiana</td><td>839</td><td>14</td><td>Vermont</td><td>946</td></tr>
<tr><td>4</td><td>Iowa</td><td>1,044</td><td>15</td><td>New Jersey</td><td>927</td></tr>
<tr><td>23</td><td>Kansas</td><td>856</td><td>16</td><td>Delaware</td><td>918</td></tr>
<tr><td>17</td><td>Kentucky</td><td>907</td><td>17</td><td>Kentucky</td><td>907</td></tr>
<tr><td>18</td><td>Louisiana</td><td>894</td><td>18</td><td>Louisiana</td><td>894</td></tr>
<tr><td>5</td><td>Maine</td><td>1,041</td><td>19</td><td>Alabama</td><td>872</td></tr>
<tr><td>26</td><td>Maryland</td><td>849</td><td>20</td><td>Wisconsin</td><td>870</td></tr>
<tr><td>2</td><td>Massachusetts</td><td>1,187</td><td>21</td><td>Tennessee</td><td>869</td></tr>
<tr><td>27</td><td>Michigan</td><td>840</td><td>22</td><td>Mississippi</td><td>866</td></tr>
<tr><td>10</td><td>Minnesota</td><td>962</td><td>23</td><td>Kansas</td><td>856</td></tr>
<tr><td>22</td><td>Mississippi</td><td>866</td><td>23</td><td>New York</td><td>856</td></tr>
<tr><td>12</td><td>Missouri</td><td>950</td><td>25</td><td>West Virginia</td><td>850</td></tr>
<tr><td>34</td><td>Montana</td><td>770</td><td>26</td><td>Maryland</td><td>849</td></tr>
<tr><td>11</td><td>Nebraska</td><td>955</td><td>27</td><td>Michigan</td><td>840</td></tr>
<tr><td>49</td><td>Nevada</td><td>564</td><td>28</td><td>Indiana</td><td>839</td></tr>
<tr><td>13</td><td>New Hampshire</td><td>948</td><td>28</td><td>North Carolina</td><td>839</td></tr>
<tr><td>15</td><td>New Jersey</td><td>927</td><td>30</td><td>Florida</td><td>810</td></tr>
<tr><td>48</td><td>New Mexico</td><td>601</td><td>31</td><td>Illinois</td><td>807</td></tr>
<tr><td>23</td><td>New York</td><td>856</td><td>32</td><td>Wyoming</td><td>782</td></tr>
<tr><td>28</td><td>North Carolina</td><td>839</td><td>33</td><td>Alaska</td><td>776</td></tr>
<tr><td>3</td><td>North Dakota</td><td>1,082</td><td>34</td><td>Montana</td><td>770</td></tr>
<tr><td>9</td><td>Ohio</td><td>976</td><td>35</td><td>Oregon</td><td>761</td></tr>
<tr><td>42</td><td>Oklahoma</td><td>691</td><td>36</td><td>Washington</td><td>756</td></tr>
<tr><td>35</td><td>Oregon</td><td>761</td><td>37</td><td>Hawaii</td><td>752</td></tr>
<tr><td>6</td><td>Pennsylvania</td><td>1,017</td><td>38</td><td>Arkansas</td><td>748</td></tr>
<tr><td>7</td><td>Rhode Island</td><td>994</td><td>39</td><td>South Carolina</td><td>735</td></tr>
<tr><td>39</td><td>South Carolina</td><td>735</td><td>40</td><td>Colorado</td><td>724</td></tr>
<tr><td>1</td><td>South Dakota</td><td>1,195</td><td>40</td><td>Virginia</td><td>724</td></tr>
<tr><td>21</td><td>Tennessee</td><td>869</td><td>42</td><td>Oklahoma</td><td>691</td></tr>
<tr><td>43</td><td>Texas</td><td>669</td><td>43</td><td>Texas</td><td>669</td></tr>
<tr><td>46</td><td>Utah</td><td>640</td><td>44</td><td>Georgia</td><td>651</td></tr>
<tr><td>14</td><td>Vermont</td><td>946</td><td>45</td><td>California</td><td>646</td></tr>
<tr><td>40</td><td>Virginia</td><td>724</td><td>46</td><td>Utah</td><td>640</td></tr>
<tr><td>36</td><td>Washington</td><td>756</td><td>47</td><td>Idaho</td><td>622</td></tr>
<tr><td>25</td><td>West Virginia</td><td>850</td><td>48</td><td>New Mexico</td><td>601</td></tr>
<tr><td>20</td><td>Wisconsin</td><td>870</td><td>49</td><td>Nevada</td><td>564</td></tr>
<tr><td>32</td><td>Wyoming</td><td>782</td><td>50</td><td>Arizona</td><td>517</td></tr>
<tr><td></td><td></td><td></td><td></td><td>District of Columbia</td><td>1,354</td></tr>
</table>

Source: CQ Press using data from U.S. Department of Labor, Bureau of Labor Statistics
   "Occupational Employment and Wages, 2006" (http://www.bls.gov/oes/)
*Does not include self-employed.

Average Annual Wages of Registered Nurses in 2006

National Average = $59,730*

ALPHA ORDER

RANK	STATE	WAGES
42	Alabama	$51,230
8	Alaska	64,830
17	Arizona	58,480
41	Arkansas	51,330
1	California	75,130
16	Colorado	58,620
9	Connecticut	64,210
13	Delaware	61,310
22	Florida	56,710
27	Georgia	55,070
3	Hawaii	68,680
38	Idaho	51,550
23	Illinois	56,590
36	Indiana	52,810
50	Iowa	47,030
47	Kansas	49,170
37	Kentucky	52,080
34	Louisiana	53,070
28	Maine	55,060
4	Maryland	68,370
2	Massachusetts	70,910
15	Michigan	59,700
10	Minnesota	64,120
44	Mississippi	50,130
33	Missouri	53,150
38	Montana	51,550
40	Nebraska	51,410
12	Nevada	63,150
25	New Hampshire	55,200
5	New Jersey	66,600
21	New Mexico	57,000
6	New York	66,390
31	North Carolina	53,770
43	North Dakota	50,720
26	Ohio	55,130
49	Oklahoma	48,480
11	Oregon	63,770
20	Pennsylvania	57,040
14	Rhode Island	60,710
32	South Carolina	53,210
45	South Dakota	49,560
30	Tennessee	54,490
19	Texas	57,180
29	Utah	54,590
35	Vermont	52,990
24	Virginia	56,310
7	Washington	64,900
46	West Virginia	49,470
18	Wisconsin	57,380
48	Wyoming	48,960

RANK ORDER

RANK	STATE	WAGES
1	California	$75,130
2	Massachusetts	70,910
3	Hawaii	68,680
4	Maryland	68,370
5	New Jersey	66,600
6	New York	66,390
7	Washington	64,900
8	Alaska	64,830
9	Connecticut	64,210
10	Minnesota	64,120
11	Oregon	63,770
12	Nevada	63,150
13	Delaware	61,310
14	Rhode Island	60,710
15	Michigan	59,700
16	Colorado	58,620
17	Arizona	58,480
18	Wisconsin	57,380
19	Texas	57,180
20	Pennsylvania	57,040
21	New Mexico	57,000
22	Florida	56,710
23	Illinois	56,590
24	Virginia	56,310
25	New Hampshire	55,200
26	Ohio	55,130
27	Georgia	55,070
28	Maine	55,060
29	Utah	54,590
30	Tennessee	54,490
31	North Carolina	53,770
32	South Carolina	53,210
33	Missouri	53,150
34	Louisiana	53,070
35	Vermont	52,990
36	Indiana	52,810
37	Kentucky	52,080
38	Idaho	51,550
38	Montana	51,550
40	Nebraska	51,410
41	Arkansas	51,330
42	Alabama	51,230
43	North Dakota	50,720
44	Mississippi	50,130
45	South Dakota	49,560
46	West Virginia	49,470
47	Kansas	49,170
48	Wyoming	48,960
49	Oklahoma	48,480
50	Iowa	47,030
	District of Columbia	63,120

Source: U.S. Department of Labor, Bureau of Labor Statistics
    "Occupational Employment and Wages, 2006" (http://www.bls.gov/oes/)
*Does not include self-employed.

Licensed Practical and Licensed Vocational Nurses in 2006

National Total = 720,380 LPN/LVNs*

ALPHA ORDER

RANK	STATE	NURSES	% of USA
19	Alabama	15,020	2.1%
50	Alaska	480	0.1%
23	Arizona	10,100	1.4%
21	Arkansas	12,320	1.7%
2	California	56,170	7.8%
32	Colorado	6,730	0.9%
29	Connecticut	8,120	1.1%
45	Delaware	1,900	0.3%
3	Florida	50,670	7.0%
8	Georgia	24,090	3.3%
43	Hawaii	2,010	0.3%
37	Idaho	2,760	0.4%
7	Illinois	24,270	3.4%
12	Indiana	18,840	2.6%
31	Iowa	6,890	1.0%
30	Kansas	7,330	1.0%
22	Kentucky	11,730	1.6%
13	Louisiana	18,310	2.5%
46	Maine	1,870	0.3%
28	Maryland	9,530	1.3%
17	Massachusetts	16,910	2.3%
15	Michigan	18,140	2.5%
11	Minnesota	18,870	2.6%
27	Mississippi	9,870	1.4%
16	Missouri	17,860	2.5%
38	Montana	2,740	0.4%
34	Nebraska	5,680	0.8%
41	Nevada	2,640	0.4%
42	New Hampshire	2,510	0.3%
14	New Jersey	18,180	2.5%
35	New Mexico	4,880	0.7%
4	New York	48,230	6.7%
18	North Carolina	15,660	2.2%
36	North Dakota	2,920	0.4%
5	Ohio	38,060	5.3%
20	Oklahoma	13,170	1.8%
40	Oregon	2,720	0.4%
6	Pennsylvania	35,630	4.9%
47	Rhode Island	1,820	0.3%
23	South Carolina	10,100	1.4%
43	South Dakota	2,010	0.3%
9	Tennessee	22,520	3.1%
1	Texas	67,260	9.3%
39	Utah	2,730	0.4%
48	Vermont	1,560	0.2%
10	Virginia	19,340	2.7%
26	Washington	9,990	1.4%
33	West Virginia	6,590	0.9%
25	Wisconsin	10,040	1.4%
49	Wyoming	700	0.1%

RANK ORDER

RANK	STATE	NURSES	% of USA
1	Texas	67,260	9.3%
2	California	56,170	7.8%
3	Florida	50,670	7.0%
4	New York	48,230	6.7%
5	Ohio	38,060	5.3%
6	Pennsylvania	35,630	4.9%
7	Illinois	24,270	3.4%
8	Georgia	24,090	3.3%
9	Tennessee	22,520	3.1%
10	Virginia	19,340	2.7%
11	Minnesota	18,870	2.6%
12	Indiana	18,840	2.6%
13	Louisiana	18,310	2.5%
14	New Jersey	18,180	2.5%
15	Michigan	18,140	2.5%
16	Missouri	17,860	2.5%
17	Massachusetts	16,910	2.3%
18	North Carolina	15,660	2.2%
19	Alabama	15,020	2.1%
20	Oklahoma	13,170	1.8%
21	Arkansas	12,320	1.7%
22	Kentucky	11,730	1.6%
23	Arizona	10,100	1.4%
23	South Carolina	10,100	1.4%
25	Wisconsin	10,040	1.4%
26	Washington	9,990	1.4%
27	Mississippi	9,870	1.4%
28	Maryland	9,530	1.3%
29	Connecticut	8,120	1.1%
30	Kansas	7,330	1.0%
31	Iowa	6,890	1.0%
32	Colorado	6,730	0.9%
33	West Virginia	6,590	0.9%
34	Nebraska	5,680	0.8%
35	New Mexico	4,880	0.7%
36	North Dakota	2,920	0.4%
37	Idaho	2,760	0.4%
38	Montana	2,740	0.4%
39	Utah	2,730	0.4%
40	Oregon	2,720	0.4%
41	Nevada	2,640	0.4%
42	New Hampshire	2,510	0.3%
43	Hawaii	2,010	0.3%
43	South Dakota	2,010	0.3%
45	Delaware	1,900	0.3%
46	Maine	1,870	0.3%
47	Rhode Island	1,820	0.3%
48	Vermont	1,560	0.2%
49	Wyoming	700	0.1%
50	Alaska	480	0.1%
	District of Columbia	1,910	0.3%

Source: U.S. Department of Labor, Bureau of Labor Statistics
"Occupational Employment and Wages, 2006" (http://www.bls.gov/oes/)
*Does not include self-employed.

Rate of Licensed Practical and Licensed Vocational Nurses in 2006

National Rate = 241 LPN/LVNs per 100,000 Population*

ALPHA ORDER

RANK	STATE	RATE
10	Alabama	327
50	Alaska	71
40	Arizona	164
2	Arkansas	439
43	California	155
45	Colorado	141
28	Connecticut	232
30	Delaware	223
17	Florida	281
21	Georgia	258
41	Hawaii	157
34	Idaho	189
33	Illinois	190
13	Indiana	299
28	Iowa	232
19	Kansas	266
18	Kentucky	279
3	Louisiana	432
44	Maine	142
39	Maryland	170
20	Massachusetts	263
35	Michigan	180
6	Minnesota	366
8	Mississippi	340
12	Missouri	306
14	Montana	289
11	Nebraska	322
47	Nevada	106
32	New Hampshire	191
31	New Jersey	210
24	New Mexico	251
26	New York	250
37	North Carolina	177
1	North Dakota	458
9	Ohio	332
5	Oklahoma	368
49	Oregon	74
15	Pennsylvania	287
38	Rhode Island	171
27	South Carolina	233
22	South Dakota	255
4	Tennessee	371
15	Texas	287
47	Utah	106
24	Vermont	251
23	Virginia	253
41	Washington	157
7	West Virginia	364
35	Wisconsin	180
46	Wyoming	137

RANK ORDER

RANK	STATE	RATE
1	North Dakota	458
2	Arkansas	439
3	Louisiana	432
4	Tennessee	371
5	Oklahoma	368
6	Minnesota	366
7	West Virginia	364
8	Mississippi	340
9	Ohio	332
10	Alabama	327
11	Nebraska	322
12	Missouri	306
13	Indiana	299
14	Montana	289
15	Pennsylvania	287
15	Texas	287
17	Florida	281
18	Kentucky	279
19	Kansas	266
20	Massachusetts	263
21	Georgia	258
22	South Dakota	255
23	Virginia	253
24	New Mexico	251
24	Vermont	251
26	New York	250
27	South Carolina	233
28	Connecticut	232
28	Iowa	232
30	Delaware	223
31	New Jersey	210
32	New Hampshire	191
33	Illinois	190
34	Idaho	189
35	Michigan	180
35	Wisconsin	180
37	North Carolina	177
38	Rhode Island	171
39	Maryland	170
40	Arizona	164
41	Hawaii	157
41	Washington	157
43	California	155
44	Maine	142
45	Colorado	141
46	Wyoming	137
47	Nevada	106
47	Utah	106
49	Oregon	74
50	Alaska	71

District of Columbia   326

Source: CQ Press using data from U.S. Department of Labor, Bureau of Labor Statistics
   "Occupational Employment and Wages, 2006" (http://www.bls.gov/oes/)
*Does not include self-employed.

Average Annual Wages of Licensed Practical and Licensed Vocational Nurses in 2006
National Average = $37,560*

ALPHA ORDER

RANK	STATE	WAGES
48	Alabama	$30,140
8	Alaska	43,470
12	Arizona	40,410
44	Arkansas	31,250
6	California	45,270
19	Colorado	37,990
1	Connecticut	50,350
7	Delaware	44,350
23	Florida	37,170
39	Georgia	32,840
18	Hawaii	38,530
32	Idaho	34,760
20	Illinois	37,870
30	Indiana	35,790
38	Iowa	33,000
36	Kansas	33,720
35	Kentucky	33,790
42	Louisiana	32,150
28	Maine	35,840
4	Maryland	46,220
2	Massachusetts	47,660
16	Michigan	38,750
24	Minnesota	36,680
49	Mississippi	30,070
41	Missouri	32,630
45	Montana	30,950
37	Nebraska	33,560
9	Nevada	41,150
14	New Hampshire	39,540
3	New Jersey	47,580
13	New Mexico	40,120
15	New York	38,910
25	North Carolina	36,410
43	North Dakota	32,040
22	Ohio	37,610
46	Oklahoma	30,840
10	Oregon	41,100
17	Pennsylvania	38,600
5	Rhode Island	45,550
33	South Carolina	33,950
47	South Dakota	30,230
40	Tennessee	32,710
27	Texas	35,920
31	Utah	34,990
26	Vermont	36,160
29	Virginia	35,810
11	Washington	40,970
50	West Virginia	30,000
21	Wisconsin	37,620
34	Wyoming	33,810

RANK ORDER

RANK	STATE	WAGES
1	Connecticut	$50,350
2	Massachusetts	47,660
3	New Jersey	47,580
4	Maryland	46,220
5	Rhode Island	45,550
6	California	45,270
7	Delaware	44,350
8	Alaska	43,470
9	Nevada	41,150
10	Oregon	41,100
11	Washington	40,970
12	Arizona	40,410
13	New Mexico	40,120
14	New Hampshire	39,540
15	New York	38,910
16	Michigan	38,750
17	Pennsylvania	38,600
18	Hawaii	38,530
19	Colorado	37,990
20	Illinois	37,870
21	Wisconsin	37,620
22	Ohio	37,610
23	Florida	37,170
24	Minnesota	36,680
25	North Carolina	36,410
26	Vermont	36,160
27	Texas	35,920
28	Maine	35,840
29	Virginia	35,810
30	Indiana	35,790
31	Utah	34,990
32	Idaho	34,760
33	South Carolina	33,950
34	Wyoming	33,810
35	Kentucky	33,790
36	Kansas	33,720
37	Nebraska	33,560
38	Iowa	33,000
39	Georgia	32,840
40	Tennessee	32,710
41	Missouri	32,630
42	Louisiana	32,150
43	North Dakota	32,040
44	Arkansas	31,250
45	Montana	30,950
46	Oklahoma	30,840
47	South Dakota	30,230
48	Alabama	30,140
49	Mississippi	30,070
50	West Virginia	30,000
	District of Columbia	46,910

Source: U.S. Department of Labor, Bureau of Labor Statistics
   "Occupational Employment and Wages, 2006" (http://www.bls.gov/oes/)
*Does not include self-employed.

Physical Therapists in 2006

National Total = 156,100 Physical Therapists*

ALPHA ORDER

RANK	STATE	THERAPISTS	% of USA
29	Alabama	1,740	1.1%
49	Alaska	320	0.2%
23	Arizona	2,540	1.6%
34	Arkansas	1,100	0.7%
1	California	13,510	8.7%
19	Colorado	3,250	2.1%
21	Connecticut	3,030	1.9%
48	Delaware	450	0.3%
3	Florida	10,080	6.5%
20	Georgia	3,200	2.0%
45	Hawaii	560	0.4%
41	Idaho	790	0.5%
6	Illinois	6,340	4.1%
13	Indiana	3,650	2.3%
30	Iowa	1,510	1.0%
32	Kansas	1,270	0.8%
27	Kentucky	1,920	1.2%
24	Louisiana	2,180	1.4%
39	Maine	900	0.6%
15	Maryland	3,590	2.3%
8	Massachusetts	6,030	3.9%
10	Michigan	5,540	3.5%
22	Minnesota	2,880	1.8%
31	Mississippi	1,340	0.9%
16	Missouri	3,410	2.2%
43	Montana	720	0.5%
37	Nebraska	970	0.6%
42	Nevada	730	0.5%
38	New Hampshire	940	0.6%
9	New Jersey	5,760	3.7%
36	New Mexico	980	0.6%
2	New York	11,810	7.6%
11	North Carolina	3,950	2.5%
47	North Dakota	490	0.3%
7	Ohio	6,290	4.0%
26	Oklahoma	1,940	1.2%
28	Oregon	1,830	1.2%
5	Pennsylvania	8,630	5.5%
40	Rhode Island	870	0.6%
25	South Carolina	2,030	1.3%
46	South Dakota	530	0.3%
18	Tennessee	3,310	2.1%
4	Texas	9,040	5.8%
33	Utah	1,110	0.7%
44	Vermont	620	0.4%
17	Virginia	3,390	2.2%
14	Washington	3,620	2.3%
35	West Virginia	1,090	0.7%
12	Wisconsin	3,680	2.4%
50	Wyoming	260	0.2%

RANK ORDER

RANK	STATE	THERAPISTS	% of USA
1	California	13,510	8.7%
2	New York	11,810	7.6%
3	Florida	10,080	6.5%
4	Texas	9,040	5.8%
5	Pennsylvania	8,630	5.5%
6	Illinois	6,340	4.1%
7	Ohio	6,290	4.0%
8	Massachusetts	6,030	3.9%
9	New Jersey	5,760	3.7%
10	Michigan	5,540	3.5%
11	North Carolina	3,950	2.5%
12	Wisconsin	3,680	2.4%
13	Indiana	3,650	2.3%
14	Washington	3,620	2.3%
15	Maryland	3,590	2.3%
16	Missouri	3,410	2.2%
17	Virginia	3,390	2.2%
18	Tennessee	3,310	2.1%
19	Colorado	3,250	2.1%
20	Georgia	3,200	2.0%
21	Connecticut	3,030	1.9%
22	Minnesota	2,880	1.8%
23	Arizona	2,540	1.6%
24	Louisiana	2,180	1.4%
25	South Carolina	2,030	1.3%
26	Oklahoma	1,940	1.2%
27	Kentucky	1,920	1.2%
28	Oregon	1,830	1.2%
29	Alabama	1,740	1.1%
30	Iowa	1,510	1.0%
31	Mississippi	1,340	0.9%
32	Kansas	1,270	0.8%
33	Utah	1,110	0.7%
34	Arkansas	1,100	0.7%
35	West Virginia	1,090	0.7%
36	New Mexico	980	0.6%
37	Nebraska	970	0.6%
38	New Hampshire	940	0.6%
39	Maine	900	0.6%
40	Rhode Island	870	0.6%
41	Idaho	790	0.5%
42	Nevada	730	0.5%
43	Montana	720	0.5%
44	Vermont	620	0.4%
45	Hawaii	560	0.4%
46	South Dakota	530	0.3%
47	North Dakota	490	0.3%
48	Delaware	450	0.3%
49	Alaska	320	0.2%
50	Wyoming	260	0.2%
	District of Columbia	380	0.2%

Source: U.S. Department of Labor, Bureau of Labor Statistics
"Occupational Employment and Wages, 2006" (http://www.bls.gov/oes/)
*Does not include self-employed.

Rate of Physical Therapists in 2006

National Rate = 52 Physical Therapists per 100,000 Population*

ALPHA ORDER			RANK ORDER		
RANK	STATE	RATE	RANK	STATE	RATE
47	Alabama	38	1	Vermont	100
35	Alaska	47	2	Massachusetts	94
44	Arizona	41	3	Connecticut	87
45	Arkansas	39	4	Rhode Island	82
48	California	37	5	North Dakota	77
9	Colorado	68	6	Montana	76
3	Connecticut	87	7	New Hampshire	72
28	Delaware	53	8	Pennsylvania	70
20	Florida	56	9	Colorado	68
49	Georgia	34	9	Maine	68
41	Hawaii	44	11	South Dakota	67
25	Idaho	54	12	New Jersey	66
32	Illinois	50	12	Wisconsin	66
17	Indiana	58	14	Maryland	64
29	Iowa	51	15	New York	61
37	Kansas	46	16	West Virginia	60
37	Kentucky	46	17	Indiana	58
29	Louisiana	51	17	Missouri	58
9	Maine	68	19	Washington	57
14	Maryland	64	20	Florida	56
2	Massachusetts	94	20	Minnesota	56
22	Michigan	55	22	Michigan	55
20	Minnesota	56	22	Nebraska	55
37	Mississippi	46	22	Ohio	55
17	Missouri	58	25	Idaho	54
6	Montana	76	25	Oklahoma	54
22	Nebraska	55	25	Tennessee	54
50	Nevada	29	28	Delaware	53
7	New Hampshire	72	29	Iowa	51
12	New Jersey	66	29	Louisiana	51
32	New Mexico	50	29	Wyoming	51
15	New York	61	32	Illinois	50
40	North Carolina	45	32	New Mexico	50
5	North Dakota	77	32	Oregon	50
22	Ohio	55	35	Alaska	47
25	Oklahoma	54	35	South Carolina	47
32	Oregon	50	37	Kansas	46
8	Pennsylvania	70	37	Kentucky	46
4	Rhode Island	82	37	Mississippi	46
35	South Carolina	47	40	North Carolina	45
11	South Dakota	67	41	Hawaii	44
25	Tennessee	54	41	Virginia	44
45	Texas	39	43	Utah	43
43	Utah	43	44	Arizona	41
1	Vermont	100	45	Arkansas	39
41	Virginia	44	45	Texas	39
19	Washington	57	47	Alabama	38
16	West Virginia	60	48	California	37
12	Wisconsin	66	49	Georgia	34
29	Wyoming	51	50	Nevada	29
				District of Columbia	65

Source: CQ Press using data from U.S. Department of Labor, Bureau of Labor Statistics
   "Occupational Employment and Wages, 2006" (http://www.bls.gov/oes/)
*Does not include self-employed.

Average Annual Wages of Physical Therapists in 2006

National Average = $68,050*

ALPHA ORDER

RANK	STATE	WAGES
14	Alabama	$68,700
NA	Alaska**	NA
29	Arizona	64,890
43	Arkansas	60,790
1	California	75,710
46	Colorado	60,120
6	Connecticut	71,440
33	Delaware	63,770
13	Florida	68,930
24	Georgia	66,600
44	Hawaii	60,710
12	Idaho	69,380
23	Illinois	66,990
30	Indiana	64,740
42	Iowa	61,190
35	Kansas	63,280
26	Kentucky	65,930
7	Louisiana	71,310
31	Maine	64,100
19	Maryland	67,790
28	Massachusetts	65,030
16	Michigan	68,040
41	Minnesota	61,470
8	Mississippi	70,500
38	Missouri	62,110
49	Montana	55,670
36	Nebraska	62,810
2	Nevada	75,200
40	New Hampshire	61,790
3	New Jersey	74,770
47	New Mexico	57,770
20	New York	67,580
25	North Carolina	66,500
39	North Dakota	61,860
17	Ohio	67,900
5	Oklahoma	72,260
34	Oregon	63,730
21	Pennsylvania	67,540
11	Rhode Island	69,470
27	South Carolina	65,720
45	South Dakota	60,340
10	Tennessee	69,500
4	Texas	73,440
22	Utah	67,000
48	Vermont	56,980
18	Virginia	67,860
15	Washington	68,160
9	West Virginia	69,550
32	Wisconsin	64,090
37	Wyoming	62,300

RANK ORDER

RANK	STATE	WAGES
1	California	$75,710
2	Nevada	75,200
3	New Jersey	74,770
4	Texas	73,440
5	Oklahoma	72,260
6	Connecticut	71,440
7	Louisiana	71,310
8	Mississippi	70,500
9	West Virginia	69,550
10	Tennessee	69,500
11	Rhode Island	69,470
12	Idaho	69,380
13	Florida	68,930
14	Alabama	68,700
15	Washington	68,160
16	Michigan	68,040
17	Ohio	67,900
18	Virginia	67,860
19	Maryland	67,790
20	New York	67,580
21	Pennsylvania	67,540
22	Utah	67,000
23	Illinois	66,990
24	Georgia	66,600
25	North Carolina	66,500
26	Kentucky	65,930
27	South Carolina	65,720
28	Massachusetts	65,030
29	Arizona	64,890
30	Indiana	64,740
31	Maine	64,100
32	Wisconsin	64,090
33	Delaware	63,770
34	Oregon	63,730
35	Kansas	63,280
36	Nebraska	62,810
37	Wyoming	62,300
38	Missouri	62,110
39	North Dakota	61,860
40	New Hampshire	61,790
41	Minnesota	61,470
42	Iowa	61,190
43	Arkansas	60,790
44	Hawaii	60,710
45	South Dakota	60,340
46	Colorado	60,120
47	New Mexico	57,770
48	Vermont	56,980
49	Montana	55,670
NA	Alaska**	NA
	District of Columbia	62,030

Source: U.S. Department of Labor, Bureau of Labor Statistics
"Occupational Employment and Wages, 2006" (http://www.bls.gov/oes/)
*Does not include self-employed.
**Not available.

Dentists in 2005

National Total = 176,634 Dentists*

ALPHA ORDER					RANK ORDER			
RANK	STATE		DENTISTS	% of USA	RANK	STATE	DENTISTS	% of USA
27	Alabama		1,985	1.1%	1	California	26,502	15.0%
45	Alaska		491	0.3%	2	New York	15,060	8.5%
21	Arizona		2,948	1.7%	3	Texas	10,370	5.9%
33	Arkansas		1,133	0.6%	4	Florida	9,200	5.2%
1	California		26,502	15.0%	5	Illinois	8,130	4.6%
19	Colorado		3,048	1.7%	6	Pennsylvania	7,845	4.4%
23	Connecticut		2,663	1.5%	7	New Jersey	6,965	3.9%
46	Delaware		394	0.2%	8	Michigan	6,120	3.5%
4	Florida		9,200	5.2%	9	Ohio	6,084	3.4%
14	Georgia		4,030	2.3%	10	Massachusetts	5,362	3.0%
37	Hawaii		1,036	0.6%	11	Washington	4,406	2.5%
40	Idaho		811	0.5%	12	Virginia	4,367	2.5%
5	Illinois		8,130	4.6%	13	Maryland	4,123	2.3%
20	Indiana		2,990	1.7%	14	Georgia	4,030	2.3%
31	Iowa		1,561	0.9%	15	North Carolina	3,895	2.2%
32	Kansas		1,393	0.8%	16	Wisconsin	3,157	1.8%
25	Kentucky		2,294	1.3%	17	Minnesota	3,071	1.7%
26	Louisiana		2,075	1.2%	18	Tennessee	3,062	1.7%
42	Maine		653	0.4%	19	Colorado	3,048	1.7%
13	Maryland		4,123	2.3%	20	Indiana	2,990	1.7%
10	Massachusetts		5,362	3.0%	21	Arizona	2,948	1.7%
8	Michigan		6,120	3.5%	22	Missouri	2,799	1.6%
17	Minnesota		3,071	1.7%	23	Connecticut	2,663	1.5%
34	Mississippi		1,126	0.6%	24	Oregon	2,469	1.4%
22	Missouri		2,799	1.6%	25	Kentucky	2,294	1.3%
44	Montana		529	0.3%	26	Louisiana	2,075	1.2%
35	Nebraska		1,104	0.6%	27	Alabama	1,985	1.1%
36	Nevada		1,086	0.6%	28	South Carolina	1,906	1.1%
41	New Hampshire		799	0.5%	29	Oklahoma	1,739	1.0%
7	New Jersey		6,965	3.9%	30	Utah	1,621	0.9%
38	New Mexico		836	0.5%	31	Iowa	1,561	0.9%
2	New York		15,060	8.5%	32	Kansas	1,393	0.8%
15	North Carolina		3,895	2.2%	33	Arkansas	1,133	0.6%
49	North Dakota		314	0.2%	34	Mississippi	1,126	0.6%
9	Ohio		6,084	3.4%	35	Nebraska	1,104	0.6%
29	Oklahoma		1,739	1.0%	36	Nevada	1,086	0.6%
24	Oregon		2,469	1.4%	37	Hawaii	1,036	0.6%
6	Pennsylvania		7,845	4.4%	38	New Mexico	836	0.5%
43	Rhode Island		555	0.3%	39	West Virginia	835	0.5%
28	South Carolina		1,906	1.1%	40	Idaho	811	0.5%
47	South Dakota		384	0.2%	41	New Hampshire	799	0.5%
18	Tennessee		3,062	1.7%	42	Maine	653	0.4%
3	Texas		10,370	5.9%	43	Rhode Island	555	0.3%
30	Utah		1,621	0.9%	44	Montana	529	0.3%
48	Vermont		363	0.2%	45	Alaska	491	0.3%
12	Virginia		4,367	2.5%	46	Delaware	394	0.2%
11	Washington		4,406	2.5%	47	South Dakota	384	0.2%
39	West Virginia		835	0.5%	48	Vermont	363	0.2%
16	Wisconsin		3,157	1.8%	49	North Dakota	314	0.2%
50	Wyoming		263	0.1%	50	Wyoming	263	0.1%
						District of Columbia	627	0.4%

Source: American Dental Association
    "Distribution of Dentists, by Region and State, 2005"
*Professionally active dentists. Total includes 53 dentists for whom state is not known. Total does not include 2,168 dentists in territories nor dentists in the Armed Forces stationed overseas.

Rate of Dentists in 2005

National Rate = 60 Dentists per 100,000 Population*

ALPHA ORDER

RANK	STATE	RATE
46	Alabama	44
8	Alaska	73
32	Arizona	50
49	Arkansas	41
6	California	74
11	Colorado	65
5	Connecticut	76
39	Delaware	47
27	Florida	52
46	Georgia	44
2	Hawaii	82
21	Idaho	57
13	Illinois	64
37	Indiana	48
25	Iowa	53
30	Kansas	51
24	Kentucky	55
40	Louisiana	46
32	Maine	50
6	Maryland	74
1	Massachusetts	83
16	Michigan	61
18	Minnesota	60
50	Mississippi	39
37	Missouri	48
21	Montana	57
14	Nebraska	63
42	Nevada	45
16	New Hampshire	61
3	New Jersey	80
46	New Mexico	44
4	New York	78
42	North Carolina	45
34	North Dakota	49
25	Ohio	53
34	Oklahoma	49
10	Oregon	68
14	Pennsylvania	63
27	Rhode Island	52
42	South Carolina	45
34	South Dakota	49
30	Tennessee	51
42	Texas	45
11	Utah	65
19	Vermont	59
20	Virginia	58
9	Washington	70
40	West Virginia	46
21	Wisconsin	57
27	Wyoming	52

RANK ORDER

RANK	STATE	RATE
1	Massachusetts	83
2	Hawaii	82
3	New Jersey	80
4	New York	78
5	Connecticut	76
6	California	74
6	Maryland	74
8	Alaska	73
9	Washington	70
10	Oregon	68
11	Colorado	65
11	Utah	65
13	Illinois	64
14	Nebraska	63
14	Pennsylvania	63
16	Michigan	61
16	New Hampshire	61
18	Minnesota	60
19	Vermont	59
20	Virginia	58
21	Idaho	57
21	Montana	57
21	Wisconsin	57
24	Kentucky	55
25	Iowa	53
25	Ohio	53
27	Florida	52
27	Rhode Island	52
27	Wyoming	52
30	Kansas	51
30	Tennessee	51
32	Arizona	50
32	Maine	50
34	North Dakota	49
34	Oklahoma	49
34	South Dakota	49
37	Indiana	48
37	Missouri	48
39	Delaware	47
40	Louisiana	46
40	West Virginia	46
42	Nevada	45
42	North Carolina	45
42	South Carolina	45
42	Texas	45
46	Alabama	44
46	Georgia	44
46	New Mexico	44
49	Arkansas	41
50	Mississippi	39

District of Columbia — 108

Source: CQ Press using data from American Dental Association
  "Distribution of Dentists, by Region and State, 2005"
*Professionally active dentists. National rate includes dentists for whom state is not known. National rate does not include dentists in territories nor dentists in the Armed Forces stationed overseas.

Average Annual Wages of Dentists in 2006

National Average = $140,950*

ALPHA ORDER

RANK	STATE	WAGES
39	Alabama	$133,040
6	Alaska	163,140
38	Arizona	133,150
48	Arkansas	112,280
24	California	142,190
15	Colorado	150,480
2	Connecticut	170,830
5	Delaware	164,760
35	Florida	135,030
9	Georgia	158,950
14	Hawaii	151,120
23	Idaho	142,910
49	Illinois	106,250
36	Indiana	134,750
11	Iowa	155,240
32	Kansas	136,900
46	Kentucky	121,720
50	Louisiana	95,870
1	Maine	171,440
28	Maryland	138,820
25	Massachusetts	142,030
7	Michigan	162,580
20	Minnesota	146,740
42	Mississippi	131,240
19	Missouri	146,990
47	Montana	121,610
27	Nebraska	140,590
30	Nevada	137,090
12	New Hampshire	153,660
37	New Jersey	134,130
33	New Mexico	136,740
29	New York	137,660
4	North Carolina	165,190
34	North Dakota	136,610
3	Ohio	165,510
45	Oklahoma	121,740
26	Oregon	140,900
44	Pennsylvania	121,910
31	Rhode Island	136,980
41	South Carolina	131,910
10	South Dakota	157,660
18	Tennessee	147,490
16	Texas	149,630
22	Utah	143,670
40	Vermont	132,910
13	Virginia	153,160
8	Washington	159,720
17	West Virginia	148,800
21	Wisconsin	143,710
43	Wyoming	128,100

RANK ORDER

RANK	STATE	WAGES
1	Maine	$171,440
2	Connecticut	170,830
3	Ohio	165,510
4	North Carolina	165,190
5	Delaware	164,760
6	Alaska	163,140
7	Michigan	162,580
8	Washington	159,720
9	Georgia	158,950
10	South Dakota	157,660
11	Iowa	155,240
12	New Hampshire	153,660
13	Virginia	153,160
14	Hawaii	151,120
15	Colorado	150,480
16	Texas	149,630
17	West Virginia	148,800
18	Tennessee	147,490
19	Missouri	146,990
20	Minnesota	146,740
21	Wisconsin	143,710
22	Utah	143,670
23	Idaho	142,910
24	California	142,190
25	Massachusetts	142,030
26	Oregon	140,900
27	Nebraska	140,590
28	Maryland	138,820
29	New York	137,660
30	Nevada	137,090
31	Rhode Island	136,980
32	Kansas	136,900
33	New Mexico	136,740
34	North Dakota	136,610
35	Florida	135,030
36	Indiana	134,750
37	New Jersey	134,130
38	Arizona	133,150
39	Alabama	133,040
40	Vermont	132,910
41	South Carolina	131,910
42	Mississippi	131,240
43	Wyoming	128,100
44	Pennsylvania	121,910
45	Oklahoma	121,740
46	Kentucky	121,720
47	Montana	121,610
48	Arkansas	112,280
49	Illinois	106,250
50	Louisiana	95,870

District of Columbia   134,040

Source: U.S. Department of Labor, Bureau of Labor Statistics
   "Occupational Employment and Wages, 2006" (http://www.bls.gov/oes/)
*Does not include self-employed.

Percent of Population Lacking Access to Dental Care in 2007

National Percent = 9.6% of Population*

ALPHA ORDER

RANK	STATE	PERCENT
3	Alabama	26.8
40	Alaska	5.2
29	Arizona	7.8
41	Arkansas	5.1
44	California	3.3
43	Colorado	4.0
27	Connecticut	7.9
12	Delaware	16.6
13	Florida	15.2
23	Georgia	9.6
35	Hawaii	6.5
9	Idaho	17.9
16	Illinois	12.1
47	Indiana	3.2
26	Iowa	8.3
10	Kansas	16.8
44	Kentucky	3.3
2	Louisiana	31.7
10	Maine	16.8
37	Maryland	5.8
30	Massachusetts	7.7
22	Michigan	10.4
44	Minnesota	3.3
1	Mississippi	32.0
7	Missouri	18.0
7	Montana	18.0
49	Nebraska	1.6
14	Nevada	14.2
42	New Hampshire	4.5
50	New Jersey	1.4
4	New Mexico	26.5
39	New York	5.3
20	North Carolina	10.9
32	North Dakota	7.4
33	Ohio	7.3
36	Oklahoma	6.0
15	Oregon	13.2
25	Pennsylvania	8.8
21	Rhode Island	10.6
5	South Carolina	20.9
17	South Dakota	11.6
6	Tennessee	19.4
19	Texas	11.0
38	Utah	5.7
48	Vermont	3.1
24	Virginia	9.3
27	Washington	7.9
34	West Virginia	7.1
31	Wisconsin	7.6
18	Wyoming	11.4

RANK ORDER

RANK	STATE	PERCENT
1	Mississippi	32.0
2	Louisiana	31.7
3	Alabama	26.8
4	New Mexico	26.5
5	South Carolina	20.9
6	Tennessee	19.4
7	Missouri	18.0
7	Montana	18.0
9	Idaho	17.9
10	Kansas	16.8
10	Maine	16.8
12	Delaware	16.6
13	Florida	15.2
14	Nevada	14.2
15	Oregon	13.2
16	Illinois	12.1
17	South Dakota	11.6
18	Wyoming	11.4
19	Texas	11.0
20	North Carolina	10.9
21	Rhode Island	10.6
22	Michigan	10.4
23	Georgia	9.6
24	Virginia	9.3
25	Pennsylvania	8.8
26	Iowa	8.3
27	Connecticut	7.9
27	Washington	7.9
29	Arizona	7.8
30	Massachusetts	7.7
31	Wisconsin	7.6
32	North Dakota	7.4
33	Ohio	7.3
34	West Virginia	7.1
35	Hawaii	6.5
36	Oklahoma	6.0
37	Maryland	5.8
38	Utah	5.7
39	New York	5.3
40	Alaska	5.2
41	Arkansas	5.1
42	New Hampshire	4.5
43	Colorado	4.0
44	California	3.3
44	Kentucky	3.3
44	Minnesota	3.3
47	Indiana	3.2
48	Vermont	3.1
49	Nebraska	1.6
50	New Jersey	1.4

District of Columbia   10.1

Source: CQ Press using data from U.S. Dept. of Health and Human Services, Div. of Shortage Designation
"Selected Statistics on Health Professional Shortage Areas" (as of June 30, 2007)
*Percent of population considered under-served by dental practitioners. An under-served population does not have primary
medical care within reasonable economic and geographic bounds.

Pharmacists in 2006

National Total = 239,920 Pharmacists*

ALPHA ORDER

RANK	STATE	PHARMACISTS	% of USA
21	Alabama	4,360	1.8%
50	Alaska	370	0.2%
20	Arizona	4,550	1.9%
29	Arkansas	2,590	1.1%
1	California	23,700	9.9%
23	Colorado	3,890	1.6%
31	Connecticut	2,530	1.1%
47	Delaware	670	0.3%
2	Florida	17,020	7.1%
10	Georgia	7,180	3.0%
40	Hawaii	1,210	0.5%
39	Idaho	1,320	0.6%
7	Illinois	9,380	3.9%
15	Indiana	5,460	2.3%
29	Iowa	2,590	1.1%
33	Kansas	2,240	0.9%
25	Kentucky	3,580	1.5%
24	Louisiana	3,740	1.6%
41	Maine	1,170	0.5%
22	Maryland	4,160	1.7%
12	Massachusetts	5,930	2.5%
8	Michigan	8,370	3.5%
19	Minnesota	4,620	1.9%
32	Mississippi	2,290	1.0%
17	Missouri	4,900	2.0%
44	Montana	920	0.4%
35	Nebraska	1,950	0.8%
34	Nevada	2,060	0.9%
42	New Hampshire	1,040	0.4%
9	New Jersey	7,580	3.2%
38	New Mexico	1,360	0.6%
4	New York	13,970	5.8%
11	North Carolina	6,990	2.9%
46	North Dakota	680	0.3%
6	Ohio	9,970	4.2%
27	Oklahoma	3,000	1.3%
28	Oregon	2,980	1.2%
5	Pennsylvania	11,690	4.9%
45	Rhode Island	910	0.4%
26	South Carolina	3,500	1.5%
43	South Dakota	990	0.4%
13	Tennessee	5,680	2.4%
3	Texas	16,580	6.9%
36	Utah	1,890	0.8%
48	Vermont	470	0.2%
14	Virginia	5,570	2.3%
16	Washington	4,920	2.1%
37	West Virginia	1,800	0.8%
18	Wisconsin	4,630	1.9%
49	Wyoming	430	0.2%

RANK ORDER

RANK	STATE	PHARMACISTS	% of USA
1	California	23,700	9.9%
2	Florida	17,020	7.1%
3	Texas	16,580	6.9%
4	New York	13,970	5.8%
5	Pennsylvania	11,690	4.9%
6	Ohio	9,970	4.2%
7	Illinois	9,380	3.9%
8	Michigan	8,370	3.5%
9	New Jersey	7,580	3.2%
10	Georgia	7,180	3.0%
11	North Carolina	6,990	2.9%
12	Massachusetts	5,930	2.5%
13	Tennessee	5,680	2.4%
14	Virginia	5,570	2.3%
15	Indiana	5,460	2.3%
16	Washington	4,920	2.1%
17	Missouri	4,900	2.0%
18	Wisconsin	4,630	1.9%
19	Minnesota	4,620	1.9%
20	Arizona	4,550	1.9%
21	Alabama	4,360	1.8%
22	Maryland	4,160	1.7%
23	Colorado	3,890	1.6%
24	Louisiana	3,740	1.6%
25	Kentucky	3,580	1.5%
26	South Carolina	3,500	1.5%
27	Oklahoma	3,000	1.3%
28	Oregon	2,980	1.2%
29	Arkansas	2,590	1.1%
29	Iowa	2,590	1.1%
31	Connecticut	2,530	1.1%
32	Mississippi	2,290	1.0%
33	Kansas	2,240	0.9%
34	Nevada	2,060	0.9%
35	Nebraska	1,950	0.8%
36	Utah	1,890	0.8%
37	West Virginia	1,800	0.8%
38	New Mexico	1,360	0.6%
39	Idaho	1,320	0.6%
40	Hawaii	1,210	0.5%
41	Maine	1,170	0.5%
42	New Hampshire	1,040	0.4%
43	South Dakota	990	0.4%
44	Montana	920	0.4%
45	Rhode Island	910	0.4%
46	North Dakota	680	0.3%
47	Delaware	670	0.3%
48	Vermont	470	0.2%
49	Wyoming	430	0.2%
50	Alaska	370	0.2%
	District of Columbia	550	0.2%

Source: U.S. Department of Labor, Bureau of Labor Statistics
   "Occupational Employment and Wages, 2006" (http://www.bls.gov/oes/)
*Does not include self-employed.

Rate of Pharmacists in 2006

National Rate = 80 Pharmacists per 100,000 Population*

ALPHA ORDER			RANK ORDER		
RANK	STATE	RATE	RANK	STATE	RATE
6	Alabama	95	1	South Dakota	126
50	Alaska	55	2	Nebraska	111
40	Arizona	74	3	North Dakota	107
11	Arkansas	92	4	West Virginia	100
49	California	65	5	Montana	97
29	Colorado	82	6	Alabama	95
45	Connecticut	72	6	Hawaii	95
33	Delaware	79	8	Florida	94
8	Florida	94	8	Pennsylvania	94
37	Georgia	77	10	Tennessee	93
6	Hawaii	95	11	Arkansas	92
13	Idaho	90	11	Massachusetts	92
42	Illinois	73	13	Idaho	90
17	Indiana	87	13	Minnesota	90
17	Iowa	87	15	Maine	89
30	Kansas	81	16	Louisiana	88
22	Kentucky	85	17	Indiana	87
16	Louisiana	88	17	Iowa	87
15	Maine	89	17	New Jersey	87
40	Maryland	74	17	Ohio	87
11	Massachusetts	92	21	Rhode Island	86
26	Michigan	83	22	Kentucky	85
13	Minnesota	90	23	Missouri	84
33	Mississippi	79	23	Oklahoma	84
23	Missouri	84	23	Wyoming	84
5	Montana	97	26	Michigan	83
2	Nebraska	111	26	Nevada	83
26	Nevada	83	26	Wisconsin	83
33	New Hampshire	79	29	Colorado	82
17	New Jersey	87	30	Kansas	81
48	New Mexico	70	30	Oregon	81
45	New York	72	30	South Carolina	81
33	North Carolina	79	33	Delaware	79
3	North Dakota	107	33	Mississippi	79
17	Ohio	87	33	New Hampshire	79
23	Oklahoma	84	33	North Carolina	79
30	Oregon	81	37	Georgia	77
8	Pennsylvania	94	37	Washington	77
21	Rhode Island	86	39	Vermont	76
30	South Carolina	81	40	Arizona	74
1	South Dakota	126	40	Maryland	74
10	Tennessee	93	42	Illinois	73
47	Texas	71	42	Utah	73
42	Utah	73	42	Virginia	73
39	Vermont	76	45	Connecticut	72
42	Virginia	73	45	New York	72
37	Washington	77	47	Texas	71
4	West Virginia	100	48	New Mexico	70
26	Wisconsin	83	49	California	65
23	Wyoming	84	50	Alaska	55
				District of Columbia	94

Source: CQ Press using data from U.S. Department of Labor, Bureau of Labor Statistics
    "Occupational Employment and Wages, 2006" (http://www.bls.gov/oes/)
*Does not include self-employed.

Average Annual Wages of Pharmacists in 2006

National Average = $93,500*

ALPHA ORDER

RANK	STATE	WAGES
28	Alabama	$91,250
3	Alaska	101,290
34	Arizona	89,870
32	Arkansas	90,440
1	California	106,150
21	Colorado	93,480
11	Connecticut	96,470
30	Delaware	90,680
27	Florida	92,030
17	Georgia	94,370
35	Hawaii	89,240
10	Idaho	96,670
6	Illinois	97,770
37	Indiana	88,510
40	Iowa	86,590
46	Kansas	83,420
5	Kentucky	98,910
44	Louisiana	84,520
2	Maine	102,300
33	Maryland	90,100
45	Massachusetts	83,510
16	Michigan	94,450
4	Minnesota	99,800
39	Mississippi	87,840
22	Missouri	93,370
49	Montana	81,300
47	Nebraska	82,820
18	Nevada	94,070
14	New Hampshire	94,690
26	New Jersey	92,300
36	New Mexico	88,760
25	New York	92,560
13	North Carolina	94,720
50	North Dakota	75,340
29	Ohio	90,710
43	Oklahoma	84,800
24	Oregon	92,640
42	Pennsylvania	85,050
38	Rhode Island	87,890
20	South Carolina	93,630
48	South Dakota	82,180
7	Tennessee	97,600
12	Texas	96,290
15	Utah	94,580
9	Vermont	96,700
23	Virginia	92,660
31	Washington	90,600
19	West Virginia	94,050
8	Wisconsin	97,250
41	Wyoming	85,740

RANK ORDER

RANK	STATE	WAGES
1	California	$106,150
2	Maine	102,300
3	Alaska	101,290
4	Minnesota	99,800
5	Kentucky	98,910
6	Illinois	97,770
7	Tennessee	97,600
8	Wisconsin	97,250
9	Vermont	96,700
10	Idaho	96,670
11	Connecticut	96,470
12	Texas	96,290
13	North Carolina	94,720
14	New Hampshire	94,690
15	Utah	94,580
16	Michigan	94,450
17	Georgia	94,370
18	Nevada	94,070
19	West Virginia	94,050
20	South Carolina	93,630
21	Colorado	93,480
22	Missouri	93,370
23	Virginia	92,660
24	Oregon	92,640
25	New York	92,560
26	New Jersey	92,300
27	Florida	92,030
28	Alabama	91,250
29	Ohio	90,710
30	Delaware	90,680
31	Washington	90,600
32	Arkansas	90,440
33	Maryland	90,100
34	Arizona	89,870
35	Hawaii	89,240
36	New Mexico	88,760
37	Indiana	88,510
38	Rhode Island	87,890
39	Mississippi	87,840
40	Iowa	86,590
41	Wyoming	85,740
42	Pennsylvania	85,050
43	Oklahoma	84,800
44	Louisiana	84,520
45	Massachusetts	83,510
46	Kansas	83,420
47	Nebraska	82,820
48	South Dakota	82,180
49	Montana	81,300
50	North Dakota	75,340
	District of Columbia	78,690

Source: U.S. Department of Labor, Bureau of Labor Statistics
   "Occupational Employment and Wages, 2006" (http://www.bls.gov/oes/)
*Does not include self-employed.

Optometrists in 2006

National Total = 24,220 Optometrists*

ALPHA ORDER

RANK	STATE	OPTOMETRISTS	% of USA
27	Alabama	300	1.2%
46	Alaska	90	0.4%
22	Arizona	390	1.6%
25	Arkansas	330	1.4%
1	California	2,470	10.2%
17	Colorado	440	1.8%
31	Connecticut	260	1.1%
44	Delaware	100	0.4%
6	Florida	1,140	4.7%
15	Georgia	460	1.9%
42	Hawaii	120	0.5%
36	Idaho	160	0.7%
2	Illinois	1,810	7.5%
9	Indiana	800	3.3%
26	Iowa	320	1.3%
27	Kansas	300	1.2%
27	Kentucky	300	1.2%
34	Louisiana	180	0.7%
48	Maine	80	0.3%
15	Maryland	460	1.9%
18	Massachusetts	430	1.8%
5	Michigan	1,160	4.8%
12	Minnesota	650	2.7%
36	Mississippi	160	0.7%
11	Missouri	680	2.8%
46	Montana	90	0.4%
31	Nebraska	260	1.1%
34	Nevada	180	0.7%
41	New Hampshire	130	0.5%
10	New Jersey	700	2.9%
33	New Mexico	210	0.9%
3	New York	1,370	5.7%
13	North Carolina	560	2.3%
36	North Dakota	160	0.7%
7	Ohio	1,050	4.3%
24	Oklahoma	380	1.6%
21	Oregon	410	1.7%
8	Pennsylvania	960	4.0%
36	Rhode Island	160	0.7%
36	South Carolina	160	0.7%
44	South Dakota	100	0.4%
20	Tennessee	420	1.7%
4	Texas	1,360	5.6%
30	Utah	280	1.2%
50	Vermont	70	0.3%
14	Virginia	540	2.2%
18	Washington	430	1.8%
43	West Virginia	110	0.5%
22	Wisconsin	390	1.6%
48	Wyoming	80	0.3%

RANK ORDER

RANK	STATE	OPTOMETRISTS	% of USA
1	California	2,470	10.2%
2	Illinois	1,810	7.5%
3	New York	1,370	5.7%
4	Texas	1,360	5.6%
5	Michigan	1,160	4.8%
6	Florida	1,140	4.7%
7	Ohio	1,050	4.3%
8	Pennsylvania	960	4.0%
9	Indiana	800	3.3%
10	New Jersey	700	2.9%
11	Missouri	680	2.8%
12	Minnesota	650	2.7%
13	North Carolina	560	2.3%
14	Virginia	540	2.2%
15	Georgia	460	1.9%
15	Maryland	460	1.9%
17	Colorado	440	1.8%
18	Massachusetts	430	1.8%
18	Washington	430	1.8%
20	Tennessee	420	1.7%
21	Oregon	410	1.7%
22	Arizona	390	1.6%
22	Wisconsin	390	1.6%
24	Oklahoma	380	1.6%
25	Arkansas	330	1.4%
26	Iowa	320	1.3%
27	Alabama	300	1.2%
27	Kansas	300	1.2%
27	Kentucky	300	1.2%
30	Utah	280	1.2%
31	Connecticut	260	1.1%
31	Nebraska	260	1.1%
33	New Mexico	210	0.9%
34	Louisiana	180	0.7%
34	Nevada	180	0.7%
36	Idaho	160	0.7%
36	Mississippi	160	0.7%
36	North Dakota	160	0.7%
36	Rhode Island	160	0.7%
36	South Carolina	160	0.7%
41	New Hampshire	130	0.5%
42	Hawaii	120	0.5%
43	West Virginia	110	0.5%
44	Delaware	100	0.4%
44	South Dakota	100	0.4%
46	Alaska	90	0.4%
46	Montana	90	0.4%
48	Maine	80	0.3%
48	Wyoming	80	0.3%
50	Vermont	70	0.3%
	District of Columbia	100	0.4%

Source: U.S. Department of Labor, Bureau of Labor Statistics
"Occupational Employment and Wages, 2006" (http://www.bls.gov/oes/)
*Does not include self-employed.

Rate of Optometrists in 2006

National Rate = 8 Optometrists per 100,000 Population*

<table>
<tr><td colspan="3">ALPHA ORDER</td><td colspan="3">RANK ORDER</td></tr>
<tr><td>RANK</td><td>STATE</td><td>RATE</td><td>RANK</td><td>STATE</td><td>RATE</td></tr>
<tr><td>30</td><td>Alabama</td><td>7</td><td>1</td><td>North Dakota</td><td>25</td></tr>
<tr><td>6</td><td>Alaska</td><td>13</td><td>2</td><td>Wyoming</td><td>16</td></tr>
<tr><td>41</td><td>Arizona</td><td>6</td><td>3</td><td>Nebraska</td><td>15</td></tr>
<tr><td>10</td><td>Arkansas</td><td>12</td><td>3</td><td>Rhode Island</td><td>15</td></tr>
<tr><td>30</td><td>California</td><td>7</td><td>5</td><td>Illinois</td><td>14</td></tr>
<tr><td>24</td><td>Colorado</td><td>9</td><td>6</td><td>Alaska</td><td>13</td></tr>
<tr><td>30</td><td>Connecticut</td><td>7</td><td>6</td><td>Indiana</td><td>13</td></tr>
<tr><td>10</td><td>Delaware</td><td>12</td><td>6</td><td>Minnesota</td><td>13</td></tr>
<tr><td>41</td><td>Florida</td><td>6</td><td>6</td><td>South Dakota</td><td>13</td></tr>
<tr><td>48</td><td>Georgia</td><td>5</td><td>10</td><td>Arkansas</td><td>12</td></tr>
<tr><td>24</td><td>Hawaii</td><td>9</td><td>10</td><td>Delaware</td><td>12</td></tr>
<tr><td>13</td><td>Idaho</td><td>11</td><td>10</td><td>Missouri</td><td>12</td></tr>
<tr><td>5</td><td>Illinois</td><td>14</td><td>13</td><td>Idaho</td><td>11</td></tr>
<tr><td>6</td><td>Indiana</td><td>13</td><td>13</td><td>Iowa</td><td>11</td></tr>
<tr><td>13</td><td>Iowa</td><td>11</td><td>13</td><td>Kansas</td><td>11</td></tr>
<tr><td>13</td><td>Kansas</td><td>11</td><td>13</td><td>Michigan</td><td>11</td></tr>
<tr><td>30</td><td>Kentucky</td><td>7</td><td>13</td><td>New Mexico</td><td>11</td></tr>
<tr><td>49</td><td>Louisiana</td><td>4</td><td>13</td><td>Oklahoma</td><td>11</td></tr>
<tr><td>41</td><td>Maine</td><td>6</td><td>13</td><td>Oregon</td><td>11</td></tr>
<tr><td>27</td><td>Maryland</td><td>8</td><td>13</td><td>Utah</td><td>11</td></tr>
<tr><td>30</td><td>Massachusetts</td><td>7</td><td>13</td><td>Vermont</td><td>11</td></tr>
<tr><td>13</td><td>Michigan</td><td>11</td><td>22</td><td>Montana</td><td>10</td></tr>
<tr><td>6</td><td>Minnesota</td><td>13</td><td>22</td><td>New Hampshire</td><td>10</td></tr>
<tr><td>41</td><td>Mississippi</td><td>6</td><td>24</td><td>Colorado</td><td>9</td></tr>
<tr><td>10</td><td>Missouri</td><td>12</td><td>24</td><td>Hawaii</td><td>9</td></tr>
<tr><td>22</td><td>Montana</td><td>10</td><td>24</td><td>Ohio</td><td>9</td></tr>
<tr><td>3</td><td>Nebraska</td><td>15</td><td>27</td><td>Maryland</td><td>8</td></tr>
<tr><td>30</td><td>Nevada</td><td>7</td><td>27</td><td>New Jersey</td><td>8</td></tr>
<tr><td>22</td><td>New Hampshire</td><td>10</td><td>27</td><td>Pennsylvania</td><td>8</td></tr>
<tr><td>27</td><td>New Jersey</td><td>8</td><td>30</td><td>Alabama</td><td>7</td></tr>
<tr><td>13</td><td>New Mexico</td><td>11</td><td>30</td><td>California</td><td>7</td></tr>
<tr><td>30</td><td>New York</td><td>7</td><td>30</td><td>Connecticut</td><td>7</td></tr>
<tr><td>41</td><td>North Carolina</td><td>6</td><td>30</td><td>Kentucky</td><td>7</td></tr>
<tr><td>1</td><td>North Dakota</td><td>25</td><td>30</td><td>Massachusetts</td><td>7</td></tr>
<tr><td>24</td><td>Ohio</td><td>9</td><td>30</td><td>Nevada</td><td>7</td></tr>
<tr><td>13</td><td>Oklahoma</td><td>11</td><td>30</td><td>New York</td><td>7</td></tr>
<tr><td>13</td><td>Oregon</td><td>11</td><td>30</td><td>Tennessee</td><td>7</td></tr>
<tr><td>27</td><td>Pennsylvania</td><td>8</td><td>30</td><td>Virginia</td><td>7</td></tr>
<tr><td>3</td><td>Rhode Island</td><td>15</td><td>30</td><td>Washington</td><td>7</td></tr>
<tr><td>49</td><td>South Carolina</td><td>4</td><td>30</td><td>Wisconsin</td><td>7</td></tr>
<tr><td>6</td><td>South Dakota</td><td>13</td><td>41</td><td>Arizona</td><td>6</td></tr>
<tr><td>30</td><td>Tennessee</td><td>7</td><td>41</td><td>Florida</td><td>6</td></tr>
<tr><td>41</td><td>Texas</td><td>6</td><td>41</td><td>Maine</td><td>6</td></tr>
<tr><td>13</td><td>Utah</td><td>11</td><td>41</td><td>Mississippi</td><td>6</td></tr>
<tr><td>13</td><td>Vermont</td><td>11</td><td>41</td><td>North Carolina</td><td>6</td></tr>
<tr><td>30</td><td>Virginia</td><td>7</td><td>41</td><td>Texas</td><td>6</td></tr>
<tr><td>30</td><td>Washington</td><td>7</td><td>41</td><td>West Virginia</td><td>6</td></tr>
<tr><td>41</td><td>West Virginia</td><td>6</td><td>48</td><td>Georgia</td><td>5</td></tr>
<tr><td>30</td><td>Wisconsin</td><td>7</td><td>49</td><td>Louisiana</td><td>4</td></tr>
<tr><td>2</td><td>Wyoming</td><td>16</td><td>49</td><td>South Carolina</td><td>4</td></tr>
<tr><td></td><td></td><td></td><td></td><td>District of Columbia</td><td>17</td></tr>
</table>

Source: CQ Press using data from U.S. Department of Labor, Bureau of Labor Statistics
  "Occupational Employment and Wages, 2006" (http://www.bls.gov/oes/)
*Does not include self-employed.

Average Annual Wages of Optometrists in 2006

National Average = $98,550*

ALPHA ORDER				RANK ORDER		
RANK	STATE	WAGES		RANK	STATE	WAGES
44	Alabama	$84,440		1	Vermont	$165,990
3	Alaska	138,100		2	Delaware	147,510
46	Arizona	82,690		3	Alaska	138,100
9	Arkansas	116,740		4	Georgia	137,890
24	California	99,350		5	North Carolina	135,720
49	Colorado	69,990		6	Washington	133,160
11	Connecticut	110,960		7	Minnesota	123,040
2	Delaware	147,510		8	Nevada	117,650
29	Florida	93,940		9	Arkansas	116,740
4	Georgia	137,890		10	South Dakota	111,820
42	Hawaii	85,390		11	Connecticut	110,960
50	Idaho	48,600		12	Louisiana	110,340
33	Illinois	92,100		13	Ohio	109,390
47	Indiana	81,480		14	Nebraska	108,950
20	Iowa	101,130		15	New York	108,890
34	Kansas	91,970		16	Kentucky	105,570
16	Kentucky	105,570		17	Maine	103,940
12	Louisiana	110,340		18	Rhode Island	101,910
17	Maine	103,940		19	Michigan	101,550
36	Maryland	91,340		20	Iowa	101,130
48	Massachusetts	72,780		21	Wyoming	100,770
19	Michigan	101,550		22	South Carolina	100,400
7	Minnesota	123,040		23	Virginia	100,240
26	Mississippi	98,790		24	California	99,350
41	Missouri	86,070		25	New Jersey	99,170
37	Montana	90,370		26	Mississippi	98,790
14	Nebraska	108,950		27	New Hampshire	98,150
8	Nevada	117,650		28	West Virginia	95,990
27	New Hampshire	98,150		29	Florida	93,940
25	New Jersey	99,170		30	Wisconsin	93,890
31	New Mexico	93,150		31	New Mexico	93,150
15	New York	108,890		32	Utah	92,760
5	North Carolina	135,720		33	Illinois	92,100
38	North Dakota	87,810		34	Kansas	91,970
13	Ohio	109,390		35	Tennessee	91,710
43	Oklahoma	85,300		36	Maryland	91,340
45	Oregon	82,960		37	Montana	90,370
40	Pennsylvania	87,360		38	North Dakota	87,810
18	Rhode Island	101,910		39	Texas	87,460
22	South Carolina	100,400		40	Pennsylvania	87,360
10	South Dakota	111,820		41	Missouri	86,070
35	Tennessee	91,710		42	Hawaii	85,390
39	Texas	87,460		43	Oklahoma	85,300
32	Utah	92,760		44	Alabama	84,440
1	Vermont	165,990		45	Oregon	82,960
23	Virginia	100,240		46	Arizona	82,690
6	Washington	133,160		47	Indiana	81,480
28	West Virginia	95,990		48	Massachusetts	72,780
30	Wisconsin	93,890		49	Colorado	69,990
21	Wyoming	100,770		50	Idaho	48,600
					District of Columbia	73,840

Source: U.S. Department of Labor, Bureau of Labor Statistics
    "Occupational Employment and Wages, 2006" (http://www.bls.gov/oes/)
*Does not include self-employed.

Emergency Medical Technicians and Paramedics in 2006

National Total = 196,190 Technicians and Paramedics*

<u>ALPHA ORDER</u>

RANK	STATE	PARAMEDICS	% of USA
24	Alabama	2,830	1.4%
49	Alaska	180	0.1%
28	Arizona	2,530	1.3%
30	Arkansas	1,960	1.0%
4	California	11,920	6.1%
23	Colorado	3,000	1.5%
26	Connecticut	2,670	1.4%
41	Delaware	740	0.4%
8	Florida	7,660	3.9%
11	Georgia	6,400	3.3%
44	Hawaii	520	0.3%
40	Idaho	830	0.4%
5	Illinois	11,640	5.9%
15	Indiana	4,870	2.5%
29	Iowa	2,140	1.1%
31	Kansas	1,890	1.0%
18	Kentucky	3,790	1.9%
27	Louisiana	2,630	1.3%
36	Maine	1,260	0.6%
21	Maryland	3,150	1.6%
16	Massachusetts	4,860	2.5%
9	Michigan	6,820	3.5%
20	Minnesota	3,620	1.8%
34	Mississippi	1,590	0.8%
10	Missouri	6,470	3.3%
43	Montana	610	0.3%
45	Nebraska	490	0.2%
37	Nevada	1,050	0.5%
38	New Hampshire	900	0.5%
14	New Jersey	5,440	2.8%
39	New Mexico	870	0.4%
3	New York	12,270	6.3%
7	North Carolina	7,890	4.0%
46	North Dakota	480	0.2%
6	Ohio	10,020	5.1%
18	Oklahoma	3,790	1.9%
35	Oregon	1,420	0.7%
2	Pennsylvania	12,920	6.6%
NA	Rhode Island**	NA	NA
17	South Carolina	4,000	2.0%
42	South Dakota	710	0.4%
12	Tennessee	6,270	3.2%
1	Texas	13,060	6.7%
33	Utah	1,760	0.9%
47	Vermont	470	0.2%
22	Virginia	3,120	1.6%
25	Washington	2,690	1.4%
32	West Virginia	1,860	0.9%
13	Wisconsin	6,150	3.1%
48	Wyoming	360	0.2%

<u>RANK ORDER</u>

RANK	STATE	PARAMEDICS	% of USA
1	Texas	13,060	6.7%
2	Pennsylvania	12,920	6.6%
3	New York	12,270	6.3%
4	California	11,920	6.1%
5	Illinois	11,640	5.9%
6	Ohio	10,020	5.1%
7	North Carolina	7,890	4.0%
8	Florida	7,660	3.9%
9	Michigan	6,820	3.5%
10	Missouri	6,470	3.3%
11	Georgia	6,400	3.3%
12	Tennessee	6,270	3.2%
13	Wisconsin	6,150	3.1%
14	New Jersey	5,440	2.8%
15	Indiana	4,870	2.5%
16	Massachusetts	4,860	2.5%
17	South Carolina	4,000	2.0%
18	Kentucky	3,790	1.9%
18	Oklahoma	3,790	1.9%
20	Minnesota	3,620	1.8%
21	Maryland	3,150	1.6%
22	Virginia	3,120	1.6%
23	Colorado	3,000	1.5%
24	Alabama	2,830	1.4%
25	Washington	2,690	1.4%
26	Connecticut	2,670	1.4%
27	Louisiana	2,630	1.3%
28	Arizona	2,530	1.3%
29	Iowa	2,140	1.1%
30	Arkansas	1,960	1.0%
31	Kansas	1,890	1.0%
32	West Virginia	1,860	0.9%
33	Utah	1,760	0.9%
34	Mississippi	1,590	0.8%
35	Oregon	1,420	0.7%
36	Maine	1,260	0.6%
37	Nevada	1,050	0.5%
38	New Hampshire	900	0.5%
39	New Mexico	870	0.4%
40	Idaho	830	0.4%
41	Delaware	740	0.4%
42	South Dakota	710	0.4%
43	Montana	610	0.3%
44	Hawaii	520	0.3%
45	Nebraska	490	0.2%
46	North Dakota	480	0.2%
47	Vermont	470	0.2%
48	Wyoming	360	0.2%
49	Alaska	180	0.1%
NA	Rhode Island**	NA	NA
	District of Columbia**	NA	NA

Source: U.S. Department of Labor, Bureau of Labor Statistics
  "Occupational Employment and Wages, 2006" (http://www.bls.gov/oes/)
*Does not include self-employed.
**Not available.

Rate of Emergency Medical Technicians and Paramedics in 2006

National Rate = 66 Technicians and Paramedics per 100,000 Population*

ALPHA ORDER

RANK	STATE	RATE
33	Alabama	62
49	Alaska	27
43	Arizona	41
21	Arkansas	70
47	California	33
31	Colorado	63
16	Connecticut	76
13	Delaware	87
40	Florida	42
24	Georgia	69
43	Hawaii	41
35	Idaho	57
9	Illinois	91
15	Indiana	77
20	Iowa	72
24	Kansas	69
10	Kentucky	90
33	Louisiana	62
7	Maine	96
36	Maryland	56
16	Massachusetts	76
27	Michigan	68
21	Minnesota	70
38	Mississippi	55
1	Missouri	111
29	Montana	64
48	Nebraska	28
40	Nevada	42
24	New Hampshire	69
31	New Jersey	63
39	New Mexico	45
29	New York	64
12	North Carolina	89
19	North Dakota	75
13	Ohio	87
3	Oklahoma	106
46	Oregon	38
4	Pennsylvania	104
NA	Rhode Island**	NA
8	South Carolina	92
10	South Dakota	90
5	Tennessee	103
36	Texas	56
27	Utah	68
16	Vermont	76
43	Virginia	41
40	Washington	42
5	West Virginia	103
2	Wisconsin	110
21	Wyoming	70

RANK ORDER

RANK	STATE	RATE
1	Missouri	111
2	Wisconsin	110
3	Oklahoma	106
4	Pennsylvania	104
5	Tennessee	103
5	West Virginia	103
7	Maine	96
8	South Carolina	92
9	Illinois	91
10	Kentucky	90
10	South Dakota	90
12	North Carolina	89
13	Delaware	87
13	Ohio	87
15	Indiana	77
16	Connecticut	76
16	Massachusetts	76
16	Vermont	76
19	North Dakota	75
20	Iowa	72
21	Arkansas	70
21	Minnesota	70
21	Wyoming	70
24	Georgia	69
24	Kansas	69
24	New Hampshire	69
27	Michigan	68
27	Utah	68
29	Montana	64
29	New York	64
31	Colorado	63
31	New Jersey	63
33	Alabama	62
33	Louisiana	62
35	Idaho	57
36	Maryland	56
36	Texas	56
38	Mississippi	55
39	New Mexico	45
40	Florida	42
40	Nevada	42
40	Washington	42
43	Arizona	41
43	Hawaii	41
43	Virginia	41
46	Oregon	38
47	California	33
48	Nebraska	28
49	Alaska	27
NA	Rhode Island**	NA
	District of Columbia**	NA

Source: CQ Press using data from U.S. Department of Labor, Bureau of Labor Statistics
"Occupational Employment and Wages, 2006" (http://www.bls.gov/oes/)
*Does not include self-employed.
**Not available.

Average Annual Wages of
Emergency Medical Technicians and Paramedics in 2006
National Average = $29,390*

ALPHA ORDER

ALPHA ORDER

RANK	STATE	WAGES
42	Alabama	$24,920
1	Alaska	46,970
38	Arizona	25,960
46	Arkansas	24,370
16	California	30,580
10	Colorado	33,970
8	Connecticut	34,740
7	Delaware	35,250
20	Florida	29,200
22	Georgia	28,970
5	Hawaii	39,230
14	Idaho	31,750
19	Illinois	29,930
26	Indiana	28,020
36	Iowa	26,450
47	Kansas	23,590
45	Kentucky	24,560
40	Louisiana	25,440
27	Maine	28,010
4	Maryland	39,740
9	Massachusetts	34,690
24	Michigan	28,620
21	Minnesota	29,010
41	Mississippi	25,360
17	Missouri	30,430
50	Montana	21,280
35	Nebraska	26,910
2	Nevada	43,000
15	New Hampshire	31,450
13	New Jersey	32,610
23	New Mexico	28,710
6	New York	35,530
28	North Carolina	27,880
29	North Dakota	27,650
37	Ohio	26,280
49	Oklahoma	21,620
11	Oregon	33,270
34	Pennsylvania	27,210
12	Rhode Island	32,630
31	South Carolina	27,470
43	South Dakota	24,840
25	Tennessee	28,410
33	Texas	27,240
32	Utah	27,260
30	Vermont	27,620
18	Virginia	30,020
3	Washington	42,200
48	West Virginia	21,780
39	Wisconsin	25,670
44	Wyoming	24,590

RANK ORDER

RANK	STATE	WAGES
1	Alaska	$46,970
2	Nevada	43,000
3	Washington	42,200
4	Maryland	39,740
5	Hawaii	39,230
6	New York	35,530
7	Delaware	35,250
8	Connecticut	34,740
9	Massachusetts	34,690
10	Colorado	33,970
11	Oregon	33,270
12	Rhode Island	32,630
13	New Jersey	32,610
14	Idaho	31,750
15	New Hampshire	31,450
16	California	30,580
17	Missouri	30,430
18	Virginia	30,020
19	Illinois	29,930
20	Florida	29,200
21	Minnesota	29,010
22	Georgia	28,970
23	New Mexico	28,710
24	Michigan	28,620
25	Tennessee	28,410
26	Indiana	28,020
27	Maine	28,010
28	North Carolina	27,880
29	North Dakota	27,650
30	Vermont	27,620
31	South Carolina	27,470
32	Utah	27,260
33	Texas	27,240
34	Pennsylvania	27,210
35	Nebraska	26,910
36	Iowa	26,450
37	Ohio	26,280
38	Arizona	25,960
39	Wisconsin	25,670
40	Louisiana	25,440
41	Mississippi	25,360
42	Alabama	24,920
43	South Dakota	24,840
44	Wyoming	24,590
45	Kentucky	24,560
46	Arkansas	24,370
47	Kansas	23,590
48	West Virginia	21,780
49	Oklahoma	21,620
50	Montana	21,280
	District of Columbia**	NA

Source: U.S. Department of Labor, Bureau of Labor Statistics
   "Occupational Employment and Wages, 2006" (http://www.bls.gov/oes/)
*Does not include self-employed.
**Not available.

Employment in Health Care Support Industries in 2006

National Total = 3,483,270 Aides and Assistants*

ALPHA ORDER

RANK	STATE	EMPLOYEES	% of USA
25	Alabama	47,670	1.4%
50	Alaska	6,220	0.2%
21	Arizona	58,410	1.7%
32	Arkansas	31,320	0.9%
1	California	318,080	9.1%
29	Colorado	41,610	1.2%
22	Connecticut	51,510	1.5%
47	Delaware	9,770	0.3%
4	Florida	200,440	5.8%
13	Georgia	79,160	2.3%
43	Hawaii	13,290	0.4%
41	Idaho	16,590	0.5%
7	Illinois	137,740	4.0%
18	Indiana	67,190	1.9%
27	Iowa	43,990	1.3%
31	Kansas	39,880	1.1%
24	Kentucky	47,880	1.4%
23	Louisiana	49,440	1.4%
39	Maine	19,340	0.6%
20	Maryland	63,670	1.8%
11	Massachusetts	94,700	2.7%
9	Michigan	124,550	3.6%
14	Minnesota	77,290	2.2%
33	Mississippi	30,190	0.9%
15	Missouri	72,730	2.1%
45	Montana	10,960	0.3%
35	Nebraska	25,090	0.7%
38	Nevada	19,440	0.6%
42	New Hampshire	14,860	0.4%
10	New Jersey	106,650	3.1%
37	New Mexico	20,640	0.6%
2	New York	308,290	8.9%
8	North Carolina	126,360	3.6%
44	North Dakota	11,590	0.3%
6	Ohio	175,320	5.0%
26	Oklahoma	45,060	1.3%
30	Oregon	40,640	1.2%
5	Pennsylvania	175,450	5.0%
40	Rhode Island	17,520	0.5%
28	South Carolina	43,310	1.2%
46	South Dakota	10,500	0.3%
19	Tennessee	65,620	1.9%
3	Texas	231,520	6.6%
34	Utah	25,860	0.7%
48	Vermont	9,470	0.3%
16	Virginia	70,630	2.0%
17	Washington	67,720	1.9%
36	West Virginia	23,870	0.7%
12	Wisconsin	80,480	2.3%
49	Wyoming	6,350	0.2%

RANK ORDER

RANK	STATE	EMPLOYEES	% of USA
1	California	318,080	9.1%
2	New York	308,290	8.9%
3	Texas	231,520	6.6%
4	Florida	200,440	5.8%
5	Pennsylvania	175,450	5.0%
6	Ohio	175,320	5.0%
7	Illinois	137,740	4.0%
8	North Carolina	126,360	3.6%
9	Michigan	124,550	3.6%
10	New Jersey	106,650	3.1%
11	Massachusetts	94,700	2.7%
12	Wisconsin	80,480	2.3%
13	Georgia	79,160	2.3%
14	Minnesota	77,290	2.2%
15	Missouri	72,730	2.1%
16	Virginia	70,630	2.0%
17	Washington	67,720	1.9%
18	Indiana	67,190	1.9%
19	Tennessee	65,620	1.9%
20	Maryland	63,670	1.8%
21	Arizona	58,410	1.7%
22	Connecticut	51,510	1.5%
23	Louisiana	49,440	1.4%
24	Kentucky	47,880	1.4%
25	Alabama	47,670	1.4%
26	Oklahoma	45,060	1.3%
27	Iowa	43,990	1.3%
28	South Carolina	43,310	1.2%
29	Colorado	41,610	1.2%
30	Oregon	40,640	1.2%
31	Kansas	39,880	1.1%
32	Arkansas	31,320	0.9%
33	Mississippi	30,190	0.9%
34	Utah	25,860	0.7%
35	Nebraska	25,090	0.7%
36	West Virginia	23,870	0.7%
37	New Mexico	20,640	0.6%
38	Nevada	19,440	0.6%
39	Maine	19,340	0.6%
40	Rhode Island	17,520	0.5%
41	Idaho	16,590	0.5%
42	New Hampshire	14,860	0.4%
43	Hawaii	13,290	0.4%
44	North Dakota	11,590	0.3%
45	Montana	10,960	0.3%
46	South Dakota	10,500	0.3%
47	Delaware	9,770	0.3%
48	Vermont	9,470	0.3%
49	Wyoming	6,350	0.2%
50	Alaska	6,220	0.2%
	District of Columbia	7,420	0.2%

Source: U.S. Department of Labor, Bureau of Labor Statistics
   "Occupational Employment and Wages, 2006" (http://www.bls.gov/oes/)
*Does not include self-employed. Includes various health care assistants and aides not included in the category of health care practitioners and technicians. Among the included occupations are home health aides, nursing aides, psychiatric aides, dental assistants, and pharmacy aides.

Rate of Employees in Health Care Support Industries in 2006

National Rate = 1,166 Aides and Assistants per 100,000 Population*

<u>ALPHA ORDER</u>

RANK	STATE	RATE
39	Alabama	1,039
46	Alaska	918
44	Arizona	947
30	Arkansas	1,115
47	California	877
48	Colorado	873
8	Connecticut	1,474
25	Delaware	1,146
31	Florida	1,110
49	Georgia	847
39	Hawaii	1,039
28	Idaho	1,133
34	Illinois	1,078
35	Indiana	1,066
7	Iowa	1,480
11	Kansas	1,447
26	Kentucky	1,139
23	Louisiana	1,165
10	Maine	1,471
27	Maryland	1,137
9	Massachusetts	1,472
21	Michigan	1,233
6	Minnesota	1,499
38	Mississippi	1,041
19	Missouri	1,246
24	Montana	1,158
14	Nebraska	1,423
50	Nevada	780
28	New Hampshire	1,133
22	New Jersey	1,231
36	New Mexico	1,063
3	New York	1,599
13	North Carolina	1,425
1	North Dakota	1,818
4	Ohio	1,529
18	Oklahoma	1,260
32	Oregon	1,101
15	Pennsylvania	1,415
2	Rhode Island	1,650
42	South Carolina	1,000
16	South Dakota	1,332
33	Tennessee	1,080
43	Texas	989
41	Utah	1,003
5	Vermont	1,526
45	Virginia	924
37	Washington	1,062
17	West Virginia	1,320
12	Wisconsin	1,444
20	Wyoming	1,238

<u>RANK ORDER</u>

RANK	STATE	RATE
1	North Dakota	1,818
2	Rhode Island	1,650
3	New York	1,599
4	Ohio	1,529
5	Vermont	1,526
6	Minnesota	1,499
7	Iowa	1,480
8	Connecticut	1,474
9	Massachusetts	1,472
10	Maine	1,471
11	Kansas	1,447
12	Wisconsin	1,444
13	North Carolina	1,425
14	Nebraska	1,423
15	Pennsylvania	1,415
16	South Dakota	1,332
17	West Virginia	1,320
18	Oklahoma	1,260
19	Missouri	1,246
20	Wyoming	1,238
21	Michigan	1,233
22	New Jersey	1,231
23	Louisiana	1,165
24	Montana	1,158
25	Delaware	1,146
26	Kentucky	1,139
27	Maryland	1,137
28	Idaho	1,133
28	New Hampshire	1,133
30	Arkansas	1,115
31	Florida	1,110
32	Oregon	1,101
33	Tennessee	1,080
34	Illinois	1,078
35	Indiana	1,066
36	New Mexico	1,063
37	Washington	1,062
38	Mississippi	1,041
39	Alabama	1,039
39	Hawaii	1,039
41	Utah	1,003
42	South Carolina	1,000
43	Texas	989
44	Arizona	947
45	Virginia	924
46	Alaska	918
47	California	877
48	Colorado	873
49	Georgia	847
50	Nevada	780

	District of Columbia	1,267

Source: CQ Press using data from U.S. Department of Labor, Bureau of Labor Statistics
  "Occupational Employment and Wages, 2006" (http://www.bls.gov/oes/)
*Does not include self-employed. Includes various health care assistants and aides not included in the category of health care practitioners and technicians. Among the included occupations are home health aides, nursing aides, psychiatric aides, dental assistants, and pharmacy aides.

Average Annual Wages of Employees in Health Care Support Industries in 2006

National Average = $24,610*

ALPHA ORDER				RANK ORDER		
RANK	STATE	WAGES		RANK	STATE	WAGES
46	Alabama	$20,320		1	Alaska	$31,160
1	Alaska	31,160		2	Connecticut	29,500
20	Arizona	24,410		3	Massachusetts	28,670
47	Arkansas	19,920		4	Hawaii	28,400
7	California	28,060		5	Nevada	28,280
12	Colorado	27,150		6	Washington	28,200
2	Connecticut	29,500		7	California	28,060
8	Delaware	27,460		8	Delaware	27,460
24	Florida	23,940		9	New Hampshire	27,250
33	Georgia	22,780		10	Rhode Island	27,240
4	Hawaii	28,400		11	New Jersey	27,200
35	Idaho	22,710		12	Colorado	27,150
19	Illinois	24,680		13	Maryland	27,010
21	Indiana	24,390		14	Minnesota	26,690
29	Iowa	23,160		15	Oregon	26,250
37	Kansas	22,420		16	New York	25,910
32	Kentucky	22,940		17	Michigan	25,780
50	Louisiana	18,890		18	Wisconsin	25,030
26	Maine	23,670		19	Illinois	24,680
13	Maryland	27,010		20	Arizona	24,410
3	Massachusetts	28,670		21	Indiana	24,390
17	Michigan	25,780		22	Pennsylvania	24,080
14	Minnesota	26,690		23	Virginia	23,980
49	Mississippi	19,010		24	Florida	23,940
39	Missouri	22,100		25	Ohio	23,920
43	Montana	21,550		26	Maine	23,670
28	Nebraska	23,320		27	Vermont	23,570
5	Nevada	28,280		28	Nebraska	23,320
9	New Hampshire	27,250		29	Iowa	23,160
11	New Jersey	27,200		30	Wyoming	23,010
34	New Mexico	22,740		31	Tennessee	22,970
16	New York	25,910		32	Kentucky	22,940
42	North Carolina	21,950		33	Georgia	22,780
38	North Dakota	22,140		34	New Mexico	22,740
25	Ohio	23,920		35	Idaho	22,710
45	Oklahoma	21,030		36	Utah	22,590
15	Oregon	26,250		37	Kansas	22,420
22	Pennsylvania	24,080		38	North Dakota	22,140
10	Rhode Island	27,240		39	Missouri	22,100
40	South Carolina	22,070		40	South Carolina	22,070
41	South Dakota	21,960		41	South Dakota	21,960
31	Tennessee	22,970		42	North Carolina	21,950
44	Texas	21,480		43	Montana	21,550
36	Utah	22,590		44	Texas	21,480
27	Vermont	23,570		45	Oklahoma	21,030
23	Virginia	23,980		46	Alabama	20,320
6	Washington	28,200		47	Arkansas	19,920
48	West Virginia	19,550		48	West Virginia	19,550
18	Wisconsin	25,030		49	Mississippi	19,010
30	Wyoming	23,010		50	Louisiana	18,890

District of Columbia   28,600

Source: U.S. Department of Labor, Bureau of Labor Statistics
"Occupational Employment and Wages, 2006" (http://www.bls.gov/oes/)
*Does not include self-employed. Includes various health care assistants and aides not included in the category of health care practitioners and technicians. Among the included occupations are home health aides, nursing aides, psychiatric aides, dental assistants, and pharmacy aides.

VII. Physical Fitness

Users of Exercise Equipment in 2006 495
Participants in Golf in 2006 496
Participants in Running/Jogging in 2006 497
Participants in Swimming in 2006 498
Participants in Tennis in 2006 499
Alcohol Consumption in 2005 500
Adult Per Capita Alcohol Consumption in 2005 501
Apparent Beer Consumption in 2005 502
Adult Per Capita Beer Consumption in 2005 503
Wine Consumption in 2005 504
Adult Per Capita Wine Consumption in 2005 505
Distilled Spirits Consumption in 2005 506
Adult Per Capita Distilled Spirits Consumption in 2005 . . 507
Percent of Adults Who Do Not Drink Alcohol: 2006 508
Percent of Adults Who Are Binge Drinkers: 2006 509
Percent of Adults Who Smoke: 2006 510
Percent of Men Who Smoke: 2006 511
Percent of Women Who Smoke: 2006 512
Percent of Adults Who Are Former Smokers: 2006 513
Percent of Adults Who Have Never Smoked: 2006 514
Percent of Population Who Are Illicit Drug Users: 2005 . 515
Percent of Adults Overweight: 2006 516
Percent of Adults Obese: 2006 517
Percent of Adults Overweight or Obese: 2006 518
Percent of Adults Who Do Not Exercise: 2006 519
Percent of Adults Who Exercise Vigorously: 2005 520
Percent of Adults Who Are Disabled: 2005 521
Percent of Adults with High Blood Pressure: 2005 522
Percent of Adults with High Cholesterol: 2005 523
Percent of Adults Who Have Visited a Dentist or
    Dental Clinic: 2006 524
Percent of Adults 65 Years Old and Older Who Have
    Lost All Their Natural Teeth: 2006 525
Percent of Adults Who Average Five or More Servings
    of Fruits and Vegetables Each Day: 2005 526
Percent of Adults Rating Their Health as Fair or Poor
    in 2006 527
Safety Belt Usage Rate in 2006 528

Users of Exercise Equipment in 2006

National Total = 52,392,000 Users

ALPHA ORDER				RANK ORDER			
RANK	STATE	USERS	% of USA	RANK	STATE	USERS	% of USA
16	Alabama	1,086,000	2.1%	1	California	6,027,000	11.5%
NA	Alaska*	NA	NA	2	Florida	3,674,000	7.0%
26	Arizona	682,000	1.3%	3	Texas	3,446,000	6.6%
36	Arkansas	332,000	0.6%	4	New York	3,308,000	6.3%
1	California	6,027,000	11.5%	5	Illinois	2,592,000	4.9%
25	Colorado	815,000	1.6%	6	Michigan	2,183,000	4.2%
29	Connecticut	555,000	1.1%	7	Pennsylvania	2,105,000	4.0%
43	Delaware	199,000	0.4%	8	Ohio	1,979,000	3.8%
2	Florida	3,674,000	7.0%	9	Georgia	1,750,000	3.3%
9	Georgia	1,750,000	3.3%	10	New Jersey	1,482,000	2.8%
NA	Hawaii*	NA	NA	11	Virginia	1,385,000	2.6%
45	Idaho	145,000	0.3%	12	North Carolina	1,363,000	2.6%
5	Illinois	2,592,000	4.9%	13	Wisconsin	1,285,000	2.5%
20	Indiana	1,025,000	2.0%	14	Washington	1,281,000	2.4%
28	Iowa	569,000	1.1%	15	Massachusetts	1,124,000	2.1%
34	Kansas	371,000	0.7%	16	Alabama	1,086,000	2.1%
21	Kentucky	999,000	1.9%	17	Minnesota	1,072,000	2.0%
23	Louisiana	962,000	1.8%	18	Tennessee	1,049,000	2.0%
40	Maine	219,000	0.4%	19	Missouri	1,026,000	2.0%
22	Maryland	974,000	1.9%	20	Indiana	1,025,000	2.0%
15	Massachusetts	1,124,000	2.1%	21	Kentucky	999,000	1.9%
6	Michigan	2,183,000	4.2%	22	Maryland	974,000	1.9%
17	Minnesota	1,072,000	2.0%	23	Louisiana	962,000	1.8%
33	Mississippi	431,000	0.8%	24	Oklahoma	850,000	1.6%
19	Missouri	1,026,000	2.0%	25	Colorado	815,000	1.6%
35	Montana	342,000	0.7%	26	Arizona	682,000	1.3%
42	Nebraska	209,000	0.4%	27	Nevada	623,000	1.2%
27	Nevada	623,000	1.2%	28	Iowa	569,000	1.1%
38	New Hampshire	292,000	0.6%	29	Connecticut	555,000	1.1%
10	New Jersey	1,482,000	2.8%	30	Oregon	467,000	0.9%
32	New Mexico	436,000	0.8%	31	South Carolina	451,000	0.9%
4	New York	3,308,000	6.3%	32	New Mexico	436,000	0.8%
12	North Carolina	1,363,000	2.6%	33	Mississippi	431,000	0.8%
47	North Dakota	100,000	0.2%	34	Kansas	371,000	0.7%
8	Ohio	1,979,000	3.8%	35	Montana	342,000	0.7%
24	Oklahoma	850,000	1.6%	36	Arkansas	332,000	0.6%
30	Oregon	467,000	0.9%	37	Utah	301,000	0.6%
7	Pennsylvania	2,105,000	4.0%	38	New Hampshire	292,000	0.6%
46	Rhode Island	116,000	0.2%	39	West Virginia	221,000	0.4%
31	South Carolina	451,000	0.9%	40	Maine	219,000	0.4%
44	South Dakota	165,000	0.3%	41	Wyoming	218,000	0.4%
18	Tennessee	1,049,000	2.0%	42	Nebraska	209,000	0.4%
3	Texas	3,446,000	6.6%	43	Delaware	199,000	0.4%
37	Utah	301,000	0.6%	44	South Dakota	165,000	0.3%
48	Vermont	44,000	0.1%	45	Idaho	145,000	0.3%
11	Virginia	1,385,000	2.6%	46	Rhode Island	116,000	0.2%
14	Washington	1,281,000	2.4%	47	North Dakota	100,000	0.2%
39	West Virginia	221,000	0.4%	48	Vermont	44,000	0.1%
13	Wisconsin	1,285,000	2.5%	NA	Alaska*	NA	NA
41	Wyoming	218,000	0.4%	NA	Hawaii*	NA	NA
					District of Columbia*	NA	NA

Source: The National Sporting Goods Association
"NSGA Sports Participation Survey, January-December 2006 (Copyright 2007, reprinted with permission)
*Not available.

Participants in Golf in 2006

National Total = 24,428,000 Golfers

<table><tr><td colspan="4">ALPHA ORDER</td><td colspan="4">RANK ORDER</td></tr><tr><td>RANK</td><td>STATE</td><td>GOLFERS</td><td>% of USA</td><td>RANK</td><td>STATE</td><td>GOLFERS</td><td>% of USA</td></tr><tr><td>29</td><td>Alabama</td><td>258,000</td><td>1.1%</td><td>1</td><td>New York</td><td>1,849,000</td><td>7.6%</td></tr><tr><td>NA</td><td>Alaska*</td><td>NA</td><td>NA</td><td>2</td><td>California</td><td>1,767,000</td><td>7.2%</td></tr><tr><td>23</td><td>Arizona</td><td>388,000</td><td>1.6%</td><td>3</td><td>Illinois</td><td>1,503,000</td><td>6.2%</td></tr><tr><td>38</td><td>Arkansas</td><td>120,000</td><td>0.5%</td><td>4</td><td>Florida</td><td>1,458,000</td><td>6.0%</td></tr><tr><td>2</td><td>California</td><td>1,767,000</td><td>7.2%</td><td>5</td><td>Michigan</td><td>1,406,000</td><td>5.8%</td></tr><tr><td>9</td><td>Colorado</td><td>845,000</td><td>3.5%</td><td>6</td><td>Texas</td><td>1,371,000</td><td>5.6%</td></tr><tr><td>14</td><td>Connecticut</td><td>624,000</td><td>2.6%</td><td>7</td><td>Ohio</td><td>1,261,000</td><td>5.2%</td></tr><tr><td>NA</td><td>Delaware*</td><td>NA</td><td>NA</td><td>8</td><td>Pennsylvania</td><td>1,147,000</td><td>4.7%</td></tr><tr><td>4</td><td>Florida</td><td>1,458,000</td><td>6.0%</td><td>9</td><td>Colorado</td><td>845,000</td><td>3.5%</td></tr><tr><td>15</td><td>Georgia</td><td>584,000</td><td>2.4%</td><td>10</td><td>Wisconsin</td><td>754,000</td><td>3.1%</td></tr><tr><td>NA</td><td>Hawaii*</td><td>NA</td><td>NA</td><td>11</td><td>Indiana</td><td>684,000</td><td>2.8%</td></tr><tr><td>39</td><td>Idaho</td><td>115,000</td><td>0.5%</td><td>12</td><td>North Carolina</td><td>675,000</td><td>2.8%</td></tr><tr><td>3</td><td>Illinois</td><td>1,503,000</td><td>6.2%</td><td>13</td><td>Minnesota</td><td>667,000</td><td>2.7%</td></tr><tr><td>11</td><td>Indiana</td><td>684,000</td><td>2.8%</td><td>14</td><td>Connecticut</td><td>624,000</td><td>2.6%</td></tr><tr><td>25</td><td>Iowa</td><td>324,000</td><td>1.3%</td><td>15</td><td>Georgia</td><td>584,000</td><td>2.4%</td></tr><tr><td>27</td><td>Kansas</td><td>291,000</td><td>1.2%</td><td>16</td><td>Missouri</td><td>540,000</td><td>2.2%</td></tr><tr><td>31</td><td>Kentucky</td><td>243,000</td><td>1.0%</td><td>17</td><td>New Jersey</td><td>528,000</td><td>2.2%</td></tr><tr><td>33</td><td>Louisiana</td><td>198,000</td><td>0.8%</td><td>18</td><td>Virginia</td><td>469,000</td><td>1.9%</td></tr><tr><td>41</td><td>Maine</td><td>105,000</td><td>0.4%</td><td>19</td><td>Nevada</td><td>462,000</td><td>1.9%</td></tr><tr><td>26</td><td>Maryland</td><td>317,000</td><td>1.3%</td><td>20</td><td>Massachusetts</td><td>458,000</td><td>1.9%</td></tr><tr><td>20</td><td>Massachusetts</td><td>458,000</td><td>1.9%</td><td>21</td><td>Washington</td><td>454,000</td><td>1.9%</td></tr><tr><td>5</td><td>Michigan</td><td>1,406,000</td><td>5.8%</td><td>22</td><td>South Carolina</td><td>436,000</td><td>1.8%</td></tr><tr><td>13</td><td>Minnesota</td><td>667,000</td><td>2.7%</td><td>23</td><td>Arizona</td><td>388,000</td><td>1.6%</td></tr><tr><td>34</td><td>Mississippi</td><td>187,000</td><td>0.8%</td><td>24</td><td>Utah</td><td>336,000</td><td>1.4%</td></tr><tr><td>16</td><td>Missouri</td><td>540,000</td><td>2.2%</td><td>25</td><td>Iowa</td><td>324,000</td><td>1.3%</td></tr><tr><td>43</td><td>Montana</td><td>80,000</td><td>0.3%</td><td>26</td><td>Maryland</td><td>317,000</td><td>1.3%</td></tr><tr><td>35</td><td>Nebraska</td><td>184,000</td><td>0.8%</td><td>27</td><td>Kansas</td><td>291,000</td><td>1.2%</td></tr><tr><td>19</td><td>Nevada</td><td>462,000</td><td>1.9%</td><td>28</td><td>Oregon</td><td>275,000</td><td>1.1%</td></tr><tr><td>40</td><td>New Hampshire</td><td>112,000</td><td>0.5%</td><td>29</td><td>Alabama</td><td>258,000</td><td>1.1%</td></tr><tr><td>17</td><td>New Jersey</td><td>528,000</td><td>2.2%</td><td>30</td><td>Tennessee</td><td>257,000</td><td>1.1%</td></tr><tr><td>36</td><td>New Mexico</td><td>143,000</td><td>0.6%</td><td>31</td><td>Kentucky</td><td>243,000</td><td>1.0%</td></tr><tr><td>1</td><td>New York</td><td>1,849,000</td><td>7.6%</td><td>32</td><td>Oklahoma</td><td>222,000</td><td>0.9%</td></tr><tr><td>12</td><td>North Carolina</td><td>675,000</td><td>2.8%</td><td>33</td><td>Louisiana</td><td>198,000</td><td>0.8%</td></tr><tr><td>44</td><td>North Dakota</td><td>69,000</td><td>0.3%</td><td>34</td><td>Mississippi</td><td>187,000</td><td>0.8%</td></tr><tr><td>7</td><td>Ohio</td><td>1,261,000</td><td>5.2%</td><td>35</td><td>Nebraska</td><td>184,000</td><td>0.8%</td></tr><tr><td>32</td><td>Oklahoma</td><td>222,000</td><td>0.9%</td><td>36</td><td>New Mexico</td><td>143,000</td><td>0.6%</td></tr><tr><td>28</td><td>Oregon</td><td>275,000</td><td>1.1%</td><td>37</td><td>Vermont</td><td>126,000</td><td>0.5%</td></tr><tr><td>8</td><td>Pennsylvania</td><td>1,147,000</td><td>4.7%</td><td>38</td><td>Arkansas</td><td>120,000</td><td>0.5%</td></tr><tr><td>NA</td><td>Rhode Island*</td><td>NA</td><td>NA</td><td>39</td><td>Idaho</td><td>115,000</td><td>0.5%</td></tr><tr><td>22</td><td>South Carolina</td><td>436,000</td><td>1.8%</td><td>40</td><td>New Hampshire</td><td>112,000</td><td>0.5%</td></tr><tr><td>42</td><td>South Dakota</td><td>94,000</td><td>0.4%</td><td>41</td><td>Maine</td><td>105,000</td><td>0.4%</td></tr><tr><td>30</td><td>Tennessee</td><td>257,000</td><td>1.1%</td><td>42</td><td>South Dakota</td><td>94,000</td><td>0.4%</td></tr><tr><td>6</td><td>Texas</td><td>1,371,000</td><td>5.6%</td><td>43</td><td>Montana</td><td>80,000</td><td>0.3%</td></tr><tr><td>24</td><td>Utah</td><td>336,000</td><td>1.4%</td><td>44</td><td>North Dakota</td><td>69,000</td><td>0.3%</td></tr><tr><td>37</td><td>Vermont</td><td>126,000</td><td>0.5%</td><td>45</td><td>West Virginia</td><td>15,000</td><td>0.1%</td></tr><tr><td>18</td><td>Virginia</td><td>469,000</td><td>1.9%</td><td>NA</td><td>Alaska*</td><td>NA</td><td>NA</td></tr><tr><td>21</td><td>Washington</td><td>454,000</td><td>1.9%</td><td>NA</td><td>Delaware*</td><td>NA</td><td>NA</td></tr><tr><td>45</td><td>West Virginia</td><td>15,000</td><td>0.1%</td><td>NA</td><td>Hawaii*</td><td>NA</td><td>NA</td></tr><tr><td>10</td><td>Wisconsin</td><td>754,000</td><td>3.1%</td><td>NA</td><td>Rhode Island*</td><td>NA</td><td>NA</td></tr><tr><td>NA</td><td>Wyoming*</td><td>NA</td><td>NA</td><td>NA</td><td>Wyoming*</td><td>NA</td><td>NA</td></tr><tr><td></td><td></td><td></td><td></td><td></td><td>District of Columbia*</td><td>NA</td><td>NA</td></tr></table>

Source: The National Sporting Goods Association
  "NSGA Sports Participation Survey, January-December 2006 (Copyright 2007, reprinted with permission)
*Not available.

Participants in Running/Jogging in 2006

National Total = 28,787,000 Runners/Joggers

ALPHA ORDER

RANK	STATE	RUNNERS	% of USA
9	Alabama	857,000	3.0%
NA	Alaska*	NA	NA
26	Arizona	353,000	1.2%
30	Arkansas	232,000	0.8%
1	California	4,682,000	16.3%
11	Colorado	719,000	2.5%
38	Connecticut	138,000	0.5%
35	Delaware	160,000	0.6%
2	Florida	2,313,000	8.0%
16	Georgia	545,000	1.9%
NA	Hawaii*	NA	NA
46	Idaho	62,000	0.2%
7	Illinois	1,130,000	3.9%
20	Indiana	491,000	1.7%
36	Iowa	155,000	0.5%
28	Kansas	267,000	0.9%
19	Kentucky	515,000	1.8%
25	Louisiana	357,000	1.2%
34	Maine	164,000	0.6%
18	Maryland	524,000	1.8%
29	Massachusetts	261,000	0.9%
5	Michigan	1,377,000	4.8%
22	Minnesota	455,000	1.6%
39	Mississippi	129,000	0.4%
14	Missouri	631,000	2.2%
43	Montana	72,000	0.3%
40	Nebraska	110,000	0.4%
32	Nevada	186,000	0.6%
37	New Hampshire	141,000	0.5%
13	New Jersey	657,000	2.3%
31	New Mexico	228,000	0.8%
4	New York	1,612,000	5.6%
17	North Carolina	544,000	1.9%
47	North Dakota	48,000	0.2%
6	Ohio	1,218,000	4.2%
23	Oklahoma	377,000	1.3%
27	Oregon	273,000	0.9%
8	Pennsylvania	1,121,000	3.9%
41	Rhode Island	105,000	0.4%
24	South Carolina	360,000	1.3%
42	South Dakota	87,000	0.3%
15	Tennessee	612,000	2.1%
3	Texas	2,209,000	7.7%
33	Utah	177,000	0.6%
48	Vermont	19,000	0.1%
10	Virginia	828,000	2.9%
12	Washington	658,000	2.3%
44	West Virginia	71,000	0.2%
21	Wisconsin	469,000	1.6%
45	Wyoming	63,000	0.2%

RANK ORDER

RANK	STATE	RUNNERS	% of USA
1	California	4,682,000	16.3%
2	Florida	2,313,000	8.0%
3	Texas	2,209,000	7.7%
4	New York	1,612,000	5.6%
5	Michigan	1,377,000	4.8%
6	Ohio	1,218,000	4.2%
7	Illinois	1,130,000	3.9%
8	Pennsylvania	1,121,000	3.9%
9	Alabama	857,000	3.0%
10	Virginia	828,000	2.9%
11	Colorado	719,000	2.5%
12	Washington	658,000	2.3%
13	New Jersey	657,000	2.3%
14	Missouri	631,000	2.2%
15	Tennessee	612,000	2.1%
16	Georgia	545,000	1.9%
17	North Carolina	544,000	1.9%
18	Maryland	524,000	1.8%
19	Kentucky	515,000	1.8%
20	Indiana	491,000	1.7%
21	Wisconsin	469,000	1.6%
22	Minnesota	455,000	1.6%
23	Oklahoma	377,000	1.3%
24	South Carolina	360,000	1.3%
25	Louisiana	357,000	1.2%
26	Arizona	353,000	1.2%
27	Oregon	273,000	0.9%
28	Kansas	267,000	0.9%
29	Massachusetts	261,000	0.9%
30	Arkansas	232,000	0.8%
31	New Mexico	228,000	0.8%
32	Nevada	186,000	0.6%
33	Utah	177,000	0.6%
34	Maine	164,000	0.6%
35	Delaware	160,000	0.6%
36	Iowa	155,000	0.5%
37	New Hampshire	141,000	0.5%
38	Connecticut	138,000	0.5%
39	Mississippi	129,000	0.4%
40	Nebraska	110,000	0.4%
41	Rhode Island	105,000	0.4%
42	South Dakota	87,000	0.3%
43	Montana	72,000	0.3%
44	West Virginia	71,000	0.2%
45	Wyoming	63,000	0.2%
46	Idaho	62,000	0.2%
47	North Dakota	48,000	0.2%
48	Vermont	19,000	0.1%
NA	Alaska*	NA	NA
NA	Hawaii*	NA	NA
	District of Columbia*	NA	NA

Source: The National Sporting Goods Association
"NSGA Sports Participation Survey, January-December 2006 (Copyright 2007, reprinted with permission)
*Not available.

Participants in Swimming in 2006

National Total = 56,463,000 Swimmers

ALPHA ORDER

RANK	STATE	SWIMMERS	% of USA
10	Alabama	1,703,000	3.0%
NA	Alaska*	NA	NA
16	Arizona	1,199,000	2.1%
34	Arkansas	428,000	0.8%
1	California	5,801,000	10.3%
20	Colorado	1,018,000	1.8%
18	Connecticut	1,166,000	2.1%
44	Delaware	134,000	0.2%
2	Florida	4,638,000	8.2%
9	Georgia	1,782,000	3.2%
NA	Hawaii*	NA	NA
43	Idaho	163,000	0.3%
8	Illinois	2,119,000	3.8%
21	Indiana	972,000	1.7%
36	Iowa	413,000	0.7%
42	Kansas	209,000	0.4%
19	Kentucky	1,041,000	1.8%
31	Louisiana	493,000	0.9%
35	Maine	418,000	0.7%
26	Maryland	771,000	1.4%
15	Massachusetts	1,205,000	2.1%
5	Michigan	2,489,000	4.4%
23	Minnesota	914,000	1.6%
27	Mississippi	755,000	1.3%
13	Missouri	1,375,000	2.4%
48	Montana	81,000	0.1%
41	Nebraska	225,000	0.4%
30	Nevada	530,000	0.9%
37	New Hampshire	389,000	0.7%
11	New Jersey	1,564,000	2.8%
32	New Mexico	479,000	0.8%
4	New York	3,693,000	6.5%
14	North Carolina	1,238,000	2.2%
45	North Dakota	115,000	0.2%
7	Ohio	2,290,000	4.1%
25	Oklahoma	829,000	1.5%
29	Oregon	691,000	1.2%
6	Pennsylvania	2,322,000	4.1%
39	Rhode Island	248,000	0.4%
22	South Carolina	956,000	1.7%
46	South Dakota	107,000	0.2%
28	Tennessee	753,000	1.3%
3	Texas	4,124,000	7.3%
33	Utah	435,000	0.8%
40	Vermont	232,000	0.4%
12	Virginia	1,494,000	2.6%
24	Washington	908,000	1.6%
38	West Virginia	267,000	0.5%
17	Wisconsin	1,168,000	2.1%
47	Wyoming	84,000	0.1%

RANK ORDER

RANK	STATE	SWIMMERS	% of USA
1	California	5,801,000	10.3%
2	Florida	4,638,000	8.2%
3	Texas	4,124,000	7.3%
4	New York	3,693,000	6.5%
5	Michigan	2,489,000	4.4%
6	Pennsylvania	2,322,000	4.1%
7	Ohio	2,290,000	4.1%
8	Illinois	2,119,000	3.8%
9	Georgia	1,782,000	3.2%
10	Alabama	1,703,000	3.0%
11	New Jersey	1,564,000	2.8%
12	Virginia	1,494,000	2.6%
13	Missouri	1,375,000	2.4%
14	North Carolina	1,238,000	2.2%
15	Massachusetts	1,205,000	2.1%
16	Arizona	1,199,000	2.1%
17	Wisconsin	1,168,000	2.1%
18	Connecticut	1,166,000	2.1%
19	Kentucky	1,041,000	1.8%
20	Colorado	1,018,000	1.8%
21	Indiana	972,000	1.7%
22	South Carolina	956,000	1.7%
23	Minnesota	914,000	1.6%
24	Washington	908,000	1.6%
25	Oklahoma	829,000	1.5%
26	Maryland	771,000	1.4%
27	Mississippi	755,000	1.3%
28	Tennessee	753,000	1.3%
29	Oregon	691,000	1.2%
30	Nevada	530,000	0.9%
31	Louisiana	493,000	0.9%
32	New Mexico	479,000	0.8%
33	Utah	435,000	0.8%
34	Arkansas	428,000	0.8%
35	Maine	418,000	0.7%
36	Iowa	413,000	0.7%
37	New Hampshire	389,000	0.7%
38	West Virginia	267,000	0.5%
39	Rhode Island	248,000	0.4%
40	Vermont	232,000	0.4%
41	Nebraska	225,000	0.4%
42	Kansas	209,000	0.4%
43	Idaho	163,000	0.3%
44	Delaware	134,000	0.2%
45	North Dakota	115,000	0.2%
46	South Dakota	107,000	0.2%
47	Wyoming	84,000	0.1%
48	Montana	81,000	0.1%
NA	Alaska*	NA	NA
NA	Hawaii*	NA	NA
	District of Columbia*	NA	NA

Source: The National Sporting Goods Association
   "NSGA Sports Participation Survey, January-December 2006 (Copyright 2007, reprinted with permission)
*Not available.

Participants in Tennis in 2006

National Total = 10,356,000 Tennis Players

ALPHA ORDER					RANK ORDER			

RANK	STATE	PLAYERS	% of USA		RANK	STATE	PLAYERS	% of USA
19	Alabama	201,000	1.9%		1	California	1,463,000	14.1%
NA	Alaska*	NA	NA		2	Texas	721,000	7.0%
35	Arizona	55,000	0.5%		3	Michigan	631,000	6.1%
37	Arkansas	30,000	0.3%		4	New York	531,000	5.1%
1	California	1,463,000	14.1%		5	Pennsylvania	466,000	4.5%
21	Colorado	190,000	1.8%		6	Georgia	427,000	4.1%
25	Connecticut	144,000	1.4%		7	Oklahoma	425,000	4.1%
NA	Delaware*	NA	NA		8	Florida	408,000	3.9%
8	Florida	408,000	3.9%		9	Virginia	401,000	3.9%
6	Georgia	427,000	4.1%		10	Ohio	372,000	3.6%
NA	Hawaii*	NA	NA		11	Illinois	335,000	3.2%
32	Idaho	81,000	0.8%		12	South Carolina	306,000	3.0%
11	Illinois	335,000	3.2%		13	New Jersey	302,000	2.9%
16	Indiana	225,000	2.2%		14	North Carolina	281,000	2.7%
39	Iowa	24,000	0.2%		15	Kentucky	249,000	2.4%
26	Kansas	142,000	1.4%		16	Indiana	225,000	2.2%
15	Kentucky	249,000	2.4%		17	New Mexico	221,000	2.1%
28	Louisiana	125,000	1.2%		17	Wisconsin	221,000	2.1%
41	Maine	20,000	0.2%		19	Alabama	201,000	1.9%
23	Maryland	153,000	1.5%		20	Minnesota	200,000	1.9%
28	Massachusetts	125,000	1.2%		21	Colorado	190,000	1.8%
3	Michigan	631,000	6.1%		22	Nevada	171,000	1.7%
20	Minnesota	200,000	1.9%		23	Maryland	153,000	1.5%
24	Mississippi	148,000	1.4%		24	Mississippi	148,000	1.4%
27	Missouri	128,000	1.2%		25	Connecticut	144,000	1.4%
36	Montana	47,000	0.5%		26	Kansas	142,000	1.4%
40	Nebraska	21,000	0.2%		27	Missouri	128,000	1.2%
22	Nevada	171,000	1.7%		28	Louisiana	125,000	1.2%
NA	New Hampshire*	NA	NA		28	Massachusetts	125,000	1.2%
13	New Jersey	302,000	2.9%		30	Washington	104,000	1.0%
17	New Mexico	221,000	2.1%		31	Rhode Island	83,000	0.8%
4	New York	531,000	5.1%		32	Idaho	81,000	0.8%
14	North Carolina	281,000	2.7%		33	Tennessee	65,000	0.6%
NA	North Dakota*	NA	NA		34	Utah	57,000	0.6%
10	Ohio	372,000	3.6%		35	Arizona	55,000	0.5%
7	Oklahoma	425,000	4.1%		36	Montana	47,000	0.5%
NA	Oregon*	NA	NA		37	Arkansas	30,000	0.3%
5	Pennsylvania	466,000	4.5%		38	West Virginia	29,000	0.3%
31	Rhode Island	83,000	0.8%		39	Iowa	24,000	0.2%
12	South Carolina	306,000	3.0%		40	Nebraska	21,000	0.2%
NA	South Dakota*	NA	NA		41	Maine	20,000	0.2%
33	Tennessee	65,000	0.6%		NA	Alaska*	NA	NA
2	Texas	721,000	7.0%		NA	Delaware*	NA	NA
34	Utah	57,000	0.6%		NA	Hawaii*	NA	NA
NA	Vermont*	NA	NA		NA	New Hampshire*	NA	NA
9	Virginia	401,000	3.9%		NA	North Dakota*	NA	NA
30	Washington	104,000	1.0%		NA	Oregon*	NA	NA
38	West Virginia	29,000	0.3%		NA	South Dakota*	NA	NA
17	Wisconsin	221,000	2.1%		NA	Vermont*	NA	NA
NA	Wyoming*	NA	NA		NA	Wyoming*	NA	NA
					District of Columbia*		NA	NA

Source: The National Sporting Goods Association
"NSGA Sports Participation Survey, January-December 2006 (Copyright 2007, reprinted with permission)
*Not available.

Alcohol Consumption in 2005

National Total = 538,268,000 Gallons*

<u>ALPHA ORDER</u>

RANK	STATE	GALLONS	% of USA
26	Alabama	7,083,000	1.3%
47	Alaska	1,391,000	0.3%
16	Arizona	11,673,000	2.2%
35	Arkansas	4,022,000	0.7%
1	California	64,120,000	11.9%
20	Colorado	10,169,000	1.9%
28	Connecticut	6,401,000	1.2%
43	Delaware	2,245,000	0.4%
2	Florida	40,013,000	7.4%
10	Georgia	14,642,000	2.7%
41	Hawaii	2,624,000	0.5%
38	Idaho	2,759,000	0.5%
5	Illinois	23,244,000	4.3%
19	Indiana	10,170,000	1.9%
30	Iowa	5,178,000	1.0%
34	Kansas	4,161,000	0.8%
29	Kentucky	6,124,000	1.1%
23	Louisiana	8,774,000	1.6%
39	Maine	2,679,000	0.5%
21	Maryland	9,577,000	1.8%
12	Massachusetts	13,313,000	2.5%
8	Michigan	17,796,000	3.3%
18	Minnesota	10,284,000	1.9%
31	Mississippi	5,047,000	0.9%
17	Missouri	10,895,000	2.0%
45	Montana	2,047,000	0.4%
37	Nebraska	3,246,000	0.6%
27	Nevada	6,879,000	1.3%
32	New Hampshire	4,452,000	0.8%
9	New Jersey	16,189,000	3.0%
36	New Mexico	3,752,000	0.7%
4	New York	31,225,000	5.8%
11	North Carolina	13,680,000	2.5%
48	North Dakota	1,388,000	0.3%
7	Ohio	18,414,000	3.4%
33	Oklahoma	4,290,000	0.8%
25	Oregon	7,345,000	1.4%
6	Pennsylvania	22,911,000	4.3%
44	Rhode Island	2,183,000	0.4%
24	South Carolina	8,339,000	1.5%
46	South Dakota	1,582,000	0.3%
22	Tennessee	9,382,000	1.7%
3	Texas	39,422,000	7.3%
42	Utah	2,355,000	0.4%
49	Vermont	1,338,000	0.2%
14	Virginia	12,744,000	2.4%
15	Washington	11,954,000	2.2%
40	West Virginia	2,632,000	0.5%
13	Wisconsin	13,246,000	2.5%
50	Wyoming	1,002,000	0.2%

<u>RANK ORDER</u>

RANK	STATE	GALLONS	% of USA
1	California	64,120,000	11.9%
2	Florida	40,013,000	7.4%
3	Texas	39,422,000	7.3%
4	New York	31,225,000	5.8%
5	Illinois	23,244,000	4.3%
6	Pennsylvania	22,911,000	4.3%
7	Ohio	18,414,000	3.4%
8	Michigan	17,796,000	3.3%
9	New Jersey	16,189,000	3.0%
10	Georgia	14,642,000	2.7%
11	North Carolina	13,680,000	2.5%
12	Massachusetts	13,313,000	2.5%
13	Wisconsin	13,246,000	2.5%
14	Virginia	12,744,000	2.4%
15	Washington	11,954,000	2.2%
16	Arizona	11,673,000	2.2%
17	Missouri	10,895,000	2.0%
18	Minnesota	10,284,000	1.9%
19	Indiana	10,170,000	1.9%
20	Colorado	10,169,000	1.9%
21	Maryland	9,577,000	1.8%
22	Tennessee	9,382,000	1.7%
23	Louisiana	8,774,000	1.6%
24	South Carolina	8,339,000	1.5%
25	Oregon	7,345,000	1.4%
26	Alabama	7,083,000	1.3%
27	Nevada	6,879,000	1.3%
28	Connecticut	6,401,000	1.2%
29	Kentucky	6,124,000	1.1%
30	Iowa	5,178,000	1.0%
31	Mississippi	5,047,000	0.9%
32	New Hampshire	4,452,000	0.8%
33	Oklahoma	4,290,000	0.8%
34	Kansas	4,161,000	0.8%
35	Arkansas	4,022,000	0.7%
36	New Mexico	3,752,000	0.7%
37	Nebraska	3,246,000	0.6%
38	Idaho	2,759,000	0.5%
39	Maine	2,679,000	0.5%
40	West Virginia	2,632,000	0.5%
41	Hawaii	2,624,000	0.5%
42	Utah	2,355,000	0.4%
43	Delaware	2,245,000	0.4%
44	Rhode Island	2,183,000	0.4%
45	Montana	2,047,000	0.4%
46	South Dakota	1,582,000	0.3%
47	Alaska	1,391,000	0.3%
48	North Dakota	1,388,000	0.3%
49	Vermont	1,338,000	0.2%
50	Wyoming	1,002,000	0.2%
	District of Columbia	1,885,000	0.4%

Source: U.S. Department of Health and Human Services, National Institute on Alcohol Abuse and Alcoholism "Volume Beverage and Ethanol Consumption for States" (http://www.niaaa.nih.gov/Resources/)
*This is apparent consumption of actual alcohol, not entire volume of an alcoholic beverage (e.g. wine is roughly 11% absolute alcohol content). Apparent consumption is based on several sources which together approximate sales but do not actually measure consumption. Accordingly, figures for some states may be skewed by purchases by nonresidents.

Adult Per Capita Alcohol Consumption in 2005

National Per Capita = 2.6 Gallons Consumed per Adult 21 Years and Older*

ALPHA ORDER

RANK	STATE	PER CAPITA
40	Alabama	2.2
5	Alaska	3.1
12	Arizona	2.8
46	Arkansas	2.0
24	California	2.6
5	Colorado	3.1
30	Connecticut	2.5
3	Delaware	3.7
8	Florida	3.0
37	Georgia	2.3
12	Hawaii	2.8
12	Idaho	2.8
24	Illinois	2.6
37	Indiana	2.3
35	Iowa	2.4
40	Kansas	2.2
46	Kentucky	2.0
12	Louisiana	2.8
22	Maine	2.7
35	Maryland	2.4
12	Massachusetts	2.8
30	Michigan	2.5
12	Minnesota	2.8
30	Mississippi	2.5
24	Missouri	2.6
8	Montana	3.0
24	Nebraska	2.6
2	Nevada	4.0
1	New Hampshire	4.7
24	New Jersey	2.6
12	New Mexico	2.8
40	New York	2.2
40	North Carolina	2.2
5	North Dakota	3.1
40	Ohio	2.2
49	Oklahoma	1.7
12	Oregon	2.8
30	Pennsylvania	2.5
12	Rhode Island	2.8
12	South Carolina	2.8
10	South Dakota	2.9
40	Tennessee	2.2
30	Texas	2.5
50	Utah	1.5
10	Vermont	2.9
37	Virginia	2.3
24	Washington	2.6
48	West Virginia	1.9
4	Wisconsin	3.3
22	Wyoming	2.7

RANK ORDER

RANK	STATE	PER CAPITA
1	New Hampshire	4.7
2	Nevada	4.0
3	Delaware	3.7
4	Wisconsin	3.3
5	Alaska	3.1
5	Colorado	3.1
5	North Dakota	3.1
8	Florida	3.0
8	Montana	3.0
10	South Dakota	2.9
10	Vermont	2.9
12	Arizona	2.8
12	Hawaii	2.8
12	Idaho	2.8
12	Louisiana	2.8
12	Massachusetts	2.8
12	Minnesota	2.8
12	New Mexico	2.8
12	Oregon	2.8
12	Rhode Island	2.8
12	South Carolina	2.8
22	Maine	2.7
22	Wyoming	2.7
24	California	2.6
24	Illinois	2.6
24	Missouri	2.6
24	Nebraska	2.6
24	New Jersey	2.6
24	Washington	2.6
30	Connecticut	2.5
30	Michigan	2.5
30	Mississippi	2.5
30	Pennsylvania	2.5
30	Texas	2.5
35	Iowa	2.4
35	Maryland	2.4
37	Georgia	2.3
37	Indiana	2.3
37	Virginia	2.3
40	Alabama	2.2
40	Kansas	2.2
40	New York	2.2
40	North Carolina	2.2
40	Ohio	2.2
40	Tennessee	2.2
46	Arkansas	2.0
46	Kentucky	2.0
48	West Virginia	1.9
49	Oklahoma	1.7
50	Utah	1.5

District of Columbia 4.3

Source: CQ Press using data from U.S. Dept of Health and Human Services, National Institute on Alcohol Abuse and Alcoholism
"Volume Beverage and Ethanol Consumption for States" (http://www.niaaa.nih.gov/Resources/)
*This is apparent consumption of actual alcohol, not entire volume of an alcoholic beverage (e.g. wine is roughly 11% absolute alcohol content). Apparent consumption is based on several sources which together approximate sales but do not actually measure consumption. Accordingly, figures for some states may be skewed by purchases by nonresidents.

Apparent Beer Consumption in 2005

National Total = 6,354,809,000 Gallons of Beer Consumed*

ALPHA ORDER

RANK	STATE	GALLONS	% of USA
24	Alabama	96,750,000	1.5%
49	Alaska	14,421,000	0.2%
14	Arizona	139,966,000	2.2%
33	Arkansas	52,425,000	0.8%
1	California	651,825,000	10.3%
23	Colorado	108,666,000	1.7%
31	Connecticut	57,377,000	0.9%
45	Delaware	21,859,000	0.3%
3	Florida	437,474,000	6.9%
9	Georgia	182,250,000	2.9%
39	Hawaii	30,644,000	0.5%
42	Idaho	27,645,000	0.4%
6	Illinois	278,362,000	4.4%
19	Indiana	125,098,000	2.0%
28	Iowa	74,025,000	1.2%
32	Kansas	55,897,000	0.9%
27	Kentucky	79,152,000	1.2%
20	Louisiana	117,675,000	1.9%
40	Maine	30,510,000	0.5%
25	Maryland	94,370,000	1.5%
17	Massachusetts	126,500,000	2.0%
8	Michigan	207,675,000	3.3%
21	Minnesota	109,109,000	1.7%
30	Mississippi	72,405,000	1.1%
15	Missouri	136,382,000	2.1%
43	Montana	26,213,000	0.4%
36	Nebraska	44,423,000	0.7%
29	Nevada	73,421,000	1.2%
38	New Hampshire	41,468,000	0.7%
13	New Jersey	149,035,000	2.3%
34	New Mexico	50,532,000	0.8%
5	New York	316,546,000	5.0%
10	North Carolina	177,157,000	2.8%
47	North Dakota	17,564,000	0.3%
7	Ohio	272,475,000	4.3%
35	Oklahoma	49,789,000	0.8%
26	Oregon	81,675,000	1.3%
4	Pennsylvania	328,939,000	5.2%
44	Rhode Island	22,275,000	0.4%
22	South Carolina	108,765,000	1.7%
46	South Dakota	20,925,000	0.3%
16	Tennessee	128,806,000	2.0%
2	Texas	566,913,000	8.9%
41	Utah	28,811,000	0.5%
48	Vermont	15,458,000	0.2%
12	Virginia	155,041,000	2.4%
18	Washington	125,896,000	2.0%
37	West Virginia	41,558,000	0.7%
11	Wisconsin	156,375,000	2.5%
50	Wyoming	11,190,000	0.2%

RANK ORDER

RANK	STATE	GALLONS	% of USA
1	California	651,825,000	10.3%
2	Texas	566,913,000	8.9%
3	Florida	437,474,000	6.9%
4	Pennsylvania	328,939,000	5.2%
5	New York	316,546,000	5.0%
6	Illinois	278,362,000	4.4%
7	Ohio	272,475,000	4.3%
8	Michigan	207,675,000	3.3%
9	Georgia	182,250,000	2.9%
10	North Carolina	177,157,000	2.8%
11	Wisconsin	156,375,000	2.5%
12	Virginia	155,041,000	2.4%
13	New Jersey	149,035,000	2.3%
14	Arizona	139,966,000	2.2%
15	Missouri	136,382,000	2.1%
16	Tennessee	128,806,000	2.0%
17	Massachusetts	126,500,000	2.0%
18	Washington	125,896,000	2.0%
19	Indiana	125,098,000	2.0%
20	Louisiana	117,675,000	1.9%
21	Minnesota	109,109,000	1.7%
22	South Carolina	108,765,000	1.7%
23	Colorado	108,666,000	1.7%
24	Alabama	96,750,000	1.5%
25	Maryland	94,370,000	1.5%
26	Oregon	81,675,000	1.3%
27	Kentucky	79,152,000	1.2%
28	Iowa	74,025,000	1.2%
29	Nevada	73,421,000	1.2%
30	Mississippi	72,405,000	1.1%
31	Connecticut	57,377,000	0.9%
32	Kansas	55,897,000	0.9%
33	Arkansas	52,425,000	0.8%
34	New Mexico	50,532,000	0.8%
35	Oklahoma	49,789,000	0.8%
36	Nebraska	44,423,000	0.7%
37	West Virginia	41,558,000	0.7%
38	New Hampshire	41,468,000	0.7%
39	Hawaii	30,644,000	0.5%
40	Maine	30,510,000	0.5%
41	Utah	28,811,000	0.5%
42	Idaho	27,645,000	0.4%
43	Montana	26,213,000	0.4%
44	Rhode Island	22,275,000	0.4%
45	Delaware	21,859,000	0.3%
46	South Dakota	20,925,000	0.3%
47	North Dakota	17,564,000	0.3%
48	Vermont	15,458,000	0.2%
49	Alaska	14,421,000	0.2%
50	Wyoming	11,190,000	0.2%
	District of Columbia	15,098,000	0.2%

Source: U.S. Department of Health and Human Services, National Institute on Alcohol Abuse and Alcoholism
"Volume Beverage and Ethanol Consumption for States" (http://www.niaaa.nih.gov/Resources/)
*This is apparent consumption and is based on several sources which together approximate sales but do not actually measure consumption. Reported state volumes reflect only in-state purchases. Accordingly, figures for some states may be skewed by purchases by nonresidents.

Adult Per Capita Beer Consumption in 2005

National Per Capita = 30.2 Gallons Consumed per Adult 21 Years and Older*

ALPHA ORDER

RANK	STATE	PER CAPITA
31	Alabama	29.8
23	Alaska	31.9
16	Arizona	33.8
42	Arkansas	26.5
44	California	26.0
22	Colorado	32.7
48	Connecticut	22.7
11	Delaware	36.3
18	Florida	33.3
34	Georgia	28.7
20	Hawaii	33.1
38	Idaho	28.2
25	Illinois	31.0
38	Indiana	28.2
15	Iowa	34.9
32	Kansas	29.0
43	Kentucky	26.2
8	Louisiana	37.6
24	Maine	31.1
46	Maryland	23.7
41	Massachusetts	26.9
32	Michigan	29.0
29	Minnesota	29.9
12	Mississippi	36.0
21	Missouri	32.9
4	Montana	38.7
12	Nebraska	36.0
2	Nevada	42.7
1	New Hampshire	43.6
45	New Jersey	23.8
7	New Mexico	37.9
47	New York	22.8
36	North Carolina	28.6
4	North Dakota	38.7
19	Ohio	33.2
49	Oklahoma	19.9
26	Oregon	30.8
9	Pennsylvania	36.4
34	Rhode Island	28.7
14	South Carolina	35.9
6	South Dakota	38.4
29	Tennessee	29.9
9	Texas	36.4
50	Utah	18.1
16	Vermont	33.8
37	Virginia	28.5
40	Washington	27.8
27	West Virginia	30.7
3	Wisconsin	39.4
27	Wyoming	30.7

RANK ORDER

RANK	STATE	PER CAPITA
1	New Hampshire	43.6
2	Nevada	42.7
3	Wisconsin	39.4
4	Montana	38.7
4	North Dakota	38.7
6	South Dakota	38.4
7	New Mexico	37.9
8	Louisiana	37.6
9	Pennsylvania	36.4
9	Texas	36.4
11	Delaware	36.3
12	Mississippi	36.0
12	Nebraska	36.0
14	South Carolina	35.9
15	Iowa	34.9
16	Arizona	33.8
16	Vermont	33.8
18	Florida	33.3
19	Ohio	33.2
20	Hawaii	33.1
21	Missouri	32.9
22	Colorado	32.7
23	Alaska	31.9
24	Maine	31.1
25	Illinois	31.0
26	Oregon	30.8
27	West Virginia	30.7
27	Wyoming	30.7
29	Minnesota	29.9
29	Tennessee	29.9
31	Alabama	29.8
32	Kansas	29.0
32	Michigan	29.0
34	Georgia	28.7
34	Rhode Island	28.7
36	North Carolina	28.6
37	Virginia	28.5
38	Idaho	28.2
38	Indiana	28.2
40	Washington	27.8
41	Massachusetts	26.9
42	Arkansas	26.5
43	Kentucky	26.2
44	California	26.0
45	New Jersey	23.8
46	Maryland	23.7
47	New York	22.8
48	Connecticut	22.7
49	Oklahoma	19.9
50	Utah	18.1

District of Columbia 34.7

Source: CQ Press using data from U.S. Dept of Health and Human Services, National Institute on Alcohol Abuse and Alcoholism
"Volume Beverage and Ethanol Consumption for States" (http://www.niaaa.nih.gov/Resources/)

*This is apparent consumption and is based on several sources which together approximate sales but do not actually measure consumption. Reported state volumes reflect only in-state purchases. Accordingly, figures for some states may be skewed by purchases by nonresidents.

Wine Consumption in 2005

National Total = 662,255,000 Gallons of Wine Consumed*

ALPHA ORDER

RANK	STATE	GALLONS	% of USA
30	Alabama	5,826,000	0.9%
46	Alaska	1,741,000	0.3%
15	Arizona	14,406,000	2.2%
40	Arkansas	2,749,000	0.4%
1	California	117,842,000	17.8%
16	Colorado	12,112,000	1.8%
17	Connecticut	11,953,000	1.8%
37	Delaware	3,117,000	0.5%
2	Florida	53,439,000	8.1%
14	Georgia	14,501,000	2.2%
32	Hawaii	3,703,000	0.6%
27	Idaho	6,421,000	1.0%
6	Illinois	27,113,000	4.1%
24	Indiana	8,584,000	1.3%
39	Iowa	2,952,000	0.4%
38	Kansas	3,021,000	0.5%
31	Kentucky	3,757,000	0.6%
26	Louisiana	6,744,000	1.0%
35	Maine	3,516,000	0.5%
18	Maryland	11,311,000	1.7%
7	Massachusetts	24,129,000	3.6%
11	Michigan	18,068,000	2.7%
21	Minnesota	10,488,000	1.6%
44	Mississippi	2,139,000	0.3%
22	Missouri	9,783,000	1.5%
45	Montana	2,063,000	0.3%
43	Nebraska	2,232,000	0.3%
23	Nevada	9,330,000	1.4%
29	New Hampshire	5,924,000	0.9%
5	New Jersey	28,179,000	4.3%
36	New Mexico	3,503,000	0.5%
3	New York	52,838,000	8.0%
13	North Carolina	14,829,000	2.2%
49	North Dakota	757,000	0.1%
12	Ohio	16,714,000	2.5%
33	Oklahoma	3,586,000	0.5%
19	Oregon	11,238,000	1.7%
9	Pennsylvania	18,816,000	2.8%
34	Rhode Island	3,539,000	0.5%
28	South Carolina	6,359,000	1.0%
48	South Dakota	936,000	0.1%
25	Tennessee	7,017,000	1.1%
4	Texas	34,303,000	5.2%
41	Utah	2,257,000	0.3%
41	Vermont	2,257,000	0.3%
10	Virginia	18,290,000	2.8%
8	Washington	21,726,000	3.3%
47	West Virginia	1,203,000	0.2%
20	Wisconsin	10,715,000	1.6%
50	Wyoming	732,000	0.1%

RANK ORDER

RANK	STATE	GALLONS	% of USA
1	California	117,842,000	17.8%
2	Florida	53,439,000	8.1%
3	New York	52,838,000	8.0%
4	Texas	34,303,000	5.2%
5	New Jersey	28,179,000	4.3%
6	Illinois	27,113,000	4.1%
7	Massachusetts	24,129,000	3.6%
8	Washington	21,726,000	3.3%
9	Pennsylvania	18,816,000	2.8%
10	Virginia	18,290,000	2.8%
11	Michigan	18,068,000	2.7%
12	Ohio	16,714,000	2.5%
13	North Carolina	14,829,000	2.2%
14	Georgia	14,501,000	2.2%
15	Arizona	14,406,000	2.2%
16	Colorado	12,112,000	1.8%
17	Connecticut	11,953,000	1.8%
18	Maryland	11,311,000	1.7%
19	Oregon	11,238,000	1.7%
20	Wisconsin	10,715,000	1.6%
21	Minnesota	10,488,000	1.6%
22	Missouri	9,783,000	1.5%
23	Nevada	9,330,000	1.4%
24	Indiana	8,584,000	1.3%
25	Tennessee	7,017,000	1.1%
26	Louisiana	6,744,000	1.0%
27	Idaho	6,421,000	1.0%
28	South Carolina	6,359,000	1.0%
29	New Hampshire	5,924,000	0.9%
30	Alabama	5,826,000	0.9%
31	Kentucky	3,757,000	0.6%
32	Hawaii	3,703,000	0.6%
33	Oklahoma	3,586,000	0.5%
34	Rhode Island	3,539,000	0.5%
35	Maine	3,516,000	0.5%
36	New Mexico	3,503,000	0.5%
37	Delaware	3,117,000	0.5%
38	Kansas	3,021,000	0.5%
39	Iowa	2,952,000	0.4%
40	Arkansas	2,749,000	0.4%
41	Utah	2,257,000	0.3%
41	Vermont	2,257,000	0.3%
43	Nebraska	2,232,000	0.3%
44	Mississippi	2,139,000	0.3%
45	Montana	2,063,000	0.3%
46	Alaska	1,741,000	0.3%
47	West Virginia	1,203,000	0.2%
48	South Dakota	936,000	0.1%
49	North Dakota	757,000	0.1%
50	Wyoming	732,000	0.1%
	District of Columbia	3,501,000	0.5%

Source: U.S. Department of Health and Human Services, National Institute on Alcohol Abuse and Alcoholism
"Volume Beverage and Ethanol Consumption for States" (http://www.niaaa.nih.gov/Resources/)
*This is apparent consumption and is based on several sources which together approximate sales but do not actually measure consumption. Reported state volumes reflect only in-state purchases. Accordingly, figures for some states may be skewed by purchases by nonresidents.

Adult Per Capita Wine Consumption in 2005

National Per Capita = 3.1 Gallons Consumed per Adult 21 Years and Older

ALPHA ORDER

RANK	STATE	PER CAPITA
38	Alabama	1.8
15	Alaska	3.9
19	Arizona	3.5
44	Arkansas	1.4
8	California	4.7
17	Colorado	3.6
8	Connecticut	4.7
4	Delaware	5.2
13	Florida	4.1
30	Georgia	2.3
14	Hawaii	4.0
1	Idaho	6.5
21	Illinois	3.0
37	Indiana	1.9
44	Iowa	1.4
42	Kansas	1.6
48	Kentucky	1.2
31	Louisiana	2.2
17	Maine	3.6
24	Maryland	2.8
5	Massachusetts	5.1
27	Michigan	2.5
23	Minnesota	2.9
49	Mississippi	1.1
28	Missouri	2.4
21	Montana	3.0
38	Nebraska	1.8
3	Nevada	5.4
2	New Hampshire	6.2
11	New Jersey	4.5
26	New Mexico	2.6
16	New York	3.8
28	North Carolina	2.4
40	North Dakota	1.7
35	Ohio	2.0
44	Oklahoma	1.4
12	Oregon	4.2
33	Pennsylvania	2.1
10	Rhode Island	4.6
33	South Carolina	2.1
40	South Dakota	1.7
42	Tennessee	1.6
31	Texas	2.2
44	Utah	1.4
6	Vermont	4.9
20	Virginia	3.4
7	Washington	4.8
50	West Virginia	0.9
25	Wisconsin	2.7
35	Wyoming	2.0

RANK ORDER

RANK	STATE	PER CAPITA
1	Idaho	6.5
2	New Hampshire	6.2
3	Nevada	5.4
4	Delaware	5.2
5	Massachusetts	5.1
6	Vermont	4.9
7	Washington	4.8
8	California	4.7
8	Connecticut	4.7
10	Rhode Island	4.6
11	New Jersey	4.5
12	Oregon	4.2
13	Florida	4.1
14	Hawaii	4.0
15	Alaska	3.9
16	New York	3.8
17	Colorado	3.6
17	Maine	3.6
19	Arizona	3.5
20	Virginia	3.4
21	Illinois	3.0
21	Montana	3.0
23	Minnesota	2.9
24	Maryland	2.8
25	Wisconsin	2.7
26	New Mexico	2.6
27	Michigan	2.5
28	Missouri	2.4
28	North Carolina	2.4
30	Georgia	2.3
31	Louisiana	2.2
31	Texas	2.2
33	Pennsylvania	2.1
33	South Carolina	2.1
35	Ohio	2.0
35	Wyoming	2.0
37	Indiana	1.9
38	Alabama	1.8
38	Nebraska	1.8
40	North Dakota	1.7
40	South Dakota	1.7
42	Kansas	1.6
42	Tennessee	1.6
44	Arkansas	1.4
44	Iowa	1.4
44	Oklahoma	1.4
44	Utah	1.4
48	Kentucky	1.2
49	Mississippi	1.1
50	West Virginia	0.9

District of Columbia 8.0

Source: CQ Press using data from U.S. Dept of Health and Human Services, National Institute on Alcohol Abuse and Alcoholism
"Volume Beverage and Ethanol Consumption for States" (http://www.niaaa.nih.gov/Resources/)
*This is apparent consumption and is based on several sources which together approximate sales but do not actually measure consumption. Reported state volumes reflect only in-state purchases. Accordingly, figures for some states may be skewed by purchases by nonresidents.

Distilled Spirits Consumption in 2005

National Total = 406,012,000 Gallons of Distilled Spirits Consumed*

ALPHA ORDER

RANK	STATE	GALLONS	% of USA
29	Alabama	4,812,000	1.2%
47	Alaska	1,260,000	0.3%
17	Arizona	8,556,000	2.1%
34	Arkansas	3,184,000	0.8%
1	California	47,655,000	11.7%
16	Colorado	9,044,000	2.2%
26	Connecticut	5,541,000	1.4%
38	Delaware	2,090,000	0.5%
2	Florida	32,684,000	8.1%
10	Georgia	11,120,000	2.7%
40	Hawaii	1,868,000	0.5%
43	Idaho	1,670,000	0.4%
5	Illinois	17,568,000	4.3%
20	Indiana	8,354,000	2.1%
33	Iowa	3,566,000	0.9%
35	Kansas	3,056,000	0.8%
28	Kentucky	5,055,000	1.2%
24	Louisiana	6,347,000	1.6%
39	Maine	2,073,000	0.5%
14	Maryland	9,420,000	2.3%
11	Massachusetts	10,969,000	2.7%
6	Michigan	14,889,000	3.7%
12	Minnesota	9,785,000	2.4%
32	Mississippi	3,681,000	0.9%
18	Missouri	8,506,000	2.1%
45	Montana	1,462,000	0.4%
37	Nebraska	2,334,000	0.6%
25	Nevada	5,771,000	1.4%
30	New Hampshire	4,432,000	1.1%
7	New Jersey	14,228,000	3.5%
36	New Mexico	2,496,000	0.6%
3	New York	24,729,000	6.1%
15	North Carolina	9,234,000	2.3%
48	North Dakota	1,217,000	0.3%
13	Ohio	9,725,000	2.4%
31	Oklahoma	3,861,000	1.0%
27	Oregon	5,401,000	1.3%
8	Pennsylvania	13,823,000	3.4%
42	Rhode Island	1,763,000	0.4%
23	South Carolina	6,384,000	1.6%
46	South Dakota	1,264,000	0.3%
22	Tennessee	6,523,000	1.6%
4	Texas	23,080,000	5.7%
40	Utah	1,868,000	0.5%
50	Vermont	855,000	0.2%
21	Virginia	8,292,000	2.0%
19	Washington	8,481,000	2.1%
44	West Virginia	1,475,000	0.4%
9	Wisconsin	11,744,000	2.9%
49	Wyoming	984,000	0.2%

RANK ORDER

RANK	STATE	GALLONS	% of USA
1	California	47,655,000	11.7%
2	Florida	32,684,000	8.1%
3	New York	24,729,000	6.1%
4	Texas	23,080,000	5.7%
5	Illinois	17,568,000	4.3%
6	Michigan	14,889,000	3.7%
7	New Jersey	14,228,000	3.5%
8	Pennsylvania	13,823,000	3.4%
9	Wisconsin	11,744,000	2.9%
10	Georgia	11,120,000	2.7%
11	Massachusetts	10,969,000	2.7%
12	Minnesota	9,785,000	2.4%
13	Ohio	9,725,000	2.4%
14	Maryland	9,420,000	2.3%
15	North Carolina	9,234,000	2.3%
16	Colorado	9,044,000	2.2%
17	Arizona	8,556,000	2.1%
18	Missouri	8,506,000	2.1%
19	Washington	8,481,000	2.1%
20	Indiana	8,354,000	2.1%
21	Virginia	8,292,000	2.0%
22	Tennessee	6,523,000	1.6%
23	South Carolina	6,384,000	1.6%
24	Louisiana	6,347,000	1.6%
25	Nevada	5,771,000	1.4%
26	Connecticut	5,541,000	1.4%
27	Oregon	5,401,000	1.3%
28	Kentucky	5,055,000	1.2%
29	Alabama	4,812,000	1.2%
30	New Hampshire	4,432,000	1.1%
31	Oklahoma	3,861,000	1.0%
32	Mississippi	3,681,000	0.9%
33	Iowa	3,566,000	0.9%
34	Arkansas	3,184,000	0.8%
35	Kansas	3,056,000	0.8%
36	New Mexico	2,496,000	0.6%
37	Nebraska	2,334,000	0.6%
38	Delaware	2,090,000	0.5%
39	Maine	2,073,000	0.5%
40	Hawaii	1,868,000	0.5%
40	Utah	1,868,000	0.5%
42	Rhode Island	1,763,000	0.4%
43	Idaho	1,670,000	0.4%
44	West Virginia	1,475,000	0.4%
45	Montana	1,462,000	0.4%
46	South Dakota	1,264,000	0.3%
47	Alaska	1,260,000	0.3%
48	North Dakota	1,217,000	0.3%
49	Wyoming	984,000	0.2%
50	Vermont	855,000	0.2%
	District of Columbia	1,834,000	0.5%

Source: U.S. Department of Health and Human Services, National Institute on Alcohol Abuse and Alcoholism
"Volume Beverage and Ethanol Consumption for States" (http://www.niaaa.nih.gov/Resources/)
*This is apparent consumption and is based on several sources which together approximate sales but do not actually measure consumption. Reported state volumes reflect only in-state purchases. Accordingly, figures for some states may be skewed by purchases by nonresidents.

Adult Per Capita Distilled Spirits Consumption in 2005

National Per Capita = 1.9 Gallons Consumed per Adult 21 Years and Older*

ALPHA ORDER

RANK	STATE	PER CAPITA
41	Alabama	1.5
5	Alaska	2.8
18	Arizona	2.1
39	Arkansas	1.6
27	California	1.9
6	Colorado	2.7
16	Connecticut	2.2
2	Delaware	3.5
10	Florida	2.5
35	Georgia	1.7
35	Idaho	1.7
23	Illinois	2.0
27	Indiana	1.9
35	Iowa	1.7
39	Kansas	1.6
35	Kentucky	1.7
23	Louisiana	2.0
18	Maine	2.1
11	Maryland	2.4
12	Massachusetts	2.3
18	Michigan	2.1
6	Minnesota	2.7
33	Mississippi	1.8
18	Missouri	2.1
16	Montana	2.2
27	Nebraska	1.9
3	Nevada	3.4
1	New Hampshire	4.7
12	New Jersey	2.3
27	New Mexico	1.9
33	New York	1.8
41	North Carolina	1.5
6	North Dakota	2.7
48	Ohio	1.2
41	Oklahoma	1.5
23	Oregon	2.0
41	Pennsylvania	1.5
12	Rhode Island	2.3
18	South Carolina	2.1
12	South Dakota	2.3
41	Tennessee	1.5
41	Texas	1.5
48	Utah	1.2
27	Vermont	1.9
41	Virginia	1.5
27	Washington	1.9
50	West Virginia	1.1
4	Wisconsin	3.0
6	Wyoming	2.7

RANK ORDER

RANK	STATE	PER CAPITA
1	New Hampshire	4.7
2	Delaware	3.5
3	Nevada	3.4
4	Wisconsin	3.0
5	Alaska	2.8
6	Colorado	2.7
6	Minnesota	2.7
6	North Dakota	2.7
6	Wyoming	2.7
10	Florida	2.5
11	Maryland	2.4
12	Massachusetts	2.3
12	New Jersey	2.3
12	Rhode Island	2.3
12	South Dakota	2.3
16	Connecticut	2.2
16	Montana	2.2
18	Arizona	2.1
18	Maine	2.1
18	Michigan	2.1
18	Missouri	2.1
18	South Carolina	2.1
23	Hawaii	2.0
23	Illinois	2.0
23	Louisiana	2.0
23	Oregon	2.0
27	California	1.9
27	Indiana	1.9
27	Nebraska	1.9
27	New Mexico	1.9
27	Vermont	1.9
27	Washington	1.9
33	Mississippi	1.8
33	New York	1.8
35	Georgia	1.7
35	Idaho	1.7
35	Iowa	1.7
35	Kentucky	1.7
39	Arkansas	1.6
39	Kansas	1.6
41	Alabama	1.5
41	North Carolina	1.5
41	Oklahoma	1.5
41	Pennsylvania	1.5
41	Tennessee	1.5
41	Texas	1.5
41	Virginia	1.5
48	Ohio	1.2
48	Utah	1.2
50	West Virginia	1.1

District of Columbia 4.2

Source: CQ Press using data from U.S. Dept of Health and Human Services, National Institute on Alcohol Abuse and Alcoholism
"Volume Beverage and Ethanol Consumption for States" (http://www.niaaa.nih.gov/Resources/)
*This is apparent consumption and is based on several sources which together approximate sales but do not actually measure consumption. Reported state volumes reflect only in-state purchases. Accordingly, figures for some states may be skewed by purchases by nonresidents.

Percent of Adults Who Do Not Drink Alcohol: 2006

National Median = 44.6% of Adults*

ALPHA ORDER			RANK ORDER		
RANK	STATE	PERCENT	RANK	STATE	PERCENT
6	Alabama	63.0	1	Utah	73.6
40	Alaska	41.4	2	Tennessee	70.5
21	Arizona	46.6	3	Kentucky	67.3
7	Arkansas	59.6	4	West Virginia	66.2
23	California	46.0	5	Mississippi	63.6
44	Colorado	38.4	6	Alabama	63.0
47	Connecticut	36.6	7	Arkansas	59.6
42	Delaware	40.8	8	Oklahoma	58.3
22	Florida	46.4	9	North Carolina	57.1
10	Georgia	54.5	10	Georgia	54.5
18	Hawaii	49.5	11	Louisiana	54.0
14	Idaho	51.8	12	South Carolina	53.9
35	Illinois	42.2	13	Indiana	52.0
13	Indiana	52.0	14	Idaho	51.8
30	Iowa	43.6	15	Texas	51.5
16	Kansas	51.1	16	Kansas	51.1
3	Kentucky	67.3	17	New Mexico	50.5
11	Louisiana	54.0	18	Hawaii	49.5
36	Maine	42.0	19	Missouri	49.3
25	Maryland	44.8	20	Virginia	47.6
45	Massachusetts	37.2	21	Arizona	46.6
30	Michigan	43.6	22	Florida	46.4
38	Minnesota	41.6	23	California	46.0
5	Mississippi	63.6	24	New Jersey	45.1
19	Missouri	49.3	25	Maryland	44.8
33	Montana	43.0	26	Ohio	44.6
39	Nebraska	41.5	27	Nevada	44.3
27	Nevada	44.3	28	Wyoming	44.1
45	New Hampshire	37.2	29	South Dakota	43.7
24	New Jersey	45.1	30	Iowa	43.6
17	New Mexico	50.5	30	Michigan	43.6
32	New York	43.1	32	New York	43.1
9	North Carolina	57.1	33	Montana	43.0
41	North Dakota	41.0	33	Pennsylvania	43.0
26	Ohio	44.6	35	Illinois	42.2
8	Oklahoma	58.3	36	Maine	42.0
36	Oregon	42.0	36	Oregon	42.0
33	Pennsylvania	43.0	38	Minnesota	41.6
48	Rhode Island	35.1	39	Nebraska	41.5
12	South Carolina	53.9	40	Alaska	41.4
29	South Dakota	43.7	41	North Dakota	41.0
2	Tennessee	70.5	42	Delaware	40.8
15	Texas	51.5	43	Washington	40.2
1	Utah	73.6	44	Colorado	38.4
48	Vermont	35.1	45	Massachusetts	37.2
20	Virginia	47.6	45	New Hampshire	37.2
43	Washington	40.2	47	Connecticut	36.6
4	West Virginia	66.2	48	Rhode Island	35.1
50	Wisconsin	31.2	48	Vermont	35.1
28	Wyoming	44.1	50	Wisconsin	31.2
				District of Columbia	40.7

Source: U.S. Department of Health and Human Services, Centers for Disease Control and Prevention
   "2006 Behavioral Risk Factor Surveillance Summary Prevalence Data" (http://apps.nccd.cdc.gov/brfss/)
*Persons 18 and older reporting not having at least one drink of alcohol in the past 30 days.

Percent of Adults Who Are Binge Drinkers: 2006

National Median = 15.4% of Adults*

ALPHA ORDER

RANK	STATE	PERCENT
45	Alabama	11.2
13	Alaska	17.0
27	Arizona	15.2
42	Arkansas	12.4
25	California	15.4
18	Colorado	16.4
31	Connecticut	14.5
5	Delaware	19.0
36	Florida	13.8
43	Georgia	12.1
8	Hawaii	17.9
29	Idaho	14.8
4	Illinois	19.3
21	Indiana	16.0
3	Iowa	20.6
25	Kansas	15.4
49	Kentucky	8.6
40	Louisiana	13.3
20	Maine	16.1
35	Maryland	13.9
9	Massachusetts	17.7
9	Michigan	17.7
11	Minnesota	17.6
47	Mississippi	9.5
17	Missouri	16.5
21	Montana	16.0
7	Nebraska	18.1
24	Nevada	15.7
27	New Hampshire	15.2
32	New Jersey	14.3
41	New Mexico	13.2
23	New York	15.8
44	North Carolina	11.3
2	North Dakota	21.2
19	Ohio	16.3
39	Oklahoma	13.4
34	Oregon	14.1
16	Pennsylvania	16.6
11	Rhode Island	17.6
37	South Carolina	13.5
6	South Dakota	18.2
49	Tennessee	8.6
30	Texas	14.7
48	Utah	9.3
14	Vermont	16.8
37	Virginia	13.5
33	Washington	14.2
45	West Virginia	11.2
1	Wisconsin	24.3
15	Wyoming	16.7

RANK ORDER

RANK	STATE	PERCENT
1	Wisconsin	24.3
2	North Dakota	21.2
3	Iowa	20.6
4	Illinois	19.3
5	Delaware	19.0
6	South Dakota	18.2
7	Nebraska	18.1
8	Hawaii	17.9
9	Massachusetts	17.7
9	Michigan	17.7
11	Minnesota	17.6
11	Rhode Island	17.6
13	Alaska	17.0
14	Vermont	16.8
15	Wyoming	16.7
16	Pennsylvania	16.6
17	Missouri	16.5
18	Colorado	16.4
19	Ohio	16.3
20	Maine	16.1
21	Indiana	16.0
21	Montana	16.0
23	New York	15.8
24	Nevada	15.7
25	California	15.4
25	Kansas	15.4
27	Arizona	15.2
27	New Hampshire	15.2
29	Idaho	14.8
30	Texas	14.7
31	Connecticut	14.5
32	New Jersey	14.3
33	Washington	14.2
34	Oregon	14.1
35	Maryland	13.9
36	Florida	13.8
37	South Carolina	13.5
37	Virginia	13.5
39	Oklahoma	13.4
40	Louisiana	13.3
41	New Mexico	13.2
42	Arkansas	12.4
43	Georgia	12.1
44	North Carolina	11.3
45	Alabama	11.2
45	West Virginia	11.2
47	Mississippi	9.5
48	Utah	9.3
49	Kentucky	8.6
49	Tennessee	8.6

| | District of Columbia | 15.9 |

Source: U.S. Department of Health and Human Services, Centers for Disease Control and Prevention
"2006 Behavioral Risk Factor Surveillance Summary Prevalence Data" (http://apps.nccd.cdc.gov/brfss/)
*Persons 18 and older reporting consumption of five or more alcoholic drinks on one or more occasions during the previous month.

Percent of Adults Who Smoke: 2006

National Median = 20.1% of Adults*

<table>
<tr><td colspan="3">ALPHA ORDER</td><td colspan="3">RANK ORDER</td></tr>
<tr><td>RANK</td><td>STATE</td><td>PERCENT</td><td>RANK</td><td>STATE</td><td>PERCENT</td></tr>
<tr><td>9</td><td>Alabama</td><td>23.2</td><td>1</td><td>Kentucky</td><td>28.5</td></tr>
<tr><td>6</td><td>Alaska</td><td>24.0</td><td>2</td><td>West Virginia</td><td>25.7</td></tr>
<tr><td>37</td><td>Arizona</td><td>18.2</td><td>3</td><td>Mississippi</td><td>25.1</td></tr>
<tr><td>7</td><td>Arkansas</td><td>23.7</td><td>3</td><td>Oklahoma</td><td>25.1</td></tr>
<tr><td>49</td><td>California</td><td>14.9</td><td>5</td><td>Indiana</td><td>24.1</td></tr>
<tr><td>41</td><td>Colorado</td><td>17.9</td><td>6</td><td>Alaska</td><td>24.0</td></tr>
<tr><td>47</td><td>Connecticut</td><td>17.0</td><td>7</td><td>Arkansas</td><td>23.7</td></tr>
<tr><td>17</td><td>Delaware</td><td>21.7</td><td>8</td><td>Louisiana</td><td>23.4</td></tr>
<tr><td>21</td><td>Florida</td><td>21.0</td><td>9</td><td>Alabama</td><td>23.2</td></tr>
<tr><td>28</td><td>Georgia</td><td>19.9</td><td>9</td><td>Missouri</td><td>23.2</td></tr>
<tr><td>45</td><td>Hawaii</td><td>17.5</td><td>11</td><td>Tennessee</td><td>22.6</td></tr>
<tr><td>48</td><td>Idaho</td><td>16.8</td><td>12</td><td>Michigan</td><td>22.4</td></tr>
<tr><td>24</td><td>Illinois</td><td>20.5</td><td>12</td><td>Ohio</td><td>22.4</td></tr>
<tr><td>5</td><td>Indiana</td><td>24.1</td><td>14</td><td>South Carolina</td><td>22.3</td></tr>
<tr><td>20</td><td>Iowa</td><td>21.4</td><td>15</td><td>Nevada</td><td>22.2</td></tr>
<tr><td>27</td><td>Kansas</td><td>20.0</td><td>16</td><td>North Carolina</td><td>22.1</td></tr>
<tr><td>1</td><td>Kentucky</td><td>28.5</td><td>17</td><td>Delaware</td><td>21.7</td></tr>
<tr><td>8</td><td>Louisiana</td><td>23.4</td><td>18</td><td>Wyoming</td><td>21.6</td></tr>
<tr><td>22</td><td>Maine</td><td>20.9</td><td>19</td><td>Pennsylvania</td><td>21.5</td></tr>
<tr><td>44</td><td>Maryland</td><td>17.7</td><td>20</td><td>Iowa</td><td>21.4</td></tr>
<tr><td>43</td><td>Massachusetts</td><td>17.8</td><td>21</td><td>Florida</td><td>21.0</td></tr>
<tr><td>12</td><td>Michigan</td><td>22.4</td><td>22</td><td>Maine</td><td>20.9</td></tr>
<tr><td>36</td><td>Minnesota</td><td>18.3</td><td>23</td><td>Wisconsin</td><td>20.8</td></tr>
<tr><td>3</td><td>Mississippi</td><td>25.1</td><td>24</td><td>Illinois</td><td>20.5</td></tr>
<tr><td>9</td><td>Missouri</td><td>23.2</td><td>25</td><td>South Dakota</td><td>20.3</td></tr>
<tr><td>32</td><td>Montana</td><td>18.9</td><td>26</td><td>New Mexico</td><td>20.1</td></tr>
<tr><td>33</td><td>Nebraska</td><td>18.7</td><td>27</td><td>Kansas</td><td>20.0</td></tr>
<tr><td>15</td><td>Nevada</td><td>22.2</td><td>28</td><td>Georgia</td><td>19.9</td></tr>
<tr><td>33</td><td>New Hampshire</td><td>18.7</td><td>29</td><td>North Dakota</td><td>19.5</td></tr>
<tr><td>39</td><td>New Jersey</td><td>18.0</td><td>30</td><td>Virginia</td><td>19.3</td></tr>
<tr><td>26</td><td>New Mexico</td><td>20.1</td><td>31</td><td>Rhode Island</td><td>19.2</td></tr>
<tr><td>37</td><td>New York</td><td>18.2</td><td>32</td><td>Montana</td><td>18.9</td></tr>
<tr><td>16</td><td>North Carolina</td><td>22.1</td><td>33</td><td>Nebraska</td><td>18.7</td></tr>
<tr><td>29</td><td>North Dakota</td><td>19.5</td><td>33</td><td>New Hampshire</td><td>18.7</td></tr>
<tr><td>12</td><td>Ohio</td><td>22.4</td><td>35</td><td>Oregon</td><td>18.5</td></tr>
<tr><td>3</td><td>Oklahoma</td><td>25.1</td><td>36</td><td>Minnesota</td><td>18.3</td></tr>
<tr><td>35</td><td>Oregon</td><td>18.5</td><td>37</td><td>Arizona</td><td>18.2</td></tr>
<tr><td>19</td><td>Pennsylvania</td><td>21.5</td><td>37</td><td>New York</td><td>18.2</td></tr>
<tr><td>31</td><td>Rhode Island</td><td>19.2</td><td>39</td><td>New Jersey</td><td>18.0</td></tr>
<tr><td>14</td><td>South Carolina</td><td>22.3</td><td>39</td><td>Vermont</td><td>18.0</td></tr>
<tr><td>25</td><td>South Dakota</td><td>20.3</td><td>41</td><td>Colorado</td><td>17.9</td></tr>
<tr><td>11</td><td>Tennessee</td><td>22.6</td><td>41</td><td>Texas</td><td>17.9</td></tr>
<tr><td>41</td><td>Texas</td><td>17.9</td><td>43</td><td>Massachusetts</td><td>17.8</td></tr>
<tr><td>50</td><td>Utah</td><td>9.8</td><td>44</td><td>Maryland</td><td>17.7</td></tr>
<tr><td>39</td><td>Vermont</td><td>18.0</td><td>45</td><td>Hawaii</td><td>17.5</td></tr>
<tr><td>30</td><td>Virginia</td><td>19.3</td><td>46</td><td>Washington</td><td>17.1</td></tr>
<tr><td>46</td><td>Washington</td><td>17.1</td><td>47</td><td>Connecticut</td><td>17.0</td></tr>
<tr><td>2</td><td>West Virginia</td><td>25.7</td><td>48</td><td>Idaho</td><td>16.8</td></tr>
<tr><td>23</td><td>Wisconsin</td><td>20.8</td><td>49</td><td>California</td><td>14.9</td></tr>
<tr><td>18</td><td>Wyoming</td><td>21.6</td><td>50</td><td>Utah</td><td>9.8</td></tr>
<tr><td></td><td></td><td></td><td></td><td>District of Columbia</td><td>17.9</td></tr>
</table>

Source: U.S. Department of Health and Human Services, Centers for Disease Control and Prevention
"2006 Behavioral Risk Factor Surveillance Summary Prevalence Data" (http://apps.nccd.cdc.gov/brfss/)
*Persons 18 and older who have smoked more than 100 cigarettes during their lifetime and who currently smoke every day or some days.

Percent of Men Who Smoke: 2006

National Median = 22.2% of Men*

ALPHA ORDER

RANK ORDER

RANK	STATE	PERCENT		RANK	STATE	PERCENT
6	Alabama	26.1		1	Kentucky	29.1
11	Alaska	25.2		2	Oklahoma	27.9
28	Arizona	21.7		3	Mississippi	27.8
7	Arkansas	25.8		4	Louisiana	26.7
47	California	18.5		5	Indiana	26.4
38	Colorado	19.3		6	Alabama	26.1
43	Connecticut	18.9		7	Arkansas	25.8
19	Delaware	23.3		8	South Carolina	25.6
18	Florida	23.5		9	West Virginia	25.4
24	Georgia	22.4		10	North Carolina	25.3
41	Hawaii	19.2		11	Alaska	25.2
46	Idaho	18.7		12	Ohio	24.9
15	Illinois	24.2		13	Michigan	24.8
5	Indiana	26.4		14	Missouri	24.5
21	Iowa	23.1		15	Illinois	24.2
26	Kansas	22.2		16	Wyoming	23.8
1	Kentucky	29.1		17	Tennessee	23.7
4	Louisiana	26.7		18	Florida	23.5
27	Maine	22.0		19	Delaware	23.3
42	Maryland	19.0		19	Wisconsin	23.3
38	Massachusetts	19.3		21	Iowa	23.1
13	Michigan	24.8		22	Nevada	22.9
47	Minnesota	18.5		23	New Mexico	22.6
3	Mississippi	27.8		24	Georgia	22.4
14	Missouri	24.5		25	Pennsylvania	22.3
49	Montana	18.4		26	Kansas	22.2
35	Nebraska	19.6		27	Maine	22.0
22	Nevada	22.9		28	Arizona	21.7
38	New Hampshire	19.3		29	South Dakota	21.6
31	New Jersey	20.7		30	North Dakota	21.0
23	New Mexico	22.6		31	New Jersey	20.7
43	New York	18.9		32	Texas	20.5
10	North Carolina	25.3		33	Virginia	20.2
30	North Dakota	21.0		34	Oregon	19.8
12	Ohio	24.9		35	Nebraska	19.6
2	Oklahoma	27.9		36	Rhode Island	19.5
34	Oregon	19.8		37	Vermont	19.4
25	Pennsylvania	22.3		38	Colorado	19.3
36	Rhode Island	19.5		38	Massachusetts	19.3
8	South Carolina	25.6		38	New Hampshire	19.3
29	South Dakota	21.6		41	Hawaii	19.2
17	Tennessee	23.7		42	Maryland	19.0
32	Texas	20.5		43	Connecticut	18.9
50	Utah	10.4		43	New York	18.9
37	Vermont	19.4		43	Washington	18.9
33	Virginia	20.2		46	Idaho	18.7
43	Washington	18.9		47	California	18.5
9	West Virginia	25.4		47	Minnesota	18.5
19	Wisconsin	23.3		49	Montana	18.4
16	Wyoming	23.8		50	Utah	10.4

District of Columbia		21.3

Source: U.S. Department of Health and Human Services, Centers for Disease Control and Prevention
"2006 Behavioral Risk Factor Surveillance System" (http://apps.nccd.cdc.gov/brfss/)
*Males age 18 and older who have smoked more than 100 cigarettes during their lifetime and who currently smoke every day or some days.

Percent of Women Who Smoke: 2006

National Median = 18.4% of Women*

ALPHA ORDER				RANK ORDER		
RANK	STATE	PERCENT		RANK	STATE	PERCENT
12	Alabama	20.5		1	Kentucky	28.0
3	Alaska	22.6		2	West Virginia	26.1
48	Arizona	14.7		3	Alaska	22.6
8	Arkansas	21.7		3	Mississippi	22.6
49	California	11.4		5	Oklahoma	22.5
39	Colorado	16.5		6	Missouri	22.0
46	Connecticut	15.2		7	Indiana	21.9
14	Delaware	20.3		8	Arkansas	21.7
25	Florida	18.7		9	Tennessee	21.5
34	Georgia	17.6		10	Nevada	21.4
42	Hawaii	15.9		11	Pennsylvania	20.7
47	Idaho	15.0		12	Alabama	20.5
37	Illinois	17.0		12	Louisiana	20.5
7	Indiana	21.9		14	Delaware	20.3
17	Iowa	19.9		15	Michigan	20.1
31	Kansas	18.0		15	Ohio	20.1
1	Kentucky	28.0		17	Iowa	19.9
12	Louisiana	20.5		17	Maine	19.9
17	Maine	19.9		19	Montana	19.4
39	Maryland	16.5		19	Wyoming	19.4
41	Massachusetts	16.4		21	South Carolina	19.2
15	Michigan	20.1		22	South Dakota	19.1
28	Minnesota	18.2		23	North Carolina	19.0
3	Mississippi	22.6		24	Rhode Island	18.9
6	Missouri	22.0		25	Florida	18.7
19	Montana	19.4		26	Virginia	18.4
32	Nebraska	17.8		26	Wisconsin	18.4
10	Nevada	21.4		28	Minnesota	18.2
29	New Hampshire	18.1		29	New Hampshire	18.1
43	New Jersey	15.6		29	North Dakota	18.1
32	New Mexico	17.8		31	Kansas	18.0
34	New York	17.6		32	Nebraska	17.8
23	North Carolina	19.0		32	New Mexico	17.8
29	North Dakota	18.1		34	Georgia	17.6
15	Ohio	20.1		34	New York	17.6
5	Oklahoma	22.5		36	Oregon	17.2
36	Oregon	17.2		37	Illinois	17.0
11	Pennsylvania	20.7		38	Vermont	16.8
24	Rhode Island	18.9		39	Colorado	16.5
21	South Carolina	19.2		39	Maryland	16.5
22	South Dakota	19.1		41	Massachusetts	16.4
9	Tennessee	21.5		42	Hawaii	15.9
44	Texas	15.4		43	New Jersey	15.6
50	Utah	9.3		44	Texas	15.4
38	Vermont	16.8		45	Washington	15.3
26	Virginia	18.4		46	Connecticut	15.2
45	Washington	15.3		47	Idaho	15.0
2	West Virginia	26.1		48	Arizona	14.7
26	Wisconsin	18.4		49	California	11.4
19	Wyoming	19.4		50	Utah	9.3
				District of Columbia		14.9

Source: U.S. Department of Health and Human Services, Centers for Disease Control and Prevention
   "2006 Behavioral Risk Factor Surveillance System" (http://apps.nccd.cdc.gov/brfss/)
*Females age 18 and older who have smoked more than 100 cigarettes during their lifetime and who currently smoke every day or some days.

Percent of Adults Who Are Former Smokers: 2006

National Median = 24.7% of Adults*

ALPHA ORDER

RANK	STATE	PERCENT
42	Alabama	23.4
7	Alaska	27.6
22	Arizona	24.9
20	Arkansas	25.1
32	California	24.2
27	Colorado	24.5
5	Connecticut	28.2
9	Delaware	27.3
13	Florida	26.1
47	Georgia	21.2
20	Hawaii	25.1
44	Idaho	23.0
38	Illinois	23.7
43	Indiana	23.3
38	Iowa	23.7
33	Kansas	24.1
30	Kentucky	24.3
49	Louisiana	20.1
2	Maine	30.4
45	Maryland	22.6
6	Massachusetts	27.7
18	Michigan	25.4
7	Minnesota	27.6
48	Mississippi	21.1
10	Missouri	26.8
10	Montana	26.8
37	Nebraska	23.8
16	Nevada	25.6
3	New Hampshire	29.7
33	New Jersey	24.1
25	New Mexico	24.7
27	New York	24.5
33	North Carolina	24.1
33	North Dakota	24.1
30	Ohio	24.3
38	Oklahoma	23.7
15	Oregon	25.7
17	Pennsylvania	25.5
4	Rhode Island	28.8
27	South Carolina	24.5
24	South Dakota	24.8
41	Tennessee	23.5
46	Texas	21.7
50	Utah	16.6
1	Vermont	30.9
19	Virginia	25.2
12	Washington	26.4
25	West Virginia	24.7
14	Wisconsin	26.0
22	Wyoming	24.9

RANK ORDER

RANK	STATE	PERCENT
1	Vermont	30.9
2	Maine	30.4
3	New Hampshire	29.7
4	Rhode Island	28.8
5	Connecticut	28.2
6	Massachusetts	27.7
7	Alaska	27.6
7	Minnesota	27.6
9	Delaware	27.3
10	Missouri	26.8
10	Montana	26.8
12	Washington	26.4
13	Florida	26.1
14	Wisconsin	26.0
15	Oregon	25.7
16	Nevada	25.6
17	Pennsylvania	25.5
18	Michigan	25.4
19	Virginia	25.2
20	Arkansas	25.1
20	Hawaii	25.1
22	Arizona	24.9
22	Wyoming	24.9
24	South Dakota	24.8
25	New Mexico	24.7
25	West Virginia	24.7
27	Colorado	24.5
27	New York	24.5
27	South Carolina	24.5
30	Kentucky	24.3
30	Ohio	24.3
32	California	24.2
33	Kansas	24.1
33	New Jersey	24.1
33	North Carolina	24.1
33	North Dakota	24.1
37	Nebraska	23.8
38	Illinois	23.7
38	Iowa	23.7
38	Oklahoma	23.7
41	Tennessee	23.5
42	Alabama	23.4
43	Indiana	23.3
44	Idaho	23.0
45	Maryland	22.6
46	Texas	21.7
47	Georgia	21.2
48	Mississippi	21.1
49	Louisiana	20.1
50	Utah	16.6
	District of Columbia	22.1

Source: U.S. Department of Health and Human Services, Centers for Disease Control and Prevention
"2006 Behavioral Risk Factor Surveillance Summary Prevalence Data" (http://apps.nccd.cdc.gov/brfss/)
*Persons 18 and older who have smoked more than 100 cigarettes during their lifetime and who currently do not smoke.

Percent of Adults Who Have Never Smoked: 2006

National Median = 54.3% of Adults*

ALPHA ORDER			RANK ORDER		
RANK	STATE	PERCENT	RANK	STATE	PERCENT
30	Alabama	53.5	1	Utah	73.6
49	Alaska	48.5	2	California	60.8
12	Arizona	56.9	3	Texas	60.4
42	Arkansas	51.2	4	Idaho	60.2
2	California	60.8	5	Maryland	59.7
8	Colorado	57.6	6	Georgia	58.8
21	Connecticut	54.8	7	New Jersey	57.9
45	Delaware	50.9	8	Colorado	57.6
36	Florida	52.9	9	Nebraska	57.5
6	Georgia	58.8	10	Hawaii	57.3
10	Hawaii	57.3	10	New York	57.3
4	Idaho	60.2	12	Arizona	56.9
17	Illinois	55.8	13	Washington	56.6
37	Indiana	52.7	14	Louisiana	56.4
21	Iowa	54.8	14	North Dakota	56.4
16	Kansas	55.9	16	Kansas	55.9
50	Kentucky	47.2	17	Illinois	55.8
14	Louisiana	56.4	17	Oregon	55.8
48	Maine	48.7	19	Virginia	55.5
5	Maryland	59.7	20	New Mexico	55.1
24	Massachusetts	54.5	21	Connecticut	54.8
39	Michigan	52.2	21	Iowa	54.8
26	Minnesota	54.1	21	South Dakota	54.8
29	Mississippi	53.8	24	Massachusetts	54.5
46	Missouri	50.0	25	Montana	54.3
25	Montana	54.3	26	Minnesota	54.1
9	Nebraska	57.5	27	North Carolina	53.9
38	Nevada	52.3	27	Tennessee	53.9
41	New Hampshire	51.6	29	Mississippi	53.8
7	New Jersey	57.9	30	Alabama	53.5
20	New Mexico	55.1	30	Wyoming	53.5
10	New York	57.3	32	Ohio	53.3
27	North Carolina	53.9	32	South Carolina	53.3
14	North Dakota	56.4	34	Wisconsin	53.2
32	Ohio	53.3	35	Pennsylvania	53.0
42	Oklahoma	51.2	36	Florida	52.9
17	Oregon	55.8	37	Indiana	52.7
35	Pennsylvania	53.0	38	Nevada	52.3
40	Rhode Island	52.0	39	Michigan	52.2
32	South Carolina	53.3	40	Rhode Island	52.0
21	South Dakota	54.8	41	New Hampshire	51.6
27	Tennessee	53.9	42	Arkansas	51.2
3	Texas	60.4	42	Oklahoma	51.2
1	Utah	73.6	44	Vermont	51.1
44	Vermont	51.1	45	Delaware	50.9
19	Virginia	55.5	46	Missouri	50.0
13	Washington	56.6	47	West Virginia	49.6
47	West Virginia	49.6	48	Maine	48.7
34	Wisconsin	53.2	49	Alaska	48.5
30	Wyoming	53.5	50	Kentucky	47.2
				District of Columbia	60.0

Source: U.S. Department of Health and Human Services, Centers for Disease Control and Prevention
   "2006 Behavioral Risk Factor Surveillance Summary Prevalence Data" (http://apps.nccd.cdc.gov/brfss/)
*Persons 18 and older who have not smoked more than 100 cigarettes during their lifetime.

Percent of Population Who Are Illicit Drug Users: 2005

National Percent = 8.0% of Population*

ALPHA ORDER

RANK	STATE	PERCENT
36	Alabama	7.3
1	Alaska	12.2
36	Arizona	7.3
29	Arkansas	7.6
11	California	8.9
4	Colorado	9.9
10	Connecticut	9.0
18	Delaware	8.3
18	Florida	8.3
32	Georgia	7.5
16	Hawaii	8.4
42	Idaho	7.0
32	Illinois	7.5
35	Indiana	7.4
50	Iowa	5.9
40	Kansas	7.2
16	Kentucky	8.4
21	Louisiana	8.2
7	Maine	9.5
46	Maryland	6.6
8	Massachusetts	9.4
14	Michigan	8.7
21	Minnesota	8.2
45	Mississippi	6.7
27	Missouri	7.7
5	Montana	9.8
47	Nebraska	6.5
18	Nevada	8.3
11	New Hampshire	8.9
40	New Jersey	7.2
11	New Mexico	8.9
9	New York	9.2
36	North Carolina	7.3
49	North Dakota	6.2
26	Ohio	7.8
23	Oklahoma	8.1
6	Oregon	9.6
25	Pennsylvania	7.9
2	Rhode Island	10.7
36	South Carolina	7.3
47	South Dakota	6.5
24	Tennessee	8.0
43	Texas	6.8
29	Utah	7.6
2	Vermont	10.7
43	Virginia	6.8
15	Washington	8.5
27	West Virginia	7.7
32	Wisconsin	7.5
29	Wyoming	7.6

RANK ORDER

RANK	STATE	PERCENT
1	Alaska	12.2
2	Rhode Island	10.7
2	Vermont	10.7
4	Colorado	9.9
5	Montana	9.8
6	Oregon	9.6
7	Maine	9.5
8	Massachusetts	9.4
9	New York	9.2
10	Connecticut	9.0
11	California	8.9
11	New Hampshire	8.9
11	New Mexico	8.9
14	Michigan	8.7
15	Washington	8.5
16	Hawaii	8.4
16	Kentucky	8.4
18	Delaware	8.3
18	Florida	8.3
18	Nevada	8.3
21	Louisiana	8.2
21	Minnesota	8.2
23	Oklahoma	8.1
24	Tennessee	8.0
25	Pennsylvania	7.9
26	Ohio	7.8
27	Missouri	7.7
27	West Virginia	7.7
29	Arkansas	7.6
29	Utah	7.6
29	Wyoming	7.6
32	Georgia	7.5
32	Illinois	7.5
32	Wisconsin	7.5
35	Indiana	7.4
36	Alabama	7.3
36	Arizona	7.3
36	North Carolina	7.3
36	South Carolina	7.3
40	Kansas	7.2
40	New Jersey	7.2
42	Idaho	7.0
43	Texas	6.8
43	Virginia	6.8
45	Mississippi	6.7
46	Maryland	6.6
47	Nebraska	6.5
47	South Dakota	6.5
49	North Dakota	6.2
50	Iowa	5.9

District of Columbia	9.5

Source: U.S. Department of Health and Human Services, Substance Abuse and Mental Health Services Administration
"2004-2005 National Survey on Drug Use and Health" (February 2007, http://www.oas.samhsa.gov/2k5state/TOC.cfm)
*Population 12 years and older who used any illicit drug at least once within month of survey.

Percent of Adults Overweight: 2006

National Median = 36.5% of Adults*

ALPHA ORDER

RANK ORDER

RANK	STATE	PERCENT	RANK	STATE	PERCENT
49	Alabama	34.5	1	Rhode Island	39.6
10	Alaska	38.0	2	North Dakota	39.1
20	Arizona	36.7	3	South Dakota	38.7
17	Arkansas	36.9	4	Nevada	38.6
40	California	35.5	5	Kentucky	38.4
20	Colorado	36.7	6	New Hampshire	38.3
7	Connecticut	38.2	7	Connecticut	38.2
12	Delaware	37.8	8	Montana	38.1
25	Florida	36.5	8	Wyoming	38.1
48	Georgia	34.6	10	Alaska	38.0
40	Hawaii	35.5	10	Minnesota	38.0
39	Idaho	35.6	12	Delaware	37.8
23	Illinois	36.6	13	New Jersey	37.3
46	Indiana	35.0	13	Pennsylvania	37.3
15	Iowa	37.2	15	Iowa	37.2
28	Kansas	36.4	16	Nebraska	37.0
5	Kentucky	38.4	17	Arkansas	36.9
35	Louisiana	35.9	17	New Mexico	36.9
23	Maine	36.6	19	Wisconsin	36.8
37	Maryland	35.8	20	Arizona	36.7
45	Massachusetts	35.2	20	Colorado	36.7
31	Michigan	36.0	20	Virginia	36.7
10	Minnesota	38.0	23	Illinois	36.6
44	Mississippi	35.3	23	Maine	36.6
38	Missouri	35.7	25	Florida	36.5
8	Montana	38.1	25	Tennessee	36.5
16	Nebraska	37.0	25	Washington	36.5
4	Nevada	38.6	28	Kansas	36.4
6	New Hampshire	38.3	29	Texas	36.3
13	New Jersey	37.3	30	North Carolina	36.2
17	New Mexico	36.9	31	Michigan	36.0
43	New York	35.4	31	Oklahoma	36.0
30	North Carolina	36.2	31	South Carolina	36.0
2	North Dakota	39.1	31	West Virginia	36.0
40	Ohio	35.5	35	Louisiana	35.9
31	Oklahoma	36.0	35	Oregon	35.9
35	Oregon	35.9	37	Maryland	35.8
13	Pennsylvania	37.3	38	Missouri	35.7
1	Rhode Island	39.6	39	Idaho	35.6
31	South Carolina	36.0	40	California	35.5
3	South Dakota	38.7	40	Hawaii	35.5
25	Tennessee	36.5	40	Ohio	35.5
29	Texas	36.3	43	New York	35.4
50	Utah	33.0	44	Mississippi	35.3
47	Vermont	34.8	45	Massachusetts	35.2
20	Virginia	36.7	46	Indiana	35.0
25	Washington	36.5	47	Vermont	34.8
31	West Virginia	36.0	48	Georgia	34.6
19	Wisconsin	36.8	49	Alabama	34.5
8	Wyoming	38.1	50	Utah	33.0

	District of Columbia	32.1

Source: U.S. Department of Health and Human Services, Centers for Disease Control and Prevention
   "2006 Behavioral Risk Factor Surveillance Summary Prevalence Data" (http://apps.nccd.cdc.gov/brfss/)
*Persons 18 and older. Does not include obese adults. Overweight is defined as a Body Mass Index (BMI) of 25.0 to 29.9
regardless of sex. BMI is a ratio of height to weight. As an example, a person 5' 8" and weighing 171 pounds has a BMI of 26.
See http://www.cdc.gov/nccdphp/dnpa/bmi/bmi-adult.htm.

Percent of Adults Obese: 2006

National Median = 25.1% of Adults*

ALPHA ORDER

RANK	STATE	PERCENT
3	Alabama	30.5
18	Alaska	26.2
38	Arizona	22.9
14	Arkansas	26.9
34	California	23.3
50	Colorado	18.2
47	Connecticut	20.6
20	Delaware	26.0
36	Florida	23.1
12	Georgia	27.1
47	Hawaii	20.6
32	Idaho	24.1
25	Illinois	25.1
10	Indiana	27.8
22	Iowa	25.7
21	Kansas	25.9
9	Kentucky	28.0
12	Louisiana	27.1
36	Maine	23.1
28	Maryland	24.9
49	Massachusetts	20.3
5	Michigan	28.8
30	Minnesota	24.7
1	Mississippi	31.4
11	Missouri	27.2
45	Montana	21.2
14	Nebraska	26.9
27	Nevada	25.0
42	New Hampshire	22.4
41	New Jersey	22.6
38	New Mexico	22.9
38	New York	22.9
16	North Carolina	26.6
23	North Dakota	25.4
8	Ohio	28.4
5	Oklahoma	28.8
29	Oregon	24.8
33	Pennsylvania	24.0
44	Rhode Island	21.4
4	South Carolina	29.4
23	South Dakota	25.4
5	Tennessee	28.8
19	Texas	26.1
43	Utah	21.9
45	Vermont	21.2
25	Virginia	25.1
31	Washington	24.2
2	West Virginia	31.0
16	Wisconsin	26.6
34	Wyoming	23.3

RANK ORDER

RANK	STATE	PERCENT
1	Mississippi	31.4
2	West Virginia	31.0
3	Alabama	30.5
4	South Carolina	29.4
5	Michigan	28.8
5	Oklahoma	28.8
5	Tennessee	28.8
8	Ohio	28.4
9	Kentucky	28.0
10	Indiana	27.8
11	Missouri	27.2
12	Georgia	27.1
12	Louisiana	27.1
14	Arkansas	26.9
14	Nebraska	26.9
16	North Carolina	26.6
16	Wisconsin	26.6
18	Alaska	26.2
19	Texas	26.1
20	Delaware	26.0
21	Kansas	25.9
22	Iowa	25.7
23	North Dakota	25.4
23	South Dakota	25.4
25	Illinois	25.1
25	Virginia	25.1
27	Nevada	25.0
28	Maryland	24.9
29	Oregon	24.8
30	Minnesota	24.7
31	Washington	24.2
32	Idaho	24.1
33	Pennsylvania	24.0
34	California	23.3
34	Wyoming	23.3
36	Florida	23.1
36	Maine	23.1
38	Arizona	22.9
38	New Mexico	22.9
38	New York	22.9
41	New Jersey	22.6
42	New Hampshire	22.4
43	Utah	21.9
44	Rhode Island	21.4
45	Montana	21.2
45	Vermont	21.2
47	Connecticut	20.6
47	Hawaii	20.6
49	Massachusetts	20.3
50	Colorado	18.2

	District of Columbia	22.5

Source: U.S. Department of Health and Human Services, Centers for Disease Control and Prevention
"2006 Behavioral Risk Factor Surveillance Summary Prevalence Data" (http://apps.nccd.cdc.gov/brfss/)
*Persons 18 and older. Obese is defined as a Body Mass Index (BMI) of 30.0 or more regardless of sex. BMI is a ratio of
height to weight. As an example, a person 5' 8" and weighing 197 pounds has a BMI of 30. See
http://www.cdc.gov/nccdphp/dnpa/bmi/bmi-adult.htm.

Percent of Adults Overweight or Obese: 2006

National Median = 61.8% of Adults*

ALPHA ORDER				RANK ORDER		
RANK	STATE	PERCENT		RANK	STATE	PERCENT
6	Alabama	64.9		1	West Virginia	67.0
10	Alaska	64.2		2	Mississippi	66.7
40	Arizona	59.6		3	Kentucky	66.4
14	Arkansas	63.8		4	South Carolina	65.4
43	California	58.8		5	Tennessee	65.3
49	Colorado	54.9		6	Alabama	64.9
43	Connecticut	58.8		7	Michigan	64.8
14	Delaware	63.8		8	Oklahoma	64.7
41	Florida	59.5		9	North Dakota	64.5
26	Georgia	61.8		10	Alaska	64.2
46	Hawaii	56.1		10	South Dakota	64.2
37	Idaho	59.7		12	Nebraska	63.9
28	Illinois	61.7		12	Ohio	63.9
22	Indiana	62.8		14	Arkansas	63.8
18	Iowa	63.0		14	Delaware	63.8
24	Kansas	62.3		16	Nevada	63.6
3	Kentucky	66.4		17	Wisconsin	63.4
18	Louisiana	63.0		18	Iowa	63.0
37	Maine	59.7		18	Louisiana	63.0
32	Maryland	60.7		20	Missouri	62.9
48	Massachusetts	55.5		20	North Carolina	62.9
7	Michigan	64.8		22	Indiana	62.8
23	Minnesota	62.7		23	Minnesota	62.7
2	Mississippi	66.7		24	Kansas	62.3
20	Missouri	62.9		24	Texas	62.3
42	Montana	59.3		26	Georgia	61.8
12	Nebraska	63.9		26	Virginia	61.8
16	Nevada	63.6		28	Illinois	61.7
32	New Hampshire	60.7		29	Pennsylvania	61.3
36	New Jersey	59.9		29	Wyoming	61.3
37	New Mexico	59.7		31	Rhode Island	61.0
45	New York	58.4		32	Maryland	60.7
20	North Carolina	62.9		32	New Hampshire	60.7
9	North Dakota	64.5		32	Oregon	60.7
12	Ohio	63.9		32	Washington	60.7
8	Oklahoma	64.7		36	New Jersey	59.9
32	Oregon	60.7		37	Idaho	59.7
29	Pennsylvania	61.3		37	Maine	59.7
31	Rhode Island	61.0		37	New Mexico	59.7
4	South Carolina	65.4		40	Arizona	59.6
10	South Dakota	64.2		41	Florida	59.5
5	Tennessee	65.3		42	Montana	59.3
24	Texas	62.3		43	California	58.8
49	Utah	54.9		43	Connecticut	58.8
47	Vermont	56.0		45	New York	58.4
26	Virginia	61.8		46	Hawaii	56.1
32	Washington	60.7		47	Vermont	56.0
1	West Virginia	67.0		48	Massachusetts	55.5
17	Wisconsin	63.4		49	Colorado	54.9
29	Wyoming	61.3		49	Utah	54.9
					District of Columbia	54.6

Source: CQ Press using data from U.S. Department of Health and Human Services, Centers for Disease Control and Prevention
"2006 Behavioral Risk Factor Surveillance Summary Prevalence Data" (http://apps.nccd.cdc.gov/brfss/)
*Persons 18 and older. Overweight is defined as a Body Mass Index (BMI) of 25.0 to 29.9 regardless of sex. Obese is a BMI of
30.0 or greater. BMI is a ratio of height to weight. As an example, a person 5' 8" and weighing 165 pounds has a BMI of 25. The
same height at 197 pounds has a BMI of 30. See http://www.cdc.gov/nccdphp/dnpa/bmi/bmi-adult.htm.

Percent of Adults Who Do Not Exercise: 2006

National Median = 22.6% of Adults*

ALPHA ORDER

RANK	STATE	PERCENT
5	Alabama	29.2
35	Alaska	21.4
29	Arizona	22.3
7	Arkansas	28.7
22	California	23.0
47	Colorado	17.4
40	Connecticut	19.8
34	Delaware	21.6
14	Florida	25.1
15	Georgia	24.7
44	Hawaii	19.3
39	Idaho	20.8
28	Illinois	22.4
13	Indiana	25.3
29	Iowa	22.3
26	Kansas	22.6
3	Kentucky	30.4
2	Louisiana	31.0
38	Maine	20.9
22	Maryland	23.0
36	Massachusetts	21.1
25	Michigan	22.8
50	Minnesota	14.2
1	Mississippi	31.1
21	Missouri	23.2
42	Montana	19.4
37	Nebraska	21.0
9	Nevada	27.1
41	New Hampshire	19.6
10	New Jersey	27.0
26	New Mexico	22.6
11	New York	26.0
20	North Carolina	23.8
31	North Dakota	22.0
17	Ohio	24.5
4	Oklahoma	29.8
49	Oregon	16.4
24	Pennsylvania	22.9
15	Rhode Island	24.7
18	South Carolina	24.3
19	South Dakota	24.0
6	Tennessee	28.8
8	Texas	28.4
42	Utah	19.4
46	Vermont	17.9
33	Virginia	21.7
48	Washington	17.3
12	West Virginia	25.6
44	Wisconsin	19.3
32	Wyoming	21.9

RANK ORDER

RANK	STATE	PERCENT
1	Mississippi	31.1
2	Louisiana	31.0
3	Kentucky	30.4
4	Oklahoma	29.8
5	Alabama	29.2
6	Tennessee	28.8
7	Arkansas	28.7
8	Texas	28.4
9	Nevada	27.1
10	New Jersey	27.0
11	New York	26.0
12	West Virginia	25.6
13	Indiana	25.3
14	Florida	25.1
15	Georgia	24.7
15	Rhode Island	24.7
17	Ohio	24.5
18	South Carolina	24.3
19	South Dakota	24.0
20	North Carolina	23.8
21	Missouri	23.2
22	California	23.0
22	Maryland	23.0
24	Pennsylvania	22.9
25	Michigan	22.8
26	Kansas	22.6
26	New Mexico	22.6
28	Illinois	22.4
29	Arizona	22.3
29	Iowa	22.3
31	North Dakota	22.0
32	Wyoming	21.9
33	Virginia	21.7
34	Delaware	21.6
35	Alaska	21.4
36	Massachusetts	21.1
37	Nebraska	21.0
38	Maine	20.9
39	Idaho	20.8
40	Connecticut	19.8
41	New Hampshire	19.6
42	Montana	19.4
42	Utah	19.4
44	Hawaii	19.3
44	Wisconsin	19.3
46	Vermont	17.9
47	Colorado	17.4
48	Washington	17.3
49	Oregon	16.4
50	Minnesota	14.2

	District of Columbia	22.1

Source: U.S. Department of Health and Human Services, Centers for Disease Control and Prevention
"2006 Behavioral Risk Factor Surveillance Summary Prevalence Data" (http://apps.nccd.cdc.gov/brfss/)
*Persons 18 and older who, in the previous month, did not participate in any physical activities.

Percent of Adults Who Exercise Vigorously: 2005

National Median = 27.5% of Adults*

ALPHA ORDER

RANK	STATE	PERCENT
47	Alabama	20.3
2	Alaska	35.9
22	Arizona	28.9
36	Arkansas	24.8
1	California	36.2
9	Colorado	32.6
12	Connecticut	31.0
35	Delaware	24.9
38	Florida	24.6
40	Georgia	23.7
17	Hawaii	30.2
11	Idaho	31.1
30	Illinois	25.7
29	Indiana	27.1
42	Iowa	22.9
34	Kansas	25.0
50	Kentucky	16.8
46	Louisiana	20.7
13	Maine	30.8
20	Maryland	29.6
19	Massachusetts	29.7
24	Michigan	28.1
23	Minnesota	28.3
45	Mississippi	20.9
32	Missouri	25.3
4	Montana	33.1
37	Nebraska	24.7
9	Nevada	32.6
7	New Hampshire	32.9
31	New Jersey	25.5
21	New Mexico	29.0
27	New York	27.3
44	North Carolina	22.2
25	North Dakota	27.5
28	Ohio	27.2
43	Oklahoma	22.5
14	Oregon	30.7
26	Pennsylvania	27.4
18	Rhode Island	29.9
38	South Carolina	24.6
41	South Dakota	23.5
49	Tennessee	17.4
32	Texas	25.3
3	Utah	34.3
4	Vermont	33.1
16	Virginia	30.4
15	Washington	30.6
48	West Virginia	17.6
8	Wisconsin	32.8
4	Wyoming	33.1

RANK ORDER

RANK	STATE	PERCENT
1	California	36.2
2	Alaska	35.9
3	Utah	34.3
4	Montana	33.1
4	Vermont	33.1
4	Wyoming	33.1
7	New Hampshire	32.9
8	Wisconsin	32.8
9	Colorado	32.6
9	Nevada	32.6
11	Idaho	31.1
12	Connecticut	31.0
13	Maine	30.8
14	Oregon	30.7
15	Washington	30.6
16	Virginia	30.4
17	Hawaii	30.2
18	Rhode Island	29.9
19	Massachusetts	29.7
20	Maryland	29.6
21	New Mexico	29.0
22	Arizona	28.9
23	Minnesota	28.3
24	Michigan	28.1
25	North Dakota	27.5
26	Pennsylvania	27.4
27	New York	27.3
28	Ohio	27.2
29	Indiana	27.1
30	Illinois	25.7
31	New Jersey	25.5
32	Missouri	25.3
32	Texas	25.3
34	Kansas	25.0
35	Delaware	24.9
36	Arkansas	24.8
37	Nebraska	24.7
38	Florida	24.6
38	South Carolina	24.6
40	Georgia	23.7
41	South Dakota	23.5
42	Iowa	22.9
43	Oklahoma	22.5
44	North Carolina	22.2
45	Mississippi	20.9
46	Louisiana	20.7
47	Alabama	20.3
48	West Virginia	17.6
49	Tennessee	17.4
50	Kentucky	16.8

| | District of Columbia | 31.5 |

Source: U.S. Department of Health and Human Services, Centers for Disease Control and Prevention
"2005 Behavioral Risk Factor Surveillance Summary Prevalence Data" (http://apps.nccd.cdc.gov/brfss/)
*Persons 18 and older. Activity that caused large increases in breathing or heart rate at least 20 minutes three or more times per week (such as running, aerobics, or heavy yard work).

Percent of Adults Who Are Disabled: 2005

National Median = 18.6%*

ALPHA ORDER				RANK ORDER		
RANK	**STATE**	**PERCENT**		**RANK**	**STATE**	**PERCENT**
3	Alabama	22.4		1	West Virginia	27.4
17	Alaska	19.3		2	Kentucky	22.6
16	Arizona	19.4		3	Alabama	22.4
8	Arkansas	21.0		3	Oregon	22.4
33	California	17.5		5	Oklahoma	22.2
44	Colorado	16.2		6	Mississippi	22.1
46	Connecticut	15.2		7	Washington	21.8
36	Delaware	17.2		8	Arkansas	21.0
23	Florida	19.0		9	Missouri	20.9
23	Georgia	19.0		10	Idaho	20.5
49	Hawaii	14.7		10	Minnesota	20.5
10	Idaho	20.5		10	Montana	20.5
50	Illinois	13.9		13	Tennessee	20.1
36	Indiana	17.2		14	Michigan	19.8
40	Iowa	16.9		15	Maine	19.5
29	Kansas	18.2		16	Arizona	19.4
2	Kentucky	22.6		17	Alaska	19.3
26	Louisiana	18.6		17	Nevada	19.3
15	Maine	19.5		17	New Mexico	19.3
45	Maryland	15.7		20	South Carolina	19.2
42	Massachusetts	16.8		20	Utah	19.2
14	Michigan	19.8		20	Vermont	19.2
10	Minnesota	20.5		23	Florida	19.0
6	Mississippi	22.1		23	Georgia	19.0
9	Missouri	20.9		23	South Dakota	19.0
10	Montana	20.5		26	Louisiana	18.6
34	Nebraska	17.3		27	Pennsylvania	18.4
17	Nevada	19.3		27	Wyoming	18.4
34	New Hampshire	17.3		29	Kansas	18.2
47	New Jersey	15.1		30	North Carolina	17.8
17	New Mexico	19.3		30	Ohio	17.8
36	New York	17.2		32	Virginia	17.6
30	North Carolina	17.8		33	California	17.5
48	North Dakota	14.8		34	Nebraska	17.3
30	Ohio	17.8		34	New Hampshire	17.3
5	Oklahoma	22.2		36	Delaware	17.2
3	Oregon	22.4		36	Indiana	17.2
27	Pennsylvania	18.4		36	New York	17.2
40	Rhode Island	16.9		36	Wisconsin	17.2
20	South Carolina	19.2		40	Iowa	16.9
23	South Dakota	19.0		40	Rhode Island	16.9
13	Tennessee	20.1		42	Massachusetts	16.8
42	Texas	16.8		42	Texas	16.8
20	Utah	19.2		44	Colorado	16.2
20	Vermont	19.2		45	Maryland	15.7
32	Virginia	17.6		46	Connecticut	15.2
7	Washington	21.8		47	New Jersey	15.1
1	West Virginia	27.4		48	North Dakota	14.8
36	Wisconsin	17.2		49	Hawaii	14.7
27	Wyoming	18.4		50	Illinois	13.9
					District of Columbia	13.7

Source: U.S. Department of Health and Human Services, Centers for Disease Control and Prevention
"2005 Behavioral Risk Factor Surveillance Summary Prevalence Data" (http://apps.nccd.cdc.gov/brfss/)
*Persons 18 and older. Adults who are limited in any activities because of physical, mental, or emotional problems.

Percent of Adults with High Blood Pressure: 2005

National Median = 25.5% of Adults*

<table>
<tr><td colspan="3">ALPHA ORDER</td><td colspan="3">RANK ORDER</td></tr>
<tr><td>RANK</td><td>STATE</td><td>PERCENT</td><td>RANK</td><td>STATE</td><td>PERCENT</td></tr>
<tr><td>4</td><td>Alabama</td><td>31.2</td><td>1</td><td>Mississippi</td><td>33.3</td></tr>
<tr><td>48</td><td>Alaska</td><td>21.5</td><td>2</td><td>South Carolina</td><td>31.4</td></tr>
<tr><td>46</td><td>Arizona</td><td>22.3</td><td>2</td><td>West Virginia</td><td>31.4</td></tr>
<tr><td>9</td><td>Arkansas</td><td>29.0</td><td>4</td><td>Alabama</td><td>31.2</td></tr>
<tr><td>22</td><td>California</td><td>25.7</td><td>5</td><td>Tennessee</td><td>30.2</td></tr>
<tr><td>49</td><td>Colorado</td><td>20.1</td><td>6</td><td>Oklahoma</td><td>29.8</td></tr>
<tr><td>38</td><td>Connecticut</td><td>23.8</td><td>7</td><td>Louisiana</td><td>29.4</td></tr>
<tr><td>11</td><td>Delaware</td><td>28.0</td><td>8</td><td>North Carolina</td><td>29.2</td></tr>
<tr><td>13</td><td>Florida</td><td>27.7</td><td>9</td><td>Arkansas</td><td>29.0</td></tr>
<tr><td>18</td><td>Georgia</td><td>26.5</td><td>10</td><td>Kentucky</td><td>28.2</td></tr>
<tr><td>33</td><td>Hawaii</td><td>24.2</td><td>11</td><td>Delaware</td><td>28.0</td></tr>
<tr><td>40</td><td>Idaho</td><td>23.6</td><td>12</td><td>Michigan</td><td>27.8</td></tr>
<tr><td>24</td><td>Illinois</td><td>25.5</td><td>13</td><td>Florida</td><td>27.7</td></tr>
<tr><td>20</td><td>Indiana</td><td>26.2</td><td>14</td><td>Missouri</td><td>27.3</td></tr>
<tr><td>30</td><td>Iowa</td><td>24.5</td><td>15</td><td>Pennsylvania</td><td>27.2</td></tr>
<tr><td>33</td><td>Kansas</td><td>24.2</td><td>16</td><td>Ohio</td><td>27.0</td></tr>
<tr><td>10</td><td>Kentucky</td><td>28.2</td><td>17</td><td>Virginia</td><td>26.8</td></tr>
<tr><td>7</td><td>Louisiana</td><td>29.4</td><td>18</td><td>Georgia</td><td>26.5</td></tr>
<tr><td>23</td><td>Maine</td><td>25.6</td><td>19</td><td>Rhode Island</td><td>26.3</td></tr>
<tr><td>21</td><td>Maryland</td><td>26.0</td><td>20</td><td>Indiana</td><td>26.2</td></tr>
<tr><td>29</td><td>Massachusetts</td><td>24.8</td><td>21</td><td>Maryland</td><td>26.0</td></tr>
<tr><td>12</td><td>Michigan</td><td>27.8</td><td>22</td><td>California</td><td>25.7</td></tr>
<tr><td>47</td><td>Minnesota</td><td>21.9</td><td>23</td><td>Maine</td><td>25.6</td></tr>
<tr><td>1</td><td>Mississippi</td><td>33.3</td><td>24</td><td>Illinois</td><td>25.5</td></tr>
<tr><td>14</td><td>Missouri</td><td>27.3</td><td>24</td><td>New York</td><td>25.5</td></tr>
<tr><td>37</td><td>Montana</td><td>24.0</td><td>26</td><td>New Jersey</td><td>25.4</td></tr>
<tr><td>30</td><td>Nebraska</td><td>24.5</td><td>27</td><td>South Dakota</td><td>25.1</td></tr>
<tr><td>35</td><td>Nevada</td><td>24.1</td><td>28</td><td>Wisconsin</td><td>25.0</td></tr>
<tr><td>42</td><td>New Hampshire</td><td>23.3</td><td>29</td><td>Massachusetts</td><td>24.8</td></tr>
<tr><td>26</td><td>New Jersey</td><td>25.4</td><td>30</td><td>Iowa</td><td>24.5</td></tr>
<tr><td>45</td><td>New Mexico</td><td>22.8</td><td>30</td><td>Nebraska</td><td>24.5</td></tr>
<tr><td>24</td><td>New York</td><td>25.5</td><td>32</td><td>Texas</td><td>24.3</td></tr>
<tr><td>8</td><td>North Carolina</td><td>29.2</td><td>33</td><td>Hawaii</td><td>24.2</td></tr>
<tr><td>42</td><td>North Dakota</td><td>23.3</td><td>33</td><td>Kansas</td><td>24.2</td></tr>
<tr><td>16</td><td>Ohio</td><td>27.0</td><td>35</td><td>Nevada</td><td>24.1</td></tr>
<tr><td>6</td><td>Oklahoma</td><td>29.8</td><td>35</td><td>Washington</td><td>24.1</td></tr>
<tr><td>40</td><td>Oregon</td><td>23.6</td><td>37</td><td>Montana</td><td>24.0</td></tr>
<tr><td>15</td><td>Pennsylvania</td><td>27.2</td><td>38</td><td>Connecticut</td><td>23.8</td></tr>
<tr><td>19</td><td>Rhode Island</td><td>26.3</td><td>39</td><td>Vermont</td><td>23.7</td></tr>
<tr><td>2</td><td>South Carolina</td><td>31.4</td><td>40</td><td>Idaho</td><td>23.6</td></tr>
<tr><td>27</td><td>South Dakota</td><td>25.1</td><td>40</td><td>Oregon</td><td>23.6</td></tr>
<tr><td>5</td><td>Tennessee</td><td>30.2</td><td>42</td><td>New Hampshire</td><td>23.3</td></tr>
<tr><td>32</td><td>Texas</td><td>24.3</td><td>42</td><td>North Dakota</td><td>23.3</td></tr>
<tr><td>50</td><td>Utah</td><td>18.4</td><td>42</td><td>Wyoming</td><td>23.3</td></tr>
<tr><td>39</td><td>Vermont</td><td>23.7</td><td>45</td><td>New Mexico</td><td>22.8</td></tr>
<tr><td>17</td><td>Virginia</td><td>26.8</td><td>46</td><td>Arizona</td><td>22.3</td></tr>
<tr><td>35</td><td>Washington</td><td>24.1</td><td>47</td><td>Minnesota</td><td>21.9</td></tr>
<tr><td>2</td><td>West Virginia</td><td>31.4</td><td>48</td><td>Alaska</td><td>21.5</td></tr>
<tr><td>28</td><td>Wisconsin</td><td>25.0</td><td>49</td><td>Colorado</td><td>20.1</td></tr>
<tr><td>42</td><td>Wyoming</td><td>23.3</td><td>50</td><td>Utah</td><td>18.4</td></tr>
<tr><td></td><td></td><td></td><td></td><td>District of Columbia</td><td>27.1</td></tr>
</table>

Source: U.S. Department of Health and Human Services, Centers for Disease Control and Prevention
"2005 Behavioral Risk Factor Surveillance Summary Prevalence Data" (http://apps.nccd.cdc.gov/brfss/)
*Persons 18 and older who have been told by a doctor, nurse, or other health professional that they have high blood pressure.

Percent of Adults with High Cholesterol: 2005

National Median = 35.6% of Adults*

ALPHA ORDER

RANK	STATE	PERCENT
7	Alabama	38.3
46	Alaska	32.8
37	Arizona	33.8
12	Arkansas	37.5
30	California	35.2
44	Colorado	33.1
37	Connecticut	33.8
4	Delaware	38.9
2	Florida	39.7
48	Georgia	32.3
33	Hawaii	34.6
19	Idaho	36.3
21	Illinois	36.2
9	Indiana	38.0
26	Iowa	35.6
40	Kansas	33.4
8	Kentucky	38.1
50	Louisiana	30.3
21	Maine	36.2
43	Maryland	33.2
25	Massachusetts	35.7
4	Michigan	38.9
47	Minnesota	32.6
11	Mississippi	37.6
6	Missouri	38.7
40	Montana	33.4
30	Nebraska	35.2
3	Nevada	39.2
29	New Hampshire	35.3
17	New Jersey	36.7
49	New Mexico	30.6
27	New York	35.5
19	North Carolina	36.3
32	North Dakota	35.0
13	Ohio	37.2
10	Oklahoma	37.8
24	Oregon	35.8
16	Pennsylvania	37.0
33	Rhode Island	34.6
13	South Carolina	37.2
35	South Dakota	34.0
45	Tennessee	32.9
35	Texas	34.0
42	Utah	33.3
39	Vermont	33.7
15	Virginia	37.1
17	Washington	36.7
1	West Virginia	39.9
27	Wisconsin	35.5
23	Wyoming	35.9

RANK ORDER

RANK	STATE	PERCENT
1	West Virginia	39.9
2	Florida	39.7
3	Nevada	39.2
4	Delaware	38.9
4	Michigan	38.9
6	Missouri	38.7
7	Alabama	38.3
8	Kentucky	38.1
9	Indiana	38.0
10	Oklahoma	37.8
11	Mississippi	37.6
12	Arkansas	37.5
13	Ohio	37.2
13	South Carolina	37.2
15	Virginia	37.1
16	Pennsylvania	37.0
17	New Jersey	36.7
17	Washington	36.7
19	Idaho	36.3
19	North Carolina	36.3
21	Illinois	36.2
21	Maine	36.2
23	Wyoming	35.9
24	Oregon	35.8
25	Massachusetts	35.7
26	Iowa	35.6
27	New York	35.5
27	Wisconsin	35.5
29	New Hampshire	35.3
30	California	35.2
30	Nebraska	35.2
32	North Dakota	35.0
33	Hawaii	34.6
33	Rhode Island	34.6
35	South Dakota	34.0
35	Texas	34.0
37	Arizona	33.8
37	Connecticut	33.8
39	Vermont	33.7
40	Kansas	33.4
40	Montana	33.4
42	Utah	33.3
43	Maryland	33.2
44	Colorado	33.1
45	Tennessee	32.9
46	Alaska	32.8
47	Minnesota	32.6
48	Georgia	32.3
49	New Mexico	30.6
50	Louisiana	30.3

District of Columbia — 31.5

Source: U.S. Department of Health and Human Services, Centers for Disease Control and Prevention
"2005 Behavioral Risk Factor Surveillance Summary Prevalence Data" (http://apps.nccd.cdc.gov/brfss/)
*Persons 18 and older who have had their cholesterol checked and have been told that they have high blood cholesterol.

Percent of Adults Who Have Visited a Dentist or Dental Clinic: 2006

National Median = 70.3%*

ALPHA ORDER			RANK ORDER		
RANK	STATE	PERCENT	RANK	STATE	PERCENT
34	Alabama	68.0	1	Connecticut	80.5
37	Alaska	66.9	2	Rhode Island	80.4
30	Arizona	68.5	3	Minnesota	78.7
48	Arkansas	60.2	4	Massachusetts	78.1
30	California	68.5	5	New Hampshire	77.1
25	Colorado	70.3	6	Delaware	76.3
1	Connecticut	80.5	6	Wisconsin	76.3
6	Delaware	76.3	8	Michigan	75.1
28	Florida	68.7	9	Maryland	75.0
22	Georgia	70.7	10	New Jersey	74.5
11	Hawaii	73.7	11	Hawaii	73.7
37	Idaho	66.9	11	Iowa	73.7
27	Illinois	68.8	13	Vermont	73.5
34	Indiana	68.0	14	Ohio	73.4
11	Iowa	73.7	15	Virginia	73.2
24	Kansas	70.4	16	Nebraska	72.6
45	Kentucky	63.3	17	North Dakota	72.2
43	Louisiana	63.5	18	New York	71.8
21	Maine	70.9	19	Washington	71.6
9	Maryland	75.0	20	Pennsylvania	71.3
4	Massachusetts	78.1	21	Maine	70.9
8	Michigan	75.1	22	Georgia	70.7
3	Minnesota	78.7	23	Utah	70.6
49	Mississippi	59.4	24	Kansas	70.4
46	Missouri	61.7	25	Colorado	70.3
32	Montana	68.3	26	South Dakota	69.5
16	Nebraska	72.6	27	Illinois	68.8
39	Nevada	66.2	28	Florida	68.7
5	New Hampshire	77.1	29	Oregon	68.6
10	New Jersey	74.5	30	Arizona	68.5
41	New Mexico	64.9	30	California	68.5
18	New York	71.8	32	Montana	68.3
36	North Carolina	67.0	33	Wyoming	68.2
17	North Dakota	72.2	34	Alabama	68.0
14	Ohio	73.4	34	Indiana	68.0
50	Oklahoma	58.0	36	North Carolina	67.0
29	Oregon	68.6	37	Alaska	66.9
20	Pennsylvania	71.3	37	Idaho	66.9
2	Rhode Island	80.4	39	Nevada	66.2
39	South Carolina	66.2	39	South Carolina	66.2
26	South Dakota	69.5	41	New Mexico	64.9
42	Tennessee	64.8	42	Tennessee	64.8
43	Texas	63.5	43	Louisiana	63.5
23	Utah	70.6	43	Texas	63.5
13	Vermont	73.5	45	Kentucky	63.3
15	Virginia	73.2	46	Missouri	61.7
19	Washington	71.6	47	West Virginia	61.4
47	West Virginia	61.4	48	Arkansas	60.2
6	Wisconsin	76.3	49	Mississippi	59.4
33	Wyoming	68.2	50	Oklahoma	58.0
				District of Columbia	71.4

Source: U.S. Department of Health and Human Services, Centers for Disease Control and Prevention
"2006 Behavioral Risk Factor Surveillance Summary Prevalence Data" (http://apps.nccd.cdc.gov/brfss/)
*Persons 18 and older who have visited a dentist within the past year for any reason.

Percent of Adults 65 Years Old and Older
Who Have Lost All Their Natural Teeth: 2006
National Median = 19.3%*

ALPHA ORDER

RANK ORDER

RANK	STATE	PERCENT		RANK	STATE	PERCENT
7	Alabama	27.2		1	West Virginia	40.5
12	Alaska	23.6		2	Kentucky	38.9
46	Arizona	14.3		3	Tennessee	34.9
15	Arkansas	22.7		4	Mississippi	31.5
47	California	14.0		5	Louisiana	28.9
48	Colorado	12.9		6	Oklahoma	28.3
49	Connecticut	12.8		7	Alabama	27.2
35	Delaware	17.8		8	Maine	26.2
37	Florida	17.4		9	Missouri	24.1
18	Georgia	21.5		10	Pennsylvania	23.9
50	Hawaii	9.6		11	New Mexico	23.8
23	Idaho	19.7		12	Alaska	23.6
25	Illinois	19.3		13	South Carolina	23.0
20	Indiana	21.2		14	North Dakota	22.9
22	Iowa	19.8		15	Arkansas	22.7
26	Kansas	19.1		16	North Carolina	22.6
2	Kentucky	38.9		17	Ohio	21.6
5	Louisiana	28.9		18	Georgia	21.5
8	Maine	26.2		19	South Dakota	21.4
41	Maryland	16.2		20	Indiana	21.2
39	Massachusetts	17.2		21	Wyoming	20.1
38	Michigan	17.3		22	Iowa	19.8
27	Minnesota	18.6		23	Idaho	19.7
4	Mississippi	31.5		23	Vermont	19.7
9	Missouri	24.1		25	Illinois	19.3
32	Montana	18.2		26	Kansas	19.1
27	Nebraska	18.6		27	Minnesota	18.6
31	Nevada	18.4		27	Nebraska	18.6
27	New Hampshire	18.6		27	New Hampshire	18.6
32	New Jersey	18.2		27	Texas	18.6
11	New Mexico	23.8		31	Nevada	18.4
36	New York	17.5		32	Montana	18.2
16	North Carolina	22.6		32	New Jersey	18.2
14	North Dakota	22.9		34	Rhode Island	17.9
17	Ohio	21.6		35	Delaware	17.8
6	Oklahoma	28.3		36	New York	17.5
42	Oregon	15.9		37	Florida	17.4
10	Pennsylvania	23.9		38	Michigan	17.3
34	Rhode Island	17.9		39	Massachusetts	17.2
13	South Carolina	23.0		40	Wisconsin	16.9
19	South Dakota	21.4		41	Maryland	16.2
3	Tennessee	34.9		42	Oregon	15.9
27	Texas	18.6		43	Washington	15.4
44	Utah	14.8		44	Utah	14.8
23	Vermont	19.7		45	Virginia	14.4
45	Virginia	14.4		46	Arizona	14.3
43	Washington	15.4		47	California	14.0
1	West Virginia	40.5		48	Colorado	12.9
40	Wisconsin	16.9		49	Connecticut	12.8
21	Wyoming	20.1		50	Hawaii	9.6
					District of Columbia	20.8

Source: U.S. Department of Health and Human Services, Centers for Disease Control and Prevention
  "2006 Behavioral Risk Factor Surveillance Summary Prevalence Data" (http://apps.nccd.cdc.gov/brfss/)
*Those who have had all their natural teeth extracted.

Percent of Adults Who Average Five or More Servings of Fruits and Vegetables Each Day: 2005
National Median = 23.2%*

RANK	STATE	PERCENT
44	Alabama	20.1
16	Alaska	24.8
23	Arizona	23.7
40	Arkansas	21.0
3	California	28.9
18	Colorado	24.5
7	Connecticut	27.4
38	Delaware	21.3
10	Florida	26.2
24	Georgia	23.2
18	Hawaii	24.5
24	Idaho	23.2
21	Illinois	24.0
34	Indiana	22.0
47	Iowa	19.5
46	Kansas	19.9
48	Kentucky	16.8
42	Louisiana	20.2
4	Maine	28.7
4	Maryland	28.7
6	Massachusetts	28.6
26	Michigan	22.8
18	Minnesota	24.5
49	Mississippi	16.5
27	Missouri	22.6
17	Montana	24.7
42	Nebraska	20.2
30	Nevada	22.5
2	New Hampshire	29.1
13	New Jersey	25.9
37	New Mexico	21.5
12	New York	26.0
30	North Carolina	22.5
35	North Dakota	21.8
27	Ohio	22.6
50	Oklahoma	15.7
13	Oregon	25.9
22	Pennsylvania	23.9
8	Rhode Island	26.8
39	South Carolina	21.2
41	South Dakota	20.5
9	Tennessee	26.5
27	Texas	22.6
33	Utah	22.1
1	Vermont	30.8
10	Virginia	26.2
15	Washington	25.2
45	West Virginia	20.0
32	Wisconsin	22.2
35	Wyoming	21.8

RANK	STATE	PERCENT
1	Vermont	30.8
2	New Hampshire	29.1
3	California	28.9
4	Maine	28.7
4	Maryland	28.7
6	Massachusetts	28.6
7	Connecticut	27.4
8	Rhode Island	26.8
9	Tennessee	26.5
10	Florida	26.2
10	Virginia	26.2
12	New York	26.0
13	New Jersey	25.9
13	Oregon	25.9
15	Washington	25.2
16	Alaska	24.8
17	Montana	24.7
18	Colorado	24.5
18	Hawaii	24.5
18	Minnesota	24.5
21	Illinois	24.0
22	Pennsylvania	23.9
23	Arizona	23.7
24	Georgia	23.2
24	Idaho	23.2
26	Michigan	22.8
27	Missouri	22.6
27	Ohio	22.6
27	Texas	22.6
30	Nevada	22.5
30	North Carolina	22.5
32	Wisconsin	22.2
33	Utah	22.1
34	Indiana	22.0
35	North Dakota	21.8
35	Wyoming	21.8
37	New Mexico	21.5
38	Delaware	21.3
39	South Carolina	21.2
40	Arkansas	21.0
41	South Dakota	20.5
42	Louisiana	20.2
42	Nebraska	20.2
44	Alabama	20.1
45	West Virginia	20.0
46	Kansas	19.9
47	Iowa	19.5
48	Kentucky	16.8
49	Mississippi	16.5
50	Oklahoma	15.7

	District of Columbia	32.3

Source: U.S. Department of Health and Human Services, Centers for Disease Control and Prevention
  "2005 Behavioral Risk Factor Surveillance Summary Prevalence Data" (http://apps.nccd.cdc.gov/brfss/)
*Persons 18 and older.

Percent of Adults Rating Their Health as Fair or Poor in 2006

National Median = 14.6% of Adults*

ALPHA ORDER			RANK ORDER		
RANK	STATE	PERCENT	RANK	STATE	PERCENT
4	Alabama	21.2	1	Kentucky	23.1
39	Alaska	12.6	2	Mississippi	22.5
19	Arizona	16.3	3	West Virginia	22.4
6	Arkansas	19.6	4	Alabama	21.2
7	California	19.0	5	Oklahoma	20.2
44	Colorado	11.7	6	Arkansas	19.6
45	Connecticut	11.5	7	California	19.0
43	Delaware	12.1	8	Tennessee	18.8
15	Florida	16.8	9	Louisiana	18.5
23	Georgia	14.8	9	Nevada	18.5
24	Hawaii	14.7	11	North Carolina	18.1
30	Idaho	13.9	12	New Mexico	17.8
20	Illinois	16.2	13	Texas	17.4
18	Indiana	16.4	14	South Carolina	17.0
36	Iowa	13.0	15	Florida	16.8
27	Kansas	14.2	15	Missouri	16.8
1	Kentucky	23.1	17	New York	16.7
9	Louisiana	18.5	18	Indiana	16.4
32	Maine	13.8	19	Arizona	16.3
40	Maryland	12.5	20	Illinois	16.2
41	Massachusetts	12.4	20	New Jersey	16.2
22	Michigan	15.3	22	Michigan	15.3
50	Minnesota	10.8	23	Georgia	14.8
2	Mississippi	22.5	24	Hawaii	14.7
15	Missouri	16.8	24	Pennsylvania	14.7
34	Montana	13.2	26	Ohio	14.6
37	Nebraska	12.9	27	Kansas	14.2
9	Nevada	18.5	27	Oregon	14.2
48	New Hampshire	11.1	29	Rhode Island	14.1
20	New Jersey	16.2	30	Idaho	13.9
12	New Mexico	17.8	30	Wyoming	13.9
17	New York	16.7	32	Maine	13.8
11	North Carolina	18.1	33	Washington	13.5
45	North Dakota	11.5	34	Montana	13.2
26	Ohio	14.6	35	Virginia	13.1
5	Oklahoma	20.2	36	Iowa	13.0
27	Oregon	14.2	37	Nebraska	12.9
24	Pennsylvania	14.7	37	Utah	12.9
29	Rhode Island	14.1	39	Alaska	12.6
14	South Carolina	17.0	40	Maryland	12.5
45	South Dakota	11.5	41	Massachusetts	12.4
8	Tennessee	18.8	42	Wisconsin	12.2
13	Texas	17.4	43	Delaware	12.1
37	Utah	12.9	44	Colorado	11.7
49	Vermont	11.0	45	Connecticut	11.5
35	Virginia	13.1	45	North Dakota	11.5
33	Washington	13.5	45	South Dakota	11.5
3	West Virginia	22.4	48	New Hampshire	11.1
42	Wisconsin	12.2	49	Vermont	11.0
30	Wyoming	13.9	50	Minnesota	10.8
				District of Columbia	13.0

Source: U.S. Department of Health and Human Services, Centers for Disease Control and Prevention
   "2006 Behavioral Risk Factor Surveillance Summary Prevalence Data" (http://apps.nccd.cdc.gov/brfss/)
*Persons 18 and older.

Safety Belt Usage Rate in 2006

National Rate = 81.0% Use Safety Belts*

ALPHA ORDER				RANK ORDER		
RANK	STATE	PERCENT		RANK	STATE	PERCENT
20	Alabama	82.9		1	Washington	96.3
18	Alaska	83.2		2	Michigan	94.3
NA	Arizona**	NA		3	Oregon	94.1
38	Arkansas	69.3		4	California	93.4
4	California	93.4		5	Hawaii	92.5
23	Colorado	80.3		6	Texas	90.4
16	Connecticut	83.5		7	New Jersey	90.0
13	Delaware	86.1		8	Iowa	89.6
NA	Florida**	NA		8	New Mexico	89.6
NA	Georgia**	NA		10	Utah	88.6
5	Hawaii	92.5		11	North Carolina	88.5
24	Idaho	79.8		12	Illinois	87.8
12	Illinois	87.8		13	Delaware	86.1
14	Indiana	84.3		14	Indiana	84.3
8	Iowa	89.6		15	Oklahoma	83.7
35	Kansas	73.5		16	Connecticut	83.5
39	Kentucky	67.2		17	Minnesota	83.3
33	Louisiana	74.8		18	Alaska	83.2
29	Maine	77.2		19	New York	83.0
NA	Maryland**	NA		20	Alabama	82.9
40	Massachusetts	66.9		21	Vermont	82.4
2	Michigan	94.3		22	Ohio	81.7
17	Minnesota	83.3		23	Colorado	80.3
34	Mississippi	73.6		24	Idaho	79.8
32	Missouri	75.2		25	Montana	79.0
25	Montana	79.0		25	North Dakota	79.0
30	Nebraska	76.0		27	Virginia	78.7
NA	Nevada**	NA		28	Tennessee	78.6
NA	New Hampshire**	NA		29	Maine	77.2
7	New Jersey	90.0		30	Nebraska	76.0
8	New Mexico	89.6		31	Wisconsin	75.4
19	New York	83.0		32	Missouri	75.2
11	North Carolina	88.5		33	Louisiana	74.8
25	North Dakota	79.0		34	Mississippi	73.6
22	Ohio	81.7		35	Kansas	73.5
15	Oklahoma	83.7		36	South Carolina	72.5
3	Oregon	94.1		37	South Dakota	71.3
NA	Pennsylvania**	NA		38	Arkansas	69.3
NA	Rhode Island**	NA		39	Kentucky	67.2
36	South Carolina	72.5		40	Massachusetts	66.9
37	South Dakota	71.3		41	Wyoming	63.5
28	Tennessee	78.6		NA	Arizona**	NA
6	Texas	90.4		NA	Florida**	NA
10	Utah	88.6		NA	Georgia**	NA
21	Vermont	82.4		NA	Maryland**	NA
27	Virginia	78.7		NA	Nevada**	NA
1	Washington	96.3		NA	New Hampshire**	NA
NA	West Virginia**	NA		NA	Pennsylvania**	NA
31	Wisconsin	75.4		NA	Rhode Island**	NA
41	Wyoming	63.5		NA	West Virginia**	NA
					District of Columbia	85.4

Source: U.S. Department of Transportation, National Highway Traffic Safety Administration
"Safety Belt Use in 2006" (http://www-nrd.nhtsa.dot.gov/pdf/nrd-30/NCSA/RNotes/2007/810690.pdf)
*National estimate is from the National Occupant Protection Use Survey (NOPUS) using a different methodology.
**Not available.

VIII. Appendix

Population in 2007 530
Population in 2006 531
Male Population in 2006 532
Female Population in 2006 533

Population in 2007

National Total = 301,621,157*

ALPHA ORDER

RANK	STATE	POPULATION	% of USA
23	Alabama	4,627,851	1.5%
47	Alaska	683,478	0.2%
16	Arizona	6,338,755	2.1%
32	Arkansas	2,834,797	0.9%
1	California	36,553,215	12.1%
22	Colorado	4,861,515	1.6%
29	Connecticut	3,502,309	1.2%
45	Delaware	864,764	0.3%
4	Florida	18,251,243	6.1%
9	Georgia	9,544,750	3.2%
42	Hawaii	1,283,388	0.4%
39	Idaho	1,499,402	0.5%
5	Illinois	12,852,548	4.3%
15	Indiana	6,345,289	2.1%
30	Iowa	2,988,046	1.0%
33	Kansas	2,775,997	0.9%
26	Kentucky	4,241,474	1.4%
25	Louisiana	4,293,204	1.4%
40	Maine	1,317,207	0.4%
19	Maryland	5,618,344	1.9%
14	Massachusetts	6,449,755	2.1%
8	Michigan	10,071,822	3.3%
21	Minnesota	5,197,621	1.7%
31	Mississippi	2,918,785	1.0%
18	Missouri	5,878,415	1.9%
44	Montana	957,861	0.3%
38	Nebraska	1,774,571	0.6%
35	Nevada	2,565,382	0.9%
41	New Hampshire	1,315,828	0.4%
11	New Jersey	8,685,920	2.9%
36	New Mexico	1,969,915	0.7%
3	New York	19,297,729	6.4%
10	North Carolina	9,061,032	3.0%
48	North Dakota	639,715	0.2%
7	Ohio	11,466,917	3.8%
28	Oklahoma	3,617,316	1.2%
27	Oregon	3,747,455	1.2%
6	Pennsylvania	12,432,792	4.1%
43	Rhode Island	1,057,832	0.4%
24	South Carolina	4,407,709	1.5%
46	South Dakota	796,214	0.3%
17	Tennessee	6,156,719	2.0%
2	Texas	23,904,380	7.9%
34	Utah	2,645,330	0.9%
49	Vermont	621,254	0.2%
12	Virginia	7,712,091	2.6%
13	Washington	6,468,424	2.1%
37	West Virginia	1,812,035	0.6%
20	Wisconsin	5,601,640	1.9%
50	Wyoming	522,830	0.2%

RANK ORDER

RANK	STATE	POPULATION	% of USA
1	California	36,553,215	12.1%
2	Texas	23,904,380	7.9%
3	New York	19,297,729	6.4%
4	Florida	18,251,243	6.1%
5	Illinois	12,852,548	4.3%
6	Pennsylvania	12,432,792	4.1%
7	Ohio	11,466,917	3.8%
8	Michigan	10,071,822	3.3%
9	Georgia	9,544,750	3.2%
10	North Carolina	9,061,032	3.0%
11	New Jersey	8,685,920	2.9%
12	Virginia	7,712,091	2.6%
13	Washington	6,468,424	2.1%
14	Massachusetts	6,449,755	2.1%
15	Indiana	6,345,289	2.1%
16	Arizona	6,338,755	2.1%
17	Tennessee	6,156,719	2.0%
18	Missouri	5,878,415	1.9%
19	Maryland	5,618,344	1.9%
20	Wisconsin	5,601,640	1.9%
21	Minnesota	5,197,621	1.7%
22	Colorado	4,861,515	1.6%
23	Alabama	4,627,851	1.5%
24	South Carolina	4,407,709	1.5%
25	Louisiana	4,293,204	1.4%
26	Kentucky	4,241,474	1.4%
27	Oregon	3,747,455	1.2%
28	Oklahoma	3,617,316	1.2%
29	Connecticut	3,502,309	1.2%
30	Iowa	2,988,046	1.0%
31	Mississippi	2,918,785	1.0%
32	Arkansas	2,834,797	0.9%
33	Kansas	2,775,997	0.9%
34	Utah	2,645,330	0.9%
35	Nevada	2,565,382	0.9%
36	New Mexico	1,969,915	0.7%
37	West Virginia	1,812,035	0.6%
38	Nebraska	1,774,571	0.6%
39	Idaho	1,499,402	0.5%
40	Maine	1,317,207	0.4%
41	New Hampshire	1,315,828	0.4%
42	Hawaii	1,283,388	0.4%
43	Rhode Island	1,057,832	0.4%
44	Montana	957,861	0.3%
45	Delaware	864,764	0.3%
46	South Dakota	796,214	0.3%
47	Alaska	683,478	0.2%
48	North Dakota	639,715	0.2%
49	Vermont	621,254	0.2%
50	Wyoming	522,830	0.2%
	District of Columbia	588,292	0.2%

Source: U.S. Bureau of the Census
  "Population Estimates" (December 21, 2007, http://www.census.gov/popest/estimates.php)
*Resident population.

Population in 2006

National Total = 298,754,819*

ALPHA ORDER

RANK	STATE	POPULATION	% of USA
23	Alabama	4,590,240	1.5%
47	Alaska	677,450	0.2%
16	Arizona	6,165,689	2.1%
32	Arkansas	2,809,111	0.9%
1	California	36,249,872	12.1%
22	Colorado	4,766,248	1.6%
29	Connecticut	3,495,753	1.2%
45	Delaware	852,747	0.3%
4	Florida	18,057,508	6.0%
9	Georgia	9,342,080	3.1%
42	Hawaii	1,278,635	0.4%
39	Idaho	1,463,878	0.5%
5	Illinois	12,777,042	4.3%
15	Indiana	6,302,646	2.1%
30	Iowa	2,972,566	1.0%
33	Kansas	2,755,817	0.9%
26	Kentucky	4,204,444	1.4%
25	Louisiana	4,243,288	1.4%
40	Maine	1,314,910	0.4%
19	Maryland	5,602,017	1.9%
13	Massachusetts	6,434,389	2.2%
8	Michigan	10,102,322	3.4%
21	Minnesota	5,154,586	1.7%
31	Mississippi	2,899,112	1.0%
18	Missouri	5,837,639	2.0%
44	Montana	946,795	0.3%
38	Nebraska	1,763,765	0.6%
35	Nevada	2,492,427	0.8%
41	New Hampshire	1,311,821	0.4%
11	New Jersey	8,666,075	2.9%
36	New Mexico	1,942,302	0.7%
3	New York	19,281,988	6.5%
10	North Carolina	8,869,442	3.0%
48	North Dakota	637,460	0.2%
7	Ohio	11,463,513	3.8%
28	Oklahoma	3,577,536	1.2%
27	Oregon	3,691,084	1.2%
6	Pennsylvania	12,402,817	4.2%
43	Rhode Island	1,061,641	0.4%
24	South Carolina	4,330,108	1.4%
46	South Dakota	788,467	0.3%
17	Tennessee	6,074,913	2.0%
2	Texas	23,407,629	7.8%
34	Utah	2,579,535	0.9%
49	Vermont	620,778	0.2%
12	Virginia	7,640,249	2.6%
14	Washington	6,374,910	2.1%
37	West Virginia	1,808,699	0.6%
20	Wisconsin	5,572,660	1.9%
50	Wyoming	512,757	0.2%

RANK ORDER

RANK	STATE	POPULATION	% of USA
1	California	36,249,872	12.1%
2	Texas	23,407,629	7.8%
3	New York	19,281,988	6.5%
4	Florida	18,057,508	6.0%
5	Illinois	12,777,042	4.3%
6	Pennsylvania	12,402,817	4.2%
7	Ohio	11,463,513	3.8%
8	Michigan	10,102,322	3.4%
9	Georgia	9,342,080	3.1%
10	North Carolina	8,869,442	3.0%
11	New Jersey	8,666,075	2.9%
12	Virginia	7,640,249	2.6%
13	Massachusetts	6,434,389	2.2%
14	Washington	6,374,910	2.1%
15	Indiana	6,302,646	2.1%
16	Arizona	6,165,689	2.1%
17	Tennessee	6,074,913	2.0%
18	Missouri	5,837,639	2.0%
19	Maryland	5,602,017	1.9%
20	Wisconsin	5,572,660	1.9%
21	Minnesota	5,154,586	1.7%
22	Colorado	4,766,248	1.6%
23	Alabama	4,590,240	1.5%
24	South Carolina	4,330,108	1.4%
25	Louisiana	4,243,288	1.4%
26	Kentucky	4,204,444	1.4%
27	Oregon	3,691,084	1.2%
28	Oklahoma	3,577,536	1.2%
29	Connecticut	3,495,753	1.2%
30	Iowa	2,972,566	1.0%
31	Mississippi	2,899,112	1.0%
32	Arkansas	2,809,111	0.9%
33	Kansas	2,755,817	0.9%
34	Utah	2,579,535	0.9%
35	Nevada	2,492,427	0.8%
36	New Mexico	1,942,302	0.7%
37	West Virginia	1,808,699	0.6%
38	Nebraska	1,763,765	0.6%
39	Idaho	1,463,878	0.5%
40	Maine	1,314,910	0.4%
41	New Hampshire	1,311,821	0.4%
42	Hawaii	1,278,635	0.4%
43	Rhode Island	1,061,641	0.4%
44	Montana	946,795	0.3%
45	Delaware	852,747	0.3%
46	South Dakota	788,467	0.3%
47	Alaska	677,450	0.2%
48	North Dakota	637,460	0.2%
49	Vermont	620,778	0.2%
50	Wyoming	512,757	0.2%
	District of Columbia	585,459	0.2%

Source: U.S. Bureau of the Census
"Population Estimates" (December 21, 2007, http://www.census.gov/popest/estimates.php)
*Resident population. Revised estimates.

Male Population in 2006

National Total = 147,512,152 Males

<table>
<tr><td colspan="4">ALPHA ORDER</td><td colspan="4">RANK ORDER</td></tr>
<tr><th>RANK</th><th>STATE</th><th>MALES</th><th>% of USA</th><th>RANK</th><th>STATE</th><th>MALES</th><th>% of USA</th></tr>
<tr><td>23</td><td>Alabama</td><td>2,229,469</td><td>1.5%</td><td>1</td><td>California</td><td>18,224,444</td><td>12.4%</td></tr>
<tr><td>47</td><td>Alaska</td><td>346,411</td><td>0.2%</td><td>2</td><td>Texas</td><td>11,714,068</td><td>7.9%</td></tr>
<tr><td>16</td><td>Arizona</td><td>3,085,755</td><td>2.1%</td><td>3</td><td>New York</td><td>9,355,020</td><td>6.3%</td></tr>
<tr><td>32</td><td>Arkansas</td><td>1,377,711</td><td>0.9%</td><td>4</td><td>Florida</td><td>8,884,135</td><td>6.0%</td></tr>
<tr><td>1</td><td>California</td><td>18,224,444</td><td>12.4%</td><td>5</td><td>Illinois</td><td>6,317,460</td><td>4.3%</td></tr>
<tr><td>22</td><td>Colorado</td><td>2,393,004</td><td>1.6%</td><td>6</td><td>Pennsylvania</td><td>6,047,537</td><td>4.1%</td></tr>
<tr><td>29</td><td>Connecticut</td><td>1,706,188</td><td>1.2%</td><td>7</td><td>Ohio</td><td>5,597,677</td><td>3.8%</td></tr>
<tr><td>45</td><td>Delaware</td><td>414,244</td><td>0.3%</td><td>8</td><td>Michigan</td><td>4,969,692</td><td>3.4%</td></tr>
<tr><td>4</td><td>Florida</td><td>8,884,135</td><td>6.0%</td><td>9</td><td>Georgia</td><td>4,611,078</td><td>3.1%</td></tr>
<tr><td>9</td><td>Georgia</td><td>4,611,078</td><td>3.1%</td><td>10</td><td>North Carolina</td><td>4,341,298</td><td>2.9%</td></tr>
<tr><td>42</td><td>Hawaii</td><td>643,328</td><td>0.4%</td><td>11</td><td>New Jersey</td><td>4,262,291</td><td>2.9%</td></tr>
<tr><td>39</td><td>Idaho</td><td>738,366</td><td>0.5%</td><td>12</td><td>Virginia</td><td>3,756,771</td><td>2.5%</td></tr>
<tr><td>5</td><td>Illinois</td><td>6,317,460</td><td>4.3%</td><td>13</td><td>Washington</td><td>3,189,630</td><td>2.2%</td></tr>
<tr><td>15</td><td>Indiana</td><td>3,110,503</td><td>2.1%</td><td>14</td><td>Massachusetts</td><td>3,117,205</td><td>2.1%</td></tr>
<tr><td>30</td><td>Iowa</td><td>1,472,810</td><td>1.0%</td><td>15</td><td>Indiana</td><td>3,110,503</td><td>2.1%</td></tr>
<tr><td>33</td><td>Kansas</td><td>1,371,446</td><td>0.9%</td><td>16</td><td>Arizona</td><td>3,085,755</td><td>2.1%</td></tr>
<tr><td>26</td><td>Kentucky</td><td>2,061,310</td><td>1.4%</td><td>17</td><td>Tennessee</td><td>2,950,890</td><td>2.0%</td></tr>
<tr><td>25</td><td>Louisiana</td><td>2,085,761</td><td>1.4%</td><td>18</td><td>Missouri</td><td>2,854,715</td><td>1.9%</td></tr>
<tr><td>41</td><td>Maine</td><td>646,427</td><td>0.4%</td><td>19</td><td>Wisconsin</td><td>2,760,942</td><td>1.9%</td></tr>
<tr><td>20</td><td>Maryland</td><td>2,716,854</td><td>1.8%</td><td>20</td><td>Maryland</td><td>2,716,854</td><td>1.8%</td></tr>
<tr><td>14</td><td>Massachusetts</td><td>3,117,205</td><td>2.1%</td><td>21</td><td>Minnesota</td><td>2,568,869</td><td>1.7%</td></tr>
<tr><td>8</td><td>Michigan</td><td>4,969,692</td><td>3.4%</td><td>22</td><td>Colorado</td><td>2,393,004</td><td>1.6%</td></tr>
<tr><td>21</td><td>Minnesota</td><td>2,568,869</td><td>1.7%</td><td>23</td><td>Alabama</td><td>2,229,469</td><td>1.5%</td></tr>
<tr><td>31</td><td>Mississippi</td><td>1,409,348</td><td>1.0%</td><td>24</td><td>South Carolina</td><td>2,103,713</td><td>1.4%</td></tr>
<tr><td>18</td><td>Missouri</td><td>2,854,715</td><td>1.9%</td><td>25</td><td>Louisiana</td><td>2,085,761</td><td>1.4%</td></tr>
<tr><td>44</td><td>Montana</td><td>472,660</td><td>0.3%</td><td>26</td><td>Kentucky</td><td>2,061,310</td><td>1.4%</td></tr>
<tr><td>38</td><td>Nebraska</td><td>876,754</td><td>0.6%</td><td>27</td><td>Oregon</td><td>1,839,688</td><td>1.2%</td></tr>
<tr><td>35</td><td>Nevada</td><td>1,268,894</td><td>0.9%</td><td>28</td><td>Oklahoma</td><td>1,764,514</td><td>1.2%</td></tr>
<tr><td>40</td><td>New Hampshire</td><td>648,568</td><td>0.4%</td><td>29</td><td>Connecticut</td><td>1,706,188</td><td>1.2%</td></tr>
<tr><td>11</td><td>New Jersey</td><td>4,262,291</td><td>2.9%</td><td>30</td><td>Iowa</td><td>1,472,810</td><td>1.0%</td></tr>
<tr><td>36</td><td>New Mexico</td><td>964,808</td><td>0.7%</td><td>31</td><td>Mississippi</td><td>1,409,348</td><td>1.0%</td></tr>
<tr><td>3</td><td>New York</td><td>9,355,020</td><td>6.3%</td><td>32</td><td>Arkansas</td><td>1,377,711</td><td>0.9%</td></tr>
<tr><td>10</td><td>North Carolina</td><td>4,341,298</td><td>2.9%</td><td>33</td><td>Kansas</td><td>1,371,446</td><td>0.9%</td></tr>
<tr><td>48</td><td>North Dakota</td><td>319,427</td><td>0.2%</td><td>34</td><td>Utah</td><td>1,282,401</td><td>0.9%</td></tr>
<tr><td>7</td><td>Ohio</td><td>5,597,677</td><td>3.8%</td><td>35</td><td>Nevada</td><td>1,268,894</td><td>0.9%</td></tr>
<tr><td>28</td><td>Oklahoma</td><td>1,764,514</td><td>1.2%</td><td>36</td><td>New Mexico</td><td>964,808</td><td>0.7%</td></tr>
<tr><td>27</td><td>Oregon</td><td>1,839,688</td><td>1.2%</td><td>37</td><td>West Virginia</td><td>890,588</td><td>0.6%</td></tr>
<tr><td>6</td><td>Pennsylvania</td><td>6,047,537</td><td>4.1%</td><td>38</td><td>Nebraska</td><td>876,754</td><td>0.6%</td></tr>
<tr><td>43</td><td>Rhode Island</td><td>516,213</td><td>0.3%</td><td>39</td><td>Idaho</td><td>738,366</td><td>0.5%</td></tr>
<tr><td>24</td><td>South Carolina</td><td>2,103,713</td><td>1.4%</td><td>40</td><td>New Hampshire</td><td>648,568</td><td>0.4%</td></tr>
<tr><td>46</td><td>South Dakota</td><td>390,578</td><td>0.3%</td><td>41</td><td>Maine</td><td>646,427</td><td>0.4%</td></tr>
<tr><td>17</td><td>Tennessee</td><td>2,950,890</td><td>2.0%</td><td>42</td><td>Hawaii</td><td>643,328</td><td>0.4%</td></tr>
<tr><td>2</td><td>Texas</td><td>11,714,068</td><td>7.9%</td><td>43</td><td>Rhode Island</td><td>516,213</td><td>0.3%</td></tr>
<tr><td>34</td><td>Utah</td><td>1,282,401</td><td>0.9%</td><td>44</td><td>Montana</td><td>472,660</td><td>0.3%</td></tr>
<tr><td>49</td><td>Vermont</td><td>307,023</td><td>0.2%</td><td>45</td><td>Delaware</td><td>414,244</td><td>0.3%</td></tr>
<tr><td>12</td><td>Virginia</td><td>3,756,771</td><td>2.5%</td><td>46</td><td>South Dakota</td><td>390,578</td><td>0.3%</td></tr>
<tr><td>13</td><td>Washington</td><td>3,189,630</td><td>2.2%</td><td>47</td><td>Alaska</td><td>346,411</td><td>0.2%</td></tr>
<tr><td>37</td><td>West Virginia</td><td>890,588</td><td>0.6%</td><td>48</td><td>North Dakota</td><td>319,427</td><td>0.2%</td></tr>
<tr><td>19</td><td>Wisconsin</td><td>2,760,942</td><td>1.9%</td><td>49</td><td>Vermont</td><td>307,023</td><td>0.2%</td></tr>
<tr><td>50</td><td>Wyoming</td><td>261,002</td><td>0.2%</td><td>50</td><td>Wyoming</td><td>261,002</td><td>0.2%</td></tr>
<tr><td></td><td></td><td></td><td></td><td></td><td>District of Columbia</td><td>272,664</td><td>0.2%</td></tr>
</table>

Source: CQ Press using data from U.S. Bureau of the Census
  "SC-EST2006-AGESEX_RES - State Characteristic Estimates"
  (http://www.census.gov/popest/datasets.html)

Female Population in 2006

National Total = 151,886,332 Females

RANK	STATE	FEMALES	% of USA
22	Alabama	2,369,561	1.6%
47	Alaska	323,642	0.2%
17	Arizona	3,080,563	2.0%
32	Arkansas	1,433,161	0.9%
1	California	18,233,105	12.0%
23	Colorado	2,360,373	1.6%
29	Connecticut	1,798,621	1.2%
45	Delaware	439,232	0.3%
4	Florida	9,205,753	6.1%
9	Georgia	4,752,863	3.1%
42	Hawaii	642,170	0.4%
39	Idaho	728,099	0.5%
5	Illinois	6,514,510	4.3%
15	Indiana	3,203,017	2.1%
30	Iowa	1,509,275	1.0%
33	Kansas	1,392,629	0.9%
26	Kentucky	2,144,764	1.4%
25	Louisiana	2,202,007	1.4%
40	Maine	675,147	0.4%
19	Maryland	2,898,873	1.9%
13	Massachusetts	3,319,988	2.2%
8	Michigan	5,125,951	3.4%
21	Minnesota	2,598,232	1.7%
31	Mississippi	1,501,192	1.0%
18	Missouri	2,987,998	2.0%
44	Montana	471,972	0.3%
38	Nebraska	891,577	0.6%
35	Nevada	1,226,635	0.8%
41	New Hampshire	666,327	0.4%
11	New Jersey	4,462,269	2.9%
36	New Mexico	989,791	0.7%
3	New York	9,951,163	6.6%
10	North Carolina	4,515,207	3.0%
49	North Dakota	316,440	0.2%
7	Ohio	5,880,329	3.9%
28	Oklahoma	1,814,698	1.2%
27	Oregon	1,861,070	1.2%
6	Pennsylvania	6,393,084	4.2%
43	Rhode Island	551,397	0.4%
24	South Carolina	2,217,536	1.5%
46	South Dakota	391,341	0.3%
16	Tennessee	3,087,913	2.0%
2	Texas	11,793,715	7.8%
34	Utah	1,267,662	0.8%
48	Vermont	316,885	0.2%
12	Virginia	3,886,113	2.6%
14	Washington	3,206,168	2.1%
37	West Virginia	927,882	0.6%
20	Wisconsin	2,795,564	1.8%
50	Wyoming	254,002	0.2%

RANK	STATE	FEMALES	% of USA
1	California	18,233,105	12.0%
2	Texas	11,793,715	7.8%
3	New York	9,951,163	6.6%
4	Florida	9,205,753	6.1%
5	Illinois	6,514,510	4.3%
6	Pennsylvania	6,393,084	4.2%
7	Ohio	5,880,329	3.9%
8	Michigan	5,125,951	3.4%
9	Georgia	4,752,863	3.1%
10	North Carolina	4,515,207	3.0%
11	New Jersey	4,462,269	2.9%
12	Virginia	3,886,113	2.6%
13	Massachusetts	3,319,988	2.2%
14	Washington	3,206,168	2.1%
15	Indiana	3,203,017	2.1%
16	Tennessee	3,087,913	2.0%
17	Arizona	3,080,563	2.0%
18	Missouri	2,987,998	2.0%
19	Maryland	2,898,873	1.9%
20	Wisconsin	2,795,564	1.8%
21	Minnesota	2,598,232	1.7%
22	Alabama	2,369,561	1.6%
23	Colorado	2,360,373	1.6%
24	South Carolina	2,217,536	1.5%
25	Louisiana	2,202,007	1.4%
26	Kentucky	2,144,764	1.4%
27	Oregon	1,861,070	1.2%
28	Oklahoma	1,814,698	1.2%
29	Connecticut	1,798,621	1.2%
30	Iowa	1,509,275	1.0%
31	Mississippi	1,501,192	1.0%
32	Arkansas	1,433,161	0.9%
33	Kansas	1,392,629	0.9%
34	Utah	1,267,662	0.8%
35	Nevada	1,226,635	0.8%
36	New Mexico	989,791	0.7%
37	West Virginia	927,882	0.6%
38	Nebraska	891,577	0.6%
39	Idaho	728,099	0.5%
40	Maine	675,147	0.4%
41	New Hampshire	666,327	0.4%
42	Hawaii	642,170	0.4%
43	Rhode Island	551,397	0.4%
44	Montana	471,972	0.3%
45	Delaware	439,232	0.3%
46	South Dakota	391,341	0.3%
47	Alaska	323,642	0.2%
48	Vermont	316,885	0.2%
49	North Dakota	316,440	0.2%
50	Wyoming	254,002	0.2%
	District of Columbia	308,866	0.2%

Source: CQ Press using data from U.S. Bureau of the Census
"SC-EST2006-AGESEX_RES - State Characteristic Estimates"
(http://www.census.gov/popest/datasets.html)

Sources

American Academy of Physician Assistants
950 North Washington Street
Alexandria, VA 22314-1552
703-836-2272
www.aapa.org

American Cancer Society, Inc.
1599 Clifton Road, NE.
Atlanta, GA 30329-4251
800-227-2345
www.cancer.org

American Dental Association
211 E. Chicago Ave.
Chicago, IL 60611-2678
312-440-2500
www.ada.org

American Hospital Association
One North Franklin
Chicago, IL 60606-3421
312-422-3000
www.aha.org

American Medical Association
515 North State Street
Chicago, IL 60610
800-621-8335
www.ama-assn.org

American Osteopathic Association
142 East Ontario Street
Chicago, IL 60611
800-621-1773
www.osteopathic.org

Bureau of Labor Statistics
2 Massachusetts Ave., NE
Washington, D.C. 20212-0001
202-691-5200
www.bls.gov

Census Bureau
4700 Silver Hill Road
Washington, D.C. 20233-0001
301-457-2800
www.census.gov

Centers for Disease Control and Prevention
1600 Clifton Road, NE.
Atlanta, GA 30333
800-311-3435
www.cdc.gov

Centers for Medicare and Medicaid Services
7500 Security Boulevard
Baltimore, MD 21244-1850
877-267-2323
www.cms.hhs.gov

Federation of Chiropractic Licensing Boards
5401 W 10th Street, Ste 101
Greeley, CO 80634-4400
970-356-3500
www.fclb.org

Health Resources and Services Administration
Division of Practitioner Data Banks
5600 Fishers Lane
Rockville, MD 20857
800-767-6732
www.hrsa.gov

HealthLeaders/InterStudy
One Vantage Way, B-300
Nashville, TN 37228
615-385-4131
www.hmodata.com

Medical Expenditure Panel Survey
Agency for Healthcare Research and Quality
540 Gaither Road
Rockville, MD   20850
301-427-1364
www.meps.ahrq.gov

National Association of State Budget Officers
444 N Capitol St., NW, Ste 642
Washington, D.C.   20001-1551
202-624-5382
www.nasbo.org

National Center for Health Statistics
U.S. Department of Health and Human Services
3311 Toledo Road
Hyattsville, MD   20782
800-232-4636
www.cdc.gov/nchs/

National Institute on Alcohol Abuse and Alcoholism
National Institutes of Health
5635 Fishers Lane, MSC 9304
Bethesda, MD   20892-9304
301-443-3860
www.niaaa.nih.gov/

National Highway Traffic Safety Administration
1200 New Jersey Ave., SE
West Building
Washington, D.C.   20590
888-327-4236
www.nhtsa.dot.gov

National Sporting Goods Association
1601 Feehanville Drive, Ste 300
Mt. Prospect, IL   60056
800-815-5422
www.nsga.org

Substance Abuse and Mental Health Services Administration
1 Choke Cherry Road, Room 8-1036
Rockville, MD   20857
240-276-2130
www.samhsa.gov

Index

A

Abortion
    by age of woman, 81–85
    by stage of gestation, 86–89
    first time, percent, 75
    numbers of, 70
    rate of, 73
    ratio of, 72
    to out-of-state residents, 74
    to teenagers, 81–85
Accidents, deaths by, 170–172
Admissions to community hospitals, 205
AIDS
    cases, 364–367
    children cases, 367
    deaths, 137–139
Alcohol consumption, 500, 501
Alcohol-induced deaths, 185–187
Anesthesiologists, 450, 451
Alzheimer's Disease, deaths by, 140–142
Arthritis, percent with, 406
Assisted reproductive technology
    births from, 58–61
    multiple births from, 61
    procedures, 57
Asthma, percent with, 405

B

Beds, hospital
    average number per hospital, 204
    children's hospital, 216
    community hospital, 202–204
    nursing home, 229, 230
    psychiatric hospital, 220
    rehabilitation hospital, 218
Beer consumption, 502, 503
Binge drinkers, 509
Births
    by age of mother, 34–49
    by assisted reproductive technology, 58–61
    by method of delivery, 50–54
    by race of mother, 9–12, 17–20, 25–28, 40–43

Hispanic, 13, 14, 21
    low birthweight, 15–22, 22, 29, 30
    number of, 3, 6
    pre-term, 55
    rates, 2, 7
    to teenagers, 34–47
    to unmarried women, 23–30
    to young teens, 46, 47
    twin rate, 56
Bladder cancer, cases, 340, 341
Blood pressure, percent with high, 522
Brain cancer, deaths by, 117, 118
Breast cancer
    cases, 329, 330
    deaths, 118, 119

C

Cancer
    bladder cases, 340, 341
    brain deaths, 117, 118
    breast (female), 119, 120, 342, 343
    cases, total and by cause, 336–363
    cervical cases, 359, 360
    colon and rectum, 121, 122, 345, 346
    deaths by, 113–116
    leukemia, 123, 124
    liver deaths, 125, 126
    lung, 127, 128, 350, 351
    lymphoma, 129, 130, 352, 353
    ovarian deaths, 131, 132
    pancreatic deaths, 133, 134
    prostate, 135, 136, 354, 355
    skin melanoma cases, 357, 358
    uterine cases, 362, 363
Cerebrovascular disease, deaths by, 143–145
Cervical cancer cases, 359, 360
Cesarean births, 52–54
Children's hospitals, 215, 216
Children's insurance, 267–272
Chiropractors, 462, 463
Chlamydia cases, 399, 400
Cholesterol, percent with high, 523
Chronic liver disease, deaths by, 146–148

Chronic lower respiratory disease, deaths by, 149–151
Colon and rectum cancer
    cases, 345, 346
    deaths, 121, 122
Community hospitals
    beds in, 202–204
    number of, 192
    per square miles, 194
    rate of, 193
Community mental health centers, 222

D

Deaths
    by cause, 113–187
    infant, 101–106
    neonatal, 107–112
    numbers of, 92, 94, 98
    occupational, 188, 189
    rates, 93, 95–97, 99, 100
Dentists
    access to, 480
    expenditures for, 315–318
    number of, 477
    rate of, 478
    visits to, 524
Diabetes mellitus
    deaths by, 152–154
    percent of adults with, 407
Distilled spirits, consumption of, 506, 507
Doctors. See physicians
Drinkers, binge, 509
Drugs
    expenditures for, 327–329
    use of illicit, 515

E

Emergency medical technicians, 487–489
Emergency outpatient visits, 211
Employment, health industries, 411, 412, 490, 491
Exercise, 519, 520
Exercise equipment, use of, 495
Expenditures, personal health care, 305–307

F

Fatalities, occupational, 188, 189
Fertility, rate of, 8
Finance, health care, 237–333
Firearm injury, deaths from, 176–178
For-profit hospitals, 200

G

General surgeons, 438, 439
General/family practice physicians, 425, 426
Golf, participants in, 496
Gonorrhea, cases and rates, 401, 402
Government health expenditures, 298–303
Government health insurance, 258, 264
Graduates of international medical schools, 455, 456
Gynecologists and obstetricians, 440, 441

H

Health care support industries
    employment, 490, 491
    wages, 492
Health insurance. See insurance
Health Maintenance Organizations (HMOs), 273–277
Health practitioners
    employment, 411, 412
    wages of, 413
Health programs, government expenditures for, 301–303
Heart disease, deaths by, 155–157
Hepatitis, cases and rates, 372, 373
HMOs, 273–277
Home health agencies, 225
Homicide, deaths by, 179–181
Hospices, 226, 227
Hospital
    admissions, 205
    average stay in, 208
    beds, 202–204, 214, 216, 218, 220, 229, 230
    community, 192–211
    expenditures for care in, 309–311
    for profit, 200
    government expenditures for, 298–300
    in rural areas, 197, 198
    in urban areas, 195, 196
    non-government not-for-profit, 199
    number of, 192, 199–201, 213, 215, 217, 219,
    221–226, 228
    occupancy rate, 209
    psychiatric, 219, 220
    state and local government-owned, 201

I

Immunizations, 394
Infant deaths, 101–106
Influenza and pneumonia, deaths by, 164–166
Injury, deaths by, 167–169
Inpatient days, community hospitals, 206

Insurance
    children's health, 267–272
    coverage, 247–266
    employment-based, 256, 262
    government, 258, 264
    Medicaid, 266, 286–297
    Medicare, 278–285
    military health, 259, 265
    premiums, 241–246
    private health, 255, 261
    uninsured, 247–252
Internal medicine physicians, 431, 432
International medical school graduates, 455, 456
Investor-owned hospitals, 200

J

Jogging/running, participants in, 497

K

Kidney disease, deaths from, 161–163

L

Legionellosis, cases and rates, 374, 375
Leukemia, 123, 124, 348, 349
Licensed practical and vocational nurses, 471–473
Liquor, consumption of, 506, 507
Liver cancer, deaths, 125, 126
Liver disease, deaths by, 146, 147
Low birth weight births, 15–22
Lung cancer
    cases, 350, 351
    deaths, 127, 128
Lyme disease, cases and rates, 376, 377

M

Malaria, cases and rates, 378, 379
Malignant neoplasms (cancers) deaths, 158–160
Malpractice, medical payments, 237
Mammograms, prevalence of, 344
Managed health care, 273–277, 281, 288, 289
Medicaid
    children covered by, 266
    enrollees, 286, 288
    expenditures, 290–296
    facilities, 212–230
    federal match, 297
Medicare
    enrollees, 278–281
    facilities, 212–230
    managed care enrollees, 281
    payments, 283–285
    physicians, 282
Melanoma (skin cancer) cases, 357, 358
Meningitis, cases and rates, 380, 381
Mental health
    access to, 454
    community centers, 222
    percent with serious psychological
        distress, 408

Military health insurance, 259, 265
Mortality, 92–189
Mothers, teenage, 34–47
Motor vehicle accidents, deaths by, 173–175

N

Natality, 3–69
Neonatal deaths
    by race, 107–112
    number of, 107, 109, 111
    rate of , 108, 110, 112
Nephritis, deaths by, 161–163
Nondrinkers, 508
Non-government not-for-profit hospitals, 199
Nurses, 468–473
Nursing homes
    beds, 229, 230
    expenditures for care, 321–323
    numbers of, 228
    occupancy rate, 231
    resident rate, 232
    population, 233
Nutrition, fruit and vegetable intake, 526

O

Obese adults, 517, 518
Obstetricians and gynecologists, 440, 441
Occupancy rates, hospital, 209
Occupational fatalities, 188, 189
Ophthalmologists, 442, 443
Optometrists, 484–486
Osteopathic physicians, 457, 458
Outpatient visits, 210
Ovarian cancer deaths, 131, 132
Overweight or obese
    percent of adults, 516, 518

P

Pap smears, frequency of, 361
Paramedics, 487–489
Pediatric physicians, 433, 434
Pertussis, cases and rates, 392, 393
Pharmacists, 481–483
Physical therapists, 474–476
Physical therapy facilities, 223
Physician assistants, 465–467
Physicians
    Chiropractic, 462–464
    expenditures for services, 312–314
    M.D. by age, 417, 418
    M.D. by sex, 416
    M.D. by specialty, 425–453
    M.D. in patient care, 419, 420
    M.D. in primary care, 421–423
    Medicare participation, 282
    Osteopathic, 457, 458
    Podiatric, 459–461
Plastic surgeons, 446, 447
Pneumonia and influenza, deaths by, 164–166
Pneumonia vaccinations, 396

Podiatrists, 459–461
Pregnancy rate
    overall, 31
    teenage, 32, 33
Premiums, average for health insurance,
    241, 244
Prenatal care, 62–69
Prescription drugs, expenditures for,
    327–329
Pre-term births, 55
Primary care
    access to, 424
    physicians in, 421–423
Private health insurance, 255, 261
Prostate cancer
    cases, 354, 355
    deaths, 135, 136
Providers, health care, 411–492
PSA test, percent receiving, 356
Psychiatric hospitals, 219, 220
Psychiatrists, 452, 453

R
Rabies (animal), cases and rates, 382, 383
Rectum and colon cancer
    cases, 345, 346
    deaths, 121, 122
Registered nurses, 468–470

Rehabilitation hospitals, 217, 218
Respiratory diseases, deaths from, 149–151
Running/jogging, participants, 497
Rural health clinics, 224

S
Salmonellosis, cases and rates, 386, 387
SCHIP, 267–272
Seatbelt use, 528
Sexually transmitted diseases, 397–404
Shigellosis, cases and rates, 388, 389
Skin melanoma cases, 357, 358
Smokers
    by sex, 511, 512
    former, 513
    never have smoked, 514
    percent of adult population, 510
Specialists, medical, 429–453
Sports participation, 495–499
State and local government expenditures for
    health, 301–303
State and local government expenditures for
    hospitals, 298–300
State and local government-owned
    hospitals, 195
Suicide, deaths by, 201
Surgeons, 435–447
Surgery centers, 221

Swimming, participants, 498
Syphilis, cases and rates, 403, 404

T
Teenage births
    by race, 40–45
    number of, 34, 38
    rate of, 36, 39
    to young teens, 46, 47
Tennis, participants, 499
Tobacco settlement, state funds from, 304
Tooth loss, 525

U
Uninsured, 247–252
Unmarried women, births to, 23–30

V
Vaccinations, 394–396
Vaginal births, 50, 51

W
West Nile Disease, cases and rates, 390, 391
Whooping cough, cases and rates, 392, 393
Wine consumption, 504, 505

Y
Young teens, births to, 46, 47